Investment Management Equations

1. Rate of return on an asset or portfolio
   Return = (End-of-period wealth – beginning-of-period wealth) / (beginning-of-period wealth)

2. Actual margin in a stock purchase
$$am = \frac{(n \times mp) - \left[(1 - im) \times pp \times n\right]}{n \times mp}$$

3. Market price at which a margin purchaser will receive a margin call
$$mp = \frac{(1 - im) \times pp}{1 - mm}$$

4. Actual margin in a short sale
$$am = \frac{\left[(sp \times n) \times (1 + im)\right] - (mp \times n)}{mp \times n}$$

5. Market price at which a short seller will receive a margin call
$$mp = \frac{sp \times (1 + im)}{1 + mm}$$

6. Expected return on a portfolio
$$\bar{r}_p = \sum_{i=1}^{N} X_i r_i$$

7. Covariance between two securities
$$\sigma_{ij} = \rho_{ij}\sigma_i\sigma_j$$

8. Standard deviation of a portfolio
$$\sigma_p = \left[\sum_{i=1}^{N}\sum_{j=1}^{N} X_i X_j \sigma_{ij}\right]^{1/2}$$

9. Standard deviation of a two-asset portfolio
$$\sigma_p = \left[X_1^2\sigma_1^2 + X_2^2\sigma_2^2 + 2X_1 X_2 \rho_{12}\sigma_1\sigma_2\right]^{1/2}$$

10. The market model
$$r_i = \alpha_i + \beta_i r_I + \varepsilon_i$$

11. Beta from the market model
$$\beta_i = \frac{\sigma_{iI}}{\sigma_I^2}$$

12. Security variance from the market model
$$\sigma_i^2 = \beta_i^2\sigma_I^2 + \sigma_{\varepsilon i}^2$$

13. Security covariance from the market model
$$\sigma_{ij} = \beta_i\beta_j\sigma_I^2$$

14. Variance of a portfolio (by market and unique risk)
$$\sigma_p^2 = \beta_p^2\sigma_I^2 + \sigma_{\varepsilon p}^2$$

15. Market risk of a portfolio
$$\beta_p = \sum_{i=1}^{N} x_i\beta_i$$

16. Unique risk of a portfolio
$$\sigma_{\varepsilon p}^2 = \sum_{i=1}^{N} X_i^2\sigma_{\varepsilon i}^2$$

17. Capital Market Line
$$r_p = r_f + \left[\frac{(r_M - r_f)}{\sigma_M}\right]\sigma_p$$

18. Variance of the market portfolio
$$\sigma_M^2 = \sum_{i=1}^{N}\sum_{j=1}^{N} X_{iM} X_{jM}\sigma_{ij}$$

19. Security Market Line (covariance and beta versions)
$$\bar{r}_i = r_f + \left[\frac{(r_M - r_f)}{\sigma_M^2}\right]\sigma_{iM}$$

$$r_i = r_f + (r_M - r_f)\beta_i$$

20. Beta from the CAPM
$$\beta_i = \frac{\sigma_{iM}}{\sigma_M^2}$$

21. Two-factor model
$$r_i = a_i + b_{i1}F_1 + b_{i2}F_2 + e_i$$

22. Variance of a security (by factor and non-factor risk, two-factor model)
$$\sigma_i^2 = b_{i1}^2\sigma_{F1}^2 + b_{i2}^2\sigma_{F2}^2 + 2b_{i1}b_{i2}Cov(F_1, F_2) + \sigma_{ei}^2$$

23. Covariance between two securities (two-factor model)
$$\sigma_{ij} = b_{i1}b_{j1}\sigma_{F1}^2 + b_{i2}b_{j2}\sigma_{F2}^2$$
$$+ (b_{i1}b_{j2} + b_{i2}b_{j1})Cov(F_1 F_2)$$

24. Arbitrage Pricing Theory (two-factor model)
$$\bar{r}_i = \lambda_0 + \lambda_1 b_{i1} + \lambda_2 b_{i2}$$
$$\bar{r}_i = r_f + (\delta_1 - r_f)b_{i1} + (\delta_2 - r_f)b_{i2}$$

25. Break-even tax rate for equivalence of tax-exempt and taxable bond yields
$$t = 1 - \text{ratio of tax-exempt to taxable bond yields}$$

26. Geometric mean (compound) annual growth rate of an index's value
$$g = \left(\frac{C_e}{C_b}\right)^{1/y} - 1$$

27. Real rate of return on an asset or portfolio
$$RR = \left[\frac{1 + NR}{1 + CCL}\right] - 1$$
$$RR > NR - CCL$$

28. Yield-to-maturity
$$P_b = \frac{C_1}{(1 + y)^1} + \frac{C_2}{(1 + y)^2} + \cdots + \frac{C_N + M}{(1 + y)^N}$$

29. Discount factor
$$d_t = \frac{1}{(1 + s_t)^t}$$

30. Forward rate between years $t-1$ and t
$$f_{t-1, t} = \frac{(1 + s_t)^t}{(1 + s_{t-1})^{t-1}} - 1$$

31. Duration
$$D = \frac{\sum_{t=1}^{T} PV(C_t) \times t}{P_0}$$

32. Modified duration
$$D_m = \frac{D}{1 + y}$$

33. Effective duration
$$D_e = \frac{P^+ - P^-}{2P\Delta y}$$

34. Relationship of duration to bond price changes
$$\frac{\Delta P}{P} = -D\frac{\Delta y}{1 + y} = -D_m\Delta y$$

35. Number of shares required to elect d directors under cumulative voting
$$n = \frac{d \times s}{D + 1} + 1$$

36. Value of a right, rights-on
$$R = \frac{C_o - S}{N + 1}$$

37. Value of a right, ex-rights
$$R = \frac{C_e - S}{N}$$

38. Beta from a simple linear regression

$$\beta = \frac{\left(T \times \sum_{i=1}^{N} X_i Y_i\right) - \left(\sum_{i=1}^{N} Y_i \times \sum_{i=1}^{N} X_i\right)}{\left(T \times \sum_{i=1}^{N} X_i^2\right) - \left(\sum_{i=1}^{N} X_i\right)}$$

39. Alpha from a simple linear regression

$$\alpha = \frac{\sum_{i=1}^{N} Y_i}{T} - \frac{\beta \times \sum_{i=1}^{N} X_i}{T}$$

40. Standard deviation of the random error term from a simple linear regression

$$\sigma_e = \left[\frac{\sum_{i=1}^{N} Y_i^2 - \left(\alpha \times \sum_{i=1}^{N} Y_i\right) - \left(\beta \times \sum_{i=1}^{N} X_i Y_i\right)}{T-2}\right]^{1/2}$$

41. Standard error of beta from a simple linear regression

$$\sigma_\beta = \frac{\sigma_e}{\left[\sum_{i=1}^{N} X_i^2 - \frac{\left(\sum_{i=1}^{N} X_i\right)^2}{T}\right]^{1/2}}$$

42. Standard error of alpha from a simple linear regression

$$\sigma_\alpha = \frac{\sigma_e}{\left[T - \frac{\left(\sum_{i=1}^{N} X_i\right)^2}{\sum_{i=1}^{N} X_i^2}\right]^{1/2}}$$

43. Correlation coefficient

$$\rho = \frac{\left(T \times \sum_{i=1}^{N} X_i Y_i\right) - \left(\sum_{i=1}^{N} Y_i \times \sum_{i=1}^{N} X_i\right)}{\left\langle\left[\left(T \times \sum_{i=1}^{N} Y_i^2\right) - \left(\sum_{i=1}^{N} Y_i\right)^2\right] \times \left[\left(T \times \sum_{i=1}^{N} X_i^2\right) - \left(\sum_{i=1}^{N} X_i\right)^2\right]\right\rangle^{1/2}}$$

44. Beta of the firm

$$\beta_{\text{firm}} = \beta_{\text{debt}}\left[\frac{(1-\tau)D}{V_u}\right] + \beta_{\text{equity}}\left(\frac{E}{V_u}\right)$$

45. Beta of the firm's equity

$$\beta_{\text{equity}} = \beta_{\text{firm}} + \left(\beta_{\text{firm}} - \beta_{\text{debt}}\right)\left(\frac{D}{E}\right)(1-\tau)$$

46. Adjusted historical beta

$$\beta_a = a + b\beta_h$$

47. Capitalization-of-income method of valuation

$$V = \sum_{t=1}^{\infty} \frac{C_t}{(1+k)^e}$$

48. Zero-growth DDM

$$V = \frac{D_1}{k}$$

49. Constant-growth DDM

$$V = \frac{D_1}{k-g}$$

50. Multiple-growth DDM

$$V = \left[\sum_{t=1}^{T} \frac{D_t}{(1+k)^t}\right] + \left[\frac{D_{T+1}}{(k-g)(1+k)^T}\right]$$

51. "Normal" price-earnings ratio with constant growth

$$\frac{V}{E_0} = p\left(\frac{1 + r(1-p)}{k - r(1-p)}\right)$$

52. Lintner dividend payout model

$$D_t = ap^\star E_t + (1-a)D_{t-1}$$

53. Annual earnings as a random walk

$$E_t = E_{r-1} + \varepsilon_t$$

54. Quarterly earnings as an autoprogressive process

$$QE_t = QE_{t-4} + a\left(QE_{t-1} - QE_{t-5}\right) + b + e_t$$

55. Intrinsic value of puts and calls

$$IV_C = MAX\left(0, P_S - E\right)$$
$$IV_P = MAX\left(0, E - P_S\right)$$

56. Put call parity

$$P_P + P_S = P_C + \frac{E}{e^{RT}}$$

57. Black-Scholes formula for the fair value of a call option

$$V_C = N(d_1)P_S - \frac{E}{e^{RT}}N(d_2)$$

$$d_1 = \frac{\ln\left(\frac{P_S}{E}\right) + (R + 5\sigma^2)T}{\sigma\sqrt{T}}$$

$$d_2 = \frac{\ln\left(\frac{P_S}{E}\right) + (R - 5\sigma^2)T}{\sigma\sqrt{T}} = d_1 - \sigma\sqrt{T}$$

58. Black-Scholes formula for the fair value of a put option

$$P_P = \left(\frac{E}{e^{RT}}\right)N(-d_2) - P_S N(-d_1)$$

59. Fair value of a futures contract

$$P_f = P_S + I - B + C$$

60. Fair value of an index futures contract

$$P_f = P_S + RP_S - yP_S$$

61. Investment company's net asset value

$$NAV_r = \frac{MVA_t - LIAB_t}{NSO_t}$$

62. Return on an investment company's shares

$$r_t = \frac{(NAV_t - NAV_{t-1}) + I_t + G_t}{NAV_{t-1}}$$

63. Risk tolerance (as implied by a choice of a portfolio)

$$\tau = \frac{2\left(r_C - r_f\right)\sigma_S^2}{\left(r_S - r_f\right)^2}$$

64. Certainty equivalent return

$$u_i = r_p - \left(\frac{1}{\tau}\right)\sigma_p^2$$

65. *Ex post* alpha

$$\alpha_p = ar_p - ar_{bp}$$

66. *Ex post* alpha based on the CAPM

$$\alpha_p = ar_p - \left[ar_f + \left(ar_M - ar_f\right)\beta_p\right]$$

67. *Ex post* characteristic line

$$r_p - r_f = \alpha_p + \beta_p\left(r_M - r_f\right)$$

68. Reward-to-volatility ratio (Treynor ratio)

$$RVOL_p = \frac{ar_p - ar_f}{\beta_p}$$

69. Sharpe ratio

$$SR_p = \frac{ar_p - ar_f}{\sigma_p}$$

70. M²

$$M_p^2 = ar_f + \left(\frac{ar_p - ar_f}{\sigma_p}\right)\sigma_M$$

71. *Ex post* characteristic curve

$$r_p - r_f = a + b\left(r_M - r_f\right) + c\left[\left(r_M - r_f\right)^2\right]$$

72. *Ex post* characteristic lines

$$r_p - r_f = a + b\left(r_M - r_f\right) + c\left[D\left(r_M - r_f\right)\right]$$
where: $D = 0$ if $r_M > r_f$
$\qquad\quad D = -1$ if $r_M < r_f$

73. Return on a foreign investment

$$r_F = r_d + r_c + r_d r_c$$

74. Standard deviation of a foreign investment

$$\sigma_F = \left(\sigma_d^2 + \sigma_c^2 + 2\rho_{dc}\sigma_d\sigma_c\right)^{1/2}$$

SIXTH EDITION

INVESTMENTS

WILLIAM F. SHARPE
STANFORD UNIVERSITY

GORDON J. ALEXANDER
UNIVERSITY OF MINNESOTA

JEFFERY V. BAILEY
DAYTON HUDSON CORPORATION

709

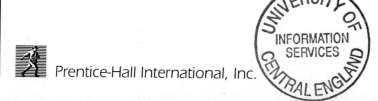
Prentice-Hall International, Inc.

Senior Acquisitions Editor: Paul Donnelly
VP/Editorial Director: Jim Boyd
Assistant Editor: Gladys Soto
Editorial Assistant: Jodi Hirsh
Marketing Manager: Patrick Lynch
Senior Production Editor: Anne Graydon
Production Manager: Susan Rifkin
Managing Editor: Dee Josephson
Production Coordinator: Carol Samet
Senior Manufacturing Supervisor: Paul Smolenski
Manufacturing Manager: Vincent Scelta
Design Manager: Pat Smythe
Cover Design: Cheryl Asherman
Cover Photo: George Diebold, The Stock Market
Full-Service Production & Composition: Preparè Inc. / Emilcomp s.r.l.

 © 1999, 1995 by Prentice Hall, Inc.
A Simon & Schuster Company
Upper Saddle River, New Jersey 07458

Printed in the United States of America

10   9   8   7   6   5   4

ISBN 0-13-011507-X

Prentice-Hall International (UK) Limited, London
Prentice-Hall of Australia Pty. Limited, Sydney
Prentice-Hall of Canada, Inc., Toronto
Prentice-Hall Hispanoamericana, S.A., Mexico
Prentice-Hall of India Private Limited, New Delhi
Prentice-Hall of Japan, Inc., Tokyo
Simon & Schuster Asia Pte. Ltd., Singapore
Editora Prentice-Hall do Brasil, Ltda., Rio de Janeiro
Prentice-Hall, Inc., Upper Saddle River, New Jersey

To Kathy
WFS

To my mother and in memory
of my father
GJA

In memory of Sudhaker Rao Aiyagari,
a brilliant economist and a good friend
JVB

BRIEF CONTENTS

CONTENTS

Page 189

Investment management once seemed a simple process. Well-heeled investors would hold portfolios composed, for the most part, of stocks and bonds of blue chip U. S. industrial companies, as well as U.S. Treasury bonds, notes, and bills. The choices available to less well-off investors were much more limited, confined primarily to passbook savings accounts and U.S. Savings Bonds. If the investment environment can be thought of as an ice cream parlor, then the customers of past decades were offered only chocolate and vanilla.

Mirroring the diversity of modern society, the investment ice cream parlor now makes available a myriad of flavors to the investing public. Investors face a dizzying array of choices. The stocks and bonds of large U.S.-based companies and the debt securities of the U.S. Treasury remain the predominant favorites. However, to mention only a few additional choices, investors can now own the stocks of small U.S.-based companies, the stocks and bonds of companies headquartered from London to Auckland, high-yield bonds, collateralized mortgage obligations, floating rate notes, swaps, puts, calls, and futures contracts. The list is seemingly endless, and it continues to grow. Furthermore, the ability to purchase these securities has become both less expensive and more convenient with the advent of advanced communications and computer networks, along with the proliferating market for mutual funds that has developed to serve large and small investors alike.

The difficulty of writing a textbook on investing has increased as the investment environment has become more complex. Virtually all types of securities, be they traditional or of recent origin, merit at least some discussion. The challenge to us as textbook writers, therefore, is daunting. We must enumerate and describe the various securities and markets in a clear and concise manner that accurately blends theory and practice. However, with the rapid evolution that the investment industry is undergoing, we must also present a discussion of new investment management techniques. Preventing the textbook from reaching encyclopedic proportions thus becomes a difficult project in itself.

The subject matter for this edition of *Investments* has evolved considerably since 1978 when the first edition was published. For example, in the last several years international investing has expanded rapidly, securities such as swaps and mortgage derivatives have become increasingly popular, and investors have placed much more emphasis on investment styles. Our task has been to keep *Investments* fresh and stimulating and to continue to offer students and instructors the most thorough survey of the investment environment available. We believe that we have accomplished these objectives and hope that you agree.

We designed *Investments*, Sixth Edition for advanced undergraduate and graduate students. In doing so, we assumed that such students would have been exposed to basic economics, accounting, statistics, and algebra. Furthermore, it is our belief that serious students of investments should receive a balanced presentation of theory and practical information without being burdened by excessive details. A textbook that focuses solely on institutional features leaves students unable to appreciate the subtle and important issues faced by investment professionals.

Some people will wonder how *Investments*, Sixth Edition compares with the textbook entitled *Fundamentals of Investments* that we have also written. Although both are intended to be comprehensive, they are dissimilar in three significant ways. First, they are organized differently. *Investments* is written in an integrated fashion, whereas *Fundamentals* is more modular in design. Second, *Investments* is somewhat more theoretical and technical than *Fundamentals*. Third, *Investments* is more extensive in its coverage of material, whereas *Fundamentals* tends to be more concentrated.

As any textbook author will attest, a previous work can always be improved—even one that has been in existence as long as this one. Over the years we have received many helpful suggestions from instructors and reviewers regarding ways in which we can make *Investments* better. In each new edition we have tried to enhance the book's breadth and presentation style. In this, the sixth edition, we have made numerous improvements from the previous edition. Of particular note are:

- **Updated coverage of material.** Where appropriate, we have updated the text to keep students abreast of the latest developments in investments. More specifically, we have revised tables and graphs and added discussions in order to incorporate current information and recent academic research.
- **A new chapter on efficient markets.** We have added an entire chapter devoted to discussing the notion of market efficiency that underlies much of current investment thinking.
- **Statistical concepts appendix.** We have added to Chapter 6 an appendix that explains certain basic statistical concepts that are fundamental to understanding the quantitative side of investing.
- **Coverage of financial analysis expanded and revised.** The discussion of financial analysis has been notably expanded and now includes a real-life corporate example.
- **New "Institutional Issues."** Students typically want to know how the concepts presented in the text are applied in the real world. In each chapter we have updated and in some cases added more of the Institutional Issues features that offer discussions concerning issues that face large institutional investors, such as pension funds and mutual funds.
- **Additional end-of-chapter problems and CFA examination questions.** These have been added to give students a better opportunity to learn the material and prepare for the CFA examinations.
- **Additional annotated references.** For those students who are interested in further study of subjects presented in the text, we have updated our extensive set of references organized by topic at the end of each chapter.

We are particularly proud of the "Institutional Issues" features in each chapter. Specifically written for *Investments*, they are designed to give students a sense of how various investment issues and techniques are applied by practitioners. For example, the Chapter 2 features discuss how institutional investors create market neutral portfolios utilizing short selling and introduces readers to hedge funds. One of the Chapter 23 features considers how pension funds go about structuring groups of money managers to achieve specific investment objectives while one of the Chapter 25 features describes the controversial issue of whether or not to hedge the currency risk of an international portfolio. Furthermore, Ann Guenther Sherman of the Hong Kong University of Science and Technology has written two "Institutional Issues" features that deal with investing in the People's Republic of China, which we view as the ultimate emerging market—particularly now that Hong Kong is part of the PRC. In summary, we believe that the "Institutional Issues" features will provide both interesting reading for the students and a stimulating source of classroom discussion material.

A new supplements package for the instructor has been designed for this edition of *Investments*. Many of these password protected supplements such as the **Power-Point Lecture Presentations, Spreadsheet Solutions**, and **Transparency Masters** can be downloaded easily from the Prentice Hall Finance Center web site: **www.prenhall.com/financecenter**. A password is available from your local Prentice Hall Representative. Included in the supplement package are:

- **The Instructor's Manual**. Written by the authors, it provides detailed solutions to all end-of-chapter problems as well as a set of course outlines designed to accommodate a variety of teaching approaches and course emphases.
- An all new **Test Item File**. Compiled by Joseph Vu of DePaul University, the Test Item File includes a bank of over 1,000 multiple-choice and true/false questions. All questions are marked for level of difficulty. Questions relating to the CFA examination are highlighted.
- **Prentice Hall Custom Test Manager.** This Windows-based computerized test program allows the instructor to edit, add, and delete questions to create their own classroom exams.
- **PowerPoint Lecture Presentations.** Prepared by Joseph Greco of California State University, Fullerton, these electronic transparencies give detailed outlines of each chapter and highlight examples from the text using graphs and tables.
- **Spreadsheet Solutions.** Excel spreadsheet solutions are provided for many of the quantitative end-of-chapter questions.
- **Transparency Masters.** Black and white of all the figures and tables in the text can also be downloaded from our Web site.

For the student:

- **Excel Worksheets.** Students can download these templates of Excel spreadsheets from www.prenhall.com/financecenter (no password required).

Many people have assisted us in preparing the sixth edition of this book, and we would like to acknowledge them as well as those who helped us with earlier editions. Specifically, we would like to thank Seth Anderson, Ted Aronson, Ann Bailey, Ed Baker, Michael Barclay, Kenneth S. Bartunek, Jeffrey Born, E. Taylor Claggett, James Conley, Thomas Eyssell, Joe Finnerty, Charlie Freund, Ping Hsiao, Terrence Jalbert, Robert Jennings, Lee Jones, Steven L. Jones, Dougles R. Kahi, Ed Keon, Robert Kleinman, Jaroslaw Komarynsky, Linda Kramer, Stephen Leroy, K.C. Ma, S. Maheswaren, Linda J. Martin, Carl McGowan, Ronald Melicher, John Nagorniak, Chee Ng, Tom Nohel, Thomas O'Brien, Martha Ortiz, James A. Overdahl, Lynne Pi, Maggie Queen, Sailesh Ramamurtie, Peter Robbins, Anthony Sanders, Frederick P. Schadler, Jandhyala L. Sharma, Arlene Spiegel, Len Washko, Tony Wilkins, Robert Wolf, Steve Wunsch, Fernando Zapatero, Emilio Zarruk, and Ken Zumwalt.

We would like to give special thanks Doug Scovanner for his many constructive comments and sharp-eyed catches and to Ann Guenther Sherman for writing the two previously mentioned "Institutional Issues" features. We are also especially grateful to the people at Preparè Inc. / Emilcomp s.r.l. Italia, Fran Daniele and Frank Weihenig, and at Prentice Hall, particularly Paul Donnelly, acquisition editor, Gladys Soto, assistant editor, Jodi Hirsh, editorial assistant, Patrick Lynch, marketing manager, and Susan Rifkin, production editor, for their work in preparing the text for publication.

We have learned much by writing this book and hope that you will learn much by reading it. Although we have done our best to eliminate errors from the book, experience tells us that perfection is unattainable. Thus we encourage those students and instructors with constructive comments to send them to us at either <wfsharpe@leland.stanford.edu>, <galexander@csom.umn.edu>, or <oldbail@winternet.com.>

WFS
GJA
JVB

William F. Sharpe

William F. Sharpe is presently the STANCO 25 Professor of Finance at Stanford University, and is also Chairman of the Board of Financial Engines, Incorporated, a firm that provides electronic investment advice for individual retirement savings. He has published articles in a number of professional journals, including *Management Science, Journal of Business, Journal of Finance, Journal of Financial Economics, Journal of Financial and Quantitative Analysis, Journal of Portfolio Management,* and the *Financial Analysts Journal.* Dr. Sharpe is past President of the American Finance Association, and in 1990 received the Nobel Prize in Economic Sciences. He received his Ph.D., M.A., and B.A. in Economics from the University of California, Los Angeles.

Gordon J. Alexander

Gordon J. Alexander is presently Professor of Finance at the University of Minnesota, having recently completed a two-year stint working in the Office of Economic Analysis at the Securities and Exchange Commission. Dr. Alexander has published articles in *Financial Management, Journal of Banking and Finance, Journal of Finance, Journal of Financial Economics, Journal of Financial and Quantitative Analysis, and Journal of Portfolio Management.* He received his Ph.D. in Finance, M.A. in Mathematics, and M.B.A. from The University of Michigan, and his B.S. in Business Administration from the State University of New York at Buffalo.

Jeffery V. Bailey

Jeffery V. Bailey is Director of Benefits Finance at Dayton Hudson Corporation. Previously he was a Principal at the pension fund consulting firm of Richards & Tierney, Inc. Before that he was the Assistant Executive Director of the Minnesota State Board of Investment. Mr. Bailey has published articles in the *Financial Analysts Journal* and the *Journal of Portfolio Management.* He has contributed articles to several practitioner handbooks and has co-authored a monograph published by the Research Foundation of the Institute of Chartered Financial Analysts. Mr. Bailey received his B.A. from Oakland University and his M.A. in Economics and his M.B.A. in Finance from the University of Minnesota. He is a Chartered Financial Analyst.

INTRODUCTION

This book is about investing in marketable securities. Accordingly, it focuses on the investment environment and process. The **investment environment** encompasses the kinds of marketable securities that exist and where and how they are bought and sold. The **investment process** is concerned with how an investor should proceed in making decisions about what marketable securities to invest in, how extensive the investments should be, and when the investments should be made. Before discussing the investment environment and process in more detail, the term **investment** will be described.

Investment, in its broadest sense, means the sacrifice of current dollars for future dollars. Two different attributes are generally involved: *time* and *risk*. The sacrifice takes place in the present and is certain. The reward comes later, if at all, and the magnitude is generally uncertain. In some cases the element of time predominates (for example, government bonds). In other cases risk is the dominant attribute (for example, call options on common stocks). In yet others, both time and risk are important (for example, shares of common stock).

A distinction is often made between investment and **savings**. Savings is defined as foregone consumption; investment is restricted to "real" investment of the sort that increases national output in the future. Although this distinction may prove useful in other contexts, it is not especially helpful here. However, it is useful to make a distinction between real and financial investments. **Real investments** generally involve some kind of tangible asset, such as land, machinery, or factories. **Financial investments** involve contracts written on pieces of paper, such as common stocks and bonds. The financing of an apartment building provides a good example. Apartments are sufficiently tangible ("bricks and mortar") to be considered real investments. But where do the resources come from to pay for the land and the construction of the apartments? Some may come from direct investment. For example, a wealthy doctor who wants to build an apartment house may use some of his or her own money to finance the project. The rest of the resources may be provided by a mortgage. In essence, someone loans money to the doctor, with repayment promised in fixed amounts on a specified schedule over many years. In the typical case the "someone" is not a person but an institution acting as a financial intermediary. Thus the doctor has made a real investment in the apartment house, and the institution has made a financial investment in the doctor.

For a second example, consider what happens when General Motors (GM) needs money to pay for plant construction. This real investment may be financed by the sale of new common stock in the **primary market** (the market in which securities are sold at the time of their initial issuance). The common stock itself represents a financial investment to the purchasers, who may subsequently trade these shares in the **secondary market** (the market in which previously issued securities are traded). Although transactions in the secondary market do not generate money for GM, the fact that such a market exists makes the common stock more attractive and thus facilitates real investment. Investors would pay less for new shares of common stock if there were no way to subsequently sell them quickly and inexpensively.

These examples have introduced the three main elements of the investment environment: securities (also known as financial investments or financial assets), security markets (also known as financial markets), and financial intermediaries (also known as financial institutions).

1.1 THE INVESTMENT ENVIRONMENT

1.1.1 Securities

When someone borrows money from a pawnbroker, the borrower must leave some item of value as security. If the borrower fails to repay the loan (plus interest), the pawnbroker can sell the pawned item to recover the amount of the loan (plus interest) and perhaps make a profit. The terms of the agreement are recorded on pawn tickets. When a college student borrows money to buy a car, the lender usually holds formal title to the car until the loan is repaid. In the event of default, the lender can repossess the car and sell it to recover costs. In this case the official certificate of title, issued by the state, serves as the security for the loan. A person who borrows money for a vacation may simply sign a piece of paper promising repayment with interest. The loan is unsecured in the sense that there is no collateral, meaning that no specific asset has been promised to the lender in the event of default. In such a situation the lender would have to take the borrower to court to try to recover the amount of the loan. Only a piece of paper called a promissory note stands as evidence of such a loan.

When a firm borrows money, it may or may not offer collateral. For example, some loans may be secured (backed) with specific pieces of property (buildings or equipment). Such loans are recorded by means of mortgage bonds, which indicate the terms of repayment and the particular assets pledged to the lender in the event of default. However, it is much more common for a corporation to simply pledge all of its assets, perhaps with some provision for the manner in which the division will take place in the event of default. Such a promise is known as a debenture bond.

Finally, a firm may promise a right to share in its profits in return for an investor's funds. Nothing is pledged, and no irrevocable promises are made. The firm simply pays whatever its directors deem reasonable from time to time. However, the investor is given the right to participate in the determination of who will be members of the board of directors. This right protects the investor against serious malfeasance. The investor's property right is represented by a share of common stock, which can be sold to someone else, who will then be able to exercise that right. The holder of common stock is said to be an *owner* of the corporation and can, in theory, exercise control over its operation through the board of directors.

In general, only a piece of paper represents the investor's rights to certain prospects or property and the conditions under which he or she may exercise those rights. This piece of paper, serving as evidence of property rights, is called a security. It may be transferred to another investor, and with it will go all its rights and conditions. Thus everything from a pawn ticket to a share of GM common stock is a security. Hereafter the term **security** will be used to refer to *a legal representation of the right to receive prospective future benefits under stated conditions*. The primary task of security analysis is to identify mispriced securities by determining these prospective future benefits, the conditions under which they will be received, and the likelihood of such conditions.

By and large the focus here is on securities that may be easily and efficiently transferred from one owner to another. Thus the concern is with common stocks and bonds rather than with pawn tickets, although much of the material in this book applies to all three types of instruments.

Figure 1.1 and Table 1.1 show the year-by-year results obtained from investing in four types of securities over the 71-year period from 1926 through 1996. In each case the percentage change in a hypothetical investor's wealth from the beginning to the end of the year is shown. This amount, known as the **rate of return** (or simply the *return*), is calculated as follows:

$$\text{Return} = \frac{\text{end-of-period wealth} - \text{beginning-of-period wealth}}{\text{beginning-of-period wealth}} \tag{1.1}$$

In the calculation of the return on a security, it is assumed that a hypothetical investor purchased one unit of the security (for example, one bond or one share of common stock) at the beginning of the period. The cost of such an investment is the value entered in the denominator of Equation (1.1). Then the value in the numerator is the answer to a simple question: How much better (or worse) off is the investor at the end of the period? For example, assume that Widget Corporation's common stock was selling for $40 per share at the beginning of the year and for $45 at the end of the year and paid dividends of $3 per share during the year. The return on Widget for the year would then be calculated as [($45 + $3) − $40]/$40 = .20, or 20%.[1]

Treasury Bills

The first type of security listed in Figure 1.1 and Table 1.1 involves loaning money on a short-term basis to the U.S. Treasury. Such a loan carries little (if any) risk that payment will not be made as promised. Moreover, although the rate of return varies from period to period, at the beginning of any single period it is known with certainty. These investments, called Treasury bills, produced returns ranging from a high of 14.71% per year (in 1981) to a low of virtually zero (actually −.02% in 1938), with an average value of 3.79% during the entire 71-year period.

Long-Term Bonds

The second and third types of securities shown in Figure 1.1 and Table 1.1 are bonds and thus also involve loaning money. Each type of bond represents a fairly long-term commitment on the part of the issuer (that is, the borrower) to the investor (that is, the lender). This commitment is to make cash payments each year (the coupon amount) up to some point in time (the maturity date), when a single final cash payment (the principal) will also be made. The amount for which such bonds can be bought and sold varies from time to time. Thus, whereas coupon payments are easily predicted, the end-of-period selling price of the security is quite uncertain at the beginning of the period, making it difficult to predict the return in advance.

The second type of security (long-term government bonds) involves approximately 20-year loans to the U.S. Treasury and is known as Treasury bonds. The third

Institutional Investors

The past 30 years have witnessed a concentration of financial power in the hands of a relatively few organizations collectively known as *institutional investors*. The economic and social consequences of this consolidation have been enormous. Because this book is about investing, we will discuss not only the basic concepts but also how they are applied by, and apply to, these immensely influential organizations.

The term *institutional investors* is used nebulously by practitioners. In a very broad sense, institutional investors are simply financial intermediaries of any type. This definition sets them apart from *retail investors*, who are individuals owning portfolios for which they are the direct beneficiaries.

At times, however, practitioners refer to institutional investors in a narrower context. For example, in discussions of the consequences of increased institutional investor participation in the U.S. common stock market, the focus is primarily on pension funds, mutual funds, insurance companies, and bank trust departments. These organizations, in aggregate, own over half of the outstanding market value of U.S. corporations.

Unquestionably, the most dynamic institutional investors today are pension funds and mutual funds. Pension funds are a relatively recent phenomenon. General Motors created the first modern U.S. pension fund in 1950. Since then, participation in pension funds has mushroomed, with approximately 40% of the working population enrolled in some type of pension plan today. Pension fund assets, which were only $170 billion in 1970, now total over $7 trillion.

Until the 1970s most U.S. pension funds were invested conservatively in U.S. bonds and common stocks. Since that time these organizations have become the driving force behind many investment industry innovations. They have moved into international stocks and bonds, derivative securities, and various "alternative equity" investments, such as oil and gas, venture capital, and timberland. Furthermore, they have popularized a variety of investment management techniques, such as passive management and market timing.

In terms of sheer growth, mutual funds have been even more impressive than pension funds. As late as 1980, investors had placed only $135 billion in mutual funds. Many investors viewed mutual funds skeptically as speculative investments. The industry still suffered a hangover from the collapse of many "go-go" equity funds in the 1973–1974 recession. Today over $4 trillion is invested in mutual fund shares.

The financial deregulation of the 1980s led to an explosion of mutual fund products. Mutual fund sponsors expanded their offerings in terms of both types of assets and investment styles. Whereas previously most mutual funds concentrated on investments in U.S. stocks, investors can now own mutual funds investing in foreign stocks, U.S. and foreign bonds, U.S. and foreign short-term fixed-income securities, options, futures, and real estate. Funds may emphasize value or growth stocks, mortgage or Treasury bonds, passive or active management. The variations are seemingly endless and continue to grow. Today almost 9,000 funds ply their services to investors. By comparison, in 1980 investors had a scant 564 funds from which to make their choices.

Willie Sutton remarked that he robbed banks because "that's where the money is." Institutional investors command attention because they are now "where the money is." In 1996, the world's largest investment managers held over $17 trillion in assets.

type of security (long-term corporate bonds) involves 20-year loans to high-quality U.S. corporations and is simply referred to as corporate bonds. To date, both types of bonds had their highest annual returns in 1982, reaching 40.36% for government bonds and 42.56% for corporate bonds. However, the lowest annual returns were reached in different years. For government bonds the lowest return occurred in 1967 (−9.18%), whereas the lowest return for corporate bonds was reached in 1969 (−8.09%). Note that, on average, government bonds had a higher return (5.45%) than Treasury bills (3.79%), and corporate bonds had a higher return (5.96%) than government bonds (5.45%). Thus, whereas the second and third types of securities have considerable variability, on average they provide somewhat larger returns than Treasury bills.

The top 50 firms controlled over $9 trillion. By comparison, as the importance of retail investors has declined, the traditional investment services provided to individuals have been reduced in number and increased in price.

The growth in institutional investor portfolios has had a bearing on many of the financial instruments and investment management techniques discussed in this text. Consider the following examples:

Security Markets. Institutional investors now dominate security trading. They control over 70% of the daily trading on the NYSE. Furthermore, 20 years ago fewer than 25% of NYSE trades involved share amounts over 5,000 shares. Today that figure is over 65%. This growth in large common stock trades has threatened to overwhelm the traditional specialist system. In response, new market mechanisms have been created, including block trading houses and crossing networks (see Chapter 3).

Corporate Control. As a consequence of their size, institutional investors collectively own a controlling interest in virtually every large publicly traded U.S. corporation. Only in the last decade have institutional investors made a concerted effort to exercise their influence on corporations, but that effort has already had a noticeable impact. Numerous corporate boards have been altered and businesses have been restructured in response to pressure from institutional investors (see Chapter 16).

Futures. Institutional investors have largely avoided commodity futures. However, their involvement with financial futures (which were not even in existence 20 years ago) has helped generate effective dollar trading volume in common stock index futures that is frequently larger than the dollar value of trading in the underlying common stocks (see Chapter 20).

Investment Management. Institutional investors have demanded new types of investment management techniques. For example, by allocating large sums to passive management, they single-handedly created an industry that now manages well over half a trillion dollars (see Chapter 23).

Portfolio Performance Evaluation. Institutional investors have placed considerable emphasis on understanding how well their investments have performed and identifying the sources of those results. This emphasis has led to the development of sophisticated portfolio monitoring and performance analysis systems (see Chapter 24).

Quantitative Techniques. Institutional investors have pioneered the application of quantitative security valuation techniques, such as dividend discount models (see Chapter 17). They have explicitly sought to maintain adequate portfolio diversification and to control systematic and unsystematic risk using complex risk models (see Chapters 7, 10, and 23).

Fixed-Income Securities. In large part because of the diverse needs of institutional investors, bond trading firms have created an array of complex fixed-income securities. Collateralized mortgage obligations (CMOs), putable bonds, and floating-rate notes are but a few examples (see Chapter 13).

Given current demographic trends, the growth in assets controlled by institutional investors seems unlikely to abate. For example, as "baby boomers" reach their peak savings years (ages 40–60) over the next two decades, purchases of mutual fund shares and contributions to pension funds will continue to rise. Consequently, the influence of institutional investors on security markets can be expected to increase further in the years ahead.

Common Stocks

The fourth and final type of security is common stocks, which represents a commitment on the part of a corporation to pay periodically whatever its board of directors deems appropriate as a cash dividend. Although the amount of cash dividends to be paid during the next year is subject to some uncertainty, it is generally relatively easy to accurately predict. However, the amount for which a stock can be bought or sold varies considerably, making the annual return difficult to accurately predict. Figure 1.1 shows the return from a portfolio of stocks (currently 500 firms) selected by Standard & Poor's Corporation to represent the average performance of large well-established common stocks. Returns ranged from an exhilarating 53.99% in 1933 to a depressing −43.34% in 1931 and averaged 12.67% per year over the entire period.

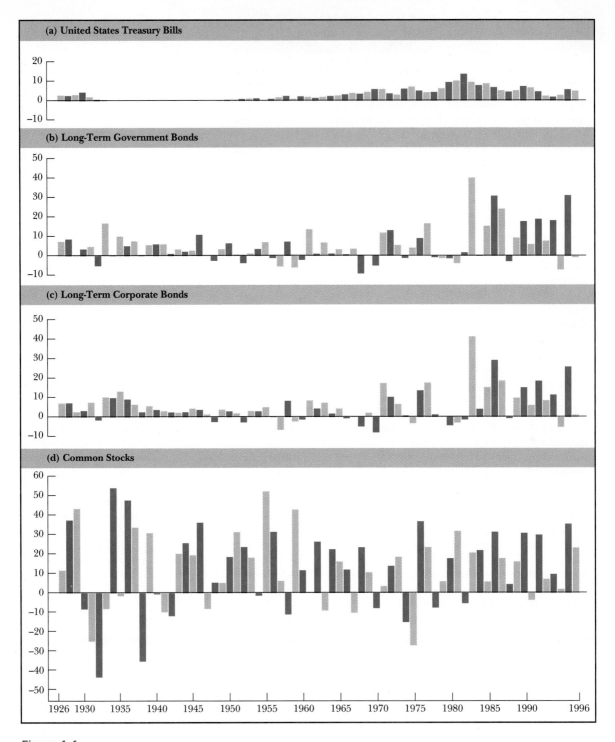

Figure 1.1
Annual Returns, 1926–1996
Source: *Stocks, Bonds, Bills, and Inflation 1997 Yearbook* (Chicago: Ibbotson Associates, 1997). All rights reserved.

Such investments can provide substantial returns, being much larger on average than the returns provided by corporate bonds. However, they also have substantial variability as they are much more volatile than either type of long-term bond.

TABLE 1.1 Annual Returns: Stocks, Bonds, Treasury Bills, and Changes in the Consumer Price Index (CPI)

Year	Treasury Bills	Long-Term Government Bonds	Long-Term Corporate Bonds	Common Stocks	Change in CPI
1926	3.27%	7.77%	7.37%	11.62%	−1.49%
1927	3.12	8.93	7.44	37.49	−2.08
1928	3.56	.10	2.84	43.61	−.97
1929	4.75	3.42	3.27	−8.42	.20
1930	2.41	4.66	7.98	−24.90	−6.03
1931	1.07	−5.31	−1.85	−43.34	−9.52
1932	.96	16.84	10.82	−8.19	−10.30
1933	.30	−.07	10.38	53.99	.51
1934	.16	10.03	13.84	−1.44	2.03
1935	.17	4.98	9.61	47.67	2.99
1936	.18	7.52	6.74	33.92	1.21
1937	.31	.23	2.75	−35.03	3.10
1938	−.02	5.53	6.13	31.12	−2.78
1939	.02	5.94	3.97	−.41	−.48
1940	.00	6.09	3.39	−9.78	.96
1941	.06	.93	2.73	−11.59	9.72
1942	.27	3.22	2.60	20.34	9.29
1943	.35	2.08	2.83	25.90	3.16
1944	.33	2.81	4.73	19.75	2.11
1945	.33	10.73	4.08	36.44	2.25
1946	.35	−.10	1.72	−8.07	18.16
1947	.50	−2.62	−2.34	5.71	9.01
1948	.81	3.40	4.14	5.50	2.71
1949	1.10	6.45	3.31	18.79	−1.80
1950	1.20	.06	2.12	31.71	5.79
1951	1.49	−3.93	−2.69	24.02	5.87
1952	1.66	1.16	3.52	18.37	.88
1953	1.82	3.64	3.41	−.99	.62
1954	.86	7.19	5.39	52.62	−.50
1955	1.57	−1.29	.48	31.56	.37
1956	2.46	−5.59	−6.81	6.56	2.86
1957	3.14	7.46	8.71	−10.78	3.02
1958	1.54	−6.09	−2.22	43.36	1.76
1959	2.95	−2.26	−.97	11.96	1.50
1960	2.66	13.78	9.07	.47	1.48
1961	2.13	.97	4.82	26.89	.67
1962	2.73	6.89	7.95	−8.73	1.22
1963	3.12	1.21	2.19	22.80	1.65
1964	3.54	3.51	4.77	16.48	1.19
1965	3.93	.71	−.46	12.45	1.92
1966	4.76	3.65	.20	−10.06	3.35
1967	4.21	−9.18	−4.95	23.98	3.04
1968	5.21	−.26	2.57	11.06	4.72
1969	6.58	−5.07	−8.09	−8.50	6.11
1970	6.52	12.11	18.37	4.01	5.49
1971	4.39	13.23	11.01	14.31	3.36
1972	3.84	5.69	7.26	18.98	3.41

		Long-Term Government	Long-Term Corporate		
Year	Treasury Bills	Bonds	Bonds	Common Stocks	Change in CPI
1973	6.93%	−1.11%	1.14%	−14.66%	8.80%
1974	8.00	4.35	−3.06	−26.47	12.20
1975	5.80	9.20	14.64	37.20	7.01
1976	5.08	16.75	18.65	23.84	4.81
1977	5.12	−.69	1.71	−7.18	6.77
1978	7.18	−1.18	−.07	6.56	9.03
1979	10.38	−1.23	−4.20	18.44	13.31
1980	11.24	−3.95	−2.76	32.42	12.40
1981	14.71	1.86	−1.24	−4.91	8.94
1982	10.54	40.36	42.56	21.41	3.87
1983	8.80	.65	6.26	22.51	3.80
1984	9.85	15.48	16.86	6.27	3.95
1985	7.72	30.97	30.09	32.16	3.77
1986	6.16	24.53	19.85	18.47	1.33
1987	5.47	−2.71	−.27	5.23	4.41
1988	6.35	9.67	10.70	16.81	4.42
1989	8.37	18.11	16.23	31.49	4.65
1990	7.81	6.18	6.78	−3.17	6.11
1991	5.60	19.30	19.89	30.55	3.06
1992	3.51	8.05	9.39	7.67	2.90
1993	2.90	18.24	13.19	9.99	2.75
1994	3.90	−7.77	−5.76	1.31	2.67
1995	5.60	31.67	27.20	37.43	2.54
1996	5.21	−.93	1.40	23.07	3.32
Average return	3.79%	5.45%	5.96%	12.67%	3.22%
Standard deviation	3.26%	9.21%	8.69%	20.32%	4.54%

TABLE 1.1 (cont.) Annual Returns: Stocks, Bonds, Treasury Bills, and Changes in the Consumer Price Index (CPI)

1.1.2 Risk, Return, and Diversification

Table 1.1 provides year-by-year annual returns for the four types of securities shown in Figure 1.1. The table also includes the annual percentage change in the Consumer Price Index (CPI) as an indicator of variations in the cost of living. Average annual returns are shown at the bottom of the table. Below these values are the standard deviations of annual returns, which serve as measures of the variability of the returns on the respective securities.[2] Table 1.2 provides average annual returns and standard deviations for securities from the United States, Japan, Germany, and the United Kingdom during the period from 1970 to 1996. The historical record revealed in Figure 1.1, Table 1.1, and Table 1.2 illustrates a general principle: When sensible investment strategies are compared with one another, risk and return tend to go together. That is, securities that have higher average returns tend to have greater amounts of risk.

It is important to note that historical variability is not necessarily an indication of prospective risk. The former deals with the record over some past period; the latter has to do with uncertainty about the future. The pattern of returns on Treasury

TABLE 1.2 Summary Statistics for U.S., Japanese, German, and U.K. Securities, 1970–1996								
	Average Return *				Standard Deviation			
	U.S.	Japan	Germany	U.K.	U.S.	Japan	Germany	U.K.
Short-term interest rates	6.93%	5.95%	6.35%	10.69%	2.71%	3.21%	2.39%	3.10%
Government bonds	9.88	7.34	8.05	11.96	12.18	5.15	5.23	12.82
Common stocks	13.47	13.32	10.59	18.45	16.14	29.25	25.62	33.02
Inflation	5.52	4.48	3.65	8.43	3.26	5.13	2.05	5.73

* Foreign returns are calculated in local currencies. Foreign stock returns include dividend income adjusted for the tax rate applicable to U.S. investors. Government bonds include maturities greater than one year.

Source: U.S. financial market data adapted from *Stocks, Bonds, Bills, and Inflation 1997 Yearbook* (Chicago: Ibbotson Associates, 1997). All rights reserved. Foreign financial market data provided by Brinson Partners, Morgan Stanley Capital International, International Financial Statistics, and DRI/McGraw-Hill.

bills provides one example. Although the values have varied from period to period, in any given period the amount to be earned is known in advance and is thus riskless. On the other hand, the annual return on a common stock is very difficult to predict accurately. For such an investment, variability in the past may provide a fairly good measure of the uncertainty surrounding the future return.[3]

To see how difficult it is to predict common stock returns, cover the portion of Table 1.1 from 1941 on, and then try to guess the return in 1941. Having done this, uncover the value for 1941, and try to guess the return for 1942. Proceed in this manner a year at a time, keeping track of your overall predictive accuracy. Unless you are very clever or very lucky, you will conclude that the past pattern of stock returns provides little help in predicting the next year's return. It will later be seen that this apparent randomness in security returns is a characteristic of an **efficient market:** that is, a market in which security prices fully reflect information immediately.

Is one of these four types of securities obviously the best? No. To oversimplify, the right security or combination of securities depends on the investor's situation and preferences for return relative to his or her distaste for risk. There may be "right" or "wrong" securities for a particular person or purpose. However, it would be surprising indeed to find a security that is clearly wrong for everyone and every purpose. Such situations are simply not present in an efficient market. Figure 1.2 illustrates the tradeoffs involved between risk and return. Note that the types of securities with higher historical returns also have had higher levels of risks, suggesting that no type of security dominates any other by having both higher return and lower risk. Also shown in the figure under "Blend" is the risk-return performance of a portfolio that at the beginning of each year was reconfigured to have one-half of its funds invested in corporate bonds and the other half in common stocks. Careful examination reveals that the portfolio's average return equals one-half of the average return of corporate bonds and one-half the average returns of common stocks. However, the risk of the portfolio is less than half the risk of corporate bonds plus half the risk of common stocks. This outcome illustrates a fundamental principle of **diversification**: When securities are combined into a portfolio, the resulting portfolio will have a lower level of risk than a simple average of the risks of the securities. Intuitively, the reason is that when some securities are doing poorly, others are doing well. This pattern tends to reduce the extremes in the portfolio's returns, thereby lowering the portfolio's volatility.

1.1.3 Security Markets

Security markets exist in order to bring together buyers and sellers of securities, meaning that they are mechanisms created to facilitate the exchange of financial as-

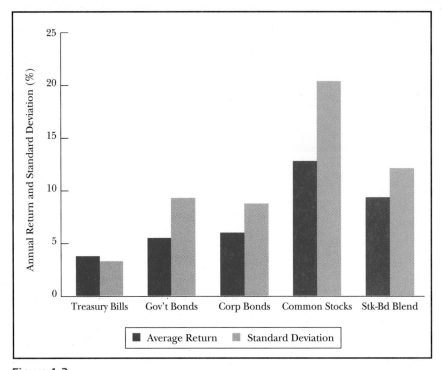

Figure 1.2
Risk and Return, 1926–1996

sets. There are many ways in which security markets can be distinguished. One way has already been mentioned: primary and secondary markets. Here the key distinction is whether the securities are being offered for sale by the issuer. Interestingly, the primary market itself can be subdivided into seasoned and unseasoned new issues. A seasoned new issue refers to the offering of an additional amount of an already existing security, whereas an unseasoned new issue involves the initial offering of a security to the public. *Unseasoned* new equity issues are often referred to as *initial public offerings,* or *ipos.*

Another way of distinguishing between security markets considers the life span of financial assets. **Money markets** typically involve financial assets that expire in one year or less, whereas **capital markets** typically involve financial assets with life spans of greater than one year. Thus Treasury bills are traded in a money market, and Treasury bonds are traded in a capital market.

1.1.4 Financial Intermediaries

Financial intermediaries, also known as financial institutions, are organizations that issue financial claims against themselves (meaning that they sell financial assets representing claims on themselves in return for cash) and use the proceeds from this issuance to purchase primarily the financial assets of others. Financial claims simply represent the right-hand side of the balance sheet for any organization, so the key distinction between financial intermediaries and other types of organizations involves what is on the left-hand side of the balance sheet.

For example, a typical commercial bank issues financial claims against itself in the form of debt (such as checking and savings accounts) and equity, but then again so does a typical manufacturing firm. However, looking at the assets held by a commercial bank reveals that most of the bank's money is invested in loans to individuals and corporations as well as in U.S. government securities such as Treasury bills,

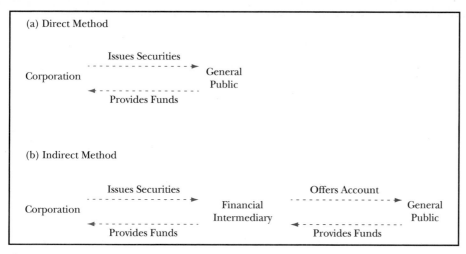

Figure 1.3
Corporate Funds Acquisition

whereas the typical manufacturing firm has its money invested mostly in land, buildings, machinery, and inventory. Thus the bank has invested primarily in financial assets, whereas the manufacturing firm has invested primarily in real assets. Accordingly, banks are classified as financial intermediaries, and manufacturing firms are not. Other types of financial intermediaries include savings and loan associations, savings banks, credit unions, life insurance companies, mutual funds, and pension funds.

Financial intermediaries provide an indirect method for corporations to acquire funds. As illustrated in Figure 1.3(a), corporations can obtain funds directly from the general public by the use of the primary market, as mentioned earlier. Alternatively, they can obtain funds indirectly from the general public by using financial intermediaries, as shown in Figure 1.3(b). Here the corporation gives a security to the intermediary in return for funds. In turn, the intermediary acquires funds by allowing the general public to maintain such investments as checking and savings accounts with it.

1.2   THE INVESTMENT PROCESS

As mentioned previously, the investment process describes how an investor should go about making decisions with regard to what marketable securities to invest in, how extensive the investments should be, and when the investments should be made. A five-step procedure for making these decisions forms the basis of the investment process:

1. Set investment policy.
2. Perform security analysis.
3. Construct a portfolio.
4. Revise the portfolio.
5. Evaluate the performance of the portfolio.

1.2.1   Investment Policy

The initial step, setting **investment policy,** involves determining the investor's objectives and the amount of his or her investable wealth. Because there is a positive relationship between risk and return for sensible investment strategies, it is not appropriate for an investor to say that his or her objective is to "make a lot of money."

What is appropriate for an investor in this situation is to state that the objective is to attempt to make a lot of money while recognizing that there is some chance that large losses may be incurred. Investment objectives should be stated in terms of both risk and return.

This step in the investment process concludes with the identification of the potential categories of financial assets for inclusion in the portfolio. This identification will be based on, among other things, the investment objectives, amount of investable wealth, and tax status of the investor. For example, as shall be seen later, usually it does not make sense for individual investors to purchase preferred stock or for tax-exempt investors (such as pension funds) to invest in tax-exempt securities (such as municipal bonds).

Investment policy is the cornerstone of the investment process. However, it is often the step that receives the least attention from investors. The *Institutional Issues* section entitled "Investment Policy" describes in greater detail the basic elements of investment policy.

1.2.2 Security Analysis

The second step in the investment process, performing **security analysis**, involves examining several individual securities (or groups of securities) within the broad categories of financial assets previously identified. One purpose for conducting such examinations is to identify those securities that currently appear to be mispriced. There are many approaches to security analysis. However, most of these approaches fall into one of two classifications. The first classification is known as **technical analysis**; analysts who use this approach to security analysis are known as technicians or technical analysts. The second classification is known as **fundamental analysis**; those who use it are known as fundamentalists or fundamental analysts. In discussing these two approaches to security analysis, the focus at first will be on common stocks. Later they will be discussed in terms of other types of financial assets.

In its simplest form, technical analysis involves the study of stock market prices in an attempt to predict future price movements for the common stock of a particular firm. Initially, past prices are examined in order to identify recurring trends or patterns in price movements. Then more recent stock prices are analyzed in order to identify emerging trends or patterns that are similar to past ones. This analysis is done in the belief that these trends or patterns repeat themselves. Thus by identifying an emerging trend or pattern, the analyst hopes to predict accurately future price movements for that particular stock.

In its simplest form, fundamental analysis begins with the assertion that the "true" (or "intrinsic") value of any financial asset equals the present value of all cash flows that the owner of the asset expects to receive. Accordingly, the fundamental stock analyst attempts to forecast the timing and size of these cash flows and then converts them to their equivalent present value by using an appropriate discount rate. More specifically, the analyst must attempt not only to estimate this discount rate but also to forecast the stream of dividends that a particular stock will provide in the future; this process is equivalent to forecasting the firm's earnings per share and payout ratios. Furthermore, the discount rate must be estimated. Once the true value of the common stock of a particular firm has been determined, it is compared with the current market price of the common stock in order to see whether the stock is fairly priced. Stocks that have a true value less than their current market price are known as overvalued, or overpriced, stocks, whereas those that have a true value greater than their current market price are known as undervalued, or underpriced, stocks. The magnitude of the difference between the true value and the current market price is also important information, because the strength of the analyst's conviction

Investment Policy

The old adage "If you don't know where you're going, any road will do" aptly applies to investing. Whether an investor is an individual or represents an institution, without a clear sense of why investments are being made and how long-run goals are to be achieved, he or she is likely to pursue inefficient approaches that lead to unsatisfactory results. An investor needs a plan that directs his or her efforts. That plan is called an *investment policy*.

Investment policy is a combination of philosophy and planning. On the one hand, it expresses the investor's attitudes toward important investment management issues such as, "Why am I investing in the first place?" or "To what extent am I willing to accept the possibility of large losses?" The answers to those questions will vary among investors in accordance with their financial circumstances and temperaments.

Investment policy is also a form of long-range strategic planning. It delineates the investor's specific goals and how the investor expects those goals to be realized. In this sense, investment policy comprises the set of guidelines and procedures that direct the long-term management of the investor's assets.

Essentially, any relatively permanent set of procedures that guide the management of a plan's assets fall under the rubric of investment policy. Nevertheless, a comprehensive investment policy should address a group of issues that includes (but is not restricted to):

- **Mission statement.** A description of long-run financial goals. For example, an individual might be focusing on savings for a child's college education. A pension fund might be intended to accumulate sufficient assets to fund promised benefits.
- **Risk tolerance.** The amount of risk that an investor is willing to bear in pursuit of the designat-ed investment missions. An elderly retiree may have a relatively low risk tolerance. Conversely, a well-funded pension fund with a young workforce may have a relatively high risk tolerance.
- **Investment objectives.** The specific investment results that will indicate when the investment program has been successful. For example, an investor's common stock portfolio might be expected to perform at least as well as a broad stock market index over a multiyear period.
- **Policy asset mix.** The investor's long-run allocation to broad asset classes, such as stocks and bonds. This choice is by far the most important decision that the investor makes and should be consistent with the investor's mission, risk tolerance, and investment objectives.
- **Active management.** The extent to which the investor attempts to "beat" the market by hiring investment management firms that analyze and select individual securities or groups of securities expected to exceed the performance of specified benchmarks.

A critical part of any investment policy involves the preparation of a written Investment Policy Statement (IPS). An IPS summarizes the investor's key investment policy decisions and explains the rationale for each decision. The level of IPS detail will vary among investors. Institutional investors, who typically have complex investment programs, should generally prepare more-detailed statements than individual investors. Nevertheless, an IPS serves the same role for all investors: It enforces logical, disciplined investment decision making, and it limits the temptation to make counterproductive changes to an investment program during periods of market stress.

---

that a given stock is mispriced will depend, in part, on it. Fundamental analysts believe that any notable cases of mispricing will be corrected by the market in the near future, meaning that prices of undervalued stocks will show unusual appreciation and prices of overvalued stocks will show unusual depreciation.

1.2.3 Portfolio Construction

The third step in the investment process, **portfolio construction**, involves identifying those specific assets in which to invest, as well as determining the proportions of the investor's wealth to put into each one. Here the issues of selectivity, timing, and diversification need to be addressed by the investor. **Selectivity**, also known as micro-forecasting, refers to security analysis and thus focuses on forecasting price movements of individual securities. **Timing**, also known as macroforecasting, involves the forecasting of price movements of common stocks in general relative to fixed-income securities, such as corporate bonds and Treasury bills. Diversification involves constructing the investor's portfolio in such a manner that risk is minimized, subject to certain restrictions.

1.2.4 Portfolio Revision

The fourth step in the investment process, **portfolio revision**, concerns the periodic repetition of the previous three steps. That is, over time the investor may change his or her investment objectives, which, in turn, may cause the currently held portfolio to be less than optimal. Perhaps the investor should form a new portfolio by selling certain securities that are currently held and purchasing certain others that are not currently held. Another motivation for revising a given portfolio is that over time the prices of securities change, meaning that some securities that initially were not attractive may become attractive and others that were attractive at one time may no longer be so. Thus the investor may want to add the former to his or her portfolio, while simultaneously deleting the latter. Such a decision will depend upon, among other things, the size of the transaction costs incurred in making these changes and the magnitude of the perceived improvement in the investment outlook for the revised portfolio.

1.2.5 Portfolio Performance Evaluation

The fifth step in the investment process, **portfolio performance evaluation**, involves determining periodically how the portfolio performed, in terms of not only the return earned but also the risk experienced by the investor. Thus appropriate measures of return and risk as well as relevant standards (or "benchmarks") are needed.

1.3   INVESTMENTS AS A CAREER

In one way or another, investments affect virtually everyone. Investments both reflect and influence the health of the economy. Direct contact with investing may be as simple as participation in an employer's retirement plan. Or it may involve investing personal assets in mutual funds or individual securities.

For persons interested in making investments a career, the long-term outlook appears bright. As shown in Table 1.3, employment in the industry has continued to grow faster than the overall economy. In 1996, roughly 1 out of every 16 nonagricultural workers dealt with investments, broadly defined. As the U.S. population ages, one can expect savings rates to rise and demand for investment services to continue to grow.

Within the investment industry, there exists a wide range of career options. Using the outline of the investment industry shown in Table 1.3 as a starting point, those options are briefly discussed next.

Grouped together, *insurance*-related jobs constitute a very large sector of the investment industry. One can view the insurance sector as two parts. The first includes agents and brokers who deliver insurance products to individuals and businesses. The second includes insurance companies who invest the funds generated by the premiums paid on the insurance products. The insurance companies' combined investment portfolios are worth trillions of dollars and are invested among a variety of asset types. The insurance industry employs thousands of security analysts and portfolio managers to invest these funds.

TABLE 1.3	Number of Employees: Finance, Insurance, and Real Estate (Thousands)				
	1960	1970	1980	1990	1996
Insurance carriers	832	1,030	1,224	1,462	1,550
Insurance agents, brokers, service	196	288	464	663	709
Financial institutions	934	1,404	2,141	2,624	2,541
Security and commodity brokers	114	205	227	424	541
Real estate	517	661	989	1,315	1,394
Other	76	57	115	221	242
Total	2,669	3,645	5,160	6,709	6,977
Employees in this industry as a percentage of total employees in nonfarm industries					
	4.9%	5.1%	5.7%	6.1%	5.8%

Source: U.S. Bureau of the Census, *Statistical Abstract of the United States 1996* (Washington, DC: GPO, 1997) pp. 411, 505; also various earlier issues.

The *banking* sector (financial institutions on Table 1.3) provides such traditional services as collecting deposits, providing access to deposited funds through check writing, and lending. Banks also provide custodial services to institutional investors and trust services to individuals. In this latter capacity, banks employ security analysts and portfolio managers to invest their clients' funds in the stock, bond, and money markets. In recent years, banks have moved aggressively to offer investment services such as discount brokerage, mutual funds, and investment banking. Legal limitations on banks' involvement in the investment industry are being dismantled at an accelerating rate. In the future, both money center and regional banks hope to become major participants in many financial services from which they have been excluded in the past. If they do, investment-related employment at banks could increase significantly.

The *brokerage* sector facilitates investors' purchases and sales of securities by providing investment advice, execution and processing of trades, record keeping, and market making. Brokerage firms also provide investment banking to corporations and governmental organizations as well as portfolio management for institutions and individuals through mutual funds and separately managed accounts. These firms also trade for their own accounts in the domestic and foreign capital markets. Although it is the most lucrative and high-profile sector of the investment industry, the brokerage business is very cyclical and employment has taken wide swings in tandem with the profitability of the business.

Persons working in the *real estate* sector engage in land acquisition, facilitating the financing and construction of residential and commercial properties, property management, and the purchase and sale of properties. The real estate industry has followed a volatile path in which it grew strongly in the early and mid-1980s, survived a devastating downturn in the late 1980s and early 1990s and more recently has regained much of its growth potential.

Other investment sectors involve a wide range of investment occupations including pension fund administrators, consultants, and independent investment managers. Pension fund administrators oversee the management of corporate and public pension funds. Consultants offer specialized research and advice to institutions and individuals on a wide range of investment issues. Independent investment management firms provide asset management services through mutual funds and separately managed accounts.

What type of training can best prepare one for a career in investments? There is no rigid formula. Most current entrants to the industry have received undergraduate degrees (although not necessarily in business), and many have earned or plan to soon acquire M.B.A. degrees. The Chartered Financial Analyst certification (see Chapter 22) has become an increasingly common requirement for advancement in the investment industry.

Despite these common denominators, the backgrounds of successful investors are quite varied, ranging from art history majors to nuclear physicists. Investing requires a blend of verbal, writing, math, and cognitive skills. In the last 25 years the investment industry has become more "quantitative" and highly computer-oriented. However, the need for "qualitative" skills (particularly intuition, insight, and initiative) remains critical.

1.4 GLOBALIZATION

The "globalization" of the investment business has become a recurring theme in recent years. The U.S. economy is now much more integrated with the rest of the world than it was several decades ago. Similarly, U.S. financial markets are now more sensitive to events abroad than they were previously. The growth in foreign security markets has significantly increased international opportunities for U.S. investors.

Figure 1.4 compares the distribution of total market value of common stock markets around the world in 1970 and in 1996. Most striking is the tremendous growth in the market value of common stocks worldwide. Since 1970, the total value of the world's major equity markets has grown from less than $1 trillion to over $17 trillion. Although the U.S. stock market has participated in this growth, non-U.S. stock markets have expanded even faster. As a result, the total proportion of the world's common stocks represented by the United States has declined over the last 25 years from almost two-thirds to roughly 45% today. With the formation of vibrant stock markets in Eastern Europe, Latin America, and the Far East, non-U.S. capital markets may continue to grow in relative importance.

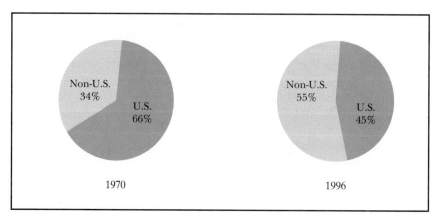

Figure 1.4
World Market Capitalization, Major Markets.

1. Because this book is about investing, it focuses on the investment environment and the investment process.
2. An investment involves the sacrifice of current dollars for future dollars.
3. Investments may be made in real assets or in financial assets (securities) through either primary markets or secondary markets.
4. The primary task of security analysis is to identify mispriced securities by determining the future benefits of owning those securities, the conditions under which those benefits will be received, and the likelihood that such conditions will occur.
5. The rate of return on an investment measures the percentage change in the investor's wealth due to owning the investment.
6. Studies of the historical rates of return on various types of securities demonstrate that common stocks produce relatively high but variable returns. Bonds generate lower returns with less variability. Treasury bills provide the lowest returns with the least variability.
7. In an efficient market, security prices reflect information immediately. Security analysis will not enable investors to earn abnormally high returns.
8. Security markets exist in order to bring together buyers and sellers of securities.
9. Financial intermediaries (financial institutions) are organizations that issue financial claims against themselves and use the proceeds to purchase primarily the financial assets of others.
10. The investment process describes how an investor makes decisions about what securities to invest in, how extensive these investments should be, and when they should be made.
11. The investment process involves five steps: set investment policy, perform security analysis, construct a portfolio, revise the portfolio, and evaluate portfolio performance.
12. Although the investment industry is of modest importance relative to total employment figures, it has a profound impact on everyone's life.

QUESTIONS AND PROBLEMS

1. Why do secondary security markets not generate capital for the issuers of securities traded in those markets?
2. After the overthrow of communist regimes in Eastern Europe, many of the fledgling democracies placed the development of security markets near the top of their economic agendas. Why do you think that they did so?
3. Colfax Glassworks stock currently sells for $36 per share. One year ago the stock sold for $33. The company recently paid a $3 per share dividend. What was the rate of return for an investor in Colfax stock over the last year?
4. Flit Cramer owns a portfolio of common stocks that was worth $150,000 at the beginning of the year. At the end of the year, Flit's portfolio was worth $162,000. What was the return on the portfolio during the year?
5. At the beginning of the year, Ray Fisher decided to take $50,000 in savings out of the bank and invest it in a portfolio of stocks and bonds; $20,000 was placed into common stocks and $30,000 into corporate bonds. A year later, Ray's stock and bond holdings were worth $25,000 and $23,000, respectively. During the year $1,000 in cash dividends was received on the stocks, and $3,000 in coupon payments was received on the bonds. (The stock and bond income was not reinvested in Ray's portfolio.)

a. What was the return on Ray's stock portfolio during the year?

b. What was the return on Ray's bond portfolio during the year?

c. What was the return on Ray's total portfolio during the year?

6. Explain why the rate of return on an investment represents the investor's relative increase in wealth from that investment.

7. Why are Treasury bills considered to be a riskfree investment? In what way do investors bear risk when they own Treasury bills?

8. Why are corporate bonds riskier than U.S. government bonds?

9. In 1951 the Treasury Department and the Federal Reserve System (the Fed) came to an agreement known as the "Accord," whereby the Fed was no longer obligated to peg interest rates on Treasury securities. What were the average returns and standard deviations on Treasury bills for the ten-year periods from 1942 to 1951 and from 1952 to 1961? From these data, does it appear that the Fed did indeed stop pegging interest rates? (See endnote 2 for the formula for standard deviation.)

10. The following table shows the annual returns on a portfolio of small stocks during the 20-year period from 1976 to 1995. What are the average return and standard deviation of this portfolio? How do they compare with the 1976–1995 average return and standard deviation of the common stock portfolio whose annual returns are shown in Table 1.1?

1976:	57.38%	1981:	13.88%	1986:	6.85%	1991:	44.63%
1977:	25.38	1982:	28.01	1987:	−9.30	1992:	23.35
1978:	23.46	1983:	39.67	1988:	22.87	1993:	20.98
1979:	43.46	1984:	−6.67	1989:	10.18	1994:	3.11
1980:	39.88	1985:	24.66	1990:	−21.56	1995:	34.46

11. Does it seem reasonable that higher return securities historically have exhibited higher risk than have securities that yielded lower returns? Why?

12. Give an example, outside of the financial markets, in which you commonly face a trade-off between risk and return.

13. Examining Table 1.1, you can find many years in which Treasury bills produced greater returns than common stocks. How can you reconcile this fact with the statements made in the text citing a positive relationship between risk and return?

14. Again referring to Table 1.1, in terms of total returns, what was the worst single calendar year for common stock investors? What was the worst year in the 1970s? Compare these two years in terms of return in "constant dollars" (that is, purchasing power). Does this comparison show that the stock market slump of the 1970s was not as disastrous as the "crash" associated with the Great Depression? Explain.

15. Calculate the average annual return on common stocks, government bonds, and Treasury bills during the six decades from the 1930s through the 1980s. Which period was clearly the "decade of the financial asset"?

16. Why might it be reasonable to believe that including securities issued in foreign countries will improve the risk-reward performance of your portfolio?

17. Describe how life insurance companies, mutual funds, and pension plans each act as financial intermediaries.

18. What are the five steps to the investment process? What is the importance of each step to the entire process?

19. Why does it not make sense to establish an investment objective of "making a lot of money"?

20. Financial advisers often contend that elderly people should invest their portfolios more conservatively than younger people. Should a conservative investment policy for an elderly person call for owning no common stocks? Discuss the reasons for your answer.

21. What factors might an individual investor take into account in determining his or her investment policy?

22. Distinguish between technical and fundamental security analysis.

CFA EXAM QUESTIONS

23. Donovan believes that the Board should emphasize the fundamental long-term considerations related to investment for BI's plan and deemphasize the short-term performance aspects. Recognizing that a well-structured investment policy is an essential element in investing, Donovan requests your help in drafting such a document.

    a. Discuss why the investment time horizon is of particular importance when setting investment policy for a corporate pension plan.

    b. Briefly explain the importance of specifying each of the following when constructing an effective pension investment policy.

       (i) an appropriate risk tolerance

       (ii) appropriate asset mix guidelines

       (iii) the benchmarks to be used for measuring progress toward plan objectives

24. Ambrose Green, 63, is a retired engineer and a client of Clayton Asset Management Associates ("Associates"). His accumulated savings are invested in Diversified Global Fund ("the Fund"), an in-house investment vehicle with multiple portfolio managers through which Associates manage nearly all client assets on a pooled basis. Dividend and capital gain distributions have produced an annual average return to Green of about 8% on his $900,000 original investment in the Fund, made six years ago. The $1,000,000 current value of his Fund interest represents virtually all of Green's net worth.

    Green is a widower whose daughter is a single parent living with her young son. Although Green is not an extravagant person, his spending has exceeded his after-tax income by a considerable margin since his retirement. As a result, his non-Fund financial resources have steadily diminished and now amount to $10,000. Green does not have retirement income from a private pension plan, but he does receive taxable government benefits of $1,000 a month. His marginal tax rate is 40%. He lives comfortably in a rented apartment, travels extensively, and makes frequent cash gifts to his daughter and grandson, to whom he wants to leave an estate of at least $1,000,000.

    Green realizes that he needs more income to maintain his lifestyle. He also believes his assets should provide an after-tax cash flow sufficient to meet his present $80,000 annual spending needs, which he is unwilling to reduce. He is uncertain as to how to proceed and has engaged you, a CFA charterholder with an independent advisory practice, to counsel him.

    Your first task is to review Green's investment policy statement.

AMBROSE GREEN'S INVESTMENT POLICY STATEMENT

Objectives

- "I need a maximum return that includes an income element large enough to meet my spending needs, so about a 10% total return is required."
- "I want low risk, to minimize the possibility of large losses and to preserve the value of my assets for eventual use by my daughter and grandson."

Constraints

- With my spending needs averaging about $80,000 a year and only $10,000 of cash remaining, I will probably have to sell something soon."
- "I am in good health and my noncancelable health insurance will cover my future medical expenses."

a. Identify and briefly discuss four key constraints present in Green's situation not adequately treated in his investment policy statement

b. On the basis of your assessment of his situation and the information presented in the Introduction, create and justify appropriate return and risk objectives for Green.

[1] In general any cash received during the period is treated as if it were received at the end of the period. However, this treatment typically causes the actual return to be understated. For example, if the dividends on Widget had been received at midyear, the investor could have put them in a bank savings account and earned, say, 5% interest on them for the rest of the year. This interest then would have amounted to $.15 (= .05 × $3.00), resulting in the annual return being equal to 20.375% {= [($45 + $3 + $.15) − $40]/$40 = $8.15/$40}.

[2] The standard deviation was calculated as being equal to the square root of

$$\sum_{t=1}^{71} (r_t - \bar{r})^2 / 70$$

where r_t is the return for year t (so $t = 1$ corresponds to 1926, $t = 2$ to 1927, and so on) and $\bar{r}$ is the average return over the 71-year period. A larger standard deviation means a greater amount of dispersion in the 71 returns and, hence, indicates more risk.

[3] Studies have found that (1) stocks have not become more volatile recently and (2) stocks have tended to be more volatile during recessions (particularly during the Great Depression of 1929 to 1939) than during nonrecessionary periods.

KEY TERMS

investment environment	money markets
investment process	capital markets
investment	financial intermediares
savings	investment policy
real investments	security analysis
financial investments	technical analysis
primary market	fundamental analysis
secondary market	portfolio construction
security	selectivity
rate of return	timing
efficient market	portfolio revision
diversification	portfolio performance evaluation

REFERENCES

1. The following two publications are major sources of historical returns on U.S. security markets.
   Roger G. Ibbotson and Rex A. Sinquefield, *Stocks, Bonds, Bills, and Inflation: The Past and the Future* (Charlottesville, VA: Financial Analysts Research Foundation, 1983). The Financial

Analysts Research Foundation has since been renamed the Research Foundation of the Institute of Chartered Financial Analysts. It can be contacted by calling (804) 980–3655.

Stocks, Bonds, Bills, and Inflation 1998 Yearbook (Chicago: Ibbotson Associates, 1998). This annual yearbook of monthly and annual data can be purchased for a fee by calling (312) 616–1620.

2. Additional historical data on U.S. common stock returns can be found in:

Jack W. Wilson and Charles P. Jones, "A Comparison of Annual Common Stock Returns: 1871–1925 and 1926–1985," *Journal of Business* 60, no. 2 (April 1987): 239–258.

Jeremy J. Siegel, *Stocks for the Long Run: A Guide to Selecting Markets for Long-Term Growth,* (Homewood, IL: Irwin, 1994).

Charles P. Jones and Jack W. Wilson, "Probabilities Associated with Common Stock Returns," *Journal of Portfolio Management* 22, no. 1 (Fall 1995): 21–32.

3. The historical relative returns of U.S. stocks versus bonds are studied in:

Jeremy J. Siegel, "The Equity Premium: Stock and Bond Returns Since 1802," *Financial Analysts Journal* 48, no. 1 (January/February 1992): 28–38.

Peter L. Bernstein, "What Rate of Return Can You Reasonably Expect...or What Can the Long Run Tell Us about the Short Run?" *Financial Analysts Journal* 53, no. 2 (March/April 1997): 20–28.

4. Comparable Japanese data for a more limited time period are presented in:

Yasushi Hamao, "A Standard Data Base for the Analysis of Japanese Security Markets," *Journal of Business* 64, no. 1 (January 1991): 87–102.

5. Historical data on bond market returns are presented in:

Roger G. Ibbotson and Laurence B. Siegel, "The World Bond Market: Market Values, Yields, and Returns," *Journal of Fixed Income* 1, no. 1 (June 1991): 90–99.

Jack W. Wilson and Charles P. Jones, "Long-Term Returns and Risk for Bonds," *Journal of Portfolio Management* 23, no. 3 (Spring 1997): 9–14.

6. The volatility of common stocks is examined in:

G. William Schwert, "Why Does Stock Market Volatility Change over Time?" *Journal of Finance* 44, no. 5 (December 1989): 1115–1153.

Peter Fortune, "An Assessment of Financial Market Volatility: Bills, Bonds, and Stocks," *New England Economic Review* (November/December 1989): 13–28.

7. For a discussion of using historical capital markets return data in making portfolio decisions, see:

Maria Crawford Scott, "Planning Assumptions: Will the Real Long-Term Return Please Stand Up?" *AAII Journal* 19, no. 10 (November 1997): 10–12.

8. Investment policy is discussed in:

Charles D. Ellis, *Investment Policy* (Homewood, IL: Dow Jones-Irwin, 1985).

Keith D. Ambachtsheer, *Pension Funds and the Bottom Line: Managing the Corporate Pension Fund As a Financial Business* (Homewood, IL: Dow Jones-Irwin, 1986).

Keith D. Ambachtsheer, "Pension Fund Asset Allocation: In Defense of the 60/40 Equity/Debt Asset Mix," *Financial Analysts Journal* 43, no. 5 (September/October 1987): 14–24.

Wayne H. Wagner, "The Many Dimensions of Risk," *Journal of Portfolio Management* 15, no. 2 (Winter 1988): 35–39.

Editorial Board, "Investment Policy Statement," *Financial Analysts Journal* 46, no. 5 (September/October 1990): 14–15.

Walter R. Good and Douglas A. Love, "Reactions to the Pension Investment Policy Statement," *Financial Analysts Journal* 47, no. 2 (March/April 1991): 7–10.

Jeffery V. Bailey, "Investment Policy: The Missing Link," in Frank J. Fabozzi (ed.), *Pension Fund Management* New Hope, PA: Frank I. Fabozzi Associates, 1997, pp. 17–30.

BUYING AND SELLING SECURITIES

When a security is sold, many people are likely to be involved. Although it is possible for two investors to trade with each other directly, the usual transaction employs the services provided by brokers, dealers, and markets.

A **broker** acts as an agent for an investor and is compensated via commission. Many individual investors deal with brokers in large retail, or "wire," houses—firms with many offices that are connected by private wires with their own headquarters and, through the headquarters, with the major markets. The people in these brokerage firms with prime responsibility for individual investors are termed **account executives** or **registered representatives**.

Institutional investors, such as commercial banks and pension funds, also deal with these large retail brokerage firms, but they typically do so through separate divisions designed to handle their specific trading needs. Institutional investors also conduct business with smaller firms that maintain only one or two offices and specialize in institutional business.

Two other types of brokerage firms are **regional brokerage firms** and **discount brokers**. The former concentrate on transactions within a geographic area; the securities being traded in a regional brokerage firm have a special following in that area of the country, perhaps because the issuers of the securities are located in that area. Discount brokers offer "bare-bones" services at low cost; that is, they provide fewer services than "full-service" brokerage firms such as Merrill Lynch and Salomon Smith Barney. Investors who simply want to have their orders executed and do not seek investment advice can substantially reduce the commissions they pay by using a discount broker. Lately a special type of discount broker has emerged who accepts, executes, and confirms orders electronically over the Internet for even lower commissions than those of the generic discount broker.

An account executive's compensation is typically determined largely by the **commissions** paid by his or her customers: an amount that is directly related to the amount of turnover (that is, trading) in an investor's account. This arrangement provides some temptation to recommend frequent changes in investors' holdings. Furthermore, because the commission rates on various types of investments differ, there is also an incentive to recommend changes in those types of investments with the highest rates. In the long run, account executives who encourage excessive turnover (or "churning") will often lose customers and may even encounter lawsuits.[1] Nonetheless, such behavior may be advantageous for them in the short run.

It is a simple matter to open an account with a brokerage firm: Simply appear at (or call) the local office. An account executive will be assigned to you and will help you fill out some forms.[2] After the initial forms have been signed, everything else can be done by mail or telephone or via the Internet. Transactions will be posted to your account just as they would to a bank account. For example, you can deposit money, purchase securities using money from the account, and add the proceeds from security sales to the account. Brokers exist (and charge fees) to make security transactions as simple as possible. All that the investor has to do is to provide the broker with what is referred to here as **order specifications**.

In discussing order specifications it will be assumed that the investor's order involves common stock. In this situation the investor must specify:

1. The name of the firm
2. Whether the order is to buy or sell shares
3. The size of the order
4. How long the order is to be outstanding
5. What type of order is to be used

The last three specifications will be discussed next in more detail.

2.1 ORDER SIZE

When buying or selling common stock, the investor places an order involving a round lot, an odd lot, or both. In general, **round lot** means that the order is for 100 shares, or a multiple of 100 shares.[3] **Odd lot** orders generally are for 1 to 99 shares. Orders that are for more than 100 shares, but are not a multiple of 100, should be viewed as a mixture of round and odd lots. Thus an order for 259 shares should be viewed as an order for two round lots and an odd lot of 59 shares.

2.2 TIME LIMIT

The investor must specify a time limit on his or her order—that is, the time within which the broker should attempt to fill the order. For **day orders** the broker will attempt to fill the order only during the day in which it was entered. If the order is not filled by the end of the day, it is canceled. If a time limit is not specified by the investor, the broker will treat an order as a day order. Week and month orders expire at the end of the respective calendar week or month during which they were entered, provided that they have not been filled by then.

Open orders, also known as **good-till-canceled** (GTC) **orders**, remain in effect until they are either filled or canceled by the investor. However, during the time period before the order has been filled, the broker may periodically ask the investor to confirm the order. In contrast to GTC orders there are **fill-or-kill orders**, also known as FOK orders. These orders are canceled if the broker is unable to fully execute them immediately.

Discretionary orders allow the broker to set the specifications for the order. The broker may have virtually complete discretion, in which case he or she decides on all the order specifications, or limited discretion, in which case he or she decides only on the price and timing of the order.

There are several types of orders that investors can place with their brokers. By far the most common types are market and limit orders. Although used to a lesser degree, stop and stop limit orders can also be used. Last, there are special types of orders that are rarely used; readers interested in them should contact their broker.[4]

2.3.1 Market Orders

By far the most common type of order is the **market order**. Here the broker is instructed to buy or sell a stated number of shares immediately. In this situation the broker is obligated to act on a "best-efforts" basis to get the best possible price (as low as possible for a purchase order, as high as possible for a sell order) at the time the order is placed. Consequently, an investor placing a market order can be fairly certain that the order will be executed but will be uncertain of the price. However, there is generally fairly good information available beforehand concerning the likely price at which such an order will be executed. Not surprisingly, market orders are day orders.

2.3.2 Limit Orders

A second type of order is the **limit order**. Here a **limit price** is specified by the investor when the order is placed with the broker. If the order is to purchase shares, then the broker is to execute the order only at a price that is less than or equal to the limit price. If the order is to sell shares, then the broker is to execute the order only at a price that is greater than or equal to the limit price. Thus for limit orders to purchase shares the investor specifies a ceiling on the price, and for limit orders to sell shares the investor specifies a floor on the price. In contrast to a market order, an investor using a limit order cannot be certain that the order will be executed. Hence there is a trade-off between these two types of orders—immediacy of execution with uncertain price versus uncertain execution with bounded price.

For example, assume that the common stock of ABC Corporation is currently selling for $25 a share. An investor placing a limit order to sell 100 shares of ABC with a limit price of $30 per share and a time limit of one day is not likely to have the order executed, because this price is notably above the current price of $25. Only if today's price becomes much more favorable (meaning in this case that the stock price rises by at least $5 per share) will the limit order be executed.

2.3.3 Stop Orders

Two special kinds of orders are stop orders (also known as stop-loss orders) and stop limit orders. For a **stop order** the investor must specify what is known as a **stop price**. If it is a sell order, the stop price must be below the market price at the time the order is placed. Conversely, if it is a buy order, the stop price must be above the market price at the time the order is placed. If later someone else trades the stock at a price that reaches or passes the stop price, then the stop order becomes, in effect, a market order. Hence a stop order can be viewed as a conditional market order.

Continuing with the $25 ABC Corporation example, a stop sell order at $20 would not be executed until a trade involving others had taken place at a price of $20 or lower. Conversely, a stop buy order at $30 would not be executed until a trade involving others had taken place at a price of $30 or more. If the price did not fall to $20, then the stop sell order would not be executed. Similarly, if the price did not rise to $30, the stop buy order would not be executed. In contrast, a limit order to sell at $20 or a limit order to buy at $30 would be executed immediately, because the current market price is $25.

One potential use of stop orders is to "lock in" paper profits. For example, assume that an investor had purchased ABC stock at $10 per share two years ago and thus has paper profits of $15 (=$25 − $10) per share. Entering a stop sell order at $20 per share means that the investor will be sure of making roughly $10 (=$20 − $10) per share if the stock falls in price to $20. If instead of falling the stock price rises, then the investor's stop sell order will be ignored and the investor's paper profits will increase in size. Thus the stop sell order will provide the investor with a degree of profit protection.[5]

One of the dangers of stop orders is that the actual price at which the order is executed may be some distance from the stop price. This discrepancy can occur if the stock price moves very rapidly in a given direction. For example, ABC may have an industrial accident that results in a spate of lawsuits and causes the stock price to fall very rapidly to $12 per share. In this situation a stop sell order at $20 may be executed at, say, $16 instead of near the stop price of $20.

2.3.4 Stop Limit Orders

The **stop limit order** is a type of order that is designed to overcome the uncertainty of the execution price associated with a stop order. With a stop limit order the investor specifies not one but two prices: a stop price and a limit price. Once someone else trades the stock at a price that reaches or passes the stop price, then a limit order is created at the limit price. Hence a stop limit order can be viewed as a conditional limit order.

Continuing with the example, the investor could place a stop limit order to sell ABC stock where the stop price is $20 and the limit price is $19. In effect, a limit order to sell ABC stock at a price of $19 or higher would be activated for the investor only if others trade ABC at a price of $20 or less. Conversely, the investor could enter a stop limit order to buy ABC stock where the stop price is $30 and the limit price is $31. In this case, a limit order to buy ABC stock at a price of $31 or lower would be activated for the investor only if others trade ABC at a price of $30 or more.

Note that if the stop price is reached, execution is assured for a stop order but not for a stop limit order. Continuing with the ABC example, the industrial accident may cause the stock price to fall to $12 so rapidly that the stop limit order to sell (where the stop price was $20 and the limit price was $19) might not have been executed, whereas the stop order (where the stop price was $20) would have been executed at $16. Hence there is a trade-off between these two types of orders that is very similar to the trade-off between market and limit orders. Once activated, the stop order provides certain execution at an uncertain price, whereas a stop limit order provides uncertain execution at a bounded price.

2.4   MARGIN ACCOUNTS

A **cash account** with a brokerage firm is like a regular checking account: Deposits (cash and the proceeds from selling securities) must cover withdrawals (cash and the costs of purchasing securities). A **margin account** is like a checking account that has overdraft privileges: If more money is needed than is in the account, a loan (within limits on its size) is automatically made by the broker.[6]

When opening a margin account with a brokerage firm, an investor must sign a **hypothecation agreement**, also known as a customer's agreement. This agreement grants the brokerage firm the right to pledge the investor's securities as collateral for bank loans, provided that the securities were purchased using a margin account. Most brokerage firms also expect investors to allow them to lend their securities to others who wish to "sell them short." Both securities lending and short selling will be described later in this chapter.

In order to facilitate either the pledging or the lending of securities, brokerage firms request that securities purchased through a margin account be held in **street name**.[7] This means that the owner of the security, as far as the original issuer is concerned, is the brokerage firm; that is, the registered owner is the brokerage firm. As a result, in the case of common stock the issuer will send all dividends, financial reports, and voting rights to the brokerage firm, not to the investor. The brokerage firm will serve as a conduit and forward these items to the investor.[8] Accordingly, holding a security in street name will not result in the investor's being treated in a substantively different manner than holding the security in his or her own name.[9]

With a margin account an investor may undertake certain types of transactions that are not allowed with a cash account. These transactions are known as margin purchases and short sales.

2.4.1 Margin Purchases

With a cash account an investor who purchases a security must pay the entire cost of the purchase with cash. However, with a margin account the investor must come up with cash for only a percentage of the cost and can borrow the rest from the broker.[10] The amount borrowed from the broker as a result of such a **margin purchase** is referred to as the investor's **debit balance**. The interest charged on loans advanced by a broker for a margin purchase is usually calculated by adding a service charge (for example, 1%) to the broker's **call money rate**. In turn, the call money rate is the rate paid by the broker to the bank that loaned the broker the cash that ultimately went to the investor to pay for part of the purchase.

For example, the bank may loan money to the broker at a rate of 10%, and then the broker may loan this money to the investor at a rate of 11%. The call money rate will change over time as the prevailing level of market interest rates changes. The interest rate that investors are charged for loans used to finance margin purchases will change correspondingly.

The securities purchased by the investor serve as collateral on the loan made by the broker. In turn, the broker uses these securities as collateral on the loan made by the bank. Thus the broker is, in a sense, acting as a financial intermediary in the lending process by facilitating a loan from the bank to the investor. Sometimes, however, the broker will use the brokerage firm's own funds to make the loan. Nevertheless, the investor will still be treated as if a bank was behind the loan.

Initial Margin Requirement

The minimum percentage of the purchase price that must come from the investor's own funds is known as the **initial margin requirement**. Regulations T, U, G, and X, prescribed in accordance with the Securities Exchange Act of 1934, give the Federal Reserve Board the responsibility for setting this percentage when either common stocks or convertible bonds are being purchased.[11] However, the exchanges where the purchase orders are filled are allowed to set a percentage higher than the one set by the Federal Reserve Board, and brokers are allowed to set it even higher. Thus, hypothetically, the Federal Reserve Board could set the initial margin requirement at 50%, the New York Stock Exchange could then make it 55%, and the broker could ultimately make it 60%. As shown in Table 2.1, the initial margin requirement since 1934 as set by the Federal Reserve Board ranged from 25% to 100%. In 1998 it was 50%.[12]

Consider, as an example, an investor who purchases on margin 100 shares of Widget Corporation for $50 per share. With an initial margin requirement of 60%,

TABLE 2.1 Initial Margin Requirements of the Federal Reserve Board

| Period | | Initial Margin Requirement (%) | | |
Beginning Date	Ending Date	Margin Stocks	Short Sales	Convertible Bonds
Oct. 15, 1934	Jan. 31, 1936	25–45	(a)	(b)
Feb. 1, 1936	Mar. 31, 1936	25–55	(a)	(b)
Apr. 1, 1936	Oct. 31, 1937	55	(a)	(b)
Nov. 1, 1937	Feb. 4, 1945	40	50	(b)
Feb. 5, 1945	Jul. 4, 1945	50	50	(b)
Jul. 5, 1945	Jan. 20, 1946	75	75	(b)
Jan. 21, 1946	Jan. 31, 1947	100	100	(b)
Feb. 1, 1947	Mar. 29, 1949	75	75	(b)
Mar. 30, 1949	Jan. 16, 1951	50	50	(b)
Jan. 17, 1951	Feb. 19, 1953	75	75	(b)
Feb. 20, 1953	Jan. 3, 1955	50	50	(b)
Jan. 4, 1955	Apr. 22, 1955	60	60	(b)
Apr. 23, 1955	Jan. 15, 1958	70	70	(b)
Jan. 16, 1958	Aug. 4, 1958	50	50	(b)
Aug. 5, 1958	Oct. 15, 1958	70	70	(b)
Oct. 16, 1958	Jul. 27, 1960	90	90	(b)
Jul. 28, 1960	Jul. 9, 1962	70	70	(b)
Jul. 10, 1962	Nov. 5, 1963	50	50	(b)
Nov. 6, 1963	Mar. 10, 1968	70	70	(b)
Mar. 11, 1968	Jun. 7, 1968	70	70	50
Jun. 8, 1968	May 5, 1970	80	80	60
May 6, 1970	Dec. 5, 1971	65	65	50
Dec. 6, 1971	Nov. 23, 1972	55	55	50
Nov. 24, 1972	Jan. 2, 1974	65	65	50
Jan. 3, 1974	Present	50	50	50

Source: *Federal Reserve Bulletin*, various issues.

[a] Requirement was the margin "customarily required" by the broker.

[b] Initial margin requirements for convertible bonds were not adopted by the Federal Reserve Board until March 11, 1968.

the investor must pay the broker $3,000 (=.6 × 100 shares × $50 per share). The remainder of the purchase price, $2,000 [=(1 − .6) × 100 shares × $50 per share], is funded by a loan from the broker to the investor.

Actual Margin

The **actual margin** in the account of an investor who has purchased stocks is calculated as:

$$\text{Actual margin} = \frac{\text{market value of assets} - \text{loan}}{\text{market value of assets}} \quad (2.1)$$

The daily calculation of the actual margin in an investor's account is known as having the account **marked to the market**. Upon examination of Equation (2.1) it can be seen that at the time of the margin purchase, the actual margin and the initial margin are the same. However, subsequent to the purchase, the actual margin can be either greater than or less than the initial margin.[13] In this example, if Widget stock fell to $25 per share, then the actual margin would drop to 20% [=($2,500 − $2,000)/$2,500].

TABLE 2.2	Investor's Balance Sheet after Margin Purchase		
Assets		**Liabilities and Net Worth**	
Widget stock	$5,000	Margin loan	$2,000
		Equity	$3,000
Total assets	$5,000	Total liabilities and net worth	$5,000

Table 2.2 presents the investor's balance sheet immediately after the margin purchase. The investor has assets of $5,000 corresponding to the value of Widget stock. Those assets are partially offset by liabilities of $2,000 representing the margin loan, leaving $3,000 in equity.

Keep in mind that the 100 shares of Widget are being kept as collateral on the loan of $2,000 to the investor. If the price of Widget drops further, the broker may become nervous because an additional sudden price decline could bring the value of the collateral below the amount of the loan. For example, if the price dropped to $15 per share, the broker would have collateral worth $1,500 [=$15 $\times$ 100 shares], whereas the amount of the loan is $2,000. If the investor skipped town, the broker would still have to make good on the bank loan of $2,000 but would have only $1,500 worth of the investor's assets to seize in order to pay off the loan. The broker would have to bear the $500 difference and hope to track down the investor and recoup this amount at a later date.

Maintenance Margin Requirement

To prevent such an occurrence, brokers require investors to keep the actual margin in their accounts at or above a certain percentage. This percentage is known as the **maintenance margin requirement**. It is set by the exchanges, not by the Federal Reserve Board, and brokers have the right to set it as high as they want. As of 1998, the New York Stock Exchange had set this percentage for common stock and convertible bond purchases at 25%.

If an account's actual margin falls below the maintenance margin requirement, the account is said to be **undermargined**. Accordingly, the broker will issue a **margin call**, requesting the investor to either (1) deposit cash or securities into the account, (2) pay off part of the loan, or (3) sell some securities currently held in the account and use the proceeds to pay off part of the loan. Any of these actions will raise the numerator or lower the denominator on the right-hand side of Equation (2.1), thereby increasing the actual margin.[14] If the investor does not act (or cannot be reached), then, in accordance with the terms of the account, the broker will sell some (or all of the) securities from the account in order to restore the actual margin to (at least) the maintenance margin requirement.

If instead of falling the stock price rises, then the investor can take part of the increase out of the account in the form of cash, because the actual margin in the account will have risen above the initial margin requirement.[15] In this situation the account is said to be **unrestricted** or **overmargined**.

The foregoing discussed the cases in which the stock price of the shares purchased on margin either (1) fell to such a degree that the actual margin was below the maintenance margin requirement, meaning that the account was undermargined, or (2) increased, resulting in the actual margin being above the initial margin requirement and the account being classified as unrestricted, there remains one case to consider. This case involves the situation in which the stock price falls but

TABLE 2.3   Potential Margin Account Conditions and Actions for Margin Purchaser

Purchase price = $50
Initial margin requirement = 60%
Maintenance margin requirement = 30%

	Current Price		
	$25	**$45**	**$60**
Actual margin	.20	.56	.67
Condition	Undermargined	Restricted	Overmargined
Potential actions	1. Add cash or securities 2. Add cash to pay off part of loan 3. Sell securities to pay off part of loan	1. Do nothing	1. Do nothing 2. Withdraw excess cash

not by enough to make the actual margin drop below the maintenance margin requirement. That is, the actual margin in the account is below the initial margin requirement but above the maintenance margin requirement. In this situation no action by the investor is necessary. However, the account will be **restricted**, meaning that any transaction having the effect of decreasing the actual margin further (such as withdrawing cash) will not be allowed.[16]

Table 2.3 shows possible margin account conditions in which the investor in Widget stock might find himself or herself. In the example, Widget stock has been purchased on margin for $50 per share, with an initial margin requirement of 60%. Assume further that the maintenance margin requirement is 30%. Three possible current prices for the stock are presented along with the resulting outcomes for the margin account and possible actions that the investor might take.

Rate of Return

The use of margin purchases allows the investor to engage in **financial leverage**. That is, by using debt to fund part of the purchase price, the investor can increase the expected rate of return of the investment. However, there is a complicating factor in the use of margin: The effect on the risk of the investment.

Consider Widget again. If the investor believes that the stock will rise by $15 per share over the next year, then the expected rate of return on a cash purchase of 100 shares of Widget at $50 per share will be 30% [= ($15 × 100 shares)/($50 × 100 shares) = $1,500/$5,000], assuming that no cash dividends are paid. A margin purchase, on the other hand, would have an expected return of 42.7% {= [($15 × 100 shares) − (.11 × $2,000)]/(.6 × $50 × 100 shares) = $1,280/$3,000}, where the interest rate on margin loans is 11% and the initial margin requirement is 60%. Thus the investor has increased the expected rate of return from 30% to 42.7% by the use of margin.

But what will happen to the rate of return if the stock falls by $10 per share? In this case the investor who made a cash purchase would have a rate of return equal to −20% [=(−$10 × 100 shares)/$5,000 = −$1,000/$5,000]. The margin purchaser, on the other hand, would have a rate of return equal to −40.7% {=[(−$10 × 100) − (.11 × $2,000)]/$3,000 = −$1,220/$3,000}. Thus the margin purchaser will experience a much larger loss than the cash purchaser for a given dollar decline in the price of the stock.

Margin purchases are usually made in the expectation that the stock price will rise in the near future, meaning that the investor thinks that the stock's current price is too low. An investor who thinks that a given stock is not too low but too high may engage in what is known as a short sale.

2.4.2 Short Sales

An old adage from Wall Street is "buy low, sell high." Most investors hope to do just that by buying securities first and selling them later.[17] However, with a **short sale** this process is reversed: The investor sells a security first and buys it back later. In this case the Wall Street adage might be reworded as "sell high, buy low."

Short sales are accomplished by borrowing stock certificates for use in the initial trade, then repaying the loan with certificates obtained in a later trade. Note that the loan here involves certificates, not dollars and cents (although it is true that the certificates at any point in time have a certain monetary value). This means that the borrower must repay the lender by returning certificates, not dollars and cents (although it is true that an equivalent monetary value, determined on the date the loan is repaid, can be remitted instead as it will be used to buy the requisite number of shares). It also means that there are no interest payments to be made by the borrower.

Rules Governing Short Sales

Any order for a short sale must be identified as such. The Securities and Exchange Commission has ruled that short sales may not be made when the market price for the security is falling, on the assumption that the short seller could exacerbate the situation, cause a panic, and profit therefrom—an assumption inappropriate for an efficient market with astute, alert traders. The precise rule, known as the **up-tick rule**, states that a short sale must be made on a **plus** (or "**up**")-**tick** (for a price higher than that of the previous trade) or on a **zero-plus tick** (for a price equal to that of the previous trade but higher than that of the last trade at a different price).[18]

Within three business days after a short sale has been made, the short seller's broker must borrow and deliver the appropriate securities to the purchaser. The borrowed securities may come from

- the inventory of securities owned by the brokerage firm itself,
- the inventory of another brokerage firm,
- the holdings of an institutional investor (such as a pension fund) that is willing to lend its securities, or
- the inventory of securities held in street name by the brokerage firm for investors who have margin accounts with the firm.

The life of the loan is indefinite, meaning that there is no specific time limit on it.[19] If the lender wants to sell the securities, then the short seller will not have to repay the loan if the brokerage firm can borrow shares elsewhere, thereby transferring the loan from one source to another. However, if the brokerage firm cannot find a place to borrow the shares, then the short seller will have to repay the loan immediately. Interestingly, the identities of the borrower and the lender are known only to the brokerage firm; that is, the lender does not know who the borrower is and the borrower does not know who the lender is.

An Example

An example of a short sale is indicated in Figure 2.1. At the start of the day, Mr. Lane owns 100 shares of *XYZ* Company, which are being held for him in street name by Brock, Inc., his broker. During this particular day, Ms. Smith places an order with her

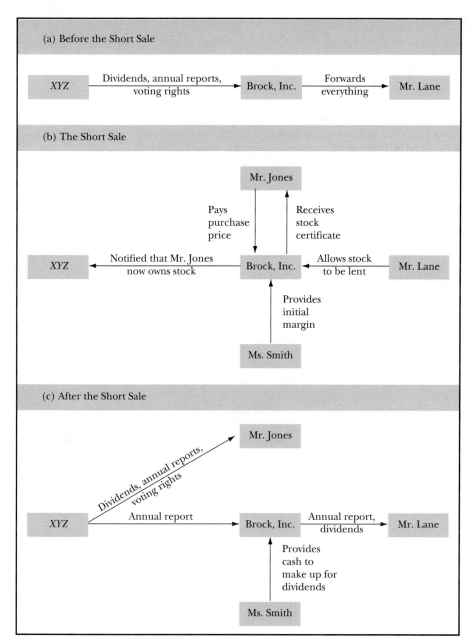

Figure 2.1
Short Selling of Common Stock

broker at Brock to short sell 100 shares of *XYZ*. (Mr. Lane believes that the price of *XYZ* stock is going to rise in the near future, whereas Ms. Smith believes that it is going to fall.) In this situation Brock takes the 100 shares of *XYZ* that it is holding in street name for Mr. Lane and sells them for Ms. Smith to some other investor, in this case Mr. Jones. At this point *XYZ* will receive notice that the ownership of 100 shares of its stock has changed hands, going from Brock (remember that Mr. Lane held his stock in street name) to Mr. Jones. At some later date Ms. Smith will tell her broker at Brock to purchase 100 shares of *XYZ* (perhaps from Ms. Poole) and to use these shares to pay off her debt to Mr. Lane. At this point *XYZ* will receive another notice

Market Neutral Strategies

Institutional investors have traditionally viewed management of common stock portfolios as a one-sided problem: Buy underpriced stocks that are likely to appreciate in value relative to an established benchmark. However, that perspective is changing as these investors explore techniques that involve purchases *and* short sales of stocks so as to systematically control portfolio risk and profit from insights into mispriced securities. Collectively, these techniques are known as "market neutral" strategies.

The logic underlying market neutral strategies is simple. If on average all securities are fairly priced, then mispricing must be a zero-sum game; underpriced securities must be accompanied by overpriced securities. Therefore, why should an investor who can discover mispriced securities restrict himself or herself to just buying the underpriced securities? Instead of merely avoiding overpriced securities, why not profit by short selling them?

The basic process of implementing market neutral strategies is similarly straightforward. The investor holds a portfolio consisting of three investments: short-term riskfree securities (for example, 90-day Treasury bills), long positions in stocks, and short positions in stocks. The market values of all the investments are the same. Furthermore, the long and short stock positions have equal exposures to common causes of stock market variability. (See Chapter 10 for a discussion of factors affecting stock returns.) The resulting portfolio, therefore, is fully hedged (that is, protected) against any type of stock market movement.

Why should this hedged portfolio be of interest? After all, it should earn only the riskfree return. The answer lies with the stock selection skills of the market neutral investor. An investor who possesses valuable knowledge of mispriced securities will purchase underpriced stocks whose unique circumstances will cause them to increase in value *relative* to the market. Conversely, this investor will short sell overpriced stocks whose unique circumstances will cause them to decrease in value *relative* to the market. The net result is that the investor benefits from the ability to identify mispriced stocks, without exposure to the vagaries of the stock market.

As a simple example, consider an investor who begins the year with $100 in cash. The investor uses the cash to purchase $100 of stocks. At the same time the investor short sells $100 of stocks. These purchases

and short sales have been carefully designed to exhibit no net exposure to any industry or other factor influencing stock market returns. (For example, the investor might form long-short pairs within industries—buy $5 of GM stock and short sell $5 of Ford stock, buy $5 of Exxon and short $5 of Texaco, and so on.) At the beginning of the year the investor's portfolio appears as follows:

Long	Short	Cash	Total
$100	−$100	$100	$100

Assume that the investor selects wisely and the long portfolio is worth $110 at year-end, for a 10% return. (By comparison, the stock market's return was 8%.) Furthermore, the short portfolio also has risen in value (but not by as much as the long portfolio or the stock market) to $105 (a 5% return), and the cash holdings have earned $2 in interest (a 2% return). At year-end the investor's portfolio appears as follows:

Long	Short	Cash	Total
$110	−$105	$102	$107

This investor has earned $7 on a $100 portfolio, or a 7% return, without assuming any market risk. The only risk the investor has taken lies in the ability to identify mispriced stocks. The abnormal return from adroit stock selection is known as "alpha" (see Chapter 24). In fact, the market neutral investor earns a "double alpha" derived from insights into both underpriced and overpriced stocks.

Of course, the real world, with its unaccommodating nature, makes the implementation of market neutral strategies much more complex than our simple example implies. Consider the following steps that the market neutral investor must follow:

1. **Establish a margin account.** As the text describes, short selling must be conducted in a margin account. Thus the investor must select a broker to hold the stocks and cash involved in the market neutral strategy.
2. **Make long and short transactions simultaneously.** Long positions must always equal short positions, or the portfolio may be exposed to unintended risks. The New York Stock Exchange's up-tick rule and the limited availability of appropriate stocks for short selling complicates this task.

3. **Maintain collateral with the broker.** The stocks from the long positions, cash from the short sales, and a small amount of initial cash (to serve as a liquidity reserve for daily marks to market on the short positions) must be deposited with the broker.
4. **Reimburse for dividends paid and substitute for recalled borrowed stocks.** The investor must compensate the stock lender for any dividends paid on the borrowed stocks. Also, if the borrowed securities are sold by the lender and cannot be replaced, the investor must find appropriate substitutes.
5. **Continuously monitor portfolio positions.** Security price movements will affect the long-short balance in the portfolio. Only careful daily monitoring can prevent the portfolio from moving away from a market neutral stance.

Institutional investors pay special attention to selecting a broker for their market neutral strategies. They invariably choose large, established brokers with impeccable credit ratings. These brokers have the best access to securities for short sales, either through their street name holdings or through security lending networks. Institutional investors also consider the interest income rebates (2% in the example) provided by the brokers. Unlike small investors, who typically receive no interest on their short sale proceeds, institutional investors can negotiate to receive anywhere from 75% to 90% of the income earned by the broker on the short sale proceeds.

Any investment organization can implement market neutral strategies. However, investors using quantitative investment processes (for example, dividend discount models; see Chapter 17) are the primary purveyors of this approach. Their processes typically rank a large number of stocks from highly attractive to highly unattractive; a step necessary to develop a diversified collection of long and short opportunities. Moreover these investors' portfolio construction methods usually are very structured, thus facilitating the intricate design and maintenance of offsetting long and short positions.

Some institutional investors extend the market neutral strategies and "equitize" the cash held in their portfolios; that is, they purchase common stock futures contracts (see Chapter 20), effectively creating stock market exposure equal to the value of their cash holdings. Their portfolio returns then become the return on the stock market plus the returns produced by their insights into attractive long and short stocks.

This equitization technique opens up a vast range of investment strategies that permit the market neutral investor to "transport" his or her skills to other markets (see the *Institutional Issues* section of Chapter 20 entitled "Transportable Alpha.") For example, consider a pension fund with an investment policy requiring investment of a portion of its assets in fixed-income securities. It could simply buy a portfolio of bonds to satisfy the policy guidelines. However, suppose that the pension fund had access to skillful market neutral stock managers. The pension fund could use those managers' investment talents, while at the same time purchasing Treasury bond futures contracts to give it the required fixed-income market exposure. Thus the pension fund's investment policy is satisfied and, if the market neutral managers are successful, then the pension fund profits from their skill as well. In essence, the pension fund has "transported" the market neutral stock managers' skills to the bond market.

Market neutral strategies offer no guarantee of success, and they are far from a "free lunch." They rely entirely on the stock selection abilities of the investor. As market neutral strategies usually involve high portfolio turnover (that is, high volume of buys and sells), a poor investor can generate substantial transaction costs (see Chapter 3) while adding no "alpha" or even producing negative "alpha" for the portfolio. Moreover, compared with traditional investment strategies, market neutral strategies usually involve higher management fees and they incur brokers' charges for borrowing securities.

In addition, while properly implemented market neutral strategies do not expose a portfolio to risk associated with stock market movements, they typically take on a considerable amount of risk associated with individual security price changes. Further, the mathematical models often used to ensure "market neutrality" may not always work to perfection, injecting another source of risk into the investment process.

Despite these caveats, market neutral strategies represent an intriguing combination of portfolio risk control and security selection. These strategies have been employed on a large scale for only a few years. Nevertheless they are making their influence felt as institutional investors examine the very essence of how value is added to their portfolios through active management.

that the ownership of 100 shares has changed hands, going from Ms. Poole to Brock, restoring Brock to its original position.

Cash Dividends

What happens when *XYZ* declares and subsequently pays a cash dividend to its stockholders? *Before the short sale*, Brock would receive a check for cash dividends on 100 shares of stock. After depositing this check in its own account at a bank, Brock would write a check for an identical amount and give it to Mr. Lane. Thus neither Brock nor Mr. Lane has been made worse off by having the shares held in street name. *After the short sale*, *XYZ* will see that the owner of those 100 shares is no longer Brock but is now Mr. Jones. Thus *XYZ* will now mail the dividend check to Mr. Jones, not to Brock. However, Mr. Lane will still be expecting his dividend check from Brock. Indeed, if there was a risk that he would not receive it, he would not have agreed to have his securities held in street name. Brock would like to mail him a check for the same amount of dividends that Mr. Jones received from *XYZ*—that is, for the amount of dividends that Mr. Lane would have received from *XYZ* had he held his stock in his own name. If Brock does mail Mr. Lane such a check, then it will be losing an amount of cash equal to the amount of dividends paid. What does Brock do to avoid incurring this loss? It makes Ms. Smith, the short seller, give it a check for an equivalent amount.

Consider all the parties involved in the short sale now. Mr. Lane is content because he has received his dividend check from his broker. Brock is content because its net cash outflow is still zero, just as it was before the short sale. Mr. Jones is content because he received his dividend check directly from *XYZ*. What about Ms. Smith? She should not be upset with having to reimburse Brock for the dividend check given by Brock to Mr. Lane, because the price of *XYZ*'s common stock can be expected to fall by an amount roughly equal to the cash dividend, thereby reducing the dollar value of her loan from Brock by an equivalent amount.

Financial Reports and Voting Rights

What about financial reports and voting rights? Before the short sale these were sent to Brock, who then forwarded them to Mr. Lane. After the short sale Brock will no longer be receiving them, so what happens? Financial reports are easily procured by brokerage firms free of charge, so Brock will probably get copies of them from *XYZ* and mail a copy to Mr. Lane. However, voting rights are different. These are limited to the registered stockholders (in this case Mr. Jones) and cannot be replicated in the manner of cash dividends by Ms. Smith, the short seller. Thus when voting rights are issued, the brokerage firm (Brock) will try to find voting rights to give to Mr. Lane if he asks for them. (Perhaps Brock owns shares, or manages a portfolio that owns shares of *XYZ*, and will give the voting rights from these shares to Mr. Lane.) Unless he is insistent, however, there is a chance that Mr. Lane will not get his voting rights once his shares have been borrowed and used in a short sale. In all other matters he will be treated just as if he were holding the shares of *XYZ* in his own name.

Initial Margin Requirement

As mentioned previously, a short sale involves a loan. Thus there is a risk that the borrower (in the example, Ms. Smith) will not repay the loan. What would happen in this situation? The brokerage firm would be left without the 100 shares that the short seller, Ms. Smith, owes the firm. Either the brokerage firm, Brock, is going to lose money or else the lender, Mr. Lane, is going to lose money. This loss is prevented by

TABLE 2.4	Investor's Balance Sheet after Short Sale		
Assets		**Liabilities and Net Worth**	
Cash proceeds of short sale	$10,000	Market value of short sold stock	$10,000
Initial margin	$ 6,000	Equity	$ 6,000
Total assets	$16,000	Total liabilities and net worth	$16,000

not giving the cash proceeds from the short sale, paid by Mr. Jones, to the short seller, Ms. Smith. Instead, they are held in her account with Brock until she repays her loan. Will holding the proceeds assure the brokerage firm that the loan will be repaid? No, unfortunately it will not.

In the example assume that the 100 shares of *XYZ* were sold at a price of $100 per share. In this case the proceeds of $10,000 from the short sale are held in Ms. Smith's account, but she is prohibited from withdrawing them until the loan is repaid. Now imagine that at some date after the short sale, *XYZ* stock rises by $20 per share. In this situation Ms. Smith owes Brock 100 shares of *XYZ* with a current market value of $12,000 (=100 shares × $120 per share), but she has only $10,000 in her account. If she skips town, Brock will have collateral of $10,000 (in cash) but a loan of $12,000, resulting in a loss of $2,000. How will Brock protect itself from experiencing losses from short sellers who do not repay their loans? By the use of margin requirements. In this example, Ms. Smith must not only leave the short sale proceeds with her broker, but she must also give her broker initial margin applied to the amount of the short sale.[20] If the initial margin requirement was 60%, she must give her broker $6,000 (=.6 × $10,000) in cash.[21]

Table 2.4 shows the investor's balance sheet immediately after the short sale. The investor's assets total $16,000, made up of the cash proceeds from the short sale and the initial margin. The investor has liabilities of $10,000 representing the market value of the short sold stock, leaving $6,000 in equity.

Actual and Maintenance Margin

In this example *XYZ* stock would have to rise in value to a price above $160 per share in order for Brock to be in jeopardy of not being repaid. Thus initial margin provides the brokerage firm with a certain degree of protection. However, this protection is not complete because it is not unheard of for stocks to rise in value by more than 60% [= ($160 − $100)/$100]. It is maintenance margin that protects the brokerage firm from losing money in such situations. In order to examine the use of maintenance margin in short sales, the actual margin in a short sale will be defined as:

$$\text{Actual margin} = \frac{(\text{short sale proceeds} + \text{initial margin}) - \text{loan}}{\text{loan}} \quad (2.2)$$

The numerator in Equation (2.2) is similar to the numerator for calculating actual margin for margin purchases, as shown in Equation (2.1); both represent the investor's equity. However, the denominator is different. For short sales it is equal to the current dollar value of the loan, whereas for margin purchases it is equal to the current market value of the assets held in the account.

In this example, if *XYZ* stock rises to $130 per share, the actual margin in Ms. Smith's account will be 23% {= [($100 × 100 shares) × (1 + .6) − ($130 × 100 shares)]/($130 × 100 shares) = $3,000/$13,000}. Assuming that the maintenance margin requirement is 30%, the account is undermargined, thereby causing Ms. Smith to receive a margin call. Just as with margin calls on margin purchases, she will be asked to put up more margin, meaning that she will be asked to add cash or securities to her account. If instead of rising the stock price falls, then the short seller can take a bit more than the drop in the price out of the account in the form of cash, because in this case the actual margin has risen above the initial margin requirement and the account is thus unrestricted.[22]

The foregoing discussed the cases for short sales in which the stock price either (1) fell and the account was thereby unrestricted or (2) went up to such a degree that the maintenance margin requirement was violated and the account was thereby undermargined. There is one more case left to be considered. This is the case in which the stock price goes up but not to such a degree that the maintenance margin requirement is violated. In this case the initial margin requirement has been violated, which means that the account is restricted. Here *restricted* has a meaning similar to its meaning for margin purchases; that is, any transaction that has the effect of further decreasing the actual margin in the account will be prohibited.

Table 2.5 shows possible margin account conditions in which the investor in *XYZ* stock might find himself or herself. In the example, *XYZ* stock has been sold short for $100 per share with initial margin and maintenance margin requirements of 60% and 30%, respectively. Three possible current prices for the stock are presented along with the resulting outcomes for the margin account and potential actions that the investor might take.

An interesting question is: What happens to the cash in the short seller's account? When the loan is repaid, the short seller will have access to the cash. (Actually, the cash is typically used to buy the shares that are needed to repay the loan.) Before the loan is repaid, however, the short seller may be able to earn interest on the portion of the cash balance that represents margin. (Brokerage firms will typically accept certain securities, such as Treasury bills, in lieu of cash for meeting margin requirements.)

In regard to the cash proceeds from the short sale, sometimes the securities may be borrowed only on the payment of a premium by the short seller, meaning that the short seller not only does not earn interest on the cash proceeds but must *pay a fee* for borrowing the shares. In contrast, when large institutional investors short sell stock, they typically negotiate a split with the brokerage firm of the interest earnings on the cash proceeds, thereby *receiving a fee*. However, securities are generally loaned "flat" to small investors; the brokerage firm keeps the cash proceeds from the short sale and enjoys the use of this money, and neither the short seller nor the lender receives any direct compensation. In this case the brokerage firm makes money not only from the commission paid by the short seller but also on the cash proceeds from the

TABLE 2.5	Potential Margin Account Conditions and Actions for Short Seller		
Short sale price = $100			
Initial margin requirement = 60%			
Maintenance margin requirement = 30%			
		Current Price	
	$130	$105	$90
Actual margin	.23	.52	.78
Condition	Undermargined	Restricted	Overmargined
Potential actions	1. Add cash or securities 2. Buy back stock to pay off part of short position	1. Do nothing	1. Do nothing 2. Withdraw excess cash

sale. (The brokerage firm may, for example, earn interest by purchasing Treasury bills with these proceeds.)

Rate of Return

The use of short selling results in rates of return to the investor that are of opposite sign to what would be earned if the shares were purchased on margin [ignoring interest on the margin loan and assuming that (1) the initial margin requirement for the short sale is met by depositing cash and (2) the short loan is flat]. Hence short sales also involve the use of financial leverage.

Consider XYZ once again, where Ms. Smith short sold its stock at a price of $100 per share. If she later repays the short loan when the stock is selling for $75 per share and just after XYZ has paid a $1 per share cash dividend, then her rate of return will equal 40% [= ($100 − $75 − $1)/(.6 × $100) = $24/$60]. In contrast, note that the return for someone who had purchased the stock of XYZ on margin would be equal to −40% [= ($75 + $1 − $100)/(.6 × $100) = −$24/$60], whereas the rate of return for someone who had purchased the stock without using margin would be equal to −24% [= ($75 + $1 − $100)/$100 = −$24/$100].

However, if Ms. Smith incorrectly predicted the future price movement of XYZ and it went up to $120 per share just after paying a $1 per share cash dividend, then her rate of return would equal −35% [= ($100 − $120 − $1)/(.6 × $100) = −$21/$60]. Conversely, if the stock had been purchased on margin, her rate of return would have been equal to 35% [= ($120 + $1 − 100)/(.6 × $100) = $21/$60]. Without margin, the rate of return on the stock would be equal to 21% [= ($120 + $1 − $100)/$100 = $21/$100].

What happens to these rate of return calculations if interest is earned on both the initial margin and on the short proceeds? The rate of return to the short seller increases. Consider the example in which XYZ fell to $75, and assume that the short seller earned 5% on the initial margin deposit and 4% on the short proceeds. In this case the return to the short seller would be equal to 51.7% {= [$100 − $75 − $1 + (.05 × .6 × $100) + (.04 × $100)]/(.6 × $100) = $31/$60}, which is notably higher than the 40% previously calculated. Hence financial leverage is even more apparent when either form of interest is paid to the short seller.

2.4.3 Securities Lending

In the example of Ms. Smith's short sale, Brock Inc. used Mr. Lane's shares of XYZ Company held in street name to facilitate the transaction. In some situations, a broker will not hold the security that a client wishes to sell short in its street name inventory. In that case, another method to obtain the securities for short selling is through **securities lending**. More than $250 billion of securities lending takes place annually. Three parties usually participate in a securities lending transaction: the lender, the lender's agent, and the borrower. Lenders usually are institutional investors, such as pension or endowment funds, which hold large portfolios of securities in the normal course of their investing activities. The lender's agent is usually a bank which acts as a custodian and record keeper for the lender. Finally, the borrower is a broker, which may be borrowing the securities on behalf of its clients.

Figure 2.2 displays the steps involved in securities lending. The lender, through its agent, makes available the desired securities to the borrower. The borrower, in turn, provides collateral for the loan, usually in the form of cash. The amount of collateral equals from 102% to 105% of the borrowed securities' market values and is adjusted daily on the basis of changes in these securities' values. The lender's agent

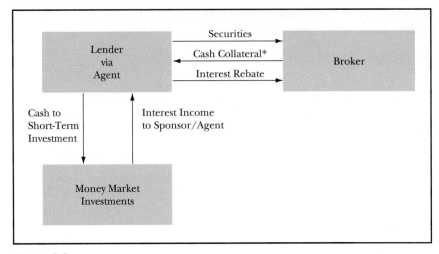

Figure 2.2
Securities Lending Process
* Noncash collateral (for example, bank letters of credit or government securities) may be used. In that case, the borrower pays a fee to the lender in lieu of the lender's investing cash.

invests the collateral in short-term fixed-income investments and rebates a portion of the interest earnings to the borrower. The retained portion represents securities lending income, which is shared by the lender and its agent. The percentage split between the rebated and retained portions depends on the supply and demand for the borrowed securities.

Legal ownership of borrowed securities passes to the borrower during a loan's life, although the lender continues to receive all dividend or interest income from the borrower. Such loans usually have no maturity date, although occasionally a fixed period of time such as a month may be attached to a loan agreement. In an open-ended loan, the lender has the right to cancel the loan at any time and demand return of the borrowed securities. In that case the lender's agent will search among its other clients' security holdings to find an identical security. If the agent is unsuccessful, the borrower must return the security to the lender.

2.4.4   Aggregation

An investor with a margin account may purchase several different securities on margin or may short sell several different securities. Alternatively, he or she may purchase some on margin and short sell others. The determination of whether an account is undermargined, restricted, or overmargined depends on the total activity in the account. For example, if one stock is undermargined and another is overmargined, then the overmargined stock can be used to offset the undermargined stock, provided that it is overmargined to a sufficiently large degree. How these multiple transactions are aggregated in one account in order to determine whether the account is undermargined, restricted, or overmargined on any given day will be shown next.

Multiple Margin Purchases

In the case of multiple margin purchases, aggregation is straightforward. The investor's balance sheet is restated by recalculating the market value of all the stocks held using current market prices. Here the "current market price" of any particular security usually means the price at which the last trade was made in the market involving that security on that day. Next the total amount of the investor's liabilities is carried over from the previous day because the amounts of the margin loans do not change from day to day. Equation (2.1) can then be used to recalculate the actual margin in the account.

Multiple Short Sales

In a similar manner, the actual margin of an investor who has short sold more than one stock can be determined. In this case, however, it is not the assets that are reevaluated every day as the account is marked to the market. Instead, it is the liabilities that are reevaluated on the basis of current market prices, because the short seller's liabilities are shares whose market values are changing every day. Once the dollar values of the liabilities are recalculated, the actual margin in the account can be determined using Equation (2.2).

Both Margin Purchases and Short Sales

The situation in which the investor has purchased some stocks, perhaps on margin, and has short sold others is more complicated than either of the situations just described. The reason is that the equation used to calculate actual margin for margin purchases, Equation (2.1), and the equation used to calculate actual margin for short sales, Equation (2.2), are different. This difference can be seen by simply noting what is in the denominator in each equation. For margin purchases the market value of the *assets* appears in the denominator; for short sales the market value of the *loan* appears in the denominator. If both kinds of transactions are appearing in the same account, neither equation can be used to calculate the overall actual margin in the account. However, the account can be analyzed in terms of the dollar amount of assets that are necessary for the account to meet the maintenance margin requirement, as illustrated in the following example.

Consider an investor who short sells 100 shares of Widget on July 1 at $50 per share and purchases 100 shares of *XYZ* on margin at $100 per share on July 15. The initial and maintenance margin requirements are 60% and 30%, respectively. Furthermore, assume that Widget is selling for $60 and *XYZ* for $80 per share on July 31. Table 2.6 shows the investor's balance sheet on that date. The investor's assets total $16,000, composed of *XYZ* stock, the cash proceeds from the short sale, and initial margin on the short sale. Liabilities are $10,000, composed of the market value of the short sold Widget stock, and the margin loan on *XYZ* stock, leaving $6,000 in equity.

In this situation the broker will require the investor to have assets of sufficient value to protect the short sale loan of Widget stock and the margin loan that was used to purchase *XYZ*. In general, the amount required as collateral against a short sale is equal to the current market value of the stock short sold times the quantity of 1 plus the maintenance margin requirement. For the short sale loan of Widget stock,

TABLE 2.6	Investor's Aggregate Balance Sheet As of July 31		
Assets		**Liabilities and Net Worth**	
XYZ stock	$ 8,000	Market value of short sold stock	$ 6,000
Cash proceeds of short sale	$ 5,000	Margin loan	$ 4,000
Initial margin on short sale	$ 3,000	Equity	$ 6,000
Total assets	$16,000	Total liabilities and net worth	$16,000

Hedge Funds

Hedge funds captured the attention of institutional investors and the financial press in the 1990s. During the extended bull market for financial assets, these organizations became synonymous with an aggressive, freewheeling investment style that produced some extraordinary successes and some spectacular failures.

Years ago, the classic hedge fund focused on buying and selling short stocks and bonds issued in U.S. markets. The term *hedge* came from the fact that much of the market exposure associated with owning stocks and bonds was offset by the corresponding short positions. These hedge funds were designed to make money regardless of the direction of the overall market, although in practice that objective was not always achieved. Leverage (that is, borrowed funds) was often used, but primarily to obtain the margin needed to sell short. Hedge funds were few in number, and participation was limited almost entirely to high-net-worth individuals.

Today, although hedge funds still use a combination of long and short positions, much else has changed, and generally these changes have been toward a more aggressive posture. Hedge funds now invest in a broad spectrum of securities around the globe, ranging from traditional stocks and bonds to options, futures, currencies, and commodities. Leverage is used to bolster profits by increasing the assets available for investment, in some cases by up to 20–30 times. The clientele has also changed, as has the number of funds available. Institutional investors now constitute the largest source of new monies entering hedge funds. It is estimated that more than $100 billion is now invested in over 3,000 hedge funds.

A new breed of hedge fund manager has also emerged. Whereas hedge funds used to attempt to profit largely from pricing discrepancies between individual securities, many hedge funds now seek to identify mispricings among whole asset classes. These "macro" hedge funds may take large bets that U.S. interest rates are going to fall or that the German mark is going to rise relative to the British pound. When correct, these macro bets can generate enormous returns for the funds, but they also run the risk of sizable losses. Macro hedge funds have been blamed for roiling the international financial markets with their aggressive speculation.

Hedge funds are usually organized as private partnerships. They avoid government regulation in one of two ways. Either they limit the number of partners to no more than 100 or they require investing individuals to own at least $5 million in financial assets and institutions to have more than $25 million under management. In either case, hedge funds are not allowed to promote themselves to the investing public. Consequently, they are not required to disclose performance results, expenses, or portfolio composition as are registered investment companies (see Chapter 21). Nor are they restricted in terms of diversification, so they can hold more-concentrated portfolios than can investment companies.

Performance (unadjusted for risk) has always been the name of the game for hedge funds. Hedge fund clients expect their managers to produce positive double-digit returns, regardless of the market environment. As one would expect in a highly efficient market (see Chapter 4), few hedge funds are able to

this amounts to $7,800 [=$6,000 $\times$ (1 + .3)], where .3 corresponds to the maintenance margin requirement.

The amount required as collateral against a margin purchase is, in general, equal to the dollar value of the margin loan divided by the quantity of 1 minus the maintenance margin requirement. For the cash loan to purchase *XYZ*, this amounts to $5,714 [=$4,000/(1 − .3)].

The total amount required in this example is thus $13,514 (=$7,800 + $5,714). The assets in the account are currently worth $16,000, so the investor will not receive a margin call. To see whether the account is restricted, repeat the previous calculations using the initial margin requirement of 60% instead of the maintenance margin requirement of 30%. For the Widget stock loan the amount required for the account to be unrestricted is $9,600 [=$6,000 $\times$ (1 + .6)]. The corresponding amount for the *XYZ* margin loan is $10,000 [=$4,000/(1 − .6)]. Summing these amounts gives a total of $19,600 (=$9,600 + $10,000), indicating that this account is restricted.

satisfy such lofty return expectations. Still, although comprehensive performance data are hard to come by, informally at least, returns of up to 120% in a good year and consistent annual returns of over 20% have been reported for successful funds. Unfortunately, "survivor bias" contaminates what aggregate performance data are available on hedge funds. That is, poorly performing funds simply close up shop, and their returns are expunged from consultants' databases, giving the impression of better overall performance than actually occurred.

Although some hedge funds pursue conservative, tightly risk-controlled strategies, in general, hedge fund investing is a highly risky proposition. Macro hedge funds in particular have produced highly variable results. Many such funds lost billions in 1994 betting that U.S. interest rates would fall and that the Japanese yen would decline relative to the U.S. dollar. The most infamous hedge fund collapse occurred in 1994 at a $600 million fund run by Askin Capital Management. In that debacle, investors (including several large sophisticated institutions) saw their holdings wiped out through the failure of a highly leveraged, mortgage derivatives strategy.

The lack of information about hedge funds' portfolios and performance results makes it difficult for investors to monitor their risks and evaluate results. Appropriate benchmarks (see Chapter 24) for most hedge funds are difficult to construct. Investors typically have very little understanding of how their hedge fund holdings fit with their other investments in a total portfolio context.

The unregulated nature of hedge funds and their increasing size has begun to draw the attention of regulators. Central banks, in particular, have become concerned about the impact of hedge funds on the stability of international financial markets. In the United States, as hedge funds have become more daring in their solicitations of potential clients, the Securities and Exchange Commission has started to question just how much leeway hedge funds should be allowed in promoting themselves. Whether hedge funds can continue to escape government supervision in the years ahead is unknown.

Still interested in investing in a hedge fund? Be sure to have substantial assets on hand. Initial investments are typically $500,000 and up. Fees range between 1% and 2% of assets under management, and the fund's general partners typically keep 20% of all fund profits. (Note, however, that the general partners do not similarly share in losses. Thus the incentive system is heavily skewed toward aggressive risk taking.) Withdrawals are usually restricted. Investors may have to commit funds for months or even years and afterward may be limited to quarterly or semiannual redemptions.

Despite these risks and limitations, institutional investors and high-net-worth individuals continue to pour money into hedge funds of various types. The lure of high returns is always tantalizing. Successful hedge fund managers, both past and present, are the stuff of Wall Street legend, including Michael Steinhardt, Julian Robertson, and George Soros, among others. Hedge funds provide an interesting study of the techniques of aggressive investment managers, a perspective one cannot usually find in more traditionally managed equity funds.

2.5 SUMMARY

1. Investors typically buy or sell securities through brokers who are compensated for their services with commissions.
2. When transacting in a security, investors must specify the following: the security's name, buy or sell, order size, time limit, and type of order.
3. The four standard types of orders are market, limit, stop, and stop limit. Market orders, followed by limit orders, are the most common types of orders.
4. Investors may purchase securities with cash or may borrow from brokerage firms to buy securities on margin.
5. Investors must make down payments on their margin purchases, maintain minimum levels of collateral in their margin accounts, and pay interest on margin loans.
6. If an investor's actual margin falls below the maintenance margin requirement, the investor's account is undermargined. The investor will receive a margin call and must increase the actual margin level in the account.

7. Buying on margin results in financial leverage, thereby magnifying (positively or negatively) the impact of a security's return on the investor's wealth.
8. Short sales involve the sale of securities that are not owned, but rather are borrowed by the sellers. The borrowed securities must ultimately be purchased in the market and returned to the lenders.
9. A short seller must deposit the proceeds of the short sale and initial margin with his or her broker. The short seller must also maintain a minimum actual margin level in his or her margin account or face a margin call.
10. For investors who purchase on margin or short sell several securities or do both, the determination of whether an account is undermargined, restricted, or overmargined depends on the aggregated activity in their accounts.

QUESTIONS AND PROBLEMS

1. Describe the conflict of interest that typically exists in the investment advisory relationship between a brokerage firm and its clients.
2. How many round lots and what odd lot size are in an order for 511 shares?
3. Discuss the advantages and disadvantages to the investor of the following:
   a. Market order
   b. Limit order
   c. Stop order
4. Why are margin account securities held in street name?
5. Lollypop Killefer purchases on margin 200 shares of Landfall Corporation stock at $75 per share. The initial margin requirement is 55%. Prepare Lollypop's balance sheet for this investment at the time of purchase.
6. Buck Ewing opened a margin account at a local brokerage firm. Buck's initial investment was to purchase 200 shares of Woodbury Corporation on margin at $40 per share. Buck borrowed $3,000 from a broker to complete the purchase.
   a. At the time of the purchase, what was the actual margin in Buck's account?
   b. If Woodbury stock subsequently rises in price to $60 per share, what is the actual margin in Buck's account?
   c. If Woodbury stock subsequently falls in price to $35 per share, what is the actual margin in Buck's account?
7. Distinguish between the initial margin requirement and the maintenance margin requirement.
8. Snooker Arnovich buys on margin 1,000 shares of Rockford Systems stock at $60 per share. The initial margin requirement is 50% and the maintenance margin requirement is 30%. If the Rockford stock falls to $50, will Snooker receive a margin call?
9. Cap Anson originally purchased 100 shares of Avalon Company's stock for $13 per share on margin. The initial margin requirement is 60% and the maintenance margin requirement is 35%. To what price must the stock fall for Cap to receive a margin call?
10. Lizzie Arlington has deposited $15,000 in a margin account with a brokerage firm. If the initial margin requirement is 50%, what is the maximum dollar amount of stock that Lizzie can purchase on margin?
11. Explain the purpose of the maintenance margin requirement.
12. Penny Bailey bought on margin 500 shares of South Beloit Inc. at $35 per share. The initial margin requirement was 45% and the annual interest on margin loans was 12%. Over the next year the stock rose to $40. What was Penny's return on investment?

13. Calculate Buck Ewing's rate of return in parts (b) and (c) of Problem 6 under the assumptions that the margin loan was outstanding for one year and carried an interest rate of 10% and that the prices of $60 and $35 were observed after one year during which the firm did not pay any cash dividends.

14. Ed Delahanty purchased 500 shares of Niagara Corporation stock on margin at the beginning of the year for $30 per share. The initial margin requirement was 55%. Ed paid 13% interest on the margin loan and never faced a margin call. Niagara paid dividends of $1 per share during the year.
    a. At the end of the year, if Ed sold the Niagara stock for $40 per share, what would Ed's rate of return be for the year?
    b. At the end of the year, if Ed sold the Niagara stock for $20 per share, what would Ed's rate of return be for the year?
    c. Recalculate your answers to parts (a) and (b) assuming that Ed made the Niagara stock purchase for cash instead of on margin.

15. Individual investors are sometimes contacted by their brokers and told that they have "unused buying power" in their brokerage accounts. What do the brokers mean by this statement?

16. Beauty Bancroft short sells 500 shares of Rockdale Manufacturing at $25 per share. The initial margin requirement is 50%. Prepare Beauty's balance sheet as of the time of the transaction.

17. Through a margin account, Candy Cummings short sells 200 shares of Madison Inc. stock for $50 per share. The initial margin requirement is 45%.
    a. If Madison stock subsequently rises to $58 per share, what is the actual margin in Candy's account?
    b. If Madison stock subsequently falls to $42 per share, what is the actual margin in Candy's account?

18. Dinty Barbare short sells 500 shares of Naperville Products at $45 per share. The initial margin and maintenance margin requirements are 55% and 35%, respectively. If Naperville stock rises to $50, will Dinty receive a margin call?

19. Willie Keeler short sold 300 shares of Sun Prairie Foods stock for $42 per share. The initial margin requirement is 50% and the maintenance margin requirement is 40%. To what price can the stock rise before Willie receives a margin call?

20. Eddie Gaedel is an inveterate short seller. Is it true that Eddie's potential losses are infinite? Why? Conversely, is it true that the maximum return that Eddie can earn on his investment is 100%? Why?

21. The stock of DeForest Inc. traded at the beginning of the year for $70 per share. At that time Deerfoot Barclay short sold 1,000 shares of the stock. The initial margin requirement was 50%. DeForest stock has risen to $75 at year-end, and Deerfoot faced no margin calls in the interim. Further, the stock paid a $2 dividend at year-end. What was Deerfoot's return on this investment?

22. Calculate Candy Cummings's rate of return in parts (a) and (b) of Problem 17, assuming that the short loan was flat but the initial margin deposit earned interest at a rate of 8% and that the prices of $58 and $42 were observed after one year during which the firm did not pay any dividends.

23. What aspects of short selling do brokerage houses typically find to be especially profitable?

24. Distinguish between an investor's receiving a margin call and having his or her margin account restricted.

25. Pooch Barnhart purchases 100 shares of Batavia Lumber Company stock on margin at $50 per share. Simultaneously, Pooch short sells 200 shares of Geneva Shelter stock at $20 per share. With an initial margin requirement of 60%:
    a. What is the initial equity (in dollars) in Pooch's account?

b. If Batavia and Geneva rise to $55 and $22 per share, respectively, what is Pooch's equity position (in dollars)?

26. On May 1, Ivy Olson sold short 100 shares of Minnetonka Minerals stock at $25 per share and bought on margin 200 shares of St. Louis Park Company stock for $40 per share. The initial margin requirement was 50%. On June 30, Minnetonka stock sold for $36 per share and St. Louis Park stock sold for $45 per share.

    a. Prepare a balance sheet showing the aggregate financial position on Ivy's margin account as of June 30.

    b. Determine whether Ivy's account is restricted as of June 30.

ENDNOTES

[1] For more on churning, see Seth C. Anderson, Sue L. Visscher, and Donald A. Winslow, "Guidelines for Detecting Churning in an Account," *AAII Journal* 11, no. 9 (October 1989): 12–14. Rewards in the brokerage business are heavily skewed toward those brokers who can generate the largest trading volumes from their customers. In general, brokers earn the greatest compensation by selling products affiliated with their employers.

[2] For more on opening an account, see Bruce Sanking, "The Brokerage Account Form: Handle with Care," *AAII Journal* 13, no. 6 (July 1991): 15–16.

[3] Occasionally, a round lot is for fewer than 100 shares. Most of these cases involve stocks that are either high-priced or traded infrequently.

[4] An example of a "special" type of order is a "market on close" order, which is executed at the close of trading at the best price available at the time.

[5] Stop buy orders can be used to lock in paper profits from what are known as short sales, which will be discussed later in this chapter.

[6] There are other types of accounts. Furthermore, an investor may have more than one type of account with a brokerage firm. An interesting variation is the "wrap" account (started in 1980 by E. F. Hutton & Co.) in which the broker, for an annual fee, helps the investor select an appropriate professional money manager. See Albert J. Golly Jr., "The Pros and Cons of Brokerage Wrap Accounts," *AAII Journal* 15, no. 2 (February 1993): 8–11.

[7] Investors with cash accounts may voluntarily elect to have their securities held in street name. Reasons offered for doing so include reduced risk of theft and improved record keeping. Typically the brokerage firm will send monthly statements detailing the investor's holdings. See J. Michael Bishop and Henry Sanchez Jr. "Reading and Understanding Brokerage Account Statements," *AAII Journal* 14, no. 10 (November 1992): 7–10.

[8] The investor may not receive the voting rights, particularly if the stock has been loaned to a short seller. This situation will be discussed later in this chapter.

[9] The investor whose securities are held in street name may be concerned about what would happen if the brokerage firm were to go bankrupt. In this case, the Securities Investor Protection Corporation (SIPC), a government-chartered firm that insures investors' accounts against brokerage firm failure, would step in and cover each individual investor's losses up to $500,000. Some brokerage firms have gone further and purchased private insurance in addition to the insurance offered by SIPC. See Henry Sanchez Jr., "SIPC: What Happens If Your Brokerage Firm Fails," *AAII Journal* 12, no. 10 (November 1990): 13–16.

[10] With either a cash or a margin account, the investor usually has up to three business days after an order is executed to provide the broker with the necessary cash. Accordingly, the third business day after execution is known as the **settlement date**. For margin purchases, the loan value of certain other securities can be used instead of cash as a down payment, in which case these securities must be provided by the settlement date. Sellers of securities must also provide their brokers with their securities by the settlement date. If requested, an investor may be able to get an extension of the settlement date.

[11] Regulation T covers credit extended by brokers and dealers; Regulation U covers credit extended by banks; Regulation G covers credit extended by anyone other than brokers, dealers, or banks; and Regulation X covers borrowers. All common stocks and convertible bonds that are listed on a national securities exchange (for example, the New York Stock Exchange,

the American Stock Exchange, or the National Market System of Nasdaq) can be purchased on margin. Furthermore, four times a year the Federal Reserve Board publishes a roster of other securities that can be purchased on margin. The determination of which firms are put on this roster is based on such factors as number of shareholders and firm size.

[12] Initial margin requirements on nonconvertible bonds are set in a similar fashion, except that the Federal Reserve Board is not involved. Typically the investor wishing to purchase non-convertible bonds on margin will face a much lower initial margin requirement (for example, 10% for purchases of U.S. Treasury securities).

[13] In general, at the end of each month the interest on the loan will be calculated and added to the amount of the loan. For ease of exposition, this fact is ignored in the examples given here.

[14] The broker may ask the investor to immediately (in some cases within three business days, in other cases even sooner) bring the actual margin up to a level corresponding to the maintenance margin requirement, or to a level that is even higher, ranging up to the initial margin requirement.

[15] Alternatively, the cash could be used as part of the initial margin requirement on an additional margin purchase by the investor. In fact, if it was large enough, it could be used to meet the entire requirement.

[16] There is an exception to this rule if the account was overmargined before it became restricted. In such a situation, the broker will create a special memorandum account for the investor; the balance in this account can be withdrawn in cash or used to purchase more securities.

[17] After purchasing a security, an investor is said to have established a *long position* in the security.

[18] A version of the up-tick rule, known as the Nasdaq Short Sale Rule, currently covers the larger stocks in the over-the-counter market. In this market, under the Nasdaq Short Sale Rule, short selling is prohibited at or below the current bid when that bid is lower than the previous different bid. Here the bids that are referred to are the "best bids," meaning the highest ones being quoted. This market will be discussed in Chapter 3.

[19] The New York Stock Exchange, the American Stock Exchange, and Nasdaq publish monthly lists of the **short interest** in their stocks. (Short interest refers to the number of shares of a given company that have been short sold where, as of a given date, the loan remains outstanding.) To be on the NYSE or AMEX list, either the total short interest must be equal to or greater than 100,000 shares or the change in the short interest from the previous month must be equal to or greater than 50,000 shares. The respective figures for Nasdaq are 50,000 and 25,000.

[20] Table 2.1 presents the initial margin requirement for short sales. Note that it has been set at the same level as for margin purchases of common stocks in the postwar period.

[21] There are other forms of collateral that can be substituted instead of cash.

[22] Alternatively, the short seller could short sell a second security and not have to put up all (or perhaps any) of the initial margin.

KEY TERMS

broker	day orders
account executives	open orders
registered representatives	good-till-canceled orders
regional brokerage firms	fill-or-kill orders
discount brokers	discretionary orders
commissions	market order
order specifications	limit order
round lot	limit price
odd lot	stop order

stop price   undermargined
stop limit order   margin call
cash account   unrestricted
margin account   overmargined
hypothecation agreement   restricted
street name   financial leverage
margin purchase   short sale
debit balance   up-tick rule
call money rate   plus-tick
initial margin requirement   zero-plus tick
actual margin   settlement date
marked to the market   short interest
maintenance margin requirement   securities lending

REFERENCES

1. For a discussion of the mechanics of purchasing and selling securities, along with margin purchasing and short selling, see:

   George Sofianos, "Margin Requirements on Equity Instruments," *Federal Reserve Bank of New York Quarterly Review* 13, no. 2 (Summer 1988): 47–60.

   DeWitt M. Foster, *The Stockbroker's Manual* (Miami: Pass, 1990). Copies can be obtained by calling (305) 270-2550.

   James J. Angel, "An Investor's Guide to Placing Stock Orders," *AAII Journal* 15, no. 4 (April 1993): 7–10.

   J. Randall Woolridge and Amy Dickinson, "Short Selling and Common Stock Prices," *Financial Analysts Journal* 50, no. 1 (January/February 1994): 20–28.

2. An interesting discussion of margin requirements and their impact on market volatility is contained in:

   David A. Hsieh and Merton H. Miller, "Margin Requirements and Market Volatility," *Journal of Finance* 45, no. 1 (March 1990): 3–29.

3. A recent study that examines levels and changes in short interest is:

   Averil Brent, Dale Morse, and E. Kay Stice, "Short Interest: Explanations and Tests," *Journal of Financial and Quantitative Analysis* 25, no. 2 (June 1990): 273–289.

4. Market neutral investment strategies are discussed in:

   Bruce I. Jacobs and Kenneth N. Levy, "Long/Short Equity Investing," *Journal of Portfolio Management* 20, no. 1 (Fall 1993): 52–63.

   Richard O. Michaud, "Are Long-Short Equity Strategies Superior?" *Financial Analysts Journal* 49, no. 6 (November/December 1993): 44–49.

   Bruce I. Jacobs and Kenneth N. Levy, "More on Long-Short Strategies," *Financial Analysts Journal* 51, no. 2 (March/April 1995): 88–90.

   Jess Lederman and Robert A. Klein (eds.), *Market Neutral* (Chicago: Irwin, 1996).

   Bruce I. Jacobs and Kenneth N. Levy, "20 Myths about Long-Short," *Financial Analysts Journal* 52, no. 5 (September/October 1996): 81–85.

   John S. Brush, "Comparisons and Combinations of Long and Long/Short Strategies," *Financial Analysts Journal* 53, no. 3 (May/June 1997): 81–89.

5. For a thorough description of the basic security lending concepts and mechanics, see:

   Paul C. Lipson, Bradley K. Sabel, and Frank Keane, "Securities Lending, Part 1: Basic Transactions and Participants," *Journal of Commercial Bank Lending* 20, no. 2 (February 1990): 4–18.

   Paul C. Lipson, Bradley K. Sabel, and Frank Keane, "Securities Lending, Part 2: Basic Transactions and Participants," *Journal of Commercial Bank Lending* 20, no. 3 (March 1990): 18–31.

SECURITY MARKETS

A **security market**, or **financial market**, can be defined as a mechanism for bringing together buyers and sellers of financial assets in order to facilitate trading. One of its main functions is "price discovery"—that is, to cause security prices to reflect currently available information. The more quickly and accurately price discovery is achieved, the more efficiently financial markets will direct capital to its most productive opportunities, thereby leading to greater improvement in public welfare. Secondary security markets involve the trading of financial assets that were issued at some previous point in time. This chapter is devoted to such markets. Chapter 16 discusses the initial issuance of securities in the primary security market.

3.1 CALL AND CONTINUOUS MARKETS

3.1.1 Call Markets

In **call markets**, trading is allowed only at certain specified times. In such a market, when a security is "called," those individuals who are interested in either buying or selling it are physically brought together.[1] At this point there may be an explicit auction in which prices are announced until the quantity demanded is as close as possible to the quantity supplied. Alternatively, orders may be left with a clerk, and periodically an official of the exchange will set a price that allows the maximum number of shares from the previously accumulated orders to be traded.

3.1.2 Continuous Markets

In **continuous markets**, trades may occur at any time. Although only investors are needed for such a market to operate, it generally would not be very effective without intermediaries also being present. In a continuous market without intermediaries, an investor who wanted to buy or sell a security quickly might have to either spend a great deal of money searching for a good offer or run the risk of accepting a poor one. Because orders from investors arrive more or less randomly, prices in such a market would vary considerably, depending on the flow of buy orders relative to the flow of sell orders. However, anyone willing to take temporary positions in securities could potentially make a profit by ironing out these transitory variations in supply and demand. This is the role of intermediaries known as dealers (also known as market-makers) and specialists. In the pursuit of personal gain, they generally reduce fluctuations in security prices that are unrelated to changes in value and in doing so provide **liquidity** (or marketability) for investors. Here *liquidity* refers to the ability of investors to convert securities into cash at a price that is similar to the price of the previous trade, assuming that no new information has arrived since the previous trade.

Secondary security markets for common stocks (as well as for certain other securities) in the United States typically involve dealers or specialists. The next topic in this chapter involves a detailed description of how these markets function and the role played by dealers and specialists. Whereas the focus is on markets for common stocks, many of the features of such markets are applicable to the markets for other types of financial assets (such as bonds). **Organized exchanges**, which are central physical locations where trading is done under a set of rules and regulations, will be discussed first. Examples of such exchanges for common stocks are the New York Stock Exchange, the American Stock Exchange, and various regional exchanges.

3.2 MAJOR MARKETS IN THE UNITED STATES

3.2.1 New York Stock Exchange

The New York Stock Exchange (NYSE) is a corporation that has 1,366 full members. It has a charter and a set of rules and regulations that govern its operation and the activities of its members. A board of 26 directors that is elected by the membership supervises the exchange. Of the directors, 12 are members and 12 are not; the latter are known as "public directors." The remaining two directors are full-time employees: a chairperson who also functions as the chief executive officer and a vice-chairperson who also functions as president.

In order to become a member, a person must purchase a **seat** (comparable to a membership card) from a current member.[2] By holding a seat, the member has the privilege of being able to execute trades using the facilities provided by the exchange. Because most trades of common stocks, in both dollar size and number of shares, take place on the NYSE, this privilege is valuable.[3] Not surprisingly, many brokerage firms are members, meaning that an officer (if the brokerage firm is a corporation) or a general partner (if the brokerage firm is a partnership) or an employee of the firm is a member. Indeed, many brokerage firms have more than one member. A brokerage firm with one or more NYSE memberships is often referred to as a **member firm**.

A stock that is available for trading on the NYSE is known as a **listed security**. In order for a company's stock to be listed, the company must apply to the NYSE. The initial application is usually informal and confidential. If approved, the company then makes a formal application that is announced publicly. Given an earlier approval on the informal application, approval at this stage is almost certain. The general criteria used by the NYSE in approving an application are:

- The degree of national interest in the company
- The company's relative position and stability in the industry
- Whether the company is engaged in an expanding industry, with prospects of at least maintaining its relative position[4]

Companies that are approved for listing must agree to pay a nominal annual fee and provide certain information to the public. After listing, if trading interest in a company's stock declines substantially, the NYSE may decide to **delist** the company, meaning that its stock is no longer available for trading on the exchange. Delisting

TABLE 3.1   New York Stock Exchange Criteria for Listing and Delisting a Security

(a) Initial Listing Requirements of the NYSE[a]

1. Either (a) the pretax income for the most recent year must be at least $2,500,000 and the pretax income over each of the preceding two years must be at least $2,000,000 or (b) the pretax income over the most recent three years must be at least $6,500,000 in total with a minimum of $4,500,000 in the most recent year, and all three years must have been profitable.

2. Net tangible assets must be worth at least $40,000,000.

3. There must be a least 1,100,000 shares outstanding that are publicly held, and these shares must have an aggregate market value of at least $40,000,000 (this amount is subject to periodic adjustment based on market conditions).

4. There must be either (a) at least 2,000 stockholders who each own a minimum of 100 shares or (b) at least 2,200 stockholders with the monthly trading volume averaging at least 100,000 shares over the most recent six months or (c) at least 500 stockholders with monthly trading volume averaging at least 1,000,000 shares over the most recent 12 months.

(b) NYSE Conditions for Delisting a Security[b]

1. The number of stockholders that each own at least 100 shares falls below 1,200.

2. The number of shares that are publicly held falls below 600,000.

3. The aggregate market value of publicly held shares falls below $8,000,000 (this amount is subject to periodic adjustment based on market conditions).

Source: Adapted from *Fact Book 1996 Data*, (New York Stock Exchange, 1997).

[a] In general, all these requirements must be met for initial listing.

[b] Normally a security will be considered for delisting if any one of these conditions occur. However, under certain circumstances a security may be delisted even though none of the conditions occur.

also occurs when a listed company is acquired by another company or is merged into another company, since the originally listed company no longer exists in such situations. A company may also voluntarily ask to have its stock delisted even though it is still eligible for listing, but in order to do so the company must first acquire approval from its audit committee and a majority of its directors, according to NYSE Rule 500. Having secured approval, the company must notify its shareholders and wait 45–60 days in order to allow them to react by, for example, asking the board to reconsider its decision.

Table 3.1 shows the specific criteria that are used by the NYSE to determine whether to list or delist a stock. Because companies may apply for listing on more than one exchange, the NYSE has some companies listed on it that are also listed on either other U.S. exchanges or on foreign exchanges. Typically, those companies that are listed on other U.S. exchanges are U.S. companies and those listed on foreign exchanges are foreign companies. In addition, under certain conditions an exchange may set up "unlisted trading privileges" for transactions in a stock already listed on another exchange.

Trading Halts and Circuitbreakers

Whereas delisting refers to the permanent suspension of exchange trading for a particular firm's shares, occassionally the need arises for a **trading halt**, which is a temporary suspension of trading in a firm's shares. Trading halts typically are issued by the NYSE when trading in a stock is roiled because of rumors or a recent news announcement (such as a rumor of a takeover attempt or an announcement of unexpected low quarterly earnings). The opening of trading can be delayed for similar reasons or if a large imbalance of orders has accumulated since the previous close.

The NYSE also has the ability to temporarily halt trading simultaneously in all its listed stocks (or a large number of them). This is done automatically by the use of **circuitbreakers** when circumstances indicate that there is a need to reduce market volatility and to promote investor confidence. Under Rule 80A, whenever the Dow Jones Industrial Average moves 50 or more points from the previous day's close, all subsequent index arbitrage orders (a form of program trading discussed in Chapter 20) involving the 500 stocks in the Standard & Poors 500 Stock Index are subject to a tick test. (Both of these widely quoted indices are discussed in Chapter 24; a *tick* is the standard unit in which prices are quoted, current 1/16th of a dollar on the NYSE.) The NYSE defines an index arbitrage order as an order simultaneously involving at least 15 stocks with an aggregate market value of at least $1 million. The tick test means that in a down market, the sell orders can be executed only on either a plus tick (for a price higher than that of the previous trade) or a zero-plus tick (for a price equal to that of the previous trade but higher than that of the last trade at a different price); in an up market, the buy orders can be executed only on either a **minus tick** (for a price lower than that of the previous trade) or a **zero-minus tick** (for a price equal to that of the previous trade but lower than that of the last trade at a different price).[5]

Under Rule 80B, as revised in April 1998, if the Dow Jones Industrial Average (DJIA) declines by 10% in a day before 2 P.M. Eastern time, the NYSE shuts down for one hour (if the decline occurs after 2:30 P.M., then the market is not shut down; if it occurs between 2:00 and 2:30, then the market is closed for 30 minutes). If the market continues to decline after it reopens so that its aggregate decline that day is at least 20% and occurs by 1:00 P.M. Eastern time, then the market closes for two hours. (If the decline occurs after 2:00 P.M., then the market is closed for the rest of the day; if it occurs between 1:00 P.M. and 2:00 P.M., then the market is closed for one hour.) If the market continues to decline after it reopens, so that its aggregate decline that day reaches 30%, then the market shuts down for the rest of the day.[6]

In summary, the current trigger points and market reactions for the Rule 80B circuitbreaker are:

DJIA Trigger	When Reached	Reaction
10% decline	Before 2:00 P.M.	One-hour halt
20% decline	Before 1:00 P.M.	Two-hour halt
30% decline	Any time	Closed for rest of day

These trigger points are converted into points at the beginning of each quarter based on the average closing price of the DJIA during the last month of the previous quarter, and are rounded to the nearest 50 points. Thus, if in June the average closing price of the DJIA was 8900, then the trigger points for the July–August–September quarter would be 900 (note 10% of 8900 is 890), 1800 (note that 20% of 8900 is 1780), and 2650 (note that 30% of 8900 is 2670).

A 50-point move in the Dow Jones Industrial Average implies less than a 1% change in its value. As a result, Rule 80A is frequently triggered. Whether the rule actually reduces market volatility, as its originators intended, is open to considerable debate. The much larger intraday price decline implied by Rule 80B has occurred only once since the rule's inception. On October 27, 1997, the Dow plunged 554.25 points (7.2%). Under Rule 80B's provisions at that time, a one-half hour shutdown was triggered, followed quickly thereafter by a one hour shutdown. Because the last trading halt took place at 3:30 P.M., the NYSE closed for the rest of the day. The next day the Dow rose 337 points. Critics claimed that the existence of the circuitbreakers actually destabilized the market. They argued that after the first trading halt, investors rushed to submit sell orders to beat the anticipated next shutdown, thereby accelerating the market's decline. Despite recent changes in Rule 80B, many market participants continue to call for elimination or substantial restructuring of the circuitbreakers.

New York Stock Exchange Members

Members in the NYSE fall into one of four categories, depending on the type of trading activity in which they engage. These categories are commission brokers, floor brokers, floor traders, and specialists. Of the 1,366 members of the NYSE, roughly 700 are commission brokers, 400 are specialists, 225 are floor brokers, and 41 are floor traders. The trading activities of members in these categories are as follows:

1. Commission brokers. These members take orders that customers have placed with their respective brokerage firms and see to it that those orders are executed on the exchange. The brokerage firms that they work for are paid commissions by the customers for their services.

2. Floor brokers, also known as two-dollar brokers. These members assist commission brokers when there are too many orders flowing into the market for the commission brokers to handle alone. For their assistance, they receive part of the commission paid by the customer. (Sometimes floor brokers, as defined here, are lumped together with commission brokers and together are called floor brokers.)

3. Floor traders. These members trade solely for themselves and are prohibited by exchange rules from handling public orders. They hope to make money by taking advantage of perceived trading imbalances that result in temporary mispricings, thereby allowing them to "buy low and sell high." These members are also known as registered competitive market-makers, competitive traders, or registered traders.

4. Specialists. These members perform two roles. First, any limit order that the commission broker cannot execute immediately because the current market price is not at or better than the specified limit price will be left with the specialist for possible execution in the future. If this order is subsequently executed, the specialist is paid part of the customer's commission. The specialist keeps these orders in what is known as the **limit order book** (or specialist's book). Stop and stop limit orders are also left with the specialist, who then enters them in the same book. In this capacity the specialist is acting as a broker (that is, agent) for the customer's broker and can be thought of as a "broker's broker."

Second, the specialist acts as a **dealer**, or **market-maker**, in certain stocks (in particular, for the same stocks in which he or she acts as a broker). This means that the specialist buys and sells certain stocks for his or her own account and is allowed to seek a profit in doing so. However, in acting as a dealer, the specialist is required by the NYSE to maintain a "fair and orderly market" in those stocks in which he or she is registered as a specialist. Thus the NYSE expects the specialist to buy or sell shares from his or her own account when there is a temporary imbalance between the number of buy and sell orders. (In doing so, specialists are allowed to short sell their assigned stocks, but they still must abide by the up-tick rule.) Even though the NYSE monitors the trading activities of the specialists, this requirement is so ill-defined that it is difficult, if not impossible, to enforce.

As might be inferred from the preceding discussion, specialists are at the center of the trading activity on the NYSE. Each stock that is listed on the NYSE currently has one specialist assigned to it.[7] (In a few instances in the past, two or more specialists were assigned to the same stock.) There are almost 3,000 common stocks listed on the NYSE and only about 400 specialists. As those numbers suggest, each specialist is assigned more than one stock.

All orders involving a given stock must be taken physically or electronically to a **trading post**, a spot on the floor of the NYSE where the specialist for that stock stands at all times during the hours the NYSE is open.[8] It is here that an order is either executed or left with the specialist.

Placing a Market Order

The operation of the New York Stock Exchange is best described by an example. Mr. B asks his broker for the current price of General Motors (GM) shares. The broker punches a few buttons on a PC-like quotation machine and finds that the current **bid** and **asked prices** on the NYSE are as favorable as the prices available on any other market, being equal to \$61 and \$61-$\frac{1}{4}$, respectively. In addition, the quotation machine indicates that these bid and asked prices are good for orders of at least 100 and 500 shares, respectively. This means that the NYSE specialist is willing to buy at least 100 shares of GM at a price of \$61 (the bid price) and is willing to sell at least 500 shares of GM at \$61-$\frac{1}{4}$ (the asked price).[9] After being given this information, Mr. B instructs his broker to "buy 300 at market," meaning that he wishes to place a market order with his broker for 300 shares of GM. At this point the broker transmits the order to his or her firm's New York headquarters, where the order is subsequently relayed to the brokerage firm's "booth" on the side of the exchange floor. Upon receiving the order, the firm's commission broker goes to the trading post for GM.

The existence of a standing order to buy at \$61 means that no lower price need be accepted, and the existence of a standing order to sell at \$61-$\frac{1}{4}$ means that no higher price need be paid. All that is left for possible negotiation is the spread between the two prices. If Mr. B is lucky, another broker (for example, one with a market order to sell 300 shares for Ms. S) will "take" the order at a price "between the quotes," here at \$61-$\frac{1}{8}$, resulting in "price improvement." (This happens often, as about one-third of the volume in NYSE-listed stocks is traded between the bid and asked quotes.) Information will be exchanged between the two brokers and the sale made. Figure 3.1 illustrates the procedure used to fill Mr. B's order.

If the gap between the quoted bid and asked prices is wide enough, an auction may occur among various commission brokers, with sales made at one or more prices between the specialist's quoted values. This auction is known as a **double** (or two-way) **auction**, because both buyers and sellers are participating in the bidding process.

What if no response came forth from the floor when Mr. B's order arrived? In such a case the specialist would "take the other side," selling 300 shares to Mr. B's broker at a price of \$61-$\frac{1}{4}$ per share. The actual seller might be the specialist or another investor whose limit order is being executed by the specialist. Sometimes the specialist will "stop" the order, meaning that the order will not be immediately filled but that the specialist will guarantee that a price that is no worse than his or her quote will be obtained for the investor before the day is over. Often such orders are later filled at prices that are better than the quotes that were posted at the time the order was initially received. It is also possible that the specialist will take the other side at \$61-$\frac{1}{8}$ for strategic reasons even though the quote is \$61-$\frac{1}{4}$. (Sometimes a specialist wants an order to be recorded at a specific price at a given time; for example, a trade at \$61-$\frac{1}{8}$ would make it subsequently easier to execute a short order under the up-tick rule than if the trade were executed at \$61-$\frac{1}{4}$.)

If the bid-ask spread on a stock is no larger than the standard unit in which prices are quoted (typically $\frac{1}{16}$ of a point, or 6.25 cents, on the NYSE), market orders are generally executed directly by the specialist at the prevailing quote because there is little room for price improvement. In the previous example, if the specialist had quoted bid and asked prices of \$61 and \$61-$\frac{1}{16}$, then there would have been little incentive for Mr. B's commission broker to try to obtain a better price for the purchase order than \$61-$\frac{1}{16}$, because any seller could have obtained a price of \$61 from the specialist. That is, to entice someone other than the specialist to sell GM to Mr. B, his com-

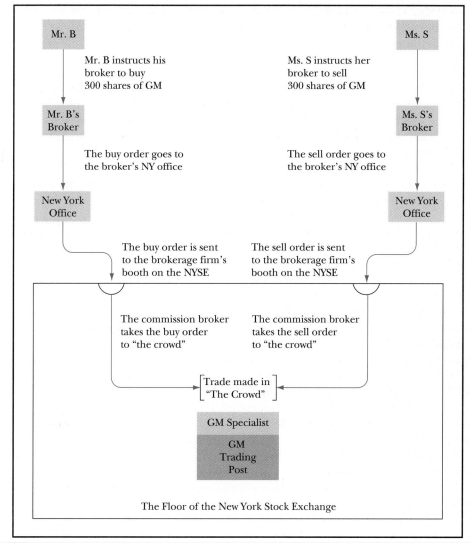

Figure 3.1
Order Flow for a NYSE-Listed Security

mission broker would have to offer a better price than $61—the price the seller could obtain from the specialist. Given that the next highest price is $61-\frac{1}{16}$, and that the specialist is willing to sell at that price, Mr. B's commission broker will typically deal with the specialist at the specialist's bid quote rather than deal with "the crowd." (In some instances, the specialist will provide price improvement in $\frac{1}{16}$-point markets— perhaps for strategic reasons—by executing the trade at the opposite side quote, which is $61 in the example.[10])

Placing a Limit Order

So far the discussion has been concerned with what would happen to a market order that was placed by Mr. B. What if Mr. B placed a limit order instead of a market order? Consider a buy limit order in which the specialist is quoting GM at $61 bid and $61-\frac{1}{4}$ asked with order quantities of 100 and 500 shares, respectively (the concepts to be illustrated also apply, but in reverse, for a sell order). Three possible situations exist; the limit price associated with a limit buy can be:

- At or above the asked price of $61-\frac{1}{4}$, or
- Below the asked price of $61-\frac{1}{4}$ but at or above the bid price of $61, or
- Below the bid price of $61.

The first case involves a "marketable limit order," meaning that the limit price is not a constraint given the existing bid and asked price quotations. Hence, it will be handled just like a market order because the specialist is willing to fill the order at a price that is at least as favorable as the limit price. For example, a limit buy of 300 shares at $62 would be filled immediately by the specialist at $61-\frac{1}{4}$ (or perhaps at an even better price by someone in "the crowd.")

In the second case, in which the specialist is quoting prices of $61 and $61-\frac{1}{4}$, assume that Mr. B has placed a limit order with his broker to buy 300 shares of GM at a limit price of $61-\frac{1}{8}$ (or $61). When this order is carried to the trading post, the commission broker could execute it for the limit price of $61-\frac{1}{8}$ if someone in the crowd (or even the specialist) were willing to take the other side of the transaction. After all, anyone with a sell order can transact with the specialist at the specialist's price of $61. To these people, the limit price of $61-\frac{1}{8}$ looks more attractive, because it represents a higher selling price to them. Thus they would prefer doing business with Mr. B's commission broker rather than with the specialist. However, if nobody is willing to trade with Mr. B's commission broker, then his order is recorded in the limit order book by the specialist within 30 seconds of receipt and the bid quote is increased from $61 to $61-\frac{1}{8}$. (If the limit buy order had a limit price matching the specialist's bid of $61, then the quote would now be good for not 100 but 400 shares.)

In the third case, assume that Mr. B has placed a limit order to buy 300 shares of GM with a limit price of $60. When this order is carried to the trading post, the commission broker will not even attempt to fill it, because the limit price is below the specialist's current bid price. That is, because anyone with a sell order can deal with the specialist at a price of $61, there is no chance that anyone will want to sell to Mr. B for the lower limit price of $60. Thus the order will be given to the specialist to be entered in the limit order book for possible execution in the future. (As in the second case, any limit orders that cannot be immediately executed must be entered by the specialist in the book within 30 seconds of receipt.) Limit orders in the book are executed in order of price. For example, all purchase orders with limit prices of $60-\frac{1}{2}$ will be executed before Mr. B's order is executed. If there are several limit orders in the book at the same price, they are executed in order of time of arrival (that is, first in first out). Furthermore, public limit orders take priority over the specialist's order if they are at the same price.

It may not be possible to fill an entire order at a single price. For example, a broker with a market order to buy 500 shares might obtain 300 shares at $61-\frac{1}{8}$ and have to pay $61-\frac{1}{4}$ for the remaining 200. Similarly, a limit order to buy 500 shares at $61-\frac{1}{8}$ or better might result in the purchase of 300 shares at $61-\frac{1}{8}$ and the entry of a limit order in the specialist's book for the other 200 shares.

Large and Small Orders

The NYSE has developed special procedures to handle both routine small orders and exceptionally large orders. In 1976 the NYSE developed an electronic system known as Designated Order Turnaround (or DOT) to handle small orders, defined at that time as market orders involving 199 or fewer shares and limit orders involving 100 or fewer shares. Subsequent developments led to DOT's being replaced by a procedure known as the **Super Designated Order Turnaround** system (or Super-DOT), which now accepts market orders involving 30,999 or fewer shares and limit orders involving 99,999 or fewer shares. In order to use SuperDOT, the member firm must be a participating subscriber. With this system, the New York office of the customer's brokerage firm can send the customer's order directly to the specialist, whereupon it will be exposed to the crowd and executed immediately (if possible), with a confirmation of the execution sent to the brokerage firm. Although SuperDOT usually sends relatively small market orders directly to the specialist for execution, it has been programmed to send certain other orders directly to the firm's floor brokers for execution.[11] In deciding where to send the order, SuperDOT looks at such things as order size and type of order. For example, market orders and limit orders whose limit price is far from the current quotes of the specialist would be sent directly to the specialist. Each member firm sets the parameters that it wants SuperDOT to use in making such decisions.

SuperDOT has greatly facilitated the execution of "basket" trades (a form of "program trading"), in which a member firm submits orders in a number of securities all at once. Before SuperDOT, brokers from member firms would carry trade tickets with preprinted amounts that were to be used if the firm suddenly launched a basket trade. These tickets had to be brought by hand to the appropriate trading posts for execution. With SuperDOT, all trades in a basket can be sent simultaneously to the various trading posts on the floor for immediate execution.

Exceptionally large orders, which are known as **blocks**, are generally defined as orders involving at least 10,000 shares or $200,000, whichever is smaller. Typically, these orders are placed by institutional customers and may be handled in a variety of ways. One way of handling a block order is to take it directly to the specialist and negotiate a price for it. However, if the block is large enough, it is quite likely that the specialist will lower the bid price (for sell orders) or raise the asked price (for buy orders) by a substantial amount. This change will be made because specialists are prohibited by the exchange from soliciting offsetting orders from the public and, thus, do not know how easily they can obtain an offsetting order. Even with these disadvantages, this procedure is used on occasion, generally for relatively small blocks, and is referred to as a **specialist block purchase** or **specialist block sale**, depending on whether the institution is selling or buying shares.[12]

Larger blocks can be handled by the use of an **exchange distribution** (for sell orders) or **exchange acquisition** (for buy orders). Here a brokerage firm attempts to execute the order by finding enough offsetting orders from its customers. The block seller or buyer pays all brokerage costs, and the trade price is within the current bid and asked prices as quoted by the specialist. A similar procedure, known as a **special offering** (for sell orders) or a **special bid** (for buy orders), involves letting all brokerage firms solicit offsetting orders from their customers.

Another way of selling blocks is to conduct a **secondary distribution**, in which the shares are sold off the exchange after the close of trading in a manner similar to the sale of new issues of common stock. The exchange must give approval for such distributions and usually does so if it appears that the block could not be absorbed easily in normal trading on the exchange. Accordingly, secondary distributions generally involve the sale of exceptionally large blocks.

Whereas all of these methods of handling block orders are used at one time or another, most block orders are handled in what is known as the **upstairs dealer market**. By using **block houses**, which are set up to deal with large orders, institutions have been able to get better prices for their orders. A block house, when informed that an institution wants to place a block order, will proceed to line up trading partners (including itself) to take the other side of the order. Once the trading partners have been identified, the block house will attempt to reach a mutually acceptable price with the original institution. If such a price is reached, the order will be "crossed" on the floor of the exchange, meaning that the specialist will be given the opportunity to fill any limit orders that are in the specialist's book at the block's selling price.[13] (If such a price is not reached, the institution can take the order to a different block house.) However, there is a limit on the number of shares (1,000 shares or 5% of the size of the block, whichever is greater) that can be taken by the specialist to fill these limit orders.

For example, suppose that the PF Pension Fund informs a block house that it wishes to sell 20,000 shares of General Motors common stock. The block house then proceeds to find three institutional investors that want to buy, say, 5,000 shares apiece; the block house decides that it too will buy 5,000 shares of GM from PF. Noting that the buyers have said that they would be willing to pay $70 per share, the block house subsequently informs PF that it will buy the 20,000 shares for $69.75 each, less a commission of $8,000. If PF accepts the deal, the block house now becomes the owner of the shares but must first "cross" them on the NYSE because the block house is a member of the exchange. In this example assume that when the block is crossed at $69.75, the specialist buys 500 shares at this price for a limit order that is in his or her book. After the cross, the block house gives 5,000 shares to each of the institutional buyers in exchange for $350,000 (=5,000 shares × $70 per share) and hopes that the remaining 4,500 shares that it now owns can be sold in the near future at a favorable price. Needless to say, the possibility of not being able to sell them at a favorable price is one of the risks involved in operating a block house.

3.2.2 Other Exchanges

Table 3.2 shows the total trading volume of the securities listed on each of the active stock exchanges in the United States in 1996. Not surprisingly, the New York Stock Exchange dominates the list. Second in importance is the American Stock Exchange (AMEX), which lists shares of somewhat smaller companies of national interest (a few of which are also listed on the New York Stock Exchange). All the others are termed **regional exchanges**, because historically each served as the sole location for trading

TABLE 3.2	Trading Volume of the Stock Exchanges				
(a) 1996 Trading Volume					
	Shares (millions)		**Dollars (millions)**		
	Annual	**Daily**	**Annual**	**Daily**	
NYSE	104,636	412	$4,063,655	$15,999	
AMEX	5,627	22	91,330	360	
Regionals	9,794	39	380,345	1,497	
Nasdaq	138,112	544	3,301,777	12,999	
Third market	7,486	29	290,727	1,145	

(b) Five-Year Comparison						
	NYSE			**Nasdaq**		
Year	**Number of Companies**	**Number of Issues**	**Daily Share Volume (millions)**	**Number of Companies**	**Number of Issues**	**Daily Share Volume (millions)**
1996	2,907	3,285	412	5,556	6,384	544
1995	2,675	3,126	346	5,122	5,955	401
1994	2,570	3,060	291	4,902	5,761	295
1993	2,361	2,904	265	4,611	5,393	263
1992	2,088	2,658	202	4,113	4,764	191

Source: Adapted from *Fact Book: 1996 Data* (New York Stock Exchange, 1997) and *The Nasdaq Stock Market 1997 Fact Book and Company Directory* (National Association of Security Dealers, 1997).

securities primarily of interest to investors in its region. However, the major regional exchanges now depend to a substantial extent on transactions in securities that are also listed on a national exchange. Interestingly, the regional exchanges are now larger, in aggregate, than the AMEX. There are five major regional exchanges currently in existence—the Boston, Cincinnati, Chicago, Pacific, and Philadelphia exchanges—and they all use procedures similar to those of the New York Stock Exchange. The role of specialists and the extent of automation may differ slightly, but the approach is basically the same.

Options exchanges and futures exchanges utilize some procedures that differ significantly from those employed by stock exchanges. Futures exchanges often have daily price limits instead of having specialists with directions to maintain "fair and orderly markets." The Chicago Board Options Exchange separates the two functions of the specialist: An order book official is charged with the maintenance of the book of limit orders, and one or more registered market-makers are assigned the role of dealer. These exchanges will be discussed in more detail in Chapters 19 and 20.

3.2.3 Over-the-Counter Market

In the early days of the United States, banks acted as the primary dealers for stocks and bonds, and investors literally bought and sold securities "over the counter" at the banks. Transactions are more impersonal now, but the designation remains in use for transactions that are not executed on an organized exchange but, instead, involve the use of a dealer. Most bonds are sold over the counter, as are the securities of small (and some not so small) companies.

Nasdaq

The over-the-counter (OTC) market for stocks is highly automated. In 1971 the **National Association of Securities Dealers** (NASD), which serves as a self-regulating agency for its members, put into operation the **National Association of Securities Dealers Automated Quotations** system (Nasdaq). This nationwide communications network allows brokers to know instantly the terms currently offered by all major dealers in securities covered by the system.

Dealers who subscribe to Level III of Nasdaq are given terminals with which to enter bid and asked prices for any stock in which they "make a market." Such dealers must be prepared to execute trades for at least one "normal unit of trading" (depending on the security, this can be as large as 1,000 shares) at the prices quoted. As soon as a bid or an asked price is entered for a security, it is placed in a central computer file and may be seen by other subscribers (including other dealers) on their own terminals. When new quotations are entered, they replace the dealer's former prices.

When there is competition among dealers, those who are not well informed either price themselves out of the market by having too wide a bid-ask spread, or go out of business after incurring heavy losses.[14] In the first situation, nobody does business with such a dealer, because there are better prices available with other dealers. The second situation occurs when the dealer accumulates a large inventory at too high a price or disposes of inventory at too low a price. Thus the dealer will be doing the opposite of the familiar advice of "buy low, sell high."

It is argued that the interests of investors are best served by a market in which multiple dealers with unlimited access to all sources of information compete with one another, thereby leading to narrow bid-ask spreads around the "intrinsic" value of the security that provide investors with the "best" prices. However, organized exchanges counter with the argument that their system produces the "best" prices because all orders are sent to a central location for execution where they can be matched and bid on. Whereas trades in the over-the-counter market take place at the "best" quoted prices, the exchanges note that, although they have only one source of quoted prices (from the specialist), trades can (and often do) take place "inside" these prices. Thus, the exchanges argue that, unlike Nasdaq, they provide investors with the chance for "price improvement."

Most brokerage firms subscribe to Level II of Nasdaq for their trading rooms, obtaining terminals that can display the current quotations on any security in the system. All bid and asked quotations are displayed, with the dealer offering each quotation being identified, so that orders can be routed to the dealer with the best price. Imagine how difficult it would be to get the best price for a customer in the absence of such a terminal (as was the case before Nasdaq existed). A broker would have to contact dealers one by one to try to find the best price. After determining what appeared to be the best price, the broker would then proceed to contact that dealer again. However, by the time the dealer was contacted, the price might have gone up or down and the previously quoted price might no longer be the best one.

Level I of Nasdaq is used by individual account executives to get a feel for the market. It shows the **inside quotes**, meaning the highest bid and the lowest asked price for each security, along with last-sale reports and market summary data. Sometimes the inside quotes are known as the **NBBO**, an abbreviation for "national best bid or offer." (**Offer price** is often used instead of *asked price* in reference to the price at which dealers are willing to sell, or "offer," a specific security.)

Nasdaq classifies stocks with larger trading volumes (which also meet certain other requirements) as belonging to the **National Market System** (Nasdaq/NMS). Every transaction made by a dealer for such a stock is reported directly, providing up-to-date detailed trading information to Nasdaq users. Furthermore, any stock included in Nasdaq/NMS is automatically eligible for margin purchases and short selling. Less active issues belong to the **Small Cap Issues** (Nasdaq Small Cap) section of Nasdaq; these issues generally are automatically "phased into" the National Market System when they meet the higher listing standards of NMS. For these issues, dealers report only the total transactions at the close of each day, and only certain ones are eligible for margin purchases and short sales. (The Federal Reserve Board determines which ones are eligible four times a year.)

As its name indicates, Nasdaq is primarily a quotation system. The price paid by a customer buying shares is likely to be higher than the amount paid by the broker to procure the shares, with the difference being known as a **markup** when the broker's firm is acting as a principal (that is, the broker's firm is also a dealer who sells the shares out of inventory). Conversely, when selling shares, the customer receives a price less than that received by the broker, with the difference being known as a **markdown** when the broker's firm is acting as a principal. However, if the broker's firm is acting as an agent, meaning the broker is executing the order with a dealer who works for a different firm, then the customer will be charged a commission. The sizes of these markups, markdowns, and commissions are examined periodically by the Securities and Exchange Commission to see that they are "reasonable."

To be included in Nasdaq, a security must have at least two registered market-makers (that is, dealers) and a minimum number of publicly held shares. Moreover, the issuing firm must meet stated capital and asset requirements. As shown in Table 3.2, at the end of 1996, 6,384 issues were included in the system.[15] Although this total is more than double the total for the NYSE, trading volume is less than that of the NYSE, especially when measured in dollars.

SOES

During the market crash of October 19, 1987, many investors who placed orders involving Nasdaq stocks were unable to receive execution because their brokers were unable to get in touch by telephone with the appropriate dealers. As a result, NASD established the **Small Order Execution System (SOES)**, an electronic order-routing system in which all Nasdaq dealers must participate. With SOES, brokers can electronically route a customer's order to the appropriate dealer for quick execution and confirmation. Large orders are typically not handled through SOES, as dealers are required only to accept orders as large as 1,000 shares. (Currently, the limit is 100 shares for 50 large Nasdaq/NMS stocks but 1,000, 500, and 200 shares for the remainder of the Nasdaq stocks, depending on trading volume, number of dealers, and best bid price.) Instead, most large orders involving Nasdaq stocks are handled by negotiation over the telephone with one of the dealers.

OTC Bulletin Board and Pink Sheets Stocks

The Nasdaq system covers only a portion of the outstanding OTC stocks. Brokers with orders to buy or sell other OTC securities rely on quotations that are published daily either on Nasdaq's OTC Bulletin Board or in what are known as **Pink Sheets** (there are also less formal communication networks) in order to obtain "best execution" for their clients. The OTC Bulletin Board is essentially an electronic quotation forum run by Nasdaq, where brokers and dealers can find current price quotes, trading data, and a list of market-makers in several thousand securities. Although companies that are on the Bulletin Board typically cannot meet Nasdaq's listing standards (they still must meet some less-demanding standards), they must file quarterly financial statements with the SEC, banking, or insurance regulators (such filing was made mandatory only in late 1997). Pink Sheets are published daily by the National Quotation Bureau, an organization unaffiliated with Nasdaq. They also contain dealer quotations in thousands of unlisted stocks but, unlike the OTC Bulletin Board, they do not contain any trading data. Trading in both OTC Bulletin Board and Pink Sheet stocks takes place over the phone rather than electronically.

3.2.4 Third and Fourth Markets

Until the 1970s the New York Stock Exchange required its member firms to trade all NYSE-listed stocks at the exchange and to charge fixed commissions. For large institutions, meeting this requirement was expensive. In particular, the existence of a required minimum commission rate created a serious problem, because it exceeded the marginal cost of arranging large trades. Brokerage firms that were not members of the exchange faced no restrictions on the commissions they could charge and thus could compete effectively for large trades in NYSE-listed stocks. Such transactions were said to take place in the **third market**. More generally, the term *third market* now refers to the trading of any exchange-listed security in the over-the-counter market. The existence of such a market is enhanced by the fact that its trading hours are not fixed (unlike exchanges) and sometimes it can continue to trade securities even when trading is halted on an exchange. As can be seen in Table 3.2, on average, 29 million shares were traded in the third market during each day of 1996.

Instinet and SelectNet

Many institutions have dispensed with brokers and exchanges altogether for transactions in exchange-listed stocks and other securities. Trades of this type, in which the buyer and seller deal directly with each other, are sometimes said to take place in the **fourth market**. In the United States some of these transactions are facilitated by an automated computer communications system called **Instinet**, which provides quotations and execution automatically.[16] A subscriber can enter a limit order in the computerized "book," where it can be seen by other subscribers who can, in turn, signal their desire to take it. Whenever two orders are matched, the system automatically records the transaction and sets up the paperwork for its completion. Subscribers can also use the system to find likely partners for a trade, then conduct negotiations by telephone. This facility grew in popularity because it allowed institutions to trade securities inside the bid-ask quotes established by dealers. Interestingly, many dealers trade through either Instinet, or a dealer-only computer network called Select-Net, in order to cheaply manage their inventories while at the same time maintaining standard bid-ask quotes for their customers. In order to enhance the competitiveness of dealers' quoted prices, since 1997 orders posted on Instinet and SelectNet have also been made available to the public.

Crossing Systems

In recent years automated electronic facilities have been developed to permit institutional investors to trade *portfolios* of stocks, rather than individual securities, directly with each other. The two largest such systems are POSIT and the Crossing Network. They are discussed in this chapter's *Institutional Issues: Crossing Systems*.

Some large investment managers maintain their own internal crossing systems. These managers invest billions of dollars for many institutional clients. On any given day, some clients will be withdrawing funds from such a manager and other clients will be contributing funds. The manager simply exchanges the contributing client's cash for shares from the withdrawing client, with the shares typically valued at closing market prices on the day of the "cross." A nominal commission is charged to handle the transactions.

3.2.5 Preferencing

Preferencing is a practice that can be thought of as taking orders and sending them for execution along a predetermined route. More specifically, whenever a preferencing broker receives an order involving a particular stock, he or she has a standing arrangement with a dealer to send the order to him or her for execution.

Payment for Order Flow

Payment for order flow refers to the practice of preferencing in which a dealer pays cash to a broker in order to have that broker's order flow sent to the dealer for execution. If Ms. Beyer places an order to buy 100 shares of Widget with her broker, the broker will send the order to Acme Brokerage for execution, provided there is a preexisting arrangement with Acme to preference all orders involving Widget to Acme. How does this arrangement benefit Ms. Beyer's broker? The broker will receive a cash payment for the order of, generally, about $.01 or $.02 per share. This amount may seem small, but when aggregated over many orders it can accumulate to a sizable sum.

Payment for order flow can be thought of as *paid-for* preferencing.[17] Often when listed securities are involved, the order is executed on a regional exchange (Cincinnati, Boston, and Chicago are popular ones for preferencing). When Ms. Beyer's order to buy 100 shares of Widget is sent to Acme for execution, her broker will receive $1 from Acme because of their payment-for-order-flow arrangement. In return, Acme will check the NYSE quotes in order to determine the current ask and then will execute the order from its own inventory at that price on, for example, the Cincinnati Stock Exchange. Alternatively, if Widget is listed on Nasdaq instead of the NYSE, then Acme will execute the order at the inside quote (that is, the lowest ask).

Given that the bid and asked prices are competitively set, one might wonder how Acme can afford to pay for order flow. The answer can be found in the Glosten-Milgrom adverse selection model, which will be presented shortly. For the moment, note that preferenced orders usually are small retail orders, and the dealer has little worry about transacting with informed traders who might possess valuable information about the particular stocks being bought or sold. By "cream skimming" these low-risk orders, Acme can afford to pay for order flow, as the current bid-ask spread more than compensates it for the risk involved. Acme can settle for a lower net spread (that is, the spread after payment for order flow) than the spread being quoted on the NYSE (or Nasdaq) and still make money.

Internalization

Until 1976 NYSE member firms were prohibited by Rule 394 from either acting as dealers in the third market or executing orders involving NYSE-listed securities for their customers in the third market. In 1976 Rule 394 was replaced by Rule 390, which permits the execution of orders for NYSE-listed stocks in the third market but still prohibits member firms from acting as dealers in the third market. In 1979 the Securities and Exchange Commission issued Rule 19c-3, permitting member firms to act as dealers in securities that became listed on the NYSE after April 26, 1979. This rule has lead to the practice of **internalization**, in which broker-dealers who are NYSE members take their customers' orders in 19c-3 stocks and fill them internally instead of sending them to an exchange floor for execution. Internalization can also involve broker-dealers who are not NYSE members and who can execute their customers' orders in any NYSE-listed stock internally. Furthermore, Nasdaq stocks can be internalized when customers' orders are filled by a brokerage firm in its dual role as a dealer instead of sending the trades to other dealers. Thus, internalization can be thought of as *preferencing orders to oneself* since the orders never make it out of the customer's brokerage firm for execution.[18]

Controversy still exists over Rules 394 and 19c-3. Some people argue that they should be abolished completely to spur competition between the NYSE and the over-the-counter market. Others argue that having all orders funneled to the NYSE will lead to the most competitive marketplace possible.

Criticisms of Preferencing

Laws concerning best execution require the dealer who receives a preferenced order to at least match the best price that is currently being publicly quoted. Nevertheless, critics of preferencing contend that the customer may still be disadvantaged. If the order were taken to the exchange floor instead of being preferenced, the trade might be executed within the specialist's quotes. However, because the dealer executes a preferenced order at the current market quotes, no opportunity exists for the customer to benefit from price improvement.

There is a potential social cost to preferencing as well. A preferenced order contributes nothing to the process of price discovery; that is, the incorporation of new and valuable information about a security into its price. It is the interplay of market participants that leads to price discovery. Brokers seeking the best prices for their orders determine the supply and demand functions, and ultimately the market-

Crossing Systems: Evolution of the Fourth Market

Scientists define the evolution of a species as its gradual adoption of features that facilitate its long-term survival. In this context it is fitting to refer to the evolution of the fourth market. From its rudimentary beginnings, the fourth market has evolved into a sophisticated trading mechanism in which millions of shares change hands daily. Furthermore, the fourth market is posing a threat to existing species, in this case the organized security exchanges. How this competition plays out will influence the nature of trading well into the twenty-first century.

The fourth market, where large institutional investors deal directly with one another, began as a response to the high commission rates charged by brokerage firms. As discussed in the text, the original fourth market trading mechanism, run by Instinet, allows investors to trade with each other through an automated communications system at commissions that were originally only a small fraction of those charged by brokers.

However, this trading process (which is still very much alive and well) has significant limitations. Investors submit buy or sell limit orders (see Chapter 2) on individual securities at irregular times. If an interested investor on the "other side" of the trade happens to access the system at the right time, the trade may be completed. Although the commission costs of trading on the original fourth market are quite low (about $.03 to $.04 per share), the odds of being able to complete large trades in numerous securities are small. What was needed was a system to allow institutional investors to trade entire portfolios instead of individual stocks. The fourth market evolved to accommodate this need through a mechanism generically known as a "crossing system." Several electronic crossing systems now conduct regular market sessions in which investors may submit large packages of securities for trade. More specifically, current crossing systems work as follows:

1. Periodic trading sessions are established and widely announced.

2. Before these trading sessions, investors anonymously submit lists of stocks they wish to buy or sell and the associated quantities.
3. At scheduled times during the day, the lists of desired trades are compared automatically by computer.
4. Trade prices are based on current market prices as set on the organized security exchanges or the OTC market.
5. Offsetting buys and sells are matched. When buy orders do not equal sell orders for a security, matches are allocated on the basis of the total dollar value of trades entered by each investor. Thus investors are encouraged to submit large trading volume requests.
6. Investors are notified of the completed trades, and the system handles the transfer of stocks.
7. Unmatched trades are returned to the investors for resubmission or execution elsewhere.

Crossing systems offer investors several key advantages over traditional trading methods. First, they provide anonymity. Investors' identities or intentions are not revealed, making it extremely difficult for other investors or market-makers to strategize against them. Second, as discussed, investors can trade entire portfolios at one time instead of individual securities on a piecemeal basis. Third, and most important, crossing networks are low-cost portfolio trading mechanisms.

The primary users of crossing networks are institutional investors with no urgent need to trade. Index funds (see chapter 23), for example, trade only to adjust their portfolios so as to track the performance of a specific market index most effectively. Whether they trade this morning or this afternoon usually has little bearing on their results. Therefore, transaction costs are their primary concern. Crossing systems charge only $.01 to $.02 per share (as opposed to the $.03 to $.12 charged to institutional investors by brokerage firms). Furthermore, because trades are carried out at prevailing market prices, crossing systems

clearing price, for a particular security. (Price discovery is further discussed in Chapter 4). A preferencing broker, however, plays a purely passive role, letting others set the security's price. The situation is somewhat analogous to voting in an election. Each individual's vote, by itself, has little meaning. In aggregate, however, all the votes cast determine the election's outcome. A nonvoter passively accepts this outcome, without adding his or her opinion to the contest.

permit investors to avoid both the costs associated with the bid-ask spread as well as the price impacts (discussed later in this chapter) of their trades.

Crossing systems present some serious disadvantages as well. They do not offer liquidity in many stocks. Investors may not be able to complete trades in certain securities even after days of submitting those securities to the crossing networks. This problem is particularly acute for smaller-capitalization OTC stocks. In addition, the crossing systems require a certain amount of technological sophistication. Investors must submit trades computer to computer. Trading packages must be readied for entry at the appropriate times, and arrangements must be made for handling trades that cannot be completed through the crossing systems.

Currently, the two largest crossing systems are POSIT (run by Investment Technology Group) and the Crossing Network (run by Instinet). The two systems work under the same basic procedures described earlier, although there are differences. For example, the Crossing Network conducts one session daily, in the early evening on the basis of NYSE closing market prices. POSIT, on the other hand, conducts six daily crosses, three in the morning [with one of those devoted solely to trades in a type of foreign security known as American Depositary Receipts (see Chapter 25)] and three in the afternoon, based on prices prevailing in the market at the time of the crosses.

When both began operations in 1987, their trading volumes were insignificant. In subsequent years, however, volumes have increased. In 1996, more than 10 million shares a day on average changed hands through the crossing systems. (POSIT's trading volume was roughly twice that of the Crossing Network.) Although this figure translates into only about 2% of the New York Stock Exchange's daily volume, the potential for the crossing systems' long-term growth has created concern among members of the organized exchanges and OTC dealers.

The success of POSIT and the Crossing Network prompted several brokerage firms to attempt their own crossing operations. The NYSE has also entered the fray with two after-hours crossing systems. However, none of these organizations have been able to attract anywhere near the volume achieved by the original crossing systems. Trading systems tend to be natural monopolies. Traders loathe fragmented markets, which reduce their chances of finding the other side. Instead they prefer that trading be concentrated in a small number of markets, thereby enhancing liquidity. The NYSE dominates the continuous auction market. POSIT and the Crossing Network (and perhaps eventually only one of them) dominate the crossing system market.

Many institutional investors have become sophisticated users of alternative trading mechanisms. For example, just after the NYSE's opening, an investor might send limit orders for a large set of stocks via the SuperDOT system (see this chapter) for immediate execution. The investor shortly thereafter withdraws uncompleted orders and submits them to POSIT for late morning and early afternoon crosses. Orders still unfilled are placed on the Crossing Network for that evening's session. Finally, the investor directs any orders still outstanding through traditional broker networks the next day.

The trading mechanisms available to institutional investors continue to grow as their per unit trading costs continue to fall. Crossing systems have played an important role in these declining costs. Crossing systems are beginning to conduct global operations. Given that transaction costs on foreign markets are usually many times greater than they are in the United States, the room for crossing system growth in those markets appears enormous. Opportunities for growth also exist in the retail market, where investors typically pay much higher commission costs than do institutional investors. Brokers may eventually bundle their clients' trades and submit them through the crossing systems, thus saving commissions and allowing trades within the dealers' spreads rather than at the bid or asked prices. Inexorably, the evolution of the fourth market continues.

3.2.6 Foreign Markets

The two largest stock markets in the world outside New York are located in London and Tokyo. Both of these markets have recently undergone major changes in their rules and operating procedures. Furthermore, both of them have active markets in foreign securities. In particular, at the end of 1996 the London Stock Exchange listed 533 foreign companies (in addition to 2,171 U.K. and Irish companies), and the Tokyo Stock Exchange listed 63 foreign stocks (in addition to 1,805 Japanese stocks).

Also of interest is the Toronto Stock Exchange, which by market value of securities listed is the fifth largest foreign stock market in the world (after Tokyo, London, Paris, and Frankfurt, according to the *Tokyo Stock Exchange 1993 Fact Book*, p. 83). Its electronic trading system has been adopted by many foreign markets, either directly (by Paris) or indirectly (by Tokyo). At the end of 1996 the Toronto Stock Exchange listed 1,626 stocks, about 100 of which were foreign stocks.

London

In October 1986 the "Big Bang" introduced several major reforms to the London Stock Exchange. Fixed brokerage commissions were eliminated, membership was opened up to corporations, and foreign firms were allowed to purchase existing member firms. Furthermore, an automated dealer quotation system similar to Nasdaq was introduced. This system, known as **SEAQ** (Stock Exchange Automated Quotations), involves competing market-makers whose quotes are displayed over a computer network. Small orders can be executed by using **SAEF** (SEAQ Automated Execution Facility), which functions like Nasdaq's SOES; large orders are handled over the telephone. Limit orders are not handled centrally but instead are handled by individual brokers or dealers who note when prices have moved sufficiently that they can be executed.

The London Stock Exchange's reforms have proved highly successful. The exchange has attracted trading in many non-U.K. stocks, thereby enhancing its status as the dominant European stock market. Even the U.S. stock markets have felt the competition. In an attempt to recapture some of the lost trading in U.S. securities from the London Stock Exchange, the NASD received approval from the SEC for a computer system like Nasdaq, which involves trading of many of the stocks listed on either the NYSE, AMEX, or Nasdaq/NMS. This system, known as **Nasdaq International**, opens for trading six hours before the NYSE, which corresponds to the opening time of the London Stock Exchange, and closes a half-hour before the NYSE opens.

Tokyo

Similar to the London Stock Exchange, the Tokyo Stock Exchange has recently experienced major reforms. **CORES** (Computer-assisted Order Routing and Execution System), a computer system for trading all but the 150 most active securities, was introduced in 1982. Then in 1986 the exchange began to admit foreign firms as members, and in 1990 **FORES** (Floor Order Routing and Execution System) was introduced as a computer system to facilitate trading in the most active stocks.

Interestingly, the system of trading both the most active and the relatively less active securities is quite different from any system found in either the United States or the United Kingdom. It is centered on members known as *saitori* who act, in a sense, as auctioneers in that they are neither dealers nor specialists. Instead they are intermediaries who accept orders from member firms and are not allowed to trade in any stocks for their own account.

At the opening of the exchange (because the exchange is open from 9 A.M. to 11 A.M. and from 12:30 P.M. to 3 P.M., there are two openings each day) the *saitori* members follow a method called *itayose*, which operates like a call market in that the *saitori* seeks to set a single price so that the amount of trading is maximized (subject to certain constraints). Setting the price effectively involves constructing supply and demand schedules for the market and limit orders that have been received and noting where the two schedules intersect. (How this is done is described and illustrated in Chapter 4.) After the opening of the exchange, the *saitori* follows a method known as *zaraba*, wherein orders are processed continually as they are received; that is, market orders are offset against previously unfilled limit orders. New limit orders are filled, if possible, against previously unfilled limit orders. New limit orders that cannot be filled are entered in the limit order book for possible future execution. Unlike the limit order book on the NYSE, the limit order book in Tokyo is available for inspection by member firms. Furthermore, unlike the NYSE, the Tokyo Stock Exchange prohibits trading at prices outside a given range based on the previous day's closing price. Hence there can be situations in which trading in a stock ceases until the next day (when the price range is readjusted) unless two parties decide to trade within the current range.

Toronto

In 1977 the Toronto Stock Exchange began to use **CATS** (Computer-Assisted Trading System) on a trial basis with 30 stocks. Two years later CATS was expanded to cover about 700 stocks and was made permanent. All other listed stocks were traded in a specialist-driven system like the one in New York. However, the success of CATS led to more and more stocks being included so that, now, all listed stocks are traded on it. Furthermore, CATS now utilizes decimal pricing; stocks priced above $5 trade in $.05 increments and those priced below $5 trade in $.01 increments.

With CATS, orders are entered electronically in brokers' offices and then routed to a computer file. This computer file displays limit orders against which other investors may trade. Market orders are matched against the limit order with the best price that is in the file (that is, a market order to buy is matched against the lowest priced limit order to sell, and a market order to sell is matched against the highest priced limit order to buy). If insufficient volume is available in the file at the best price, the remainder of the market order is then put in the file as a limit order at that price. However, brokers, responding to the wishes of the investor, can change this price at any time.

At the daily opening CATS uses a different procedure. Like *itayose* in Tokyo, CATS sets an opening price so as to maximize the number of shares that are traded. Although both market and limit orders are accepted, there are constraints on the size of each market order, and these orders must be from the public (meaning that member firms are not allowed to submit opening market orders).

3.3 INFORMATION-MOTIVATED AND LIQUIDITY-MOTIVATED TRADERS

Perhaps the single major concern of a dealer is the adverse consequences he or she experiences as a result of buying or selling from an informed trader. When a trader approaches a dealer, the dealer cannot tell whether the trader knows something about the stock that he or she does not know. That is, the dealer cannot tell whether the trader has an information advantage. However, the dealer understands that if the trader is informed, then it is likely that any information will soon be disseminated that is good news for the stock if the informed trader bought it and is bad news if the informed trader sold it.

For example, assume that the bid and asked quotes for Widget are $20 and $21 and an informed trader (remember that at this point the dealer does not know whether the trader is informed) arrives and sells 1,000 shares to the dealer at $20. Typically, a negative piece of information about the company will be released shortly thereafter that will cause the dealer to lower his or her quotes to, say, $18 and $19. Thus, the dealer has just bought 1,000 shares for $20 but now is offering and likely will sell them for $19, a potential loss of $1,000. (In this example it is also assumed that the dealer cannot quote an asked price of $20 because there are other dealers who would undercut him or her at that price.) Conversely, if an informed trader arrives and buys 1,000 shares at $21, typically there will be a positive piece of information announced shortly thereafter that will cause the dealer to raise his or her quotes to, say, $22 and $23, resulting in an opportunity loss of $1,000. In both of these cases, the dealer has been "picked off" by informed traders, losing money in the process.

So how does the dealer earn a profit? By transacting with uninformed traders, because their trades are not consistently followed by news of any particular type. After an uninformed trader buys 1,000 shares when the quotes are $20 and $21, it is equally possible that good or bad information (if any) about the stock will be released. The dealer, on average, will not be adversely affected by transacting with an uninformed trader. Consequently, the dealer will set a spread so that his or her expected losses from dealing with informed traders equals his or her expected gains from dealing with uninformed traders. In the language of financial economists, the dealer copes with this *adverse selection problem* by setting a spread so that the losses from trading with *information-motivated traders* are offset by the gains from trading with *liquidity-motivated traders* (so called because they either have excess cash to invest in stocks or else need cash and hence sell stocks to raise it).[19]

The Glosten-Milgrom adverse selection model illustrates just how the spread is set. Imagine that the dealer believes there is a 40% probability that Widget stock is worth $10 and a 60% probability that it is worth $20. Hence, its expected value is $16 [=(.4 × $10) + (.6 × $20)]. Furthermore, 10% of all traders are information-motivated in that they know what the stock is worth (they know whether it is worth $10 or $20), while the remaining 90% are not information-motivated. The dealer must set his or her asked price A at a level that will ensure that expected losses equal expected gains:

$$.1 \times .6 \times (\$20 - A) = .9 \times .5 \times (A - \$16)$$

or

$$A = \$16.47$$

The left-hand side of this equation shows that there is a 10% chance that an information-motivated trader will arrive and a 60% chance that he or she will buy. The loss on the trade with such an investor is $20 − A, so the expected loss with an asked price of $16.47 is $.21 [=.1 × .6 × ($20 − $16.47)]. On the right-hand side, there is a 90% chance that a liquidity-motivated trader will show up, and a 50% chance that he or she will buy. The gain on the trade with this investor is A − $16, so the expected gain with an ask price of $16.47 is $.21 [=.9 × .5 × ($16.47 − $16)]. Thus, the $.21 expected loss from selling to an information-motivated trader is exactly offset by the $.21 expected gain from selling to a liquidity-motivated trader when the asked price is set at $16.47.

Similarly, the bid price B is set so that the expected losses from buying from the information-motivated investor equals the expected gains from buying from the liquidity-motivated trader:

$$.1 \times .4 \times (B - \$10) = .9 \times .5 \times (\$16 - B)$$

or

$$B = \$15.51$$

Thus, the spread is $16.47–$15.51, or $.96. If it is wider, the dealer will not get any business because of competition from other dealers (or will get business on just one side—either buying a lot of shares or selling a lot of shares). If it is narrower, then the dealer will likely be put out of business by too many losses from transacting with information-motivated traders.[20] Although this model does not explicitly provide for the dealer's making a profit, that feature is easily accommodated by simply expanding the $.96 spread by an amount sufficient for the dealer to cover costs and earn a reasonable profit on his or her investment in inventory. However, competition among dealers will continue to limit the size of the spread and, hence, profits.

One feature of this model is that the larger the proportion of informed traders, the larger the spread. For example, in the above example if that proportion is 20% instead on 10%, then the asked and bid prices will be $16.92 and $15.00, respectively, for a spread of $1.92 instead of $.96. Intuitively, this makes sense because there is now a greater likelihood that the dealer will be "picked off" by an informed trader.

3.4   CENTRAL MARKET

The Securities Acts Amendments of 1975 mandated that the U.S. Securities and Exchange Commission move as rapidly as possible toward the implementation of a truly nationwide competitive central security market:

> The linking of all markets for qualified securities through communication and data processing facilities will foster efficiency, enhance competition, increase the information available to brokers, dealers, and investors, facilitate the offsetting of investors' orders, and contribute to best execution of such orders.[21]

Implementation of these objectives has proceeded in steps. In 1975 a **consolidated tape** began to report trades in stocks listed on the New York and American stock exchanges that took place on the two exchanges, on major regional exchanges, in the over-the-counter market using the Nasdaq system, and in the fourth market using the Instinet system. Since 1976 this information has been used to produce the **composite stock price tables** published in the daily press.

The second step involved the setting of commissions charged to investors by brokerage firms that are members of the NYSE. Before 1975 the NYSE required its members to charge all investors the same commission for a given order. However, as a result of the Securities Acts Amendments of 1975, this system of fixed commissions was abolished and all brokerage firms were free to set their commissions at whatever level they desired.

The next step involved quotations. To obtain the best possible terms for a client, a broker must know the prices currently available on all major markets. To facilitate this objective, the Securities and Exchange Commission instructed stock exchanges to make their quotations available for use in the **Consolidated Quotations System** (CQS). With the implementation of this system in 1978, bid and asked prices (along with the corresponding volume limits) were made more accessible to subscribers to quotation services. Increasingly a broker is able to rely on electronics to determine the best available terms for a trade, thus avoiding the need for extensive "shopping around."

In 1978 the **Intermarket Trading System** (ITS) was inaugurated. This electronic communications network links eight exchanges (NYSE, AMEX, the Boston, Cincinnati, Chicago, Pacific, and Philadelphia stock exchanges, and the Chicago Board Options Exchange) and certain over-the-counter security dealers, thereby enabling commission and floor brokers, specialists, and dealers at various locations to interact with one another. Intermarket Trading System display monitors provide the bid and asked prices quoted by market-makers (these quotes are obtained from CQS), and the system allows the commission and floor brokers, specialists, and dealers to route orders electronically to where the best price exists at that moment. However, the market-maker providing the best price may withdraw it on receipt of an order. Another drawback is that the customer's broker is not required to route the order to the market-maker providing the best price. At the end of 1996, according to the NYSE *Fact Book 1996 Data* (p. 28), 4,001 exchange-listed stocks were included on the system, and daily trading volume averaged 12.7 million shares.

In 1996 the SEC passed a series of initiatives known as order handling rules. Among other things, these rules required that (1) the NASD establish a central limit order book for investors and (2) quotations posted on electronic communication networks (ECNs) be made available to all investors; previously, ECNs such as Instinet and SelectNet had made their quotations available to only certain investors such as institutions or dealers.

3.5   CLEARING PROCEDURES

Most stocks are sold the "regular way," which requires delivery of certificates within three business days. On rare occasions a sale may be made as a "cash" transaction, requiring delivery the same day, or as a "seller's option," giving the seller the choice of any delivery day within a specified period (typically, no more than 60 days). On other occasions extensions to the three-day time limit are granted.

It would be extremely inefficient if every security transaction had to end with a physical transfer of stock certificates from the seller to the buyer. A brokerage firm might sell 500 shares of AT&T stock for one client, Mr. S, and later that day buy 500 shares for Ms. B, another client. Mr. S's 500 shares could be delivered to his buyer, and Ms. B's shares could be obtained by accepting delivery from her seller. However, it would be much easier to transfer Mr. S's shares to Ms. B and instruct Ms. B's seller to deliver 500 shares directly to Mr. S's buyer. This route would be especially helpful if the brokerage firm's clients, Mr. S and Ms. B, held their securities in street name. Then the 500 shares would not have to be moved and their ownership would not have to be changed on the books of AT&T.

The process can be facilitated even more by a **clearinghouse**, the members of which are brokerage firms, banks, and other financial institutions. Records of transactions made by members during the day are sent there shortly afterward. At the end of the day, both sides of the trades are verified for consistency, then all transactions are netted out. Each member receives a list of the net amounts of securities to be delivered or received along with the net amount of money to be paid or collected. Every day each member settles with the clearinghouse instead of with various other firms.

By holding securities in street name and using clearinghouses, brokers can reduce the cost of transfer operations. But even more can be done: Certificates can be immobilized almost completely. The **Depository Trust Company** (DTC) immobilizes certificates by maintaining computerized records of the securities "owned" by its member firms (brokers, banks, and so on). Members' stock certificates are credited to their accounts at the DTC, while the certificates are transferred to the DTC on the books of the issuing corporation and remain registered in its name unless a member subsequently withdraws them. Whenever possible, one member will "deliver" securities to another by initiating a simple bookkeeping entry in which one account is credited and the other is debited for the shares involved. Dividends paid on securities held by the DTC are simply credited to members' accounts on the basis of their holdings and may be subsequently withdrawn from the DTC in cash.

INSURANCE

The Securities Investor Protection Act of 1970 established the **Securities Investor Protection Corporation** (SIPC), a quasigovernmental agency that insures the accounts of clients of all brokers and members of exchanges registered with the **Securities and Exchange Commission (SEC)** against loss due to a brokerage firm's failure. Each account is insured up to a stated amount ($500,000 per customer in 1998). The cost of the insurance is supposed to be borne by the covered brokers and members through premiums. Should this amount be insufficient, the SIPC can borrow up to $1 billion from the U.S. Treasury. A number of brokerage firms have gone further, arranging for additional coverage from private insurance companies.

3.7   COMMISSIONS

3.7.1   Fixed Commissions

In the 1770s people interested in buying and selling stocks and bonds met under a buttonwood tree near present-day 68 Wall Street in New York City. In May 1792 a group of brokers pledged "not to buy or sell from this day for any person whatsoever, any kind of public stock at a less rate than one quarter percent commission on the specie value, and that we will give preference to each other in our negotiations."[22] A visitor to the New York Stock Exchange today can see a copy of this "buttonwood agreement" publicly displayed. This is not surprising, since the exchange is a lineal descendant of the group that met under the buttonwood tree. Also, until 1968 the exchange required its member brokers to charge fixed minimum commissions for stocks, with no "rebates, returns, discounts or allowances in 'any shape or manner,' direct or indirect."[23] The terms had changed, but the principle established 180 years earlier remained in effect.

In the United States most cartels designed to limit competition by fixing prices are illegal. This one, however, was exempted from prosecution under the antitrust laws. Before 1934 the exchange was, in essence, considered a private club for its members. This view of the exchange changed with passage of the Securities Exchange Act of 1934, which required most exchanges to be registered with the SEC. The commission, in turn, encouraged exchanges to "self-regulate" their activities, including the setting of minimum commissions.

3.7.2   Competitive Commissions

As mentioned earlier in this chapter, the system of fixed commissions was finally terminated by the Securities Acts Amendments of 1975 (but only after repeated challenges by the NYSE). Since May 1, 1975 (known in the trade as **May Day**), brokers have been free to set commissions at any desired rate or to negotiate with customers concerning the fees charged for particular trades. The former procedure is more commonly employed in "retail" trades executed for small investors, whereas the latter is used more often when handling large trades involving institutional investors.

Experience after May Day reveals that commissions for large trades have fallen substantially. So have those charged for small trades by firms offering only "barebones" brokerage services. On the other hand, broad-line firms that provided extensive services to small investors for no additional fee have continued to charge commissions similar to those specified in the earlier fixed schedules. In succeeding years, as costs have risen, charges for smaller transactions have increased, whereas those for large trades have not.

During the 1960s and 1970s a number of procedures were used to subvert the fixed commission rates. In particular, the third and fourth markets expanded their

Soft Dollars

Suppose that you have decided to build a new home. As your first step you hire a general contractor to oversee the different construction phases. The general contractor, in turn, hires various subcontractors to lay the foundation, frame the house, install electrical wiring, and so on.

You compensate the general contractor in large part on the basis of the charges billed by the subcontractors. Now assume that the general contractor allowed the subcontractors to charge more than the true costs of their services. The difference between the billed costs and the true costs was then rebated to the general contractor in the form of payments for goods and services only indirectly related to the general contractor's work on your home, such as accounting services or transportation vehicles. For example, the electrician buys the general contractor a new pickup truck after being requested to do so by the contractor.

Presumably you would find such an arrangement objectionable. After all, fairness dictates that the general contractor's charges to you include only the actual cost of the subcontractors' labor and materials. The general contractor should pay for the pickup truck directly out of his or her own pocket. The efficiency and equity of such an arrangement seem unquestionable, except perhaps in the investment management business, where each year institutional investors pay hundreds of millions of "soft" dollars to brokerage firms in a situation analogous to our hypothetical home-building example.

Soft dollars are brokerage commissions paid by institutional investors in excess of amounts required to compensate brokers for simply executing trades; they had their origin in the fixed commission rates imposed by the New York Stock Exchange before May 1, 1975. Large institutional investors paid the same commission rates as small retail investors, despite the obvious economies of scale present in carrying out large trades as opposed to small trades.

Brokerage firms competed with one another, not by lowering commission rates, but by rebating a portion of the commissions to large investors. These brokerage firms did so by offering a plethora of "free" services to the investors. These services typically involved various types of investment research, although on occasion they included such ethically questionable items as airline tickets and lodging for trips abroad.

After the deregulation of commission rates in 1975, it was widely assumed that soft dollars would disappear. Investors would pay brokers only for executing their trades in the most cost-effective manner. Other services, such as investment research, would be purchased directly from the supplying firms. This decoupling of payments for trade execution from other services is known as "unbundling."

Surprisingly, the soft dollar industry, despite some initial rough going after May Day, did not wither away. In fact, it flourished. Its prosperity was facilitated by two factors. First, Congress legislated in 1975 that commissions could continue to be used to pay for investment research, not just for trade execution. The conditions under which soft dollars could be used and the general types of investment research that can be purchased are specified (and occasionally modified) by the Securities and Exchange Commission (SEC). Although the legislation had the effect of curbing some of the most egregious soft dollar abuses, it left soft dollar users with wide latitude.

operations while regional exchanges invented ways to serve as conduits to return a portion of the fixed commissions to institutional investors.

No legal restriction gave the NYSE its monopoly power in the first instance. Instead, the situation has been attributed to the natural monopoly arising from economies of scale in bringing together many people (either physically or via modern communications technology) to trade with one another. The potential profits from such a monopoly are limited by the advantages it confers. The increasing institutionalization of security holdings and progress in communications and computer technology have diminished the advantages associated with a centralized physical exchange. Thus the removal of legal protection for this particular type of price fixing may have accelerated a trend already under way.

Increased competition among brokerage firms has resulted in a wide range of alternatives for investors. After May Day, some firms "unbundled," meaning that they

The second factor was the general trend of institutional investors toward hiring external investment managers to invest their assets. These managers, in a loose sense, act as the general contractor referred to earlier. The managers have discretion over the allocation of their clients' commissions. They are permitted (and, in fact, have a strong incentive) to use soft dollars to pay for various forms of investment research. That research includes primarily fundamental company analyses, data on expected earnings, and economic forecasts. It also includes computer software and hardware, performance measurement, and educational services. By using soft dollars to pay for such research, the managers are effectively shifting the costs to their clients, rather than paying for them themselves.

Establishing the size of the soft dollar industry is difficult, but estimates of total soft dollar commissions in the range of $500 million to $1 billion annually appear reasonable. The soft dollar industry is large and lucrative enough to support a number of brokerage firms devoted solely to supplying third-party research services to investors in exchange for soft dollars. These brokerage firms make arrangements with providers of investment research to funnel payments for services rendered to investment managers in exchange for having the managers' execute trades through the brokerage firms.

In the investment industry, prices for research services are often quoted on two levels: hard (straight cash payment) or soft (price in commission dollars). The ratio of the two prices implies a conversion rate. Although this conversion rate is negotiable, a standard figure is 1.6 commission dollars paid to receive one dollar in services.

The stated rationale behind managers' use of soft dollars is that their clients benefit from the research services purchased. Presumably, in the absence of soft dollars managers would raise their fees to enable them to purchase the necessary research directly, yet maintain their current profit margins. However, managers are not required to provide their clients with a detailed accounting of their soft dollar use. Thus it is difficult for clients to assess whether their commission dollars are being wisely allocated by their managers. One is hard-pressed to imagine how clients are better off under a system of unidentified, implicit fees than they would be if commission payments were completely unbundled.

Why don't institutional clients insist that soft dollar use be prohibited or at least be fully divulged? Inertia and ignorance appear to be two explanations. For another reason, many institutional investors have themselves become beneficiaries of soft dollars. They use soft dollars by directing their managers to purchase various services for their immediate benefit. (Soft dollars generated in this manner are sometimes called "directed commissions.") For example, a corporate pension fund staff may use their managers' soft dollars to purchase performance measurement services that the corporate budget would not normally allow.

Over the years, soft dollars have been criticized as inefficient and ripe for abuse. Calls for prohibition of soft dollars have occasionally been heard. The SEC has periodically rattled its regulatory saber and threatened to crack down on inappropriate practices. However, the status quo likely will prevail. The soft dollar industry is powerful and to date has been able to ward off any substantive changes.

priced their services separately from their pricing of order execution. Other firms "went discount," meaning that they dropped almost all ancillary services and cut commissions accordingly. Still others "bundled" new services into comprehensive packages. Some of these approaches have not stood the test of time, but just as mail-order firms, discount houses, department stores, and expensive boutiques coexist in the retail clothing trade, many different combinations are viable in the brokerage industry.

3.8   TRANSACTION COSTS

3.8.1 Bid-Ask Spread

Commission costs are only a portion of the total cost associated with buying or selling a security. Consider a "round-trip" transaction, in which a stock is purchased and then sold during a period in which no new information is released that would cause investors to collectively reassess the value of the stock (more concretely, the bid and asked prices quoted by dealers do not change). The stock will be purchased typically at the dealers' asked price and sold at the bid price, which is lower. The **bid-ask spread** thus constitutes a portion of the round-trip transaction costs.

How large is the spread between bid and asked prices for a typical stock? The spread generally amounts to less than 1% of the price per share for large actively traded stocks of this type—a reasonably small amount to pay for the ability to buy or sell in a hurry. However, not all securities enjoy this type of liquidity. Shares of smaller firms tend to sell at lower prices but at similar bid-ask spreads. As a result, the percentage transaction cost is considerably larger.

Spreads are inversely related to the amount of trading activity in a stock. That is, stocks with more trading activity (that is, trading volume) tend to have lower spreads.[24] The inverse relationship between the amount of trading activity (or market value) and spread size can be explained once it is recognized that the spread is the dealer's compensation for providing investors with liquidity. The smaller the amount of trading, the less frequently the dealer will capture the spread (by buying at the bid and selling at the asked). Hence the dealer will need a wider spread in order to generate a level of compensation commensurate with more frequently traded securities.

3.8.2 Price Impact

Brokerage commissions and bid-ask spreads represent transaction costs for small orders (typically 100 shares). For larger orders the possibility of **price impacts** must also be considered. Owing to the law of supply and demand, the larger the size of the order, the more likely the investor's purchase price will be higher (or sale price lower). Furthermore, the more rapidly the order is to be completed and the more knowledgeable the individual or organization placing the order, the higher the purchase price (or lower the sale price) set by the dealer.

Table 3.3 offers a profile of trading activity conducted by a sample of institutional investors over the 12-month period ending June 30, 1996. The table presents information encompassing 1.3 million trades on both the NYSE and the Nasdaq/NMS markets. Stocks traded are divided into three groups based on their **market capitalization**, which equals the market value of the firm's outstanding equity (that is, its share price times the number of shares outstanding). For example, large capitalization stocks are classified as those with market capitalizations greater than $10 billion. The table also segments the trades themselves into three groups based on the number of shares involved in the transactions. For example, large trades are classified as those involving over 50,000 shares.

Table 3.3 indicates that the commissions charged on NYSE trades are relatively similar regardless of the stocks' market capitalizations. However, because average price per share tends to be inversely related to market capitalization, commissions, stated as a percentage of the dollar value of a trade, increase as market capitalization declines. Further, the smaller is the market capitalization of a traded stock, the greater is the price impact of the trade. Similarly, the larger is the trade in terms of shares traded, the greater is the price impact.

Figure 3.2 provides estimates of the average cost of institutional trading. All three sources of costs are included: brokerage commissions, bid-ask spreads, and price impacts. The figure refers to the total cost of a "round trip" for a purchase followed by a sale. It illustrates the round-trip cost for stocks with varying market capitalizations and varying trade sizes, with the trade size expressed relative to the daily volume of trading carried out in that stock on a typical day. Transaction costs increase as both market capitalization declines and the proportion of a day's trading volume consumed by the trade rises.

TABLE 3.3 Price Impact Analysis, 12 Months Ending June 30, 1996

(a) New York Stock Exchange Trades

	Size	Percent of Total	Avg. Price Impact	Avg. Commision	Avg. Market Capitalization (billions)	Avg. No. of Traded Shares	Percent of Daily Volume	Avg. Price/Share
Large market capitalization	More than $10 billion	28	$.10 (.17%)	$.045	$34.4	24,000	15	$75
Mid-market capitalization	$1–$10 billion	51	$.09 (.25%)	$.046	$ 4.4	24,000	32	$35
Small market capitalization	Less than $1 billion	21	$.07 (.36%)	$.044	$ 0.6	17,000	54	$19
Small trades	0–10,000 shares	63	$.04 (.10%)	$.040	$15.2	2,000	4	$41
Medium trades	10–50,000 shares	26	$.055 (.14%)	$.044	$13.6	23,000	14	$39
Large trades	More than 50,000 shares	11	$.105 (.27%)	$.046	$18.7	133,000	34	$39

(b) Nasdaq/NMS Trades

	Size	Percent of Total	Avg. Price Impact	Avg. Commision	Avg. Market Capitalization (billions)	Avg. No. of Traded Shares	Percent of Daily Volume	Avg. Price/Share
Large market capitalization	More than $10 billion	7	$.17 (.35%)	N.A.	$34.5	38,000	11	$48
Mid-market capitalization	$1–$10 billion	32	$.19 (.52%)	N.A.	$ 3.4	28,000	24	$37
Small market Capitalization	Less than $1 billion	61	$.16 (.80%)	N.A.	$ 0.5	17,000	48	$20
Small trades	0–10,000 shares	58	$.06 (.23%)	N.A.	$ 5.5	3,000	13	$28
Medium trades	10–50,000 shares	32	$.125 (.43%)	N.A.	$ 4.6	22,000	23	$29
Large trades	More than 50,000 shares	10	$.22 (.68%)	N.A.	$11.1	128,000	33	$32

Source: Plexus Group, 1997. All rights reserved.

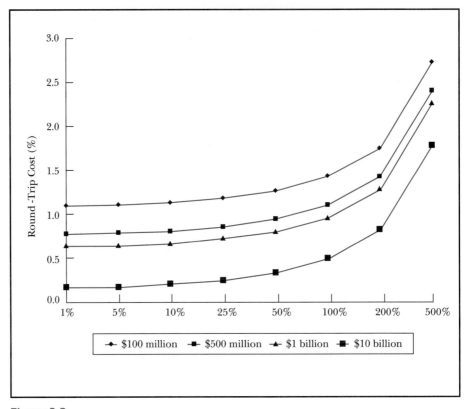

Figure 3.2
Transaction Costs versus Percent of Daily Trading Volume (by market capitalization)
Source: Plexus Group, 1997. All rights reserved.

3.9 REGULATION OF SECURITY MARKETS

Directly or indirectly, security markets in the United States are regulated under both federal and state laws. Figure 3.3 denotes the four main laws that regulate U.S security markets.

1. The Securities Act of 1933 was the first major legislation at the federal level. Sometimes called the "truth in securities" law, it requires registration of new issues and disclosure of relevant information by the issuer. Furthermore, the act prohibits misrepresentation and fraud in security sales.

2. The Securities Exchange Act of 1934 extended the principles of the earlier act to cover secondary markets and required national exchanges, brokers, and dealers to be registered. It also made possible the establishment of self-regulatory organizations (SROs) to oversee the securities industry. Since 1934 both acts (and subsequent amendments to them, such as the Securities Acts Amendments of 1975 that were discussed earlier in the chapter) have been administered by the Securities and Exchange Commission (SEC), a quasijudicial agency of the U.S. government established by the 1934 Act.[25]

3. The Investment Company Act of 1940 extended disclosure and registration requirements to investment companies, whose total assets at the end of 1997 amounted to more than $4 trillion. (Investment companies use their funds primarily to purchase securities issued by the U.S. government, state governments, and corporations; they are discussed in Chapter 21.)

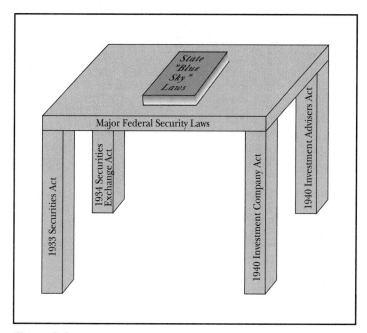

Figure 3.3
Pillars of Security Legislation

4. The Investment Advisers Act of 1940 required the registration of those individuals who provide others with advice about security transactions. Advisers were also required to disclose any potential conflicts of interest.

As mentioned earlier, federal securities legislation relies heavily on the principle of **self-regulation**. The SEC has delegated its power to control trading practices for listed securities to the registered exchanges. However, the SEC has retained the power to alter or supplement any of the resulting rules or regulations. The SEC's power to control trading practices in over-the-counter securities has been similarly delegated to the National Association of Securities Dealers (NASD), a private association of brokers and dealers in OTC securities.[26] In practice, the SEC staff usually discusses proposed changes with both the NASD and the registered exchanges in advance. Consequently, the SEC formally alters or rejects few rules.

An important piece of legislation that makes security markets in the United States different from those in many other countries is the Banking Act of 1933, also known as the Glass-Steagall Act. This act prohibited commercial banks from participating in investment banking activities because it was felt that there was an inherent conflict of interest in allowing banks to engage in both commercial and investment banking. Consequently, banks have not played as prominent a role in security markets in the United States as they do elsewhere. Recently, however, their role has increased, as the federal government has taken action to spur competition among various types of financial institutions. Many banks now offer security brokerage services, retirement funds, and the like via subsidiaries of their holding companies. Furthermore, long-standing limitations on rates paid on deposits and checking accounts were removed. As a result, the line between commercial banking and investment banking is becoming more blurred every day.

Initially, security regulation in the United States was the province of state governments. Beginning in 1911, state *blue sky laws* were passed to prevent "speculative schemes which have no more basis than so many feet of blue sky."[27] Although such statutes vary substantially from state to state, most of them outlaw fraud in security sales and require the registration of certain securities as well as brokers and dealers (and, in some cases, investment advisers). Some order has been created by the passage in many states of all or part of the Uniform Securities Acts proposed by the National Conference of Commissions on Uniform State Laws in 1956. Furthermore, the North American Securities Administrators Association (NASAA), an organzation of state securities regulators based in Washington, D.C., monitors federal regulation and attempts to coordinate state regulation.

Securities that are traded across state lines, as well as the brokers, dealers, and exchanges involved in such trading, typically fall under the purview of federal legislation. However, a considerable domain still comes under the exclusive jurisdiction of the states. Generally, federal legislation only supplements state legislation; it does not supplant it. Some critics argue that the investor is overprotected as a result. Others suggest that the regulatory agencies (especially those that rely on "self-regulation" by powerful industry organizations) in fact protect the members of the regulated industry against competition, thereby damaging the interests of their customers instead of protecting them. Both positions undoubtedly contain some elements of truth.

3.10 SUMMARY

1. Security markets facilitate the trading of securities by providing a means of bringing buyers and sellers of financial assets together.
2. Common stocks are traded primarily on organized security exchanges or on the over-the-counter market.
3. Organized security exchanges provide central physical locations where trading is done under a set of rules and regulations.
4. The primary organized security exchange is the New York Stock Exchange. Various regional exchanges also operate.
5. Trading on organized security exchanges is conducted only by members who transact in a specified group of securities.
6. Exchange members fall into one of four categories, depending on the type of trading activity in which they engage. Those categories are commission broker, floor broker, floor trader, and specialist.
7. Specialists are charged with maintaining an orderly market in their assigned stocks. In this capacity they perform two roles. They act as brokers, maintaining limit order books for unexecuted trades, and they act as dealers, trading in their stocks for their own accounts.
8. In the OTC market, individuals act as dealers in a manner similar to specialists. However, unlike specialists, OTC dealers face competition from other dealers.
9. Most of the trading in the OTC market is done through a computerized system known as Nasdaq.
10. Trading in listed securities may take place outside the various exchanges on the third and fourth markets.
11. Foreign security markets each have their own particular operating procedures, rules, and customs.
12. Dealers typically make money trading with liquidity-motivated traders and lose money trading with adept information-motivated traders. A dealer must set a bid-ask spread that attracts sufficient revenue from the former group to offset losses to the latter.

13. Since legislation in 1975, the Securities and Exchange Commission has mandated procedures designed to create a truly nationwide central security market.

14. Clearinghouses facilitate the transfer of securities and cash between buyers and sellers. Most U.S. security transactions are now cleared electronically.

15. The SIPC is a quasigovernmental agency that insures the accounts of clients of all brokers and members of exchanges registered with the SEC against loss due to a brokerage firm's failure.

16. Since May Day (May 1, 1975), commissions have been negotiated between brokerage firms and their larger clients. In a competitive environment, commission rates typically vary inversely with the size of the order.

17. Transaction costs are a function of the stock's bid-ask spread, the price impact of the trade, and the commission.

18. The most prominent security market regulator is the SEC, a federal agency. Regulation of the U.S. security markets involves both federal and state laws.

19. The SEC has delegated to the various exchanges and the NASD the power to control trading practices through a system of self-regulation with federal government oversight.

QUESTIONS AND PROBLEMS

1. Virtually all secondary trading of securities takes place in continuous markets as opposed to call markets. What aspects of continuous markets causes them to dominate call markets?

2. Circuitbreakers were first instituted after the market crash of October 1987. Some observers argue that the rapid increase in the stock market's value since 1987 has diminished whatever value the rules may originally have possessed. Why?

3. Discuss the advantages and disadvantages of the NYSE specialist system.

4. Differentiate between the role of a specialist on the NYSE and the role of a dealer on the OTC market.

5. Give several reasons why a corporation might desire to have its stock listed on the NYSE.

6. Describe the functions of commission brokers, floor brokers, and floor traders.

7. Pigeon Falls Fertilizer Company is listed on the NYSE. Gabby Hartnett, the specialist handling Pigeon Falls stock, is currently bidding $35\frac{3}{8}$ and asking $35\frac{5}{8}$. What would be the likely outcomes of the following trading orders?

   a. Through a broker, Eppa Rixey places a market order to buy 100 shares of Pigeon Falls stock. No other broker from the crowd takes the order.

   b. Through a broker, Eppa places a limit order to sell 100 shares of Pigeon Falls stock at 36.

   c. Through a broker, Eppa places a limit order to buy 100 shares of Pigeon Falls stock at $35\frac{1}{2}$. Another broker offers to sell 100 shares at $35\frac{1}{2}$.

8. Bosco Snover is the NYSE specialist in Eola Enterprises' stock. Bosco's limit order book for Eola appears as follows:

Limit-Sell		Limit-Buy	
Price	Shares	Price	Shares
$30.250	200	$29.750	100
30.375	500	29.000	100
30.500	300	28.500	200
30.875	800	27.125	100
31.000	200	26.875	200

The last trade in the stock took place at $30.

    a. If a market order to sell 200 shares arrives, what will happen?

    b. If another market order to sell 100 shares arrives just moments later, what will happen?

    c. Do you think that Bosco would prefer to accumulate shares or to reduce inventory, given the current orders in the limit order book?

9. Because specialists such as Chick Gandil are charged with maintaining a "fair and orderly" market, at times they will be required to sell when others are buying and to buy when others are selling. How can Chick earn a profit when required to act in such a manner?

10. Why can't all trade orders on the NYSE, no matter how large, be handled through the SuperDOT system?

11. Why is Nasdaq so important to the success of the OTC market?

12. If the NYSE moved to decimal pricing with prices moving in at $.05 increments, would there be greater opportunities for price improvement over the current pricing system? Explain.

13. Distinguish between two forms of preferencing: payment for order flow and internalization.

14. Using the model described in the text, calculate the appropriate bid-ask spread for a dealer making a market in a security under the conditions that 15% of all traders are information-motivated and there is a 30% chance that the stock is worth $30 per share and a 70% change that it is worth $50 per share.

15. How might a dealer attempt to discern whether a trader is information motivated?

16. What are some of the major steps that have been taken toward the ultimate emergence of a truly nationwide security market?

17. The NYSE has strongly opposed the creation of alternative market trading structures such as off-exchange crossing systems. The NYSE claims that these alternative structures undermine its ability to offer "best execution" to all investors. Discuss the merits of the NYSE's contention.

18. Distinguish between the third and fourth markets.

19. Why was May Day such an important event for the NYSE?

20. What is the purpose of SIPC insurance? Given the late 1980s experience of the banking and savings and loan deposit insurance programs, under what conditions might SIPC insurance be expected to be effective? Under what conditions might it fail to accomplish its objectives?

21. After May Day, why did commission rates fall so sharply for large investors but decline so little (or even increase) for small investors?

22. Transaction costs can be thought of as being derived from three sources. Identify and describe those sources.

23. Why does the price impact of a trade seem to be directly related to the size of the trade?

24. What functions does a clearinghouse perform?

ENDNOTES

[1] Enough time is allowed to elapse between calls (for example, an hour or more) so that a substantial number of orders to buy and sell will accumulate by the time of the auction.

[2] The applicant for membership must also pass a written examination, be sponsored by two current members of the exchange, and be approved by the board. Recently the NYSE began allowing members to lease their seats to individuals acceptable to the exchange. As of the end of 1996 there were 781 leased seats. In addition to the 1,366 full memberships, at the

end of 1996 there were 61 individuals who held special memberships. In return for an annual fee, these members are granted access to the trading floor.

[3] During 1996, trading volume on the NYSE averaged, on a daily basis, 412.0 million shares, worth nearly $7 billion. The American Stock Exchange, the second largest organized exchange, had daily values of less than one-tenth those amounts.

[4] *Fact Book 1997 Data* (New York Stock Exchange, 1997), p. 37.

[5] Note that the tick test for a down market is the same as the up-tick rule discussed in Chapter 2 with respect to short sales.

[6] There is another circuitbreaker known as the Sidecar that halts certain trades on Super-DOT (discussed later in this chapter) for five minutes whenever the primary Standard & Poor's 500 futures contract (see Chapter 20) drops 12 points. Readers are encouraged to check the NYSE's Web page ⟨www.nyse.com⟩ for the current status of the various circuit-breakers, as they are subject to change.

[7] The assignment is made by the board of directors and also includes any preferred stock or warrants that the company has listed on the exchange. At the end of 1996 there were 2,907 companies listed on the NYSE, with 3,285 stock issues being traded, meaning that there were over 300 different issues of preferred stock and other classes of common stock being traded on the NYSE. There were also 116 warrants on these companies' stock that were traded. Bonds are also listed on the NYSE but are traded in an entirely different manner that does not involve the use of specialists. At the end of 1996 there were 563 companies that had 2,064 issues of bonds listed on the NYSE.

[8] The NYSE is currently open from 9:30 A.M. until 4 P.M. However, the NYSE often considers extending its hours of operation in order to overlap with the London and Tokyo stock markets. The NYSE does allow certain computerized trading to take place after close in Crossing Session I (4:15 P.M. to 5 P.M.) and Crossing Session II (4 P.M. to 5:15 P.M.). Trades in Crossing Session I are based on 4 P.M. closing prices, whereas each trade in Crossing Session II must involve a "basket" of at least 15 NYSE-listed stocks and an aggregate price of $15 million (prices are set for the baskets not for individual stocks).

[9] These quotations may represent either orders for the specialist's own account or public orders. These quotations may not be the "best" ones, because under certain circumstances specialists are not required to display them on the screens of quotation machines. However, such "hidden orders" would appear in the limit order book and would be revealed on the exchange floor. As a matter of NYSE policy, only the specialist is allowed to see the contents of the limit order book. However, in 1991 the NYSE began to allow the specialists to disclose some information about buying and selling interest to others on the floor.

[10] Evidence of price improvement in minimum spread markets (as well as in markets with larger spreads) is provided in Lawrence Harris and Joel Hasbrouck, "Market vs. Limit Orders: The SuperDOT Evidence on Order Submission Strategy," *Journal of Financial and Quantitative Analysis* 31, no. 2 (June 1996): 213–231, and Katharine D. Ross, James E. Shapiro, and Katherine A. Smith, "Price Improvement of SuperDOT Market Orders on the NYSE," NYSE Working Paper 96-02.

[11] Odd lot market orders are executed immediately by the specialist at the quoted bid or asked price. Odd lot limit orders are held by the specialist and executed immediately after there has been another trade at the limit price. Typically, odd lot orders utilize the facilities of SuperDOT. There are special features of SuperDot that are used to execute opening orders; that is, orders that are received up to the time the NYSE opens in the morning.

[12] One alternative for the institution that is thinking of placing the block order is to place many small orders sequentially. However, institutions generally do not want to do this because it means that their block order will not be executed with due speed. Furthermore, other traders may anticipate these additional transactions and develop strategies to take advantage of them.

[13] The order must be crossed on an exchange where the stock is listed, provided that the block house is a member of that exchange.

[14] In 1996 the Department of Justice and the Securities and Exchange Commission reached settlements with NASD after concluding that NASD had engaged in anticompetitive behavior by, for example, colluding in the setting of spreads in large Nasdaq stocks. Interestingly, the investigation was triggered by an academic paper by William G. Christie and Paul H. Schultz, "Why Do NASDAQ Market Makers Avoid Odd-Eighth Quotes?" *Journal of Finance* 49, no. 5 (December 1994): 1813–1840. For press articles describing the Settlement, see Anita Raghavan and Jeffrey Taylor, "Will NASD Accord Transform Nasdaq Market?" *The Wall Street Journal*, August 8 1996, pp. C1, C6; and Floyd Norris, "Tough Crackdown on NAS-DAQ Market Announced by US," *New York Times*, August 9, 1996, pp. A1, D16.

[15] Of this total, 460 were foreign securities consisting of 142 American Depositary Receipts (ADRs) and 318 non-ADRs. (Many of the non-ADRs were Canadian securities.) ADRs are discussed in Chapter 25.

[16] The use of an intermediary such as a computer system, makes it difficult to categorize such trades. Some people would refer to the market where trades involving a "matchmaker" take place as the "3.5 market." The term *fourth market* would then be used only when referring to the market where no matchmaker is involved.

[17] See James B Cloonan, "Payment for Order Flow Is No Deal for Investors," *AAII Journal* 13, no. 3 (March 1991): 28–29.

[18] There is a another way that internalization can take place. Broker-dealers can also be specialists in NYSE-listed securities on either the NYSE itself or on a regional exchange. Hence, they can take their customers' orders and send them to their own specialists for execution. This practice is particularly common on certain regional exchanges where the specialists can make markets in many stocks (often several specialists will make a market in the same stock).

[19] A similar classification of traders that has often been used by financial economists involves (1) informed speculative traders who possess both public and private information, (2) uninformed speculative traders who possess just public information, and (3) noise traders whose trades are not based on information. Hence the first two types can be viewed as information-motivated traders, and the third as liquidity-motivated traders. See Sanford J. Grossman and Joseph E. Stiglitz, "On the Impossibility of Informationally Efficient Markets," *American Economic Review* 70, no. 3 (June 1980): 393–408.

[20] There are a number of implicit assumptions associated with this model that have not been spelled out here. The interested reader is directed to Lawrence R. Glosten and Paul R. Milgrom, "Bid, Ask, and Transaction Prices in a Specialist Market with Heterogeneously Informed Traders," *Journal of Financial Economics* 14 no. 1 (March 1985): 71–100.

[21] From *Securities Acts Amendments of 1975*, section 11A.

[22] See Wilford J. Eiteman, Charles A. Dice, and David K. Eiteman, *The Stock Market* (New York: McGraw-Hill, 1969), p. 19.

[23] Eitemen, Dice, and Eiteman, *The Stock Market*, p. 138.

[24] Roger D. Huang and Hans R. Stoll, *Major World Equity Markets: Current Structure and Prospects for Change*, Monograph Series in Finance and Economics 1991–93, (New York: New York University Salomon Center, 1991), p. 11.

[25] The Commodity Futures Trading Commission (CFTC) was established in 1974 by Congress to regulate futures markets, and the Municipal Securities Rulemaking Board (MSRB) was established in 1975 to regulate trading in municipal securities. A brief discussion of federal regulation in those two markets can be found in Chapters 20 and 13, respectively.

[26] The Maloney Act of 1938 extended the SEC's jurisdiction to include the over-the-counter market and recognized the National Association of Security Dealers as a self-regulatory organization (SRO).

[27] See Hall v. Geiger-Jones Co., 242 U.S. 539 (1917).

security market

financial market

call markets

continuous markets

liquidity

organized exchanges

seat

member firm

listed security

delist

trading halt

circuitbreakers

minus tick

zero-minus tick

commission brokers

floor brokers

floor traders

specialists

limit order book

dealer

market-maker

trading post

bid price

asked price

double auction

Super Designated Order Turnaround

blocks

specialist block purchase

specialist block sale

exchange distribution

exchange acquisition

special offering

special bid

secondary distribution

upstairs dealer market

block houses

regional exchanges

National Association of Securities
    Dealers

National Association of Securities Dealers
    Automated Quotations

inside quotes

NBBO

offer price

National Market System

Small Cap Issues

markup

markdown

Small Order Execution System
    (SOES)

Pink Sheets

third market

fourth market

Instinet

preferencing

payment for order flow

internalization

SEAQ

SAEF

Nasdaq International

CORES

FORES

CATS

consolidated tape

composite stock price tables

Consolidated Quotations System

Intermarket Trading System

clearinghouse

Depository Trust Company

Securities Investor Protection
    Corporation

Securities and Exchange Commission (SEC)

May Day

soft dollars

bid-ask spread

price impacts

market capitalization

self-regulation

R E F E R E N C E S

1. A good reference source for U.S. stock markets is:
   Robert A. Schwartz, *Equity Markets* (New York: Harper & Row, 1988).

2. Other valuable sources are the following fact books, which are updated annually, and
   Web sites:
   New York Stock Exchange, *Fact Book: 1997 Data*, 1998; ⟨www.nyse.com⟩.

American Stock Exchange, *American Stock Exchange 1997 Fact Book*, 1998; ⟨wwww.amex.com⟩.

National Association of Security Dealers, *The Nasdaq Stock Market 1997 Fact Book & Company Directory*, 1997; ⟨www.nasd.com⟩ or ⟨www.nasdaq.com⟩ or ⟨www.nasdr.com⟩.

London Stock Exchange, *Stock Exchange Official Yearbook*; ⟨www.londonstockex.co.uk⟩.

Toronto Stock Exchange Press, *1997 Official Trading Statistics*; ⟨www.tse.com⟩.

Tokyo Stock Exchange, *Tokyo Stock Exchange 1997 Fact Book*; ⟨www.tse.or.jp/eindex.html⟩.

The Securities and Exchange Commission's Web site: ⟨www.sec.gov⟩.

3. For a description of foreign stock markets, see:

Guiseppe Tullio and Giorgio P. Szego (eds.), "Equity Markets: An International Comparison: Part A," *Journal of Banking and Finance* 13, nos. 4/5 (September 1989): 479–782.

Guiseppe Tullio and Giorgio P. Szego (eds.), "Equity Markets: An International Comparison: Part B," *Journal of Banking and Finance* 14, nos. 2/3 (August 1990): 231–672.

Roger D. Huang and Hans R. Stoll, *Major World Equity Markets: Current Structure and Prospects for Change*, Monograph Series in Finance and Economics 1991–1993 (New York: New York University Salomon Center, 1991).

Roger D. Huang and Hans R. Stoll, "The Design of Trading Systems: Lessons from Abroad," *Financial Analysts Journal* 48, no. 5 (September/October 1992): 49–54.

Bruce N. Lehman and David M. Modest, "Trading and Liquidity on the Tokyo Stock Exchange: A Bird's Eye View," *Journal of Finance* 49, no. 3 (July 1994): 951–984.

Alexandros Benos and Michel Crouhy, "Changes in the Structure and Dynamics of European Securities Markets," *Financial Analysts Journal* 52, no. 3 (May/June 1996): 37–50.

4. Other useful sources for information on market microstructure are:

James L. Hamilton, "Off-Board Trading of NYSE-Listed Stocks: The Effects of Deregulation and the National Market System," *Journal of Finance* 42, no. 5 (December 1987): 1331–1345.

Ian Domowitz, "The Mechanics of Automated Execution Systems," *Journal of Financial Intermediation* 1, no. 2 (June 1990): 167–194.

Lawrence E. Harris, *Liquidity, Trading Rules, and Electronic Trading Systems*, Monograph Series in Finance and Economics 1990–1994, (New York: New York University Salomon Center, 1990).

Peter A. Abken, "Globalization of Stock, Futures, and Options Markets," *Federal Reserve Bank of Atlanta Economic Review* 76, no. 4 (July/August 1991): 1–22.

Joel Hasbrouck, George Sofianos, and Deborah Sosebee, "New York Stock Exchange Systems and Procedures," NYSE Working Paper 93-01, 1993.

Maureen O'Hara, *Market Microstructure Theory* (Cambridge, MA: Blackwell, 1995).

5. For a discussion of the effects of listing and delisting on a firm's stock, see:

Gary C. Sanger and John J. McConnell, "Stock Exchange Listings, Firm Value, and Security Market Efficiency: The Impact of NASDAQ," *Journal of Financial and Quantitative Analysis* 21, no. 1 (March 1986): 1–25.

John J. McConnell and Gary C. Sanger, "The Puzzle in Post-Listing Common Stock Returns," *Journal of Finance* 42, no. 1 (March 1987): 119–140.

Gary C. Sanger and James D. Peterson, "An Empirical Analysis of Common Stock Delistings," *Journal of Financial and Quantitative Analysis* 25, no. 2 (June 1990): 261–272.

6. Empirical studies that examine the costs of trading include:

Harold Demsetz, "The Cost of Transacting," *Quarterly Journal of Economics* 82, no. 1 (February 1968): 33–53.

Walter Bagehot, "The Only Game in Town," *Financial Analysts Journal* 27, no. 2 (March/April 1971): 12–14, 22.

Larry J. Cuneo and Wayne H. Wagner, "Reducing the Cost of Stock Trading," *Financial Analysts Journal* 31, no. 6 (November/December 1975): 35–44.

Gilbert Beebower and William Priest, "The Tricks of the Trade," *Journal of Portfolio Management* 6, no. 2 (Winter 1980): 36–42.

Jack L. Treynor, "What Does It Take to Win the Trading Game?" *Financial Analysts Journal* 37, no. 1 (January/February 1981): 55–60.

Thomas F. Loeb, "Trading Cost: The Critical Link between Investment Information and Results," *Financial Analysts Journal* 39, no. 3 (May/June 1983): 39–44.

Wayne H. Mikkelson and M. Megan Partch, "Stock Price Effects and Costs of Secondary Distributions," *Journal of Financial Economics* 14, no. 2 (June 1985): 165–194.

Robert W. Holthausen, Richard W. Leftwich, and David Mayers, "The Effect of Large Block Transactions on Security Prices," *Journal of Financial Economics* 19, no. 2 (December 1987): 237–267.

Stephen A. Berkowitz, Dennis E. Logue, and Eugene E. Noser Jr., "The Total Cost of Transactions on the NYSE," *Journal of Finance* 43, no. 1 (March 1988): 97–112.

André F. Perold, "The Implementation Shortfall: Paper versus Reality," *Journal of Portfolio Management* 14, no. 3 (Spring 1988): 4–9.

Lawrence R. Glosten and Lawrence E. Harris, "Estimating the Components of the Bid/Ask Spread," *Journal of Financial Economics* 21, no. 1 (May 1988): 123–142.

Joel Hasbrouck, "Trades, Quotes, Inventories, and Information," *Journal of Financial Economics* 22, no. 2 (December 1988): 229–252.

Hans R. Stoll, "Inferring the Components of the Bid-Ask Spread: Theory and Empirical Tests," *Journal of Finance* 44, no. 1 (March 1989): 115–134.

Robert W. Holthausen, Richard W. Leftwich, and David Mayers, "Large-Block Transactions, the Speed of Response, and Temporary and Permanent Stock-Price Effects," *Journal of Financial Economics* 26, no. 1 (July 1990): 71–95.

F. Douglas Foster and S. Viswanathan, "Variations in Trading Volume, Return Volatility, and Trading Costs: Evidence on Recent Price Formation Models," *Journal of Finance* 48, no. 1 (March 1993): 187–211.

Hans R. Stoll, "Equity Trading Costs In-the-Large," *Journal of Portfolio Management* 19, no. 4 (Summer 1993): 41–50.

Joel Hasbrouck and George Sofianos, "The Trades of Market Makers: An Empirical Analysis of NYSE Specialists," *Journal of Finance* 48, no. 5 (December 1993): 1565–1593.

Ananth Madhavan and Seymour Smidt, "An Analysis of Changes in Specialist Inventories and Quotations" *Journal of Finance* 48, no. 5 (December 1993): 1595–1628.

Mitchell A. Petersen and David Fialkowski, "Posted versus Effective Spreads: Good Prices or Bad Quotes?" *Journal of Financial Economics* 35, no. 3 (June 1994): 269–292.

Jack L. Treynor, "The Invisible Costs of Trading," *Journal of Portfolio Management* 22, no. 1 (Fall 1995): 71–78.

7. For a comparison of trading costs on Nasdaq and the NYSE, see:

Roger D. Huang and Hans R. Stoll, "Competitive Trading of NYSE Listed Stocks: Measurement and Interpretation of Trading Costs," *Financial Markets, Institutions & Instruments* 5, no. 2 (1996).

Roger D. Huang and Hans R. Stoll, "Dealer versus Auction Markets: A Paired Comparison of Execution Costs on NASDAQ and NYSE," *Journal of Financial Economics* 41, no. 3 (July 1996): 313–357.

Michele LaPlante and Chris J. Muscarella, "Do Institutions Receive Comparable Execution in the NYSE and Nasdaq Markets? A Transaction Study of Block Trades," *Journal of Financial Economics* 45, no. 1 (July 1997): 97–134.

8. For a historical essay on the development of American capital markets, which includes a significant discussion of regulation, see:

George David Smith and Richard Sylla, "The Transformation of Financial Capitalism: An Essay on the History of American Capital Markets," *Financial Markets, Institutions & Instruments* 2, no. 2 (1993).

9. For more on the adverse selection problem that dealers face in setting spreads, see:

Lawrence R. Glosten and Paul R. Milgrom, "Bid, Ask, and Transaction Prices in a Specialist Market with Heterogeneously Informed Traders," *Journal of Financial Economics* 14, no. 1 (March 1985): 71–100.

Albert S. Kyle, "Continuous Auctions and Insider Trading," *Econometrica* 53, no. 6 (November 1985): 1315–1335.

Murugappa Krishnan, "An Equivalence between the Kyle (1985) and the Glosten-Milgrom (1985) Models, " *Economic Letters* 40, (1992): 333–338.

Steven V. Mann, "How Do Security Dealers Protect Themselves from Traders with Private Information: A Pedagogical Note," *Financial Practice and Education* 5, no. 1 (Spring/Summer 1995): 38–44.

Michael J. Brennan and Avanidhar Subrahmanyam, "Investment Analysis and Price Formation in Securities Markets," *Journal of Financial Economics* 38, no. 3 (July 1995): 361–381.

10. Articles on soft dollars include:

Keith P. Ambachtsheer, "The Soft Dollar Question: What Is the Answer?" *Financial Analysts Journal* 49, no. 1 (January/February 1993): 8–10.

Marshall E. Blume, "Soft Dollars and the Brokerage Industry," *Financial Analysts Journal* 49, no. 2 (March/April 1993): 36–44.

Miles Livingston and Edward S. O'Neal, "Mutual Fund Brokerage Commissions," *Journal of Financial Research* 19, no. 2 (Summer 1996): 273–292.

EFFICIENT MARKETS, INVESTMENT VALUE, AND MARKET PRICE

Payments provided by securities may differ in size, timing, and riskiness. Thus a security analyst must estimate the size of such payments along with when, and under what conditions, these payments will be received. This estimate typically requires detailed analysis of the firm involved, the industry (or industries) in which the firm operates, and the economy (either regionally, nationally, or internationally) as a whole.

Once such estimates have been made, the overall investment value of the security must be determined. This determination generally requires conversion of uncertain future values to certain present values. The current prices of other securities can often be utilized in this process. If it is possible to obtain a similar set of payments in some other way, the market price of doing so provides a benchmark for the investment value of the security being analyzed, because an investor would neither want to pay more than this for the security nor want to sell it for less. In some cases, however, equivalent alternatives may not exist, or the mere act of buying or selling the security in question in the quantities being considered might affect the price substantially. Under these conditions the preferences of the investor may have to be utilized explicitly in the process of estimating the security's investment value.

Later chapters discuss in detail the manner in which estimated future payments can be used to determine investment value. Methods for estimating the payments and finding equivalent alternatives will be discussed after the characteristics of the securities have been introduced. In this chapter some general principles of investment value and how it is related to market prices in an efficient market are presented, leaving valuation methodology for specific types of securities for later.

4.1 DEMAND AND SUPPLY SCHEDULES

Although there are over 1 billion shares of AT&T common stock outstanding, on a typical day only a few million shares will be traded. What determines the prices at which such trades take place? A simple (and correct) answer is: demand and supply. A more fundamental (and also correct) answer is: investors' estimates of AT&T's future earnings and dividends, for such estimates greatly influence demand and supply. Before dealing with such influences, it is useful to examine the role of demand and supply in the determination of security prices.

As shown in the previous chapter, securities are traded by many people in many different ways. Although the forces that determine prices are similar in all markets, they are slightly more obvious in markets using periodic "calls." One such market corresponds to the *itayose* method of price determination that is used by the *saitori* at the twice-a-day openings of the Tokyo Stock Exchange, as discussed in Chapter 3.

4.1.1 Demand-to-Buy Schedule

At a designated time all brokers holding orders to buy or sell a given stock for customers gather at a specified location on the floor of the exchange. Some of the orders are market orders. For example, Mr. A may have instructed his broker to buy 100 shares of Minolta at the lowest possible price, whatever it may be. His personal **demand-to-buy schedule** at that time is shown in Figure 4.1(a): He wishes to buy 100 shares no matter what the price. Although this schedule captures the contractual nature of Mr. A's market order at a specific point in time, Mr. A undoubtedly has a good idea that his ultimate purchase price will be near the price for which orders were executed just before he placed his order. Thus his true demand schedule might be sloping downward from the upper left portion to the lower right portion of the graph. This schedule is shown by the dashed line in the figure. It indicates his desire to buy more shares if the price is lower. However, to simplify his own tasks as well as his broker's tasks, he has estimated that the price for which his order will be ultimately executed will be in the range at which he would choose to hold 100 shares. In the example shown here, this price is 945 yen per share.

Other customers may place limit orders with their brokers. Thus Ms. B may have instructed her broker to buy 200 shares of Minolta at the lowest possible price if and only if that price is less than or equal to 940 yen per share. Her demand schedule is shown in Figure 4.1(b).

Some customers may give their broker two or more orders for the same security. Thus Mr. C may wish to buy 100 shares of Minolta at a price of 955 or less, plus an additional 100 shares if the price is at or below 945. To do this, Mr. C places a limit order for 100 shares at 955 and a second limit order for 100 shares at 945. Figure 4.1(c) portrays his demand schedule.

If one could look at all the brokers' books and aggregate all the orders to buy Minolta (both market and limit orders), it would be possible to determine how many shares would be bought at every possible price. Assuming that only Mr. A, Ms. B, and Mr. C have placed buy orders, the resulting aggregate demand-to-buy schedule will look like line *DD* in Figure 4.1(d). Note that at lower prices more shares would be demanded.

4.1.2 Supply-to-Sell Schedule

Brokers will also hold market orders to sell shares of Minolta. For example, Ms. X may have placed a market order to sell 100 shares of Minolta at the highest possible price. Figure 4.2(a) displays her **supply-to-sell schedule**. As with market orders to buy, customers generally place such orders on the supposition that the actual price will be in the range in which their true desire would be to sell the stated number of shares. Thus Ms. X's actual supply schedule might appear more like the dashed line in Figure 4.2(a), indicating her willingness to sell more shares at higher prices.

Customers may also place limit orders to sell shares of Minolta. For example, Mr. Y may have placed a limit order to sell 100 shares at a price of 940 or higher, and

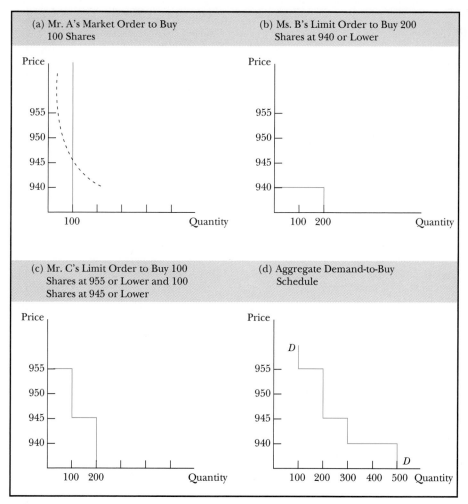

Figure 4.1
Individual Investors' Demand-to-Buy Schedules

Ms. Z may have placed a limit order to sell 100 shares at a price of 945 or higher. Panels (b) and (c) of Figure 4.2 illustrate these two supply-to-sell schedules.

Similar to the buy orders, if one could look at all the brokers' books and aggregate all the orders to sell Minolta (both market and limit orders), it would be possible to determine how many shares would be sold at every possible price. Assuming that only Ms. X, Mr. Y, and Ms. Z have placed sell orders, the resulting aggregate supply-to-sell schedule will look like line *SS* in Figure 4.2(d). Note that at higher prices more shares would be supplied.

4.1.3   Interaction of Schedules

The aggregate demand and supply schedules are shown on one graph in Figure 4.3. In general no one would have enough information to draw the actual schedules. However, this limitation in no way diminishes the schedules' usefulness as representations of the underlying forces that are interacting to determine the market clearing price of Minolta.

What actually happens when all the brokers gather together with their order books in hand? A clerk of the exchange "calls out" a price—for example, 940 yen per

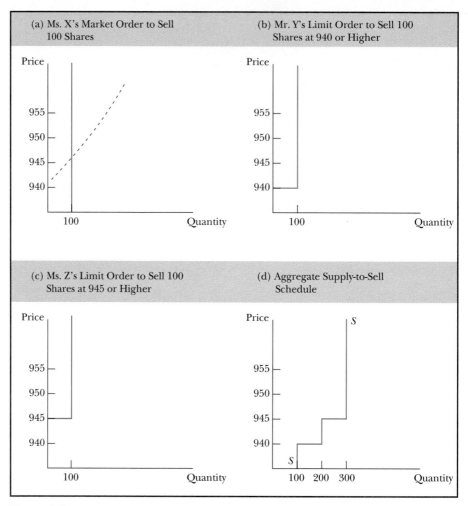

Figure 4.2
Individual Investors' Supply-to-Sell Schedules

share. The brokers then try to complete transactions with one another at that price. Those with orders to buy at that price signify the number of shares they wish to buy. Those with orders to sell do likewise. Some deals will be tentatively made, but as Figure 4.3 shows, more shares will be demanded at 940 than will be supplied. In particular, 300 shares will be demanded, but only 200 shares will be supplied. When trading is completed (meaning that all possible tentative deals have been made), there will be a number of brokers calling "buy," but nobody will stand ready to sell to them. The price of 940 was too low.

Seeing this outcome, the clerk will cry out a different price, for example, 950. As the previous trades are all canceled at this point, the brokers will consult their order books once again and signify the extent to which they are willing to buy or sell shares at this new price. In this case, as Figure 4.3 shows, when trading is completed, there will be a number of brokers calling "sell," but nobody will stand ready to buy from them. In particular, 300 shares will be supplied, but there will be a demand for only 200 shares. The price of 950 was too high.

Undaunted, the clerk will try again. And again, if necessary. Only when there are relatively few unsatisfied brokers will the price (and the associated tentative deals) be

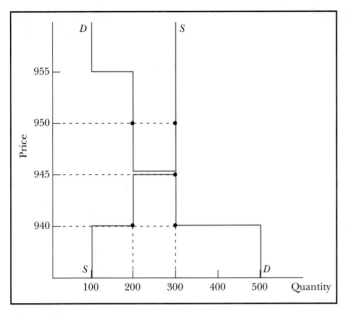

Figure 4.3
Determining a Security's Price by the Interaction of the Aggregate Demand-to-Buy and Supply-to-Sell Schedules

declared final. As Figure 4.3 shows, 945 is such a price. At 945, customers collectively wish to sell 300 shares. Furthermore, there is a collective demand for 300 shares at this price. Thus quantity demanded equals quantity supplied. The price is "just right."

4.1.4 Elasticity of the Demand-to-Buy Schedule

How elastic (that is, flat) will be the aggregate demand-to-buy schedule for a security? The answer depends in part on the extent to which the security is regarded as "unique." Securities are considered more unique when they have few close substitutes. Securities are considered less unique when they have more close substitutes. This relation means that the aggregate demand-to-buy schedule will be more elastic (that is, flatter) for less unique securities. Equivalently, the less unique a security is, the greater will be the increase in the quantity demanded for a given fall in price because these shares will produce a smaller increase in the typical portfolio's risk when substituted for other shares. At one extreme, other securities are viewed as perfect substitutes for the one being analyzed. In this case the security's demand-to-buy schedule will be horizontal, or perfectly elastic. At the other extreme, where there are no substitutes, the security has an almost vertical (or almost perfectly inelastic) demand schedule.

4.1.5 Shifts of the Demand-to-Buy and Supply-to-Sell Schedules

If one investor becomes more optimistic about the prospects for a security while another investor becomes more pessimistic about the same security, they may very likely trade with one another with no effect on the aggregate demand-to-buy and supply-to-sell schedules. In this situation there will be no change in the market price

The Arizona Stock Exchange: A Better Mousetrap

So you think that supply and demand curves are merely esoteric figments of ivory-tower thinking. Perhaps a valid concept, you say, but they cannot possibly be of any practical use in establishing security prices. Well, don't tell that to the owners of AZX Inc. (AZX). Since early 1991 that organization (or its predecessor, Wunsch Auction Systems, Inc.) has been conducting regular security auctions among institutional investors for a broad list of common stocks. Market clearing prices in those auctions are determined by the explicit interaction of the investors' supply and demand preferences.

Step back for a moment and recall how prices are set on organized security exchanges or the OTC market (see Chapter 3). Dealers (whether specialists or OTC dealers) "make markets" in particular securities; that is, acting as intermediaries, they buy and sell from other investors for their own accounts. The dealers quote prices (bid and asked) to sellers and buyers on a continuous basis. They adjust prices as they sense supply and demand building and ebbing. It is the competitive efforts of these intermediaries that determine security prices.

AZX has developed a market mechanism quite different from that of the conventional dealer markets. AZX calls this mechanism the Arizona Stock Exchange, although it bears no resemblance to any existing stock exchange. (The name derives from financial support provided to AZX by the State of Arizona.) The concept behind the Arizona Stock Exchange is simple. Auctions are scheduled on a regular basis. (Originally an auction was held once a day

at 5 P.M. EST, after the New York Stock Exchange closes. More recently, a second auction was added at 9:15 A.M. for Nasdaq National Market Sytsem issues, and an additional morning auction is being planned.) Before a scheduled auction, investors submit orders electronically to buy or sell specified quantities of a security at specified prices (essentially limit orders; see Chapter 2).

At the time of the auction, the orders of all participating investors are aggregated by computer; that is, the computer calculates supply and demand curves for each security being auctioned. The intersection of these curves determines the market clearing price for a security. At that price the maximum number of shares of stock will be exchanged. (All buy orders above and all sell orders below the equilibrium price are matched; orders at the equilibrium price are matched on a time priority basis.)

Investors are able to access the auction order information (in graphic or tabular form) up to the time of the auction through an open limit order book. As opposed to a specialist's use of a proprietary closed limit order book, the Arizona Stock Exchange permits investors to examine the current supply and demand for a stock. Having this information enables investors to raise their bid prices (or lower their asked prices) to adjust to the current market conditions. Manipulative behavior is discouraged by the imposition of a penalty charge for withdrawn orders.

The Arizona Stock Exchange possesses some intriguing advantages over traditional dealer markets:

for the security. However, if more investors become optimistic rather than pessimistic, the demand-to-buy schedule will shift to the right (for example, to $D'D'$ in Figure 4.4) and the supply-to-sell schedule will shift to the left (for example, to $S'S'$ in Figure 4.4), causing an increase in price (to P'). Correspondingly, if more investors become pessimistic rather than optimistic, the demand-to-buy schedule will shift to the left and the supply-to-sell schedule will shift to the right, causing a decrease in price.

A factor that complicates an analysis of this type is the tendency for some investors to regard sudden and substantial price changes in a security as indicators of changes in the future prospects of the issuer. In the absence of further information, an investor may interpret such a change as an indication that "someone knows something that I don't know." While exploring the situation, the investor may at least temporarily revise his or her own assessment of the issuer's prospects and, in doing so, may alter his or her demand-to-buy or supply-to-sell schedule. For this reason, few investors place limit orders at prices substantially different from the current price for

1. It is simple and fair. All investors have access to the same auction information, and all investors trade at the same price.
2. Investors have direct access to the market. This feature removes the inherent conflicts of interest present in dealer markets.
3. Investors' orders are anonymous. Orders and trade executions are handled by computer.
4. It matches "natural" buyers and sellers (those with an explicit desire to transact), thereby perhaps establishing more robust and stable prices.
5. Transaction costs are low (about $.01 per share versus $.10 to $.20 per share or more in dealer markets).

This last point warrants elaboration. Traditional dealer markets are continuous; trading can occur at any time during the trading day. Continuous trading mechanisms are expensive and require dealers because the "other side" of a trade is not always immediately available. Dealers provide liquidity to investors who wish to transact immediately.

With more frequent large trades having been made by institutional investors in the last decade, the ability of dealer markets to provide continuous liquidity has been severely tested. The market crash of October 1987 was an extreme, but not singular, example.

Many (and perhaps most) institutional investors do not require immediate liquidity. They can wait several hours to trade, particularly if by waiting they can significantly reduce transaction costs. In lieu of the continuous intervention of the dealer, the Arizona Stock Exchange substitutes a periodic call to market (akin to the crossing systems discussed in Chapter 3). Without the expensive overhead of the dealer, the Arizona Stock Exchange can afford to match buyers and sellers at a small fraction of the cost of the dealer market.

What are the disadvantages of the Arizona Stock Exchange? Conceptually, there are none to investors who do not require immediate liquidity. However, if you throw a party and no one comes, the party is a failure no matter how elaborate the preparations. Likewise, to be successful, AZX must attract enough institutional investors to generate sufficient liquidity and to contribute to the "discovery" of market prices. Consequently, AZX must overcome investor inertia and ignorance. As does any fledgling trading mechanism, the Arizona Stock Exchange faces a difficult dilemma: Institutional investors want to see large trading volumes before they will participate, but those large volumes can occur only if institutional investors participate.

To date, traders have not beaten a path to AZX's door. Currently 20 to 25 institutional investors use the system on any given day, and daily trading volume runs around several hundred thousand shares. Although these figures pale in comparison to the activity on the New York Stock Exchange, participating investors and trading volumes have been growing over the last few years. Whether or not the Arizona Stock Exchange succeeds in its present form, the concept of an electronic call to market is likely to gain increasing attention in the years ahead.

fear that such orders would be executed only if the security's prospects changed significantly. If such a large price change actually occurred, it would imply the need for a careful reevaluation of the security before buying or selling shares.

4.1.6 Summary

Trading procedures employed in security markets vary from auction markets to dealer markets and from call markets to continuous markets. However, the similarities are more important than the differences. In the United States, for example, specialists at the New York Stock Exchange and dealers in the over-the-counter market provide some of the functions of the *saitori* at the Tokyo Stock Exchange, and trades can take place at any time. Nevertheless, the basic principles of security price determination still apply. In general, market price equates quantity demanded with quantity supplied.

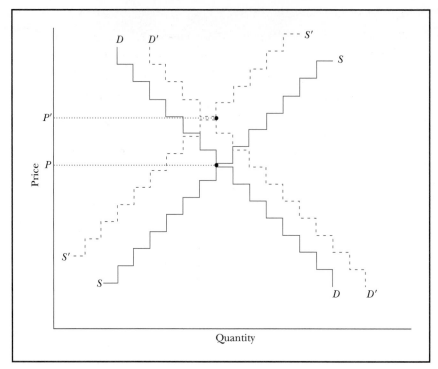

Figure 4.4
Shifts in the Aggregate Demand-to-Buy and Supply-to-Sell Schedules

MARKET EFFICIENCY

The topic of market efficiency has been and is likely to continue to be a matter of intense debate in the investment community. In order to understand and participate in this debate, one must understand just what is meant by market efficiency. First of all, most financial economists would agree that it is desirable to see that capital is channeled to the place where it will do the most good. That is, a reasonable goal of government policy is to encourage the establishment of **allocationally efficient markets**, in which the firms with the most promising investment opportunities have access to the needed funds. However, in order for markets to be allocationally efficient, they need to be both internally and externally efficient. In an **externally efficient market**, information is quickly and widely disseminated, thereby allowing each security's price to adjust rapidly in an unbiased manner to new information so that it reflects investment value (a term that will be discussed shortly). In comparison, an **internally efficient market** is one in which brokers and dealers compete fairly so that the cost of transacting is low and the speed of transacting is high. External market efficiency has been the subject of much research since the 1960s, but internal market efficiency has only recently become a popular area of research.[1] Indeed, the Securities and Exchange Commission has adopted polices aimed at improving the internal efficiency of markets, primarily by setting rules and regulations that affect the design and operations of security markets. Nevertheless, from now on the term *market efficiency* will denote external market efficiency, because this is the subject that has generated the most interest among practitioners and academics.

4.2.1 The Efficient Market Model

Imagine a world in which (1) all investors have costless access to currently available information about the future, (2) all investors are capable analysts, and (3) all investors pay close attention to market prices and adjust their holdings appropriately.[2] In such a market a security's price will be a good estimate of its **investment value**, where investment value is the present value of the security's future prospects, as estimated by well-informed and skillful analysts who use the information that is currently at hand. (Investment value is often referred to as the security's "fair" or "intrinsic" value.) That is, an **efficient market**, defined as one in which every security's price equals its investment value at all times, will exist.

In an efficient market a set of information is fully and immediately reflected in market prices. But what information? A popular distinction, offered by Eugene Fama, is the following:[3]

Form of Efficiency	Set of Information Reflected in Security Prices
Weak	Previous prices of securities
Semistrong	All publicly available information
Strong	All information, both public and private

This distinction leads to an equivalent definition of an efficient market as follows:

A market is efficient with respect to a particular set of information if it is impossible to make abnormal profits (other than by chance) by using this set of information to formulate buying and selling decisions.

That is, in an efficient market investors should expect to make only normal profits by earning a normal rate of return on their investments. For example, a market would be described as being **weak-form efficient** if it is impossible to make abnormal profits (other than by chance) by using past prices to formulate buying and selling decisions. Similarly, a market would be described as being **semistrong-form efficient** if it is impossible to make abnormal profits (other than by chance) by using publicly available information to formulate buying and selling decisions. Last, a market would be described as being **strong-form efficient** if it is impossible to make abnormal profits (other than by chance) by using any information whatsoever to make buying and selling decisions. Typically, when people refer to efficient markets, they really mean semistrong-form efficient markets, because the United States has strict laws about the use of insider information (a form of private information) to formulate buying and selling decisions. Hence, it is interesting to investigate whether markets are semistrong-form efficient since that involves the set of publicly available information that analysts are restricted to using in preparing their recommendations.

Why have the above statements included the qualifying phrase "other than by chance" in the definition of an efficient market? Simply because some people, for example, may invest on the basis of patterns in past prices and end up making extraordinarily high returns. However, in an efficient market this outcome would have had nothing to do with the investor's use of past price information. Instead, it would have been merely due to luck, just as someone who wins a lottery after using a method for picking a number does not necessarily have a successful method for picking winning lottery numbers.

Figure 4.5 illustrates these three forms of efficiency. Note how in moving from weak to semistrong to strong-form efficiency, the set of information expands. Thus,

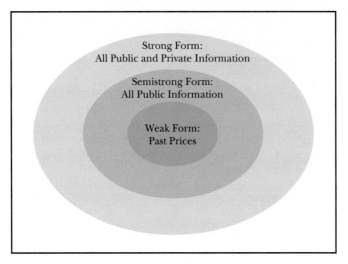

Figure 4.5
Information and the Levels of Market Efficiency

if markets are strong-form efficient, then they are also semistrong and weak-form efficient. Similarly, if markets are semistrong-form efficient, then they are also weak-form efficient.

4.2.2 Fama's Formulation of the Efficient Market Model

Fama presented a general notation describing how investors generate price expectations for securities. That is:

$$E(p_{j,\,t+1}|\Phi_t) = \left[1 + E(r_{j,\,t+1}|\Phi_t)\right]p_{jt} \qquad (4.1)$$

where:

E = expected value operator

$p_{j,\,t+1}$ = price of security j at time $t + 1$

$r_{j,\,t+1}$ = return on security j during period $t + 1$

Φ_t = the set of information available to investors at time t

so $E(p_{j,\,t+1}|\Phi_t)$ denotes the expected end-of-period price on security j, given the information available at the beginning of the period. Continuing, the term $1 + E(r_{j,\,t+1}|\Phi_t)$ denotes the expected return over the forthcoming time period on securities having the same amount of risk as security j, given the information available at the beginning of the period. Last, $p_{j,\,t}$ denotes the price of security j at the beginning of the period. Thus, Equation (4.1) states that the expected price for any security at the end of the period $(t + 1)$ is based on the security's expected normal (or equilibrium) rate of return during that period. In turn, the expected rate of return is determined by (or is conditional on) the information set available at the start of the period, Φ_t. Investors are assumed to make full and accurate use of this available information set. That is, they do not ignore or misinterpret this information in setting their return projections for the coming period.

What is contained in the available information set Φ_t? The answer depends on the particular form of market efficiency being considered. In the case of weak-form efficiency, the information set includes past price data. In the case of semistrong-form efficiency, the information set includes all publicly available information relevant to establishing security values, including the weak-form information set. This information would include published financial data about companies, government data about the state of the economy, earnings estimates disseminated by companies and securities analysts, and so on. Finally, in the case of strong-form efficiency, the information set includes all relevant valuation data, including information known only to corporate insiders, such as imminent corporate takeover plans and extraordinary positive or negative future earnings announcements.

If markets are efficient, then investors cannot earn abnormal profits trading on the available information set Φ_t other than by chance. Again employing Fama's notation, the level of over- or undervaluation of a security is defined as:

$$x_{j,\,t+1} = p_{j,\,t+1} - E\left(p_{j,\,t+1}\,|\,\Phi_t\right) \tag{4.2}$$

where $x_{j,\,t+1}$ indicates the extent to which the actual price for security j at the end of the period differs from the price expected by investors based on the information available at the beginning of the period. As a result, in an efficient market it must be true that:

$$E\left(x_{j,\,t+1}\,|\,\Phi_t\right) = 0 \tag{4.3}$$

That is, there will be no expected under- or overvaluation of securities based on the available information set. That information is always impounded in security prices.

4.2.3   Security Price Changes As a Random Walk

What happens when *new* information arrives that changes the information set Φ_t, such as an announcement that a company's earnings have just experienced a significant and unexpected decline? In an efficient market, investors will incorporate any new information immediately and fully in security prices. New information is just that: new, meaning a surprise. (Anything that is not a surprise is predictable and should have been anticipated before the fact.) Because happy surprises are about as likely as unhappy ones, price changes in an efficient market are about as likely to be positive as negative. A security's price can be expected to move upward by an amount that provides a reasonable return on capital (when considered in conjunction with dividend payments), but anything above or below such an amount would, in an efficient market, be unpredictable.

In a perfectly efficient market, price changes are random.[4] This does not mean that prices are irrational. On the contrary, prices are quite rational. Because information arrives randomly, changes in prices that occur as a consequence of that information will appear to be random, sometimes being positive and sometimes being negative. However, these price changes are simply the consequence of investors' reassessing a security's prospects and adjusting their buying and selling appropriately. Hence the price changes are random but rational.

As mentioned earlier, in an efficient market a security's price will be a good estimate of its investment value, where investment value is the present value of the security's future prospects as estimated by well-informed and capable analysts. In a well-developed and free market, major disparities between price and investment value will be noted by alert analysts who will seek to take advantage of their discoveries. Securities priced below investment value (known as underpriced or undervalued securities) will be purchased, creating pressure for price increases due to the increased demand to buy. Securities priced above investment value (known as overpriced or overvalued securities) will be sold, creating pressure for price decreases due to the increased supply to sell. As investors seek to take advantage of opportunities created by temporary inefficiencies, they will cause the inefficiencies to be reduced, denying the less alert and the less informed a chance to obtain large abnormal profits. As a consequence of the efforts of such highly alert investors, at any time a security's price can be assumed to equal the security's investment value, implying that security mispricing will not exist.

4.2.4 Observations about Perfectly Efficient Markets

Some interesting observations can be made about perfectly efficient markets.

1. Investors should expect to make a fair return on their investment but no more. This statement means that looking for mispriced securities with either technical analysis (whereby analysts examine the past price behavior of securities) or fundamental analysis (whereby analysts examine earnings and dividend forecasts) will not prove to be fruitful. Investing money on the basis of either type of analysis will not generate abnormal returns (other than for those few investors who turn out to be lucky).

2. Markets will be efficient only if enough investors believe that they are not efficient. The reason for this seeming paradox is straightforward; it is the actions of investors who carefully analyze securities that make prices reflect investment values. However, if everyone believed that markets are perfectly efficient, then everyone would realize that nothing is to be gained by searching for undervalued securities, and hence nobody would bother to analyze securities. Consequently, security prices would not react instantaneously to the release of information but instead would respond more slowly. Thus, in a classic "Catch-22" situation, markets would become inefficient if investors believed that they are efficient, yet they are efficient because investors believe them to be inefficient.

3. Publicly known investment strategies cannot be expected to generate abnormal returns. If somebody has a strategy that generated abnormal returns in the past and subsequently divulges it to the public (for example, by publishing a book or article about it), then the usefulness of the strategy will be destroyed. The strategy, whatever it is based on, must provide some means to identify mispriced securities. The reason that it will not work after it is made public is that the investors who know the strategy will try to capitalize on it, and in doing so will force prices to equal investment values the moment the strategy indicates a security is mispriced. The action of investors following the strategy will eliminate its effectiveness at identifying mispriced securities.

4. Some investors will display impressive performance records. However, their performance is merely due to chance (despite their assertions to the contrary). Think of a simple model in which half of the time the stock market has an annual return greater than Treasury bills (an "up" market) and the other half of the time its return is less than T-bills (a "down" market). With many investors attempting to forecast whether the stock market will be up or down each year and acting accordingly, in an efficient market about half the investors will be right in any given year and half will be wrong. The next year, half of those who were right the first year will be right the second year too. Thus, $1/4$ ($= 1/2 \times 1/2$) of all the investors will have been right both years. About half of the surviving investors will be right in the third year, so in total $1/8$ ($= 1/2 \times 1/2 \times 1/2$) of all the investors can show that they were right all three years. Thus, it can be seen that $(1/2)^T$ investors will be correct every year over a span of T years. Hence if $T = 6$, then $1/64$ of the investors will have been correct all five years, but only because they were lucky, not because they were skillful. Consequently, anecdotal evidence about the success of certain investors is misleading. Indeed, any fees paid for advice from such investors would be wasted.

5. Professional investors should fare no better in picking securities than ordinary investors. Prices always reflect investment value, and hence the search for mispriced securities is futile. Consequently, professional investors do not have an edge on ordinary investors when it comes to identifying mispriced securities and generating abnormally high returns.

6. Past performance is not an indicator of future performance. Investors who have done well in the past are no more likely to do better in the future than are investors who have done poorly in the past. Those who did well in the past were merely lucky, and those who did poorly merely had a streak of misfortune. Because past luck and misfortune do not have a tendency to repeat themselves, historical performance records are useless in predicting future performance records. (Of course, if the poor performance was due to incurring high operating expenses, then poor performers are likely to remain poor performers.)

4.2.5 Observations about Perfectly Efficient Markets with Transactions Costs

The efficient market model discussed earlier assumed that investors had free access to all information relevant to setting security prices. In reality, it is expensive to collect and process such information. Furthermore, investors cannot adjust their portfolios in response to new information without incurring transaction costs. How does the existence of these costs affect the efficient market model? Sanford Grossman and Joseph Stiglitz considered this issue and arrived at two important conclusions.[5]

1. In a world where it costs money to analyze securities, analysts will be able to identify mispriced securities. However, their gain from doing so will be exactly offset by the increased costs (perhaps associated with the money needed to procure data and analytical software) that they incur. Hence, their gross returns will indicate that they have made abnormal returns, but their net returns will show that they have earned a fair return and nothing more. Of course, they can earn less than a fair return in such an environment if they fail to properly use the data. For example, by rapidly buying and selling securities, they may generate large transactions costs that would more than offset the value of their superior security analysis.

2. Investors will do just as well using a passive investment strategy where they simply buy the securities in a particular index and hold onto that investment. Such a strategy will minimize transaction costs and can be expected to do as well as any professionally managed portfolio that actively seeks out mispriced securities and incurs costs in doing so. Indeed, such a strategy can be expected to outperform any professionally managed portfolio that incurs unnecessary transaction costs (by, for example, trading too often). Note that the gross returns of professionally managed portfolios will exceed those of passively managed portfolios having similar investment objectives but that the two kinds of portfolios can be expected to have similar net returns.

4.3   TESTING FOR MARKET EFFICIENCY

Now that the method for determining prices in a perfectly efficient market has been described, it is useful to take a moment to consider how to conduct tests to determine if markets actually are perfectly efficient, reasonably efficient, or not efficient at all. There are a multitude of methodologies, but three stand out. They involve conducting event studies, looking for patterns in security prices, and examining the investment performance of professional money managers.

The Active versus Passive Debate

The issue of market efficiency has clear and important ramifications for the investment management industry. At stake are billions of dollars in investment management fees, professional reputations, and, some would argue, even the effective functioning of our capital markets.

Greater market efficiency implies a lower probability that an investor will be able to consistently identify mispriced securities. Consequently, the more efficient is a security market, the lower is the expected payoff to investors who buy and sell securities in search of abnormally high returns. In fact, when research and transaction costs are factored into the analysis, greater market efficiency increases the chances that investors "actively" managing their portfolios will underperform a simple technique of holding a portfolio that resembles the composition of the entire market. Institutional investors have responded to evidence of significant efficiency in the U.S. stock and bond markets by increasingly pursing an investment approach referred to as *passive management*. Passive management involves a long-term, buy-and-hold approach to investing. The investor selects an appropriate target and buys a portfolio designed to closely track the performance of that target. Once the portfolio is purchased, little additional trading occurs, beyond reinvesting income or minor rebalancings necessary to accurately track the target. Because the selected target is usually (although not necessarily) a broad, diversified market index (for example, the S&P 500 for domestic common stocks), passive management (see Chapter 23) is commonly referred to as "indexation," and the passive portfolios are called "index funds."

Active management, on the other hand, involves a systematic effort to exceed the performance of a selected target. A wide array of active management investment approaches exists—far too many to summarize in this space. Nevertheless, all active management entails the search for mispriced securities or for mispriced groups of securities. Accurately identifying and adroitly purchasing or selling these mispriced securities provides the active investor with the potential to outperform the passive investor.

Passive management is a relative newcomer to the investment industry. Before the mid-1960s, it was axiomatic that investors should search for mispriced stocks. Some investment strategies had passive overtones, such as buying "solid, blue-chip" companies for the "long term." Nevertheless, even these strategies implied an attempt to outperform some nebulously specified market target. The concepts of broad diversification and passive management were, for practical purposes, nonexistent.

Attitudes changed in the 1960s with the popularization of Markowitz's portfolio selection concepts (see Chapter 6), the introduction of the efficient market hypothesis (see this chapter), the emphasis on "the market portfolio" derived from the Capital Asset Pricing Model (see Chapter 9), and various academic studies proclaiming the futility of active management. Many investors, especially large institutional investors, began to question the wisdom of actively managing all of their assets. The first domestic common stock index fund was introduced in 1971. By the end of the decade, roughly $100 million was invested in index funds. Today, hundreds of billions of dollars are invested in domestic and international stock and bond index funds. Even individual investors have become enamored of index funds. Passively managed portfolios are some of the fastest growing products offered by many large mutual fund organizations.

Proponents of active management argue that capital markets are inefficient enough to justify the

4.3.1 Event Studies

Event studies can be carried out to see just how fast security prices actually react to the release of information. Do they react rapidly or slowly? Are the returns after the announcement date abnormally high or low, or are they simply normal? Note that the answer to the second question requires a definition of a "normal return" for a given security. Typically "normal" is defined by the use of some equilibrium-based asset pricing model, two of which will be discussed in Chapters 9 and 11. An improperly specified asset pricing model can invalidate a test of market efficiency. Thus, event studies are really joint tests, as they simultaneously involve tests of the asset pricing

search for mispriced securities. They may disagree on the degree of the markets' inefficiencies. Technical analysts (see Chapter 16), for example, tend to view markets as dominated by emotionally driven and predictable investors, thereby creating numerous profit opportunities for the creative and disciplined investor. Conversely, managers who use highly quantitative investment tools often view profit opportunities as smaller and less persistent. Nevertheless, all active managers possess a fundamental belief in the existence of consistently exploitable security mispricings. As evidence they frequently point to the stellar track records of certain successful managers and various studies identifying market inefficiencies (see Appendix A, Chapter 16, which discusses empirical regularities).

Some active management proponents also introduce into the active-passive debate what amounts to a moralistic appeal. They contend that investors have virtually an obligation to seek out mispriced securities, because their actions help remove these mispricings and thereby lead to a more efficient allocation of capital. Moreover, some proponents derisively contend that passive management implies settling for mediocre, or average, performance.

Proponents of passive management do not deny that exploitable profit opportunities exist or that some managers have established impressive performance results. Rather, they contend that the capital markets are efficient enough to prevent all but a few with inside information from consistently being able to earn abnormal profits. They claim that examples of past successes are more likely the result of luck rather than skill. If 1,000 people flip a coin ten times, the odds are that one of them will flip all heads. In the investment industry, this person is crowned a brilliant money manager.

Passive management proponents also argue that the expected returns from active management are actually less than those for passive management. The fees charged by active managers are typically much higher than those levied by passive managers. (The difference averages anywhere from .30% to 1.00% of the managers' assets under management.) Further, passively managed portfolios usually experience very small transaction costs, whereas, depending on the amount of trading involved, active management transaction costs can be quite high. Thus it is argued that passive managers will outperform active managers because of cost differences. Passive management thus entails settling for superior, as opposed to mediocre, results.

The active-passive debate will never be totally resolved. The random "noise" inherent in investment performance tends to drown out any systematic evidence of investment management skill on the part of active managers. Subjective issues therefore dominate the discussion, and as a result neither side can convince the other of the correctness of its viewpoint.

Despite the rapid growth in passively managed assets, most domestic and international stock and bond portfolios remain actively managed. Many large institutional investors, such as pension funds, have taken a middle ground on the matter, hiring both passive and active managers. In a crude way, this strategy may be a reasonable response to the unresolved active-passive debate. Assets cannot all be passively managed—who would be left to maintain security prices at "fair" value levels? On the other hand, it may not take many skillful active managers to ensure an adequate level of market efficiency. Further, the evidence is overwhelming that managers with above-average investment skills are in the minority of the group currently offering their services to investors.

model's validity and tests of market efficiency. A finding that prices react slowly to information might be due to markets' being inefficient, or it might be due to the use of an improper asset pricing model, or it might be due to both.

As an example of an event study, consider what happens in a perfectly efficient market when information is released. When the information arrives in the marketplace, prices will react instantaneously and, in doing so, will immediately move to their new investment values. Figure 4.6(a) shows what happens in such a market when good news arrives; Figure 4.6(b) shows what happens when bad news arrives. Note that in both cases the horizontal axis is a time line and the vertical axis is the security's price, so the figure reflects the security's price over time. At time 0 ($t = 0$),

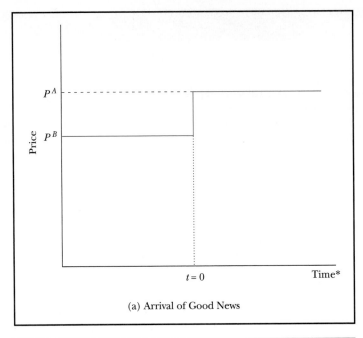

(a) Arrival of Good News

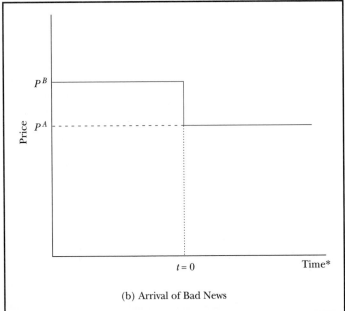

(b) Arrival of Bad News

Figure 4.6
The Effect of Information on a Firm's Stock Price in a Perfectly Efficient Market.
*Information is assumed to arrive at time $t = 0$.

information is released about the firm. Observe that, shortly before the news arrived, the security's price was at a price P^B. With the arrival of the information the price immediately moves to its new equilibrium level of P^A, where it stays until some additional piece of information arrives. (To be more precise, the vertical axis would represent the security's abnormal return, which in an efficient market would be zero until $t = 0$, when it would briefly be either significantly positive, in the case of good news,

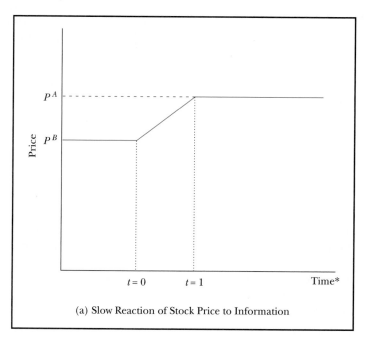

(a) Slow Reaction of Stock Price to Information

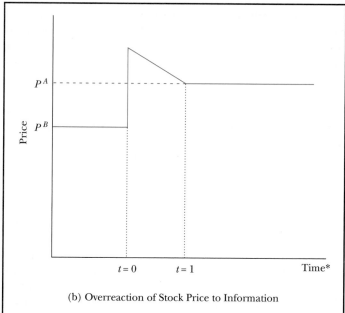

(b) Overreaction of Stock Price to Information

Figure 4.7
Possible Effects of Information on a Firm's Stock Price in an Inefficient Market.
* Information is assumed to arrive at time $t = 0$.

or significantly negative, in the case of bad news. Afterward, it would return to zero. For simplicity, prices are used instead of returns, because over a short time period surrounding $t = 0$ the results are essentially the same.)

Figure 4.7 displays two situations that cannot occur with regularity in an efficient market when good news arrives. (A similar situation, although not illustrated here, cannot occur when bad news arrives.) In Figure 4.7(a) the security reacts slowly to the information, so it does not reach its equilibrium price P^A until $t = 1$. This situation cannot occur regularly in an efficient market, because analysts will realize after $t = 0$ but before $t = 1$ that the security is not priced fairly and will rush to buy it. Consequently, they will force the security to reach its equilibrium price before $t = 1$. Indeed, they will force the security to reach its equilibrium price moments after the information is released at $t = 0$.

In Figure 4.7(b) the security's price overreacts to the information and then slowly settles down to its equilibrium value. Again, this situation cannot occur with regularity in an efficient market. Analysts will realize that the security is selling above its fair value and will proceed to sell it if they own it or to short sell it if they do not own it. As a consequence of their actions, they will prevent its price from rising above its equilibrium value, P^A, after the information is released.

Many event studies have been made about the reaction of security prices, particularly stock prices, to the release of information, such as news (usually referred to as "announcements") pertaining to earnings and dividends, share repurchase programs, stock splits and dividends, stock and bond sales, stock listings, bond rating changes, mergers and acquisitions, and divestitures. Indeed, this area of academic research has become a virtual growth industry.

4.3.2   Looking for Patterns

A second method to test for market efficiency is to investigate whether there are any patterns in security price movements attributable to something other than what one would expect. Securities can be expected to provide a rate of return over a given time period in accord with an asset pricing model. Such a model asserts that a security's expected rate of return is equal to a riskfree rate of return plus a "risk premium" whose magnitude is based on the riskiness of the security. Hence, if the riskfree rate and risk premium are both unchanging over time, then securities with high average returns in the past can be expected to have high returns in the future. However, the risk premium, for example, may be changing over time, making it difficult to see if there are patterns in security prices. Indeed, any tests that are conducted to test for the existence of price patterns are once again joint tests of both market efficiency and the asset pricing model that is used to estimate the risk premiums on securities.

In recent years, a large number of these patterns have been identified and labeled as "empirical regularities" or "market anomalies." For example, one of the most prominent market anomalies is the January effect. Security returns appear to be abnormally high in the month of January. Other months show no similar type returns. This pattern has a long and consistent track record, and no convincing explanations have been proposed. (The January effect and other market anomalies are discussed in Chapter 16.)

4.3.3   Examining Performance

The third approach is to examine the investment record of professional investors. Are more of them able to earn abnormally high rates of return than one would expect in a perfectly efficient market? Are more of them able to consistently earn abnormally high returns period after period than one would expect in an efficient market? Again, problems are encountered in conducting such tests because they require the determination of abnormal returns, which, in turn, requires the determination of just what are "normal returns." Because normal returns can be determined only by assuming that a particular asset pricing model is applicable, all such tests are joint tests of market efficiency and an asset pricing model.

Many tests have been conducted over the years examining the degree to which security markets are efficient. Rather than laboriously review the results of those tests here, the most prominent studies are discussed in later chapters, where the specific investment activities associated with the studies are considered. However, a few comments about the general conclusions drawn from those studies are appropriate here.

4.4.1 Weak-Form Tests

Early tests of weak-form market efficiency failed to find any evidence that abnormal profits could be earned trading on information related to past prices. That is, knowing how security prices had moved in the past could not be translated into accurate predictions of future security prices. These tests generally concluded that technical analysis, which relies on forecasting security prices on the basis of past prices, was ineffective. More recent studies, however, have indicated that investors may overreact to certain types of information, driving security prices temporarily away from their investment values. As a result, it may be possible to earn abnormal profits buying securities that have been "oversold" and selling securities whose prices have been bid up excessively. It should be pointed out, however, that these observations are debatable and have not been universally accepted.

4.4.2 Semistrong-Form Tests

The results of tests of semistrong-form market efficiency have been mixed. Most event studies have failed to demonstrate sufficiently large inefficiencies to overcome transaction costs. However, various market "anomalies" have been discovered whereby securities with certain characteristics or during certain time periods appear to produce abnormally high returns. For example, as mentioned, common stocks in January have been shown to offer returns much higher than those earned in the other 11 months of the year.

4.4.3 Strong-Form Tests

One would expect that investors with access to private information would have an advantage over investors who trade only on publicly available information. In general, corporate insiders and stock exchange specialists, who have information not readily available to the investing public, have been shown to be able to earn abnormally high profits. Less clear is the ability of security analysts to produce such profits. At times, these analysts have direct access to private information, and in a sense they also "manufacture" their own private information through their research efforts. Some studies have indicated that certain analysts are able to discern mispriced securities, but whether this ability is due to skill or chance is an open issue.

4.4.4 Summary of Efficient Markets

Tests of market efficiency demonstrate that U.S. security markets are highly efficient, impounding relevant information about investment values into security prices quickly and accurately. Investors cannot easily expect to earn abnormal profits trading on publicly available information, particularly once the costs of research and transactions are considered. Nevertheless, numerous pockets of unexplained abnormal returns have been identified, guaranteeing that the debate over the degree of market efficiency will continue.

1. The forces of supply and demand interact to determine a security's market price.
2. An investor's demand-to-buy schedule indicates the quantity of a security that the investor wishes to purchase at various prices.
3. An investor's supply-to-sell schedule indicates the quantity of a security that the investor wishes to sell at various prices.
4. The demand and supply schedules for individual investors can be aggregated to create aggregate demand and supply schedules for a security.
5. The intersection of the aggregate demand and supply schedules determines the market clearing price of a security. At that price, the quantity traded is maximized.
6. The market price of a security can be thought of as representing a consensus opinion about the future prospects for the security.
7. An allocationally efficient market is one in which firms with the most promising investment opportunities have access to needed funds.
8. Markets must be both internally and externally efficient in order to be allocationally efficient. In an externally efficient market, information is quickly and widely disseminated, thereby allowing each security's price to adjust rapidly in an unbiased manner to new information so that it reflects investment value. In an internally efficient market, brokers and dealers compete fairly so that the cost of transacting is low and the speed of transacting is high.
9. A security's investment value is the present value of the security's future prospects, as estimated by well-informed and capable analysts, and can be thought of as the security's fair or intrinsic value.
10. In an efficient market a security's market price will fully reflect all available information relevant to the security's value at that time.
11. The concept of market efficiency can be expressed in three forms: weak, semistrong, and strong.
12. The three forms of market efficiency make different assumptions about the set of information reflected in security prices.
13. Tests of market efficiency are really joint tests about whether markets are efficient and whether security prices are set according to a specific asset pricing model.
14. Evidence suggests that U.S. financial markets are highly efficient.

QUESTIONS AND PROBLEMS

1. What is the difference between call security markets and continuous security markets?
2. Using demand-to-buy or supply-to-sell schedules, explain and illustrate the effect of the following events on the equilibrium price and quantity traded of Fairchild Corporation's stock.
   a. Fairchild officials announce that next year's earnings are expected to be significantly higher than analysts had previously forecast.
   b. A wealthy shareholder initiates a large secondary offering of Fairchild stock.
   c. Another company, quite similar to Fairchild in all respects except for being privately held, decides to offer its outstanding shares for sale to the public.
3. Imp Begley is pondering this statement: "The pattern of security price behavior might appear the same whether markets were efficient or security prices bore no relationship whatsoever to investment value." Explain to Imp the meaning of the statement.

4. We all know that investors have widely diverse opinions about the future course of the economy and earnings forecasts for various industries and companies. How then is it possible for all these investors to arrive at an equilibrium price for any particular security?

5. Distinguish between the three forms of market efficiency.

6. Does the fact that a market exhibits weak-form efficiency necessarily imply that it is also strong-form efficient? How about the converse statement? Explain.

7. Consider the following types of information. If this information is immediately and fully reflected in security prices, what form of market efficiency is implied?
   a. A company's recent quarterly earnings announcement
   b. Historical bond yields
   c. Deliberations of a company's board of directors concerning a possible merger with another company
   d. Limit orders in a specialist's book
   e. A brokerage firm's published research report on a particular company
   f. Movements in the Dow Jones Industrial Average as plotted in *The Wall Street Journal*

8. Would you expect that fundamental security analysis makes security markets more efficient? Why?

9. Would you expect that NYSE specialists should be able to earn an abnormal profit in a semistrong efficient market? Why?

10. Is it true that in a perfectly efficient market no investor would consistently be able to earn a profit?

11. Although security markets may not be perfectly efficient, what is the rationale for expecting them to be highly efficient?

12. When a corporation announces its earnings for a period, the volume of transactions in its stock may increase, but frequently that increase is not associated with significant moves in the price of its stock. How can this situation be explained?

13. What are the implications of the three forms of market efficiency for technical and fundamental analysis (discussed in Chapter 1)?

14. In 1986 and 1987 several high-profile insider trading scandals were exposed.
   a. Is successful insider trading consistent with the three forms of market efficiency? Explain.
   b. Play the role of devil's advocate and present a case outlining the benefits to financial markets of insider trading.

15. The text states that tests for market efficiency involving an asset pricing model are really joint tests. What is meant by that statement?

16. In perfectly efficient markets with transaction costs, why should analysts be able to find mispriced securities?

17. When investment managers present their historical performance records to potential and existing customers, market regulators require the managers to qualify those records with the comment that "past performance is no guarantee of future performance." In a perfectly efficient market, why would such an admonition be particularly appropriate?

CFA EXAM QUESTIONS

18. Discuss the role of a portfolio manager in a perfectly efficient market.

19. Fairfax asks for information concerning the benefits of active portfolio management. She is particularly interested in the question of whether active managers can be expected to consistently exploit inefficiencies in the capital markets to produce above-average returns without assuming higher risk.

   The semistrong form of the efficient market hypothesis (EMH) asserts that all publicly available information is rapidly and correctly reflected in securities prices. This assertion implies that investors cannot expect to derive above-average profits from purchases made after the information has become public because security prices already reflect the information's full effects.

    a. **(i)** Identify and explain two examples of empirical evidence that tend to support the EMH implication stated above.

        (ii) Identify and explain two examples of empirical evidence that tend to refute the EMH implication stated above.

    b. Discuss two reasons why an investor might choose an active manager even if the markets were, in fact, semistrong-form efficient.

ENDNOTES

[1] A burgeoning field of research in finance is known as *market microstructure*, which involves the study of internal market efficiency.

[2] Actually, not all investors need to meet these three conditions in order for security prices to equal their investment values. Instead, what is needed is for marginal investors to meet these conditions, since their trades would correct the mispricing that would occur in their absence.

[3] Eugene F. Fama, "Efficient Capital Markets: A Review of Theory and Empirical Work," *Journal of Finance* 25, no. 5 (May 1970): 383–417.

[4] Some people assert that daily stock prices follow a **random walk**, meaning that stock price changes (say, from one day to the next) are independently and identically distributed. That is, the price change from day t to day $t + 1$ is not influenced by the price change from day $t - 1$ to day t, and the size of the price change from one day to the next can be viewed as being determined by the spin of a roulette wheel (with the same roulette wheel being used every day). Statistically, in a random walk $P_t = P_{t-1} + e_t$ where e_t is a random error term whose expected outcome is zero but whose actual outcome is like the spin of a roulette wheel. A more reasonable characterization is to describe daily stock prices as following a **random walk with drift**, where $P_t = P_{t-1} + d + e_t$ where d is a small positive number, since stock prices have shown a tendency over time to go up. However, since it can be reasonably argued that the random error term e_t is not independent and identically distributed over time (that is, evidence suggests that the same roulette wheel is not used every period), the most accurate characterization of stock prices is to say they follow a *submartingale process*. This simply means that a stock's expected price in period $t + 1$, given the information that is available at time t, is greater than the stock's price at time t.

[5] Sanford J. Grossman and Joseph E. Stiglitz, "On the Impossibility of Informationally Efficient Markets," *American Economic Review* 70, no. 3 (June 1980).

KEY TERMS

demand-to-buy schedule	efficient market
supply-to-sell schedule	weak-form efficient
allocationally efficient market	semistrong-form efficient
externally efficient market	strong-form efficient
internally efficient market	random walk
investment value	random walk with drift

REFERENCES

1. Discussion and examination of the demand curves for stocks are contained in:

Andrei Shleifer, "Do Demand Curves Slope Down?" *Journal of Finance* 41, no. 3 (July 1986): 579–590.

Lawrence Harris and Eitan Gurel, "Price and Volume Effects Associated with Changes in the S&P 500: New Evidence for the Existence of Price Pressures," *Journal of Finance* 41, no. 4 (September 1986): 815–829.

Stephen W. Pruitt and K. C. John Wei, "Institutional Ownership and Changes in the S&P 500," *Journal of Finance* 44, no. 2 (June 1989): 509–513.

2. For articles presenting arguments that securities are "overpriced" owing to short sale restrictions, see:

Edward M. Miller, "Risk, Uncertainty, and Divergence of Opinion," *Journal of Finance* 32, no. 4 (September 1977): 1151–1168.

Douglas W. Diamond and Robert E. Verrecchia, "Constraints on Short-Selling and Asset Price Adjustment to Private Information," *Journal of Financial Economics* 18, no. 2 (June 1987): 277–311.

3. Allocational, external, and internal market efficiency are discussed in:

Richard R. West, "Two Kinds of Market Efficiency," *Financial Analysts Journal* 31, no. 6 (November/December 1975): 30–34.

4. Many people believe that the following articles are the seminal pieces on efficient markets:

Paul Samuelson, "Proof That Properly Anticipated Prices Fluctuate Randomly," *Industrial Management Review* 6 (1965): 41–49.

Harry V. Roberts, "Stock Market 'Patterns' and Financial Analysis: Methodological Suggestions," *Journal of Finance* 14, no. 1 (March 1959): 1–10.

Eugene F. Fama, "Efficient Capital Markets: A Review of Theory and Empirical Work," *Journal of Finance* 25, no. 5 (May 1970): 383–417.

Eugene F. Fama, "Efficient Capital Markets: II," *Journal of Finance* 46, no. 5 (December 1991): 1575–1617.

5. For an extensive discussion of efficient markets and related evidence, see:

George Foster, *Financial Statement Analysis* (Englewood Cliffs, NJ: Prentice Hall, 1986), Chapters 9 and 11.

Stephen F. LeRoy, "Capital Market Efficiency: An Update," *Federal Reserve Bank of San Francisco Economic Review* no. 2 (Spring 1990): 29–40. A more detailed version of this paper can be found in: Stephen F. LeRoy, "Efficient Capital Markets and Martingales," *Journal of Economic Literature* 27, no. 4 (December 1989): 1583–1621.

Peter Fortune, "Stock Market Efficiency: An Autopsy?" *New England Economic Review* (March/April 1991): 17–40.

Richard A. Brealey and Stewart C. Myers, *Principles of Corporate Finance* (New York: McGraw-Hill, 1996), Chapter 13.

Stephen A. Ross, Randolph W. Westerfield, and Jeffrey F. Jaffe, *Corporate Finance* (Boston: Irwin/McGraw Hill, 1996), Chapter 13.

6. Interesting overviews of efficient market concepts are presented in:

Robert Ferguson, "An Efficient Stock Market? Ridiculous!" *Journal of Portfolio Management* 9, no. 4 (Summer 1983): 31–38.

Bob L. Boldt and Harold L. Arbit, "Efficient Markets and the Professional Investor," *Financial Analysts Journal* 40, no. 4 (July/August 1984): 22–34.

Fischer Black, "Noise," *Journal of Finance* 41, no. 3 (July 1986): 529–543.

Keith C. Brown, W. V. Harlow, and Seha M. Tinic, "How Rational Investors Deal with Uncertainty (Or, Reports of the Death of Efficient Markets Theory Are Greatly Exaggerated)," *Journal of Applied Corporate Finance* 2, no. 3 (Fall 1989): 45–58.

Ray Ball, "The Theory of Stock Market Efficiency: Accomplishments and Limitations," *Journal of Applied Corporate Finance* 8, no. 1 (Spring 1995): 4–17.

THE VALUATION OF RISKLESS SECURITIES

Auseful first step in understanding security valuation is to consider riskless securities, which are those fixed-income securities that are certain of making their promised payments in full and on time. Subsequent chapters will be devoted to valuing risky securities, for which the size and timing of payments to investors are uncertain. Whereas common stocks and corporate bonds are examples of risky securities, the obvious candidates for consideration as riskless securities are the securities that represent the debt of the federal government. Because the government can print money whenever it chooses, the promised payments on such securities are virtually certain to be made on schedule. However, there is a degree of uncertainty as to the purchasing power of the promised payments. Although government bonds may be riskless in terms of their nominal payments, they may be quite risky in terms of their real (or inflation-adjusted) payments. This chapter begins with a discussion of the relationship between nominal and real interest rates.

Despite the concern with inflation risk, it will be assumed that there are fixed-income securities whose nominal and real payments are certain. Specifically, it will be assumed that the magnitude of inflation can be accurately predicted. Such an assumption makes it possible to focus on the impact of *time* on bond valuation. The influences of other attributes on bond valuation can be considered afterward.

5.1 NOMINAL VERSUS REAL INTEREST RATES

Modern economies gain much of their efficiency through the use of money—a generally agreed-upon medium of exchange. Instead of trading present corn for a future Toyota, as in a barter economy, the citizen of a modern economy can trade his or her corn for money (that is, "sell it"), trade the money for future money (that is, "invest it"), and finally trade the future money for a Toyota (that is, "buy it"). The rate at which he or she can trade present money for future money is the **nominal** (or "monetary") **interest rate**—usually simply called the interest rate.

In periods of changing prices, the nominal interest rate may prove a poor guide to the real return obtained by the investor. Although there is no completely satisfactory way to summarize the many price changes that take place in such periods, most governments attempt to do so by measuring the cost of a specified bundle of major items. The "overall" price level computed for this representative combination of items is usually called a **cost-of-living index** or **consumer price index**.

Whether the index is relevant for a given individual depends to a major extent on the similarity of his or her purchases to the bundle of goods and services used to construct the index. Moreover, such indices tend to overstate increases in the cost of living for people who do purchase the chosen bundle of items for two reasons. First, improvements in quality are seldom taken adequately into account. Perhaps more important, little or no adjustment is made in the composition of items in the bundle as relative prices change. The rational consumer can reduce the cost of attaining a given standard of living as prices change by substituting relatively less expensive items for those that have become relatively more expensive.

Despite these drawbacks, cost-of-living indices provide at least rough estimates of changes in prices. And such indices can be used to determine an overall real rate of interest. For example, assume that during a year in which the nominal rate of interest is 7%, the cost-of-living index increases from 121 to 124. This means that the bundle of goods and services that cost $100 in some base year and $121 at the beginning of the year now cost $124 at year-end. The owner of such a bundle could have sold it for $121 at the start of the year, invested the proceeds at 7% to obtain $129.47 (= $121 × 1.07) at the end of the year, and then immediately purchased 1.0441 (= $129.47/$124) bundles. The real rate of interest was, thus, 4.41% (= 1.0441 − 1). Effectively then, the **real interest rate** represents the percentage increase in an investor's consumption level from one period to another.

These calculations can be summarized in the following formula:

$$\frac{C_0(1 + NIR)}{C_1} = 1 + RIR \qquad (5.1)$$

where:

C_0 = level of the cost-of-living index at the beginning of the year
C_1 = level of the cost-of-living index at the end of the year
NIR = the nominal interest rate
RIR = the real interest rate

Alternatively, Equation (5.1) can be written as:

$$\frac{1 + NIR}{1 + CCL} = 1 + RIR \qquad (5.2)$$

where CCL equals the rate of change in the cost of living index, or $(C_1 - C_0)/C_0$. In this case, $CCL = .02479 = (124 - 121)/121$, so prices increased by about 2.5%.

For quick calculation, the real rate of interest can be estimated by simply subtracting the rate of change in the cost of living index from the nominal interest rate:

$$RIR \cong NIR - CCL \qquad (5.3)$$

where $\cong$ means "is approximately equal to." In this case the quick calculation results in an estimate of 4.5% (= 7% − 2.5%), which is reasonably close to the true value of 4.41%.

Equation (5.2) can be applied on either a historical or a forward-looking basis. The economist Irving Fisher argued in 1930 that the nominal interest rate ought to be related to the *expected* real interest rate and the *expected* inflation rate through an equation that became known as the Fisher equation. That is:

Almost Riskfree Securities

Riskfree securities play a central role in modern financial theory, providing the baseline against which to evaluate risky investment alternatives. It is perhaps surprising therefore that no riskfree financial asset has historically been available to U.S. investors. Recent developments in the U.S. Treasury bond market, however, have made important strides toward bringing that deficiency to an end.

A riskless security provides an investor with a guaranteed (certain) return over the investor's time horizon. As the investor is ultimately interested in the purchasing power of his or her investments, the riskless security's return should be certain, not just on a nominal but on a real (or inflation-adjusted) basis.

Although U.S. Treasury securities have zero risk of default, even they have not traditionally provided riskless real returns. Their principal and interest payments are not adjusted for inflation over the securities' lives. As a result, unexpected inflation may produce real returns quite different from those expected at the time the securities were purchased.

However, assume for the moment that U.S. inflation remains low and fairly predictable so that we can effectively ignore inflation risk. Will Treasury securities provide investors with riskless returns? The answer is generally no.

An investor's time horizon usually will not coincide with the life of a particular Treasury security. If the investor's time horizon is longer than the security's life, then the investor must purchase another Treasury security when the first security matures. If interest rates have changed in the interim, the investor will earn a different return than he or she originally anticipated. (This risk is known as reinvestment-rate risk; see Chapter 8.)

If the Treasury security's life exceeds the investor's time horizon, then the investor will have to sell the security before it matures. If interest rates change before the sale, the price of the security will change, thereby causing the investor to earn a different return from the one originally anticipated. (This risk is known as interest-rate or price risk; see Chapter 8.)

Even if the Treasury security's life matches the investor's time horizon, it generally will not provide a riskless return. With the exception of Treasury bills and STRIPS, all Treasury securities make periodic interest payments (see Chapter 13), which the investor must reinvest. If interest rates change over the security's life, then the investor's reinvestment rate will change, causing the investor's return to differ from that originally anticipated at the time the security was purchased.

Clearly, what investors need are Treasury securities that make only one payment (which includes principal and all interest) when those securities mature. Investors could then select a security whose life matched their investment time horizons. These securities would be truly riskless, at least on a nominal basis.

A fixed-income security that makes only one payment at maturity is called a zero-coupon (or pure-discount) bond. Until the 1980s, however, zero-coupon Treasury bonds did not exist, except for Treasury bills (which have a maximum maturity of one year). However, a coupon-bearing Treasury security can be viewed as a *portfolio* of zero-coupon bonds, with each interest payment, as well as the principal, considered a separate bond. In 1982, several brokerage firms came to a novel realization: A Treasury security's payments could be segregated and sold piecemeal through a process known as **coupon stripping**.

For example, brokerage firm *XYZ* purchases a newly issued 20-year Treasury bond and deposits the bond with a custodian bank. Assuming semiannual interest payments, *XYZ* creates 41 separate zero-coupon bonds (40 interest payments plus one principal repayment). Naturally, *XYZ* can create larger zero-coupon bonds by buying and depositing more securities of the same Treasury issue.

$$NIR = \left[1 + E(RIR)\right] \times \left[1 + E(CCL)\right] - 1$$

where $E(\cdot)$ indicates the expectation of the variable.

If the real interest rate is fairly stable over time and relatively small in size, then the nominal interest rate should increase approximately one-for-one with changes in the expected inflation rate. Unfortunately, the precise magnitude of inflation is hard to forecast much in advance. Some people believe that with the U.S. Treasury Department's recent introduction of Treasury Inflation Indexed Securities it will be

These zero-coupon bonds, in turn, are sold to investors (for a fee, of course). As the Treasury makes its required payments on the bond, the custodian bank remits the payments to the zero-coupon bondholders of the appropriate maturity and effectively retires that particular bond. The process continues until all interest and principal payments have been made and all of the zero-coupon bonds associated with this Treasury bond have been extinguished.

Brokerage firms have issued zero-coupon bonds based on Treasury securities under a number of exotic names, such as LIONs (Lehman Investment Opportunity Notes), TIGRs (Merrill Lynch's Treasury Investment Growth Receipts), and CATs (Salomon Brothers' Certificates of Accrual on Treasury Securities). Not surprisingly, these securities have become known in the trade as "animals."

Brokerage firms and investors benefit from coupon stripping. The brokerage firms found that the sum of the parts was worth more than the whole, as the zero-coupon bonds could be sold to investors at a higher combined price than could the source Treasury security. Investors benefited from the creation of a liquid market in riskless securities.

The U.S. Treasury only belatedly recognized the popularity of stripped Treasury securities. In 1985, the Treasury introduced a program called STRIPS (Separate Trading of Registered Interest and Principal Securities). This program allows purchasers of certain interest-bearing Treasury securities to keep whatever cash payments they want and to sell the rest. The stripped bonds are "held" in the Federal Reserve System's computer (called the *book entry system*), and payments on the bonds are made electronically. Any financial institution that is registered on the Federal Reserve System's computer may participate in the STRIPS program. Brokerage firms soon found that it was much less expensive to create zero-coupon bonds through STRIPS than to use bank custody accounts.

They subsequently switched virtually all of their activity to that program.

The introduction of stripped Treasuries still did not solve the inflation risk problem faced by investors seeking a truly riskfree security. Finally, in 1997 the U.S. Treasury offered the first U.S. securities whose principal and interest payments were indexed to inflation, officially named Treasury Inflation Indexed Securities. With the introduction of these securities, the United States joined Australia, Canada, Israel, New Zealand, Sweden, and the United Kingdom in issuing debt that is indexed to the rate of inflation.

To date, the Treasury has issued three maturities (5, 10, and 30 years). The principal amounts of these "indexed" bonds are adjusted semiannually on the basis of the cumulative change in the Consumer Price Index (CPI) since issuance of the bonds. A fixed rate of interest, determined at the time of the bonds' issuance, is paid on the adjusted principal, thereby producing inflation-adjusted interest payments as well. Coupon stripping is allowed so that investors can purchase zero-coupon inflation-protected U.S. bonds—apparently the real McCoy of riskfree securities.

Only a nitpicker would note several flaws in this arrangement. The bonds' issuer (the U.S. government) controls the definition and calculation of the CPI. In light of concerns over whether the CPI accurately measures inflation, there is some risk that the government might change the index in ways detrimental to inflation-indexed securityholders (although the Treasury could adjust the bond terms to compensate for such an adverse change). Further, for taxable investors, the adjustments to the bonds' principal values immediately become taxable income, reducing (perhaps significantly, depending on the investor's tax rate) the inflation protection provided by the bonds. Despite these complications, it appears that the Treasury has finally introduced a security that can truly claim the title of (almost) riskfree.

much easier to arrive at a consensus forecast of inflation in the United States by simply looking at their market prices. (These securities are discussed further in "Institutional Issues: Almost Riskfree Securities" and in Chapter 12.) Further consideration of real versus nominal interest rates and forecasting the rate of inflation is deferred until Chapter 12. Suffice it to say that it may be best to view the expected real interest rate as being determined by the interaction of numerous underlying economic forces, with the nominal interest rate approximately equal to the expected real interest rate plus the expected rate of change in prices.

There are many interest rates, not just one. Furthermore, there are many ways that interest rates can be calculated. One such method results in an interest rate that is known as the yield-to-maturity. Another results in an interest rate known as the spot rate, which will be discussed in the next section.

5.2.1   Calculating Yield-to-Maturity

In describing yields-to-maturity and spot rates, three hypothetical Treasury securities that are available to the public for investment will be considered. Treasury securities are widely believed to be free from default risk, meaning that investors have no doubts about being paid fully and on time. Thus the impact of differing degrees of default risk on yields-to-maturity and spot rates is removed.

The three Treasury securities to be considered will be referred to as bonds A, B, and C. Bonds A and B are called pure-discount bonds because they make no interim interest (or "coupon") payments before maturity. Any investor who purchases this kind of bond pays a market-determined price and in return receives the principal (or "face") value of the bond at maturity. In this case, bond A matures in a year, at which time the investor will receive $1,000. Similarly, bond B matures in two years, at which time the investor will receive $1,000. Finally, bond C is not a pure-discount bond. Rather, it is a coupon bond that pays the investor $50 one year from now and matures two years from now, paying the investor $1,050 at that time. The prices at which these bonds are currently being sold in the market are:

Bond A (the one-year pure-discount bond): $934.58
Bond B (the two-year pure-discount bond): $857.34
Bond C (the two-year coupon bond): $946.93

The **yield-to-maturity** on any fixed-income security is the single interest rate (with interest compounded at some specified interval) that, if paid by a bank on the amount invested, would enable the investor to obtain all the payments promised by the security in question. It is simple to determine the yield-to-maturity on a one-year pure-discount security such as bond A. Because an investment of $934.58 will pay $1,000 one year later, the yield-to-maturity on this bond is the interest rate r_A that a bank would have to pay on a deposit of $934.58 in order for the account to have a balance of $1,000 after one year. Thus the yield-to-maturity on bond A is the rate r_A that solves the following equation:

$$(1 + r_A) \times \$934.58 = \$1,000 \tag{5.4}$$

which is 7%.

In the case of bond B, assuming annual compounding at a rate r_B, an account with $857.34 invested initially (the cost of B) would grow to $(1 + r_B) \times \$857.34$ in one year. If this total is left intact, the account will grow to $(1 + r_B) \times [(1 + r_B) \times \$857.34]$ by the end of the second year. The yield-to-maturity is the rate r_B that makes this amount equal to $1,000. In other words, the yield-to-maturity on bond B is the rate r_B that solves the following equation:

$$(1 + r_B) \times [(1 + r_B) \times \$857.34] = \$1,000 \tag{5.5}$$

which is 8%.

For bond *C*, consider investing $946.93 in a bank account. At the end of one year, the account would grow in value to $(1 + r_C) \times \$946.93$. Then the investor would remove $50, leaving a balance of $\left[(1 + r_C) \times \$946.93\right] - \$50$. At the end of the second year this balance would have grown to an amount equal to $(1 + r_C) \times \{[(1 + r_C) \times \$946.93] - \$50\}$. The yield-to-maturity on bond *C* is the rate r_C that makes this amount equal to $1,050:

$$(1 + r_C) \times \{[(1 + r_C) \times \$946.93] - \$50\} = \$1,050 \qquad (5.6)$$

which is 7.975%.

Equivalently, yield-to-maturity is the discount rate that makes the present value of the promised future cash flows equal in sum to the current market price of the bond.[1] When viewed in this manner, yield-to-maturity is analogous to internal rate of return, a concept used for making capital budgeting decisions and often described in introductory finance textbooks. This equivalence can be seen for bond *A* by dividing both sides of Equation (5.4) by $(1 + r_A)$, resulting in:

$$\$934.58 = \frac{\$1,000}{(1 + r_A)} \qquad (5.7)$$

Similarly, for bond *B* both sides of Equation (5.5) can be divided by $(1 + r_B)^2$, resulting in:

$$\$857.34 = \frac{\$1,000}{(1 + r_B)^2} \qquad (5.8)$$

whereas for bond *C* both sides of Equation (5.6) can be divided by $(1 + r_C)^2$:

$$\$946.93 - \frac{\$50}{(1 + r_C)} = \frac{\$1,050}{(1 + r_C)^2}$$

or:

$$\$946.93 = \frac{\$50}{(1 + r_C)} + \frac{\$1,050}{(1 + r_C)^2} \qquad (5.9)$$

Because Equations (5.7), (5.8), and (5.9) are equivalent to Equations (5.4), (5.5), and (5.6), respectively, the solutions must be the same as before, with $r_A = 7\%$, $r_B = 8\%$, and $r_C = 7.975\%$.

For coupon-bearing bonds, the procedure for determining yield-to-maturity involves trial and error. In the case of bond *C*, a discount rate of 10% could be tried initially, resulting in a value for the right-hand side of Equation (5.9) of $913.22, a value that is too low. This result indicates that the number in the denominator is too high, so a lower discount rate is used next—say 6%. In this case, the value on the right-hand side is $981.67, which is too high and indicates that 6% is too low. The solution is somewhere between 6% and 10%, and the search could continue until the answer, 7.975%, is found.

Fortunately, computers are good at trial-and-error calculations. One can enter a very complex series of cash flows into a properly programmed computer and instantaneously find the yield-to-maturity. In fact, many hand-held calculators and spreadsheets come with built-in programs to find yield-to-maturity; you simply enter the number of days to maturity, the annual coupon payments, and the current market price, then press the key that indicates yield-to-maturity.

5.3 SPOT RATES

A **spot rate** is measured at a given point in time as the yield-to-maturity on a pure-discount security and can be thought of as the interest rate associated with a spot contract. Such a contract, when signed, involves the immediate loaning of money from one party to another. The loan, along with interest, is to be repaid in its entirety at a specific time in the future. The interest rate that is specified in the contract is the spot rate.

Bonds A and B in the previous example were pure-discount securities, meaning that an investor who purchased either one would expect to receive only one cash payment from the issuer. Accordingly, in this example the one-year spot rate is 7% and the two-year spot rate is 8%. In general, the t-year spot rate s_t is the solution to the following equation:

$$P_t = \frac{M_t}{\left(1 + s_t\right)^t} \tag{5.10}$$

where P_t is the current market price of a pure-discount bond that matures in t years and has a maturity value of M_t. For example, the values of P_t and M_t for bond B would be $857.34 and $1,000, respectively, with $t = 2$.

Spot rates can also be determined in another manner if only coupon-bearing Treasury bonds are available for longer maturities by using a procedure known as *bootstrapping*. The one-year spot rate $\left(s_1\right)$ generally is known, as there typically is a one-year pure-discount Treasury security available for making this calculation. However, it may be that no two-year pure-discount Treasury security exists. Instead, only a two-year coupon-bearing bond may be available for investment, having a current market price of P_2, a maturity value of M_2, and a coupon payment one year from now equal to C_1. In this situation, the two-year spot rate $\left(s_2\right)$ is the solution to the following equation:

$$P_2 = \frac{C_1}{\left(1 + s_1\right)} + \frac{M_2}{\left(1 + s_2\right)^2} \tag{5.11}$$

Once the two-year spot rate has been calculated, then it and the one-year spot rate can be used in a similar manner to determine the three-year spot rate by examining a three-year coupon-bearing bond. By applying this procedure iteratively in a similar fashion over and over again, one can calculate an entire set of spot rates from a set of coupon-bearing bonds.

For example, assume that only bonds A and C exist. In this situation it is known that the one-year spot rate, s_1, is 7%. Now Equation (5.11) can be used to determine the two-year spot rate, s_2, where $P_2 = \$946.93$, $C_1 = \$50$, and $M_2 = \$1,050$:

$$\$946.93 = \frac{\$50}{(1 + .07)} + \frac{\$1,050}{\left(1 + s_2\right)^2}$$

The solution to this equation is $s_2 = .08 = 8\%$. Thus, the two-year spot rate is determined to be the same in this example, regardless of whether it is calculated directly by analyzing pure-discount bond B or indirectly by analyzing coupon-bearing bond C in conjunction with bond A. Although the rate will not always be the same in both calculations when actual bond prices are examined, typically the differences are insignificant.

5.4	DISCOUNT FACTORS

Once a set of spot rates has been determined, it is a straightforward matter to determine the corresponding set of **discount factors**. A discount factor d_t is equivalent to the present value of $1 to be received t years in the future from a Treasury security and is equal to:

$$d_t = \frac{1}{\left(1 + s_t\right)^t} \qquad (5.12)$$

The set of these factors is sometimes referred to as the **market discount function**, and it changes from day to day as spot rates change. In the example, $d_1 = 1/(1 + .07)^1 = .9346$; and $d_2 = 1/(1 + .08)^2 = .8573$.

Once the market discount function has been determined, it is fairly straightforward to find the present value of any Treasury security (or, for that matter, any default-free security). Let C_t denote the cash payment to be made to the investor at year t by the security being evaluated. The multiplication of C_t by d_t is termed **discounting**: converting the given future value into an equivalent present value. The latter is equivalent in the sense that P present dollars can be converted into C_t dollars in year t via available investment instruments, given the currently prevailing spot rates. An investment paying C_t dollars in year t with certainty should sell for $P = d_t C_t$ dollars today. If it sells for more, it is overpriced; if it sells for less, it is underpriced. These statements rest solely on comparisons with equivalent opportunities in the marketplace. Valuation of default-free investments thus requires no assessment of individual preferences; instead, it requires only careful analysis of the available opportunities in the marketplace.

The simplest and, in a sense, most fundamental characterization of the market structure for default-free bonds is given by the current set of discount factors, referred to earlier as the market discount function. With this set of factors, it is a simple matter to evaluate a default-free bond that provides more than one payment, for it is, in effect, a package of bonds, each of which provides a single payment. Each amount is simply multiplied by the appropriate discount factor, and the resultant present values are summed.

For example, assume that the Treasury is preparing to offer for sale a two-year coupon-bearing security that will pay $70 in one year and $1,070 in two years. What is a fair price for such a security? It is the present value of $70 and $1,070. How can this value be determined? By multiplying the $70 and $1,070 by the one-year and two-year discount factors, respectively. Doing so results in ($70 × .9346) + ($1,070 × .8573), which equals $982.73.

No matter how complex the pattern of payments, this procedure can be used to determine the value of any default-free bond of this type. The general formula for a bond's present value (PV) is:

$$PV = \sum_{t=1}^{n} d_t C_t \qquad (5.13)$$

where the bond has promised cash payments C_t for each year from year 1 through year n.

At this point, it has been shown how spot rates and, in turn, discount factors can be calculated. However, no link between different spot rates (or different discount factors) has been established. For example, it has yet to be shown how the one-year spot rate of 7% is related to the two-year spot rate of 8%. The concept of forward rates makes that link.

5.5   FORWARD RATES

In the example, the one-year spot rate was determined to be 7%. This means that the market has determined that the present value of $1 to be paid by the United States Treasury in one year is $1/1.07, or $.9346. That is, the relevant discount rate for converting a cash flow one year from now to its present value is 7%. Because, as was also noted, the two-year spot rate was 8%, the present value of $1 to be paid by the Treasury in two years is $1/1.08^2, or $.8573.

An alternative view of $1 to be paid in two years is that it can be discounted in two steps. The first step determines its equivalent one-year value. That is, $1 to be received in two years is equivalent to $1/(1 + f_{1,2})$ to be received in one year. The second step determines the present value of this equivalent one-year amount by discounting it at the one-year spot rate of 7%. Thus its current value is:

$$\frac{\$1/(1 + f_{1,2})}{(1 + .07)}$$

However, this value must be equal to $.8573, as it was mentioned earlier that, according to the two-year spot rate, $.8573 is the present value of $1 to be paid in two years. That is,

$$\frac{\$1/(1 + f_{1,2})}{(1 + .07)} = \$.8573 \tag{5.14}$$

which has a solution for $f_{1,2}$ of 9.01%.

The discount rate $f_{1,2}$ is known as the **forward rate** from year one to year two. That is, it is the discount rate for determining the equivalent value one year from now of a dollar that is to be received two years from now. In the example, $1 to be received two years from now is equivalent in value to $1/1.0901 = $.9174 to be received one year from now (in turn, note that the present value of $.9174 is $.9174/1.07 = $.8573).

Symbolically, the link between the one-year spot rate, two-year spot rate, and one-year forward rate is:

$$\frac{\$1/(1 + f_{1,2})}{(1 + s_1)} = \frac{\$1}{(1 + s_2)^2} \tag{5.15}$$

which can be rewritten as:

$$(1 + f_{1,2}) = \frac{(1 + s_2)^2}{(1 + s_1)} \tag{5.16}$$

or:

$$(1 + s_1)(1 + f_{1,2}) = (1 + s_2)^2 \tag{5.17}$$

Figure 5.1 illustrates this relation by referring to the example and then generalizing from it.

More generally, for year $t - 1$ and year t spot rates, the link to the forward rate between years $t - 1$ and t is:

$$(1 + f_{t-1,t}) = \frac{(1 + s_t)^t}{(1 + s_{t-1})^{t-1}} \tag{5.18}$$

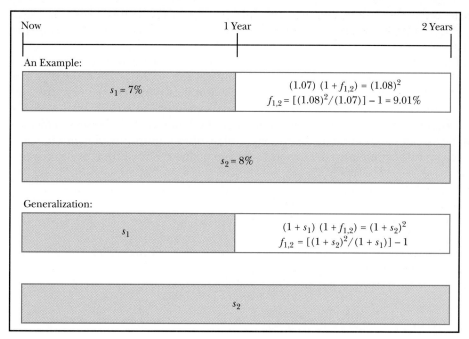

Figure 5.1
Spot and Forward Rates

or:

$$\left(1 + s_{t-1}\right)^{t-1} \times \left(1 + f_{t-1,\,t}\right) = \left(1 + s_t\right)^t \qquad (5.19)$$

There is another interpretation that can be given to forward rates. Consider a contract made now wherein money will be loaned a year from now and paid back two years from now. Such a contract is known as a *forward contract*. The interest rate specified on the one-year loan (note that the interest will be paid when the loan matures in two years) is known as the forward rate.

It is important to distinguish this rate from the rate for one-year loans that will prevail for deals made a year from now (the spot rate at that time). A forward rate applies to contracts made now but relating to a period "forward" in time. By the nature of the contract the terms are certain now, even though the actual transaction will occur later. If instead one were to wait until next year and sign a contract to borrow money in the spot market at that time, the terms might turn out to be better or worse than today's forward rate, because the future spot rate is not perfectly predictable.

In the example, the marketplace has priced Treasury securities such that a representative investor making a two-year loan to the government would demand an interest rate equal to the two-year spot rate, 8%. Equivalently, the investor would be willing to simultaneously (1) make a one-year loan to the government at an interest rate equal to the one-year spot rate, 7%, and (2) sign a forward contract with the government to loan the government money one year from now, being repaid two years from now with the interest rate to be paid being the forward rate, 9.01%.

When viewed in this manner, forward contracts are implicit. However, forward contracts are sometimes made explicitly. For example, a contractor might obtain a commitment from a bank for a one-year construction loan a year hence at a fixed rate of interest. Financial futures markets (discussed in Chapter 20) provide standardized forward contracts of this type. For example, in September an investor could contract to pay approximately $970 in December to purchase a 90-day Treasury bill that would pay $1,000 in the following March.

The Valuation of Riskless Securities

In Equation (5.12) it was shown that a discount factor for t years could be calculated by adding one to the t-year spot rate, raising this sum to the power t, and then taking the reciprocal of the result. For example, it was shown that the two-year discount factor associated with the two-year spot rate of 8% was equal to $1/(1 + .08)^2 = .8573$.

Equation (5.17) suggests an equivalent method for calculating discount factors. In the case of the two-year factor, this method involves multiplying one plus the one-year spot rate by one plus the forward rate and taking the reciprocal of the result:

$$d_2 = \frac{1}{\left(1 + s_1\right) \times \left(1 + f_{1,2}\right)} \tag{5.20}$$

which in the example is:

$$d_2 = \frac{1}{(1 + .07) \times (1 + .0901)}$$

$$= .8573.$$

More generally, the discount factor for year t that is shown in Equation (5.12) can be restated as follows:

$$d_t = \frac{1}{\left(1 + s_{t-1}\right)^{t-1} \times \left(1 + f_{t-1,t}\right)} \tag{5.21}$$

Thus, given a set of spot rates, one can determine the market discount function in either of two ways, both of which will provide the same figures. First, the spot rates can be used in Equation (5.12) to arrive at a set of discount factors. Alternatively, the spot rates can be used to determine a set of forward rates, and then the spot rates and forward rates can be used in Equation (5.21) to arrive at a set of discount factors.

5.7   COMPOUNDING

Thus far, the discussion has concentrated on annual interest rates by assuming that cash flows are compounded (or discounted) annually. This assumption is often appropriate, but for more precise calculations a shorter period may be more desirable. Moreover, some lenders explicitly compound funds more often than once each year.

Compounding is the payment of "interest on interest." At the end of each compounding interval, interest is computed and added to principal. This sum becomes the principal on which interest is computed at the end of the next interval. The process continues until the end of the final compounding interval is reached.

No problem is involved in adapting the previously stated formulas to compounding intervals other than a year. The simplest procedure is to count in units of the chosen interval. For example, yield-to-maturity can be calculated using any chosen compounding interval. If payment of P dollars now will result in the receipt of F dollars 10 years from now, the yield-to-maturity can be calculated using annual compounding by finding a value r_a that satisfies the equation:

$$P(1 + r_a)^{10} = F \qquad (5.22)$$

since F will be received ten annual periods from now. The result, r_a, will be expressed as an annual rate with annual compounding.

Alternatively, yield-to-maturity can be calculated using semiannual compounding by finding a value r_s that satisfies the equation:

$$P(1 + r_s)^{20} = F \qquad (5.23)$$

since F will be received 20 semiannual periods from now. The result, r_s, will be expressed as a semiannual rate with semiannual compounding. It can be doubled to give an annual rate with semiannual compounding. Alternatively, the annual rate with annual compounding can be computed for a given value of r_s by using the following equation:

$$1 + r_a = (1 + r_s)^2 \qquad (5.24)$$

For example, consider an investment costing $2,315.97 that will pay $5,000 ten years later. Applying Equations (5.22) and (5.23) to this security results in, respectively:

$$\$2,315.97(1 + r_a)^{10} = \$5,000$$

and:

$$\$2,315.97(1 + r_s)^{20} = \$5,000$$

where the solutions are $r_a = 8\%$ and $r_s = 3.923\%$. Thus this security can be described as having an annual rate with annual compounding of 8%, a semiannual rate with semiannual compounding of 3.923%, and an annual rate with semiannual compounding of 7.846% (= 2 × 3.923%).[2]

Semiannual compounding is commonly used to determine the yield-to-maturity for bonds, because coupon payments are usually made twice each year. Most pre-programmed calculators and spreadsheets use this approach.[3]

5.8 THE BANK DISCOUNT METHOD

One time-honored method to summarize interest rates is a procedure called the *bank discount method*. If someone "borrows" $100 from a bank, to be repaid a year later, the bank may subtract the interest payment of, for instance, $8, and give the borrower $92. According to the bank discount method, this is an interest rate of 8%. However, this method understates the effective annual interest rate that the borrower pays. That is, the borrower receives only $92, for which he or she must pay $8 in interest after one year. The true interest rate must be based on the money the borrower actually gets to use, which in this case is $92, making the true interest rate 8.70% (= $8/$92).

It is simple to convert an interest rate quoted on the bank discount method to a true interest rate. (In this situation, the true interest rate is often called the *bond equivalent yield*.) If the bank discount rate is denoted BDR, the true rate is simply $BDR/(1 - BDR)$. Because $BDR > 0$, the bank discount rate understates the true cost of borrowing [that is, $BDR < BDR/(1 - BDR)$]. The previous example provides an illustration: 8.70% = .08/(1 − .08). Note how the bank discount rate of 8% understates the true cost of borrowing by .70% in this example.

5.9 YIELD CURVES

At any point in time, Treasury securities will be priced approximately in accord with the existing set of spot rates and the associated discount factors. Although there have been times when all the spot rates are roughly equal in size, generally they have different values. Often the one-year spot rate is less than the two-year spot rate, which in turn is less than the three-year spot rate, and so on (that is, s_t increases as t increases). At other times, the one-year spot rate is greater than the two-year spot rate, which in turn is greater than the three-year spot rate, and so on (that is, s_t decreases as t increases). It is wise for the security analyst to know which case currently prevails, as this is a useful starting point in valuing fixed-income securities.

Unfortunately, specifying the current situation is easier said than done. Only the bonds of the U.S. government are clearly free from default risk. However, government bonds differ in tax treatment, as well as in callability, liquidity, and other features. Despite these problems, a summary of the approximate relationship between yields-to-maturity on Treasury securities of various terms-to-maturity is presented in each issue of the *Treasury Bulletin*. This summary is given in the form of a graph illustrating the current yield curve. Figure 5.2 provides an example.

A **yield curve** is a graph that shows the yields-to-maturity (on the vertical axis) for Treasury securities of various maturities (on the horizontal axis) as of a particular date. This graph provides an estimate of the current **term structure** of interest rates and will change daily as yields-to-maturity change. Figure 5.3 illustrates some of the commonly observed shapes that the yield curve has taken in the past.[4]

Although not shown in Figures 5.2 and 5.3, this relationship between yields and maturities is less than perfect. That is, not all Treasury securities lie exactly on the yield curve. Part of this variation is because of the previously mentioned differences in tax treatment, callability, liquidity, and the like. Part is because of the fact that the yield-to-maturity on a coupon-bearing security is not clearly linked to the set of spot rates currently in existence. Because the set of spot rates is a fundamental determinant of the price of any Treasury security, there is no reason to expect yields to lie exactly on the curve. Indeed, a more meaningful graph would be one on which spot rates instead of yields-to-maturity are measured on the vertical axis. With this caveat in mind, ponder these two interesting questions: Why are the spot rates of different magnitudes? And why do the differences in these rates change over time, in that long-term spot rates usually are greater than short-term spot rates but sometimes the opposite occurs? Attempts to answer such questions can be found in various term structure theories.

5.10 TERM STRUCTURE THEORIES

Four primary theories are used to explain the term structure of interest rates. In discussing them, the focus will be on the term structure of spot rates, because these rates (not yields-to-maturity) are critically important in determining the price of any Treasury security.

5.10.1 The Unbiased Expectations Theory

The **unbiased expectations theory** (or pure expectations theory, as it is sometimes called) holds that the forward rate represents the average opinion of what the expected future spot rate for the period in question will be. Thus, a set of spot rates that is rising can be explained by arguing that the marketplace (that is, the general opinion of investors) believes that spot rates will be rising in the future. Conversely, a set of decreasing spot rates is explained by arguing that the marketplace expects spot rates to fall in the future.[5]

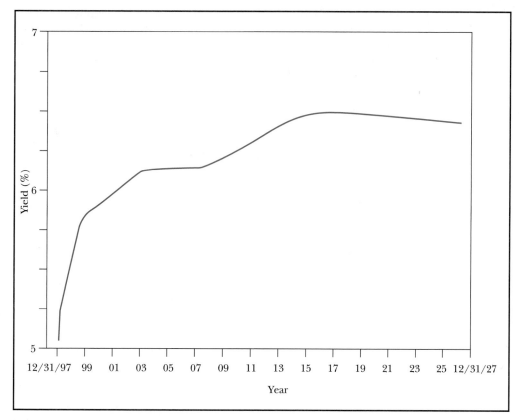

Figure 5.2
Yield Curve of Treasury Securities. September 30, 1997 (based on closing bid quotations in percentages)

Source: *Treasury Bulletin*, December 1997, p. 51

Note: The curve is based only on the most actively traded issues. Market yields on coupon issues due in less than 3 months are excluded.

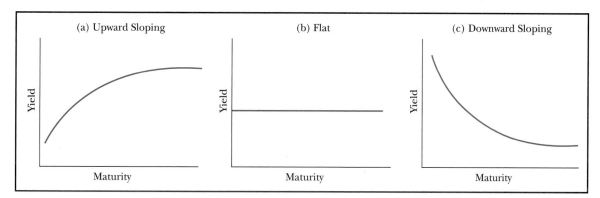

Figure 5.3
Typical Yield Curve Shapes

Upward-Sloping Yield Curves

In order to understand this theory more fully, consider the earlier example in which the one-year spot rate was 7% and the two-year spot rate was 8%. The basic question is this: Why are these two spot rates different? Equivalently, why is the yield curve upward-sloping?

The Valuation of Riskless Securities   **121**

Consider an investor with $1 to invest for two years (for ease of exposition, it will be assumed that any amount of money can be invested at the prevailing spot rates). This investor could follow a "maturity strategy," investing the money now for the full two years at the two-year spot rate of 8%. With this strategy, at the end of two years the dollar will have grown in value to $1.1664 (= $1 × 1.08 × 1.08). Alternatively, the investor could invest the dollar now for one year at the one-year spot rate of 7%, so that the investor knows that one year from now he or she will have $1.07 (= $1 × 1.07) to reinvest for one more year. Although the investor does not know what the one-year spot rate will be one year from now, the investor has an *expectation* about what it will be (this expected future spot rate will hereafter be denoted $es_{1,2}$). If the investor thinks that it will be 10%, then his or her $1 investment has an expected value two years from now of $1.177 (= $1 × 1.07 × 1.10). In this case, the investor would choose a "rollover strategy," meaning that the investor would choose to invest in a one-year security at 7% rather than in the two-year security, because he or she would expect to have more money at the end of two years by doing so ($1.177 > $1.1664).

However, an expected future spot rate of 10% cannot represent the general view in the marketplace. If it did, people would not be willing to invest money at the two-year spot rate, as a higher return would be expected from investing money at the one-year rate and using the rollover strategy. Thus the two-year spot rate would quickly rise as the supply of funds for two-year loans at 8% would be less than the demand. Conversely, the supply of funds for one year at 7% would be more than the demand, causing the one-year rate to fall quickly. Thus, a one-year spot rate of 7%, a two-year spot rate of 8%, and an expected future spot rate of 10% cannot represent an equilibrium situation.

What if the expected future spot rate is 6% instead of 10%? In this case, according to the rollover strategy the investor would expect $1 to be worth $1.1342 (= $1 × 1.07 × 1.06) at the end of two years. This is less than the value the dollar will have if the maturity strategy is followed ($1.1342 < $1.664), so the investor would choose the maturity strategy. Again, however, an expected future spot rate of 6% cannot represent the general view in the marketplace because if it did, people would not be willing to invest money at the one-year spot rate.

Earlier, it was shown that the forward rate in this example was 9.01%. What if the expected future spot rate was of this magnitude? At the end of two years the value of $1 with the rollover strategy would be $1.1664 (= $1 × 1.07 × 1.0901), the same as the value of $1 with the maturity strategy. In this case, equilibrium would exist in the marketplace because the general view would be that the two strategies have the same expected return. Accordingly, investors with a two-year holding period would not have an incentive to choose one strategy over the other.

Note that an investor with a one-year holding period could follow a maturity strategy by investing $1 in the one-year security and receiving $1.07 after one year. Alternatively, a "naive strategy" could be followed, where a two-year security could be purchased now and sold after one year. If that were done, the expected selling price would be $1.07 (= $1.1664/1.0901), for a return of 7% (the security would have a maturity value of $1.1664 = $1 × 1.08 × 1.08, but since the spot rate is expected to be 9.01% in a year, its expected selling price is just the discounted value of its maturity value). Because the maturity and naive strategies have the same expected return, investors with a one-year holding period would not have an incentive to choose one strategy over the other.

Thus the unbiased expectations theory asserts that the expected future spot rate is equal in magnitude to the forward rate. In the example, the current one-year spot rate is 7%, and, according to this theory, the general opinion is that it will rise to a rate of 9.01% in one year. This expected rise in the one-year spot rate is the reason behind the upward-sloping term structure where the two-year spot rate (8%) is greater than the one-year spot rate (7%).

Equilibrium

In equation form, the unbiased expectations theory states that in equilibrium the expected future spot rate is equal to the forward rate:

$$es_{1,2} = f_{1,2} \tag{5.25}$$

Thus Equation (5.17) can be restated with $es_{1,2}$ substituted for $f_{1,2}$ as follows:

$$(1 + s_1)(1 + es_{1,2}) = (1 + s_2)^2 \tag{5.26}$$

which can be conveniently interpreted to mean that the expected return from a maturity strategy must equal the expected return on a rollover strategy.[6]

The previous example dealt with an upward-sloping term structure; the longer the term, the higher the spot rate. It is a straightforward matter to deal with a downward-sloping term structure, where the longer the term, the lower the spot rate. Whereas the explanation for an upward-sloping term structure was that investors expect spot rates to rise in the future, the reason for the downward-sloping curve is that investors expect spot rates to fall in the future.

Changing Spot Rates and Inflation

Why do investors expect spot rates to change, either rising or falling, in the future? A possible answer can be found by noting that the spot rates that are observed in the marketplace are nominal rates. That is, they are a reflection of the underlying real rate and the expected inflation rate.[7] If either (or both) of these rates is expected to change in the future, then the spot rate will be expected to change.

For example, assume a constant real rate of 3%. Because the current one-year spot rate is 7%, a constant real rate of 3% means that the general opinion in the marketplace is that the expected rate of inflation over the next year is approximately 4% (the nominal rate is approximately equal to the sum of the real rate and the expected inflation rate; see Equation (5.3)). Now, according to the unbiased expectations theory, the expected future spot rate is 9.01%, an increase of 2.01% from the current one-year spot rate of 7%. On the assumption of a constant real rate, this increase can be attributed to investors, on average, expecting the inflation rate to rise by 2.01%. That is, the expected inflation rate over the next 12 months is approximately 4%, and over the following 12 months it is expected to be higher, at approximately 6.01%.

To recapitulate, the two-year spot rate (8%) is greater than the one-year spot rate (7%) because investors expect the future one-year spot rate to be greater than the current one-year spot rate. They expect it to be greater because of an anticipated rise in the rate of inflation, from approximately 4% to approximately 6.01%.

In general, when current economic conditions make short-term spot rates abnormally high (owing, say, to a relatively high current rate of inflation), according to the unbiased expectations theory, the term structure should be downward-sloping because inflation would be expected to abate in the future. Conversely, when current conditions make short-term rates abnormally low (owing, say, to a relatively low current rate of inflation), the term structure should be upward-sloping because inflation would be expected to rise in the future. Examination of historical term structures suggests that this is what has actually happened; the structure has been upward-sloping in periods of lower interest rates and downward-sloping in periods of higher interest rates.

However, examining historical term structures uncovers a problem. In particular, it is logical to expect that over time there will be roughly as many occurrences of investors expecting spot rates to rise as there are occurrences of investors expecting spot rates to fall. Therefore the unbiased expectations theory should imply that there will be as many instances of upward-sloping term structures as downward-sloping term structures. In reality, upward-sloping term structures occur much more frequently than downward-sloping term structures. The unbiased expectations theory would have to explain this phenomenon by suggesting that the majority of the time investors expect spot rates to rise. The liquidity preference theory (also known as the liquidity premium theory) provides a more plausible explanation for the observed prevalence of upward-sloping term structures.

5.10.2 The Liquidity Preference Theory

The **liquidity preference theory** starts with the notion that investors are primarily interested in purchasing short-term securities. That is, even though some investors may have longer holding periods, there is a tendency for them to prefer short-term securities. These investors realize that they may need their funds earlier than anticipated and recognize that they face less "price risk" (that is, "interest rate risk") if they invest in shorter-term securities.

Price Risk

For example, an investor with a two-year holding period would tend to prefer the rollover strategy because he or she would be certain of having a given amount of cash at the end of one year when it may be needed. An investor who followed a maturity strategy would have to sell the two-year security after one year if cash were needed. However, it is not known now what price that investor would get for the two-year security in one year. Thus there is an extra element of risk associated with the maturity strategy that is absent from the rollover strategy.[8]

The upshot is that investors with a two-year holding period will not choose the maturity strategy if it has the same expected return as the rollover strategy because it is riskier. The only way investors will follow the maturity strategy and buy the two-year securities is if the expected return is higher. That is, borrowers are going to have to pay the investors a risk premium in the form of a greater expected return in order to get them to purchase two-year securities.

Will borrowers be inclined to pay such a premium when issuing two-year securities? Yes, they will, according to the liquidity preference theory. First, frequent refinancing may be costly in terms of registration, advertising, and paperwork. These costs can be lessened by issuing relatively long-term securities. Second, some borrowers will realize that relatively long-term bonds are a less risky source of funds than relatively short-term bonds because borrowers who use them will not have to be as concerned about the possibility of refinancing in the future at higher interest rates. Thus borrowers may be willing to pay more (via higher expected interest costs) for relatively long-term funds.

In the example, the one-year spot rate was 7% and the two-year spot rate was 8%. According to the liquidity preference theory, the only way investors will agree to follow a maturity strategy is if the expected return from doing so is higher than the expected return from following the rollover strategy. So the expected future spot rate must be something *less* than the forward rate of 9.01%; perhaps it is 8.6%. At 8.6% the value of a $1 investment in two years is expected to be $1.1620 (= $1 $\times$ 1.07 $\times$ 1.086), if the rollover strategy is followed. Because the value of a $1 investment with the maturity strategy is $1.1664 (= $1 $\times$ 1.08 $\times$ 1.08), it can be seen that the maturity strategy has a higher expected return for the two-year period that can be attributed to its greater degree of price risk.

Liquidity Premium

The difference between the forward rate and the expected future spot rate is known as the **liquidity premium**.[9] It is the "extra" return given investors in order to entice them to purchase the riskier longer-maturity two-year security. In the example, it is equal to .41% (= 9.01% $-$ 8.6%). More generally,

$$f_{1,2} = es_{1,2} + L_{1,2} \tag{5.27}$$

where $L_{1,2}$ is the liquidity premium for the period starting one year from now and ending two years from now.[10]

How does the liquidity preference theory explain the slope of the term structure? In order to answer this question, note that with the rollover strategy the expected value of a dollar at the end of two years is $1 $\times$ $(1 + s_1)$ $\times$ $(1 + es_{1,2})$. Alternatively, with the maturity strategy, the expected value of a dollar at the end of two years is $1 $\times$ $(1 + s_2)^2$. According to the liquidity preference theory, there is more risk with the maturity strategy, which in turn means that it must have a higher expected return. That is, the following inequality must hold:

$$\$1(1 + s_1)(1 + es_{1,2}) < \$1(1 + s_2)^2 \tag{5.28}$$

or:

$$(1 + s_1)(1 + es_{1,2}) < (1 + s_2)^2 \tag{5.29}$$

This inequality is the key to understanding how the liquidity preference theory explains the term structure.[11]

Downward-Sloping Yield Curves

Consider the downward-sloping case first, where $s_1 > s_2$. The above inequality will hold in this situation only if the expected future spot rate $(es_{1,2})$ is substantially lower than the current one-year spot rate (s_1).[12] Thus a downward-sloping yield curve will be observed only when the marketplace believes that interest rates are going to decline substantially.

As an example, assume that the one-year spot rate (s_1) is 7% and the two-year spot rate (s_2) is 6%. Because 7% is greater than 6%, this is a situation in which the term structure is downward-sloping. Now, according to the liquidity preference theory, Equation (5.29) indicates that,

$$(1 + .07)(1 + es_{1,2}) < (1.06)^2$$

which can be true only if the expected future spot rate $(es_{1,2})$ is substantially less than 7%. Given the one-year and two-year spot rates, the forward rate $(f_{1,2})$ is equal to 5.01%. Assuming the liquidity premium $(L_{1,2})$ is .41%, then, according to Equation (5.27), $es_{1,2}$ must be 4.6% (= 5.01% − .41%). Thus, the term structure is downward-sloping because the current one-year spot rate of 7% is expected to decline to 4.6% in the future.

In comparison, the unbiased expectations theory also would explain the term structure by saying it was downward-sloping because the one-year spot rate was expected to decline in the future. However, the unbiased expectations theory would expect the spot rate to decline only to 5.01%, not to 4.6%.

Flat Yield Curves

Consider next the case of a flat yield curve, where $s_1 = s_2$. Equation (5.29) will be true in this situation only if $es_{1,2}$ is less than s_1. Thus a flat term structure will occur only when the marketplace expects interest rates to decline. Indeed, if $s_1 = s_2 = 7\%$ and $L_{1,2} = .41\%$, then $f_{1,2} = 7\%$, and according to Equation (5.27), the expected future spot rate is 6.59% (= 7% − .41%), a decline from the current one-year spot rate of 7%. This outcome is in contrast to the unbiased expectations theory, which would interpret a flat term structure to mean that the marketplace expected interest rates to remain at the same level.

Upward-Sloping Yield Curves

The last case is an upward-sloping yield curve where $s_1 < s_2$. A slightly upward-sloping curve can be consistent with an expectation that interest rates are going to decline in the future. For example, if $s_1 = 7\%$ and $s_2 = 7.1\%$, then the forward rate is 7.2%. In turn, if the liquidity premium is .41%, then the expected future spot rate is 6.79% (= 7.2% − .41%), a decline from the current one-year spot rate of 7%. Thus the reason for the slight upward slope to the term structure is that the marketplace expects a small decline in the spot rate. In contrast, the unbiased expectations theory would argue that the reason for the slight upward slope was the expectation of a small increase in the spot rate.

If the term structure is more steeply sloped, then it is more likely that the marketplace expects interest rates to rise in the future. For example, if $s_1 = 7\%$ and $s_2 = 7.3\%$, then the forward rate is 7.6%. Continuing to assume a liquidity premium of .41%, Equation (5.27) indicates that the marketplace expects the one-year spot rate to rise from 7% to 7.19% (= 7.6% − .41%). The unbiased expectations theory also would explain this steep slope by saying that the spot rate was expected to rise in the future, but by a larger amount. In particular, the unbiased expectations theory would state that the spot rate was expected to rise to 7.6%, not to 7.19%.

In summary, with the liquidity preference theory, downward-sloping term structures are indicative of an expected decline in the spot rate, whereas upward-sloping term structures may indicate either an expected rise or decline, depending on how steep the slope is. In general, the steeper the slope, the more likely it is that the marketplace expects spot rates to rise. If roughly half the time investors expect that spot rates will rise and half the time investors expect that spot rates will decline, then the liquidity preference theory suggests that there should be more occurrences of upward-sloping term structures than downward-sloping ones. As mentioned earlier, this is indeed what has been observed.

5.10.3   The Market Segmentation Theory

A third explanation for the determination of the term structure rests on the assumption that there is market segmentation. Various investors and borrowers are thought to be restricted by law, preference, or custom to certain maturities. Perhaps there is a market for short-term securities, another for intermediate-term securities, and a third for long-term securities. According to the **market segmentation theory**, spot rates are determined by supply and demand conditions in each market. Furthermore, in the theory's most restrictive form, investors and borrowers will not leave their market and enter a different one even when the current rates suggest to them that there is a substantially higher expected return available by making such a move.

With this theory, an upward-sloping term structure exists when the intersection of the supply and demand curves for shorter-term funds is at a lower interest rate than the intersection for longer-term funds. This situation could be due to either a relatively greater demand for longer-term funds by borrowers or a relatively greater supply of shorter-term funds by investors, or some combination of the two. Conversely, a downward-sloping term structure would exist when the intersection for shorter-term funds was at a higher interest rate than the intersection for longer-term funds.

5.10.4   The Preferred Habitat Theory

A more moderate and realistic version of the market segmentation theory is the **preferred habitat theory**. According to this theory, investors and borrowers have segments of the market in which they prefer to operate, similar to the market segmentation theory. However, they are willing to leave their desired maturity segments if there are significant differences in yields between the various segments. These yield differences are determined by the supply and demand for funds within the segments.

As a result, as under the liquidity preference theory, the term structure under the preferred habitat theory reflects both expectations of future spot rates and a risk premium. Unlike the risk premium according to the liquidity preference theory, though, that under the preferred habitat theory does not necessarily rise directly with maturity. Instead, it is a function of the extra yield required to induce borrowers and investors to shift out of their preferred habitats. The risk premium may, therefore, be positive or negative in the various segments.

5.10.5   Empirical Evidence on the Theories

Empirical evidence provides some insight into the determinants of the term structure, but it is difficult to precisely assess the relative importance of these four theories. The market segmentation theory receives relatively slight empirical validation. This is understandable when it is realized that the theory will not hold if there are some investors and borrowers who are flexible enough to be willing to move into whatever segment has the highest expected return. By their actions, these investors and borrowers will give the term structure a continuity that is linked to expectations of future interest rates.

There does appear to be some evidence that the term structure conveys information about expected future spot rates, as hypothesized by the unbiased expectations, preferred habitat, and liquidity preference theories. The evidence tends to favor the liquidity preference theory, because liquidity premiums also appear to exist.[13] In particular, there appear to be liquidity premiums of increasing size associated with Treasury securities of up to roughly one year in maturity (meaning that, for example, $L_{.5, .75} < L_{.75, 1}$), but the premiums beyond one year do not seem to be much larger than those for one-year periods. That is, investors seem to demand a premium in order to get them to purchase a one-year security instead of, say, a six-month security. However, the premium needed to get them to purchase an 18-month security (even though the 18-month security has more price risk than a one-year security) may be no larger than the premium needed to get them to purchase the one-year security (meaning that $L_{.5,1} = L_{1,1.5}$).

A word of caution is in order here regarding estimating the size of liquidity premiums. Undoubtedly these premiums (if they exist) change in size over time. Hence trying to estimate their average size accurately is very difficult, and any observations must be made cautiously.

Examining the term structure of interest rates is important for determining the current set of spot rates, which can be used as a basis for valuing any fixed-income security. Such an examination is also important because it provides some information about what the marketplace expects regarding the level of future interest rates.

5.11   HOLDING-PERIOD RETURN

Yield-to-maturity calculations do not take into account any changes in the market value of a security before maturity. This fact might be interpreted as implying that the owner has no interest in selling the instrument before maturity, no matter what happens to its price or his or her situation. The calculation also fails to treat intermediate payments in a fully satisfactory way. An owner who does not wish to spend interest payments might choose to buy more of these securities. But the number that can be bought at any time depends on the price at that time, and yield-to-maturity calculations fail to take this consideration into account.

Although few people dispute the value of yield-to-maturity as an indicator of a bond's overall return, it should be recognized as being no more than that: an indicator. For some purposes, other measures may prove more useful. Moreover, for other types of securities there is no maturity. Common stocks provide the most important example of that situation.

A measure that can be used for any investment is its **holding-period return**. The idea is to specify a **holding period** of major interest and then assume that any payments received during that period will be reinvested. Holding period is defined as the length of time over which an investor is assumed to invest a given sum of money. Although assumptions may differ from case to case, the usual procedure assumes that any payment received from a security (for example, a dividend from a stock, a coupon payment from a bond) will be used to purchase more units of that security at the then current market price. When this procedure is applied, the performance of a security can be measured by comparing the value obtained in this manner at the end of the holding period with the value at the beginning. This **value-relative** can be converted to a holding-period return by subtracting 1 from it:[14]

$$r_{hp} = \frac{\text{value at the end of the holding period}}{\text{value at the the beginning of the holding period}} - 1$$

Holding-period return can be converted to an equivalent return for each period. Allowing for the effect of compounding, the appropriate procedure is to find the value that satisfies the relationship:

$$\left(1 + r_g\right)^N = 1 + r_{hp}$$

or:

$$r_g = \left(1 + r_{hp}\right)^{1/N} - 1$$

where:

Suppose that a Treasury bond sold for $980 at the beginning of one year, paid interest of $80 during that year, sold for $990 at the end of the year, paid interest of $80 during the next year, and sold for $1,000 at the end of that year. What was the return over the two-year holding period?

To simplify the calculations, assume that all interest payments are received at year-end. Then the $80 received during the first year could have bought .0808 (= $80/$990) additional Treasury bonds at the end of the first year. In practice, of course, this would be feasible only if the money were pooled with other similarly in-vested funds in, for example, a mutual fund (the interest from 100 bonds could have been used to buy 8.08 additional bonds). In any event, for each bond originally held, the investor would have obtained $86.46 (= 1.0808 × $80) in interest in the sec-ond year and would have had bonds with a value of $1,080.80 (= 1.0808 × $1,000) at the end of the second year. The ending value would thus have been $1,167.26 (= $1,080.80 + $86.46), giving a value-relative of:

$$\$1,167.26/\$980.00 = 1.1911$$

The holding-period return was thus 19.11% per two years. This is equivalent to $(1.1911)^{1/2} - 1 = .0914$, or 9.14% per year.

An alternative method of computation treats the overall value-relative as the product of value-relatives for the individual periods. For example, if V_0 is the value at the beginning, V_1 the value at the end of the first year, and V_2 the value at the end of the second year:

$$V_2/V_0 = V_2/V_1 \times V_1/V_0$$

Moreover, there is no need to carry the expansion in number of shares from period to period, as the factor (1.0808 in the example) will simply cancel out in the subse-quent periods' value-relatives. Each period can be analyzed in isolation, an appro-priate value-relative calculated, and the set of such value-relatives multiplied together.

In our example, during the first year, ownership of a Treasury bond with an ini-tial value of $980 led to bonds and cash with a value of $990 + $80 = $1,070 at the end of the year. Thus,

$$V_1/V_0 = \$1,070.00/\$980.00 = 1.0918$$

During the second year, ownership of the bond with an initial value of $990 led to bonds and cash with a value of $1,000 + $80 = $1,080 at year-end. Thus:

$$V_2/V_1 = \$1,080.00/\$990.00 = 1.0909$$

The two-year holding-period value-relative was therefore:

$$1.0918 \times 1.0909 = 1.1911$$

which is exactly equal to the value obtained earlier (after accounting for rounding).

The value-relative for each period can be viewed as 1 plus the return for that pe-riod. Thus the return on the Treasury bond being analyzed was 9.18% in the first year and 9.09% in the second. The holding-period value-relative is the product of 1 plus each return. If N periods are involved,

$$V_N/V_0 = (1 + r_1)(1 + r_2)...(1 + r_N)$$

To convert the result to a holding-period return stated as an amount per period, with compounding, one can find the **geometric mean return** of the periodic returns:

$$1 + r_g = \left[\left(1 + r_1 \right)\left(1 + r_2 \right) \ldots \left(1 + r_N \right) \right]^{1/N} \qquad (5.30)$$

More sophisticated calculations may be employed within this overall framework. Each interest payment can be used to purchase more bonds immediately upon receipt, or it can be allowed to earn interest in a savings account until the end of the period. Brokerage and other costs associated with reinvestment of interest can also be taken into account, although the magnitude of such costs will undoubtedly depend on the overall size of the holdings in question. The appropriate degree of complexity will, as always, be a function of the use for which the values are obtained.

Unfortunately, the most appropriate holding period is often at least as uncertain as the return over any given holding period. Neither an investor's situation nor his or her preferences can usually be predicted with certainty. Moreover, from a strategic viewpoint, an investment manager would like to hold a given security only as long as it outperforms available alternatives. Attempts to identify such periods in advance are seldom successful, but managers quite naturally continue to try to discover them. Holding-period return, like yield-to-maturity, provides a useful device for simplifying the complex reality of investment analysis. Although no panacea, it allows an analyst to focus on the most relevant horizon in a given situation and offers a good measure of performance over such a period.

5.12 SUMMARY

1. The nominal (or monetary) interest rate is the rate at which an investor can trade present money for future money.
2. The real interest rate is a function of the difference between the nominal interest rate and the inflation rate.
3. A convenient method for understanding how bonds are valued in the marketplace is to examine initially those fixed-income securities that are free from default risk—namely, Treasury securities.
4. The yield-to-maturity of a security is the discount rate that makes the present value of the security's promised future cash flows equal to the current market price of the security.
5. The spot rate is the yield-to-maturity on a pure-discount Treasury security.
6. Once spot rates (each one associated with a different maturity) have been calculated, they can be used, for example, to value coupon-bearing Treasury securities.
7. A forward rate is the interest rate, established today, that will be paid on money to be borrowed at some specific date in the future and to be repaid at a specific but even more distant date in the future.
8. The payment of interest on interest is known as compounding.
9. Increasing the number of compounding intervals within a year will increase the effective annual interest rate (see Appendix).
10. A yield curve shows the relationship between yield-to-maturity and term-to-maturity for Treasury securities. This relationship is also known as the term structure of interest rates.
11. Four theories have generally been used to explain the term structure of interest rates: the unbiased expectations theory, the liquidity preference theory, the market segmentation theory, and the preferred habitat theory.
12. The unbiased expectations theory states that forward rates represent the consensus opinion about what spot rates will be in the future.

13. The liquidity preference theory states that forward rates overstate the consensus opinion about future spot rates by an amount necessary to compensate investors for the risk involved in holding longer-maturity securities.

14. The market segmentation theory states that different spot rates have different values because of the interaction of supply and demand for funds in markets that are separated from each other by maturity.

15. The preferred habitat theory states that different spot rates occur because investors and borrowers at times must be induced to leave their preferred maturity segments (or habitats).

16. Evidence tends to favor the liquidity preference theory, at least for maturities up to roughly one year.

17. A security's holding-period return compares the expected value of all of the security's cash flows from the current date until a given future date (with those cash flows reinvested at an assumed interest rate) relative to the current market price of the security.

QUESTIONS AND PROBLEMS

1. If the real return on an investment in a given year was 6.0%, while its nominal return was 11.3%, what must have been the inflation rate during the year?

2. Equation (5.3) gives a method to approximately calculate the real rate of interest. Why is that approximation much less accurate in a hyperinflationary economy than in an economy with a relatively stable inflation rate.

3. At the end of 1974, Emil Bildilli held a portfolio of long-term U.S. government bonds valued at $14,000. At the end of 1981, Emil's portfolio was worth $16,932. Referring to Table 1.1, calculate the annualized real rate of return on Emil's bond portfolio over this seven-year period.

4. Consider two bonds, each with a $1,000 face value and each with three years remaining to maturity.

   a. The first bond is a pure-discount bond that currently sells for $816.30. What is its yield-to-maturity?

   b. The second bond currently sells for $949.37 and makes annual coupon payments at a rate of 7% (that is, it pays $70 in interest each year). The first interest payment is due one year from today. What is this bond's yield-to-maturity?

5. Camp Douglas Dirigibles has a bond outstanding with four years to maturity, a face value of $1,000, and an annual coupon payment of $100. What is the price of the Camp Douglas bond if its yield-to-maturity is 12%? If its yield-to-maturity is 8%?

6. The concept of yield-to-maturity is based on two crucial assumptions. What are those assumptions? What will happen to the bondholder's return if those assumptions are violated?

7. Patsy Dougherty bought a $1,000-face-value bond with a 9% annual coupon and three years to maturity that makes its first interest payment one year from today. Patsy bought the bond for $975.13. What is the bond's yield-to-maturity?

8. Consider three pure-discount bonds with maturities of one, two, and three years and prices of $930.23, $923.79, and $919.54, respectively. Each bond has a $1,000 face value. On the basis of this information, what are the one-year, two-year, and three-year spot rates?

9. What are the discount factors associated with three-year, four-year, and five-year $1,000-face-value pure-discount bonds that sell for $810.60, $730.96, and $649.93, respectively?

10. Distinguish between spot rates and forward rates.

The Valuation of Riskless Securities

11. Given the following spot rates for various periods of time from today, calculate forward rates from years 1 to 2, 2 to 3, and 3 to 4.

Years from Today	Spot Rate
1	5.0%
2	5.5%
3	6.5%
4	7.0%

12. Given the following forward rates, calculate the one-, two-, three-, and four-year spot rates.

Forward Time Period	Forward Rate
$f_{0,1}$	10.0%
$f_{1,2}$	9.5%
$f_{2,3}$	9.0%
$f_{3,4}$	8.5%

13. Assume that the current one-year spot rate is 6% and the forward rates for one year hence and two years hence are, respectively:

$$f_{1,2} = 9\%$$

$$f_{2,3} = 10\%$$

What should be the market price of an 8% coupon bond, with a $1,000 face value, maturing three years from today? The first interest payment is due one year from today. Interest is payable annually.

14. Assume that the government has issued three bonds. The first, which pays $1,000 one year from today, is now selling for $909.09. The second, which pays $100 one year from today and $1,100 one year later, is now selling for $991.81. The third, which pays $100 one year from today, $100 one year later, and $1,100 one year after that, is now selling for $997.18.
    a. What are the current discount factors for dollars paid one, two, and three years from today?
    b. What are the forward rates?
    c. Honus Wagner, a friend, offers to pay you $500 one year from today, $600 two years from today, and $700 three years from today in return for a loan today. Assuming that Honus will not default on the loan, how much should you be willing to loan?

15. Mercury National Bank offers a passbook savings account that pays interest at a stated annual rate of 6%. Calculate the effective annual interest rate paid by Mercury National if it compounds interest:
    a. Semiannually
    b. Daily (365 days in a year)

16. Marty Marion is considering placing $30,000 in a three-year, default-free fixed-income investment that promises to provide interest at the rate of 8% during the first year, 10% in the second year, and 12% in the third year. Coupon payments can be reinvested at the rate in effect for the following year.
    a. Assuming annual compounding and repayment of principal at the end of the third year, to what value is Marty's investment expected to grow after three years?
    b. Recalculate your answer to part (a) assuming semiannual compounding.

17 A finance company offers you a loan of $8,000 for two years. Interest on the loan of $1,500 is subtracted from the loan proceeds immediately. What is the bank discount rate on the loan? What is the true interest rate?

18. Turn to the table in *The Wall Street Journal* entitled "Treasury Bonds, Notes & Bills." Find the yield-to-maturity for Treasury securities maturing in one month, three months, one year, five years, ten years, and twenty years. With this information, construct the yield curve as of the paper's publication date.

19. Is it true that an observed downward-sloping yield curve is inconsistent with the liquidity preference theory of the term structure of interest rates? Explain.

20. Assume that the current structure of forward interest rates is upward-sloping. Which will have a lower yield-to-maturity:
    a. A 15-year pure-discount bond or a 10-year pure-discount bond?
    b. A 10-year 5% coupon bond or a 10-year 6% coupon bond?

21. How would your answers to Question 20 change if the forward interest rate structure were downward-sloping?

22. Four theories explaining the term structure of interest rates are described in the chapter. Which theory do you believe best explains the relationship between spot rates and term-to-maturity? Provide supporting arguments for your answer.

23. Assume that the current spot rates are as follows:

Years from Today	Spot Rate
1	8%
2	9%
3	10%

If the unbiased expectations theory holds, what should be the yields-to-maturity on one- and two-year pure discount bonds one year from today?

24. The one-year spot rate is 9%, and the two-year spot rate is 7%. If the one-year spot rate expected in one year is 4.5%, according to the liquidity preference theory, what must be the one-year liquidity premium commencing one year from now?

25. If an investment returns 7% per year, how long does it take for the investment's value to double?

26. Pol Perritt purchased 100 shares of Waunakee Inc. and held the stock for four years. Pol's holding-period returns over these four years were:

Year	Return
1	+20%
2	+30%
3	+50%
4	−90%

    a. What was the value-relative of Pol's investment over the four-year period?
    b. What was Pol's geometric mean return for the four-year period?

27. Assume that you own a bond that you purchased three years ago for $10,300. The bond has made three annual interest payments of $700 to you, the last of which was just paid. At the end of year 1 the bond sold for $10,100. At the end of year 2, it sold for $9,900. The bond now sells for $9,500. Assuming that you could have reinvested your interest income in fractional portions of the bond, what was your holding-period return over the three-year period?

28. (Appendix Question) Recalculate the answers to Questions 15 and 16 assuming that interest compounds continuously.

---

29. (Appendix Question) What is the intrinsic value of a pure-discount bond with a $1,000 face value maturing one year from today and having an 8% discount rate with continuous compounding?

CFA EXAM QUESTIONS

30. The following are the average yields on U.S. Treasury bonds at two points in time.

	Yield-to-Maturity	
Term to Maturity	**January 15, 19XX**	**May 15, 19XX**
1 year	7.25%	8.05%
2 years	7.50%	7.90%
3 years	7.90%	7.70%
10 years	8.30%	7.45%
15 years	8.45%	7.30%
20 years	8.55%	7.20%
25 years	8.60%	7.10%

a. Assuming a pure expectations hypothesis, define a forward rate. Describe how you would calculate the forward rate for a three-year U.S. Treasury bond two years from May 15, 19XX, using the actual term structure above.

b. Discuss how each of the three major term structure hypotheses could explain the January 15, 19XX term structure shown above. (Note: the CFA exam question does not take into account the preferred habitat theory.)

c. Discuss what happened to the term structure over the time period and the effect of this change on the U.S. Treasury bonds of two and ten years.

d. Assume that you invest solely on the basis of yield spreads, and in January 19XX acted upon the expectation that the yield spread between one-year and 25-year U.S. Treasuries would return to a more typical spread of 170 basis points. Explain what you would have done on January 15, 19XX, and describe what happened between January 15, 19XX and May 15, 19XX.

31. a. Calculate the two-year spot rate implied by the U.S. Treasury yield curve data given below. Assume that interest is paid annually for purposes of this calculation. Show all calculations.

Years to Maturity	Current Coupon Yield-to-Maturity	Spot Rate
1	7.5%	7.5%
2	8.0%	—

b. Explain why a spot rate curve can be derived entirely from the current coupon (yield-to-maturity) yield curve.

c. Given a U.S. Treasury one-year spot rate of 9.0% and a U.S. Treasury two-year spot rate of 9.5%, calculate the implied one-year forward rate for the two-year U.S. Treasury security with one year remaining to maturity. Explain why a one-year forward rate of 9.6% would not be expected to prevail in a market given these spot rates.

d. Describe one practical application of the spot rate concept and one practical application of the forward rate concept.

APPENDIX

CONTINUOUS COMPOUNDING

In the computation of an investment's return, the compounding interval can make a difference. For example, regulations may limit a savings institution to paying a fixed rate of interest but make no specifications about the compounding interval. This was the situation in early 1975, when the legal limit on interest paid by savings and loan companies on deposits committed from six to ten years was 7.75% per year. Initially, most savings and loans paid "simple interest." Thus $1 deposited at the beginning of the year would grow to $1.0775 by the end of the year. Later, in an attempt to attract depositors, some enterprising savings and loans announced that they would pay 7.75% per year, compounded semiannually at a rate of 3.875% (= 7.75%/2). This meant that $1 deposited at the beginning of the year would grow to $1.03875 at the end of six months, and this total would then grow to $1.079 (= $1.03875 × 1.03875) by the end of the year, for an effective annual interest rate of 7.9%. This procedure was considered within the letter, if not the spirit, of the law.

Before long, other competitors offered 7.75% per year compounded quarterly (that is, 7.75%/4 = 1.938% per quarter), giving an effective annual interest rate of 7.978%. Then others offered to compound the 7.75% rate on a monthly basis (at 7.75%/12 = .646% per month), for an effective annual interest rate of 8.031%. The end was reached when one company offered continuous compounding of the 7.75% annual rate. This rather abstract procedure represents the limit as interest is compounded more and more frequently. If r represents the annual rate of interest (in this case, 7.75%) and n the number of times compounding takes place each year, the effective annual rate, r_e, is given by:

$$\left(1 + \frac{r}{n}\right)^n = 1 + r_e \tag{5.31}$$

Thus, with semiannual compounding of 7.75%,

$$\left(1 + \frac{.0775}{2}\right)^2 = (1 + .03875)^2 = 1.079$$

and with quarterly compounding,

$$\left(1 + \frac{.0775}{4}\right)^4 = (1 + .01938)^4 = 1.07978$$

and so on. Note that as the compounding interval grows shorter, the number of times compounding takes place (n) grows larger and the effective interest rate (r_e) becomes higher.

Mathematicians can prove that as n grows larger, the quantity $\left[1 + (r/n)\right]^n$ becomes increasingly close to e^r where e stands for the number 2.71828 (rounded to five-place accuracy). In this case, $e^{.0775} = 1.0806$, indicating an effective annual rate of 8.06%.[15]

A more general formula for continuous compounding can also be derived. At an annual rate of r, with continuous compounding, P dollars will grow to F_t dollars t years from now, where the relationship between P, r, and F_t is:

$$Pe^{rt} = F_t \tag{5.32}$$

Similarly, the present value of F_t dollars received t years later at an annual rate of r that is continuously compounded will be:

$$P = \frac{F_t}{e^{rt}} \tag{5.33}$$

Thus if spot rates are expressed as annual rates with continuous compounding, then the discount factors d_t can be calculated as:

$$d_t = \frac{1}{e^{rt}} \tag{5.34}$$

These last three formulas can be used for any value of t, including fractional amounts (for example, if F_t is to be received in $2\frac{1}{2}$ years, then $t = 2.5$).

ENDNOTES

[1] This calculation assumes that the bond will not be called before maturity. If it is assumed that the bond will be called as soon as possible, then the discount rate that makes the present value of the corresponding cash flows equal to the current market price of the bond is known as the bond's **yield-to-call**.

[2] Note how, when Equation (5.24) is used, $r_a = (1.03923)^2 - 1 = 8\%$, a solution that is the same as the one provided by Equation (5.22).

[3] Consider what would happen if the number of compounding intervals in a year became arbitrarily large so that each interval was very small. In the limit there would be an infinite number of infinitely small intervals; such a situation involves *continuous compounding*, which is discussed in the Chapter appendix.

[4] Occasionally, the yield curve will be "humped." It rises for a short while and then declines, perhaps leveling off for intermediate to long-term maturities. For more on yield curves and term structure, see Carol Lancaster and Jerry L. Stevens, "Debt Term Structures: Beyond Yield to Maturity Assumptions," *Financial Practice and Education* 5, no. 2 (Fall/Winter 1995): 125–137.

[5] Recently, a "modern" expectations theory has been developed that is economically more logical than the "unbiased" expectations theory. However, it provides approximately the same empirical implications and explanations of the term structure as those given by the unbiased expectations theory. Given the similarities of the two theories, only the unbiased expectations theory is presented.

[6] Equation (5.25) can be expressed more generally as $es_{t-1, t} = f_{t-1, t}$. Thus, using Equation (5.19), the unbiased expectations theory states that, in general, $\left(1 + s_{t-1}\right)^{t-1} \times \left(1 + es_{t-1, t}\right) = \left(1 + s_t\right)^t$.

[7] See Equations (5.1) through (5.3) and Chapter 12 for a discussion of the nature of the relationship between nominal rates, real rates, and expected inflation rates.

[8] Unfortunately, this risk is often referred to as "liquidity risk" when it more appropriately should be called "price risk," because it is the price volatility associated with longer-term securities that is of concern to investors. Partially offsetting this price risk is a risk that is present in the rollover strategy and absent from the maturity strategy; namely, the risk associated

with the uncertainty of the reinvestment rate at the end of the first year when the rollover strategy is chosen. The liquidity preference theory assumes that this risk is of relatively little concern to investors.

[9] Sometimes the difference is referred to as the *term premium*. See Bradford Cornell, "Measuring the Term Premium: An Empirical Note," *Journal of Economics and Business* 42, no. 1 (February 1990): 89–92.

[10] Although the forward rate can be determined, neither the expected future spot rate nor the liquidity premium can be observed. All that can be done is to estimate their respective values.

[11] Equation (5.27) can be expressed more generally as $f_{t-1,t} = es_{t-1,t} + L_{t-1,t}$. Thus, using Equation (5.19), the liquidity preference theory states that:

$$\left(1 + s_{t-1}\right)^{t-1} \times \left(1 + es_{t-1,t} + L_{t-1,t}\right) = \left(1 + s_t\right)^t$$

Since $L_{t-1,t} > 0$, it follows that, in general:

$$\left(1 + s_{t-1}\right)^{t-1} \times \left(1 + es_{t-1,t}\right) < \left(1 + s_t\right)^t$$

[12] If $es_{1,2}$ were equal to or greater than s_1, then the inequality would not hold in the correct direction because it was assumed that $s_1 > s_2$.

[13] The empirical evidence is not without dispute. Fama has argued that the evidence is inconsistent with both the unbiased expectations and liquidity preference theories, whereas McCulloch refutes Fama's findings and argues in favor of the latter theory. See Eugene F. Fama, "Term Premiums in Bond Returns," *Journal of Financial Economics* 13, no. 4 (December 1984): 529–546; and J. Huston McCulloch, "The Monotonicity of the Term Premium: A Closer Look," *Journal of Financial Economics* 18, no. 1 (March 1987): 185–192, and "An Estimate of the Liquidity Premium," *Journal of Political Economy* 83, no. 1 (February 1975): 95–119. McCulloch's findings are supported by Matthew Richardson, Paul Richardson, and Tom Smith in "The Monotonicity of the Term Premium: Another Look," *Journal of Financial Economics* 31, no. 1 (February 1992): 97–105.

[14] The term *price-relative* refers to the ratio of a security's price on a given day relative to its price on some previous day. Hence, it is the same as the *value-relative* if there are no cash flows associated with the security between the two days.

[15] Tables of natural logarithms may be used for such calculations. The natural logarithm of 1.0806 is .0775, and the antilogarithm of .0775 is 1.0806.

KEY TERMS

nominal interest rate	yield curve
cost-of-living index	term structure
consumer price index	unbiased expectations theory
real interest rate	liquidity preference theory
coupon stripping	liquidity premium
yield-to-maturity	market segmentation theory
spot rate	preferred habitat theory
discount factors	yield-to-call
market discount function	holding-period return
discounting	holding-period
forward rate	value-relative
compounding	geometric mean return

REFERENCES

1. Many of the fundamental concepts having to do with bonds are discussed in:
   Homer Sidney and Martin L. Leibowitz, *Inside the Yield Book: New Tools for Bond Market Strategy* (Upper Saddle River, NJ: Prentice Hall, 1972).

Marcia Stigum, *The Money Market,* 3rd ed. (Homewood, IL: Business One Irwin, 1990).

Frank J. Fabozzi (ed.) *The Handbook of Fixed-Income Securities* 5th ed. (Homewood, IL: Irwin Professional Publishing, 1997).

2. A discussion of the zero-coupon Treasury bond market is presented in:

Deborah W. Gregory and Miles Livingston, "Development of the Market for U.S. Treasury STRIPS," *Financial Analysts Journal* 48, no. 2 (March/April 1992): 68–74.

3. A brief overview of the term structure of interest rates is contained in:

Mark Kritzman, "...About the Term Structure of Interest Rates," *Financial Analysts Journal* 19, no. 4 (July/August 1993): 14–18.

4. For a thorough review of term structure theories and the associated empirical evidence, see:

John H. Wood and Norma L. Wood, *Financial Markets* (San Diego: Harcourt Brace Jovanovich, 1985), Chapter 19.

Peter A. Abken, "Innovations in Modeling the Term Structure of Interest Rates," Federal Reserve Bank of Atlanta, *Economic Review* 75, no. 4 (July/August 1990): 2–27.

Steven Russell, "Understanding the Term Structure of Interest Rates: The Expectations Theory," Federal Reserve Bank of St. Louis, *Review* 74, no. 4 (July/August 1992): 36–50.

Frederic S. Mishkin, *Financial Markets, Institutions, and Money* (New York: HarperCollins, 1995), Chapter 6.

Frank J. Fabozzi, Franco Modigliani, and Michael G. Ferri, *Foundations of Financial Markets and Institutions* (Upper Saddle River, NJ: Prentice Hall, 1998), Chapter 12.

James C. Van Horne, *Financial Market Rates and Flows* (Upper Saddle River, NJ: Prentice Hall, 1998), Chapter 6.

5. For an intriguing tax-based explanation of why the yield curve has usually been upward-sloping, see:

Richard Roll, "After-Tax Investment Results from Long-Term vs. Short-Term Discount Coupon Bonds," *Financial Analysts Journal* 40, no. 1 (January/February 1984): 43–54.

Ricardo J. Rodriguez, "Investment Horizon, Taxes and Maturity Choice for Discount Coupon Bonds," *Financial Analysts Journal* 44, no. 5 (September/October 1988): 67–69.

THE PORTFOLIO SELECTION PROBLEM

Most securities available for investment have uncertain outcomes and are thus risky. The basic problem facing each investor is to determine which particular risky securities to own. Because a portfolio is a collection of securities, this problem is equivalent to the investor selecting the optimal portfolio from a set of possible portfolios. Hence it is often referred to as the *portfolio selection problem*. One solution to this problem was put forth in 1952 by Harry M. Markowitz, when he published a landmark paper that is generally viewed as the origin of the *modern portfolio theory* approach to investing.

Markowitz's approach begins by assuming that an investor has a given sum of money to invest at the present time. This money will be invested for a particular length of time known as the investor's holding period. At the end of the holding period, the investor will sell the securities that were purchased at the beginning of the period and then will either spend the proceeds on consumption or reinvest the proceeds in various securities (or do some of both). Thus Markowitz's approach can be viewed as a single-period approach, wherein the beginning of the period is denoted $t = 0$ and the end of the period is denoted $t = 1$. At $t = 0$, the investor must decide which particular securities to purchase and hold until $t = 1$.[1]

In making this decision at $t = 0$, the investor should recognize that security returns (and thus portfolio returns) over the forthcoming holding period are unknown. Nevertheless, the investor could estimate the **expected** (or mean) **returns** on the various securities under consideration and then invest in the one with the highest expected return. (Methods for estimating expected returns will be discussed in Chapter 17.) Markowitz notes that this would generally be an unwise decision because the typical investor, although wanting "returns to be high," also wants "returns to be as certain as possible." Thus the investor, in seeking to both maximize expected return and minimize uncertainty (that is, **risk**), has two conflicting objectives that must be balanced against each other when making the purchase decision at $t = 0$. The Markowitz approach for how the investor should go about making this decision gives full consideration to both of these objectives.

One interesting consequence of having these two conflicting objectives is that the investor should diversify by purchasing not just one security but several. The ensuing discussion of Markowitz's approach to investing begins by defining more specifically what is meant by initial and terminal wealth.

In Equation (1.1) of Chapter 1 it was noted that the one-period rate of return on a security could be calculated as:

$$\text{Return} = \frac{\text{end-of-period wealth} - \text{beginning-of-period wealth}}{\text{beginning-of-period wealth}} \tag{1.1}$$

where beginning-of-period wealth is the purchase price of one unit of the security at $t = 0$ (for example, one share of a firm's common stock), and end-of-period wealth is the market value of the unit at $t = 1$, along with the value of any cash (and cash equivalents) paid to the owner of the security between $t = 0$ and $t = 1$.

6.1.1 Determining the Rate of Return on a Portfolio

Because a portfolio is a collection of securities, its return r_p can be calculated in a similar manner:

$$r_p = \frac{W_1 - W_0}{W_0} \tag{6.1}$$

Here W_0 denotes the aggregate purchase price at $t = 0$ of the securities contained in the portfolio; W_1 denotes the aggregate market value of these securities at $t = 1$ as well as the aggregate cash (and cash equivalents) received between $t = 0$ and $t = 1$ from owning these securities. Equation (6.1) can be manipulated algebraically, resulting in:

$$W_0(1 + r_p) = W_1 \tag{6.2}$$

From Equation (6.2) it can be seen that beginning-of-period or **initial wealth** (as W_0 is sometimes called), when multiplied by 1 plus the rate of return on the portfolio, equals end-of-period, or **terminal wealth** (as W_1 is sometimes called).

Earlier it was noted that the investor must make a decision regarding what portfolio to purchase at $t = 0$. In doing so, the investor does not know what the value of W_1 will be for most of the various alternative portfolios under consideration because the investor does not know what the rate of return will be for most of these portfolios.[2] Thus, according to Markowitz, the investor should view the rate of return associated with any one of these portfolios as what is called in statistics a **random variable**; such variables can be "described" by their moments, two of which are **expected** (or **mean**) **value** and **standard deviation**.[3]

Markowitz asserts that investors should base their portfolio decisions solely on expected returns and standard deviations. That is, the investor should estimate the expected return and standard deviation of each portfolio and then choose the "best" one on the basis of the relative magnitudes of these two parameters. The intuition behind this assertion is actually quite straightforward. Expected return can be viewed as a measure of the potential reward associated with any portfolio, and standard deviation can be viewed as a measure of the risk associated with any portfolio. Thus, once each portfolio has been examined in terms of its potential rewards and risks, the investor is in a position to identify the one portfolio that appears most desirable to him or her.

TABLE 6.1	A Comparison of Terminal Wealth Levels for Two Hypothetical Portfolios	
	Percent Chance of Being Below This Level of Terminal Wealth	
Level of Terminal Wealth	Portfolio A^a	Portfolio B^b
$70,000	0	2
80,000	0	5
90,000	4	14
100,000	21	27
110,000	57	46
120,000	88	66
130,000	99	82

Note: Initial wealth is assumed to be $100,000, and both portfolios are assumed to have normally distributed returns.

[a] The expected return and standard deviation of A are 8% and 10%, respectively.

[b] The expected return and standard deviation of B are 12% and 20%, respectively.

6.1.2 Example

Consider the two alternative portfolios denoted A and B, shown in Table 6.1. Portfolio A has an expected annual return of 8%, and portfolio B has an expected annual return of 12%. Assuming that the investor has initial wealth of $100,000 and a one-year holding period, the expected levels of terminal wealth associated with A and B are $108,000 and $112,000, respectively. It would appear, then, that B is the more desirable portfolio. However, A and B have annual standard deviations of 10% and 20%, respectively. Table 6.1 shows that this means that there is a 2% chance that the investor will end up with terminal wealth of $70,000 or less if he or she purchases B, whereas there is virtually no chance that the investor's terminal wealth will be less than $70,000 if A is purchased. Similarly, B has a 5% chance of being worth less than $80,000, whereas A again has no chance. Continuing, B has a 14% chance of being worth less than $90,000, whereas A has only a 4% chance. Going on, B has a 27% chance of being worth less than $100,000, whereas A has only a 21% chance. Because the investor has initial wealth of $100,000, this last observation means that there is a greater probability of having a negative return if B (27%) is purchased instead of A (21%). Overall, it can be seen from Table 6.1 that A is less risky than B, meaning that on this dimension A would be more desirable. The ultimate decision about whether to purchase A or B will depend on this particular investor's attitude toward risk and return.

6.2 NONSATIATION AND RISK AVERSION

6.2.1 Nonsatiation

Two assumptions are implicit in this discussion of the portfolio selection problem. First, it is assumed that investors, when given a choice between two otherwise identical portfolios, will always choose the one with the higher level of expected return. More fundamentally, an assumption of **nonsatiation** is made in the Markowitz approach; that is, investors are assumed to always prefer higher levels of terminal wealth to lower levels of terminal wealth. The reason is that higher levels of terminal wealth allow the investor to spend more on consumption at $t = 1$ (or in the more distant future). Thus, given two portfolios with the same standard deviation, the investor will choose the portfolio with the higher expected return.

However, it is not quite so obvious what the investor will do when having to choose between two portfolios having the same level of expected return but different levels of standard deviation. This is where the second assumption enters the discussion.

6.2.2   Risk Aversion

In general, it is assumed that investors are **risk-averse**, which means that the investor will choose the portfolio with the smaller standard deviation.[4] What does it mean to say that an investor is risk-averse? It means that the investor, when given the choice, will not want to take *fair gambles* (or fair bets), where a fair gamble is defined to be one that has an expected payoff of zero. For example, consider flipping a coin, with "heads" meaning that you win $5 and "tails" meaning that you lose $5. Because the coin has a 50:50 chance of being heads or tails, the expected payoff is $0 $\left[= (.5 \times \$5) + (.5 \times -\$5)\right]$. Accordingly, the risk-averse investor will choose to avoid this gamble. The concept of investor utility helps explain why.

6.3   UTILITY

Economists use the term **utility** to quantify the relative enjoyment or satisfaction that people derive from economic activity such as work, consumption, or investment. Satisfying activities generate positive utility; dissatisfying activities produce negative utility (or disutility). Because tastes (or preferences) differ among individuals, one person may experience more utility from a particular activity than another person does. Nevertheless, people are presumed to be rational and to allocate their resources (such as time and money) in ways that maximize their own utilities. The Markowitz portfolio selection problem can be viewed as an effort to maximize the expected utility associated with the investor's terminal wealth.

6.3.1   Marginal Utility

The exact relationship between utility and wealth is called the investor's *utility of wealth function*. Under the assumption of nonsatiation, all investors prefer more wealth to less wealth. (Money is indeed assumed to buy happiness.) Every extra dollar of wealth enhances an investor's utility. But by how much?

Each investor has a unique utility of wealth function. As a result, each investor may derive a unique increment of utility from an extra dollar of wealth. That is, the **marginal utility** of wealth may differ among investors. Further, that marginal utility may depend on the level of wealth that the investor possesses before receiving the extra dollar. (A rich investor may value an extra dollar of wealth less than a poor investor does.)

A common assumption is that investors experience diminishing marginal utility of wealth. Each extra dollar of wealth always provides positive additional utility, but the added utility produced by each extra dollar becomes successively smaller. Figure 6.1(a) illustrates the utility of wealth function of an investor. Higher levels of wealth (read off the horizontal axis) produce higher levels of utility (read off the vertical axis). The assumption of nonsatiation requires that the utility of wealth function is always positively sloped no matter what the level of wealth. However, this utility of wealth function is concave (bowed downward). As wealth increases, the corresponding increase in utility becomes smaller. That is, marginal utility diminishes.

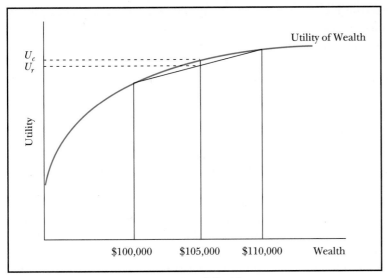

(a) Utility of Wealth

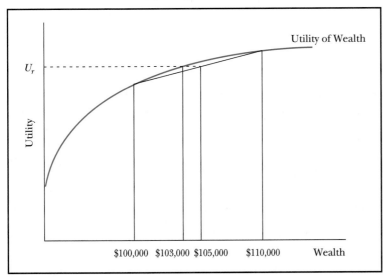

(b) Certainty Equivalent

Figure 6.1
Investor's Utility of Wealth Function and Certainty Equivalent Wealth.

An investor with diminishing marginal utility is necessarily risk-averse. This risk-averse investor is unwilling to accept a fair bet. The utility of wealth function can now be used to explain that preference.

Smith has been offered the choice of two investments. One is to invest $100,000 and earn a certain return of 5%. The expected terminal wealth of this investment is $105,000. The alternative investment also requires an outlay of $100,000. It has a 50% probability of returning a $10,000 gain (a 10% return) and a 50% probability of returning only the original investment (a 0% return). The expected terminal wealth of the risky investment is the same as that of the certain investment: $105,000 (= .5 × $100,000 + .5 × $110,000), or a 5% expected return. Which investment will Smith prefer?

The Portfolio Selection Problem

The answer is shown in Figure 6.1(a). The utility associated with the certain investment is found by moving up from the terminal wealth axis at $105,000 to the utility of wealth function and then moving across to the utility axis. The utility of the certain investment is identified as U_c. The expected utility of the risky investment is found by connecting the utility of the upper and lower possible outcomes on the investment ($100,000 and $110,000) with a straight line and then moving up from the expected terminal wealth of the investment ($105,000) on the terminal wealth axis to that line and then moving across to the utility axis. The expected utility of the risky investment is labeled U_r. Because U_c is greater than U_r, Smith will choose the certain investment.[5] This conclusion can be generalized for any pair of certain and risky investments with the same expected terminal wealth: A risk-averse investor will derive greater satisfaction by selecting the certain investment over the risky investment.

The reasoning for this preference is straightforward. A risk-averse investor displays diminishing marginal utility of wealth. Thus the negative utility (or disutility) associated with a $1 (or $5,000) loss is more than the positive utility of earning $1 (or $5,000). That is, at any point along a concave utility of wealth function, if one moves $1 (or $5,000) to the right, the corresponding increase in utility is smaller than the decline in utility if one were to move $1 (or $5,000) to the left.

6.3.2 Certainty Equivalents and Risk Premiums

Figure 6.1(b) introduces two additional concepts. Smith is given the chance to enter into the same risky investment as described in the previous example. Moving horizontally from the utility axis at the expected utility of the risky investment to the utility of wealth function and then moving down to the terminal wealth axis indicates the **certainty equivalent** wealth associated with this risky investment. In this case that wealth is $103,000. This is the amount of terminal wealth that, if offered with certainty, would provide the same amount of expected utility as the risky investment. Smith will be indifferent between a $100,000 investment that offers a terminal wealth of $103,000 with certainty (a 3% certain return) and this risky investment, with an expected terminal wealth of $105,000 (a 5% risky return). Further, the additional $2,000 in expected terminal wealth (or additional 2% in expected return) offered by the risky investment over the certain investment is termed a **risk premium**: It is the expected increase in terminal wealth (or expected return) over the certain investment required to compensate the investor for the risk incurred. For a risky investment with a given expected terminal wealth, investors who are more risk-averse will have lower certainty equivalents and commensurately higher risk premiums than will investors who are less risk-averse.

Risk-averse investors are willing to forego some expected terminal wealth (that is, accept lower expected returns) in exchange for less risk. Thus various combinations of expected terminal wealth (or expected returns) and risk will produce the same level of expected utility for an investor. This relationship leads to the concept of indifference curves.

6.4 INDIFFERENCE CURVES

An **indifference curve** represents a set of risk and expected return combinations that provide an investor with the same amount of utility. The investor is said to be indifferent between any of the risk-expected return combinations on the same indifference curve. Because indifference curves indicate an investor's preferences for risk and expected return, they can be drawn on a two-dimensional figure where the horizontal axis indicates risk as measured by standard deviation (denoted σ_p) and the vertical axis indicates reward as measured by expected return (denoted $\bar{r}_p$).

Figure 6.2 illustrates a "map" of indifference curves that a hypothetical risk-averse investor might possess. Each curved line indicates one indifference curve for the investor and represents all combinations of portfolios that provide the investor with a given level of utility. For example, the investor with the indifference curves in Figure 6.2 would find portfolios A and B (the same two portfolios that were shown in Table 6.1) equally desirable, even though they have different expected returns and standard deviations, because they both lie on the same indifference curve, I_2. Portfolio B has a higher standard deviation (20%) than portfolio A (10%) and is therefore less desirable on that dimension. However, exactly offsetting this loss in desirability is the gain in desirability provided by the higher expected return of B (12%) relative to A (8%).

Because all portfolios that lie on a given indifference curve are equally desirable to the investor, by implication *indifference curves cannot intersect*. To see that this is so, consider two curves that do intersect, such as those that are shown in Figure 6.3. Here, the point of intersection is represented by X. Remember that all the portfolios

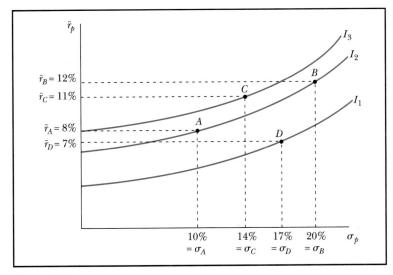

Figure 6.2
Map of Indifference Curves for a Risk-Averse Investor

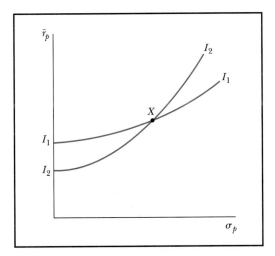

Figure 6.3
Intersecting Indifference Curves

Behavioral Finance

The bedrock on which theories of risky security valuation rest is the presumed existence of rational investors who respond in a predictable manner to the opportunities for gain and the risks of loss. As the text discusses, these investors are assumed to assess potential investments on the basis of expected returns and standard deviations that are derived from estimates of the investments' probability distributions of returns. Furthermore, the investors' estimates are assumed to exhibit no systematic biases relative to the "true" probability distributions. That is, investors do not consistently make mistakes in one direction or another when examining potential investments.

If such assumptions of rationality make sense for individual investors, then we might reasonably believe that they apply even more appropriately to institutional investors. After all, institutional investors bring to bear extensive analytical resources on the investment management problem. Moreover, the decision-making structures of institutional investors—such as hierarchies of personnel, committees, and performance reviews—are all designed to promote consistent and rational investment choices.

The view of investors as objective decision makers has traditionally gone unchallenged in the academic world. Although many professional investors have argued that investing is dominated by the emotions of fear and greed, their opinions have been dismissed by many academics as anecdotal and self-serving. More recently, however, a school of thought has developed among certain academics that argues that investors may not deal with risky choices in a totally rational manner. This line of reasoning is based on a branch of psychology known as *cognitive psychology*, which studies the capacity of human beings for perception and judgment.

Applied to the study of economic decision making, and investments in particular, cognitive psychology draws some intriguing conclusions. Most fundamentally, people do not appear to be consistent in how they treat economically equivalent choices if the choices are presented in significantly different contexts. These differences are referred to as *framing effects*. Two prominent cognitive psychology researchers, Daniel Kahneman and Amos Tversky, cite a simple example of framing effects (see "The Psychology of Preferences," *Scientific American*, January 1982).

Suppose that you are walking to a Broadway play carrying a ticket that cost $100. On reaching the theater you discover that you have lost your ticket. Would you pay another $100 for a ticket at the door? Now suppose that you were planning to buy the ticket at the door. On arriving you find that you have lost $100 on the way. Would you still buy a ticket?

The economic consequences of these two situations are identical. You have lost $100 and now must decide whether to spend another $100. Interestingly, however, most people would buy a ticket in the second case but not in the first. People therefore appear to "frame" the choices differently. They treat the loss of cash differently from the loss of a ticket.

In terms of investing, these framing effects have been suggested to cause deviations from rational decision making. For example, it appears that people react differently to situations involving the prospects

on I_1 are equally desirable. This means they are all as desirable as X, because X is on I_1. Similarly, all the portfolios on I_2 are equally desirable and are as desirable as X, because X is also on I_2. Given that X is on both indifference curves, all the portfolios on I_1 must be as desirable as those on I_2. But this interpretation presents a contradiction, because I_1 and I_2 are two curves that are supposed to represent different levels of utility. Thus, in order for there to be no contradiction, these curves cannot intersect.

Although the investor represented in Figure 6.2 would find portfolios A and B equally desirable, he or she would find portfolio C, with an expected return of 11% and a standard deviation of 14%, preferable to both of them. This is because portfolio C happens to be on an indifference curve, I_3, that is located to the "northwest" of I_2. Now C has a sufficiently larger expected return relative to A to more than offset its higher standard deviation and, on balance, to make it more desirable than A. Equivalently, C has a sufficiently smaller standard deviation than B to more than off-for large gains as opposed to large losses. That is, investors are assumed to choose a riskier investment over a less risky one only if the expected return of the riskier investment is greater than that of the less risky investment. (This trait is known as risk aversion, as mentioned earlier in the chapter.) Indeed, this assumption seems to hold well for situations involving large gains. For example, consider a situation in which you have invested in a start-up company and have a 90% chance of receiving $1 million and a 10% chance of receiving nothing. Hence the expected payoff is $900,000 $\left[= (.9 \times \$1 \text{ million}) + (.1 \times \$0)\right]$. If somebody offered to buy you out for $850,000, most likely you would accept the offer, because it has nearly the same expected payoff but much less risk. That is, you would be exhibiting risk-averse behavior.

Now, however, consider a situation involving large losses. Suppose that you had invested in another start-up company. Things are going poorly, and if nothing changes there is a 90% chance of losing $1 million but a 10% chance that things might work out well enough to not lose (or gain) anything. Thus the expected loss is $900,000 $\left[= (.9 \times -\$1 \text{ million}) + (.1 \times \$0)\right]$. Another investor offers to take over the company if you pay him or her $850,000; a certain $850,000 loss. Most people would reject the offer and choose to remain with the risky option even though it has a lower expected value (−$900,000 versus −$850,000). Thus in a situation involving large expected losses, people do not seem to exhibit risk-averse behavior—a framing effect.

People also seem to overestimate the probability of unlikely events occurring and to underestimate the probability of moderately likely events occurring. These traits may explain the popularity of lotteries but may also have direct ramifications for the pricing of investments when the chances of success are low—such as bonds and stocks of bankrupt companies, start-up companies, and options whose strike prices are far above the underlying securities' prices.

Framing effects may also be involved in the observed tendency of investors to overreact to good and bad news. (see Chapter 16.) That is, some studies suggest that investors bid up the prices of companies reporting unexpectedly good earnings beyond the amount fairly warranted by the improved earnings. The converse seems to occur for companies reporting unexpectedly poor earnings.

Are the observations of cognitive psychologists relevant to the study of financial markets? Do these framing effects produce market anomalies that produce exploitable investment opportunities or even undermine commonly accepted theories of security valuation? Or are these framing effects merely interesting stories whose impacts are overwhelmed by the sophistication and profit motive of avaricious investors? Certainly, investors as a whole are far from irrational, for large and persistent disparities between "fair" values and market values are difficult to find. Nevertheless, the behavioral observations of cognitive psychologists are likely to provide a better understanding of how investors make decisions and help to explain certain apparent market inefficiencies. Indeed, it has opened up a whole new field known as *behavioral finance.*

set its smaller expected return and, on balance, to make it more desirable than *B*. This comparison leads to the second important feature of indifference curves: *A risk-averse investor will find any portfolio that is lying on an indifference curve that is "farther northwest" to be more desirable (that is, to provide greater utility) than any portfolio lying on an indifference curve that is "not as far northwest."*

Last, it should be noted that *an investor has an infinite number of indifference curves.* This statement simply implies that whenever two indifference curves have been plotted on a graph, it is possible to plot a third indifference curve that lies between them. As can be seen in Figure 6.4, given indifference curves I_1 and I_2, it is possible to graph a third curve, I^*, lying between them. It also implies that another indifference curve can be plotted above I_2 and yet another below I_1.

How does an investor determine what his or her indifference curves look like? After all, each investor has a map of indifference curves that, although having the previously noted features, is nevertheless unique to that individual. One method, as will

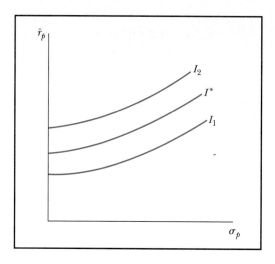

Figure 6.4
Plotting a Third Indifference Curve
between Two Others

be shown in Chapter 23, involves presenting the investor with a set of hypothetical portfolios, along with their expected returns and standard deviations.[6] Then he or she would be asked to choose the most desirable one. Given the choice that is made, the shape and location of the investor's indifference curves can be estimated because it is presumed that the investor would have acted as if he or she had explicit knowledge of his or her own indifference curves in making this choice, even though those indifference curves would not have been directly referenced.

In summary, every investor has an indifference map representing his or her preferences for expected returns and standard deviations.[7] This means that the investor should determine the expected return and standard deviation for each potential portfolio, plot them on a graph such as Figure 6.2, and then select the one portfolio that lies on the indifference curve that is farthest northwest. As shown in this example, from the set of the four potential portfolios—*A, B, C,* and *D*—the investor should select *C.*

The two assumptions of nonsatiation and risk aversion cause indifference curves to be positively sloped and convex.[8] Although it is assumed that all investors are risk-averse, it is not assumed that they have identical degrees of risk aversion. Some investors may be highly risk-averse, whereas others may be only slightly so. Consequently, different investors will have different maps of indifference curves. Figure 6.5 displays maps for three investors who are highly risk-averse (a), moderately risk-averse (b), and slightly risk-averse (c). As can be seen in the figure, the more risk-averse an investor is, the more steeply sloped the indifference curves will be.

6.5	CALCULATING EXPECTED RETURNS AND STANDARD DEVIATIONS FOR PORTFOLIOS

The previous section introduced the portfolio selection problem that every investor faces. It also introduced the investment approach of Harry Markowitz as a method of solving that problem. With this approach, an investor should evaluate alternative portfolios on the basis of their expected returns and standard deviations by using indifference curves. In the case of a risk-averse investor, the portfolio on the indifference curve that is farthest northwest would be the one selected for investment. However, certain questions remain unanswered. In particular, how does the investor calculate the expected return and standard deviation for a portfolio?

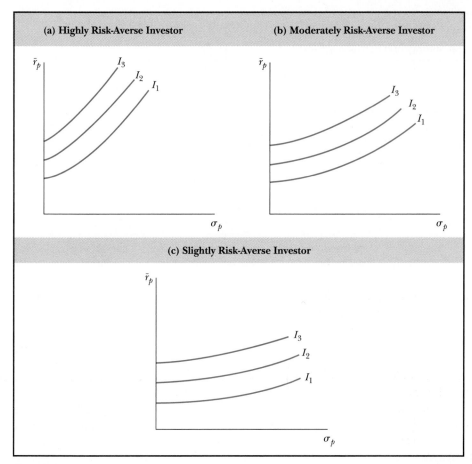

Figure 6.5
Indifference Curves for Three Types of Risk-Averse Investors

6.5.1 Expected Returns

With the Markowitz approach to investing, the focus of the investor is on terminal (or end-of-period) wealth, W_1. That is, in deciding which portfolio to purchase with his or her initial (or beginning-of-period) wealth, W_0, the investor should focus on the effect of the various portfolios on W_1. This effect can be measured by the expected return and standard deviation of each portfolio.

As mentioned previously, a portfolio is a collection of securities. Thus the expected return and standard deviation of a portfolio depend on the expected return and standard deviation of each security contained in the portfolio. Furthermore, the amount invested in each security is important.

In order to show how the expected return on a portfolio depends on both the expected return on the individual securities and the amount invested in these securities, consider the three-security portfolio shown in Table 6.2(a). Assume that the investor has a one-year holding period and that for this period the expected returns on Able, Baker, and Charlie stock are estimated to be 16.2%, 24.6%, and 22.8%, respectively. The investor has, in effect, estimated the end-of-period values of these three stocks to be, respectively, $46.48 $\big[= \$40 \times (1 + .162)\big]$, $43.61 $\big[= \$35 \times (1 + .246)\big]$, and $76.14 $\big[= \$62 \times (1 + .228)\big]$.[9] Furthermore, assume that this investor has initial wealth of $17,200.

TABLE 6.2   Calculating the Expected Return on a Portfolio

(a) Security and Portfolio Values

Security Name	Number of Shares in Portfolio	Initial Market Price per Share	Total Investment	Proportion of Initial Market Value of Portfolio
Able Co.	100	$40	$4,000	$4,000/$17,200 = .2325
Baker Co.	200	35	7,000	7,000/17,200 = .4070
Charlie Co.	100	62	6,200	6,200/17,200 = .3605

Initial market value of portfolio $= W_0 = \$17,200$ Sum of proportions $= 1.0000$

(b) Calculating the Expected Return for a Portfolio Using End-of-Period Values

Security Name	Number of Shares in Portfolio	Expected End-of-Period Value per Share	Aggregate Expected End-of-Period Value
Able Co.	100	$46.48	$46.48 \times 100 = \$4,648$
Baker Co.	200	43.61	$43.61 \times 200 = 8,722$
Charlie Co.	100	76.14	$76.14 \times 100 = 7,614$

Expected end-of-period value of portfolio $= W_1 = \$20,984$

Portfolio expected return $= \bar{r}_p = (\$20,984 - \$17,200)/\$17,200 = 22.00\%$

(c) Calculating the Expected Return for a Portfolio Using Security Expected Returns

Security Name	Proportion of Initial Market Value of Portfolio	Security Expected Returns	Contribution to Portfolio Expected Return
Able Co.	.2325	16.2%	$.2325 \times 16.2\% = 3.77\%$
Baker Co.	.4070	24.6	$.4070 \times 24.6 = 10.01$
Charlie Co.	.3605	22.8	$.3605 \times 22.8 = 8.22$

Portfolio expected return $= \bar{r}_p = 22.00\%$

Using End-of-Period Values

The expected return on this portfolio can be calculated in several ways, all of which give the same answer. Consider the method shown in Table 6.2(b). This method involves calculating the expected end-of-period value of the portfolio and then using the formula for calculating the rate of return that was shown in Chapter 1. That is, first the initial portfolio value (W_0) is subtracted from the expected end-of-period value of the portfolio (W_1), and then this difference is divided by the initial portfolio value (W_0), the result of which is the portfolio's expected return. Although the example shown in Table 6.2(b) involves three securities, the procedure can be generalized to any number of securities.

Using Security Expected Returns

An alternative method for calculating the expected return on this portfolio is shown in Table 6.2(c). This procedure involves calculating the expected return on a portfolio as the weighted average of the expected returns on its component securities. The relative market values of the securities in the portfolio are used as weights. In symbols, the general rule for calculating the expected return on a portfolio consisting of N securities is:

$$\bar{r}_p = \sum_{i=1}^{N} X_i \bar{r}_i \qquad\qquad (6.3a)$$

$$= X_1 \bar{r}_1 + X_2 \bar{r}_2 + \cdots + X_N \bar{r}_N \qquad (6.3b)$$

where:

> $\bar{r}_p$ = the expected return of the portfolio
> X_i = the proportion of the portfolio's initial value invested in security i
> $\bar{r}_i$ = the expected return of security i
> N = the number of securities in the portfolio[10]

Thus, an **expected return vector** can be used to calculate the expected return for any portfolio formed from the N securities. This vector consists of one column of numbers, where the entry in row i contains the expected return of security i. In the previous example, the expected return vector was estimated by the investor to be:

$$\begin{array}{l} \text{Row 1} \\ \text{Row 2} \\ \text{Row 3} \end{array} \begin{bmatrix} 16.2\% \\ 24.6\% \\ 22.8\% \end{bmatrix}$$

where the entries in rows 1, 2, and 3 denote the expected returns for securities Able, Baker, and Charlie, respectively.

Because a portfolio's expected return is a weighted average of the expected returns of its securities, the contribution of each security to the portfolio's expected return depends on its expected return and its proportionate share of the initial portfolio's market value. Nothing else is relevant. It follows from Equation (6.3a) that an investor who simply wants the greatest possible expected return should hold one security: the one he or she considers to have the greatest expected return. Very few investors do this, and very few investment advisers would counsel such an extreme policy. Instead, investors should diversify; their portfolios should include more than one security because diversification can reduce risk, as measured by standard deviation.

6.5.2 Standard Deviations

A useful measure of risk should somehow take into account both the probabilities of various possible bad outcomes and their associated magnitudes. Instead of measuring the probability of a number of different possible outcomes, the measure of risk should somehow estimate the extent to which the actual outcome is likely to diverge from the expected outcome. Standard deviation is a measure that does this, because it is an estimate of the likely divergence of an *actual* return from an *expected* return.

It may seem that any single measure of risk would provide at best a very crude summary of the bad possibilities. But in the common situation in which a portfolio's prospects are being assessed, standard deviation may prove to be a very good measure of the degree of uncertainty. The clearest example arises when the **probability distribution** for a portfolio's returns can be approximated by the familiar bell-shaped curve known as a **normal distribution**. This is often considered a plausible assumption for analyzing returns on diversified portfolios when the holding period being studied is relatively short (say, a quarter or less).

An obvious question about standard deviation as a measure of risk is: Why count "happy" surprises (those above the expected return) at all in a measure of risk? Why not just consider the deviations *below* the expected return? Measures that do so have merit. However, the results will be the same if the probability distribution is symmetric, as is the normal distribution. Why? Because the left side of a symmetric distribution is a mirror image of the right side. Thus a list of portfolios ordered on the basis of "downside risk" will not differ from one ordered on the basis of standard deviation if returns are normally distributed.[11]

Formula for Standard Deviation

Now just how is the standard deviation of a portfolio calculated? For the three-security portfolio consisting of Able, Baker, and Charlie, the formula is:

$$\sigma_p = \left[\sum_{i=1}^{3} \sum_{j=1}^{3} X_i X_j \sigma_{ij} \right]^{1/2} \qquad (6.4)$$

where σ_{ij} denotes the **covariance** of the returns between security i and security j.

Covariance

Covariance is a statistical measure of the relationship between two random variables. That is, it is a measure of how two random variables, such as the returns on securities i and j, "move together." A positive value for covariance indicates that the securities' returns tend to move in the same direction; for example, a better-than-expected return for one is likely to occur along with a better-than-expected return for the other. A negative covariance indicates a tendency for the returns to offset one another; for example, a better-than-expected return for one security is likely to occur along with a worse-than-expected return for the other. A relatively small or zero value for the covariance indicates that there is little or no relationship between the returns for the two securities.

Correlation

Closely related to covariance is the statistical measure known as correlation. In fact, the covariance between two random variables is equal to the correlation between the two random variables times the product of their standard deviations:

$$\sigma_{ij} = \rho_{ij} \sigma_i \sigma_j \qquad (6.5)$$

where ρ_{ij} (the Greek letter *rho*) denotes the **correlation coefficient** between the return on security i and the return on security j. The correlation coefficient rescales the covariance to facilitate comparison with corresponding values for other pairs of random variables.

Correlation coefficients always lie between -1 and $+1$. A value of -1 represents perfect negative correlation, and a value of $+1$ represents perfect positive correlation. Most cases lie between those two extreme values.

Figure 6.6(a) presents a scatter diagram for the returns on hypothetical securities A and B when the correlation between these two securities is perfectly positive. Note how all the points lie precisely on a straight upward-sloping line.

This slope indicates that, when one of the two securities has a relatively high return, then so will the other. Similarly, when one of the two securities has a relatively low return, then so will the other.

Alternatively, the returns on the two securities will have a perfectly negative correlation when the scatter diagram indicates that the points lie precisely on a straight downward-sloping line, as shown in Figure 6.6(b). In such a case the returns on the two securities can be seen to move opposite each other. That is, when one security has a relatively high return, the other will have a relatively low return.

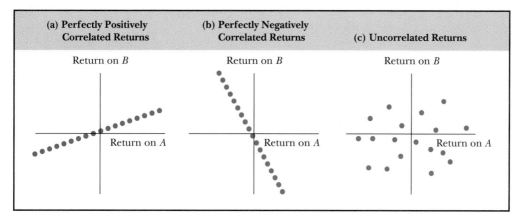

Figure 6.6
Returns on Two Securities

A case of special importance arises when the scatter diagram of security returns shows a dispersion that cannot be represented even approximately by an upward-sloping or a downward-sloping line. In such an instance, the returns are uncorrelated, meaning that the correlation coefficient is zero. Figure 6.6(c) provides an example. In this situation, when one security has a relatively high return, the other can have a relatively high, low, or average return.

Double Summation

Given an understanding of covariance and correlation, it is important to understand how the *double summation* indicated in Equation (6.4) is computed. Although there are many ways of computing double summation, all of which lead to the same answer, one way is perhaps more intuitive than the others. It starts with the first summation and sets i at its initial value of 1. Then the second summation is performed for j going from 1 to 3. At this point, i in the first summation is increased by 1, so that now $i = 2$. Again the second summation is performed by letting j go from 1 to 3, except that now $i = 2$. Continuing, i in the first summation is again increased by 1, so that $i = 3$. Then the second summation is once again performed by letting j go from 1 to 3. At this point, note that i and j are each at their upper limits of 3. This means that it is time to stop, as the double summation has been finished. This process can be shown algebraically as follows:

$$\sigma_p = \left[\sum_{j=1}^{3} X_1 X_j \sigma_{1j} + \sum_{j=1}^{3} X_2 X_j \sigma_{2j} + \sum_{j=1}^{3} X_3 X_j \sigma_{3j} \right]^{1/2} \qquad (6.6a)$$

$$= \left[X_1 X_1 \sigma_{11} + X_1 X_2 \sigma_{12} + X_1 X_3 \sigma_{13} \right.$$
$$+ X_2 X_1 \sigma_{21} + X_2 X_2 \sigma_{22} + X_2 X_3 \sigma_{23} \qquad (6.6b)$$
$$\left. + X_3 X_1 \sigma_{31} + X_3 X_2 \sigma_{32} + X_3 X_3 \sigma_{33} \right]^{1/2}$$

Each term in the double sum involves the product of the weights for two securities, X_i and X_j, and the covariance between these two securities. Note how there are nine terms to be added together in order to calculate the standard deviation of a portfolio consisting of three securities. It is no coincidence that the number of terms to be added together (9) equals the number of securities squared (3^2).

In general, calculating the standard deviation for a portfolio consisting of N securities involves performing the double sum indicated in Equation (6.4) over N securities, thereby involving the addition of N^2 terms:

$$\sigma_p = \left[\sum_{i=1}^{N} \sum_{j=1}^{N} X_i X_j \sigma_{ij} \right]^{1/2} \tag{6.7}$$

An interesting feature of the double sum occurs when the subscripts i and j refer to the same security. In Equation (6.6), this occurs in the first $\left(X_1 X_1 \sigma_{11} \right)$, fifth $\left(X_2 X_2 \sigma_{22} \right)$, and ninth $\left(X_3 X_3 \sigma_{33} \right)$ terms. What does it mean to have the subscripts for covariance refer to the same security? For example, consider security 1 (Able) so that $i = j = 1$. Since σ_{11} denotes the covariance of security 1 (Able) with security 1 (Able), Equation (6.5) indicates that:

$$\sigma_{11} = \rho_{11} \sigma_1 \sigma_1 \tag{6.8}$$

Now the correlation of any security with itself, in this case ρ_{11}, can be shown to be equal to $+1$.[12] This means that Equation (6.8) reduces to:

$$\sigma_{11} = 1 \times \sigma_1 \times \sigma_1$$
$$= \sigma_1^2$$

which is just the standard deviation of security one squared, known as the *variance* of security one. Thus the double sum involves both variance and covariance terms.

Variance-Covariance Matrix

As an example, consider the following **variance-covariance matrix** for the stocks of Able, Baker, and Charlie:

	Column 1	Column 2	Column 3
Row 1	146	187	145
Row 2	187	854	104
Row 3	145	104	289

The matrix can be thought of as the cells in a computer spreadsheet. Each cell is formed by the combination of a specific row and a specific column. The entry in cell (i, j) denotes the covariance between security i and security j. For example, the entry in $(1,3)$ denotes the covariance between the first and third securities, which in this case is 145. Also, the entry in cell (i, i) denotes the variance of security i. For example, the variance of security 2 appears in cell $(2,2)$ and is equal to 854. Using this variance-covariance matrix along with the formula given in Equation (6.6b), one can now compute the standard deviation of any portfolio that consists of investments in Able, Baker, and Charlie.

For example, consider the portfolio given in Table 6.2 that had proportions $X_1 = .2325$, $X_2 = .4070$, and $X_3 = .3605$:

$$\sigma_p = \left[X_1 X_1 \sigma_{11} + X_1 X_2 \sigma_{12} + X_1 X_3 \sigma_{13} \right.$$
$$+ X_2 X_1 \sigma_{21} + X_2 X_2 \sigma_{22} + X_2 X_3 \sigma_{23}$$
$$\left. + X_3 X_1 \sigma_{31} + X_3 X_2 \sigma_{32} + X_3 X_3 \sigma_{33} \right]^{1/2}$$
$$= \left[(.2325 \times .2325 \times 146) + (.2325 \times .4070 \times 187) \right.$$
$$+ (.2325 \times .3605 \times 145) + (.4070 \times .2325 \times 187)$$
$$+ (.4070 \times .4070 \times 854) + (.4070 \times .3605 \times 104)$$

$$+ \ (.3605 \times .2325 \times 145) + (.3605 \times .4070 \times 104)$$

$$+ \ (.3605 \times .3605 \times 289) \big]^{1/2}$$

$$= [277.13]^{1/2}$$

$$= 16.65\%$$

Several interesting features about variance-covariance matrices deserve mention. First, such matrices are square, meaning that the number of columns equals the number of rows and that the total number of cells for N securities equals N^2.

Second, the variances of the securities appear on the diagonal of the matrix, which are the cells that lie on a line going from the upper left-hand corner to the lower right-hand corner of the matrix. In the previous example, the variance of security 1 (146) appears in row one of column one. Similarly, the variances of securities 2 and 3 appear in row two of column two (854) and row three of column three (289), respectively.

Third, the matrix is symmetric, meaning that the number appearing in row i of column j also appears in row j of column i. That is, the elements in the cells above the diagonal also appear in the corresponding cells below the diagonal. In the previous example, note that the element in row one of column two, 187, also appears in row two of column one. Similarly, 145 appears in both row one of column three and row three of column one, and 104 appears in both row two of column three and row three of column two. The reason for this feature is quite simple; the covariance between two securities does not depend on the order in which the two securities are specified. For example, the covariance between the first and second securities is the same as the covariance between the second and first securities.[13]

SUMMARY

1. The Markowitz approach to portfolio selection assumes that investors seek both maximum expected return for a given level of risk and minimum uncertainty (risk) for a given level of expected return.
2. Expected return serves as the measure of potential reward associated with a portfolio. Standard deviation is viewed as the measure of a portfolio's risk.
3. The relationship between an investor's utility (satisfaction) and wealth is described by the investor's utility of wealth function. The assumption of nonsatiation requires the utility of wealth function to be upward-sloping.
4. Risk-averse investors will have diminishing marginal utility. Each extra unit of wealth provides the risk-averse investor with additional, but increasingly smaller, amounts of utility.
5. An indifference curve represents the various combinations of risk and return that the investor finds equally desirable.
6. Risk-averse investors are assumed to consider any portfolio lying on an indifference curve farther to the northwest to be more desirable than any portfolio lying on an indifference curve that is not as far northwest.
7. The assumptions of investor nonsatiation and risk aversion cause indifference curves to be positively sloped and convex.
8. The expected return on a portfolio is a weighted average of the expected returns of its component securities, with the relative portfolio proportions of the component securities serving as weights.

Alternative Risk Measures

Virtually all investment textbooks (this one being no exception) define a portfolio's investment risk to be its volatility of returns, measured by the standard deviation (or, equivalently, the variance) of the portfolio's return distribution. This definition's pedagogical dominance reflects the practice of academics and, to a lesser extent, those investment professionals steeped in quantitative portfolio management techniques. Yet ask the average person on the street to define investment risk, and he or she will invariably refer to the chances that something "bad" will happen. To suggest to this person that risk also has some association with the possible occurrence of good outcomes will almost certainly draw a disbelieving look.

If, on the surface, the textbook definition of risk appears to have only an indirect relationship with an intuitive sense of risk, why has this "risk as standard deviation" definition so thoroughly dominated investment research? Further, why have alternative risk measures that directly address the likelihood of experiencing undesirable outcomes not been more widely considered and applied?

The straightforward answer to the first question is that standard deviation is computationally easier to work with than any alternative. Proofs and applications of various risk-return investment principles are typically simplest to derive using standard deviation as the measure of risk. For example, Harry Markowitz originally suggested a risk measure involving only negative outcomes when he developed his pioneering work on efficient sets (see Chapters 6–8). He rejected that approach in favor of standard deviation in order to simplify the calculations.

As our average person on the street intuitively understands, the biggest problem with standard deviation is that it "discriminates" against investments with volatility on the "upside." As the text describes, we assume that investors dislike risk. Therefore, if we define risk to incorporate both good and bad results, then our risk-reward evaluation of potential invest-

ments penalizes investments that might give us positive surprises just as we penalize those investments for the possibility of giving us negative surprises.

All of this concern is moot if investment returns are symmetrically distributed, particularly in the form of a normal distribution (or "bell-shaped" curve). In that case, the chances of a positive outcome that is a certain distance away from the center of the distribution are just as great as the chances of a negative outcome that is an equal distance in the opposite direction. The fact that results above the expected value are included with those below the expected value becomes irrelevant. The standard deviation accurately summarizes the "bad" part of an investment's return distribution.

However, what if investment returns are not normally distributed? For example, we have good reason to believe that common stock returns do not conform to this pattern. Consider that common stock investors face limited liability (see Chapter 16); the most that they can lose is their original investment. Further, the potential upside gains on their investments are unlimited. Finally, most common stock returns are expected to fall near the market average. What we have just described is a "right-skewed" distribution rather than a normal distribution. Standard deviation insufficiently characterizes the risk of a right-skewed security, ignoring the fact that most of the security's volatility is on the "good" side of the security's expected return.

Interestingly, a simple mathematical transformation can often convert a right-skewed distribution to a normal distribution. If we add 1.0 to a security's return and then compute the natural logarithm of this value, the resulting transformed return distribution may appear to be normally distributed. Consequently, researchers are often concerned with whether security returns are "lognormally" distributed rather than normally distributed. Although the empirical evidence is open to debate, most observers

---

9. Covariance and correlation measure the extent to which two random variables "move together."
10. The standard deviation of a portfolio depends on the standard deviations and proportions of the component securities as well as their covariances with one another.

---

consider lognormality to adequately characterize common stock returns.

Unfortunately, the returns on certain types of securities are neither normally nor lognormally distributed. The most obvious are options (see Chapter 19). For example, a call option allows the owner, for a price, to participate in positive returns on an underlying asset but to avoid the asset's negative returns. Essentially, a call option truncates the underlying asset's return distribution at the point where losses begin. The investor then owns only the "good," or right, side of the return distribution. The returns on a call option are definitely not normally distributed.

Moreover, some securities have options embedded in them. For example, callable bonds (see Chapter 14) allow issuers to redeem them at the issuers' discretion. They do so only if interest rates move in their favor. Home mortgages (which are often packaged and sold in pass-through securities; see Chapter 13) have similar prepayment features. Therefore, their returns are also not normally distributed.

If we wish to explicitly focus only on the likelihood of undesirable investment results in defining and measuring risk, what alternatives are available? The simplest answer is called *shortfall probability*. It measures the chances that a security's return will fall short of the expected return. Essentially, it is the proportion of the probability distribution lying to the left of the expected return.

More complex downside risk measures are provided by a family of statistics known as *lower partial moments*, or LPMs. For example, *mean shortfall* measures the average deviation of a security's returns below the expected return. Mean shortfall is more useful than shortfall probability because it takes into account the distance of each downside return from the expected return. That is, shortfall probability tells us only how likely it is that a security's return may fall below the expected return. Mean shortfall tells us how far below the expected return that shortfall is likely to be.

Semivariance is analogous to variance, but only those potential returns below the expected return are used in its calculation. Because semivariance is the average squared deviation below the expected return, it penalizes securities with relatively large potential shortfalls.

Applied to securities with non-normal (and non-lognormal) return distributions, these downside risk measures are not only more intuitively appealing but are also more flexible in their application than the traditional risk measures. Standard deviation is measured from the mean of the return distribution. However, an investor may want to evaluate investments using some other value as a target, such as the return on a market index or an absolute number such as 0%. Downside risk measures can accommodate these preferences.

However, downside risk measures have their own problems. In particular, they ignore the nature of an investment's possible outcomes above the target return. An alternative to using downside risk measures is to directly bring skewness into the evaluation of an investment. That is, we might assume that investors analyze potential investments not only on the basis of their expected returns and standard deviations but also on their amount of right-skewness. In essence, risk becomes multidimensional; it includes both standard deviation and skewness. If two investments had the same expected return and standard deviation, the most right-skewed investment would be preferred.

No one measure can be expected to function well in all circumstances. Standard deviation has proved effective in the majority of the situations encountered by practitioners. In cases for which it is inadequate, alternatives must be considered not only in light of how well they describe the return distribution but also in terms of the complexity that they add to the analysis.

QUESTIONS AND PROBLEMS

1. Why must it be the case that an investor with diminishing marginal utility of wealth is risk-averse?
2. Listed below are a number of portfolios and expected returns, standard deviations, and the amount of satisfaction (measured in utils) these portfolios provide

Arky Vaughn. Given this information, graph Arky's identifiable indifference curves.

Portfolio	Expected Return	Standard Deviation	Utility
1	5%	0%	10 utils
2	6	10	10
3	9	20	10
4	14	30	10
5	10	0	20
6	11	10	20
7	14	20	20
8	19	30	20
9	15	0	30
10	16	10	30
11	19	20	30
12	24	30	30

3. Why are the indifference curves of typical investors assumed to slope upward to the right?
4. What does a set of convex indifference curves imply about an investor's trade-off between risk and return as the amount of risk varies?
5. Why are typical investors assumed to prefer portfolios on indifference curves lying to the northwest?
6. What is meant by the statement that "risk-averse investors exhibit diminishing marginal utility of income"? Why does diminishing marginal utility cause an investor to refuse to accept a "fair bet"?
7. Explain why an investor's indifference curves cannot intersect.
8. Why are the indifference curves of more risk-averse investors more steeply sloped than those of investors with less risk aversion?
9. Consider the following two sets of indifference curves for investors Hack Wilson and Kiki Cuyler. Determine whether Hack or Kiki:
   a. Is more risk-averse
   b. Prefers investment A to investment B
   c. Prefers investment C to investment D
   Explain the reasons for your answers.

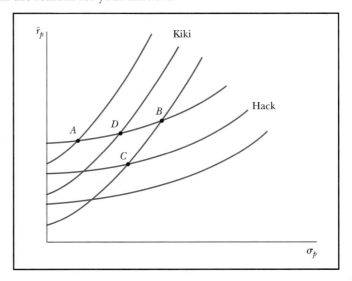

10. Consider four stocks with the following expected returns and standard deviations.

Stock	Expected Return	Standard Deviation
A	15%	12%
B	13	8
C	14	7
D	16	11

Are any of these stocks preferred over another by a risk-averse investor?

11. Do you agree with the assumptions of nonsatiation and risk aversion? Make a case for or against these assumptions.

12. At the beginning of the year, Corns Bradley owned four securities in the following amounts and with the following current and expected end-of-year prices:

Security	Share Amount	Current Price	Expected Year-End Price
A	100	$50	$60
B	200	35	40
C	50	25	50
D	100	100	110

What is the expected return on Corns's portfolio for the year?

13. Given the following information about four stocks comprising a portfolio, calculate each stock's expected return. Then, using these individual securities' expected returns, calculate the portfolio's expected return.

Stock	Initial Investment Value	Expected End-of-Period Investment Value	Proportion of Portfolio Initial Market Value
A	$500	$700	19.2%
B	200	300	7.7
C	1,000	1,000	38.5
D	900	1,500	34.6

14. Squeaky Bluege has been considering an investment in Oakdale Merchandising. Squeaky has estimated the following probability distribution of returns for Oakdale stock:

Return	Probability
−10%	.10
0	.25
10	.40
20	.20
30	.05

On the basis of Squeaky's estimates, calculate the expected return and standard deviation of Oakdale stock.

---

15. The expected returns and standard deviations of stocks A and B are:

Stock	Expected Return	Standard Deviation
A	13%	10%
B	5	18

Mox McQuery buys $20,000 of stock A and sells short $10,000 of stock B, using *all* of the proceeds to buy more of stock A. The correlation between the two securities is .25. What are the expected return and standard deviation of Mox's portfolio?

16. Both the covariance and the correlation coefficient measure the extent to which the returns on securities move together. What is the relationship between the two statistical measures? Why is the correlation coefficient a more convenient measure?

17. Give an example of two common stocks that you would expect to exhibit a relatively low correlation. Then give an example of two that would have a relatively high correlation.

18. Gibby Brock has estimated the following joint probability distribution of returns for investments in the stock of Lakeland Halfway Homes and Afton Brewery:

Lakeland	Afton	Probability
−10%	15%	.15
5	10	.20
10	5	.30
20	0	.35

On the basis of Gibby's estimates, calculate the covariance and correlation coefficient between the two investments.

19. Calculate the correlation matrix that corresponds to the variance-covariance matrix given in the text for Able, Baker, and Charlie.

20. Given the following variance-covariance matrix for three securities, as well as the percentage of the portfolio for each security, calculate the portfolio's standard deviation.

	Security **A**	Security **B**	Security **C**
Security A	459		
Security B	−211	312	
Security C	112	215	179
	$X_A = .50$	$X_B = .30$	$X_C = .20$

21. Rube Bressler owns three stocks and has estimated the following joint probability distribution of returns:

Outcome	Stock **A**	Stock **B**	Stock **C**	Probability
1	−10	10	0	.30
2	0	10	10	.20
3	10	5	15	.30
4	20	−10	5	.20

Calculate the portfolio's expected return and standard deviation if Rube invests 20% in stock A, 50% in stock B, and 30% in stock C. Assume that each security's return is completely uncorrelated with the returns of the other securities.

22. If a portfolio's expected return is equal to the weighted average of the expected returns of the component securities, why is a portfolio's risk not generally equal to the weighted average of the component securities' standard deviations?

23. When is the standard deviation of a portfolio equal to the weighted average of the standard deviation of the component securities? Show this mathematically for a two-security portfolio. (Hint: Some algebra is necessary to solve this problem. Remember that $\sigma_{ij} = \rho_{ij}\sigma_i\sigma_j$. Try different values of ρ_{ij}.)

24. Consider two securities, A and B, with expected returns of 15% and 20%, respectively, and standard deviations of 30% and 40%, respectively. Calculate the standard deviation of a portfolio weighted equally between the two securities if their correlation is:

 a. 0.9
 b. 0.0
 c. −0.9

25. Listed here are estimates of the standard deviations and correlation coefficients for three stocks.

Stock	Standard Deviation	Correlation with Stock: A	B	C
A	12%	1.00	−1.00	0.20
B	15	−1.00	1.00	−0.20
C	10	0.20	−0.20	1.00

 a. If a portfolio is composed of 20% of stock A and 80% of stock C, what is the portfolio's standard deviation?
 b. If a portfolio is composed of 40% of stock A, 20% of stock B, and 40% of stock C, what is the portfolio's standard deviation?
 c. If you were asked to design a portfolio using stocks A and B, what percentage investment in each stock would produce a zero standard deviation? [Hint: Some algebra is necessary to solve this problem. Remember that $X_B = (1 - X_A)$.]

26. (Appendix Question) Calculate the expected return, mode, and median for a stock having the following probability distribution:

Return	Probability of Occurrence
−40%	.03
−10	.07
0	.30
+15	.10
+30	.05
+40	.20
+50	.25

27. (Appendix Question) Bear Tracks Schmitz has estimated the following probability distribution of next year's dividend payments for Mauston Inc.'s stock. According to Bear Tracks, what is the standard deviation of Mauston's dividend?

Dividend	Probability
$1.90	.05
1.95	.15
2.00	.30
2.05	.30
2.10	.15
2.15	.05

28. (Appendix Question) Given the following joint probability distribution of returns for Securities *A* and *B*, calculate the covariance between the two securities.

State	Security *A*	Security *B*	Probability
1	10%	20%	.10
2	12	25	.25
3	8	33	.35
4	14	27	.20
5	19	22	.10

29. (Appendix Question) Using the data given in Tables 6.3 and 6.4, calculate the correlation coefficient between the returns on Alpha and Omega stock.

APPENDIX A

CHARACTERISTICS OF PROBABILITY DISTRIBUTIONS

This chapter introduces the concepts of expected return and risk for a portfolio of securities. That discussion presumes that the reader has some familiarity with probability distributions and the measures of central tendency and dispersion. This appendix is designed to provide a brief overview of these and other statistical concepts. Additional information can be obtained by consulting an introductory statistics textbook.

A.1 PROBABILITY DISTRIBUTIONS

A probability distribution describes the possible values that a random variable might take on and the associated probabilities of those values occurring. A discrete probability distribution displays a finite number of possible values that the random variable might assume. For example, in a classroom the possible amounts of money that students might have in their pockets would constitute a discrete probability distribution, as the smallest unit of currency that any student might hold is $.01. A continuous probability distribution, on the other hand, contains an infinite number of values for the random variable. For example, the distribution of temperatures that might occur during the day is described by a continuous probability distribution, as one can always divide temperature into smaller and smaller fractions of a degree.

Table 6.3 presents information regarding the probability distribution for Alpha Company's common stock returns, where there are assumed to be seven different "states of nature," or simply "states" [column (1)]. In this example, Alpha stock can

TABLE 6.3						
(1)	(2)	(3)	(4)	(5)	(6)	(7)
State	Possible Return	Return Probability	(2) × (3)	Deviation from Expected Return	Squared Deviation	(3) × (6)
1	−10%	.07	−.7%	−15.0%	225	15.8
2	−5	.10	−.5	−10.0	100	10.0
3	0	.18	0	−5.0	25	4.5
4	5	.30	1.5	0.0	0	0.0
5	10	.18	1.8	5.0	25	4.5
6	15	.10	1.5	10.0	100	10.0
7	20	.07	1.4	15.0	225	15.8
		Expected return = 5.0%				Variance = 60.6%²

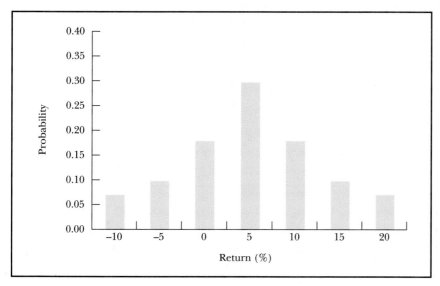

Figure 6.7
Probability Distribution of Alpha Stock Returns

produce seven different returns [column (2)], depending on the state that occurs. The probability of each return occurring is also shown in the table [column (3)]. Note that the sum of the probabilities is 1.0; there is a 100% chance that one of these returns will occur. The probability distribution of Alpha's stock returns is graphed in Figure 6.7; typically distributions such as this one are estimated (in reality, distributions of economic variables are almost never known) by using either past data or intuition or both.

A probability distribution is characterized by a number of measures. Two of the most important such characteristics are related to the central tendency and dispersion of the probability distribution.

A.2   CENTRAL TENDENCY

The center of a probability distribution is measured by several statistics. The **median** is the middle outcome of the distribution when the possible values of the random variable are arranged according to size. The **mode** is the most likely value.

Finally, the expected value (or mean) is the weighted average value of the distribution, where all possible values are weighted by their respective probabilities of occurrence.

In Table 6.3, the median and the mode of Alpha Company stock both can quickly be identified as 5%. The expected value (or mean) is less obvious. It is calculated as the sum of the products of each of the possible values times their associated probabilities. That is:

$$EV = \sum_{i=1}^{N} p_i X_i$$

where:

$X_i = i^{th}$ possible value for the random variable

$p_i =$ probability of the ith value occurring

$N =$ number of possible values that the random variable might take on (that is, the number of states)

The expected return on Alpha Company stock is found by multiplying each possible return by its associated probability [column (4)]. The expected return for Alpha stock is:

$$\bar{r}_{Alpha} = \sum_{i=1}^{7} p_i r_i$$

Table 6.3 displays the results of this calculation, with the expected return on Alpha's stock equal to 5%. (Note that the equality of the median, mode, and expected value is a feature of a random variable having a normal distribution.)

A.3   DISPERSION

The dispersion of possible values around the expected value is measured by the variance (and equivalently, the standard deviation) of the probability distribution. The probability distributions of two random variables can have the same expected value, yet one can have a smaller variance (or standard deviation) than the other. This means that the values of the less dispersed random variable are less likely to stray from the expected value of its probability distribution than are those of the random variable with the higher variance (or standard deviation).

The variance of a random variable is calculated as the weighted average of the squared deviations from the expected value of the random variable. The weights assigned to those deviations are the probabilities of the particular values' occurring. That is:

$$\sigma^2 = \sum_{i=1}^{N} p_i (X_i - EV)^2$$

The variance of returns of Alpha Company's stock is found by solving:

$$\sigma^2_{Alpha} = \sum_{i=1}^{7} p_i (r_i - \bar{r}_{Alpha})^2$$

The results of that calculation are shown in columns (5) through (7) of Table 6.3. The expected return of 5% is subtracted from each of the seven possible Alpha returns [column (5)]. The resulting value is squared [column (6)] and multiplied by the probability of that particular return's occurring [column (7)]. Finally, the sum of the squared deviations is computed to arrive at a variance of 60.6%^{2}.

The variance is calculated in units that are similar to those used to calculate the expected value of the random variable. However, because the variance is an average squared deviation, these units are squared. Conceptually, this idea causes some difficulty for users attempting to interpret variance, as the units of "return squared" or "percent return squared" are not readily understood by most people. The standard deviation overcomes this problem by simply taking the square root of the variance, thus producing a statistic expressed in the same units as the expected value. That is:

$$\sigma_i = \sqrt{\sum_{i=1}^{N} p_i (X_i - EV)^2}$$

Taking the square root of the variance of returns for Alpha Company gives:

$$\sigma_{Alpha} = \sqrt{\sigma_{Alpha}^2}$$
$$= \sqrt{60.6\%^2} = 7.8\%$$

Note that the units of measurement are "percent," just as the units used to measure Alpha's expected return are.

A.4   COMOVEMENT

Covariance measures the tendency for two random variables to move together (to covary). Instead of referring to the probability distribution for a single random variable, covariance considers the joint probability distribution of two random variables. That is, in a given state the two random variables assume particular values. The joint probability distribution describes what those pairs of values are for each possible state and the probabilities of those outcomes' occurring. Covariance is found by computing the weighted average of the product of the deviations of two random variables from their respective expected values. The weights assigned to these joint deviations are the probabilities of the two random variable taking on their associated joint values. That is:

$$\sigma_{xy} = \sum_{i=1}^{N} p_i (X_i - EV_X)(Y_i - EV_Y)$$

In the case of variance, the ith outcome refers to the value the random variable takes on when the ith state occurs. In the case of covariance, the ith outcome refers to the values that both random variables X and Y take on when the ith state occurs.

Continuing with the example of Alpha Company, consider now a second company's stock, that of Omega Company. Table 6.4 shows that corresponding to each

				TABLE 6.4			
(1)	(2)	(3)	(4)	(5)	(6)	(7)	(8)
State	Alpha Possible Return	Omega Possible Return	Outcome Probability	Alpha Deviations	Omega Deviations	(5) × (6) Deviation Products	(4) × (7)
1	−10%	25%	.07	−15.0%	13.3%	−199.5	−14.0
2	−5	15	.10	−10.0	3.3	−33.0	−3.3
3	0	18	.18	−5.0	6.3	−31.5	−5.7
4	5	10	.30	0.0	−1.8	0.0	0.0
5	10	7	.18	5.0	−4.8	−24.0	−4.3
6	15	10	.10	10.0	−1.8	−18.0	−1.8
7	20	0	.07	15.0	−11.8	−177.0	−12.4
	Expected return of Alpha = 5.0%			Expected return of Omega = 11.8%		Covariance = −41.5%²	

of the seven possible returns on Alpha stock [column (2)], Omega stock has its own corresponding return [column (3)]. As an exercise, the reader can calculate the expected returns and standard deviation of returns for Omega Company, which are respectively, 11.8% and 5.9%. Computing the deviations of both Alpha and Omega's returns from their expected values for each of the seven possible outcomes [columns (5) and (6)], taking the product of those two deviations for each possible outcome [column (7)], multiplying the product by the probability of the outcome occurring [column (8)], and finally summing across all seven states gives the covariance between Alpha and Omega stock. That is, the covariance of Alpha and Omega's returns equals:

$$\sigma_{Alpha, Omega} = \sum_{i=1}^{7} p_i \left(r_{Alpha, i} - \overline{r}_{Alpha} \right) \left(r_{Omega, i} - \overline{r}_{Omega} \right)$$

which, as shown in the table, equals $-41.5\%^2$. Note that the units of measurement here are "percent return squared," just as the units used to measure variance are.

Once the covariance of Alpha and Omega's returns have been calculated, it is a simple matter to compute the correlation between their returns. In general, this calculation is given by:

$$\rho_{xy} = \frac{\sigma_{xy}}{\sigma_x \sigma_y}$$

In the case of Alpha and Omega, the correlation is calculated to be

$$\rho_{Alpha, Omega} = \frac{-41.5}{7.8 \times 5.9} = -.90$$

APPENDIX B

RISK-NEUTRAL AND RISK-SEEKING INVESTORS

Earlier, it was mentioned that the Markowitz approach assumes that investors are risk-averse. Although this is a reasonable assumption to make, it is not necessary to do so. Alternatively, it can be assumed that investors are either risk-neutral or risk-seeking.

Consider the **risk-seeking investor** first. This investor, when faced with a fair gamble, will want to take the gamble. Furthermore, larger gambles will be more desirable than smaller gambles, because the utility (or "pleasure") derived from winning is greater than the disutility (or "displeasure") derived from losing. Because there is an equal chance of winning and losing, on balance the risk-seeking investor will want to take the gamble. Such investors have utility functions that are upward-sloping and convex.

For example, in choosing between two portfolios with the same expected return but different standard deviations, the risk-seeking investor will choose the portfolio with the higher standard deviation. This choice suggests that the risk-seeking investor will have negatively sloped indifference curves.[14] In addition, risk-seeking investors will prefer to be on the indifference curve that is farthest northeast. Figure 6.8 illustrates a map of the indifference curves for a hypothetical risk-seeking investor. As shown in the figure, when choosing from A, B, C, and D (the same four portfolios shown in Figure 6.2), this investor will choose B.

The **risk-neutral** case lies between the risk-seeking and risk-averse cases. Whereas the risk-averse investor does not want to take fair gambles and the risk-seeking investor does want to take such gambles, the risk-neutral investor does not care whether or not the gamble is taken. Risk, or more specifically, standard deviation, is unimportant to the risk-neutral investor in evaluating portfolios. Accordingly, the indifference curves for such investors are horizontal lines as shown in Figure 6.9. These investors prefer to be on the indifference curve that is farthest north. When faced with the choice of A, B, C, and D, such an investor will choose B, because it has the highest expected return. Such investors have utility functions that are upward-sloping straight lines.

Whereas investors can be either risk-seeking or risk-neutral, there is evidence to suggest that they are more accurately characterized as being, in general, risk-averse. One piece of evidence is the observation that equities have historically had higher

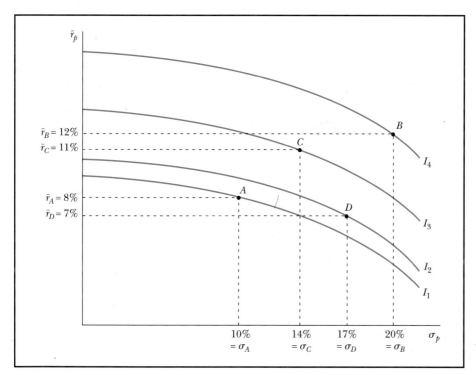

Figure 6.8
Map of Indifference Curves for a Risk-Seeking Investor

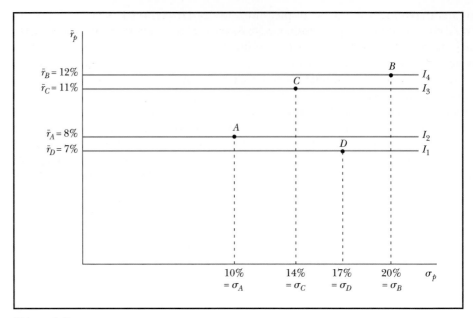

Figure 6.9
Map of Indifference Curves for a Risk-Neutral Investor

average returns than bonds, suggesting that investors have had to be induced with higher rewards in order to get them to make riskier purchases.

E N D N O T E S

[1] Markowitz recognized that investing was generally a multiperiod activity in which, at the end of each period, part of the investor's wealth was consumed and part was reinvested. Nevertheless, his one-period approach is optimal under a variety of reasonable circumstances. See Edwin J. Elton and Martin J. Gruber, *Finance As a Dynamic Process* (Upper Saddle River, NJ: Prentice Hall, 1975), particularly Chapter 5.

[2] One portfolio that would not have an uncertain rate of return would involve the investor's putting all of his or her initial wealth in a pure-discount government security that matures at $t = 1$. See Chapter 5 for a discussion of this riskfree security. However, for almost all other portfolios the rate of return would be uncertain.

[3] A random variable's expected value is, in a sense, its "average" value. Thus the expected value for the return of a portfolio can be thought of as its expected, or average, return. The standard deviation of a random variable is a measure of the dispersion (or "spread") of possible values the random variable can take on. Accordingly, the standard deviation of a portfolio is a measure of the dispersion of possible returns that could be earned on the portfolio. Sometimes **variance** is used as a measure of the dispersion instead of standard deviation. However, because variance is simply the squared value of the standard deviation of the random variable, this distinction is not of importance here. These concepts are discussed in more detail in Appendix A.

[4] Investors can also be risk-seeking or risk-neutral. Appendix B to this chapter discusses both risk-neutral and risk-seeking investors.

[5] Equivalently, in order to determine U_r, one could calculate the utility of $100,000 and the utility of $110,000 and then take a weighted average of them, where the weights

correspond to the probabilities of the outcomes' occurring, which in this case is .50 for each one of them. That is, the expected utility of the risky investment is equal to $U_r = [.5 \times U(\$100,000)] + [.5 \times U(\$110,000)]$.

[6] For an alternative procedure, see Ralph O. Swalm, "Utility Theory: Insights into Risk Taking," *Harvard Business Review* 44, no. 6 (November–December 1966): 123–136.

[7] At some point the reader may wonder why an investor's preferences are based only on expected returns and standard deviations. For example, it may seem logical that the investor's preferences should be based on expected returns, standard deviations, and the probability that a portfolio will lose money. The assertion that an investor's preferences are not based on anything other than expected returns and standard deviations follows from some specific assumptions coupled with *utility theory*. See Gordon J. Alexander and Jack Clark Francis, *Portfolio Analysis* (Upper Saddle River, NJ: Prentice Hall, 1986), particularly Chapters 2 and 3, for more details. There is some dispute about the validity of using utility theory to describe people's behavior. Those holding the view that utility theory is not applicable are often referred to as behaviorists. For a discussion of their views, see the entire second part of the October 1986 issue of the *Journal of Business* and *Institutional Issues: Behavioral Finance* in this chapter.

[8] Convexity of indifference curves means that their slopes increase when moving from left to right along any particular one. That is, they "bend upward." The underlying rationale for convexity lies in utility theory.

[9] The figures given for the expected end-of-period values include both the expected prices and the expected dividends for the period. For example, Able has an expected end-of-period value of $46.48, which could consist of a hypothetical expected cash dividend of $2 and share price of $44.48. These expected returns and values are estimated by use of security analysis, which will be discussed in Chapter 17.

[10] Security weights in a portfolio can be either positive (indicating a long position) or negative (indicating a short position). However, because of margin requirements, an investor does not have direct access to the proceeds of a short sale (see Chapter 2). As a result, the return on a stock sold short is not the opposite of the return on a stock held in a long position. This implies that a negative sign cannot simply be inserted into Equation (6.3a) to indicate a short position without adjusting the security's expected return for the effects of the short selling margin requirements.

[11] If returns are not normally distributed, the use of standard deviation can still be justified in an approximate sense, provided that there are small probabilities of extremely high and low returns. See H. Levy and H. M. Markowitz, "Approximating Expected Utility by a Function of Mean and Variance," *American Economic Review* 69, no. 3 (June 1979): 308–317; and Yoram Kroll, Haim Levy, and Harry M. Markowitz, "Mean-Variance versus Direct Utility Maximization," *Journal of Finance* 39, no. 1 (March 1984): 47–61. Some researchers have argued that the best model for a stock's returns is a mixture of normal distributions; for a discussion and references, see Richard Roll, "R^2," *Journal of Finance* 43, no. 3 (July 1988): 541–566, particularly footnote 11 on p. 561.

[12] Remember that correlation refers to how two random variables move together. If the two random variables are the same, then they must move exactly together with each other. This movement can be visualized by graphing the values of the same random variable on both the *X*-axis and the *Y*-axis. In such a graph, all points would lie on a straight 45 degree line passing through the origin, thereby implying a correlation of +1.

[13] For any variance-covariance matrix there is an implied correlation matrix that can be determined by using the data in the variance-covariance matrix and Equation (6.5). Specifically, this equation can be used to show that the correlation between any two securities i and j is equal to $\sigma_{ij}/\sigma_i\sigma_j$. The values for σ_{ij}, σ_i, and σ_j can be obtained from the variance-covariance matrix. For example, $\rho_{12} = 187/(\sqrt{146} \times \sqrt{854}) = .53$.

[14] It can also be shown that for a risk-seeking investor, these indifference curves will be concave, meaning that their slopes decrease when moving from left to right along any particular one. The underlying rationale for concavity lies in utility theory.

---

expected returns	certainty equivalent
risk	risk premium
initial wealth	indifference curve
terminal wealth	expected return vector
random variable	probability distribution
expected value	normal distribution
mean	covariance
standard deviation	correlation coefficient
variance	variance-covariance matrix
nonsatiation	median
risk-averse investor	mode
utility	risk-seeking investor
marginal utility	risk-neutral investor

REFERENCES

1. The seminal work developing the mean-variance model is credited to Harry Markowitz, co-winner of the 1990 Nobel Prize in economics, who developed his ideas in a paper and later in a book:

   Harry M. Markowitz, "Portfolio Selection," *Journal of Finance* 7, no. 1 (March 1952): 77–91.

   Harry M. Markowitz, *Portfolio Selection: Efficient Diversification of Investments* (New York: Wiley, 1959). (A reprint of this book that also contains some new material is available from Basil Blackwell, Cambridge, MA; its copyright date is 1991.)

2. Although utility theory can be traced back to the work of Daniel Bernoulli in the early part of the eighteenth century, the modern notion of utility theory was developed in:

   John von Neumann and Oskar Morgenstern, *Theory of Games and Economic Behavior* (New York: Wiley, 1944).

   Kenneth J. Arrow, *Essays in the Theory of Risk-Bearing* (Chicago: Markham, 1971).

3. Significant other work in utility theory is reviewed in:

   Paul J. H. Schoemaker, "The Expected Utility Model: Its Variants, Purposes, Evidence and Limitations," *Journal of Economic Literature* 20, no. 2 (June 1982): 529–563.

4. For an introduction to uncertainty and utility theory, see:

   Mark P. Kritzman, "…About Uncertainty," *Financial Analysts Journal* 47, no. 2 (March/April 1991): 17–21.

   Mark Kritzman, "…About Utility," *Financial Analysts Journal* 48, no. 3 (May/June 1992): 17–20.

5. For a description of various alternative measures of risk, see:

   Mark Kritzman, "… About Higher Moments," *Financial Analysts Journal* 50, no. 5 (September/October 1994): 10–17.

   Leslie A. Balzer, "Measuring Investment Risk: A Review," *Journal of Investing* 4, no. 3 (Fall 1995): 5–16.

   Frank A. Sortino and Hal J. Forsey, "On the Use and Misuse of Downside Risk," *Journal of Portfolio Management* 22, no. 2 (Winter 1996): 35–43.

   Robert A. Olsen, "Investment Risk: The Experts' Perspective," *Financial Analysts Journal* 53, no. 2 (March/April 1997): 62–66.

PORTFOLIO ANALYSIS

The previous chapter introduced the portfolio selection problem that every investor faces. It also introduced the investment approach of Harry Markowitz as a method of solving that problem. With this approach, an investor should evaluate alternative portfolios on the basis of their expected returns and standard deviations by using indifference curves. A risk-averse investor would select for investment the portfolio with the indifference curve that is farthest northwest.

The previous chapter, however, left certain questions unanswered. In particular, how can Markowitz's approach be used once it is recognized that there are an infinite number of portfolios available for investment? What happens when the investor considers investing in a set of securities, one of which is riskless? What happens if the investor is allowed to buy securities on margin? This chapter and the next one will provide the answers to those questions, beginning with the first one.

7.1   THE EFFICIENT SET THEOREM

As mentioned earlier, an infinite number of portfolios can be formed from a set of N securities. Consider the situation with Able, Baker, and Charlie companies, where N is equal to 3. The investor could purchase just shares of Able, or just shares of Baker. Alternatively, the investor could purchase a combination of shares of Able and Baker. For example, the investor could put 50% of his or her money in each company, or 25% in one company and 75% in the other, or 33% in one and 67% in the other, or any percent (between 0% and 100%) in one company with the rest going into the other company. Without even considering investing in Charlie, there are already an infinite number of possible portfolios that could be purchased.[1]

Does the investor need to evaluate all these portfolios? Fortunately, the answer is no. The key to why the investor needs to look at only a subset of the available portfolios lies in the **efficient set theorem**, which states that:

An investor will choose his or her optimal portfolio from the set of portfolios that

    1. *Offer maximum expected return for varying levels of risk, and*
    2. *Offer minimum risk for varying levels of expected return.*

The set of portfolios meeting these two conditions is known as the **efficient set** (also known as the efficient frontier).

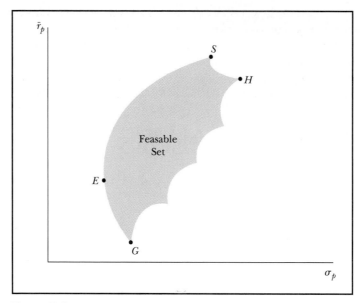

Figure 7.1
Feasible and Efficient Sets

7.1.1 The Feasible Set

Figure 7.1 provides an illustration of the location of the **feasible set** (also known as the opportunity set) from which the efficient set can be identified. The feasible set simply represents all portfolios that could be formed from a group of N securities. That is, all possible portfolios that could be formed from the N securities lie either on or within the boundary of the feasible set. (The points denoted G, E, S, and H in the figure are examples of such portfolios.) In general, this set will have an umbrella-type shape similar to the one shown in the figure. Depending on the particular securities involved, it may be more to the right or left, or higher or lower, or fatter or skinnier than indicated here. The point is that its shape will, except in perverse circumstances, look similar to what appears here.

7.1.2 The Efficient Set Theorem Applied to the Feasible Set

The efficient set can now be located by applying the efficient set theorem to this feasible set. To begin with, the set of portfolios that meet the first condition of the efficient set theorem must be identified. Looking at Figure 7.1, there is no portfolio offering less risk than that of portfolio E because if a vertical line were drawn through E, there would be no point in the feasible set that was to the left of the line. Also, there is no portfolio offering more risk than that of portfolio H because if a vertical line were drawn through H, there would be no point in the feasible set to the right of the line. Thus the set of portfolios offering maximum expected return for varying levels of risk is the set of portfolios lying on the northern boundary of the feasible set between points E and H.

Considering the second condition next, there is no portfolio offering an expected return greater than portfolio S, because no point in the feasible set lies above a horizontal line going through S. Similarly, there is no portfolio offering a lower expected return than portfolio G, because no point in the feasible set lies below a horizontal line going through G. Thus the set of portfolios offering minimum risk for varying levels of expected return is the set of portfolios lying on the western boundary of the feasible set between points G and S.

Remember that both conditions have to be met in order to identify the efficient set. It can be seen that only those portfolios lying on the northwest boundary between points E and S do so. Accordingly, these portfolios form the efficient set, and it is from this set of **efficient portfolios** that the risk-averse investor will find his or her optimal one.[2] All the other feasible portfolios are **inefficient portfolios** and can be ignored.

7.1.3   Selection of the Optimal Portfolio

How will the investor select an **optimal portfolio?** As shown in Figure 7.2, the investor should plot his or her indifference curves on the same figure as the efficient set and then proceed to choose the portfolio that is on the indifference curve that is farthest northwest. This portfolio will correspond to the point at which an indifference curve is just tangent to the efficient set. As can be seen in the figure, this is portfolio O^* on indifference curve I_2. Although the investor would prefer a portfolio on I_3, no such portfolio exists; wanting to be on this indifference curve is just wishful thinking. In regard to I_1, there are several portfolios that the investor could choose (for example, O). However, the figure shows that portfolio O^* dominates such portfolios, because it is on an indifference curve that is farther northwest. Figure 7.3 shows that the highly risk-averse investor will choose a portfolio close to E. Figure 7.4 shows that the investor who is only slightly risk-averse will choose a portfolio close to S.[3]

Upon reflection, the efficient set theorem is quite rational. In Chapter 6, it was shown that the investor should select the portfolio that put him or her on the indifference curve that is farthest northwest. The efficient set theorem, stating that the investor needs to be concerned only with portfolios that lie on the northwest boundary of the feasible set, is a logical consequence.

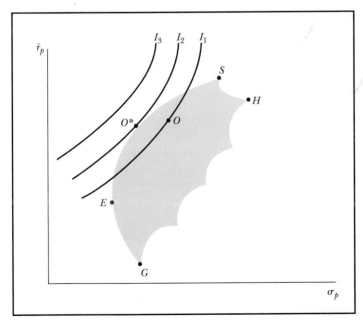

Figure 7.2
Selecting an Optimal Portfolio

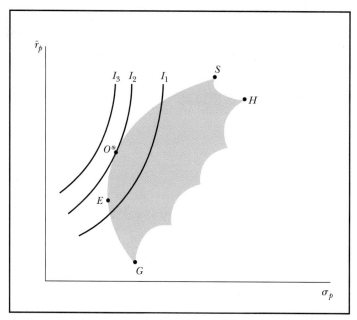

Figure 7.3
Portfolio Selection for a Highly Risk-Averse Investor

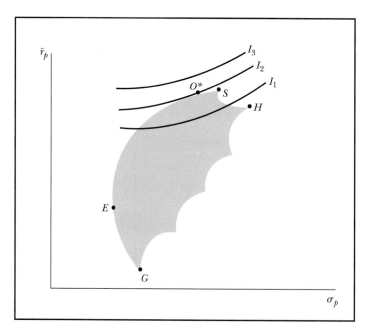

Figure 7.4
Portfolio Selection for a Slightly Risk-Averse Investor

Indifference curves for the risk-averse investor were shown to be positively sloped and convex in Chapter 6. Now it will be shown that the efficient set is generally positively sloped and concave, meaning that if a straight line is drawn between any two points on the efficient set, the straight line will lie below the efficient set. This feature of the efficient set is important because it means that there will be only one tangency point between the investor's indifference curves and the efficient set.

In order to see why the efficient set is concave, consider the following two-security example. Security 1, the Ark Shipping Company, has an expected return of 5% and a standard deviation of 20%. Security 2, the Gold Jewelry Company, has an expected return of 15% and a standard deviation of 40%. Their respective locations are indicated by the letters A and G in Figure 7.5.

7.2.1   Bounds on the Location of Portfolios

Now consider all possible portfolios that an investor could purchase by combining these two securities. Let X_1 denote the proportion of the investor's funds invested in Ark Shipping and $X_2(= 1 - X_1)$ the proportion invested in Gold Jewelry. Thus, if the investor purchased just Ark Shipping, then $X_1 = 1$ and $X_2 = 0$. Alternatively, if the investor purchased just Gold Jewelry, then $X_1 = 0$ and $X_2 = 1$. A combination of .17 in Ark Shipping and .83 in Gold Jewelry is also possible, as are the respective combinations of .33 and .67, and .50 and .50. Although there are many other possibilities, only the following seven portfolios will be considered:

	Portfolio **A**	Portfolio **B**	Portfolio **C**	Portfolio **D**	Portfolio **E**	Portfolio **F**	Portfolio **G**
X_1	1.00	.83	.67	.50	.33	.17	.00
X_2	.00	.17	.33	.50	.67	.83	1.00

In order to consider these seven portfolios for possible investment, their expected returns and standard deviations must be calculated. All the necessary information to calculate the expected returns for these portfolios is at hand, because all that is needed in order to utilize Equation (6.3a) has been provided:

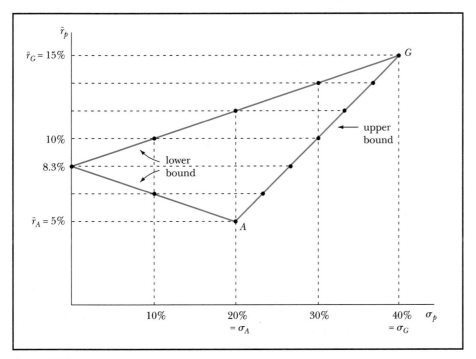

Figure 7.5
Upper and Lower Bounds to Combinations of Securities A and G

The Trouble with Optimizers

Suppose that the captain of a modern luxury liner chose not to use the ship's state-of-the-art navigational system (a system that employs computers to triangulate off geostationary-orbiting satellites, thereby estimating the ship's position accurately to within a few feet). Instead, suppose that the captain chose to rely on the old-fashioned method of navigating by the stars, an antiquated method fraught with problems and imprecision. Most people would view the captain's choice as, at best, eccentric and, at worst, highly dangerous.

When it comes to constructing portfolios, many investment managers make a choice analogous to that of the ship's captain. They reject computer-based portfolio construction methods in favor of traditional approaches. Are their decisions as foolhardy as the captain's? Or is there a method to their apparent madness?

As this chapter discusses, the concepts of the efficient set and the investor's optimal portfolio are central to modern investment theory. But how can investors actually go about estimating the efficient set and selecting their optimal portfolios? Harry Markowitz first described the solution in the early 1950s. Using a mathematical technique called *quadratic programming*, investors can process expected returns, standard deviations, and covariances to calculate the efficient set. (See Appendix A to this chapter.) Given an estimate of their indifference curves (as reflected in their individual risk tolerances; see Chapter 23), they can then select a portfolio from the efficient set.

Simple, right? Certainly not in the 1950s. Given the data-processing facilities available to investors at that time, calculating the efficient set for even a few hundred securities was essentially impossible. However, in the 1980s, with the advent of low-cost, high-speed computers and the development of sophisticated risk models (see Chapter 10), an efficient set can be created for thousands of securities in a matter of minutes. The necessary computer hardware and software are available to virtually every institutional investor at a relatively low cost. In fact, the process has become so commonplace that it has acquired its own terminology. Using a computer to identify the efficient set and select an optimal portfolio is known as using an "optimizer." Portfolios are "optimized," and investors are said to apply "optimization techniques."

Despite the technology's widespread availability, relatively few investment managers actually use an optimizer to build portfolios of individual securities (although optimizers are often used for allocating funds among major asset classes). Instead, they rely for the most part on a series of qualitative rules and judgments.

Why do investment managers resist applying optimization techniques to portfolio building? Ignorance is not the answer. Most investment managers are well aware of Markowitz's portfolio selection concepts and the available technology, having graduated from business schools where these ideas are discussed in detail. Instead, the resistance derives from two sources: territorial concerns and implementation inadequacies.

From a territorial perspective, many investment managers simply are not comfortable with a quantitative approach to investing. Their decision making emphasizes intuition and complex subjective judgments. The application of optimization techniques to

$$\bar{r}_p = \sum_{i=1}^{N} X_i \bar{r}_i \tag{6.3a}$$

$$= \sum_{i=1}^{2} X_i \bar{r}_i$$

$$= X_1 \bar{r}_1 + X_2 \bar{r}_2$$

$$= \left(X_1 \times 5\% \right) + \left(X_2 \times 15\% \right)$$

For portfolios A and G, this calculation is trivial, because the investor is purchasing shares of just one company. Thus their expected returns are 5% and 15%, respectively. For portfolios B, C, D, E, and F, the expected returns are, respectively:

$$\bar{r}_B = (.83 \times 5\%) + (.17 \times 15\%)$$

$$= 6.70\%$$

portfolio construction imposes a very systematic and formal decision-making structure. Security analysts become responsible for generating quantifiable expected return and risk forecasts. Portfolio managers must implement the decisions of a computer. As a result, the optimizer destroys the "artistry and grace" of investment management.

Further, with the introduction of an optimizer, a new breed of investment professional gains influence—the quantitative analyst (derisively called a "quant")—who coordinates the collection and application of risk and return estimates. Authority gained by quantitative analysts diminishes the influence of traditional security analysts and portfolio managers, much to their consternation.

From the implementation perspective, serious problems have arisen with optimizers in practice. In particular, they tend to produce counterintuitive, uninvestable portfolios. This situation is not so much a problem with optimizers as it is the fault of the human operators supplying inputs to the optimizers. Here the GIGO (garbage in, garbage out) paradigm rules.

By their design, optimizers are attracted to securities with high expected returns, low standard deviations, and low covariances with other securities. Often this information is derived from historical databases covering thousands of securities. Unless the risk and return data are carefully checked, errors (for example, understating a security's standard deviation) can easily lead the optimizer to recommend purchases of securities for erroneous reasons. Even if the data are "clean," extreme historical values for some securities may lead the optimizer astray.

Optimizers also display a nasty habit of generating high turnover and recommending investments in relatively illiquid securities. *High turnover* refers to significant changes in portfolio composition from one period to the next. High turnover can result in unacceptably large transaction costs (see Chapter 3), thereby hindering portfolio performance. *Liquidity* refers to the ability to actually buy the securities selected by the optimizer. Selected securities may possess desirable risk-return characteristics but may not trade in sufficient volume to permit institutional investors to purchase them without incurring sizable transaction costs.

Solutions to these implementation problems do exist, ranging from careful data checking to placing realistic limits (or "constraints") on maximum turnover or minimum liquidity allowed in the solution designed by the optimizer. In the end, however, nothing can substitute for skillful judgmental forecasts of security returns and risks, balanced by properly applied notions of market equilibrium.

Territorial and implementation problems have given investment managers convenient reasons to avoid optimizers and to stick to traditional portfolio construction methods. Nevertheless, the outlook for quantitative portfolio construction techniques is quite bright. The increasing efficiency of capital markets has forced institutional investment managers to process more information about more securities more rapidly than ever before. In response, they have generally increased their use of quantitative investment tools. Although most do not directly integrate optimizers into their portfolio construction procedures, virtually all have become more sensitive to the objective of creating diversified portfolios that display the highest levels of expected return at acceptable levels of risk.

$$\bar{r}_C = (.67 \times 5\%) + (.33 \times 15\%)$$
$$= 8.30\%$$
$$\bar{r}_D = (.50 \times 5\%) + (.50 \times 15\%)$$
$$= 10\%$$
$$\bar{r}_E = (.33 \times 5\%) + (.67 \times 15\%)$$
$$= 11.70\%$$
$$\bar{r}_F = (.17 \times 5\%) + (.83 \times 15\%)$$
$$= 13.30\%$$

In calculating the standard deviation of these seven portfolios, Equation (6.7) must be used:

$$\sigma_p = \left[\sum_{i=1}^{N} \sum_{j=1}^{N} X_i X_j \sigma_{ij} \right]^{1/2} \qquad (6.7)$$

$$= \left[\sum_{i=1}^{N} \sum_{j=1}^{N} X_i X_j \sigma_{ij} \right]^{1/2}$$

$$= \left[X_1 X_1 \sigma_{11} + X_1 X_2 \sigma_{12} + X_2 X_1 \sigma_{21} + X_2 X_2 \sigma_{22} \right]^{1/2}$$

$$= \left[X_1^2 \sigma_1^2 + X_2^2 \sigma_2^2 + 2X_1 X_2 \sigma_{12} \right]^{1/2}$$

$$= \left[X_1^2 \times 20\%^2 + X_2^2 \times 40\%^2 + 2X_1 X_2 \sigma_{12} \right]^{1/2}$$

Again, for portfolios A and G, this calculation is trivial, because the investor is purchasing shares of just one company. Thus their standard deviations are 20% and 40%, respectively.

For portfolios B, C, D, E, and F, application of Equation (6.7) indicates that the standard deviations depend on the magnitude of the covariance between the two securities. As shown in Equation (6.5), this covariance term is equal to the correlation between the two securities multiplied by the product of their standard deviations:

$$\sigma_{ij} = \rho_{ij} \times \sigma_i \times \sigma_j \qquad (6.5)$$

so letting $i = 1$ and $j = 2$,

$$\sigma_{12} = \rho_{12} \times \sigma_1 \times \sigma_2$$

$$= \rho_{12} \times 20\% \times 40\%$$

$$= 800\rho_{12}$$

This means that the standard deviation of any portfolio consisting of Ark Shipping and Gold Jewelry can be expressed as:

$$\sigma_p = \left[X_1^2 \times 20\%^2 + X_2^2 \times 40\%^2 + 2X_1 X_2 \times 800\rho_{12} \right]^{1/2} \qquad (7.1)$$

$$= \left[400X_1^2 + 1{,}600X_2^2 + 1{,}600X_1 X_2 \rho_{12} \right]^{1/2}$$

Consider portfolio D first. The standard deviation of this portfolio will be somewhere between 10% and 30%, the exact value depending upon the size of the correlation coefficient. How were these bounds of 10% and 30% determined? First, note that for portfolio D, Equation (7.1) reduces to:

$$\sigma_D = \left[(400 \times .25) + (1{,}600 \times .25) + (1{,}600 \times .5 \times .5\rho_{12}) \right]^{1/2} \qquad (7.2)$$

$$= \left[500 + 400\rho_{12} \right]^{1/2}$$

Inspection of Equation (7.2) indicates that σ_D will be at a minimum when the correlation coefficient, ρ_{12}, is at a minimum. Now, remembering that the minimum value for any correlation coefficient is -1, the lower bound on σ_D is:

$$\sigma_D = [500 + (400 \times -1)]^{1/2}$$

$$= [500 - 400]^{1/2}$$

$$= [100]^{1/2}$$

$$= 10\%$$

Similarly, inspection of Equation (7.2) indicates that σ_D will be at a maximum when the correlation coefficient is at a maximum, which is $+1$. Thus the upper bound on σ_D is:

$$\sigma_D = [500 + (400 \times 1)]^{1/2}$$
$$= [500 + 400]^{1/2}$$
$$= [900]^{1/2}$$
$$= 30\%$$

In general, it can be seen from Equation (7.1) that for any given set of weights X_1 and X_2, the lower and upper bounds will occur when the correlation between the two securities is -1 and $+1$, respectively. Applying the same analysis to the other portfolios reveals that their lower and upper bounds are:

Portfolio	Standard Deviation of Portfolio	
	Lower Bound	Upper Bound
A	20.00%	20.00%
B	10.00	23.33
C	0.00	26.67
D	10.00	30.00
E	20.00	33.33
F	30.00	36.67
G	40.00	40.00

These values are shown in Figure 7.5.

Interestingly, the upper bounds all lie on a straight line connecting points A and G. This means that any portfolio consisting of these two securities cannot have a standard deviation that plots to the right of a straight line connecting the two securities. Instead, the standard deviation must lie on or to the left of the straight line. This observation suggests a motivation for diversifying a portfolio. Namely, *diversification generally leads to risk reduction*, because the standard deviation of a portfolio will generally be less than a weighted average of the standard deviations of the securities in the portfolio.

Also interesting is the observation that the lower bounds all lie on one of two line segments that go from point A to a point on the vertical axis corresponding to 8.30% and then to point G. This means that any portfolio consisting of these two securities cannot have a standard deviation that plots to the left of either of these two line segments. For example, portfolio B must lie on the horizontal line going through the vertical axis at 6.70% but bounded between the values of 10% and 23.33%.

In sum, any portfolio consisting of securities A and G will lie within or on the boundary of the triangle shown in Figure 7.5, with its actual location depending on the magnitude of the correlation coefficient between the two securities.

7.2.2   Actual Locations of the Portfolios

What would happen if the correlation were zero? In this case, Equation (7.1) reduces to:
$$\sigma_p = \left[\left(400X_1^2\right) + \left(1{,}600X_2^2\right) + \left(1{,}600X_1X_2 \times 0\right)\right]^{1/2}$$
$$= \left[\left(400X_1^2\right) + \left(1{,}600X_2^2\right)\right]^{1/2}$$

Applying the appropriate weights for X_1 and X_2, the standard deviation for portfolios B, C, D, E, and F is as follows:
$$\sigma_B = \left[(400 \times .83^2) + (1{,}600 \times .17^2)\right]^{1/2}$$
$$= 17.94\%$$

$$\sigma_C = \left[\left(400 \times .67^2\right) + \left(1{,}600 \times .33^2\right)\right]^{1/2}$$
$$= 18.81\%$$
$$\sigma_D = \left[\left(400 \times .50^2\right) + \left(1{,}600 \times .50^2\right)\right]^{1/2}$$
$$= 22.36\%$$
$$\sigma_E = \left[\left(400 \times .33^2\right) + \left(1{,}600 \times .67^2\right)\right]^{1/2}$$
$$= 27.60\%$$
$$\sigma_F = \left[\left(400 \times .17^2\right) + \left(1{,}600 \times .83^2\right)\right]^{1/2}$$
$$= 33.37\%$$

Figure 7.6 indicates the location of these portfolios, along with the upper and lower bounds that were shown in Figure 7.5. As can be seen, these portfolios, as well as all other possible portfolios consisting of Ark Shipping and Gold Jewelry, lie on a line that is curved, or bowed, to the left. Although not shown here, if the correlation were less than zero, the line would curve more to the left. If the correlation were greater than zero, it would not curve quite as much to the left. The important point about this figure is that as long as the correlation is less than +1 and greater than −1, the line representing the set of portfolios consisting of various combinations of the two securities will have some degree of curvature to the left. Furthermore, the northwest portion will be concave.

Similar analysis can be applied to a situation in which there are more than two securities under consideration. As long as the correlations are less than +1 and greater than −1, the northwest portion must be concave, just as it is in the two-security example.[4] Thus, in general, the efficient set will be concave.[5]

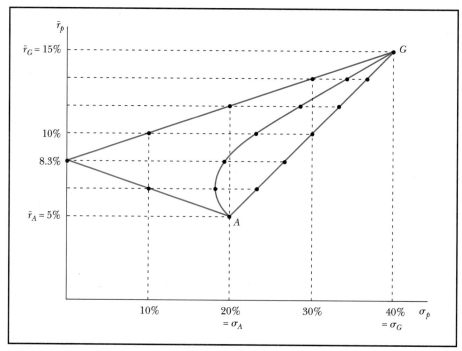

Figure 7.6
Portfolios Formed by Combining Securities *A* and *G*

Suppose that the return on a common stock over a given time period (say, a month) is related to the return over the same period that is earned on a market index such as the widely cited S&P 500.[6] That is, if the market has gone up then it is likely that the stock has gone up, and if the market has gone down then it is likely that the stock has gone down. One way to capture this relationship is with the **market model**:

$$r_i = \alpha_{iI} + \beta_{iI}r_I + \varepsilon_{iI} \tag{7.3}$$

where:

r_i = return on security i for some given period
r_I = return on market index I for the same period
α_{iI} = intercept term
β_{iI} = slope term
ε_{iI} = random error term

Assuming that the slope term β_{iI} is positive, Equation (7.3) indicates that the higher the return on the market index, the higher the return on the security is likely to be (note that the expected value of the random error term is zero). Consider stock A, for example, which has $\alpha_{iI} = 2\%$ and $\beta_{iI} = 1.2$. This means that the market model for stock A is:

$$r_A = 2\% + 1.2r_I + \varepsilon_{AI} \tag{7.4}$$

so that if the market index has a return of 10%, the return on the security is expected to be 14% [= 2% + (1.2 × 10%)]. Similarly, if the market index's return is −5%, then the return on security A is expected to be −4% [= 2% + (1.2 × (−5%))].

7.3.1 Random Error Terms

The term ε_{iI}, known as the **random error term** in Equation (7.3), simply shows that the market model does not explain security returns perfectly. That is, when the market index goes up by 10% or down by 5%, the return on security A is not going to be exactly 14% or −4%, respectively. The difference between what the return actually is and what it is expected to be, given the return on the market index, is attributed to the effect of the random error term. Hence, if the security's return were 9% instead of 14%, the 5% difference would be attributed to the random error term (that is, $\varepsilon_{AI} = -5\%$; this concept will be illustrated shortly in Figure 7.7). Similarly, if the security return were −2% instead of −4%, the 2% difference would be attributed to the random error term (that is, $\varepsilon_{AI} = +2\%$).

The random error term can be viewed as a random variable that has a probability distribution with a mean of zero and a standard deviation denoted $\sigma_{\varepsilon i}$.[7] That is, it can be viewed as the outcome that results from the spin of a special kind of roulette wheel.

For example, security A might be thought of as having a random error term corresponding to a roulette wheel with integer values on it that range from −10% to +10%, with the values evenly spaced.[8] This wheel would have 21 possible outcomes, all of which have an equal probability of occurring. In addition, given the range of numbers, the expected outcome of the random error term would be zero:

$$[-10 \times 1/21] + [-9 \times 1/21] + \ldots + [9 \times 1/21] + [10 \times 1/21] = 0$$

As can be seen, this calculation involves multiplying each outcome by its probability of occurring and then summing up the resulting products. The standard deviation of this random error term can now be shown to equal 6.06%:

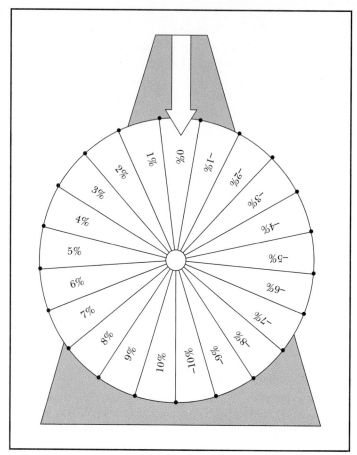

Figure 7.7
Security as Random Error Term

$$\{[(-10-0)^2 \times 1/21] + [(-9-0)^2 \times 1/21] + \ldots + [(9-0)^2 \times 1/21] +$$
$$[(10-0)^2 \times 1/21]\}^{1/2} = 6.06\%$$

This calculation involves subtracting the expected outcome from each possible outcome, then squaring each one of those differences, multiplying each square by the probability of the corresponding outcome's occurring, adding the products, and finally taking the square root of the resulting sum.[9]

Figure 7.7 illustrates the roulette wheel corresponding to this random error term. In general, securities will have random error terms whose corresponding roulette wheels have different ranges and different forms of uneven spacing. All of them will have an expected value of zero, but they will typically have different standard deviations. For example, security B may have a random error term whose expected value is equal to zero and whose standard deviation is equal to 4.76%.[10]

7.3.2 Graphical Representation of the Market Model

The solid line in Figure 7.8(a) provides a graph of the market model for security A. This line corresponds to Equation (7.4), but without the random error term. Accordingly, the line that is graphed for security A is:

$$r_A = 2\% + 1.2r_I \tag{7.5}$$

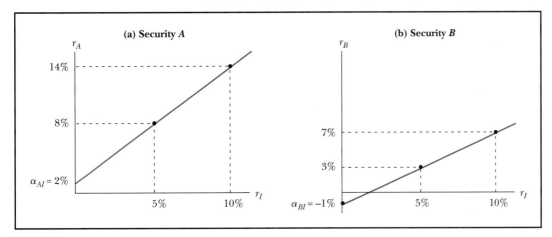

Figure 7.8
Market Model

Here the vertical axis measures the return on the particular security (r_A), whereas the horizontal axis measures the return on the market index (r_I). The line goes through the point on the vertical axis corresponding to the value of α_{AI}, which in this case is 2%. In addition, the line has a slope equal to β_{AI}, or 1.2.

Figure 7.8(b) presents the graph of the market model for security B. The line can be expressed as the following equation:

$$r_B = -1\% + .8r_I \qquad (7.6)$$

This line goes through the point on the vertical axis corresponding to the value of α_{BI}, which in this case is -1%. Note that its slope is equal to β_{BI}, or .8.

7.3.3 Beta

At this point it can be seen that the slope in a security's market model measures the sensitivity of the security's returns to the market index's returns. Both lines in Figure 7.8 have positive slopes, indicating that the higher the returns of the market index, the higher the returns of the two securities. However, the two securities have different slopes, indicating that they have different sensitivities to the returns of the market index. Specifically, A has a higher slope than B, indicating that the returns of A are more sensitive than the returns of B to the returns of the market index.

For example, assume that the market index's expected return is 5%. If the market index subsequently has an actual return of 10%, it will have returned 5% more than expected. Figure 7.8(a) shows that security A should have a return that is 6% $(= 14\% - 8\%)$ greater than initially expected. Similarly, Figure 7.8(b) shows that security B should have a return that is 4% $(= 7\% - 3\%)$ greater than initially expected. The reason for the 2% $(= 6\% - 4\%)$ difference is that security A has a higher slope than security B; that is, A is more sensitive than B to returns on the market index.

The slope term in the market model is often referred to as **beta** and is equal to:

$$\beta_{iI} = \frac{\sigma_{iI}}{\sigma_I^2} \qquad (7.7)$$

where σ_{iI} denotes the covariance of the returns on stock i and the market index, and σ_I^2 denotes the variance of returns on the market index. A stock that has a return that mirrors the return on the market index will have a beta equal to 1 (and an intercept of zero, resulting in a market model that is $r_i = r_I + \varepsilon_{iI}$). Hence stocks with

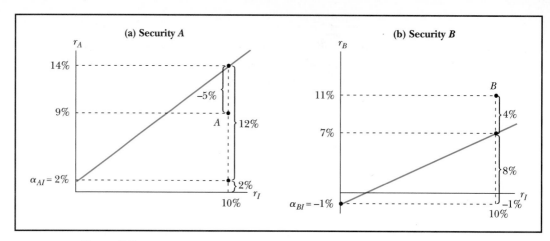

Figure 7.9
Market Model and Actual Returns

betas greater than 1 (such as *A*) are more volatile than the market index and are known as **aggressive stocks**. In contrast, stocks with betas less than one (such as *B*) are less volatile than the market index and are known as **defensive stocks**.[11]

7.3.4 Actual Returns

The random error term suggests that for a given return on the market index, the actual return on a security will usually lie off its market model line.[12] If the actual returns on securities *A* and *B* turn out to be 9% and 11%, respectively, and the market index's actual return turns out to be 10%, then the actual return on *A* and *B* could be viewed as having the following three components:

	Security A	Security B
Intercept	2%	−1%
Actual return on the market index × beta	12% = 10% × 1.2	8% = 10% × .8
Random error outcome	−5% = 9% − (2% + 12%)	4% = 11% − (−1% + 8%)
Actual return	9%	11%

In this case, the roulette wheels for *A* and *B* can be thought of as having been "spun," resulting in values (that is, random error outcomes) of −5% for *A* and +4% for *B*. These values can be viewed as being equal to the vertical distance by which each security's actual return ended up being off its market model line, as shown in Figure 7.9.

7.4   DIVERSIFICATION

According to the market model, the total risk of any security *i*, measured by its variance and denoted σ_i^2, consists of two parts: (1) **market** (or systematic) **risk** and (2) **unique** (or unsystematic or specific) **risk**. That is, σ_i^2 equals the following:

$$\sigma_i^2 = \beta_{iI}^2 \sigma_I^2 + \sigma_{\varepsilon i}^2 \tag{7.8}$$

where σ_I^2 denotes the variance of returns on the market index. Thus $\beta_{iI}^2 \sigma_I^2$ denotes the market risk of security i, and $\sigma_{\varepsilon i}^2$ denotes the unique risk of security i as measured by the variance of the random error term, ε_{iI}, appearing in Equation (7.3).

7.4.1 Portfolio Total Risk

When the return on every risky *security* in a portfolio is related to the return on the market index as specified by the market model, what can be said about the total risk of the *portfolio*? If the proportion of funds invested in security i for a given portfolio p is denoted X_i, then the return on this portfolio will be:

$$r_p = \sum_{i=1}^{N} X_i r_i \tag{7.9}$$

Substituting the right-hand side of Equation (7.3) for r_i in Equation (7.9) results in the following market model for the portfolio:

$$r_p = \sum_{i=1}^{N} X_i\left(\alpha_{iI} + \beta_{iI} r_I + \varepsilon_{iI}\right)$$

$$= \sum_{i=1}^{N} X_i \alpha_{iI} + \left(\sum_{i=1}^{N} X_i \beta_{iI}\right) r_I + \sum_{i=1}^{N} X_i \varepsilon_{iI}$$

$$= \alpha_{pI} + \beta_{pI} r_I + \varepsilon_{pI} \tag{7.10a}$$

where:

$$\alpha_{pI} = \sum_{i=1}^{N} X_i \alpha_{iI} \tag{7.10b}$$

$$\beta_{pI} = \sum_{i=1}^{N} X_i \beta_{iI} \tag{7.10c}$$

$$\varepsilon_{pI} = \sum_{i=1}^{N} X_i \varepsilon_{iI} \tag{7.10d}$$

In Equations (7.10b) and (7.10c), the portfolio's vertical intercept $\left(\alpha_{pI}\right)$ and beta $\left(\beta_{pI}\right)$ are shown to be weighted averages of the intercepts and betas of the securities, respectively, using their relative proportions in the portfolio as weights. Similarly, in Equation (7.10d), the portfolio's random error term $\left(\varepsilon_{pI}\right)$ is a weighted average of the random error terms of the securities, again using the relative proportions in the portfolio as weights. Thus the portfolio's market model is a straightforward extension of the market model for individual securities given in Equation (7.3).[13]

From Equation (7.10a), it follows that the total risk of a portfolio, measured by the variance of the portfolio's returns and denoted σ_p^2, will be:

$$\sigma_p^2 = \beta_{pI}^2 \sigma_I^2 + \sigma_{\varepsilon p}^2 \tag{7.11a}$$

where:

$$\beta_{pI}^2 = \left[\sum_{i=1}^{N} X_i \beta_{iI}\right]^2 \tag{7.11b}$$

and, assuming the random error components of security returns are uncorrelated:[14]

$$\sigma_{\varepsilon p}^2 = \sum_{i=1}^{N} X_i^2 \sigma_{\varepsilon i}^2 \tag{7.11c}$$

Equation (7.11a) shows that the total risk of any portfolio can be viewed as having two components, similar to the two components of the total risk of an individual security. Accordingly, these components are also referred to as market risk $(\beta_{pI}^2 \sigma_I^2)$ and unique risk $(\sigma_{\varepsilon p}^2)$.

Next, it will be shown that increased diversification can lead to the reduction of a portfolio's total risk. Risk is reduced because the size of the portfolio's unique risk is reduced while the portfolio's market risk remains approximately the same size.

7.4.2 Portfolio Market Risk

In general, the more diversified a portfolio (that is, the larger the number of securities in the portfolio), the smaller will be each proportion X_i. The portfolio's beta, β_{pI}, will neither decrease nor increase significantly unless a deliberate attempt is made to do so by adding either relatively low or high beta securities, respectively, to the portfolio. That is, because a portfolio's beta is an average of the betas of its securities, there is no reason to suspect that increasing the amount of diversification will cause the portfolio beta, and thus the market risk of the portfolio, to change in a particular direction. Accordingly,

Diversification leads to an averaging *of market risk.*

This concept makes sense because when prospects for the economy turn sour (or rosy), most securities will fall (or rise) in price. Regardless of the amount of diversification, portfolio returns will always be susceptible to such marketwide influences.

7.4.3 Portfolio Unique Risk

The situation is entirely different for unique risk. In a portfolio, some securities will go up as a result of unexpected good news specific to the company that issued the securities (such as an unexpected approval of a patent). Other securities will go down as a result of unexpected company-specific bad news (such as an industrial accident). Looking forward, approximately as many companies will have good news as have bad news, so there will be little anticipated net impact on the return of a "well-diversified" portfolio. In other words, as a portfolio becomes more diversified, the smaller will be its unique risk and, in turn, its total risk.

This relation can be quantified precisely if the random error components of security returns are assumed to be uncorrelated, as was done when Equation (7.11c) was written. Consider the following situation. If the amounts invested in all the securities are equal, then the proportion X_i will equal $1/N$, and the level of unique risk, as shown in Equation (7.11c), will be equal to:

$$\sigma_{\varepsilon p}^2 = \sum_{i=1}^{N} \left[\frac{1}{N} \right]^2 \sigma_{\varepsilon i}^2 \tag{7.12a}$$

$$= \frac{1}{N} \left[\frac{\sigma_{\varepsilon 1}^2 + \sigma_{\varepsilon 2}^2 + \dots + \sigma_{\varepsilon N}^2}{N} \right] \tag{7.12b}$$

The value inside the square brackets in Equation (7.12b) is simply the average unique risk of the component securities. But the portfolio's unique risk is only one-Nth as large, because the term $1/N$ appears outside the square brackets. Now as the portfolio becomes more diversified, the number of securities in it (that is, N) becomes larger. In turn, $1/N$ will become smaller, and the portfolio will have less unique risk.[15] That is,

Diversification can substantially reduce *unique risk.*

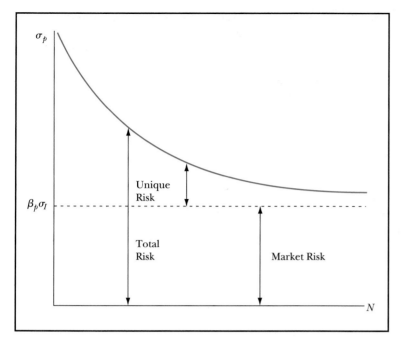

Figure 7.10
Risk and Diversification

Roughly speaking, a portfolio that has equal proportions of 30 or more randomly selected securities in it will have a relatively small amount of unique risk. Its total risk will be only slightly greater than the amount of market risk that is present. Thus such portfolios are well diversified. Figure 7.10 illustrates how diversification results in the reduction of unique risk but the averaging of market risk.

7.4.4 An Example

Consider the two securities, A and B, that were referred to earlier. These two securities had betas of 1.2 and .8, respectively; the standard deviations of their random error terms were, respectively, 6.06% and 4.76%. Thus, given that $\sigma_{\varepsilon A} = 6.06\%$ and $\sigma_{\varepsilon B} = 4.76\%$, it follows that $\sigma_{\varepsilon A}^2 = 6.06^2 = 37$ and $\sigma_{\varepsilon B}^2 = 4.76^2 = 23$. Now assume that the standard deviation of the market index, σ_I, is 8%, which implies that the variance of the market index is $8^2 = 64$. Using Equation (7.8), this means that the variances of securities A and B are as follows:

$$\sigma_A^2 = \left(1.2^2 \times 64\right) + 37$$

$$= 129$$

$$\sigma_B^2 = \left(.8^2 \times 64\right) + 23$$

$$= 64$$

A Two-Security Portfolio

Consider combining securities A and B into a portfolio, with an equal amount of the investor's money going into each security. That is, consider a portfolio that has $X_A = .5$ and $X_B = .5$. Since $\beta_{AI} = 1.2$ and $\beta_{BI} = .8$, the beta of this portfolio can be calculated using Equation (7.10c):

Portfolio Analysis **187**

The Active Manager Portfolio Selection Problem

The classic formulation of the portfolio selection problem depicts an investor who must choose a portfolio on the efficient set that exhibits the optimal combination of expected return and standard deviation, given the investor's risk-return preferences. In practice, however, this description inadequately characterizes the situation faced by most organizations that manage money for institutional investors. We want to consider how the portfolio selection problem can be modified to fit the concerns of institutional investors.

Certain types of institutional investors, such as pension and endowment funds (we will call them the "clients"), typically hire outside firms (we will call them the "managers") as agents to invest their assets. These managers usually specialize in a particular asset class, such as common stocks or fixed-income securities. The clients establish performance benchmarks for their managers. These benchmarks may be market indices (such as the S&P 500) or specialized benchmarks that reflect specific investment styles (such as small-capitalization growth stocks).

The clients hire some managers to simply match the performance of the benchmarks. These managers are called *passive managers* (see Chapter 23). The clients hire other managers to exceed the returns produced by the benchmarks. These managers are called *active managers.*

In the case of passive managers, the portfolio selection problem is trivial. They simply buy and hold those securities that constitute their assigned benchmarks. Their portfolios are called *index funds.* Passive managers need make no reference to the efficient set or to risk-return preferences. Those issues must be dealt with by their clients. (Whether the benchmarks chosen by the clients are efficient is a separate, although important, subject that we will not address in this discussion.)

Active managers face a much more difficult task. They must create portfolios that produce returns exceeding the returns on their assigned benchmarks in sufficient magnitude and consistency to satisfy their clients. The greatest obstacle confronting active managers is their lack of omniscience. Even the most capable of them make numerous errors in their security selections. Despite fables about managers who outperform the market's return every year by 10 percentage points, common stock managers who consistently exceed their benchmarks' returns (after all fees and expenses) by 1–2 percentage points per annum are considered exceptional performers. Managers lacking skill (with *skill* defined in this case as the ability to accurately forecast security returns) will lose to their benchmarks as their fees and trading costs diminish their returns.

We refer to the returns that active managers earn above those of their benchmarks as *active returns.* For example, a manager whose portfolio and benchmark generate returns of 7% and 4%, respectively, has earned a 3% active return (= 7% − 4%). The expected active return for highly skillful managers exceeds that of less talented managers. Nevertheless, in any given period, through sheer chance, the less capable manager's active return may exceed that of the highly skillful manager.

Because the results of active managers' investment decisions are uncertain, their returns relative to their benchmarks exhibit variability over time. We refer to the standard deviation of active return as *active risk.*

Active managers (at least those with some investment forecasting ability) can increase their ex-

$$\beta_{pI} = (.5 \times 1.2) + (.5 \times .8)$$

$$= 1.0$$

Using Equation (7.11c), the variance of the portfolio's random error term, $\sigma_{\varepsilon p}^2$ equals:

$$\sigma_{\varepsilon p}^2 = (.5^2 \times 37) + (.5^2 \times 23)$$

$$= 15$$

From Equation (7.11a), it can be seen that this portfolio will have the following variance:

$$\sigma_p^2 = (1.0^2 \times 64) + 15$$

$$= 79$$

This represents the total risk of the two-security portfolio.

pected active returns by taking on more active risk. Suppose that Manager X forecasts that IBM stock will earn a return above that of the benchmark. IBM constitutes 2% of the benchmark. Manager X could "bet" on IBM by holding a portfolio with a 4% position in IBM stock. The difference between the actual portfolio's position in IBM and the benchmark's position (+2% = 4% − 2%) we call an *active position*. If IBM does perform well, Manager X's active return will be enhanced by the positive active position in IBM. However, if IBM performs poorly, then Manager X's active return will be diminished. The larger Manager X's active position is in IBM, the greater is his or her expected active return. However, the larger also is Manager X's active risk.

Active risk (and, hence, expected active return) can be eliminated by owning every benchmark security at weights matching those of the same securities in the benchmark. Passive managers follow this approach. Active managers assume active risk when they deviate in their portfolio holdings relative to their benchmarks. Rational and skillful active managers will take on active risk only with the expectation of earning positive active return.

The outline of the portfolio selection problem for an active manager now becomes clear. The manager is not concerned with the trade-off between portfolio expected return and standard deviation. Rather, the manager chooses between higher expected active return and lower active risk.

This process requires that we make an assumption about the manager's ability to forecast security returns. With that information, we can construct a manager's **active efficient set** that exhibits the highest combination of expected active return per unit of

active risk and the lowest active risk per unit of expected active return. Managers with greater skill will have active efficient sets that lie farther to the northwest than managers with less skill.

Indifference curves, analogous to those applied in the classical portfolio selection problem, indicate various combinations of active return and active risk that the manager finds equally desirable. The steepness of these indifference curves reflects the manager's degree of risk aversion, which is directly related to the manager's assessment of how his or her clients will respond to various investment outcomes.

The manager's optimal combination of active return and risk is that point on the active efficient set which is tangent to one of the indifference curves. We can view this point as the manager's desired level of aggressiveness in implementing his or her security return forecasts. Managers (and their clients) with higher risk aversion will choose portfolios with lower levels of active risk. Conversely, managers (and their clients) with lower risk aversion will choose portfolios with higher levels of active risk.

It is easy to argue that this type of approach may lead to an inefficient combination of total risk and expected return for a client who has hired several active managers. That is, if the client could direct his or her managers to hold particular portfolios, the combined portfolio might be more efficient than letting each manager make independent decisions about the composition of his or her portfolio. However, the complexity of the task of coordinating managers' portfolio decisions makes the decentralized decision-making arrangement attractive to both institutional investors and their managers.

A Three-Security Portfolio

Consider what would happen if a third security (C) was combined with the other two to form a three-security portfolio having $X_A = X_B = X_C = .33$. This third security has a beta of 1.0 and a random error term whose standard deviation $(\sigma_{\varepsilon C})$ is 5.50%. Thus the variance of the random error term is $\sigma_{\varepsilon C}^2 = 5.5^2 = 30$ and the security's variance is:

$$\sigma_C^2 = \left(1.0^2 \times 64\right) + 30$$

$$= 94$$

First of all, note that the three-security portfolio has the same amount of market risk as the two-security portfolio, because both portfolios have a beta of 1.0:

$$\beta_{pI} = (.33 \times 1.2) + (.33 \times .8) + (.33 \times 1.0)$$
$$= 1.0$$

Thus increased diversification has not led to a change in the level of market risk. Instead it has led to an averaging of market risk.

Using Equation (7.11c), the variance of the portfolio's random error term equals:

$$\sigma_{\varepsilon p}^2 = (.33^2 \times 37) + (.33^2 \times 23) + (.33^2 \times 30)$$
$$= 10$$

Note that the variance of this three-security portfolio's random error term is less than the variance of the two-security portfolio's random error term (that is, $10 < 15$). Thus, in this example, increased diversification has indeed reduced unique risk. From Equation (7.11a), it can be seen that this three-security portfolio will have the following variance:

$$\sigma_p^2 = (1.0^2 \times 64) + 10$$
$$= 74$$

This represents the total risk of the portfolio and is less than the total risk of the two-security portfolio ($74 < 79$). Thus increased diversification has led to a reduction in total risk.

7.4.5 Random versus Efficient Diversification

Equation (7.12b) demonstrates how adding randomly selected securities, and combining them in equal proportions, reduces a portfolio's unique risk. That analysis explicitly assumes that the random error components of the securities' returns are uncorrelated. In more general terms, this **random diversification** implicitly assumes that an investor has no knowledge of the standard deviations and correlations of the available securities. This situation contrasts with the Markowitz approach to portfolio construction. Using estimates of securities' risks allows an investor to make maximum use of the diversification potential of a group of securities, as is reflected in the efficient set, by explicitly considering their standard deviations and correlations. Diversifying a portfolio in this way is referred to as **efficient diversification**.

7.5   **SUMMARY**

1. The efficient set contains those portfolios that offer both maximum expected return for varying levels of risk and minimum risk for varying levels of expected return.
2. Investors are assumed to select their optimal portfolios from among the portfolios lying on the efficient set.
3. An investor's optimal portfolio is located at the tangency point between the investor's indifference curves and the efficient set.
4. The proposition that the efficient set is concave follows from the definition of portfolio standard deviation and the existence of assets whose returns are not perfectly positively or perfectly negatively correlated.
5. Diversification usually leads to risk reduction, because the standard deviation of a portfolio generally will be less than a weighted average of the standard deviations of the component securities.
6. The relationship between the return on a security and the return on a market index is known as the market model.

CHAPTER 7

7. The market index's return does not completely explain the return on a security. The unexplained elements are captured by the random error term of the market model.

8. The slope in a security's market model measures the sensitivity of the security's return to the market index's return. The slope term is known as the security's beta.

9. According to the market model, the total risk of a security consists of market risk and unique risk.

10. A portfolio's vertical intercept, beta, and random error term are weighted averages of the component securities' intercepts, betas, and random error terms, respectively, with the securities' relative proportions in the portfolio serving as weights.

11. Diversification leads to an averaging of market risk.

12. Diversification can substantially reduce unique risk.

QUESTIONS AND PROBLEMS

1. Why would you expect individual securities to generally lie in the eastern portion of the feasible set, whereas only portfolios would lie in the northwestern portion?

2. Explain why most investors prefer to hold a diversified portfolio of securities as opposed to placing all of their wealth in a single asset. Use an illustration of the feasible and efficient sets to explain your answer.

3. Why would you expect most U.S. common stocks to have positive covariances? Give an example of two stocks that you would expect to have a very high positive covariance. Give an example of two stocks that you would expect to have a very low positive (or even negative) covariance.

4. Discuss why the concepts of covariance and diversification are closely related.

5. Mule Haas is a portfolio manager. On average, the expected returns on all securities that Mule is researching are positive. Under what conditions might Mule be willing to purchase a security with a negative expected return?

6. In terms of the Markowitz model, explain, using words and graphs, how an investor goes about identifying his or her optimal portfolio. What specific information does an investor need to identify this portfolio?

7. Dode Brinker owns a portfolio of two securities with the following expected returns, standard deviations, and weights:

Security	Expected Return	Standard Deviation	Weight
A	10%	20%	.35
B	15	25	.65

What correlation between the two securities produces the maximum portfolio standard deviation? What correlation between the two securities produces the minimum portfolio standard deviation. Show your calculations.

8. Explain why the efficient set must be concave. (Hint: Think about the ramifications of the efficient set having a "dent" in it.)

9. Leslie Nunamaker owns a portfolio whose market model is expressed as:

$$r_p = 1.5\% + 0.90 r_I + \varepsilon_{pI}$$

If the expected return on the market index is 12%, what is the expected return on Leslie's portfolio?

10. How is beta derived from a security's market model? Why are high beta securities termed "aggressive"? Why are low beta securities termed "defensive"?

11. The following table presents ten years of return data for the stock of Glenwood City Properties and for a market index. Plot the returns of Glenwood City and

---

Portfolio Analysis   **191**

the market index on a graph, with the market index's returns on the horizontal axis and Glenwood City's returns on the vertical axis. Draw your best guess of the market model through these points. Examining the graph, estimate the beta of Glenwood City stock.

Year	Glenwood City	Market Index
1	8.1%	8.0%
2	3.0	0.0
3	5.3	14.9
4	1.0	5.0
5	−3.1	14.1
6	−3.0	18.9
7	5.0	10.1
8	3.2	5.0
9	1.2	1.5
10	1.3	2.4

12. Consider the stocks of two companies, Woodville Weasel Farms and New Richmond Furriers.
    a. If you are told that the slope of Woodville's market model is 1.20 and that the slope of New Richmond's market model is 1.00, which stock would you say is likely to be riskier in a portfolio context? Why?
    b. If you are now also told that the standard deviation of the random error term for Woodville stock is 10.0%, whereas for New Richmond stock it is 21.5%, does your answer change? Explain.
13. The market model specifies a very simple relationship between a security's return and the return on the market index. Discuss some real-world complexities that might diminish the predictive power of the market model.
14. Each of two stocks, one the stock of an electric utility company and the other the stock of a gold mining company, has a beta of 0.60. Why would a security analyst be interested to know that the gold mining stock has a much larger standard deviation of the random error term (unique risk) than the electric utility stock?
15. Lyndon Station stock has a beta of 1.20. Over five years, the following returns were produced by Lyndon stock and a market index. Assuming a market model intercept term of 0%, calculate the standard deviation of the market model random error term over this period.

Year	Lyndon Return	Market Index
1	17.2%	14.0%
2	−3.1	−3.0
3	13.3	10.0
4	28.5	25.0
5	9.8	8.0

16. Why does diversification lead to a reduction in unique risk but not in market risk? Explain, both intuitively and mathematically.
17. Siggy Boskie owns a portfolio composed of three securities with the following characteristics:

Security	Beta	Standard Deviation Random Error Term	Proportion
A	1.20	5%	.30
B	1.05	8	.50
C	0.90	2	.20

If the standard deviation of the market index is 18%, what is the total risk of Siggy's portfolio?

18. Consider two portfolios, one composed of four securities and the other of ten securities. All the securities have a beta of 1 and unique risk of 30%. Each portfolio distributes weight equally among its component securities. If the standard deviation of the market index is 20%, calculate the total risk of both portfolios.

19. (Appendix Question) What is a corner portfolio? Why are corner portfolios important for identifying the composition of the efficient set?

20. (Appendix Question) Why is the market model approach a simpler technique than the original Markowitz approach for constructing the efficient set?

21. (Appendix Question) If the variance of the market index is 490 and the covariance between securities A and B is 470, what is the beta of security B, knowing that security A's beta is 1.20?

22. (Appendix Question) How many parameters must be estimated to analyze the risk-return profile of a 50-stock portfolio using (a) the original Markowitz approach and (b) the market model approach?

CFA EXAM QUESTIONS

23. Explain the concepts of specific (or unique) risk, systematic risk, variance, covariance, standard deviation, and beta as they are related to investment management.

APPENDIX A

THE MARKOWITZ MODEL

A.1 DETERMINING THE COMPOSITION AND LOCATION OF THE EFFICIENT SET

Previously, it was noted that there are an infinite number of possible portfolios available to the investor but that the investor needs to be concerned with only those portfolios that are on the efficient set. However, Markowitz's efficient set is a curved line, which means that there are an infinite number of points along it. In turn, there must then be an infinite number of efficient portfolios! How can Markowitz's approach be used if an investor needs to identify the composition of each one of an infinite number of portfolios? Fortunately, there is no need to despair. Markowitz saw this potential problem and, in a major contribution, presented a method for solving it.[16] It involves the use of a quadratic programming algorithm known as the *critical-line method.*

Although the algorithm is beyond the scope of this book, it is important to recognize what it does. To begin with, the investor must estimate the expected return vector and variance-covariance matrix. For example, consider the three-security example presented earlier in the chapter.[17] The expected return vector, denoted by *ER*, and the variance-covariance matrix, denoted by *VC*, were estimated to be:

$$ER = \begin{bmatrix} 16.2 \\ 24.6 \\ 22.8 \end{bmatrix} \qquad VC = \begin{bmatrix} 146 & 187 & 145 \\ 187 & 854 & 104 \\ 145 & 104 & 289 \end{bmatrix}$$

The algorithm then identifies a number of *corner portfolios* that are associated with these securities and completely describe the efficient set. A **corner portfolio** is an efficient portfolio with the following property:

Any combination of two adjacent corner portfolios will result in a portfolio that lies on the efficient set between the two corner portfolios. However, any combination of two non-adjacent corner portfolios will not result in a portfolio that lies on the efficient set.

Just what this statement means is illustrated in the example. The algorithm begins by identifying the portfolio with the highest expected return. This portfolio corresponds to point *S* in Figure 7.1 and is an efficient portfolio. It is composed of just one security: the security with the highest expected return.[18] That is, an investor who wants to purchase that portfolio, need only purchase shares of the company whose stock has the highest expected return. Any other portfolio would have a lower expected return, because at least part of the investor's funds would be placed in shares of other companies that have an expected return lower than *S*.

In the example, the company whose shares have the highest expected return is the second one, Baker Company. The corresponding efficient portfolio is the first of several corner portfolios that the algorithm will identify. Its composition is given by the following weight vector, denoted by $X(1)$:

$$X(1) = \begin{bmatrix} .00 \\ 1.00 \\ .00 \end{bmatrix}$$

Its expected return and standard deviation correspond to the expected return and standard deviation of Baker, which are equal to 24.6% and $(854)^{1/2} = 29.22\%$, respectively. In Figure 7.11, this corner portfolio is denoted by $C(1)$.

The algorithm then identifies the second corner portfolio. This portfolio is on the efficient set below the first corner portfolio and has a composition given by the following weight vector, denoted by $X(2)$:

$$X(2) = \begin{bmatrix} .00 \\ .22 \\ .78 \end{bmatrix}$$

That is, the second corner portfolio is a portfolio in which the investor puts 22% of his or her funds into Baker common stock and the remainder, 78%, into Charlie common stock. When these weights are applied to Equations (6.3a) and (6.7), the expected return and standard deviation of this corner portfolio are found to be 23.20% and 15.90%, respectively. In Figure 7.11, this corner portfolio is denoted by $C(2)$.

What is important about the first and second corner portfolios is that they are *adjacent* efficient portfolios, and any efficient portfolio lying on the efficient set between them has a composition that is just a combination of their compositions. For example, the efficient portfolio lying halfway between them has the following composition:

$$[.5 \times X(1)] + [.5 \times X(1)] = .5 \times \begin{bmatrix} .00 \\ 1.00 \\ .00 \end{bmatrix} + .5 \times \begin{bmatrix} .00 \\ .22 \\ .78 \end{bmatrix} = \begin{bmatrix} .00 \\ .61 \\ .39 \end{bmatrix}$$

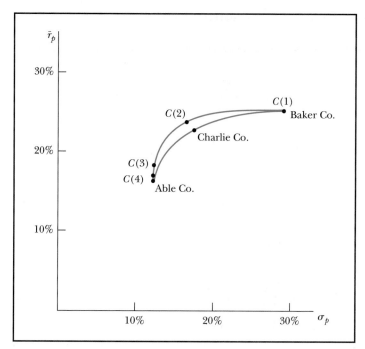

Figure 7.11
Corner Portfolios

That is, the portfolio has weights of .61 in Baker stock and .39 in Charlie stock. Using Equations (6.3a) and (6.7), the expected return and standard deviation of this portfolio turn out to be 23.9% and 20.28%, respectively.

Having identified the second corner portfolio, the algorithm then identifies the third one. Its composition is:

$$X(3) = \begin{bmatrix} .84 \\ .00 \\ .16 \end{bmatrix}$$

These weights can now be used to calculate the expected return and standard deviation of this portfolio, which are 17.26% and 12.22%, respectively. As was noted for the previous two corner portfolios, this corner portfolio is an efficient portfolio and is denoted by $C(3)$ in Figure 7.11.

Because they are adjacent, combinations of the second and third corner portfolios result in efficient portfolios that lie on the efficient set between them. For example, if the investor puts 33% of his or her money in the second corner portfolio and 67% in the third corner portfolio, then the resulting efficient portfolio has the following composition (rounded to the nearest hundredth):

$$[.33 \times X(2)] + [.67 \times X(3)] = .33 \times \begin{bmatrix} .00 \\ .22 \\ .78 \end{bmatrix} + .67 \times \begin{bmatrix} .84 \\ .00 \\ .16 \end{bmatrix} = \begin{bmatrix} .56 \\ .07 \\ .37 \end{bmatrix}$$

Using Equations (6.3a) and (6.7), this portfolio can be shown to have an expected return of 19.10% and a standard deviation of 12.88%.[19]

If only combinations of *adjacent* corner portfolios will be efficient then portfolios formed by combining *nonadjacent* corner portfolios will not lie on the efficient set. For example, the first and third corner portfolios are nonadjacent, which means that any portfolio formed by combining them will not be efficient. For example, if the investor put 50% of his or her funds in the first corner portfolio and 50% in the third corner portfolio, the resulting portfolio would have the following composition:

$$[.5 \times X(1)] + [.5 \times X(3)] = .5 \times \begin{bmatrix} .00 \\ 1.00 \\ .00 \end{bmatrix} + .5 \times \begin{bmatrix} .84 \\ .00 \\ .16 \end{bmatrix} = \begin{bmatrix} .42 \\ .50 \\ .08 \end{bmatrix}$$

With these weights, the expected return and standard deviation of this portfolio are equal to 20.93% and 18.38%, respectively. However, this is an inefficient portfolio. Because its expected return (20.93%) lies between the expected return of the second (23.20%) and third (17.26%) corner portfolios, by combining these two adjacent corner portfolios the investor will be able to form an efficient portfolio that has the same expected return but lower standard deviation.[20]

Continuing, the algorithm now identifies the composition of the fourth corner portfolio:

$$X(4) = \begin{bmatrix} .99 \\ .00 \\ .01 \end{bmatrix}$$

Its expected return and standard deviation can be calculated to be 16.27% and 12.08%, respectively. Having identified this portfolio as the one corresponding to point E in Figure 7.1 [and $C(4)$ in Figure 7.11], meaning that it is the portfolio that has the smallest standard deviation of all efficient portfolios, the algorithm stops. The four corner portfolios, summarized in Table 7.1 completely describe the efficient set associated with the stocks of Able, Baker, and Charlie.

It is a simple matter for the computer, using its capability for graphics, now to draw the graph of the efficient set. Perhaps it will find the composition, and in turn the expected return and standard deviation, for each of 20 efficient portfolios that are evenly spaced between the first and second corner portfolios. Then it will "connect the dots," tracing a straight line along all of the 20 successive portfolios. Connecting the dots will give the graph the appearance of a curved line, as shown in Figure 7.11, since these portfolios are located close to each other.

In a similar fashion, 20 efficient portfolios between the second and third corner portfolios will be located and the corresponding segment of the efficient set traced.

TABLE 7.1	Corner Portfolios for a Three-Security Example				
	Weight			Corner Portfolio	
Corner Portfolio	Able Co.	Baker Co.	Charlie Co.	Expected Return	Standard Deviation
$C(1)$	.00	1.00	.00	24.60%	29.22%
$C(2)$	.00	.22	.78	23.20	15.90
$C(3)$	.84	.00	.16	17.26	12.22
$C(4)$	.99	.00	.01	16.27	12.08

Then the same procedure will be followed for the region between the third and fourth corner portfolios, at which point the graph has been completely drawn.

| A.2 | DETERMINING THE COMPOSITION OF THE OPTIMAL PORTFOLIO |

Once the location and composition of Markowitz's efficient set have been determined, the composition of the investor's optimal portfolio can be determined. This portfolio, indicated by $O*$ in Figure 7.2, corresponds to the tangency point between the efficient set and one of the investor's indifference curves. The procedure for determining its composition starts by the investor's noting graphically the level of its expected return. That is, from the graph the investor can note where $O*$ is located and then can calibrate its expected return simply by using a ruler and extending a line from it to the vertical axis (with computers, more precise ways exist for doing this; see Appendix B in Chapter 8 for one method).

The investor can now identify the two corner portfolios having expected returns "surrounding" this level. That is, the investor can identify the corner portfolio with the expected return nearest to but greater than this level (the surrounding corner portfolio that is "above" $O*$) and the corner portfolio with the expected return nearest to but less than this level (the surrounding corner portfolio that is "below" $O*$).

If the expected return of the optimal portfolio is denoted by $r*$ and the expected returns of these two surrounding portfolios are denoted by r^a and r^b, respectively, then the composition of the optimal portfolio can be determined by solving the following equation for Y:

$$\bar{r}* = (\bar{r}^a \times Y) + [\bar{r}^b \times (1 - Y)] \qquad (7.13)$$

The optimal portfolio will consist of a proportion Y of the "above" surrounding corner portfolio and a proportion $1 - Y$ of the "below" surrounding corner portfolio.

In the example, if the optimal portfolio had an expected return of 20%, then it can be noted that the second and third corner portfolios are the above and below surrounding corner portfolios, since they have expected returns of 23.20% and 17.26%, respectively. Equation (7.13) thus looks like:

$$20\% = (23.20\% \times Y) + [17.26\% \times (1 - Y)]$$

Solving this equation for Y results in $Y = .46$, meaning that the optimal portfolio consists of a proportion of .46 in the second corner portfolio and .54 in the third corner portfolio. In terms of the amount of investment in the securities of Able, Baker, and Charlie companies, this result translates to:

$$[.46 \times X(2)] + [.54 \times X(3)] = .46 \times \begin{bmatrix} .00 \\ .22 \\ .78 \end{bmatrix} + .54 \times \begin{bmatrix} .84 \\ .00 \\ .16 \end{bmatrix} = \begin{bmatrix} .45 \\ .10 \\ .45 \end{bmatrix}$$

Thus the investor should put 45%, 10%, and 45% of his or her funds in shares of Able, Baker, and Charlie, respectively.

More generally, if the weight vectors of the above and below surrounding corner portfolios are denoted by X^a and X^b, respectively, then the weights for the individual securities contained in the optimal portfolio will be equal to $(Y \times X^a) + [(1 - Y) \times X^b]$.

APPENDIX B

DETERMINING THE INPUTS NEEDED FOR LOCATING THE EFFICIENT SET

In order to construct the efficient set, the investor must estimate the expected returns for all the securities under consideration, as well as all of the variances and covariances. Subsequently, the optimal portfolio can be identified by noting where one of the investor's indifference curves is tangent to the efficient set, as shown in Figure 7.2.

Considerable effort is needed to construct this efficient set. First, the expected return for each security must be estimated. Given that there are N risky securities, N parameters must be estimated. Second, the variance for each one of these securities must be estimated. Again, because there are N risky securities, another N parameters must be estimated. Third, the covariance between each pair of risky securities must be estimated. There are $(N^2 - N)/2$ of these parameters to be estimated.[21] Consequently, the total number of parameters that need to be estimated is equal to $(N^2 + 3N)/2$ determined as follows:

Expected returns	N
Variances	N
Covariances	$(N^2 - N)/2$
Total	$(N^2 + 3N)/2$

For example, if there were 100 risky securities under consideration, then $[100^2 + (3 \times 100)]/2 = 5{,}150$ parameters would need to be estimated, consisting of 100 expected returns, 100 variances, and 4,950 covariances. These parameters can be estimated one by one, a task that will be quite time-consuming if not, practically speaking, impossible. Fortunately, alternatives exist, including one that is based on the market model.[22]

With the market model approach, the expected return on the market index must be estimated initially. Then, the vertical intercept and beta for each security must be estimated. At this point, $(1 + 2N)$ parameters have been estimated (1 for $\bar{r}_I$; $2N$ for the vertical intercept and beta for each of the N risky securities). In turn, these figures can be used to estimate the expected return for each security using Equation (7.3), restated as follows:

$$\bar{r}_i = \alpha_{iI} + \beta_{iI}\bar{r}_I \tag{7.14}$$

Earlier, the expected return on the market index was estimated to be 5%. Given these figures, the expected return for security A was estimated to be 8%, because the vertical intercept and beta of this security were estimated to be 2% and 1.2, respectively:

$$\bar{r}_A = 2\% + (5\% \times 1.2)$$

$$= 8\%$$

Similarly, the expected return for security B was estimated to be 3%, because its vertical intercept and beta were estimated to be 11% and .8, respectively:

$$\bar{r}_B = -1\% + (5\% \times .8)$$

$$= 3\%$$

With the market model approach, the variance of any security i can be estimated by multiplying the squared value of the security's beta by the variance of the market index and then adding the variance of the random error term to the product. The equation for doing this was given earlier:

$$\sigma_i^2 = \beta_{iI}^2 \sigma_I^2 + \sigma_{\varepsilon i}^2 \tag{7.8}$$

where σ_I^2 denotes the variance of the market index and $\sigma_{\varepsilon i}^2$ denotes the variance of the random error term for security i.

If the variance on the market index is 49, the respective variances of securities A and B can be estimated as follows:

$$\sigma_A^2 = \left(1.2^2 \times 49\right) + 6.06^2$$

$$= 107.28$$

$$\sigma_B^2 = \left(.8^2 \times 49\right) + 4.76^2$$

$$= 54.02$$

The standard deviations of these securities are estimated to be equal to 10.36% = $(107.28)^{1/2}$ and 7.35% = $(54.02)^{1/2}$, respectively.

Last, the covariance between any two securities i and j can be estimated by the product of the three numbers: the beta of security i, the beta of security j, and the variance of the market index. That is, the following formula can be used:

$$\sigma_{ij} = \beta_{iI}\beta_{jI}\sigma_I^2 \tag{7.15}$$

Thus for securities A and B, the estimated covariance would be:

$$\sigma_{AB} = 1.2 \times .8 \times 49$$

$$= 47.04$$

In summary, if the market model approach is used to estimate expected returns, variances, and covariances, then the following parameters must first be estimated:

For the market index:	
Expected return $(\bar{r}_I)$	1
Variance (σ_I^2)	1
For each security:	
Vertical intercept (α_{iI})	N
Beta (β_{iI})	N
Variance of random error term $(\sigma_{\varepsilon i}^2)$	N
Total	$3N + 2$

Thus for 100 risky securities, $(3 \times 100) + 2 = 302$ parameters need to be estimated when the market model approach is used to determine the efficient set and tangency portfolio. With this approach, once these 302 parameters have been estimated, then it is a simple matter to use Equations (7.14), (7.8), and (7.15) to estimate the expected returns, variances, and covariances for the risky securities. Alternatively, the expected returns, variances, and covariances could be estimated one by one as noted earlier, in which case 5,150 parameters would need to be estimated. As can be seen with this example, the market model approach results in a notable reduction in the number of parameters that need to be estimated.

With the market model approach (or alternatively the one-by-one approach), after the expected returns, variances, and covariances have been estimated, a computer can be given these values. Then, using a "quadratic programming algorithm" the computer can proceed to identify the efficient set.[23] At this juncture, the investor's optimal portfolio can be determined by finding the point at which one of the indifference curves is tangent to the efficient set.

ENDNOTES

[1] This fact can be seen by noting that there are an infinite number of points on the real number line between 0 and 100. If these numbers are thought of as representing the percentage of the investor's funds going into shares of Able, with 100 minus that percentage going into Baker, it can be seen that there are an infinite number of portfolios that could be formed from just two different securities. In this assertion, however, it is assumed that an investor can buy a fraction of a share. For example, the investor can buy not only one share of Able, but also 1.1 or 1.01 or 1.001 shares.

[2] In order to determine the compositions of the portfolios on the efficient set, the investor must solve a quadratic programming problem. See Markowitz's book entitled *Portfolio Selection*, particularly pp. 176–185. (See Reference 1 at the end of the chapter.)

[3] The risk-neutral investor will choose portfolio *S*, while the risk-seeking investor will choose either *S* or *H*. See Appendix B in Chapter 6.

[4] This "curvature property" can also be used to explain why the right-hand side of the feasible set has the umbrella shape noted in Figure 7.1.

[5] For a demonstration of why there cannot be a convex region on the efficient set, see Gordon J. Alexander and Jack Clark Francis, *Portfolio Analysis* (Upper Saddle River, NJ: Prentice Hall, 1986), pp. 50–55.

[6] This is an example of a single-factor model wherein the factor is the return on a market index (see Chapter 10 for more on factor models; see Chapters 24 and 25 for more on market indices). The model is actually more general than indicated here in that the return need not be on a market index. It can be on any variable that is believed to have a major influence on individual stock returns, such as the predicted rate of increase in industrial production or gross domestic product.

[7] To be technically correct, the standard deviation of the random error term should be denoted $\sigma_{\varepsilon iI}$, because it is measured relative to market index *I*. The subscript *I* is not shown here for ease of exposition.

[8] Because the range refers to the possible outcomes and the spacing refers to the probabilities of the various outcomes occurring, it can be seen that the roulette wheel is just a convenient way of referring to the random error term's probability distribution. Typically, it is assumed that a random error term has a normal distribution with a mean of zero.

[9] Appendix A of Chapter 6 discusses several basic statistical concepts, including expected value (or outcome) and standard deviation.

[10] This would be the case if security *B* had a random error term whose roulette wheel had integers from −9% to +9% on it, but the spacing for each integer between −5% and +5% was twice as large as the spacing for each integer from −9% to −6% and from +6% to +9%. This means that the probability that any specific integer between −5% and +5% will occur is equal to 2/30, whereas the probability that any specific integer from −9% to −6% and from +6% to +9% will occur is equal to 1/30.

[11] Just how beta is estimated will be addressed in Chapter 16.

[12] If the random error term takes on a value of zero, then the security will lie *on* the line. However, the probability of this occurring is very small for most securities.

[13] Appendix B shows how the market model can be used to estimate expected returns, variances, and covariances for the securities in the feasible set; with these estimates in hand, one can subsequently determine the efficient set. (See Endnote 2.)

[14] The assumption of uncorrelated random error components is an approximation. The market-weighted sum of all the residuals must be zero. Therefore, on average, the residuals must have a slight negative correlation. However, the average correlation is so small that it can safely be assumed to equal zero.

[15] Actually, all that is necessary for this reduction in unique risk to occur is for the maximum amount invested in any one security to continually decrease as N increases.

[16] See Harry M. Markowitz, "The Optimization of a Quadratic Function Subject to Linear Constraints," *Naval Research Logistics Quarterly* 3, nos. 1, 2 (March–June 1956):111–133.

[17] This example is based on one from Markowitz's book entitled *Portfolio Selection*, pp. 176–185. (See Reference 1.)

[18] If two or more securities have the same highest return, then one can be given a slightly higher expected return to break the tie.

[19] The portfolio's expected return and standard deviation were computed without rounding the securities' weights to the nearest one hundredth.

[20] In this example, the efficient portfolio having an expected return of 20.93% can be determined by solving the following equation for Y: $(23.20\% \times Y) + [17.26\% \times (1 - Y)] = 20.93\%$. Because this is a linear equation with one unknown, it can easily be solved. The solution, $Y = .62$, indicates that by putting .62 of his or her funds in the second corner portfolio and .38 $(= 1.00 - .62)$ in the third corner portfolio, the investor will have an efficient portfolio with the same expected return but lower standard deviation (specifically, 14.09%) than the portfolio involving a 50-50 combination of the first and third corner portfolios.

[21] This number was arrived at in the following manner. The variance-covariance matrix has N rows and N columns, meaning that it contains N^2 cells whose corresponding parameters need to be estimated. The cells on the diagonal contain the N variances mentioned earlier, leaving $(N^2 - N)$ covariances to be estimated. Because the variance-covariance matrix is symmetric, only those covariances below the diagonal need be estimated (because they also appear in corresponding locations above the diagonal), leaving a total of $(N^2 - N)/2$ parameters to be estimated.

[22] The market model approach is an approximate one (as are all the other alternatives) because it makes some simplifying assumptions. For example, this approach assumes that the random error terms for any two securities are uncorrelated [an assumption that was needed in deriving Equation (7.11c) and later in (7.15)]. This assertion means that the outcome from a spin of the roulette wheel for one security (such as Mobil) has no bearing on the outcome from a spin of the roulette wheel for any other security (such as Exxon). It has been argued that this zero correlation is not true for securities within certain industries. See Benjamin F. King, "Market and Industry Factors in Stock Price Behavior," *Journal of Business* 39, no. 1 (January 1966): 139–170; and James L. Farrell Jr., "Analyzing Covariation of Returns to Determine Homogeneous Stock Groupings," *Journal of Business* 47, no. 2 (April 1974): 186–207.

[23] See Appendix B to Chapter 8 for a description of an algorithm that can be used in conjunction with the market model to determine the composition of the efficient set.

KEY TERMS

efficient set theorem
efficient set
feasible set
efficient portfolios
inefficient portfolios
optimal portfolio
market model
random error term
beta

aggressive stocks
defensive stocks
market risk
unique risk
active efficient set
random diversification
efficient diversification
corner portfolio

1. As mentioned in Chapter 6, the seminal work developing the mean-variance model is credited to Harry Markowitz, who presented his ideas in a paper and later in a book:

   Harry M. Markowitz, "Portfolio Selection," *Journal of Finance* 7, no. 1 (March 1952): 77–91.

   Harry M. Markowitz, *Portfolio Selection: Efficient Diversification of Investments* (New York: Wiley, 1959). (A reprint of this book that also contains some new material is available from Basil Blackwell, in Cambridge, MA; its copyright date is 1991.)

2. The technique used for determining the location of the efficient set, along with the composition of the "corner portfolios" that lie on it, was developed in:

   Harry M. Markowitz, "The Optimization of a Quadratic Function Subject to Linear Constraints," *Naval Research Logistics Quarterly* 3, nos. 1, 2 (March–June 1956): 111–133.

3. The market model, initially mentioned by Markowitz in a footnote on p. 100 of his book, was developed in:

   William F. Sharpe, "A Simplified Model for Portfolio Analysis," *Management Science* 9, no. 2 (January 1963): 277–293.

4. An extensive discussion of the market model can be found in chapters 3 and 4 of:

   Eugene F. Fama, *Foundations of Finance* (New York: Basic Books, 1976).

5. For discussions of how diversification reduces market risk, see:

   John L. Evans and Stephen H. Archer, "Diversification and the Reduction of Dispersion: An Empirical Analysis," *Journal of Finance* 23, no. 5 (December 1968): 761–767.

   W. H. Wagner and S. C. Lau, "The Effect of Diversification on Risk," *Financial Analysts Journal*, 27, no. 6 (November/December 1971): 48–53.

   Meir Statman, "How Many Stocks Make a Diversified Portfolio?" *Journal of Financial and Quantitative Analysis* 22, no. 3 (September 1987): 353–363.

   Gerald D. Newbould and Percy S. Poon, "The Minimum Number of Stocks Needed for Diversification," *Financial Practice and Education* 3, no. 2 (Fall 1993): 85–87.

6. A discussion of some statistical problems that are encountered in partitioning total risk is contained in:

   Bert Stine and Dwayne Key, "Reconciling Degrees of Freedom When Partitioning Risk: A Teaching Note," *Journal of Financial Education*, 19 (Fall 1990): 19–22.

7. Some of the statistical problems encountered in using optimization techniques to manage portfolios (specifically, the problem of how to cope with *estimation risk*) are discussed in:

   J. D. Jobson and Bob Korkie, "Putting Markowitz Theory to Work," *Journal of Portfolio Management* 7, no. 4 (Summer 1981): 70–74.

   Gordon J. Alexander and Jack Clark Francis, *Portfolio Analysis* (Upper Saddle River, NJ: Prentice Hall, 1986), Chapter 6.

   Peter A. Frost and James E. Savarino, "Portfolio Size and Estimation Risk," *Journal of Portfolio Management* 12, no. 4 (Summer 1986): 60–64.

   Peter A. Frost and James E. Savarino, "For Better Performance: Constrain Portfolio Weights," *Journal of Portfolio Management*, 15, no. 1 (Fall 1988): 29–34.

   Richard O. Michaud, "The Markowitz Optimization Enigma: Is `Optimized' Optimal?" *Financial Analysts Journal* 45, no. 1 (January/February 1989): 31–42.

   Philippe Jorion, "Portfolio Optimization in Practice," *Financial Analysts Journal* 48, no. 1 (January/February 1992): 68–74.

   Vijay K. Chopra and William T. Ziemba, "The Effects of Errors in Means, Variances, and Covariances on Optimal Portfolio Choice," *Journal of Portfolio Management* 19, no. 2 (Winter 1993): 6–11.

Kenneth L. Fisher and Meir Statman, "The Mean-Variance-Optimization Puzzle: Security Portfolios and Food Portfolios," *Financial Analysts Journal* 53, no. 4 (July/August 1997): 41–50.

8. The active manager portfolio selection problem is addressed in:

Richard C. Grinold, "The Fundamental Law of Active Management," *Journal of Portfolio Management* 16, no. 4 (Summer 1989): 30–37.

Richard Roll, "A Mean/Variance Analysis of Tracking Error," *Journal of Portfolio Management* 19, no. 4 (Summer 1992): 13–22.

George Chow, "Portfolio Selection Based on Return, Risk, and Relative Performance," *Financial Analysts Journal* 51, no. 2 (March/April 1995): 54–60.

RISKFREE LENDING AND BORROWING

The previous two chapters focused on how an investor should go about determining what portfolio to select for investment. Markowitz's approach assumes that the investor has a certain amount of initial wealth (W_0) to invest for a given holding period. Of all the portfolios that are available, the optimal one is shown to correspond to the point at which one of the investor's indifference curves is tangent to the efficient set. At the end of the holding period, the investor's initial wealth will have either increased or decreased depending on the portfolio's rate of return. The resulting end-of-period wealth (W_1) can then be completely reinvested, completely spent on consumption, or partially reinvested and partially consumed.

The Markowitz approach assumes that the assets considered for investment are individually risky; that is, each one of the N risky assets is assumed to have an uncertain return over the investor's holding period. Because none of the assets has a perfectly negative correlation with any other asset, all the portfolios also have uncertain returns over the investor's holding period and thus are risky. Furthermore, the investor is not allowed to use borrowed money along with his or her initial wealth to purchase a portfolio of assets. This means that the investor is not allowed to use financial leverage, or margin.

In this chapter, the Markowitz approach to investing is expanded by first allowing the investor to consider investing not only in risky assets but also in a riskfree asset. There will now be N assets available for purchase, consisting of $N - 1$ risky assets and one riskfree asset. Second, the investor is allowed to borrow money but has to pay a given rate of interest on the loan. The next section considers the effect of adding a riskfree asset to the set of risky assets.

8.1   DEFINING THE RISKFREE ASSET

What exactly is a **riskfree asset** in the context of Markowitz's approach? Because this approach involves investing for a single holding period, the return on the riskfree asset is certain. An investor who purchases a riskfree asset at the beginning of a holding period knows exactly what the value of the asset will be at the end of the holding period. Because there is no uncertainty about the terminal value of the riskfree asset, the standard deviation of the riskfree asset is, by definition, zero.

In turn, the covariance between the rate of return on the riskfree asset and the rate of return on any risky asset is zero. Remember that the covariance between the returns on any two assets i and j is equal to the product of the correlation coefficient between the assets and the standard deviations of the two assets: $\sigma_{ij} = \rho_{ij}\sigma_i\sigma_j$. Given that $\sigma_i = 0$ if i is the riskfree asset, it follows that $\sigma_{ij} = 0$.

Because a riskfree asset has by definition a certain return, this type of asset must be some kind of fixed-income security with no possibility of default. All corporate securities in principle have some chance of default, so the riskfree asset cannot be issued by a corporation. Instead it must be a security issued by the federal government. However, not just any security issued by the U.S. Treasury qualifies as a riskfree security.

Consider an investor with a three-month holding period who purchases a Treasury security maturing in 20 years. Such a security is risky because the investor does not know what this security will be worth at the end of the holding period. Because interest rates will very likely change in an unpredictable manner during the investor's holding period, the market price of the security will likewise change in an unpredictable manner. The presence of such **interest-rate risk** (also known as *price risk*) makes the value of the Treasury security uncertain, disqualifying it as a riskfree asset. Indeed any Treasury security with a maturity date greater than the investor's holding period cannot qualify as a riskfree asset.

Next consider a Treasury security that matures before the end of the investor's holding period, such as a 30-day Treasury bill in the case of the investor with the three-month holding period. In this situation, the investor does not know at the beginning of the holding period what interest rates will be in 30 days. In other words, the investor does not know the interest rate at which the proceeds from the maturing Treasury bill can be reinvested for the remainder of the holding period. The presence of such **reinvestment-rate risk** in all Treasury securities of shorter maturity than the investor's holding period means that these securities do not qualify as riskfree assets.

Only one type of Treasury security is left to qualify as a riskfree asset: a Treasury security with a maturity that matches the length of the investor's holding period. For example, the investor with the three-month holding period would find that a Treasury bill with a three-month maturity date had a certain return. Because this security matures at the end of the investor's holding period, it provides the investor with an amount of money at the end of the holding period that is known for certain at the beginning of the holding period when an investment decision has to be made.[1] Investing in the riskfree asset is often referred to as **riskfree lending** because such an investment involves the purchase of Treasury bills and thus involves a loan by the investor to the federal government.

8.2   ALLOWING FOR RISKFREE LENDING

With the introduction of a riskfree asset, the investor is now able to put part of his or her money in this asset and the remainder in any of the risky portfolios contained in Markowitz's feasible set. Adding these new opportunities expands the feasible set significantly and, more important, changes the location of a substantial part of Markowitz's efficient set. The nature of these changes needs to be analyzed, because investors are concerned with selecting a portfolio from the efficient set. In this analysis, initial consideration is given to determining the expected return and standard deviation for a portfolio that consists of an investment in the riskfree asset combined with an investment in a single risky security.

8.2.1 Investing in Both a Riskfree Asset and a Risky Asset

In Chapter 6, the companies of Able, Baker, and Charlie were assumed to have expected returns, variances, and covariances as indicated in the following expected return vector and variance-covariance matrix:

$$ER = \begin{bmatrix} 16.2 \\ 24.6 \\ 22.8 \end{bmatrix} \quad VC = \begin{bmatrix} 146 & 187 & 145 \\ 187 & 854 & 104 \\ 145 & 104 & 289 \end{bmatrix}$$

Defining the riskfree asset as security number 4, consider all portfolios that involve investing in just the common stock of Able and the riskfree asset. Let X_1 denote the proportion of the investor's funds invested in Able and $X_4 = 1 - X_1$ denote the proportion invested in the riskfree asset. If the investor put all of his or her money in the riskfree asset, then $X_1 = 0$ and $X_4 = 1$. Alternatively, the investor could put all of his or her money in just Able, in which case $X_1 = 1$ and $X_4 = 0$. A combination of .25 in Able and .75 in the riskfree asset is also possible, as are respective combinations of .50 and .50 or .75 and .25. Although there are many other possibilities, the focus here will be on these five portfolios:

	Portfolio A	Portfolio B	Portfolio C	Portfolio D	Portfolio E
X_1	.00	.25	.50	.75	1.00
X_4	1.00	.75	.50	.25	.00

On the assumption that the riskfree asset has a rate of return (often denoted r_f) of 4%, all the necessary information for calculating the expected returns and standard deviations for these five portfolios is at hand. Equation (6.3a) from Chapter 6 can be used to calculate the expected returns for these portfolios:

$$\bar{r}_p = \sum_{i=1}^{N} X_i \bar{r}_i \tag{6.3a}$$

$$= \sum_{i=1}^{4} X_i \bar{r}_i$$

Portfolios A, B, C, D, and E do not involve investing in the second and third securities (that is, Baker and Charlie companies), meaning that $X_2 = 0$ and $X_3 = 0$ in these portfolios. Thus, the previous equation reduces to:

$$\bar{r}_p = X_1 \bar{r}_1 + X_4 \bar{r}_4$$

$$= (X_1 \times 16.2\%) + (X_4 \times 4\%)$$

where the riskfree rate is now denoted $\bar{r}_4$.

For portfolios A and E this calculation is trivial because all the investor's funds are being placed in just one security. Thus their expected returns are just 4% and 16.2%, respectively. For portfolios B, C, and D, the expected returns are, respectively:

$$\bar{r}_B = (.25 \times 16.2\%) + (.75 \times 4\%)$$

$$= 7.05\%$$

$$\bar{r}_C = (.50 \times 16.2\%) + (.50 \times 4\%)$$

$$= 10.10\%$$

$$\bar{r}_D = (.75 \times 16.2\%) + (.25 \times 4\%)$$

$$= 13.15\%$$

The standard deviations of portfolios A and E are simply the standard deviations of the riskfree asset and Able, respectively. Thus $\sigma_A = 0\%$ and $\sigma_E = 12.08\%$. In the calculation of the standard deviations of portfolios B, C, and D, Equation (6.7) from Chapter 6 must be used:

$$\sigma_p = \left[\sum_{i=1}^{N} \sum_{j=1}^{N} X_i X_j \sigma_{ij} \right]^{1/2} \qquad (6.7)$$

$$= \left[\sum_{i=1}^{4} \sum_{j=1}^{4} X_i X_j \sigma_{ij} \right]^{1/2}$$

Because $X_2 = 0$ and $X_3 = 0$ in these portfolios, this equation reduces to:

$$\sigma_p = \left[X_1 X_1 \sigma_{11} + X_1 X_4 \sigma_{14} + X_4 X_1 \sigma_{41} + X_4 X_4 \sigma_{44} \right]^{1/2}$$

$$= \left[X_1^2 \sigma_1^2 + X_4^2 \sigma_4^2 + 2 X_1 X_4 \sigma_{14} \right]^{1/2}$$

This equation can be reduced even further, because security number 4 is the riskfree security, which, by definition, has $\sigma_4 = 0$ and $\sigma_{14} = 0$. Accordingly, it reduces to:

$$\sigma_p = \left[X_1^2 \sigma_1^2 \right]^{1/2}$$

$$= \left[X_1^2 \times 146 \right]^{1/2}$$

$$= X_1 \times 12.08\%$$

Thus the standard deviations of portfolios B, C, and D are:

$$\sigma_B = .25 \times 12.08\%$$

$$= 3.02\%$$

$$\sigma_C = .50 \times 12.08\%$$

$$= 6.04\%$$

$$\sigma_D = .75 \times 12.08\%$$

$$= 9.06\%$$

In summary, the five portfolios have the following expected returns and standard deviations:

Portfolio	X_1	X_4	Expected Return	Standard Deviation
A	.00	1.00	4.00%	0.00%
B	.25	.75	7.05	3.02
C	.50	.50	10.10	6.04
D	.75	.25	13.15	9.06
E	1.00	.00	16.20	12.08

These portfolios are plotted in Figure 8.1. It can be seen that they all lie on a straight line connecting the points representing the location of the riskfree asset and Able.

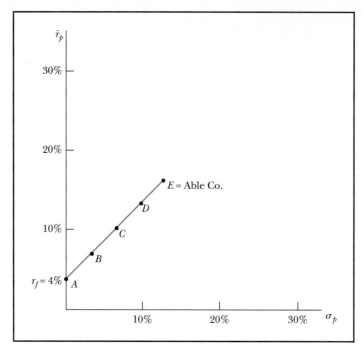

Figure 8.1
Combining Riskfree Lending with Investing in a Risky Asset

Although only five particular combinations of the riskfree asset and Able have been examined here, it can be shown that any combination of the riskfree asset and Able will lie somewhere on the straight line connecting them; the exact location will depend on the relative proportions invested in these two assets. Furthermore, this observation can be generalized to combinations of the riskfree asset and any risky asset. Thus, any portfolio consisting of a combination of the riskfree asset and a risky asset will have an expected return and standard deviation such that it plots somewhere on a straight line connecting them.

8.2.2 Investing in Both the Riskfree Asset and a Risky Portfolio

Next consider what happens when a portfolio consisting of more than just one risky security is combined with the riskfree asset. For example, consider the risky portfolio PAC that consists of Able and Charlie in proportions of .80 and .20, respectively. Its expected return (denoted $\bar{r}_{PAC}$) and standard deviation (denoted σ_{PAC}) are equal to:

$$\bar{r}_{PAC} = (.80 \times 16.2\%) + (.20 \times 22.8\%)$$
$$= 17.52\%$$
$$\sigma_{PAC} = \left[(.80 \times .80 \times 146) + (.20 \times .20 \times 289) + \right.$$
$$\left. (2 \times .80 \times .20 \times 145) \right]^{1/2}$$
$$= 12.30\%$$

Any portfolio that consists of an investment in both PAC and the riskfree asset will have an expected return and standard deviation that can be calculated in a manner identical to that previously shown for combinations of an individual asset and the riskfree asset. A portfolio that has the proportion X_{PAC} invested in the portfolio PAC and the proportion $X_4 = 1 - X_{PAC}$ in the riskfree asset will have an expected return and standard deviation that are equal to, respectively:

$$\overline{r}_{PAC} = \left(X_{PAC} \times 17.52\%\right) + \left(X_4 \times 4\%\right)$$

$$\sigma_{PAC} = X_{PAC} \times 12.30\%$$

For example, consider investing in a portfolio that consists of PAC and the riskfree asset in proportions of .25 and .75, respectively.[2] This portfolio will have an expected return of:

$$\overline{r}_p = (.25 \times 17.52\%) + (.75 \times 4\%)$$

$$= 7.38\%$$

and a standard deviation of:

$$\sigma_p = .25 \times 12.30\%$$

$$= 3.08\%$$

Figure 8.2 shows that this portfolio lies on a straight line connecting the riskfree asset and PAC. In particular, it is indicated by the point P on this line. Other portfolios consisting of various combinations of PAC and the riskfree asset will also lie on this line, with their exact locations depending on the relative proportions invested in PAC and the riskfree asset. For example, a portfolio that involves investing a proportion of .50 in the riskfree asset and a proportion of .50 in PAC lies on this line exactly halfway between the two endpoints.

In summary, combining the riskfree asset with any risky portfolio can be viewed as being no different from combining the riskfree asset with an individual risky security. In both cases, the resulting portfolio has an expected return and standard deviation such that it lies somewhere on a straight line connecting the two endpoints.

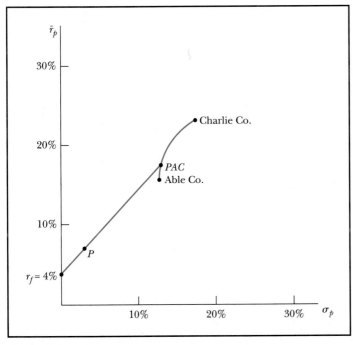

Figure 8.2
Combining Riskfree Lending with Investing in a Risky Portfolio

---

Riskfree Lending and Borrowing

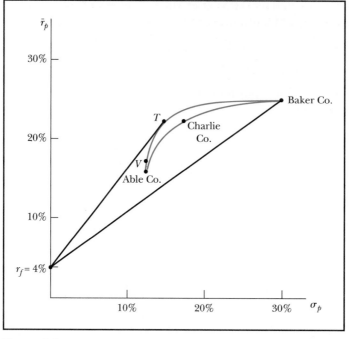

Figure 8.3
Feasible and Efficient Sets When Riskfree Lending Is Introduced

8.2.3 The Effect of Riskfree Lending on the Efficient Set

As mentioned earlier, the feasible set is changed significantly as a result of the introduction of riskfree lending. Figure 8.3 shows how it changes the feasible set for the example at hand. Here all risky assets and portfolios, not just Able and *PAC*, are considered in all possible combinations with the riskfree asset. In particular, note that there are two boundaries that are straight lines emanating from the riskfree asset. The bottom line connects the riskfree asset with Baker. Thus it represents portfolios formed by combining Baker and the riskfree asset.

The other straight line emanating from the riskfree asset represents combinations of the riskfree asset and a particular risky portfolio on the efficient set of the Markowitz model. It is a line that is just tangent to this efficient set, with the tangency point being denoted *T*. This tangency point represents a risky portfolio consisting of Able, Baker, and Charlie in proportions equal to, respectively, .12, .19, and .69. Substituting these proportions into Equations (6.3a) and (6.7) indicates that the expected return and standard deviation of *T* are 22.4% and 15.2%, respectively.

Although other risky efficient portfolios from the Markowitz model can also be combined with the riskfree asset, portfolio *T* deserves special attention. Why? Because there is no other portfolio consisting purely of risky assets that, when connected by a straight line to the riskfree asset, lies northwest of it. In other words, of all the lines that can be drawn emanating from the riskfree asset and connecting with either a risky asset or a risky portfolio, none has a greater slope than the line that goes to *T*.

This fact is important because part of the efficient set of the Markowitz model is dominated by this line. In particular, the portfolios on the Markowitz model efficient set going from the minimum-risk portfolio, denoted *V*, to *T* are no longer efficient when a riskfree asset is made available for investment. Instead the efficient set now consists of a straight-line segment and a curved segment. The straight-line segment is the straight line going from the riskfree asset to T and thus consists of portfolios made up of various combinations of the riskfree asset and T. The curved segment consists of those portfolios to the northeast of T on the Markowitz model efficient set.

8.2.4 The Effect of Riskfree Lending on Portfolio Selection

Figure 8.4 shows how an investor would go about selecting an optimal efficient portfolio when there is a riskfree asset available for investment in addition to a number of risky assets. If the investor's indifference curves look like those shown in Figure 8.4(a), the investor's optimal portfolio O^* will involve investing part of his or her initial wealth in the riskfree asset and the rest in T because his or her indifference curves are tangent to the efficient set between the riskfree asset and T.[3] Alternatively, if the investor is less risk-averse and has indifference curves that look like those shown in Figure 8.4(b), then the investor's optimal portfolio O^* will not involve any riskfree lending because his or her indifference curves are tangent to the curved segment of the efficient set that lies to the northeast of T.

8.3   ALLOWING FOR RISKFREE BORROWING

The analysis that was presented in the previous section can be expanded by allowing the investor to borrow money. This investor is no longer restricted to his or her initial wealth when it comes time to decide how much money to invest in risky assets.[4] However, if the investor borrows money, then interest must be paid on the loan. Because the interest rate is known and there is no uncertainty about repaying the loan, this practice is often referred to as **riskfree borrowing**.

It will be assumed that the rate of interest charged on the loan is equal to the rate of interest that could be earned from investing in the riskfree asset.[5] The investor from the earlier example now not only has the opportunity to invest in a riskfree asset that earns a rate of return of 4% but also may borrow money, for which the investor must pay a rate of interest equal to 4%.

Earlier, the proportion invested in the riskfree asset was denoted X_4, and this proportion was constrained to be a nonnegative number between 0 and 1. Now with the opportunity to borrow at the same rate, X_4 will no longer be so constrained. In the earlier example, the investor had initial wealth of $17,200. If the investor borrows money, then he or she will have in excess of $17,200 to invest in the risky securities of Able, Baker, and Charlie.

For example, if the investor borrows $4,300, then he or she will have a total of $21,500 (=$17,200 + $4,300) to invest in these securities. In this situation, X_4 can be viewed as being equal to $-.25$ (=$-$4,300/$17,200). However, the sum of the proportions must still equal 1. This means that if the investor has borrowed money, the sum of the proportions invested in risky assets would be greater than one. For example, borrowing $4,300 and investing $21,500 in Able means that the proportion in Able, X_1, equals 1.25 (= $21,500/$17,200). Note that in this case $X_1 + X_4 = 1.25 + (-.25) = 1$.

8.3.1 Borrowing and Investing in a Risky Security

The example presented in the previous section will be expanded to evaluate the effect that the introduction of riskfree borrowing has on the efficient set. In particular, consider portfolios F, G, H, and I; for these portfolios the investor will invest all

---

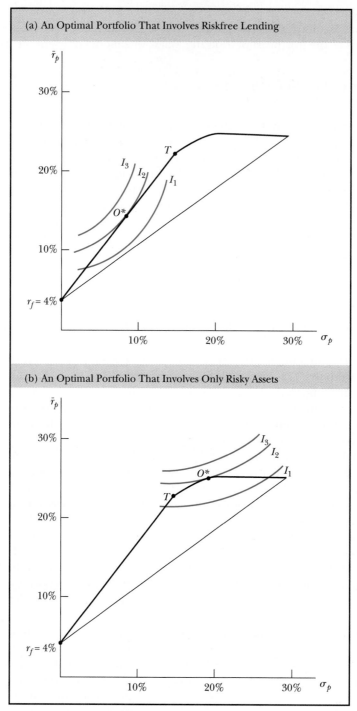

Figure 8.4
Portfolio Selection with Riskfree Lending

the borrowed funds as well as his or her own funds in Able. Thus the proportions for these portfolios can be summarized as follows:

	Portfolio *F*	Portfolio *G*	Portfolio *H*	Portfolio *I*
X_1	1.25	1.50	1.75	2.00
X_4	−.25	−.50	−.75	−1.00

The expected returns of these portfolios are calculated in the same manner as was shown in the previous section. Equation (6.3a) is still used:

$$\bar{r}_p = \sum_{i=1}^{N} X_i \bar{r}_i \tag{6.3a}$$

$$= \sum_{i=1}^{4} X_i \bar{r}_i.$$

$$= X_1 \bar{r}_1 + X_4 \bar{r}_4$$

$$= (X_1 \times 16.2\%) + (X_4 \times 4\%)$$

Thus portfolios F, G, H, and I have the following expected returns:

$$\bar{r}_F = (1.25 \times 16.2\%) + (-.25 \times 4\%)$$

$$= 19.25\%$$

$$\bar{r}_G = (1.50 \times 16.2\%) + (-.50 \times 4\%)$$

$$= 22.30\%$$

$$\bar{r}_H = (1.75 \times 16.2\%) + (-.75 \times 4\%)$$

$$= 25.35\%$$

$$\bar{r}_I = (2.00 \times 16.2\%) + (-1.00 \times 4\%)$$

$$= 28.40\%$$

Similarly, the standard deviations of these portfolios are calculated by using Equation (6.7) as was done in the previous section:

$$\sigma_p = \left[\sum_{i=1}^{N} \sum_{j=1}^{N} X_i X_j \sigma_{ij} \right]^{1/2} \tag{6.7}$$

$$= \left[\sum_{i=1}^{4} \sum_{j=1}^{4} X_i X_j \sigma_{ij} \right]^{1/2}$$

which was shown to reduce to:

$$\sigma_p = X_1 \times 12.08\%$$

Thus the standard deviations of the four portfolios are:

$$\sigma_F = 1.25 \times 12.08\%$$

$$= 15.10\%$$

$$\sigma_G = 1.50 \times 12.08\%$$

$$= 18.12\%$$

$$\sigma_H = 1.75 \times 12.08\%$$

$$= 21.14\%.$$

$$\sigma_I = 2.00 \times 12.08\%$$

$$= 24.16\%$$

In summary, these four portfolios, as well as the five portfolios that involve riskfree lending, have the following expected returns and standard deviations:

Portfolio	X_1	X_4	Expected Return	Standard Deviation
A	.00	1.00	4.00%	0.00%
B	.25	.75	7.05	3.02
C	.50	.50	10.10	6.04
D	.75	.25	13.15	9.06
E	1.00	.00	16.20	12.08
F	1.25	−.25	19.25	15.10
G	1.50	−.50	22.30	18.12
H	1.75	−.75	25.35	21.14
I	2.00	−1.00	28.40	24.16

In Figure 8.5, it can be seen that the four portfolios that involve riskfree borrowing (*F, G, H*, and *I*) all lie on the same straight line that goes through the five portfolios that involve riskfree lending (*A, B, C, D*, and *E*). Furthermore, the larger the amount of borrowing, the farther out on the line the portfolio lies; equivalently, the smaller the value of X_4, the farther out on the line the portfolio lies.

Although only four particular combinations of borrowing and investing in Able have been examined here, it can be shown that any combination of borrowing and investing in Able will lie somewhere on this line, with the exact location depending on the amount of borrowing. Furthermore, this observation can be generalized to combinations of riskfree borrowing and an investment in any particular risky asset: Borrowing at the riskfree rate and investing all the borrowed money and the investor's own money in a risky asset will result in a portfolio that has an expected return and standard deviation such that it lies on the extension of the straight line connecting the riskfree rate and the risky asset.

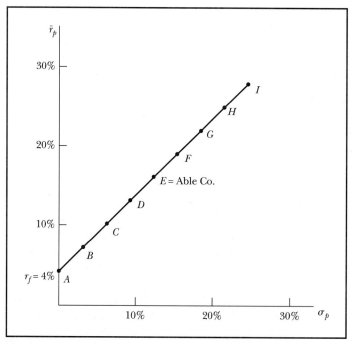

Figure 8.5
Combining Riskfree Borrowing and Lending with Investing in a Risky Asset

8.3.2 Borrowing and Investing in a Risky Portfolio

Next consider what happens when a portfolio of more than one risky asset is purchased with both the investor's own funds and borrowed funds. Earlier it was shown that the portfolio having proportions invested in Able and Charlie equal to .80 and .20, respectively, had an expected return of 17.52% and a standard deviation of 12.30%. This portfolio was referred to as *PAC*. Any portfolio that involves borrowing money at the riskfree rate and then investing these funds and the investor's own funds in *PAC* will have an expected return and standard deviation that can be calculated in a manner identical to that which was previously shown when borrowing was incurred and Able was purchased. A portfolio that involves borrowing the proportion X_4 and investing these funds and all the investor's own funds in *PAC* will have an expected return and standard deviation that are equal to, respectively:

$$\bar{r}_{PAC} = \left(X_{PAC} \times 17.52\% \right) + \left(X_4 \times 4\% \right)$$

$$\sigma_{PAC} = X_{PAC} \times 12.30\%$$

For example, consider borrowing an amount of money equal to 25% of the investor's initial wealth and then investing all the investor's own funds and these borrowed funds in *PAC*. Thus, $X_{PAC} = 1 - X_4 = 1 - (-.25) = 1.25$.[6] This portfolio will have an expected return of:

$$\bar{r}_p = (1.25 \times 17.52\%) + (-.25 \times 4\%)$$

$$= 20.90\%$$

and a standard deviation of:

$$\sigma_p = 1.25 \times 12.30\%$$

$$= 15.38\%$$

Figure 8.6 shows that this portfolio (denoted P) lies on the extension of the line that connects the riskfree rate with *PAC*. Other portfolios consisting of *PAC* and borrowing at the riskfree rate will also lie somewhere on this extension, with their exact location depending on the amount of the borrowing. Thus borrowing to purchase a risky portfolio is no different from borrowing to purchase an individual risky asset. In both cases, the resulting portfolio lies on an extension of the line connecting the riskfree rate with the risky investment.

| 8.4 | ALLOWING FOR BOTH RISKFREE BORROWING AND LENDING |

8.4.1 The Effect of Riskfree Borrowing and Lending on the Efficient Set

Figure 8.7 shows how the feasible set is changed when both borrowing and lending at the same riskfree rate are allowed. Here all risky assets and portfolios, not just Able and *PAC*, are considered. The feasible set is the entire area between the two lines emanating from the riskfree rate that go through the location of Baker and the portfolio denoted *T*. These two lines extend indefinitely to the right if it is assumed that there is no limit to the amount of borrowing that the investor can incur.

The straight line that goes through portfolio *T* is of special importance because it represents the efficient set. This means that it represents the set of portfolios that offer the best opportunities, because it represents the set of feasible portfolios lying farthest northwest. Portfolio *T*, as was mentioned earlier, consists of investments in Able, Baker, and Charlie in proportions equal to, respectively, .12, .19, and .69.[7]

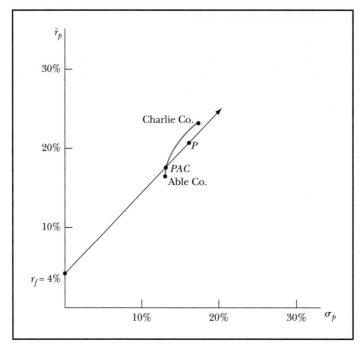

Figure 8.6
Combining Riskfree Borrowing and Lending with Investing in a Risky Portfolio

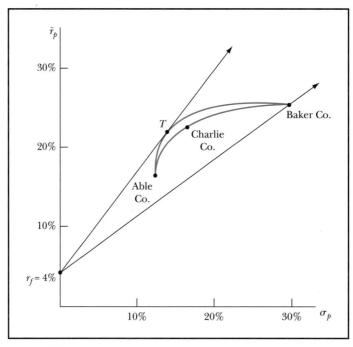

Figure 8.7
Feasible and Efficient Sets When Riskfree Borrowing and Lending Are Introduced

As before, the line going through T is just tangent to the Markowitz model efficient set. None of the portfolios, except for T, that were on the Markowitz model efficient set are efficient when riskfree borrowing and lending are introduced. This outcome can be seen by noting that every portfolio (except T) that lies on the Markowitz model efficient set is dominated by a portfolio on this straight line having the same standard deviation along with a higher expected return.

8.4.2 The Effect of Riskfree Borrowing and Lending on Portfolio Selection

Given the opportunity to either borrow or lend at the riskfree rate, an investor would proceed to identify the optimal portfolio by plotting his or her indifference curves on this graph and noting where one of them is tangent to the linear efficient set.[8] Figure 8.8 shows two alternative situations. If the investor's indifference curves look like

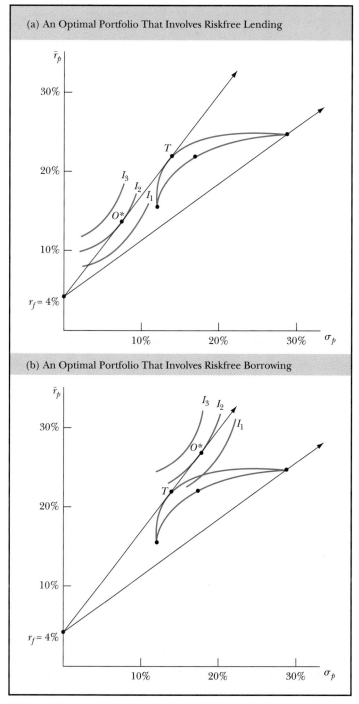

Figure 8.8
Portfolio Selection with Riskfree Borrowing and Lending

The Cost of Short-Term Borrowing

The extension of the Markowitz model to incorporate borrowing and lending assumes that investors can borrow or lend at the riskfree rate. Certainly, every investor has the opportunity to lend at the riskfree rate by simply purchasing U.S. Treasury securities whose maturities correspond to the length of his or her investment holding period.

Borrowing at the riskfree rate is another matter. In reality, only one entity has the option to borrow at the riskfree rate: the U.S. Treasury. Other investors, be they individuals or institutional investors, must borrow at interest rates exceeding those paid by the Treasury.

Just what level of interest rates do investors pay to borrow? To provide some perspective on this issue, we briefly survey some of the interest rates available in the market for short-term financial assets known as the *money market*.

The standard of comparison for all money market interest rates is the rate paid on short-term U.S. Treasury securities called U.S. Treasury bills (see Chapter 1). The return on Treasury bills is completely certain over the short term because the federal government will never default on its obligations. It always has the option to print money or to raise taxes to pay off its debts.

Other borrowers, no matter how strong their current financial position, run at least some risk of defaulting on their short-term debts. Largely owing to this fact, virtually all non-Treasury borrowers must pay interest rates exceeding those paid by the Treasury. The difference between what the Treasury pays to borrow money and what other borrowers pay is known as the *yield spread*. How large is the spread for non-Treasury borrowers?

If you as an individual investor wish to finance your investment in securities, you typically purchase them on margin from your broker. The same holds true for institutional investors. In such transactions the broker actually borrows money elsewhere in the money market (usually drawing down a line of credit at a bank and pledging securities as collateral). The interest rate paid by the broker is known as the *broker call money rate*, or broker call loan rate (see Chapter 2). Brokers add anywhere from 1% to 2% to the call money rate to determine the interest rate charged their margin purchase customers. Larger investors can usually negotiate more favorable borrowing terms than smaller investors.

Over the 12-month period ending March 1997, the broker call money rate averaged roughly 7.02%.

the ones in panel (a), then the investor's optimal portfolio O^* will consist of an investment in the riskfree asset as well as in T. Alternatively, if the investor is less risk-averse and has indifference curves that look like those shown in panel (b), then the investor's optimal portfolio O^* will consist of borrowing at the riskfree rate and investing these funds as well as his or her own funds in T.[9]

8.5 | SUMMARY

1. The return on a riskfree asset is certain. The riskfree asset's standard deviation is zero as is its covariance with other assets.
2. In extending the Markowitz feasible set to include riskfree lending, investors are assumed to allocate their funds among a riskfree asset and a portfolio of risky assets.
3. With riskfree lending, the efficient set becomes a straight line from the riskfree rate to a point tangent to the curved Markowitz efficient set, in addition to the portion of the Markowitz efficient set that lies northeast of this tangency point.
4. Introducing riskfree borrowing permits an investor to engage in financial leverage. The investor may use all of his or her money, plus money borrowed at the riskfree rate, to purchase a portfolio of risky assets.

By comparison, the U.S. Treasury paid an average interest rate on 90-day Treasury bills of 5.19%. Thus the broker call money spread was 1.83 percentage points. Assuming a 1 percentage point markup over the broker call money rate, margin investors faced an average spread over 90-day Treasuries of 2.83 percentage points during the 12-month period in 1996–1997.

Large, financially strong corporations usually borrow in the money market through an instrument known as *commercial paper*. Commercial paper represents the negotiable, short-term, unsecured promissory notes of finance, industrial, utility, insurance, and bank holding companies. The financial strength of these corporations allows them to borrow at money market rates very near those of Treasury bills. For the 12-month period, three-month commercial paper interest rates averaged 5.34%, a spread of only .15 percentage points over similar-maturity 90-day Treasury bills.

Corporations without the size and financial strength to borrow in the commercial paper market must obtain their short-term financing from banks. The interest rate officially quoted by banks on short-term unsecured loans to their best customers is known as the *prime rate*. The prime rate is not always an accurate measure of short-term borrowing costs, because banks often discount from it on loans to their financially strong borrowers. Financially weaker clients, on the other hand, may be charged a premium above the prime rate. For the 12-month period, the prime rate averaged 8.27%, a 3.08 percentage point spread over 90-day Treasuries.

Banks themselves borrow in the money market through large-denomination certificates of deposit (of usually $1 million or larger). Although these loans are unsecured and do not carry federal deposit insurance, the strong financial standing of most banks requires them to pay little more than the government for short-term borrowing. For the 12-month period, rates for large, three-month certificates of deposit averaged 5.44%, only .25 percentage points above 90-day Treasuries.

From this brief money market survey, it is apparent that the Treasury bill rate is relevant to investor borrowing only as a base of comparison. Investors actually have to pay more, sometimes much more, to borrow in the money market, but then, of course, such borrowing is not considered riskfree, at least by the lenders.

5. With riskfree lending and borrowing, the efficient set becomes a straight line from the riskfree rate through a point tangent to the curved Markowitz efficient set.
6. With riskfree lending and borrowing, the efficient set consists of combinations of a single risky portfolio and various proportions of riskfree lending or borrowing.
7. The investor's optimal portfolio is determined by plotting his or her indifference curves against the efficient set.
8. The investor's optimal portfolio will include an investment in the risky portfolio and borrowing or lending at the riskfree rate.
9. Investors with higher levels of risk aversion will engage in less borrowing (or more lending) than investors with less risk aversion.

QUESTIONS AND PROBLEMS

1. Why is a pure-discount government security (that is, one that does not make coupon payments, pays interest at maturity, and hence sells at a discount from par) with no risk of default still risky to an investor whose holding period does not coincide with the maturity date of the security?
2. Distinguish between reinvestment-rate risk and interest-rate risk.
3. The covariance between a riskfree asset and a risky asset is zero. Explain why this is the case and demonstrate it mathematically.

Riskfree Lending and Borrowing

4. Lindsay Brown owns a risky portfolio with a 15% expected return. The riskfree return is 5%. What is the expected return on Lindsay's total portfolio if Lindsay invests the following proportions in the risky portfolio and the remainder in the riskfree asset?
   a. 120%
   b. 90%
   c. 75%
5. Consider a risky portfolio with an expected return of 18%. With a riskfree return of 5%, how could you create a portfolio with a 24% expected return?
6. Happy Buker owns a risky portfolio with a 20% standard deviation. If Happy invests the following proportions in the riskfree asset and the remainder in the risky portfolio, what is the standard deviation of Happy's total portfolio?
   a. 130%
   b. 10%
   c. 30%
7. Oyster Burns's portfolio is composed of an investment in a risky portfolio (with a 12% expected return and a 25% standard deviation) and a riskfree asset (with a 7% return). If Oyster's total portfolio has a 20% standard deviation, what is its expected return?
8. Hick Cady argues that buying a risky portfolio with riskfree borrowing is equivalent to a purchase of the risky portfolio on margin. Patsy Cahill contends that such an investment can be viewed as selling the riskfree asset short and using proceeds to invest in the risky portfolio. Who is correct? Explain.
9. How does the efficient set change when riskfree borrowing and lending are introduced into the Markowitz model? Explain with words and graphs.
10. Why does the efficient set with the Markowitz model extended to include riskfree borrowing and lending have only one point in common with the efficient set of the Markowitz model without riskfree borrowing and lending? Why are the other points on the "old" efficient set no longer desirable? Explain with words and graphs.
11. On the basis of the assumptions developed in this chapter, is it true that all investors will hold the same risky portfolio? Explain.
12. How does the feasible set change when riskfree borrowing and lending are introduced into the Markowitz model? Explain with words and graphs.
13. With the Markowitz model extended to include riskfree borrowing and lending, draw the indifference curves, efficient set, and optimal portfolio for an investor with high risk aversion and an investor with low risk aversion.
14. Given the following expected return vector and variance-covariance matrix for three assets:

$$ER = \begin{bmatrix} 10.1 \\ 7.8 \\ 5.0 \end{bmatrix} \quad VC = \begin{bmatrix} 210 & 60 & 0 \\ 60 & 90 & 0 \\ 0 & 0 & 0 \end{bmatrix}$$

   and given the fact that Pie Traynor's risky portfolio is split 50-50 between the two risky assets:
   a. Which security of the three must be the riskfree asset? Why?
   b. Calculate the expected return and standard deviation of Pie's portfolio.
   c. If the riskfree asset makes up 25% of Pie's total portfolio, what are the total portfolio's expected return and standard deviation?
15. What does the efficient set look like if riskfree borrowing is permitted but no lending is allowed? Explain with words and graphs.
16. What will be the effect on total portfolio expected return and risk if you borrow money at the riskfree rate and invest in the optimal risky portfolio?

---

17. Suppose that your level of risk aversion decreased as you grew richer. In a world of riskfree borrowing and lending, how would your optimal portfolio change? Would the types of risky securities you hold change? Explain with words and graphs.

18. (Appendix Question) How does the efficient set change when the condition of borrowing and lending at the same riskfree rate is changed to borrowing at a rate greater than the rate at which riskfree lending can be conducted? Explain with words and graphs.

19. (Appendix Question) Pickles Gerken owns a tangency portfolio composed of four securities held in the following proportions:

$$X(T) = \begin{bmatrix} .18 \\ .30 \\ .24 \\ .28 \end{bmatrix}$$

The riskfree rate is 4%. The expected return and standard deviation of the tangency portfolio are respectively, 12% and 18%. What is the composition of Pickles' optimal portfolio if Pickles has a risk aversion coefficient of 2.47?

APPENDIX A

ALLOWING FOR DIFFERENT BORROWING AND LENDING RATES

In this chapter it was assumed that the investor could borrow funds at the same rate that could be earned on an investment in the riskfree asset. As a result, the feasible set became the area bounded by two straight lines emanating from the riskfree rate. The upper line represented the efficient set and had one portfolio in common with the curved efficient set of the Markowitz model. This portfolio was located where the straight line from the riskfree rate was tangent to the curved efficient set. Now the concern will be with what happens if it is assumed that the investor can borrow but at a rate that is greater than the rate that can be earned by an investment in the riskfree asset. The rate on the riskfree asset will be denoted r_{fL}, where L indicates lending, because, as mentioned earlier, an investment in the riskfree asset is equivalent to lending money to the government. The rate at which the investor can borrow money will be denoted r_{fB} and is of a magnitude such that $r_{fB} > r_{fL}$.

One way to understand the effect on the efficient set of assuming that these two rates are different is as follows. First, consider what the efficient set would look like if riskfree borrowing and lending were possible at the same rate, r_{fL}. The resulting efficient set would be the straight line shown in Figure 8.9 that goes through the points r_{fL} and T_L.

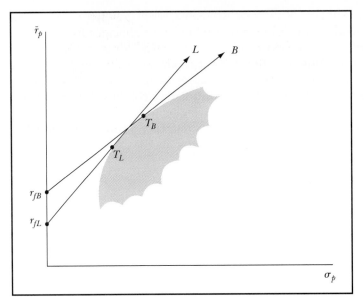

Figure 8.9
Evaluating Different Riskfree Rates

Second, consider what the efficient set would look like if riskfree borrowing and lending were possible at the higher rate, r_{fB}. The resulting efficient set would be the straight line shown in Figure 8.9 that goes through the points r_{fB} and T_B. Note that the portfolio T_B lies on Markowitz's efficient set above the portfolio T_L, because it corresponds to a tangency point associated with a higher riskfree rate.

Third, because the investor cannot borrow at r_{fL}, the part of the line emanating from r_{fL} that extends to the right of T_L is not available to the investor and can be removed from consideration.

Fourth, because the investor cannot lend at the riskfree rate r_{fB}, the part of the line emanating from r_{fB} and going through T_B but lying to the left of T_B is not available to the investor and can be removed from consideration. The northwest boundary of what remains, shown in Figure 8.10, is the resulting efficient set.

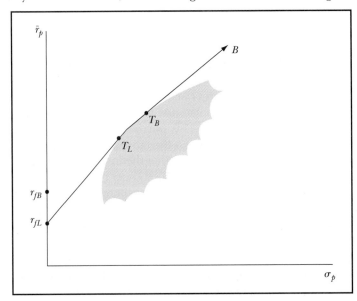

Figure 8.10
Efficient Set When the Riskfree Rates Are Different

This efficient set consists of three distinct but connected segments. The first segment is the straight line going from r_{fL} to T_L, which represents various amounts of riskfree lending combined with investing in the portfolio of risky assets denoted T_L. The second segment is the curved line going from T_L to T_B, which represents various risky portfolios that were also on Markowitz's curved efficient set. The third segment is the straight line extending outward from T_B, which represents various amounts of borrowing combined with an investment in the risky portfolio denoted T_B.

The optimal portfolio for an investor will be, as before, the portfolio that corresponds to the point at which an indifference curve is tangent to the efficient set. Depending on the investor's indifference curves, this tangency point could be on any one of the three segments that define the efficient set.

APPENDIX B

DETERMINING THE COMPOSITION OF THE INVESTOR'S OPTIMAL PORTFOLIO O^*

Once the investor has identified the straight line efficient set by locating the tangency portfolio T, he or she can move on to determine the composition of his or her optimal portfolio. This portfolio, denoted O^* in Figure 8.8, corresponds to the tangency point between the efficient set and one of the investor's indifference curves. It will be a combination of the tangency portfolio and riskfree borrowing or lending. The question is: What is that combination?

One procedure for determining the composition of the optimal portfolio assumes that the investor's indifference curves are of the following general form:

$$S = \bar{r} - a\sigma^2 \tag{8.1}$$

where $\bar{r}$ and σ^2 denote the expected return and variance of a particular portfolio, respectively.[10] The term S is a constant that indicates the level of utility associated with an indifference curve.[11] Various combinations of expected return and standard deviation can provide the investor with the same utility. Higher values of S correspond to indifference curves that are farther northwest. Last, the term a is a positive constant that indicates the investor's degree of risk aversion, where larger values indicate greater degrees of risk aversion.[12] (Note that when $a = 0$, the investor is risk-neutral because the amount of satisfaction a given portfolio provides is not dependent upon its riskiness, which is measured by σ^2. In the limit, when $a = \infty$, the investor is completely risk-averse and will not invest in any asset that has risk.) The investor's optimal portfolio O^* will provide a level of utility given by:

$$S = \bar{r}^* - a\sigma^{*2} \tag{8.2}$$

---

where $\bar{r}^*$ and σ^* denote the optimal portfolio's expected return and standard deviation, respectively.

Next, remember that the expected return of the investor's optimal portfolio is a weighted average of the riskfree rate, r_f, and the expected return of the tangency portfolio T, $\bar{r}_T$:

$$\bar{r}^* = \left(\bar{r}_T \times Y\right) + \left[r_f \times (1 - Y)\right] \tag{8.3}$$

where Y is the proportion invested in the tangency portfolio and thus $(1 - Y)$ is the proportion invested in the riskfree rate. Furthermore, the standard deviation of this portfolio is simply:

$$\sigma^* = Y\sigma_T \tag{8.4}$$

because the standard deviation of the riskfree rate is zero. Inserting the right-hand sides of Equations (8.3) and (8.4) into the appropriate places in Equation (8.2) results in:

$$S^* = \left(\bar{r}_T \times Y\right) + \left[r_f \times (1 - Y)\right] - aY^2\sigma_T^2 \tag{8.5}$$

which indicates that the utility that an investor will get from his or her optimal portfolio will depend on the proportions invested in T and r_f.

A bit of differential calculus is needed to determine the optimal values for these proportions. In particular, the value of Y is sought that maximizes the value of S^* in Equation (8.5). This can be determined by taking the derivative of S^* with respect to Y in Equation (8.5) and setting the result equal to zero:

$$0 = \bar{r}_T - r_f - 2aY\sigma_T^2 \tag{8.6a}$$

which can be solved for Y:

$$Y = \frac{\left(\bar{r}_T - r_f\right)}{2a\sigma_T^2} \tag{8.6b}$$

Because the term a is positive, a greater difference between the expected return on the tangency portfolio and the riskfree rate will cause the investor to purchase more of the tangency portfolio and less of the riskfree rate, an intuitively pleasing result. A similar result will also occur when either the investor is less risk-averse (meaning the term a is smaller) or the standard deviation of the tangency portfolio is smaller, which also squares with our intuition.

As an example, consider again the situation illustrated in Figure 8.8a, where the tangency portfolio associated with Able, Baker, and Charlie companies had an expected return of 22.4% and a standard deviation of 15.2%, given the riskfree rate was 4%. If it is assumed that the risk-aversion coefficient for the investor was $a = 7.96$, Equation (8.6b) will indicate that:

$$Y = \frac{.224 - .04}{\left(2 \times 7.96 \times .152^2\right)}$$

$$= .50$$

Thus, the investor will allocate his or her investable wealth so as to use 50% of it to purchase the tangency portfolio. In terms of the amount of investment in Able, Baker, and Charlie companies, this proportion translates to:

$$\left[.50 \times X(T)\right] = .50 \times \begin{bmatrix} .12 \\ .19 \\ .69 \end{bmatrix} = \begin{bmatrix} .060 \\ .095 \\ .345 \end{bmatrix}$$

Thus the investor should invest an amount of money that is equal to 6%, 9.5%, and 34.5% of his or her initial wealth in shares of Able, Baker, and Charlie, respectively. Furthermore, 50% of the investor's initial wealth should be used to buy the risk-free asset.

Alternatively, consider the example displayed in Figure 8.8b, where the investor is less risk-averse, having $a = 3.19$. In this situation, Equation (8.6b) indicates that:

$$Y = \frac{.224 - .04}{(2 \times 3.19 \times .152^2)}$$

$$= 1.25$$

Thus, the less risk-averse investor will allocate his or her investable wealth so as to use 125% of it to purchase the tangency portfolio, with the extra 25% coming from borrowing at the riskfree rate. In terms of the amount of investment in the securities of Able, Baker, and Charlie companies, this decision translates to:

$$\begin{bmatrix} 1.25 \times X(T) \end{bmatrix} = 1.25 \times \begin{bmatrix} .12 \\ .19 \\ .69 \end{bmatrix} = \begin{bmatrix} .150 \\ .238 \\ .862 \end{bmatrix}$$

As a result, the less risk-averse investor should invest an amount of money that is equal to 15%, 23.8%, and 86.2% of his or her initial wealth in shares of Able, Baker, and Charlie, respectively.

ENDNOTES

[1] To be truly riskfree, the security must not provide the investor with any coupon payments during the holding period. Instead it must provide the investor with only one cash inflow, and that inflow must occur at the end of the investor's holding period. Any intervening coupon payments would subject the investor to reinvestment-rate risk because he or she would not know the rate at which the coupon payments could be invested for the remainder of the holding period. It should also be noted that the discussion has focused on an asset that is riskfree in nominal terms because the presence of uncertain inflation means that nearly all U.S. Treasury securities are risky in real terms (although the Treasury has recently begun to issue inflation-protected securities). These topics were considered in *Institutional Issues: Almost Riskfree Securities* in Chapter 5 and are also discussed in Chapter 12.

[2] Note that investing the proportion .25 in portfolio *PAC* is equivalent to investing the proportion .20 (=.25 × .80) in Able and the proportion .05 (=.25 × .20) in Charlie.

[3] A more risk-averse investor (meaning an investor whose indifference curves have greater slopes) would choose an optimal portfolio that is closer to the riskfree asset on the line that connects the riskfree asset to *T*. Only if the investor is infinitely risk-averse will the optimal portfolio consist of an investment in just the riskfree asset.

[4] Allowing for borrowing can be viewed as giving the investor the opportunity to engage in margin purchases if he or she so desires. Thus the investor is allowed to use financial leverage.

[5] Appendix A discusses what happens to the efficient set when the investor is able to borrow but at a rate that is greater than the rate that can be earned by investing in the riskfree asset.

[6] Note that investing the proportion 1.25 in portfolio *PAC* is equivalent to investing the proportion 1.00 (=1.25 × .80) in Able and the proportion .25 (=1.25 × .20) in Charlie.

[7] The composition of the tangency portfolio *T* can be found by use of commonly available mathematical algorithms. One such algorithm is available on the Internet at <www-sharpe.stanford.edu>. Further, on a historical note, an early simple approach to determining the composition of *T* that did not require the identification of corner portfolios was presented in Edwin J. Elton, Martin J. Gruber, and Manfred D. Padberg, "Simple Criteria for Optimal Portfolio Selection," *Journal of Finance* 31, no. 5 (December 1976): 1341–1357.

[8] Appendix B illustrates how the composition of the investor's optimal portfolio $O*$ is determined.

[9] The less risk-averse the investor is, the smaller the proportion invested in the riskfree rate and the larger the proportion invested in T.

[10] Equation (8.1) is linear in form because the variance (σ^2) of the portfolio is used instead of the standard deviation (σ). If standard deviation were used, then the equation would be expressed in the more commonly recognized form of a parabola that opens upward.

[11] The concept of investor utility is discussed in Chapter 6.

[12] Risk aversion is discussed further in the appendix to Chapter 23.

KEY TERMS

riskfree asset
interest-rate risk
reinvestment-rate risk

riskfree lending
riskfree borrowing

REFERENCES

1. Credit for extending Markowitz's model to include riskfree lending and borrowing belongs to:

   James Tobin, "Liquidity Preference As Behavior Towards Risk," *Review of Economic Studies* 26, no. 1 (February 1958): 65–86.

   James Tobin, "The Theory of Portfolio Selection," in F. H. Hahn and F. P. R. Brechling (eds.), *The Theory of Interest Rates* (London: Macmillan, 1965).

2. For a discussion of various mean-variance models that involve different sets of assumptions regarding riskfree lending and borrowing, margin purchasing, and short selling, see:

   Eugene F. Fama, *Foundations of Finance* (New York: Basic Books, 1976), Chapters 7 and 8.

   Gordon J. Alexander and Jack Clark Francis, *Portfolio Analysis* (Upper Saddle River, NJ: Prentice Hall, 1986), Chapter 4.

3. For a discussion of how to determine the composition of portfolios on the efficient set under a variety of different assumptions, see:

   Edwin J. Elton, Martin J. Gruber, and Manfred D. Padberg, "Simple Criteria for Optimal Portfolio Selection," *Journal of Finance* 31, no. 5 (December 1976): 1341–1357.

   Gordon J. Alexander, "Short Selling and Efficient Sets," *Journal of Finance* 48, no. 4 (September 1993): 1497–1506.

   Edwin J. Elton and Martin J. Gruber, *Modern Portfolio Theory and Investment Analysis* (New York: Wiley, 1995), Chapters 6 and 9.

THE CAPITAL ASSET PRICING MODEL

Chapters 6, 7, and 8 presented a method for identifying an investor's optimal portfolio. With this method, the investor needs to estimate the expected returns and variances for all securities under consideration. Furthermore, all the covariances among these securities need to be estimated, and the riskfree rate needs to be determined. Once this is done, the investor can identify the composition of the tangency portfolio as well as its expected return and standard deviation. At this juncture the investor can proceed to identify the optimal portfolio by noting where one of his or her indifference curves touches but does not intersect the efficient set. This portfolio involves an investment in the tangency portfolio along with a certain amount of either riskfree borrowing or lending because the efficient set is linear (that is, a straight line).

Such an approach to investing can be viewed as an exercise in **normative economics**, wherein investors are told what they should do. Thus, the approach is prescriptive in nature. This chapter enters the realm of **positive economics** by presenting a descriptive model of how assets are priced. The model assumes among other things that all investors use the approach to investing given in Chapters 6, 7, and 8. The major implication of the model is that the expected return of an asset will be related to a measure of risk for that asset known as *beta*. The exact manner in which expected return and beta are related is specified by the **capital asset pricing model** (CAPM). This model provides the intellectual basis for a number of the current practices in the investment industry. Although many of these practices are based on various extensions and modifications of the CAPM, a sound understanding of the original version is necessary in order to understand them. Accordingly, this chapter presents the original version of the CAPM.[1]

9.1 ASSUMPTIONS

To see how assets are priced, one must construct a model (that is, a theory). This process requires simplification in that the model-builder must abstract from the full complexity of the situation and focus only on the most important elements. This focus is achieved by making certain assumptions about the environment. The assumptions need to be simplistic in order to provide the degree of abstraction necessary for success in building the model. The *reasonableness* of the assumptions (or lack thereof) is of little concern. Instead the test of a model is its ability to help one understand and predict the process being modeled. As Milton Friedman, recipient of the 1976 Nobel Prize in Economics, stated in a famous essay:

> *The relevant question to ask about the "assumptions" of a theory is not whether they are descriptively "realistic," for they never are, but whether they are sufficiently good approximations for the purpose in hand. And this question can be answered only by seeing whether the theory works, which means whether it yields sufficiently accurate predictions.*[2]

Some of the assumptions behind the CAPM are also behind the normative approach to investing described in the previous three chapters. These assumptions are as follows:

1. Investors evaluate portfolios by looking at the expected returns and standard deviations of the portfolios over a one-period horizon.
2. Investors are never satiated, so when given a choice between two portfolios with identical standard deviations, they will choose the one with the higher expected return.
3. Investors are risk-averse, so when given a choice between two portfolios with identical expected returns, they will choose the one with the lower standard deviation.
4. Individual assets are infinitely divisible, meaning that an investor can buy a fraction of a share if he or she so desires.
5. There is a riskfree rate at which an investor may either lend (that is, invest) or borrow money.
6. Taxes and transaction costs are irrelevant.

To those assumptions the following ones are added:

7. All investors have the same one-period horizon.
8. The riskfree rate is the same for all investors.
9. Information is freely and instantly available to all investors.
10. Investors have **homogeneous expectations**, meaning that they have the same perceptions in regard to the expected returns, standard deviations, and covariances of securities.

As can be seen by examining these assumptions, the CAPM reduces the situation to an extreme case. Everyone has the same information and agrees about the future prospects for securities. Implicitly this means that investors analyze and process information in the same way. The markets for securities are **perfect markets**, meaning that there are no *frictions* to impede investing. Potential impediments such as finite divisibility, taxes, transaction costs, and different riskfree borrowing and lending rates have been assumed away. This approach allows the focus to change from how an individual should invest to what would happen to security prices if everyone invested in a similar manner. Examining the collective behavior of all investors in the marketplace enables one to develop the resulting equilibrium relationship between each security's risk and return.

9.2 THE CAPITAL MARKET LINE

9.2.1 The Separation Theorem

Having made these ten assumptions, the resulting implications can now be examined. First, investors would analyze securities and determine the composition of the tangency portfolio. In so doing, *everyone would obtain in equilibrium the same tangency portfolio.* This result is not surprising because there is complete agreement among investors on the estimates of the securities' expected returns, variances, and covariances, as well as on the level of the riskfree rate. Also, the linear efficient set (described in Chapter 8) is the same for all investors because it simply involves combinations of the agreed-upon tangency portfolio and either riskfree borrowing or riskfree lending.

Because all investors face the same efficient set, the only reason they will choose dissimilar portfolios is that they have different indifference curves, resulting in distinct preferences toward risk and return. For example, the investor in Figure 8.8(a) will choose a different portfolio than the investor in Figure 8.8(b). Note, however, that although the chosen portfolios will be different, *each investor will choose the same combination of risky securities*, denoted *T* in Figure 8.8. This means that each investor will spread his or her funds among risky securities in the same relative proportions, adding riskfree borrowing or lending in order to achieve a personally preferred overall combination of risk and return. This feature of the CAPM is often referred to as the **separation theorem**:

> *The optimal combination of risky assets for an investor can be determined without any knowledge of the investor's preferences toward risk and return.*

In other words, the optimal combination of risky assets can be determined without any knowledge of the shape of an investor's indifference curves.

The reasoning behind the separation theorem involves a property of the linear efficient set introduced in Chapter 8. There it was shown that all portfolios located on the linear efficient set involved an investment in a tangency portfolio combined with varying degrees of riskfree borrowing or lending. With the CAPM everyone faces the same linear efficient set, meaning that each person will be investing in the same tangency portfolio in which everyone else is investing. (There will also be a certain amount of either riskfree borrowing or lending that depends upon that person's indifference curves.) It therefore follows that the risky portion of all investors' portfolios will be the same.

In the example from Chapter 8, three securities were considered, corresponding to the stock of Able, Baker, and Charlie companies. With a riskfree rate of return of 4%, the tangency portfolio *T* was shown to consist of investments in Able, Baker, and Charlie in proportions equal to .12, .19, and .69, respectively. If the ten assumptions of the CAPM are made, then the investor shown in Figure 8.8(a) will invest approximately half of his or her money in the riskfree asset and the remainder in *T*. The investor shown in Figure 8.8(b), on the other hand, will borrow an amount of money equal to approximately one-quarter the value of his or her initial wealth and proceed to invest these borrowed funds as well as his or her own funds in *T*.[3] Thus the proportions invested in the three stocks for investors in Figure 8.8 would equal:[4]

$$.5 \times \begin{bmatrix} .12 \\ .19 \\ .69 \end{bmatrix} = \begin{bmatrix} .060 \\ .095 \\ .345 \end{bmatrix} \text{ for the investor in panel (a) and}$$

$$1.25 \times \begin{bmatrix} .12 \\ .19 \\ .69 \end{bmatrix} = \begin{bmatrix} .150 \\ .238 \\ .862 \end{bmatrix} \text{ for the investor in panel (b)}$$

Note that, although the proportions to be invested in each of these three risky securities for the Figure 8.8 (a) investor (.060, .095, .345) are different in size from their values for the Figure 8.8(b) investor (.150, .238, .862), the relative proportions are the same, being equal to .12, .19, and .69, respectively.

9.2.2 The Market Portfolio

Another important feature of the CAPM is that in equilibrium each security must have a nonzero proportion in the composition of the tangency portfolio.[5] That is, no security can in equilibrium have a proportion in T that is zero. The reasoning behind this feature lies in the previously mentioned separation theorem, which asserts that the risky portion of every investor's portfolio is independent of the investor's risk-return preferences. The justification for the theorem was that the risky portion of each investor's portfolio is simply an investment in T. If every investor is purchasing T and T does not involve an investment in each security, then nobody is investing in those securities with zero proportions in T. Consequently, the prices of these zero-proportion securities must fall, thereby causing the expected returns of these securities to rise until the resulting tangency portfolio has a nonzero proportion associated with them.

In the previous example, Charlie had a current price of $62 and an expected end-of-period price of $76.14, so the expected return for Charlie was 22.8% [= ($76.14 − $62)/$62]. Now imagine that the current price of Charlie is $72, not $62, meaning that its expected return is 5.8% [= ($76.14 − $72)/$72]. If this were the case, the tangency portfolio associated with a riskfree rate of 4% would involve just Able and Baker in proportions of .90 and .10, respectively.[6] Because Charlie has a proportion of zero, nobody would want to hold shares of Charlie. Consequently, orders to sell would be received in substantial quantities with virtually no offsetting orders to buy being received. As a result, Charlie's price would fall as brokers would try to find someone to buy the shares. However, as Charlie's price fell, its expected return would rise because the same end-of-period price of $76.14 would be forecast for Charlie as before and it would now cost less to buy one share. Eventually, as the price fell, investors would change their minds and want to buy shares of Charlie. Ultimately, at a price of $62 investors would want to hold shares of Charlie, so in aggregate the number of shares demanded would equal the number of shares outstanding. Thus in equilibrium Charlie would have a nonzero proportion in the tangency portfolio.

Another interesting situation could also arise. What if each investor concludes that the tangency portfolio should involve a proportionate investment in the stock of Baker equal to .40, but at the current price of Baker there are not enough shares outstanding to meet the demand? In this situation orders to buy Baker will flood in, and brokers will raise the price in search of sellers. The higher price will cause the expected return of Baker to fall, making it less attractive and thereby reducing its proportion in the tangency portfolio to a level at which the number of shares demanded equals the number of shares outstanding.

Ultimately, everything will balance out. When all the price adjusting stops, the market will have been brought into equilibrium. First, each investor will want to hold a certain positive amount of each risky security. Second, the current market price of each security will be at a level where the number of shares demanded equals the number of shares outstanding.[7] Third, the riskfree rate will be at a level where the total amount of money borrowed equals the total amount of money lent. As a result, in equilibrium the proportions of the tangency portfolio will correspond to the proportions of what is known as the **market portfolio**, defined as follows:

The market portfolio is a portfolio consisting of all securities in which the proportion invested in each security corresponds to its relative market value. The relative market value of a security is simply equal to the aggregate market value of the security divided by the sum of the aggregate market values of all securities.[8]

The reason the market portfolio plays a central role in the CAPM is that the efficient set consists of an investment in the market portfolio, coupled with a desired amount of either riskfree borrowing or riskfree lending. Thus it is common practice to refer to the tangency portfolio as the market portfolio and to denote it as M instead of T. In theory, M consists not only of common stocks but also of such other kinds of investments as bonds, preferred stocks, and real estate. However, in practice some people restrict M to just common stocks—a procedure that may give inappropriate results in some applications.

9.2.3 The Efficient Set

In the world of the capital asset pricing model it is a simple matter to determine the relationship between risk and expected return for efficient portfolios. Figure 9.1 portrays it graphically. Point M represents the market portfolio, and r_f represents the riskfree rate of return. Efficient portfolios, which plot along the line starting at r_f and going through M, and consist of alternative combinations of risk and expected return obtainable by combining the market portfolio with riskfree borrowing or lending. This linear efficient set of the CAPM is known as the **capital market line** (CML). All portfolios other than those employing the market portfolio and riskfree borrowing or lending would lie below the CML, although some might plot very close to it.

The slope of the CML is equal to the difference between the expected return of the market portfolio and that of the riskfree security $(\bar{r}_M - r_f)$ divided by the difference in their risks $(\sigma_M - 0)$, or $(\bar{r}_M - r_f)/\sigma_M$.[9] Because the vertical intercept of the CML is r_f, the straight line characterizing the CML has the following equation:

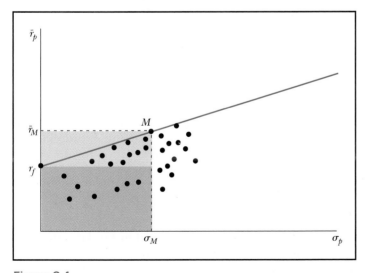

Figure 9.1
The Capital Market Line

The Elusive Market Portfolio

The market portfolio holds a special place in modern investment theory and practice. It is central to the CAPM, which assumes that the market portfolio lies on the efficient set and that all investors hold the market portfolio in combination with a desired amount of riskfree borrowing and riskfree lending. Furthermore, the market portfolio represents the ultimate in diversification. Consequently, passive investors (or index fund managers; see Chapter 23), who do not *bet* on the performance of particular securities but rather desire broad diversification, seek to hold the market portfolio. The market portfolio also serves as a universal performance evaluation standard. Investment managers and their clients often compare the managers' results against the returns on the market portfolio.

Despite its widespread application, the market portfolio is surprisingly ill-defined. In theory, the composition of the market portfolio is simple: All assets are weighted in proportion to their respective market values. In reality, actually identifying the *true* market portfolio (or even a close approximation) is beyond the capability of any individual or organization.

Consider how we might go about specifying the market portfolio. The process would involve two steps: enumerating the assets to be included and calculating the market values of those assets.

First, we must list the various types of assets that constitute the market portfolio. These days we should think globally by considering assets held by investors in both the United States and foreign countries. Of course we want to include all securities representing the assets of businesses. Therefore we should include common stocks, preferred stocks, and corporate bonds. In that vein we should also consider the value of proprietorships and partnerships. How about government debt? This should be considered if the debt is backed by real assets such as buildings. (Because of deficit spending, much of the government's debt is actually backed by future taxes and thus does not represent current wealth—a technical matter often overlooked.) We should also include real estate, cash holdings, monetary metals (primarily gold), and art. But we have not finished yet. We should also include consumer durable assets, such as autos, furniture, and major appliances. Last but certainly not least, we should include the largest asset of all, the training and education in which people have invested vast sums, called *human capital.*

Merely listing the composition of the market portfolio is a complex undertaking. Measuring its value is even more problematic. Given the sophistication of U.S. capital markets, the values of domestic publicly traded assets are relatively easy to collect. (We should be careful, however, to avoid double-counting—for example, when one corporation owns part of another corporation.) Data availability in foreign

$$\bar{r}_p = r_f + \left[\frac{\bar{r}_M - r_f}{\sigma_M} \right] \sigma_p \tag{9.1}$$

where $\bar{r}_p$ and σ_p refer to the expected return and standard deviation of an efficient portfolio.[10] In the previous example, the market portfolio associated with a riskfree rate of 4% consisted of Able, Baker, and Charlie (these stocks are assumed to be the only ones that exist) in the proportions of .12, .19, and .69, respectively. It was shown in Chapter 8 that the expected return and standard deviation for a portfolio with these proportions was 22.4% and 15.2%, respectively. The equation for the resulting CML is:

$$\bar{r}_p = 4 + \left[\frac{22.4 - 4}{15.2} \right] \sigma_p = 4 + 1.21 \sigma_p$$

Equilibrium in the security market can be characterized by two key numbers. The first is the vertical intercept of the CML (that is, the riskfree rate), which is often referred to as the *reward for waiting.* The second is the slope of the CML, which is often referred to as the *reward per unit of risk borne.* In essence, the security market provides a place where time and risk can be traded, with their prices determined by the

markets varies from country to country. In some markets, such as those in the United Kingdom and Japan, security data collection systems are just as sophisticated as those in the United States. In other markets, such as those in emerging markets countries, comprehensive security valuation data are difficult to acquire.

A similar situation exists with respect to non-publicly traded asset values. In some countries, such as the United States, the government attempts to make accurate estimates of myriad asset values from real estate to consumer durable goods. In other countries, little or no effort is made to compile these data.

Finally, with respect to estimating the value of human capital—well, good luck.

The difficulties involved in determining the composition and value of the *true* market portfolio have led to the use of market portfolio proxies. In dealing with common stocks, for example, most researchers and practitioners arbitrarily define the market portfolio to be a broad stock market index, such as the S&P 500 or Russell 3000 or the Wilshire 5000.

What are the ramifications of not knowing the market portfolio's true composition? From a theoretical perspective, the potential problems are significant. In two controversial articles (*Journal of Financial Economics*, March 1977, and *Journal of Finance*, September 1978), Richard Roll argued that the ambiguity of the market portfolio leaves the CAPM untestable. He contended that only if one knows the true market portfolio can one test whether it actually lies on the efficient set. Considering that the CAPM linear relationship between expected return and beta depends on the efficiency of the market portfolio, Roll's argument should not be taken lightly. Furthermore, Roll argued that the practice of using proxies for the market portfolio is loaded with problems. Different proxies, even if their returns are highly correlated, could lead to different beta estimates for the same security. Roll's arguments, it should be noted, were strongly contested by prominent CAPM defenders.

From a practical perspective, investors have generally been willing to overlook the market portfolio's ambiguity. Passive managers typically segment the market into various asset classes, such as stocks and bonds, or into even finer subclasses, such as large and small stocks. They then define somewhat arbitrarily a market portfolio for each of those asset classes and construct portfolios to track the performance of the respective asset class market portfolios. Similarly, active managers frequently refer to a designated market portfolio when they devise their investment strategies. Performance evaluators employ market proxies in their CAPM-risk-adjusted return calculations (see Chapter 24). For now these uses appear to be the best that can be done in using the market portfolio for portfolio management and evaluation.

forces of supply and demand. Thus the intercept and slope of the CML can be thought of as the *price of time* and the *price of risk*, respectively. In the example, they are equal to 4% and 1.21, respectively.

9.3 THE SECURITY MARKET LINE

9.3.1 Implications for Individual Risky Assets

The capital market line represents the equilibrium relationship between the expected return and standard deviation for efficient portfolios. Individual risky securities will always plot below the line because a single risky security when held by itself is an inefficient portfolio. The capital asset pricing model does not imply any particular relationship between the expected return and the standard deviation (that is, total risk) of an individual security. To say more about the expected return of an individual security requires deeper analysis.

In Chapter 6 the following equation was given for calculating the standard deviation of any portfolio:

$$\sigma_p = \left[\sum_{i=1}^{N} \sum_{j=1}^{N} X_i X_j \sigma_{ij} \right]^{1/2} \tag{6.7}$$

where X_i and X_j denoted the proportions invested in securities i and j, respectively, and σ_{ij} denoted the covariance of returns between security i and j. Now consider using this equation to calculate the standard deviation of the market portfolio:

$$\sigma_M = \left[\sum_{i=1}^{N} \sum_{j=1}^{N} X_{iM} X_{jM} \sigma_{ij} \right]^{1/2} \tag{9.2}$$

where X_{iM} and X_{jM} denote the proportions invested in securities i and j in forming the market portfolio, respectively. It can be shown that another way to write Equation (9.2) is as follows:

$$\sigma_M = \left[X_{1M} \sum_{j=1}^{N} X_{jM} \sigma_{1j} + X_{2M} \sum_{j=1}^{N} X_{jM} \sigma_{2j} + X_{3M} \sum_{j=1}^{N} X_{jM} \sigma_{3j} + \cdots + X_{NM} \sum_{j=1}^{N} X_{jM} \sigma_{Nj} \right]^{1/2} \tag{9.3}$$

At this point a property of covariance can be used: The covariance of security i with the market portfolio (σ_{iM}) can be expressed as the weighted average of every security's covariance with security i:

$$\sum_{j=1}^{N} X_{jM} \sigma_{ij} = \sigma_{iM} \tag{9.4}$$

This property, when applied to each one of the N risky securities in the market portfolio, results in the following:

$$\sigma_M = \left[X_{1M} \sigma_{1M} + X_{2M} \sigma_{2M} + X_{3M} \sigma_{3M} + \cdots + X_{NM} \sigma_{NM} \right]^{1/2} \tag{9.5}$$

where σ_{1M} denotes the covariance of security 1 with the market portfolio, σ_{2M} denotes the covariance of security 2 with the market portfolio, and so on. Thus the standard deviation of the market portfolio is equal to the square root of a weighted average of the covariances of all the securities with it, where the weights are equal to the proportions of the respective securities in the market portfolio.

At this juncture an important point can be observed. Under the CAPM, each investor holds the market portfolio and is concerned with its standard deviation because this will influence the slope of the CML and hence the magnitude of his or her investment in the market portfolio. The contribution of each security to the standard deviation of the market portfolio can be seen in Equation (9.5) to depend on the size of its covariance with the market portfolio. Accordingly each investor will note that *the relevant measure of risk for a security is its covariance with the market portfolio, σ_{iM}.* This statement means that securities with larger values of σ_{iM} will be viewed by investors as contributing more to the risk of the market portfolio. It also means that securities with larger standard deviations should not be viewed as necessarily adding more risk to the market portfolio than those securities with smaller standard deviations.[11] From this analysis it follows that securities with larger values for σ_{iM} have to provide proportionately larger expected returns to interest investors in purchasing them. To see why, consider what would happen if such securities did not provide investors with proportionately larger levels of expected return. In this situation, these securities would contribute to the risk of the market portfolio while not contributing proportionately to the expected return of the market portfolio. Deleting such securities from the market portfolio would cause the expected return of the market portfolio relative to its standard deviation to rise. Because investors would view this as a favorable change, the market portfolio would no longer be the optimal risky portfolio to hold. Thus security prices would be out of equilibrium.

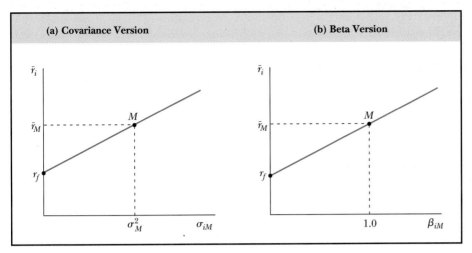

Figure 9.2
The Security Market Line

The exact form of the equilibrium relationship between risk and return can be written as follows:

$$\bar{r}_i = r_f + \left[\frac{\bar{r}_M - r_f}{\sigma_M^2}\right]\sigma_{iM} \tag{9.6}$$

As can be seen in Figure 9.2(a), Equation (9.6) represents a straight line having a vertical intercept of r_f and a slope of $\left[(\bar{r}_M - r_f)/\sigma_M^2\right]$. Because the slope is positive, the equation indicates that securities with larger covariances with the market (σ_{iM}) will be priced so as to have larger expected returns $(\bar{r}_i)$. This relationship between covariance and expected return is known as the **security market line** (SML).[12]

Interestingly, a risky security with $\sigma_{iM} = 0$ will have an expected return equal to the rate on the riskfree security, r_f. Why? Because this risky security, just like the riskfree security, will not affect the risk of the market portfolio when a marginal change is made in its weight. This is so even though the risky security has a positive standard deviation, whereas the riskfree security has a standard deviation of zero.

It is even possible for some risky securities (meaning securities with positive standard deviations) to have expected returns less than the riskfree rate. According to the CAPM, this will occur if $\sigma_{iM} < 0$, thereby indicating that they contribute a negative amount of risk to the market portfolio (meaning that they cause the risk of the market portfolio to be lower than it would be if less money were invested in them).

Also of interest is the observation that a risky security with $\sigma_{iM} = \sigma_M^2$ will have an expected return equal to the expected return on the market portfolio, $\bar{r}_M$. Such a security contributes an average amount of risk to the market portfolio.

Another way of expressing the SML is as follows:

$$\bar{r}_i = r_f + (\bar{r}_M - r_f)\beta_{iM} \tag{9.7}$$

where the term β_{iM} is defined as:

$$\beta_{iM} = \frac{\sigma_{iM}}{\sigma_M^2} \tag{9.8}$$

The term β_{iM} is known as the **beta coefficient** (or simply the beta) for security i, and is an alternative way of representing the covariance of a security. Equation (9.7) is a different version of the SML as can be seen in Figure 9.2(b). Although having the same intercept as the earlier version shown in Equation (9.6), r_f, it has a different slope. The slope of this version is $(\overline{r}_M - r_f)$, whereas the slope of the earlier version was $[(\overline{r}_M - r_f)/\sigma_M^2]$.

One property of beta is that the beta of a portfolio is simply a weighted average of the betas of its component securities, where the proportions invested in the securities are the respective weights. That is, the beta of a portfolio can be calculated as:

$$\beta_{pM} = \sum_{i=1}^{N} X_i \beta_{iM} \qquad (9.9)$$

Earlier it was shown that the expected return of a portfolio is a weighted average of the expected returns of its component securities, where the proportions invested in the securities are the weights. Therefore, every portfolio plots on the SML because every security plots on the SML. To put it more broadly, not only every security but also every portfolio must plot on an upward-sloping straight line in a diagram with expected return on the vertical axis and beta on the horizontal axis. So efficient portfolios plot on both the CML and the SML, although inefficient portfolios plot on the SML but below the CML.

Also of interest is that the SML must go through the point representing the market portfolio itself. Its beta is 1 and its expected return is $\overline{r}_M$, so its coordinates are $(1, \overline{r}_M)$. Because riskfree securities have beta values of 0, the SML will also go through a point with an expected return of r_f and coordinates of $(0, r_f)$. As a result, the SML will have a vertical intercept equal to r_f and a slope equal to the vertical distance between these two points $(\overline{r}_M - r_f)$ divided by the horizontal distance between these two points $(1 - 0)$, or $(\overline{r}_M - r_f)/(1 - 0) = (\overline{r}_M - r_f)$. Thus these two points suffice to fix the location of the SML, indicating the appropriate expected returns for securities and portfolios with different beta values.

The equilibrium relationship shown by the SML comes to exist through the combined effects of investors' adjustments in holdings and the resulting pressures on security prices (as shown in Chapter 4). Given a set of security prices, investors calculate expected returns and covariances and then determine their optimal portfolios. If the number of shares of a security collectively desired differs from the number available, there will be upward or downward pressure on its price. Given a new set of prices, investors will reassess their desires for the various securities. The process will continue until the number of shares collectively desired for each security equals the number available.

For the individual investor, security prices and prospects are fixed while the quantities held can be altered. For the market as a whole, however, these quantities are fixed (at least in the short run), and prices are variable. As in any competitive market, equilibrium requires the adjustment of each security's price until there is consistency between the quantity desired and the quantity available.

It may seem logical to examine historical returns on securities to determine whether securities have been priced in equilibrium as suggested by the CAPM. However, the issue of whether such testing of the CAPM can be done in a meaningful manner is controversial. For at least some purposes, affirmative test results may not be necessary to make practical use of the CAPM.

9.3.2 An Example

In the example that was used earlier, Able, Baker, and Charlie were shown to form the market portfolio in proportions equal to .12, .19, and .69, respectively. With these proportions, the market portfolio was shown to have an expected return of 22.4% and a standard deviation of 15.2%. The riskfree rate in the example was 4%. Thus for this example the SML as indicated in Equation (9.6) is:

$$\bar{r}_i = r_f + \left[\frac{\bar{r}_M - r_f}{\sigma_M^2}\right]\sigma_{iM} \tag{9.6}$$

$$= 4 + \left[\frac{22.4 - 4}{(15.2)^2}\right]\sigma_{iM}$$

$$= 4 + .08\sigma_{iM} \tag{9.10}$$

The following expected return vector and variance-covariance matrix that were used in the examples shown in Chapters 6, 7, and 8 are also used here:

$$ER = \begin{bmatrix} 16.2 \\ 24.6 \\ 22.8 \end{bmatrix} \qquad VC = \begin{bmatrix} 146 & 187 & 145 \\ 187 & 854 & 104 \\ 145 & 104 & 289 \end{bmatrix}$$

At this point, the covariance of each security with the market portfolio can be calculated by using Equation (9.4). More specifically, the covariances with the market portfolio for Able, Baker, and Charlie are equal to:

$$\sigma_{1M} = \sum_{j=1}^{3} X_{jM}\sigma_{1j}$$

$$= (.12 \times 146) + (.19 \times 187) + (.69 \times 145)$$

$$= 153$$

$$\sigma_{2M} = \sum_{j=1}^{3} X_{jM}\sigma_{2j}$$

$$(.12 \times 187) + (.19 \times 854) + (.69 \times 104)$$

$$= 257$$

$$\sigma_{3M} = \sum_{j=1}^{3} X_{jM}\sigma_{3j}$$

$$= (.12 \times 145) + (.19 \times 104) + (.69 \times 289)$$

$$= 236$$

Note that the SML as given in Equation (9.10) states that the expected return for Able should be equal to $4 + (.08 \times 153) = 16.2\%$. Similarly, the expected return for Baker should be $4 + (.08 \times 257) = 24.6\%$, and the expected return for Charlie should be $4 + (.08 \times 236) = 22.8\%$. Each of these expected returns corresponds to the respective value given in the expected return vector.

Alternatively, Equation (9.8) can be used to calculate the betas for the three companies. More specifically, the betas for Able, Baker, and Charlie are equal to:

$$\beta_{1M} = \frac{\sigma_{1M}}{\sigma_M^2}$$

$$= \frac{153}{(15.2)^2}$$

$$= .66$$

$$\beta_{2M} = \frac{\sigma_{2M}}{\sigma_M^2}$$

$$= \frac{257}{(15.2)^2}$$

$$= 1.11$$

$$\beta_{3M} = \frac{\sigma_{3M}}{\sigma_M^2}$$

$$= \frac{236}{(15.2)^2}$$

$$= 1.02$$

Now, Equation (9.7) indicated that the SML could be expressed in a form wherein the measure of risk for an asset was its beta. For the example under consideration, this reduces to:

$$\bar{r}_i = r_f + (\bar{r}_M - r_f)\beta_{iM}$$

$$= 4 + (22.4 - 4)\beta_{iM}$$

$$= 4 + 18.4\beta_{iM} \tag{9.11}$$

Note that the SML as given in this equation states that the expected return for Able should be equal to $4 + (18.4 \times .66) = 16.2\%$. Similarly, the expected return for Baker should be $4 + (18.4 \times 1.11) = 24.6\%$, and the expected return for Charlie should be $4 + (18.4 \times 1.02) = 22.8\%$. Each of these expected returns corresponds to the respective value given in the expected return vector.

It is important to realize that if any other portfolio is assumed to be the market portfolio, meaning that if any set of proportions other than .12, .19, and .69 is used, then such an equilibrium relationship between expected returns and betas (or covariances) will not hold. Consider a hypothetical market portfolio with equal proportions (that is, .333) invested in Able, Baker, and Charlie. Because this portfolio has an expected return of 21.2% and a standard deviation of 15.5%, the hypothetical SML would be as follows:

$$\bar{r}_i = r_f + \left[\frac{\bar{r}_M - r_f}{\sigma_M^2}\right]\sigma_{iM}$$

$$= r_f + \left[\frac{21.2 - 4}{(15.5)^2}\right]\sigma_{iM}$$

$$= 4 + .07\sigma_{iM}$$

Able has a covariance with this portfolio of:

$$\sigma_{1M} = \sum_{j=1}^{3} X_{jM}\sigma_{1j}$$

$$= (.333 \times 146) + (.333 \times 187) + (.333 \times 145)$$

$$= 159$$

which means that Able's expected return according to the hypothetical SML should be equal to $15.1\% = 4 + (.07 \times 159)$. However, because this does not correspond to the 16.2% figure that appears in the expected return vector, a portfolio with equal proportions invested in Able, Baker, and Charlie cannot be the market portfolio.[13]

| **9.4** | ## THE MARKET MODEL |

Chapter 7 introduced the market model, wherein the return on a common stock was assumed to be related to the return on a market index in the following manner:

$$r_i = \alpha_{iI} + \beta_{iI} r_I + \varepsilon_{iI} \qquad (7.3)$$

where:

> r_i = return on security i for some given period
> r_I = return on market index for the same period
> α_{iI} = intercept term
> β_{iI} = slope term
> ε_{iI} = random error term

It is natural to think about the relationship between the market model and the capital asset pricing model. After all, both models have a slope term called "beta" in them, and both models somehow involve the market. However, there are two significant differences between the models.

First, the market model is a *factor model*, or to be more specific, a single-factor model in which the factor is a market index. Unlike the CAPM, however, it is not an *equilibrium model* that describes how prices are set for securities.

Second, the market model utilizes a *market index* such as the S&P 500, whereas the CAPM involves the *market portfolio*. The market portfolio is a collection of all the securities in the marketplace, whereas a market index is based on a sample of the market broadly construed (for example, 500 in the case of the S&P 500). Therefore, conceptually the beta of a stock based on the market model, β_{iI}, differs from the beta of the stock according to the CAPM, β_{iM} because the market model beta is measured relative to a market index whereas the CAPM beta is measured relative to the market portfolio. In practice, however, the composition of the market portfolio is not precisely known, so a market index is used. Thus, although conceptually different, betas determined with the use of a market index are often treated as if they were determined with the use of the market portfolio. That is, β_{iI} is used as an estimate of β_{iM}.

In the example, only three securities were in existence: the common stocks of Able, Baker, and Charlie. Subsequent analysis indicated that the CAPM market portfolio consisted of these stocks in the proportions of .12, .19, and .69, respectively. It is against this portfolio that the betas of the securities should be measured. However, in practice they are likely to be measured against a market index (for example, one that is based on just the stocks of Able and Charlie in proportions of .20 and .80, respectively).

9.4.1 Market Indices

One of the most widely known indices is the Standard & Poor's Stock Price Index (referred to earlier as the S&P 500), a value-weighted average price of 500 large stocks. Complete coverage of the stocks listed on the New York Stock Exchange is provided by the NYSE Composite Index, which is broader than the S&P 500 in that it considers more stocks. The American Stock Exchange computes a similar index (the Amex Composite) for the stocks it lists, and the National Association of Security Dealers provides an index of over-the-counter stocks traded on the Nasdaq system (the Nasdaq Composite). The Russell 3000 and Wilshire 5000 stock indices are the most comprehensive indices of U.S. common stock prices published regularly in the United States. Because they consist of both listed and over-the-counter stocks, they are closer than the others to representing the overall performance of U.S. stocks.[14]

Without question the most widely quoted market index is the Dow Jones Industrial Average (DJIA). Although based on the performance of only 30 stocks and utilizing a less satisfactory averaging procedure than the other indices use, the DJIA provides at least a fair idea of what is happening to stock prices.[15] Table 9.1 provides a listing of the 30 stocks whose prices are reflected in the DJIA.

The Capital Asset Pricing Model

TABLE 9.1	Stocks in the Dow Jones Industrial Average
Alcoa	IBM
Allied Signal	International Paper
American Express	Johnson & Johnson
AT&T	McDonald's
Boeing	Merck
Caterpillar	Minnesota Mining and Manufacturing (3M)
Chevron	J. P. Morgan
Coca-Cola	Philip Morris
DuPont	Procter & Gamble
Eastman Kodak	Sears, Roebuck
Exxon	Traveler's Group
General Electric	Union Carbide
General Motors	United Technologies
Goodyear Tire	Wal-Mart Stores
Hewlett-Packard	Walt Disney

Source: Web site ⟨http://djia100.dowjones.com/frameset.html⟩, June 3, 1997.

9.4.2   Market and Non-Market Risk

In Chapter 7 it was shown that the total risk of a security, σ_i^2, could be partitioned into two components as follows:

$$\sigma_i^2 = \beta_{iI}^2 \sigma_I^2 + \sigma_{\varepsilon i}^2 \tag{7.8}$$

where the components are:

$$\beta_{iI}^2 \sigma_I^2 = \text{market risk}$$
$$\sigma_{\varepsilon i}^2 = \text{unique risk}$$

Because beta, or covariance, is the relevant measure of risk for a security according to the CAPM, it is only appropriate to explore the relationship between it and the total risk of the security. It turns out that the relationship is identical to that given in Equation (7.8) *except that the market portfolio is involved instead of a market index:*

$$\sigma_i^2 = \beta_{iM}^2 \sigma_M^2 + \sigma_{\varepsilon i}^2 \tag{9.12}$$

As in the market model, the total risk of security i, measured by its variance and denoted σ_i^2, is shown to consist of two parts. The first component is the portion related to moves of the market portfolio. It is equal to the product of the square of the beta of the stock and the variance of the market portfolio and also is often referred to as the **market risk** of the security. The second component is the portion not related to moves of the market portfolio. It is denoted $\sigma_{\varepsilon i}^2$ and can be considered **non-market risk.** Under the assumptions of the market model, it is also unique to the security in question and hence is also termed *unique risk*. Note that if β_{iI} is treated as an estimate of β_{iM} then the decomposition of σ_i^2 is the same in Equations (7.8) and (9.12).

9.4.3   An Example

From the earlier example, the betas of Able, Baker, and Charlie were calculated to be .66, 1.11, and 1.02, respectively. Because the standard deviation of the market portfolio was equal to 15.2%, the market risk of the three firms is equal to $(.66^2 \times 15.2^2) = 100$, $(1.11^2 \times 15.2^2) = 285$, and $(1.02^2 \times 15.2^2) = 240$, respectively.

The non-market risk of any security can be calculated by solving Equation (9.12) for $\sigma_{\varepsilon i}^2$:

$$\sigma_{\varepsilon i}^2 = \sigma_i^2 - \beta_{iM}^2 \sigma_M^2 \qquad (9.13)$$

Thus, Equation (9.13) can be used to calculate the non-market risk of Able, Baker, and Charlie, respectively:

$$\sigma_{\varepsilon 1}^2 = 146 - 100$$
$$= 46$$
$$\sigma_{\varepsilon 2}^2 = 854 - 285$$
$$= 569$$
$$\sigma_{\varepsilon 3}^2 = 289 - 240$$
$$= 49$$

Non-market risk is sometimes expressed as a standard deviation. This is calculated by taking the square root of $\sigma_{\varepsilon i}^2$ and would be equal to $\sqrt{46} = 6.8\%$ for Able, $\sqrt{569} = 23.9\%$ for Baker, and $\sqrt{49} = 7\%$ for Charlie.

9.4.4 Motivation for the Partitioning of Risk

At this point one may wonder: Why partition total risk into two parts? For the investor, it would seem that risk is risk—whatever its source. The answer lies in the domain of expected returns.

Market risk is related to the risk of the market portfolio and to the beta of the security in question. Securities with larger betas will have larger amounts of market risk. In the world of the CAPM, securities with larger betas will have larger expected returns. These two relationships together imply that securities with larger market risks should have larger expected returns.

Non-market risk is not related to beta. There is no reason why securities with larger amounts of non-market risks should have larger expected returns. Thus according to the CAPM, investors are rewarded for bearing market risk but not for bearing non-market risk.

9.5 SUMMARY

1. The capital asset pricing model (CAPM) is based on a specific set of assumptions about investor behavior and the existence of perfect security markets.
2. On the basis of these assumptions, it can be stated that all investors will hold the same efficient portfolio of risky assets.
3. Investors will differ only in the amounts of riskfree borrowing or lending they undertake.
4. The risky portfolio held by all investors is known as the market portfolio.

---

5. The market portfolio consists of all securities, each weighted in proportion to its market value relative to the market value of all securities.

6. The linear efficient set of the CAPM is known as the capital market line (CML). The CML represents the equilibrium relationship between the expected return and standard deviation of efficient portfolios.

7. Under the CAPM the relevant measure of risk for determining a security's expected return is its covariance with the market portfolio.

8. The linear relationship between market covariance and expected return is known as the security market line (SML).

9. The beta of a security is an alternative way of measuring the risk that a security adds to the market portfolio. Beta is a measure of the covariance between the security and the market portfolio relative to the market portfolio's variance.

10. The beta from the CAPM is similar in concept to the beta from the market model. However, the market model is not an equilibrium model of security prices as is the CAPM. Furthermore, the market model uses a market index, which is a subset of the CAPM's market portfolio.

11. Under the CAPM, the total risk of a security can be separated into market risk and non-market risk. Each security's non-market risk is unique to that security and hence is also termed its unique risk.

QUESTIONS AND PROBLEMS

1. Describe the key assumptions underlying the CAPM.

2. Many of the underlying assumptions of the CAPM are violated to some degree in the real world. Does that fact invalidate the model's conclusions? Explain.

3. What is the separation theorem? What implications does it have for the optimal portfolio of risky assets held by investors?

4. What constitutes the *market portfolio*? What problems does one confront in specifying the composition of the true market portfolio? How have researchers and practitioners circumvented these problems?

5. In the equilibrium world of the CAPM, is it possible for a security not to be part of the market portfolio? Explain.

6. Describe the price adjustment process that equilibrates the market's supply and demand for securities. What conditions will prevail under such an equilibrium?

7. Will an investor who owns the market portfolio have to buy and sell units of the component securities every time the relative prices of those securities change? Why?

8. Given an expected return of 12% for the market portfolio, a riskfree rate of 6%, and a market portfolio standard deviation of 20%, draw the capital market line.

9. Explain the significance of the capital market line.

10. Assume that two securities constitute the market portfolio. Those securities have the following expected returns, standard deviations, and proportions:

Security	Expected Return	Standard Deviation	Proportion
A	10%	20%	.4
B	15	28	.6

On the basis of this information, and given a correlation of .30 between the two securities and a riskfree rate of 5%, specify the equation for the capital market line.

11. Distinguish between the capital market line and the security market line.

12. The market portfolio is assumed to be composed of four securities. Their co-variances with the market portfolio and their proportions are shown below:

Security	Covariance with Market	Proportion
A	242	.2
B	360	.3
C	155	.2
D	210	.3

Given these data, calculate the market portfolio's standard deviation.

13. Explain the significance of the slope of the SML. How might the slope of the SML change over time?

14. Why should the expected return for a security be directly related to the security's covariance with the market portfolio?

15. The risk of a well-diversified portfolio to an investor is measured by the standard deviation of the portfolio's returns. Why shouldn't the risk of an individual security be calculated in the same manner?

16. The riskfree rate is 5% while the market portfolio's expected return is 12%. If the standard deviation of the market portfolio is 13%, what is the equilibrium expected return on a security that has a covariance with the market portfolio of 186?

17. A security with a high standard deviation of returns is not necessarily highly risky to an investor. Why might you suspect that securities with above-average standard deviations tend to have above-average betas?

18. Oil Smith, an investments student, argued, "A security with a positive standard deviation must have an expected return greater than the riskfree rate. Otherwise, why would anyone be willing to hold the security?" On the basis of the CAPM, is Oil's statement correct? Why?

19. The standard deviation of the market portfolio is 15%. Given the covariances with the market portfolio of the following securities, calculate their betas.

Security	Covariance
A	292
B	180
C	225

20. Kitty Bransfield owns a portfolio composed of three securities. The betas of those securities and their proportions in Kitty's portfolio are shown here. What is the beta of Kitty's portfolio?

Security	Beta	Proportion
A	.90	.3
B	1.30	.1
C	1.05	.6

21. Assume that the expected return on the market portfolio is 15% and its standard deviation is 21%. The riskfree rate is 7%. What is the standard deviation of a well-diversified (no non-market-risk) portfolio with an expected return of 16.6%?

22. Given that the expected return on the market portfolio is 10%, the riskfree rate of return is 6%, the beta of stock A is .85, and the beta of stock B is 1.20:

a. Draw the SML.
b. What is the equation for the SML?
c. What are the equilibrium expected returns for stocks A and B?
d. Plot the two risky securities on the SML.

23. You are given the following information on two securities, the market portfolio, and the riskfree rate:

	Expected Return	Correlation with Market Portfolio	Standard Deviation
Security 1	15.5%	0.9	20.0%
Security 2	9.2	0.8	9.0
Market portfolio	12.0	1.0	12.0
Riskfree rate	5.0	0.0	0.0

a. Draw the SML.
b. What are the betas of the two securities?
c. Plot the two securities on the SML.

24. The SML describes an equilibrium relationship between risk and expected return. Would you consider a security that plotted above the SML to be an attractive investment? Why?

25. Assume that two securities, A and B, constitute the market portfolio. Their proportions and variances are .39, 160, and .61, 340, respectively. The covariance of the two securities is 190. Calculate the betas of the two securities.

26. The CAPM permits the standard deviation of a security to be segmented into market and non-market risk. Distinguish between the two types of risk.

27. Is an investor who owns any portfolio of risky assets other than the market portfolio exposed to some non-market risk? Explain.

28. On the basis of the risk and return relationships of the CAPM, supply values for the seven missing numbers in the following table.

Security	Expected Return	Beta	Standard Deviation	Non-market Risk $(\sigma_{\varepsilon i}^2)$
A	____ %	0.8	____ %	81
B	19.0	1.5	____	36
C	15.0	____	12	0
D	7.0	0	8	____
E	16.6	____	15	____

29. (Appendix Question) Describe how the SML is altered when the riskfree borrowing rate exceeds the riskfree lending rate.

CFA EXAM QUESTIONS

30. The following information describes the expected return and risk relationship for the stocks of two of WAH's competitors.

	Expected Return	Standard Deviation	Beta
Stock X	12.0%	20%	1.3
Stock Y	9.0	15	0.7
Market index	10.0	12	1.0
Riskfree rate	5.0		

Using only the data shown above:

a. Draw and label a graph showing the security market line and position stocks *X* and *Y* relative to it.
b. Compute the alphas both for stock *X* and for stock *Y*. Show your work. (Hint: Alpha is the difference between the stock's expected return and the equilibrium expected return given by the SML.)
c. Assume that the riskfree rate increases to 7% with the other data remaining unchanged. Select the stock providing the higher expected risk-adjusted return and justify your selection. Show your calculations.

APPENDIX A

SOME EXTENDED VERSIONS OF THE CAPM

The original capital asset pricing model makes strong assumptions and gives strong implications. In the years since it was developed, more complex models have been proposed. These models generally involve relaxing some of the assumptions associated with the original CAPM and are often referred to as *extended versions of the CAPM*, or extended capital asset pricing models. Some of them are described in this appendix.

A.1 IMPOSING RESTRICTIONS ON RISKFREE BORROWING

A.1.1 The Capital Market Line

The original CAPM assumes that investors can lend or borrow at the same riskfree rate of interest. In reality, such borrowing is likely to be either unavailable or restricted in amount. What impact might the relaxation of this riskfree borrowing assumption have on the CAPM?

A useful way to answer the question makes the following assumptions: (1) Investors can lend money risklessly—that is, they can purchase assets that provide a riskfree return of r_{fL}, and (2) investors can borrow money without limit at a higher rate of interest, r_{fB}. These riskfree rates are shown on the vertical axis of Figure 9.3; the umbrella area represents risk-return combinations available from investment solely in risky assets.[16]

If there were no opportunities to borrow or lend at the riskfree rate, the efficient set would be the curve $WT_L T_B Y$, and many combinations of risky securities would be efficient. However, the availability of riskfree lending at the rate r_{fL} makes the risky portfolios between *W* and T_L inefficient, because combinations of riskfree lending and the portfolio plotting at T_L provide more return for the same risk.

Similarly, the ability to borrow money at rate r_{fB} makes another portfolio, denoted by T_B, of special interest. Risky portfolios between T_B and *Y* are now ineffi-

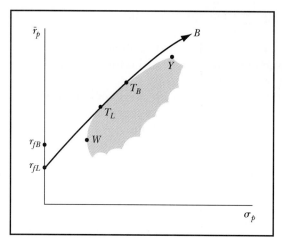

Figure 9.3
Efficient Set When the Riskfree Rates Are Different

cient, because leveraged holdings of T_B dominate them by providing more return for the same risk.

Investors with attitudes toward risk that suggest neither borrowing nor lending should hold efficient combinations of risky securities plotting along curve $T_L T_B$. Accordingly, their holdings should be tailored to be consistent with differences in their degrees of aversion to risk.

In this situation the CML is now two lines and a curve, corresponding to the line going from r_{fL} to T_L, then the curve from T_L to T_B, and then the line from T_B on out to the northeast in Figure 9.3.

A.1.2   The Security Market Line

What becomes of the security market line when the riskfree borrowing rate exceeds the riskfree lending rate? The answer depends on whether the market portfolio is in fact one of the efficient combinations of risky securities along the boundary between T_L and T_B in Figure 9.3.[17] If it is not, little can be said other than that the CAPM does not hold. If it is, a great deal can be said.

Figure 9.4 shows a case in which the market portfolio (shown by point M) is efficient. In panel (a) a line has been drawn that is tangent to the efficient set at point M. When this line is extended to the vertical axis, the resulting intercept is denoted $\bar{r}_z$. In panel (b) only this tangency line is shown.

A striking characteristic of Figure 9.4(b) is this: It is precisely the same picture that would be produced in a market in which investors could borrow and lend without limit at a hypothetical riskfree rate equal in value to $\bar{r}_z$. Whereas only point M along the line emanating from $\bar{r}_z$ would be attainable, the expected returns of risky securities would be the same as they would be in a hypothetical market with borrowing and lending at $\bar{r}_z$. That is, all risky securities (and portfolios consisting of those securities) would plot along an SML going through point $\bar{r}_z$, as shown in Figure 9.5.

The vertical intercept of the SML indicates the expected return on a security or portfolio with a beta of zero. Accordingly, this extension of the CAPM is termed the *zero-beta capital asset pricing model*. This version of the CAPM implies that the SML will be flatter than implied by the original version, because $\bar{r}_z$ will be above r_{fL}. As a practical matter, it means that $\bar{r}_z$ must be inferred from the prices of risky securities, because it cannot simply be found in the quotations of current prices on, for example,

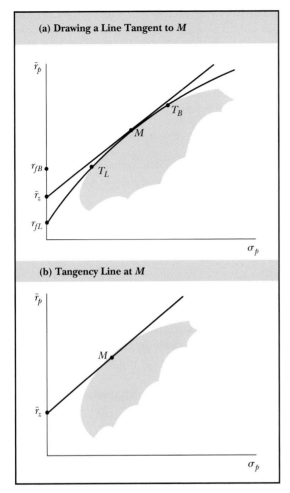

(a) Drawing a Line Tangent to M

(b) Tangency Line at M

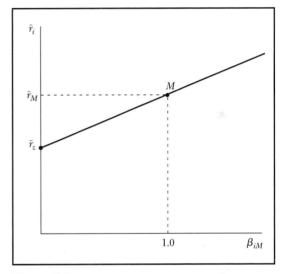

Figure 9.4
Risk and Return When the Market Portfolio Is Efficient

Figure 9.5
The Zero-Beta Security Market Line

Treasury bills. Many organizations that estimate the SML generally find that it conforms more to the zero-beta CAPM than to the original CAPM.

Cases in which borrowing is either impossible or costs more as one borrows larger amounts lead to only minor modifications in the conclusions. As long as the market portfolio is efficient, all securities will plot along an SML, but the "zero-beta return" will exceed the riskfree rate at which funds can be invested.

A.2   INTRODUCING HETEROGENEOUS EXPECTATIONS

A number of researchers have examined the implications of assuming that different investors have different perceptions about expected returns, standard deviations, and covariances. More specifically, the assumption of homogeneous expectations has been replaced by these researchers with an assumption of *heterogeneous expectations*.

In one such study, it was noted that each investor would face an efficient set that was unique to him or her.[18] This means that the tangency portfolio (denoted by T in Chapter 8) is unique to each investor, because the optimal combination of risky assets for an investor depends on that investor's perceptions about expected returns, standard deviations, and covariances. Furthermore, an investor will likely determine that his or her tangency portfolio does not involve an investment in some securities (that is, certain securities may have zero proportions in the tangency portfolio). Nevertheless, in equilibrium each security's price still has to be at a level where the amount of the security demanded equals the supply of the security. Now, however, the equilibrium expected return for each security will be a complex weighted average of all investors' perceptions of its expected return.

A.3	LIQUIDITY

The original CAPM assumes that investors are concerned only with risk and return. However, other characteristics may also be important to investors. For example, *liquidity* may be important. Here, liquidity refers to the cost of selling or buying a security "in a hurry." A house is regarded as a relatively illiquid investment, because usually a "fair" price for it cannot be obtained quickly. In terms of securities, liquidity may be estimated by the size of the spread between the bid and asked prices, with smaller spreads suggesting greater liquidity. Furthermore, it is reasonable to assume that many investors would find more liquid securities to be more attractive, keeping everything else the same. However, investors undoubtedly differ in their attitudes toward liquidity. For some it is very important; for others, somewhat important; and for yet others, of little importance.

Under these conditions, security prices would adjust until, overall, investors would be content to hold all of the outstanding securities. The expected return of a security would be based on two characteristics of the security:

1. The marginal contribution of the security to the risk of an efficient portfolio. This would be measured by the familiar beta (β_{iM}) of the security.
2. The marginal contribution of the security to the liquidity of an efficient portfolio. This would be measured by the liquidity (L_i) of the security.

Now, other things being equal, investors dislike large values of β_{iM} but like large values of L_i. This means that two securities with the same beta but different liquidities would not have the same level of expected return. To understand why they would have different levels of expected return, consider what would happen if they had the same level of expected return. In such a situation investors would buy the security with the greater liquidity and sell the one with the lesser liquidity. The price of the first security would be pushed up, and that of the second one down. Ultimately, in equilibrium the quantity demanded would equal the quantity supplied, and the security with the greater liquidity would have a relatively lower expected return. Similarly, two securities with the same liquidity but different betas would not have the same level of expected return. Instead, the security with the higher beta would have a higher expected return.[19]

Figure 9.6 shows the equilibrium relationship one might expect among $\bar{r}_i$, β_{iM}, and L_i. For a given level of β_{iM}, securities that are more liquid have lower expected returns. And for a given level of L_i, riskier securities have higher expected returns, as in the original CAPM. Last, there are securities with various levels of β_{iM}, and L_i that provide the same level of $\bar{r}_i$. The figure is three-dimensional, because now expected returns are related to two characteristics of securities. Accordingly, it is sometimes referred to as a *Security Market Plane*.[20]

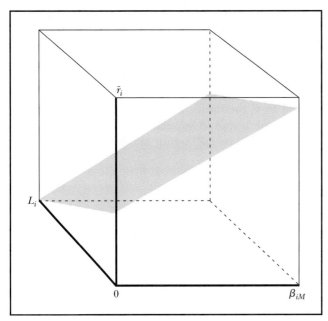

Figure 9.6
Security Market Plane

If expected returns are based on beta, liquidity, and a third characteristic, then a four-dimensional CAPM would be necessary to describe the corresponding equilibrium.[21] Although a diagram cannot be drawn for this type of extended CAPM, an equation can be written for it. Such an equation, by analogy to the three-dimensional plane, is termed a *hyperplane*.

> *In equilibrium, all securities will plot on a security market hyperplane, where each axis measures the contribution of a security to a characteristic of efficient portfolios that matters (on average) to investors.*

The relationship between the expected return of a security and its contribution to a particular characteristic of efficient portfolios depends on the attitudes of investors to the characteristic:

> *If, on the average, a characteristic (such as liquidity) is liked by investors, then those securities that contribute more to that characteristic will, other things being equal, offer lower expected returns. Conversely, if a characteristic (such as beta) is disliked by investors, then those securities that contribute more to that characteristic will offer higher expected returns.*

In a capital market with many relevant characteristics, the task of tailoring a portfolio for a specific investor is more complicated, because only an investor with average attitudes and circumstances should hold the market portfolio. In general:

> *If an investor likes a characteristic more (or dislikes it less) than the average investor, he or she should generally hold a portfolio with relatively more of that characteristic than is provided by holding the market portfolio. Conversely, if an investor likes a characteristic less (or dislikes it more) than the average investor, he or she should generally hold a portfolio with relatively less of that characteristic than is provided by holding the market portfolio.*

For example, consider an investor who likes having a relatively liquid portfolio. Such an investor should hold a portfolio consisting of relatively liquid securities.

The Capital Asset Pricing Model

Conversely, an investor who has relatively little need for liquidity should hold a portfolio of relatively illiquid securities.

The right combination of "tilt" away from market proportions will depend on the extent of the differences between the investor's attitudes and those of the average investor and on the added risk involved in such a strategy. A complex capital market requires all the tools of modern portfolio theory for managing the money of any investor who is significantly different from the "average investor." On the other hand, in such a world, investment management should be relatively passive: After the selection of an initial portfolio, there should be only minor and infrequent changes.

APPENDIX B

A DERIVATION OF THE SECURITY MARKET LINE

Figure 9.7 shows the location of the feasible set of the Markowitz model along with the riskfree rate and the associated efficient set that represents the capital market line. Within the feasible set of the Markowitz model lies every individual risky security. An arbitrarily chosen risky security, denoted i, has been selected for analysis and is shown on the figure.

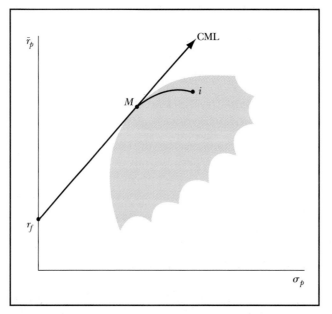

Figure 9.7
Deriving the Security Market Line

Consider any portfolio, denoted p, that consists of the proportion X_i invested in security i and the proportion $(1 - X_i)$ invested in the market portfolio M. Such a portfolio will have an expected return equal to:

$$\bar{r}_p = X_i \bar{r}_i + (1 - X_i) \bar{r}_M \tag{9.14}$$

and a standard deviation equal to:

$$\sigma_p = \left[X_i^2 \sigma_i^2 + (1 - X_i)^2 \sigma_M^2 + 2X_i(1 - X_i)\sigma_{iM} \right]^{1/2} \tag{9.15}$$

All such portfolios will lie on a curved line connecting i and M such as the one shown in Figure 9.7.

Of concern is the slope of this curved line. Because it is a curved line, its slope is not a constant. However, its slope can be determined with the use of calculus. First, using Equation (9.14), the derivative of $\bar{r}_p$ with respect to X_i is taken:

$$\frac{d\bar{r}_p}{dX_i} = \bar{r}_i - \bar{r}_M \tag{9.16}$$

Second, using Equation (9.15), the derivative of σ_p with respect to X_i is taken:

$$\frac{d\sigma_p}{dX_i} = \frac{X_i\sigma_i^2 - \sigma_M^2 + X_i\sigma_M^2 + \sigma_{iM} - 2X_i\sigma_{iM}}{\left[X_i^2\sigma_i^2 + (1 - X_i)^2\sigma_M^2 + 2X_i(1 - X_i)\sigma_{iM} \right]^{1/2}} \tag{9.17}$$

Third, it can be noted that the slope of the curved line iM, $d\bar{r}_p/d\sigma_p$, can be written as:

$$\frac{d\bar{r}_p}{d\sigma_p} = \frac{d\bar{r}_p/dX_i}{d\sigma_p/dX_i} \tag{9.18}$$

This means that the slope of iM can be calculated by substituting Equations (9.16) and (9.17) into the numerator and denominator of Equation (9.18), respectively:

$$\frac{d\bar{r}_p}{d\sigma_p} = \frac{[\bar{r}_i - \bar{r}_M]\left[X_i^2\sigma_i^2 + (1 - X_i)^2\sigma_M^2 + 2X_i(1 - X_i)\sigma_{iM} \right]^{1/2}}{X_i\sigma_i^2 - \sigma_M^2 + X_i\sigma_M^2 + \sigma_{iM} - 2X_i\sigma_{iM}} \tag{9.19}$$

Of interest is the slope of the curved line iM at the endpoint M. Because the proportion X_i is zero at this point, the slope of iM can be calculated by substituting zero for X_i in Equation (9.19). After that substitution has been done, many terms drop out, leaving:

$$\frac{d\bar{r}_p}{d\sigma_p} = \frac{[\bar{r}_i - \bar{r}_M][\sigma_M]}{\sigma_{iM} - \sigma_M^2} \tag{9.20}$$

At M the slope of the CML, $(\bar{r}_M - r_f)/\sigma_M$, must equal the slope of the curved line iM. The reason is that the slope of the curved line iM increases when moving from the endpoint i, converging with the slope of the CML at the endpoint M. Accordingly, the slope of the curve iM at M, as shown on the right-hand side of Equation (9.20), is set equal to the slope of the CML:

$$\frac{[\bar{r}_i - \bar{r}_M][\sigma_M]}{\sigma_{iM} - \sigma_M^2} = \frac{\bar{r}_M - r_f}{\sigma_M} \tag{9.21}$$

Solving Equation (9.21) for $\bar{r}_i$ results in the covariance version of the SML:

$$\overline{r}_i = r_f + \left[\frac{\overline{r}_M - r_f}{\sigma_M^2} \right] \sigma_{iM} \qquad (9.6)$$

The beta version of the SML is derived by substituting β_{iM} for σ_{iM}/σ_M^2 in Equation (9.6).

ENDNOTES

[1] Some extended versions of the CAPM are discussed in Appendix A.

[2] Milton Friedman, *Essays in the Theory of Positive Economics* (Chicago: University of Chicago Press, 1953), p. 15.

[3] If the investor had initial wealth of $40,000, he or she would borrow $10,000 and then invest $50,000 (=$40,000 + $10,000) in *T*.

[4] Note how the proportions in these three stocks sum to .5 for the panel (a) investor and 1.25 for the panel (b) investor. Because the respective proportions for the riskfree asset are .5 and −.25, the aggregate proportions for the stocks and riskfree asset sum to 1.0 for each investor. See Appendix B to Chapter 8.

[5] Securities that have zero net amounts outstanding will not appear in the tangency portfolio. Options and futures, discussed in Chapters 19 and 20, are examples of such securities.

[6] Although the expected return of Charlie has been changed, all the variances and covariances as well as the expected returns for Able and Baker are assumed to have the same values that were given in Chapters 6, 7 and 8. The singular change in the expected return of Charlie alters not only the composition of the tangency portfolio but, more generally, the location and shape of the efficient set.

[7] In this situation the market for each security is said to have *cleared*.

[8] The aggregate market value for the common stock of a company is equal to the current market price of the stock multiplied by the number of shares outstanding.

[9] The slope of a straight line can be determined if the location of two points on the line are known. It is determined by *rise over run*, meaning that it is determined by dividing the vertical distance between the two points by the horizontal distance between the two points. In the case of the CML, two points are known, corresponding to the riskfree rate and the market portfolio, so its slope can be determined in this manner.

[10] The equation of a straight line is of the form: $y = a + bx$, where a is the vertical intercept and b is the slope. Because the vertical intercept and slope of the CML are known, its equation can be written as shown here by making the appropriate substitutions for a and b.

[11] More precisely, σ_{iM} is the relevant measure of a security's risk because $\partial \sigma_M / \partial X_{iM} = \sigma_{iM}/\sigma_M$. That is, a marginal change in the weight in security i will result in a marginal change in the variance of the market portfolio that is a linear function of the security's covariance with the market portfolio. Accordingly, the relevant measure of the security's risk is its covariance, σ_{iM}.

[12] A more rigorous derivation of the SML is provided in Appendix B.

[13] In this situation, Baker and Charlie have covariances with the market portfolio of 382 and 179, respectively, which means that their expected returns should be equal to 30.7% = 4 + (.07 × 382) and 16.5% = 4 + (.07 × 179). However, these figures do not correspond to the respective ones (24.6% and 22.8%) appearing in the expected return vector, indicating that there are discrepancies for all three securities. Although this example has used the covariance version of the SML, the analysis is similar for the beta version of SML that is shown in Equation (9.7).

[14] Other indices of common stocks are commonly reported in the daily press. Many of these are components of the major indices mentioned here. For example, the *Wall Street Journal* reports on a daily basis not only the level of the S&P 500 but also the levels of four of its components: Industrials, Transportations, Utilities, and Financials. Standard & Poor's also reports the level of a 400 MidCap index based on the stock prices of middle-sized companies. See Chapters 24 and 25 for a more thorough discussion of stock market indices.

[15] Charles Dow created this index in 1884 by simply adding the prices of 11 companies and then dividing the sum by 11. In 1928 securities were added to bring the total number up to 30. Since then the composition of these 30 has been changed periodically. Owing to corporate actions such as stock dividends and splits as well as changes in the index's companies, the divisor is no longer simply equal to the number of stocks in the index.

[16] A more rigorous development of this figure is presented in Appendix A to Chapter 8.

[17] Assume that (1) initial margin requirements for short sales do not exist; (2) investors can obtain the proceeds from short sales; and (3) neither riskfree borrowing nor lending is possible. In such a situation the feasible set would be bounded by a hyperbola that opens to the right. Furthermore, the efficient set would be the upper half of this boundary. Introducing riskfree borrowing and lending changes the shape and location of the efficient set to one that is similar to what appears in Figure 9.3. In such a situation the market portfolio would definitely plot on the efficient set between T_L and T_B. See Fischer Black, "Capital Market Equilibrium with Restricted Borrowing," *Journal of Business* 45, no. 3 (July 1972): 444–455.

[18] See John Lintner, "The Aggregation of Investor's Diverse Judgements and Preferences in Purely Competitive Markets," *Journal of Financial and Quantitative Analysis* 4, no. 4 (December 1969): 347–400.

[19] The ability of an investor to produce a stream of income by working shows that the investor possesses an asset known as human capital and that different investors have different amounts of human capital. As slavery is outlawed, this asset cannot be sold and hence is nonmarketable and completely illiquid. Nevertheless, because human capital is an asset, certain researchers have argued that it is relevant to each investor in identifying his or her optimal portfolio. Accordingly, the market portfolio should consist of all marketable and nonmarketable assets (such as human capital), and each security's beta should be measured relative to it. See David Mayers, "Nonmarketable Assets and Capital Market Equilibrium under Uncertainty," in Michael C. Jensen (ed.), *Studies in the Theory of Capital Markets,* (New York: Praeger, 1972), and "Nonmarketable Assets and the Determination of Capital Asset Prices in the Absence of a Riskless Asset," *Journal of Business* 46, no. 2 (April 1973): 258–267.

[20] The term *security market plane* is a trademark of Wells Fargo Bank. For more on the relationship between liquidity and stock returns, see Yakov Amihud and Haim Mendelson, "Liquidity and Stock Returns," *Financial Analysts Journal* 42, no. 3 (May/June 1986): 43–48; "Asset Pricing and the Bid-Ask Spread," *Journal of Financial Economics* 17, no. 2 (December 1986): 223–249; and "Liquidity, Asset Prices and Financial Policy," *Financial Analysts Journal* 47, no. 6 (November/December 1991): 56–66.

[21] Taxes might be such a third characteristic if the tax rate on income from capital gains is less than the tax rate on dividend income. In considering such taxes, one study found that the before-tax expected return of a security was a positive linear function of its beta and dividend yield. Securities with higher betas or dividend yields tended to have higher before-tax expected returns than securities with lower betas or dividend yields. The reason securities with higher dividend yields would have had higher before-tax expected returns was that they would be taxed more heavily. See M. J. Brennan, "Taxes, Market Valuation and Corporate Financial Policy," *National Tax Journal* 23, no. 4 (December 1970): 417–427. The issue of whether dividends influence before-tax expected returns has been debated. It is discussed in Chapters 15 and 16 of Thomas E. Copeland and J. Fred Weston, *Financial Theory and Corporate Policy* (Reading, MA: Addison-Wesley, 1988).

KEY TERMS

normative economics	market portfolio
positive economics	capital market line
capital asset pricing model	security market line
homogeneous expectations	beta coefficient
perfect markets	market risk
separation theorem	non-market risk

1. Credit for the initial development of the CAPM is usually given to:

   William F. Sharpe, "Capital Asset Prices: A Theory of Market Equilibrium under Conditions of Risk," *Journal of Finance* 19, no. 3 (September 1964): 425–442.

   John Lintner, "The Valuation of Risk Assets and the Selection of Risky Investments in Stock Portfolios and Capital Budgets," *Review of Economics and Statistics*, 47, no. 1 (February 1965): 13–37; and "Security Prices, Risk, and Maximal Gains from Diversification," *Journal of Finance* 20, no. 4 (December 1965): 587–615.

   Jan Mossin, "Equilibrium in a Capital Asset Market," *Econometrica* 34, no. 4 (October 1966): 768–783.

2. The Sharpe and Lintner papers were compared in:

   Eugene F. Fama, "Risk, Return, and Equilibrium: Some Clarifying Comments," *Journal of Finance* 23, no. 1 (March 1968): 29–40.

3. Some extended versions of the CAPM are described in:

   Gordon J. Alexander and Jack Clark Francis, *Portfolio Analysis* (Upper Saddle River, NJ: Prentice Hall, 1986), Chapter 8.

   Edwin J. Elton and Martin J. Gruber, *Modern Portfolio Theory and Investment Analysis* (New York: Wiley, 1995), Chapter 14.

4. For a comparison of the market model and CAPM betas, see:

   Harry M. Markowitz, "The 'Two Beta' Trap," *Journal of Portfolio Management* 11, no. 1 (Fall 1984): 12–20.

5. It has been argued that the CAPM is virtually impossible to test because (a) the only testable hypothesis of the CAPM is that the "true" market portfolio lies on the efficient set (when this happens securities' expected returns and betas have a positive linear relationship) and (b) the "true" market portfolio cannot be meaningfully measured. See:

   Richard Roll, "A Critique of the Asset Pricing Theory's Tests; Part I. On Past and Potential Testability of the Theory," *Journal of Financial Economics* 4, no. 2 (March 1977): 129–176.

6. Despite Roll's critique, several tests of the CAPM have been conducted. Some of them are summarized in:

   Gordon J. Alexander and Jack Clark Francis, *Portfolio Analysis* (Upper Saddle River, NJ: Prentice Hall, 1986), Chapter 10.

   Edwin J. Elton and Martin J. Gruber, *Modern Portfolio Theory and Investment Analysis* (New York: Wiley, 1995), Chapter 15.

7. Recently some people have concluded that the CAPM is no longer relevant on the basis of the following test results that show that the relationship between beta and average stock returns is flat:

   Eugene F. Fama and Kenneth R. French, "The Cross-Section of Expected Stock Returns," *Journal of Finance* 47, no. 2 (June 1992): 427–465.

   Eugene F. Fama and Kenneth R. French, "Common Risk Factors in the Returns on Stocks and Bonds," *Journal of Financial Economics* 33, no. 1 (February 1993): 3–56.

   James L. Davis, "The Cross-Section of Realized Stock Returns: The Pre-COMPUSTAT Evidence," *Journal of Finance* 49, no. 5 (December 1994): 1579–1593.

   Eugene F. Fama and Kenneth R. French, "The CAPM Is Wanted, Dead or Alive," *Journal of Finance* 51, no. 5 (December 1996): 1947–1958.

8. However, these test results have been challenged by others, such as those listed below. For example, the Jagannathan and Wang study shows that average returns and betas have a positive linear relationship when the market portfolio includes human capital (see endnote 19) and betas are allowed to vary over the business cycle:

   Louis K. C. Chan and Josef Lakonishok, "Are the Reports of Beta's Death Premature?" *Journal of Portfolio Management* 19, no. 4 (Summer 1993): 51–62.

Fischer Black, "Beta and Return," *Journal of Portfolio Management* 20, no. 1 (Fall 1993): 8–18.

S. P. Kothari, Jay Shanken, and Richard D. Sloan, "Another Look at the Cross-Section of Expected Stock Returns," *Journal of Finance* 50, no. 1 (March 1995): 185–224.

Ravi Jagannathan and Ellen R. McGrattan, "The CAPM Debate," Federal Reserve Bank of Minneapolis *Quarterly Review* 19, no. 4 (Fall 1995): 2–17

Kevin Grundy and Burton Makiel, "Report of Beta's Death Have Been Greatly Exaggerated," *Journal of Portfolio Management* 22, no. 3 (Spring 1996): 36–44.

Ravi Jagannathan and Zhenyu Wang, "The Conditional CAPM and the Cross-Section of Expected Returns," *Journal of Finance* 51, no. 1 (March 1996): 3–53.

9. For an assertion that the use of modern portfolio theory does not depend upon successful testing of the CAPM, see:

Harry M. Markowitz, "Nonnegative or Not Nonnegative: A Question about CAPMs," *Journal of Finance* 38, no. 2 (May 1983): 283–295.

10. An interesting Web site that presents a wealth of information on the Dow Jones Averages can be found at:

⟨http://averages.dowjones.com/home.html⟩.

FACTOR MODELS

The objective of modern portfolio theory is to provide a means by which the investor can identify his or her optimal portfolio when there are an infinite number of possibilities. Using a framework involving expected returns and standard deviations shows that the investor needs to estimate the expected return and standard deviation for each security under consideration for inclusion in the portfolio along with all the covariances between securities. With these estimates the investor can derive the curved efficient set of Markowitz. Then for a given riskfree rate the investor can identify the tangency portfolio and determine the location of the linear efficient set. Finally, the investor can proceed to invest in this tangency portfolio and borrow or lend at the riskfree rate, with the amount of borrowing or lending depending on the investor's risk-return preferences.

10.1   FACTOR MODELS AND RETURN-GENERATING PROCESSES

The task of identifying the curved Markowitz efficient set can be greatly simplified by introducing a **return-generating process**. A return-generating process is a statistical model that describes how the return on a security is produced. Chapter 7 presented a type of return-generating process known as the market model. The market model states that a security's return is a function of the return on a market index. However, there are many other types of return-generating processes for securities.

10.1.1   Factor Models

Factor models, or index models, assume that the return on a security is sensitive to the movements of various factors, or indices. The market model assumes that there is one factor—the return on a market index. However, in attempting to accurately estimate expected returns, variances, and covariances for securities, multiple-factor models are potentially more useful than the market model. They have this potential because it appears that security returns are sensitive to more than movements in a market index. That is, there probably is more than one pervasive factor in the economy that affects security returns.

    As a return-generating process, a factor model attempts to capture the major economic forces that systematically move the prices of all securities. Implicit in the construction of a factor model is the assumption that the returns on two securities will be correlated—that is, will move together—only through common reactions to one or more of the factors specified in the model. Any aspect of a security's return unexplained by the factor model is assumed to be unique or specific to the security and therefore uncorrelated with the unique elements of returns on other securities. As a result, a factor model is a powerful tool for portfolio management. It can supply the information needed to calculate expected returns, variances, and covariances for every security—a necessary condition for determining the curved Markowitz efficient set. It can also be used to characterize a portfolio's sensitivity to movements in the factors.

10.1.2 Application

As a practical matter, all investors employ factor models whether they do so explicitly or implicitly. It is impossible to consider separately the interrelationship of every security with every other. Numerically, the problem of calculating covariances among securities rises exponentially as the number of securities analyzed increases.[1]

Conceptually, the tangled web of security variances and covariances becomes mind-boggling as the number of securities increases beyond just a few securities, let alone hundreds or thousands. Even the vast data-processing capabilities of high-speed computers are strained when they are called upon to construct efficient sets from a large number of securities.

Abstraction is therefore an essential step in identifying the curved Markowitz efficient set. Factor models supply the necessary level of abstraction. They provide investment managers with a framework to identify important factors in the economy and the marketplace and to assess the extent to which different securities and portfolios will respond to changes in those factors.

Given the belief that one or more factors influence security returns, a primary goal of security analysis is to determine these factors and the sensitivities of security returns to movements in them. A formal statement of such a relationship is termed a *factor model of security returns*. The discussion begins with the simplest form of such a model, a one-factor model.

10.2 ONE-FACTOR MODELS

Some investors argue that the return-generating process for securities involves a single factor. For example, they may contend that the returns on securities respond to the growth rate in the gross domestic product (GDP). Table 10.1 and Figure 10.1 illustrate one way of providing substance for such statements.

TABLE 10.1	Factor Model Data		
Year	Growth Rate in GDP	Rate of Inflation	Return on Widget Stock
1	5.7%	1.1%	14.3%
2	6.4	4.4	19.2
3	7.9	4.4	23.4
4	7.0	4.6	15.6
5	5.1	6.1	9.2
6	2.9	3.1	13.0

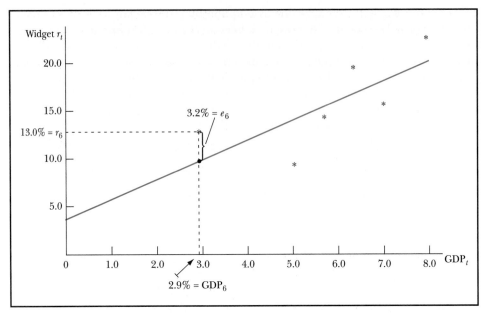

Figure 10.1
A One-Factor Model

10.2.1 An Example

On the horizontal axis of Figure 10.1 is the growth rate in GDP; the vertical axis measures the return on Widget's stock. Each point in the graph represents the combination of Widget's return and GDP growth rate for a particular year as reported in Table 10.1. A line has been statistically fitted to the data by using a technique known as *simple linear regression analysis*. (*Simple* refers to the fact that there is one variable—GDP in this example—on the right-hand side of the equation.)[2] This line has a positive slope of 2, indicating that there exists a positive relationship between GDP growth rates and Widget's returns. Higher rates of GDP growth are associated with higher returns.[3]

In equation form, the relationship between GDP growth and Widget's return can be expressed as follows:

$$r_t = a + b\text{GDP}_t + e_t \tag{10.1}$$

where:

r_t = the return on Widget in period t
GDP_t = the rate of growth in GDP in period t
e_t = the unique or specific return on Widget in period t
b = **sensitivity** of Widget to GDP growth[4]
a = the zero factor for GDP

In Figure 10.1 the zero factor is 4% per period. This is the return that would be expected for Widget if GDP growth equaled zero. The sensitivity of Widget to predicted GDP growth is 2 and is the same as the slope of the line in Figure 10.1. This value indicates that, in general, higher growth in GDP is associated with higher returns for Widget. If GDP growth equaled 5%, Widget should generate a return of 14% [= 4% + (2 × 5%)]. If GDP growth were 1% higher—that is, 6%—Widget's return should be 2% higher, or 16%.

In this example, GDP growth in year 6 was 2.9%, and Widget actually returned 13%. Therefore Widget's unique return (given by e_t) in this particular year was +3.2%. This was determined by subtracting an amount that represents Widget's expected return, given that GDP grew by 2.9%, from Widget's actual return of 13%. In this case, Widget was expected to return of 9.8% [= 4 + (2 × 2.9%)], thereby resulting in a unique return of +3.2% (= 13% − 9.8%).

In effect, the one-factor model presented in Figure 10.1 and Equation (10.1) attributes Widget's return in any particular period to three elements:

1. An effect common in any period (the term a)
2. An effect that differs across periods depending on the factor, the growth rate of GDP (the term $b\text{GDP}_t$)
3. An effect specific to the particular period observed that is not attributable to the factor (the term e_t)

10.2.2   Generalizing the Example

This example of a one-factor model can be generalized in equation form for any security i in period t:

$$r_{it} = a_i + b_i F_t + e_{it} \tag{10.2}$$

where F_t is the value of the factor in period t, and b_i is the sensitivity of security i to this factor. If the value of the factor were zero, the return on the security would equal $a_i + e_{it}$. Note that e_{it} is a random error term just like the random error term discussed in Chapter 7. This means that it is a random variable with an expected value of zero and a standard deviation σ_{ei}. It can be thought of as the outcome occurring from a spin of a roulette wheel in the same manner as described in Chapter 7.

Expected Return

According to the one-factor model, the expected return on security i can be written as:

$$\bar{r}_i = a_i + b_i \bar{F} \tag{10.3}$$

where $\bar{F}$ denotes the expected value of the factor.

This equation can be used to estimate the expected return on the security. For example, if the expected growth rate in GDP is 3%, then the expected return for Widget equals 10% [= 4% + (2 × 3%)].

Variance

With the one-factor model, it can also be shown that the variance of any security i is equal to:

$$\sigma_i^2 = b_i^2 \sigma_F^2 + \sigma_{ei}^2 \tag{10.4}$$

where σ_F^2 is the variance of the factor F and σ_{ei}^2 is the variance of the random error term e_i. Thus if the variance of the factor σ_F^2 equals 3 and the residual variance σ_{ei}^2 equals 15.2, then according to this equation Widget's variance equals:

$$\sigma_i^2 = \left(2^2 \times 3\right) + 15.2$$

$$= 27.2$$

Covariance

With a one-factor model the covariance between any two securities i and j can be shown to equal:

$$\sigma_{ij} = b_i b_j \, \sigma_F^2 \qquad\qquad (10.5)$$

In the example of Widget, Equation (10.5) can be used to estimate the covariance between Widget and another hypothetical security, such as the stock of Whatever Company. Assuming that the factor sensitivity of Whatever is 4.0, the covariance between Widget and Whatever equals:

$$\sigma_{ij} = 2 \times 4 \times 3$$
$$= 24$$

Assumptions

Equations (10.4) and (10.5) are based on two critical assumptions. The first assumption is that the random error term and the factor are uncorrelated. This means that the outcome of the factor has no bearing on the outcome of the random error term.

The second assumption is that the random error terms of any two securities are uncorrelated. This means that the outcome of the random error term of one security has no bearing on the outcome of the random error term of any other security. As a result, the returns of two securities will be correlated only through common responses to the factor. If either of these two assumptions is invalid, then the model is an approximation, and a different factor model (perhaps one with more factors) theoretically will be a more accurate representation of the return-generating process.

10.2.3   The Market Model

The market model can now be shown to be a specific example of a one-factor model in which the factor is the return on a market index. In Chapter 7, the market model appeared as:

$$r_i = \alpha_{iI} + \beta_{iI} r_I + \varepsilon_{iI} \qquad\qquad (7.3)$$

Comparison of Equation (7.3) with the general form of the one-factor model in Equation (10.2) makes readily apparent the similarity between the two equations. The intercept α_{iI} from the market model equation corresponds to the zero factor term a_i from Equation (10.2). Furthermore, the slope term β_{iI} from the market model equates to the sensitivity term b_i from the generalized one-factor model. Each equation has a random error term: e_{iI} in the factor model and ε_{iI} in the market model.[5] Finally, the market index return plays the role of the single factor.

However, as mentioned earlier, the concept of a one-factor model does not restrict the investor to using a market index as the factor. Many other single factors are plausible. Macroeconomic variables such as growth in the economy, interest rates, and the inflation rate offer a fertile ground in the search for pervasive factors.

10.2.4   Two Important Features
of One-Factor Models

Two features of one-factor models are of particular interest: the tangency portfolio and diversification.

The Tangency Portfolio

First, the assumption that the returns on all securities respond to a single common factor greatly simplifies the task of identifying the tangency portfolio. To determine the composition of the tangency portfolio, the investor needs to estimate all of the securities' expected returns, variances, and covariances. This task can be accomplished with a one-factor model by estimating a_i, b_i, and σ_{ei} for each of the N risky securities.[6]

Also needed are the expected value of the factor $\overline{F}$ and its standard deviation σ_F. With these estimates, Equations (10.3), (10.4), and (10.5) can subsequently be used to calculate expected returns, variances, and covariances for the securities. When these values are used, the curved efficient set of Markowitz can be derived. Finally, the tangency portfolio can be determined for a given riskfree rate.

The common responsiveness of securities to the factor eliminates the need to estimate directly the covariances between the securities. Those covariances are captured by the securities' sensitivities to the factor and the factor's variance.

Diversification

The second interesting feature of one-factor models has to do with diversification. Earlier it was shown that diversification leads to an averaging of market risk and a reduction in unique risk. This feature is true of any one-factor model except that instead of market and unique risk, the terms *factor risk* and *nonfactor risk* are used. In Equation (10.4) the first term on the right-hand side $\left(b_i^2 \sigma_F^2\right)$ is known as the **factor risk** of the security, and the second term $\left(\sigma_{ei}^2\right)$ is known as the **nonfactor** (or unique) **risk** of the security.

With a one-factor model, the variance of a portfolio is given by:

$$\sigma_p^2 = b_p^2 \sigma_F^2 + \sigma_{ep}^2 \qquad (10.6a)$$

where:

$$b_p = \sum_{i=1}^{N} X_i b_i \qquad (10.6b)$$

$$\sigma_{ep}^2 = \sum_{i=1}^{N} X_i^2 \sigma_{ei}^2 \qquad (10.6c)$$

Equation (10.6a) shows that the total risk of any portfolio can be viewed as having two components similar to the two components of the total risk of an individual security shown in Equation (10.4). In particular, the first and second terms on the right-hand side of Equation (10.6a) are the factor risk and nonfactor risk of the portfolio, respectively.

As a portfolio becomes more diversified (meaning that it contains more securities), each proportion X_i will become smaller. However, this change will not cause b_p to either decrease or increase significantly unless a deliberate attempt is made to do so by continually adding securities with values of b_i that are either relatively low or high, respectively. As Equation (10.6b) shows, the reason is that b_p is simply a weighted average of the sensitivities of the securities b_i, with the values of X_i serving as the weights. Thus *diversification leads to an averaging of factor risk.*

However, as a portfolio becomes more diversified, there is reason to expect σ_{ep}^2, the nonfactor risk, to decrease. This change can be shown by examining Equation (10.6c). On the assumption that the same amount is invested in each security, then this equation can be rewritten by substituting $1/N$ for X_i:

$$\sigma_{ep}^2 = \sum_{i=1}^{N} \left(\frac{1}{N}\right)^2 \sigma_{ei}^2$$

$$= \left(\frac{1}{N}\right)\left[\frac{\sigma_{e1}^2 + \sigma_{e2}^2 + \cdots + \sigma_{eN}^2}{N}\right]$$

The value inside the square brackets is the average nonfactor risk for the individual securities. But the portfolio's nonfactor risk is only one-Nth as large because the term $1/N$ appears outside the brackets. As the portfolio becomes more diversified, the number of securities in it, N, becomes larger. Consequently, $1/N$ becomes smaller, and the nonfactor risk of the portfolio is, in turn, reduced. Simply stated, *diversification reduces nonfactor risk.*[7]

10.3 MULTIPLE-FACTOR MODELS

The health of the economy affects most firms. Thus changes in expectations concerning the future of the economy will generally have profound effects on the returns of most securities. However, the economy is not a simple, monolithic entity. Several common influences with pervasive effects might be identified.

1. The growth rate of gross domestic product
2. The level of interest rates on short-term Treasury securities
3. The yield spread between long-term and short-term Treasury securities
4. The yield spread between long-term corporate and Treasury securities
5. The inflation rate
6. The level of oil prices

10.3.1 Two-Factor Models

Instead of a one-factor model, a multiple-factor model for security returns that considers these various influences may be more accurate. As an example of a multiple-factor model, consider a two-factor model which assumes that the return-generating process contains two factors.

In equation form, the two-factor model for period t is:

$$r_{it} = a_i + b_{i1}F_{1t} + b_{i2}F_{2t} + e_{it} \qquad (10.7)$$

where F_{1t} and F_{2t} are the two factors that are pervasive influences on security returns, and b_{i1} and b_{i2} are the sensitivities of security i to those two factors. As with the one-factor model, e_{it} is a random error term and a_i is the expected return on security i if each factor has a value of zero.

Figure 10.2 provides an illustration of Widget Company's stock, whose returns are affected by expectations concerning both the growth rate in GDP and the rate of inflation. As was the case in the one-factor example, each point in the figure corresponds to a particular year. (Only one point has been shown to avoid cluttering the figure.) This time, however, each point is a combination of Widget's return, the rate of inflation, and the growth in GDP in that year as given in Table 10.1. To this scatter of points is fit a two-dimensional plane by using the statistical technique of *multiple-regression analysis.* (*Multiple* refers to the fact that there is more than one variable on the right-hand side of the equation, in this case F_1 and F_2, explaining the variable on the left-hand side of the equation, in this case r_t.) The plane for a given security is described by the following adaptation of Equation (10.7):

$$r_t = a + b_1 \text{GDP}_t + b_2 \text{INF}_t$$

The slope of the plane in the GDP growth-rate direction (the term b_1) represents Widget's sensitivity to changes in GDP growth, assuming no change in inflation. The slope of the plane in the inflation rate direction (the term b_2) is Widget's sensitivity to changes in the inflation rate, assuming no change in GDP growth. Note that the sen-

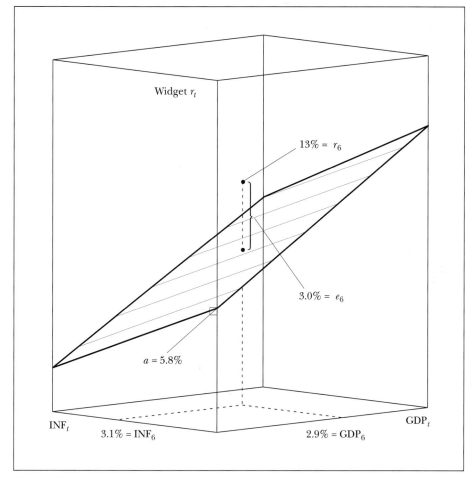

Figure 10.2
A Two-Factor Model

sitivities b_1 and b_2 in this example are positive and negative, respectively, having corresponding values of 2.2 and $-.7$.[8] This slope indicates that as GDP growth rises Widget's return should increase, and as inflation rises Widget's return should decrease.

The intercept term (the zero factor) in Figure 10.2 of 5.8% indicates Widget's expected return if both GDP growth and inflation are zero. Finally, in a given year, the distance from Widget's actual point to the plane indicates its unique return (e_{it}), the portion of Widget's return not attributed to either GDP growth or inflation. For example, given that GDP grew by 2.9% and inflation was 3.1%, Widget's expected return in year 6 equals 10% [= 5.8% + (2.2 $\times$ 2.9%) $-$ (.7 $\times$ 3.1%)]. Hence its unique return for that year is equal to +3% (= 13% $-$ 10%).

Four parameters need to be estimated for each security with the two-factor model: a_i, b_{i1}, b_{i2}, and the standard deviation of the random error term, denoted σ_{ei}. For each of the factors, two parameters need to be estimated. These parameters are the expected value of each factor $\left(\overline{F}_1 \text{ and } \overline{F}_2 \right)$ and the variance of each factor $\left(\sigma_{F1}^2 \text{ and } \sigma_{F2}^2 \right)$. Finally, the covariance between the factors $COV(F_1, F_2)$ needs to be estimated.

Expected Return

With these estimates, the expected return for any security i can be determined by specifying the expected values for the two factors and using the following formula:

$$\bar{r}_i = a_i + b_{i1}\bar{F}_1 + b_{i2}\bar{F}_2 \tag{10.8}$$

For example, the expected return for Widget equals 8.9% [= 5.8% + (2.2 × 3%) − (.7 × 5%)] provided that the expected increases in GDP and inflation are 3% and 5%, respectively.

Variance

According to the two-factor model, the variance for any security i is:

$$\sigma_i^2 = b_{i1}^2\sigma_{F1}^2 + b_{i2}^2\sigma_{F2}^2 + 2b_{i1}b_{i2}COV(F_1, F_2) + \sigma_{ei}^2 \tag{10.9}$$

If, in the example, the variances of the first (σ_{F1}^2) and second (σ_{F2}^2) factors are equal to 3 and 2.9, respectively, their covariance $[COV(F_1, F_2)]$ equals .65, and the random error term has a variance σ_{ei}^2 of 18.2, then the variance of Widget equals 32.1 [= (2.2² × 3) + (−.7² × 2.9) + (2 × 2.2 × −.7 × .65) + 18.2], because its two sensitivities are 2.2 and −.7, respectively.

Covariance

Similarly, according to the two-factor model the covariance between any two securities i and j can be determined by:

$$\sigma_{ij} = b_{i1}b_{j1}\sigma_{F1}^2 + b_{i2}b_{j2}\sigma_{F2}^2 + (b_{i1}b_{j2} + b_{i2}b_{j1})COV(F_1, F_2) \tag{10.10}$$

Thus continuing with the example, the covariance between Widget and Whatever is estimated to equal 39.9 {= (2.2 × 6 × 3) + (−.7 × −5 × 2.9) + [(2.2 × −5) + (−.7 × 6)] × .65} because the sensitivities of Whatever to the two factors are 6 and −5, respectively.

The Tangency Portfolio

As with the one-factor model, once the expected returns, variances, and covariances have been determined using these equations, the investor can proceed to use an *optimizer* (a special kind of mathematical routine discussed in Chapter 7) to derive the curved efficient set of Markowitz. Then for a given riskfree rate, the tangency portfolio can be identified, after which the investor can determine his or her optimal portfolio.

Diversification

Everything said earlier regarding one-factor models and the effects of diversification applies here as well.

1. Diversification leads to an averaging of factor risk.
2. Diversification can substantially reduce nonfactor risk.
3. For a *well-diversified portfolio*, nonfactor risk will be insignificant.

As with a one-factor model, the sensitivity of a portfolio to a particular factor in a multiple-factor model is a weighted average of the sensitivities of the securities where the weights are equal to the proportions invested in the securities. This relation can be seen by remembering that the return on a portfolio is a weighted average of the returns of its component securities:

$$r_{pt} = \sum_{i=1}^{N} X_i r_{it} \tag{10.11}$$

Substituting the right-hand side of Equation (10.7) for r_{it} on the right-hand side of Equation (10.11) results in:

$$r_{pt} = \sum_{i=1}^{N} X_i \left(a_i + b_{i1} F_{1t} + b_{i2} F_{2t} + e_{it} \right)$$

$$= \left[\sum_{i=1}^{N} X_i a_i \right] + \left[\sum_{i=1}^{N} X_i b_{i1} F_{1t} \right] + \left[\sum_{i=1}^{N} X_i b_{i2} F_{2t} \right] + \left[\sum_{i=1}^{N} X_i e_{it} \right]$$

$$= a_p + b_{p1} F_{1t} + b_{p2} F_{2t} + e_{pt} \tag{10.12}$$

where:

$$a_p = \sum_{i=1}^{N} X_i a_i$$

$$b_{p1} = \sum_{i=1}^{N} X_i b_{i1}$$

$$b_{p2} = \sum_{i=1}^{N} X_i b_{i2}$$

$$e_{pt} = \sum_{i=1}^{N} X_i e_{it}$$

Note that the portfolio sensitivities b_{p1} and b_{p2} are weighted averages of the respective individual sensitivities b_{i1} and b_{i2}.

The Importance of Expectations

Security prices reflect investors' estimates of the present values of firms' future prospects. At any given time the price of Widget stock is likely to respond to the *projected* values of such factors as the growth rate of GDP or the rate of inflation, as opposed to depending on the *historical* values of those factors. If investors' projections of such fundamental economic conditions change, so too will the price of Widget. Because the return on a stock is influenced heavily by changes in its price, stock returns are expected to be more highly correlated with changes in expected future values of fundamental economic variables than with the actual changes that occur contemporaneously.

For example, a large increase in inflation that was fully anticipated might have no effect on the stock price of a company whose earnings are highly sensitive to inflation. However, if the consensus expectation was for a low inflation rate, then the subsequent large unanticipated increase would have a significant effect on the company's stock price, particularly if investors believed that the unexpected increase was a harbinger of larger than previously anticipated future inflation.

For this reason, whenever possible it is desirable to select factors that measure changes in expectations rather than realizations, as the latter typically include both changes that were anticipated and those that were not. One way to accomplish this goal is to rely on variables that involve changes in market prices. Thus the difference in the returns on two portfolios—one consisting of stocks thought to be unaffected by inflation and the other consisting of stocks thought to be affected by inflation—can be used as a factor that measures revisions in inflation expectations.

10.3.2 Sector-Factor Models

The prices of securities in the same industry or economic sector often move together in response to changes in prospects for that sector. Some investors acknowledge this relation by using a special kind of multiple-factor model referred to as a **sector-factor model**. A sector-factor model is created by assigning to a sector each security under consideration. For a two-sector-factor model, there are two sectors, and each security must be assigned to one of them.

For example, let sector factor 1 consist of all industrial companies and sector factor 2 consist of all nonindustrial companies (such as utility, transportation, and financial companies). Thus F_1 and F_2 can be thought of as representing the returns on an industrial stock index and on a nonindustrial stock index, respectively. (They could, for example, be components of the S&P 500.) It should be kept in mind, however, that both the number of sectors and what each sector consists of is an open matter that is left to the investor to decide.[9]

For this two-sector-factor model, the return-generating process for securities is of the same general form as for the two-factor model, given in Equation (10.7). However, with the two-sector-factor model, F_1 and F_2 now denote sector factors 1 and 2, respectively. Furthermore, any particular security belongs to either sector factor 1 or sector factor 2 but not to both. By definition, a value of zero is given to the sensitivity term corresponding to the sector factor to which the security is not assigned. This means that either b_{i1} or b_{i2} is set equal to zero, depending on the sector factor to which security i is not assigned. The value of the other sensitivity term must be estimated. (To make matters simple, some people simply give it a value of 1.)

As an illustration, consider General Motors (GM) and Delta Air Lines (DAL). The two-sector-factor model for GM (the time subscript t has been deleted for ease of exposition here) would be:

$$r_{GM} = a_{GM} + b_{GM1}F_1 + b_{GM2}F_2 + e_{GM} \qquad (10.13)$$

However, because GM belongs to sector factor 1 as an industrial security, the coefficient b_{GM2} is assigned a value of zero. Once this assignment is made, Equation (10.13) reduces to:

$$r_{GM} = a_{GM} + b_{GM1}F_1 + e_{GM} \qquad (10.14)$$

Thus only the values of a_{GM}, b_{GM1}, and σ_{eGM} need to be estimated for GM with the two-sector-factor model. In comparison with the two-factor model, values of a_{GM}, b_{GM1}, b_{GM2}, and σ_{eGM} need to be estimated.

Similarly, because DAL belongs to the nonindustrial sector, it would have the following two-sector-factor model:

$$r_{DAL} = a_{DAL} + b_{DAL1}F_1 + b_{DAL2}F_2 + e_{DAL} \qquad (10.15)$$

which would reduce to:

$$r_{DAL} = a_{DAL} + b_{DAL2}F_2 + e_{DAL} \qquad (10.16)$$

because b_{DAL1} would be assigned a value of zero. Thus only the values of a_{DAL}, b_{DAL2}, and σ_{eDAL} need to be estimated with the two-sector-factor model.

In general, whereas four parameters need to be estimated for each security with a two-factor model (a_i, b_{i1}, b_{i2}, and σ_{ei}), only three parameters need to be estimated with a two-sector-factor model (a_i, either b_{i1} or b_{i2}, and σ_{ei}). With these estimates in hand, along with estimates of $\overline{F}_1$, $\overline{F}_2$, σ_{F1}, and σ_{F2}, the investor can use Equations (10.8) and (10.9) to estimate expected returns and variances for each security. Pairwise covariances can be estimated using Equation (10.10). The investor will then be able to derive the curved efficient set of Markowitz from which the tangency portfolio can be determined for a given riskfree rate.

10.3.3 Extending the Model

To extend the discussion to more than two factors requires the abandonment of diagrams as the analysis moves beyond three dimensions. Nevertheless, the concepts are the same. If there are k factors, the multiple-factor model can be written as:

$$r_{it} = a_i + b_{i1}F_{1t} + b_{i2}F_{2t} + \cdots + b_{ik}F_{kt} + e_{it} \tag{10.17}$$

where each security has k sensitivities, one for each of the k factors.

It is possible to have both factors and sector factors represented in Equation (10.17). For example, F_1 and F_2 could represent GDP and inflation as in Table 10.1, whereas F_3 and F_4 could represent the returns on industrial stocks and nonindustrial stocks, respectively. Hence each stock would have three sensitivities: b_{i1}, b_{i2}, and b_{i3} for industrials and b_{i1}, b_{i2}, and b_{i4} for nonindustrials.[10]

10.3.4 An Alternative

As an alternative to Equation (10.17), factor models are sometimes written as follows:

$$r_{it} = \overline{r}_{it} + c_{i1}FD_{1t} + c_{i2}FD_{2t} + \cdots + c_{ik}FD_{kt} + e_{it} \tag{10.18}$$

Here $\overline{r}_i$ denotes the expected return of stock i in period t and the terms $FD_{1t} \ldots FD_{kt}$ denote the deviations of factors 1 through k from their expected values in period t. For example, in the case of the first factor, $FD_{1t} = F_{1t} - \overline{F}_{1t}$, which represents the difference between the actual value of the first factor and its expected value. Hence, if this factor is the rate of inflation, then FD_{1t} would denote the unexpected rate of inflation because it is equivalent to the difference between the actual rate of inflation and the expected rate of inflation. Last, the terms $c_{i1} \ldots c_{ik}$ denote the response coefficients in the rate of return of stock i to these factor deviations. Note that the random error term e_{it} and the factor deviation terms $FD_{1t} \ldots FD_{kt}$ all have expected values of zero.[11]

As an example, assume that there are two factors: the growth rate in gross domestic product and the rate of inflation. Thus, the factor model would describe Widget's rate of return in period t as follows:

$$r_t = \overline{r}_t + c_{GDP}FD_{GDPt} + c_{INF}FD_{INFt} + e_t \tag{10.19}$$

indicating that there are four components to Widget's actual return:

1. Widget's expected return, $\overline{r}_t$, which is determined by Equation (10.8)
2. Widget's response to the growth rate in gross domestic product turning out to be different from what was expected, $c_{GDP}FD_{GDPt}$
3. Widget's response to the rate of inflation turning out to be different from what was expected, $c_{INF}FD_{INFt}$
4. Widget's random error return, e_t

Imagine that the expected growth rate in GDP was 2% and the expected inflation rate was 4% but that the actual growth rate in GDP turned out to be 1% and the actual inflation rate was 5%. Hence, $FD_{GDPt} = 1\% - 2\% = -1\%$, and $FD_{INFt} = 5\% - 4\% = 1\%$. Assume that c_{GDP} and c_{INF} are equal to 3 and -2, respectively, and that Widget had an expected return at the beginning of the period of 10%. If its actual return for the period ended up being 8%, then this return would have the following four components:

1. An expected return of 10%
2. A return attributable to GDP turning out to be different than initially expected, amounting to $-3\% = (3 \times -1\%)$

The BARRA U.S. Equity Multiple-Factor Model

For the quantitatively inclined investment professional, multiple-factor models are intuitively appealing tools. They capture the essence of the fundamental economic and financial forces that affect security returns in a concise and readily testable form. However, moving from abstract discussions to the development of factor models that are sufficiently comprehensive and robust to serve the varied needs of institutional investors is a difficult task. An overview of the BARRA U.S. equity multiple-factor model offers insights into the complex elements of factor model implementation.

The BARRA model is based on the pioneering work of Barr Rosenberg, an econometrician and former finance professor. In the early 1970s, while at the University of California, Berkeley, he and Vinay Marathe formulated a sophisticated factor model. The model related common stock returns to a variety of factors derived primarily from the underlying companies' business operations.

Rosenberg is more than your typical ivory tower academic. Instead of being content to publish his results and receive the accolades of his colleagues, he recognized the commercial applications of his model. He formed a firm, now called BARRA, to enhance and sell the model to institutional investors.

Both the model and the firm proved successful beyond anyone's imagination. BARRA has grown into a worldwide consulting organization with annual revenues exceeding $100 million. Its stock is publicly traded and today has a market capitalization of over $300 million. Although Rosenberg left the firm in 1985 to pursue his own investment management ambitions, BARRA has continued to leverage off of its factor-model expertise by designing additional factor models for the global equity market and various foreign stock markets. The firm has also built factor models for the U.S. and several foreign bond markets.

Rosenberg's original U.S. equity multiple-factor model underwent major revisions in 1982 and 1997 and is referred to by factor-model aficionados as the E3 model. Currently, hundreds of institutional investors (more than half of them outside of the United States) subscribe to the E3 model service (and its predecessor, the E2 model). These investors range from large investment managers to pension funds, and in total they manage over $1 trillion dollars of U.S. common stocks.

All factor models are based on the assumption that securities with similar exposures to specific factors will exhibit similar investment behavior. The factor-model builder must translate this basic concept into practice. The process of constructing factor models is far from an exact science. Although certain statistical tests can be applied to gauge the explanatory power of a particular factor model, the model builder retains wide latitude to include or exclude potential factors.

It is instructive, therefore, to review how BARRA developed the E3 model. The process by which the model was specified is summarized by five steps.

1. Data collection and checking
2. Factor selection
3. Creation of composite factors
4. Estimation of factor returns and the factor variance-covariance matrix
5. Model testing

The E3 model's construction began with the collection of relevant security data. BARRA gathered monthly components of security returns, such as prices, dividends, and shares outstanding over an extended period of time for stocks to constitute the "estimation universe." This group included the largest 1,500 U.S. common stocks, with another roughly 400 stocks added to ensure adequate industry representation. BARRA also acquired a wide array of income and balance sheet information on the underlying companies. These financial data came largely from the annual and quarterly financial statements issued by the companies.

In this collection process, BARRA checked the data for quality. Although this task may seem mundane, it was a critical step, because a small amount of bad data can have a disproportionately large impact on a factor model's accuracy.

The second step involved factor selection. Hundreds of potential factors were available for inclusion in the model. BARRA sought to identify those factors that had a pervasive influence on the returns and risks of individual securities. Using historical security return data, BARRA isolated 39 market-related income statement and balance sheet factors that demonstrated statistically significant relationships with security prices.

The particular factors selected by BARRA ranged from the obvious to the novel. Examples included a company's historical equity beta, its consensus forecast earnings growth, its historical variability in earnings, the relative performance of its stock, its stock's book-to-price and earnings-to-price ratios, its debt to total assets, its earnings payout ratio, and the sensitivity of its stock to movements in foreign currency values.

The third step in the E3 model's construction entailed creating a set of composite fundamental factors from the individual factors. BARRA employed 13 composite factors: Volatility, Momentum, Size, Size Non-Linearity, Trading Activity, Growth, Earnings/Yield, Value, Earnings Variability, Leverage, Currency Sensitivity, Dividend Yield, and Non-Estimation Universe Estimator. The individual factors were assigned to and weighted within the composite factors on the basis of both judgment and statistical analyses. The weights of the factors may change over time as BARRA refits the model periodically.

The purpose of creating these composite fundamental factors was largely statistical convenience. As the text describes, a factor-model builder must estimate the variance of each factor and the covariances among all the factors. The number of variances and covariances grows exponentially as the number of factors increases. Therefore, instead of having to calculate variances and covariances for dozens of factors, BARRA's task was considerably reduced by combining the individual factors into a handful of composite factors.

To these 13 composite factors, BARRA added 13 sector factors. Like the composite fundamental factors, the sector factors are composed of smaller items, in this case 52 individual industries. (In the E3 model, a security can be assigned to as many as six industries, with total weights summing to 1, on the basis of analysis of the company's sales, earnings, and assets. Although the defined sectors remain constant over time, the number and definitions of the industries evolve as economic forces dictate. For example, the computer software industry was unimportant in the 1970s but is a large industry today.) Thus in its final form, the BARRA E3 factor model contains 26 fundamental and industry factors.

The fourth step involved estimating factor returns for each of the 26 factors and developing forecasts of nonfactor risk. Given return data on the model's estimation universe, for every month in its test period, BARRA effectively estimated the returns on 26 portfolios that each had unit exposure to one particular factor and zero exposure to all other 25 factors. The returns to these unit-exposure portfolios represented the monthly returns to the respective fac-

tors. Using these factor returns, BARRA computed the factor variance-covariance matrix. Further, nonfactor returns were separated from the factor returns, and a nonfactor risk forecasting model was estimated.

The last step involved testing the performance of the E3 model. BARRA was concerned with how effective its forecasts of security risk were outside of the test period. Cutting through the statistical jargon, BARRA found that the model performed well.

The BARRA E3 model and its predecessors are applied by institutional investors in a variety of situations. Investment managers use the model to forecast the variability of their portfolios' returns, both in an absolute sense and relative to a benchmark. The model allows the managers to dissect this forecast risk into factor and nonfactor components.

Managers can make informed judgments about the expected rewards offered by their particular portfolio strategies relative to the forecast risks. Managers and their clients also use the E3 model for performance attribution (see Chapter 24). Here an analyst uses the model to calculate a portfolio's historical exposure to the various factors. Then, using BARRA's calculated factor returns, the analyst computes the contribution of each of those exposures to the portfolio's total return. Finally, comparing the portfolio's exposures and the contributions of those exposures to the portfolio's performance against a relevant benchmark provides clues to the success or failure of the manager's strategies.

Institutional investors also use the E3 model to characterize the investment styles of their managers. Similar investment styles tend to exhibit similar E3 factor exposures. For example, large-capitalization growth managers typically have large Size and Growth exposures and low Value exposures. By analyzing a series of past returns for various portfolios with the E3 model, a client can accurately identify the investment styles of its current and potential managers. This process aids in both performance evaluation (see Chapter 24) and manager structuring (see Chapter 23).

The BARRA U.S. equity multiple-factor model has contributed to the rigor and sophistication with which institutional investors approach the task of managing large pools of U.S. common stocks. Perhaps the most impressive testament to the model's utility and robustness is that, in the highly competitive and fickle world of investments, no alternative factor model has gained the widespread acceptance that the BARRA models have achieved.

3. A return attributable to inflation turning out to be different than initially expected, amounting to $-2\% = (-2 \times 1\%)$

4. A random error return of $+3\%$

Note that the 8% actual return equals the sum of its components, $10\% - 3\% - 2\% + 3\%$ (actually, the random error return of 3% is determined in order for the sum to equal 8%).

10.4 ESTIMATING FACTOR MODELS

Although many methods of estimating factor models are used, these methods can be grouped into three primary approaches:

1. Time-series approaches
2. Cross-sectional approaches
3. Factor-analytic approaches

10.4.1 Time-Series Approaches

Time-series approaches are perhaps the most intuitive to investors.[12] The model builder begins with the assumption that he or she knows in advance the factors that influence security returns. Identification of the relevant factors typically proceeds from an economic analysis of the firms involved. Aspects of macroeconomics, microeconomics, industrial organization, and fundamental security analysis will play a major role in the process.

For example, as discussed earlier, certain macroeconomic variables might be expected to have a pervasive impact on security returns, including such things as predicted growth in GDP, inflation, interest rates, and oil prices. With these factors specified, the model builder collects information concerning the historical values of the factors and security returns from period to period. Using these data, the model builder calculates the sensitivities of the securities' returns to the factors, the securities' zero factors and unique returns, and the standard deviations of the factors and their correlations. In this approach, accurate measurement of factor values is crucial. In practice, this can be quite difficult.

An Example

Table 10.1 and Figure 10.2 presented an example of how to use the time-series approach to estimate a two-factor model. In this example, returns on individual stocks such as Widget were related to two factors—gross domestic product and inflation—by comparing over time each stock's returns with the values of the factors.

Recently, Fama and French conducted a study that used a time-series approach to identify the factors that explain stock and bond returns.[13] Their study found monthly stock returns to be related to three factors: a market factor, a size factor, and a book-to-market equity factor. In equation form, their factor model for stocks appears as:

$$r_{it} - r_{ft} = a_i + b_{i1}(r_{Mt} - r_{ft}) + b_{i2}\mathrm{SMB}_t + b_{i3}\mathrm{HML}_t + e_{it} \qquad (10.20)$$

The first factor $(r_{Mt} - r_{ft})$ is simply the monthly return on a broad stock market index over and above the return on one-month Treasury bills. The size factor (SMB_t) can be thought of as the difference in the monthly return on two stock indices: a small-stock index and a big-stock index. (Here a stock's size is measured by its stock price at the end of the previous June each year times the number of shares it has outstanding at that time. The small-stock index consists of stocks that are below the median NYSE size, and the big-stock index consists of stocks that are above the median.) The book-to-market equity factor $\left(\text{HML}_t\right)$ is also the difference in the monthly return on two stock indices: an index of stocks with high book-to-market equity ratios and an index of stocks with low book-to-market equity ratios. (Here book equity is stockholders' equity taken from the firm's balance sheet, and market equity is the same as the stock's size used in determining the previous factor. The high-ratio index consists of stocks that are in the top third, and the low-ratio index consists of stocks that are in the bottom third.)

Fama and French also identified two factors that seem to explain monthly bond returns. In equation form, their factor model for bonds appears as:

$$r_{it} - r_{ft} = a_i + b_{i1}\text{TERM}_t + b_{i2}\text{DEF}_t + e_{it} \qquad (10.21)$$

These two factors are a term-structure factor and a default factor.[14] The term-structure factor $\left(\text{TERM}_t\right)$ is simply the difference in the monthly returns on long-term Treasury bonds and one-month Treasury bills. The default factor $\left(\text{DEF}_t\right)$ is the difference in the monthly returns on a portfolio of long-term corporate bonds and long-term Treasury bonds.[15]

Note that by creating factors using the return differences between two portfolios, Fama and French are able to indirectly capture investors' expectations. For example, when the DEF_t factor has a positive value, investors are expressing their optimistic expectations about the trend in corporate creditworthiness. They have bid up the price of securities exposed to default (corporate bonds) relative to securities free of default risk (Treasury bonds).

10.4.2   Cross-Sectional Approaches

Cross-sectional approaches are less intuitive than time-series approaches but can often be just as powerful a tool. The model builder begins with estimates of securities' sensitivities to certain factors. Then in a particular time period, the values of the factors are estimated on the basis of securities' returns and their sensitivities to the factors. This process is repeated over multiple time periods, thereby providing estimates of the factors' values. In turn these values can be used to estimate the factors' standard deviations and correlations.

Note that the cross-sectional approach is entirely different from the time-series approach. With the time-series approach, the values of the factors are known and the sensitivities are estimated. Furthermore, the analysis is conducted for one security over multiple time periods, then another security, then another, and so on. With the cross-sectional approach the sensitivities are known and the values of the factors are estimated. Accordingly, the sensitivities in the cross-sectional approach are sometimes referred to as *attributes*. Furthermore, the analysis is conducted over one time period for a group of securities, then another time period for the same group, then another, and so on. Examples of one-factor and two-factor models will be shown next to illustrate the cross-sectional approach.[16]

One-Factor Cross-Sectional Models

Figure 10.3 provides a hypothetical example of the relationship between the returns for a number of different stocks in a given time period and one security attribute—dividend yield—for each stock. Each point represents one particular stock, showing its return and dividend yield for the time period under evaluation. In this case, stocks with higher dividend yields tended to do better—that is, to have higher returns—than

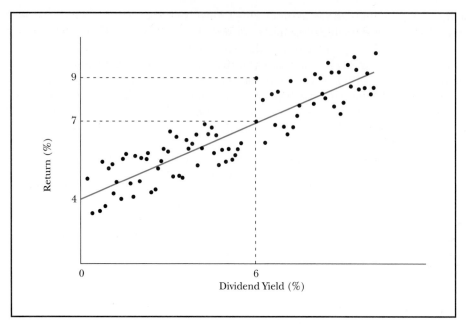

Figure 10.3
A Cross-Sectional One-Factor Model

those with lower dividend yields. Whereas Figure 10.3 (an example of the cross-sectional approach) is based on many stocks for one time period, Figure 10.1 (an example of the time-series approach) is based on one stock for many time periods.

The relationship shown in Figure 10.3 was quantified by fitting a straight line to the diagram by using the statistical technique of simple linear regression analysis. The equation of the line in Figure 10.3 is:

$$\bar{r}_{it} = 4 + .5b_{it} \tag{10.22}$$

or, more generally

$$\bar{r}_{it} = a_t + b_{it}F_t \tag{10.23}$$

where:

$\bar{r}_{it}$ = the expected return on stock i in period t, given that the factor had an actual value of F_t
a_t = the zero factor in period t
b_{it} = the dividend yield of stock i in period t
F_t = the actual value of the factor in period t

The vertical intercept a_t indicates the expected return on a typical stock with a dividend yield of zero. Hence it is called the zero factor as in Equation (10.1). In Figure 10.3 it is equal to 4%. The slope of .5 indicates the increase in expected return for each percent of dividend yield. Hence it represents the actual value of the dividend yield factor (F_t) in this time period.

From this example it can be seen that the cross-sectional approach uses sensitivities to provide estimates of the values of the factors. Hence these factors are known as *empirical factors*. In comparison it was shown earlier that the time-series approach uses known values of factors to provide estimates of a security's sensitivities. Hence these factors are known as *fundamental factors*.

The actual return on any given security may lie above or below the line because of its nonfactor return. A complete description of the relationship for this one-factor model is:

$$r_{it} = 4 + .5b_{it} + e_{it} \qquad (10.24)$$

where e_{it} denotes the nonfactor return during period t on security i. In Figure 10.3, security x had a dividend yield of 6%. Hence from Equation (10.20) it had an expected return during this time period of 7% [= 4 + (.5 × 6)]. Because it actually had a return of 9%, its nonfactor return was +2% (= 9% − 7%).

In periods such as the one shown in Figure 10.3, high-yield stocks tended to outperform low-yield stocks. This result indicates that the yield factor F_t was positive at the time. However, it is possible that in another time period low-yield stocks will tend to outperform high-yield stocks. The regression line in the corresponding diagram would be downward-sloping, and the yield factor would be negative. In still other time periods, there will be no relationship between yield and return, resulting in a flat regression line and a yield factor of zero.

Two-Factor Cross-Sectional Models

In some time periods small stocks tend to outperform large stocks. In other months the converse is true. Hence many cross-sectional models use a *size attribute* that is often computed by taking the logarithm of the total market value of the firm's outstanding equity measured in millions, which is, in turn, calculated by taking the firm's stock price and multiplying it by the number of shares outstanding and then dividing the resulting figure by 1 million.[17] Thus a $1 million stock would be assigned a size attribute value of zero; a $10 million stock a size attribute value of one; a $100 million stock a size attribute value of two, and so on. This convention is based on the empirical observation that the impact of the size factor on a security with a large total market value is likely to be twice as great as that on a security with one-tenth the value. More succinctly, the size effect appears to be *linear in the logarithms*.

The procedure used in Figure 10.3 to estimate the yield factor can be used to estimate the size factor in a given month. The size attributes of securities can be plotted on the horizontal axis, and their returns for the given time period plotted (as in Figure 10.3) on the vertical axis. The slope of the resultant regression line provides an estimate of the size factor for the time period.

This procedure has drawbacks, however. Large stocks tend to have high yields. Thus differences in returns between large and small stocks may be due to some extent to differences in yield, not size. The estimated size factor may be in part a reflection of a true yield factor. The problem is symmetric in that the estimated yield factor may also be in part a reflection of the true size factor.

This problem can be mitigated by comparing returns with both size and yield attributes simultaneously by using the statistical technique of multiple linear regression analysis. Figure 10.4 provides an illustration. Each security is represented by a point in a three-dimensional graph, with return during the time period shown on the vertical axis, dividend yield for the time period shown on one of the horizontal axes, and size for the period shown on the other.

Multiple-regression analysis fits a plane to the data. In the example shown in Figure 10.4, this process results in the following regression equation:

$$r_{it} = 7 + .4b_{i1t} - .3b_{i2t} + e_{it} \qquad (10.25)$$

where b_{i1t} and b_{i2t} denote, respectively, the dividend yield and size of stock i in time period t. In general, the regression equation for a two-factor model is:

$$r_{it} = a_t + b_{i1t}F_{1t} + b_{i2t}F_{2t} + e_{it} \qquad (10.26)$$

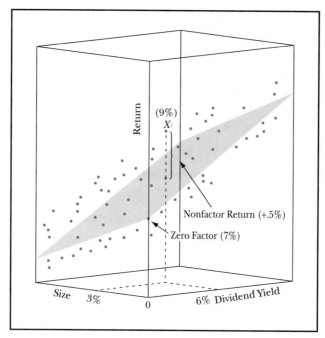

Figure 10.4
A Cross-Sectional Two-Factor Model

where a_t denotes the zero factor in time period t and the two factors are denoted F_{1t} and F_{2t}.

The equation of the plane shown in Figure 10.4 is:

$$\bar{r}_{it} = 7 + .4b_{i1t} - .3b_{i2t} \tag{10.27}$$

or, more generally,

$$\bar{r}_{it} = a_t + b_{i1t}\bar{F}_{1t} + b_{i2t}\bar{F}_{2t} \tag{10.28}$$

This means that the zero factor a_t was 7%, indicating that a stock with zero-dividend yield and zero size (meaning a market value of $1 million) would have been expected to have a return of 7%. Note that the estimated expected values of the dividend yield factor $\left(\bar{F}_{1t}\right)$ and size factor $\left(\bar{F}_{2t}\right)$ are .4 and −.3, respectively. Thus during this time period, higher dividend yields and smaller sizes were both associated with larger returns.

In Equations (10.25) and (10.27), a given security x with a dividend yield of 6% and a size of 3 would have been expected to have a return of 8.5% [= 7 + (.4 × 6) − (.3 × 3)]. With an actual return of 9% its nonfactor return e_{it} is thus +.5% (= 9% − 8.5%) during this time period, as shown in Figure 10.4.

The inclusion of size and dividend yield along with the use of multiple-regression analysis can help sort out the effects of differences in yield and size on differences in security returns. It cannot deal adequately with influences that are not represented at all, nor can it guarantee that the included attributes are not simply serving as *proxies* for other, more fundamental, attributes. Statistical tests can indicate the ability of the variables included in the analysis to explain or predict past security returns. But judgment and luck are required to identify variables that can help predict future security returns, risks, and covariances. The extension to more than two variables follows in a straightforward manner from what has been indicated in Equations (10.25) through (10.28).[18]

10.4.3 Factor-Analytic Approaches

Finally, with factor-analytic approaches the model builder knows neither the factor values nor the securities' sensitivities to those factors. A statistical technique called *factor analysis* is used to extract the number of factors and securities' sensitivities based simply on a set of securities' past returns. Factor analysis takes the returns over many time periods on a sample of securities and attempts to identify one or more statistically significant factors that could have generated the covariances of returns observed within the sample. In essence, the return data tell the model builder about the structure of the factor model. Unfortunately, factor analysis does not specify what economic variables the factors represent.

10.4.4 Limitations

There is no reason to assume that a good factor model for one period will be a good one for the next period. Key factors—such as the effect of energy prices on security markets—change, as they did in the 1970s and more recently during the war in the Persian Gulf. The risks and returns associated with various factors and the sensitivities of securities to factors can change over time.[19]

It would be convenient if neither the relevant factors nor their magnitudes were to change from period to period. If neither changed, mechanical procedures could be applied to security returns over an extended past period and the factor model inferred along with all the needed magnitudes. As it is, statistical estimation methods should be tempered with the judgment of the model builder to account for the dynamic nature of the investment environment.

10.5   FACTOR MODELS AND EQUILIBRIUM

It should be kept in mind that a factor model is not an equilibrium model of asset pricing. Compare, for example, the expected return on a stock using a one-factor model from Equation (10.3) with that of the capital asset pricing model (CAPM) from Equation (9.7):[20]

$$\overline{r}_i = a_i + b_i \overline{F} \tag{10.3}$$

$$\overline{r}_i = r_f + (\overline{r}_M - r_f)\beta_{iM} \tag{9.7}$$

Both equations show that the expected return on the stock is related to a characteristic of the stock, b_i or β_i. If the expected return on both the factor $\overline{F}$ and the market risk premium $(\overline{r}_M - r_f)$ are positive, the larger the size of the characteristic, the larger the security's expected return. Hence at this point there appears to be little to differentiate these two equations of expected return.

The key is in the other term on the right-hand side of each equation: a_i and r_f. The only characteristic of the stock that determines its expected return according to the CAPM is β_i, because r_f denotes the riskfree rate and is the same for all securities. However, with the factor model there is a second characteristic of the stock that needs to be estimated to determine the stock's expected return: namely, a_i. Because the size of a_i differs from one stock to another, it prevents the factor model from being an equilibrium model.

Stated differently, two stocks with the same value of b_i can have dramatically different expected returns according to a factor model. For example, if GDP is expected to rise by 5%, then the expected return on Widget is 14% because a_i and b_i for Widget are 4 and 2 [14% = 4% + (2 × 5%)]. In comparison, even though ABC has the same sensitivity to GDP as Widget $(b_i = 2)$, it has an expected return of only 8% because its value of a_i is 12% [8% = −2% + (2 × 5%)].

In contrast, two stocks with the same value of β_i will have the same expected return according to the equilibrium-based CAPM. If Widget and XYZ both have a beta of 1.2, then they both will have an expected return of 14%, given that the riskfree rate is 8% and the expected return on the market is 13% [14% = 8% + (13% − 8%) × 1.2].

Having established that a factor model is not an equilibrium model, it seems appropriate to investigate the relationship between the parameters a_i and b_i of the one-factor model and the single parameter β_i of the CAPM.

For example, if actual returns can be viewed as being generated by a one-factor model, where the factor F is the return on the market portfolio r_M, then according to Equation (10.3), expected returns will be equal to:

$$\bar{r}_i = a_i + b_i \bar{r}_M \tag{10.29}$$

because $\bar{F} = \bar{r}_M$. But if equilibrium exists according to the CAPM, then Equation (9.7) can be rewritten to state that expected returns will also be equal to :

$$\bar{r}_i = \left(1 - \beta_{iM}\right)r_f + \bar{r}_M \beta_{iM} \tag{10.30}$$

This means that the parameters of the one-factor model and the CAPM must have the following relationships:

$$a_i = \left(1 - \beta_{iM}\right)r_f \tag{10.31}$$

$$b_i = \beta_{iM} \tag{10.32}$$

Therefore, if expected returns are determined according to the CAPM and actual returns are generated by the one-factor market model, then a_i and b_i must be related to β_{iM}.[21]

10.6   SUMMARY

1. A factor model is a return-generating process that relates returns on securities to the movement in one or more common factors.
2. Any aspect of a security's return unexplained by the factor model is assumed to be unique to the security and therefore uncorrelated with the unique element of returns on other securities.
3. The market model is a specific example of a factor model where the factor is the return on a market index.
4. The assumption that the returns on securities respond to common factors greatly simplifies the task of calculating the curved Markowitz efficient set.
5. The sensitivity of a portfolio to a factor is the weighted average of the sensitivities of the component securities, with the securities' proportions in the portfolio serving as weights.
6. The total risk of a security is composed of factor risk and nonfactor risk.
7. Diversification leads to an averaging of factor risk.
8. Diversification reduces nonfactor risk.
9. Three basic methods are used to estimate factor models: the time-series approach, the cross-sectional approach, and the factor-analytic approach.
10. A factor model is not an equilibrium model of asset prices as is the CAPM. However, if equilibrium exists, certain relationships will hold between the factor model and the equilibrium asset pricing model.

QUESTIONS AND PROBLEMS

1. Included among the factors that might be expected to be pervasive are expectations regarding growth in real GDP, real interest rates, inflation, and oil prices. For each factor, provide an example of an industry that is expected to have a high (either positive or negative) sensitivity to the factor.

2. Why do factor models greatly simplify the process of deriving the curved Markowitz efficient set?

3. Many investment management firms assign each of their security analysts to research a particular group of stocks. (Usually these assignments are organized by industry.) How are these assignments an implicit recognition of the validity of factor-model relationships?

4. What are two critical assumptions underlying any factor model? Cite hypothetical examples of violations of those assumptions.

5. Cupid Childs, a wise investment statistician, once said with respect to factor models, "Similar stocks should display similar returns." What did Cupid mean by this statement?

6. On the basis of a one-factor model, consider a security with a zero-factor value of 4% and a sensitivity to the factor of .50. The factor takes on a value of 10%. The security generates a return of 11%. What portion of the return is related to nonfactor elements?

7. On the basis of a one-factor model, consider a portfolio of two securities with the following characteristics:

Security	Factor Sensitivity	Nonfactor Risk (σ_{ei}^2)	Proportion
A	.20	49	.40
B	3.50	100	.60

   a. If the standard deviation of the factor is 15%, what is the factor risk of the portfolio?
   b. What is the nonfactor risk of the portfolio?
   c. What is the portfolio's standard deviation?

8. Recalculate the answers to Problem 7 assuming that the portfolio is also invested in a riskfree asset so that its investment proportions are:

Security	Proportion
Riskfree	.10
A	.36
B	.54

9. On the basis of a one-factor model, security A has a sensitivity of $-.50$, whereas security B has a sensitivity of 1.25. If the covariance between the two securities is -312.50, what is the standard deviation of the factor?

10. On the basis of a one-factor model, for two securities A and B:

$$r_{At} = 5\% + .8F_t + e_{At}$$
$$r_{Bt} = 7\% + 1.2F_t + e_{Bt}$$
$$\sigma_F = 18\%$$
$$\sigma_{eA} = 25\%$$
$$\sigma_{eB} = 15\%$$

   Calculate the standard deviation of each security.

11. On the basis of a one-factor model, if the average nonfactor risk (σ_{ei}^2) of all securities is 225, what is the nonfactor risk of a portfolio with equal weights assigned to its 10 securities? 100 securities? 1,000 securities?

12. On the basis of the discussion of factor and nonfactor risk and given a set of securities that can be combined into various portfolios, what might be a useful measure of the relative diversification of each of the alternative portfolios?

13. With a five-factor model (assuming uncorrelated factors) and a 30-stock portfolio, how many parameters must be estimated to calculate the expected return and standard deviation of the portfolio? How many additional parameter estimates are required if the factors are correlated?

14. Beyond the factors discussed in the text, speculate as to other factors that could reasonably be expected to pervasively affect security returns.

15. On the basis of a three-factor model, consider a portfolio composed of three securities with the following characteristics:

Security	Factor 1 Sensitivity	Factor 2 Sensitivity	Factor 3 Sensitivity	Proportion
A	−.20	3.60	.05	.60
B	.50	10.00	.75	.20
C	1.50	2.20	.30	.20

What are the sensitivities of the portfolio to factors 1, 2, and 3?

16. Smiler Murray, a quantitative security analyst, remarked, "The structure of any factor model concerns surprise, in particular the nature of correlations between surprises in different securities' returns." What does Smiler mean by this statement?

17. Dode Cicero owns a portfolio of two securities. On the basis of a two-factor model, the two securities have the following characteristics:

Security	Zero 1 Factor	Factor 1 Sensitivity	Factor 2 Sensitivity	Nonfactor Risk (σ_{ei}^2)	Proportion
A	2%	.30	2.0	196	.70
B	3	.50	1.8	100	.30

The factors are uncorrelated. Factor 1 has an expected value of 15% and a standard deviation of 20%. Factor 2 has an expected value of 4% and a standard deviation of 5%. Calculate the expected return and standard deviation of Dode's portfolio. [Hint: Think about how Equation (10.6a) could be extended to a two-factor model by considering Equation (10.9).]

18. Compare and contrast the three approaches to estimating factor models.

19. Why are investor expectations about future factor values more relevant to security returns than are the historical value of the factors?

20. The return on security A can be expressed as a one-factor model of the form:

$$r_{At} = -4\% + 2.6F_t + e_{At}$$

The response coefficient of security A (c_A) to unanticipated changes in the factor is $+1.5$. During the period security A returned 13%. If the expected value of the factor was 8% and security A's random error term (e_{At}) during the period was $+1\%$, what must have been the unexpected change in the factor (FD_t)?

21. Consider a factor model with earnings yield (or earnings/price ratio) and book-price (or book value/market price ratio) as the two factors. Stock A has an earnings yield of 10% and a book-price of 2. Stock B's earnings yield is 15% and its book-price is .90. The zero factors of stocks A and B are 7% and 9%, respectively. If the expected returns of stocks A and B are 18% and 16.5%, respectively, what are the expected earnings-yield and book-price factor values?

22. On the basis of a two-factor model, consider two securities with the following characteristics:

Characteristic	Security A	Security B
Factor 1 sensitivity	1.5	.7
Factor 2 sensitivity	2.6	1.2
Nonfactor risk (σ_{ei}^2)	25.0	16.0

The standard deviations of factor 1 and factor 2 are 20% and 15%, respectively, and the factors have a covariance of 225. What are the standard deviations of securities A and B? What is their covariance?

23. Are factor models consistent with the CAPM? If returns are determined by a one-factor model (where that factor is the return on the market portfolio) and the CAPM holds, what relationships must exist between the two models?

ENDNOTES

[1] See Appendix B in Chapter 7.

[2] Only six data points are shown in the figure for ease of exposition. The standard statistical procedure of simple linear regression is discussed in Chapter 16 and in Mark Kritzman, "…About Regression," *Financial Analysts Journal* 47, no. 3 (May/June 1991), 12–15. It can be found in most statistics books, such as James T. McClave and P. George Benson, *Statistics for Business and Economics* (New York: Macmillan, 1994), Chapter 10.

[3] It is more appropriate to state that security returns respond to expectations (and deviations from those expectations) about the future values of factors such as GDP growth as opposed to merely the realized values of those factors. This subtle (but important) distinction will be addressed later in the chapter.

[4] Sometimes b is referred to as the **factor loading** or attribute of the security.

[5] The time subscript t was deleted from the market model simply for ease of exposition. Technically the random error term should be written as ε_{ilt}.

[6] This calculation is shown in more detail in Appendix B in Chapter 7.

[7] Actually, all that is necessary for this reduction in nonfactor risk to occur is for the maximum amount invested in any one security to continually decrease as N increases. An example based on the market model is given in Chapter 7.

[8] These values were arrived at by applying multiple regression (see McClave and Benson, *Statistics for Business and Economics*, Chapter 11) to the data given in Table 10.1.

[9] Attempts have been made to identify stock groups, or clusters, where stocks within any group have returns that are more highly correlated with one another than with the returns of stocks from different groups. See, for example, Benjamin F. King, "Market and Industry factors in Stock Price Behavior," *Journal of Business* 39, no. 1 (January 1966): 139–170; James L. Farrell Jr., "Analyzing Covariation of Returns to Determine Stock Groupings," *Journal of Business* 47, no. 2 (April 1974): 186–207; "Homogeneous Stock Groupings: Implications for Portfolio Management," *Financial Analysts Journal* 31, no. 3 (May/June 1975): 50–62; and Robert D. Arnott, "Cluster Analysis and Stock Price Comovement," *Financial Analysts Journal* 36, no. 6 (November/December 1980): 56–62.

[10] Another example of such a model expands the market model to include sector factors where the sectors are selected to represent "industries." Hence each stock has two sensitivities that indicate how the stock responds to returns on the stock index and an industry index to which the stock belongs. See Gordon J. Alexander and Jack Clark Francis, *Portfolio Analysis* (Upper Saddle River, NJ: Prentice Hall, 1986), 83–92.

[11] Equations (10.17) and (10.18) can be reconciled as follows; for ease of exposition, the analysis deletes the time subscript t and assumes that there is one factor. Note that Equation (10.17) implies $\bar{r}_i = a_i + b_i \bar{F}_1$, where $\bar{r}_i$ and $\bar{F}_1$ are the expected return for security i and

the expected value of the factor, respectively. Substituting $\bar{r}_i - b_i \bar{F}_1$ for a_i results in: $r_i = \bar{r}_i + b_i(F_1 - \bar{F}_1) + e_i$. Letting $FD_1 = F_1 - \bar{F}_1$ produces an alternative formulation of a one-factor model that corresponds to Equation (10.18): $r_i = \bar{r}_i + b_i FD_1 + e_i$.

[12] The examples given earlier in the chapter based on Table 10.1 use this approach.

[13] Eugene F. Fama and Kenneth R. French, "Common Risk Factors in the Returns on Stocks and Bonds," *Journal of Financial Economics* 33, no. 1 (February 1993): 3–56. Other time-series examples are presented in Chapter 11. It should be noted that attempts to relate the Fama-French factor model to an asset pricing model of market equilibrium have been controversial. See, for example, A. Craig MacKinlay, "Multifactor Models Do Not Explain Deviations from the CAPM," *Journal of Financial Economics* 38, no. 1 (May 1995): 3–28.

[14] Speculative-grade bonds were found to also be related to the three stock factors.

[15] Interestingly, Fama and French also found that the market factor $(r_{Mt} - r_{ft})$ was related to these two bond factors. In light of this finding, they constructed a revised market factor that basically consisted of the market factor less the influence of the two bond factors and the two other stock factors, and they found that stock returns were related to five factors: the revised market factor, SML_t, HML_t, $TERM_t$, and DEF_t. Bond returns continued to be related to just the two bond factors.

[16] Note that in the time-series approach, a security's sensitivity to a factor is its "attribute," and the factor is a given macroeconomic variable. Hence the attribute's value is unknown and must be estimated, whereas the value of the factor is known. In the cross-sectional approach, a security's attribute is usually some microeconomic variable measuring the security's exposure to the factor (a stock's dividend yield and market capitalization can be thought of as examples of attributes). Hence the attribute's value is known, whereas the factor is unknown and must be estimated.

[17] Size has also been used as a factor in the time-series approach but in a different manner. See the previous discussion of the Fama and French study that is mentioned in endnote 13.

[18] One of the first studies to use the cross-sectional approach with more than two factors is William F. Sharpe, "Factors in New York Stock Exchange Security Returns, 1931–1979," *Journal of Portfolio Management* 8, no. 4 (Summer 1982): 5–19. A subsequent application is presented in Blake R. Grossman and William F. Sharpe, "Financial Implications of South African Divestment," *Financial Analysts Journal* 42, no. 4 (July/August 1986): 15–29.

[19] One study found that the factors that appear to explain security returns on even dates generally do not explain security returns on odd dates. See Dolores A. Conway and Marc R. Reinganum, "Stable Factors in Security Returns: Identification Using Cross Validation," *Journal of Business and Economic Statistics* 6, no. 1 (January 1988): 1–15.

[20] Time subscripts have been removed for ease of exposition. In section 11.5. of Chapter 11, the relationship between a factor model's sensitivities and the CAPM's beta is examined.

[21] If the factor in a one-factor world is the return on the market portfolio (as shown here), then technically the random error term for any security cannot be completely uncorrelated with the factor because the market portfolio consists of all securities and hence is influenced by the nonfactor return of each security. Hence, Equation (10. 30) is not exactly true but is a close approximation. See Eugene F. Fama, *Foundations of Finance* (New York: Basic Books, 1976), Chapter 3.

KEY TERMS

return-generating process	factor risk
factor models	nonfactor risk
sensitivity	sector-factor model
factor loading (attribute)	sector factor

REFERENCES

1. General discussions of factor models can be found in:

   William F. Sharpe, "Factors in New York Stock Exchange Security Returns, 1931–1979," *Journal of Portfolio Management* 8, no. 4 (Summer 1982): 5–19; and "Factor Models, CAPMs, and the ABT [sic]," *Journal of Portfolio Management* 11, no. 1 (Fall 1984): 21–25.

   Mark Kritzman, "... About Factor Models," *Financial Analysts Journal* 49, no. 1 (January/February 1993): 12–15.

   Gregory Connor, "The Three Types of Factor Models: A Comparison of Their Explanatory Power," *Financial Analysts Journal* 51, no. 3 (May/June 1995): 42–46.

   Richard C. Grinold and Ronald N. Kahn, *Active Portfolio Management* (Chicago: Probus Publishing, 1995), Chapter 3.

2. Empirical papers that attempt to identify relevant factors and to estimate the magnitudes of the associated values include:

   Benjamin F. King, "Market and Industry Factors in Stock Price Behavior," *Journal of Business* 39, no. 1 (January 1966): 139–170.

   George J. Feeney and Donald D. Hester, "Stock Market Indices: A Principal Components Analysis," in Donald D. Hester and James Tobin (eds.), *Risk Aversion and Portfolio Choice* (New York: Wiley, 1967).

   Edwin J. Elton and Martin J. Gruber, "Estimating the Dependence Structure of Share Prices—Implications for Portfolio Selection," *Journal of Finance* 28, no. 5 (December 1973): 1203–1232.

   James J. Farrell Jr., "Analyzing Covariation of Returns to Determine Homogeneous Stock Groupings," *Journal of Business* 47, no. 2 (April 1974): 186–207.

   Barr Rosenberg and Vinay Marathe, "The Prediction of Investment Risk: Systematic and Residual Risk," in *Proceedings of the Seminar on the Analysis of Security Prices* (Center for Research in Security Prices, Graduate School of Business, University of Chicago, November 1975).

   Robert D. Arnott, "Cluster Analysis and Stock Price Movement," *Financial Analysts Journal* 36, no. 6 (November/December 1980): 56–62.

   Tony Estep, Nick Hanson, and Cal Johnson, "Sources of Value and Risk in Common Stocks," *Journal of Portfolio Management* 9, no. 4 (Summer 1983): 5–13.

   Nai-Fu Chen, Richard Roll, and Stephen A. Ross, "Economic Forces and the Stock Market," *Journal of Business* 59, no. 3 (July 1986): 383–403.

   Robert D. Arnott, Charles M. Kelso Jr., Stephen Kiscadden, and Rosemary Macedo, "Forecasting Factor Returns: An Intriguing Possibility," *Journal of Portfolio Management* 16, no. 1 (Fall 1989): 28–35.

   Eugene F. Fama and Kenneth R. French, "The Cross-Section of Expected Stock Returns," *Journal of Finance* 47, no. 2 (June 1992): 427–465.

   Eugene F. Fama and Kenneth R. French, "Common Risk Factors in the Returns on Stocks and Bonds," *Journal of Financial Economics* 33, no. 1 (February 1993): 3–56.

   James L. Davis, "The Cross-Section of Realized Stock Returns: The Pre-COMPUSTAT Evidence," *Journal of Finance* 49, no. 5 (December 1994): 1579–1593.

   Eugene F. Fama and Kenneth R. French, "Size and Book-to-Market Factors in Earnings and Returns," *Journal of Finance* 50, no. 1 (March 1995): 131–155.

   S. P. Kothari, Jay Shanken, and Richard G. Sloan, "Another Look at the Cross-Section of Expected Stock Returns," *Journal of Finance* 50, no. 1 (March 1995): 185–224.

   Eugene F. Fama and Kenneth R. French, "Multifactor Explanations of Asset Pricing Anomalies," *Journal of Finance* 51, no. 1 (March 1996): 55–84.

   William C. Barbee Jr., Sandip Mukherji, and Gary A. Raines, "Do Sales-Price and Debt-Equity Explain Stock Returns Better Than Book-Market and Firm Size?" *Financial Analysts Journal* 52, no. 2 (March/April 1996): 56–60.

Kent Daniel and Sheridan Titman, "Evidence on the Characteristics of Cross Sectional Variation in Stock Returns," *Journal of Finance* 52, no. 1 (March 1997): 1–33.

3. Several recent papers have argued that a factor model that distinguishes value stocks from growth (or "glamour") stocks is more appropriate than the Fama-French model:

Josef Lakonishok, Andrei Shleifer, and Robert W. Vishny, "Contrarian Investment, Extrapolation, and Risk," *Journal of Finance* 49, no. 5 (December 1994): 1541–1578.

Louis K. C. Chan, Narasimhan Jegadeesh, and Josef Lakonishok, "Evaluating the Performance of Value versus Glamour Stocks: The Impact of Selection Bias," *Journal of Financial Economics* 38, no. 3 (July 1995): 269–296.

Rafael La Porta, Josef Lakonishok, Andrei Shleifer, and Robert Vishny, "Good News for Value Stocks: Further Evidence on Market Efficiency," *Journal of Finance* 52, no. 2 (June 1997): 859–874.

4. Fixed-income factor models are discussed in:

Ronald N. Kahn and Deepak Gulrajani, "Risk and Return in the Canadian Bond Market," *Journal of Portfolio Management* 19, no. 3 (Spring 1993): 86–92.

CHAPTER 11

ARBITRAGE PRICING THEORY

The capital asset pricing model (CAPM) is an equilibrium model that describes why different securities have different expected returns. In particular, this economic model of asset pricing asserts that securities have different expected returns because they have different betas. However, there exists an alternative model of asset pricing that was developed by Stephen Ross. It is known as **arbitrage pricing theory** (APT), and in some ways it is less complicated than the CAPM.

The CAPM requires a number of assumptions, including those initially made by Harry Markowitz when he developed the basic mean-variance model that was presented in Chapters 6 and 7. For example, each investor is assumed to choose his or her optimal portfolio by the use of indifference curves based on portfolio expected returns and standard deviations. In contrast, APT makes different assumptions. One primary APT assumption is that each investor, when given the opportunity to increase the return of his or her portfolio without increasing its risk, will proceed to do so. The mechanism for doing so involves the use of arbitrage portfolios.

11.1 FACTOR MODELS

Arbitrage pricing theory starts by making the assumption that security returns are related to an unknown number of unknown factors.[1] For ease of exposition, imagine that there is only one factor, and that factor is the rate of increase in industrial production. In this situation, security returns are related to the following one-factor model:

$$r_i = a_i + b_i F_1 + e_i \qquad (11.1)$$

where:

r_i = rate of return on security i
a_i = the zero factor
F_1 = the value of the factor, which in this case is the rate of growth in industrial production
e_i = random error term[2]

In this equation, b_i is known as the sensitivity of security i to the factor. (It is also known as the factor loading for security i or the attribute of security i.)

Imagine that an investor owns three stocks, and the current market value of his or her holdings in each one is $4,000,000. In this case, the investor's current investable wealth W_0 is equal to $12,000,000. Everyone believes that these three stocks have the following expected returns and sensitivities:

i	$\bar{r}_i$	b_i
Stock 1	15%	.9
Stock 2	21	3.0
Stock 3	12	1.8

Do these expected returns and factor sensitivities represent an equilibrium situation? If not, what will happen to stock prices and expected returns to restore equilibrium?

11.1.1   Principle of Arbitrage

In recent years, baseball card conventions have become commonplace events. Collectors gather to exchange baseball cards with one another at negotiated prices. Suppose that Ms. A attends such a gathering, where in one corner she finds S offering to sell a 1951 Mickey Mantle rookie card for $400. Exploring the convention further, she finds B bidding $500 for the same card. Recognizing a financial opportunity, Ms. A agrees to sell the card to B, who gives her $500 in cash. She races back to give $400 to S, receives the card, and returns with it to B, who takes possession of the card. Ms. A pockets the $100 in profit from the two transactions and moves on in search of other opportunities. Ms. A has engaged in a form of arbitrage.

Arbitrage is the process of earning riskless profits by taking advantage of differential pricing for the same physical asset or security. As a widely applied investment tactic, arbitrage typically entails the sale of a security at a relatively high price and the simultaneous purchase of the same security (or its functional equivalent) at a relatively low price.

Arbitrage activity is a critical element of modern, efficient security markets. Because arbitrage profits are by definition riskless, all investors have an incentive to take advantage of them whenever they are discovered. Granted, some investors have greater resources and inclination to engage in arbitrage than others. However, it takes relatively few of these active investors to exploit arbitrage situations and, by their buying and selling actions, eliminate these profit opportunities.

The nature of arbitrage is clear when discussing different prices for an individual security. However, "almost arbitrage" opportunities can involve "similar" securities or portfolios. That similarity can be defined in many ways. One interesting way is the exposure to pervasive factors that affect security prices.

A factor model implies that securities or portfolios with equal factor sensitivities will behave in the same way except for nonfactor risk. Therefore, securities or portfolios with the same factor sensitivities should offer the same expected returns. If they do not, then "almost arbitrage" opportunities exist. Investors will take advantage of these opportunities, causing their elimination. That is the essential logic underlying APT.

11.1.2   Arbitrage Portfolios

According to APT, an investor will explore the possibility of forming an **arbitrage portfolio** in order to increase the expected return of his or her current portfolio without increasing its risk. Just what is an arbitrage portfolio? First of all, it is a portfolio that does not require any additional funds from the investor. If X_i denotes the *change* in the investor's holdings of security *i* (and hence the weight of security *i* in the arbitrage portfolio), this requirement of an arbitrage portfolio can be written as:

$$X_1 + X_2 + X_3 = 0 \tag{11.2}$$

Second, an arbitrage portfolio has no sensitivity to any factor. (In the terminology of factor models, an arbitrage portfolio has "zero factor exposures.") Because the sensitivity of a portfolio to a factor is just a weighted average of the sensitivities of the securities in the portfolio to that factor, this requirement of an arbitrage portfolio when there is one factor can be written as:

$$b_1 X_1 + b_2 X_2 + b_3 X_3 = 0 \tag{11.3a}$$

or, in the current example:

$$.9X_1 + 3.0X_2 + 1.8X_3 = 0 \tag{11.3b}$$

Thus, in this example, an arbitrage portfolio will have no sensitivity to the growth rate of industrial production.

Strictly speaking, an arbitrage portfolio should also have zero nonfactor risk. However, the APT assumes that such risk is small enough to be ignored.

At this point many potential arbitrage portfolios can be identified. These candidates are simply portfolios that meet the conditions given in Equations (11.2) and (11.3b). Note that there are three unknowns (X_1, X_2, and X_3) and two equations in this situation, which means that there is an infinite number of combinations of values for X_1, X_2, and X_3 that satisfy these two equations.[3] As a way of finding one combination, consider arbitrarily assigning a value of .1 to X_1. Doing so results in two equations and two unknowns:

$$.1 + X_2 + X_3 = 0 \tag{11.4a}$$

$$.09 + 3.0X_2 + 1.8X_3 = 0 \tag{11.4b}$$

The solution to Equations (11.4a) and (11.4b) is $X_2 = .075$ and $X_3 = -.175$. Hence a potential arbitrage portfolio is one with these weights.

To see if this candidate portfolio is indeed an arbitrage portfolio, one must determine its expected return. If its expected return is positive, then an arbitrage portfolio will have been identified.[4] Mathematically, this third and last requirement for an arbitrage portfolio is:

$$X_1 \bar{r}_1 + X_2 \bar{r}_2 + X_3 \bar{r}_3 > 0 \tag{11.5a}$$

or, for this example,

$$15X_1 + 21X_2 + 12X_3 > 0 \tag{11.5b}$$

The solution for this candidate shows that its expected return is $(15\% \times .1) + (21\% \times .075) + (12\% \times -.175) = .975\%$. Because this is a positive number, an arbitrage portfolio has indeed been identified.

The arbitrage portfolio just identified involves buying \$1,200,000 of stock 1 and \$900,000 of stock 2. How were these dollar figures arrived at? The solution comes from taking the current market value of the portfolio ($W_0 = \$12,000,000$) and multiplying it by the weights for the arbitrage portfolio of $X_1 = .1$ and $X_2 = .075$. Where does the money come from to make these purchases? It comes from selling \$2,100,000 of stock 3. (Note that $X_3 W_0 = -.175 \times \$12,000,000 = -\$2,100,000$.)

In summary, this arbitrage portfolio is attractive to any investor who desires a higher return and is not concerned with nonfactor risk. It requires no additional dollar investment, it has no factor risk, and it has a positive expected return.

TABLE 11.1	How an Arbitrage Portfolio Affects an Investor's Position		
	Old Portfolio +	Arbitrage Portfolio =	New Portfolio
Weight			
X_1	.333	.100	.433
X_2	.333	.075	.408
X_3	.333	−.175	.158
Property:			
r_p	16.000%	.975%	16.975%
b_p	1.900	.000	1.900
σ_p	11.000	Small	Approx. 11.000

11.1.3 The Investor's Position

At this juncture the investor can evaluate his or her position from either one of two equivalent viewpoints: (1) holding both the old portfolio and the arbitrage portfolio or (2) holding a new portfolio. Consider, for example, the weight in stock 1. The old portfolio weight was .333 and the arbitrage portfolio weight was .10, with the sum of these two weights being equal to .433. Note that the dollar value of the holdings of stock 1 in the new portfolio rises to $5,200,000 (=$4,000,000 + $1,200,000), so its weight is .433 (=$5,200,000/$12,000,000), equivalent to the sum of the old and arbitrage portfolio weights.

Similarly, the portfolio's expected return is equal to the sum of the expected returns of the old and arbitrage portfolios, or 16.975% (=16% + .975%). Equivalently, the new portfolio's expected return can be calculated using the new portfolio's weights and the expected returns of the stocks, or 16.975% $[= (.433 \times 15\%) + (.408 \times 21\%) + (.158 \times 12\%)]$.

The sensitivity of the new portfolio is 1.9 $[= (.433 \times .9) + (.408 \times 3.0) + (.158 \times 1.8)]$. This is the same as the sum of the sensitivities of the old and arbitrage portfolios (=1.9 + 0.0).

What about the risk of the new portfolio? Assume that the standard deviation of the old portfolio was 11%. The variance of the arbitrage portfolio will be small because its only source of risk is nonfactor risk. Similarly, the variance of the new portfolio will differ from that of the old only as a result of changes in its nonfactor risk. Thus it can be concluded that the risk of the new portfolio will be approximately 11%.[5] Table 11.1 summarizes these observations.

11.2 PRICING EFFECTS

What are the consequences of buying stocks 1 and 2 and selling stock 3? Because everyone will be doing so, the stocks' prices will be affected and, accordingly, their expected returns will adjust. Specifically, the prices of stocks 1 and 2 will rise because of increased buying pressure. In turn, this rise will cause their expected returns to fall. Conversely, the selling pressure put on stock 3 will cause its stock price to fall and its expected return to rise.

This outcome can be seen by examining the equation for estimating a stock's expected return:

$$\bar{r} = \frac{\overline{P_1}}{P_0} - 1 \tag{11.6}$$

where P_0 is the stock's current price and $\overline{P}_1$ is the stock's expected end-of-period price. Buying a stock such as stock 1 or 2 will push up its current price P_0 yet will have no impact on the stock's expected end-of-period price $\overline{P}_1$. As a result, its expected return $\overline{r}$ will decline. Conversely, selling a stock such as stock 3 will push down its current price and result in a rise in its expected return.

This buying-and-selling activity will continue until *all* arbitrage possibilities are significantly reduced or eliminated. That is, all possible portfolio adjustments that require no additional funds and that have zero factor exposures will all have zero expected returns. At this point there will exist an approximately linear relationship between expected returns and sensitivities of the following sort:

$$\overline{r}_i = \lambda_0 + \lambda_1 b_i \tag{11.7}$$

where λ_0 and λ_1 are constants. This equation is the asset pricing equation of the APT when returns are generated by one factor.[6] Note that it is the equation of a straight line, meaning that in equilibrium there will be a linear relationship between expected returns and sensitivities.

In the example, one possible equilibrium setting could have $\lambda_0 = 8$ and $\lambda_1 = 4$.[7] Consequently, the pricing equation is:

$$\overline{r}_i = 8 + 4b_i \tag{11.8}$$

This would result in the following equilibrium levels of expected returns for stocks 1, 2, and 3:

$$\overline{r}_1 = 8 + (4 \times .9) = 11.6\%$$

$$\overline{r}_2 = 8 + (4 \times 3.0) = 20.0\%$$

$$\overline{r}_3 = 8 + (4 \times 1.8) = 15.2\%$$

As a result, the expected returns for stocks 1 and 2 will have fallen from 15% and 21%, respectively, to 11.6% and 20% because of increased buying pressure. Conversely, increased selling pressure will have caused the expected return on stock 3 to rise from 12% to 15.2%. The bottom line is that the expected return on any security is, in equilibrium, a linear function of the security's sensitivity to the factor b_i.[8]

11.2.1   A Graphical Illustration

Figure 11.1 illustrates the asset pricing equation of Equation (11.7). Any security that has a factor sensitivity and expected return such that it lies off the line will be mispriced according to the APT and will present investors with the opportunity of forming arbitrage portfolios. Security B is an example. An investor who buys security B and sells security S in equal dollar amounts will have formed an arbitrage portfolio.[9] How?

First of all, by selling an amount of security S to pay for the long position in security B, the investor will not have committed any new funds. Second, because securities B and S have the same sensitivity to the factor, the selling of security S and buying of security B will constitute a portfolio with no sensitivity to the factor. Finally, the arbitrage portfolio will have a positive expected return because the expected return of security B is greater than the expected return of security S.[10] As a result of investors' buying security B, its price will rise and, in turn, its expected return will fall until it is located on the APT asset pricing line.[11]

In the three-security example presented earlier, it can be shown that the securities do not initially all lie on a straight line. Instead, any line that is drawn will have at least one of them lying above or below the line. However, after stocks 1, 2, and 3's expected returns have adjusted from 15%, 21%, and 12% to 11.6%, 20%, and 15.2%,

---

Arbitrage Pricing Theory

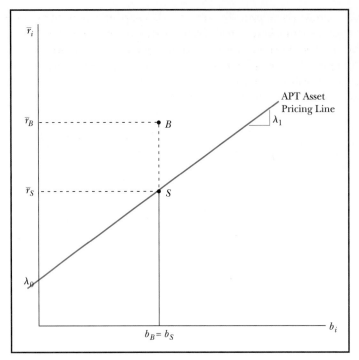

Figure 11.1
APT Asset Pricing Line

respectively, they will all lie on a line with a vertical intercept of 8% and a slope of 4. This result will be shown next.

11.2.2   Interpreting the APT Pricing Equation

How can the constants λ_0 and λ_1 that appear in the APT pricing Equation (11.7) be interpreted? On the assumption that there is a riskfree asset in existence, such an asset will have a rate of return that is a constant. Therefore this asset will have no sensitivity to the factor. From Equation (11.7) it can be seen that $\bar{r}_i = \lambda_0$ for any asset with $b_i = 0$. In the case of the riskfree asset, it is also known that $\bar{r}_i = r_f$, implying that $\lambda_0 = r_f$. Hence the value of λ_0 in Equation (11.7) must be r_f, allowing this equation to be rewritten as:

$$\bar{r}_i = r_f + \lambda_1 b_i \qquad (11.9)$$

The value of λ_1 can be determined by considering a **pure factor portfolio** (or pure factor play) denoted p^* that has unit sensitivity to the factor, meaning $b_{p^*} = 1.0$. (If there were other factors, such a portfolio would be constructed so as to have no sensitivity to them.) According to Equation (11.9), such a portfolio will have the following expected return:

$$\bar{r}_{p^*} = r_f + \lambda_1 \qquad (11.10a)$$

Note that this equation can be rewritten as:

$$\bar{r}_{p^*} - r_f = \lambda_1 \qquad (11.10b)$$

Thus λ_1 is the expected excess return (meaning the expected return over and above the riskfree rate) on a portfolio that has unit sensitivity to the factor. Accordingly, it is known as a **factor risk premium** (or factor-expected return premium). Letting $\delta_1 = \bar{r}_{p*}$ denote the expected return on a portfolio that has unit sensitivity to the factor, Equation (11.10b) can be rewritten as:

$$\delta_1 - r_f = \lambda_1 \qquad (11.10c)$$

Inserting the left-hand side of Equation (11.10c) for λ_1 in Equation (11.9) results in a second version of the APT pricing equation:

$$\bar{r}_i = r_f + \left(\delta_1 - r_f\right)b_i \qquad (11.11)$$

In the example, because $r_f = 8\%$ and $\lambda_1 = \delta_1 - r_f = 4\%$, it follows that $\delta_1 = 12\%$. This means that the expected return on a portfolio that has unit sensitivity to the first factor is 12%. This outcome can also be seen by considering the formation of a pure factor portfolio from securities 1 and 3. Because the securities have sensitivities of .9 and 1.8, respectively, their weights in the pure factor portfolio will be 8/9 and 1/9, respectively. [Note that $(.9 \times 8/9) + (1.8 \times 1/9) = 1$]. Accordingly, the portfolio's expected return will be 12% $[= (11.6\% \times 8/9) + (15.2\% \times 1/9)]$, as indicated earlier.

In order to generalize the pricing equation of APT, one needs to examine the case in which security returns are generated by more than one factor. This examination is done by considering a two-factor model and then expanding the analysis to k factors where $k > 2$.

11.3   TWO-FACTOR MODELS

In the case of two factors, denoted F_1 and F_2 and representing, for example, industrial production and inflation, each security will have two sensitivities, b_{i1} and b_{i2}. Thus security returns are generated by the following factor model:

$$r_i = a_i + b_{i1}F_1 + b_{i2}F_2 + e_i \qquad (11.12)$$

Consider a situation in which there are four securities that have the following expected returns and sensitivities.

i	$\bar{r}_i$	b_{i1}	b_{i2}
Stock 1	15%	.9	2.0
Stock 2	21	3.0	1.5
Stock 3	12	1.8	.7
Stock 4	8	2.0	3.2

In addition, consider an investor who has $5,000,000 invested in each of the securities. (Thus the investor has initial wealth W_0 of $20,000,000.) Are these securities priced in equilibrium?

11.3.1   Arbitrage Portfolios

To answer that question, one must explore the possibility of forming an arbitrage portfolio. First of all, an arbitrage portfolio must have weights that satisfy the following equations:

$$X_1 + X_2 + X_3 + X_4 = 0 \tag{11.13}$$

$$.9X_1 + 3X_2 + 1.8X_3 + 2X_4 = 0 \tag{11.14}$$

$$2X_1 + 1.5X_2 + .7X_3 + 3.2X_4 = 0 \tag{11.15}$$

These conditions mean that the arbitrage portfolio must not involve an additional commitment of funds by the investor [Equation (11.13)] and must have zero sensitivity to each factor [Equations (11.14) and (11.15)].

Note that there are three equations that need to be satisfied and that each equation involves four unknowns. Because there are more unknowns than equations, there are an infinite number of solutions. One solution can be found by setting X_1 equal to .1 (an arbitrarily chosen amount) and then solving for the remaining weights. Doing so results in the following weights: $X_2 = .088$, $X_3 = -.108$, and $X_4 = -.08$.

These weights represent a potential arbitrage portfolio. What remains to be done is to see if this portfolio has a positive expected return. Calculating the expected return of the portfolio reveals that it is equal to 1.41% $[= (.1 \times 15\%) + (.088 \times 21\%) + (-.108 \times 12\%) + (-.08 \times 8\%)]$. Hence an arbitrage portfolio has been identified.

This arbitrage portfolio involves the purchase of stocks 1 and 2, funded by selling stocks 3 and 4. Consequently, the buying-and-selling pressures will drive the prices of stocks 1 and 2 up and of stocks 3 and 4 down. In turn, the expected returns of stocks 1 and 2 will fall and of stocks 3 and 4 will rise.

Investors will continue to create such arbitrage portfolios until equilibrium is reached. Equilibrium will be attained when any portfolio that satisfies the conditions given by Equations (11.13), (11.14), and (11.15) has an expected return of zero. This expected return will occur when the following linear relationship between expected returns and sensitivities exists:

$$\overline{r}_i = \lambda_0 + \lambda_1 b_{i1} + \lambda_2 b_{i2} \tag{11.16}$$

As in Equation (11.7), this is a linear equation except that it now has three dimensions $(\overline{r}_i, b_{i1}, \text{ and } b_{i2})$ instead of two $(\overline{r}_i \text{ and } b_i)$ and hence corresponds to the equation of a plane instead of a line.

In the example, one possible equilibrium setting is where $\lambda_0 = 8$, $\lambda_1 = 4$, and $\lambda_2 = -2$. Thus the pricing equation is:

$$\overline{r}_i = 8 + 4b_{i1} - 2b_{i2} \tag{11.17}$$

As a result, the four stocks have the following equilibrium levels of expected returns:

$$\overline{r}_i = 8 + (4 \times .9) - (2 \times 2) = 7.6\%$$

$$\overline{r}_i = 8 + (4 \times 3) - (2 \times 1.5) = 17.0\%$$

$$\overline{r}_i = 8 + (4 \times 1.8) - (2 \times .7) = 13.8\%$$

$$\overline{r}_i = 8 + (4 \times 2) - (2 \times 3.2) = 9.6\%$$

The expected returns of stocks 1 and 2 have fallen from 15% and 21% while the expected returns of stocks 3 and 4 have risen from 12% and 8%, respectively. Given the buying-and-selling pressures generated by investing in arbitrage portfolios, these changes are in the predicted direction.

One consequence of Equation (11.17) is that a stock with higher sensitivity to the first factor than another stock will have a higher expected return if the two stocks also have the same sensitivity to the second factor because $\lambda_1 > 0$. Conversely, because $\lambda_2 < 0$, a stock with higher sensitivity to the second factor will have a lower expected return than another stock with a lower sensitivity to the second factor, provided that the two stocks have the same sensitivity to the first factor. However, the effect of two stocks having different sensitivities to both factors can be confounding. For example, stock 4 has a lower expected return than stock 3 even though both of its sensitivities are larger. The reason is that the advantage of having a higher sensitivity to the first factor ($b_{41} = 2.0 > b_{31} = 1.8$) is not of sufficient magnitude to offset the disadvantage of having a higher sensitivity to the second factor ($b_{42} = 3.2 > b_{32} = .7$).

11.3.2   Pricing Effects

Extending the one-factor APT pricing Equation (11.7) to this two-factor situation is relatively uncomplicated. As before, λ_0 is equal to the riskfree rate because the riskfree asset has no sensitivity to either factor, meaning that its values of b_{i1} and b_{i2} are both zero. Hence it follows that $\lambda_0 = r_f$. Thus Equation (11.16) can be rewritten more generally as:

$$\overline{r}_i = r_f + \lambda_1 b_{i1} + \lambda_2 b_{i2} \tag{11.18}$$

In the example given in Equation (11.16), it can be seen that $r_f = 8\%$.

Next consider a well-diversified portfolio that has unit sensitivity to the first factor and zero sensitivity to the second factor. As mentioned earlier, such a portfolio is known as a pure factor portfolio (or pure factor play) because it has: (1) unit sensitivity to one factor, (2) no sensitivity to any other factor, and (3) zero nonfactor risk. Specifically, it has $b_1 = 1$ and $b_2 = 0$. It can be seen from Equation (11.18) that the expected return on this portfolio, denoted δ_1, will be equal to $r_f + \lambda_1$. As it follows that $\delta_1 - r_f = \lambda_1$, Equation (11.18) can be rewritten as:

$$\overline{r}_i = r_f + (\delta_1 - r_f) b_{i1} + \lambda_2 b_{i2} \tag{11.19}$$

In the example given in Equation (11.16), it can be seen that $\delta_1 - r_f = 4$. This means that $\delta_1 = 12$ because $r_f = 8$. In other words, a portfolio that has unit sensitivity to industrial production (the first factor) and zero sensitivity to inflation (the second factor) will have an expected return of 12%, or 4% more than the riskfree rate of 8%.

Finally, consider a portfolio that has zero sensitivity to the first factor and unit sensitivity to the second factor, meaning that it has $b_1 = 0$ and $b_2 = 1$. It can be seen from Equation (11.18) that the expected return on this portfolio, denoted δ_2, will be equal to $r_f + \lambda_2$. Accordingly, $\delta_2 - r_f = \lambda_2$, thereby allowing Equation (11.19) to be rewritten as:

$$\overline{r}_i = r_f + (\delta_1 - r_f) b_{i1} + (\delta_2 - r_f) b_{i2} \tag{11.20}$$

In the example given in Equation (11.16), it can be seen that $\delta_2 - r_f = -2$. This means that $\delta_2 = 6$ since $r_f = 8$. In other words, a portfolio that has zero sensitivity to industrial production (the first factor) and unit sensitivity to inflation (the second factor) will have an expected return of 6%, or 2% less than the riskfree rate of 8%.

11.4   MULTIPLE-FACTOR MODELS

When returns were generated by a two-factor model instead of a one-factor model, APT pricing Equations (11.7) and (11.11) were simply expanded to accommodate the additional factor in Equations (11.16) and (11.20). What happens to these APT pricing equations when returns are generated by a multiple-factor model where the number of factors k is greater than 2? It turns out that the basic pricing equations are expanded once again in a relatively straightforward manner.

In the case of k factors $(F_1, F_2, ..., F_k)$ each security will have k sensitivities $(b_{i1}, b_{i2}, ..., b_{ik})$ in the following k-factor model:

$$r_i = a_i + b_{i1}F_1 + b_{i2}F_2 + ... + b_{ik}F_k + e_i \tag{11.21}$$

In turn, securities will be priced by the following equation, which is similar to Equations (11.7) and (11.16):

$$\bar{r}_i = \lambda_0 + \lambda_1 b_{i1} + \lambda_2 b_{i2} + ... + \lambda_k b_{ik} \tag{11.22}$$

As before, this is a linear equation, except now it is in $k + 1$ dimensions, with the dimensions being $\bar{r}_i, b_{i1}, b_{i2}, ...,$ and b_{ik}.

Extending the APT pricing Equations (11.11) and (11.20) to this situation is relatively uncomplicated. As before, λ_0 is equal to the riskfree rate because the riskfree asset has no sensitivity to any factor. Each value of δ_j represents the expected return on a portfolio of stocks that has unit sensitivity to factor j and zero sensitivity to all the other factors. As a result, Equations (11.11) and (11.20) can be expanded as follows:

$$\bar{r}_i = r_f + (\delta_1 - r_f)b_{i1} + (\delta_2 - r_f)b_{i2} + ... + (\delta_k - r_f)b_{ik} \tag{11.23}$$

Hence a stock's expected return is equal to the riskfree rate plus k risk premiums based on the stock's sensitivities to the k factors.

11.5   A SYNTHESIS OF THE APT AND THE CAPM

Unlike the APT, the CAPM does not assume that returns are generated by a factor model. However, this does not mean that the CAPM is inconsistent with a world in which returns are generated by a factor model. Indeed, it is possible to have a world in which returns are generated by a factor model, where the remaining assumptions of the APT hold, and where all the assumptions of the CAPM hold. This situation will now be examined.

11.5.1   One-Factor Models

Consider what will happen if returns are generated by a one-factor model and that factor is the market portfolio. In such a situation, δ_1 will correspond to the expected return on the market portfolio and b_i will represent the beta of stock i measured relative to the market portfolio. Hence the CAPM will hold.

What if returns are generated by a one-factor model and that factor is *not* the market portfolio? Now δ_1 will correspond to the expected return on a portfolio with unit sensitivity to the factor, and b_i will represent the sensitivity of stock i measured relative to the factor.[12] However, if the CAPM also holds, then security i's expected return will be a function of both its beta *and* its factor sensitivity:

$$\bar{r}_i = r_f + (\bar{r}_M - r_f)\beta_{iM} \tag{11.24}$$

$$\bar{r}_i = r_f + (\delta_1 - r_f)b_i \tag{11.25}$$

These relationships suggest that betas and sensitivities must somehow be related to each other.

Beta Coefficients and Factor Sensitivities

It can be demonstrated that betas and factor sensitivities will be linearly related to each other in the following manner:

$$\beta_{iM} = \frac{COV(F_1, r_M) + COV(e_i, r_M)}{\sigma_M^2} b_i \qquad (11.26a)$$

$$= (\beta_{F_1 M} + \beta_{e_i M}) b_i \qquad (11.26b)$$

where $COV(F_1, r_M)$ denotes the covariance between the factor and the market portfolio, $COV(e_i, r_M)$ denotes the covariance between the residual return of the factor model for security i and the return on the market portfolio, σ_M^2 denotes the variance of the return on the market portfolio, and $\beta_{F_1 M}$ and $\beta_{e_i M}$ are defined as being equal to $COV(F_1, r_M)/\sigma_M^2$ and $COV(e_i, r_M)/\sigma_M^2$, respectively.[13] Hence, $\beta_{F_1 M}$ denotes the beta of the factor, and $\beta_{e_i M}$ denotes the beta of security i's residual returns; both of these betas are measured relative to the market portfolio. What if each security's residual return is uncorrelated with the market's return? In this situation, $COV(e_i, r_M) = 0$, which in turn means that $\beta_{e_i M} = 0$. Thus, Equation (11.26b) reduces to:

$$\beta_{iM} = \beta_{F_1 M} b_i \qquad (11.27)$$

Because the quantity $\beta_{F_1 M}$ is a constant and does not change from one security to another, Equation (11.27) is equivalent to saying that β_{iM} will be equal to a constant times b_i when Equations (11.24) and (11.25) both hold. Hence if the factor is industrial production, then Equation (11.27) states that each security's beta is equal to a constant times the security's sensitivity to industrial production, when the security's residual return is uncorrelated with the market's return. The constant will be a positive number if industrial production and the returns on the market portfolio are positively correlated because then $\beta_{F_1 M}$ will be positive.[14] Conversely, the constant will be negative if the correlation is negative because then $\beta_{F_1 M}$ will be negative.

Factor Risk Premiums

Note what happens if the right-hand side of Equation (11.27) is substituted for β_{iM} on the right-hand side of Equation (11.24):

$$\overline{r}_i = r_f + [(\overline{r}_M - r_f)\beta_{F_1 M}] b_i \qquad (11.28)$$

Comparing this equation with Equation (11.9) reveals that if the assumptions of both APT (with one factor) and the CAPM hold and each security's residual return is uncorrelated with the market's return, then the following relationship must hold:

$$\lambda_1 = (\overline{r}_M - r_f)\beta_{F_1 M} \qquad (11.29)$$

By itself, APT says nothing about the size of the factor risk premium λ_1. However, if the CAPM also holds, it can provide some guidance. This guidance is given in Equation (11.29), which has been shown to hold if the assumptions of both APT and the CAPM are taken as given and each security's residual return is uncorrelated with the market's return.

Imagine that the factor moves with the market portfolio, meaning that it is positively correlated with the market portfolio so that $\beta_{F_1 M}$ is positive.[15] Because $(\overline{r}_M - r_f)$ is positive, it follows that the right-hand side of Equation (11.29) is positive and hence λ_1 is positive. Furthermore, because λ_1 is positive, it can be seen in Equation (11.9) that the higher the value of b_i, the higher will be the expected return of the security.[16] To generalize, if a factor is positively correlated with the market portfolio but the residual return of each security is uncorrelated with the market return, then each security's expected return will be a positive function of the security's sensitivity to that factor.

Applying Arbitrage Pricing Theory

Since its inception in the mid-1970s, arbitrage pricing theory (APT) has provided researchers and practitioners with an intuitive and flexible framework through which to address important investment management issues. As opposed to the capital asset pricing model (CAPM), with its specific assumptions concerning investor preferences as well as the critical role played by the market portfolio, APT operates under relatively weaker assumptions. Because of its emphasis on multiple sources of systematic risk, APT has attracted considerable interest as a tool for better explaining investment results and more effectively controlling portfolio risk.

Despite its attractive features, APT has not been widely applied by the investment community. The reason lies largely with APT's most significant drawback: the lack of specificity regarding the multiple factors that systematically affect security returns as well as the long-term return associated with each of these factors. Rightly or wrongly, the CAPM unambiguously states that a security's covariance with the market portfolio is the only systematic source of its investment risk within a well-diversified portfolio. Arbitrage pricing theory, conversely, is conspicuously silent regarding the particular systematic factors affecting a security's risk and return. Investors must fend for themselves in determining those factors.

Few institutional investors actually use APT to manage assets. The most prominent organization that does use it is Roll & Ross Asset Management Corporation (R&R). Because Stephen Ross invented the APT, it is interesting to briefly review how R&R translates this theory into practice.

R&R begins with a statement of the systematic sources of risk (or factors) that it believes are *currently* relevant in the capital markets. Specifically, R&R has identified five factors that pervasively affect common stock returns:

- The business cycle
- Interest rates
- Investor confidence
- Short-term inflation
- Long-term inflationary expectations

R&R quantifies these factors by designating certain measurable macroeconomic variables as proxies. For example, the business-cycle factor is represented by real (inflation-adjusted) percentage changes in the index of industrial production, whereas short-term inflation is measured by monthly percentage changes in the consumer price index.

At the heart of the R&R approach are several assumptions. First, each source of systematic risk has a certain current volatility and expected reward. Factor volatilities and expected rewards, and even the

---

The same kind of argument can be used to show that if the factor moves against the market portfolio, meaning that F_1 is negatively correlated with $\bar{r}_M$, then λ_1 will be negative. This statement means that the higher the value of b_i, the lower will be the expected return on the security. Generalizing, if a factor is negatively correlated with the market portfolio, then a security's expected return will be a negative function of the security's sensitivity to that factor.

A Market Index As the Factor

What if returns are generated by a one-factor model and, instead of industrial production, the factor is the return on a market index such as the S&P 500? Consider a situation in which the following two conditions are met: (1) The returns on the index and market portfolio are perfectly correlated, and (2) the variances of the returns on the market portfolio and on the market index are identical.

First of all, a stock's beta will be equal to its sensitivity. This equality can be seen by examining Equation (11.26b). Given the two conditions just described, $COV(F_1, r_M) = \rho_{F_1} \sigma_{F_1} \sigma_M = \sigma_M^2$ so that $COV(F_1, r_M)/\sigma_M^2 = \beta_{F_1 M} = 1$ and $\beta_{e_i M} = 0$. Hence Equation (11.26b) would reduce to $\beta_{iM} = b_i$.

Second, λ_1 will equal $\bar{r}_M - r_f$ under these two conditions. This relation can be seen

factors themselves, may change over time. Second, individual securities and portfolios possess different sensitivities to each factor. These sensitivities may also vary through time. Third, a well-diversified portfolio's exposures to the factors will determine its expected return and total risk. Fourth, a portfolio should be constructed that offers the most attractive total expected reward-to-risk ratio, given the current expected rewards and volatilities exhibited by the factors.

R&R has developed a security database (updated monthly) that covers roughly 15,000 individual common stocks in 17 countries. For each country's stock market, R&R applies the database to create a pure factor portfolio (discussed in this chapter) for each of the five factors. R&R uses the historical returns on these pure factor portfolios not only to estimate the sensitivity of every security in its database to each of the factors but also to estimate factor standard deviations, correlations, and risk premiums as well as to calculate nonfactor returns and risk for every security.

Attention at this point turns to a client's benchmark. Typically, a U.S. institutional investor will select a market index such as the S&P 500 as its common stock benchmark. R&R's standard assignment is to devise a more efficient portfolio that exceeds the benchmark's expected return by a prespecified (reasonable) amount, yet maintains a similar standard deviation. R&R does this by employing portfolio optimization techniques (see Chapter 7) that combine securities in a way that attempts to set portfolio standard deviation near that of the benchmark; reduce nonfactor risk to minimal levels; emphasize stocks with high market-to-book and market-to-earnings ratios as well as positive recent returns relative to other stocks; increase exposure to risk factors with attractive reward-to-risk; and minimize buying and selling of securities (to control transaction costs). The process is repeated monthly to keep the portfolio properly aligned with the benchmark.

The R&R approach is highly quantitative and, intriguingly, involves no judgmental forecasts of factor returns or risks. Rather, historical data on the factors and securities' factor sensitivities are mechanically manipulated to determine the desired portfolio composition. This approach may prove effective if the future mimics the past, but it can produce disappointing results if past factor data display no stable relationship with future values.

R&R captured considerable U.S. institutional investor interest when the firm was organized in 1986, although it never has gained a large U.S. clientele. The firm has expanded to take on foreign partners who now apply its techniques abroad. R&R provides an interesting example of converting theoretical investment concepts into practical investment products.

by again noting that $\beta_{F_1M} = COV(F_1, r_M)/\sigma_M^2 = 1$, which in turn means that Equation (11.29) reduces to $\lambda_1 = \bar{r}_M - r_f$. Because Equation (11.10c) states that $\delta_1 - r_f = \lambda_1$, then $\delta_1 = \bar{r}_M$. Hence the expected return on a portfolio that has unit sensitivity to the returns on the S&P 500 equals the expected return on the market portfolio.

In summary, if a proxy for the market portfolio could be found such that the two conditions given previously were met, then the CAPM would hold where the role of the market portfolio could be replaced by the proxy. Unfortunately, because the market portfolio is unknown, it cannot be verified whether any proxy even roughly meets the two conditions.

11.5.2 Multiple-Factor Models

It is possible for the CAPM to hold even though returns are generated by a multiple-factor model such as a two-factor model. Again, Equations (11.24) and (11.25) can be extended to show that security i's expected return will be related to its beta and two sensitivities:

$$\bar{r}_i = r_f + (\bar{r}_M - r_f)\beta_{iM} \tag{11.30}$$

$$\bar{r}_i = r_f + (\delta_1 - r_f)b_{i1} + (\delta_2 - r_f)b_{i2} \tag{11.31}$$

In this situation, Equation (11.26a) can be extended to show that betas will be related to sensitivities in the following linear manner (when each security's residual return is uncorrelated with the market return):

$$\beta_{iM} = \frac{COV(F_1, r_M)}{\sigma_M^2} b_{i1} + \frac{COV(F_2, r_M)}{\sigma_M^2} b_{i2} \qquad (11.32a)$$

$$= \beta_{F_1 M} b_{i1} + \beta_{F_2 M} b_{i2} \qquad (11.32b)$$

Here $COV(F_1, r_M)$ and $COV(F_2, r_M)$ denote the covariance between the first factor and the market portfolio and the covariance between the second factor and the market portfolio, respectively. As the quantities $COV(F_1, r_M)/\sigma_M^2 = \beta_{F_1 M}$ and $COV(F_2, r_M)/\sigma_M^2 = \beta_{F_2 M}$ are constants, it can be seen from Equation (11.32b) that β_{iM} will be a function of b_{i1} and b_{i2} when Equations (11.30) and (11.31) hold and each security's residual return is uncorrelated with the market return. Consequently, a stock's beta will be a linear combination of its sensitivities to the two factors, which means that, in this example, the size of a stock's beta will be dependent of the size of its sensitivities to industrial production and inflation.

Note what happens if the right-hand side of Equation (11.32b) is substituted for β_{iM} on the right-hand side of Equation (11.30):

$$\bar{r}_i = r_f + (\bar{r}_M - r_f)[\beta_{F_1 M} b_{i1} + \beta_{F_2 M} b_{i2}] \qquad (11.33a)$$

which can be rewritten as:

$$\bar{r}_i = r_f + [(\bar{r}_M - r_f)\beta_{F_1 M}]b_{i1} + [(\bar{r}_M - r_f)\beta_{F_2 M}]b_{i2} \qquad (11.33b)$$

Comparing this equation with Equation (11.18) reveals that if the assumptions of both APT (with two factors) and the CAPM hold and each security's residual return is uncorrelated with the market return, then the following relationships must hold:

$$\lambda_1 = (\bar{r}_M - r_f)\beta_{F_1 M} \qquad (11.34a)$$

$$\lambda_2 = (\bar{r}_M - r_f)\beta_{F_2 M} \qquad (11.34b)$$

Hence the size of λ_1 and λ_2 will be dependent upon both the market premium $(\bar{r}_M - r_f)$, a positive number, and the beta of the factor with the market portfolio, which may be positive or negative. This relation means that λ_1 and λ_2 will have positive values if the factors are positively correlated with the returns on the market portfolio.[17] However, if either factor is negatively correlated with the returns on the market portfolio, then the corresponding value of λ will be negative (as was the case with λ_2 in the example).

11.6   IDENTIFYING THE FACTORS

Left unanswered by APT are the number and identity of the factors that have values of lambda (λ) that are sufficiently positive or negative in magnitude so that they need to be included when estimating expected returns. Several researchers have investigated stock returns and have estimated that there are anywhere from three to five factors that are "priced." Subsequently, various people attempted to identify those factors.[18] In one paper by Nai-Fu Chen, Richard Roll, and Stephen Ross, the following factors were identified:

1. Growth rate in industrial production
2. Rate of inflation (both expected and unexpected)
3. Spread between long-term and short-term interest rates
4. Spread between low-grade and high-grade bonds[19]

Another paper by Michael Berry, Edwin Burmeister, and Marjorie McElroy identifies five factors. Of these five factors, three correspond closely to the last three identified by Chen, Roll, and Ross. The other two are the growth rate in aggregate sales in the economy and the rate of return on the S&P 500.[20]

Finally, consider the five factors used by Salomon Brothers (now Salomon Smith Barney) in what they refer to as their fundamental factor model. Only one factor, inflation, is in common with the factors identified by the others. The remaining factors are as follows:

1. Growth rate in gross domestic product
2. Rate of interest
3. Rate of change in oil prices
4. Rate of growth in defense spending [21]

It is interesting to note that the three sets of factors have some common characteristics. First, they contain some indication of aggregate economic activity (industrial production, aggregate sales, and GDP). Second, they contain inflation. Third, they contain some type of interest rate factor (either spreads or a rate itself). When one considers the fact that stock prices can be thought of as being equal to the discounted value of future dividends, the factors make intuitive sense.[22] Future dividends will be related to aggregate economic activity, and the discount rate used to determine present value will be related to inflation and interest rates.

11.7   SUMMARY

1. Arbitrage pricing theory (APT) is an equilibrium model of security prices, as is the capital asset pricing model (CAPM).
2. APT makes different assumptions than does the CAPM.
3. APT assumes that security returns are generated by a factor model but does not identify the factors.
4. An arbitrage portfolio includes long and short positions in securities. It must have a net market value of zero, no sensitivity to any factor, and a positive expected return.
5. Investors will invest in arbitrage portfolios, provided they exist, driving up the prices of the securities held in long positions and driving down the prices of securities held in short positions until all arbitrage possibilities have been eliminated.
6. When all arbitrage possibilities have been eliminated, the equilibrium expected return on a security will be a linear function of its sensitivities to the factors.
7. A factor-risk premium is the equilibrium return over the riskfree rate expected to be generated by a portfolio with a unit sensitivity to the factor and no sensitivity to any other factor.
8. APT and the CAPM are not necessarily inconsistent with each other. If security returns are generated by a factor model and the CAPM holds, then a security's beta will depend on the security's sensitivities to the factors and the beta values of the factors with the market portfolio.
9. APT does not specify the number or identity of the factors that affect expected returns or the magnitudes or signs of the risk premiums. Most research into factors has focused on indicators of aggregate economic activity, inflation, and interest rates.

1. In what significant ways does the APT differ from the CAPM?
2. Why would an investor wish to form an arbitrage portfolio?
3. What three conditions define an arbitrage portfolio?
4. Assuming a one-factor model, consider a portfolio composed of three securities with the following factor sensivities:

Security	Factor Sensitivity
1	0.90
2	3.00
3	1.80

If the proportion of security 1 in the portfolio is increased by .2, how must the proportions of the other two securities change if the portfolio is to maintain the same factor sensitivity?

5. Assuming a one-factor model of the form:

$$r_i = 4\% + b_i F + e_i$$

consider three well-diversified portfolios (zero nonfactor risk). The expected value of the factor is 8%.

Portfolio	Factor Sensitivity	Expected Return
A	0.80	10.4%
B	1.00	10.0
C	1.20	13.6

Is one of the portfolio's expected return not in line with the factor model relationship? Which one? Can you construct a combination of the other two portfolios that has the same factor sensitivity as the "out-of-line" portfolio? What is the expected return of that combination? What action would you expect investors to take with respect to these three portfolios?

6. Socks Seybold owns a portfolio with the following characteristics. (Assume that returns are generated by a one-factor model.)

Security	Factor Sensitivity	Proportion	Expected Return
A	2.0	.2	20%
B	3.5	.4	10
C	0.5	.4	5

Socks decides to create an arbitrage portfolio by increasing the holdings of security A by .2. (Hint: Remember, X_B must equal $-X_C - X_A$.)
   a. What must be the weights of the other two securities in Socks' arbitrage portfolio?
   b. What is the expected return on the arbitrage portfolio?
   c. If everyone follows Socks' buy-and-sell decisions, what will be the effects on the prices of the three securities?

7. Assume that security returns are generated by a one-factor model. Hap Morse holds a portfolio whose component securities have the following characteristics:

Security	Factor Sensitivity	Proportion	Expected Return
A	.60	.40	12%
B	.30	.30	15
C	1.20	.30	8

Specify an arbitrage portfolio in which Hap might invest. (Remember that there are an infinite number of possibilities; choose one.) Demonstrate that this portfolio satisfies the conditions of an arbitrage portfolio.

8. Why must the variance of a well-diversified arbitrage portfolio be small?

9. Why is the concept of arbitrage central to the asset-pricing mechanism of the APT?

10. On the basis of a one-factor model, Wyeville Labs' stock has a factor sensitivity of 3. Given a riskfree rate of 5% and a factor risk premium of 7%, what is the equilibrium expected return on Wyeville stock?

11. According to APT, why must the relationship between a security's equilibrium return and its factor sensitivities be linear?

12. On the basis of a one-factor model, two portfolios, A and B, have equilibrium expected returns of 9.8% and 11.0%, respectively. If the factor sensitivity of portfolio A is 0.8 and that of portfolio B is 1.0, what must be the riskfree rate?

13. What is a pure factor portfolio? How may such a portfolio be constructed?

14. On the basis of a one-factor model, assume that the riskfree rate is 6% and the expected return on a portfolio with unit sensitivity to the factor is 8.5%. Consider a portfolio of two securities with the following characteristics:

Security	Factor Sensitivity	Proportion
A	4.0	.3
B	2.6	.7

According to the APT, what is the portfolio's equilibrium expected return?

15. Assume that security returns are generated by a factor model in which two factors are pervasive. The sensitivities of two securities and of the riskfree asset to each of the two factors are shown below, along with the expected return on each security.

Security	b_{i1}	b_{i2}	Expected Return
A	0.5	0.8	16.2%
B	1.5	1.4	21.6
r_f	0.0	0.0	10.0

a. If Dots Miller has $100 to invest and sells short $50 of security B and purchases $150 of security A, what is the sensitivity of Dots's portfolio to the two factors? (Ignore margin requirements.)

b. If Dots now borrows $100 at the riskfree rate and invests the proceeds of the loan along with the original $100 in securities A and B in the same proportions as described in part (a), what is the sensitivity of this portfolio to the two factors?

c. What is the expected return on the portfolio created in part (b)?

d. What is the expected return premium of factor 2?

16. Dandelion Pfeffer owns a portfolio with the following characteristics:

Security	Factor 1 Sensitivity	Factor 2 Sensitivity	Proportion	Expected Return
A	2.5	1.4	.3	13%
B	1.6	0.9	.3	18
C	0.8	1.0	.2	10
D	2.0	1.3	.2	12

Assume that the returns are generated by a two-factor model. Dandelion decides to create an arbitrage portfolio by increasing the holding of security B by .05.

a. What must be the weights of the other three securities in Dandelion's portfolio?

b. What is the expected return on the arbitrage portfolio?

17. Is it true that if the APT is a correct theory of asset pricing, then the risk-return relationship derived from the CAPM is necessarily incorrect? Why?

18. If the CAPM and APT both hold, why must it be the case that the factor-risk premium is negative for a factor that is negatively correlated with the market portfolio? Explain both mathematically and intuitively.

19. Some people have argued that the market portfolio can never be measured and that the CAPM, therefore, is untestable. Others have argued that APT specifies neither the number of factors nor their identity and, hence, is also untestable. If these views are correct, does this mean that the theories are of no value? Explain.

20. Although APT does not specify the identity of the relevant factors, most empirical APT research has focused on certain types of factors. What are some of the common characteristics of those factors?

21. Assume that the CAPM holds and that returns on securities are generated by a single-factor model. You are given the following information:

$$\sigma^2_M = 400 \quad b_A = 0.7 \quad b_B = 1.1 \quad COV(F, r_M) = 370$$

a. Calculate the beta coefficients of securities A and B.

b. If the riskfree rate is 6% and the expected return on the market portfolio is 12%, what is the equilibrium expected return on securities A and B?

22. Assume that the CAPM holds and that returns are generated by a two-factor model. You are given the following information:

$$\sigma^2_M = 324 \quad b_{A1} = .8 \quad b_{B1} = 1.0 \quad COV(F_1, r_M) = 156$$

$$b_{A2} = 1.1 \quad b_{B2} = .7 \quad COV(F_2, r_M) = 500$$

Calculate the beta coefficients of securities A and B.

CFA EXAM QUESTIONS

23. As the manager of a large, broadly diversified portfolio of stocks and bonds, you realize that changes in certain macroeconomic variables may directly affect the performance of your portfolio. You are considering using an arbitrage pricing theory (APT) approach to strategic portfolio planning and want to analyze the possible impacts of the following four factors:

- Industrial production
- Inflation
- Risk premiums or quality spreads
- Yield curve shifts

a. Indicate how each of these four factors influences the cash flows and the discount rates in the traditional discounted cash flow valuation model. Explain how unanticipated changes in each of these four factors could affect portfolio returns.

b. You now use a constant-proportion allocation strategy of 60% stock and 40% bonds, which you rebalance monthly. Compare and contrast an active portfolio approach that incorporates macroeconomic factors, such as the four factors listed above, with the constant-proportion strategy currently in use.

ENDNOTES

[1] Factor models are discussed in detail in Chapter 10.

[2] As noted in Equation (10.18) of Chapter 10, there are other ways to write the equation for a factor model.

[3] There will always be an infinite number of solutions whenever there are more unknowns than equations. For example, consider a situation in which there is one equation with two unknowns: $Y = 3X$. Note that there is an infinite number of paired values of X and Y that solve this equation, such as $(1, 3)$, $(2, 6)$, and $(3, 9)$.

[4] If its expected return is negative, then simply changing the signs of the weights will cause the expected return to become positive. Note that the new weights will also sum to zero and will still represent a portfolio that has zero sensitivity to the factor. Thus the new weights will represent an arbitrage portfolio.

[5] The APT ignores nonfactor risk. Because the total risk of a portfolio σ_p^2 is equal to $b_p^2 \sigma_F^2 + \sigma_{ep}^2$ according to the one-factor model [see Equation (10.6a) in Chapter 10], and given that the arbitrage portfolio has no factor risk by design, meaning that $b_p^2 \sigma_F^2 = 0$ because $b_p = 0$, the arbitrage portfolio must be sufficiently diversified so as to have insignificant nonfactor risk and, consequently, insignificant total risk.

[6] Technically, this pricing equation is only approximately true and may be significantly wrong for a small number of assets.

[7] Why choose 8 and 4 for λ_0 and λ_1, respectively? The magnitudes of these two parameters in equilibrium will depend on many things, such as investors' relative degrees of risk aversion, wealth, and time preferences.

[8] To demonstrate that Equation (11.8) is indeed an equilibrium situation, the reader is encouraged to try setting various values for X_1, X_2, and X_3 and show that the resulting potential arbitrage portfolios will all have expected returns of zero.

[9] If B were to plot below the APT asset pricing line, then investors would do just the opposite of what is described here. They would buy S and sell B.

[10] A simpler way of viewing this transaction is as a stock swap where S is being swapped for B. Because it is a swap, no new funds are needed. Furthermore, because B and S have the same factor sensitivity, the swap will not alter the sensitivity of the currently held portfolio. Finally, the replacement of S with B will increase the currently held portfolio's expected return because B has a higher level of expected return than S.

[11] Technically, the APT asset pricing line would shift upward a bit because of the selling of S.

[12] If the factor is a market index (instead of the market portfolio) such as the S&P 500, then δ_1 will correspond to the expected return on the index and b_i will represent the beta of stock i measured relative to the index, denoted previously in Chapter 7 as β_{iI}.

[13] This can be seen by noting that $COV(r_i, r_M) = COV(a_i + b_i F_1 + e_i, r_M)$, which simplifies to $COV(r_i, r_M) = b_i COV(F_1, r_M) + COV(e_i, r_M)$. Dividing both sides by σ_M^2 and recognizing from Chapter 9 that $COV(r_i, r_M)/\sigma_M^2 = \beta_{iM}$ produces Equation (11.26a).

[14] The term $COV(F_1, r_M)$ will be positive if the correlation is positive because it is equal to the product of the correlation and the standard deviations of F_1 and r_M.

[15] See endnote 14.

[16] The greater the extent to which the factor moves with the market portfolio (meaning the higher the correlation between F_1 and r_M), the greater will be the associated expected return premium λ_1.

[17] For the reasoning behind this assertion, see endnote 14.

[18] In Chapter 10 a three-factor model that was developed by Fama and French was described. In their model, the factors represented returns on (1) a general market index, (2) the difference between small and large stock indices, and (3) the difference between high and low book-to-market equity ratio stock indices. Fama and French argue that these factors are consistent with a 3-factor APT. See "Multi-Factor Explanations of Asset Pricing Anamolies," *Journal of Finance* 51, no. 1 (March 1996): 55–83.

[19] Note that the third factor can be interpreted as a measure of the term structure of interest rates, and the fourth factor can be interpreted as a measure of the default risk premium that investors demand for holding risky corporate bonds instead of Treasury bonds.

[20] Technically, the authors used the part of the rate of return of the S&P 500 that could not be attributed to the other four factors.

[21] Technically, the authors used inflation-adjusted figures for all the variables except the rate of interest.

[22] Dividend discount models are discussed in depth in Chapter 17.

KEY TERMS

arbitrage pricing theory

arbitrage

arbitrage portfolio

pure factor portfolio

factor risk premium

REFERENCES

1. Credit for the initial development of APT belongs to:

   Stephen A. Ross, "The Arbitrage Theory of Capital Asset Pricing," *Journal of Economic Theory* 13, no. 3 (December 1976): 341–360, and "Risk, Return, and Arbitrage," in Irwin Friend and James L. Bicksler (eds.), *Risk and Return in Finance*, vol. 1 (Cambridge, MA: Ballinger Publishing, 1977), section 9.

2. Ross's initial presentation of APT was clarified in:

   Gur Huberman, "A Simple Approach to Arbitrage Pricing Theory," *Journal of Economic Theory* 28, no. 1 (October 1982): 183–191.

   Jonathan E. Ingersoll Jr., "Some Results in the Theory of Arbitrage Pricing," *Journal of Finance* 39, no. 4 (September 1984): 1021–1039.

3. The fundamental asset pricing equation of Ross's APT is approximately correct for all but a small number of assets. When additional assumptions are made, all assets will be priced with, at most, negligible error. Some of the papers (also see the papers cited in references 7 and 8) that address this issue are:

   Nai-Fu Chen and Jonathan E. Ingersoll Jr., "Exact Pricing in Linear Factor Models with Finitely Many Assets: A Note," *Journal of Finance* 38, no. 3 (June 1983): 985–988.

   Gary Chamberlain and Michael Rothschild, "Arbitrage, Factor Structure, and Mean-Variance Analysis on Large Asset Markets," *Econometrica* 51, no. 5 (September 1983): 1281–1304.

   Gary Chamberlain, "Funds, Factors, and Diversification in Arbitrage Pricing Models," *Econometrica* 51, no. 5 (September 1983): 1305–1323.

   Philip H. Dybvig, "An Explicit Bound on Individual Assets' Deviations from APT Pricing in a Finite Economy," *Journal of Financial Economics* 12, no. 4 (December 1983): 483–496.

   Mark Grinblatt and Sheridan Titman, "Factor Pricing in a Finite Economy" *Journal of Financial Economics* 12, no. 4 (December 1983): 497–507.

   Gregory Connor, "A Unified Beta Pricing Theory," *Journal of Economic Theory* 34, no. 1 (October 1984): 13–31.

   Robert A. Jarrow, "Preferences, Continuity, and the Arbitrage Pricing Theory," *Review of Financial Studies* 2, no. 1 (Summer 1988): 159–172.

4. Nontechnical descriptions of APT can be found in:

Richard W. Roll and Stephen A. Ross, "Regulation, the Capital Asset Pricing Model, and the Arbitrage Pricing Theory," *Public Utilities Fortnightly* 111, no. 11 (May 26, 1983): 22–28.

Richard Roll and Stephen A. Ross, "The Arbitrage Pricing Theory Approach to Strategic Portfolio Planning," *Financial Analysts Journal* 40, no. 3 (May/June 1984): 14–26.

Dorothy H. Bower, Richard S. Bower, and Dennis E. Logue, "A Primer on Arbitrage Pricing Theory," *Midland Corporate Finance Journal* 2, no. 3 (Fall 1984): 31–40.

Richard C. Grinold and Ronald N. Kahn, *Active Portfolio Management* (Chicago: Probus Publishing, 1995), Chapter 7.

5. Some of the attempts to identify the number of factors that are priced are:

Richard Roll and Stephen A. Ross, "An Empirical Investigation of the Arbitrage Pricing Theory," *Journal of Finance* 35, no. 5 (December 1980): 1073–1103.

Stephen J. Brown and Mark I. Weinstein, "A New Approach to Testing Asset Pricing Models: The Bilinear Paradigm," *Journal of Finance* 38, no. 3 (June 1983): 711–743.

Phoebus J. Dhrymes, Irwin Friend, and N. Bulent Gultekin, "A Critical Reexamination of the Empirical Evidence on the Arbitrage Pricing Theory," *Journal of Finance* 39, no. 2 (June 1984): 323–346.

Richard Roll and Stephen A. Ross, "A Critical Reexamination of the Empirical Evidence on the Arbitrage Pricing Theory: A Reply," *Journal of Finance* 39, no. 2 (June 1984): 347–350.

Phoebus J. Dhrymes, Irwin Friend, Mustafa N. Gultekin, and N. Bulent Gultekin, "New Tests of the APT and Their Implications," *Journal of Finance* 40, no. 3 (July 1985): 659–674.

Charles Trzcinka, "On the Number of Factors in the Arbitrage Pricing Model," *Journal of Finance* 41, no. 2 (June 1986): 347–368.

Gur Huberman, Samuel Kandel, and Robert F. Starbaugh, "Mimicking Portfolios and Exact Arbitrage Pricing," *Journal of Finance* 42, no. 1 (March 1987): 1–9.

Dolores A. Conway and Marc R. Reinganum, "Stable Factors in Security Returns: Identification Using Cross Validation," *Journal of Business and Economic Statistics* 6, no. 1 (January 1988): 1–15.

Edwin Burmeister and Marjorie B. McElroy, "Joint Estimation of Factor Sensitivities and Risk Premia for the Arbitrage Pricing Theory," *Journal of Finance* 43, no. 3 (July 1988): 721–735.

Bruce N. Lehmann and David M. Modest, "The Empirical Foundations of the Arbitrage Pricing Theory," *Journal of Financial Economics* 21, no. 2 (September 1988): 213–254.

Gregory Connor and Robert A. Korajczyk, "Risk and Return in an Equilibrium APT: Application of a New Test Methodology," *Journal of Financial Economics* 21, no. 2 (September 1988): 255–289.

Stephen J. Brown, "The Number of Factors in Security Returns," *Journal of Finance* 44, no. 5 (December 1989): 1247–1262.

Ravi Shukla and Charles Trzcinka, "Sequential Tests of the Arbitrage Pricing Theory: A Comparison of Principal Components and Maximum Likelihood Factors," *Journal of Finance* 45, no. 5 (December 1990): 1541–1564.

Eugene F. Fama and Kenneth R. French, "Common Risk Factors in the Returns on Stocks and Bonds," *Journal of Financial Economics* 33, no. 1 (February 1993): 3–56.

Jianping Mei, "A Semiautoregression Approach to the Arbitrage Pricing Theory," *Journal of Finance* 48, no. 2 (June 1993): 599–620.

Gregory Connor and Robert A. Korajczyk, "A Test for the Number of Factors in an Approximate Factor Model," *Journal of Finance* 48, no. 4 (September 1993): 1263–1291.

Jianping Mei, "Explaining the Cross-Section of Returns via a Multi-Factor APT Model," *Journal of Financial and Quantitative Analysis* 28, no. 3 (September 1993): 331–345.

John Geweke and Guofu Zhou, "Measuring the Pricing Error of the Arbitrage Pricing Theory," *Review of Financial Studies* 9, no. 2 (Summer 1996): 557–587.

6. A few of the papers listed in reference 5 identified factors. Some other papers that also identified factors are:

Tony Estep, Nick Hansen, and Cal Johnson, "Sources of Value and Risk in Common Stocks," *Journal of Portfolio Management* 9, no. 4 (Summer 1983): 5–13.

Nai-Fu Chen, Richard Roll, and Stephen A. Ross, "Economic Forces and the Stock Market," *Journal of Business* 59, no. 3 (July 1986): 383–403.

Marjorie B. McElroy and Edwin Burmeister, "Arbitrage Pricing Theory As a Restricted Nonlinear Multivariate Regression Model," *Journal of Business and Economic Statistics* 6, no. 1 (January 1988): 29–42.

Michael A. Berry, Edwin Burmeister, and Marjorie B. McElroy, "Sorting Out Risks Using Known APT Factors," *Financial Analysts Journal* 44, no. 2 (March/April 1988): 29–42.

Eugene F. Fama and Kenneth R. French, "Multi-Factor Explanations of Asset Pricing Anamolies," *Journal of Finance* 51, no. 1 (March 1996): 55–83.

7. It has been argued that the APT cannot be meaningfully tested and hence is of questionable practical use. These arguments and their rebuttals have been provided by:

Jay Shanken, "The Arbitrage Pricing Theory: Is It Testable?" *Journal of Finance* 37, no. 5 (December 1982): 1129–1140.

Phoebus J. Dhrymes, "The Empirical Relevance of Arbitrage Pricing Models," *Journal of Portfolio Management* 10, no. 4 (Summer 1984): 35–44.

Stephen A. Ross, "Reply to Dhrymes: APT Is Empirically Relevant," *Journal of Portfolio Management* 11, no.1 (Fall 1984): 54–56.

Phoebus J. Dhrymes, "On the Empirical Relevance of APT: Comment," *Journal of Portfolio Management* 11, no. 4 (Summer 1985): 70–71.

Stephen A. Ross, "On the Empirical Relevance of APT: Reply," *Journal of Portfolio Management* 11, no. 4 (Summer 1985): 72–73.

Philip H. Dybvig and Stephen A. Ross, "Yes, The APT Is Testable," *Journal of Finance* 40, no. 4 (September 1985): 1129–1140.

Christian Gilles and Stephen F. LeRoy, "On the Arbitrage Pricing Theory," *Economic Theory* 1, no. 3 (1991): 213–229.

Jay Shanken, "The Current State of Arbitrage Pricing Theory," *Journal of Finance* 47, no. 4 (September 1992): 1569–1574.

8. For a discussion of the relationships between the APT and the CAPM, see:

Robert Jarrow and Andrew Rudd, "A Comparison of the APT and CAPM: A Note," *Journal of Banking and Finance* 7, no. 2 (June 1983): 295–303.

William F. Sharpe, "Factor Models, CAPMs, and the ABT(sic)," *Journal of Portfolio Management* 11, no. 1 (Fall 1984): 21–25.

Jay Shanken, "Multi-Beta CAPM or Equilibrium-APT?: A Reply," *Journal of Finance* 40, no. 4 (September 1985): 1189–1196.

K. C. John Wei, "An Asset-Pricing Theory Unifying the CAPM and APT," *Journal of Finance* 43, no. 4 (September 1988): 881–892.

9. For a discussion of the APT in an international context, see:

Bruno Solnik, "International Arbitrage Pricing Theory," *Journal of Finance* 38, no. 2 (May 1982): 449–457.

TAXES AND INFLATION

Neither taxation nor inflation should be regarded as an unmitigated evil. Each provides benefits to some individuals that may outweigh the associated costs that others have to bear. Regardless of whether the benefits outweigh the costs, however, both taxes and inflation have a significant impact on investment decisions and results. This chapter provides an overview of some of the more important aspects of taxation and inflation from the viewpoint of the investor.

Federal and state tax laws play a major role in the way securities are priced in the marketplace because investors are understandably concerned with after-tax returns, not before-tax returns. Accordingly, the investor should determine the applicable tax rate before making any investment decision. This tax rate is not the same for all securities for a given individual investor: It can be from as low as 0% in the case of certain tax-exempt securities issued by states and municipalities to well over 40% for corporate bonds when both federal and state taxes are considered. After determining the applicable tax rate, the investor can estimate a security's expected after-tax return and risk. Upon doing so, the investor can make a wise investment decision.

12.1   TAXES IN THE UNITED STATES

Many of the specific tax rates and provisions in the United States were enacted with the Tax Reform Act of 1986, the Omnibus Budget Reconciliation Acts of 1990 and 1993, and the Orwellian-named Taxpayer Relief Act of 1997. Changes do occur from year to year, and current regulations should, of course, be consulted when preparing tax returns or considering major investment decisions. However, the material given here can be considered broadly representative of current taxation (primarily federal) in the United States.

In general, the most important taxes for investment decision making are personal and corporate income taxes. The essential elements of each will be described, and the manner in which they influence the pricing of securities will be considered.

12.1.1 Corporate Income Taxes

There are three forms of business organizations in the United States and in most other countries:

1. Corporations
2. Partnerships
3. Proprietorships

The corporate form of organization is the largest in terms of the dollar value of assets owned, even though there are more firms organized as partnerships or as single proprietorships. Legally, a corporation is regarded as a separate entity, whereas a proprietorship or partnership is considered an extension of its owner or owners. Income earned by proprietorships and partnerships is taxed primarily through the personal income tax levied on their owners. Income earned by a corporation may be taxed twice: once when it is earned, via the corporate income tax, and again when it is received as dividends by holders of the firm's securities, via the personal income tax.[1]

This double taxation of corporate income may at first seem inefficient, if not unfair. It also raises questions about the efficiency of the corporate form of organization. Suffice it to say that limited liability and the ability to transfer shares of subdivided ownership appear to be of sufficient value to more than offset the tax law disadvantages. Moreover, without the corporate income tax, personal tax rates would have to be increased if the level of government expenditures were to remain constant without increasing the national debt.

Corporate Tax Rates

Before 1993 the corporate income tax was relatively simple in one respect; there were only a few basic rates. However, in 1993 even this feature was made more complex, as there are now eight basic rates. The rates and applicable levels of taxable annual income are as follows:

1. A tax rate of 15% is applicable to the first $50,000
2. A tax rate of 25% to the next $25,000
3. A tax rate of 34% to the next $25,000
4. A tax rate of 39% to the next $235,000
5. A tax rate of 34% to the next $9,665,000
6. A tax rate of 35% to the next $5,000,000
7. A tax rate of 38% to the next $3,333,333
8. A tax rate of 35% on all additional income

Figure 12.1 illustrates what are known as the **marginal tax rate** and **average tax rate** schedules for corporations. A corporation's marginal tax rate is the tax rate that it would pay on an additional dollar of income. For example, a corporation earning $85,000 would pay $17,150 in income taxes:

$$
\begin{aligned}
0.15 \times \$50,000 &= \$7,500 \\
0.25 \times 25,000 &= 6,250 \\
0.34 \times 10,000 &= 3,400 \\
\text{Total income tax} &= \$17,150
\end{aligned}
$$

For this corporation, the marginal tax rate is 34% because an additional dollar of income would be taxed at this rate. In other words, if this firm's income were $85,001 instead of $85,000, its tax bill would be $17,150.34 instead of $17,150. Thus $.34

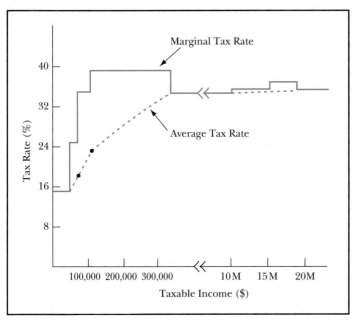

Figure 12.1
Marginal and Average Corporate Tax Rates, 1997

(= $17,150.34 − $17,150.00) more in taxes would be paid as a result of earning $1 (= $85,001 − $85,000) more in income.

The average tax rate is equal to the total amount of taxes paid divided by the total income subject to tax. The average tax rate for the previous example would thus be 20.18% (= $17,150/$85,000). That is, 20.18% of this firm's total income would be taken by the government in the form of corporate income taxes. As can be seen in Figure 12.1, the average rate is exactly equal to the marginal rate at three places: (1) The rates are equal to 15% for incomes below $50,000; (2) the rates are equal to 34% for incomes between $335,000 and $10,000,000; and (3) the rates are equal to 35% for incomes above $18,333,333.

The average rate measures the overall impact of taxes, but the marginal rate is more relevant for most decisions. For example, if a corporation were considering an investment that would increase its income from $85,000 to $90,000 each year, the increase in income after taxes would be $3,300 [= (1 − .34) × $5,000], not $3,991 [= (1 − .2018) × $5,000].

Corporate Income from Dividends, Interest, and Capital Gains

Congress has provided that 80% of the dividends received by a corporation can be excluded from income when calculating the corporation's income tax liability.[2] The effective tax rate on an additional dollar of dividends received by a corporation with an income in the 35% range is thus 7% [= (1 − .80) × .35]. The reason for this special treatment of dividends is to avoid the triple taxation of income. Consider how dividends would be taxed if this 80% exclusion did not exist. Corporation *A* is taxed on its income and then pays dividends to one of its stockholders, corporation *B*. Corporation *B* then pays taxes on its income, which includes the dividends received from *A*. Finally, the stockholders of *B* pay income taxes on the dividends received from *B*. Thus a dollar of income earned by *A* would be taxed three times—a tax on *A*, then a tax on *B*, then a tax on the stockholders of *B*—if the dividend exclusion did not exist. With the dividend exclusion, a dollar of income earned by *A* is taxed, for all practical purposes, "only" a little more than twice.

Taxes and Inflation

TABLE 12.1	Comparison of Yields of Preferred Stocks and Corporate Bonds	
	Investment	
	Preferred Stock	Corporate Bond
(a) Feature		
Price	$10 per share	$1,000 per bond
Annual dollar yield	$.70 per share	$80 per bond
Aggregate investment	100 shares	1 bond
Cost of aggregate investment	$1,000	$1,000
Aggregate annual dollar yield	$70	$80
Before-tax percentage yield	7% = $70/$1,000	8% = $80/$1,000
(b) Corporate investor[a]		
After-tax dollar yield	$65.10 = $70[1 − (.20 × .35)]	$52 = $80 (1 − .35)
After-tax percentage yield	6.51% = $65.10/$1,000	5.20% = $52/$1,000
(c) Individual investor[b]		
After-tax dollar yield	$50.40 = $70 (1 − .28)	$57.60 = $80 (1 − .28)
After-tax percentage yield	5.04% = $50.40/$1,000	5.76% = $57.60/$1,000

[a] Assuming a marginal corporate income tax rate of 35%.

[b] Assuming a marginal individual income tax rate of 28%.

Bonds versus Preferred Stocks

No deduction is allowed for interest received on bonds bought by a corporate investor. It is simply added to income and taxed at the regular rates. This means that the maximum effective tax rate on interest received from bonds is 35%, an amount substantially greater than the 7% effective tax rate on common and preferred stock dividends. This differential tax treatment has an effect on the relative prices that corporate and individual investors are willing to pay for these securities, because their concern is with relative after-tax yields.

Table 12.1 provides an example of preferred stock that illustrates the before-tax and after-tax yields for both a corporate investor with a marginal tax rate of 35% and an individual investor with a marginal personal tax rate of 28%. Note that the preferred stock has a lower before-tax yield despite of being riskier than the bond. The table shows that the individual investor will be better off purchasing the bond, because its after-tax yield of 5.76% exceeds the after-tax yield of 5.04% on the preferred stock. (Careful scrutiny reveals that this is true for *any* marginal tax rate for the individual investor because dividend and interest income of any individual are taxed equally.) However, the corporate investor will be better off purchasing the preferred stock, because its after-tax yield of 6.51% exceeds the after-tax yield on bonds of 5.20%.

Tax-Exempt Organizations

Many organizations are wholly or partly exempt from federal income taxes. Nonprofit religious, charitable, or educational foundations generally qualify. A small tax (2% in 1998) is levied on the net investment income of such a foundation. In addition, the foundation should pay out either all income received by the end of the year in which it was received or a minimum percentage of its assets (5% in 1998), whichever is higher. Failure to pay the higher amount can result in a confiscatory tax on the difference between the two.

Investment companies, often called *mutual funds*, may elect to be treated as regulated investment companies for tax purposes. This privilege is granted if certain conditions are met. For example, the funds of the investment company must be invested primarily in securities, without undue concentration in any one. Thus its income takes the form of dividends and interest received on its investments, as well as capital gains from price appreciation realized when investments are sold at a price that is higher than their purchase price. A regulated investment company pays income tax only on income and capital gains not distributed to its shareholders. As a result of this tax treatment, such companies distribute substantially all income and gains, and in doing so end up not having to pay any taxes.

Employee pension, profit-sharing, and stock-bonus plans may also qualify for tax-exempt status. Such a plan may entrust its assets, which are usually securities, to a *fiduciary* (for example, a bank; a fiduciary is a person who is entrusted with the securities of another and is to act in that person's best interests). The fiduciary receives new contributions, makes required payments, and manages the investments owned by the plan. A fiduciary under a qualified plan (that is, a plan that meets all the requirements of applicable legislation) pays no taxes on either income or capital gains.

Another example of a tax-exempt entity is the *personal trust*. Here, funds are provided for the benefit of one or more individuals by another individual or individuals, with a fiduciary serving as a trustee. Some trusts are created by wills, others by contracts among living persons. Whatever the origin, trusts generally pay taxes only on income that is not distributed to the designated beneficiaries.

Income and capital gains earned by investment companies, pension funds, and personal trusts do not go untaxed forever. Payments made to investment company shareholders, pension fund beneficiaries, and the beneficiaries of personal trusts are subject to applicable personal income tax rules. The exemptions apply only to taxes that might otherwise be levied at the previous stage.

12.1.2 Personal Income Taxes

Although the corporate income tax is an important feature of the investment scene, its impact on most individuals is indirect. Individuals, on the other hand, directly bear the personal income tax. Few investors avoid dealing with it in detail, at both an economic and an emotional level. Its provisions have major and direct effects on investment behavior.

Personal Tax Rates

Taxes must be paid on an individual's income, defined as "all wealth which flows to the taxpayer other than as a mere return of capital. It includes gains and profits from any source, including gains from the sale or other disposition of capital assets."[3] Certain items are excluded from the definition of income; others are deducted from income before the tax due is computed. Moreover, capital gains and losses are subject to special procedures, which will be described in a later section. Deductions and exclusions of special importance for investment purposes are described in this section as well as in later sections.

Personal taxes are based on an individual's or family's taxable income. Taxable income is found by initially computing gross income. From that point, adjusted gross income is obtained by subtracting certain allowed adjustments (for example, business expenses and contributions to certain retirement funds). This amount, less a number

Taxing Pension Funds

In the late1990s, the federal government succeeded at least temporarily in eliminating its chronic budget deficits. Nevertheless, concern still exists over the government's long-run ability to match revenues and expenditures. Further spending cuts seem unlikely because politicians make few friends by chopping favored programs. Although additional tax increases may be more palatable, the choice of targets for those increases will be a volatile issue. The well-to-do were tapped for the 1993 increases, leaving politicians the unpleasant task of asking middle-class voters to pay more. Where else can the government look for revenue "enhancements"?

One of the last unexploited sources of significant tax revenue is pension plans. Currently, private and public pension plans hold over $5 trillion in assets. Virtually all of those pension plans conform to specific government regulations and as a result are "qualified." These qualified pension plans offer their sponsors and participants several important tax advantages:

1. Employers may treat their pension fund contributions immediately as tax-deductible expenses.
2. Employees defer paying taxes on contributions that their employers make to the pension funds on their behalf.
3. Pension fund investment earnings are not taxed until they are withdrawn.

Under present laws, employers (and in some cases employees) make tax-deductible contributions to a pension plan to prefund pension benefits that are to be paid upon employees' subsequent retirements. These employer contributions clearly represent a form of income to employees. After all, employers could just as easily increase the employees' paychecks by the amount of the contributions and let the employees invest those dollars for themselves. Moreover, this income is invested and grows untaxed over the employees' working lives. Eventually the employees pay taxes on their invested pension contributions, but not until they receive their pension benefits during their retirement years.

This tax-advantaged status of pension funds is quite valuable. The U.S. Treasury estimates that the exclusion of pension contributions and plan earnings from taxation results in an annual loss to government coffers of over $55 billion. The exclusion of employer contributions from the payroll tax base adds several billion dollars more to that figure. These lost taxes constitute the second largest source of forgone revenues experienced by the federal government and considerably exceed the losses associated with such higher profile tax subsidies as mortgage interest deductions and accelerated depreciation. Only the exclusion of employer contributions for medical insurance surpasses the tax "expenditures" associated with pension funds. (Of course, these figures conveniently ignore the fact that pension fund participants ultimately are taxed when they receive their benefits.)

Proponents of taxing pension plans contend that the costs of exempting pension plans from taxation far exceed the benefits (for example, Alicia Munnell, "Current Taxation of Qualified Pension Plans: Has the Time Come?" *New England Economic Review*, March/April 1992). Their primary argument is that pension funds do not increase national savings sig-

of personal expense deductions, equals taxable income. The amount of tax must be paid unless the taxpayer is able to claim tax credits, which may be subtracted directly from the tax liability to obtain a final amount due the government. In summary, after-tax income is determined as follows:

Gross income
—adjustments
Adjusted gross income
—deductions
Taxable income
—taxes
+tax credits
After-tax income

nificantly. This contention may seem counterintuitive at first. After all, annual contributions to U.S. pension plans total roughly $150 billion. For a nation with a puny personal savings rate of under 5%, this $150 billion would seem to be an important source of funds for investment. But pension fund taxation proponents believe that employees save less outside of their pension funds because of their savings accumulated inside the pension funds. That is, pension savings offset other personal savings. Proponents estimate that this offset, although not dollar-for-dollar, effectively reduces net savings from pension plans to "only" about $50 billion per year (see the Munnell article)—roughly the same amount as the Treasury forgoes in lost tax revenues each year.

Taxation proponents also contend that exempting pension funds from taxation violates fundamental tax fairness principles. Not quite half of the U.S. working population is covered by pension plans. Moreover, those persons covered tend to be in the higher income categories. Further, as these higher income persons are subject to higher marginal tax rates, the benefit of tax-exempt pension funds is greatest for them.

Most proposals to tax pension funds involve levying a tax on each pension plan expressed as a percentage of the plan's annual contributions and investment earnings. Benefits would then not be subject to tax. As a transition to the tax scheme, a one-time tax on the plans' assets would be charged, thus taxing employees who have already accrued benefits tax-free.

Opponents of taxing pension funds contend that pension savings are a critical source of total U.S. savings. They take issue with the crowding-out theory of taxation proponents. That theory is difficult to substantiate empirically, and the crowding-out effect may be much less than proponents contend.

Moreover, even if some personal savings are crowded out by pension savings, adding $50 billion or more to U.S. savings represents roughly one-quarter of the country's annual personal savings. Because savings ultimately have a multiplier effect on national income, accepting a $1 revenue loss for $1 of additional savings may be a sound long-term tradeoff.

As for the equity issue, taxation opponents point out that higher income persons in all economies always provide the bulk of the economies' savings. It may be unrealistic and counterproductive to add to the existing disincentives to save in the name of wealth equity.

Opponents also point to the technical difficulties of taxing pension plans. Lost tax revenues are split about evenly between private and public pension funds. Constitutionally, it may be difficult to tax public plans. Even if it can be accomplished, cash-strapped state and local governments may respond to taxation by lowering their contributions to pension plans—surely an undesirable outcome.

Taxation of pension funds, if it ever occurs, may not take the form of radical legislation. Rather, it may begin with seemingly innocuous dips into pension fund coffers. In recent years, for example, taxes on pension fund holdings of foreign securities above a certain threshold have been proposed. Also discussed have been taxes on pension funds' security transactions as well as on their short-term capital gains.

Although the Tax Reform Act of 1986 (as amended in 1990 and 1993) brought sweeping changes aimed at simplification, the Taxpayer Relief Act of 1997 brought many complications. Consequently, most people are of the opinion that almost nothing about personal income taxes in the United States is simple. Four different schedules of tax rates are currently in effect. Which one is applicable depends on whether the particular taxpayer is single, married and filing a joint return with his or her spouse, married but filing a separate return, or a head of a household. Table 12.2 shows the tax rates in effect for income earned in 1996 for the first two types of taxpayers. (The figures shown here—and elsewhere—are indexed to inflation, and hence will change over time.) The rates are plotted in Figure 12.2.[4] For comparison, the 1913 federal tax form applicable to individuals, the first one ever needed by U.S. taxpayers, is shown in Figure 12.3. Its relative simplicity is striking and emphasizes the complexity of modern personal income taxation.

TABLE 12.2 Personal Income Tax Marginal Rates, 1996

Taxable Income		Amount of Taxes
At Least	**But Not More Than**	
Single Taxpayers		
$ 0	$ 24,000	$ 0 + 15% of income over $ 0
24,000	58,150	3,600 + 28 of income over 24,000
58,150	121,300	13,162 + 31 of income over 58,150
121,300	263,750	32,738 + 36 of income over 121,300
263,750	...	84,020 + 39.6 of income over 263,750
Married Taxpayers Filing Jointly		
$ 0	$ 40,100	$ 0 + 15% of income over $ 0
40,100	96,900	6,015 + 28 of income over 40,100
96,900	147,700	21,919 + 31 of income over 96,900
147,700	263,750	37,667 + 36 of income over 147,700
263,750	...	79,445 + 39.6 of income over 263,750

The top line in each panel of Figure 12.2 shows the marginal tax rate, which was defined earlier when corporate income taxes were discussed. A similar definition applies here: The marginal tax rate is the tax rate an individual would pay on an additional dollar of taxable income. Although this rate is constant over certain ranges of income, it increases as the taxpayer moves to higher taxable income brackets, topping out at 39.6% for income over $263,750 for both individuals and married couples filing jointly. Interestingly, Figure 12.3 indicates that the highest marginal tax rate in 1913 was 6% and was applicable to any income over $500,000 that was earned by individuals.

The lower line in both panels of Figure 12.2 shows the average tax rate, which was also defined earlier when corporate income taxes were being discussed. Again, a similar definition applies here: The average tax rate is the ratio of total tax paid to total taxable income and is generally smaller than the marginal tax rate. Although the average rate is less than the marginal rate for all levels of income above that specified for the lowest tax bracket of 15%, it becomes very close in size to the top marginal rate of 39.6% as income becomes very high.

Earlier, it was mentioned that, for corporations, the marginal tax rate is generally more relevant than the average tax rate in making certain kinds of decisions. This observation is also true for individuals and married couples. For example, consider a married couple with taxable income of $80,000 who are evaluating an investment opportunity that is expected to increase their taxable income by $3,000. This increase in taxable income will result in an increase of $840 (= $3,000 × .28) in taxes, leaving a net increase in spendable income of $2,160 (=$3,000 − $840). The calculations for this particular example are simple because the change in taxable income left the taxpayer in the same bracket. Thus 28% of the additional income will be taxed away, leaving 72% to be spent. The average tax rate before and after the increase is irrelevant to this couple in deciding whether to make the investment.

When an investment moves income into a higher bracket, the computations are more complex. For example, assume that the opportunity in question would increase the couple's income by $20,000. This increase in taxable income will result in an increase of $5,693 [= (.28 × $16,900) + (.31 × $3,100)] in taxes, leaving a net increase in spendable income of $14,307 (= $20,000 − $5,693). Thus 28.5% (=$5,693/$20,000) of the additional income will be taxed away, an amount greater

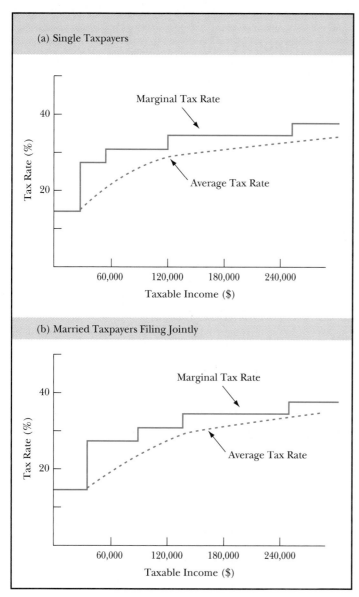

Figure 12.2
Marginal and Average Personal Tax Rates, 1997

than the 28% figure that was applicable to the previous example. As before, average tax rates are irrelevant to the couple in making their decision.

Tax-Exempt Bonds

A major consideration for investors with large taxable incomes is the possibility of obtaining tax-exempt income. The simplest way to accomplish this goal is to purchase **tax-exempt bonds.** These securities exist because the notion of federalism has been interpreted to imply that the federal government should not tax states and municipalities or the income produced from their bonds.[5] Although the legal basis is complex, the facts are simple. Interest income from most bonds issued by states, municipalities, and their agencies need not be included in taxable income in determining the amount of federal taxes that are owed. The benefit for a high-bracket taxpayer is significant.

FORM 1040

INCOME TAX

List No...........................

THE PENALTY
FOR FAILURE TO HAVE THIS RETURN IN
THE HANDS OF THE COLLECTOR OF
INTERNAL REVENUE ON OR BEFORE
MARCH 1 IS $20 TO $1,000
(SEE INSTRUCTIONS ON PAGE 4.)

File No...

..................*District of*..

Assessment List...

Date received...

Page.................... *Line*........................

UNITED STATES INTERNAL REVENUE.

RETURN OF ANNUAL NET INCOME OF INDIVIDUALS.

(As provided by Act of Congress, approved October 3, 1913.)

RETURN OF NET INCOME RECEIVED OR ACCRUED DURING THE YEAR ENDED DECEMBER 31, 191....
(FOR THE YEAR 1913, FROM MARCH 1, TO DECEMBER 31.)

Filed by (or for) --- *of* ---
(Full name of individual)   (Street and No.)

in the City, Town, or Post Office of --- *State of* ---
(Fill in page 2 and 3 before making entries below.)

1. Gross Income (see page 2, line 12) --- $----------------

2. General Deductions (see page 3, line 7) ----------------------------- $----------------

3. Net Income --- $----------------

Deductions and exemptions allowed in computing income subject to the normal tax of 1 percent.

4. Dividends and net earnings received or accrued, of corporations, etc. subject to like tax. (See page 2, line 11) ---------- $----------------

5. Amount of income on which the normal tax has been deducted and withheld at the source. (See page 2, line 9, column A) --

6. Specific exemptions of $3,000 or $4,000, as the case may be. (See Instructions 3 and 19) --------------

Total deductions and exemptions. (Items 4,5 and 6)------- $----------------

7. Taxable Income on which the normal tax of 1 per cent is to be calculated (See Instruction 3). $----------------

8. When the net income shown above on line 3 exceeds $20,000, the additional tax thereon must be calculated as per schedule below:

	INCOME	TAX
1 per cent on amount over $20,000 and not exceeding $50,000	$----------------	$----------------
2 " " $50,000 " " $75,000		
3 " " $75,000 " " $100,000		
4 " " $100,000 " " $250,000		
5 " " $250,000 " " $500,000		
6 " " $500,000		
Total additional or super tax		$----------------
Total normal tax (1 per cent of amount entered on line 7)		
Total tax liability		

Figure 12.3
1913 Federal Income Tax Form 1040

Consider again the couple in the previous example. Assume that for the same cost they can obtain an increase in taxable income of $20,000 per year by investing in corporate bonds or a tax-free increase in income of $16,000 per year by purchasing tax-exempt bonds. As shown earlier, their effective tax rate on an increase of $20,000 in taxable income would be 28.5%, leaving 71.5%, or $14,307, to be spent. But all $16,000 in tax-exempt income could be spent—clearly a preferable investment opportunity.

This relationship is no secret. Not surprisingly, tax-exempt bonds offer lower before-tax rates of interest than taxable bonds. Thus they are not attractive for investors with low marginal tax rates. For example, if the couple had a marginal tax rate of 15% instead of 28.5%, they would prefer the corporate bonds because their after-tax return would be $17,000 [=$20,000 × (1 − .15)], an amount greater than the $16,000 provided by the tax-exempt bonds.

If couples with a marginal tax rate of 28.5% find the tax-exempt bonds more attractive, and couples with a marginal tax rate of 15% find the corporate bonds more attractive, then there should be a marginal tax rate in between these two rates that makes couples in that bracket indifferent between the two types of bonds. In this example, if the couple had a marginal tax rate of 20%, they would be indifferent between the corporate bonds and the tax-exempt bonds, because both would provide an after-tax return of $16,000. However, a 20% marginal tax rate does not currently exist. What this means is that couples with rates equal to or greater than the next highest tax rate (28%) would prefer the tax-exempt bonds; couples with rates equal to or less than the next lowest tax rate (15%) would prefer the corporate bonds (unless the additional income from the bond pushed them into the 28% bracket).

The 20% marginal tax rate figure was determined by solving the following equation for t:

$$\$20,000 \times (1 - t) = \$16,000$$

More generally, the marginal tax rate that makes an investor indifferent between a taxable and a tax-exempt investment can be arrived at by solving the following equation for t:

$$\text{taxable bond yield} \times (1 - t) = \text{tax-exempt bond yield} \qquad (12.1\text{a})$$

or:

$$1 - t = \frac{\text{tax-exempt bond yield}}{\text{taxable bond yield}} \qquad (12.1\text{b})$$

or:

$$t = 1 - \text{ratio of tax-exempt to taxable bond yields} \qquad (12.1\text{c})$$

Figure 12.4 shows the ratio, over time, of the yield-to-maturity for a group of tax-exempt bonds issued by municipalities to that of a group of taxable bonds issued by public utilities.[6] On this basis, tax-exempt bonds appear to be competitive with taxable bonds for investors subject to marginal tax rates between 20% (when the ratio of bond yields is 80%) and 40% (when the ratio of bond yields is 60%). For those wealthy enough to be considering investments that provide income subject to the higher ranges, tax-exempt bonds are well worth investigation. Less wealthy investors are likely to find them unattractive.

Capital Gains and Losses

The provisions of the personal income tax laws that deal with the treatment of capital gains and losses have had a great impact on investor behavior. Only the basic elements of these provisions can be described here. Complete understanding of the details would require an effort sufficient to keep many lawyers, tax accountants, and investment advisers busy, especially with the complexities introduced in the Taxpayer Relief Act of 1997.

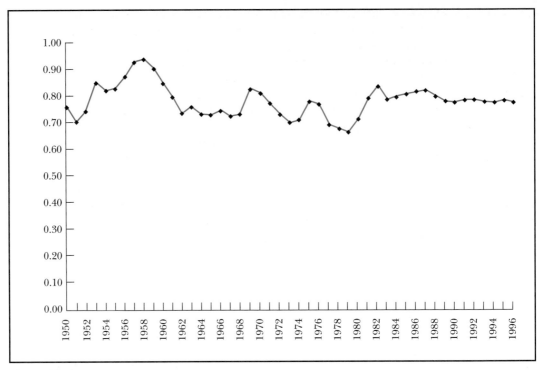

Figure 12.4
Ratio of High-Grade Municipal Bond Yields to High-Grade Corporate Bond Yields
(1950–1996)
Source: *1997 Economic Report of the President* (Washington, DC: GPO, 1997); p. 382.

A change in the market value of a capital asset is not relevant for tax purposes until it is **realized** as a **capital gain** (or loss) by sale or exchange. If a security purchased for $50 appreciates to a value of $100 in a year, no tax is due on the **unrealized capital gain**. But if it is sold for $120 two years after purchase, the difference of $70 must be declared as capital gains realized at the time of sale, and tax must be paid at the rate applicable to it.

This rule makes the end of the year an interesting time for stockbrokers. Depending on their situations, taxpayers may be either eager or reluctant to realize capital gains or losses before a new tax year begins. Consider, for example, a taxpayer who earlier in the year had sold 1,000 shares of stock *A* for $50 per share, having purchased it three years ago for $20 per share. This investor has a capital gain of $30,000 [= 1,000 × ($50 − $20)] and will have to pay taxes on this gain if nothing is done. However, it is now December, and the investor currently owns 1,000 shares of stock *B*, which is selling for $65 per share. Having purchased it four years ago for $95 per share, the investor has an unrealized loss of $30,000 [= 1,000 × ($65 − $95)] on the investment in *B*. Nevertheless, the investor believes that stock *B* will rebound in the near future and, hence, wants to continue owning it. It might seem at first glance that the investor should sell *B* on December 31 and then buy it back on January 1, thereby establishing a capital loss of $30,000 on *B* to offset the capital gain on *A*. This action would remove the tax liability associated with the investor's gain on *A*, while essentially maintaining the position in *B*. However, the same stock cannot be bought and sold simultaneously in such tax exchanges because the tax laws preclude a deduction associated with a loss on a **wash sale**, in which a security is sold and a "substantially identical" one is bought within 30 days.

Brokerage firms publish lists pairing similar stocks for investors who wish to sell a particular stock for tax purposes. By selling a stock and simultaneously purchasing the matching stock, the investor may be able to continually maintain a portfolio with similar investment characteristics. In the previous example, a brokerage firm may have stocks B and C matched together. These two stocks have different issuers but may be in the same industry and, in the opinion of the brokerage firm, be poised for a similar rebound next year. Accordingly, the investor might sell B and purchase C.

End-of-year sales and purchases motivated by tax considerations are fairly common. At this time, securities that experienced substantial price changes during the year tend to have large numbers of trades as investors sell to realize gains or losses. If buyers recognize that the sellers are motivated by knowledge of the tax laws, and not some previously unrecognized bad news affecting the company in question, such "selling pressure" should not seriously depress the company's stock price.

Capital gains and losses involve, of course, capital assets, but the regulations define capital assets rather narrowly. Capital assets include all kinds of property, except that held in conjunction with the taxpayer's trade or business (for example, inventories). Gains (or losses) on property that is an integral part of a taxpayer's business are considered regular income. Pro rata appreciation of a fixed-income security issued at a significant discount (for example, a 90-day Treasury bill) may also be considered income, as it is more like interest than capital gains.

The capital gain or loss realized when an asset is sold or exchanged is the difference between the value received and the asset's basis. For an asset purchased outright, the (initial) basis is equal to the actual cost of the asset. For an asset received as a gift or inheritance, the recipient's basis may be the donor's basis or the value at the time of receipt, depending on the relationship between the two and the value at the time of the sale. Gains and losses are categorized as short-term if the asset is held for a year or less and long-term if the asset is held for more than a year. The treatment of long-term gains and losses is complex owing to the existence of several categories of long-term gains and losses, depending on the length of time the assets were held and when they were bought.

The ability to control the realization of capital gains and losses has a number of obvious advantages. Most important, tax can be paid at the most opportune time. The clearest case involves the realization of capital gains around the time of retirement. Shortly before retirement is usually a time when the taxpayer's income is relatively high, which in turn means that the taxpayer's marginal tax rate is relatively high. After retirement the taxpayer's income and, in turn, marginal tax rate are usually substantially lower. Accordingly, it is generally advantageous for the taxpayer who is near retirement to wait until after retirement to realize any capital gains.

The tax treatment of capital gains begins by bringing all short-term capital gains and losses together to obtain either a net short-term capital gain or a loss. Similarly, all long-term gains and losses are brought together for each category to obtain either a net long-term capital gain or a loss for that category. For the tax year 1998, here are the various categories and the tax rates involved, assuming there is a net gain:

1. Holding period: Less than one year

   Taxation: The aggregate gain is taxed as ordinary income.

2. Holding period: More than 12 months.

   Taxation: The aggregate gain is taxed at a rate of 20%, unless the taxpayer is in the 15% income tax bracket, in which case the rate is 10%.

3. Holding period: Five years or more; asset must be purchased in 2001 or later.

   Taxation: The aggregate gain is taxed at a rate of 18%. An exception is allowed for any taxpayer who is in the 15% income tax bracket, in which case the 2001 restriction on when the asset was purchased is replaced with a restriction that the asset must have been sold in 2001 or later. For these taxpayers, the rate is 8%.

As an example, assume that Mr. and Mrs. Smith have taxable income of $400,000, which includes $50,000 of capital gains. Their tax bill can be determined by first noting in Table 12.2 that the marginal tax rate for $400,000 of income appears to be 39.6%. Because this rate is greater than the marginal rates for long-term gains given in cases 2 through 4, their tax bill will depend on the nature of the $50,000 capital gain. Note that if the $50,000 is attributable to short-term capital gains, then the full $400,000 will be treated as ordinary income, resulting in a tax bill of $133,400 [=$79,445 + .396 × ($400,000 − $263,750)]. In this case, the net capital gain is taxed at a rate of 39.6% and amounts to $19,800 because the Smiths are unable to take advantage of the lower long-term capital gains tax rates.

In case 2, the $50,000 is associated with the sale of capital assets after owning them for at least 12 months. Table 12.2 shows that the Smiths' taxable income before the long-term capital gains equals to $350,000 (=$400,000 − $50,000) and will be taxed at a marginal rate of 39.6% with taxes amounting to $113,600 [=$79,445 + .396 × ($350,000 − $263,750)]. However, the long-term capital gains will now be taxed at a rate of only 20%, producing taxes of $10,000 (=.20 × $50,000). Hence the Smiths' total tax bill comes to $123,600 (=$113,600 + $10,000).

In case 3, the $50,000 is derived from selling of capital assets after holding them at least five years and having initially purchased them in 2001 or later. Once again, the Smiths' marginal income tax rate is 39.6%, resulting in taxes of $113,600. Now, the long-term capital gains tax rate is only 18%, and the capital gains taxes are $9,000 (=.18 × $50,000), resulting in a total tax bill of $122,600 (=$113,600 + $9,000). (It goes without saying that Congress changes the tax laws frequently. As a result, it might be unwise to count on the current rules' applying to assets purchased after 2001 and held for five years).

In summary, note that the total tax bill of the Smiths is different in all three cases because of the difference in the amount of tax paid on the $50,000 capital gain.

	Total Taxes Paid	Income Taxes Paid	Capital Gains Taxes Paid
Case 1	$133,400	$113,600	$19,800
Case 2	123,600	113,600	10,000
Case 3	122,600	113,600	9,000

The total tax bill amounts to either $133,400 or $123,600 or $122,600, depending upon how long the asset was owned and, in the last case, when it was initially bought. The best situation from the Smiths' viewpoint is if the $50,000 is due entirely to five-year long-term capital gains (the tax bill would thus be minimized at $122,600), whereas the worst situation is if the $50,000 is due to short-term capital gains (the tax bill would thus be maximized at $133,400).

State Income Taxes

Most states levy personal income taxes, following a format similar to that of the federal government. Although lower, state taxes are also likely to be progressive. The impact of these taxes is not quite as large as it might first appear, because income taxes paid to state governments may be deducted from income before computing federal income tax. For example, consider an investor whose marginal rates for state and federal income taxes are 10% and 31%, respectively. Assume in this example that federal taxes are not deductible in computing state taxes. An additional $100 of income will result in $10 of state tax. This leaves $90 subject to federal income tax, thereby increasing the investor's federal income taxes by $27.90. Overall, $37.90 will be taxed away, giving an effective combined marginal rate of 37.9%. More generally:

$$\text{Combined marginal tax rate} = s + (1 - s)f \qquad (12.2)$$

where s and f denote the marginal state and federal tax rates, respectively.

The situation becomes a bit more complicated if the state allows the taxpayer to deduct the amount of federal taxes paid in determining the amount of taxable income. In this situation there is **cross-deductibility**, because state taxes are deductible for federal tax purposes and federal taxes are deductible for state tax purposes. Now, using the previous $100 example, $7.12 $\{= \$100 \times [.1 - (.1 \times .31)]/[1 - (.1 \times .31)]\}$ will be paid in state income taxes, and $28.79 $\{= \$100 \times [.31 - (.1 \times .31)]/[1 - (.1 \times .31)]\}$ will be paid in federal income taxes, for a combined total of $35.91. Thus the effective combined marginal tax rate is 35.91%. More generally, the amount of state tax paid for each additional dollar earned equals $[s - (s \times f)]/[1 - (s \times f)]$, and the corresponding amount of federal tax paid equals $[f - (s \times f)]/[1 - (s \times f)]$. Therefore:

$$\text{Combined marginal tax rate} = \frac{s + f - (2 \times s \times f)}{1 - (s \times f)} \qquad (12.3)$$

Another interesting feature of state taxation is that the interest income from bonds issued by municipalities within a state may be exempt from that state's income tax. Some states extend this exemption to include dividends from certain corporations domiciled within the state. Furthermore, cities that levy personal income taxes typically exempt from taxation the interest income on any municipal bonds they have issued. In this situation, the resident of the city who purchases such a bond escapes taxation on three levels: federal, state, and local.

12.1.3   Before-Tax Investing

There are features of the tax code that virtually all investors should consider. Specifically, investors should take advantage of the opportunities available to invest their money on a before-tax basis where, in addition, the income earned on the initial investment grows tax-free. If this strategy is not possible, then they should consider doing only the latter—investing in such a manner that the income earned on the initial investment can grow tax-free.

Two examples can be used to illustrate the point. First, the tax code allows individuals who are self-employed to set aside as much as 25% of their income each year on a before-tax basis, subject to a maximum of $30,000, in what is known as a **Keogh plan** (also known as an H.R. 10 plan). This money can be invested according to the investor's desires and can be withdrawn after the investor reaches an age of 59-$\frac{1}{2}$ (such withdrawals must begin by the age of 70-$\frac{1}{2}$; penalties exist if withdrawals do not take place between the ages of 59-$\frac{1}{2}$ and 70-$\frac{1}{2}$). The key feature of Keogh plans is that neither the amount invested nor the income earned on this investment is subject to taxation until funds are withdrawn from the plan, at which point the funds are taxed as ordinary income.[7] Hence the investor benefits by deferring the payment of income taxes on both the amount invested and the income earned on the investment until a later date.

Adjusting Capital Gains Taxes for Inflation

A look back at recent U.S. taxation of capital gains reveals a picture of vacillating economic and social policies. Tax rates on long-term capital gains (hereafter, simply "capital gains") have fluctuated radically as various political groups and ideologies have come and gone in Washington, D.C. Over the last 20 years, capital gains tax rates on individuals in the *highest* personal income tax brackets have ranged from a high of 49% in 1977 to a low of 18% today. Despite the current relatively low tax rates, only the most naive investor would assume that they will remain in place for long.

Economists agree that taxing any commodity or activity reduces the output of that commodity or activity. Taxing gains on capital assets, therefore, reduces the amount of capital assets "produced." Other things remaining the same (always a tenuous assumption), lower capital gains tax rates will encourage savings, increase investment, and thus enhance economic productivity. However, because the vast proportion of taxable capital assets is directly or indirectly held by a minority of relatively affluent people, proponents of wealth redistribution view capital gains taxes as symbolic of their effort to create a more egalitarian society.

No particular capital gains tax rate will satisfy all interested groups. The politics of the issue are much too entangled with the economics. Despite this conflict, at least one inequitable aspect of the current capital gains tax structure calls for a remedy: the taxation of returns to capital that merely compensates investors for inflation experienced over the periods in which they hold their capital assets.

Suppose that you purchased a share of *XYZ* Corporation for $100. One year later you sell the stock for $110, giving you a 10% [= ($110 − $100)/$100] before-tax nominal return. With a 20% capital gains tax rate, your after-tax nominal return is 8.0% {= [($110 − $100) − (.20 × $10)]/$100}. (As the text described, the current tax rate structure is complex, with the rate in effect being a function of income and the length of time that the asset is held. Taxpayers in the highest tax bracket holding an asset for at least 12 months pay a 20% capital gains tax rate.)

Now assume that the inflation rate was 5% during the year. Presuming that you are concerned with real returns, then you require a 5% return simply to make yourself "whole" in a purchasing power sense. The first 5% of your 10% before-tax nominal return is effectively a return of capital, not a source of profit. Therefore your before-tax real return should be calculated from a base value of $105, not $100, to take into account the 5% inflation rate. Consequently, your before-tax real return is 4.8% [= ($110 − $105)/$105].

However, the government levies capital gains taxes on both the inflation-compensation component of investment returns and the real profit component. Therefore your after-tax real return is 2.9% {= [($110 − $105) − (.20 × $10)]/$105}. From an-

---

The second example is what is known as an **individual retirement account**, or IRA, which can be set up by anyone. According to the tax code, an individual can contribute up to $2,000 per year to an IRA and a married couple can set aside up to $4,000. Although the amount contributed to an IRA is not tax-deductible for those whose income exceeds a certain limit (unless their employer does not offer a pension plan), the earnings on the investment are allowed to grow without the payment of taxes until withdrawn.[8]

The Taxpayer Relief Act of 1997 created a new type of IRA knows as an IRA Plus, or Roth IRA.[9] With this type of IRA, contributions are not tax-deductible regardless of income level, but withdrawals are tax-free, provided the taxpayer is at least 59-$\frac{1}{2}$ when they are made and the account has been open for at least five years. Earlier withdrawals are also tax-free provided they are used for either the purchase of a first home or for educational expenses or are taken from the amount initially contributed. Consider an individual who is thinking about investing $2,000 of gross income in a 20-year bond. This investor is in the 31% marginal tax bracket and anticipates being in it for life. Bonds currently earn 10% and are anticipated to continue earning this amount indefinitely. If the investor deposits the $2,000 in either a Keogh plan or a deductible

---

other perspective, because your before-tax real profits are $5 and the government has collected $2.00 in capital gains taxes from you, the effective tax rate on your capital gains is 40% (=$2.00/$5), not 20%.

The tax assessed on your capital, as distinguished from the tax imposed on the profits from your capital, is more akin to a property tax than an income tax. Moreover, the level of that tax changes with the inflation rate, producing an arbitrary and capricious tax structure. Over some holding periods, a capital asset's value may actually suffer a decline in real terms, yet inflation boosts its nominal value sufficiently to generate a gain for tax reporting purposes. An investor selling this asset could end up paying capital gains taxes on an inflation-adjusted capital loss.

The solution to this inequity involves indexing the base value (that is, the original cost) of the capital asset to the inflation rate. The base value is adjusted upward by the inflation rate experienced over the period the capital asset is held. Only gains above this adjusted base are subject to tax.

In our earlier example, the inflation-adjusted base value of *XYZ* common stock after one year is $105 (= $100 × 1.05), so your taxable gain is now $5 (=$110 − $105) instead of $10. Thus your after-tax nominal return is 9.0% {= [($110 − $100) − (.20 × $5)]/$100}. Furthermore, your after-tax real return is 3.8% {= [($110 − $105) − (.20 × $5)]/$105}, for an effective tax rate of 20% (=$1.00/$5).

The fairness and simplicity of adjusting capital gains taxes for inflation seem indisputable. There was considerable support in Congress to incorporate such an adjustment in the Taxpayer Relief Act of 1997. However, the legislation failed to pass. Why has there not been more public demand for an inflation-adjusted capital gains tax? Several explanations are plausible. First, in periods of relatively low inflation, such as has been witnessed since the early 1980s, the inflation-compensation component of capital gains is relatively small, making the issue less pressing. Second, in periods when balancing the federal budget is of concern, any cut in taxes, even in the name of equity and increased long-term investment, causes short-term problems. Current government spending would have to be reduced or other taxes increased if the budget deficit were not to grow in the short term owing to the effective capital gains tax cut. Finally, there is the slippery-slope problem. That is, if one accepts the argument for adjusting capital gains for inflation, should not the same logic apply to interest income as well? After all, this investment income has its own inflation-compensation component. However, the tax revenue lost over the short term from such a change in the taxation of interest income would far exceed the revenue losses caused by altering the capital gains tax structure.

IRA, which in turn buys the bonds, the investment will grow to be worth $13,455 [=$2,000 × (1.10)^{20}] at the end of 20 years. If the money is withdrawn at that time, the investor will receive $9,284 [=$13,455 × (1 − .31)] after taxes.

Alternatively, the investor could consider investing in a nondeductible IRA, which, in turn, buys the bonds. However, taxes on the $2,000 amounting to $620 (=$2,000 × .31) must be paid first, assuming the investor does not qualify for a tax-deductible IRA. Depositing the remaining $1,380 (=$2,000 − $620) results in the IRA's having a balance of $9,284 [=$1,380 × (1.10)^{20}] at the end of 20 years. If the money is withdrawn at that time, the investor will receive $6,834 {= $1,380 + [($9,284 − $1,380) × (1 − .31)]} after taxes. However, if a Roth IRA had been used instead, the investor would have received $9,284 [=$1,380 × (1.10)^{20}] in after-tax money, assuming the investor was over 59-$\frac{1}{2}$ and initially was qualified for the Roth IRA.

As a basis for comparison, consider what would happen if the investor avoided using either a Keogh plan or an IRA and invested directly in bonds. In that case, only $1,380 would be available for investment, and each year the investor would get to keep earnings amounting to only 6.9% [=10% × (1 − .31)] of the amount invested. Hence after 20 years the investor would have an amount available after taxes equal to $5,241 [=$1,380 \times (1.069)^{20}]$.

In summary, the after-tax payoffs for the three alternatives discussed are:

Keogh plan, deductible IRA, and Roth IRA:	$9,284
Nondeductible IRA:	6,834
Direct investment:	5,241

Note that the Keogh plan, deductible IRA, and Roth IRA provide the investor with 77% more money after taxes than could be earned by investing directly. Another way to view these payoffs is to note that the direct investment would have to earn 14.5% before taxes in order to provide the same after-tax payoff provided by investing in a Keogh plan, deductible IRA, or Roth IRA that earns 10%. Similarly, the direct investment would have to earn 12% before taxes in order to provide the same after-tax payoff provided by the nondedectible IRA. It is no surprise that a popular book on investing advises readers that "one of the best ways to obtain extra investment funds is to avoid taxes legally."[10]

12.2   INFLATION IN THE UNITED STATES

The story is told of the modern-day Rip Van Winkle who awoke in the year 2050 and immediately called his broker. (Fortunately, pay phones at the time permitted a call of up to three minutes without charge.) He first asked what had happened to the $10,000 he had instructed the broker to put in Treasury bills, continually reinvesting the proceeds. The broker promptly informed him that because of high interest rates and the power of compounding, his initial $10,000 investment had grown to be worth over $1 million. Stunned, Mr. Van Winkle inquired about his stocks, which were also worth about $10,000 when he dozed off. The broker told him that he was in for an even more pleasant surprise: They were now worth $2.5 million. "In short, Mr. Van Winkle," said the broker, "you are a millionaire 3.5 times over." At this point an operator cut in: "Your three minutes are over, please deposit $100 for an additional three minutes." Although this story clearly overstates the case, there is no doubt that inflation is a major concern for investors. By and large, people have come to fear significant inflation, particularly when it is unpredictable.

This section begins by describing how **inflation** is typically measured. Then the benefits and costs of inflation are discussed, along with who gains and who loses when it is present.

12.2.1   Measuring Inflation

There is no completely satisfactory way to summarize the price changes that have occurred over a given time period for the large number of goods and services available in the United States. Nevertheless, the federal government has attempted to do so by measuring the cost of a specific mix of major items (a "basket of goods") at various points in time. The "overall" price level computed for this representative combination of items is termed a **cost-of-living index.** The percentage change in this index over a given time period can be viewed as a measure of the inflation (or deflation) that took place from the beginning of the period to the end of the period.

As Chapter 5 discussed, whether this measure of inflation is relevant for a given individual depends to a major extent on the similarity of the individual's purchases to the mix of items used to construct the index. Even if the individual finds the mix to be appropriate at the beginning of a period, the rate of increase in the price of the mix over the time period is likely to overstate the increase in the cost of living for the individual for two reasons. First, improvements in the quality of the items in the mix are seldom taken adequately into account. Consequently, the end-of-period price for a good is not comparable to the beginning-of-period price, because the good is different. For example, a new Toyota may have a 5% higher sticker price than a similar model had the previous year, but the newer model may have better tires than the older model. Hence it would be inaccurate to conclude that the price of this particular model rose by 5% over the year.

Second, and perhaps more important, little or no adjustment is made in the mix as relative prices change. The rational customer can reduce the cost of attaining a given standard of living as prices change by substituting relatively less expensive goods for those that have become relatively more expensive. For example, if the price of beef rises 20% over a given year while the price of chicken rises only 10% over the same year, then the customer may start to eat more chicken and less beef. Failure to take into account this change in the mix will result in an overstatement in the rate of inflation. Despite these two drawbacks, cost-of-living indices provide at least rough estimates of changes in prices.[11]

12.2.2 Price Indices

Most governments compute a number of alternative price indices in order to provide a wider choice for analysis. Nevertheless, many people tend to focus on one index as an indicator of the price level. In the United States the **Consumer Price Index** (CPI) often fills this role, despite some attempts by government officials to discourage such widespread use.[12] Because the CPI is so widely used, the composition of the market basket of goods that make up the CPI has been changed from time to time in order to provide a more representative basket. Furthermore, the process by which the relevant data are gathered and verified has periodically been improved. Currently the CPI is calculated monthly by the U.S. Bureau of Labor Statistics in the Department of Labor.

In Chapter 1, Table 1.1 provided some historical perspective on the rate of inflation in the United States. It showed the annual rate of increase in the CPI from 1926 through 1996. As an aid to interpretation, these rates are plotted on a graph shown in Figure 12.5(a). As can be seen in the figure, the CPI did not grow at a constant rate over the period of 1926 to 1996. After substantial deflation from 1926 to 1933, prices increased in almost every year. In general, there were four subsequent subperiods with different rates of inflation: mild (but notably uneven) inflation from 1934 to 1952, negligible inflation from 1953 to 1965, and fairly rapid (but somewhat uneven) inflation from 1966 to 1981, followed again by mild inflation from 1982 to 1996. Interestingly, the recent moderation in U.S. inflation has occurred almost simultaneously in most other countries as well, leading some observers to contend (perhaps erroneously) that inflation is no longer a serious macroeconomic problem.

Table 12.3 shows the average annual rate of growth of the CPI for each of these subperiods, measured by what is known as the *geometric mean growth rate* of the CPI. This growth rate, when compounded over the subperiod and applied to the beginning index value, results in the ending index value. For example, at the end of 1965 the CPI was 95.5, and at the end of 1981 it was at 281.5 (here the CPI is adjusted so that its value in 1967 was 100). Thus the geometric mean growth rate was 7.0%, because 95.5, when growing at this compounded rate over 16 years, equals 281.5:

$$281.5 = 95.5 \times (1 + .070)^{16}$$

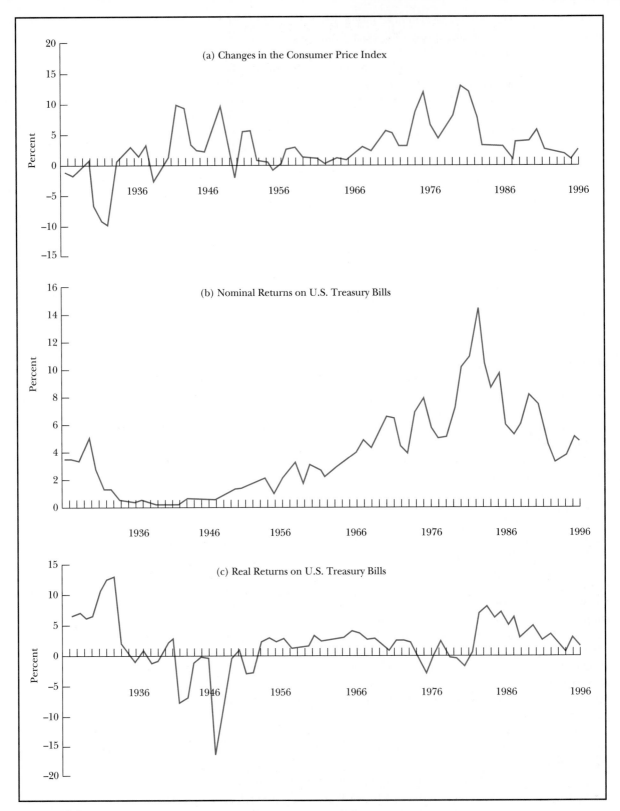

Figure 12.5

Nominal and Real Returns on Short-Term Default-Free Investments, 12-month Periods Ending December, from 1926 to 1996

Source: *Stocks, Bonds, Bills, and Inflation 1997 Yearbook* (Chicago: Ibbotson Associates, 1997). All rights reserved.

TABLE 12.3	Geometric Mean Growth Rates of the U.S. Consumer Price Index	
From	To	Rate of Growth (% per Year)
1926	1933	−3.8
1934	1952	3.8
1953	1965	1.4
1966	1981	7.0
1982	1996	3.6
Overall:		
1926	1996	3.1

More generally, the geometric mean growth rate (g) can be calculated by solving the following equation for g:

$$C_e = C_b(1 + g)^y \qquad (12.4)$$

which results in

$$g = \left(\frac{C_e}{C_b}\right)^{1/y} - 1 \qquad (12.5)$$

where y denotes the number of years and C_e and C_b denote the ending and beginning CPI values, respectively.

12.3   NOMINAL AND REAL RETURNS

12.3.1   Nominal Returns

Modern economies gain much of their efficiency through the use of money—a generally agreed-upon medium of exchange. Instead of trading corn for a stereo to be delivered in one year, as in a barter economy, the citizen of a modern economy can trade corn for money, then trade this "current" money for "future" money by investing it. Later, the future money can be used to buy a stereo. The rate at which the citizen can trade current money for future money depends on the investment made and is known as the **nominal return** (also known as the *nominal rate*).

12.3.2   Fisher Model of Real Returns

In times of changing prices, the nominal return on an investment may be a poor indicator of the **real return** (also known as the *real rate*) obtained by the investor.[13] This is because part of the additional dollars received from the investment may be needed to recoup the investor's lost purchasing power due to inflation that has occurred over the investment period. As a result, adjustments to the nominal return are needed to remove the effect of inflation in order to determine the real return. Frequently, the CPI is used for this purpose.

For example, assume that at the start of a given year the CPI is at a level of 150, and that at the end of the year it is at a level of 160. This means that it costs $160 at the end of the year to buy the same amount of the CPI market basket of goods that at the start of the year could have been purchased for $150. Assuming that the nominal return is 9% for this year, the investor who started the year with $150 and invested it would have $150 × 1.09 = $163.50 at year-end. At this point, the investor could purchase ($163.50/$160) $- 1 = .0218 = 2.18\%$ more of the CPI market basket of goods than at the beginning of the year. Thus the real return for this investment was 2.18%.

These calculations can be summarized in the following formula:

$$\left[C_0 \times \frac{1 + NR}{C_1} \right] - 1 = RR \qquad (12.6)$$

where:

> $C_0 = $ CPI at the beginning of the year
> $C_1 = $ CPI at the end of the year
> $NR = $ the nominal return for the year
> $RR = $ the real return for the year

Alternatively, the citizen could note that an increase in the CPI from 150 to 160 can be translated into an inflation rate of $(160/150) - 1 = .0667$, or 6.67%. This inflation rate can be denoted as CCL (change in the cost of living), and the real return can be calculated using the following formula, known as the Fisher model:[14]

$$\left[\frac{1 + NR}{1 + CCL} \right] - 1 = RR \qquad (12.7)$$

Note that for the example, $RR = (1.09/1.0667) - 1 = .0218$, or 2.18%.

For quick calculation involving the Fisher model, the real return can be estimated by simply subtracting the inflation rate (CCL) from the nominal return:

$$NR - CCL \cong RR \qquad (12.8)$$

where $\cong$ means "is approximately equal to." In this example, the "quick method" results in an estimate of the real return of $.09 - .0667 = .0233$, or 2.33%. Thus the error resulting from use of this method is $.0233 - .0218 = .0015$, or .15%.[15]

12.3.3 The Effect of Investor Expectations

The simplest view of investors' attitudes toward inflation is that they are concerned with real returns, not nominal returns, and that a single price index is adequate to characterize the difference. Looking to the future, investors do not know what the rate of inflation will be, nor do they know what the nominal return on an investment will be. However, in both cases they have expectations about what these figures will be, which are denoted as $E(CCL)$ (expected inflation rate) and $E(NR)$ (expected nominal return), respectively. Thus the Fisher model implies that $E(RR)$ (the expected real return on an investment) can be approximated by:

$$E(RR) \cong E(NR) - E(CCL) \qquad (12.9)$$

If a security is to provide a given expected real return, the expected nominal return must be larger by the expected rate of inflation for the relevant holding period. This condition can be seen by rearranging Equation (12.9):

$$E(NR) \cong E(RR) + E(CCL) \qquad (12.10)$$

For example, if the expected rate of inflation is 4% and a given security is to provide investors with an expected real return of 6%, then the security must be priced in the marketplace so that its expected nominal return is approximately 10%. Furthermore, if the expected real rate remains constant, then a 1% increase in the expected rate of inflation from 4% to 5% will result in a 1% increase in the expected nominal rate of return from 10% to 11%. In summary, if investors are concerned with real returns, then securities will be priced in the marketplace so that expected nominal returns incorporate the expected rate of inflation.[16]

12.4   INTEREST RATES AND INFLATION

At the start of a given investment holding period, nominal interest rates for securities having no risk of default should cover both a requisite expected real return and the expected rate of inflation for the period in question. At the end of the period, the real return actually received will be the difference between the nominal return and the rate of inflation actually experienced. Only when actual inflation equals expected inflation will the actual real return equal the expected real return on such securities. As mentioned earlier, Figure 12.5(a) indicates the annual rate of inflation, as measured by changes in the Consumer Price Index, over the 71-year time period from 1926 to 1996. Figure 12.5(b) shows how short-term nominal interest rates varied over this time period; Treasury bill rates, taken from Table 1.1, are used for this purpose. Figure 12.5(c), derived by subtracting panel (a) from panel (b), represents real returns.

One cannot help being struck by the fact that those who invested in short-term securities over this period frequently ended up with less purchasing power (particularly if taxes are taken into account) than they started with because the real return was negative in 25 of the 71 years. Perhaps even more surprising is the fact that the average real return over the period was close to zero.

Although expected real returns may vary from year to year, this variation may be relatively small. If it is, investors may have been willing to invest in short-term highly liquid securities even though they expected to earn very little in real terms. If they are currently willing to do so, such securities will be priced to give a very low expected real return.[17]

If this assumption is made, the "market's" predicted rate of inflation over the near future can be estimated by simply subtracting an estimate of the low expected real rate, say 1%, from the nominal interest rate (also known as the yield) on short-term government securities, namely, Treasury bills. In a sense, the resulting figure represents a consensus prediction of inflation—a prediction that an "average" investor in this market would make and one that is likely to be more accurate over time than the predictions of any single forecaster.

12.5   THE EFFECT OF INFLATION ON BORROWERS AND LENDERS

Although deviations of actual inflation from expected inflation may have relatively little effect on the real return on investments in general, they may have a significant effect on specific investments. In fact, one would expect a direct impact on the real returns associated with investments whose payments are fixed in terms of dollars to be received.

A simple example will illustrate the relationship. Assume that everyone currently expects the rate of inflation to be 5% over the next year and that a lender has agreed to make loans at a nominal rate of 5% (that is, the lender is content with having an expected real return of zero). Thus one can borrow $100 now and pay back one year later $105 (=$100 × 1.05) for a one-year loan. Note that if actual inflation equals expected inflation, a one-year loan would require a payment equivalent to $100 in constant (that is, today's purchasing power) dollars a year hence. In this case, the real rate of interest would turn out to be zero.

Now, imagine that an individual takes advantage of the lender's offer, borrowing $100 for one year. How will the borrower and lender be affected if the actual rate of inflation differs from the expected rate of inflation?

Assume that in the first year prices rise by 9% instead of the expected 5%, meaning that unexpected inflation is 4% (=9% − 5%). In this situation, the short-term borrower gains at the expense of the lender. Why? The borrower must still repay $105, but in terms of constant dollars, this is only $96.33 (= $105/1.09), a figure that is less than the amount of the loan. As a result, the lender receives a real rate of interest of −3.67% [= ($96.33 − $100)/$100], instead of the anticipated rate of 0%.

What if first-year prices had risen by only 3%, meaning that unexpected inflation was −2% (=3% − 5%)? In this situation, the short-term lender would gain at the expense of the borrower. The borrower would have to repay $105, which in terms of constant dollars amounts to $101.94 (= $105/1.03), a figure that is greater than the amount of the loan. As a result, the lender would receive a real rate of interest of 1.94% [= ($101.94 − $100)/$100], instead of the anticipated rate of 0%.

These results can be generalized: When the actual rate of inflation exceeds the expected rate of inflation, those with commitments to make payments that are fixed in nominal terms (debtors) gain in real terms at the expense of those to whom payments are to be made (creditors). Conversely, when actual inflation is less than expected inflation, creditors gain and debtors lose.[18] This uncertainty in the real return on fixed-income securities that is due to uncertain inflation is frequently referred to as **purchasing-power risk.**

12.6   INDEXATION

The previous section suggests that in a world of uncertain inflation, even default-free bonds are subject to purchasing-power risk. Contractual nominal interest rates can cover expected inflation, but the subsequent real return from any investment with fixed nominal payments will depend on the actual amount of inflation. As long as the two inflation rates differ, the expected real return will be uncertain. However, there is a way to design a bond so that its expected real return is certain. It involves the use of indexation.

12.6.1   Government Bonds

If a specified price index can adequately measure purchasing power, there is no reason why a contract, such as a government bond, cannot be written with specified real payments instead of specified nominal payments. Thus, if the CPI currently stands at C_0, and will be C_1 one year later, C_2 two years later, and so on, in return for a loan of $100, the government could promise to pay amounts that are currently unknown but will be equal to $4 \times C_1/C_0$ one year later, $4 \times C_2/C_0$ two years later, ..., and $104 \times C_{10}/C_0$ ten years later. The values $C_1/C_0, C_2/C_0, ..., C_{10}/C_0$ are known as *index ratios* and represent the quantity of 1 + the rate of inflation from the time that the bond was issued (time 0) to the time a given payment is to be made. Conversion of these payments to constant (or real) dollars requires that each one be divided by the corresponding quantity of 1 + the rate of inflation since the bond was issued, which is equivalent to C_t/C_0 for a payment made at time t.

Time	Amount in Nominal Dollars	Price Level (CPI)	Amount in Real Dollars
1	$4 \times C_1/C_0$	C_1	4
2	$4 \times C_2/C_0$	C_2	4
$\vdots$	$\vdots$	$\vdots$	$\vdots$
10	$104 \times C_{10}/C_0$	C_{10}	104

The real value of each payment is the amount shown in the final column. These payments will have the indicated purchasing power expressed in time 0 prices regardless of what happens to prices in the future (that is, regardless of the actual values of C_1, C_2, and so on). Thus the bond is said to be fully indexed, because all amounts are tied to a stated price index on a one-for-one basis; when the price index goes up by 10%, for example, all of the subsequent payments go up by 10%. Thus, any investor who buys this bond at issuance for $100 and then holds it until maturity will receive an annual *real* return of 4%.

What happens if inflation the first year turns out to be 5% and the investor sells the bond at year-end for $103? This investor's return will be 7.2% $\{=[(\$4 \times 1.05) + \$103]/\$100\}$, for a real return of approximately 2.2% (=7.2% − 5%). The new buyer will be facing an inflation-protected stream of annual cash inflows amounting to $4.20 (= $4 × 1.05) for the next eight years and $109.20 [= ($100 × 1.05) + ($4 × 1.05)] in nine years. Having paid $103 for this stream, the buyer will receive an annual *real* return of 4.3% if the bond is held to maturity.[19]

In January of 1997 the U.S. Treasury started a program in which bonds of this nature, dubbed *Treasury inflation-indexed securities*, are to be sold quarterly. (Inflation-indexed securities were discussed in *Institutional Issues: Almost Riskfree Securities*, Chapter 5). One of the interesting features of such securities is that a comparison of their yields with those of conventional Treasury securities of similar maturities provides a rough measure of the representative investor's expected rate of inflation over the life of the security. In the previous example, when the 10-year inflation-indexed security was first sold it provided the investor with a real yield-to-maturity of 4%. If at the same time a 10-year conventional Treasury note was sold with a nominal yield-to-maturity of 7%, then a rough estimate of the expected rate of inflation over the forthcoming 10-year period is 3% (=7% − 4%).[20]

Table 12.4 indicates the experience of six other countries with similar securities. Note that Israel has made the greatest use of such securities, which is not surprising given its history of relatively high inflation.

TABLE 12.4	Inflation-Indexed Securities in Other Countries					
	Israel	U.K.	Sweden	Australia	Canada	New Zealand
	Year First Issued					
	1955	1981	1994	1985	1991	1995
Amount outstanding (in billions of U.S. dollars)	$27.9	$71.1	$5.7	$2.7	$4.3	$.1
Indexed debt as percent of country's total marketable debt	79.0%	17.8%	4.5%	3.8%	1.4%	.7%

Source: Jeffrey M. Wrase, "Inflation-Indexed Bonds: How Do They Work?" *Federal Reserve Bank of Philadelphia Business Review* (July–August 1997): 7.

12.6.2 Indexing Other Contracts

It should be kept in mind that not only government bonds can be tied to inflation. In some countries (two notable examples are Israel and Brazil), a great many contracts besides bonds are tied to standard price indices. Returns on savings accounts, wage contracts, pension plans, insurance contracts—all have been indexed at various times and places. In the United States, Social Security payments are indexed, as are pension payments of retired federal employees. Some of these payments are fully indexed; others are only partially indexed, meaning that, for example, they might be increased by 7% when the price index increases by 10%.

The key advantage of indexation is its role in reducing or eliminating purchasing-power risk. Typically, higher expected inflation is accompanied by increased uncertainty about the actual rate of inflation. This increased uncertainty means that the potential gains and losses to both nonindexed borrowers and nonindexed lenders are larger. Because both borrowers and lenders dislike the prospect of losses more than they like the prospect of gains, there will be increased pressure for indexation by both borrowers and lenders when a country moves into periods of high inflationary expectations.

Thus when uncertainty about inflation is substantial, one would expect indexation to become widespread. However, laws regulating interest rates may prevent the issuance of fully indexed debt if these laws place a ceiling on the nominal rate but not on the real rate. Such laws lead to predictable inefficiencies when expected inflation increases, because credit rationing might be required. Rationing may be necessary because a ceiling on the nominal rate causes the real rate to decline as inflationary expectations increase. The decline in the real rate, in turn, increases the demand for credit and reduces the supply, leading to credit rationing.[21] A notable example occurred in the 1970s in the United States. At that time, ceilings placed on nominal rates paid by savings and loan companies, coupled with increased inflationary expectations, caused a substantial outflow of funds from such companies and a corresponding reduction in the amount of money made available by them for home mortgages. On the other side were issuers of securities that were not subject to rate ceilings and that offered an appropriate nominal rate and, thus, had little difficulty in attracting funds. The term **disintermediation** was invented to describe this pattern of funds flow.

Because inflation is generally hard to predict for long time periods, uncertainty about inflation often leads to a reduction in the average term-to-maturity of newly issued fixed-income securities. For example, the average term-to-maturity of fixed-coupon debt issued in periods of great inflationary uncertainty is usually shorter than in more stable times.

Alternatively, debt with long maturities can be written with **variable rates** (also known as **floating rates**) of interest. Such instruments provide long-term debt at short-term rates. Interest payments are allowed to vary, with each one determined by adding a fixed number of percentage points (say, 2%) to a specified base rate that changes periodically. Two base rates frequently used are the prime rate and the yield on 90-day U.S. Treasury bills. If short-term interest rates anticipate inflation reasonably well, such a variable-rate security is an effective substitute for a fully indexed bond.

12.7 STOCK RETURNS AND INFLATION

12.7.1 Long-Term Historical Relationships

It is reasonable to assume that investors are more concerned with real returns than with nominal returns because real returns reflect how much better off they are in terms of the purchasing power of their wealth. Accordingly, real returns of securities need to

TABLE 12.5 Rates of Real Return on Common Stocks and Treasury Bills and the Equity Premium

Period (1)	Real Return on Stocks (2)	Real Return on Bills (3)	Equity Premium (2) − (3) = (4)
1802–1996[a,b]	8.03%	3.14%	4.89%
1802–1888[a]	7.52	5.62	1.90
1889–1996[a,b]	8.59	1.18	7.41
1926–1996[b]	9.35	.67	8.68
1950–1996[b]	9.65	.99	8.66

[a] **Source:** Andrew B. Abel, "The Equity Premium Puzzle," *Federal Reserve Bank of Philadelphia Business Review* (September–October 1991), p. 8.
[b] **Source:** Table 1.1.

be analyzed. This analysis is done in Table 12.5 for common stocks and Treasury bills for the long-term period of 1802 to 1996 and four relatively long subperiods.

Column (2) of the table shows that, on average, the rate of return on common stocks has substantially exceeded the rate of inflation, providing a real return of nearly 8% for the entire period examined and in excess of 7% in all of the subperiods. In comparison, the rate of return on Treasury bills exceeded the rate of inflation by over 3% in the entire period. However, the subperiods show substantial variation, as the real return on Treasury bills ranged from .67% over the period from 1926 to 1996 to 5.62% in the period from 1802 to 1888.

Also of interest is the **equity premium** shown in column (4), which is simply the difference between the real rate of return on stocks and bills. Although less than 2% from 1802 to 1888, it has since then been nearly 7%, an amount that some researchers believe is inexplicably large. In summary, Table 12.5 shows that common stocks have historically returned substantially more than the rate of inflation and Treasury bills. That is, in the long run, common stocks have had a large positive real return.

12.7.2 Short-Term Historical Relationships

Another interesting question to investigate is the relationship between the short-term rate of return on stocks and the rate of inflation. Conventional wisdom suggests that stock returns should be relatively high when inflation is relatively high and relatively low when inflation is relatively low. Why? Because stocks represent claims on real assets that should increase in value with inflation.

Figure 12.6 displays the relationship between annual stock returns and rates of inflation for the period from 1926 to 1996. The figure shows that there is no discernible relationship between the rate of inflation and stock returns. Indeed, the correlation coefficient between these two variables is −.01, which for all practical purposes is equal to zero.[22] That is, when inflation is relatively high, there is no tendency for stock returns to be either relatively high or low. Similarly, when inflation is relatively low, there is no tendency for stock returns to be either relatively high or low.[23] Accordingly, stocks are not good hedges against inflation in the short term.

12.7.3 Relationships Involving Expected Inflation

The previous results used historical (or *ex post*) rates of inflation and stock returns. Also of interest are tests of the relationship between expected (or *ex ante*) rates

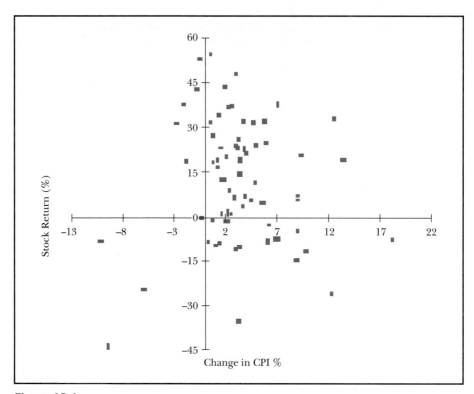

Figure 12.6
Annual Stock Returns and Rates Inflation, 1926–1996
Source: *Stocks, Bonds, Bills, and Inflation 1997 Yearbook* (Chicago: Ibbotson Associates, 1997). All rights reserved.

of inflation and stock returns. For example, what effect does a relatively high expected inflation for the forthcoming year have on stock returns over the year?

One study explored this relationship by using time horizons of one and five years.[24] The major difficulty in performing such a test is that expected inflation rates are not observable; only subsequent actual inflation rates can be observed. This obstacle was overcome by constructing and testing four models for arriving at estimates of expected inflation. These models used past inflation rates and interest rates as "instrumental variables" to estimate expected inflation.

To simplify, the tests involved the following model:

$$r_t = \alpha + \beta\pi_t + e_t \qquad (12.11)$$

where r_t and π_t denote, respectively, the rate of return on stocks and the expected inflation rate over time period t. In this equation the variable of interest is the coefficient β. If there is a one-for-one relationship between expected inflation and stock returns, then the estimated value of β will be approximately equal to 1.0. In such a situation, an increase of 1% in the expected inflation rate would result in a 1% increase in stock returns, indicating that the Fisher model is appropriate when stated in terms of expectations.

Equation (12.11) was first tested using one-year stock returns and inflation rates from 1802 to 1990 and then was tested again using overlapping five-year returns and rates.[25] Table 12.6 presents the results. In two of the four cases involving one-year expectations, the value of β appears to be significantly less than 1.0. This result suggests that, in the short term, stock returns do not respond to changes in expected rates of inflation. However, in all four cases involving five-year expectations, the value of β is not significantly different from 1.0, suggesting that stock returns do respond to

TABLE 12.6 Testing the Relationship Between Expected Inflation Rates and Stock Returns, 1802–1990

Instrumental Variables Used[a]		Estimated Value of β	
One-Year	Five-Year	One-Year	Five-Year
ST int rates	LT int rates	−2.781	1.394
ST inf rates	LT inf rates	−.048*	1.820
ST int rates	ST, LT int rates	−2.531	2.072
ST inf rates	ST, LT int rates	.061*	.380

Source: Jacob Boudoukh and Matthew Richardson, "Stock Returns and Inflation: A Long-Horizon Perspective," *American Economic Review* 83, no. 5 (December 1993): 1352.

[a] ST = past year; LT = past five years; int = interest; inf = inflation.

* Denotes number is significantly different from 1.0 at .10 level of significance.

changes in expected rates of inflation over long horizons. Hence the Fisher model appears to be validated when applied over long horizons but not when applied over short horizons.[26] That is, there appears to be a positive relation between expected rates of inflation and stock returns over long periods of time but not over short periods. These findings are consistent with those observed when actual rates of inflation were compared with stock returns.

12.8   SUMMARY

1. Because investors concern themselves with after-tax returns, federal and state tax laws play a major role in the way securities are priced.
2. Income earned by a corporation may be taxed twice: once when it is earned, via the corporate income tax, and again when it is received as dividends by the stockholders, via the personal income tax.
3. In the case of both individuals and corporations, the marginal tax rate is more relevant than the average tax rate for making investment decisions.
4. Tax-exempt bonds generally pay lower interest rates than equivalent-risk taxable bonds. Comparable tax-exempt and taxable bonds should be evaluated on an after-tax basis.
5. Long-term capital gains taxes are lower than short-term capital gains taxes; the size of the tax depends on the investor's tax bracket, the length of time the investor owns the asset before selling it, and when it was bought.
6. Because state taxes are deductible on a federal level and vice versa for some states, the combined marginal tax rate is not the sum of the state and federal marginal tax rates.
7. Some tax shelters, such as Keogh plans and IRAs, permit the deferral of taxes on part of the investor's wage income and all of the investment earnings, subject to certain conditions.
8. Inflation measures the percentage change in a specific cost-of-living index at various points in time.
9. Whether a measure of inflation is relevant for a given individual depends to a large extent on the similarity of the person's purchases to the composition of the price index.
10. An investor's real return is a function of the difference between the investor's nominal return and the inflation rate.

11. Real returns are important to an investor because they represent how much the investor's purchasing power has increased (or decreased) and thus how much better (or worse) off the investor is.

12. If investors are concerned with real returns, securities will be priced so that expected nominal returns incorporate the expected inflation rate.

13. When the actual inflation rate exceeds the expected inflation rate, debtors gain in real terms at the expense of creditors. The opposite is the case when actual inflation is less than expected inflation.

14. Investment returns can be indexed by tying security payments to changes in the price level. Indexation reduces or removes an investment's purchasing-power risk.

15. Over long periods of time, common stocks have generated large, positive real returns. Treasury bills have produced much lower, but still positive, real returns.

16. Over short periods of time, stock returns are not positively related to either actual or expected rates of inflation. However, over long periods of time, stock returns are positively related to both actual and expected rates of inflation.

QUESTIONS AND PROBLEMS

1. Why is the marginal tax rate more relevant to investment decision making than the average tax rate is?

2. Given the following income tax schedule, draw a graph illustrating the marginal and average tax rates as a function of income level.

Income	Tax Rate
$0–$10,000	10%
$10,001–$20,000	13
$20,001–$30,000	15
$30,001–$50,000	20
$50,001 and above	25

3. Minneapolis Pipelines pays an annual dividend of $0.80 per share on its preferred stock. The stock currently sells for $12 per share. Maplewood Chemicals is considering investing idle cash in either Minneapolis's preferred stock or a bond yielding 9.8%. If Maplewood's marginal tax rate is 34%, which investment is more attractive?

4. U.S. federal personal income tax rates are progressive in that the marginal tax rate increases with income (see Figure 12.2). What is the justification for this tax structure? Make a case for or against progressive tax rates.

5. Footsie Belardi earned $60,000 last year. Using the single filer tax schedule in Table 12.2, calculate Footsie's income tax.

6. Heine Groh expects consumer prices to rise at a 7% rate next year and has negotiated a 9.5% pay increase. Given a 35% marginal income tax bracket, will this pay increase cause Heine's real income (that is, purchasing power) to grow? Explain.

7. A corporate bond is selling for $950. It matures in a year, at which time the holder will receive $1,000. In addition, the bond will pay $50 in interest during the year. What would be the after-tax return on the bond to an investor in the 50% marginal income tax bracket? (Assume that capital gains do not receive preferential tax treatment.) What would be the after-tax return if the bond had been a tax-free municipal bond?

8. Consider a tax-exempt municipal bond yielding 6%. To an investor in the following marginal tax brackets, what is the equivalent before-tax interest rate that

a taxable bond would have to offer to be considered equivalent to the municipal bond?

a. 10%

b. 28%

c. 33%

9. Spot Bethea must choose between investing in a tax-free municipal bond yielding 5% and a taxable bond yielding 7.5%. Spot's marginal tax rate is 30%. Which bond should Spot choose?

10. Pinky Higgins and spouse had taxable income of $100,000 last year, which includes a capital gain of $20,000. What is their tax bill if the gain is entirely short-term? What is their tax bill if the gain is derived from assets held for 13 months?

11. Jean Dubuc lives in a state where the tax schedule lists an 8% marginal tax rate. The federal tax schedule lists a 25% marginal tax rate. Accounting for cross-deductibility:

a. What is Jean's effective state marginal tax rate?

b. What is Jean's effective federal marginal tax rate?

c. What is Jean's effective combined marginal tax rate?

12. Would you expect tax shelters to be as attractive to lower-income persons as to higher-income persons? Should lower-income persons invest in tax shelters at all? Why?

13. Given the following beginning and ending values for a particular price index and the respective number of years between the measurement of the two values, calculate the annual compounded (geometric mean) inflation rates during the three periods.

Price Index Beginning Value	Price Index Ending Value	Number of Years Covered
100	120	1
120	175	3
175	150	2

14. Calculate the arithmetic (that is, the simple) mean rate of inflation using the data in Table 1.1 for the same time periods given in Table 12.3. What is the relationship between the arithmetic and geometric means?

15. Given the following average compound annual inflation rates, how much would $1 be worth in terms of purchasing power five years from today expressed in today's dollars?

a. 5%

b. 10%

c. 15%

16. Bingo Binks's portfolio earned an 8% average compound annual return over an eight-year period. The average compound annual inflation rate over this time period was 4%. Bingo's portfolio was worth $15,000 at the beginning of the period. At the end of the period, what was the portfolio worth, expressed in beginning-of-period dollars?

17. Kirby Higbe started the year with investments valued at $11,500. At the end of two years those same investments were worth $16,000. During the same time period the price index rose from 210 to 250. What was Kirby's annual real rate of return over the two-year period?

18. How are economywide inflation rates calculated? Are all consumers affected equally by the increase in overall prices measured by the price index? Explain.

19. Assume that your portfolio grows 9% in value per year and annual inflation is 5%. How many years will it take for the nominal value of your portfolio to triple? How many years will it take for the real value of your portfolio to triple?

20. Why is it reasonable to assume that rational investors will build an expected inflation premium into the returns they require from their investments?

21. In the late 1970s and early 1980s, a period of unexpectedly high inflation, Happy Felsch referred to long-term bonds issued by U.S. corporations and the Treasury as "certificates of confiscation." Why would Happy make such a comment?

22. Also in the late 1970s and early 1980s, there was considerable discussion concerning the "quality" of corporate earnings. Straight-line depreciation and the FIFO inventory valuation methods were often cited as the causes of "poor quality" earnings. Further, it was argued that these accounting methods effectively resulted in tax overpayments. Discuss the reasons for both contentions.

23. From the perspective of after-tax returns, what is typically the problem with fully inflation-indexed securities?

24. Explain why the returns on bonds are found to be negatively correlated with unexpected inflation. Why does this relationship become progressively more negative as one considers longer-lived bonds?

25. Common stocks, in general, do not appear to be effective hedges against either expected or unexpected short-run inflation. Explain why the stocks of some companies might be better hedges against inflation than the stocks of other companies.

ENDNOTES

1 Certain corporations with 35 or fewer shareholders may elect to be treated as partnerships for tax purposes. Such firms, often called "Subchapter S corporations" (after the enabling provision of the Internal Revenue Code), constitute an exception to the general rule.

2 This provision assumes that the corporate investor owns between 20% and 80% of the stock of the firm issuing the dividends. If less than 20% is owned, then only 70% of the dividends are excluded from income. If 80% or more is owned, then 100% of the dividend is excluded.

3 1988 Federal Tax Course (Upper Saddle River, NJ: Prentice Hall, 1987), p. 89.

4 Some subtle yet complicated changes made in 1990 and 1993 cause the tax rate schedules to be slightly different from what is shown here.

5 Chapter 13 describes various types of bonds that are available for investment and gives a more detailed discussion of how they are taxed.

6 These yields are also compared in Chapter 13 (see, in particular, Figure 13.11).

7 Other plans that are treated similarly with respect to taxation are known as 401(k) plans, run by corporations, 403(b) plans, run by certain nonprofit organizations and school districts, and 457 plans, run by state and local governments.

8 Variable annuities, available from many insurance companies, are treated similarly for tax purposes. See *Institutional Issues: Variable Annuities* in Chapter 21.

9 The Education IRA was also introduced with the Taxpayers Relief Act of 1997. With this IRA a maximum of $500 per child can be set aside annually. This amount is not tax-deductible for those whose income exceeds a certain limit, but withdrawals are tax-exempt if used to pay for college expenses.

10 Burton G. Malkiel, *A Random Walk Down Wall Street* (New York: W. W. Norton, 1990), p. 279.

11 In 1996, a commission headed by former White House chief economist Barry Boskin examined the accuracy of the CPI in measuring inflation. The Boskin commission estimated that the CPI overstates inflation by roughly 1% to 1.5% per year. This conclusion generated considerable controversy. How it will affect public policy remains to be seen. For a summary of the report, see Michael J. Boskin, "Prisoner of Faulty Statistics," *Wall Street Journal*,

December 5, 1996, p. A20. See also the entire issue of the May/June 1997 *Federal Reserve Bank of St. Lous Review*, which is devoted to discussing the Boskin report and its implications.

[12] A number of authorities prefer "deflators" derived from gross domestic product figures, but such indices have not received the publicity accorded the Consumer Price Index.

[13] Here *real return* refers to the increase (or decrease) in purchasing power that the investor has received as a result of making a particular investment.

[14] The Fisher model is named after its creator, Irving Fisher, who derived the model in *The Theory of Interest* (New York: Macmillan, 1930).

[15] This error will be larger for higher rates of inflation. Thus, in countries with "hyperinflation," the quick method will have a substantial amount of error associated with it. For example, if the nominal return is 110% and the inflation rate is 100%, then the true real return is 5%, but the quick method will indicate that it is twice as large, 10%.

[16] The model given in Equation (12.10) can be written more precisely as $E(NR) \cong E(RR) + E(CCL) + IRP$, where *IRP* denotes inflation risk premium. Investors will demand to be compensated not only for the expected inflation rate but also for the risk they bear in that the inflation rate is uncertain, that is, for inflation risk. Thus, if the expected rate of inflation is 4% and a given security is to provide investors with an expected real return of 6%, then the security must be priced in the marketplace so that its expected nominal return is more than 10%, such as 10.5% if the inflation risk premium is .5%. Similar adjustments can also be made to Equations (12.6) through (12.8) by replacing *RR* with $RR + IRP$. It should be noted that the "Fisher effect", reflected in equations (12.9) and (12.10), tends to underestimate the expected rate of inflation; see Robert G. Schwebach and Thomas S. Zorn, "A Simple Derivation of the Fisher Equation Under Uncertainty," *Journal of Financial Education* 23 (Fall 1997): 84–87, and the references cited therein.

[17] However, there apparently are periods of time when such securities have an expected real return that is relatively large. For example, in the 1981–1986 period, Treasury bill returns actually exceeded the rate of change in the CPI by over 5%. The implication is that investors expected a positive real return over the latter part of the period.

[18] More specifically, it can be shown that long-term borrowers are likely to gain somewhat more than short-term borrowers when actual inflation exceeds expected inflation and to lose somewhat more when actual inflation falls below expectations. Similarly, long-term lenders are likely to lose somewhat more than short-term lenders when actual inflation exceeds expectations and to gain somewhat more when actual inflation falls below expectations.

[19] To see that 4.3% is the investor's new real rate of return, begin with a purchase price of $103. Given cash inflows each year for eight years of $4.20 in real dollars and a final payment after nine years of $109.20 in real dollars, the internal rate of return of the investment can be shown to equal 4.3%.

[20] A more accurate determination of the expected rate of inflation would involve comparison of the yields on two stripped bonds. For more on determining expected inflation rates from comparing Treasury inflation-indexed securities with conventional Treasury securities, see Jeffrey M. Wrase, "Inflation-Indexed Bonds: How Do They Work?" *Federal Reserve Bank of Philadelphia Business Review* (July–August 1997): 3–16.

[21] Rationing might not occur because lenders may simply refuse to make the kinds of loans that are subject to ceilings when inflationary expectations are high.

[22] The correlation coefficient for the period from 1950 to 1996 is equal to $-.26$. Similar results occur when monthly data are used. Hence some people argue that there is an inverse relationship between historical rates of inflation and stock returns.

[23] Interestingly, there appears to be a significantly negative relationship between the real return on stocks and the rate of inflation. That is, higher rates of inflation seem to be accompanied by lower real stock returns. A number of explanations (some of them conflicting) have been offered to account for this observation. For a survey, see David P. Ely and Kenneth J. Robinson, "The Stock Market and Inflation: A Synthesis of the Theory and Evidence," *Federal Reserve Bank of Dallas Economic Review* (March 1989): 17–29.

[24] Jacob Boudoukh and Matthew Richardson, "Stock Returns and Inflation: A Long-Horizon Perspective," *American Economic Review* 83, no. 5 (December 1993): 1346–1355.

[25] Equation (12.11) was also tested using actual inflation rates and stock returns from 1802 through 1990. The estimated value of β when one-year rates were used was .07, which was significantly less than 1.0 and not significantly different from zero. When five-year rates were used, its estimated value was .52, which was not significantly different from 1.0. These results are consistent with the earlier results about the observed short-term and long-term relationship between inflation rates and stock returns.

[26] Similar results were obtained when both subperiods and U.K. data were analyzed.

KEY TERMS

marginal tax rate	inflation
average tax rate	nominal return
tax-exempt bonds	real return
realized capital gain	purchasing-power risk
unrealized capital gain	indexation
wash sale	inflation-indexed securities
capital gains and losses	disintermediation
cross-deductibility	variable rates
Keogh plan	floating rates
individual retirement account	equity premium

REFERENCES

1. A good reference source for reading about the federal tax code is:

   John L. Kramer and Lawrence C. Phillips (eds.), *Prentice Hall's Federal Taxation, 1992* (Upper Saddle River, NJ: Prentice Hall, 1991).

2. For a valuable book that provides a framework for analyzing how tax rules affect decision making, see:

   Myron S. Scholes and Mark A. Wolfson, *Taxes and Business Strategy* (Upper Saddle River, NJ: Prentice Hall, 1992).

3. Portfolio management and taxation are discussed in:

   Robert H. Jeffrey and Robert D. Arnott, "Is Your Alpha Big Enough to Cover Its Taxes?" *Journal of Portfolio Management* 19, no. 3 (Spring 1993): 15–25.

   Laurence B. Siegel and David Montgomery, "Stocks, Bonds, and Bills after Taxes and Inflation," *Journal of Portfolio Management* 21, no. 2 (Winter 1995): 17–25.

   Roberto Apelfeld, Gordon B. Fowler Jr., and James P. Gordon Jr., "Tax-Aware Equity Investing," *Journal of Portfolio Management* 22, no. 2 (Winter 1996): 18–28.

   William Ghee and Willaim Reichenstein, "The After-Tax Returns from Different Savings Vehicles," *Financial Analysts Journal* 52, no. 4 (July/August 1996): 62–72.

4. The seminal work linking interest rates and inflationary expectations is:

   Irving Fisher, *The Theory of Interest* (New York: Macmillan, 1930).

5. For a review article and test of this linkage, see, respectively:

   Herbert Taylor, "Interest Rates: How Much Does Expected Inflation Matter?" *Federal Reserve Bank of Philadelphia Business Review* (July/August 1982): 3–12.

   Jacob Boudoukh and Matthew Richardson, "Stock Returns and Inflation: A Long-Horizon Perspective," *American Economic Review* 83, no. 5 (December 1993): 1346–1355.

6. The relationship between real interest rates and inflation is discussed in:

   George G. Pennachi, "Identifying the Dynamics of Real Interest Rates and Inflation: Evidence Using Survey Data," *Review of Financial Studies* 4, no. 1 (1991): 53–86.

7. The following papers present an analysis of the effect of inflation on the accounting treatment of corporate earnings:

Franco Modigliani and Richard A. Cohn, "Inflation and the Stock Market," *Financial Analysts Journal* 35, no. 2 (March/April 1979): 24–44.

Kenneth R. French, Richard S. Ruback, and G. William Schwert, "Effects of Nominal Contracting on Stock Returns," *Journal of Political Economy* 91, no. 1 (February 1983): 70–96.

William H. Beaver, Paul A. Griffin, and Wayne R. Landsman, "How Well Does Replacement Cost Income Explain Stock Return [sic]?" *Financial Analysts Journal* 39, no. 2 (March/April 1983): 26–30, 39.

William C. Nordby, "Applications of Inflation-Adjusted Accounting Data," *Financial Analysts Journal* 39, no. 2 (March/April 1983): 33–39.

Charles G. Callard and David C. Kleinman, "Inflation-Adjusted Accounting: Does It Matter?" *Financial Analysts Journal* 41, no. 3 (May/June 1985): 51–59.

8. For a discussion of the U.S. Treasury's inflation-indexed securities, see:

Richard Roll, "U.S. Treasury Inflation-Indexed Bonds: The Design of a New Security," *Journal of Fixed Income* 6, no. 3 (December 1996): 28.

Jeffrey M. Wrase, "Inflation-Indexed Bonds: How Do They Work?" *Federal Reserve Bank of Philadelphia Business Review* (July–August 1997): 3–16.

Robert J. Angell and Alonzo L. Redmon, "Inflation-Indexed Treasures: How Good Are They?" *AAII Journal* 20, no. 3 (April 1998): 22–24.

9. A Web site that contains tax information is:

⟨http://www.irs.ustreas.gov⟩.

10. For a discussion of the relationship of the inflation rate to the returns on stocks, bonds, and real estate, see:

Eugene F. Fama and G. William Schwert, "Asset Returns and Inflation," *Journal of Financial Economics* 5, no. 2 (November 1977): 115–146.

11. Other papers dealing with the relationship between inflation and stock returns can be found at the end of the following survey articles:

David P. Ely and Kenneth J. Robinson, "The Stock Market and Inflation: A Synthesis of the Theory and Evidence," *Federal Reserve Bank of Dallas Economic Review* (March 1989): 17–29.

Andrew B. Abel, "The Equity Premium Puzzle," *Federal Reserve Bank of Philadelphia Business Review* (September/October 1991): 3–14.

12. The equity premium has also been reviewed and analyzed in:

Jeremy J. Siegel, "The Equity Premium: Stock and Bond Returns Since 1802," *Financial Analysts Journal* 48, no. 1 (January/February 1992): 28–38, 46.

Narayana Kocherlakota, "The Equity Premium: It's Still a Puzzle," *Journal of Economic Literature* 34, no. 1 (March 1996): 42–71.

13. The tendency of certain types of common stocks to offer better inflation hedges is discussed in:

Douglas K. Pearce and V. Vance Roley, "Firm Characteristics, Unanticipated Inflation, and Stock Returns," *Journal of Finance* 43, no. 4 (September 1988): 965–981.

Christopher K. Ma and M. E. Ellis, "Selecting Industries As Inflation Hedges," *Journal of Portfolio Management* 15, no. 4 (Summer 1989): 45–48.

Yaman Asikoglu and Metin R. Ercan, "Inflation Flow-Through and Stock Prices," *Journal of Portfolio Management* 18, no. 3 (Spring 1992): 63–68.

14. International evidence on the relationship between stock returns and inflation is provided by:

Bruno Solnik, "The Relation between Stock Prices and Inflationary Expectations: The International Evidence," *Journal of Finance* 38, no. 1 (March 1983): 35–48.

N. Bulent Gultekin, "Stock Market Returns and Inflation: Evidence from Other Countries," *Journal of Finance* 38, no. 1 (March 1983): 49–65.

FIXED-INCOME SECURITIES

This chapter surveys the major types of fixed-income securities, with an emphasis on those currently popular in the United States. Such a survey cannot be exhaustive. A security is, after all, a contract giving the investor certain rights to the future prospects of the issuer. Because the rights given to the investor can differ from one security to another, and because the future prospects of issuers can differ substantially, the number of different types of fixed-income securities is quite large (and growing), making a complete survey virtually impossible.

The term *fixed-income* is commonly used to cover the types of securities discussed in this chapter, but is a bit misleading. Typically, these securities promise the investor that he or she will receive certain specified cash flows at certain specified times in the future. It may be one cash flow, in which case the security is known as a **pure-discount security** (or zero-coupon security). Alternatively, it may involve multiple cash flows. If all of these cash flows (except for the last one) are of the same size, they are generally referred to as **coupon payments**. The specified date beyond which the investor will no longer receive cash flows is known as the **maturity date**. On this date, the investor receives the **principal** (also known as the par value or face value) associated with the security, along with the last coupon payment. However, all the cash flows are *promised* and thus may not be received. That is, in many cases there is at least some risk that a promised payment will not be made in full and on time.

13.1   SAVINGS DEPOSITS

Perhaps the most familiar type of fixed-income investment is the personal savings account at a bank, savings and loan company, or credit union. Such an account provides substantial (if not complete) safety of principal and interest, high liquidity, and a relatively low return.

13.1.1   Commercial Banks

Many people maintain a checking account at a commercial bank. Formally, these accounts are termed **demand deposits**, because money can be withdrawn on demand by the depositors. Although the bookkeeping required to keep track of withdrawals and deposits is costly to the bank, the balance in such an account is available to support interest-earning loans made by the bank. Within bounds set by regulations, banks offer terms for checking accounts that reflect these aspects. Customers with small balances who write many checks pay the bank, whereas those with large balances who write few checks are paid by the bank. Often, the two elements are identified separately, with service charges assessed for check writing and interest paid on average balances. In some cases the rate of interest paid increases substantially if a larger minimum balance is maintained.

An alternative to a checking account is a standard savings account. Although a written request for a withdrawal may be required up to 30 days in advance, in practice, requests for withdrawals are almost always honored immediately. Almost any amount may be invested in a savings account.

Almost all banks also offer money market accounts, which pay interest and on which checks may be written. Credit unions offer services similar to these accounts, via share draft accounts, and many investment companies (described in Chapter 21) provide at least limited check-writing services.

The standard ("passbook") savings account is only one of many types of **time deposits**. A single-maturity deposit may be withdrawn at a stated maturity date (for example, one year after the initial deposit). A multiple-maturity deposit may be withdrawn at a stated date or left for one or more periods of equal length (thus, a 90-day multiple-maturity deposit can be withdrawn roughly every three months after the date of the initial deposit). In practice, most single-maturity and multiple-maturity deposits can be withdrawn at any time. However, a penalty must be paid when a deposit is withdrawn before maturity. Often, the penalty takes the form of recomputing the interest earned using a lower rate. Sometimes, an additional penalty may be deducted from the recomputed account balance.

Some types of time deposits may be made in almost any amount, whereas others may be made only in units of, say, $1,000 each. The latter may be represented by **certificates of deposit** (CDs), which clearly qualify to be called securities. Large-denomination CDs (generally $100,000 or more and known as "jumbos") may be negotiable; that is, the original depositor may sell the certificate to someone else before maturity. In most cases all interest is paid, along with the principal, at maturity.[1] The top part of Figure 13.1 shows average yields of CDs with various maturities issued by major banks, as published each Wednesday in *The Wall Street Journal.*

Most bank accounts in the United States are insured by the Federal Deposit Insurance Corporation (FDIC), a government agency that guarantees the payment of principal on any account up to a stated limit ($100,000 in 1998) if the bank is closed and liquidated. The FDIC, created in 1933, levies insurance premiums on its member banks and is authorized to borrow funds from the U.S. Treasury, if needed, although it has never done so. By opening certain kinds of multiple accounts, each under the limit, an investor can have a considerable amount covered by deposit insurance.

13.1.2 Other Types of Personal Savings Accounts

In the United States, a number of institutions similar to commercial banks are chartered to accept federally insured deposits and to use the proceeds to make consumer loans. These institutions include savings and loan companies, mutual savings banks, and credit unions. In other countries, the government-run post office often accepts savings deposits. Certain kinds of life insurance policies include a savings component, because payments often exceed the amount strictly required to pay for just the insurance involved. The "cash value" of such a policy may be obtained by cancella-

BANXQUOTE® MONEY MARKETS

Tuesday, October 7, 1997

AVERAGE YIELDS OF MAJOR BANKS

	MMI*	One Month	Two Months	Three Months	Six Months	One Year	Two Years	Five Years
NEW YORK								
Savings	2.92%			4.59%	4.83%	5.07%	5.04%	5.41%
Jumbos	4.08%	3.79%	3.78%	4.71%	4.95%	5.08%	5.17%	5.48%
CALIFORNIA								
Savings	2.59%			4.62%	5.14%	5.31%	5.48%	5.74%
Jumbos	3.72%	5.20%	5.21%	5.37%	5.44%	5.53%	5.72%	5.99%
PENNSYLVANIA								
Savings	3.15%			3.68%	4.40%	4.70%	4.93%	5.15%
Jumbos	4.06%	5.28%	5.31%	5.36%	5.43%	5.51%	5.64%	5.90%
ILLINOIS								
Savings	3.75%			5.03%	5.22%	5.39%	5.51%	5.78%
Jumbos	3.71%	5.24%	5.25%	5.41%	5.53%	5.65%	5.70%	6.01%
TEXAS								
Savings	3.99%			3.45%	4.63%	4.87%	4.97%	5.51%
Jumbos	4.77%	4.67%	4.66%	4.83%	5.07%	5.38%	5.35%	5.69%
FLORIDA								
Savings	2.67%			3.73%	4.05%	4.40%	5.02%	5.22%
Jumbos	4.55%	3.82%	3.81%	4.38%	4.73%	5.07%	5.70%	5.85%
U.S. BANK AVERAGE								
Savings	3.47			4.12	4.81	5.07	5.30	5.54
Jumbos	4.18	4.53	4.56	4.80	5.18	5.36	5.53	5.80
WEEKLY CHANGE (in percentage points)								
Savings	....			−0.01	+0.03	+0.01	−0.01	−0.01
Jumbos	+0.01	−0.01	−0.02	−0.01	−0.01	−0.01	−0.03	−0.03

SAVINGS CD YIELDS OFFERED THROUGH LEADING BROKERS

	Three Months	Six Months	One Year	Two Years	Five Years
BROKER AVERAGE	5.38%	5.42%	5.68%	5.70%	5.90%
WEEKLY CHANGE	+0.03	....	+0.07	−0.15	−0.15

*Money Market Investments include MMDA, NOW, savings deposits, passbook and other liquid accounts.

Each depositor is insured by the Federal Deposit Insurance Corp. (FDIC) up to $100,000 per issuing institution.

COMPOUND METHODS: c-Continuously. d-Daily. w-Wkly. m-Mthly. q-Qrtly. s-Semi-annually. a-Annually.

SIMPLE INTEREST: si-Paid Monthly. e-Paid Semi-annually. y-Paid at Maturity.

OTHER SYMBOLS: APY-Annual percentage yield. F-Floating rate P-Prime CD. T-T-Bill CD.

BD-Broker-Dealer. pp-Priced below par.
Day BASIS: A-Actual/Actual. B-30/360. C-Actual/360.
The information included in this table has been obtained directly from broker-dealers, banks and savings institutions, but the accuracy and validity cannot be guaranteed. Rates are subject to change. Yields, terms and capital adequacy should be verified before investing. Only well capitalized or adequately capitalized depository institutions are quoted.
z-Unavailable.

HIGH YIELD SAVINGS

Small minimum balance/opening deposit, generally $500 to $25,000

Money Market Investments*	Rate		APY
Chase Manhttn USA, Wilmgtn DE ..	5.59%	dA	5.75
Bluebonnet Savings, Dallas TX	5.55%	mA	5.69
Advanta Natl, Wilmington DE	5.50%	dA	5.65
First Deposit, Tilton NH	5.45%	dA	5.60
Telebank, Arlington VA	5.28%	dA	5.42

Six Months CDs	Rate		APY
Southn Pac Bk, Los Angeles CA	5.85%	dA	6.02
Sterling Bk, Newport Beach CA	5.86%	siA	5.95
Advanta Financial, Draper UT	5.78%	dA	5.95
Safra National, New York NY	5.76%	dA	5.93
Providian Bk, Salt Lake City UT	5.69%	dA	5.85

One Month CDs	Rate		APY
New South FSB, Birminghm AL	5.50%	siA	5.64
Bluebonnet Savings, Dallas TX	5.50%	siA	5.64
Southn Pac Bk, Los Angeles CA	5.30%	dA	5.44
Bar Harbor Bank, Bar Harbor ME .	5.05%	mA	5.17
Pacific Crest, San Diego CA	4.88%	dA	5.00

One Year CDs	Rate		APY
Advanta Natl, Wilmingtn DE	5.97%	dA	6.15
Advanta Financial, Draper UT	5.97%	dA	6.15
First Deposit, Tilton NH	5.97%	dA	6.15
Southn Pac Bk, Los Angeles CA	5.95%	dA	6.13
MBNA America, Wilmington DE	5.90%	dA	6.08

Two Months CDs	Rate		APY
New South FSB, Birminghm AL	5.55%	siA	5.68
Bluebonnet Savings, Dallas TX	5.55%	siA	5.68
Southn Pac Bk, Los Angeles CA	5.40%	dA	5.55
Bar Harbor Bank, Bar Harbor ME .	5.05%	mA	5.17
Michigan Natl, Farmingtn Hill MI .	4.89%	mA	5.00

Two Years CDs	Rate		APY
Advanta Natl, Wilmington DE	6.16%	dA	6.35
Advanta Financial, Draper UT	6.11%	dA	6.30
Southn Pac Bk, Los Angeles CA	6.10%	dA	6.29
Capital One FSB, Richmond VA	6.06%	dA	6.25
First Deposit, Tilton NH	6.06%	dA	6.25

Three Months CDs	Rate		APY
New South FSB, Birminghm AL	5.60%	siA	5.72
Bluebonnet Savings, Dallas TX	5.60%	siA	5.72
Southn Pac Bk, Los Angeles CA	5.55%	dA	5.71
Keybank USA, Albany NY	5.50%	dA	5.65
Imperial Thrift, Glendale CA	5.40%	dA	5.55

Five Years CDs	Rate		APY
Advanta Natl, Wilmington DE	6.49%	dA	6.70
Capital One FSB, Richmond VA	6.44%	dA	6.65
Providian Bk, Salt Lake City UT	6.40%	dA	6.61
First Deposit, Tilton NH	6.40%	dA	6.61
MBNA America, Wilmington DE	6.35%	dA	6.56

HIGH YIELD JUMBOS

Large minimum balance/opening deposit, generally $95,000 to $100,000

Money Market Investments*	Rate		APY
Stearns County NB, St Cloud MN ...	5.77%	mA	5.93
Heritage Bank, Willmar MN	5.77%	mA	5.93
Advanta Natl, Wilmingtn DE	5.75%	dA	5.92
First Signature, Portsmouth NH	5.72%	dA	5.89
Bluebonnet Savings, Dallas TX	5.70%	mA	5.85

Six Months Jumbo CDs	Rate		APY
Advanta Natl, Wilmington DE	5.90%	siA	5.99
Mountainwest Fincl, Sandy UT	5.85%	siA	5.94
Hurley St BK, Sioux Falls SD	5.85%	siA	5.94
Advanta Financial, Draper UT	5.85%	siA	5.94
Providian National, Concord NH	5.73%	dA	5.90

One Month Jumbo CDs	Rate		APY
Advanta Natl, Wilmington DE	5.55%	siA	5.69
Mountainwest Fincl, Sandy UT	5.55%	siA	5.69
Hurley St BK, Sioux Falls SD	5.55%	siA	5.69
New South FSB, Birminghm AL	5.50%	siA	5.64
Bluebonnet Savings, Dallas TX	5.50%	siA	5.64

One Year Jumbo CDs	Rate		APY
Providian National, Concord NH	5.97%	dA	6.15
First Deposit, Tilton NH	5.97%	dA	6.15
First Federal SB, Huntington IN	6.00%	qA	6.14
Advanta Natl, Wilmington DE	6.10%	dA	6.10
MBNA America, Wilmington DE	5.90%	dA	6.08

Two Months Jumbo CDs	Rate		APY
Equitable Federal, Wheaton MD ...	5.65%	siA	5.78
Advanta Natl, Wilmington DE	5.60%	siA	5.73
Mountainwest Fincl, Sandy UT	5.60%	siA	5.73
Hurley St BK, Sioux Falls SD	5.60%	siA	5.73
Advanta Financial, Draper UT	5.60%	siA	5.73

Two Years Jumbo CDs	Rate		APY
Advanta Natl, Wilmington DE	6.30%	siA	6.30
Capital One FSB, Richmond VA	6.06%	dA	6.25
Advanta Financial, Draper UT	6.25%	siA	6.25
MBNA America, Wilmington DE	6.05%	dA	6.24
Providian National, Concord NH	6.02%	dA	6.20

Three Months Jumbo CDs	Rate		APY
Advanta Natl, Wilmington DE	5.75%	siA	5.88
Mountainwest Fincl, Sandy UT	5.70%	siA	5.82
Hurley St BK, Sioux Falls SD	5.70%	siA	5.82
Advanta Financial, Draper UT	5.70%	siA	5.82
Equitable Federal, Wheaton MD ...	5.65%	siA	5.77

Five Years Jumbo CDs	Rate		APY
Capital One FSB, Richmond VA	6.44%	dA	6.65
Providian National, Concord NH	6.40%	dA	6.61
First Deposit, Tilton NH	6.40%	dA	6.61
Eastern Sav, Hunt Valley MD	6.41%	mA	6.60
MBNA America, Wilmington DE	6.35%	dA	6.56

WSJ.com Additional information on deposits and loans for all 50 states is available in the BanxQuote® Banking Center in The Wall Street Journal Interactive Edition at http://wsj.com

For BanxQuote® Dealer Market and Institutional CDs see Dow Jones Markets pages 22300-99.
Source: BanxQuote Inc., Fairfield N.J. Tel. 800-666-2000. Registered with the FDIC as a deposit broker.

Figure 13.1
Yields on Certificates of Deposit

tion; alternatively, some or all of it may be "borrowed" without canceling the policy. The implicit rate of return on the cash value of an insurance policy is typically quite low, reflecting the extremely low risk to the policyholder and the length of the insurance company's commitment.[2]

13.2   MONEY MARKET INSTRUMENTS

Certain types of short-term (meaning, arbitrarily, one year or less), highly marketable loans play a major role in the investment and borrowing activities of both financial and nonfinancial corporations. Individual investors with substantial funds may invest in such money market instruments directly, but most do so indirectly via money market accounts at various financial institutions.[3]

Some money market instruments are negotiable and are traded in active secondary dealer markets; others are not. Some may be purchased by anyone with adequate funds; others only by particular types of institutions. Many are sold on a discount basis. For example, a 90-day note with a face value of $100,000 might be sold for $98,000, where $100,000 is paid to the investor at maturity. The difference of $2,000 represents interest income.

Interest rates on such money market instruments are often reported on what is known as a **bank discount basis**. The note in the example will be described in the media as having a discount of 2% per quarter, or 8% per year. However, the discount does not represent the true interest rate on the note. In such a situation, the true interest rate is higher; in this case it equals $2,000/$98,000 = 2.04\%$ per quarter, or the equivalent of 8.16% per year (with quarterly compounding, it would equal $8.41\% = 1.0204^4 - 1$).

The Wall Street Journal publishes on a daily basis a list of the current interest rates on a number of money market instruments. Figure 13.2 presents such a list. Some of the types of money market instruments mentioned on this list are described next.

13.2.1   Commercial Paper

Commercial paper is an unsecured short-term promissory note. Instruments of this type are issued by both financial and nonfinancial companies. The dollar amount of commercial paper outstanding exceeds the amount of any other type of money market instrument except for Treasury bills, with the majority being issued by financial companies such as bank holding companies as well as companies involved in sales and personal finance, insurance, and leasing. Such notes are often issued by large firms that have unused lines of credit at banks, making it highly likely that the loan will be paid off when it becomes due. The interest rates on commercial paper reflect this small risk by being relatively low in comparison with the interest rates on other corporate fixed-income securities.

Commercial paper is usually sold in denominations of $100,000 or more, with maturities of up to 270 days (the maximum allowed by the Securities and Exchange Commission without registration) to large institutional investors such as money market mutual funds. Typically these investors hold onto the paper until maturity, resulting in a very small secondary market. In general, the terms of commercial paper are not negotiable, but the issuer may be willing to prepay the note (perhaps by issuing another) if necessary.

13.2.2   Certificates of Deposit

Certificates of deposit represent time deposits at commercial banks or savings and loan associations that were mentioned earlier. Large-denomination (or jumbo) CDs

MONEY RATES

Monday, October 6, 1997

The key U.S. and foreign annual interest rates below are a guide to general levels but don't always represent actual transactions.

PRIME RATE: 8.50% (effective 3/26/97). The base rate on corporate loans posted by at least 75% of the nation's 30 largest banks.

DISCOUNT RATE: 5.00%. The charge on loans to depository institutions by the Federal Reserve Banks.

FEDERAL FUNDS: 5 1/2% high, 5 1/4% low, 5 3/8% near closing bid, 5 1/2% offered. Reserves traded among commercial banks for overnight use in amounts of $1 million or more. Source: Prebon Yamane (U.S.A.) Inc.

CALL MONEY: 7.25% (effective 3/27/97). The charge on loans to brokers on stock exchange collateral. Source: Dow Jones.

COMMERCIAL PAPER placed directly by General Electric Capital Corp.: 5.48% 30 to 49 days; 5.49% 50 to 67 days; 5.47% 68 to 89 days; 5.50% 90 to 149 days; 5.49% 150 to 270 days.

COMMERCIAL PAPER: High-grade unsecured notes sold through dealers by major corporations: 5.50% 30 days; 5.47% 60 days; 5.52% 90 days.

CERTIFICATES OF DEPOSIT: 5.19% one month; 5.22% two months; 5.24% three months; 5.60% six months; 5.79% one year. Average of top rates paid by major New York banks on primary new issues of negotiable C.D.s, usually on amounts of $1 million and more. The minimum unit is $100,000. Typical rates in the secondary market: 5.55% one month; 5.62% three months; 5.67% six months.

BANKERS ACCEPTANCES: 5.45% 30 days; 5.45% 60 days; 5.46% 90 days; 5.45% 120 days; 5.45% 150 days; 5.45% 180 days. Offered rates of negotiable, bank-backed business credit instruments typically financing an import order.

LONDON LATE EURODOLLARS: 5 5/8% - 5 1/2% one month; 5 21/32% - 5 17/32% two months; 5 23/32% - 5 19/32% three months; 5 3/4% - 5 5/8% four months; 5 3/4% - 5 5/8% five months; 5 25/32% - 5 21/32% six months.

LONDON INTERBANK OFFERED RATES (LIBOR): 5 5/8% one month; 5 23/32% three months; 5 25/32% six months; 5 29/32 % one year. The average of interbank offered rates for dollar deposits in the London market based on quotations at five major banks. Effective rate for contracts entered into two days from date appearing at top of this column.

FOREIGN PRIME RATES: Canada 5.25%; Germany 3.40%; Japan 1.625%; Switzerland 3.375%; Britain 7.00%. These rate indications aren't directly comparable; lending practices vary widely by location.

TREASURY BILLS: Results of the Monday, October 6, 1997, auction of short-term U.S. government bills, sold at a discount from face value in units of $10,000 to $1 million: 4.93% 13 weeks; 5.01% 26 weeks.

OVERNIGHT REPURCHASE RATE: 5.50%. Dealer financing rate for overnight sale and repurchase of Treasury securities. Source: Dow Jones.

FEDERAL HOME LOAN MORTGAGE CORP. (Freddie Mac): Posted yields on 30-year mortgage commitments. Delivery within 30 days 7.35%, 60 days 7.38%, standard conventional fixed-rate mortgages; 5.625%, 2% rate capped one-year adjustable rate mortgages. Source: Dow Jones.

FEDERAL NATIONAL MORTGAGE ASSOCIATION (Fannie Mae): Posted yields on 30 year mortgage commitments (priced at par) for delivery within 30 days 7.32%, 60 days 7.37%, standard conventional fixed rate-mortgages; 6.45%, 6/2 rate capped one-year adjustable rate mortgages. Source: Dow Jones.

MERRILL LYNCH READY ASSETS TRUST: 5.08%. Annualized average rate of return after expenses for the past 30 days; not a forecast of future returns.

Figure 13.2

Interest Rates on Money Market Instruments

Source: Reprinted by permission of *The Wall Street Journal*, Dow Jones & Company, Inc., October 7, 1997, p. C25. All rights reserved worldwide.

are issued in amounts of $100,000 or more, have a specified maturity, and generally are negotiable, meaning that they can be sold by one investor to another. Such certificates are insured by the FDIC or the National Credit Union Administration (NCUA), but only for $100,000 (in 1998).

Interestingly, foreign banks that have branches in the United States also offer dollar-denominated CDs to investors. Such CDs have been dubbed Yankee CDs by the media.

13.2.3   Bankers' Acceptances

Historically, bankers' acceptances were created to finance goods in transit; currently, they are generally used to finance foreign trade. For example, the buyer of the goods may issue a written promise to the seller to pay a given sum within a short period of time (for example, 180 days or less). A bank then "accepts" this promise, obligating itself to pay the amount when requested, and obtains in return a claim on the goods as collateral. The written promise becomes a liability of both the bank and the buyer of the goods and is known as a **bankers' acceptance**.

The seller of the goods, having received the written promise from the buyer that the bank has "accepted," need not wait until the promise is due in order to receive payment. Instead, the acceptance can be sold to someone else at a price that is less than the amount of the promised payment to be made in the future. Thus such instruments are pure-discount securities.

13.2.4 Eurodollars

In the world of international finance, large short-term CDs denominated in dollars and issued by banks outside the United States (most often in London) are known as **Eurodollar CDs** (or simply Euro CDs). Also available for investment are dollar-denominated time deposits in banks outside the United States, known as **Eurodollar deposits**. A key distinction between Euro CDs and Eurodollar deposits is that Euro CDs are negotiable, meaning that they can be traded, whereas Eurodollar deposits are nonnegotiable, meaning that they cannot be traded.

The demand and supply conditions for such instruments may differ from the conditions for other U.S. money market instruments, owing to restrictions imposed (or likely to be imposed) by the United States and other governments. However, enough commonality exists to keep interest rates from diverging too much from rates available on domestic alternatives. One difference from CDs issued by U.S. banks is that the Euro CDs do not have federal deposit insurance.

13.2.5 Repurchase Agreements

Often one investor (usually a financial institution) will sell another investor (usually another financial institution) a money market instrument and agree to repurchase it for an agreed-upon price at a later date. For example, investor A might sell investor B a number of Treasury bills that mature in 180 days for a price of $10 million. As part of the sale, investor A has signed a **repurchase agreement** (or "repo") with investor B (from the perspective of the purchaser, investor B, the agreement is referred to as a "reverse repo"). This agreement specifies that after 30 days, investor A will repurchase these Treasury bills for $10.1 million. Thus investor A will have paid investor B $100,000 in interest for 30 days' use of $10 million, meaning that investor B has, in essence, purchased a money market instrument that matures in 30 days. The annualized interest rate is known as the **repo rate**, which in this case is equal to 12% [= ($100,000/$10,000,000) $\times$ (360/30)].

Note how this repurchase agreement is like a collateralized loan from B to A, with the Treasury bills serving as the collateral. Such loans involve very little risk to the lender (B), because the money market instruments typically used in repurchase agreements are of high quality.

U.S. GOVERNMENT SECURITIES

It should come as no surprise that the U.S. government relies heavily on debt financing. Since the 1960s, revenues have seldom covered expenses, and the differences have been financed primarily by issuing debt instruments. Moreover, new debt must be issued in order to get the necessary funds to pay off old debt that comes due. Such **debt refunding** sometimes allows the holders of the maturing debt to exchange it directly for new debt, and in the process receive beneficial treatment for tax purposes.

Some idea of the magnitude and ownership structure of U.S. Treasury debt can be gained by examining Table 13.1. Through the U.S. Treasury, federal agencies, and various trust funds, the federal government itself is a large holder, as is the Federal Reserve System. However, a large amount is held by state and local governments as well as private investors of one sort or another. For example, these securities are a major factor in the portfolios of commercial banks and other financial institutions. To a lesser extent, business corporations also invest in them, primarily as outlets for relatively short-term excess working capital. The amount held by individual households is also substantial, with over half of their investment in U.S. government securities being in savings bonds and notes. Last, holdings by foreigners have become quite large in recent years.

About two-thirds of the public debt is *marketable*, meaning that it is represented by securities that can be sold at any time by the original purchaser through government security dealers.[4] The major *nonmarketable* issues are held by U.S. government agencies, foreign governments, state and local governments, and individuals (the latter in the form of U.S. Savings Bonds). Marketable issues include Treasury bills, notes, and bonds. Table 13.2 shows the amounts of interest-bearing U.S. public debt at the end of 1996. (There was an additional $6.0 billion of non-interest-bearing U.S. public debt outstanding at that time, so total U.S. public debt amounted to $5,323.2 billion.)

The relative maturity dates for U.S. government debt are influenced by a number of factors. As time passes, of course, the **term-to-maturity** (that is, the remaining time until maturity) of an outstanding issue will decrease. Moreover, the Treasury has considerable latitude in selecting maturities for new issues and can also engage in refunding operations. From time to time, congressional limits on amounts issued or interest paid on certain types of instruments may force reliance on other types of instruments. Debt operations may also be employed as a conscious instrument of

TABLE 13.1	Ownership of Outstanding Public Debt of U.S. Treasury, End of 1996		
Held By		Dollar Amount (billions)	Percent of Total Amount
U.S. Treasury, federal agencies, and trust funds		$1,497.2	28.2%
Federal Reserve banks		410.9	7.7
Private investors			
Commercial banks	$261.7		4.9
Money market funds	91.6		1.7
Insurance companies	235.9		4.4
Other companies	258.5		4.9
State and local treasuries	358.0		6.7
Individuals	356.6		6.7
Foreign and international	1,131.8		21.3
Other miscellaneous	717.1		13.5
Total private investors		3,411.2	64.1
Total gross public debt		$5,319.3	100.0%

Source: *Federal Reserve Bulletin*, September 1997, p. A27.

TABLE 13.2	Interest-Bearing U.S. Public Debt, End of 1996	
Category		Amount (billions)
Nonmarketable		
Government account series	$1,505.9	
U.S. Savings Bonds	182.4	
Foreign series	37.4	
State and local government series	101.3	
Total nonmarketable debt		$1,857.5
Marketable		
Bills	$ 777.4	
Notes	2,112.3	
Bonds	555.0	
Total marketable debt		3,459.7
Total debt[a]		$5,317.2

Source: *Federal Reserve Bulletin*, September 1997, p. A27.

[a] According to the *Federal Reserve Bulletin*, the components do not sum to the total shown because of rounding.

government economic policy in an attempt to influence the current interest rates for securities of various maturities.

Figure 13.3 shows that the maturity structure of marketable, interest-bearing U.S. public debt in December 1996 was not long. For example, about 35% was short-term debt, maturing in less than one year. Furthermore, about 76% had a maturity date within five years. The total amount of the debt shown in the figure was $3,033 billion.

Many types of debt have been issued by the U.S. government as well as by U.S. government agencies and organizations sponsored by the federal government. Figure 13.4 shows a typical list of price quotations for certain types of debt securities that have been issued by the U.S. government. These securities will be discussed next.

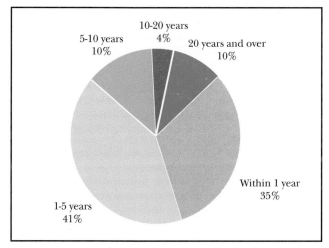

Figure 13.3
Maturity Structure of Marketable Interest-Bearing U.S. Public Debt Held by Private Investors, December 1996
Source: *Treasury Bulletin*, March 1997, p. 23.

13.3.1 U.S. Treasury Bills

Treasury bills are issued on a discount basis, with maturities of up to 52 weeks and in denominations of $1,000 or more. (Before August 1998 the minimum denomination was $10,000.) All are issued in book-entry form; the buyer receives a receipt at the time of purchase and the bill's face value at maturity. Although Treasury bills are sold at discount, their dollar yield (that is, the difference between the purchase price and the face value if the bill is held to maturity) is treated as interest income for tax purposes.

Offerings of 13-week and 26-week bills are usually made once each week; 52-week bills are usually offered every fourth week. All are sold by use of a *multiple price auction* that is held on a Monday. Bids may be entered on either a competitive or a noncompetitive basis. With a competitive bid, the investor states a price that he or she is willing to pay (which can be converted to the interest rate that would be earned if the bid is accepted). For example, an investor might enter a bid for a stated number of 13-week bills at a price of 98.512. If the bid is accepted, the investor will pay $985.12 for each $1,000 of face value, meaning that an investment of $985.12 will generate a receipt of $1,000 if held to maturity 13 weeks later. With a noncompetitive bid, the investor agrees to pay the average price of all bids that will be accepted by the Treasury.

Before each auction, the Treasury announces the total face value and the maturities of all bills that it plans to issue. At the auction itself, having received the bids, the Treasury proceeds to accept all noncompetitive bids. For example, if $6 billion of 13-week bills are to be issued, perhaps $2 billion of noncompetitive bids will have been received by the time of the auction. Because all of these bids will be accepted, the Treasury will accept only $4 billion of competitive bids, taking the highest prices offered by competitive-bidding investors. The average price on the accepted competitive bids will be charged to the noncompetitive bidders. Once the auction is completed, these newly offered Treasury securities are referred to as **on-the-run issues**, meaning that they are the most recently issued ones. Typically, on-the-run issues have more liquidity than "off-the-run" issues, which are issues offered at previous auctions.

Each Tuesday *The Wall Street Journal* publishes the results of the auction that took place on the previous day. Figure 13.5 presents the results of the auction that took place on October 6, 1997. Individuals may purchase new issues of Treasury bills directly from one of the 12 Federal Reserve banks or over the Internet or using the telephone. They can also be bought indirectly via a bank or broker. Government security dealers maintain an active secondary market in bills, and it is a simple matter to buy or sell a bill before maturity (especially if the original purchase was through a bank or a broker). Terms offered by government security dealers are reported daily in the financial press, stated on a "bank discount" basis. To determine the actual dollar prices, an investor needs to "undo" the bank discount computation.

For example, a bill with 120 days left to maturity might be listed as "7.48% bid, 7.19% ask." Both of these discounts were obtained by multiplying the actual discount by 360/120 (the inverse of the portion of a 360-day year involved). Thus, to find the actual discount associated with the 7.48% bid, multiply 7.48% by 120/360, resulting in a figure of 2.493%. This means that the dealer is bidding 97.507% (= 100% − 2.493%) of face value, or equivalently that the dealer is willing to pay $975.07 for this $1,000 Treasury bill.

Similarly, the dealer is offering to sell such a bill at a discount of 2.397% {= 100% − [7.19% × (120/360)]}, meaning that the dealer is willing to sell such a bill for $976.03 [= $1,000 × (100% − 2.397%)]. The difference between the prices—$.96 (= $976.03 − $975.07)—is known as the **dealer's spread**, and it serves

---

TREASURY BONDS, NOTES & BILLS

Monday, October 6, 1997

Representative and Indicative Over-the-Counter quotations based on $1 million or more.

Treasury bond, note and bill quotes are as of mid-afternoon. Colons in bond and note bid-and-asked quotes represent 32nds; 101:01 means 101 1/32. Net changes in 32nds. Treasury bill quotes in hundredths, quoted in terms of a rate discount. Days to maturity calculated from settlement date. All yields are based on a one-day settlement and calculated on the offer quote. Current 13-week and 26-week bills are boldfaced. For bonds callable prior to maturity, yields are computed to the earliest call date for issues quoted above par and to the maturity date for issues quoted below par. n-Treasury note. i-Inflation-Indexed. wi-When issued. iw-Inflation-Indexed when issued; daily change is expressed in basis points.

Source: Dow Jones/Cantor Fitzgerald.

U.S. Treasury strips as of 3 p.m. Eastern time, also based on transactions of $1 million or more. Colons in bid-and-asked quotes represent 32nds; 99:01 means 99 1/32. Net changes in 32nds. Yields calculated on the asked quotation. ci-stripped coupon interest. bp-Treasury bond, stripped principal. np-Treasury note, stripped principal. For bonds callable prior to maturity, yields are computed to the earliest call date for issues quoted above par and to the maturity date for issues below par.

Source: Bear, Stearns & Co. via Street Software Technology Inc.

GOVT. BONDS & NOTES

Rate	Maturity Mo/Yr	Bid	Asked	Chg.	Ask Yld.
8¾	Oct 97n	100:01	100:03	− 1	4.28
5⅝	Oct 97n	100:00	100:02	....	4.55
5¾	Oct 97n	100:00	100:02	....	4.67
7⅜	Nov 97n	100:05	100:07	− 1	5.15
8⅞	Nov 97n	100:10	100:12	− 1	5.14
5⅜	Nov 97n	99:31	100:01	....	5.07
6	Nov 97n	100:02	100:04	....	5.04
5¼	Dec 97n	99:31	100:01	....	5.04
6	Dec 97n	100:05	100:07	....	4.96
7⅞	Jan 98n	100:22	100:24	....	4.99
5	Jan 98n	99:27	99:29	....	5.25
5⅝	Jan 98n	100:01	100:03	− 1	5.27
7¼	Feb 98n	100:19	100:21	....	5.32
8⅛	Feb 98n	100:29	100:31	....	5.29
5⅛	Feb 98n	99:28	99:30	....	5.26
5⅛	Mar 98n	99:27	99:29	− 1	5.32
6⅛	Mar 98n	100:11	100:13	....	5.25
7⅞	Apr 98n	101:07	101:09	− 1	5.35
5⅛	Apr 98n	99:26	99:28	....	5.35
5⅞	Apr 98n	100:07	100:09	....	5.36
6⅛	May 98n	100:12	100:14	+ 1	5.37
9	May 98n	102:02	102:04	....	5.37

Rate	Maturity Mo/Yr	Bid	Asked	Chg.	Ask Yld.
11⅞	Nov 03	129:28	130:02	+ 5	5.93
5⅞	Feb 04n	99:23	99:25	+ 6	5.92
7¼	May 04n	107:00	107:02	+ 5	5.94
12⅜	May 04	134:17	134:23	+ 6	5.94
7¼	Aug 04n	107:05	107:07	+ 6	5.95
13¾	Aug 04	143:04	143:10	+ 6	5.96
7⅞	Nov 04n	110:26	110:30	+ 7	5.96
11⅝	Nov 04	132:04	132:10	+ 7	5.98
7½	Feb 05n	108:28	108:30	+ 7	5.98
6½	May 05n	103:01	103:03	+ 7	5.99
8¼	May 00-05	105:16	105:18	+ 3	5.91
12	May 05	136:01	136:07	+ 7	6.00
6½	Aug 05n	103:02	103:04	+ 8	5.99
10¾	Aug 05	129:05	129:11	+ 8	6.01
5⅞	Nov 05n	99:03	99:05	+ 8	6.01
5⅝	Feb 06n	97:12	97:14	+ 7	6.02
9⅜	Feb 06	121:29	122:03	+ 8	5.98
6⅞	May 06n	105:19	105:21	+ 9	6.02
7	Jul 06n	106:15	106:17	+ 9	6.03
6½	Oct 06n	103:06	103:08	+ 9	6.03
3⅜	Jan 07i	98:20	98:21	+ 4	3.55
6¼	Feb 07n	101:19	101:21	+10	6.01
7⅝	Feb 02-07	105:29	105:31	+ 5	6.04

Rate	Maturity Mo/Yr	Type	Bid	Asked	Chg.	Ask Yld.
Feb	06	ci	60:15	60:20	+ 7	6.08
Feb	06	bp	60:24	60:28	+ 7	6.03
Feb	06	np	60:30	61:02	+ 7	5.99
May	06	ci	59:16	59:21	+ 7	6.10
Aug	06	ci	58:20	58:24	+ 8	6.10
Nov	06	ci	57:22	57:26	+ 7	6.11
Feb	07	ci	56:23	56:28	+ 6	6.13
May	07	ci	55:26	55:31	+ 7	6.14
Aug	07	ci	54:31	55:04	+ 7	6.14
Nov	07	ci	54:03	54:08	+ 8	6.14
Feb	08	ci	53:05	53:10	+ 7	6.17
May	08	ci	52:09	52:14	+ 7	6.18
Aug	08	ci	51:15	51:20	+ 8	6.18
Nov	08	ci	50:18	50:23	+ 7	6.21
Feb	09	ci	49:23	49:29	+ 8	6.22
May	09	ci	48:29	49:02	+ 8	6.23
Aug	09	ci	48:05	48:10	+ 8	6.23
Nov	09	ci	47:12	47:17	+ 8	6.24
Nov	09	bp	46:31	47:05	+ 8	6.31
Feb	10	ci	46:17	46:23	+ 8	6.26
May	10	ci	45:25	45:30	+ 8	6.27
Aug	10	ci	45:00	45:06	+ 8	6.28
Nov	10	ci	44:09	44:14	+ 8	6.29
Feb	11	ci	43:18	43:24	+ 9	6.29
May	11	ci	42:27	43:01	+ 9	6.30
Aug	11	ci	42:05	42:10	+ 9	6.30
Nov	11	ci	41:15	41:20	+ 9	6.31
Feb	12	ci	40:25	40:30	+ 9	6.32
May	12	ci	40:03	40:09	+ 9	6.32
Aug	12	ci	39:15	39:20	+ 9	6.33
Nov	12	ci	38:26	38:31	+ 9	6.34
Feb	13	ci	38:05	38:10	+ 8	6.34
May	13	ci	37:17	37:23	+ 8	6.35
Aug	13	ci	36:29	37:03	+ 8	6.36
Nov	13	ci	36:10	36:16	+ 8	6.36
Feb	14	ci	35:23	35:28	+ 8	6.37
May	14	ci	35:04	35:09	+ 8	6.37
Aug	14	ci	34:18	34:23	+ 8	6.38
Nov	14	ci	33:31	34:05	+ 8	6.38
Feb	15	ci	33:14	33:20	+ 9	6.38
Feb	15	bp	34:00	34:05	+ 10	6.29
May	15	ci	32:29	33:02	+ 9	6.39
Aug	15	ci	32:11	32:17	+ 9	6.39
Aug	15	bp	32:15	32:21	+ 8	6.37
Nov	15	ci	31:26	32:00	+ 8	6.39
Nov	15	bp	31:28	32:02	+ 8	6.39

7⅛	Sep 99n	102:20	102:22	+ 2	5.67
6	Oct 99n	100:21	100:23	+ 1	5.62
7½	Oct 99n	103:14	103:16	+ 2	5.68
5⅞	Nov 99n	100:10	100:12	+ 2	5.68
7⅞	Nov 99n	104:07	104:09	+ 2	5.68
7¾	Nov 99n	104:02	104:04	+ 3	5.68
7¾	Dec 99n	104:06	104:08	+ 2	5.69
6⅜	Jan 00n	101:14	101:16	+ 3	5.66
7¾	Jan 00n	104:09	104:11	+ 1	5.71
5⅞	Feb 00n	100:08	100:10	+ 2	5.73
8½	Feb 00n	106:00	106:02	+ 2	5.71
7⅛	Feb 00n	103:01	103:03	+ 2	5.72
6⅞	Mar 00n	102:18	102:20	+ 2	5.72
5½	Apr 00n	99:14	99:16	+ 3	5.72
6¾	Apr 00n	102:10	102:12	+ 2	5.74
6⅜	May 00n	101:16	101:17	+ 4	5.73
8⅞	May 00n	107:16	107:18	+ 1	5.71
6¼	May 00n	101:06	101:08	+ 3	5.73
5⅞	Jun 00n	100:10	100:12	+ 3	5.72
6⅛	Jul 00n	100:29	100:31	+ 3	5.74
6	Aug 00n	100:21	100:22	+ 3	5.73
8¾	Aug 00n	107:24	107:26	+ 2	5.74
6¼	Aug 00n	101:07	101:09	+ 3	5.76
6⅛	Sep 00n	100:29	100:31	+ 3	5.77
5¾	Oct 00n	99:27	99:29	+ 3	5.78
8½	Nov 00n	107:18	107:20	+ 3	5.78
5⅝	Nov 00n	99:15	99:17	+ 3	5.79
5½	Dec 00n	99:03	99:05	+ 4	5.79
5¼	Jan 01n	98:14	98:16	+ 4	5.75
7¾	Feb 01n	105:27	105:29	+ 4	5.79
11¾	Feb 01	117:28	118:00	+ 3	5.77
5⅝	Feb 01n	99:13	99:15	+ 3	5.80
6⅜	Mar 01n	101:22	101:24	+ 3	5.81
6¼	Apr 01n	101:11	101:13	+ 4	5.81
8	May 01n	106:31	107:01	+ 3	5.81
13⅛	May 01	123:13	123:19	+ 3	5.78
6½	May 01n	102:05	102:07	+ 4	5.81
6⅝	Jun 01n	102:18	102:20	+ 4	5.83
6⅝	Jul 01n	102:20	102:22	+ 4	5.83
7⅞	Aug 01n	106:29	106:31	+ 4	5.83
13⅜	Aug 01	125:19	125:25	+ 4	5.81
6½	Aug 01n	102:07	102:09	+ 4	5.83
6⅜	Sep 01n	101:26	101:28	+ 4	5.84
6¼	Oct 01n	101:13	101:15	+ 4	5.84
7½	Nov 01n	105:29	105:31	+ 5	5.84
15¾	Nov 01	135:19	135:25	+ 3	5.82
5⅞	Nov 01n	100:01	100:03	+ 4	5.85
6⅛	Dec 01n	100:31	101:01	+ 4	5.84
6¼	Jan 02n	101:14	101:16	+ 4	5.85
14¼	Feb 02	131:25	131:31	+ 5	5.83
6¼	Feb 02n	101:14	101:16	+ 4	5.86
6⅝	Mar 02n	102:29	102:31	+ 4	5.86
6⅝	Apr 02n	103:05	103:07	+ 6	5.81
7½	May 02n	106:17	106:19	+ 4	5.84
6½	May 02n	102:21	102:23	+ 6	5.82
6¼	Jun 02n	101:15	101:17	+ 4	5.87
	Jul 02iw	3:59	3:58	− 2	....
3⅝	Jul 02i	100:05	100:06	+ 4	3.58
6	Jul 02n	100:18	100:20	+ 3	5.85
6⅜	Aug 02n	102:04	102:06	+ 5	5.85
6¼	Aug 02n	101:18	101:19	+ 6	5.87
5⅞	Sep 02n	100:04	100:05	+ 6	5.84
11⅝	Nov 02	125:00	125:06	+ 6	5.84
6¼	Feb 03n	101:19	101:21	+ 5	5.88
10¾	Feb 03	121:27	122:01	+ 4	5.89
10¾	May 03	122:21	122:27	+ 5	5.90
5¾	Aug 03n	99:05	99:07	+ 6	5.91
11⅛	Aug 03	125:08	125:14	+ 4	5.92

U.S. TREASURY STRIPS

Mat.		Type	Bid	Asked	Chg.	Ask Yld.
Nov	97	ci	99:15	99:15	+ 1	5.23
Nov	97	np	99:15	99:15	+ 1	5.29
Feb	98	ci	98:05	98:05	....	5.33
Feb	98	np	98:04	98:04	....	5.41
May	98	ci	96:26	96:26	+ 1	5.43
May	98	np	96:26	96:26	+ 1	5.43
Aug	98	ci	95:15	95:15	+ 1	5.51
Aug	98	np	95:13	95:14	+ 1	5.57
Nov	98	ci	94:03	94:04	+ 1	5.57
Nov	98	np	94:02	94:02	+ 1	5.61
Feb	99	ci	92:24	92:25	+ 2	5.61
Feb	99	np	92:23	92:24	+ 2	5.64
May	99	ci	91:14	91:15	+ 2	5.63
May	99	np	91:14	91:15	+ 3	5.63
Aug	99	ci	90:05	90:06	+ 3	5.64
Aug	99	np	90:05	90:06	+ 3	5.66
Nov	99	ci	88:27	88:28	+ 3	5.69
Nov	99	np	88:27	88:28	+ 3	5.69
Feb	00	ci	87:17	87:18	+ 3	5.72
Feb	00	np	87:17	87:18	+ 3	5.72
May	00	ci	86:10	86:11	+ 3	5.72
May	00	np	86:11	86:12	+ 3	5.71
Aug	00	ci	85:02	85:03	+ 4	5.74
Aug	00	np	85:00	85:02	+ 4	5.75
Nov	00	ci	83:25	83:26	+ 4	5.77
Nov	00	np	83:24	83:26	+ 4	5.77
Feb	01	ci	82:17	82:19	+ 4	5.79
Feb	01	np	82:17	82:19	+ 4	5.79
May	01	ci	81:10	81:12	+ 4	5.80
May	01	np	81:10	81:12	+ 4	5.80
Aug	01	ci	80:04	80:06	+ 5	5.81
Aug	01	np	80:02	80:04	+ 4	5.83
Nov	01	ci	78:30	79:00	+ 5	5.82
Nov	01	np	78:27	78:29	+ 4	5.85
Feb	02	ci	77:26	77:28	+ 5	5.82
May	02	ci	76:22	76:24	+ 6	5.83
May	02	np	76:21	76:23	+ 6	5.84
Aug	02	ci	75:19	75:21	+ 6	5.83
Aug	02	np	75:17	75:20	+ 5	5.84
Nov	02	ci	74:16	74:19	+ 6	5.83
Feb	03	ci	73:07	73:11	+ 6	5.88
Feb	03	np	73:07	73:11	+ 6	5.88
May	03	ci	72:02	72:06	+ 6	5.90
Aug	03	ci	71:00	71:04	+ 6	5.91
Aug	03	np	71:01	71:04	+ 6	5.90
Nov	03	ci	69:31	70:03	+ 6	5.91
Feb	04	ci	68:25	68:29	+ 6	5.95
Feb	04	np	68:30	69:02	+ 6	5.91
May	04	ci	67:21	67:25	+ 6	5.98
May	04	np	67:26	67:31	+ 6	5.94
Aug	04	ci	66:22	66:26	+ 6	5.97
Aug	04	np	66:24	66:28	+ 6	5.96
Nov	04	ci	65:17	65:22	+ 6	6.01
Nov	04	bp	65:15	65:19	+ 6	6.02
Nov	04	np	65:22	65:26	+ 6	5.98
Feb	05	ci	64:16	64:20	+ 6	6.03
Feb	05	np	64:20	64:25	+ 7	5.99
May	05	ci	63:14	63:18	+ 7	6.05
May	05	bp	63:13	63:17	+ 7	6.06
May	05	np	63:22	63:26	+ 7	5.99
Aug	05	ci	62:16	62:20	+ 7	6.05
Aug	05	bp	62:14	62:19	+ 7	6.06
Aug	05	np	62:22	62:27	+ 7	6.01
Nov	05	ci	61:18	61:23	+ 7	6.05
Nov	05	np	61:22	61:27	+ 7	6.02

May	23	ci	19:23	19:28	+ 8	6.41
Aug	23	ci	19:16	19:21	+ 8	6.39
Aug	23	bp	19:19	19:23	+ 8	6.38
Nov	23	ci	19:06	19:11	+ 8	6.39
Feb	24	ci	18:29	19:02	+ 7	6.39
May	24	ci	18:20	18:25	+ 7	6.39
Aug	24	ci	18:12	18:17	+ 7	6.38
Nov	24	ci	18:02	18:07	+ 7	6.39
Nov	24	bp	18:02	18:07	+ 7	6.39
Feb	25	ci	17:26	17:30	+ 7	6.38
Feb	25	bp	17:26	17:31	+ 7	6.38
Aug	25	ci	17:13	17:18	+ 7	6.34
Aug	25	bp	17:11	17:15	+ 7	6.36
Feb	26	ci	16:26	16:30	+ 7	6.36
Feb	26	bp	16:28	17:00	+ 7	6.34
Aug	26	ci	16:11	16:15	+ 6	6.35
Aug	26	bp	16:16	16:20	+ 7	6.32
Nov	26	ci	16:05	16:10	+ 6	6.33
Nov	26	bp	16:10	16:15	+ 7	6.30
Feb	27	bp	16:05	16:10	+ 7	6.28

TREASURY BILLS

Maturity	Days to Mat.	Bid	Asked	Chg.	Ask Yld.
Oct 09 '97	2	4.75	4.71	+0.06	4.78
Oct 16 '97	9	4.83	4.79	+0.08	4.86
Oct 23 '97	16	4.63	4.59	−0.07	4.66
Oct 30 '97	23	4.58	4.54	−0.02	4.62
Nov 06 '97	30	4.65	4.61	−0.03	4.69
Nov 13 '97	37	4.84	4.80	....	4.89
Nov 20 '97	44	4.80	4.76	+0.04	4.85
Nov 28 '97	52	4.81	4.77	−0.01	4.87
Dec 04 '97	58	4.80	4.76	−0.01	4.86
Dec 11 '97	65	4.81	4.79	....	4.90
Dec 18 '97	72	4.63	4.61	+0.01	4.72
Dec 26 '97	80	4.82	4.80	−0.04	4.92
Jan 02 '98	87	4.86	4.85	−0.03	4.98
Jan 08 '98	93	4.90	4.88	−0.01	5.01
Jan 08 '98	**93**	**4.94**	**4.93**	**+0.01**	**5.06**
Jan 15 '98	100	4.91	4.89	−0.02	5.03
Jan 22 '98	107	4.91	4.89	−0.02	5.03
Jan 29 '98	114	4.92	4.90	−0.01	5.05
Feb 05 '98	121	4.95	4.93	....	5.08
Feb 12 '98	128	4.95	4.93	....	5.09
Feb 19 '98	135	4.94	4.92	−0.01	5.08
Feb 26 '98	142	4.95	4.93	....	5.10
Mar 05 '98	149	4.99	4.97	....	5.14
Mar 12 '98	156	4.98	4.96	....	5.14
Mar 19 '98	163	4.97	4.95	−0.01	5.13
Mar 26 '98	170	4.88	4.86	....	5.04
Apr 02 '98	177	5.01	5.00	....	5.20
Apr 09 '98	**184**	**5.01**	**5.00**	....	**5.20**
Apr 30 '98	205	5.03	5.01	....	5.21
May 28 '98	233	5.04	5.02	−0.01	5.23
Jun 25 '98	261	5.06	5.04	−0.02	5.26
Jul 23 '98	289	5.10	5.08	−0.02	5.32
Aug 20 '98	317	5.13	5.11	−0.02	5.36
Sep 17 '98	345	5.10	5.09	−0.03	5.36
Oct 15 '98	373	5.12	5.11	−0.03	5.40

INFLATION-INDEXED TREASURY SECURITIES

Rate	Mat.	Bid/Asked	Chg.	*Yld.	Accr. Prin.
3.625	07/02	100-05/06	+ 04	3.566	1003
3.375	01/07	98-20/21	+ 04	3.537	1013

*-Yld. to maturity on accrued principal.

Figure 13.4
Price Quotations for U.S. Treasury Securities (Excerpts)

Source: Reprinted by permission of *The Wall Street Journal*, Dow Jones & Company, Inc., October 7, 1997, p. C20. All rights reserved worldwide.

	13-Week	26-Week
Applications	$36,515,342,000	$38,330,948,000
Accepted bids	$7,541,582,000	$7,505,102,000
Accepted at low price	57%	34%
Accepted noncompet'ly ...	$1,290,331,000	$1,166,296,000
Average price (Rate)	98.754 (4.93%)	97.467 (5.01%)
High price (Rate)	98.759 (4.91%)	97.477 (4.99%)
Low price (Rate)	98.754 (4.93%)	97.467 (5.01%)
Coupon equivalent	5.06 %	5.21 %
CUSIP number	9127944Q4	9127946K5

Both issues are dated Oct. 9. The 13-week bills mature Jan. 8, 1998, and the 26-week bills mature April 9, 1998.

Figure 13.5

Treasury Bill Auction Results for October 6, 1997

Source: Reprinted by permission of *The Wall Street Journal*, Dow Jones & Company, Inc., October 7, 1997, p. C25. All rights reserved worldwide.

as compensation for carrying inventories of bills, taking associated risks, and bearing the clerical and other costs associated with being a market-maker.

In addition to the bid and asked discounts, *The Wall Street Journal* and other media provide an **equivalent yield** that is based on the asked price. In the example, the equivalent yield would be calculated by determining the dollar discount on the security ($1,000 − $976.03 = $23.97) and then dividing this figure by the purchase price ($23.97/$976.03 = 2.455%) in order to arrive at the rate of return associated with purchasing the security. Then this rate of return would be annualized by multiplying it by 365 divided by the number of days until maturity. The resulting figure would be the equivalent yield. In the example, the equivalent yield would be 7.47% [=2.455% × (365/120)].[5]

13.3.2 U.S. Treasury Notes

Treasury notes are issued with maturities from one to ten years and generally make coupon payments semiannually. Some, issued before 1983, were in *bearer* form, with coupons attached; the owner simply submitted each coupon on its specified date to receive payment for the stated amount (hence the phrase, "clipping coupons"). Beginning in 1983, the Treasury ceased the issuance of bearer notes (and bonds). All issues since then are in *registered* form; the current owner is registered with the Treasury, which sends him or her each coupon payment when due and the principal value at maturity. When a registered note is sold, the new owner's name and address are substituted for those of the old owner on the Treasury's books.

Treasury notes are issued in denominations of $1,000 or more. Coupon payments are set at an amount so that the notes will initially sell close to par value. In most cases a *single price auction* is held monthly when two and five-year notes are sold, with both competitive and noncompetitive bids being submitted. As in a Treasury bill multiple price auction, all noncompetitive bids are accepted first, and then the competitive bids offering the highest prices (and thus the lowest yields) are accepted until the entire offering has been fully allocated. However, unlike the practice in the multiple price auction, in a single price auction all of the accepted noncompetitive and competitive bids pay the lowest price that was accepted. Every quarter the Treasury also sells three- and ten-year notes but uses a multiple price auction to allocate them.

Treasury notes are traded in an active secondary market made by dealers in U.S. government securities. For example, as shown in Figure 13.4, the October 7, 1997 issue of *The Wall Street Journal* carried the following quotation from the day before, October 6, 1997:

Rate	Mat.	Bid	Asked	Chg.	Ask Yield
$7\frac{1}{4}$	May 04n	107:00	107:02	+5	5.94

The quotation indicated that a note (n), maturing in May 2004, carried a coupon rate of $7\text{-}\frac{1}{4}\%$. It could be sold to a dealer for $107\text{-}\frac{00}{32}\%$ of par value, which is equivalent to \$1,070.00 per \$1,000 of par value. Alternatively, it could be purchased from a dealer for $107\text{-}\frac{02}{32}\%$ of par value, which is equivalent to \$1,070.625 per \$1,000 of par value. Thus the dealer's spread was equal to \$.625 (=\$1,070.00 − \$1,070.625). On October 6, 1997, the bid price was 5/32 more than it had been on the previous trading day, resulting in a reported change ("Chg.") of +5 (note that numbers are expressed in 32nds, reflecting an old tradition). The effective yield-to-maturity at the time, based on the asked price, was approximately 5.94% per year.[6]

In practice, the situation facing a potential buyer (or seller) is a little more complicated. The buyer is generally expected to pay the dealer not only the stated price (\$1,070.625) but also any **accrued interest**. For example, if 122 days have elapsed since the last coupon payment and 61 days remain, then an amount equal to 2/3 [=122/(122 + 61)] of the semiannual coupon (2/3 × 1/2 × \$72.50 = \$24.167) is added to the stated purchase price to determine the total payment required (in this case, \$24.167 + \$1,070.625 = \$1,094.792). Similarly, if an investor were to sell a note to the dealer, the dealer would pay the investor the stated bid price plus accrued interest (in this case, \$1,070.00 + \$24.167 = \$1,094.167). This procedure is commonly followed with both government and corporate bonds.[7]

In 1997 the Treasury began to issue five- and ten-year inflation-indexed Treasury notes, followed by thirty-year bonds in 1998 (see Chapter 12 for a description of how they provide the investor with a known real return but an uncertain nominal return; they are sold using a single price auction). These securities make a coupon payment every six months that is determined by multiplying one-half of the coupon rate times an inflation-adjusted amount of principal that is equal to \$1,000 multiplied by the inflation rate from the date the note was first issued to the coupon date. (Technically, there is a three-month lag where, for example, the first coupon payment reflects the rate of inflation over the six-month period beginning three months before the note was issued.) Hence, if the coupon rate was 4% and the rate of inflation over the first six months was 3%, then the principal would be increased to \$1,030 (= \$1,000 × 1.03). Consequently, the coupon payment would be \$20.60 (=\$1,030 × .04/2). At the end of the life of the note, the investor would receive not only the final coupon payment but also the inflation-adjusted principal. Furthermore, the Treasury guarantees a minimum of \$1,000 so that in a period of deflation (that is, falling prices) where the inflation-adjusted principal was less than \$1,000, the investor would nevertheless receive \$1,000. Given the record of the U.S. inflation over the last fifty years, however, it would seem quite unlikely that this guarantee would ever come into play.

13.3.3 U.S. Treasury Bonds

Treasury bonds have maturities greater than ten years at the time of issuance. Those issued before 1983 may be in either bearer or registered form; subsequent issues are all in registered form. Denominations range from \$1,000 upward. Unlike Treasury notes, some Treasury bond issues have **call provisions** that allow them to be "called" during a specified period (usually the period begins five to ten years before maturity and ends at the maturity date); at any scheduled coupon payment date during this period, the Treasury has the right to force the investor to sell the bonds back to the government at par value. Callable issues can be identified in Figure 13.4 by noting which issues have a range of years given as the maturity date (this "range of years" indicates the call period). For example, the $8\text{-}\frac{1}{4}$ bonds of May 00-05 mature in 2005 but may be called beginning in 2000 (the "$8\text{-}\frac{1}{4}$" indicates that the bonds have a coupon rate of $8\text{-}\frac{1}{4}\%$, paid semiannually, just like the Treasury notes from earlier).

For callable issues, the yield-to-maturity is calculated using the asked price. If this price is greater than par, then the yield-to-maturity is based on an assumption that the bond will be called at the earliest allowable date. Otherwise, Treasury bonds are comparable to Treasury notes, with dealers' bid and asked quotations being stated in the same form. Thirty-year bonds are sold semiannually using a multiple price auction.

13.3.4   U.S. Savings Bonds

Nonmarketable U.S. Savings Bonds are offered only to individuals and selected organizations. No more than a specified amount—currently $15,000 of issue price, which corresponds to a total face amount of $30,000 (the bonds are sold at half of their face amount)—may be purchased by any person in a single year. Two types are available. Series EE bonds are essentially pure-discount bonds, meaning that no interest is paid on them in the form of coupon payments before maturity. The term-to-maturity at the date of issuance has varied from time to time. For bonds issued in 1998, it was 17 years. However, they may continue to be held as long as an additional 13 years before they must be either redeemed or exchanged for an HH bond (if held, they will continue to earn interest during these additional years just as they did over the first 17 years). Series HH bonds mature in 20 years and pay interest semiannually but can be redeemed for their purchase price at any time. Both types are registered.

Series EE bonds are available in small denominations (the smallest one has a face amount of $50) and may be purchased from commercial banks and many other financial institutions. Some employers even allow employees to obtain them through payroll savings plans. Series HH bonds are available only in exchange for eligible Series EE bonds (that is, a Series EE bond must be purchased first and then held for a minimum of six months before it can be exchanged) and can be obtained only from the Treasury or one of the 12 Federal Reserve banks.

Series EE bonds utilize a floating market-based rate that is determined every six months (on May 1 and November 1) and is applicable for the next six months. This rate is set equal to 90% of the average market yield over the previous six months on five-year Treasury securities. The Treasury guarantees that these securities will be worth their face amount after 17 years. Thus, if an EE savings bond that was bought for $500 grows to be worth $900 after 17 years, the Treasury would step in and change its value to $1,000. This $1,000 could then be either redeemed for cash, swapped for a $1,000 HH savings bond, or kept in the EE bond, where interest would initially be based on the $1,000 value instead of the $900 (subsequent interest would be based on the ever-increasing value). Thus, should the savings bond be held for 17 years, the investor will be paid the higher of (1) the floating rates in existence since the bond was purchased or (2) 4.16% $[=($1,000/$500)^{1/17} - 1]$, since $500 growing annually at 4.16% will be worth $1,000 after 17 years. Should the bond be held for less than five years, the investor forfeits the last three months' worth of interest.

Unlike the taxation on interest of most other discount bonds, taxes are not paid on the interest as it accumulates monthly on the Series EE bonds. Only when these bonds are redeemed is the interest subject to federal income tax. In addition, no state or local income taxes are assessed.[8] Thus a $15,000 investment that grows to $25,000 in 12 years will create a tax obligation only at the end of the twelfth year, provided it is redeemed at that time. Furthermore, should a Series EE bond be exchanged for a Series HH bond, this tax obligation on the interest earned on the Series EE bond can be deferred until the Series HH bond is redeemed. However, the HH bond interest is subject to federal income tax annually. Hence, the tax obligation on the $30,000 would be deferred if the EE bond were exchanged for an HH bond, but the $1,800 (=.06 × $30,000, assuming a 6% interest rate) annual HH interest would be taxable each year after the exchange.

The terms on which Savings Bonds are offered have been revised from time to time. (The terms previously described apply only to newly issued savings bonds at the time of this book's writing.) In some cases, improved terms have been offered to holders of outstanding bonds. Terms have sometimes been inferior to those available on less well-known or less accessible instruments with similar characteristics. At such times, the Treasury sells Savings Bonds by appealing more to patriotism than to the desire for high return.

13.3.5   Zero-Coupon Treasury Security Receipts

A noncallable Treasury note or bond is, in effect, a portfolio of pure-discount bonds (or, equivalently, a portfolio of zero-coupon bonds). That is, each coupon payment, as well as the principal, can be viewed as a bond unto itself; the investor who owns the bond can therefore be viewed as holding a number of individual pure-discount bonds. In 1982, several brokerage firms began separating these components, using a process known as *coupon stripping*. (Chapter 5's *Institutional Issues: Almost Riskfree Securities* also discusses zero-coupon Treasury securities.)

With this process, Treasury bonds of a given issue are purchased and placed in trust with a custodian (for example, a bank). Sets of *receipts* are then issued, one set for each coupon date. For example, an August 15, 2005, receipt might entitle its holder to receive $1,000 on that date (and nothing on any other date). The amount required to meet the payments on all the August 15, 2005, receipts would exactly equal the total amount received on that date from coupon payments on the Treasury securities held in the trust account.

In addition to issuing sets of receipts corresponding to the particular Treasury bond issue's coupon dates, another set of receipts would be issued that mature on the date the principal of the securities held in trust is due. Thus holders of these receipts share in the principal payment.[9]

Noting the favorable market reaction to the offering of these stripped securities, in 1985 the Treasury introduced a program for investors called Separate Trading of Registered Interest and Principal Securities (STRIPS). This program allows purchasers of certain coupon-bearing Treasury securities to keep whatever cash payments they want and to sell the rest. The prices at which such pure-discount securities sold on October 6, 1997 are shown in Figure 13.4.

Figure 13.6 shows typical market prices for a set of stripped Treasury securities, where price is expressed as a percent of maturity value. As the figure shows, the longer the investor has to wait until maturity, the lower the price of the security.

The Internal Revenue Service requires that taxes be paid annually on the accrued interest earned on such securities. That is, such securities are treated for tax purposes as **original issue discount securities**, also known as OID debt instruments. They are securities that were issued at a discount from par because of their relatively small (or nonexistent) coupon payments.[10]

For example, a STRIP that matures in two years for $1,000 might be purchased currently for $900. Thus the investor would earn $100 in interest over two years, realizing it when the STRIP matures. However, the IRS would make the investor pay taxes on a portion of the $100 each year. The amount to be recognized must be calculated using the *constant interest method*, which reflects the actual economic accrual of interest. In this method the investor does not report $50 $(=\$100/2)$ per year as interest income. Instead, first the annual yield needs to be calculated, which in this case is 5.4% $[=(\$1,000/\$900)^{1/2} - 1]$. Accordingly the implied value of the STRIP at the end of the first year would be $948.60 $(=\$900 \times 1.054)$. The amount of interest income to be reported would then be $48.60 $(=\$948.60 - \$900)$. The amount of interest income to be reported in the second year, assuming that the STRIP is held to

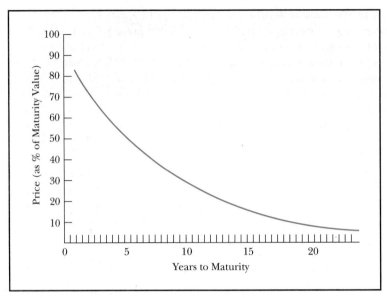

Figure 13.6
Typical Market Prices for a Set of Stripped Treasury Securities

maturity, will be $51.40 (=$1,000 − $948.60; note that $1,000 = $948.60 × 1.054). Consequently, the taxable investor has a cash outflow not only when purchasing the STRIP but also every year until it matures. Only at that time does the investor experience a cash inflow. As a result, such securities are attractive primarily for tax-exempt investors and for investors in low tax brackets. (For example, some people purchase them as investments that are held in the names of their children.)

13.4   FEDERAL AGENCY SECURITIES

Although much of the federal government's activity is financed directly, via taxes and debt issued by the Treasury, a substantial amount is financed in other ways. In some situations, various government departments provide explicit or implicit backing for the securities of quasigovernmental agencies. In other situations, the federal government has guaranteed both the principal and coupon payments on bonds issued by certain private organizations. In both cases, some of the arrangements are so convoluted that cynics suggest that the original legislative intent was to obscure the nature and extent of government backing. In any event, a wide range of bonds with different degrees of government backing has been created in this manner. Many of the bonds are considered second in safety only to the debt obligations of the U.S. government itself.

Table 13.3 lists the issuers of these securities and the amounts outstanding at the end of 1996. A partial list of typical price quotations is shown in Figure 13.7; these quotations can be interpreted in a manner similar to that used for Treasury security quotations.

13.4.1   Bonds of Federal Agencies

Bonds issued by federal agencies provide funds to support such activities as housing (through either direct loans or the purchase of existing mortgages); export and im-

TABLE 13.3 Debt Outstanding of Federal and Federally Sponsored Agencies, End of 1996

Agency	Amount of Debt (millions)
Federal Agencies	
Defense Department: Family Housing and Homeowner's Assistance	$ 6
Export-Import Bank	1,447
Federal Housing Administration	84
Tennessee Valley Authority	27,853
Total debt of federal agencies	$29,390
Federally Sponsored Agencies	
Federal Home Loan Banks	$263,404
Federal National Mortgage Association	331,270
Federal Home Loan Mortgage Corporation	156,980
Student Loan Marketing Association	44,763
Farm Credit Banks	60,053
Financing Corporation	8,170
Farm Credit Financial Assistance Corporation	1,261
Resolution Funding Corporation	29,996
Other	546
Total debt of federally sponsored agencies	$896,443

Source: *Federal Reserve Bulletin*, September 1997, p. A30.

port activities (via loans, credit guarantees, and insurance); the postal service; and the activities of the Tennessee Valley Authority. Many issues are guaranteed by the full faith and credit of the U.S. government, but some (for example, those of the Tennessee Valley Authority) are not.

13.4.2 Bonds of Federally Sponsored Agencies

Federally sponsored agencies are privately owned agencies that issue securities and use the proceeds to support the granting of certain types of loans to farmers, students, homeowners, and others. A common procedure involves the creation of a series of governmental "banks" to buy securities issued by private organizations that grant the loans in the first instance. Some or all of the initial capital for these banks may be provided by the government, but subsequent amounts typically come from bonds issued by the banks.

Although the debts of agencies of this type are usually not guaranteed by the federal government, governmental control is designed to ensure that each debt issue is backed by extremely safe assets (for example, mortgages insured by another quasigovernmental agency). Moreover, it is generally presumed that governmental assistance of one sort or another would be provided if there were any danger of default on such debt.

As shown in Table 13.3, there are eight federally sponsored agencies. Federal Home Loan Banks make loans to thrift institutions, primarily savings and loan associations. The Federal National Mortgage Association (FNMA, also known as "Fannie Mae") purchases and sells real estate mortgages—not only those insured by the Federal Housing Administration or guaranteed by the Veterans Administration but also conventional mortgages. The Federal Home Loan Mortgage Corporation (known as "Freddie Mac") deals only in conventional mortgages. The Student Loan Marketing Association (known as "Sallie Mae") purchases federally guaranteed loans

GOVERNMENT AGENCY & SIMILAR ISSUES

Monday, October 6, 1997

Over-the-Counter mid-afternoon quotations based on large transactions, usually $1 million or more. Colons in bid-and-asked quotes represent 32nds; 101:01 means 101 1/32.

All yields are calculated to maturity, and based on the asked quote. * -- Callable issue, maturity date shown. For issues callable prior to maturity, yields are computed to the earliest call date for issues quoted above par, or 100, and to the maturity date for issues below par.

Source: Bear, Stearns & Co. via Street Software Technology Inc.

FNMA Issues

Rate	Mat.	Bid	Asked	Yld.
5.35	10-97*	100:00	100:01	0.00
6.05	11-97	100:02	100:03	4.87
9.55	11-97	100:12	100:14	4.60
9.55	12-97	100:24	100:25	4.82
6.05	1-98	100:06	100:07	5.07
5.38	1-98*	99:28	99:29	5.66
8.65	2-98	101:01	101:03	5.29
5.01	2-98	99:29	99:31	5.06
5.51	2-98	100:03	100:05	5.05
8.20	3-98	101:02	101:04	5.40
5.30	3-98*	99:30	100:00	5.32
5.71	3-98	100:03	100:05	5.33
5.25	3-98	99:26	99:28	5.55
5.79	3-98	100:05	100:07	5.30
5.92	4-98	100:06	100:08	5.39
9.15	4-98	101:22	101:25	5.52
8.15	5-98	101:12	101:14	5.60
5.25	5-98*	99:23	99:25	5.62
5.40	5-98*	99:26	99:28	5.57
5.38	6-98	99:27	99:29	5.51
6.34	6-98	100:16	100:18	5.52
6.29	7-98	100:14	100:16	5.59
5.10	7-98*	99:16	99:18	5.66
5.35	8-98*	99:19	99:21	5.76
4.70	9-98*	99:02	99:04	5.68
7.85	9-98	101:31	102:01	5.55
4.95	9-98*	99:08	99:10	5.68
4.88	10-98*	99:02	99:04	5.79
5.77	11-98	100:02	100:04	5.64
5.94	11-98*	100:00	100:02	5.87
5.30	12-98*	99:08	99:10	5.89
5.75	12-98*	100:00	100:02	5.70
7.05	12-98	101:12	101:14	5.74
5.20	1-99	99:10	99:12	5.70
5.09	2-99	99:04	99:07	5.71
5.32	2-99*	99:10	99:13	5.77
5.55	2-99*	99:20	99:23	5.76
9.55	3-99	105:04	105:07	5.67
6.00	3-99	100:10	100:13	5.72
8.70	6-99	104:08	104:11	5.91
6.60	6-99	101:10	101:13	5.71
8.45	7-99	104:10	104:13	5.76
5.86	7-99	100:04	100:07	5.72
6.00	8-99*	100:04	100:07	5.73
6.35	8-99	100:01	100:04	6.27
8.55	8-99	104:27	104:30	5.76
5.98	9-99*	100:00	100:03	5.86
6.07	10-99	100:16	100:19	5.75
8.35	11-99	104:26	104:29	5.81
6.10	2-00	100:22	100:25	5.74
9.05	4-00	107:18	107:21	5.73
6.41	5-00	101:15	101:18	5.76
8.90	6-00	107:10	107:13	5.87
5.90	7-00	100:02	100:05	5.83
5.97	7-00	100:11	100:14	5.80
6.55	8-00*	100:12	100:15	5.97
6.41	9-00*	100:09	100:12	5.97
9.20	9-00	108:11	108:14	6.01
6.38	10-00*	100:04	100:07	6.13
6.30	11-00*	100:00	100:03	6.26
8.25	12-00	106:18	106:21	5.93
5.55	1-01	98:22	98:26	5.95
5.50	2-01	98:22	98:26	5.89
5.97	2-01*	99:19	99:23	6.06
5.37	2-01	98:08	98:12	5.91
5.65	2-01*	98:19	98:23	6.08

Rate	Mat.	Bid	Asked	Yld
6.80	1-03	103:06	103:12	6.03
6.40	3-03*	99:22	99:28	6.42
6.63	4-03*	100:02	100:08	6.08
6.71	5-03	102:28	103:02	6.06
6.45	6-03*	99:22	99:28	6.48
6.38	7-03*	100:00	100:06	6.34
6.20	7-03*	99:12	99:18	6.29
6.51	8-03*	100:00	100:06	6.47
6.25	8-03*	99:07	99:13	6.37
5.45	10-03	96:24	96:30	6.07
6.20	11-03*	98:24	98:30	6.41
5.80	12-03	98:08	98:14	6.11
6.40	1-04*	99:18	99:24	6.45
6.90	3-04*	100:02	100:08	3.96
6.85	4-04	103:18	103:24	6.14
7.60	4-04*	100:00	100:06	0.00
7.55	6-04*	101:03	101:09	6.72
7.40	7-04	107:10	107:16	6.02
7.70	8-04*	102:15	102:21	6.14
7.85	9-04*	102:18	102:24	6.30
8.25	10-04*	103:26	104:00	6.11
8.40	10-04*	103:28	104:02	6.24
8.63	11-04*	104:25	104:31	6.05
8.55	12-04*	100:14	100:20	4.67
8.50	2-05*	105:06	105:12	5.97
7.88	2-05	109:22	109:28	6.18
7.65	3-05	108:18	108:24	6.16
8.00	4-05*	100:28	101:02	5.83
6.35	6-05	100:20	100:26	6.21
6.55	9-05	102:04	102:10	6.18
6.85	9-05*	100:24	100:30	6.50
6.70	11-05*	101:00	101:06	6.27
5.94	12-05	97:31	98:05	6.23
5.88	2-06	97:18	97:24	6.22
6.41	3-06	101:00	101:06	6.23
6.22	3-06	99:22	99:28	6.24
6.89	4-06	103:23	103:29	6.29
6.75	5-06	103:10	103:16	6.22
7.90	6-06*	102:08	102:14	6.38
7.07	7-06	105:28	106:02	6.16
7.93	9-06*	102:31	103:05	6.18
7.59	10-06*	102:03	102:09	6.35
7.50	11-06*	102:08	102:14	6.24
6.88	11-06*	101:01	101:07	6.53
6.96	4-07	105:18	105:24	6.15
6.64	7-07	102:16	102:22	6.26
6.52	7-07	101:31	102:05	6.22
6.54	9-07	102:04	102:10	6.22
7.13	9-07*	100:27	101:01	6.73
6.59	9-07	102:16	102:22	6.22
6.39	9-07	100:23	100:29	6.27
0.00	7-14	33:15	33:23	6.60
10.35	12-15	138:21	138:29	6.63
8.20	3-16	116:10	116:18	6.63
8.95	2-18	123:03	123:11	6.81
8.10	8-19	116:00	116:08	6.68
0.00	10-19	23:23	23:31	6.60
7.13	4-26	107:04	107:10	6.55
6.09	9-27	94:02	94:10	6.52

Federal Home Loan Bank

Rate	Mat.	Bid	Asked	Yld.
5.45	11-97	100:01	100:02	4.68
5.63	12-97*	100:02	100:03	5.03
5.65	1-98*	100:03	100:04	5.07
5.75	1-98*	100:04	100:05	5.08
5.78	1-98	100:05	100:06	5.10

Rate	Mat	Bid	Asked	Yld
6.12	1-01*	99:31	100:03	6.09
5.58	2-01*	98:20	98:24	5.99
7.00	1-02*	100:06	100:10	5.95
7.01	12-03*	100:02	100:08	4.91
9.50	2-04	117:26	118:00	6.06
6.79	6-04	103:18	103:24	6.09
7.25	6-05*	100:02	100:08	5.97
6.95	2-06*	100:00	100:06	6.92
7.00	7-07*	100:16	100:22	6.72
7.00	8-07*	100:17	100:23	6.71
7.18	1-11*	100:01	100:09	5.97
8.00	1-12*	100:08	100:16	5.84
8.02	1-12*	100:08	100:16	6.24
8.00	3-12*	100:06	100:14	0.00

Federal Farm Credit Bank

Rate	Mat.	Bid	Asked	Yld.
11.90	10-97	100:07	100:09	3.27
5.50	11-97	100:00	100:01	5.00
5.60	11-97	100:00	100:01	4.81
5.68	11-97	100:00	100:01	5.10
5.51	12-97	101:12	101:13	0.00
5.62	12-97	100:02	100:03	4.88
5.40	12-97	100:01	100:02	4.89
5.63	1-98	100:00	100:01	5.41
5.53	2-98	99:31	100:00	5.47
5.65	2-98	100:04	100:06	5.00
5.90	4-98	100:05	100:07	5.43
6.05	5-98	100:09	100:11	5.41
5.90	6-98	100:07	100:09	5.44
5.75	7-98	100:04	100:06	5.47
5.27	2-99*	99:00	99:03	5.99
8.65	10-99	105:08	105:11	5.75
6.28	6-01	101:03	101:07	5.91
6.10	9-01	100:11	100:15	5.97
6.75	6-07	104:04	104:10	6.15

Student Loan Marketing

Rate	Mat.	Bid	Asked	Yld.
5.63	12-97*	100:02	100:03	5.03
5.75	1-98*	100:04	100:05	5.11
7.00	3-98	100:18	100:20	5.34
6.25	6-98	100:15	100:17	5.48
5.82	9-98	100:00	100:02	5.73
6.16	12-99*	99:20	99:23	6.30
7.50	3-00	103:22	103:25	5.79
6.05	9-00	100:14	100:17	5.85
5.88	2-01*	99:03	99:07	6.14
6.38	12-01*	100:04	100:08	6.00
7.00	12-02	104:04	104:10	6.01
7.30	8-12	108:08	108:16	6.40
0.00	5-14*	34:25	35:01	6.42
0.00	10-22	17:29	18:05	6.95

World Bank Bonds

Rate	Mat.	Bid	Asked	Yld.
8.38	10-99	105:16	105:19	5.37
8.13	3-01	107:22	107:26	5.57
6.38	5-01	102:00	102:04	5.71
6.75	1-02	102:14	102:18	6.05
12.38	10-02	125:01	125:07	6.42
5.25	9-03	97:09	97:15	5.76
6.38	7-05	101:22	101:28	6.07
6.63	8-06	103:12	103:20	6.09
8.25	9-16	116:08	116:16	6.70
8.63	10-16	120:06	120:14	6.71
9.25	7-17	127:15	127:23	6.70
7.63	1-23	113:02	113:10	6.54
8.88	3-26	126:08	126:16	6.76

Financing Corporation

Rate	Mat.	Bid	Asked	Yld.
10.70	10-17	139:12	139:20	6.99
9.80	11-17	135:00	135:08	6.61
9.40	2-18	125:26	126:02	6.98
9.80	4-18	134:18	134:26	6.66
10.00	5-18	136:09	136:17	6.70
10.35	8-18	139:29	140:05	6.73

Rate	Mat	Bid	Asked	Yld
9.65	11-18	133:05	133:13	6.67
9.90	12-18	135:15	135:23	6.71
9.60	12-18	132:05	132:13	6.71
9.65	3-19	133:00	133:08	6.70
9.70	4-19	133:11	133:19	6.72
9.00	6-19	124:23	124:31	6.78
8.60	9-19	120:19	120:27	6.76

Inter-Amer. Devel. Bank

Rate	Mat.	Bid	Asked	Yld.
9.50	10-97	100:03	100:05	1.40
9.45	9-98	103:13	103:16	5.55
7.13	9-99	102:24	102:27	5.58
8.50	5-01	107:23	107:27	6.02
6.13	3-06	99:28	100:02	6.11
6.63	3-07	102:30	103:04	6.18
12.25	12-08	144:05	144:13	6.58
8.88	6-09	118:16	118:24	6.55
8.40	9-09	115:15	115:23	6.48
8.50	3-11	116:04	116:12	6.64
7.13	3-23*	93:30	94:06	7.65
7.00	6-25	102:27	103:03	6.75
6.80	10-25	100:16	100:24	6.74

GNMA Mtge. Issues Oct97

Rate	Mat.	Bid	Asked	Yld.
6.00	30Yr	96:03	96:05	6.66
6.50	30Yr	98:18	98:20	6.78
7.00	30Yr	100:18	100:20	6.96
7.50	30Yr	102:07	102:09	7.15
8.00	30Yr	103:24	103:26	7.25
8.50	30Yr	104:28	104:30	7.01
9.00	30Yr	106:25	106:27	6.71
9.50	30Yr	108:17	108:19	6.82
10.00	30Yr	109:21	109:23	7.04
10.50	30Yr	110:01	110:03	7.40
11.00	30Yr	111:21	111:23	7.28

Tennessee Valley Authority

Rate	Mat.	Bid	Asked	Yld.
5.13	3-98	99:24	99:26	5.53
5.95	9-98	100:08	100:10	5.61
6.25	8-99*	100:16	100:19	5.89
8.38	10-99	104:26	104:29	5.71
6.00	11-00	100:10	100:13	5.85
6.50	8-01	100:00	100:04	6.46
7.45	10-01*	102:28	103:00	6.58
6.88	1-02*	101:20	101:24	6.39
6.88	8-02*	101:24	101:30	6.39
6.13	7-03*	99:19	99:25	6.17
6.38	6-05	101:06	101:12	6.15
3.38	1-07	97:20	97:26	3.66
7.63	9-22*	102:24	103:00	7.36
7.75	12-22*	103:28	104:04	7.39
8.05	7-24*	104:06	104:14	5.39
6.75	11-25	102:04	102:12	6.56
8.63	11-29*	110:02	110:10	6.11
8.25	9-34*	105:04	105:12	5.28
8.25	4-42*	111:10	111:18	7.20
7.25	7-43*	102:02	102:10	7.08
6.88	12-43*	97:24	98:00	7.02
7.85	6-44*	106:23	106:31	7.32

Farm Credit Fin. Asst. Corp.

Rate	Mat.	Bid	Asked	Yld.
9.38	7-03	115:04	115:10	6.18
9.45	11-03*	103:27	104:01	5.67
8.80	6-05	115:28	116:02	6.14
9.20	9-05*	107:27	108:01	6.20

Resolution Funding Corp.

Rate	Mat.	Bid	Asked	Yld.
8.13	10-19	116:12	116:20	6.67
8.88	7-20	124:20	124:28	6.72
9.38	10-20	129:14	129:22	6.80
8.63	1-21	121:09	121:17	6.77
8.63	1-30	121:08	121:16	6.95
8.88	4-30	123:24	124:00	6.99

Figure 13.7

Price Quotations for Government Agency Issues (Excerpts)

Source: Reprinted by permission of *The Wall Street Journal*, Dow Jones & Company, Inc., October 7, 1997, p. C20. All rights reserved worldwide.

made to students by other lenders, such as commercial banks, and may make direct student loans under special circumstances. The Farm Credit Banks lend to farmers as well as farm associations and cooperatives, and the Farm Credit Financial Assistance Corporation was created in 1987 to support the Farm Credit Bank System. The Financing Corporation was established in August 1987 to recapitalize the Federal Savings and Loan Insurance Corporation (FSLIC). Last, the Resolution Funding Corporation was created in 1989 to assist in the recovery of the thrift industry, mainly by assisting bankrupt or near-bankrupt savings and loans.

13.4.3 Participation Certificates

To support credit for home purchases, the government has authorized the issuance of **participation certificates** (or pass-throughs). In a process known as *securitization*, a group of assets (for example, mortgages) is placed in a pool, and certificates representing ownership of those assets are issued to pay for them. The holders of the certificates receive the interest and principal payments as they are made by homeowners, minus a small service charge. The most important certificates of this type are those issued by the Government National Mortgage Association (GNMA, or "Ginnie Mae") and are known as GNMA Modified Pass-Through Securities. These securities are guaranteed by GNMA and are backed by the full faith and credit of the U.S. government.

GNMA pass-through securities are created by certain private organizations such as savings and loans and mortgage bankers that bundle a package of similar (in terms of maturity date and interest rate) mortgages together. These mortgages must be individually guaranteed by either the Federal Housing Administration or the Veterans Administration (thus making them free from default risk) and have, in aggregate, a principal amount of at least $1 million. After these mortgages have been bundled together, an application is made to GNMA for a guarantee on the pass-through securities. Typically, each security represents $25,000 worth of principal. Once the guarantee is received, the securities are sold to the public through brokers. The interest rate paid on the securities is .5% less than the interest rate paid on the mortgages, with GNMA keeping .1% and the creator .4%.

Unlike most bonds, GNMA pass-through securities pay investors on a monthly basis an amount of money that represents both a pro rata return of principal and interest on the underlying mortgages. For example, the holder of a $25,000 certificate from a $1 million pool would indirectly "own" $2\text{-}\frac{1}{2}\%$ of every mortgage in the pool. Each month the homeowners make mortgage payments that consist of part principal and part interest. In turn, each month the investor receives $2\text{-}\frac{1}{2}\%$ of the aggregate amount paid by the homeowners. Because the mortgages are free from default risk, there is no default risk on the pass-through securities. (If homeowner payments are late, GNMA will either use excess cash or borrow money from the Treasury to make sure that the investors are paid in a timely fashion.)

Prepayment Risk

There is one particular risk to investors, however, that arises because homeowners are allowed to prepay their mortgages. As a result of this prepayment provision, typical pass-through securities may actually have much shorter lives then their initially stated lives of thirty years. If interest rates have fallen since the time the pass-through security was created, homeowners may start to prepay their mortgages. If the investor bought an existing pass-through that was selling at a premium and homeowners prepay, then the investor will receive par value on the security shortly after having paid a premium for it. Therefore, the investor will incur a loss. In addition, the investor will be faced with the problem of reinvesting the proceeds of the prepayments because similar risk securities will now yield a lower interest rate than had been paid by the pass-through security.

Consider a pass-through security of $25,000, initially issued with a stated interest rate of 12%. Suppose that afterward interest rates unexpectedly fall so that new pass-throughs carry a stated rate of 10%. At this time the older pass-through security has $20,000 of principal outstanding, but as a consequence of the fall in interest rates it is selling at a premium, perhaps for $22,000. Now suppose that interest rates unexpectedly fall again, this time to 8%. At this point many homeowners prepay their mortgages in order to refinance them at the current rate of 8%. As a result an investor who purchased the older pass-through security for $22,000 ends up shortly thereafter receiving $20,000, thereby quickly losing $2,000.[11] Further, the $20,000 can now be reinvested only in similar risk securities yielding 8% instead of 10%, resulting in an opportunity loss in income of $400 per year [=$20,000 × (.10 − .08)].

Innovations

The interest the investing public has shown in GNMA pass-through securities has caused a number of similar securities to be created. One, typically issued in denominations of $100,000 or more, is the "guaranteed mortgage certificate" sold by the Federal Home Loan Mortgage Corporation ("Freddie Mac"), a federally sponsored agency that was mentioned earlier. Some banks have offered similar pass-through mortgage certificates backed by private insurance companies. Some of them have repackaged the cash flows that are paid by the homeowners so that investors can receive something other than a pro rata share of them. A broad class of such securities named collateralized mortgage obligations are discussed next.

13.4.4   Collateralized Mortgage Obligations

Collateralized mortgage obligations (CMOs) are a means to allocate a mortgage pool's principal and interest payments among investors in accordance with their preferences for prepayment risk. A CMO originator (or "sponsor") transforms a traditional mortgage pool into a set of securities, called CMO *tranches* (French for "slices"), that have different priority claims on the interest and principal paid by the mortgages underlying the CMO. Sponsors of CMOs may be government agencies, such as GNMA or FNMA, or they may be private entities, such as brokerage firms.

Although there is no standard form of CMO, consider an example of a simple "sequential-pay" CMO structure that involves three tranches: A, B, and C. The tranches were formed from a pool of mortgages with a total principal value of $250 million. The mortgages in the pool all carry an interest rate of 8%. As shown in Table 13.4, each tranche is initially allocated a specific proportion of the underlying mortgage pool's principal: $150 million for tranche A, $25 million for tranche B, and $75 million for tranche C. Interest payments, as with any bond, are paid as a percentage of the outstanding principal corresponding to each tranche. (The example assumes that interest and principal are paid annually. In practice, those payments occur monthly.)

In this example, the three tranches earn the same interest rate on their principal. However, they differ in terms of how they are retired (that is, how principal payments are allocated among them). All principal payments (both scheduled and prepaid) made by the pool are funneled to the A tranche until its outstanding principal has been extinguished. The B and C tranches receive only interest payments so long as the A tranche has not been fully paid off. Once it has, the B tranche receives all principal payments until it is retired; afterward, principal payments go to the C tranche. For example, in year 1, each tranche receives an 8% interest payment on its

---

TABLE 13.4 Three-Tranche Sequential-Pay CMO

	Tranche A			Tranche B		
Year	Year-End Balance	Principal	Interest	Year-End Balance	Principal	Interest
0	$150,000,000			$25,000,000		
1	132,742,627	$17,257,372	$12,000,000	25,000,000	0	$2,000,000
2	114,104,665	18,637,962	10,619,410	25,000,000	0	2,000,000
3	93,975,667	20,128,999	9,128,373	25,000,000	0	2,000,000
4	72,236,348	21,739,319	7,518,053	25,000,000	0	2,000,000
5	48,757,884	23,478,464	5,778,908	25,000,000	0	2,000,000
6	23,401,142	25,356,741	3,900,631	25,000,000	0	2,000,000
7	0	23,401,142	1,872,091	21,015,862	$3,984,138	2,000,000
8	0	0	0	0	21,015,862	1,681,294
9	0	0	0	0	0	0
10	0	0	0	0	0	0

	Tranche C			Mortgage Pool		
Year	Year-End Balance	Principal	Interest	Year-End Balance	Principal	Interest
0	$75,000,000			$250,000,000		
1	75,000,000	0	$6,000,000	232,742,628	$17,257,372	$20,000,000
2	75,000,000	0	6,000,000	214,104,666	18,637,962	18,619,410
3	75,000,000	0	6,000,000	193,975,667	20,128,999	17,128,373
4	75,000,000	0	6,000,000	172,236,348	21,739,319	15,518,053
5	75,000,000	0	6,000,000	148,757,884	23,478,464	13,778,908
6	75,000,000	0	6,000,000	123,401,142	25,356,741	11,900,631
7	75,000,000	0	6,000,000	96,015,862	27,385,281	9,872,091
8	66,439,758	$8,560,242	6,000,000	66,439,758	29,576,103	7,681,269
9	34,497,567	31,942,192	5,315,181	34,497,567	31,942,192	5,315,181
10	0	34,497,567	2,759,805	0	34,497,567	2,759,805

principal balance at the beginning of the year. Further, in year 1 the pool's mortgages make a combined principal payment of $17,257,372, which is assigned in full to tranche A. Its principal balance falls by the amount of the payment, leaving $132,742,627 in outstanding principal to begin the second year. In year 2, tranche A's interest payment is smaller because its beginning-of-the-year principal balance has been reduced by $17,257,372. The interest payments to tranches B and C remain the same, however, because their principal balances have not yet been reduced. By the end of year 6 the outstanding principal of tranche A has been completely extinguished and it receives no further interest or principal payments. Tranche B is now the recipient of all principal payments, with tranches B and C (the two remaining tranches) earning interest based on their outstanding principal. Because of its small size, the B tranche is quickly retired. By year 8, only the C tranche is still in existence. It now receives all of the pool's interest and principal payments. By the end of year 10 it too has been retired because all of the mortgages in the pool have paid off their principal balances.

The primary purpose of dividing a mortgage pass-through pool's principal and income flows into various tranches is to create a set of securities with varying levels of interest rate and prepayment risk. Investors can match their risk preferences and predictions with the appropriate securities. The CMO originator expects that investors will pay a premium for this flexibility, with the sum of the parts being worth more than the whole.

Considerably more complex CMO structures than that involved in the simple sequential-pay CMO example are commonplace. Greater complexity allows an even greater fine-tuning of risk. Note that in the sequential-pay CMO example, investors seeking shorter-maturity mortgage-backed securities will generally hold the faster-pay tranches, whereas investors desiring longer-maturity mortgage-backed securities will hold the slower-pay tranches. Nevertheless, both types of investors are still exposed to considerable prepayment risk. If interest rates fall, prepayments will increase, shortening the maturities of all three tranches. Conversely, it interest rates rise, prepayments will decline, increasing the effective maturities of all three tranches.

Solutions to this problem involve creating tranches whose interest and principal payments respond in various ways to movements in market interest rates and the prepayment tendencies of the pool's mortgages. Some CMO structures contain dozens of tranches. Instead of fixed interest rates, certain tranches may have interest rates that vary directly with the movement of short-term interest rates. These securities are called "floaters." They are paired with "inverse floaters," whose interest payments move in the opposite direction of short-term interest rates. Other tranches, called planned amortization classes (PACs), make fixed principal and interest payments over a specified period, similar to a standard coupon bond. They are matched with support (or companion) bonds, which are exposed to high levels of prepayment risk. The seemingly endless list of CMO variations is limited only by the imaginations of CMO sponsors and the appetite of investors for different cash flow patterns and different levels of prepayment risk.

Although the risk of principal prepayments can be allocated among various tranches, in the final analysis the prepayment risk of the mortgage pool cannot be reduced. Evaluating prepayment risk can prove extremely difficult, particularly in the more complex CMO structures. Various organizations have developed prepayment models designed to simulate the behavior of mortgage prepayments under specified interest rate scenarios. These models allow CMO investors to better evaluate the riskiness and, hence, the appropriate yields of the available CMO tranches.

13.5 STATE AND LOCAL GOVERNMENT SECURITIES

The 1992 Census of Governments showed that there were 85,005 governmental units in the United States in addition to the federal government itself.[12] These nonfederal governmental units consist of:

State government		50
Local government		
County	3,043	
Municipal	19,279	
Township and town	16,656	
School district	14,422	
Special district	31,555	
Total local governmental units		84,955
Total nonfederal governmental units		85,005

A great many of these units borrow money; their securities are called **municipal bonds** or simply "municipals" or "muni's." (Only the securities of the U.S. government are referred to as "governments.") Figure 13.8 provides estimates of the amounts of

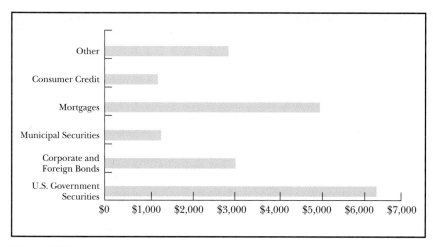

Figure 13.8
Estimated Amounts of Various Fixed-Income Securities Outstanding, Year-End 1996
($ billions)
Source: *Federal Reserve Bulletin*, September, 1997, p. A40.

various types of fixed-income securities outstanding at the end of 1996. With over
$1 trillion in outstanding value, municipals clearly warrant attention.

13.5.1   Issuing Agencies

Figure 13.9 shows the dollar values of municipal bonds issued in 1996 by various
agencies, and Figure 13.10 shows the purposes for the issuance of such debt. States
generally issue debt to finance capital expenditures, primarily for highways, housing,
and education.[13] The concept behind the issuance of such debt is that the revenue
generated by the resulting facilities will be used to make the required debt payments.
In some cases, the link is direct (for example, tolls may be used to pay for a bridge).
In other cases it is somewhat indirect (for example, gasoline taxes may be used to pay
for highway construction) or very indirect (for example, state sales taxes or income
taxes may be used to pay for the construction of new government buildings).

   States cannot be sued without their consent. Thus bondholders may have no
legal recourse in the event of default, and state-issued bonds that are dependent on

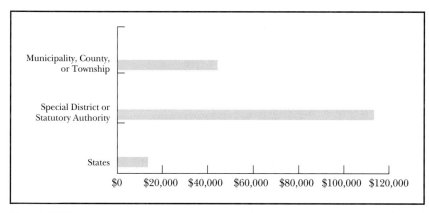

Figure 13.9
New Security Issues of State and Local Governments in 1996, Classified by Issues ($ millions)
Source: *Federal Reserve Bulletin*, September, 1997, p. A31.

Collateralized Bond Obligations

Can lead really be turned into gold? More to the point, can a set of high-yield bonds be transformed into AAA-rated securities? The answer is yes, through some sophisticated financial alchemy that produces an investment instrument known as a collateralized bond obligation (CBO). With the huge demand that has developed for high-yield bonds in the 1990s, CBOs have become a popular means of investing in that type of debt. In fact, in 1997 it has been estimated that one in every five newly issued high-yield bonds was placed in a CBO.

To understand CBOs requires some knowledge of two financial techniques: *securitization* and *cash flow prioritization*. Securitization is a two-stage process. First, assets that generate cash flows are brought together into a single pool. These assets are referred to as the collateral underlying the pool. Second, securities representing interests in the pool are sold to investors. As the collateral throws off cash flows (be they dividends, interest, royalties, principal payments, and so on), the securities entitle their owners to a pro rata share of those payments.

Cash flow prioritization involves defining a set of rules for how the cash flows generated by a pool's collateral are distributed to the pool's owners. In particular, the securities denoting ownership of the pool do not all receive the same pro rata participation in the pool's cash flows. Instead, the pool is divided into tranches, and securities are issued for each tranche. The pool's cash flows are allocated to the securityholders of the tranches according to a specified formula. This formula may be very simple or quite complex. In either case, cash flow prioritization causes the expected pattern of payments to vary from one tranche to another. This variation potentially appeals to a wider set of investors, thereby enhancing the value of the entire pool.

The concepts of securitization and cash flow prioritization should sound familiar. They are central to the creation of collateralized mortgage obligations (CMOs). Indeed, as their names imply, CBOs are very similar to CMOs. They differ, however, in terms of their underlying collateral. (Mortgages in the case of CMOs; high-yield bonds in the case of CBOs.) Just as important, they differ in terms of the types of cash flow risks that they are designed to address.

Collateralized mortgage obligations are concerned with prepayment risk: the possibility that homeowners will prepay their mortgages at a time disadvantageous to the mortgage owner. Collateralized bond obligations, on the other hand, are created with default risk in mind. Producers of CBOs package together a number of below-investment-grade debt issues (or, in some cases, the government debt of various international emerging markets). Three tranches are typically established. These tranches have prioritized

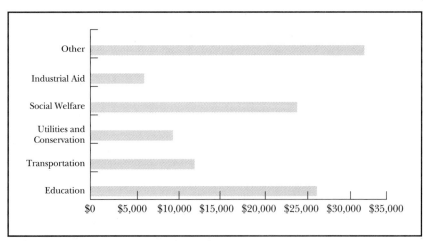

Figure 13.10
New Security Issues of State and Local Governments in 1996, Classified by Purpose ($ millions)
Source: *Federal Reserve Bulletin,* September, 1997, p. A31.

claims on the principal and interest payments made by the pool's collateral. The senior tranche receives its principal and interest in full first, followed by the senior subordinated tranche, and lastly by the junior tranche. As a result, any default affects the junior tranches first. Because defaults tend to be relatively firm-specific, the senior claims in a well-diversified CBO pool are largely insulated from default risk. The junior securities, conversely, stand to gain or lose significantly depending on the pool's default experience. Therefore, they effectively convey equity ownership in the pool.

In total, creating a CBO structure from a pool of collateral cannot alter the pool's default risk. It merely redistributes that risk. The senior tranche will have less default risk than the pool itself, whereas the junior tranche will have more default risk.

A CBO pool is actually a managed portfolio of securities. A CBO sponsor purchases the pool's collateral, establishes tranches backed by the pool, and issues securities representing pro rata ownership of the tranches. Going forward, the CBO sponsor will buy and sell securities for the pool depending on the sponsor's view of the risk-reward opportunities available in the high-yield market. For this service, the CBO sponsor receives a fee in the range of .25% to .45% of the pool's value.

Because of the prominent role played by the CBO sponsor, CBO investors should evaluate the sponsor's abilities to assess credit risk, to create and maintain a well-diversified portfolio, and to take advantage of mispriced securities. Further, CBO investors should be prepared to analyze a pool's collateral and the design of the pool's tranches. What is the credit quality of the collateral? What is the collateral's average life? How liquid is the collateral? How might the collateral respond to different economic and interest rate environments? How are the senior tranches protected relative to the junior tranches?

The major credit-rating agencies, such as Moody's and Standard & Poor's (see Chapter 14) can be of some assistance in this analysis. They provide ratings of the relative default risk of CBO tranche securities. Senior tranches in some pools have been rated as high as AAA, even though the collateral is almost entirely composed of below-investment-grade debt. Nevertheless, ratings by the credit-rating agencies do not speak to the fair market value of a CBO's securities. In that respect investors are left to fend for themselves. Despite the added complexity that CBOs bring to an existing financial instrument such as high-yield bonds (or perhaps because of that added complexity), they represent an excellent example of how the financial markets respond to the needs of suppliers and users of funds by creating flexible new securities.

particular revenues from some capital project may involve considerable risk. However, bonds backed by the "full faith and credit" of a state government are generally considered quite safe despite the inability of the bondholders to sue. It is anticipated that state legislatures will do whatever is necessary to see that such bonds are paid off in a timely manner.

Unlike state governments, local governments can be sued against their will, making it possible for bondholders to force officials to collect whatever amount is needed in order to meet required debt payments. In many cases, only revenues from specific projects may be used (for example, the tolls collected on a particular highway). In other cases, collections from a particular tax may be used, although possibly only up to some statutory limit.

Some local governments (for example, Cleveland in 1978–1979) have defaulted on their debts, and others (for example, New York City in 1975 and Orange County, California, in 1996) have "restructured" their debt, giving current bondholders new certificates offering lower or deferred interest and longer maturities in exchange for currently outstanding certificates. Thus, the right of bondholders to sue does not always mean that they will be able to collect what they are owed in a timely fashion.

Counties and municipalities are familiar to most people, but other forms of local government also exist. Examples include school districts as well as other districts and authorities that have been created to finance and operate seaports or airports. All are created by state charter and may be granted monopoly powers as well as rights to collect certain types of taxes. However, limits are often placed on the amount of taxes collected, the tax rate charged, and the amount (or type) of debt issued.

The primary source of funding for such agencies is the property tax. Because a given property may be liable for taxes levied by several agencies (such as a city, a county, a school district, a port authority, and a sewer district), the risk of an agency's bonds may depend on both the value of property subject to its taxes and the amount of other debt dependent on the same property.

13.5.2 Types of Municipal Bonds

In 1996, new municipal bonds with a par value of $177.2 billion were issued. Of this total, $60.4 billion were general obligation bonds (GOs) and $110.8 billion were revenue bonds.[14]

General obligation bonds are backed by the full faith and credit (and thus the full taxing power) of the issuing agency. Most are issued by agencies with unlimited taxing power, although in a minority of cases the issuer is subject to limits on the amount of taxes or on the tax rate (or both).

Revenue bonds are backed by revenues from a designated project, authority, or agency or by the proceeds from a specific tax. In many cases, such bonds are issued by agencies that hope to sell their services, pay the required expenses, and have enough left over to meet required payments on outstanding debt. Except for the possible granting of monopoly powers, the authorizing state and local government may provide no further assistance to the issuer. Such bonds are only as creditworthy as the enterprise associated with the issuer.

Many revenue bonds are issued to finance capital expenditures for publicly owned utilities (for example, water, electricity, or gas). Others are issued to finance quasi-utility operations (for example, public transportation). Some are financed by special assessments levied on properties benefiting from the original expenditure (for example, those connected to a new sewer system). **Industrial development bonds** (IDBs) are used to finance the purchase or construction of industrial facilities that are to be leased to firms on a favorable basis. In effect, such bonds provide cheap financing to businesses choosing to locate in the geographical area of the issuer.

Although most municipal financing involves the issuance of long-term securities, a number of different types of short-term securities have been issued in order to meet short-term demands for cash. Traditionally used types include tax anticipation notes (TANs), revenue anticipation notes (RANs), grant anticipation notes (GANs), and tax and revenue anticipation notes (TRANs). In each case, the name of the security refers to the source of repayment. Thus some can be classified as general obligation securities and others as revenue securities.

More recently, municipalities have started to issue two other kinds of short-term securities. Tax-exempt commercial paper is similar to corporate commercial paper, having a fixed interest rate and a maturity typically within 270 days. Variable-rate demand obligations have an interest rate that changes periodically (perhaps weekly) as some prespecified market interest rate changes. Furthermore, they can be redeemed at the desire of the investor within a prespecified number of days after the investor has given notice to the issuer (for example, seven days after notification of intent).

13.5.3 Tax Treatment

Through a reciprocal arrangement with the federal government, coupon payments on state and local government securities are exempt from federal taxation, and coupon payments on Treasury and agency (except FNMA) securities are exempt from state and local taxation. Similar tax treatment is accorded to the price appreciation on short-term and long-term issues that are original issue discount securities. (As mentioned earlier, OID securities are securities that were issued for a below-par price.)

However, a different tax treatment is generally given to coupon-bearing securities that were issued at par value but were subsequently bought at a discount in the marketplace. Such securities, known as **market discount bonds**, provide the investor with income not only from the coupons but also from the difference between the purchase price and the par value. Unlike the coupons, which are tax-exempt, this difference is treated as taxable interest income.

Another interesting tax feature of municipals is that an investor who resides in the state of the issuer is generally exempt not only from paying federal taxes on the coupon payments but also from paying state taxes. Furthermore, an investor who resides in a city that has an income tax and who purchases municipals issued by the city usually is exempt from paying city taxes on the coupon payments. Thus a resident of New York City who purchases a municipal security issued by the city (or one of its political subdivisions) will not have to pay federal, state, or city income taxes on the coupon payments. However, if the New York City resident were to purchase a California municipal, then both New York State and New York City income taxes would have to be paid on the coupon payments. Although state and city income tax rates are much lower than those of the federal government, this feature nevertheless tends to make local issues more advantageous from an after-tax return viewpoint (an advantage that is offset to a certain degree by the resulting lack of diversification).

The avoidance of federal income tax on interest earned on a municipal bond makes such a security attractive to wealthy individual investors as well as corporate investors. As shown in Figure 13.11, the lack of federal taxation has resulted in municipal securities having yields that are considerably lower than those on taxable securities.[15] Consequently, the cost of financing to municipal issuers is lower, suggesting that a federal subsidy has been provided to the issuers.

Over the years, this subsidy has been used to support activities deemed worthy of encouragement (even though the encouragement is somewhat hidden). For example, private universities may issue tax-exempt bonds to finance certain types of improvements, and private firms may do so to finance certain pollution-reducing activities. Such bonds are generally backed only by the resources of the issuer, with government involvement limited to the granting of favorable tax treatment. The Tax Reform Act of 1986 greatly restricted the granting of such tax treatment, leading to the emergence of **taxable municipals**, which are typically issued to finance projects that are not viewed as essential under the tax law.

13.5.4   The Market for Municipal Bonds

Municipals are usually issued as **serial bonds**; one prespecified group matures a year after issue, another two years after issue, another three years after, and so on. Alternatively, **term bonds** (that is, bonds that all mature on the same date) or a mixture of serial and term bonds may be issued. The overall package is generally offered by the issuer on a competitive basis to various underwriters. The winning bidder then reoffers the individual bonds to investors at a higher price.

Unlike corporate bonds, municipal bonds do not need to be registered with the SEC before public issuance.[16] Indeed, the federal government leaves most regulation in this market to state and local authorities and the Municipal Securities Rulemaking Board.

Municipal bonds may be callable at specified dates and prices. Occasionally, the issuing authority is obligated to make designated payments into a **sinking fund**, which

---

Figure 13.11
Average Yields of Long-Term Fixed-Income Securities (monthly average)
Source: *Treasury Bulletin,* December 1997, p. 55.

is used to buy similar bonds (or perhaps even its own bonds). As the issuing authority's bonds mature, the money for paying them off will come from having the sinking fund sell some of its holdings.

A secondary market in municipal bonds is made by various dealers. Standard & Poor's Corporation publishes on a daily basis a listing of municipal bond quotations by various dealers in the *Blue List*. In addition, the *Bond Buyer* has an electronic system that provides dealer quotations. However, the relatively small amounts of particular issues and maturities outstanding limit the size of the market. Many individuals who invest in municipals simply buy new issues and hold them to maturity.

13.5.5 Municipal Bond Insurance

An investor concerned about possible default of a municipal bond can purchase an insurance policy to cover any losses that would be incurred if coupons or principal were not paid in full and on time. That is, an investor can contract with a company to have a specific portfolio of bonds insured. Alternatively, the issuer of the bonds can purchase such insurance from one of the firms that specialize in issuing this type of insurance. The cost of this insurance is generally more than offset by the lower interest rate that the issuer has to pay as a result of insuring its bonds. Regardless of whether the investor or the issuer purchases the insurance, the cost of the insurance will depend on the bonds included and their ratings.

Corporate bonds are similar to other kinds of fixed-income securities in that they promise to make specified payments at specified times and provide legal remedies in the event of default. Restrictions are often placed on the activities of the issuing corporation in order to provide additional protection for bondholders (for example, there may be restrictions on the amount of additional bonds that can be issued in the future).

13.6.1 Tax Treatment

Corporate bonds that are original issue discount securities generally have the discount taxed as ordinary income by the federal government. The constant interest method is to be used to determine the portion of the discount that must be reported as taxable interest each year. (This method was described earlier when stripped Treasury bonds were discussed.) With this method a portion of the discount must be recognized as income each year that the security is held, thereby causing the investor to have to pay taxes on that amount.

Corporate bonds carrying coupon payments have the coupon taxed as income each year. Furthermore, if the bond was originally sold at par but was later bought at a discount in the marketplace (as mentioned earlier, such bonds are known as market discount bonds), then the investor generally will have to pay ordinary income taxes on both the coupon payments and the discount. Using either the constant interest method or straight-line method, wherein the discount is spread out evenly over the remaining life of the bond, the investor can recognize a portion of the discount as interest income each year that the bond is held and pay taxes on it. Alternatively, the investor can wait until the bond is sold and at that time recognize the market discount as taxable interest income.[17]

From the viewpoint of the issuing corporation, debt differs from equity in two crucial respects. First, principal and interest payments are obligatory. Failure to make any payment in full and on time can expose the issuer to expensive, time-consuming, and potentially disruptive legal actions. Second, unlike dividend payments, interest payments are considered expenses to the corporation and hence can be deducted from earnings before calculating the corporation's income tax liability. As a result, each dollar paid in interest reduces earnings before taxes by a dollar, thereby reducing corporate taxes by $.35 for a firm in the 35% marginal tax bracket. This reduction leads to less than a dollar decline in earnings after taxes (in the 35% tax bracket example, the decline in earnings is $.65).

13.6.2 The Indenture

An issue of bonds is generally covered by an **indenture**, in which the issuing corporation promises a specified **trustee** that it will comply with stated provisions. Chief among these is the timely payment of required coupons and principal on the issue. Other terms are often included to control the sale of pledged property, the issuance of other bonds, and the like.

The trustee for a bond issue, usually a bank or a trust company, acts on behalf of the bondholders. Some actions may be required by the indenture; others, such as acting in response to a request from specific bondholders, may be done at the trustee's discretion.

If the corporation defaults on an interest payment, then after a relatively short period of time (perhaps one to six months) the entire principal typically becomes due and payable. This procedure is designed to enhance the bondholders' status in any forthcoming bankruptcy or related legal proceedings.

13.6.3   Types of Bonds

An exhaustive list of the names used to describe bonds would be intolerably long. Different names are often used for the same type of bond, and occasionally the same name will be used for two quite different bonds. A few major types do predominate, however, with relatively standard nomenclature.

Mortgage Bonds

Mortgage bonds represent debt that is secured by the pledge of specific property. In the event of default, the bondholders are entitled to obtain the property in question and to sell it to satisfy their claims on the firm. In addition to the property itself, the holders of mortgage bonds have an unsecured claim on the corporation.

Mortgage bondholders are usually protected by terms included in the bond indenture. The corporation may be constrained from pledging the property for other bonds (or such bonds, if issued, must be "junior" or "second" mortgages, with a claim on the property only after the first mortgage is satisfied). Certain property acquired by the corporation after the bonds were issued may also be pledged to support the bonds.

Collateral Trust Bonds

Collateral trust bonds are backed by other securities that are usually held by the trustee. A common situation of this sort arises when the securities of a subsidiary firm are pledged as collateral by the parent firm.

Equipment Obligations

Known also as equipment trust certificates, **equipment obligations** are backed by specific pieces of equipment (for example, railroad cars and commercial aircraft). If necessary, the equipment can be readily sold and delivered to a new owner. The legal arrangements used to facilitate the issuance of such bonds can be very complex. The most popular procedure uses the "Philadelphia Plan," in which the trustee initially holds the equipment and issues obligations and then leases the equipment to a corporation. Money received from the lessee is subsequently used to make interest and principal payments to the holders of the obligations. Ultimately, if all payments are made on schedule, the leasing corporation takes title to the equipment.

Debentures

Debentures are general obligations of the issuing corporation and thus represent unsecured credit. To protect the holders of such bonds, the indenture will usually limit the future issuance of secured debt as well as any additional unsecured debt.

Subordinated Debentures

When more than one issue of debenture is outstanding, a hierarchy may be specified. For example, **subordinated debentures** are junior to unsubordinated debentures, meaning that in the event of bankruptcy, junior claims are to be considered only after senior claims have been fully satisfied.

Asset-backed securities are much like the participation securities that were described earlier. However, instead of mortgages being pooled and pieces of ownership in the pool being sold, debt obligations such as credit card revolving loans, automobile loans, student loans, and equipment loans are pooled to serve as collateral backing the securities. The basic concept, known as securitization, is the same, however. Originators of these loans pool them and sell securities that represent part ownership of the pool. A servicing company collects the payments made by the debtors over a period of time, such as a month, and then pays each owner the appropriate percent of the aggregate amount received. As for investors in participation certificates associated with mortgages, two concerns for investors in asset-backed securities are default risk and prepayment risk.

Other Types of Bonds

Income bonds are more like preferred stock (described in a later section) than bonds. Payment of interest in full and on schedule is not absolutely required, and failure to do so need not send the corporation into bankruptcy. Interest on income bonds may not qualify as a tax-deductible expense for the issuing corporation. This type of bond has rarely been used, except in reorganizations of bankrupt railroads.

Guaranteed bonds are issued by one corporation but backed in some way by another (for example, by a parent firm). **Participating bonds** require stated interest payments and provide additional amounts if earnings exceed some stated level. **Voting bonds**, unlike regular bonds, give the holders some voice in management. *Serial bonds*, with different portions of the issue maturing at different dates, are sometimes used by corporations for equipment financing (as mentioned earlier, they are also used by municipalities).

Convertible bonds may, at the holder's option, be exchanged for other securities, often common stock. Such bonds, which have become very popular in recent years, are discussed in more detail in the appendix to Chapter 19. **Putable bonds** also give the holders an option, but this time it is to exchange their bonds for cash equal to the bond's face value. This option generally can be exercised over a brief period of time after a stated number of years has elapsed since the bond's issuance.[18]

13.6.4 Call Provisions

Management would like to have the right to pay off the corporation's bonds at par at any time before maturity. This ability would provide management with flexibility, because debt could be reduced or its maturity altered via refunding. Most important, expensive high-coupon debt that was issued during a time of high interest rates could be replaced with cheaper low-coupon debt if rates decline.

Not surprisingly, investors hold quite a different opinion on the matter. The issuer's ability to redeem an issue at par at any time virtually precludes a substantive rise in price over par and robs the holder of potential gains from price appreciation associated with declining interest rates. Moreover, it introduces a new form of uncertainty. A bond with such a feature will almost certainly sell for less than one without it.

Despite the cost of obtaining this sort of flexibility, many corporations include call provisions in their bond indentures that give the corporation the option to call some or all of the bonds from their holders at stated prices during specified periods before maturity. In a sense, the firm sells a bond and simultaneously buys an option from the holders. The net price of the bond is thus the difference between the value of the bond and the option.

The indenture usually gives investors two kinds of call protection. First of all, during the first few years after being issued, a bond may not be callable. Secondly, a

call premium may be specified in the call provision. Such a premium indicates that if the issue is called, the issuer must pay the bondholders a **call price** that is a stated amount above par. Often, the amount above par becomes smaller as time passes and the maturity date approaches.

An entire issue may be called, or only specific bonds that are chosen randomly by the trustee. In either case, a notice of redemption will appear in advance in the financial press.

13.6.5 Sinking Funds

A bond indenture will often require the issuing corporation to make annual payments into a sinking fund. The idea is to pay part of the principal of the debt (as well as the interest) each year, thereby reducing the amount outstanding at maturity.

Sinking funds operate by having the corporation transmit cash to the trustee, who can then purchase bonds in the open market. Alternatively, the corporation may obtain the bonds itself, by either purchase or call, and deposit them with the trustee. Call prices for sinking fund purchases may differ from those specified when the entire issue is to be repaid before maturity.

Required contributions to a sinking fund may not be the same each year. In some cases, the required amount may depend on earnings, output, and so on; in others, the goal is to make the total paid for interest and principal the same each year.

13.6.6 Private Placements

Bonds intended for eventual public sale are usually issued in denominations of $1,000 each. Either bearer or registered forms may be used. Often, however, a single investor or a small group of investors will buy an entire issue known as a **private placement**. Such offerings do not involve a prospectus and are not required to be registered with the SEC provided certain conditions are met. The two most important ones prohibit general advertising and solicitation of interest and restrict the sale to only those investors who are deemed "sophisticated" as evidenced by their wealth and income. Subsequent trading after a lapse of one year from the offering date is allowed, but Rule 144A allows trading before the one year is up, provided the purchaser is a qualified institutional buyer (one with assets of at least $100 million, dubbed a "QIB").

13.6.7 Bankruptcy

When a corporation fails to make a scheduled coupon or principal payment on a bond, the corporation is said to be in default on that obligation. If the payment is not made within a relatively short period, some sort of litigation almost inevitably follows.

A corporation unable to meet its obligatory debt payments is said to be technically insolvent (or insolvent in the equity sense). If the value of the firm's assets falls below its liabilities, it is said to be insolvent (or insolvent in the bankruptcy sense).

Behind these definitions lie much legislation, many court cases, and varied legal opinions. Although the details differ, the usual situation begins with a default on one or more required coupon payments. Failure to obtain voluntary agreements with creditors usually leads to a filing of bankruptcy by the corporation itself. Subsequent developments involve courts, court-appointed officials, representatives of the firm's creditors, and the management of the firm, among others.

Liquidation

A question that arises in most bankruptcy cases is whether the firm's assets should be liquidated (that is, sold) and the proceeds divided among the creditors. Such an action is taken only if the court feels that the resulting value would exceed that likely to be obtained if the firm continued in operation (perhaps after substantial reorganization).

If the firm's assets are liquidated in a "straight bankruptcy," secured creditors receive either the property pledged for their loans or the proceeds from the sale of the secured property. If this amount falls short of their claims, the difference is considered an unsecured debt of the firm; on the other hand, any excess is made available for other creditors. Next, assets are used to pay the claims of priority creditors to the extent possible. These include claims for such items as administrative expenses, wages (up to a stated limit per person), uninsured pension claims, taxes, and rents. Anything left over is used to pay unsecured creditors in proportion to their claims on the firm.

Reorganization

If the value of a firm's assets when employed as part of a "going concern" appears to exceed the value of the assets in liquidation, a reorganization of the firm and its liabilities may be undertaken. Such proceedings, conducted under the provisions of the Federal Bankruptcy Act, may be voluntary (initiated by the firm) or involuntary (initiated by three or more creditors). A number of parties must concur in the proposed reorganization, including the holders of two-thirds of the value in each general class of creditor that is affected by the reorganization.

Among the goals of reorganization are "fair and equitable" treatment of various classes of securities and the elimination of "burdensome" debt obligations. Typically, creditors are given new claims on the reorganized firm, with the amounts of the new claims intended to be at least equal in value to the amounts that the creditors would have received in liquidation. For example, holders of debentures might receive bonds of longer maturity, holders of subordinated debentures might become stockholders, and stockholders might be left without any claims on the firm.

Arrangements

A third procedure is available to financially distressed corporations. The Federal Bankruptcy Act authorizes *arrangements*, in which debts may be extended (to longer maturities) or reduced.

Some Financial Aspects of Bankruptcy

Although the subject is far too complex for detailed treatment here, two aspects of bankruptcy deserve some discussion. First, the choice between continuation of a firm and liquidation of its assets should be unrelated to considerations of bankruptcy. If an asset can be sold for more than the present value of its future earnings, it should be. Management may have to be taken to court to be forced to sell, but the issue is not really one of solvency or lack thereof.

Second, the definition of insolvency is rather vague. Assume, for the sake of argument, that assets can be adequately valued at the larger of liquidating or going-concern value. A firm is said to be insolvent if this value is less than that of the firm's liabilities. But how should the liabilities be valued? Their current market value will inevitably be less than the value of the assets, whereas their book value can be greater than the value of the assets.

Distressed Securities

Investments in fixed-income securities have traditionally encompassed investment-grade bonds—securities rated Baa (or BBB) or higher by the major credit rating agencies. In the 1980s, the universe of popular fixed-income investments expanded to include below-investment-grade bonds, called high-yield bonds. As interest rates fell in the early and mid-1990s, high-yield bonds became increasingly inviting to portfolio managers seeking to maintain attractive interest payouts to their clients.

Even in prosperous times, a surprisingly large percentage of high-yield bond issuers default on their debt. Although the high-yield bond category technically includes securities whose issuers have defaulted on their debt, high-yield bond portfolio managers in practice do not usually purchase bonds already in default. Rather, they focus their efforts on issuers who they anticipate can avoid default and therefore make the high yields paid on the issuers' bonds attractive relative to alternative fixed-income investments.

The securities of firms that have defaulted on their debt and who either (1) have filed for legal bankruptcy protection or (2) are negotiating out of court with creditors in the hope of avoiding bankruptcy, are called *distressed securities*. These securities include publicly traded bonds as well as privately traded debt owed to commercial banks (known as bank debt) or suppliers of goods and services to the distressed companies (called trade debt). In addition, distressed securities can also include common stock, because one likely resolution to a bankruptcy is for holders of the company's debt to be compensated, in part, with newly issued equity.

Most companies that restructure their debt do so out of court. Those that do enter legal bankruptcy either reorganize their debt under Chapter 11 of the U.S. Bankruptcy Code or liquidate under Chapter 7. Investors in distressed securities will often prefer a Chapter 11 reorganization as opposed to an out-of-court restructuring because the reorganized company must file considerable financial information with the court. This disclosure makes an evaluation of the company's debt less difficult.

For those companies that do enter bankruptcy, each situation is unique. Nevertheless, there tend to be common aspects of most bankruptcies. Figure 13.12 provides an overview of the bankruptcy process from a company's initial financial problems to its ultimate reorganization.

It is often argued that distressed securities represent a more inefficient sector of the fixed-income market than either investment-grade or high-yield bonds. The reasoning is several-fold. First, there may be a market segmentation effect. Many institutional investors are prohibited from owning bankrupt securities. Thus, when a company enters bankruptcy, these investors are forced to sell their holdings, potentially driving down the price of the company's debt excessively. Second, the process of bankruptcy is time-consuming and unpredictable. Debtholders of a company near, or in, bankruptcy may wish to avoid these complications and sell their holdings cheaply to investors willing see the process through to reorganization. Third, there is a lack of research coverage on bankrupt companies. Analysts at major brokerage firms typically suspend their coverage when a company becomes bankrupt, leaving investors to secure their own information about the company's financial condition. Finally, there is the issue of limited liquidity. The reluctance of most organizations to make a market in distressed securities results in wider bid-ask spreads.

Investors use different strategies to invest in distressed securities. Some follow a nonparticipatory approach in which they do not attempt to influence the bankruptcy proceedings. They simply purchase the debt of bankrupt companies that they view to be attractively priced and hold that debt until hopefully it can be sold at a higher price later in the bankruptcy process. Other investors follow a proactive approach, serving on creditors' committees that are charged with negotiating the terms of the company's reorganization. Through these committees, they hope to secure outcomes favorable to the value of their holdings. At the most aggressive end of the spectrum are investors who attempt to impose their solutions on other creditors by acquiring "blocking" positions in certain classes of a bankrupt company's debt. Because two-thirds of each class of debt must concur with the bankruptcy settlement, holding at least a one-third position in a strategically located debt class gives an investor effective veto power over a settlement. Applied strategically, this power can be translated into an outcome that favors the holders of the position.

Some distressed securities investors prefer to own the most senior debt in a bankrupt company's financial structure. Their reasoning is that bankruptcy rules require that creditors be paid in order of seniority

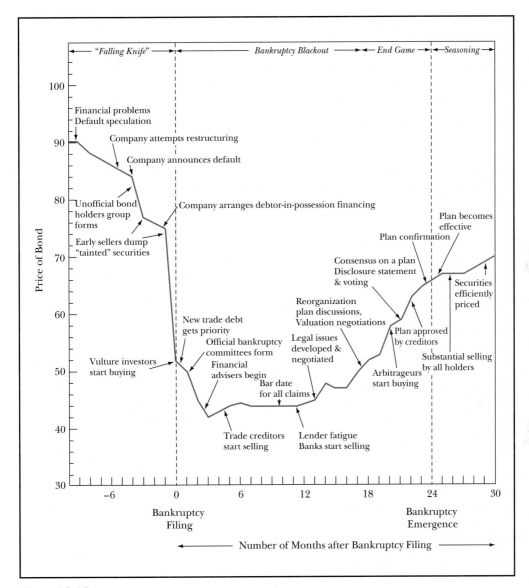

Figure 13.12
Time Line of the Bankruptcy Process
Source: Provided by T. R. Price Associates, 1998.

(although in practice this rule is not always followed to the letter). Thus, owning senior debt provides more of a valuation cushion in the event that the company's value in reorganization turns out to be worth less than originally expected. Other investors prefer to own more junior claims. Their logic is that junior debt is the most likely to appreciate significantly in value if a successful reorganization plan can be developed and implemented. In the reorganization, more senior claims tend to receive cash and newly issued debt, while more junior claims tend to receive more common stock.

The bankruptcy court is responsible for assigning a value to the company's assets and allocating that value among the creditors. The court's assigned value may not necessarily equal the value of the company's assets after the reorganization. Therefore, holders of junior claims stand to benefit more if the bankruptcy court assigns a greater value to the company's assets, because their claim is largely a residual. Holders of more senior claims, on the other hand, prefer a lower assigned asset value because that will leave more of the company's assets in their hands and reduce the proportion of assets allocated to junior claims.

A successful distressed securities investor possesses a blend of skills. First, the ability to accurately estimate the value of the company's assets that the bankruptcy court will assign is critical to determining an appropriate price to pay for different classes of the company's debt. Second, the investor must have a thorough knowledge of the bankruptcy process. Many intricate aspects of that process can easily trip up an inexperienced investor. Third, the investor must be a skillful negotiator. He or she must be able to strike deals with a disparate group of creditors, who may have financial agendas quite different from his or her own. Negotiations that become stalemated can quickly drag down returns while the investor's capital remains tied up in unproductive assets. Finally, the investor must be a savvy trader who understands the market for the company's debt and maintains access to sources of liquidity, both in initiating positions in the company's debt and in exiting those positions.

13.6.8 Trading in Corporate Bonds

Although most of the trading in corporate bonds takes place through dealers in the over-the-counter market, many corporates, as well as Treasuries, agencies, and municipals, are listed on the New York Stock Exchange's Fixed Income Market (a notably smaller number are listed on the American Stock Exchange). However, trading in corporate bonds on the NYSE takes place in a manner that is quite different from the way that common stocks are traded because neither specialists nor trading posts are involved. Instead, bonds that are listed on the NYSE are traded through a computer system known as the **Automated Bond System** (ABS). With this system, subscribers (ABS is available for a fee) enter their bid or asked prices, along with the quantities, into computer terminals. Other subscribers can see these orders by looking at display terminals and can respond by entering an order at a terminal. Thus, ABS not only provides subscribers with quotes, it also provides them with execution capability.

Because some corporate bonds are traded on the NYSE, the prices at which such trades are made can be found in the financial press. Figure 13.13 provides an example. Consider the following entry in this figure:

Bonds	Current Yield	Volume	Close	Net Change
ATT 7-$\frac{1}{2}$ 06	7.0	10	106$\frac{7}{8}$	+1/8

This entry indicates that AT&T bonds carrying a $7\frac{1}{2}\%$ coupon (paid semiannually) and maturing in 2006 last traded on October 6, 1997 at 106-$\frac{7}{8}$. Because these bonds have a par value of $1,000, the last trade was at $1,068.75. The **current yield**, meaning the annual coupon rate divided by the current closing price, was approximately 7.0% (=$75/$1,068.75). In all, 10 bonds traded hands on the exchange during the day, and the closing price was up 1/8 (=$1.25) from that of the previous trading day.

In a sense, the NYSE is the "odd lot" market for bonds, even though at the end of 1996 it had nearly 2, 064 bonds available for trading, with 1,080 of them being U.S. corporate debt issues having an aggregate par value of $250.9 billion).[19] That is,

NEW YORK EXCHANGE BONDS

Quotations as of 4 p.m. Eastern Time
Monday, October 6, 1997

Volume $13,390,000

SALES SINCE JANUARY 1
(000 omitted)

1997	1996	1995
$4,080,315	$4,372,357	$5,675,462

WHAT NYSE BONDS DID

	Domestic Mon.	Domestic Fri.	All Issues Mon.	All Issues Fri.
Issues traded	243	254	253	262
Advances	129	132	133	137
Declines	67	75	70	77
Unchanged	47	47	50	48
New highs	32	57	33	60
New lows	2	1	2	1

Dow Jones Bond Averages

–1996– High	–1996– Low	–1997– High	–1997– Low		–1997– Close	–1997– Chg.	–1997– %Yld	–1996– Close	–1996– Chg.
106.09	100.99	104.70	101.09	20 Bonds	104.52	+0.09	6.93	102.55	−0.21
102.43	97.46	102.38	97.64	10 Utilities	102.32	+0.11	6.97	99.34	−0.23
109.94	104.06	107.23	104.54	10 Industrials	106.73	+0.09	6.89	105.76	−0.20

CORPORATION BONDS
Volume, $12,884,000

Bonds	Cur Yld	Vol	Close	Net Chg
AMR 9s16	7.7	10	116¼	...
ATT 6s00	6.0	72	99⅝	...
ATT 5⅛01	5.3	15	96½	+⅜
ATT 7⅛02	6.9	2	103⅜	...
ATT 6¾04	6.6	5	102	...
ATT 7½06	7.0	10	106⅞	+⅛
ATT 8⅛22	7.7	151	105½	−⅛
ATT 8⅛24	7.7	10	106	...
AcmeM 12½02	11.4	10	109⅝	+⅝
AlaPw 9¼21	8.9	97	104½	−¼
AlskAr 6⅞14	cv	55	107¾	+½
AlldC zr99	...	40	89⅝	+¾
AlldC zr09	...	50	44½	+¼
Allwst 7¼14	cv	200	100½	...
Alza 5s06	cv	74	100	−½
Alza zr14	...	6	44	+½
ARetire 5¾02	cv	135	101¼	+½
Amresco 10s04	9.5	65	105¾	+½
Anhr 8⅝16	8.4	8	102¾	+⅜
AnnTaylr 8¾00	8.8	266	99⅜	−¼
Argosy 12s01	cv	125	90	+¼
Argosy 13¼04	12.8	395	103½	+½
Arml 8½01	8.5	7	100	...
AubrnHl 12⅜20f	...	21	160¾	+1½
AutDt zr12	...	1	63	...
BkrHgh zr08	...	30	85⅜	+⅜
BellPa 7⅛12	7.1	15	100	−⅞
BellPa 7½13	7.4	21	101½	+⅛
BellsoT 6½00	6.4	20	100⅞	−¼
BellsoT 6⅜04	6.4	25	100	+⅜
BellsoT 7s25	6.8	5	103¼	+1
BellsoT 7⅞32	7.5	25	105⅝	−⅝
BellsoT 7½33	7.3	20	103⅛	+¼
BellsoT 6¾33	7.0	50	95¾	−⅞
BstBuy 8⅝00	8.6	281	100	+⅛
BethSt 8⅜01	8.3	3	101½	−¼
BethSt 8.45s05	8.3	3	101½	...
Bevrly 7⅝03	cv	36	102	...
BorgWS 9⅛03	8.9	25	102¼	...
ChaseM 8s04	7.8	39	102¼	−1
ChespkE 9⅛06	8.9	52	103	+⅛
ChvrnC 9¾17	9.3	40	105	+½
ChckFul 7s12	cv	10	108	+2½
ChryF 13¼99	11.8	84	112¼	−⅛
ChryF 12¾99	11.4	1	111⅜	...
ChryF 9½99	8.8	5	107⅜	+2⅝
Clardge 11¾02f	...	520	94½	+⅜
ClrkOil 9½04	9.1	10	104⅜	+⅜
ClevEl 8¾05	8.6	52	101⅝	−⅜
ClevEl 8⅜11	8.2	23	101⅞	...
Coeur 6⅜04	cv	90	95¼	−¾
CmwE 7⅝03F	7.6	9	100⅛	...
CompUSA 9½00	9.2	57	103⅝	−¼
CompMgt 8s03	cv	10	125	+1
Consec 8⅛03	7.5	5	108	+2⅞
ConNG 7¼15	cv	6	114	+1
ConPort 10s06	9.9	20	100¾	−¼
CntlHm 10s06	9.4	10	106⅞	+¾
Convrse 7s04	cv	68	87¼	...
Datpnt 8⅞06f	cv	34	80	...
Dole 7⅞13	7.4	10	105⅞	+1⅞
Dow 6.85s13	6.9	4	99	+1⅝
duPnt dc6s01	6.0	31	99⅞	+⅜
DukeEn 7s00	6.9	2	101½	−1¼
DukeEn 6⅞23	7.2	5	96⅛	−⅞
DukeEn 7⅞24	7.7	8	102	−1½
Eatn dc7s11	7.1	1	98	−1⅜
EthAln 8¾01	8.6	22	102	+⅜
FairCp 13⅛06	12.8	126	102⅜	−⅜
FairCp 13s07	12.6	13	103⅛	−⅞
FedDS 8⅛02	7.7	15	106¼	+¼
FldNtl zr09	...	152	58½	+1
Fldcst 6s12	cv	62	84¼	−¼
FstRep 8s09	8.0	20	100	+1½
FUnRE 8⅞03	8.6	30	103½	...
FordCr 6⅜08	6.5	31	98⅜	+½
GHost 11½02	11.3	30	101⅞	...
GHost 8s02	cv	27	86½	−½
GMA 9⅝00	8.9	20	108⅜	+⅛
GMA 7s00	6.9	5	101½	...
GMA 5¼01	5.7	15	96⅝	...
GMA 7s02	6.8	5	102½	−¾
GMA dc6s11	6.5	133	91¾	+⅜
GMA zr12	...	12	360⅛	+⅛
GMA zr15	...	4	306	+3
GenesisH 9¾05	9.2	50	105⅞	+¾
GrandCas 10⅛03	9.5	36	106⅞	+¾
Hallwd 7s00	7.4	20	94¼	−¼
Hallw na13½09C	...	10	100½	+½
Hlthso 9½01	9.0	43	105	−½
Hills 12½03	15.0	672	83⅛	+⅞
Hilton 5s06	cv	90	120½	+4½
Hollngr 9¼06	8.9	50	104¼	...
HomeDpt 3¼01	cv	5	122	...
ICN Ph 8½99	cv	21	221½	+1
ITT Cp 7¾25	7.9	15	98⅛	−1⅞
IllBel 7⅝06	7.5	32	101⅝	...
IntgHlt 6s03	cv	10	110	+5
IBM 6⅜97	6.4	40	99 27/32	...
IBM 6⅜00	6.3	34	100⅞	−⅛
IBM 7¼02	6.9	37	104⅜	+¾
IPap dc5⅛12	6.3	10	81⅛	...
JCPL 6⅜03	6.4	15	99⅝	+1⅛
KaufB 9⅜03	9.0	30	104	...
KentE 4½04	cv	2	99	−1
Koppers 8½04	8.4	15	101⅜	−½
LibPrp 8s01	cv	10	129¾	+¾
Loews 3⅛07	cv	50	110	+6
LgIsLt 7.3s99	7.2	10	101¼	−⅛
LgIsLt 7.05s03	7.0	10	100⅜	+¼
LgIsLt 8⅝04	8.4	10	102½	+⅛
LgIsLt 8.9s19	8.4	32	105¾	−⅛
LgIsLt 9¾21	9.5	67	102½	+⅛
LgIsLt 9s22	8.1	20	111	−⅛
LgIsLt 9⅝24	9.4	50	102¼	+¼
Lucent 6.9s01	6.7	10	102¼	...
MacNS 7⅞04	cv	15	103½	...

Bonds	Cur Yld	Vol	Close	Net Chg
OwIll 11s03	9.9	21	111⅜	+1¼
PacBell 7¼02	7.0	5	104¼	+1⅛
PacBell 7⅛26	6.9	44	103⅛	−⅜
PacBell 7½33	7.4	35	101¾	...
ParkElc 5½06	cv	91	98	...
Pathmk zr03	...	20	74½	+2
PennTr 9⅝05	14.7	386	65½	+¾
Pennzl 4¾03	3.3	2	144½	+½
PepBoys 4s99	cv	15	99	...
PepBoys zr11	...	4	52	−¾
PhilEl 7¾23	7.5	100	102⅞	...
PhilEl 7⅛23	7.2	10	99⅛	+1½
PhilEl 7¼24	7.3	28	98⅞	+1½
PhilP 8.86s22	8.2	15	107½	−1
PotEl 7s18	cv	20	102	−½
PrmHsp 9¼06	8.7	5	106	+½
PSEG 7½23	7.5	45	100¼	−¼
PSvEG 7s24	7.2	113	97½	+¾
PSEG 8s37	7.4	8	107½	+6½
Quest 10¾06	9.9	40	109	−½
RJR Nb 8s00	7.8	5	102¾	+⅝
RJR Nb 8s01	7.8	35	103	−⅜
RJR Nb 8⅝02	8.1	125	106½	+⅛
RJR Nb 7⅝03	7.5	133	101⅜	+½
RJR Nb 8¾05	8.2	110	106⅝	...
RJR Nb 8¾07	8.2	70	106¾	+½
RJR Nb 9¼13	8.4	70	109¾	+½
RJR Nb 8¾04	8.2	32	106⅞	+½
Rallys 9⅞00	10.2	36	97	+⅛
RelGrp 9s00	8.6	7	104¾	+⅛
RelGrp 9¾03	9.2	20	106	+1⅜
RiteA zr06	cv	33	90½	+2½
Rohr 7s12	cv	21	99¼	−⅛
Rowan 11⅞01	11.3	33	105⅛	+⅞
Royce 5¾04	cv	15	128	−⅛
Safwy 9.35s99	8.9	11	105¼	+⅞
Safwy 10s01	8.9	23	112½	−⅛
Safwy 9.65s04	8.4	20	115	...
SallM zr14	...	110	27 3/32	−13/32
Sears 9½99	9.0	10	105	−⅜
Sequa 9⅝99	9.4	10	102¾	−¼
SvcMer 8⅜01	8.5	12	98⅜	+1⅞
SvcMer 9s04	10.1	298	89	+½
Shoney zr04	...	30	43	+1
Showboat 9¼08	8.9	35	104	+¼
SouBell 5s97	5.0	5	99⅜	+3/32
SouBell 6s04	6.2	10	96¾	−¾
SouBell 7⅝13	7.5	50	102¼	+⅝
SoCG 7½23	7.7	5	97	+¾
SPacFd 6½06	cv	7	95¼	+1½
SwBell 7¼25	7.2	30	100¾	+¼
StdCmcl 07	cv	39	92¼	...
StdPac 10½00	10.0	20	105¼	...
StoneCn 11⅞98	11.4	10	104⅝	...
StoneCn 11s99	10.6	60	104	+¼
StoneC 9⅞01	9.6	368	102⅝	+⅜
StoneC 10¾02A	10.4	170	103⅝	+⅛
StoneC 10¾02O	10.0	30	107⅛	−⅜
StoneC 11½04	10.7	75	107⅝	−⅛
StoneCn 6¾07	cv	45	89	+¼
TVA 6¼99	6.3	50	100	...
TVA 7.45s01	7.3	57	102	...
TVA 6⅞02	6.8	25	101⅝	+1¼
TVA 6⅞02	6.7	50	102	+¾
TVA 6⅛03	6.2	163	99⅛	+½
TVA 7⅝22	7.4	71	102½	...
TVA 7¾22	7.5	51	103⅛	+⅜
TVA 8.05s24	7.9	15	101⅞	+⅜
TVA 8⅝29	7.9	44	108⅞	+½
TVA 6⅞43	7.0	106	98	+⅛
TVA 7.85s44	7.4	35	105½	+¼
Texco 9s97	9.0	4	99 15/16	...
TmeWar 7.45s98	7.4	15	100⅜	+1/16
TmeWar 7.95s00	7.7	10	103⅝	+⅜
TmeWar 7¾05	7.4	1	104⅝	−¼
TmeWE 7¼08	7.1	5	101½	+¾
TmeWar 9⅛13	7.8	162	116⅞	+¼
TmeWar zr13	...	41	48½	+½
TmeWar 9.15s23	7.7	20	118⅛	+½
TitanCp 03	cv	10	220	+30
TolEd 7½02	7.5	10	99¾	−1⅛
TolEd 8s03	7.9	15	100¾	−⅞
TucEP 8⅛01	8.1	5	100⅜	...
TucEP 7.55s02	7.5	5	100⅜	+⅜
USA Wst 4s02	cv	10	112	+1½
USX 5¾01	cv	25	98¼	−¼
Unisys 8¼00	cv	217	142	−2

Bonds	Cur Yld	Vol	Close	Net Chg
Walnoco 12s02	11.5	5	104¼	+¼
Webb 9¾03	9.5	976	102¼	+¼
Webb 9s06	8.9	61	101¼	−½
Webb 9¾08	9.5	140	102½	+⅜
Weirton 10¾05	10.1	20	106⅝	+1¼
WstbrgC 11s02	10.9	36	100¾	+¼
WhlPit 9⅜03	9.0	126	103¾	+⅜
Wrldcp 7s04	cv	4	63	−¼
Zenith 6¼11	cv	48	77½	−¼

FOREIGN BONDS
Volume, $486,000

Bonds	Cur Yld	Vol	Close	Net Chg
Inco 7¾16	7.4	8	104¼	+¼
Rhone 6¾99	6.8	75	100	...
SeaCnt 12½04A	10.8	105	115¼	+1⅛
SeaCnt 9½03	9.0	152	105½	+⅝
EmplCA 5s04	...	10	84	+¼
TelArg 11⅞04	9.7	20	122	...
Ivaco 11½05	10.6	25	108½	−1½
SeaCnt 10½03	9.5	53	110	−¼
TrnMarMx 06	...	15	104¾	−¼

AMEX BONDS

Volume $870,000

SALES SINCE JANUARY 1

1997	1996	1995
$293,490,000	$383,304,000	$568,540,000

WHAT AMEX BONDS DID

	Mon.	Fri.	Thu.	Wed.
Issues traded	23	18	17	22
Advances	11	11	7	8
Declines	5	5	4	7
Unchanged	7	2	6	7
New highs	3	3	3	1
New lows	0	0	0	0

Bonds	Cur Yld	Vol	Close	Net Chg
AdvMd 7¼02	cv	7	92	+¾
AHaagn 7½01	cv	80	100½	−½
ArchCm 10⅞08f	...	75	67	−1⅛
ChckFul 8s06	cv	16	110	+1
DRS T 8½98	cv	5	102½	...
DrPep11½02f	...	8	104¼	+¼
GTE Sou 7½02	7.5	5	100½	...
Greyhnd 8½07	cv	100	99½	+½
Griffin 00f	...	4	99⅝	+⅛
JTS 5¼02	cv	105	37½	...
KelleyOG 8½00	cv	5	99	...
MercAir 7¾06	cv	35	107½	−4
MovStar 12⅞01f	...	41	84	+¼
SwBell 7⅜12	7.3	36	101	+¾
SwBell 7⅝13	7.5	30	101¾	+½
TmeWar zr12	...	1	39⅛	−⅛
TWA 12s98	11.7	56	102⅜	+⅜
Trump 11¾03f	...	120	98⅝	+¼
Trump 13⅞05f	...	12	98½	...
US Cell zr15	...	27	38½	...
Viacm 9⅛99	8.9	3	102½	...
Viacom 8s06	8.0	59	100	+½

NASDAQ

Convertible Debentures

Monday, October 6, 1997

Issue	Vol.	Close	Net Chg.
Agnico 3½04	21	84½	...
BankAtl 06	10	190	...
BellSpt 4¼00	37	88	+¼
BostChck 4½04	200	75½	−¼
BostChk zr15	700	21⅝	...
BostChck 7¾04	700	91	−¼

Figure 13.13 Price Quotations for Corporate Bonds (Excerpts)

Source: Reprinted by permission of *The Wall Street Journal*, Dow Jones & Company, Inc., October 7, 1997, p. C20. All rights reserved worldwide.

major trades of bonds are generally negotiated elsewhere by dealers and institutional investors, either directly or through brokers. Thus, reported prices on the NYSE may be poor guides to values associated with large transactions (the same can be said for quotes that are publicly supplied by bond dealers) but appear to be reasonable for small transactions.

A second bond market, run by the Nasdaq Stock Market, is known as the **Fixed Income Pricing System** (FIPS). Unlike ABS, this market is devoted to trading high-yield bonds, which are defined as bonds that are less than investment grade (bond grades are discussed in more detail in Chapter 15), meaning they are speculative and have a reasonable chance of default. All members of the National Association of Security Dealers (NASD) that hold themselves out to be dealers or brokers in high-yield bonds are required to use FIPS. However, because FIPS lists only liquid high-yield debt, brokers and dealers in less liquid issues are not required to use FIPS. Quotes are entered on FIPS by dealers and must be at least one-sided (that is, either a bid or asked quote must be given). Subsequent trades are made by contacting a dealer, typically by telephone, and depending on the bond, may have to be reported within five minutes of execution. Trade report summaries are disseminated by Nasdaq and other market data vendors on an hourly basis for the fifty most liquid issues and on a daily basis for all the others.

13.7 FOREIGN BONDS

The foreign bond market refers to bonds issued and denominated in the currency of a country other than the one in which the issuer is primarily located. For example, Inco has issued bonds that are denominated in U.S. dollars, mature in 2016, and carry a $7\text{-}\frac{3}{4}\%$ coupon rate. Although some foreign bonds (such as Inco's) appear daily at the end of the "New York Exchange Bonds" quotations section in *The Wall Street Journal*, as shown in Figure 13.13, the amount of trading is often so small that all that is reported is the total volume. Foreign bonds that are issued in the United States and are denominated in U.S. dollars are referred to as Yankee bonds, and foreign (that is, non-Japanese) bonds that are issued in Japan are referred to as Samurai bonds.

In issuing foreign bonds, the issuer must abide by the rules and regulations imposed by the government of the country in which the bonds are issued. Compliance may be relatively easy or difficult, depending on the country involved.

One of the main advantages of purchasing foreign bonds is the opportunity to obtain international diversification of the default risk of a bond portfolio while not having to be concerned about foreign exchange fluctuations. For example, a U.S. investor might be able to buy a Toyota bond in Japan that is denominated in yen, but in doing so would have to worry about the yen-dollar exchange rate. The reason is that the coupon payments and ultimately the principal would be paid to the investor in yen, which would then have to be converted into dollars at a currently unknown exchange rate. However, the investor could avoid such worries by purchasing a Toyota bond that is denominated in U.S. dollars.

13.8 EUROBONDS

Owing in part to government restrictions on investment in foreign securities, some borrowers have found it advantageous to sell securities in other countries. The term **Eurobond** is loosely applied to bonds that are offered outside the country of the borrower and outside the country in whose currency the securities are denominated.[20]

Thus a bond issued by a U.S. corporation that is denominated in Japanese yen (or U.S. dollars) and sold in Europe would be referred to as a Eurobond.

As the Eurobond market is neither regulated nor taxed, it offers substantial advantages for many issuers and buyers of bonds. For example, a foreign subsidiary of a U.S. corporation may issue a Eurobond in "bearer" form. No tax will be withheld by the corporation, and the tax (if any) paid by the purchaser will depend on his or her country of residence. For tax reasons, interest rates on Eurobonds tend to be somewhat lower than those on domestic bonds denominated in the same currency.

13.9   PREFERRED STOCK

In some respects, **preferred stock** is like a perpetual bond. A given dollar amount is to be paid each year by the issuer to the investor. This amount may be stated as a percent of the stock's par value (for example, 8% of $100, meaning $8 per year) or directly as a dollar figure (for example, $2.75 per year). Because the security is a "stock," such payments are called dividends instead of interest and hence do not qualify as a tax-deductible expense for the issuing corporation. Furthermore, failure to make such payments does not constitute grounds for bankruptcy proceedings.

A recent innovation is adjustable rate preferred stock (ARPS), where the dividend is reset periodically in terms of an applicable rate. For example, the annualized "percent of par" for the dividend might be reset every three months to be equal to the largest of the rates on (1) three-month Treasury bills, (2) ten-year Treasury bonds, and (3) 20-year Treasury bonds. Related to ARPS are Dutch auction rate preferred stocks (DARPS), where the dividend is reset periodically (more often than for ARPS) at a level determined by bidding from current and potential owners.[21] Preferred stock generally receives preferential treatment when it comes to dividends. Specified payments must be made on the preferred stock before any dividends may be paid to holders of the firm's common stock. Failure to pay a preferred dividend in full does not constitute default, but unpaid dividends are usually **cumulative**. That is, all previously unpaid preferred stock dividends must be paid (but seldom with interest) before any dividends may be paid on the common stock.

No indenture is provided with a preferred stock issue. However, various provisions protecting the preferred stockholders against potentially harmful actions may be written into the corporation's charter. For example, one provision may limit the dollar amount of senior securities that can be issued in the future. Although preferred stockholders typically do not have voting rights, there may be another provision that gives them voting rights when the corporation is in arrears on its preferred dividends.

Many issues of preferred stock are callable at a stated redemption price. *Participating preferred stock* entitles the holder to receive extra dividends when earnings permit. *Convertible preferred stock* may, at the option of the holder, be converted into another security (usually the firm's common stock) on stated terms. Some firms issue more than one class of preferred stock, with preference accorded the various classes in a specified order.

In the event of a dissolution of the firm, preferred stock often receives preferential treatment as to assets. Preferred stockholders are generally entitled to receive the stock's par value before any payment is made to common stockholders.

As indicated in Chapter 12, interest income from bonds held by a corporate investor is subject to the corporate income tax, but 80% of any dividend income received is exempt from taxation.[22] For a corporate investor this exemption makes the effective tax rate on dividends from preferred stock approximately 7% (=.35 × .20), compared with 35% for interest received on bonds. For this reason, preferred stocks tend to sell at prices that give lower before-tax returns than long-term bonds, even though bonds may be considerably lower in risk. As a result, preferred stocks are generally unattractive holdings for noncorporate investors, such as individuals and tax-exempt investors.

Because preferred stock has many features of a bond, but is without the substantial tax advantage that bonds give to the issuer, it is used less often than debt. In 1996, $33.2 billion of preferred stock was issued, compared with more than $500 billion of publicly offered domestic corporate debt.[23] A recent innovation that blurs the distinction between debt and preferred stock involves the use of *trust preferred stock*. From the issuer's perspective, the distinguishing feature of this security is that it is structured so that its dividend payments are treated as tax-deductible interest by the issuer. From the corporate investor's perspective, trust preferred stock is treated as traditional preferred stock with one exception: All of a trust preferred's dividends are taxable income, whereas, as previously mentioned, up to 80% of a traditional preferred's dividends are exempt from taxes.[24]

Just how such securities are structured is quite clever, as the following example shows. Big Widget, Inc. sets up a wholly owned subsidiary, Little Widget, Inc., who issues 10 shares of trust preferred stock, carrying an 8% dividend yield, to the public for $100 per share. The $1,000 in proceeds received by Little Widget is passed on to Big Widget in exchange for an 8% $1,000 bond. After one year, Big Widget makes a tax-deductible interest payment of $80 {thus costing Big Widget only $52 [=$80 × (1 − .35)] after-taxes} to Little Widget, who, in turn, pays $8 to each of the 10 trust preferred stockholders. Note that Little Widget receives $80 and pays out $80. Because Little Widget is organized as a limited liability corporation, it pays no taxes on the $80 received from Big Widget.[25]

Many preferred stocks are traded on major exchanges in a manner similar to common stocks. Typically, they are assigned to the same specialist that is responsible for the firm's common stock. Trading prices are reported in the financial press in the same format used for common stocks.

13.10   SUMMARY

1. The most familiar types of fixed-income securities are personal savings deposits. These include demand deposits, time deposits, and certificates of deposit issued by commercial banks, savings and loan companies, mutual savings banks, and credit unions.

2. Highly marketable, short-term securities are referred to as money market instruments. These securities include commercial paper, large-denomination certificates of deposit, bankers' acceptances, repurchase agreements, and Eurodollar CDs.

3. The U.S. Treasury issues debt securities to finance the government's borrowing needs. These securities are issued in various maturities—short-term (Treasury bills), intermediate-term (Treasury notes), and long-term (Treasury bonds). The Treasury also issues Savings Bonds to individual investors.

4. Treasury notes or bonds can be converted into a set of pure-discount bonds by issuing marketable receipts entitling the holder to a specific coupon payment or the bond's principal payment. Separating a bond into its component payments is known as coupon stripping.

5. Federal agencies also issue securities to finance their operations. In some cases this debt is explicitly backed by the U.S. Treasury. In other cases the government guarantee is implicit.

---

6. Participation certificates (pass-throughs) represent ownership of a pool of mortgages. The holders receive cash flows from the pool's mortgages in proportion to their ownership in the pool.

7. Collateralized mortgages obligations (CMOs) are classes of securities that have different claims on the payments received from a pool of mortgages.

8. State and local governments issue a wide variety of fixed-income securities. These securities may be backed solely by the full faith and credit of the issuer or by a specific revenue source.

9. Because municipal securities are generally exempt from federal taxation, they usually offer lower yields than taxable securities.

10. Corporate bonds, such as mortgage bonds or equipment obligations, may be backed by specific assets. Alternatively, corporate bonds, such as debentures, may represent general obligations of the issuing corporations.

11. Corporate bonds (and some federal government and municipal bonds) may contain call provisions, giving the issuer the right to redeem the security before maturity under specified terms.

12. Corporations entering bankruptcy may undergo liquidation or reorganization or enter into arrangements.

13. Preferred stock dividends are generally fixed but do not represent legal obligations of the issuers. Most preferred stock dividends are cumulative, requiring payment of all unpaid preferred dividends before common stock dividends can be paid.

QUESTIONS AND PROBLEMS

1. What is the annual equivalent yield on a 13-week Treasury bill selling at a price of 96?

2. Consider a 13-week Treasury bill, issued today, which is selling for $9,675. (Its face value is $10,000.)
   a. What is the annual discount based on the selling price of the security?
   b. What is the annual equivalent yield of the security?

3. If a three-month Treasury bill sells for a price of 98, whereas a six-month Treasury bill sells for 96, is the equivalent yield (unannualized) for the six-month bill twice that of the three-month bill? Why?

4. Rank the various money market instruments discussed in the text in terms of default risk. Explain the reasoning behind your rankings. Find the latest interest rates for these securities. Do they correspond with your default-risk rankings?

5. The U.S. Treasury once issued notes and bonds only in bearer form. Now its notes and bonds are issued only in registered form. Given the characteristics of bearer and registered bonds, speculate as to what reasons might have prompted the Treasury to change the form of issuance.

6. Using *The Wall Street Journal* as a data source, identify a particular Treasury note or bond. What is its coupon rate? What is its maturity date? What is the latest bid-ask spread for the security? What is the security's yield-to-maturity?

7. Describe the standard practice by which sellers of government and corporate bonds are compensated for accrued interest.

8. What is the rationale for including a call provision in the indenture of a bond issue? How do bond investors typically respond to the inclusion of a call provision?

9. How do zero-coupon fixed-income securities provide returns to investors?

---

10. Consider a ten-year zero-coupon Treasury security selling for a price of $300, with a face value of $1,000. What is the before-tax annual rate of return to an investor who buys and holds this security to maturity?

11. Why does the IRS treat the difference between the price of a bond purchased at a discount and its face value as ordinary income to the investor, as opposed to treating it as a capital gain?

12. Bonds issued by federal agencies carry an explicit or implicit promise that the federal government will ensure payment of interest and principal. Why then are these securities usually priced by the market to offer yields above Treasury securities?

13. What is a mortgage participation certificate? What is the primary risk that such securities present to investors?

14. Cozy Dolan, an amateur investor, said, "I prefer investing in GNMA pass-through securities. Their government guarantee gives me a riskfree return." Comment on Cozy's remark.

15. Distinguish between a general obligation municipal bond and a revenue bond.

16. Pigeon Falls Airlines was in difficult financial shape owing to ongoing recession and labor problems. To this point the firm had issued no debt, but management believed that borrowing in the bond market was the only way to get through the tough times. Because of its poor financial condition, Pigeon Falls's investment bankers advised management that a debenture issue would not be well received. What other bond issuance options might Pigeon Falls pursue?

17. Is any mortgage bond necessarily a more secure investment than any debenture? Explain.

18. A callable bond is sometimes described as a combination of a noncallable bond and an option. Explain why this description is appropriate. Further, explain how these two features affect the price of a callable bond.

19. Muddy Ruel is considering purchasing one of two bonds: a corporate bond with a 9% coupon interest rate, selling at par, or a tax-free municipal bond with a 6% coupon interest rate, likewise selling at par. Given that Muddy is in the 30% tax bracket, and assuming that all other relevant factors are the same between the two bonds, which bond should Muddy select?

20. Is it true that most corporations that default on their debt eventually enter bankruptcy and see their assets liquidated to repay creditors? Explain.

21. Eurobonds have become very popular forms of financing in recent years. What features of the Eurobond market make Eurobonds attractive to issuers and bondholders?

22. In trying to explain the concept of preferred stock to a novice investor, Patsy Donovan referred to it as a "hybrid" security. What did Patsy mean by this term?

23. What is the purpose of the cumulative restriction of most preferred stock?

24. The preferred stock of Clinton Foods carries a dividend of $8 per share. The stock currently sells for $50. If one year from today the Clinton preferred stock's price remains unchanged, what is the return from holding the stock for:
    a. A corporation in the 35% tax bracket?
    b. An individual in the 35% tax bracket?

CFA EXAM QUESTION

25. A portfolio manager at Superior Trust Company is structuring a fixed-income portfolio to meet the objectives of a client. The client plans on retiring in 15 years and wants a substantial lump sum at that time. The client has specified the use of AAA-rated securities.

The portfolio manager compares U.S. Treasuries with zero-coupon stripped U.S. Treasuries and observes a significant yield advantage for the stripped bonds.

Maturity	Coupon U.S. Treasuries	Zero-Coupon Stripped U.S. Treasuries
3-year	5.50%	5.80%
5-year	6.00	6.60
7-year	6.75	7.25
10-year	7.25	7.60
15-year	7.40	8.80
30-year	7.75	7.75

Briefly discuss two reasons why zero-coupon stripped U.S. Treasuries could yield more than coupon U.S. Treasuries with the same final maturity.

ENDNOTES

[1] One recent innovation is the issuance of "equity-linked CDs," which provide the investor with a return based on the performance of a given market index, coupled with a guarantee that the investor will not experience a loss (some even guarantee the investor some minimal interest rate if the market index performs poorly). See Michael D. Joehnk, "Short-Term Investing: Socking It Away in CDs," *AAII Journal* 12, no. 8 (September 1990): 7–9. See also Jeffrey Cohn and Michael E. Edieson, "Banking on the Market: Equity-Linked CDs," *AAII Journal* 15, no. 3 (March 1993): 11–15.

[2] Many insurance companies sell large-denomination *guaranteed investment contracts* (GICs) that are similar to CDs in that they typically pay a stated interest rate for a given number of years. Other types of financial institutions offer contracts similar to GICs. See Robert T. Kleiman and Anandi P. Sahu, "The ABCs of GICs for Retirement Plan Investing," *AAII Journal* 14, no. 3 (March 1992): 7–10.

[3] Short-term obligations of the U.S. government and its agencies are also considered money market instruments; they will be described in the next section.

[4] For more on trading Treasuries, see Jay Goldinger, "Trading Treasuries: Know the Risks before You Invest," *AAII Journal* 11, no. 10 (November 1989): 12–15.

[5] This approach to calculating equivalent yields for Treasury bills is applicable only if the maturity is six months or less; a more complicated approach is necessary for T-bills with longer lives. See Richard J. Kish, "Discrepancy in Treasury Bill Yield Calculations," *Financial Practice and Education* 2, no. 1 (Spring/Summer 1992): 41–45.

[6] As discussed in Chapter 5, the yield-to-maturity on a bond is the discount rate that makes the present value of the future coupon payments and par value equal to its current market price (which in this case is the asked price). Chapter 14 will discuss yields more thoroughly.

[7] The procedure for calculating accrued interest on corporate bonds is different in that it is based on an assumption that there are 30 days in each month and 180 days in each semiannual period. Specifically, (1) the number of complete months left until the next coupon payment is determined and multiplied by 30; (2) the number of days left in the current month is determined and added to the previous figure; (3) the resulting figure is subtracted from 180, thereby giving the number of days that have elapsed since the last coupon payment; (4) this figure is divided by 180, giving the fraction of the period that has elapsed; and (5) this fraction is multiplied by the semiannual coupon, resulting in the amount of accrued interest. See "Dividends and Interest: Who Gets Payments after a Trade?" *AAII Journal* 12, no. 4 (April 1990): 8–11.

[8] If the bonds are used to pay for certain educational expenses the interest may be completely tax-free. For more on savings bonds, see Paul F. Jessup, "The Purloined Investment: EE Savings Bonds Make Sense," *AAII Journal* 12, no. 8 (September 1990): 10–13; and Phillip R.

Daves and Robert A. Kunkel, "After the Fall: Savings Bonds Are Still Attractive Short Term," *AAII Journal* 15, no. 4 (April 1993): 11–12.

[9] If the underlying Treasury security is callable, this set of receipts will provide the holders with all coupon payments received after the date of first call as well as the principal.

[10] OID securities can have either no coupons (in which case they are pure-discount securities) or small coupons. The key distinguishing feature of an OID security is that, at issuance, it was sold for a significant discount from par value. *De minimus rules* indicate that, for tax purposes, small discounts can be ignored until the security is sold or matures.

[11] Determining an appropriate price for a pass-through security is quite complicated. For an analysis, see Richard J. Kish and James Greenleaf, "Teaching How Mortgage Pass-Through Securities Are Priced," *Financial Practice and Education* 3, no. 1 (Spring/Summer 1993): 85–94.

[12] This census is conducted every five years. The data reported here are from the *1996 Statistical Abstract of the United States* (Washington, DC: GPO, 1997), Table 468, p. 295.

[13] In some cases no capital expenditure is involved. (For example, the proceeds from the debt issue may be used to refund an outstanding debt issue.)

[14] *Federal Reserve Bulletin*, September 1997, p. A31.

[15] As noted in Chapter 12 (see Figure 12.4 and the related discussion), the yields on municipal bonds have historically been 20% to 40% below the yields on similar taxable bonds.

[16] However, municipal bonds that are unregistered with respect to ownership cannot be issued (this prohibition began July 1, 1983). See Hildy Richelson, "Municipal Bonds: A Guide to the Various Forms of Ownership," *AAII Journal* 13, no. 4 (April 1991): 13–16.

[17] This practice assumes that the bond was purchased on or after May 1, 1993. For more on the taxation of bonds, see Chapter 12 or Clark Blackman II and Donald Laubacher, "The Basics of Bond Discounts and Premiums," *AAII Journal* 15, no. 3 (March 1993): 24–27; or IRS Publications 550 and 1212. The taxation of securities in general and bonds in particular is a complex matter, with many exceptions and alternative procedures. Any investor would be well advised to check carefully beforehand to be certain of the method of taxation involved for any security being considered for purchase.

[18] It has been reported that 1996 was the first year that putable bond volume exceeded call bond volume. See Leland E. Crabbe and Panos Nikoulis, "The Putable Bond Market: Structure, Historical Experience, and Strategies," *Journal of Fixed Income* 7, no. 3 (December 1997): 47–60.

[19] *New York Stock Exchange Fact Book 1996 Data*, (New York Stock Exchange, 1997), p. 84.

[20] There are also fixed-income securities of this nature that have shorter lives; they are sometimes referred to as Euronotes or Euro-commercial paper. The market where they (and Eurobonds) are issued and traded is known as the Eurocredit market.

[21] For a discussion of ARPS and DARPS, see Michael J. Alderson, Keith C. Brown, and Scott L. Lummer, "Dutch Auction Rate Preferred Stock," *Financial Management* 16, no. 2 (Summer 1987), 68–73. See also Michael J. Alderson and Donald R. Fraser, "Financial Innovations and Excesses Revisited: The Case of Auction Rate Preferred Stock," *Financial Management* 22, no. 2 (Summer 1993): 61–75.

[22] This proportion is based on the assumption that the corporate investor owns between 20% and 80% of the firm's common stock. If less than 20% is owned, only 70% of the dividend is exempt from taxation, whereas if more than 80% is owned, then all of the dividend is exempt.

[23] *Federal Reserve Bulletin*, September 1997, p. A31.

[24] It has been reported that trust preferred stocks have recently "largely replaced traditional preferred stock as a source of capital"; see Ellen Engel, Merle Erickson, and Edward Maydew, "Debt-Equity Hybrid Securities," unpublished paper, University of Chicago, Graduate School of Business, August 1997, p. 2.

[25] Trust preferred stock is only one example of many financial innovations that have been created in recent years to avoid taxes. These securities may satisfy the legal letter of the law, but critics view them as devious attempts to thwart the intent of the tax code.

pure-discount security
coupon payments
maturity date
principal
demand deposits
time deposits
certificates of deposit
bank discount basis
commercial paper
bankers' acceptance
Eurodollar CDs
Eurodollar deposits
repurchase agreement
repo rate
debt refunding
term-to-maturity
on-the-run issues
dealer's spread
equivalent yield
accrued interest
call provisions
original issue discount securities
federally sponsored agencies
participation certificates
collateralized mortgage obligations
municipal bonds
general obligation bonds
revenue bonds

industrial development bonds
market discount bonds
taxable municipals
serial bonds
term bonds
sinking fund
indenture
trustee
mortgage bonds
collateral trust bonds
equipment obligations
debentures
subordinated debentures
income bonds
guaranteed bonds
participating bonds
voting bonds
convertible bonds
putable bonds
call premium
call price
private placements
Automated Bond System
current yield
Eurobond
preferred stock
cumulative dividends

REFERENCES

1. A concise summary description of the various types of money market instruments is contained in:

Timothy Q. Cook and Timothy D. Rowe, *Instruments of the Money Market* (Federal Reserve Bank of Richmond, 1993).

Gunter Dufey and Ian Giddy, *The International Money Market* (Englewood Cliffs, NJ: Prentice Hall, 1994).

2. The following contain thorough descriptions of the various types of fixed-income securities discussed in this chapter:

Suresh Sundaresan, *Fixed Income Markets and Their Derivatives* (Cincinnati: South-Western College Publishing, 1997), Chapters 1, 2, 8–10.

Frank J. Fabozzi, Franco Modigliani, and Michael G. Ferri, *Foundations of Financial Markets and Institutions* (Upper Saddle River, NJ: Prentice Hall, 1998), Chapters 16, 17, 20–25.

3. For a discussion of coupon stripping, see:

Miles Livingston and Deborah Wright Gregory, *The Stripping of U.S. Treasury Securities*, Monograph Series in Finance and Economics 1989-1 (New York University Salomon Center, Leonard N. Stern School of Business).

Deborah W. Gregory and Miles Livingston, "Development of the Market for U.S. Treasury STRIPS," *Financial Analysts Journal* 48, no. 2 (March/April 1992): 68–74.

Phillip R. Daves, Michael C. Ehrhardt, and John M. Wachowicz Jr., "A Guide to Investing in U.S. Treasury STRIPS," *AAII Journal* 15, no. 1 (January 1993): 6–10.

Phillip R. Daves and Michael C. Ehrhardt, "Liquidity, Reconstitution, and the Value of U.S. Treasury STRIPS," *Journal of Finance* 47, no. 1 (March 1993): 315–329.

4. For a discussion of the market for securities issued by the U.S. Treasury, see:

Peter Wann, *Inside the US Treasury Market* (New York: Quorum Books, 1989).

Saikat Nandi, "Treasury Auctions: What Do the Recent Models Tell Us?" *Federal Reserve Bank of Atlanta Economic Review* 82, no. 4 (Fourth Quarter 1997): 4–15.

5. A Web site for the U.S. Treasury that contains links to sites for information on Treasury securities, including U.S. Savings Bonds is:

⟨www.publicdebt.treas.gov⟩.

6. For a discussion of mortgage-backed securities, see:

Earl Baldwin and Saundra Stotts, *Mortgage-Backed Securities: A Reference Guide for Lenders and Issuers* (Chicago: Probus Publishing, 1990).

Sean Becketti and Charles S. Morris, *The Prepayment Experience of FNMA Mortgage-Backed Securities*, Monograph Series in Finance and Economics 1990-3 (New York University Salomon Center, Leonard N. Stern School of Business, 1990).

Eduardo S. Schwartz and Walter N. Torous, "Prepayment, Default, and the Valuation of Mortgage Pass-Through Securities," *Journal of Business* 65, no. 2 (April 1992): 221–239.

Andrew Carron, "Understanding CMOs, REMICs, and Other Mortgage Derivatives," *Journal of Fixed Income* 2, no. 1 (June 1992): 25–43.

Albert J. Golly Jr., "An Individual Investor's Guide to the Complex World of CMOs," *AAII Journal* 14, no. 6 (July 1992): 7–10.

Frank J. Fabozzi and Franco Modigliani, *Mortgage and Mortgage-Backed Securities Markets* (Boston: Harvard Business School Press, 1992).

Michael D. Joehnk and Matthew J. Hassett, "Getting a Grip on the Risks of CMO Prepayments," *AAII Journal* 15, no. 5 (June 1993): 8–12.

Frank J. Fabozzi, Charles Ramsey, and Frank R. Ramirez, *Collateralized Mortgage Obligations: Structure and Analysis* (Summit, NJ: Frank J. Fabozzi Associates, 1993).

7. For a discussion of municipal bonds, see:

Peter Fortune, "The Municipal Bond Market, Part I: Politics, Taxes, and Yields," *Federal Reserve Bank of Boston New England Economic Review*, (September/October 1991): 13–36.

Peter Fortune, "The Municipal Bond Market, Part II: Problems and Policies," *Federal Reserve Bank of Boston New England Economic Review* (May/June 1992): 47–64.

8. For a discussion of the foreign bond and Eurobond markets, see:

J. Orlin Grabbe, *International Financial Markets* (New York: Elsevier Science Publishing, 1996), Chapter 12.

Bruno Solnik, *International Investments* (Reading, MA: Addison-Wesley, 1991), Chapters 6, 7.

9. For a discussion of the Eurocredit market, see:

Arie L. Melnik and Steven E. Plaut, *The Short-Term Eurocredit Market*, Monograph Series in Finance and Economics 1991-1 (New York University Salomon Center, Leonard N. Stern School of Business, 1991).

10. For a discussion of how government bond markets function in the United Kingdom, Japan, and Germany, see:

Thomas J. Urich, *U.K., German and Japanese Government Bond Markets*, Monograph Series in Finance and Economics 1991-2 (New York University Salomon Center, Leonard N. Stern School of Business, 1991).

11. The accuracy of reported prices for corporate bonds is analyzed in:

Kenneth P. Nunn Jr., Joanne Hill, and Thomas Schneeweis, "Corporate Bond Price Data Sources and Risk/Return Measurement," *Journal of Financial and Quantitative Analysis* 21, no. 2 (June 1986): 197–208.

Oded Sarig and Arthur Warga, "Bond Price Data and Bond Market Liquidity," *Journal of Financial and Quantitative Analysis* 24, no. 3 (September 1989): 367–378.

Arthur D. Warga, "Corporate Bond Price Discrepancies in the Dealer and Exchange Markets," *Journal of Fixed Income* 1, no. 3 (December 1991): 7–16.

12. The market for preferred stock is discussed in:

Arthur L. Houston Jr., and Carol Olson Houston, "Financing with Preferred Stock," *Financial Management* 19, no. 3 (Autumn 1990): 42–54.

13. An extensive discussion of the private placement market for corporate debt is contained in:

Mark Carey, Stephen Prowse, John Rea, and Gregory Udell, "The Economics of Private Placements: A New Look," *Financial Markets, Institutions & Instruments* 2, no. 3 (1993).

Cynthia J. Campbell, "Private Security Placements and Resales to the Public Under SEC Rule 144," *Corporate Finance Review* (July/August, 1997): 11–16.

BOND ANALYSIS

Consider an investor who believes that there are situations in which public information can be used to identify mispriced bonds. To translate that belief into action about which bonds to buy and sell, the investor needs an analytical procedure. One procedure involves comparing a bond's yield-to-maturity with a yield-to-maturity that the investor feels is appropriate, based on the characteristics of the bond as well as on current market conditions. If the yield-to-maturity is higher than the appropriate yield-to-maturity, then the bond is said to be underpriced (or undervalued), and it is a candidate for buying. Conversely, if the yield-to-maturity is lower than the appropriate one, then the bond is said to be overpriced (or overvalued), and it is a candidate for selling (or even short selling).

Alternatively, the investor could estimate the bond's "true" or "intrinsic" value and compare it with the bond's current market price. Specifically, if the current market price is less than the bond's intrinsic value, then the bond is underpriced, and if it is greater, then the bond is overpriced. Both procedures for analyzing bonds are based on the capitalization of income method of valuation.[1] The first procedure involving yields is analogous to the internal rate of return (IRR) method that is discussed in most introductory finance textbooks, whereas the second procedure involving intrinsic value is analogous to the net present value (NPV) method, which also appears in such books. The focus in those books is on making an investment decision involving some type of real asset (such as whether to purchase a new piece of machinery); the focus here is on making an investment decision involving a particular type of financial asset—bonds.[2]

14.1 APPLYING THE CAPITALIZATION OF INCOME METHOD TO BONDS

The **capitalization of income method of valuation** states that the intrinsic value of any asset is based on the discounted value of the cash flows that the investor expects to receive in the future from owning the asset. As mentioned earlier, one way that this method has been applied to bond valuation is to compare the bond's yield-to-maturity y with the appropriate yield-to-maturity y^*. Specifically, if $y > y^*$, then the bond is underpriced, and if $y < y^*$, then the bond is overpriced. If $y = y^*$, then the bond is said to be fairly priced.

14.1.1 Promised Yield-to-Maturity

Letting P denote the current market price of a bond with a remaining life of n years, and promising cash flows to the investor of C_1 in year 1, C_2 in year 2, and so on, the yield-to-maturity (more specifically, the **promised yield-to-maturity**) of the bond is the value of y that solves the following equation:

$$P = \frac{C_1}{(1+y)^1} + \frac{C_2}{(1+y)^2} + \frac{C_3}{(1+y)^3} + \cdots + \frac{C_n}{(1+y)^n}$$

With summation notation, this equation can be rewritten as:

$$P = \sum_{t=1}^{n} \frac{C_t}{(1+y)^t} \tag{14.1}$$

For example, consider a bond that is currently selling for $900 and has a remaining life of three years. For ease of exposition, assume that it makes annual coupon payments amounting to $60 per year and has a par value of $1,000; that is, $C_1 = \$60$, $C_2 = \$60$, and $C_3 = \$1,060\ (=\$1,000 + \$60)$. Using Equation (14.1), the yield-to-maturity on this bond is the value of y that solves the following equation:

$$P = \frac{\$60}{(1+y)^1} + \frac{\$60}{(1+y)^2} + \frac{\$1,060}{(1+y)^3}$$

which is $y = 10.02\%$. If subsequent analysis indicates that the yield-to-maturity should be 9.00%, then this bond is underpriced because $y = 10.02\% > y^* = 9.00\%$.

14.1.2 Intrinsic Value

Alternatively, the intrinsic value of a bond can be calculated using the following formula:

$$V = \frac{C_1}{(1+y^*)^1} + \frac{C_2}{(1+y^*)^2} + \frac{C_3}{(1+y^*)^3} + \cdots + \frac{C_n}{(1+y^*)^n}$$

or, using summation notation,

$$V = \sum_{t=1}^{n} \frac{C_t}{(1+y^*)^t} \tag{14.2}$$

After V has been estimated, it should be compared with the bond's market price P in order to see if $V > P$, in which case the bond is underpriced, or if $V < P$, in which case the bond is overpriced.

Alternatively, the **net present value** (NPV) of the bond can be calculated as the difference between the value of the bond and the purchase price:

$$NPV = V - P = \sum_{t=1}^{n} \frac{C_t}{(1+y^*)^t} - P \tag{14.3}$$

The NPV of the bond in the previous example is the solution to the following equation:

$$NPV = \frac{\$60}{(1+.09)^1} + \frac{\$60}{(1+.09)^2} + \frac{\$1,060}{(1+.09)^3} - \$900$$

$$= \$24.06$$

Because this bond has a positive NPV, it is underpriced. This will always be the case when a bond has a yield-to-maturity that is higher than the appropriate one. (Earlier it was shown that this bond's yield-to-maturity was 10.02%, which is more than 9.00%, the appropriate yield-to-maturity.) That is, in general, any bond with $y > y*$ will always have a positive NPV and vice versa, so that under either method it would be underpriced.[3]

Alternatively, if the investor had determined that $y*$ was equal to 11.00%, then the bond's NPV would have been $-\$22.19$. This value would suggest that the bond was overpriced, just as would have been noted when the yield-to-maturity of 10.02% was compared with 11.00%. This outcome will always be the case: A bond with $y < y*$ will always have a negative NPV and vice versa, so that under either method it would be found to be overpriced.

If the investor had determined that $y*$ had a value of approximately the same magnitude as the bond's yield-to-maturity of 10%, then the NPV of the bond would be approximately zero. In such a situation the bond would be viewed as being fairly priced.

Note that in order for the capitalization of income method of valuation to be used, the values of C_t, P, and $y*$ must be determined. It is generally quite easy to determine the values for C_t and P because they are the bond's promised cash flows and current market price, respectively. However, determining the value of $y*$ is difficult because it will depend on the investor's subjective evaluation of certain characteristics of the bond and current market conditions. Given that the key ingredient in bond analysis is determining the appropriate value of $y*$, the next section will discuss what attributes should be considered in making such a determination.

14.2 BOND ATTRIBUTES

Six primary attributes of a bond are of significant importance in bond valuation:

- Length of time until maturity
- Coupon rate
- Call and put provisions
- Tax status
- Marketability
- Likelihood of default

At any time the structure of market prices for bonds differing in those dimensions can be examined and described in terms of yields-to-maturity. This overall structure is sometimes referred to as the **yield structure**. Often attention is confined to differences along a single dimension, holding the other attributes constant. For example, the set of yields of bonds of different maturities constitutes the **term structure** (discussed in Chapter 5), and the set of yields of bonds of different default risk is referred to as the **risk structure.**

Most bond analysts consider the yields-to-maturity for default-free bonds to form the term structure. "Risk differentials" are then added to obtain the relevant yields-to-maturity for bonds of lower quality. Although subject to some criticism, this procedure makes it possible to think about a complicated set of relationships sequentially.

The differential between the yields of two bonds is usually called a **yield spread**. Most often it involves the bond that is under analysis and a comparable default-free bond (that is, a Treasury security of similar maturity and coupon rate). Yield spreads are sometimes measured in **basis points**, where one basis point equals .01%. If the yield-to-maturity for one bond is 11.50% and that of another is 11.90%, the yield spread is 40 basis points.

14.2.1 Coupon Rate and Length of Time Until Maturity

The coupon rate and length of time to maturity are important attributes of a bond because they determine the size and timing of the cash flows that are promised to the bondholder by the issuer. If a bond's current market price is known, these attributes can be used to determine the bond's yield-to-maturity, which will subsequently be compared with what the investor thinks it should be. More specifically, if the market for Treasury securities is viewed as being efficient, then the yield-to-maturity on a Treasury security that is similar to the bond under evaluation can form a starting point in the analysis of the bond.

Consider the previously mentioned bond that is selling for $900 and has promised cash flows over the next three years of $60, $60, and $1,060. In this case, perhaps a Treasury security with a cash flow over the next three years of $50, $50, and $1,050 that is currently selling for $910.61 would form the starting point of the analysis. Because the yield-to-maturity on this security is 8.5%, the yield spread between the bond and the Treasury security is 10.02% − 8.50% = 1.52%, or 152 basis points. Figure 14.1 illustrates the yield spread between an index of long-term Aaa-rated corporate bonds and U.S. Treasury bonds for a two-year period ending September 1997. Note that the spread fluctuated slightly around 50 to 75 basis points during that time.

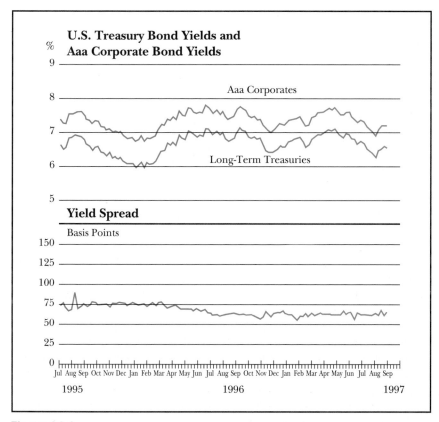

Figure 14.1

Source: *Moody's Bond Record*, September 1997, p. 916.

14.2.2 Call and Put Provisions

There are times when, by historical standards, yields-to-maturity are relatively high. Bonds issued during such times may, at first glance, appear to be unusually attractive investments. However, deeper analysis indicates that this is not necessarily the case. Why? Because most corporate bonds have a call provision that enables the issuer to redeem the bonds before maturity, usually for a price somewhat above par.[4] This price is known as the *call price*, and the difference between it and the par value of the bond is known as the *call premium*. An issuer will often find it financially advantageous to call the existing bonds if yields drop substantially after the bonds were initially sold because the issuer will be able to replace them with lower-yielding securities that are less costly.[5]

For example, consider a ten-year bond issued at par ($1,000) that has a coupon rate of 12% and is callable at $1,050 any time after it has been outstanding for five years.[6] If, after five years, yields on similar five-year bonds were 8%, the bond would probably be called. An investor who had planned on receiving annual coupon payments of $120 for ten years would instead actually receive $120 annual coupon payments for five years and the call price of $1,050 after five years. At this time the investor could take the $1,050 and reinvest it in the 8% bonds, thereby receiving $84 per year in coupon payments over the remaining five years (it is assumed here that the investor can purchase a fraction of a bond, so that the full $1,050 can be invested in the 8% bonds) and $1,050 at the end of the tenth year as a return of principal. With this pattern of cash flows, the bond's actual yield-to-maturity (otherwise known as the *realized return*) over the ten years would be 10.96% instead of the 12% that would have been its actual yield if it had not been called.

This example suggests that the higher the coupon rate of a callable bond, the greater is the likely divergence between actual and promised yields. This relation is borne out by experience. Figure 14.2 plots the coupon rate, set at the time of issue, on the horizontal axis. Because most bonds are initially sold at (or very close to) par, the coupon rate is also a measure of the yield-to-maturity that an investor may have thought was obtainable by purchasing one of the newly issued bonds.

The vertical axis in this figure plots the subsequent actual yields-to-maturity obtained up to the original maturity date by an investor, assuming that the payments received in the event of a call were reinvested in noncallable bonds with appropriate maturities. The curve is based on experience for a group of callable bonds issued by utility companies during a period of fluctuating interest rates. As can be seen, the coupon rate and actual yield are quite similar in magnitude until the coupon rate gets near 5%. At that point, higher coupon rates are no longer associated with higher actual yields because these coupon rates were relatively high during the time period examined. As a consequence, most of the bonds with coupon rates above 5% were ultimately called.

The upshot is that a bond with a greater likelihood of being called should have a higher yield-to-maturity; that is, the higher the coupon rate or the lower the call premium, the higher the yield-to-maturity should be. Equivalently, callable bonds with higher coupon rates or lower call premiums will have lower intrinsic values, keeping everything else equal.

A relatively new innovation in the issuance of bonds is the use of *put provisions*. Bonds with put provisions, known as *putable bonds*, allow the investor to return the bond to the issuer before maturity and receive the par value in return. Like call provisions, typically the put provision does not allow the bond to be "put" with the issuer until several years (for example, five) have elapsed after the issuance of the bond. Although call provisions are valuable to issuers and potentially detrimental to investors, resulting in callable bonds having a higher yield-to-maturity than non-callable bonds,

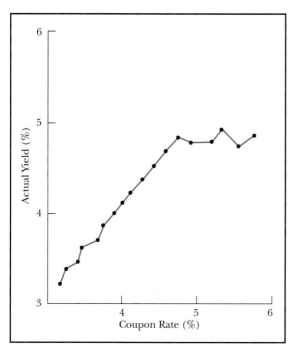

Figure 14.2
*Promised and Actual Yields of Callable Aa Utility Bonds,
1956–1964*

Source: Frank C. Jen and James E. Wert, "The Effect of Call Risk on
Corporate Bond Yields," *Journal of Finance* 22, no. 4 (December 1967): 646.

the opposite occurs with putable bonds. More specifically, the put provision is a benefit to investors and costly to issuers, since it allows investors to receive the par value of the bond after the waiting period has elapsed (unlike call provisions, the put provision will typically allow the put to be exercised only for a brief time at the end of the waiting period, not for the rest of the bond's life). Thus, if interest rates rise, an investor can turn in the bond and use the proceeds to invest in a higher yielding bond, thereby forcing the issuer to issue new bonds at a higher rate. Consequently, put provisions are likely to be used when interest rates rise whereas call provisions are likely to be used when interest rates fall. Since put provisions are potentially beneficial to investors, the result is that putable bonds will have lower yields than non-putable bonds.

14.2.3   Tax Status

In Chapter 12 it was noted that tax-exempt municipal bonds have had yields-to-maturity that were approximately 20% to 40% lower than the yields-to-maturity on similar taxable bonds because the coupon payments on muni's are exempt from federal income taxation. However, taxation can also affect bond prices and yields in other ways. For example, any low-coupon taxable bond selling at a discount provides return in two forms: coupon payments and gains from price appreciation. In the United States both are taxable as ordinary income, but taxes on the latter may be deferred until the bond either is sold or matures if the bond was initially sold at par.[7] Such *market discount bonds* seem to have a tax advantage because of this deferral. As a result, they should have slightly lower before-tax yields than high-coupon taxable bonds, other things being equal; that is, such low-coupon bonds will have a slightly higher intrinsic value than will high-coupon bonds.

14.2.4 Marketability

Marketability (sometimes also referred to as liquidity) refers to the ability of an investor to sell an asset quickly without having to make a substantial price concession. An example of an illiquid asset would be a collectible, such as a piece of artwork. An investor who owns a van Gogh painting may have to settle for a relatively low price if the painting has to be sold within an hour. If the sale could be postponed long enough for a public auction to be set up, undoubtedly a much higher price could be obtained. Alternatively, an investor who has to sell $1,000,000 worth of IBM common stock within an hour will probably be able to receive a price close to the price that other sellers of IBM stock recently received. Furthermore, it is quite unlikely that waiting would increase the expected selling price of such a security.

Because most bonds are bought and sold in dealer markets, one measure of a bond's marketability is the bid-ask spread that the dealers are quoting on the bond. Bonds that are being actively traded will tend to have lower bid-ask spreads than bonds that are inactive because the dealer is more exposed to risk when making a market in an inactive security than when making a market in an active security. The sources of this risk are the inventory that the dealer holds and the fact that interest rates in general may move in a way that causes the dealer to lose money on his or her inventory. Accordingly, bonds that are actively traded should have a lower yield-to-maturity and a higher intrinsic value than bonds that are inactive, everything else being equal.

14.2.5 Likelihood of Default

Currently several corporations—the two largest being Standard & Poor's Corporation and Moody's Investors Service, Inc.—provide ratings of the creditworthiness of thousands of corporate and municipal bonds. Such **bond ratings** are often interpreted as an indication of the likelihood of default by the issuer. Figure 14.3 provides details on the ratings assigned by Standard & Poor's, and Figure 14.4 provides similar details for Moody's.[8]

A broader set of categories is often employed, with bonds classified as being of either **investment-grade** or **speculative-grade.** Typically, investment-grade bonds are bonds that have been assigned to one of the top four ratings (AAA through BBB by Standard & Poor's; Aaa through Baa by Moody's). In contrast, speculative-grade bonds are bonds that have been assigned to one of the lower ratings (BB and below by Standard & Poor's; Ba and below by Moody's). Sometimes these low-rated securities are called high-yield bonds or, derisively, **junk bonds.**[9] Furthermore, if the junk bonds were of investment grade when originally issued, they are often called **fallen angels**.

At times certain regulated financial institutions, such as banks, savings and loans, and insurance companies, have been prohibited from purchasing bonds that were not of investment grade. As a consequence, investment-grade bonds are sometimes thought to command "superpremium" prices and, hence, disproportionately low yields. However, a major disparity in yields could attract a great many new issuers, who would increase the supply of such bonds, thereby causing bond prices to fall and yields to rise. For a significant superpremium to persist, rather substantial market segmentation on both the buying and the selling sides would be required. As there

A Standard & Poor's issue credit rating is a current opinion of the creditworthiness of an obligor with respect to a specific financial obligation, a specific class of financial obligations, or a specific financial program (including ratings on medium-term note programs and commercial paper programs). It takes into consideration the creditworthiness of guarantors, insurers, or other forms of credit enhancement on the obligation and takes into account the currency in which the obligation is denominated.

Issue credit ratings are based on current information furnished by the obligors or obtained by Standard & Poor's from other sources it considers reliable. Standard & Poor's does not perform an audit in connection with any credit rating and may, on occasion, rely on unaudited financial information. Credit ratings may be changed, suspended, or withdrawn as a result of changes in, or unavailability of, such information, or based on other circumstances.

Issue credit ratings are based, in varying degrees, on the following considerations:

  I. Likelihood of payment-capacity and willingness of the obligor to meet its financial commitment on an obligation in accordance with the terms of the obligation;

  II. Nature of and provisions of the obligation;

  III. Protection afforded by, and relative position of, the obligation in the event of bankruptcy, reorganization, or other arrangement under the laws of bankruptcy and other laws affecting creditors' rights.

'AAA' An obligation rated 'AAA' has the highest rating assigned by Standard & Poor's. The obligaor's capacity to meet its financial commitment on the obligation is extremely strong.

'AA' An obligation rated 'AA' differs from the highest rated obligations only in small degree. The obligor's capacity to meet its financial commitment on the obligation is very strong.

'A' An obligation rated 'A' is somewhat more susceptible to the adverse effects of changes in circumstances and economic conditions than obligations in higher rated categories. However, the obligor's capacity to meet its financial commitment on the obligation is still strong.

'BBB' An obligation rated 'BBB' exhibits adequate protection parameters. However, adverse economic conditions or changing circumstances are more likely to lead to a weakened capacity of the obligor to meet its financial commitment on the obligation. Obligations rated 'BB', 'B', 'CCC', 'CC', and 'C' are regarded as having significant speculative characteristics. 'BB' indicates the least degree of speculation and **'C'** the highest. While such obligations will likely have some quality and protective characteristics, these may be outweighed by large uncertainties or major exposures to adverse conditions.

'BB' An obligation rated 'BB' is less vulnerable to nonpayment than speculative issues. However, it faces major ongoing uncertainties or exposure to adverse business, financial, or economic conditions which could lead to the obligor's inadequate capacity to meet its financial commitment on the obligation.

'B' An obligation rated 'B' is more vulnerable to nonpayment than obligations rated 'BB', but the obligor currently has the capacity to meet its financial commitment on the obligation. Adverse business, financial, or economic conditions will likely impair the obligor's capacity or willingness to meet its financial commitment on the obligation.

'CCC' An obligation rated 'CCC' is currently vulnerable to nonpayment, and its dependent upon favorable business, financial, and economic conditions for the obligor to meet its financial commitment on the obligation. In the event of adverse business, financial, or economic conditions, the obligor is not likely to have the capacity to meet its financial commitment on the obligation.

'CC' An obligation rated 'CC' is currently highly vulnerable to nonpayment.

'C' The 'C' rating may be used to cover a situation where a bankruptcy petition has been filed or similar action has been taken, but payments on this obligation are being continued.

'D' An obligation rated 'D' is in payment default. The 'D' rating category is used when payments on an obligation are not made on the date due even if the applicable grace period has not expired, unless Standard & Poor's believes that such payments will be made during such grace period. The 'D' rating also will be used upon the filing of a bankruptcy petition or the taking of a similar action if payments on an obligation are jeopardized.

Figure 14.3
Standard & Poor's Rating Definitions
Source: *Standard & Poor's Bond Guide*, September 1997, p. 12.

is no clear evidence that such segmentation exists, it seems more likely that the differences in yields between investment-grade bonds and speculative-grade bonds are roughly proportional to differences in default risk.

According to Moody's, ratings are designed to provide "investors with a simple system of gradation by which the relative investment qualities of bonds may be noted."[10] Moreover:

> Since ratings involve judgments about the future, on the one hand, and since they are used by investors as a means of protection, on the other, the effort is made when assigning ratings to look at "worst" potentialities in the "visible" future, rather than solely at the past record and the status of the present. Therefore, in-

---

Aaa

Bonds which are rated **Aaa** are judged to be of the best quality. They carry the smallest degree of investment risk and are generally referred to as "gilt edged." Interest payments are protected by a large or by an exceptionally stable margin and principal is secure. While the various protective elements are likely to change, such changes as can be visualized are most unlikely to impair the fundamentally strong position of such issues.

Aa

Bonds which are rated **Aa** are judged to be of high quality by all standards. Together with the **Aaa** group they comprise what are generally known as high grade bonds. They are rated lower than the best bonds because margins of protection may not be as large as in **Aaa** securities or fluctuation of protective elements may be of greater amplitude or there may be other elements present which make the long-term risk appear somewhat larger than the **Aaa** securities.

A

Bonds which are rated **A** possess many favorable investment attributes and are to be considered as upper-medium-grade obligations. Factors giving security to principal and interest are considered adequate, but elements may be present which suggest a susceptibility to impairment some time in the future.

Baa

Bonds which are rated **Baa** are considered as medium-grade obligations, (i.e., they are neither highly protected nor poorly secured). Interest payments and principal security appear adequate for the present but certain protective elements may be lacking or may be characteristically unreliable over any great length of time. Such bonds lack outstanding investment characteristics and in fact have speculative characteristics as well.

Ba

Bonds which are rated **Ba** are judged to have speculative elements; their future cannot be considered as well-assured. Often the protection of interest and principal payments may be very moderate, and thereby not well safeguarded during both good and bad times over the future. Uncertainty of position characterizes bonds in this class.

B

Bonds which are rated **B** generally lack characteristics of the desirable investment. Assurance of interest and principal payments or of maintenance of other terms of the contract over any long period of time may be small.

Caa

Bonds which are rated **Caa** are of poor standing. Such issues may be in default or there may be present elements of danger with respect to principal or interest.

Ca

Bonds which are rated **Ca** represent obligations which are speculative in a high degree. Such issues are often in default or have other marked shortcomings.

C

Bonds which are rated **C** are the lowest rated class of bonds, and issues so rated can be regarded as having extremely poor prospects of ever attaining any real investment standing.

Figure 14.4
Moody's Rating Definitions
Source: *Moody's Bond Record*, September 1997, p. 3.

vestors using the ratings should not expect to find in them a reflection of statistical factors alone, since they are an appraisal of long-term risks, including the recognition of many non-statistical factors.[11]

Despite this disclaimer, the influence of "statistical factors" on the ratings is apparently significant. Several studies have investigated the relationship between historical measures of a firm's performance and the ratings assigned its bonds. Many of the differences in the ratings accorded various bonds can in fact be attributed to differences in the issuers' financial situations, measured in traditional ways. For corporate bonds, better ratings are generally associated with:

1. **Lower financial leverage:** for example, having a smaller debt-to-total-assets (or debt-to-equity) ratio and a larger current (or quick) ratio (that is, current assets divided by current liabilities or, in the case of the quick ratio, current assets except inventory divided by current liabilities).

2. **Larger firm size:** for example, having a larger amount of total assets.

3. **Larger and steadier profits:** for example, having a consistently high rate of return on equity or rate of return on total assets (often earnings before interest and taxes is used as the numerator in such ratios when evaluating a firm's debt) and coverage ratio, such as times interest earned (measured by dividing earnings before interest and taxes by interest).

4. Larger cash flow: for example, having a large cash flow to debt ratio.

5. Lack of subordination to other debt issues.

These observations are used in, among other things, the development of models for predicting the initial ratings that will be given to forthcoming bond issues as well as for predicting changes in the ratings of outstanding bonds.

Default Premiums

Because common stocks do not "promise" any cash flows to the investor, they are not subject to default. To assess the investment prospects for a common stock, one might consider all possible holding-period returns. Multiplying each return by its perceived probability of occurrence and then adding up the products yields, an estimate of the expected holding-period return.

A similar procedure can be employed with bonds, with the analysis usually focusing on yield-to-maturity. Formally all possible yields are considered, along with their respective probabilities, and a weighted average is computed to determine the **expected yield-to-maturity**. As long as there is any possibility of default or late payment, the expected yield will fall below the promised yield. In general, the greater the risk of default and the greater the amount of loss in the event of default, the greater will be this disparity in yields.

This relationship is illustrated in Figure 14.6 for a hypothetical risky bond. Its promised yield-to-maturity is 12% but, owing to a high default risk, the expected yield is only 9%. The 3% difference between promised and expected yields is the **default premium**. Any bond that has some probability of default should offer such a premium, and the greater the probability of default, the greater the premium should be.

Just how large should a bond's default premium be? According to one model, the answer depends on both the probability of default and the likely financial loss to the bondholder in the event of default.[12] Consider a bond that is perceived to be equally likely to default in each year (given that it did not default in the previous year), with the probability that it will default in any given year denoted by p_d. Assume that if the bond does default, a payment equal to $(1 - \lambda)$ times its market price a year earlier will be made to the owner of each bond. According to this model, a bond will be fairly priced if its promised yield-to-maturity y is:

$$y = \frac{\bar{y} + \lambda p_d}{1 - p_d} \tag{14.4}$$

where $\bar{y}$ denotes the bond's expected yield-to-maturity. The difference d between a bond's promised yield-to-maturity y and its expected yield-to-maturity $\bar{y}$ was referred to earlier as the bond's default premium. In Equation (14.4), this difference for a fairly priced bond will be equal to:

$$d = y - \bar{y}$$

$$= \left(\frac{\bar{y} + \lambda p_d}{1 - p_d} \right) - \bar{y} \tag{14.5}$$

As an example, consider the bond illustrated in Figure 14.6. Assume that this bond has a 6% annual default probability, and that it is estimated that if the bond does default, each bondholder will receive an amount equal to 60% of the bond's market price a year earlier (meaning that $1 - \lambda = .60$, which in turn means that $\lambda = .40$).

Taking Advantage of the Bond Rating Process

"Your bond rating: don't try to issue debt without it," might read the motto of U.S. bond rating agencies. Receiving a bond rating has long been a prerequisite for any U.S. debt issuer desiring easy access to the domestic bond market. Without such a rating, debt issuers are forced to seek financing from more expensive sources: banks or the market for privately placed debt.

Once they have acquired a bond rating, debt issuers strive to maintain that rating or even to improve it. The benefits of an improved rating (and the costs of a lower rating) can be substantial. The difference in yields between the highest and lowest rated investment-grade bonds fluctuates over time, but it is often well over a full percentage point (as is illustrated in Figure 14.5). Yield differences between investment-grade and below-investment-grade bonds typically are even greater. As U.S. corporations have increased the

amount of debt on their balance sheets in recent decades, the financial ramifications of bond rating changes have increased commensurately.

Most institutional bond investors focus their efforts on forecasting changes in interest rates and structuring their portfolios to benefit from those expected movements. However, the emphasis placed by the bond market on both a debt issue's initial rating and subsequent changes in that rating present insightful investors with another approach to bond management: searching for bonds whose "true" credit quality is different from their assigned ratings. In discussing those opportunities, we first consider some additional information on the bond rating process.

Two companies dominate the bond rating business: Standard & Poor's and Moody's. Virtually every corporate debt security that comes to the public market is rated by at least one of these organizations. Over

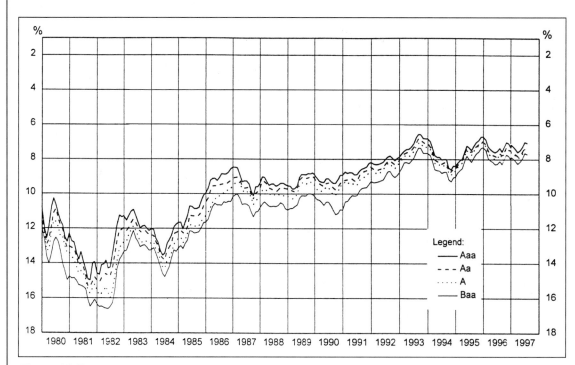

Figure 14.5

Corporate Bond Yields by Ratings, Long-Term Monthly Averages
Source: *Moody's Bond Record,* September 1997, p. 912.

2,000 debt issuers submit financial data to these organizations. For all practical purposes, no bond can be considered an investment-grade security without the acquiescence of S&P's or Moody's.

In addition, a relatively small market exists for "third opinions." Three other firms—Fitch Investors; Duff & Phelps; and McCarthy, Crisanti & Maffei—produce ratings on a portion of the bonds that are rated by the two big firms. Although their ratings rarely differ significantly from S&P's and Moody's, in some situations investors and issuers are comforted by a confirmation of the two big firms' ratings or believe that the smaller rating agencies may uncover aspects of the debt issuers' financial conditions overlooked by S&P's and Moody's.

The text describes many of the financial factors that rating agencies use in assigning bond ratings, including the issuers' leverage, earnings variability, and profitability. Research has shown that such factors systematically "explain" a large portion of bond rating differences among debt issues, implying that there is a significant "mechanical" aspect to the rating process.

Despite this dominant formulistic element of bond ratings, qualitative judgments by the rating agencies still appear to play an important role in rating assignments. Interestingly, as corporations have increased the leverage on their balance sheets, a firm's ability to generate future cash flow to meet its interest expenses has come to play a major role in setting bond ratings. However, evaluating the prospective, rather than contemporaneous, cash flow strength of an issuer is an uncertain process and requires more subjective interpretations of the financial data on the part of the rating agencies.

Some institutional bond investors attempt to take advantage of the uncertainty surrounding a bond's rating. They recognize that, all other factors being equal, a bond with a lower rating will sell for a lower price (equivalently, a higher yield) than a bond with a higher rating. If bonds can be discovered whose credit quality supports a higher rating, then these bonds will offer premium yields relative to bonds with the same "actual" credit quality. Conversely, bonds that deserve a lower rating will provide yields below those with the same "actual" credit quality. Thus an investor who purchases underrated bonds and avoids overrated bonds can construct a portfolio that will outperform a passively managed portfolio of similar risk.

Owners of underrated bonds may benefit even further if their bonds are subsequently upgraded by the rating agencies. Such upgrades are usually associated with substantial price increases, although those increases usually occur before rating changes rather than after them.

Why do such institutional bond investors expect to beat the ratings game? They believe that with intensive security analysis they can understand a debt issuer's financial condition more accurately and on a more timely basis than can the rating agencies. Essentially, these investors make their moves and wait for the market and the rating agencies to catch up to them.

Security analysis of this type is similar to fundamental stock analysis (see Chapters 17 and 22), although less emphasis is placed on an issuer's long-term growth prospects and more attention is paid to the issuer's ability to cover near- and medium-term obligations. Nevertheless, an interpretation of a debt issuer's "true" financial condition is based on a wide range of disparate variables, from the quality of the debt issuer's management to the market for its products.

To a certain extent, these bond investors also play a numbers game with the rating agencies. Both S&P and Moody's each employ fewer than 100 analysts (the smaller rating agencies employ far fewer). Thus the rating agencies cannot cover all debt issuers at all times. Further, they devote the majority of their resources to evaluating new debt offerings. It is true that significant positive or negative news about an issuer may cause the rating agencies to immediately reevaluate their bond ratings. However, at other times a debt issuer's financial condition may change slowly, without full recognition by the market and the rating agencies.

Of course, as with successful common stock analysis, identifying misrated bonds consistently and accurately requires skills possessed by few investors in an efficient market. But also as with common stock analysis, the potential profits to bond investors who correctly diverge from the current consensus can be large.

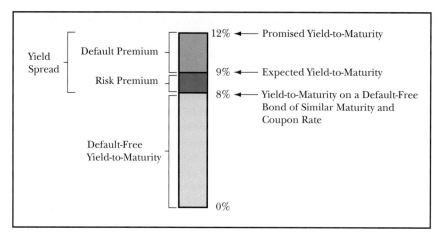

Figure 14.6
Yield-to-Maturity for a Risky Bond

Equation (14.5) can be used to determine that this bond would be fairly priced if its default premium were equal to:

$$d = \left[\frac{.09 + (.40 \times .06)}{1 - .06}\right] - .09$$

$$= .0313$$

or 3.13%. Because the actual default premium earlier was estimated to be 3%, it can be seen that the two figures are similar. This similarity suggests that the actual default premium is appropriate, according to this model.

What sort of default experience might the long-run bond investor anticipate, and how is this experience likely to be related to the ratings of the bonds held? In a massive study of all large bond issues and a sample of small bond issues, W. Braddock Hickman attempted to answer those questions.[13] He analyzed investor experience for each bond from 1900 through 1943 to determine the actual yield-to-maturity, measured from the date of issuance to the date on which the bond matured, defaulted, or was called, whichever came first. He then compared this actual yield with the promised yield-to-maturity on the basis of the price at the time of issue. Every bond was also classified according to the ratings assigned at the time of issue. Table 14.1(a) shows the major results.

As might be expected, Hickman found that, in general, the riskier the bond, the higher the promised yield at the time of issue and the higher the percentage of bonds that subsequently defaulted. However, a surprise was uncovered when the actual yields-to-maturity were compared with promised yields-to-maturity. As the last column on the right of the table shows, in four out of five rating classifications, the actual yield was found to *exceed* the promised yield. As it turns out, a convenient explanation exists for this finding; the period studied by Hickman was one in which a substantial drop in interest rates occurred. This condition is important because the drop made it attractive for issuers to call their outstanding bonds, paying the bondholders a call premium in the process, which resulted in an actual yield above the promised yield.

To see what might have happened had this not been the case, Harold Fraine and Robert Mills reanalyzed the data for large investment-grade issues.[14] Their results are shown in Table 14.1(b). The initial columns differ from those in panel (a) because smaller issues were excluded. The major difference between the panels appears in

TABLE 14.1 Actual and Realized Bond Yields-to-Maturity, 1900–1943

(a) All Large and a Sample of Small Issues

Composite Rating	Comparable Moody's Rating	Promised Yield-to-Maturity at Issue	Percent Defaulting before Maturity	Actual Yield-to-Maturity
I	Aaa	4.5%	5.9%	5.1%
II	Aa	4.6	6.0	5.0
III	A	4.9	13.4	5.0
IV	Baa	5.4	19.1	5.7
V–IX	Below Baa	9.5	42.4	8.6

(b) All Large Issues

Composite Rating	Comparable Moody's Rating	Promised Yield-to-Maturity	Actual Yield-to-Maturity	Modified Actual Yield-to-Maturity
I	Aaa	4.5%	5.1%	4.3%
II	Aa	4.5	5.1	4.3
III	A	4.9	5.0	4.3
IV	Baa	5.4	5.8	4.5

Source: (a) W. Braddock Hickman, *Corporate Bond Quality and Investor Experience* (Princeton: Princeton University Press, 1958), p. 10. (b) Harold G. Fraine and Robert H. Mills, "The Effect of Defaults and Credit Deterioration on Yields of Corporate Bonds," *Journal of Finance* 16, no. 3 (September 1961): 433.

the right-hand column, where Fraine and Mills substituted a bond's promised yield for its actual yield whenever the latter was larger, thereby removing the effects of most calls. Unlike Hickman's, their results suggest that there was little difference in actual yields within the highest rating classifications.[15]

More recently, Edward Altman examined the default experience of corporate bonds over the period from 1971 through 1990.[16] His methodology was somewhat different from Hickman's in that for each bond he noted its rating when it was originally issued and then how many years later it went into default (if at all). From this information he compiled "mortality tables," such as Table 14.2, which shows the percentage of bond issues that went into default within various numbers of years after issuance.

Several interesting observations can be made upon inspection of this table. First, in looking down any particular column, one can see that the cumulative rate of default increases as one moves farther from the date of issuance. Second, except for bonds originally rated AA, lower rated bonds had higher default rates. Third, the default rates for the speculative grades of bonds are strikingly high. This result raises a question of whether such bonds make good investments; their higher yields might not make up for their higher default rates.[17] That question will be addressed shortly.

Risk Premiums

It is useful to compare the expected return of a risky security with the certain return of a default-free security. In an efficient market, the difference in these returns will be related to the relevant systematic (or nondiversifiable) risk of the security. Consider an investor in common stocks who has a holding period of one year or less. In this situation the expected return on a share is typically compared with the yield of a Treasury bill having a maturity date corresponding to the end of the holding period. (Note that the yield on such a Treasury bill is equal to its holding period return.)

Traditionally, a risky bond's expected yield-to-maturity is compared with that of a default-free bond of similar maturity and coupon rate. The difference between

---

Bond Analysis

TABLE 14.2	Default Rates of U.S. Bonds, 1971–1990						
Number of Years After Issuance	**Original Rating**						
	AAA	**AA**	**A**	**BBB**	**BB**	**B**	**CCC**
1	.00%	.00%	.00%	.03%	.00%	.87%	1.31%
2	.00	.00	.30	.57	.93	3.22	4.00
3	.00	1.11	.60	.85	1.36	9.41	19.72
4	.00	1.42	.65	1.34	3.98	16.37	36.67
5	.00	1.70	.65	1.54	5.93	20.87	38.08
6	.14	1.70	.73	1.81	7.38	26.48	40.58
7	.19	1.91	.87	2.70	10.91	29.62	NA
8	.19	1.93	.94	2.83	10.91	31.74	NA
9	.19	2.01	1.28	2.99	10.91	39.38	NA
10	.19	2.11	1.28	3.85	13.86	40.86	NA

Source: Edward I. Altman, "Defaults and Returns on High-Yield Bonds through the First Half of 1991," *Financial Analysts Journal* 47, no. 6 (November/December 1991): Table X.

these yields is known as the bond's risk premium. In the example shown in Figure 14.6, default-free bonds of similar maturity and coupon rate offer a certain 8% yield-to-maturity. Because the risky bond's expected yield-to-maturity is 9%, its risk premium is 1% (that is, 100 basis points).

Every bond that might default will offer a default premium. But the risk premium is another matter. Any security's expected return should be related only to its systematic risk, for it is this risk that measures its contribution to the risk of a well-diversified portfolio; its total risk is not directly relevant.

For example, if a group of companies all faced the possibility of bankruptcy, but from totally unrelated causes, a portfolio that included all of their bonds would subsequently provide an actual return very close to its expected return. The default premiums earned on the bonds that did not default would offset the losses incurred from the bonds that did default. Consequently, there should be little reason for this expected return to differ significantly from that of a default-free bond, because there is little doubt concerning what its actual return will be. Accordingly, each bond should be priced to offer little or no risk premium (but each bond should have a substantive default premium).

The risks associated with bonds are not unrelated, however. Figure 14.7 shows the ratio of the par value of corporate bonds defaulting during the year to the par value outstanding at the beginning of the year for each year from 1900 to 1965. Not surprisingly, the peaks coincide with periods of economic distress.[18] When business is bad, most firms are affected. The market value of a firm's common stock will decline when an economic downturn is anticipated. If the likelihood of default on its debt also increases, the market value of its outstanding bonds will follow suit. Thus the holding-period return on a bond may be correlated with the returns of other bonds and with those of stocks. Most important, a risky bond's holding-period return is likely to be correlated, at least to some extent, with the return on a widely diversified "market portfolio" that includes both corporate bonds and stocks. It is this part of the risk of a bond that is known as systematic risk and causes a bond to have a risk premium in the form of an expected return that is greater than the default-free rate because it is not diversifiable.

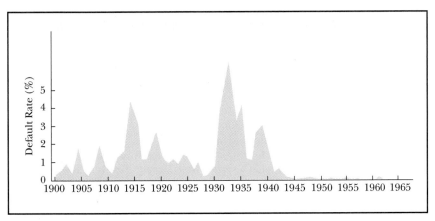

Figure 14.7
Default Rates, 1900–1965
Source: Adapted from Thomas R. Atkinson and Elizabeth T. Simpson, *Trends in Corporate Bond Quality* (New York: Columbia University Press, 1967), p. 5.

Bonds with greater likelihood of default will have greater potential sensitivity to market declines, which, in turn, represent lowered assessments of prospects for the economy as a whole. This relation is illustrated in Table 14.3, which summarizes the investment performance of three portfolios of bonds, known as bond funds, in the Keystone group.[19] All values shown in the table are based on annual returns earned over a 24-year period by each portfolio. As might be anticipated, the bond portfolio with the lowest-rated bonds (fund B4) had the highest average return and highest standard deviation, whereas the bond portfolio with the highest-rated bonds (fund B1) had the lowest average return and lowest standard deviation.

Each portfolio's returns were compared with those of Standard & Poor's 500 to estimate each portfolio's sensitivity to changes in stock prices. Specifically, a beta was calculated for each portfolio in order to measure the sensitivity of each portfolio to swings in the stock market. As can be seen in the table, the lower the bond rating of the portfolio, the higher the estimated beta, indicating that lower-rated bonds were more sensitive to stock price movements and thus should have had higher average returns.

The final row in the table shows the proportion of the year-to-year variation in bond portfolio returns that was associated with stock market swings. As indicated, relatively more of the B2 and B4 portfolios' variation was associated with the stock market than was the case with the B1 portfolio. Thus for higher-rated bonds, interest-rate risk appears to have been more important than stock market risk.[20]

TABLE 14.3 Risk and Return, Keystone Bond Funds, 1968–1991			
	Fund B1: Conservative Bonds	**Fund B2: Investment-Grade Bonds**	**Fund B4: Discount Bonds**
Average return (% per year)	7.84	8.53	8.64
Standard deviation of return (% per year)	8.27	9.35	13.68
Beta value, relative to S&P 500	.26	.38	.54
Proportion of variance explained by S&P 500	.28	.45	.42

Matrix Bond Pricing

Most institutional investors must periodically determine the market values of their bond portfolios. For example, a pension fund may wish to keep beneficiaries abreast of the value of their fixed-income investments. Further, the pension fund needs accurate market valuations to evaluate fixed-income managers' investment results and to compute their compensation. (Managers' fees are typically based on the market values of their portfolios.)

In some cases, valuing a bond portfolio is a straightforward matter. Prices of most Treasury bonds, many government agency bonds, and certain actively traded corporate bonds are available through real-time electronic quotation systems and the print media. Unlike common stocks, however, where an active market usually exists for all but the smallest issues, many bond issues (even some with large face values outstanding) do not trade frequently. It is not uncommon to find entire bond issues held to maturity by investors. The limited trading of these securities inhibits efforts to accurately determine their current market prices.

How can an institutional investor establish market prices for thinly traded fixed-income securities in its possession? It could ask its fixed-income managers to supply their best estimates of the bonds' market prices. After all, these managers constantly compare their perceptions of the bonds' intrinsic values with the bonds' estimated market prices as part of their portfolio management processes. However, a manager has an inherent conflict of interest in providing such valuations because his or her financial well-being is directly related to those values.

Alternatively, the institutional investor might canvass bond dealers who trade the bonds under question (or similar securities) and solicit representative bid prices. Unfortunately, this procedure is too time-consuming to conduct on a regular basis for hundreds of bonds. Furthermore, the dealers have no incentive to participate.

In response to this dearth of pricing data, institutional investors have turned to various commercial bond valuation services. For a fee, these organizations provide third-party security valuations for tens of thousands of fixed-income securities on a daily, weekly, or monthly basis.

Some bond pricing services "lever off" of their own trading operations. (Merrill Lynch, for example, runs one of the largest pricing services.) They use their bond traders to submit bid-side valuations daily for any securities that their traders regularly see traded in the market. This "hand pricing" by traders offers perhaps the best estimate that institutional investors can readily obtain as to the "true" market price, or liquidation value, of their bonds. Note, however, that the pricing services do not offer to transact at their price quotations. An actual bid for an institutional investor's fixed-income portfolio would involve an assessment by the trader of many factors, including the trader's current inventory, the price risk of the portfolio, the number of bonds being bought, and available hedges on the portfolio.

Often, however, a bond pricing service does not have immediate access to current prices for certain securities, either because it does not maintain a trading desk or because its traders do not deal in the securities. In those cases, various mechanical procedures, generally known as *matrix pricing*, are used to estimate market prices. The particular matrix pricing formulas vary among the pricing services and among the types of bonds valued by the services. Nevertheless, the pricing of corporate bonds provides a

14.3 THE RISK STRUCTURE OF INTEREST RATES

The greater a bond's risk of default, the greater its default premium. This fact alone will cause a bond with a higher default risk to offer a higher promised yield-to-maturity. If it is also true that the greater a bond's risk of default, the greater its risk premium, then the promised yield-to-maturity will have to be even higher. As a result, bonds with lower agency ratings should have higher promised yields-to-maturity if such ratings really do reflect the risk of default.

Figure 14.5 shows that this is indeed the case. Each of the curves plots the promised yield-to-maturity for a group of corporate bonds assigned the same ratings by Moody's. Note that the scale is "upside down," so that higher promised yields plot at lower positions on the diagram. (Such a procedure is often employed for bonds.)

good example of the essential aspects of matrix bond pricing.

The price matrix for investment grade corporate bonds is typically three-dimensional, with sector, quality, and term-to-maturity as the three primary variables. Each cell in the matrix represents a unique three-way combination of these variables. For example, one cell might contain industrial bonds with A ratings and three years to maturity.

Each cell in the matrix is assigned a yield spread over comparable maturity Treasury securities, based on an analysis of current market conditions. (For example, three-year, A-rated industrial bonds might be assigned a 100 basis point spread over Treasuries.) These spreads may change over time at the discretion of the pricing service.

Once the matrix spreads have been established, a corporate bond is priced by finding the cell in which it resides and using the associated yield to discount the bond's promised cash flows and thereby compute an estimated price. Adjustments may be made for special factors, such as coupon rates, call features, and sinking fund provisions.

Mortgage pass-through securities create particular problems for matrix pricing systems, especially complex mortgage-backed bonds, such as various forms of collateral mortgage obligations (CMOs). There exist literally thousands of variations of mortgage pass-through securities that differ in terms of coupon rate, payment terms, years since issuance (called "seasoning"), underlying collateral, and expected prepayment speed. The existing matrix pricing procedures are relatively primitive compared with the state-of-the-art, option-adjusted pricing models used by many fixed-income managers.

For standard mortgage pass-through securities, the bond pricing services may supply valuations for various generic securities. These valuations are based on issuer type, coupon rate, and seasoning (for example, GNMA single-family, moderately seasoned, 8% coupon mortgage pools). Any mortgage pass-through security that matches the characteristics of one of the generic securities is assigned the same price.

For CMOs, the matrix-pricing systems use a set of prepayment assumptions to generate a stream of expected cash flows for the particular CMO tranche under consideration (see Chapter 13 for a further discussion of CMOs). With these expected cash flows, the expected life of the security is calculated, and a yield spread from a comparable term-to-maturity Treasury security is established. The pass-through security's expected cash flows are then discounted at the assigned yield to produce an estimated market price.

Current matrix-pricing procedures for pass-through securities have been criticized for not explicitly accounting for the embedded option contained in those securities (that is, the ability of homeowners to prepay their mortgages at their discretion). This option has an implicit value, and failing to adequately incorporate it into a pass-through securities price will produce systematic errors.

As one might expect, the accuracy of matrix bond pricing depends on the uniqueness of the security under analysis. Those securities that do not deviate significantly in terms of investment characteristics from their actively traded counterparts are comparatively easy to price accurately. Securities with unique or complicated features are more difficult to price accurately, and their matrix prices are often considered suspect by fixed-income managers.

Figure 14.5 shows not only that bonds are priced so that higher promised yields go with lower ratings, it also shows that the differences between the yields in the rating categories vary considerably over time. This result suggests that agency ratings indicate *relative* levels of risk instead of *absolute* levels of risk.

If an absolute level of risk were indicated by a rating classification, then each classification would be associated with a particular probability of default (or, more accurately, a range of probabilities of default). Consequently, as the economy became more uncertain in terms of such factors as the near-term level of gross domestic product, bonds would be reclassified, with most moving to lower ratings. In this situation, yield spreads between classifications would change only slightly, because each classification would still reflect bonds having the same probability of default. However, Figure 14.5 shows that these spreads change over time, an observation that can be interpreted as evidence that the ratings do not reflect absolute levels of risk. Further evidence is provided in Table 14.4, which shows the historical difference in the returns on high-yield bonds and U.S. Treasuries for various holding periods. As shown in the table, at times these differences are positive and at other times they are negative. (For example, the average annual differences for 1978–1983 and 1984–1991 are +5.82% and −2.31%, respectively.)

It is known that rating agencies prefer to avoid making a large number of rating changes as the economy becomes more uncertain. Instead, they prefer to use the classifications to indicate relative levels of risk, so that an overall increase in economic uncertainty would not result in a significant number of reclassifications. Thus the probability of default associated with bonds in a given rating classification would be greatest at times of economic uncertainty. In turn, the yield spreads between classifications of corporate bonds and the yield spreads between corporate and government bonds would increase at such times. Indeed, there is considerable evidence that the spread between the promised yields of bonds of different rating classifications increases when the degree of uncertainty about the economy increases.

Some models have attempted to take advantage of this observation in order to predict the amount of economic uncertainty. In particular, these models use the size of the yield spread between, say, bonds rated AAA and those rated BBB by Standard & Poor's as an indication of the degree of economic uncertainty. For example, widening of this spread might be taken as an indication that the near-term future of the economy was becoming more uncertain. There are other models that look not at yield spreads but at differences in the holding-period returns of AAA and BBB bonds.

14.4   DETERMINANTS OF YIELD SPREADS

As mentioned previously, when bond analysts refer to a corporate bond's yield spread, they are typically referring to the difference between the corporate bond's promised yield-to-maturity and that of another bond (often a Treasury security) having a similar maturity and coupon rate. The greater the risk of default, the greater this spread should be. Moreover, bonds that have more marketability might command an additional "premium" in price and hence offer a lower yield-to-maturity with a corresponding lower spread. Given a large enough sample of bonds, one should be able to see whether these relationships really do exist.

One study of corporate bond prices did just this.[21] Four measures were used to assess the probability of default:

1. The extent to which the firm's net income had varied over the preceding nine years (measured by the coefficient of variation of earnings—that is, the ratio of standard deviation of earnings to average earnings)
2. The length of time that the firm had operated without forcing any of its creditors to take a loss
3. The ratio of the market value of the firm's equity to the par value of its debt
4. The market value of the firm's outstanding debt (an indication of marketability)

First, these measures were calculated, along with the yield spread, for each of 366 bonds. Second, the logarithm of every yield spread and measure was calculated. Third, statistical methods were used to analyze the relationship between a bond's yield spread and these measures. This relationship was found to be most accurately described as:

TABLE 14.4 Historical Return Differences between Junk Bonds and U.S. Treasuries

Base Period (Jan.1)	Terminal Period (December 31)													
	1978	1979	1980	1981	1982	1983	1984	1985	1986	1987	1988	1989	1990	1991
1978	8.68%	6.60%	5.01%	5.51%	3.17%	5.82%	4.13%	2.70%	1.59%	2.22%	2.41%	0.98%	(0.04%)	1.37%
1979		4.55	3.23	4.48	1.71	5.22	3.32	1.77	0.62	1.44	1.73	0.23	(0.82)	0.74
1980			1.96	4.45	0.67	5.39	3.05	1.24	(0.02)	1.01	1.38	(0.25)	(1.35)	0.37
1981				7.08	(0.13)	6.74	3.36	1.07	(0.42)	0.85	1.29	(0.54)	(1.73)	0.19
1982					(9.63)	6.49	1.93	(0.69)	(2.16)	(0.33)	0.36	(1.60)	(2.80)	(0.60)
1983						19.57	6.62	1.84	(0.56)	1.22	1.74	(0.65)	(2.11)	0.26
1984							(6.32)	(7.60)	(7.73)	(3.48)	(1.89)	(4.06)	(5.19)	(2.31)
1985								(9.03)	(8.50)	(2.50)	(0.76)	(3.60)	(5.00)	(1.70)
1986									(7.99)	0.34	1.64	2.41	(4.30)	(0.54)
1987										7.34	5.89	(0.76)	(3.49)	0.93
1988											4.27	5.16	(7.31)	(1.04)
1989												(14.37)	(12.76)	(3.11)
1990													(11.24)	4.34
1991[a]														19.01

[a] First six months of 1991.

Source: Edward I. Altman, "Defaults and Returns on High-Yield Bonds through the First Half of 1991," *Financial Analysts Journal* 47, no. 6 (November/December 1991): Table XIV.

$$\text{Yield spread} = 1.987 + (.307 \times \text{earnings variability}) - (.253 \times \text{time without default})$$
$$-(.537 \times \text{equity/debt ratio}) - (.275 \times \text{market value of debt}) \quad (14.6)$$

This form of the relationship accounted for roughly 75% of the variation in the bonds' yield spreads.

The advantage of an equation such as this is that the coefficients can be easily interpreted. Because all yield spreads and values were converted to logarithms, the effect is similar to that of using ratio scales on all axes of a diagram. Thus, a 1% increase in a bond's earnings variability can be expected to bring about an increase of .307% in the bond's yield spread, other things being equal. Similarly, a 1% increase in a bond's time without default can be expected to cause a decrease of approximately .253% in the bond's yield spread, and so on. Each coefficient is an elasticity, indicating the percentage change in a bond's yield spread likely to accompany a 1% change in the associated measure. Because every measure was found to be related in the expected direction to the yield spread, the study provides substantial support for the notion that bonds with higher default risk and less marketability have higher yield spreads.

14.5 FINANCIAL RATIOS AS PREDICTORS OF DEFAULT

For years, security analysts have used accounting ratios to indicate the probability that a firm will fail to meet its financial obligations. Specific procedures have been developed to predict default with such ratios. Univariate analysis attempts to find the best single predictor for this purpose, whereas multivariate analysis searches for the best combination of two or more predictors.

14.5.1 Univariate Methods

Cash inflows can be viewed as contributions to the firm's cash balance, whereas cash outflows can be viewed as drains on that balance. When the balance falls below zero, default is likely to occur. The probability of default will be greater for the firm when (1) the existing cash balance is smaller, (2) the expected net cash flow (measured before payments to creditors and stockholders) is smaller, and (3) the net cash flow is more variable.

In an examination of various measures used to assess these factors, it was found that the ratio of net cash flow (income before depreciation, depletion, and amortization charges) to total debt was particularly useful.[22] Figure 14.8(a) shows the mean value of this ratio for a group of firms that defaulted on a promised payment and for a companion group that did not. As early as five years before default the two groups' ratios diverged, and the spread widened as the year of default approached.

This changing spread suggests that the probability of default may not be constant through time. Instead, warning signals may indicate an increase in the probability, which should, in turn, cause a fall in the market price of the firm's bonds along with a fall in the market price of its common stock. Figure 14.8(b) shows that such signals are indeed recognized in the marketplace. The median market value of common stock in the firms that did not default went up, while that of the firms that subsequently defaulted went down as the date of default approached.

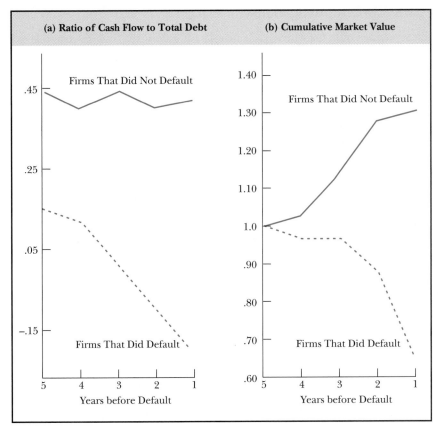

Figure 14.8
Financial Ratios and Market Prices for Firms That Defaulted and Those That Did Not
Source: William H. Beaver, "Market Prices, Financial Ratios and the Prediction of Failure," *Journal of Accounting Research* 6, no. 2 (Autumn 1968): 182, 185.

14.5.2 Multivariate Methods

Combinations of certain financial ratios and cash flow variables have been considered as possible predictors of default. In one of the first studies, statistical analysis indicated that the most accurate method of predicting default involved calculating a firm's default-risk rating, known as its *Z-score*, from some of its financial ratios as follows:

$$Z = 1.2X_1 + 1.4X_2 + 3.3X_3 + .6X_4 + .99X_5 \tag{14.7}$$

where the following five ratios were calculated from information contained in the firm's most recent income statement and balance sheet:

X_1 = (current assets − current liabilities)/total assets
X_2 = retained earnings/total assets
X_3 = earnings before interest and taxes/total assets
X_4 = market value of equity/book value of total debt
X_5 = sales/total assets

Any firm with a Z-score below 1.8 was considered a likely candidate for default, and the lower the score, the greater the likelihood.[23]

14.5.3 Investment Implications

Should the securities of firms whose cash flow-to-total debt ratio or *Z*-score has declined be avoided? Hardly. It should be remembered that the firms represented by the dashed lines in Figure 14.8 were chosen because they eventually defaulted. Had all firms with declining ratios been selected, corresponding decreases in their market prices would undoubtedly have been observed, reflecting the increased probability of future default. However, only some of these firms would have ultimately defaulted; the others would have recovered. Consequently, the gains on the firms that recovered might well have offset the losses on the firms that defaulted. In summary, the net result from purchasing a portfolio of stocks that had declining ratios or *Z*-scores could easily have been the achievement of an average return.

What about purchasing bonds of companies that have just had their ratings increased, and selling (or avoiding) bonds of companies that have just had their ratings decreased? After all, such changes in ratings should be related to a change in the default risk of the issuer. In a study that looked at the behavior of bond prices around the time of ratings changes, some evidence was found that the bond price adjustment to a rating change occurred in the period from eighteen to seven months *before* the rating change. Little or no evidence of a substantive price change was found either during the month of the rating change or in the period from six months before to six months after the rating change.[24] These findings are consistent with the notion that the bond market is semistrong-form efficient, because bond ratings are at least partly predictable from publicly available information.

The study mentioned above looked primarily at ratings changes within investment-grade categories. A recent paper also looked at what happened around the time of ratings changes for bonds that (1) were not investment-grade and were downgraded or (2) were investment-grade and were downgraded to no longer be investment-grade.[25] Care was made to ensure that there were no other firm announcements and that the downgrades were issued at the same time by both Moody's and Standard & Poor's. In both of these cases, there was a strong negative price reaction during the month of the downgrade and during the previous six months. The reaction before the downgrade is again consistent with semistrong-form market efficiency, but the reaction during the month of the downgrade might not be; it is unclear whether the reaction occurred, at least in part, on or after the day of the downgrade. A significant negative price reaction after the day of the downgrade would be evidence of an inefficiency because investors could short sell such bonds on the announcement date and make abnormal profits. However, if most of the reaction was before the announcement, then there would not be any way to profit from trading after the announcement was made.

14.6	SUMMARY

1. The capitalization of income method of valuation is a commonly used approach to identify mispriced bonds. It is based on the discounted value of the cash flows that the investor expects to receive from owning a bond.
2. Given the bond's current market price and promised cash flows, the investor can calculate the bond's promised yield-to-maturity and compare it with an appropriate discount rate.
3. Alternatively, the investor can use an appropriate discount rate to discount the bond's promised cash flows. The sum of the present value of these cash flows is compared with the bond's market price.

4. Six primary attributes are of significance in bond valuation: length of time to maturity, coupon rate, call and put provisions, tax status, marketability, and likelihood of default.

5. Time to maturity, call provisions, tax status, and likelihood of default tend to be directly related to promised yield-to-maturity. Coupon rate, put provisions, and marketability tend to be inversely related to promised yield-to-maturity.

6. Several organizations provide ratings of the creditworthiness of thousands of corporate and municipal bonds. These ratings are often interpreted as an indication of the issuer's likelihood of default.

7. Bond ratings indicate relative levels of risk instead of absolute levels of risk.

8. A bond's promised yield-to-maturity can be decomposed into a default-free yield-to-maturity and a yield spread. Furthermore, the yield spread can be decomposed into a risk premium and a default premium.

9. Various statistical models have been developed to predict the probability that a bond issuer will default. These models typically use financial ratios derived from the issuer's balance sheet and income statement.

QUESTIONS AND PROBLEMS

1. Grapefruit Yeargin is considering purchasing a 10-year Treasury STRIP with a $10,000 par value. If the Treasury yield curve indicates that 6% is the appropriate yield for such bonds, what is the fair market value of this bond? (Assume annual compounding.)

2. Bones Ely owns a $1,000 face-value bond with three years to maturity. The bond makes annual interest payments of $75, the first to be made one year from today. The bond is currently priced at $975.48. Given an appropriate discount rate of 10%, should Bones hold or sell the bond?

3. A broker has advised Jewel Ens to purchase a ten-year $10,000 face-value bond that makes 8% annual coupon payments. The appropriate discount rate is 9%. The first interest payment is due one year from today. If the bond currently sells for $8,560, should Jewel follow the broker's advice?

4. Patsy Tebeau is considering investing in a bond currently selling for $8,785.07. The bond has four years to maturity, a $10,000 face value, and an 8% coupon rate. The next annual interest payment is due one year from today. The appropriate discount rate for investments of similar risk is 10%.
   a. Calculate the intrinsic value of the bond. On the basis of this calculation, should Patsy purchase the bond?
   b. Calculate the yield-to-maturity of the bond. On the bases of this calculation, should Patsy purchase the bond?

5. Consider two bonds with $1,000 face values that carry coupon rates of 8%, make annual coupon payments, and exhibit similar risk characteristics. The first bond has five years to maturity whereas the second has ten years to maturity. The appropriate discount rate for investments of similar risk is 8%. If this discount rate rises by two percentage points, what will be the respective percentage price changes of the two bonds?

6. Why is it convenient to use Treasury securities as a starting point for analyzing bond yields?

7. Bond A's yield-to-maturity is 9.80%; bond B's yield-to-maturity is 8.73%. What is the difference in yields stated in basis points?

8. Bibb Falk recently purchased a bond with a $1,000 face value, a 10% coupon rate, and four years to maturity. The bond makes annual interest payments, the first to be received one year from today. Bibb paid $1,032.40 for the bond.

a. What is the bond's yield-to-maturity?

b. If the bond can be called two years from now at a price of $1,100, what is its yield-to-call?

9. Burleigh Grimes purchased at par a bond with a face value of $1,000. The bond had five years to maturity and a 10% coupon rate. The bond was called two years later for a price of $1,200, after making its second annual interest payment. Burleigh then reinvested the proceeds in a bond selling at its face value of $1,000, with three years to maturity and a 7% coupon rate. What was Burleigh's actual yield-to-maturity over the five-year period?

10. Nellie Fox acquired at par a bond for $1,000 that offered a 9% coupon rate. At the time of purchase, the bond had four years to maturity. Assuming annual interest payments, calculate Nellie's actual yield-to-maturity if all the interest payments were reinvested in an investment earning 15% per year. What would Nellie's actual yield-to-maturity be if all interest payments were spent immediately upon receipt?

11. Distinguish between yield-to-first-call and yield-to-maturity.

12. What is the effect of a call provision on a bond's potential for price appreciation?

13. What is the primary purpose of bond ratings? Given the importance attached to bond ratings by bond investors, why don't common stock investors focus on quality ratings of entire companies in making their investment decisions?

14. According to Lave Cross, "Agency ratings indicate *relative* levels of risk instead of *absolute* levels of risk." Explain the meaning of Lave's statement.

15. On the basis of the default premium model presented in the text, what is the fair value default premium for a bond with an expected yield-to-maturity of 8.5%, a 10% annual default probability, and an expected loss as a percent of market value of 60%?

16. Corporate default appears to be an event specific to an individual company. Yet, despite the apparent diversifiable nature of corporate default (meaning that relatively few bonds would default in a well-diversified portfolio), the bond market systematically adds default premiums when valuing corporate bonds. Explain why.

17. High-yield bonds are often viewed by investors as having financial characteristics much more akin to common stocks than to high-grade corporate bonds. Why?

18. Examining Equation (14.6), explain the rationale underlying the observed relationship (positive or negative) between each of the variables and the yield spread.

19. How would you expect yield spreads to respond to the following macroeconomic events: recession, high inflation, tax cuts, stock market decline, improved trade balance? Explain the reasoning behind each of your answers.

20. Urban Shocker has noted that the spread between the yield-to-maturity on BBB-rated bonds and that on AAA-rated bonds has recently widened considerably. Explain to Urban what this change might indicate.

CFA Exam Questions

21. [In 1990,] Barney Gray, CFA, is Director of Fixed-Income Securities at Piedmont Security Advisors. In a recent meeting, one of his major endowment clients suggested investing in corporate bonds yielding 9%, rather than U.S. government bonds yielding 8%. Two bond issues—one U.S. Treasury and one corporate—were compared to illustrate the point.

U.S. Treasury bond	8% due 6/15/2010	Priced at 100
AJAX Manufacturing	9.5% due 6/15/2015	Priced at 105
Rated AAA		
Callable @ 107.5 on 6/15/1995		

Gray wants to prepare a response based upon his expectation that long-term U.S. Treasury interest rates will fall sharply (at least 100 basis points) over the next three months.

Evaluate the return expectations for each bond under this scenario, and support an evaluation of which bond would be the superior performer. Discuss the price-yield measures that affect your conclusion.

22. One common goal among fixed-income managers is to earn high incremental returns on corporate bonds versus government bonds of comparable durations. The approach of some corporate bond portfolio managers is to find and purchase those corporate bonds having the largest initial spreads over comparable-duration government bonds. John Ames, HFS's fixed-income manager, believes that a more rigorous approach is required if incremental returns are to be maximized.

The table below presents data relating to one set of corporate/government spread relationships present in the market at a given date:

	Current and Expected Spreads and Durations of High-Grade Corporate Bonds (One-Year Horizon)			
Bond Rating	Initial Spread over Governments	Expected Horizon Spread	Initial Duration	Expected Duration One Year from Now
Aaa	31 basis points	31 basis points	4 years	3.1 years
Aa	40 basis points	50 basis points	4 years	3.1 years

a. Recommend purchase of either Aaa or Aa bonds for a one-year investment horizon given a goal of maximizing incremental returns. Show your calculations. (Base your decision only on the information presented in the table.)

Ames chooses not to rely solely on initial spread relationships. His analytical framework considers a full range of other key variables likely to affect realized incremental returns including:

- Call provisions
- Potential changes in interest rates

b. Describe two variables, in addition to those identified above, that Ames should include in his analysis, and explain how each of those two variables could cause realized incremental returns to differ from those indicated by initial spread relationships.

ENDNOTES

[1] The capitalization of income approach to valuation is also known as the discounted cash flow approach; its usefulness is discussed in Steven N. Kaplan and Richard S. Ruback, "The Valuation of Cash Flow Forecasts: An Empirical Analysis," *Journal of Finance* 50, no. 4 (September 1995): 1059–1093.

[2] With complex cash flows (such as a mix of positive and negative cash flows), the IRR method can be misleading. However, this is not a problem when it is applied to bonds (or stocks; see Chapter 17). For a discussion of potential problems in other contexts, see Richard A. Brealey and Stewart C. Myers, *Principles of Corporate Finance* (New York: McGraw-Hill, 1996), chapter 5.

[3] A more accurate method of determining a bond's intrinsic value involves the use of spot rates. That is, in determining the NPV of this bond, the investor might have determined that the relevant spot rates for the one-year, two-year, and three-year cash flows are 8.24%, 8.69%,

and 9.03%, respectively. Using these values, the investor would find that the bond's intrinsic value equals $924.06 $\{=[\$60/(1.0824)] + [\$60/(1.0869)^2] + [\$1,060/(1.0903)^3]\}$. Although V is the same in this example when either spot rates or y^* is used in the calculations, this need not always be the case.

[4] Many corporate bonds have, in addition to a call provision, a provision for a sinking fund wherein each year the issuer retires a prespecified portion of the original bond issue.

[5] The investor generally can escape having his or her bonds called if either Treasury securities or discounted corporate bonds are purchased. However, because these securities have less "call risk," they are likely to have lower yields-to-maturity than similar bonds with higher levels of "call risk." Call risk is analyzed by Duane Stock in "Par Coupon Yield Curves for Callable Bonds and Amortizing Instruments," *Financial Practice and Education* 6, no. 2 (Fall/Winter 1996): 49–59.

[6] In this example, the **yield-to-call** (or, to be more specific, the yield-to-first-call) is 12.78%. That is, 12.78% is the discount rate that makes the present value of $120 received after each of the first four years and $1,170 (=$1,050 + $120) at the end of five years equal to the issue price of the bond, $1,000. Note that the yield-to-call is greater than the bond's 12% promised yield-to-maturity at the time of issue.

[7] Any gains from price appreciation realized by an investor in municipal bonds is also taxable as ordinary income. For more on the taxation of fixed-income securities, see Chapter 12 or Clark Blackman II and Donald Laubacher, "The Basics of Amortizing Bond Premiums and Discounts," *AAII Journal* 15, no. 3 (March 1993): 24–27.

[8] Both rating agencies actually use finer gradations than those shown in the figures. Standard & Poor's sometimes places a+ or a− next to its letter rating if a bond is in a category ranging from AA to CCC. Similarly, Moody's may place a 1, 2, or 3 next to its letter rating if a bond is in a category ranging from Aa down to B. Both agencies also rate certain types of short-term debt instruments. These agencies also apply the same rating scale to the debt of more than 50 foreign goverments; see Richard Cantor and Frank Packer, "Determinants and Impact of Sovereign Credit Ratings," *Journal of Fixed Income* 6, no. 3 (December 1996): 76–91. Furthermore, preferred stock is also rated; see Lea V. Carty, "Moody's Preferred Stock Ratings and Dividend Impairment," *Journal of Fixed Income* 5, no. 3 (December 1995): 95–103.

[9] For a primer on high-yield bonds and their analysis, see Stanley Block, "High-Yielding Securities: How Appropriate Are They?" *AAII Journal* 11, no. 10 (November 1989): 7–11; and Glenn E. Atkins and Ben Branch, "A Qualitative Look at High-Yield Bond Analysis," *AAII Journal* 13, no. 12 (October 1991): 12–15.

[10] *Moody's Bond Record* (New York: Moody's Investors Service, September 1997): p. 3.

[11] *Moody's Bond Record*, p. 3.

[12] The model was developed by Gordon Pye in "Gauging the Default Premium," *Financial Analysts Journal* 30, no. 1 (January/February 1974): 49–52.

[13] W. Braddock Hickman, *Corporate Bond Quality and Investor Experience* (Princeton: Princeton University Press, 1958).

[14] Harold G. Fraine and Robert H. Mills, "The Effect of Defaults and Credit Deterioration on Yields of Corporate Bonds," *Journal of Finance* 16, no. 3 (September 1961): 423–434.

[15] Although the Fraine and Mills work may appear to be dated, the "work holds up extremely well a generation or so after its publication," according to Martin S. Fridson, "Fraine's Neglected Findings: Was Hickman Wrong?" *Financial Analysts Journal* 50, no. 5 (September/October 1994): 52.

[16] Edward I. Altman, "Defaults and Returns on High-Yield Bonds through the First Half of 1991," *Financial Analysts Journal* 47, no. 6 (November/December 1991): 67–77.

[17] Interestingly, one study found that investors who purchased the equity of B-rated firms at the time that they issued debt subsequently received relatively poor returns over the next three years, whereas those who bought the equity of Ba or higher rated firms received a normal return. See Jeff Jewell and Miles Livingston, "The Long-Run Performance of Firms Issuing Debt," *Journal of Fixed Income* 7, no. 2 (September 1997): 61–66.

[18] See Marshall E. Blume and Donald B. Keim, "Realized Returns and Defaults on Low-Grade Bonds: The Cohort of 1977 and 1978," *Financial Analysts Journal* 47, no. 2 (March/April

1991): 63–72; Marshall E. Blume, Donald B. Keim, and Sandeep A. Patel, "Returns and Volatility of Low-Grade Bonds, 1977–1989," *Journal of Finance* 46, no. 1 (March 1991): 49–74; and Marshall E. Blume and Donald B. Keim, "The Risk and Return of Low-Grade Bonds: An Update," *Financial Analysts Journal* 47, no. 5 (September/October 1991). A similar observation has been made for municipal bonds. See George H. Hempel, *The Postwar Quality of State and Local Debt* (New York: Columbia University Press, 1971).

[19] For an in-depth analysis of such bond portfolios, see Bradford Cornell and Kevin Greene, "The Investment Performance of Low-Grade Bond Funds," *Journal of Finance* 46, no. 1 (March 1991): 29–48; and Bradford Cornell, "Liquidity and the Pricing of Low-Grade Bonds," *Financial Analysts Journal* 48, no. 1 (January/February 1992): 63–67, 74.

[20] In a study of preferred stocks, it was found that the price movements of low-rated preferred stocks were related more to the price movements of common stocks than to the price movements of bonds; for high-rated preferred stocks, the findings were just the opposite. See John S. Bildersee, "Some Aspects of the Performance of Non-Convertible Preferred Stocks," *Journal of Finance* 28, no. 5 (December 1973): 1187–1201.

[21] Lawrence Fisher, "Determinants of Risk Premiums on Corporate Bonds," *Journal of Political Economy* 67, no. 3 (June 1959): 217–237.

[22] William H. Beaver, "Market Prices, Financial Ratios and the Prediction of Failure," *Journal of Accounting Research* 6, no. 2 (Autumn 1968): 179–192.

[23] Edward I. Altman, "Financial Ratios, Discriminant Analysis and the Prediction of Corporate Bankruptcy," *Journal of Finance* 23, no. 4 (September 1968): 589–609.

[24] Mark I. Weinstein, "The Effect of a Rating Change Announcement on Bond Price," *Journal of Financial Economics* 5, no. 3 (December 1977): 329–350. Another study that examined rating change announcements that were "noncontaminated by other news releases found a small but statistically significant upward movement in daily bond prices around upgrades; downgrades produced no significant movements." See John R. M. Hand, Robert W. Holthausen, and Richard W. Leftwich, "The Effect of Bond Rating Agency Announcements on Bond and Stock Prices," *Journal of Finance* 47, no. 2 (June 1992): 733–752.

[25] Gailen Hite and Arthur Warga, "The Effect of Bond-Rating Changes on Bond Price Performance," *Financial Analysts Journal* 53, no. 3 (May/June 1997): 35–51. The authors looked at other rating change scenarios in addition to the two mentioned here.

KEY TERMS

capitalization of income method of valuation	yield-to-call
promised yield-to-maturity	bond ratings
net present value	investment-grade bonds
yield structure	speculative-grade bonds
term structure	junk bonds
risk structure	fallen angels
yield spread	expected yield-to-maturity
basis points	default premium

REFERENCES

1. For a detailed discussion of bond valuation and the attributes of bonds that are important in their pricing, see:

   Karlyn Mitchell, "The Call, Sinking Fund, and Term-To-Maturity Features of Corporate Bonds: An Empirical Investigation," *Journal of Financial and Quantitative Analysis* 26, no. 2 (June 1991): 201–222.

Frank J. Fabozzi, *Valuation of Fixed Income Securities* (Summit, NJ: Frank J. Fabozzi Associates, 1994).

Frank J. Fabozzi (ed.), *Advances in Fixed Income Valuation Modeling and Risk Management* (New Hope, PA: Frank J. Fabozzi Associates, 1997).

James C. Van Horne, *Financial Market Rates and Flows* (Upper Saddle River, NJ: Prentice Hall, 1998).

2. Putable bond are discussed in:

Leland E. Crabbe and Panos Nikoulis, "The Putable Bond Market: Structure, Historical Experience, and Strategies," *Journal of Fixed Income* 7, no. 3 (December 1997): 47–60.

3. Some of the many studies that have investigated the relationship between historical measures of a firm's performance and its bond ratings are:

Thomas F. Pogue and Robert M. Soldofsky, "What's in a Bond Rating?" *Journal of Financial and Quantitative Analysis* 4, no. 2 (June 1969): 201–228.

R. R. West, "An Alternate Approach to Predicting Corporate Bond Ratings," *Journal of Accounting Research* 8, no. 1 (Spring 1970): 118–125.

George E. Pinches and Kent A. Mingo, "A Multivariate Analysis of Industrial Bond Ratings," *Journal of Finance* 30, no. 1 (March 1975): 201–206.

Robert S. Kaplan and Gabriel Urwitz, "Statistical Models of Bond Ratings: A Methodological Inquiry," *Journal of Business* 52, no. 2 (April 1979): 231–261.

Ahmed Belkaoui, *Industrial Bonds and the Rating Process* (Westport, CT: Quorum Books, 1983).

4. Bond ratings have been studied in:

Steven Katz, "The Price Adjustment Process of Bonds to Rating Reclassifications: A Test of Bond Market Efficiency," *Journal of Finance* 29, no. 2 (May 1974): 551–559.

Paul Grier and Steven Katz, "The Differential Effects of Bond Rating Changes among Industrial and Public Utility Bonds by Maturity," *Journal of Business* 49, no. 2 (April 1976): 226–239.

Mark I. Weinstein, "The Effect of a Rating Change Announcement on Bond Price," *Journal of Financial Economics* 5, no. 3 (December 1977): 329–350.

Douglas J. Lucas and John G. Lonski, "Changes in Corporate Credit Quality 1970–1990," *Journal of Fixed Income* 1, no. 4 (March 1992): 7–14.

Edward I. Altman and Duen Li Kao, "Rating Drift in High-Yield Bonds," *Journal of Fixed Income* 1, no. 4 (March 1992): 15–20.

Edward I. Altman, "The Implications of Bond Ratings Drift," *Financial Analysts Journal* 48, no. 3 (May/June 1992): 64–75.

John R. M. Hand, Robert W. Holthausen, and Richard W. Leftwich, "The Effect of Bond Rating Agency Announcements on Bond and Stock Prices," *Journal of Finance* 47, no. 2 (June 1992): 733–752.

Lea V. Carty and Jerome S. Fons, "Measuring Changes in Corporate Credit Quality," *Journal of Fixed Income* 4, no. 1 (June 1994): 27–41.

Richard Cantor and Frank Packer, "The Credit Rating Industry," *Journal of Fixed Income* 5, no. 3 (December 1995): 10–34.

Gailen Hite and Arthur Warga, "The Effect of Bond-Rating Changes on Bond Price Performance," *Financial Analysts Journal* 53, no. 3 (May/June 1997): 35–51.

Allen Michel, Israel Shaked, and Christopher McHugh, "After Bankruptcy: Can Ugly Ducklings Turn into Swans?" *Financial Analysts Journal* 54, no. 3 (May/June 1998): 31–40.

5. Municipal bond ratings are discussed in:

John E. Petersen, *The Rating Game* (New York: The Twentieth Century Fund, 1974).

Robert W. Ingram, Leroy D. Brooks, and Ronald M. Copeland, "The Information Content of Municipal Bond Rating Changes: A Note," *Journal of Finance* 38, no. 3 (June 1983): 997–1003.

George Foster, *Financial Statement Analysis* (Englewood Cliffs, NJ: Prentice Hall, 1986), Chapter 14.

6. Default premiums and risks are discussed in:

W. Braddock Hickman, *Corporate Bond Quality and Investor Experience* (Princeton: Princeton University Press, 1958).

Harold G. Fraine and Robert H. Mills, "The Effect of Defaults and Credit Deterioration on Yields of Corporate Bonds," *Journal of Finance* 16, no. 3 (September 1961): 423–434.

Thomas R. Atkinson and Elizabeth T. Simpson, *Trends in Corporate Bond Quality* (New York: Columbia University Press, 1967).

Gordon Pye, "Gauging the Default Premium," *Financial Analysts Journal* 30, no. 1 (January/February 1974): 49–52.

Ricardo J. Rodriguez, "Default Risk, Yield Spreads, and Time to Maturity," *Journal of Financial and Quantitative Analysis* 23, no. 1 (March 1988): 111–117.

Edward I. Altman, "Measuring Corporate Bond Mortality and Performance," *Journal of Finance* 44, no. 4 (September 1989): 909–922.

Paul Asquith, David W. Mullins Jr., and Eric D. Wolff, "Original Issue High Yield Bonds; Aging Analysis of Defaults, Exchanges, and Calls," *Journal of Finance* 44, no. 4 (September 1989): 923–952.

Marshall E. Blume and Donald B. Keim, "Realized Returns and Defaults on Low-Grade Bonds: The Cohort of 1977 and 1978," *Financial Analysts Journal* 47, no. 2 (March/April 1991): 63–72.

Marshall E. Blume, Donald B. Keim, and Sandeep A. Patel, "Returns and Volatility of Low-Grade Bonds, 1977–1989," *Journal of Finance* 46, no. 1 (March 1991): 49–74.

Bradford Cornell and Kevin Greene, "The Investment Performance of Low-Grade Bond Funds," *Journal of Finance* 46, no. 1 (March 1991): 29–48.

Jerome S. Fons and Andrew E. Kimball, "Corporate Bond Defaults and Default Rates 1970–1990," *Journal of Fixed Income* 1, no. 1 (June 1991): 36–47.

Marshall E. Blume and Donald B. Keim, "The Risk and Return of Low-Grade Bonds: An Update," *Financial Analysts Journal* 47, no. 5 (September/October 1991): 85–89.

Edward I. Altman, "Defaults and Returns on High-Yield Bonds through the First Half of 1991," *Financial Analysts Journal* 47, no. 6 (November/December 1991): 67–77.

Bradford Cornell, "Liquidity and the Pricing of Low-Grade Bonds," *Financial Analysts Journal* 48, no. 1 (January/February 1992): 63–67, 74.

Edward I. Altman, "Revisiting the High-Yield Bond Market," *Financial Management* 21, no. 2 (Summer 1992): 79–92.

Martin S. Fridson, "Fraine's Neglected Findings: Was Hickman Wrong?" *Financial Analysts Journal*, 50, no. 5 (September/October 1994): 43–53.

7. The classic study on yield spreads is:

Lawrence Fisher, "Determinants of Risk Premiums on Corporate Bonds," *Journal of Political Economy* 67, no. 3 (June 1959): 217–237.

8. Yield spreads are also discussed in:

George Foster, *Financial Statement Analysis* (Englewood Cliffs, NJ: Prentice Hall, 1986), pp. 510–511.

Martin S. Fridson and Jeffrey A. Bersh, "Spread versus Treasuries as a Market-Timing Tool for High-Yield Investors," *Journal of Fixed Income* 4, no. 1 (June 1994): 63–69.

Martin S. Fridson and Jon G. Jonsson, "Spread versus Treasuries and the Riskiness of High-Yield Bonds," *Journal of Fixed Income* 5, no. 3 (December 1995): 79–88.

9. Predicting and analyzing bankruptcy has been a subject of much research; see the following papers and their citations:

William H. Beaver, "Financial Ratios As Predictors of Failure," *Empirical Research in Accounting: Selected Studies, 1966*, supplement to *Journal of Accounting Research* 4, 1966: 71–111.

William H. Beaver, "Market Prices, Financial Ratios and the Prediction of Failure," *Journal of Accounting Research* 6, no. 2 (Autumn 1968): 179–192.

Edward I. Altman, "Financial Ratios, Discriminant Analysis and the Prediction of Corporate Bankruptcy," *Journal of Finance* 23, no. 4 (September 1968): 589–609.

Edward B. Deakin, "A Discriminant Analysis of Predictors of Business Failure," *Journal of Accounting Research* 10, no. 1 (Spring 1972): 167–179.

R. Charles Moyer, "Forecasting Financial Failure: A Re-examination," *Financial Management* 6, no. 1 (Spring 1977): 11–17.

Edward I. Altman, Robert G. Haldeman, and P. Narayanan, "Zeta Analysis: A New Model to Identify Bankruptcy Risk of Corporations," *Journal of Banking and Finance* 1, no. 1 (June 1977): 29–54.

James A. Ohlson, "Financial Ratios and the Probabilistic Prediction of Bankruptcy," *Journal of Accounting Research* 18, no. 1 (Spring 1980): 109–131.

Joseph Aharony, Charles P. Jones, and Itzhak Swary, "An Analysis of Risk and Return Characteristics of Corporate Bankruptcy Using Capital Market Data," *Journal of Finance* 35, no. 4 (September 1980): 1001–1016.

Ismael G. Dambolena and Sarkis J. Khoury, "Ratio Stability and Corporate Failure," *Journal of Finance* 35, no. 4 (September 1980): 1017–1026.

Edward I. Altman, "The Success of Business Failure Prediction Models: An International Survey," *Journal of Banking and Finance* 8, no. 2 (June 1984): 171–198.

Cornelius J. Casey and Norman J. Bartczak, "Cash Flow—It's Not the Bottom Line," *Harvard Business Review* 62, no. 4 (July–August 1984): 61–66.

Cornelius J. Casey and Norman J. Bartczak, "Using Operating Cash Flow Data to Predict Financial Distress: Some Extensions," *Journal of Accounting Research* 23, no. 1 (Spring 1985): 384–401.

James A. Gentry, Paul Newbold, and David T. Whitford, "Classifying Bankrupt Firms with Funds Flow Components," *Journal of Accounting Research* 23, no. 1 (Spring 1985): 146–160.

James A. Gentry, Paul Newbold, and David T. Whitford, "Predicting Bankruptcy: If Cash Flow's Not the Bottom Line, What Is?" *Financial Analysts Journal* 41, no. 5 (September/October 1985): 47–56.

Maggie Queen and Richard Roll, "Firm Mortality: Using Market Indicators to Predict Survival," *Financial Analysts Journal* 43, no. 3 (May/June 1987): 9–26.

Ismael G. Dambolena and Joel M. Shulman, "A Primary Rule for Detecting Bankruptcy: Watch the Cash," *Financial Analysts Journal* 44, no. 5 (September/October 1988): 74–78.

James M. Gahlon and Robert L. Vigeland, "Early Warning Signs of Bankruptcy Using Cash Flow Analysis," *Journal of Commercial Bank Lending* 71, no. 4 (December 1988): 4–15.

Abdul Aziz and Gerald H. Lawson, "Cash Flow Reporting and Financial Distress Models: Testing of Hypotheses," *Financial Management* 18, no. 1 (Spring 1989): 55–63.

Douglas J. Lucas, "Default Correlation and Credit Analysis," *Journal of Fixed Income* 4, no. 4 (March 1995): 76-87.

Jean Helwege and Paul Kleiman, "Understanding Aggregate Default Rates of High-Yield Bonds," *Journal of Fixed Income* 7, no. 1 (June 1997): 55–61.

Martin S. Fridson, M. Christopher Garman, and Sheng Wu, "Real Interest Rates and the Default Rate on High-Yield Bonds," *Journal of Fixed Income* 7, no. 2 (September 1997): 29–34.

Bond Portfolio Management

The methods currently in use for managing bond portfolios can be divided into two general categories: passive and active. Methods in the passive category rest on the basic assumption that bond markets are semistrong-form efficient; that is, current bond prices are viewed as accurately reflecting all publicly available information. Thus bonds are felt to be priced fairly in the marketplace, providing a return that is commensurate with the risk involved. In addition to believing that individual bonds are not mispriced, passive investors also believe that attempting to predict interest rates is, in general, futile. In summary, passive management rests on the belief that attempts at both security selection (that is, identifying mispriced bonds) and market timing (for example, buying long-term bonds when interest rates are predicted to fall and replacing them with short-term bonds when interest rates are predicted to rise) will be unsuccessful in providing the investor with above-average returns.

Active methods of bond portfolio management are based on the assumption that the bond market is not so efficient, thereby giving some investors the opportunity to earn above-average returns. That is, active management is based on the ability of the portfolio manager either to identify mispriced bonds or to "time" the bond market by accurately predicting interest rates.

This chapter will discuss these two general approaches to bond portfolio management. It begins by reviewing some of the findings regarding the efficiency of the bond market.

15.1   BOND MARKET EFFICIENCY

In this assessment of bond market efficiency, only a few of the major studies will be mentioned. The conclusion obtained from reading them is that bond markets are highly, but not perfectly, semistrong-form efficient; that is, bond prices tend to reflect almost all publicly available information. Not surprisingly, this impression is similar to the one that is obtained from studies of the efficiency of stock markets.

15.1.1 Price Behavior of Treasury Bills

An early study of bond market efficiency focused on the price behavior of Treasury bills. In particular, the prices of Treasury bills were analyzed on a weekly basis from October 1946 through December 1964, a total of 796 weeks. The study found that knowledge of how Treasury bill prices changed in the past was of little use in trying to predict how they would change in the future. Consequently, the results from this study are consistent with the notion that the market for Treasury bills is weak-form efficient.[1]

15.1.2 Expert Predictions of Interest Rates

Bond market efficiency has also been studied by examining the accuracy of interest-rate predictions that have been made by experts. These people use a wide range of techniques and many different sources of information. It is reasonable to assume that their information is publicly available, so such studies can be viewed as tests of semistrong-form efficiency.

One way these tests have been conducted involves the building of statistical models that are based on what the experts have said in regard to how interest rates should be predicted. Once these models have been constructed, their predictive accuracy can be evaluated. In one study six models were constructed, and their one-month-ahead predictions were tested over the two-year period of 1973 and 1974. Consistent with the notion of efficient markets, it was found that a simple model of "no change" was more accurate in predicting interest rates than any of the six statistical models.[2]

Another way these tests have been conducted involves comparing a set of explicit predictions with what subsequently occurred. One source of such predictions is the quarterly survey of interest-rate expectations that appears in the *Goldsmith-Nagan Bond and Money Market Newsletter*, published by Goldsmith-Nagan, Inc. Specifically, this survey reports the predictions made by roughly 50 "money market professionals" regarding three-month-ahead and six-month-ahead levels of ten different interest rates. In one study the predictions made from September 1969 through December 1972 (that is, 14 sets of quarterly predictions) were compared with those of a no-change model—that is, a model that forecasts no change from the current level of interest rates.[3] Interestingly, the professionals seemed to forecast better than the no-change model for short-term interest rates (such as forecasting what the three-month Treasury bill rate will be three months in the future) but did worse than the no-change model for longer-term interest rates (such as forecasting what the intermediate-term Treasury note rate will be three months in the future).

A subsequent study examined the Goldsmith-Nagan predictions of three-month Treasury bill rates six months in the future during the time period from March 1970 through September 1979 (39 predictions).[4] These predictions were compared with those of three "simple" models, the first one being the no-change model. The second model was based on the liquidity preference theory of the term structure of interest rates (discussed in Chapter 5). According to this theory, the forward rate implicit in current market rates should be equal to the expected future interest rate plus a liquidity premium. Thus a forecast of the expected future rate can be obtained by subtracting an estimate of the liquidity premium from the forward rate. The third model was what statisticians refer to as an *autoregressive model*. Basically, a forecast of the future Treasury bill rate was formed from the current Treasury bill rate as well as what the Treasury bill rate was one, two, three, and six quarters ago.

The study found that the professionals were more accurate than both the no-change model and the liquidity premium model, but less accurate than the autoregressive model.

Another study evaluated the six-month-ahead predictions of three-month Treasury bill rates that were made by nine economists and reported semiannually in *The Wall Street Journal*. Evaluation of the forecasts published from December 1981 through June 1986 showed that the no-change model was the most accurate.[5] An update of this study looked at six-month-ahead predictions of three-month Treasury bill and 30-year Treasury bond yields made by economists from 1982 through 1996 in surveys conducted by *The Wall Street Journal*. Yields moved in the opposite direction of the economists' consensus prediction 53% of the time for the Treasury bill forecasts and 67% of the time for the Treasury bond forecasts. Furthermore, a no-change model produced smaller forecast errors. Last, no evidence was uncovered that the best forecasters in one period were able to demonstrate superior forecasting ability in the next period.[6]

In summary, it appears from this evidence that the no-change model sometimes provides the most accurate forecasts of future interest rates, whereas at other times the experts are more accurate. On balance, a reasonable interpretation of these results is that the bond market is nearly semistrong-form efficient. Although the bond market may not be perfectly efficient, the evidence clearly suggests that it is hard to forecast interest rates consistently with greater accuracy than a no-change model.[7]

15.1.3 Price Reaction to Bond Rating Changes

A different test of market efficiency concerned the reaction of bond prices to rating changes. If ratings are based on public information, then any rating change will follow the release of such information. This fact suggests that in a semistrong-form efficient market, a bond's price will react to the release of the public information rather than to the subsequent announcement of the rating change. Thus an announcement of a rating change should not trigger a subsequent adjustment in the associated bond's price.

In a study that examined 100 rating changes that took place during the period from 1962 through 1974, no significant changes in bond prices were detected in the period from six months before through six months after the announcement of the change. However, a significant change was observed in the period from 18 months through 7 months before the announcement. Specifically, rating increases were preceded by price increases, and rating decreases were preceded by price decreases.[8]

In a second study that looked at downgrades to a below-investment-grade rating during 1985–1995, it was found that there was a large abnormal downward price movement in the bond over the six-month period before the downgrade. Furthermore, there was a smaller but still significant abnormal downward price movement during the month of the downgrade.[9] However, it is unknown whether this downward price movement occurred during the days before or after the day of the downgrade.

15.1.4 Money Supply Announcements

Every week, generally on Thursday, the Federal Reserve Board announces the current size of the money supply in the economy. It is known that interest rates are related to, among other things, the availability of credit, and that the money supply affects this availability. As a result, if the money supply figures are surprisingly high or low, then the announcement should trigger adjustments in the levels of various interest rates.[10] Furthermore, such adjustments should take place rapidly in a semi-strong-form efficient market. Studies indicate that such adjustments are indeed rapid, generally taking place within a day after the announcement.[11]

15.1.5 Performance of Bond Portfolio Managers

Perhaps the best test of bond market efficiency is to examine the performance record of those professionals who manage bond portfolios. After all, if these people who make their living by investing other people's money in fixed-income securities cannot, on average, generate abnormal returns for their clients, then it would be difficult to argue that these markets are not highly efficient. One study that examined the performance of 41 bond funds from 1979 to 1988 found that, depending on the model of performance used, between 27 (66%) and 33 (80%) of the funds had negative abnormal returns. Furthermore, the underperformance ranged from −.023% to −.069% per month (or −.3% to −.8% per year).

Despite the evidence that the average fund was not able to generate positive abnormal returns, it is still possible that some of the managers were consistently able to do so. One way of testing their investment skills is to examine whether the top-performing funds in one time period continued being top performers in the next period. More specifically, the managers were ranked on the basis of their funds' performance during the five-year period of 1979–1983 and then ranked again on the basis of their performance during the next five-year period of 1984–1988. If the top managers had a special talent for "beating the market," then these two sets of rankings should have been highly correlated. However, depending on the model used to generate the rankings, the correlations ranged from .234 to −.111; none were statistically significantly different from zero.

The issue of bond market efficiency was slightly clouded in a study that analyzed 223 bond funds over the period of 1987–1991. The average fund had negative abnormal returns of from −.077% to −.107% per month (or −.9% to −1.3% per year). However, relative performance was observed to persist; the performance rankings from the first three-year period had a significantly positive correlation ranging from .212 to .451 with the rankings for the following two years.[12]

15.1.6 Summary

In summary, the evidence on the efficiency of the bond market is consistent with the notion that it is highly, but not perfectly, semistrong-form efficient.[13] Statistical tests of past prices of Treasury bills suggest that the bond market is efficient. It appears that corporate bonds reflect the information leading to a rating change in a timely fashion and that interest rates change rapidly when there is a surprise in the announced size of the money supply—observations that are also consistent with the notion of efficiency. Furthermore, professional bond portfolio managers appear, on average, to be unable to generate abnormally high returns.

However, there is some evidence that suggests that certain professionals are occasionally able to forecast interest rates in an accurate manner and that some bond portfolio managers persist in their ability to consistently rank near the top of their peers in terms of relative performance. With this in mind, one should not be surprised to find that, although some bond managers have opted to follow a passive approach to investing, others have decided to be more active in their approach. These two approaches will be presented next, beginning with a discussion of some bond pricing theorems. In turn, these theorems will be related to a concept known as duration, which is the basis for one method of passively managing a bond portfolio.

Bond pricing theorems deal with how bond prices move in response to changes in the bonds' yields-to-maturity. Before the theorems are presented, a brief review of some terms associated with bonds will be given.

The typical bond is characterized by a promise to pay the investor two types of cash flows. The first involves the payment of a fixed dollar amount periodically (usually every six months), with the last payment being on a stated date. The second type of cash flow involves the payment of a lump sum on this stated date. The periodic payments are known as **coupon payments**, and the lump-sum payment is known as the bond's principal (or par value or face value). A bond's **coupon rate** is calculated by taking the dollar amount of the coupon payments a bondholder will receive over the course of a year and dividing this total by the par value of the bond. Finally, the amount of time left until the last promised payment is made is known as the bond's **term-to-maturity**, and the discount rate that makes the present value of all the cash flows equal to the market price of the bond is known as the bond's **yield-to-maturity** (or, simply, yield).

Note that if a bond has a market price that is equal to its par value, then its yield-to-maturity will be equal to its coupon rate. However, if the market price is less than par value (a situation in which the bond is said to be selling at a *discount*), then the bond will have a yield-to-maturity that is greater than the coupon rate. Conversely, if the market price is greater than par value (a situation in which the bond is said to be selling at a *premium*), then the bond will have a yield-to-maturity that is less than the coupon rate. In short:

Par: Market price = Par value; Yield-to-maturity = Coupon rate

Discount: Market price < Par value; Yield-to-maturity > Coupon rate

Premium: Market price > Par value; Yield-to-maturity < Coupon rate

Five theorems that deal with bond pricing have been derived on the basis of those relations.[14] For ease of exposition, it is assumed that there is one coupon payment per year (that is, coupon payments are made every 12 months), although the theorems hold in the more common case of two coupon payments per year. The theorems are as follows:

1. *If a bond's market price increases, then its yield must decrease; conversely, if a bond's market price decreases, then its yield must increase.*

    As an example, consider bond A, which has a life of five years, a par value of $1,000, and pays coupons annually of $80. Its yield is 8% because it is currently selling for $1,000. However, if its price increases to $1,100, then its yield will fall to 5.76%. Conversely, if its price falls to $900, then its yield will rise to 10.68%.

2. *If a bond's yield does not change over its life, then the size of its discount or premium will decrease as its life gets shorter.*

    This relation can be seen by examining Figure 15.1. Note how the price of a bond that is selling at either a premium or a discount today will converge over time to its par value. Ultimately the premium or discount will completely disappear at the maturity date.

    As an example, consider bond B, which has a life of five years, a par value of $1,000, and pays coupons annually of $60. Its current market price is $883.31, indicating that it has a yield of 9%. After one year, if it still has a yield

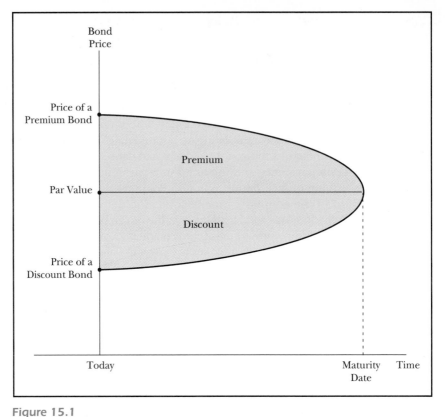

Figure 15.1
Changes in a Bond's Price over Its Life*

*Assuming that the bond's yield-to-maturity remains constant through time.

of 9%, it will be selling for $902.81. Thus its discount has decreased from $116.69 (=$1,000 − $883.31) to $97.19 (=$1,000 − $902.81), for a change of $19.50 (=$116.69 − $97.19).

An equivalent interpretation of this theorem is that if two bonds have the same coupon rate, par value, and yield, then the one with the shorter life will sell for a smaller discount or premium. Consider two bonds, one with a life of five years and the other with a life of four years. Both bonds have a par value of $1,000, pay annual coupons of $60, and yield 9%. In this situation, the bond with a five-year life has a discount of $116.69, whereas the bond with a four-year life has a smaller discount of $97.19.

3. *If a bond's yield does not change over its life, then the size of its discount or premium will decrease at an increasing rate as its life gets shorter.*

Figure 15.1 can also be used to illustrate this theorem. Note how the size of the premium or discount does not change much at first when time passes from today to tomorrow. In contrast, note how the size changes much more notably as time passes just before the maturity date.

As an example, consider bond *B* again. After two years, if it still has a yield of 9%, it will be selling for $924.06. Thus its discount has decreased to $75.94 (=$1,000 − $924.06). Now the amount of the change in the discount from five years to four years was $19.50 (= $116.69 − $97.19) for a percentage change from par of 1.950%. However, the amount of the change from four years to three years is larger, going from $97.19 to $75.94 for a dollar change of $21.25 and a percentage change from par of 2.125%.

4. *A decrease in a bond's yield will raise the bond's price by an amount that is greater in size than the corresponding fall in the bond's price that would occur if there were an equal-sized increase in the bond's yield.*

As an example, consider bond C, which has a life of five years and a coupon rate of 7%. Because it is currently selling at its par value of $1,000, its yield is 7%. If its yield rises by 1% to 8%, then it will be selling for $960.07, a change of $39.93. Alternatively, if its yield falls by 1% to 6%, then it will be selling for $1,042.12, a change of $42.12, which is of greater magnitude than the $39.93 associated with the 1% rise in the bond's yield.

5. *The percentage change in a bond's price owing to a change in its yield will be smaller if its coupon rate is higher.* (Note: This theorem assumes that there is at least one coupon payment besides the one at maturity remaining to be paid. It does not apply to bonds with a life of one year or to bonds that have no maturity date, known as *consols* or *perpetuities*.)

As an example, compare bond D with bond C. Bond D has a coupon rate of 9%, which is 2% larger than C's. However, bond D has the same life (five years) and yield (7%) as C. Thus D's current market price is $1,082.00. Now if the yield on both C and D increases to 8%, then their prices will be $960.07 and $1,039.93, respectively. This change represents a decrease in the price of C equal to $39.93 (=$1,000 − $960.07), or 3.993% (=$39.93/$1,000). For D, the decrease in price is equal to $42.07 (=$1,082 − $1,039.93), or 3.889% (=$42.07/$1,082). Because D had the higher coupon rate, it has the smaller percentage change in price.

It is important for a bond analyst to understand these properties of bond prices thoroughly because they are valuable in forecasting how bond prices will respond to changes in interest rates.

15.3 CONVEXITY

The first and fourth bond pricing theorems have led to the concept in bond valuation known as **convexity**. Consider what happens to the price of a bond if its yield increases or decreases. According to theorem 1, bond prices and yields are inversely related. However, this relationship is not linear, according to theorem 4. The size of the rise in a bond's price associated with a given decrease in its yield is greater than the drop in the bond's price for a similar-sized increase in the bond's yield.

This relationship can be seen by examining Figure 15.2. The price and the current yield-to-maturity for the bond are denoted by P and y, respectively. Consider what would happen to the bond's price if the yield increased or decreased by a fixed amount (for example, 1%), denoted y^+ and y^-. The associated bond prices are denoted by P^- and P^+, respectively.

Two observations can be made by examining this figure. First, an increase in the yield to y^+ is associated with a drop in the bond's price to P^-, and a decrease in the yield to y^- is associated with a rise in the bond's price to P^+. This movement is in accord with the first bond theorem. (Hence the symbols $+$ and $-$ are paired inversely so that, for example, y^+ is associated with P^-.) Second, note that the size of the rise in the bond's price $(P^+ - P)$ is greater than the size of the drop in the bond's price $(P - P^-)$. This relation is in accord with the fourth bond theorem.

The curved line in the figure that shows the relationship between bond prices and yields is convex because it opens upward. Accordingly, the relationship is frequently referred to as convexity. Although this relationship is true for standard types of bonds, the degree of curvature (or convexity) is not the same for all bonds. Instead,

---

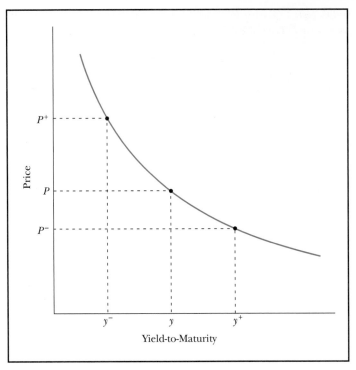

Figure 15.2
Bond Convexity

it depends on, among other things, the size of the coupon payments, the life of the bond, and its current market price. Furthermore, if the bond has a call provision, then the convexity will disappear at sufficiently low yields because such a drop in yields will trigger a call, limiting the rise in the bond's price to its call price.

15.4 DURATION

Duration is a measure of the "average maturity" of the stream of payments associated with a bond. More specifically, it is a weighted average of the lengths of time until the remaining payments are made. Consider, for example, a bond with annual coupon payments of $80, a remaining life of three years, and a par value of $1,000. Because it has a current market price of $950.25, it has a yield-to-maturity of 10.00%. As shown in Table 15.1, its duration is 2.78 years. Note that this is calculated by taking the present value of each cash flow, multiplying each one by the respective amount

TABLE 15.1	Calculation of Duration			
Time Until Receipt of Cash Flow	Amount of Cash Flow	Discount Factor	Present Value of Cash Flow	Present Value of Cash Flow × Time
1	$ 80	.9091	$ 72.73	$ 72.73
2	80	.8264	66.12	132.23
3	1,080	.7513	811.40	2,434.21
			$950.25	$2,639.17
		Duration = $2,639.17/$950.25 = 2.78 years		

of time until it is received, summing the resulting figures, and then dividing this sum ($2,639.17) by the market price of the bond ($950.25).

15.4.1 The Formula

Specifically, the formula for a bond's duration D is:

$$D = \frac{\sum_{t=1}^{T} PV(C_t) \times t}{P_0} \qquad (15.1)$$

where $PV(C_t)$ denotes the present value of the cash flow to be received at time t; P_0 denotes the current market price of the bond, and T denotes the bond's remaining life. Sometimes D is referred to as Macaulay duration, after its discoverer.[15] Although $PV(C_t)$ can be calculated using the appropriate current spot rates as the discount rates, it is more common in practice to use the bond's yield-to-maturity (the latter will be used hereafter).

Why is duration thought of as the "average maturity of the stream of payments associated with a bond"? The reason can be seen by realizing that the current market price of the bond, P_0, is equal to the sum of the present values of the cash flows, $PV(C_t)$, where the discount rate is the bond's yield-to-maturity,

$$P_0 = \sum_{t=1}^{T} PV(C_t) \qquad (15.2)$$

Thus there is an equivalent method for calculating a bond's duration that can be seen by rewriting Equation (15.1) in a slightly different manner,

$$D = \sum_{t=1}^{T} \left[\frac{PV(C_t)}{P_0} \times t \right] \qquad (15.3)$$

First, the present value of each cash flow, $PV(C_t)$, is expressed as a proportion of the market price P_0. Second, these proportions are multiplied by the respective amount of time until the cash flows are received. Third, these figures are summed, with the sum being equal to the bond's duration.

In the example shown in Table 15.1, note that .07653 (=$72.73/$950.25) of the bond's market price is to be received in one year. Similarly, .06958 (=$66.12/$950.25) is to be received in two years, and .85388 (=$811.40/$950.25) is to be received in three years. These proportions sum to 1, so they can be interpreted as weights in calculating a weighted average. Thus the average maturity of the payments associated with a bond is calculated by multiplying each weight by the respective amount of time until the corresponding cash flow is to be received and then summing the products: $(1 \times .07653) + (2 \times .06958) + (3 \times .85388) = 2.78$ years.

Note that a zero-coupon bond will have a duration equal to its remaining life T because there is only one cash flow associated with such a bond; that is, because $P_0 = PV(C_T)$ for such bonds, Equation (15.3) reduces to:

$$D = \frac{PV(C_T)}{P_0} \times T$$
$$= 1 \times T$$
$$= T$$

For any coupon-bearing bond, duration will always be less than the amount of time to its maturity date T. Again, examination of Equation (15.3) indicates why. Because the largest value that t can have is T, and each value of t is multiplied by a weight equal to $PV(C_t)/P_0$, it follows that D must be less than T.

15.4.2 Relationship to Bond Price Changes

One implication of theorem 5 is that bonds having the same maturity date but different coupon sizes may react differently to a given change in interest rates. That is, the prices of these bonds may adjust by notably different amounts when there is a given change in interest rates. However, bonds with the same duration will react quite similarly. Thus, duration can be thought of as a measure of the *price risk* of a bond. Specifically, the percentage change in a bond's price is related to its duration in the following fashion:

$$\begin{matrix}\text{Percentage} \\ \text{change in} \\ \text{price}\end{matrix} \cong -D \times \begin{matrix}\text{percentage change} \\ \text{in } (1 + \text{the} \\ \text{bond's yield})\end{matrix} \qquad (15.4a)$$

where the symbol $\cong$ means "is approximately equal to." This formula implies that when the yields of two bonds having the same duration change by the same percentage, then the prices of the two bonds will change by approximately equal percentages. Equivalently, Equation (15.4a) is written as

$$\frac{\Delta P}{P} \cong -D\left(\frac{\Delta y}{1 + y}\right) \qquad (15.4b)$$

where ΔP denotes the change in the bond's price, P is the bond's initial price, Δy is the change in the bond's yield-to-maturity, and y is the bond's initial yield-to-maturity.

As an example, consider a bond that is currently selling for $1,000 with a yield-to-maturity of 8%. Given that the bond has a duration of ten years, by how much will the bond's price change if its yield increases to 9%? Equation (15.4b) shows that $\Delta y = 9\% - 8\% = 1\% = .01$, so that $\Delta y/(1 + y) = .01/1.08 = .00926 = .926\%$ and $-D[\Delta y/(1 + y)] = -10[.926\%] = -9.26\%$. Hence the one-percentage-point rise in the yield will cause approximately a 9.26% drop in the bond's price to $907.40 [= \$1,000 - (.0926 \times \$1,000)]$.

Equation (15.4b) can be rewritten by rearranging terms, resulting in:

$$\frac{\Delta P}{P} \cong -\left[\frac{D}{(1 + y)}\right] \times \Delta y \qquad (15.4c)$$

The quantity $D/(1 + y)$ is sometimes referred to as a bond's **modified duration** (D_m); it reflects the bond's percentage change in price for a 1% change in its yield and hence is a better measure of the price risk of a bond than Macaulay D. Thus, the link between these two measures of duration is:

$$D_m = \frac{D}{(1 + y)} \qquad (15.4d)$$

As an illustration of why some people prefer D_m over D as the measure of a bond's price risk, consider the previous example. Because the bond's duration is 10 years, its modified duration is $10/(1 + .08) = 9.26$ years. Thus, a 1% change in yields will cause the bond's price to change in an opposite direction [note the minus sign in Equation (15.4c)] by approximately 9.26%, as stated earlier. That is:

$$+.01 \times (-9.26) = -.0926$$

or equivalently:

$$+1\% \times (-9.26) = -9.26\%$$

An important assumption has been made in presenting Equations (15.4a) through (15.4d). These equations reflect the price risk of a bond only when the yield curve is horizontal and any shifts in it up or down are parallel. Hence, in the example the current yield curve is assumed to initially be flat at 8% and then to shift either up to 9% or down to 7% so that it remains horizontal afterward. Yield curves are seldom horizontal and infrequently shift in a parallel manner, so these equations are best viewed as approximations. There are other reasons why they are approximations, as will be seen next.

15.4.3 Relationship between Convexity and Duration

At this point it is useful to consider just what kind of relationship the concepts of convexity and duration have to each other. After all, both have something to do with measuring the association of the change in a bond's price with a change in the bond's yield-to-maturity. Figure 15.3 shows the nature of the relationship. Like Figure 15.2, this figure represents a bond that is currently selling for P and has a yield-to-maturity of y. Note the straight line that is tangent to the curve at the point associated with the current price and yield.

If the bond's yield increases to y^+, then the associated price of the bond will fall to P^-. Conversely, if the bond's yield decreases to y^-, then the associated price of the bond will rise to P^+. However, Equation (15.4b) shows that if the yield decreases to y^-, the estimated price will be P_D^+, and if the yield increases to y^+ the estimated price will be P_D^-. The reason is that the relationship between the bond's price, yield, and duration, as mentioned earlier, is not exact. Instead, it is an approximation that assumes that the percentage change in the bond's price is a linear function of its duration. Hence the equation approximates the new price in a linear fashion represented by the straight line and leading to an error that is a consequence of convexity. [In the example, the sizes of the respective errors are $\left(P^- - P_D^-\right)$ and

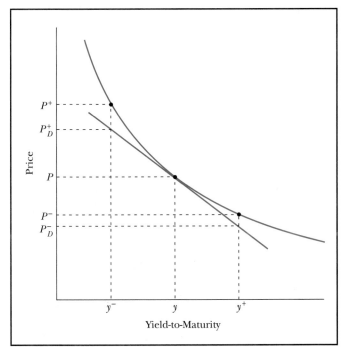

Figure 15.3
Bond Convexity and Duration

$\left(P^+ - P_D^+\right).\right]$ That is, because the relationship between yield changes and bond price changes is convex, not linear, the use of Equation (15.4b) will underestimate the new price associated with either an increase or a decrease in the bond's yield.[16] However, for small changes in yields the error is relatively small, and thus, Equation (15.4b) works reasonably well. Its usefulness can be seen by observing in Figure 15.3 that the size of the pricing error becomes smaller as the size of the yield change gets smaller. (Note that the distance between the linear approximating line and the convex curve will be smaller for smaller changes in yields from y.)

15.4.4 Changes in the Term Structure

As mentioned earlier, when yields change, most bond prices also change, but some react more than others. Even bonds with the same maturity date can react quite differently to a given change in yields. However, it was shown in Equations (15.4a) and (15.4b) that the percentage change in a bond's price is related to its duration. Hence the prices of two bonds that have the same duration will react similarly to a given change in yields.

For example, the bond shown in Table 15.1 has a duration of 2.78 and a yield of 10%. If its yield changes to 11%, then the percentage change in (1 + the bond's yield) is .91% $\left[= (1.11 - 1.10)/1.10\right]$. Thus its price should change by approximately -2.53% $(=-2.78 \times .91\%)$. With a discount rate of 11%, its price can be calculated to equal $926.69, for an actual price change of $-\$23.56$ $(=\$926.69 - \$950.25)$ and a percentage change of -2.48% $(=-\$23.56/\$950.25)$. Any other bond having a duration of 2.78 years will experience a similar price change if it has a similar percentage change in its yield. Equivalently, any other bond having a modified duration of 2.53 $(=2.78/1.10)$ will experience a similar price change for a similar change in its yield.

Consider a bond with a maturity of four years that also has a duration of 2.78 years. When there is a shift in interest rates, and the yields on the three-year and four-year bonds change by the same amount, then their prices will change similarly. For example, if the yield on the four-year bond goes from 10.8% to 11.81% at the same time the yield on the three-year bond is going from 10% to 11%, then the percentage change in the present value of the four-year bond will be approximately -2.53% $\left[= -2.78 \times (1.1181 - 1.108)/1.108 = -2.78 \times .91\%\right]$, which is the same percentage as the three-year bond. Here the difference in the two bonds' modified durations $(2.53 = 2.78/1.10$ for the three-year bond; $2.51 = 2.78/1.108$ for the four-year bond) is exactly offset by the different changes in yield (1% for the three-year bond; 1.01% for the four-year bond.)

What if the "percentage change in (1 + the bond's yield)" is different? That is, what happens if the term structure shifts in a manner so that "the percentage change in (1 + the bond's yield)" is not the same for all bonds? Perhaps when the three-year bond goes from a yield of 10% to a yield of 11% [a percentage change of .91% = $(1.11 - 1.10)/1.10$], the four-year bond will go from a yield of 10.8% to a yield of 11.5% [a percentage change of .63% = $(1.115 - 1.108)/1.108$]. In this case the percentage change in price for the four-year bond will be approximately -1.75% $\left[= -2.78 \times (1.115 - 1.108)/1.108\right]$, which is a smaller change than the -2.53% associated with the three-year bond. Accordingly, even though the two bonds have the same duration or modified duration, it does not automatically follow that their prices will react identically to *any* change in the yield curve, because the associated yield changes can be different for two bonds having the same duration.

The introduction of the concept of duration led to the development of the technique of bond portfolio management known as **immunization**. Specifically, this technique purportedly allows a bond portfolio manager to be relatively certain of being able to meet a given promised stream of cash outflows. Thus once the portfolio has been formed, it is "immunized" from any adverse effects associated with future changes in interest rates.

15.5.1 How Immunization Is Accomplished

Immunization is accomplished simply by calculating the duration of the promised outflows and then investing in a portfolio of bonds that has an identical duration.[17] In doing so, this technique takes advantage of the observation that *the duration of a portfolio of bonds is equal to the weighted average of the durations of the individual bonds in the portfolio.* For example, if a portfolio has one-third of its funds invested in bonds having a duration of six years and two-thirds in bonds having a duration of three years, then the portfolio itself has a duration of four years $[= (1/3 \times 6) + (2/3 \times 3)]$.

Consider a simple situation in which a portfolio manager has one and only one cash outflow to make from a portfolio: an amount equal to $1,000,000, which is to be paid in two years. Because there is only one cash outflow, its duration is simply two years. Now the bond portfolio manager is considering investing in two different bond issues. The first issue is the one shown in Table 15.1, with bonds that have a maturity of three years. The second issue involves a set of bonds that mature in one year, providing the holder of each bond with a single payment of $1,070 (consisting of a single coupon payment of $70 and a par value of $1,000). Because these bonds are currently selling for $972.73, their yield-to-maturity is 10%.

Consider the choices open to the portfolio manager. All of the portfolio's funds could be invested in the one-year bonds, with the intention of reinvesting the proceeds from the maturing bonds one year from now in another one-year issue. However, doing so would entail risks. In particular, if interest rates were to decline over the next year, then the funds from the maturing one-year bonds would have to be reinvested at a lower rate than the currently available 10%. Thus the portfolio manager faces reinvestment-rate risk owing to the possibility that the funds one year from now might have to be reinvested at a lower rate.[18]

A second alternative would be for the portfolio manager to invest all of the funds in the three-year issue. However, this choice also entails risks. In particular, the three-year bonds will have to be sold after two years in order to come up with the $1,000,000. The risk is that interest rates will have risen before then, meaning that bond prices, in general, will have fallen and the bonds will not have a selling price that is at least $1,000,000. Thus the portfolio manager faces interest-rate risk with this strategy.

One proposed solution is to invest part of the portfolio's funds in the one-year bonds and the rest in the three-year bonds. How much should be placed in each issue? If immunization is to be used, the solution can be found by solving simultaneously a set of two equations involving two unknowns,

$$W_1 + W_3 = 1 \qquad (15.5)$$

$$(W_1 \times 1) + (W_3 \times 2.78) = 2 \qquad (15.6)$$

Here W_1 and W_3 denote the weights (or proportions) of the portfolio's funds that are to be invested in the bonds with maturities of one and three years, respectively. Note that Equation (15.5) states that the sum of the weights must equal 1, whereas Equation (15.6) states that the weighted average of the durations of the bonds in the portfolio must equal the duration of the cash outflow, which is two years.

The solution to these two equations is easily found. First, Equation (15.5) is rewritten as:

$$W_1 = 1 - W_3 \tag{15.7}$$

Then $1 - W_3$ is substituted for W_1 in Equation (15.6), resulting in

$$\left[(1 - W_3) \times 1 \right] + (W_3 \times 2.78) = 2 \tag{15.8}$$

Because this is one equation with one unknown, W_3, it can be solved easily. Doing so results in $W_3 = .5618$. Inserting this value into Equation (15.7) indicates that $W_1 = .4382$. Thus the portfolio manager should put 43.82% of the portfolio's funds in the one-year bonds and 56.18% in the three-year bonds.

In this case, the portfolio manager would need $826,446 $\left[= \$1,000,000/(1.10)^2 \right]$ in order to purchase bonds that would create a fully immunized portfolio. With this money, $362,149 (= .4382 × $826,446) would be used to buy one-year bonds and $464,297 (=.5618 × $826,446) would be used to buy three-year bonds. Because the current market prices of the one-year and three-year bonds are $972.73 and $950.25, respectively, 372 one-year bonds (= $362,149/$972.73) and 489 three-year bonds (=$464,297/$950.25) would be purchased.

What does immunization accomplish? According to the theory, if yields rise, then the portfolio's losses owing to the selling of the three-year bonds at a discount after two years will be exactly offset by the gains from reinvesting the maturing one-year bonds (and first-year coupons on the three-year bonds) at the higher rate. Alternatively, if yields fall, then the loss from being able to reinvest the maturing one-year bonds (and first-year coupons on the three-year bonds) at a lower rate will be exactly offset by being able to sell the three-year bonds after two years at a premium. Thus the portfolio is *immunized* from the effect of any movements in interest rates in the future.

Table 15.2 shows more explicitly what would happen to the portfolio. The second column shows what the portfolio would be worth at the end of two years if yields remained at 10% over the next two years. As can be seen, the value of the portfolio

TABLE 15.2	Example of an Immunized Portfolio		
	Yield-to-Maturity at the End of One Year		
	9%	10%	11%
Value at $t = 2$ from reinvesting one-year bond proceeds: $\left[\$1,070 \times 372.3 \times (1 + y) \right] =$	$ 434,213	$438,197	$ 442,181
Value at $t = 2$ of three-year bonds: value from reinvesting coupons received at $t = 1$: $\left[\$80 \times 488.6 \times (1 + y) \right] =$	42,606	42,997	43,388
Coupons received at $t = 2$: $[\$80 \times 488.6] =$	39,088	39,088	39,088
Selling price at $t = 2$: $\left[\$1,080 \times 488.6/(1 + y) \right] =$	484,117	479,716	475,395
Aggregate portfolio value at $t = 2$	$1,000,024	$999,998	$1,000,052

of one-year and three-year bonds would be approximately equal to the promised cash outflow of $1,000,000. Alternatively, if yields fell to 9% or rose to 11% before one year had passed and remained at the new level, then the value of the portfolio would be slightly more than the needed $1,000,000.[19]

15.5.2 Problems with Immunization

The preceding section described what immunization purports to accomplish. Left open is the possibility that it might not work quite as well in practice. What can cause it to work less than perfectly? Underlying this issue is this question: Why might duration fail to measure the interest-rate risk of a bond accurately? In terms of the example, what can cause the value of the portfolio to be less than $1,000,000 at the end of two years?

Default and Call Risk

To begin with, immunization (and duration) are based on the assumptions that the bonds will not default and will not be called before maturity; that is, the bonds are assumed to be free from both call risk and default risk and will thus pay their promised cash flows in full and on time. Consequently, if a bond in the portfolio either enters into default or is called, the portfolio will not be immunized.

Because of problems with the use of the traditional measure of duration in forming immunized portfolios, an alternative measure known as **effective duration** has been introduced.[20] Specifically, this measure is of use in evaluating any bond that contains *embedded options*, meaning that either the bond issuer or the bondholder has the ability to cause the actual stream of cash payments to differ from that which would be received if the bond were paid off as promised over its entire life. Examples of embedded options include the option of the issuer to go into default or to prepay the bond before maturity by exercising the bond's call provision, and the option of bondholders of *putable bonds* to force the issuer to pay them off before maturity.

The formula for calculating a bond's effective duration D_e is:

$$D_e = \frac{P^+ - P^-}{2P\Delta y} \tag{15.9}$$

where P^+ and P^- denote the bond's price if its yield decreases or increases by a given amount Δy (say, 1%), such as shown in Figure 15.2. For example, consider a default-free bond with a 7% coupon paid annually that has 15 years left until maturity but can be called at any time for $1,050. The bond is currently selling for par, so if its yield increases by 1% to 8%, the bond's price will be $914.41 because no embedded options will be exercised. However, if its yield drops by 1% to 6%, then it is believed that the call option will be exercised, so the value of the bond will be $1,050 instead of $1,097.12. Thus, the effective duration for this bond can be approximated by using Equation (15.9), and will be ($1,050 − $914.41)/(2 × $1,000 × .01) = 6.8 years, in contrast to the traditional duration and modified duration measures of 9.75 years and 9.11 years, respectively.

Multiple Nonparallel Shifts in a Nonhorizontal Yield Curve

Immunization (and duration) are also based on the assumption that the yield curve is horizontal and that any shifts in it will be parallel and will occur before any payments are received from the bonds that were purchased. In the example, the one-year and the three-year bonds had the same 10% yield-to-maturity at the start, and the shift of

1% in yields was assumed to be the same for both bond issues. Furthermore, this shift was assumed to occur sometime before one year had passed.

In reality, the yield curve will not be horizontal at the start, and shifts in it are not likely to be either parallel or restricted when they occur. Perhaps the one-year and the three-year bonds will have initial yields of 10% and 10.5%, respectively, with the yields on the one-year and three-year bonds falling by 1% and .8%, respectively, after one year. Indeed, there is evidence of greater volatility in yields of shorter-term securities. If these kinds of shifts occur, then it is possible that the portfolio will not be immunized.[21]

If the bond portfolio manager followed a special kind of immunization known as **cash matching**, then frequent nonparallel shifts in a nonhorizontal yield curve would have no adverse effect on the portfolio. The reason is that cash matching involves the purchase of bonds so that the cash received each period from the bonds is identical in size to the promised cash outflow for that period. Such a cash-matched portfolio of bonds is often referred to as a **dedicated portfolio**. Note that there is no need to reinvest any cash inflows with a dedicated portfolio, so there is no reinvestment-rate risk. Furthermore, because bonds do not have to be sold before maturity, there is no interest-rate risk either.

In the simplest situation in which there is one promised cash outflow, the dedicated portfolio would consist of zero-coupon bonds, with each bond having a life corresponding to the date of the promised cash outflow. In the previous example, where there was a promised cash outflow of $1,000,000 after two years, this goal would be accomplished by purchasing the requisite number of zero-coupon bonds having a maturity of two years.

However, cash matching is often not so easily accomplished because the promised cash outflows may involve an uneven stream of payments for which no zero-coupon bonds exist. The growth in the stripped Treasury bond market has facilitated cash matching, but it can still be difficult and expensive to exactly match cash inflows with promised outflows.

Another potential way around the problem of nonhorizontal yield curves that experience nonparallel shifts is to use one of a variety of more complicated immunization models. These models involve various other assumptions about the current shape of the yield curve and how it will shift in the future. Consequently, the model that the bond portfolio manager personally views as being most accurate should be chosen. Interestingly, various studies have found that despite the inconsistency of its assumptions with actual movements in yields, simple immunization through duration matching works quite well in many cases. Thus some researchers argue that the portfolio manager interested in immunization would be well advised to use this version.[22]

An implication is that, regardless of the model being used, the bond portfolio manager must recognize that a risk is being incurred—the risk that the yield curve will shift in a way that does not correspond with the shift assumed by the model. For example, if the model presented here is used, then the bond portfolio is facing risk in that the yield curve will not shift in a parallel manner. Consequently, some people have argued that none of the immunization models are useful.[23] Others have argued that there are ways to use immunization in the presence of such risk, which has been called **stochastic process risk**.[24]

Rebalancing

Another problem with the use of immunization is the effect of the passage of time on the duration of the bonds held and on the duration of the promised cash outflows. As time passes and yields change, these durations can change at different rates so that the portfolio is no longer immunized. Consequently, the portfolio may need to be rebalanced fairly often.

Here *rebalancing* refers to selling some bonds currently held and replacing them with others so that afterward the duration of the portfolio matches the duration of the promised cash outflows. However, because rebalancing causes the portfolio manager to incur transaction costs, the manager might not want to rebalance whenever the durations do not match; the costs might outweigh the perceived gains from rebalancing. Ultimately, the bond portfolio manager will have to decide how frequently to rebalance the portfolio, taking into consideration the risk of being unbalanced along with the transaction costs associated with rebalancing.

Many Candidates

Finally, there are usually many portfolios that have a duration of the requisite length. Which one is the bond portfolio manager to choose? In the example, imagine that in addition to the one-year and three-year bonds, there is a zero-coupon bond having a life of four years (thus its duration is also four years) that the manager is considering. Now the manager faces a choice of which portfolio to hold; there are many that have the requisite duration of two years. In addition to the one previously described that consisted of just one-year and three-year bonds, there is also one in which two-thirds and one-third of the portfolio's funds are invested in one-year bonds and four-year bonds, respectively. [Note that the duration of this portfolio is also two years: $(2/3 \times 1) + (1/3 \times 4) = 2$.] Furthermore, there are many other candidate portfolios.

One possible solution is to choose the portfolio having the highest average yield-to-maturity (or, alternatively, the lowest cost). Here the yield of each issue is multiplied by the percentage of the portfolio's funds invested in that issue. Another possible solution is to choose the portfolio that most closely resembles a "bullet" or "focused" portfolio, because it has been argued that such a portfolio has less stochastic process risk than any other. Such a portfolio is one in which the bonds have durations (or, alternatively, terms-to-maturity) most closely matching the duration of the promised outflows. In the example, the portfolio consisting of just one-year and three-year bonds would be more focused than the one consisting of the one-year and four-year bonds.

15.6   ACTIVE MANAGEMENT

As mentioned earlier, active management of a bond portfolio is based on the belief that the bond market is not perfectly efficient. Such management can involve security selection; that is, the portfolio manager tries to identify mispriced bonds. Alternatively, it can involve market timing; the portfolio manager tries to forecast general movements in interest rates. It is also possible for an active portfolio manager to be involved in both security selection and market timing. Although there are many methods of actively managing a bond portfolio, some general types of active management can be described.

15.6.1   Horizon Analysis

The return on a bond over any given holding period, sometimes referred to as the bond's *realized return*, depends on its price at the beginning of the period and its price at the end of the period, as well as on its coupon rate. Thus the return on a bond over a one-year holding period will depend on the yield structure at the beginning of the year and the yield structure at the end of the year, because the prices of the

Surplus Management

Corporate pension funds are established to secure the funding of retirement benefits promised to employees. Therefore the primary investment objective of these funds is to accumulate sufficient assets, through contributions and investment income, to satisfy all pension obligations on a timely basis.

The management of corporate pension funds has traditionally focused solely on the asset side of the asset-liability equation. Organizations charged with the oversight of pension funds (often referred to as "plan sponsors") have typically defined their investment policies in terms of seeking maximum returns subject to their tolerance for volatility of returns (see Chapter 23). This philosophy has led many plan sponsors to invest heavily in equity assets, particularly common stocks, on the basis of stocks' perceived superior long-run risk-return characteristics (see Chapter 1).

The foundation of this investment philosophy received a jolt in 1986 when the Financial Accounting Standards Board issued FAS 87, a directive requiring corporations to more fully disclose pension obligations on their financial statements beginning in 1989. Before FAS 87, corporate reporting on pension obligations was consigned to annual report footnotes. This level of disclosure seemed inadequate, given that pension assets and liabilities would represent the largest items on many corporations' balance sheets if they were reported there and that annual pension expenses often constitute a large portion of a corporation's earnings. FAS 87 was designed to address this deficiency.

FAS 87 requires that companies report any negative difference between their pension assets and their pension liabilities on their balance sheets as liabilities. (There is no corresponding balance sheet asset if pension assets exceed pension liabilities.) Moreover, the way in which companies state pension expenses on their income statements was redefined. The expense includes costs associated with pension benefits earned in the current year, plus interest on past obligations, plus the amortization of any unfunded liabilities (that is, liabilities not offset by pension assets), less the expected earnings on the pension fund's assets.

As a result of FAS 87, a corporation's earnings have become sensitive to changes in its pension fund's surplus, which is the difference in value between the fund's assets and liabilities. A significant decrease in pension surplus will result in an earnings reduction, whereas a significant increase can boost earnings. Thus FAS 87 created for the first time a source of reported earnings variability directly attributable to changes in a pension fund's assets and liabilities.

This new source of earnings variability has caused some companies to emphasize control of pension surplus volatility through a process known as *surplus management*. Instead of focusing only on the size of the surplus (effectively, the surplus return), these plan sponsors are directly concerned with the risk of the surplus as well. Depending on their risk tolerances, plan sponsors engaged in surplus management will manage the tradeoff between expected surplus return and surplus risk. At the extreme, a plan sponsor with very low tolerance for surplus risk may want to implement an investment strategy that causes the value

bond at those two points in time will depend on those structures. It follows that possible subsequent changes to the beginning-of-period yield structure must be analyzed in order to estimate possible bond returns over a given holding period. Bond portfolio managers who believe that they are able to identify such changes will want to translate their beliefs into action.

One method, known as **horizon analysis**, involves both selection of a single holding period for analysis and consideration of possible yield structures at the end of the period (that is, at the "horizon"). The possible returns for two bonds—one currently held and one candidate to replace it—are then analyzed. In the analysis, neither bond is assumed to default up to the horizon date. In the process of the analysis, the sensitivities of the returns to changes in key assumptions regarding yields are estimated, allowing at least a rough assessment of some of the relevant risks.

Horizon analysis can be viewed as another way of implementing the capitalization-of-income method of valuation that was discussed in Chapter 14. By focusing

of the pension fund's assets to move closely with the pension fund's liabilities. That is, the plan sponsor wishes to immunize the pension fund's liabilities by creating an appropriately structured portfolio of assets. In this way the variability of changes in pension surplus will be substantially reduced, thereby minimizing the pension fund's impact on the variability of the corporation's earnings.

In order to specify the appropriate composition of the pension fund's portfolio that will immunize the fund's pension liabilities, the plan sponsor must determine what factors can cause the value of these liabilities to change. In the short run, when promised pension benefits can be viewed as fixed, only movements in interest rates will alter the value of pension liabilities. FAS 87 mandates that the value of pension liabilities be calculated as the discounted value of pension benefits earned to date by the company's employees (plus, in some cases, projected salary increases for current employees). The discount rate applied to these earned pension benefits is related to current market interest rates. Therefore, as those interest rates fluctuate, so too does the value of a company's pension liabilities. Interest-rate increases reduce the value of pension liabilities, whereas interest-rate declines increase pension liabilities.

As described in the text, a simple means of at least partially immunizing a set of interest-sensitive liabilities is to create a portfolio of bonds whose duration equals that of the liabilities. As interest rates change, the value of the assets will rise and fall more or less in line with the value of the liabilities, maintaining a relatively constant pension surplus.

Critics of immunization have two arguments. The first argument is that the model of liabilities is too simple because it ignores a pension plan's obligations that are not fixed in nominal terms. That is, from a long-run perspective, liabilities grow with inflation and worker productivity (which translate into pay increases and higher pension benefits). Thus, in the long-run, other factors may be more important than interest rates in determining changes in the value of pension liabilities, thereby undermining the effectiveness of the immunization strategy. The second argument is that the focus of immunization on minimizing surplus risk is short-sighted and counterproductive. Unless a plan sponsor has zero tolerance for surplus risk, other strategies that accept such risk in exchange for higher surplus returns are more desirable. A plan sponsor implementing an immunization approach is effectively "leaving money on the table" by investing in a portfolio of only fixed-income assets to the exclusion of assets, such as common stocks, with higher expected returns.

Despite the problems of immunization, surplus management is an important consideration for plan sponsors. If nothing else, FAS 87 has had the salutary effect of making plan sponsors aware of the surplus risk associated with their pension plans' investment programs. Plan sponsors now regularly conduct "asset-liability" studies designed to highlight the potential outcomes of various mixes of asset classes on their plans' pension surplus. In this way they can make better-informed decisions about the integration of their pension assets and liabilities within their overall financial circumstances.

on the estimated end-of-period price of a bond, it seeks to determine whether the current market price is relatively high or low. That is, for a given estimated end-of-period price, a bond will have a relatively high expected return if its current price is relatively low. Conversely, a bond will have a relatively low expected return if its current price is relatively high.

Figure 15.4 represents a page from a standard yield book for bonds with a 4% coupon. As indicated, a 4% bond with ten years remaining to maturity that is currently priced at $67.48 (for ease of exposition, a par value of $100 is used here) will have a 9% promised annual yield-to-maturity (or 4.5% semiannually). Five years into the future, such a bond's term-to-maturity will have decreased, and the relevant promised yield-to-maturity will probably have changed. Thus as time passes, the bond might follow a path "through the table" such as that shown by the dashed line. If it does, it will end up at a price of $83.78 at the *horizon* (five years hence) with an 8% promised annual yield-to-maturity (or 4% semiannually).

	YEARS TO MATURITY						
Yield to Maturity (%)	10 Yrs.	9 Yrs.	...	5 Yrs.	...	1 Yr.	0 Yrs.
7.00	78.68	80.22		87.53		97.15	100.00
7.50	75.68	77.39		85.63		96.69	100.00
y_H (8.00)	72.82	74.68		(83.78) $\leftarrow P_H$		96.23	100.00
8.50	70.09	72.09		81.98		95.77	100.00
y_0 (9.00) P_0 (67.48)	69.60			(80.22) P_A		95.32	100.00
9.50	64.99	67.22		78.51		94.87	100.00
10.00	62.61	64.92	...	76.83	...	94.42	100.00
10.50	60.34	62.74		75.21		93.98	100.00
11.00	58.17	60.64		73.62		93.54	100.00

Actual Price Pattern / Over Time — Yield Change Effect — Time Effect

Figure 15.4

The Effect of Time and Yield Change on a 4% Coupon Bond

Note: y_0 and P_0 denote the bond's annual yield-to-maturity and price at the beginning of the period; y_H and P_H denote the bond's annual yield-to-maturity and price at the horizon (that is, the end of the period); P_A denotes the bond's price at the horizon if its annual yield remained at $y_0 = 9\%$; yields are compounded semiannually.

Source: Martin L. Leibowitz, "Horizon Analysis for Managed Bond Portfolio," *Journal of Portfolio Management* 1, no. 3 (Spring 1975): 26.

Over any holding period, a bond's return will typically be affected by both the passage of time and a change in yield. Horizon analysis explicitly breaks this return into those two parts: one owing solely to the passage of time, whereby the bond's price moves toward the par value to be paid at maturity (assuming no change in yield), and the other owing solely to a change in yield (assuming no passage of time). These effects are illustrated in Figure 15.4. The total price change from $67.48 to $83.78 (or $16.30) is broken into a change from $67.48 to $80.22 (or $12.74) followed by an instantaneous change from $80.22 to $83.78 (or $3.56). The intermediate value of $80.22 is the price the bond would have commanded at the horizon if its promised yield-to-maturity had remained unchanged at its initial level of 9%. The actual price of $83.78 is that which the bond commands at its actual yield-to-maturity of 8%. In summary, the total price change can be broken into two parts, representing the two effects:

$$\text{Price change} = \text{time effect} + \text{yield change effect} \qquad (15.10)$$

Thus far, no account has been taken of the coupon payments to be received before the horizon date. In principle, one should consider all possible uses of such cash flows or at least analyze possible alternative yield structures during the period to determine likely reinvestment opportunities. In practice, this analysis is rarely done. Instead, a single reinvestment rate is assumed, and the future value of all coupon payments at the horizon date is determined by compounding each one using this rate.[25]

For example, if $2 is received every six months (as in Figure 15.4), with the first payment occurring six months from now and the last payment occurring five years from now, and if each payment is reinvested at 4.25% per six months, then the value at the end of five years will be approximately $24.29. Of this amount, $20 can be considered interest (coupon payments of $2 for ten six-month periods), with the remaining $4.29 being "interest on interest."

In summary, a bond's overall dollar return has four components: the time effect, the yield change effect, the coupons, and the interest from reinvesting the coupons. In the example, the overall dollar return is

$$
\begin{matrix}
\text{Overall} & & \text{yield} & & \text{interest} \\
\text{dollar} & = \text{time} & + \text{change} & + \text{coupons} & + \text{on} \\
\text{return} & \text{effect} & \text{effect} & & \text{coupons}
\end{matrix}
$$

$$= (\$80.22 - \$67.48) + (\$83.78 - \$80.22) + \$20.00 + \$4.29$$

$$= \$12.74 + \$3.56 + \$20.00 + \$4.29$$

$$= \$40.59$$

This overall dollar return can be converted into an overall rate of return by dividing it by the market price of the bond at the beginning of the period, $67.48. Thus it can be seen that a bond's overall rate of return consists of four components:

$$\text{Overall rate of return} = \frac{\$12.74}{\$67.48} + \frac{\$3.56}{\$67.48} + \frac{\$20.00}{\$67.48} + \frac{\$4.29}{\$67.48}$$

$$= .1888 + .0528 + .2964 + .0635$$

$$= .6015$$

or 60.15%. The first term is the return owing to the passage of time; the second term is the return owing to yield change; the third term is coupon return; and the fourth term is the return owing to the reinvestment of the coupon payments.

Because the second term is uncertain, it is important to analyze it further. In the example, a change in yield from 9.0% to 8.0% will result in a change in the market price from $80.22 to $83.78. Given that 8.0% was the expected yield at the horizon, an expected overall rate of return of 60.15% was computed. Using different end-of-period yields enables one to calculate different overall rates of return. Estimates of the probabilities of these yields occurring provide a sense of the bond's risk. Indeed, it can now be seen why bond portfolio managers devote a great deal of attention to making predictions of future yields.

15.6.2 Bond Swaps

Given a set of predictions about future bond yields, a portfolio manager can estimate holding-period returns over one or more horizons for one or more bonds. The goal of **bond swapping** is to actively manage a portfolio by exchanging bonds to take advantage of any superior ability to predict such yields.[26] In making a swap, the portfolio manager believes that an overpriced bond is being exchanged for an underpriced bond. Some swaps are based on the belief that the market will correct for its mispricing in a short period of time, whereas other types of swaps are based on a belief that corrections either will never take place or will take place, but over a long period of time.

There are several categories for classifying swaps, and the distinctions between the categories are often blurry. Nevertheless, many bond swaps can be placed in one of four general categories:

1. **Substitution swap.** Ideally, this swap is an exchange of a bond for a perfect substitute or "twin" bond. The motivation here is temporary price advantage, presumably resulting from an imbalance in the relative supply and demand conditions in the marketplace.

2. **Intermarket spread swap.** This type of swap involves a more general movement out of one market component and into another with the intention of exploiting a currently advantageous yield relationship. The idea here is to benefit from a forecasted changing relationship between the two market components. Although such swaps will almost always have some sensitivity to the direction of the overall market, the idealized focus of this type of swap is the spread relationship itself.

3. **Rate anticipation swap.** This type of swap, on the other hand, is geared toward profiting from an anticipated movement in overall market rates.

4. **Pure yield pickup swap.** This type of swap is oriented toward yield improvements over the long term, with little heed being paid to interim price movements in either the respective market components or the market as a whole.[27]

Consider a hypothetical portfolio manager who holds some of a 30-year AA utility bond issue that has a 7% coupon rate. These bonds are currently selling at par, so their yield-to-maturity is 7%. Now imagine that there is another 30-year AA utility bond issue with a 7% coupon rate that is being made available to the manager at a price that provides a yield-to-maturity of 7.10%. In a substitution swap the manager would exchange a given dollar amount of the currently held bonds for an equivalent dollar amount of the second bond issue, thereby picking up 10 basis points in yield.

Alternatively, the manager might note that there is a 10-year AA utility bond issue outstanding that carries a 6% coupon and is priced at par; thus its yield is 6%. In this case there is a 100-basis-point yield spread between the currently held 30-year bonds and the 10-year bonds. If the manager feels that this spread is too low, then an intermarket spread swap might be used; some of the 30-year bonds would be exchanged for an equivalent dollar amount of the 10-year bonds. Because the manager expects the spread to increase in the future, the yield on the 10-year bonds is expected to fall. It follows that the price on these bonds is expected to rise by an abnormal amount, resulting in an abnormally high holding-period return.

Another possibility is that the manager feels that yields in general are going to rise. In such a situation, the manager will recognize that the currently held portfolio is in a very risky position: Longer-term bonds generally move downward further in price for a given rise in yields than do shorter-term bonds, because they generally have a longer duration. Accordingly, the manager might use a rate anticipation swap to exchange a given dollar amount of the 30-year bonds for an equivalent amount of short-term bonds.

Finally, the manager might not want to make any predictions about future yields or yield spreads. Instead, it might simply be noted that some 30-year AA industrial bonds are currently priced to yield 8%. In this case the manager might want to enter a pure yield pickup swap, in which some of the 7% utility bonds would be exchanged for an equivalent dollar amount of the 8% industrial bonds, the motivation being to earn the extra 100 basis points in yield from the industrials.

15.6.3 Contingent Immunization

One method of bond portfolio management that has both passive and active elements is **contingent immunization**. In the simplest form of contingent immunization, the portfolio will be actively managed as long as favorable results are obtained. However, if unfavorable results occur, then the portfolio will be immunized immediately.

As an illustration, consider the earlier example in which the portfolio manager had to come up with $1,000,000 at the end of two years and the current yield curve was horizontal at 10%. In this situation it was mentioned that the portfolio manager could immunize the portfolio by investing $826,446 in one-year and three-year bonds. However, the portfolio manager might convince the client that the portfolio should be *contingently* immunized with $841,680. In this case, the portfolio manager must be certain that the portfolio will be worth at least $1,000,000 at the end of the two years, with any excess going to the client and the manager being compensated accordingly. Equivalently, the portfolio manager must earn a minimum average return of 9% (note that $841,680 \times 1.09^2 = $1,000,000) over the two years. Here, the client is willing to settle for a return as low as 9% but hopes that the portfolio manager will be able to exceed the 10% return that could have been locked in with an immunized portfolio.

In this situation the manager would proceed to actively manage the portfolio by engaging in either selectivity or timing, or both. Perhaps the arrangement with the client is that the status of the portfolio will be reviewed weekly, and yields that are currently available will be determined.

Consider how the review would be conducted after one year has elapsed and the yield curve is still horizontal but now is at 11%. First, it is noted that $900,901 (=$1,000,000/1.11) is needed to immunize the portfolio at this point in time. Second, the market value of the current portfolio is determined to be $930,000. In this example, the arrangement between the client and the portfolio manager is that the manager can continue to actively manage the portfolio as long as it is worth at least $10,000 more than the amount needed for immunization. Because it is worth $930,000, an amount greater than $910,901 (=$900,901 + $10,000), the portfolio manager can continue being active. However, if the portfolio had been worth less than $910,901, then, according to the agreement, the manager would immediately immunize the portfolio.

15.6.4 Riding the Yield Curve

Riding the yield curve is a method of bond portfolio management that is sometimes used by people who, having liquidity as a primary objective, invest in short-term fixed-income securities. One way of investing is to simply purchase these securities, hold them until they mature, and then reinvest the proceeds. An alternative way is to ride the yield curve, provided that certain conditions exist.

One condition is that the yield curve be upward-sloping, indicating that longer-term securities have higher yields. Another condition is that the investor believe that the yield curve will remain upward-sloping. Given these two conditions, the investor who is riding the yield curve will purchase securities that have a somewhat longer term-to-maturity than desired and then will sell them before they mature, thereby capturing some capital gains.

For example, consider an investor who prefers investing in 90-day Treasury bills. Currently such bills are selling for $98.25 per $100 of face value, indicating that they have a yield of 7.00% [note that $98.25 = $100 - (7.00 \times 90/360)]$. However, 180-day Treasury bills are currently selling for $96.00, indicating that they have a higher yield of 8.00% [note that $96 = $100 - (8.00 \times 180/360)]$. If, as this investor believes, the yield curve remains upward-sloping over the next three months, it can be shown that riding the yield curve will result in a higher return than simply buying and holding the 90-day Treasury bills.

If the investor buys and holds the 90-day Treasury bills, then the resulting annualized rate of return will be:

$$\frac{\$100 - \$98.25}{\$98.25} \times \frac{365}{90} = 7.22\%$$

Alternatively, if the investor buys the 180-day Treasury bills and subsequently sells them after 90 days, then the expected selling price will be $98.25. (Note that this is the

Modified Duration and Key Rate Durations

Issues concerning the term structure of interest rates stand at the top of most bond managers' decision-making hierarchies. Shifts in, and changes in the shape of, the yield curve affect the value of investment-grade bond portfolios to a far greater extent than do other factors. Whether bond managers follow strategies that attempt to actively benefit from interest-rate changes or simply desire to neutralize the impact of those changes on their portfolios, controlling interest-rate risk is of paramount importance.

If we were to poll bond managers and ask them what single measure best indicates their interest-rate risk exposure, they would be nearly unanimous in answering modified duration. As the text discusses, modified duration gauges the sensitivity of the market value of a bond (or a portfolio of bonds) to changes in the level of interest rates. Modified duration represents the approximate percentage change in a bond's price caused by a 100-basis-point change in the bond's yield. Thus, for example, if you own a four-year modified duration bond and its yield rises by 100 basis points, your bond's price should fall by roughly 4%.

An active bond manager attempting to outperform an assigned benchmark may adjust his or her portfolio's modified duration in anticipation of changes in interest rates. Expectations of falling interest rates call for maintaining a modified duration greater than that of the benchmark. Conversely, a bond manager anticipating rising interest rates will want to hold his or her portfolio's modified duration to less than that of the benchmark. A passive bond manager similarly pays close attention to modified duration. If the manager lets the portfolio's modified duration differ significantly from that of the index, the portfolio's returns likely will fail to track the index's returns adequately. Other passive bond management strategies, such as immunization, also rely on matching a portfolio's modified duration with that of a target.

Despite its importance to bond portfolio management, modified duration does have certain prac-tical limitations that restrict its ability to accurately measure how a bond's price will respond to a change in yields. Those limitations are related to the underlying assumptions made in calculating a bond's duration. Of particular consequence is the assumption that interest-rate changes take the form of parallel shifts along a flat yield curve. In actuality, such shifts are unusual. Various segments of the yield curve usually move by different amounts. In some instances one or more segments may move in the opposite direction of other segments. When these nonparallel shifts occur, two bonds with the same durations may respond quite differently, depending on the pattern of their cash flows. As a simple example, if long-term interest rates rise and short-term interest rates fall (referred to as a yield curve *steepening*) than a portfolio holding a single zero-coupon bond with a five-year modified duration may respond quite differently than a portfolio with an equal weighting in two zero-coupon bonds, one with a two-year and the other with an eight-year modified duration, even though the modified durations of the two portfolios are the same. What is needed are alternative measures of interest-rate risk that can account for the valuation effect of more complex changes in the yield curve. One such tool is known as *key rate durations*.

Essentially, key rate durations are a means of breaking apart a bond's modified duration. Instead of one number summarizing the bond's interest rate sensitivity, key rate durations are a set of numbers identifying the sensitivity of the bond to interest-rate changes at various points along the yield curve. As the name implies, key rate durations entail specifying certain key rates and associated terms on the yield curve. Thus, a bond manager might select four key rates at 90 days, one year, five years, and 30 years. (In practice, more are usually chosen. Regardless of the number chosen, the key rates must extend across the entire yield curve—effectively from zero to 30 years. Further, the larger the number of key rates, the greater is the ability of the key rate analysis to capture the diverse nature of yield curve shifts, but the more

same as the current price of 90-day bills, because it is assumed that the yield curve will not have changed after 90 days have elapsed.) In this case, the expected return is:

$$\frac{\$98.25 - \$96.00}{\$96.00} \times \frac{365}{90} = 9.50\%$$

In comparison, the expected return from riding the yield curve is higher. The reason is that the investor expects to benefit from a decline in yield, a decline that does

complex becomes that analysis.) The shape of a yield curve shift is indicated by measuring the yield change at each key rate and linearly interpolating the change in between key rates.

At each key rate, the sensitivity of a bond's value to a small shift in the yield curve is estimated. That is, the modified duration of the bond at that point is calculated. For example, if the yield curve at one year were to move by .01 percentage point (1 basis point) and the bond's value changed in the opposite direction by .02%, then the bond's one-year key rate duration would be 2. Carrying out this calculation at all key rates provides a *profile* of the bond's sensitivity to changes in the yield curve.

By construction, the sum of all key rate durations equals the modified duration of the entire bond. Further, key rate durations combine in a portfolio of bonds in the same way that modified duration does; that is, the key rate duration of a bond at a particular term is the weighted average of the individual bonds' key rate durations at that term, where the weights are the proportion of the portfolio invested in each bond.

Key rate durations enhance the ability of bond managers to fine-tune interest-rate risk in their portfolios. For example, XYZ Financial Management is an active bond manager who attempts to outperform a bond market index benchmark while keeping tight control over interest rate risk. XYZ maintains a modified duration close to that of the index, 4.69 years versus 4.49 years. However, the manager is willing to place small interest rate "bets" at various points along the yield curve. The table below shows how a portfolio managed by XYZ compares with the index in terms of key rate durations.

	Key Rate Duration											Modified Duration
	.25	1	2	3	5	7	10	15	20	25	30	
Portfolio	.02	.11	.33	.43	.69	.56	.99	.43	.31	.43	.40	4.69
Benchmark	.02	.15	.31	.52	.66	.71	.71	.46	.46	.34	.14	4.49
Gap	.00	(.04)	.02	(.09)	.03	(.15)	.27	(.04)	(.15)	.09	.26	0.20

The portfolio's key rate durations are greater than those of the benchmark at the long end of the yield curve. For example, at the 30-year term, the portfolio's key rate duration is .40 years against the benchmark's .14 years. A 100 basis point decline in the 30-year rate would cause the portfolio to outperform the benchmark by .26% $\left[= (.40 - .14) \times 100 \right]$. The portfolio is also tilted in favor of rates declining at the 10-year term. Because XYZ maintains a modified duration near that of the benchmark, the key rate duration bets at the long end of the yield curve and at the 10-year term must be largely offset by opposite bets at other key rates along the yield curve. This is the case, particularly at the 3-, 7-, and 20-year terms.

Use of key rate durations is not limited to active bond managers. By constructing an indexed portfolio whose key rate durations match those of the assigned index, a bond index fund manager can have greater confidence that yield curve shifts will not result in unacceptable levels of tracking error.

Key rate durations as an analytical tool are not without deficiencies. Because they involve a set of numbers, their application is more complex than is modified duration with its single summary statistic. Key rate durations also ignore potentially valuable information about the covariance of different segments of the yield curve by assuming that all the segments move independently. Nevertheless, key rate durations are a valuable additional arrow in the quiver of bond managers seeking to effectively control interest-rate risk.

not result from a shift in the yield curve but is attributable to the shortening of the maturity of the 180-day Treasury bills that were initially purchased.

It should be kept in mind that if the yield curve does change, then "riding it" might be detrimental to the investor's return.[28] That is, riding the yield curve has more risk than simply buying securities that mature at the appropriate time. Similarly, two transactions are necessary (buying and then selling the security) when riding the yield curve, whereas a maturity strategy has only one transaction (buying the security). Thus there will be larger transaction costs associated with riding the yield curve.

The previous discussion of active management assumes that there are inefficiencies in the market that can be exploited. Examples include the ability to find mispriced bonds and the ability to discern when certain market sectors are likely to outperform others (for example, when short-term Treasuries are likely to outperform long-term Treasuries and vice versa). However, if one believes that bond markets are highly efficient, then a passive approach to investing in bonds is in order.

The most common passive approach involves *indexation*. With this approach, an investor selects a bond index that is consistent with his or her risk-return preferences. The objective of indexation is to invest in a portfolio of bonds whose performance *tracks* (that is, closely follows) that of the index.[29] Three broad-based indices commonly used by investors creating indexed bond portfolios are:

1. Lehman Brothers Aggregate Index
2. Merrill Lynch Domestic Market Index
3. Salomon Brothers Broad Investment-Grade Bond Index

Each one of these indexes contains over 5,000 bonds that have maturities of greater than one year and are rated BBB or above. In addition, Lehman Brothers, Merrill Lynch, and Salomon Brothers as well as other organizations, such as Morgan Stanley and First Boston, publish narrower market indices.[30]

Investing in a portfolio of bonds whose performance tracks that of a given index is not simple. Indeed, it is quite challenging. Why? First of all, buying all the bonds in the index is impractical because, as mentioned earlier, there are thousands of bonds in each of the broad-based indices. Indeed, even the narrower bond indices are typically composed of many bonds. Second, transactions costs are not reflected in the performance of a bond index but will be incurred in buying and selling bonds in an attempt to manage a portfolio whose performance tracks the index. Third, each of the bonds held will provide the investor with coupon payments periodically that need to be reinvested. However, it is impractical to take, say $3,000 of coupon payments received during a given week and invest these coupons in all the bonds that are currently held in the portfolio.

As a consequence, most approaches to constructing indexed bond portfolios involve sampling techniques. That is, a subset of all the bonds in the index (plus, possibly, some bonds that are outside the index) is selected for investment such that *the tracking error* of the portfolio is minimal. That is, the portfolio is designed so that its rate of return has minimal deviations from the return on the bond index. If an investment-grade corporate index is to be tracked, one method known as *stratified sampling* initially involves dissecting the index by determining, for example:

1. What bonds in the index have a duration of 0–3 years, 3–6 years, and over 6 years
2. What bonds in the index are issued by companies in one of three economic sectors: industrials, utilities, and financial
3. What bonds in the index are in each of the four investment-grade rating categories (AAA, AA, A, and BBB)

Note that, in total, there are $3 \times 3 \times 4 = 36$ categories, referred to as *cells*. Next, the percent of the bond index's value associated with each cell is calculated. Finally, some but not all of the bonds in each cell are selected for purchase such that the weight in the cell for the portfolio is the same as the weight for the index. Thus, if 3% of the index consists of AAA-rated financial bonds with 3–6 year durations and the portfolio is worth $200,000,000, then $6,000,000 of the portfolio will be invested in a subset of those bonds in the index that are rated AAA, are issued by financial companies, and have a duration between 3 and 6 years.

Tracking error will be related to the number of different cells that are defined. At first, more cells leads to closer tracking, but after a point more categories lead to poorer tracking as transaction costs begin to overwhelm the benefits of more precise cell definitions. This result can be seen by considering two extreme cases. At one extreme, the number of cells is one (in the above example, the cell would be "investment-grade corporates"), which would result in large tracking errors because all that would be done would be to select randomly a subset of the bonds in the index. At the other extreme, the categories are drawn up so narrowly that the number of categories equals the number of bonds in the index, which would result in large tracking errors due to the large amount of transaction costs incurred. Somewhere in between these two extremes lies the optimal number of cells, determined by both art and science.[31]

15.8 BONDS VERSUS STOCKS

Bonds and stocks are different kinds of securities, with quite different characteristics. Making an investment decision between them should not be based on some simple one-dimensional comparison. In many cases this decision, known as **asset allocation**, will involve investing in both bonds and stocks.[32]

Although historical relationships may not be useful for predicting future relationships accurately, it is instructive to examine the average values, standard deviations, and correlations of past stock and bond returns. These statistics are presented in Table 15.3, based on annual excess returns (that is, returns over Treasury bills) during one time period, 1926–1996, and two subperiods, 1926–1945 and 1946–1996. (The returns were published by Ibbotson Associates; see Figure 1.1 and Table 1.1 in Chapter 1.)

On the basis of average returns, stocks appear to have a substantial advantage for the investor with a reasonably long horizon.[33] However, there is good reason to believe that the average returns on long-term bonds are not representative of investors' expectations for future returns. The returns show the results obtained by purchasing a long-term government bond, holding it for a period of time, then replacing it with another long-term government bond. The total returns include both income and capital gains or losses. During the postwar subperiod, bond price changes were frequently negative, averaging roughly −.7% per year.[34] A better estimate of investors' expectations might be obtained by assuming that the price would be as likely to increase as to decrease (that is, the expected price change is zero). Expected future returns on bonds might then have been roughly .7% per year greater than shown in the table.

Bond returns were less variable than stock returns in both the full period and the two subperiods. However, the standard deviation of bonds in the postwar subperiod was double that of the earlier subperiod. It is likely that the increased uncertainty

	Stocks	Bonds	Correlation
A. 1926–1996			
Average annual excess return	8.90%	1.67%	
Standard deviation	20.67	9.01	
Correlation			.21
B. 1926–1945			
Average annual excess return	9.86%	3.75%	
Standard deviation	28.43	5.07	
Correlation			.19
C. 1946–1996			
Average annual excess return	8.52%	0.85%	
Standard deviation	17.05	10.07	
Correlation			.25

TABLE 15.3 Historical Relationships between Bonds and Stocks

Source: Adapted from Meir Statman and Neal L. Ushman, "Bonds versus Stocks: Another Look," *Journal of Portfolio Management* 13, no. 2 (Winter 1987): 33–38.

concerning the rate of inflation during the postwar subperiod increased the variability of bond returns.

The correlation between stock and bond returns has been low, and during various multiyear subperiods it has even had negative values. This low correlation indicates that portfolios combining both stocks and bonds benefited considerably from diversification. More recently, however, correlations have been considerably more positive than in the past, owing in part to common reactions to changes in inflationary expectations. Consequently, the gains from diversification have recently been reduced substantially. Nevertheless, from the historical record it would be reasonable to expect that, in the future, bonds will still offer diversification benefits.

15.9   SUMMARY

1. Similar to the U.S. common stock market, the U.S. bond market appears to be highly, but not perfectly, semistrong-form efficient.
2. For a typical bond making periodic interest payments and a final principal repayment on a stated date, five bond pricing theorems apply:
    a. If a bond's market price increases, then its yield must decrease; conversely, if a bond's market price decreases, then its yield must increase.
    b. If a bond's yield does not change over its life, then the size of its discount or premium will decrease as its life gets shorter.
    c. If a bond's yield does not change over its life, then the size of its discount or premium will decrease at an increasing rate as its life gets shorter.
    d. A decrease in a bond's yield will raise the bond's price by an amount that is greater in size than the corresponding fall in the bond's price that would occur if there were an equal-sized increase in the bond's yield. (That is, the price-yield relationship is convex.)
    e. The percentage change in a bond's price owing to a change in its yield will be smaller if its coupon rate is higher.
3. Duration is a measure of the "average maturity" of the stream of payments associated with a bond. It is a weighted average of the length of time until the bond's remaining payments are made, with the weights equal to the present value of each cash flow relative to the price of the bond.

4. The duration of a portfolio of bonds is equal to the weighted average of the durations of the individual bonds in the portfolio.

5. A bond portfolio manager can be fairly confident of being able to meet a given promised stream of cash outflows by creating a bond portfolio with a duration equal to the liabilities. This procedure is known as immunization.

6. Problems with immunization include default and call risk, multiple nonparallel shifts in a nonhorizontal yield curve, costly rebalancings, and choosing from a wide range of candidate bond portfolios.

7. Active bond management may involve security selection, market timing (where attempts are made to forecast general movements in interest rates), or combinations of the two.

8. Active management strategies include horizon analysis, bond swaps, contingent immunization, and riding the yield curve.

9. The most common passive management strategy involves indexation, where a portfolio is formed whose performance tracks that of a chosen index.

10. Portfolios consisting of both stocks and bonds benefit from the resulting diversification because of the relatively low correlation of returns between the two asset classes.

QUESTIONS AND PROBLEMS

1. A $10,000 face-value bond with a ten-year term-to-maturity and an 8% coupon rate currently sells so as to produce an 8% yield-to-maturity. What is the bond's price? Calculate the bond's price if its yield rises to 10%; if its yield falls to 5%.

2. Bonds A and B both have $10,000 face values, have 10% coupon rates, and sell with yields-to-maturity of 9%. However, bond A has a 20-year term-to-maturity, whereas bond B has a five-year term-to-maturity. Calculate the prices of the two bonds. Despite having the same yields, why is one bond's price different from the other's?

3. Consider three pure-discount bonds, each with a $1,000 face value; 7% yield-to-maturity; and terms-to-maturity of 5, 10, and 20 years. Calculate each bond's price. Graph the bond's discounts versus their terms-to-maturity. Is the relationship linear? Why?

4. Consider two bonds with 10% coupon rates and $1,000 face values. One of the bonds has a term-to-maturity of four years; the other has a term-to-maturity of 15 years. Both make annual interest payments. Assuming that yields on the two bonds rise from 10% to 14%, calculate the intrinsic values of the two bonds before and after the change in interest rates. Explain the difference in percentage price changes.

5. Consider a five-year term-to-maturity bond with a $1,000 face value and $100 annual coupon interest payments. The bond sells at par. What is the bond's percentage price change if the yield-to-maturity rises to 12%; if it falls to 8%?

6. Consider two bonds, one with five years to maturity and the other with 20 years to maturity. Both have $1,000 face values and 8% coupon rates (with annual interest payments), and both sell at par. Assume that the yields of both bonds fall to 6%. Calculate the dollar increases in the bonds' prices. What percentage of this increase in each case comes from a change in the present value of the bonds' principals, and what percentage comes from a change in the present value of the bonds' interest payments?

7. Bonds A and B both have $10,000 face values, 8% yields-to-maturity, and ten-year terms-to-maturity. However, bond A has a 10% coupon rate, whereas bond

---

Bond Portfolio Management 445

B sells at par. (Both make annual interest payments.) If the yields on both bonds decline to 6%, calculate the percentage price changes of the two bonds.

8. Consider a bond selling at its par value of $1,000, with six years to maturity and a 7% coupon rate (with annual interest payments). Calculate the bond's duration.

9. What is the modified duration of the bond in Problem 8?

10. If the yield-to-maturity on the bond in Problem 8 increases to 8%, what happens to the bond's duration? Why does this change occur?

11. Why must the duration of a coupon-bearing bond always be less than the time to its maturity date?

12. Liz Funk owns a portfolio of four bonds with the following durations and proportions:

Bond	Duration	Proportion
A	4.5 years	.20
B	3.0	.25
C	3.5	.25
D	2.8	.30

What is the duration of Liz's bond portfolio?

13. Rank order the following bonds in terms of duration. Explain the rationale behind your rankings. (You do not have to actually calculate the bonds' durations. Logical reasoning will suffice.)

Bond	Term-to-Maturity	Coupon Rate	Yield-to-Maturity
1	30 years	10%	10%
2	30	0	10
3	30	10	7
4	5	10	10

14. What impact would you expect the option features of callable bonds and mortgage participation certificates to have on the expected durations of such bonds as opposed to the durations calculated on the basis of the bonds' stated maturity dates?

15. Consider a bond with a 3.5-year duration. If its yield-to-maturity increases from 8.0% to 8.3%, what is the expected percentage change in the price of the bond?

16. Distinguish between modified duration and effective duration.

17. Referring to Equation 15.9, show why a bond with no embedded options will have an effective duration equal to its modified duration. [Hint: Think about what the relationship is between $(P^+ - P^-)$ and ΔP.]

18. The price-yield relationship for a typical bond is convex, opening upward as shown in Figure 15.2. Investment professionals often describe the price-yield relationship of mortgage pass-through securities as being "negatively convex"; that is, a graph of the relationship opens downward. What features of these securities could produce such a relationship?

19. Explain why immunization permits a bond investor to be confident of meeting a given liability on a predetermined future date.

20. What are the advantages and disadvantages of meeting promised cash outflows through cash matching as opposed to duration matching?

21. Why can nonparallel shifts in the yield curve cause problems for an investor seeking to construct an immunized bond portfolio?

22. Old True Blue Richardson is planning to offset a single-payment liability with an immunized bond portfolio. Old True Blue is considering buying either bonds with durations close to that of the liability (a "bullet" strategy) or bonds with durations considerably above and below that of the liability (a "barbell" strategy).

Why is the bullet strategy a lower-risk strategy for Old True Blue? What are its disadvantages relative to the barbell strategy?

23. Describe the four components of return on a bond investment over a given holding period.

24. Consider a bond with a $1,000 face value, ten years to maturity, and $80 annual coupon interest payments. The bond sells so as to produce a 10% yield-to-maturity. That yield is expected to decline to 9% at the end of four years. Interest income is assumed to be invested at 9.5%. Calculate the bond's four-year holding period return and the four components of that return.

25. Distinguish between a substitution swap and an intermarket spread swap.

26. Compare contingent immunization with the strategy of using stop orders (discussed in Chapter 2) to protect a portfolio's value.

CFA EXAM QUESTIONS

27. Bill Peters is the investment officer of a $60 million pension fund. He has become concerned about the big price swings that have occurred lately in the fund's fixed-income securities. Peters has been told that such price behavior is only natural given the recent behavior of market yields. To deal with the problem, the pension fund's fixed-income money manager keeps track of exposure to price volatility by closely monitoring bond duration. The money manager believes that price volatility can be kept to a reasonable level as long as portfolio duration is maintained at approximately seven to eight years.

    Discuss the concepts of duration and convexity and explain how each fits into the price-yield relationship. In the situation described above, explain why the money manager should have used both duration and convexity to monitor the bond portfolio's exposure to price volatility.

28. As a continuation of your analysis of Monticello's debt you are asked to evaluate two specific bond issues held in Cavalier managed accounts, as shown in the table below.
    a. Using the duration and yield information in the table, compare the price and yield behavior of the two bonds under each of the following two scenarios:
       • Scenario 1—strong economic recovery with rising inflation expectations
       • Scenario 2—economic recession with reduced inflation expectations.
    b. Using the information in the table below, calculate the projected price change for Bond B if the yield-to-maturity for this bond falls by 75 basis points.
    c. Describe the shortcoming of analyzing Bond A strictly to call or to maturity. Explain an approach to remedy this shortcoming.

	Bond A (Callable)	Bond B (Non-Callable)
Maturity	2002	2002
Coupon	11.50%	7.25%
Current price	125.75	100.00
Yield-to-maturity	7.70%	7.25%
Modified duration to maturity	6.20	6.80
Convexity to maturity	0.50	0.60
Call date	1996	—
Call price	105	—
Yield-to-call	5.10%	—
Maturity duration to call	3.10	—
Convexity to call	0.10	—

29. Identify and briefly explain the three conditions that must be satisfied to immunize a portfolio.

APPENDIX

EMPIRICAL REGULARITIES IN THE BOND MARKET

Certain empirical regularities in the stock market are well known among investment professionals.[35] Because these regularities cannot be explained by any of the currently known asset pricing models, they are referred to as anomalies. An interesting question to ponder is this: Do such regularities also exist in the bond market? One study looked at this question by examining the daily performance from January 1963 through December 1986 of the Dow Jones Composite Bond Average. (This bond index consists of 20 investment-grade U.S. corporate bonds, divided evenly between industrials and utilities.)[36]

A.1 THE JANUARY EFFECT

Table 15.4 presents evidence that, as with common stocks, there is a January effect in bonds; that is, on average, corporate bonds have a notably higher return during the month of January than during the other 11 months of the year. Furthermore, this table also shows that this observation was true for all investment-grade (Aaa to Baa) and two speculative-grade (Ba and B) risk classes. Interestingly, the effect is extremely pronounced for the speculative classes.

TABLE 15.4	Seasonality in Bond Returns	
	Average Return in January	**Average Monthly Return in Other Months**
(a) 1963–1986[a]	4.34%	−.56%
(b) 1963–1979[b]		
Aaa	1.15%	.22%
Aa	1.21	.29
A	1.18	.30
Baa	1.55	.30
Ba	3.32	.27
B	5.09	.36

[a] **Source:** Susan D. Jordan and Bradford D. Jordan, "Seasonality in Daily Bond Returns," *Journal of Financial and Quantitative Analysis* 26, no. 2 (June 1991): table 5.
[b] **Source:** Eric C. Chang and Roger D. Huang. "Time-Varying Return and Risk in the Corporate Bond Market," *Journal of Financial and Quantitative Analysis* 25, no. 3 (September 1990): table 1.

Table 15.5 presents the average daily returns for each business day of the week over the period from 1963 to 1986. As with common stocks, the average return on Monday is negative. However, it is also negative for every day except Thursday, and the average returns for all five days are not statistically significantly different from one another.[37] Hence in contrast to common stocks, the day-of-the-week effect does not appear to exist for corporate bonds.

TABLE 15.5	Analysis of Daily Return
Day of Week	Average Daily Return
Monday	−.20%
Tuesday	−.93
Wednesday	−.00
Thursday	.44
Friday	−.00

Source: Susan D. Jordan and Bradford D. Jordan, "Seasonality in Daily Bond Returns," *Journal of Financial and Quantitative Analysis* 26, no. 2 (June 1991): table 5.

ENDNOTES

[1] For details, see Richard Roll, *The Behavior of Interest Rates* (New York: Basic Books, 1970). Interestingly, this study also produced evidence rejecting the unbiased expectations theory of the term structure of interest rates (see Chapter 5 for a discussion of this theory). Also of interest is that U.S. Treasury bonds appear to have been mispriced in May and June of 1986. See Bradford Cornell and Alan C. Shapiro, "The Mispricing of U.S. Treasury Bonds: A Case Study," *Review of Financial Studies* 2, no. 3 (1989): 297–310.

[2] J. Walter Elliott and Jerome R. Baier, "Econometric Models and Current Interest Rates: How Well Do They Predict Future Rates?" *Journal of Finance* 34, no. 4 (September 1979): 975–986. The models used by major economic forecasting firms tend to have similar amounts of accuracy. See Stephen K. McNees, "Forecasting Accuracy of Alternative Techniques: A Comparison of U.S. Macroeconomic Forecasts," *Journal of Business & Economic Statistics* 4, no. 1 (January 1986): 5–15, particularly Table 6, where 90-day Treasury bill rate forecasts are evaluated; and Dean Croushore, "Introducing The Survey of Professional Forecasters," *Federal Reserve Bank of Philadelphia Business Review*, November–December 1993: 3–15.

[3] Michael J. Prell, "How Well Do the Experts Forecast Interest Rates?" *Federal Reserve Bank of Kansas City Monthly Review*, September–October 1973: 3–13.

[4] Adrian W. Throop, "Interest Rate Forecast and Market Efficiency," *Federal Reserve Bank of San Francisco Economic Review*, Spring 1981: 29–43. This article contains a useful reference list of other studies concerning the prediction of interest rates.

[5] Forecasts implicit in the futures market (to be discussed in Chapter 20) for Treasury bills were also found to be more accurate than those of the economists, but less accurate than those of the no-change model over this time period. For a longer time period, the futures market and no-change model forecasts were of comparable accuracy; see Michael T. Belognia, "Predicting Interest Rates: A Comparison of Professional and Market-Based Forecasts," *Federal Reserve Bank of St. Louis Review* 69, no. 3 (March 1987): 9–15.

[6] See Kevin Stephenson, "Just How Bad Are Economists at Predicting Interest Rates? (And What Are the Implications for Investors?)," *Journal of Investing* 6, no. 2 (Summer 1997): 8–10.

[7] The reported accuracy of macroeconomic forecasters in regard to Treasury bill rates (see the Early Quarter results for a two-quarter horizon in Table 6 of McNees, "Forecasting

Accuracy of Alternative Techniques") can be compared with the reported accuracy of the no-change model (see Table 1 of Belognia, "Predicting Interest Rates"). Although such a comparison should be done with caution, it does suggest that the no-change model is of similar, and in some cases superior, accuracy. It also appears that the record of the experts in predicting the level of the stock market is of little value. See Werner F. De Bondt, "What Do Economists Know about the Stock Market?" *Journal of Portfolio Management* 17, no. 2 (Winter 1991): 84–91.

[8] See Mark I. Weinstein, "The Effect of a Rating Change Announcement on Bond Price," *Journal of Financial Economics* 5, no. 3 (December 1977): 329–350. A study of the prices of the common stocks associated with bonds that had rating changes reported similar results; stock prices tended to change several months before the announcement dates of the rating changes. See George E. Pinches and J. Clay Singleton, "The Adjustment of Stock Prices to Bond Rating Changes," *Journal of Finance* 33, no. 1 (March 1978): 29–44. Another study that examined rating change announcements that were "noncontaminated" by other news releases found a small but statistically significant upward movement in daily bond prices around upgrades; downgrades produced no significant movements. Oddly, these findings were reversed when stock prices were examined in that no significant movements were found around upgrades, but marginally significant downward movements were observed around downgrades. See John R. M. Hand, Robert W. Holthausen, and Richard W. Leftwich, "The Effect of Bond Rating Agency Announcements on Bond and Stock Prices," *Journal of Finance* 47, no. 2 (June 1992): 733–752. Further analysis revealed that one type of downgrade—namely, "downgrades associated with deteriorating financial prospects"—resulted in a significant downward movement in the price of the associated firm's stock. See Jeremy C. Goh and Louis H. Ederington, "Is a Bond Downgrade Bad News, Good News, or No News for Stockholders?" *Journal of Finance* 48, no. 5 (December 1993): 2001–2008.

[9] Gailen Hite and Arthur Warga, "The Effect of Bond-Rating Changes on Bond Price Performance," *Financial Analysts Journal* 53, no. 3 (May/June 1997): 35–51. The authors looked at other rating change scenarios in addition to the downgrades mentioned here.

[10] For an explanation and empirical investigation of this adjustment process, see Richard G. Sheehan, "Weekly Money Announcements: New Information and Its Effects," *Federal Reserve Bank of St. Louis Review* 67, no. 7 (August/September 1985): 25–34; and Anthony M. Santomero, "Money Supply Announcements: A Retrospective," *Journal of Economics and Business* 43, no. 1 (February 1991): 1–23.

[11] See, for example, Thomas Urich and Paul Wachtel, "Market Response to Weekly Money Supply Announcements in the 1970s," *Journal of Finance* 36, no. 5 (December 1981): 1063–1072, and "The Effects of Inflation and Money Supply Announcements on Interest Rates," *Journal of Finance* 39, no. 4 (September 1984): 1177–1188; and Bradford Cornell, "Money Supply Announcements and Interest Rates: Another View," *Journal of Business* 56, no. 1 (January 1983): 1–23.

[12] See Christopher R. Blake, Edwin J. Elton, and Martin J. Gruber, "The Performance of Mutual Bond Funds," *Journal of Business* 66, no. 3 (July 1993): 371–403.

[13] Like the stock market, the bond market has some anomalies. However, they are fewer in number and less pronounced. These anomalies are briefly discussed in the appendix.

[14] Burton G. Malkiel, "Expectations, Bond Prices, and the Term Structure of Interest Rates," *Quarterly Journal of Economics* 76, no. 2 (May 1962): 197–218.

[15] See Frederick R. Macaulay, *Some Theoretical Problems Suggested by the Movement of Interest Rates, Bond Yields, and Stock Prices in the United States Since 1856* (New York: National Bureau of Economic Research, 1938).

[16] It follows that if there are two bonds that are identical in all aspects except that one has "more convexity," then the one with more convexity would be more desirable. If yields rise, its price will drop by a smaller amount than the price of the other bond. Conversely, if yields drop, its price will rise by a larger amount than the price of the other bond. In either case, the investor is better off with the bond having more convexity.

[17] To accomplish immunization when there is more than one promised outflow, additional conditions must be met; see Frank J. Fabozzi, *Bond Markets, Analysis and Strategies* (Upper Saddle River, NJ, Prentice Hall, 1996): pp. 544–545.

---

[18] If there were two-year coupon-bearing bonds available for investment, then there would be no reinvestment-rate risk associated with the principal. However, the investor would still face reinvestment-rate risk in terms of the coupon payments received after one year. Such risk appears to be relatively minor in this example, but it becomes much more substantial in situations involving promised cash outflows that are more than two years into the future.

[19] The value is more than $1,000,000 because of the convexity property of bonds, discussed earlier.

[20] The concept of *effective convexity* has also been introduced to take into consideration such issues as default and call risk when measuring a bond's convexity. See, for example, Fabozzi, *Bond Markets, Analysis and Strategies*, pp. 344–345, 358.

[21] See Jeffrey Nelson and Stephen Schaefer, "The Dynamics of the Term Structure and Alternative Portfolio Immunization Strategies," pp. 61–101; and Jonathan E. Ingersoll Jr., "Is Immunization Feasible? Evidence from the CRSP Data," pp. 163–182 in George G. Kaufman, G. O. Bierwag, and Alden Toevs (eds.), *Innovations in Bond Portfolio Management: Duration Analysis and Immunization* (Greenwich, CT: JAI Press 1983); and Robert R. Reitano, "Non-Parallel Yield Curve Shifts and Spread Leverage," *Journal of Portfolio Management* 17, no. 3 (Spring 1991): 82–87.

[22] For a summary and set of references, see G. O. Bierwag, George G. Kaufman, Robert Schweitzer, and Alden Toevs, "The Art of Risk Management in Bond Portfolios," *Journal of Portfolio Management* 7, no. 3 (Spring 1981): 27–36; G. O. Bierwag, George G. Kaufman, and Alden Toevs, "Duration: Its Development and Use in Bond Portfolio Management," *Financial Analysts Journal* 39, no. 4 (July/August 1983): 15–35; and Stephen M. Schaefer, "Immunization and Duration: A Review of Theory, Performance and Applications," *Midland Corporate Finance Journal* 2, no. 3 (Fall 1984): 41–58.

[23] See N. Bulent Gultekin and Richard J. Rogalski, "Alternative Duration Specifications and the Measurement of Basis Risk," *Journal of Business* 57, no. 2 (April 1984): 241–264. For rebuttals and responses, see G. O. Bierwag, George G. Kaufman, Cynthia M. Latta, and Gordon S. Roberts, "Duration: Response to Critics," *Journal of Portfolio Management* 13, no. 2 (Winter 1987): 48–52; N. Bulent Gultekin and Richard J. Rogalski, "Duration: Response to Critics: Comment," *Journal of Portfolio Management* 15, no. 3 (Spring 1989): 83–87; G. O. Bierwag, George G. Kaufman, Cynthia M. Latta, and Gordon S. Roberts, "Duration As a Measure of Basis Risk: The Wrong Answer at Low Cost—Rejoinder," *Journal of Portfolio Management* 15, no. 4 (Summer 1989): 82–85; and N. Bulent Gultekin and Richard J. Rogalski, "Duration As a Measure of Basis Risk: The Wrong Answer at Low Cost—Answer to Rejoinder," *Journal of Portfolio Management* 15, no. 4 (Summer 1989): 86–87.

[24] G. O. Bierwag, George G. Kaufman, and Alden Toevs, "Bond Portfolio Immunization and Stochastic Process Risk," *Journal of Bank Research* 13 (Winter 1983), 282–291; and G. O. Bierwag, George G. Kaufman, and Cynthia M. Latta, "Duration Models: A Taxonomy," *Journal of Portfolio Management* 15, no. 1 (Fall 1988): 50–54.

[25] The longer the horizon, the greater the importance of the size of the reinvestment rate in determining a bond's return. Thus, if the investor's horizon is greater than, say, ten years, alternative reinvestment rates should be considered. See Richard W. McEnally, "Rethinking Our Thinking about Interest Rates," *Financial Analysts Journal* 41, no. 2 (March/April 1985): 62–67.

[26] Bond swaps should not be confused with interest-rate swaps, wherein two issuers of debt keep the respective amounts raised but make each other's coupon payments. That is, issuer *A* makes the coupon payments on issuer *B*'s debt, and issuer *B* makes the coupon payments on issuer *A*'s debt, perhaps because *A* has fixed-rate debt and *B* has floating-rate debt. See, for example, Stuart M. Turnbull, "Swaps: A Zero Sum Game?" *Financial Management* 16, no. 1 (Spring 1987): 15–21; Clifford W. Smith Jr., Charles W. Smithson, and D. Sykes Wilford, *Managing Financial Risk* (New York: Harper & Row, 1990), Chapters 9–12; John F. Marshall and Kenneth R. Kapner, *The Swaps Market* (Miami: Kolb Publishing, 1993); and Bernadette A. Minton, "An Empirical Examination of Basic Valuation Models for Plain Vanilla U.S. Interest Rate Swaps," *Journal of Financial Economics* 44, no. 2 (May 1997): 251–277. Interest rate swaps are discussed in Chapter 23.

[27] Martin L. Leibowitz, "Horizon Analysis for Managed Bond Portfolios," *Journal of Portfolio Management* 1, no. 3 (Spring 1975): 32–33.

[28] According to the unbiased expectations theory (discussed in Chapter 5), the yield curve would be expected to shift in such a manner that the expected return of the two strategies (in the example, buy and hold the 90-day T-bills versus buy and sell 90 days later the 180-day T-bills) would be the same.

[29] A hybrid approach is known as *enhanced indexation*. It involves managing a portfolio with the objective of earning a return that is at least equal to and sometimes slightly better than the return on a chosen index. See Fabozzi, *Bond Markets, Analysis and Strategies*, pp. 423–424.

[30] For more information on bond market indices, see Frank K. Reilly, G. Wenchi Kao, and David J. Wright, "Alternative Bond Market Indices," *Financial Analysts Journal* 48, no. 3 (May/June 1992): 44–58.

[31] For more on passive management in general and stratified sampling in particular, see Fabozzi, *Bond Markets, Analysis and Strategies*, Chapter 18.

[32] Chapter 23 presents a discussion of some methods for making the asset allocation decision. For a model on how to measure the interest-rate sensitivity of a portfolio consisting of both stocks and bonds, see Martin L. Leibowitz, "Total Portfolio Duration: A New Perspective on Asset Allocation," *Financial Analysts Journal* 42, no. 5 (September/October 1986): 18–29.

[33] Another study involving simulation found that, on the basis of historical returns, an investor with a 20-year horizon had about a 5% probability of earning less when investing in a common stock index than when investing in a long-term Treasury bond index. For a ten-year horizon the probability was 11%. See Kirt C. Butler and Dale L. Domian, "Risk, Diversification, and the Investment Horizon," *Journal of Portfolio Management* 17, no. 3 (Spring 1991): 41–47.

[34] More recent data since 1982 indicate that bond price changes have more often been positive than negative, averaging a positive 4.5% per year.

[35] Some of these anomalies are discussed in Appendix A, Chapter 16.

[36] Susan D. Jordan and Bradford D. Jordan, "Seasonality in Daily Bond Returns," *Journal of Financial and Quantitative Analysis* 26, no. 2 (June 1991): 269–285. This study did not examine the bond market in order to see whether the "size effect" (observed for common stocks) was present. Hence only two of the anomalies discussed in Appendix A, Chapter 16 are discussed here.

[37] The returns on Wednesday and Friday are shown to be zero but only because of rounding; they are slightly negative.

KEY TERMS

coupon rate	horizon analysis
convexity	bond swapping
duration	substitution swap
modified duration	intermarket spread swap
immunization	rate anticipation swap
effective duration	pure yield pickup swap
cash matching	contingent immunization
dedicated portfolio	asset allocation
stochastic process risk	

REFERENCES

1. There have been many tests of efficiency in the bond market. Endnotes 1 through 11 contain citations of several of them. Some of the others are cited in:

   Frank J. Fabozzi and T. Dessa Fabozzi, *Bond Markets, Analysis and Strategies* (Englewood Cliffs, NJ: Prentice Hall, 1989): 300–303. Chapter 4 of this book also contains an extensive discussion of the concepts of convexity and duration.

2. Books that discuss convexity, duration, and many related investment strategies are:

Gerald O. Bierwag, *Duration Analysis* (Cambridge, MA: Ballinger Publishing, 1987).

Frank J. Fabozzi, *Bond Markets, Analysis and Strategies* (Upper Saddle River, NJ: Prentice Hall, 1996).

Kenneth D. Garbade, *Fixed Income Analytics* (Cambridge, MA: MIT Press, 1996).

Suresh Sundaresan, *Fixed Income Markets and Their Derivatives* (Cincinnati: South-Western Publishing, 1997).

3. A method for measuring convexity is given by:

Robert Brooks and Miles Livingston, "A Closed-Form Equation for Bond Convexity," *Financial Analysts Journal* 45, no. 6 (November/December 1989): 78–79.

4. The concept of duration and its use to measure interest-rate risk was initially developed by:

Frederick R. Macaulay, *Some Theoretical Problems Suggested by the Movement of Interest Rates, Bond Yields, and Stock Prices in the United States Since 1856* (New York: National Bureau of Economic Research, 1938).

J. R. Hicks, *Value and Capital*, 2d ed. (Oxford, England: Clarendon Press, 1946; the first edition was published in 1939).

Michael H. Hopewell and George G. Kaufman, "Bond Price Volatility and Term to Maturity: A Generalized Respecification," *American Economic Review* 63, no. 4 (September 1973): 4749–4753.

5. For interesting articles describing the development of the concept of duration (as well as immunization), see:

Roman L. Weil, "Macaulay's Duration: An Appreciation," *Journal of Business* 46, no. 4 (October 1973): 589–592.

Frank K. Reilly and Rupinder S. Sidhu, "The Many Uses of Bond Duration," *Financial Analysts Journal* 36, no. 4 (July/August 1980): 58–72.

G. O. Bierwag, George G. Kaufman, and Alden Toevs, "Duration: Its Development and Use in Bond Portfolio Management," *Financial Analysts Journal* 39, no. 4 (July/August 1983): 15–35.

6. For alternative methods of calculating duration, see:

Jess H. Chua, "A Generalized Formula for Calculating Bond Duration," *Financial Analysts Journal* 44, no. 5 (September/October 1988): 65–67.

Sanjay K. Nawalkha and Nelson J. Lacey, "Closed-Form Solutions of Higher-Order Duration Measures," *Financial Analysts Journal* 44, no. 6 (November/December 1988): 82–84.

7. For the initial development and subsequent supportive tests of immunization, see:

F. M. Redington, "Review of the Principles of Life-Office Valuations," *Journal of the Institute of Actuaries* 78, no. 3 (1952): 286–315.

Lawrence Fisher and Roman L. Weil, "Coping with the Risk of Interest-Rate Fluctuations: Returns to Bondholders from Naive and Optimal Strategies," *Journal of Business* 44, no. 4 (October 1971): 408–431.

G. O. Bierwag and George G. Kaufman, "Coping with the Risk of Interest-Rate Fluctuations: A Note," *Journal of Business* 50, no. 3 (July 1977): 364–370.

Charles H. Gushee, "How to Immunize a Bond Investment," *Financial Analysts Journal* 37, no. 2 (March/April 1981): 44–51.

G. O. Bierwag, George G. Kaufman, Robert Schweitzer, and Alden Toevs, "The Art of Risk Management in Bond Portfolios," *Journal of Portfolio Management* 7, no. 2 (Spring 1981): 27–36.

Gerald O. Bierwag, *Duration Analysis* (Cambridge, MA: Ballinger Publishing, 1987), Chapter 12.

Donald R. Chambers, Willard T. Carleton, and Richard W. McEnally, "Immunizing Default-Free Bond Portfolios with a Duration Vector," *Journal of Financial and Quantitative Analysis* 23, no. 1 (March 1988): 89–104.

Iraj Fooladi and Gordon S. Roberts, "Bond Portfolio Immunization," *Journal of Economics and Business* 44, no. 1 (February 1992): 3–17.

8. For some interesting articles involving duration, convexity, and immunization, see:

Mark L. Dunetz and James M. Mahoney, "Using Duration and Convexity in the Analysis of Callable Bonds," *Financial Analysts Journal* 44, no. 3 (May/June 1988): 53–72.

Bruce J. Grantier, "Convexity and Bond Portfolio Performance: The Benter the Better," *Financial Analysts Journal* 44, no. 6 (November/December 1988): 79–81.

Jacques A. Schnabel, "Is Benter Better: A Cautionary Note on Maximizing Convexity," *Financial Analysts Journal* 46, no. 1 (January/February 1990): 78–79.

Robert Brooks and Miles Livingston, "Relative Impact of Duration and Convexity on Bond Price Changes," *Financial Practice and Education* 2, no. 1 (Spring/Summer 1992): 93–99.

Mark Kritzman, "…About Duration and Convexity," *Financial Analysts Journal* 48, no. 6 (November/December 1992): 17–20.

Gerald O. Bierwag, Iraj Fooladi, and Gordon S. Roberts, "Designing an Immunized Portfolio: Is M-Squared the Key?" *Journal of Banking and Finance* 17, no. 6 (December 1993): 1147–1170.

Edward J. Kane and Stephen A. Kane, "Teaching Duration of Annuities and Portfolio Net Worth from a Financial Engineering Perspective," *Financial Practice and Education* 5, no. 2 (Fall/Winter 1995): 144–148.

Don M. Chance and James V. Jordan, "Duration, Convexity, and Time As Components of Bond Returns," *Journal of Fixed Income* 6, no. 2 (September 1996): 88–96.

Nicola Carcano and Silverio Foresi, "Hedging against Interest Rate Risk: Reconsidering Volatility-Adjusted Immunization," *Journal of Banking and Finance* 21, no. 2 (February 1997): 127–141.

Antony C. Cherin and Robert C. Hanson, "Consistent Treatment of Interest Payments in Immunization Examples," *Financial Practice and Education* 7, no. 1 (Spring/Summer 1997): 122–126.

Joel R. Barber and Mark L. Copper, "Is Bond Convexity a Free Lunch?" *Journal of Portfolio Management* 24, no. 1 (Fall 1997): 113–119.

9. Some of the research that is critical of the use of duration, convexity, and immunization is mentioned in endnote 23. Other critical research includes:

Jonathan E. Ingersoll Jr., Jeffrey Skelton, and Roman L. Weil, "Duration Forty Years Later," *Journal of Financial and Quantitative Analysis* 13, no. 4 (November 1977): 627–650.

Ronald N. Kahn and Roland Lochoff, "Convexity and Exceptional Return," *Journal of Portfolio Management* 16, no. 2 (Winter 1990): 43–47.

Antti Ilmanen, "How Well Does Duration Measure Interest Rate Risk?" *Journal of Fixed Income* 1, no. 4 (March 1992): 43–51.

10. For a discussion of how to use non-default-free bonds in an immunized portfolio, see:

Gordon J. Alexander and Bruce G. Resnick, "Using Linear and Goal Programming to Immunize Bond Portfolios," *Journal of Banking and Finance* 9, no. 1 (March 1985): 35–54.

G. O. Bierwag and George G. Kaufman, "Durations of Nondefault-Free Securities," *Financial Analysts Journal* 44, no. 4 (July/August 1988): 39–46, 62.

Gerald O. Bierwag, Charles J. Corrado, and George G. Kaufman, "Computing Durations for Bond Portfolios," *Journal of Portfolio Management* 17, no. 1 (Fall 1990): 51–55.

Gerald O. Bierwag, Charles J. Corrado, and George G. Kaufman, "Durations for Portfolios of Bonds Priced on Different Term Structures," *Journal of Banking and Finance* 16, no. 4 (August 1992): 705–714.

Antti Ilmanen, Donald McGuire, and Arthur Warga, "The Value of Duration As a Risk Measure for Corporate Debt," *Journal of Fixed Income* 4, no. 1 (June 1994): 70–76.

Martin Leibowitz, Stanley Kogelman, and Lawrence N. Bader, "Spread Immunization: Portfolio Improvements through Dollar-Duration Matching," *Journal of Investing* 4, no. 3 (Fall 1995): 49–56.

Iraj J. Fooladi, Gordon S. Roberts, and Frank Skinner, "Duration for Bonds with Default Risk," *Journal of Banking and Finance* 21, no. 1 (January 1997): 1–16.

11. For a discussion of the effect of call risk on duration (and immunization), see:

Kurt Winkelmann, "Uses and Abuses of Duration and Convexity," *Financial Analysts Journal* 45, no. 5 (September/October 1989): 72–75.

12. For a discussion of how to use duration to measure the risk of foreign bonds, see:

Steven I. Dym, "Measuring the Risk of Foreign Bonds," *Journal of Portfolio Management* 17, no. 2 (Winter 1991): 56–61.

Steven Dym, "Global and Local Components of Foreign Bond Risk," *Financial Analysts Journal* 48, no. 2 (March/April 1992): 83–91.

13. Dedicated bond portfolios and contingent immunization are discussed in:

Martin L. Leibowitz and Alfred Weinberger, "Contingent Immunization—Part I: Risk Control Procedures," *Financial Analysts Journal* 38, no. 6 (November/December 1982): 17–31.

Martin L. Leibowitz and Alfred Weinberger, "Contingent Immunization—Part II: Problem Areas," *Financial Analysts Journal* 39, no. 1 (January/February 1983): 39–50.

Martin L. Leibowitz, "The Dedicated Bond Portfolio in Pension Funds—Part I: Motivations and Basics," *Financial Analysts Journal* 42, no. 1 (January/February 1986): 69–75.

Martin L. Leibowitz, "The Dedicated Bond Portfolio in Pension Funds—Part II: Immunization, Horizon Matching, and Contingent Procedures," *Financial Analysts Journal* 42, no. 2 (March/April 1986): 47–57.

14. For a discussion of horizon analysis and bond swaps, see:

Sidney Homer and Martin L. Leibowitz, *Inside the Yield Book* (Upper Saddle River, NJ: Prentice Hall, 1972), Chapters 6, 7.

Martin L. Leibowitz, "Horizon Analysis for Managed Bond Portfolios," *Journal of Portfolio Management* 1, no. 3 (Spring 1975): 23–34.

Martin L. Leibowitz, "An Analytic Approach to the Bond Market," in Sumner N. Levine (ed.), *Financial Analyst's Handbook I* (Homewood, IL: Dow Jones-Irwin, 1975), pp. 226–277.

Marcia Stigum and Frank J. Fabozzi, *The Dow Jones-Irwin Guide to Bond and Money Market Investments* (Homewood, IL: Dow Jones-Irwin, 1987), Chapter 16.

15. For a discussion of various yield curve strategies, see:

Jerome S. Osteryoung, Gordon S. Roberts, and Daniel E. McCarty, "Ride the Yield Curve When Investing Idle Funds in Treasury Bills?" *Financial Executive* 47, no. 4 (April 1979): 10–15.

Edward A. Dyl and Michael D. Joehnk, "Riding the Yield Curve: Does It Work?" *Journal of Portfolio Management* 7, no. 3 (Spring 1981): 13–17.

Marcia Stigum and Frank J. Fabozzi, *The Dow Jones-Irwin Guide to Bond and Money Market Investments* (Homewood, IL: Dow Jones-Irwin, 1987), 270–272.

Frank J. Jones, "Yield Curve Strategies," *Journal of Fixed Income* 1, no. 2 (September 1991): 43–51.

Robin Grieves and Alan J. Marcus, "Riding the Yield Curve: Reprise," *Journal of Portfolio Management* 18, no. 4 (Summer 1992): 67–76.

16. More on bond investment strategies is contained in:

Ehud I. Ronn, "A New Linear Programming Approach to Bond Portfolio Management," *Journal of Financial and Quantitative Analysis* 22, no. 4 (December 1987): 439–466.

Michael C. Ehrhardt, "A New Linear Programming Approach to Bond Portfolio Management: A Comment," *Journal of Financial and Quantitative Analysis* 24, no. 4 (December 1989): 533–537.

Randall S. Hiller and Christian Schaack, "A Classification of Structured Bond Portfolio Modeling Techniques," *Journal of Portfolio Management* 17, no. 1 (Fall 1990): 37–48.

Frank J. Fabozzi, *Bond Markets, Analysis and Strategies* (Upper Saddle River, NJ: Prentice Hall, 1996), in particular Chapters 20–22.

Antti Ilmanen, "Market Rate Expectations and Forward Rates," *Journal of Fixed Income* 6, no. 2 (September 1996): 8–22,

Antti Ilmanen, "Does Duration Extension Enhance Long-Term Expected Returns?" *Journal of Fixed Income* 6, no. 2 (September 1996): 23–36.

17. For interesting discussions of what mix of bonds and stocks is appropriate for investors, see:

Martin L. Leibowitz and William S. Krasker, "The Persistence of Risk: Stocks versus Bonds over the Long Term," *Financial Analysts Journal* 44, no. 6 (November/December 1988): 40–47.

Paul A. Samuelson, "The Judgment of Economic Science on Rational Portfolio Management: Indexing, Timing and Long-Horizon Effects," *Journal of Portfolio Management* 16, no. 1 (Fall 1989): 4–12.

Martin L. Leibowitz and Terence C. Langetieg, "Shortfall Risk and the Asset Allocation Decision: A Simulation Analysis of Stock and Bond Profiles," *Journal of Portfolio Management* 16, no. 1 (Fall 1989): 61–68.

Keith P. Ambachtscheer, "The Persistence of Investment Risk," *Journal of Portfolio Management* 16, no. 1 (Fall 1989): 69–71.

Kirt C. Butler and Dale L. Domian, "Risk, Diversification, and the Investment Horizon," *Journal of Portfolio Management* 17, no. 3 (Spring 1991): 41–47.

Peter L. Bernstein, "Are Stocks the Best Place to Be in the Long Run?" *Journal of Investing* 5, no. 2 (Summer 1996): 6–9.

Ravi Jagannathan and Narayana R. Kotcherlakota, "Why Should Older People Invest Less in Stocks Than Younger People?" *Federal Reserve Bank of Minneapolis Quarterly Review* 20, no. 3 (Summer 1996): 11–23.

18. Pension fund surplus management is discussed in:

Martin L. Leibowitz, "Total Portfolio Duration: A New Perspective on Asset Allocation," *Financial Analysts Journal* 42, no. 5 (September/October 1986): 18–29, 77.

Martin L. Leibowitz and Roy D. Henriksson, "Portfolio Optimization within a Surplus Framework," *Financial Analysts Journal* 44, no. 2 (March/April 1988): 43–51.

William F. Sharpe, "Liabilities—A New Approach," *Journal of Portfolio Management* 16, no. 2 (Winter 1990): 4–10.

19. Empirical regularities in the bond market have been investigated by:

Eric C. Chang and J. Michael Pinegar, "Return Seasonality and Tax-Loss Selling in the Market for Long-Term Government and Corporate Bonds," *Journal of Financial Economics* 17, no. 2 (December 1986): 391–415.

Eric C. Chang and Roger D. Huang, "Time-Varying Return and Risk in the Corporate Bond Market," *Journal of Financial and Quantitative Analysis* 25, no. 3 (September 1990): 323–340.

Susan D. Jordan and Bradford D. Jordan, "Seasonality in Daily Bond Returns," *Journal of Financial and Quantitative Analysis* 26, no. 2 (June 1991): 269–285.

Kam C. Chan and H. K. Wu, "Another Look on Bond Market Seasonality: A Note," *Journal of Banking and Finance* 19, no. 6 (September 1995): 1047–1054.

20. Key rate durations are discussed in:

Robert R. Reitano, "Non-Parallel Yield Curve Shifts and Durational Leverage," *Journal of Portfolio Management* 16, no. 4 (Summer 1990): 62–67.

Thomas S. Y. Ho, "Key Rate Durations: Measures of Interest Rate Risks," *Journal of Fixed Income* 2, no. 2 (September 1992): 29–44.

Bennett W. Golub and Leo M. Tilman, "Measuring Yield Curve Risk Using Principal Components Analysis, Value at Risk, and Key Rate Durations," *Journal of Portfolio Management* 23, no. 4 (Summer 1997): 72–84.

COMMON STOCKS

Common stocks are easier to describe than fixed-income securities such as bonds, but they are harder to analyze. Fixed-income securities almost always have a limited life and an upper dollar limit on cash payments to investors. Common stocks have neither. Although the basic principles of valuation apply to both, the role of uncertainty is larger for common stocks, so much so that it often dominates all other elements in their valuation.

Common stock represents equity, or an ownership position in a corporation. It is a residual claim, in the sense that creditors and preferred stockholders must be paid as scheduled before common stockholders can receive any payments. In bankruptcy, common stockholders are in principle entitled to any value remaining after all other claimants have been satisfied. (However, in practice, courts sometimes violate this principle.)

The great advantage of the corporate form of organization is the **limited liability** of its owners. Common stocks are generally "fully paid and nonassessable," meaning that common stockholders may lose their initial investment but not more. That is, if the corporation fails to meet its obligations, the stockholders cannot be forced to give the corporation the funds that are needed to pay off the obligations. However, as a result of such a failure, it is possible that the value of a corporation's shares will be negligible. This outcome will result in the stockholders' having lost an amount equal to the price paid to buy the shares.

16.1   THE CORPORATE FORM

A corporation exists only when it has been granted a **charter**, or certificate of incorporation, by a state. This document specifies the rights and obligations of stockholders. It may be amended with the approval of the stockholders, perhaps by a majority or a two-thirds vote, wherein each share of stock generally entitles its owner to one vote. Both the initial terms of the charter and the terms of any amendment must also be approved by the state in which the corporation is chartered. The state of Delaware has captured a disproportionate number of corporate charters because it is particularly hospitable in this respect as well as in levying corporate taxes.

16.1.1 Stock Certificates

The ownership of a firm's stock has typically been represented by a single certificate, with the number of shares held by the particular investor noted on it. Such a stock certificate is usually registered, with the name, address, and holdings of the investor included on the corporation's books. Dividend payments, voting material, annual and quarterly reports, and other mailings are then sent directly to the investor, taking into account the size of his or her holdings.

Shares of stock held by an investor may be transferred to a new owner with the assistance of either the issuing corporation or, more commonly, its designated **transfer agent**. This agent will cancel the old stock certificate and issue a new one in its place, made out to the new owner. Frequently, a **registrar** will make sure that this canceling and issuing of certificates has been done properly. Usually, banks and trust companies act as transfer agents and registrars. Many stockholders have chosen to avoid these rather cumbersome procedures. Instead, depository trust companies (discussed in Chapter 3) are used, which substitute computerized records for embossed certificates.

16.1.2 Voting

Because a common shareholder is one of the owners of a corporation, he or she is entitled to vote on matters brought up at the corporation's annual meeting and to vote for the corporation's directors. Any owner may attend and vote in person, but most choose instead to vote by **proxy**. That is, the incumbent directors and senior management will typically solicit all the stockholders, asking each one to sign a proxy statement. Such a statement is a power of attorney authorizing the designated party listed on the statement to cast all of the investor's votes on any matter brought up at the meeting. Occasionally, desired positions on specific issues are solicited on the proxy statement. However, most of the time the positions held by the incumbents are made known with the proxy solicitation. Because the majority of votes are generally controlled by the incumbents via proxy statements, the actual voting turns out to be perfunctory, leaving little if any controversy or excitement.[1]

16.1.3 Proxy Fight

Once in a while, however, a **proxy fight** (or contest) develops. Insurgents from outside the corporation solicit proxies to vote against the incumbents, often in order to effect a takeover of some sort. Stockholders are deluged with literature and appeals for their proxies. The incumbents usually win, but the possibility of a loss in such a skirmish tends to curb activities clearly not in the stockholders' best interests.[2]

When proposals are to be voted on, the number of votes given an investor equals the number of shares held. Thus when a yes or no vote is called for, anyone controlling a majority of the shares will be able to make sure that the outcome he or she favors will receive a majority of the votes. When directors are to be elected, however, there are two types of voting systems that can be used, one of which does not give a majority owner complete control of the outcome. This type of voting system is known as a **cumulative voting system**, whereas the other type of voting system that does allow a majority owner to control the outcome completely is known as a **majority voting system** (or straight voting system).

Under both systems, the winners of the election are those candidates who have received the highest number of votes. Thus if six candidates were running for three directorships, the three receiving the largest number of votes would be elected.

Majority Voting System

With both voting systems, a stockholder receives a total number of votes that equals the number of directors to be elected times the number of shares owned. However, with the majority voting system, the stockholder may give any one candidate, as a maximum, only a number of votes equal to the number of shares owned. Thus, in a situation in which three directors are to be elected, a stockholder with 400 shares would have 1,200 votes but could give no more than 400 of those votes to any one candidate. Note that if there are a total of 1,000 shares outstanding and one stockholder owns, or has proxies for, 501 shares, then he or she can give 501 votes to each of the three candidates he or she favors. In doing so, this stockholder will be certain that the three favored candidates will be elected, regardless of how the remaining 499 shares are voted. The majority shareholder's candidates would each have 501 votes, whereas the most any other candidate could receive is 499 votes. Thus with a majority voting system, a stockholder owning (or controlling with proxies) one share more than 50% is certain of electing all the candidates that he or she favors.

Cumulative Voting System

The cumulative voting system differs from the majority voting system in that a stockholder can cast his or her votes in any manner. As a result, a minority stockholder is certain of having some representation on the board of directors, provided that the number of shares owned is sufficiently large. In the previous example, the minority owner of the 400 shares could now cast all of his or her 1,200 votes for one candidate. Imagine that this owner wanted to elect director A, but the majority owner of 501 shares wanted to elect candidates B, C, and D. In this situation, the minority stockholder could give all 1,200 votes to A and be certain that A would be one of the three directors elected, regardless of what the majority stockholder did. Why? If the majority owner held the remaining 600 shares, he or she would have 1,800 votes. There is no way that candidate A, favored by the minority stockholder, can come in lower than second place in the vote totals; A will receive 1,200 votes, and there is no way that the 1,800 votes of the majority stockholder can be cast to give more than one of his or her favored candidates a vote total in excess of 1,200. Thus the minority stockholder is assured that A will be elected, whereas the majority stockholder is assured that only two of his or her favorites will be elected.

How many shares, at a minimum, must a stockholder own in order to be able to elect a specific number of candidates under a cumulative voting system? In general, the formula for making such a determination is

$$n = \left(\frac{ds}{D + 1} \right) + 1 \qquad (16.1)$$

where:

n = minimum number of shares that must be owned
d = number of directors the stockholder wants to be certain of electing
s = number of shares outstanding
D = number of directors to be elected

Thus the minimum number of shares a stockholder needs in order to ensure the election of one director when three are to be elected and there are 1,000 shares outstanding is

251 $\{= [(1 \times 1,000)/(3 + 1)] + 1\}$. Because in the example the minority stockholder owned 400 shares, it can be seen from the formula that he or she is certain of being able to elect one director. Note that the minimum number of shares that must be owned in order to be certain of electing two directors is 501 $\{= [(2 \times 1,000)/(3 + 1)] + 1\}$. Last, the minimum number that must be owned in order to be certain of electing all three directors is 751 $\{= [(3 + 1,000)/(3 + 1)] + 1\}$.

In summary, the cumulative voting system gives minority stockholders the right to have some representation on the board of directors, provided that the number of shares owned is sufficiently large. In contrast, the majority voting system does not give minority stockholders the right to such representation, even if 49.9% of the shares are owned by the minority stockholder.

The voting system that a corporation decides to use depends not only on the desires of the corporate founders but also on the state in which the firm is incorporated. Some states require cumulative voting systems. In Delaware, however, there is no cumulative voting unless it is specifically stated in the corporate charter.

16.1.4 Takeovers

Periodically, a firm or a wealthy individual who is convinced that the management of a corporation is not fully exploiting its business opportunities will attempt a **takeover**. This is frequently done with a **tender offer** being made by a **bidder** to a **target firm**.[3] Before this offer is announced, some of the target firm's shares are usually acquired by the bidder in the open market through the use of brokers. (Once 5% of the stock is so acquired, the bidder has ten days to report the acquisition to the SEC on a 13d form.) Then, in its quest to acquire a substantial number of the target's shares, the bidder announces the bid to the public. Advertisements to purchase shares are placed in the financial press, and material describing the bid is mailed to the target's stockholders. The bidder generally offers to buy at a stated price some or all shares offered ("tendered") by the current stockholders of the target. This buying offer is usually contingent on the tender of a minimum number of shares by the target's stockholders by a fixed date. When the buying offer is first made, the offered price ("tender price") is generally set considerably above the current market price, although the offer itself usually leads to a subsequent price increase.

Management of the target firm frequently responds to tender offers with advertisements, mailings, and the like, urging its stockholders to reject the bidder's offer. Sometimes a **white knight** will be sought, meaning that another firm that is favorably inclined toward current management will be invited to make a better offer to the target's stockholders. Another type of response by management is to pay **greenmail** to the bidder, meaning that any shares held by the bidder will be bought by the target firm at an above-market price. Still another type of response is for management of the target firm to issue a tender offer of its own, known as a **repurchase offer**, whereby the firm offers to buy back some of its own stock. (Repurchase offers are also often made by firms that have not received tender offers from outside bidders.) Other types of corporate defenses include the **Pac-Man defense**, wherein the initial target turns around and makes a tender offer for the initial acquirer; the **crown jewel defense**, wherein the target sells its most sought-after assets to make the firm less attractive; and the use of **poison pills**, wherein the target gives its shareholders certain rights that can be exercised only in the event of a subsequent takeover and that, once exercised, will be extremely onerous to the acquirer.

16.1.5 Ownership versus Control

Much has been written about the effect of the separation of ownership and control of the modern corporation.[4] This separation gives rise to what is known as a principal-agent problem. In particular, stockholders can be viewed as principals who hire management to act as their agent. The agent is to make decisions that maximize shareholder wealth as reflected in the firm's stock price. No problem would exist if stockholders could monitor the managers costlessly, because the stockholders would then be capable of determining for certain whether management had acted in their best interests. However, monitoring is not costless, and complete monitoring of every decision is, practically speaking, impossible.[5] As a result, some, but not complete, monitoring is done. This gives management considerable latitude in making decisions and leaves open the possibility that some decisions will not be in the stockholders' best interests.[6] However, the possibility of a proxy fight or tender offer provides at least some check on such decisions.

To align the interests of management with their own, stockholders frequently offer certain incentives to management. An example is the use of stock options. These options are given to certain high-level managers and allow them to purchase a specified number of shares at a stated price (often above the market price when the options are initially issued) by a stated date. Thus they motivate these managers to make decisions that will increase the stock price of the firm as much as possible because it is in the managers' own self-interest to do so. Furthermore, given their relatively long initial life span (in comparison with listed options, discussed in Chapter 19), stock options implicitly exert pressure on management to take a long-term view in making decisions.

16.1.6 Stockholders' Equity

Par Value

When a corporation is first chartered, it is authorized to issue up to a stated number of shares of common stock, each of which will often carry a specified **par value**. Legally a corporation may be precluded from making payments to common stockholders if doing so would reduce the balance sheet value of stockholders' equity below the amount represented by the par value of outstanding stock. For this reason the par value is typically low relative to the price for which the stock is initially sold. Some corporations issue no-par stock. (In that case, a stated value must be recorded in place of the par value.)

When stock is initially sold for more than its par value, the difference may be carried separately on the corporation's books under stockholders' equity. Frequently the entry is for "capital contributed in excess of par value" or "paid-in capital." The par value of the stock is carried in a separate account, generally entitled simply "common stock," with an amount that is equal to the number of shares outstanding times the par value per share (for no-par stock, the stated value).

Book Value

With the passage of time, a corporation will generate income, much of which is paid out to creditors (as interest) and to stockholders (as dividends). Any remainder is added to the amount shown as cumulative retained earnings on the corporation's books. The sum of the cumulative retained earnings and other entries (such as "common stock" and "capital contributed in excess of par value") under stockholders' equity is the **book value of the equity**:

Corporate Governance

Conflicts between corporate managements and institutional shareholders first surfaced as a major public policy issue in the 1980s. The potentially adversarial principal-agent relationship between corporate owners and managers has long been recognized. In the last decade, however, two major developments brought this issue to greater prominence.

First, corporate managements, responding to a wave of hostile corporate takeovers, instituted various defensive strategies such as poison pill provisions, the sale of key corporate assets, and staggered board of directors terms. These defenses were designed to prevent the target companies from being acquired easily, thereby protecting the jobs of existing management. Indeed, they appear to have had the intended result of making hostile takeovers more difficult. However, to the extent that they entrench inefficient corporate managements, the defenses also may have reduced the value of the companies to their existing shareholders.

Second, institutional shareholders now wield considerable corporate voting power. The growth of institutional investors has concentrated corporate ownership in the hands of a relatively few organizations. (See *Institutional Issues: Institutional Investors* in Chapter 1.) The resources of these large organizations enabled them to actively oppose management decisions that diminished the value of their investments. *Corporate governance*, a particularly bureaucratic-sounding term, has become the catchall description for institutional investor efforts to influence the fundamental relationships between corporate managements and their shareholders.

Until recently, the attitude of most company managements toward shareholders was simply, "If you don't like the way we run the company, then sell our stock and quit complaining." Institutional investors, however, came to realize that they had nowhere else to go. For example, they place hundreds of billions of dollars in *indexed* portfolios designed to track the U.S. stock market (see Chapter 23). As a result, they effectively hold permanent positions in all large U.S. corporations. Corporate governance (or "shareholder rights") activities expressed institutional investors' desires to stand and fight for their financial interests.

State and local pension funds (that is, "public" pension funds) are the leading shareholder rights proponents. Their activism can be traced to the early and mid-1980s, when many of them sponsored shareholder resolutions that urged corporations to end their involvement in South Africa. Although none of those resolutions passed, their mere introduction embarrassed the confronted corporate managements. Many prominent U.S. companies voluntarily sold their South African business investments or considerably lowered their profile in the country.

The organizational lessons acquired in this South African "divestment" debate proved valuable when the battle against corporate takeover defenses began soon after. In 1984 several public pension funds, along with various union pension funds, formed the Council of Institutional Investors (CII). The goal of the CII is to provide a forum for institutional investors to discuss and organize efforts to encourage enlightened shareholder rights policies by corporate managements. Although the CII is still dominated by public and union pension funds, several large corporate pension funds have joined. Today the CII has over 100 members who, in total, control more than $1 trillion in assets.

cumulative retained earnings

+ capital contributed in excess of par

+ common stock
_____

= book value of the equity

The **book value per share** is obtained by dividing the book value of the equity by the number of shares outstanding.

Reserved and Treasury Stock

Typically, a corporation will issue only part of its authorized stock. Some of the remainder may be specifically reserved for outstanding options, convertible securities,

The CII and other shareholder rights organizations have become forces to be reckoned with on corporate governance issues. Shareholder victories have begun to mount. In the early 1990s, under pressure from institutional investors, chief executives from such large organizations as General Motors, American Express, and Westinghouse were ousted. IBM restructured its board of directors to give more power to outsiders. Sears revamped its business strategy, eliminating unprofitable operations.

Many large corporations have come to see the handwriting on the wall and have moved to negotiate directly with their large institutional shareholders. Although direct victories by institutional investors in proxy battles remain rare, shareholder rights proponents are increasingly accomplishing their objectives away from the publicity of annual meetings. The mere threat of introducing corporate governance proposals at a company's annual meeting now often is sufficient to force concessions from corporate management. In several cases, institutional investors have produced target lists of poorly performing companies and focused their reform efforts on those companies.

Interestingly, the motives of institutional shareholders in the corporate governance debate are not always clear-cut. For example, public pension funds may be sensitive to political pressures to support companies domiciled in their states or localities, regardless of the companies' shareholder rights record. Managers of corporate pension funds may wish to avoid opposing other corporations' shareholder rights practices for fear that their own companies may face similar pressures some day. Insurance companies and mutual funds, newcomers to the corporate governance debate, may be directly employed by the companies whose shareholder policies they might oppose.

Given these potentially conflicting motivations, it is perhaps surprising that the shareholder rights movement has achieved its current prominence. Actions on the part of the federal government seem likely to ensure that the debate continues. In 1992 the Securities and Exchange Commission issued regulations making it easier for institutional investors to communicate with one another to enlist support for various shareholder proposals. Also in 1992 the Department of Labor strongly reaffirmed an early ruling that a pension fund's proxy votes are a plan asset and must be managed accordingly. Congress, on occasion, has considered legislation formalizing certain shareholder rights, although no such action is currently pending.

Institutional investors have been encouraged enough by their successes to take their corporate governance proposals abroad. They have begun to challenge corporate practices that disenfranchise shareholders and protect managements in Europe and Japan. Further, in the United States, while shareholder rights activists still oppose blatantly antishareholder takeover defenses, they have begun to focus their attention on subtler issues, such as executive compensation, independent boards of directors, and secret balloting in proxy fights. The future may see debates moving to such nonshareholder issues as product liability, health care, and the environment. To what extent institutional investors should involve themselves with corporate business decision making remains a hotly contested subject, as is the issue of whether such activities actually enhance shareholder value. One thing is certain, however: Corporate managements will never again be able to run their businesses oblivious to the wishes of their largest shareholders.

and so on. However, if a corporation wishes to issue new stock in excess of the amount originally authorized, the charter must be amended. Amending the charter requires approval by both the state and the stockholders.

Sometimes a corporation will repurchase some of its outstanding stock, either in the open market through the services of a broker or with a tender offer. Afterward, this stock may be "held in the treasury." Such **treasury stock** is not entitled to voting rights or dividends and is equivalent economically (though not legally) to unissued stock.

A major study of over 1,300 stock repurchases found that nearly 90% of the repurchases analyzed were executed in the open market, with the remainder being "self-tender offers."[7] There were two types of self-tender offers that occurred with approximately equal frequency. The first type is a "fixed-price" self-tender offer; the corporation makes an offer to repurchase a stated number of shares at a set, pre-determined price. The second type is a "Dutch-auction" self-tender offer; the corporation again makes an offer to repurchase a stated number of shares but at a price that is determined by inviting existing shareholders to submit offers to sell. The ultimate repurchase price is the lowest offered price at which the previously stated number of shares can be repurchased from those shareholders who have submitted offers.[8]

Figure 16.1 shows the average stock price behavior surrounding the announcement date for the three types of stock repurchases, just mentioned. For each repurchase, the stock's "abnormal" return was determined by relating daily returns on the stock to the corresponding returns on a stock market index. This calculation was made for the 50-day period immediately prior to the repurchase announcement and the 50-day period immediately following it. These abnormal returns were averaged across firms for each day relative to the announcement and then cumulated across time. The figure shows that open-market repurchases are typically made after the stock price has had an abnormal decline. However, fixed-price and Dutch-auction repurchases are made after a period of fairly normal returns. Also of interest is the observation that the stock price jumped upward on the announcement of the repurchase offer for all three types. (The average size of the abnormal return on the announcement date was 11% for fixed-price, 8% for Dutch-auction, and 2% for open-market repurchases.) Finally, after the repurchase offer expired, the stock price did not tend to fall back to its preannouncement level.

Interestingly, two other studies found that investors could have formed profitable investment strategies to take advantage of the announcement of a stock re-

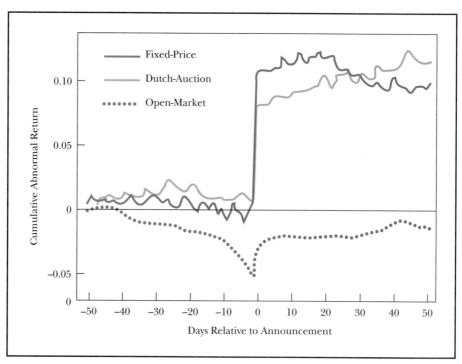

Figure 16.1
Abnormal Stock Price Behavior around Repurchase Announcements
Source: Robert Comment and Gregg A. Jarrell, "The Relative Signalling Power of Dutch-Auction and Fixed-Price Self-Tender Offers and Open-Market Share Repurchases," *Juornal of Finance* 46, no. 4 (September 1991): 1254.

purchase. In one study the strategy involved fixed-price self-tender offers where the stock was purchased by the investor in the open market shortly before the offer's expiration date if it was selling at least 3% below the repurchase price. Then the investor tendered the stock to the firm on the expiration date. If the repurchase was oversubscribed (meaning that more shares were submitted for repurchase than the corporation indicated it was buy), then the number of the investor's shares that the corporation did not buy were sold in the marketplace shortly after the expiration date. The result was that for an investment of less than a week, this strategy generated an abnormal return of more than 9%.[9]

In the second study, investors who bought shares of a firm's stock upon hearing of the firm's announcement of an open-market repurchase program would have made an abnormal return of about 12% over the next three years (or 4% per year). Furthermore, if these investors limited their purchases to those firms that had low book-value-to-market-value ratios, the abnormal returns were even higher, being about 45% over three years (or about 15% per year).[10] Clearly, both of these studies uncovered investment strategies that appear to be inconsistent with the notion of efficient markets.

Why do firms repurchase their stock? Previously it is mentioned that one motive is to repel a takeover attempt. Two other explanations have been offered. First, management may be attempting to send a *signal* to the shareholders (and the public) that the corporation's stock is undervalued in the marketplace. Second, it may be beneficial taxwise to the current shareholders for the firm to use excess cash to repurchase stock instead of using it to pay a cash dividend.

For example, consider a shareholder who bought 10 shares of stock at $40 per share that are now worth $50 per share, resulting in an unrealized capital gain of $10 per share, or $100 in total. Furthermore, the shareholder could receive a $10 per share cash dividend from the firm as part of a general disbursement of excess cash. As a result, the stock price will drop $10 per share, removing the capital gain, but all of this dividend will be treated as taxable income to the shareholder. Alternatively, the corporation could spend the same amount to repurchase its stock. If the shareholder tenders his or her pro rata share, then the investor will receive $100 for two shares of stock (=$100 cash dividend/$50 share price, assuming perfect markets) and will have to pay capital gains on only the amount of $100 that exceeds the $80 (=2 shares × $40) cost of the two shares that were repurchased (if the shareholder will not tender any shares, then no taxes of any sort are owed). Hence the shareholder will have to pay capital gains taxes on only $20 of the $100 at that time but will have unrealized capital gains of $10 per share on the eight shares still owned (because the stock price will remain at $50 per share), upon which capital gains taxes will have to be paid at some later date when they are sold. Thus the shareholder benefits taxwise from a repurchase in two ways in that a *smaller* amount is taxed at that time at a capital gains tax rate that is potentially *lower* than the ordinary income tax rate.

Classified Stock

Some corporations issue two or more classes of common stock. For example, class *A* stock might have a preferred position in regard to dividends but might not have any voting rights. In contrast, class *B* stock might have full voting rights but a lower position in regard to dividends. Often issuing two classes of stock is equivalent to an issue of preferred stock along with a normal issue of common stock.

An interesting example involves the three classes of General Motors common stock that existed until the mid-1990s. These classes were referred to as $1-\frac{2}{3}$ par value, class E, and class H stock (the E class no longer exists, but the other two still are outstanding). One share in each class had 1, 1/4, and 1/2 vote, respectively. In terms of dividends, the class E and class H stocks were allowed to receive an amount that did not exceed the "adjusted earnings" of GM's Electronic Data Systems and Hughes Electronics subsidiaries, respectively. The $1-\frac{2}{3}$ par value stock was allowed to receive dividends that did not exceed the remainder of GM's earnings.

Another example involves Canadian corporations. Because of the Canada Income Tax Act of 1971, Canadian firms are allowed to have class A and class B shares. The only difference between the two classes is that class A shares receive cash dividends, whereas class B shares receive stock dividends. Furthermore, owners of either class can swap their shares one-for-one for shares of the other class at any time.

Letter or Restricted Stock

In the United States, security regulations require that most stock be registered with the SEC before it may be sold in a public offering. Under some conditions, unregistered stock may be sold directly to a purchaser through a *private placement*, but its subsequent sale is **restricted**. Such **letter stock** must be held for at least one year and can be sold over the next year only if ample information on the company is available and the amount sold is a relatively small percentage of the total amount outstanding. (Indeed, it is called letter stock because the purchaser must provide the SEC with a letter indicating that the shares will be held as an investment and will not be for resale.) However, under certain circumstances (defined by SEC Rule 144A), large institutional investors are allowed to trade nonpublic securities issued under this rule among themselves at any time after their issuance. (Rule 144A is discussed later in this chapter.)

16.2   CASH DIVIDENDS

Payments made in cash to stockholders are termed **dividends**. These are typically declared quarterly by the board of directors and are paid to the current stockholders of record at a date specified by the board, known as the **date of record**. The dividends may be of almost any size, subject to certain restrictions such as those contained in the charter or in documents given to creditors. Thus, dividends could be even larger than the current earnings of the corporation, although they seldom are. (Such dividends are usually paid out of past earnings.)

Compiling a list of stockholders to receive the dividend is not as simple as it may initially seem, because for many firms the list changes almost constantly as shares are bought and sold. Those stockholders who are to receive the dividend are identified by use of an **ex-dividend date**. Because of the time required to record the transfer of ownership of common stock, major stock exchanges specify an ex-dividend date that is two business days prior to the date of record. Investors purchasing shares before an ex-dividend date are entitled to receive the dividend in question; those purchasing on or after the ex-dividend date are not entitled to the dividend.

For example, a dividend may be declared on May 15 with a date of record of Friday, June 15. In this situation Wednesday, June 13, would become the ex-dividend date. An investor who bought shares on Tuesday, June 12, would subsequently receive the cash dividend (unless the shares were sold late in the day on the 12th, in which case the new owner would receive the dividend). However, if the shares were bought on Wednesday, June 13, the investor would not receive the cash dividend. Besides a declaration date (May 15), an ex-dividend date (June 13), and a date of record (June 15), there is also a fourth date, the "payment date." On this date (perhaps June 25) the checks for the cash dividends are put in the mail or deposited electronically in shareholder accounts at brokerage firms or custodian banks. Summarizing the example:

May 15 ⟶ June 13 ⟶ June 15 ⟶ June 25

| Declaration | Ex-Dividend | Date of | Payment |
| Date | Date | Record | Date |

16.3 STOCK DIVIDENDS AND STOCK SPLITS

Occasionally, the board of directors decides to forgo a cash dividend and "pays" a **stock dividend** instead. For example, if a 5% stock dividend is declared, the owner of 100 shares receives five additional shares that are issued for this occasion. The accounting treatment of a stock dividend is to increase the "common stock" and "capital contributed in excess of par" accounts by an amount equal to the market value of the stock at the time of the dividend times the number of new shares issued. (The "common stock" account would increase by an amount equal to the par value times the number of new shares. The remainder of the increase would go into the "capital contributed in excess of par" account.) The total book value of stockholders' equity is kept the same by reducing the "retained earnings" account by an equivalent amount.

A **stock split** is similar to a stock dividend in that the stockholder owns more shares afterward. However, it is different in both magnitude and accounting treatment. With a stock split, all the old shares are destroyed and new ones are issued with a new par value. Afterward, the number of new shares outstanding is usually larger than the previous number of old shares by 25% or more, with the exact amount depending on the size of the split. In contrast, a stock dividend usually results in an increase of less than 25%. Whereas a stock dividend results in adjustments to the dollar figures in certain stockholders' equity accounts, no adjustments are made for a split. For example, if a $1 par value stock is split two for one, the holder of 200 old shares will receive 400 new $.50 par value shares, and none of the dollar figures in stockholders' equity will change.

A **reverse stock split** reduces the number of shares and increases the par value per share. For example, in a reverse two-for-one split, the holder of 200 $1 par value shares would exchange them for 100 $2 par value shares. Again there would not be any change in the dollar figures in stockholders' equity.

Stock dividends and splits must be taken into account when following the price of a company's shares. For example, a fall in price per share may be due solely to a large stock split. To reduce confusion, most financial services provide data adjusted for at least some of these changes. Thus if a stock split two-for-one on July 31, prices prior to that date might be divided by 2 to facilitate comparison.

16.3.1 Ex-Distribution Dates

In a manner similar to that used for the payment of cash dividends, the corporation specifies three dates associated with either stock dividends or stock splits: a declaration date, a date of record, and a payment date. However, there is now an **ex-distribution date** instead of an ex-dividend date. For stock dividends of less than 20%, the procedure is identical to the one described previously for cash dividends: The ex-distribution date is two business days before the date of record, meaning that if you buy the stock on or after that date, you do not get the additional shares.

For larger stock dividends and all stock splits, the procedure is a bit different in that the ex-distribution date is usually the business day after the payment date (which, in turn, is after the date of record). Hence if a 25% stock dividend is declared on May 15 with a date of record of June 15 and a payment date of June 25, then anyone buying the stock before June 26 will receive the stock dividend. However, those who wait until June 26 to buy the stock will not receive the stock dividend.[11]

16.3.2   Reasons for Stock Dividends and Splits

Why do corporations issue stock dividends and split their stocks? Nothing of importance would appear to be changed because such actions do not increase revenues or reduce expenses. All that happens is that there is a change in the size of the units in which ownership may be bought and sold. Moreover, because the process involves administrative effort, and costs something to execute, one wonders why it is done.

It is sometimes argued that stockholders respond positively to "tangible" evidence of the growth of their corporation. A related argument states that stock splits, like repurchases, are used by management to *signal* investors that they believe the firm's stock is undervalued in the marketplace. Another view holds that splits and stock dividends, by decreasing the price per share, may bring the stock's price into a more desirable trading range and hence, by increasing the liquidity of the stock and subsequently its price, increase the total value of the amount outstanding. A related view is that there is a desirable trading range for the stock that is based on the minimum tick size that is allowed (currently 1/16 for all stocks priced over $1). Lower prices result in larger spreads relative to the stock's price, thereby benefiting brokers and dealers but costing investors.[12] Figure 16.2 presents the average behavior of stock returns for 1,275 two-for-one stock splits that occurred between 1975 and 1990.[13] For each split, the stock's "abnormal" return was determined by relating monthly returns on the stock to the corresponding returns in the stock market. This calculation

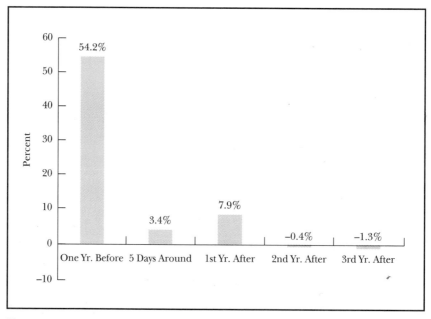

Figure 16.2

Average Abnormal Returns of Stocks around the Time That They Announce Stock Splits

Source: Adapted from David Ikenberry, Graeme Rankine, and Earl K. Stice, "What Do Stock Splits Really Signal?" *Journal of Financial and Quantitative Analysis* 31, no. 3 (September 1996): 360, 362, 367.

was done for (1) the 12-month period before the split announcement month, (2) the five-day period running from two days before to two days after the split announcement, and (3) the three years after the split announcement. These abnormal returns were first averaged across firms for each day relative to the announcement of the firm's split and then were cumulated across time.

As the figure shows, the stocks tended to have a positive abnormal return of about 54% during the year before announcement of the split. Thus, it appears that unexpected positive developments (such as unexpected large increases in earnings) caused abnormal increases in the stock prices of these firms, after which the firms decided to split their stock. The announcement of the stock split appears to have triggered a boost in the firm's stock; it had an abnormal increase of a bit over 3% in the period from two days before to two days after the announcement. The behavior of the postsplit prices indicates that over the following year investors continued to receive significantly positive abnormal returns amounting to about 8% and that thereafter no notable abnormal returns occurred.[14] Apparently the prices of firms whose stocks split did rise, but they did not rise to an equilibrium level on the announcement date. Such an underreaction to the announcement of a stock split can be interpreted as evidence of a market inefficiency. However, other studies, using different stocks and time periods have found slightly negative abnormal returns, no abnormal returns, or slightly positive abnormal returns after the split.[15]

The evidence also suggests that stock splits are associated with increased transaction costs. A study of presplit and postsplit behavior showed that after splits, trading volume rose less than proportionately, and both commission costs and bid-ask spreads, expressed as a percentage of value, increased—hardly reactions that are favorable to stockholders.[16] For example, after a two-for-one stock split there will be twice as many shares outstanding, so it is reasonable to expect the daily number of shares that are traded to double. It is also reasonable to expect the commission for buying 200 shares after the split to be the same as the commission for buying 100 shares before the split. Instead, it was found that after the split the number of shares traded daily was less than twice as large and the commission costs per share traded were proportionately larger.

Another study of stock splits and stock dividends uncovered an apparent market inefficiency.[17] This study examined the performance of stocks around the "ex" dates associated with their stock splits and dividends. If an investor bought shares of a firm the day before its ex date and sold them the day after the ex date, then on average the investor would make an abnormal return of roughly 2% for stock dividends and 1% for stock splits. Such a result appears to violate the notion of efficient markets because it suggests that an investor can make abnormal returns by trading stocks using a simple strategy based on publicly available information.

16.4 PREEMPTIVE RIGHTS

Under common law (and most state laws), a stockholder has an inherent right to maintain his or her proportionate ownership of the corporation. The existence of these **preemptive rights** means that when new shares are to be sold, the current stockholders must be given the right of first refusal in regard to the purchase of the new shares.[18] Each current stockholder is issued a certificate that indicates the number of new shares he or she is authorized to purchase. This number will be proportional to the number of existing shares currently owned by the stockholder. Usually, the new shares will be priced below the current market price of the stock, making such

rights valuable. The stockholder can exercise the rights by purchasing his or her allotted amount of new shares, thereby maintaining his or her proportional ownership in the firm, but at the cost of providing additional capital. Alternatively, the rights can be sold to someone else.[19]

For example, if a firm needs $10,000,000 for new equipment, it may decide to sell new shares in order to raise the capital. Given that the current market price of the stock is $60 per share, a **rights offering** may be used to raise the capital, where the **subscription price** is set at $50 per share.[20] Accordingly, 200,000 (=$10,000,000/$50) new shares are to be sold. If the firm has 4,000,000 shares outstanding, the owner of one share will receive the right to buy 1/20 (=200,000/4,000,000) of a new share. Because the number of rights received is equal to the number of shares owned, it can be seen that 20 shares must be owned in order to be able to buy one new share. Thus a stockholder who owns 100 shares will receive 100 rights allowing him or her to buy 5 (= 100 × 1/20) new shares. These rights are valuable because their owner can buy stock at $50 a share when the market price is significantly higher. The current owner of 100 shares can either use the 100 rights by coming up with cash equal to $250 (=5 × $50) or sell the 100 rights to someone else. But what is a fair price for the rights?

Rights are distributed in a manner similar to cash dividends. That is, there is a date of record and, two business days earlier, an **ex-rights date**. Before the ex-rights date, the value of a right can be calculated by using the following equation:

$$C_0 - (RN + S) = R \qquad (16.2)$$

where:

C_0 = "rights-on" market price of stock
R = value of a right
N = number of rights needed to buy one share
S = subscription price

Equation (16.2) can be interpreted in the following manner. If an investor purchases one share before the ex-rights date, by definition he or she pays the *rights-on* market price of C_0, shown on the left-hand side of the equation. Alternatively, the investor could purchase the number of rights necessary to buy one share of the new stock at a cost of RN and set aside an amount of money equal to the subscription price S. The total cost of this transaction is $(RN + S)$. The only difference between the two alternatives is that the first one gives the investor not only one share of stock but also one right. Thus, the difference in the cost of the two alternatives, $C_0 - (RN + S)$, must equal the value of a right R, as shown in Equation (16.2).

Equation (16.2) can be rewritten as:

$$R = \frac{C_0 - S}{N + 1} \qquad (16.3)$$

Thus in the previous example, the value of a right when the stock is selling for $60 would be equal to approximately $.48 $\left[= (\$60 - \$50)/(20 + 1)\right]$.

On or after the ex-rights date, the value of a right can be calculated by using the following equation:

$$C_e - (RN + S) = 0 \qquad (16.4)$$

where C_e is the *ex-rights* market price of the stock. The reasoning behind this equation is similar to the reasoning behind Equation (16.2). That is, an investor can purchase one share by either buying it in the open market at a cost of C_e or purchasing the requisite number of rights and setting aside the subscription price, for a total cost of $RN + S$. Because the purchase of one share ex-rights means that the investor does not receive a right, the two alternatives provide the investor with the same item. Thus the cost of these two alternatives should be equivalent, so the difference in their cost should be zero.

Equation (16.4) can be rewritten as:

$$R = \frac{C_e - S}{N} \qquad (16.5)$$

In the previous example, if the stock were selling for $56 after the ex-rights date, then the value of a right at that time would be approximately $.30 $\left[= (\$56 - \$50)/20\right]$.

16.5 STOCK QUOTATIONS

Figures 16.3 through 16.5 provide examples of quotations summarizing a day's transactions in stocks traded over the counter and on various stock exchanges.

16.5.1 Nasdaq

Active stocks traded with the aid of the National Association of Securities Dealers' Automated Quotation system (Nasdaq) are summarized in the forms shown in Figure 16.3. Transactions in securities designated "National Market Issues" are summarized in detail, as shown in Figure 16.3(a). High and low prices for trades over the preceding 52 weeks are given, along with the annual per share amount of dividends, in dollars, based on the latest declared amount. (Letters refer to footnotes providing details concerning extra or special dividends and yields. The footnotes also explain the sporadic entries in the extreme left column and why certain rows are either emboldened or underlined.) This dollar amount is divided by the **closing price** (the price at which the last trade of the day was made) to obtain the figure shown for **dividend yield**. The price-earnings ratio (the closing price divided by the last 12 months' earnings per share) is given next. The remaining entries summarize the day's transactions in the major markets in which the stock is traded. Sale volume, in hundreds of shares, are indicated, followed by the highest and lowest prices at which trades were completed during the day. The next entry is the closing price, and the final entry shows the difference between the day's closing price and that of the preceding day.

Over-the-counter Nasdaq stocks with somewhat less activity are referred to as "Small-Cap Issues"; transactions in these stocks are summarized in Figure 16.3(b). Annual per share dividends are reported first, followed by trading volume (in hundreds of shares) and the price at which the last trade of the day took place. The net change in the last price from the previous day is shown in the right-hand column. Investors in these securities, like investors in National Market Issues, transact with dealers paying the asked price when purchasing shares and receiving the bid price when selling shares. Hence the last price and net change figures may reflect bid or asked prices. Investors may also have to bear markdowns or markups and commissions, which may be added by retail brokers.[21]

16.5.2 U.S. Stock Exchanges

Activity in stocks traded on U.S. stock exchanges is shown in Figure 16.4. Stocks listed on the New York Stock Exchange are shown in Figure 16.4(a). Those listed on the American Stock Exchange are shown in panel (b). The information provided for

---

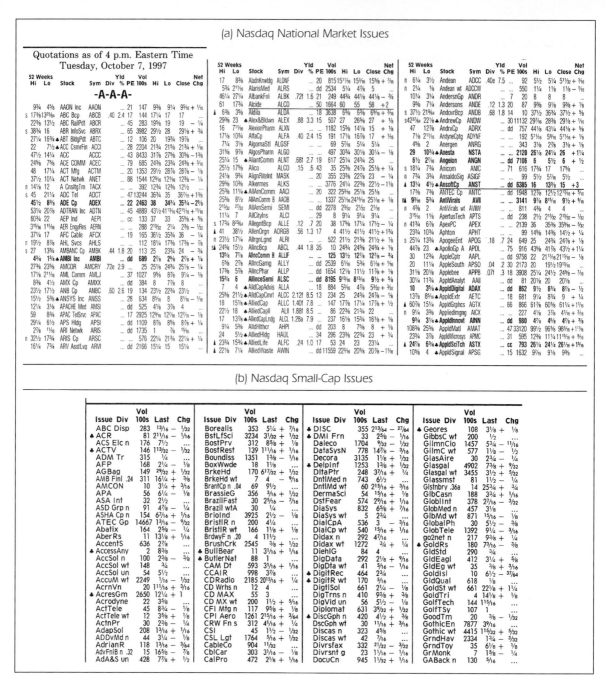

Figure 16.3

Summary of Stocks Traded with the Aid of the Nasdaq System (Excerpts)

Source: Reprinted by permission of *The Wall Street Journal*, Dow Jones & Company, October 8, 1997, pp. C9, C10. All rights reserved worldwide.

both of these exchanges is identical in format to the information provided for Nasdaq National Market Issues shown in Figure 16.3(a).

Figure 16.4(c) describes the activity in various regional stock exchanges in the United States. However, any trading that involves securities that are also listed on either the NYSE or AMEX ("dually listed securities") is excluded, because those trades are reflected in either panel (a) or panel (b). Less information is provided for trading on the regional exchanges than on organized exchanges; all that is reported are

(a) Stocks Listed on the New York Stock Exchange

Quotations as of 5 p.m. Eastern Time
Thursday, October 9, 1997

-A-A-A-

	52 Weeks Hi	52 Weeks Lo	Stock	Sym	Div	Yld %	PE	Vol 100s	Hi	Lo	Close	Net Chg
	38 7/16	23 7/8	AAR	AIR	.48	1.4	24	429	34 13/16	34 1/2	34 5/8	...
	29 3/16	15 1/2	ABM Indus	ABM	.40	1.4	25	481	29 1/8	28 15/16	29 1/16	...
n	24 7/16	18 3/8	ABN AMRO ADR	AAN	.25p	...	...	889	20 15/16	20 5/8	20 7/8	– 5/8
	11	9 7/8	ACM Gvt Fd	ACG	.90a	8.3	...	645	10 15/16	10 7/8	10 7/8	– 1/16
	8 1/4	6 7/8	ACM OppFd	AOF	.63	8.0	...	130	7 15/16	7 7/8	7 7/8	...
	10 1/4	8 7/8	ACM SecFd	GSF	.90	8.9	...	610	10 1/8	10 1/16	10 1/8	+ 1/16
	7	6 1/4	ACM SpctmFd	SI	.57	8.8	...	1678	6 1/2	6 7/16	6 1/2	...
	15	11 1/2	ACM MgmdInc	ADF	1.35	9.3	...	473	14 11/16	14 9/16	14 9/16	– 1/16
	10 1/2	9 1/4	ACM MgdIncFd	AMF	.90	8.7	...	276	10 5/16	10 1/4	10 5/16	– 1/16
	14 1/4	12 1/4	ACM MuniSec	AMU	.90	6.4	...	174	14 1/4	14 1/8	14 1/8	– 1/16
	27 7/16	16 3/4	♣ACX Tch A	ACX		...	dd	78	26 15/16	26 9/16	26 9/16	– 5/16
s	49 5/8	20 3/16	♣AES Cp	AES		...	51	5599	48	46 7/8	47 3/4	+ 3/4
	57 7/8	35 3/4	♣AFLAC	AFL	.46	.9	12	1509	54 7/16	53 1/4	54	– 9/16
	36 5/16	23 3/4	AGCO Cp	AG	.04	.1	13	3748	31 1/2	31	31 3/8	+ 1/4
	22	18 3/8	AGL Res	ATG	1.08	5.7	13	841	19	18 13/16	18 7/8	– 1/8
	20 1/4	11 1/2	AgSvcAm	ASV		...	20	70	19	18 9/16	18 7/8	+ 1/8
n	25 3/4	25	AICI CapTr pf		.35p	...	...	113	25 7/16	25 1/4	25 5/16	– 1/16
	19 5/8	13 1/4	AJL PepsTr	AJP	1.44	8.5	...	150	17 3/16	16 7/16	16 15/16	+ 3/8
	24 3/4	20 1/4	♣AMLI Resdntl	AML	1.72	7.3	19	384	23 13/16	23 1/2	23 1/2	– 7/16
	56 11/16	32 7/8	♣AMP	AMP	1.04	1.9	45	1990	53 15/16	52 5/8	53 3/4	+ 1/8
▲	118 1/2	78 1/4	AMR	AMR		...	10	5030	119 1/8	115 5/16	119 1/8	+ 2 3/4
	50 5/8	40 7/8	♣ARCO Chm	RCM	2.80	5.7	20	935	49 1/2	48 5/8	49 1/2	+ 3/4
	41	28 5/16	ASA	ASA	1.20	3.9	...	748	31 5/8	30 13/16	30 15/16	– 9/16
	47 7/16	30 3/4	AT&T	T	1.32	2.9	15	54070	46 3/4	45 1/2	46 3/16	– 5/16
	35 3/16	28 1/4	AXA-UAP ADR	AXA	.65p	...	...	193	34 7/8	34 5/16	34 5/8	– 9/16
s	37 1/8	10 1/2	AamesFnl	AAM	.13	.8	11	3728	16 3/4	16 1/8	16 11/16	...
n	26 5/16	24 1/2	AbbeyNtl		2.19	8.3	...	46	26 1/4	26 1/16	26 1/4	+ 1/16
	68 15/16	48 3/4	AbbotLab	ABT	1.08	1.7	25	9143	65 7/16	63 7/8	64 15/16	– 5/8
	28	12 1/2	Abercrombie A	ANF		...	...	869	24 11/16	24	24 7/16	– 1/2
	21	12 5/8	Abitibi g	ABY	.40	...	...	1105	16 5/8	16 5/16	16 5/8	+ 1/16
	28	17 3/4	♣AcceptIns	AIF		...	14	129	27 9/16	27 3/8	27 9/16	+ 3/16
	32	15 3/4	AccuStaff	ASI		...	53	1246	31 3/4	31 5/16	31 3/8	– 1/2
▲	65 5/8	31 1/4	♣AppldPwr	APW	.12	.2	23	1612	67 1/2	65	66 1/2	+ 1 1/2
	22 1/8	12 3/4	ApriaHlthcr	AHG		...	dd	5158	14 1/8	13 3/4	14	...
n	16	9 7/8	APT Satellite	ATS		...	...	276	14 3/4	14 1/4	14 5/8	+ 1/2
	59 1/8	30 1/2	♣AptarGp	ATR		...	25	67	56 7/8	56 1/2	56 7/8	– 1/8
	28 3/4	24 3/8	Aquarion	WTR	1.64f	5.9	20	89	27 5/8	27 3/16	27 5/8	+ 1/8
	16 1/2	9 5/16	♣AquilaGasPip	AQP	.05	.4	11	289	12 7/8	12 1/2	12 5/8	+ 1/8
s	22 9/16	15 1/2	Aracruz	ARA	.19e	.9	...	513	20 3/4	20 5/8	20 5/8	+ 1/16
	11 1/16	6 1/2	ArborProp	ABR	.70	6.5	43	1480	10 3/4	10 1/2	10 3/4	– 1/8
	23 1/2	6 3/4	♣ArcadiaFnl	AAC		...	dd	2223	12 1/8	11 11/16	12 1/16	– 1/16
n	30 1/2	26 7/8	ArchCoal	ACI	.35	1.2	...	22	28 1/8	27 15/16	28	– 1/8
	24 5/8	16 3/16	ArcherDan	ADM	.20b	.8	36	9104	24 1/8	23 7/8	23 15/16	– 1/16
	32 5/16	22	ArdenRlty	ARI	1.60	5.1	...	691	31 13/16	31	31 1/8	– 13/16
	32	19 1/4	Argentaria	AGR	.75e	2.6	...	39	28 1/2	28 1/4	28 1/2	– 1/4
n	25 1/2	24	ArgnCapTr pfA		.49p	...	...	591	25	24 13/16	25	...
	16 3/4	11 1/8	ArgntnaFd	AF	.33e	2.2	...	410	15	14 3/4	14 7/8	– 1/16
	7 1/8	2 3/4	ArgosyGaming	AGY		...	dd	225	5 1/2	5 1/4	5 3/8	– 1/8
	26 1/8	24	ArizPubSvc pfW		1.81	7.0	...	2	25 13/16	25 13/16	25 13/16	...
	28	26 1/4	ArizPubSvc un	AZD	2.50	9.0	...	42	27 13/16	27 9/16	27 3/4	+ 1/8
	6 3/8	3 3/8	Armco	AS		...	15	1949	5 15/16	5 3/4	5 7/8	+ 1/16
	26 3/16	21	Armco pf		2.10	8.2	...	13	25 3/4	25 1/2	25 1/2	...
	51 3/4	45 3/8	Armco pfA		4.50	9.0	...	2	50 3/16	50 3/16	50 3/16	...
	52 1/8	39	Armco pfB		3.63	7.2	...	44	50 1/2	49 1/4	50 1/2	+ 3/16
	75 1/4	61 1/2	ArmstrngWld	ACK	1.76	2.6	14	1234	67 1/4	66 7/16	66 7/8	– 3/8
	64 1/8	43	♣ArrowElec	ARW		...	16	2038	59 7/8	59 5/16	59 3/4	+ 7/8
	6 3/4	3 1/2	ArtraGp	ATA		...	49	88	3 15/16	3 3/4	3 15/16	+ 1/16
	41 1/2	21	♣ArvinInd	ARV	.76	1.9	15	739	39 7/8	39 3/16	39 11/16	– 3/16
	34 1/4	23 7/8	Asarco	AR	.80	2.6	11	3479	30 3/4	30 5/16	30 3/8	– 7/16
	17 1/8	9 7/16	AshntGldfld	ASL	.38e	3.4	...	2299	11 11/16	11 3/16	11 1/4	+ 1/16
	55	39 1/4	Ashland	ASH	1.10	2.0	19	2442	53 15/16	53 1/8	53 11/16	+ 7/16
	13 5/8	10 1/4	AsiaPacFd	APB	.94e	9.0	...	1906	10 9/16	10 5/16	10 7/16	– 1/8
	6	3 1/8	AsiaPacif A	ARH		...	...	62	4	4	4	– 1/16
FD			AsiaPacRes rt wi			...	...	150	1/8	1/8	1/8	...
n	14 1/16	9 1/4	AsiaPacWrCbl	AWC		...	...	17	11 1/2	11 3/8	11 1/2	...
	17 1/8	9 3/4	AsiaPulp	PAP	.05e	.3	...	2840	15 13/16	15 1/8	15 3/4	– 3/16
	31 5/8	21 1/2	AsiaSatTelcm	SAT	.20e	.7	...	47	26 7/8	26 3/4	26 7/8	– 11/16
	11 11/16	9 1/8	AsiaTigers	GRR	.04e	.4	...	1869	9 13/16	9 9/16	9 9/16	– 1/4

(b) Stocks Listed on the American Stock Exchange

Quotations as of 5 p.m. Eastern Time
Tuesday, October 7, 1997

-A-A-A-

	52 Weeks Hi	52 Weeks Lo	Stock	Sym	Div	Yld %	PE	Vol 100s	Hi	Lo	Close	Net Chg
	38 7/16	23 3/8	AAR	AIR	.48	1.4	24	284	35	34 7/16	34 9/16	– 5/16
▲	27 1/2	15 1/2	ABM Indus	ABM	.40	1.4	25	328	28 7/8	27 11/16	28 3/4	+ 1 5/16
n	24 7/16	18 3/8	ABN AMRO ADR	AAN	.25p	...	...	915	22 1/16	21 13/16	22	– 3/16
	11	9 7/8	ACM Gvt Fd	ACG	.90a	8.2	...	699	10 15/16	10 13/16	10 15/16	+ 1/8
	8 1/4	6 7/8	ACM OppFd	AOF	.63	7.9	...	177	8 1/16	8	8	– 1/16
	10 1/4	8 7/8	ACM SecFd	GSF	.90	9.0	...	1405	10 1/8	10	10	– 1/16
	7	6 1/4	ACM SpctmFd	SI	.57	8.7	...	836	6 9/16	6 1/2	6 9/16	+ 1/16
	15	11 1/2	ACM MgmdInc	ADF	1.35	9.1	...	768	14 13/16	14 3/4	14 13/16	+ 1/8
	10 1/2	9 1/4	ACM MgdIncFd	AMF	.90	8.7	...	345	10 7/16	10 3/8	10 3/8	...
▲	14 1/8	12 1/4	ACM MuniSec	AMU	.90	6.3	...	491	14 1/4	14	14 1/4	+ 1/4
	27 7/16	16 3/4	♣ACX Tch A	ACX		...	dd	43	27	26 7/8	26 15/16	+ 1/16
s	49 5/8	20 3/16	♣AES Cp	AES		...	50	2413	47 3/8	46 7/16	47 1/16	+ 3/16
	57 7/8	35 3/4	♣AFLAC	AFL	.46	.8	13	786	56 5/16	55 1/2	56 1/4	+ 3/8
	36 5/16	23 3/4	AGCO Cp	AG	.04	.1	12	4741	31 3/8	30 13/16	30 13/16	– 1/8
	22	18 3/8	AGL Res	ATG	1.08	5.7	14	782	19 1/8	18 15/16	18 15/16	– 1/16
	20 1/4	11 1/2	AgSvcAm	ASV		...	20	152	18 3/4	18 1/4	18 3/8	– 3/16
n	25 3/4	25	AICI CapTr pf		.35p	...	...	131	25 11/16	25 9/16	25 5/8	– 1/16
	19 5/8	13 1/4	AJL PepsTr	AJP	1.44	9.0	...	368	16 1/16	15 13/16	16	+ 1/16
	24 3/4	20 1/4	♣AMLI Resdntl	AML	1.72	7.1	20	488	24 3/16	24 1/16	24 1/8	– 1/16
	56 11/16	32 7/8	♣AMP	AMP	1.04	1.9	45	4126	54 1/4	53 9/16	54 1/8	+ 5/16
	118 1/2	78 1/4	AMR	AMR		...	10	3515	117 3/16	115 1/4	116 5/8	+ 3/8
	50 5/8	40 7/8	♣ARCO Chm	RCM	2.80	5.7	19	1282	48 15/16	47 15/16	48 15/16	+ 13/16
	41	28 5/16	ASA	ASA	1.20	3.8	...	756	31 1/4	30 9/16	31 3/16	...
	46 1/8	30 3/4	AT&T	T	1.32	2.9	14	59526	45 9/16	44 1/4	45 7/16	+ 1 1/2
	35 1/8	28 1/4	AXA-UAP ADR	AXA	.65p	...	...	275	34 13/16	34 9/16	34 3/4	+ 1/4
s	**40 3/4**	**10 1/2**	**AamesFnl**	**AAM**	**.13**	**.8**	**11**	**4086**	**17 1/8**	**16 1/8**	**17 1/8**	**+ 15/16**
n▲	26 1/4	24 1/2	AbbeyNtl		2.19	8.3	...	32	26 5/16	26 1/4	26 5/16	+ 1/16
	68 15/16	48 3/4	AbbotLab	ABT	1.08	1.6	26	8005	65 15/16	64 11/16	65 7/8	+ 7/8
	28	12 1/2	Abercrombie A	ANF		...	...	651	26 7/8	25 7/8	26	– 1
	21	12 5/8	Abitibi g	ABY	.40	...	...	611	17	16 119/256	16 9/16	– 1/2
	28	17 3/4	♣AcceptIns	AIF		...	13	68	27 1/2	26 1/2	27 1/2	+ 3/4
	32	15 3/4	AccuStaff	ASI		...	53	3867	31 1/2	31 1/16	31 3/8	+ 3/8
n	16	9 7/8	APT Satellite	ATS		...	...	270	14 3/4	14 5/8	14 5/8	– 1/8
	59 1/8	30 1/2	♣AptarGp	ATR		...	25	347	57 1/8	56 13/16	56 7/8	+ 1/8
	28 3/4	24 3/8	Aquarion	WTR	1.64f	5.9	20	154	28 1/4	27 9/16	27 11/16	– 5/8
	16 1/2	9 5/16	♣AquilaGasPip	AQP	.05	.4	12	218	13	12 5/8	13	+ 5/16
s	22 9/16	15 1/2	Aracruz	ARA	.19e	.9	...	1456	20 11/16	20 9/16	20 11/16	...
▲	**10 3/8**	**6 1/2**	**ArborProp**	**ABR**	**.70**	**6.5**	**43**	**1893**	**10 11/16**	**9 15/16**	**10 11/16**	**+ 9/16**
	24 7/8	6 3/4	♣ArcadiaFnl	AAC		...	dd	3098	12 5/16	11 15/16	12 1/4	– 1/16
n	30 1/2	26 7/8	ArchCoal	ACI	.35	1.2	...	143	28 15/16	28 1/16	28 1/8	– 13/16
	24 5/8	16 3/16	ArcherDan	ADM	.20b	.8	37	10414	24 7/16	24 1/16	24 3/16	+ 1/8
n▲	32 1/8	22	ArdenRlty	ARI	1.60	5.0	...	1278	32 5/16	32	32 3/16	+ 3/16
	32	19 1/4	Argentaria	AGR	.75e	2.5	...	105	29 13/16	29	29 3/4	+ 1/2
n	25 1/2	24	ArgnCapTr pfA		.49p	...	...	647	25 1/4	24 7/8	25 3/16	+ 1/4
	16 3/4	11 1/8	ArgntnaFd	AF	.33e	2.2	...	1016	15	14 3/4	14 15/16	+ 3/16
	7 1/8	2 3/4	ArgosyGaming	AGY		...	dd	365	5 1/16	4 15/16	5	– 1/16
	26 1/8	24	ArizPubSvc pfW		1.81	7.0	...	2	25 13/16	25 11/16	25 13/16	+ 1/8
	28	26 1/4	ArizPubSvc un	AZD	2.50	9.0	...	23	27 13/16	27 11/16	27 13/16	+ 1/16
	6 3/8	3 3/8	Armco	AS		...	15	1806	5 15/16	5 7/8	5 7/8	...
	26 3/16	21	Armco pf		2.10	8.2	...	7	25 3/4	25 7/16	25 3/4	...
	51 3/4	45 3/8	Armco pfA		4.50	9.0	...	5	50 1/8	50	50 1/8	+ 3/16
	52 1/8	39	Armco pfB		3.63	7.2	...	1	50 5/8	50 5/8	50 5/8	– 5/16
	75 1/4	61 1/2	ArmstrngWld	ACK	1.76	2.6	14	1320	68 3/8	67 7/8	68	+ 1/8
	64 1/8	43	♣ArrowElec	ARW		...	16	1210	59 15/16	58 13/16	59 5/8	+ 13/16
	6 3/4	3 1/2	ArtraGp	ATA		...	49	202	4	3 7/8	3 15/16	– 1/16
	41 1/2	21	♣ArvinInd	ARV	.76	1.9	15	533	41	39 9/16	40 1/16	– 1 3/16
	34 1/4	23 7/8	Asarco	AR	.80	2.6	11	2811	31 1/2	30 3/4	30 15/16	– 1/8
	17 1/8	9 7/16	AshntGldfld	ASL	.38e	3.5	...	2083	11	10 15/16	11	– 1/16
	55	39 1/4	Ashland	ASH	1.10	2.0	19	2183	54 3/16	53 7/16	54	+ 5/16
	13 5/8	10 1/4	AsiaPacFd	APB	.94e	8.9	...	2104	10 3/4	10 1/2	10 9/16	– 3/16
	6	3 1/8	AsiaPacif A	ARH		...	...	210	4 7/8	4 3/4	4 3/4	...
n	14 1/16	9 1/4	AsiaPacWrCbl	AWC		...	...	61	11 3/8	11 1/4	11 3/8	...
	17 1/8	9 3/4	AsiaPulp	PAP	.05e	.3	...	1562	17	16 7/16	16 9/16	– 1/8
	31 5/8	21 1/2	AsiaSatTelcm	SAT	.20e	.7	...	6	27 3/8	27 3/8	27 3/8	– 1/4
	11 11/16	9 1/8	AsiaTigers	GRR	.04e	.4	...	390	10	9 3/4	9 3/4	– 3/8
	4 1/2	3 1/8	AssetInvest	AIC	.26f	6.3	7	1502	4 5/16	4 1/16	4 1/8	– 1/8
	24 3/4	20	♣AssocEstate	AEC	1.86	7.8	20	703	24 1/16	23 15/16	24	...
	27 1/4	24 1/2	♣AssocEstate pf		2.44	9.1	...	32	27	26 7/8	26 15/16	+ 1/8
	66 1/4	41 1/4	AssocFstCap A	AFS	.40	.6	23	3738	63 1/8	61	63 1/8	+ 3/16

(c) Stocks Listed on the Regional Exchanges

Dually Listed Issues Excluded. Sales in Hundreds.
Thursday, October 9, 1997

CHICAGO

Sales	Stock	High	Low	Close	Chg
13	BlueFish	4 7/8	4 5/8	4 7/8	+ 1/4
7	NAIC Gt	14 7/16	14 3/8	14 7/16	+ 1/4
10	PionRail	1 9/16	1 9/16	1 9/16	+ 1/16

PACIFIC

Sales	Stock	High	Low	Close	Chg
20	AFn pfF	22 9/16	22 9/16	22 9/16	...
2	AFin Ent	41	41	41	...
2	AncorCm	9 7/16	9 7/16	9 7/16	– 13/16
45	CanSoPt g	9 3/4	9 9/16	9 3/4	...
5	ChiefCM	5 5/8	5 5/8	5 5/8	– 1/8
12	GeoTek	4 3/8	4 1/4	4 3/8	...
76	GoldCyc	7 3/4	7 3/4	7 3/4	– 1/8

Sales	Stock	High	Low	Close	Chg
100	GrNthGs	1 5/8	1 5/8	1 5/8	...
25	MagelPt	3 9/16	3 7/16	3 9/16	+ 1/16
5	MendoBr	4	3 3/4	4	+ 1/2
53	MesaOffsh	1/4	7/32	1/4	+ 1/32
8	OrigSix	3	3	3	...
24	SCGs pfC	25 1/8	25 1/8	25 1/8	– 1/8
5	Z Sevn s	19 1/2	19 1/2	19 1/2	...

PHILADELPHIA

Sales	Stock	High	Low	Close	Chg
1	BltGE pfI	101	101	101	...
258	IRT Inds	2	1 7/8	1 7/8	...

BOSTON

Sales	Stock	High	Low	Close	Chg
50	All Comm	3 7/16	3 7/16	3 7/16	...
380	CstlCarib	2 5/16	2 1/16	2 1/8	+ 1/8

Sales	Stock	High	Low	Close	Chg
5	Exolon	33	33	33	+ 1/2
3	VSI Ent	2 7/16	2 7/16	2 7/16	+ 9/32

CBOE

Sales	Stock	High	Low	Close	Chg
30	SmBarSP02 n	17 5/16	17 3/16	17 5/16	+ 1/16
167	SB S&P03	15 1/16	15	15	– 1/16

TOTAL SALES

BOSTON	7,235,000
CBOE	19,700
CHICAGO	26,544,000
PHILADELPHIA	5,762,000
PACIFIC	11,150,000

Figure 16.4
Summary of Activities in Stocks Traded on U.S. Exchanges (Excerpts)

Source: Reprinted by permission of *The Wall Street Journal*, Dow Jones & Company, October 10, 1997, pp. C5, C13, C20. All rights reserved worldwide.

the daily sales volume and the high, low, and closing prices, along with the change in the close from the previous day.

16.5.3 Foreign Stock Exchanges

Figure 16.5 displays the trading activities in various foreign stock markets. The figure shows the trading activities in the two major Canadian markets (Toronto and Montreal) and the major Mexican market (Mexico City) and then proceeds to cover the trading activities in several other foreign markets based on the area of the world in which they are located. In the figure, the prices given are stated in the local currency of the country in which the exchange is located.

16.6   EX ANTE AND EX POST VALUES

Equilibrium theories such as the capital asset pricing model and arbitrage pricing theory imply that, in the opinion of well-informed investors, securities with different attributes will have different expected returns. Thus the focus of these theories is on future, or *ex ante* (Latin for "before the fact"), expected returns. However, only historical, or *ex post* (Latin for "after the fact"), actual returns are subsequently observed. Because these historical returns are undoubtedly different from the expected returns, it is extremely difficult to tell whether security attributes and expected returns do in fact go together in the manner implied by either the CAPM or APT. Moreover, such theories are relatively silent concerning simple ways in which a security's future expected return and attributes might be estimated by examining historical returns.

To bridge this gap, investigators have used the average historical return of a security as an estimate of its expected return. This approach requires an assumption that the expected return did not change over some arbitrary time period and that this time period contains a sufficient number of historical returns to make a reasonably accurate estimate of the expected return. However, an objection may be made in that expectations almost certainly would have changed over the time period needed to obtain a useful estimate of the expected return for any given security.[22] Despite this objection, it is worthwhile to examine historical returns to see how they might be used to come up with meaningful predictions about the future.[23] The next section explores the prediction of a firm's beta. It begins by discussing the estimation of the firm's historical beta by use of the market model.

16.7   COMMON STOCK BETAS

For purposes of portfolio management, the relevant risk of a security concerns its impact on the risk of a well-diversified portfolio. In the world of the CAPM, such portfolios would be subject primarily to market risk. This fact suggests the importance of a security's beta, which measures its sensitivity to future market movements. In principle the possible sources of such movements should be considered to estimate beta. Then the reaction of the security's price to each of these sources should be estimated, along with the probability of each reaction. In the process, the economics of the relevant industry and firm, the impact of both operating and financial leverage on the firm, and other fundamental factors should be taken into account.

Americas

MONTREAL in Canadian dollars

	CLOSE	NET CHG.
Bio Pha	42.25	- 0.65
BombrdrB	27.05	- 0.60
Cambior	14.60	- 0.30
Cascades	10.65	+ 0.15
DomTxtA	12.50	+ 0.20
Donohue A	31.00	+ 0.05
NatBk Cda	20.30	+ 0.80
Power Corp	44.90	+ 1.40
Provigo	7.65	- 0.20
Quebecr B	27.00	+ 0.80
Quebecr P	24.80	+ 0.15
SNC-Lavalin	14.95	+ 0.10
Teleglobe	52.00	+ 1.50
Videotron	10.40	- 0.50

TORONTO in Canadian dollars

	CLOSE	NET CHG.
Abitibi C	22.75	- .45
AirCanada	13.25	- .25
Alcan	45.80	- .55
AltEnergy	33.45	+ .20
Anderson	17.10	- .15
Atco I f	31.50	...
Aur Res	5.40	+ .10
Avenor	24.80	- .30
BC Gas	25.40	- .10
BCE Inc	44.35	+ 1.30
BCE Mobl	46.30	- .40
BCTelcom	35.75	+ .45
BGR A	14.25	- .30
Bank Mtl	60.65	- .50
Bank N S	66.85	- .35
Barick gld	32.80	- .30
Baton	17.25	...
C Util B	39.40	+ .30
CAE	12.60	+ .05
CCL B f	16.60	- .10
CIBkCom	41.25	- .05
CP Ltd	41.60	+ .60
CTire A f	29.40	- .40
Cambior	14.55	- .30
Cambridg	16.20	+ .70
Cameco	54.85	- .35
Canfor	13.25	- .25
Cdn Airlne	3.95	- .18
Cdn Tire	31.00	...
CdnNatRes	43.00	...
Cfracmstr	24.60	+ 1.25
Chauvco	31.60	+ .10
Co Steel	21.85	- .15
Cominco L	33.00	- .25
Crestar	27.00	...
Dia a o f	27.50	+ .25
Dofasco	25.65	- .55
Domtar	11.80	- .15
DundeeAf	40.45	- .25
Dupont A	34.50	...
Dylex Ltd	9.00	...
ELANEng	10.25	- .30
Euro Nev	24.70	+ .65
FSesnHlf	53.50	- 1.25
Fairfax f	379.00	+ 2.00
Falcnbrg	24.70	- .60
Finning	20.15	+ .05
FletCCanA	23.05	- .15
Franco	33.00	+ 1.00
GeacComp	85.00	- 2.00
Gendis A	22.75	- .25
GoldcorpAf	8.80	- .20
Gulf Can	12.90	+ .15
H Bay Co	37.25	+ .50
I Comfort	11.45	+ .35
IForestAf	8.80	- .20
IPL eng	54.75	+ .65
Imasco L	45.10	+ .85
ImperialOil	89.50	+ 5.30
Inco	32.85	- .95
Ipsco	66.25	+ 1.25
Ivaco A f	5.25	- .15
Jannock	19.35	+ .05
Loblaw Co	21.20	- .65
MDS B	34.75	+ .25
Mackenzie	41.00	+ 1.65
Macmilan	19.75	+ .05
Maritime f	30.75	+ .50
Mind Wlyn	23.00	- .15
MolsonAf	25.50	+ .25
Moore	24.90	- .65
NS Power	15.20	+ .05
NatBkCan	20.35	+ .85
Noma A f	5.40	+ .10
Noranda F	9.30	+ .05
Noranda I	26.50	- .40
Norcen	34.65	+ .65
Nova Corp	11.40	- .05
Onex C f	36.55	- .20
OshawaAf	23.90	- .35
PanCan P	24.65	- .10
PetroCCV	27.65	+ .95
PlacerDm	25.35	- .25
Poco Pete	13.90	+ .10
Ptash Cor	112.50	+ .65
Ranger	13.25	- .30
Renisanc	35.40	- .15
RogersBf	8.50	...
Royal Bnk	70.90	+ .05
Russel A	5.50	+ .10
Sears Can	25.65	+ .90
ShawC B f	12.40	- .20
Shell Can	26.25	+ .55
Southam	27.70	+ .45
Spar Aero	11.75	...
Stelco A	11.00	- .35
TIPS	37.45	+ .15
Talisman	52.15	- 1.10
Teck B f	26.00	- .50
Telus Corp	28.40	- .30
ThomCor	34.90	+ .65
TorDmBk	51.60	+ .35
TorstarBf	49.00	+ .35
TrAlt corp	19.35	+ .10
TrCan PL	27.30	+ .10
Trilon A	10.85	- .15
Trimac	12.00	+ .25
TrizecHaf	37.45	- .25
Wcoast E	29.35	+ .05
Westmin	5.85	- .25
Weston	107.50	+ 1.00

MEXICO CITY in pesos

	CLOSE	NET CHG.
Alfa A	73.30	+ 0.70
Apasco A	57.90	+ 1.10
Banacci B	23.55	+ 0.70
Bimbo A	73.00	+ 0.10
Cemex B	44.70	+ 0.30
Cifra B	18.00	- 0.16
Cifra C	16.64	- 0.04
Femsa B	68.50	+ 1.40
Gcarso A1	62.10	- 0.40
Kimber A	40.30	- 0.50
Tamsa	221.00	+ 8.00
Telecom A1	32.40	- 0.35
Televisa	153.80	+ 0.80
Tolmex B2	50.00	....
Vitro	40.60	+ 1.45

Europe

AMSTERDAM in guilders

	CLOSE	NET CHG.
ABN Amro	43.50	- 0.70
Aegon	171.20	- 0.70
Ahold	55.40	- 1.60
Akzo Nobel	370.20	+ 5.20
AMEV	90.50	+ 1.70
Bols Wessanen	37.00	+ 0.20
DSM	196.50	- 3.50
Elsevier	28.30	- 0.10
Fokker	0.52	+ 0.01
Gist-Brocades	55.70	- 1.10
Hagemeyer	102.40	- 1.10
Heineken	347.10	- 9.30
Hoogovens	127.80	- 2.60
Hunter Douglas	89.20	+ 3.20
ING Groep N.V.	97.30	- 0.30
KLM	74.80	- 0.60
KNP BT	53.40	....
Nedlloyd	69.90	- 1.00
Oce-van Grntn	255.00	- 4.90
Pakhoed Hldg	71.00	+ 0.30
Philips	166.90	- 4.90
RandStad	82.50	- 0.50
Robeco	194.70	- 3.00
Rodamco	61.40	....
Rolinco	196.60	- 0.40
Rorento	118.70	+ 0.10
Royal Dutch	115.50	+ 0.20
Royal PTT	76.10	- 3.20
Unilever	441.00	- 1.20
Van Ommeren	86.20	- 0.20
VNU	46.40	- 1.70
Wolters Kluwer	264.00	- 5.70

BRUSSELS in Belgian francs

	CLOSE	NET CHG.
Arbed	5360	+ 10
BarcoNV	7700	+ 20
BBL	9410	- 40
Bekaert	25325	- 675
CBR	3240	- 25
Delhaize	1835	- 5
Electrabel	7660	- 30
Fortis	7780	+ 40
Gen de Bnque	15025	+ 25
Gevaert	1650	- 20
GIB	1865	+ 35
Kredietbank	15850	+ 50
Petrofina	14800	- 250
Royale Belge	10425	- 100
Soc Gen Belg	3520	- 20
Solvay	2230	- 20
Tractebel	15075	+ 100

FRANKFURT in marks

	CLOSE	NET CHG.
Adidas	240.00	+ 2.50
Allianz	452.00	- 1.50
BASF	65.40	- 0.20
Bayer	73.60	+ 1.20
Beiersdorf	84.00	- 1.00
BMW	1462.00	- 8.00
Byr Vereinsbk	109.50	- 2.30
Commerzbank	67.00	- 0.10
Continental	47.80	- 0.50
Daimler Benz	142.55	- 2.45
Degussa	97.00	....
Deutsche Bank	128.75	+ 1.60
Deutsche Tel	34.90	- 0.05
Dresdner Bank	82.30	- 0.90
Gehe	95.30	- 1.50
Heidlbg Zemnt	157.50	- 4.00
Henkel	106.00	+ 2.50
Hochtief	79.70	- 2.50
Hoechst	79.60	+ 0.90
Hypo Bank	85.00	- 0.30
Karstadt	630.00	....
Linde	1281.00	+ 16.00
Lufthansa	35.75	- 0.65
MAN	575.00	....
Mannesmnn	849.50	+ 1.50
Metallges	40.00	+ 1.60
Metro AG	87.40	+ 0.50
Munchen Rk	634.00	- 1.00
Porsche	3225.00	+ 76.00
Preussag	515.50	+ 9.50
RWE	88.20	+ 1.10
SAP	485.50	+ 5.50
SAP Pfd	503.70	+ 5.70
Schering	187.80	- 3.20
SchwarzPhar	127.50	....
Siemens	120.00	....
Thyssen	417.80	- 3.70
Veba	107.10	- 0.80
VEW	580.00	- 5.00
Viag	824.00	- 6.00
Volkswagen	1285.00	+ 37.50

LONDON in pound/pence

	CLOSE	NET CHG.
3-I Group Plc	5.195	+ 0.030
Abbey National	9.470	+ 0.075
Allied-Domecq	4.930	+ 0.085
Arjo Wiggins	1.995	- 0.010
Assoc Brit Fds	5.450	+ 0.035
BAA Plc	5.830	+ 0.110
Barclays	16.925	+ 0.125
Bass	8.390	+ 0.030
BAT Indus	5.540	....
BG	2.675	....
Blue Circle	3.760	+ 0.060
BOC Group	11.075	- 0.075
Body Shop	1.800	....
Boots	9.035	+ 0.010
BPB Indus	3.635	+ 0.020
Brit Sky Brd	4.645	- 0.010
British Aero	17.920	+ 0.405
British Airwys	6.605	+ 0.060
British Land	7.035	+ 0.145
British Pete	9.390	....
British Steel	1.793	+ 0.005
British Telcom	4.515	- 0.070
BTR	2.435	+ 0.035
Burmah Castrol	11.065	- 0.085
Cable&Wireless	5.745	+ 0.105
Cadbury Schwp	6.100	+ 0.100
Caradon	1.995	- 0.005
Charter Plc	8.425	+ 0.135
Christielnt	2.715	+ 0.065
Coats Viyella	1.190	+ 0.005
Commercial Un	7.965	- 0.035
Cookson Group	2.515	....
Courtaulds	3.350	- 0.025
EMI	5.995	- 0.010
Eng Ch Clay	2.715	- 0.040
Enterprise Oil	6.885	- 0.030
Euro Tunnel	0.670	- 0.005
Gen Accident	11.240	+ 0.170
Gen Electric	4.030	....
GKN	14.195	+ 0.105
Glaxo Wellcome	13.995	- 0.065
Granada	8.795	+ 0.130
Grand Metrop	5.895	+ 0.015
Great Universl	7.185	+ 0.140
Guardian Royal	3.275	+ 0.085
Guinness	5.855	+ 0.035
Hanson Plc	2.980	- 0.040
Hillsdown	1.755	+ 0.060
Imp Chem Ind	10.060	- 0.005
Imperl Tobac	3.725	+ 0.060
Inchcape Plc	2.865	- 0.025
Jefferson Smurf	2.145	....
Johnson Mathy	6.845	- 0.050
Kingfisher	8.470	+ 0.020
Ladbroke Grp	2.915	+ 0.080
Land Securs	10.550	+ 0.205
LASMO	2.820	- 0.015
Legal & Genl	4.925	+ 0.010
Lloyds TSB Grp	8.070	- 0.095
Lonrho	1.150	- 0.010
Lucas Varity	2.340	- 0.050
Marks & Spencr	6.475	- 0.165
MEPC	5.450	+ 0.025
Nat Power Plc	5.585	....
Nat Wstmn Bk	9.855	+ 0.005
Next Plc	7.395	+ 0.115
NFC	1.480	- 0.005
P & O	6.975	+ 0.175
Pearson	8.240	+ 0.255
Pilkgtn Bros	1.580	+ 0.010
PowerGen Plc	7.635	+ 0.050
Prudential	6.880	+ 0.075
Rank Org	3.545	- 0.040
Reckit&Colman	10.100	+ 0.120
Redland	2.480	+ 0.015
Reed Intl	5.210	- 0.075
Rentokil	2.580	- 0.010
Reuters	7.640	+ 0.020
Rexam Plc	3.230	- 0.095
Rio Tinto	9.850	- 0.025
RMC	10.110	+ 0.185
Rolls Royce	2.380	- 0.045
Royal and Sun	6.110	+ 0.040
Royl Bk Scot	6.800	- 0.125
Safeway	3.775	+ 0.045
Sainsbury J	4.605	+ 0.045
Scottish Pwr	4.835	+ 0.005
Sears	0.600	+ 0.010
Sedgwick Grp	1.240	- 0.020
Severn Trent	9.275	+ 0.010
Shell	4.830	+ 0.030
Siebe Plc	12.985	+ 0.085
Smith & Nephew	1.880	- 0.018
SmithKline B	6.070	- 0.095
Smiths Ind	9.375	- 0.010
Std Chartrd	8.195	- 0.145
SunLife & Prov	4.185	+ 0.050
Tarmac	1.305	- 0.010
Tate & Lyle	4.510	+ 0.025
Tesco	4.610	+ 0.040
Thames Wtr	8.815	+ 0.035
TI Group	6.720	+ 0.015
Tomkins	3.370	- 0.040
Unilever	18.925	+ 0.195
United Util	7.535	- 0.075
Utd Biscuits	2.090	- 0.010
Utd Newsprs	7.940	+ 0.065
Vodafone	3.440	- 0.005
Williams	3.670	- 0.010
WPP Group	2.870	- 0.025
Zeneca Grp	21.190	+ 0.365

MADRID in pesetas

	CLOSE	NET CHG.
ACESA	1955	- 20
Argentaria	8760	+ 60
BANESTO	1475	+ 20
Bco Bil Viz	4630	+ 40
Bco Cntrl Hisp	6160	+ 10
Bco de Sntdr	4745	- 25
Bco Inter Esp	8590	- 30
Bco Populr Esp	9460	+ 40
Centr Com Pry	2720	+ 15
Crp Mapfre	8140	+ 40
ENDESA	3085	+ 20
Fomnto Constr	23410	+ 160
Gas Natrl SDG	7450	- 150
Iberdrola I	1795	+ 15
Petroleos	4590	- 50
Repsol	6560	+ 50
Sevillana Elec	1395	+ 10
Tabacalera A	9900	- 90
Telefonica Esp	4495	+ 45
Valen Cem Port	2990	+ 10

MILAN in lire

	CLOSE	NET CHG.
Alleanza	16010	....
Banca Com	4780	+ 60
Benetton	27550	- 300
CIGA	1031	- 12
CIR	1318	- 12
Cred Ital Ord	4340	- 35
ENI	10475	- 75
FIAT Com	6010	+ 10
FIAT Pref	3010	+ 10
Generali	38300	+ 500
IMI	17200	+ 10
Instituto Naz	2640	- 5
Mediobanca	12800	- 100
Montedison	1315	- 12
Olivetti Com	946	- 8
Olivetti NC	995	- 12
Pirelli Co	2760	+ 80
Pirelli SpA	4935	- 25
RAS	15070	+ 100
Rinascente	13550	+ 360
Rolo Banca	24900	+ 400
Saipem	10210	+ 80
Snia	1788	- 32
Telecm Ital	6780	- 40
Telecm Itl Ord	11030	+ 20

PARIS in French francs

	CLOSE	NET CHG.
Accor	1111.00	+ 7.00
Air Liquide	1006.00	- 10.00
Alcatel Alstm	804.00	- 10.00
AXA Group	406.60	+ 2.00
Bic	454.00	+ 3.00
BNP	311.50	+ 1.20
Carrefour	3660.00	- 70.00
Club Med	476.80	- 2.20
Danone	969.00	- 4.00
Dassault Avitn	1330.00	+ 32.00
Elf Aquitaine	790.00	- 10.00
Euro Disneyld	8.05	....
Generale Eaux	734.00	+ 3.00
Havas	411.20	- 2.80
Imetal	760.00	+ 1.00
L'Oreal	2427.00	- 30.00
Lafarge	441.40	- 3.10
Lagardere Grp	189.40	- 4.60

Figure 16.5 Summary of Trading Activities on Selected Foreign Exchanges (Excerpts)

Source: Reprinted by permission of *The Wall Street Journal*, Dow Jones & Company Inc., October 8, 1997, p. C14. All rights reserved worldwide.

But what about investigating the extent to which the security's price moved with the market in the past? Such an approach ignores myriad possible differences between the past and the future. However, it is easily done and provides a useful starting point.

As shown in Chapter 7, a security's beta can be regarded as the slope of the market model. If this line were constant over time, meaning that it was not changing from period to period, then the **historical beta** for a security could be estimated by examining the historical relationship between the returns on the security and on a market index. The statistical procedure used for making such estimates of *ex post* betas is **simple linear regression,** also known as ordinary least squares (OLS).[24]

As an example, consider estimating the *ex post* beta for Widget Manufacturing (WM) using a hypothetical market index. Table 16.1 presents the most recent 16 quarterly returns on both WM and the index and the calculations necessary to determine WM's *ex post* beta and alpha, as well as certain other statistical parameters. As can be seen, WM's beta and alpha were equal to .63 and .79%, respectively, over this period.[25]

Given these values for alpha and beta, the market model for WM is:

$$r_{WM} = .79\% + .63r_I + \varepsilon_{WM} \tag{16.6}$$

Figure 16.6 presents a scatter diagram of the returns on WM (r_{WM}) and the index r_I. Also shown in the figure is a graph of the market model except that the random error term is deleted; that is, the figure has a graph of the following line:

$$r_{WM} = .79\% + .63r_I \tag{16.7}$$

The vertical distance of each point in the scatter diagram from this line represents an estimate of the size of the random error term for the corresponding quarter. The exact distance can be found by rewriting Equation (16.6) as:

$$r_{WM} - (.79\% + .63r_I) = \varepsilon_{WM} \tag{16.8}$$

For example, look at Table 16.1(a). In quarter 14 the returns on WM and the index were 7.55% and 2.66%, respectively. The value of ε_{WM} for that quarter can be calculated by using Equation (16.8) as follows:

$$7.55\% - [.79\% + (.63 \times 2.66\%)] = 5.08\%$$

The values of ε_{WM} can be similarly calculated for the other 15 quarters of the estimation period. The standard deviation of the resulting set of 16 numbers is an estimate of the **standard deviation of the random error term** (or residual standard deviation) and is shown in Table 16.1(b) to be equal to 6.67%. This number can be viewed as an estimate of the historical unique risk of WM.

The market model for WM that is shown in Figure 16.6 corresponds to the regression line for the scatter diagram. Recall that a straight line is defined by its intercept and slope; it can be shown that there are no other values for alpha and beta that will define a straight line that fits the scatter diagram any better than the regression line. This means that there is no line that could be drawn that would result in a smaller standard deviation of the random error term. Thus the regression line is often referred to as the line of "best fit."

Equivalently, the line of best fit is the line that has the smallest sum of squared values of the random error terms. That is, the 16 random error terms associated with the regression line can each be squared and then summed. This sum (the sum of squared errors) is smaller for the line of best fit than is the sum associated with any other line.

For example, if alpha equaled 1.5% and beta equaled .8, then the random error term ε_{WM} could be calculated for each of the 16 quarters by using Equation (16.8).

TABLE 16.1 Market Model for Widget Manufacturing

(a) Data

Year	Quarter	WM Returns = Y (1)	Index Returns = X (2)	Y^2 (3)	X^2 (4)	$Y \times X$ (5)
1	1	−13.38%	2.52%	178.92	6.35	−33.71
	2	16.79	5.45	282.00	29.71	91.54
	3	−1.67	0.76	2.77	0.57	−1.26
	4	−3.46	2.36	11.99	5.58	−8.18
2	5	10.22	8.56	104.53	73.36	87.57
	6	7.13	8.67	50.79	75.19	61.80
	7	6.71	10.80	45.07	116.59	72.49
	8	7.84	3.33	61.47	11.08	26.10
3	9	2.15	−5.07	4.62	25.66	−10.89
	10	7.95	7.10	63.22	50.42	56.46
	11	−8.05	−11.57	64.74	133.87	93.09
	12	7.68	4.65	58.97	21.58	35.67
4	13	4.75	14.59	22.55	212.97	69.29
	14	7.55	2.66	57.03	7.05	20.05
	15	−2.36	3.81	5.58	14.54	−9.01
	16	4.98	7.99	24.78	63.85	39.78
Sum (Σ) =		54.83%	66.61%	1039.03	848.37	590.79
		$= \Sigma Y$	$= \Sigma X$	$= \Sigma Y^2$	$= \Sigma X^2$	$= \Sigma XY$

(b) Calculations

1. Beta:

$$\frac{(T \times \Sigma XY) - (\Sigma Y \times \Sigma X)}{(T \times \Sigma X^2) - (\Sigma X)^2} = \frac{(16 \times 590.79) - (54.83 \times 66.61)}{(16 \times 848.37) - (66.61)^2} = .63$$

2. Alpha:

$$[\Sigma Y/T] - [\text{Beta} \times (\Sigma X/T)] = [54.83/16] - [.63 \times (66.61/16)] = .79\%$$

3. Standard deviation of random error term:

$$\{[\Sigma Y^2 - (\text{Alpha} \times \Sigma Y) - (\text{Beta} \times \Sigma XY)]/[T - 2]\}^{1/2}$$
$$\{[1039.03 - (.79 \times 54.83) - (.63 \times 590.79)]/[16 - 2]\}^{1/2} = 6.67\%$$

4. Standard error of beta:

Standard deviation of random error term$/\{\Sigma X^2 - [(\Sigma X)^2/T]\}^{1/2}$
$$= 6.67/\{848.37 - [(66.61)^2/16]\}^{1/2} = .28$$

5. Standard error of alpha:

Standard deviation of random error term$/\{T - [(\Sigma X)^2/\Sigma X^2]\}^{1/2}$
$$= 6.67/\{16 - [(66.61)^2/848.37]\}^{1/2} = 2.03$$

6. Correlation coefficient:

$$\frac{(T \times \Sigma XY) - (\Sigma Y \times \Sigma X)}{\{[(T \times \Sigma Y^2) - (\Sigma Y)^2] \times [(T \times \Sigma X^2) - (\Sigma X)^2]\}^{1/2}}$$
$$= \frac{(16 \times 590.79) - (54.83 \times 66.61)}{\{[(16 \times 1039.03) - (54.83)^2] \times [(16 \times 848.37) - (66.61)^2]\}^{1/2}} = .52$$

7. Coefficient of determination:

$$(\text{Correlation Coefficient})^2 = (.52)^2 = .27$$

8. Coefficient of nondetermination:

$$1 - \text{coefficient of determination} = 1 - .27 = .73$$

Note: All summations are to be carried out over t, where t goes from 1 to T (in this example, $t = 1, 2, \ldots, 16$).

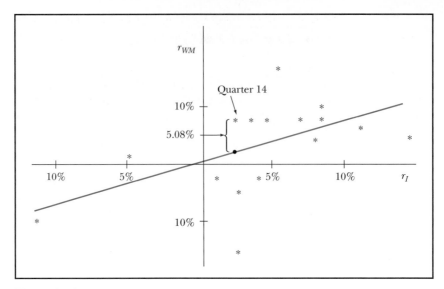

Figure 16.6
Market Model for WM

With these 16 values, the standard deviation of the random error term could be calculated by squaring each value, summing up the squared values, and dividing the sum by $14 \left[= (16 - 2) \right]$. The standard deviation of the random error term would then be the square root of this number. However, it would be larger than 6.67%, which is the standard deviation of the random error term associated with the line of best fit—that is, the line with an alpha of .79% and a beta of .63.

It should be remembered that a security's "true" historical beta cannot be observed. All that can be done is to estimate its value. Thus even if a security's "true" beta remained the same forever, its estimated value, obtained in the manner shown in Table 16.1, would still change from time to time because of mistakes (known as sampling errors) in estimating it. For example, if a different set of 16 quarters were examined, the resulting estimated beta for WM would almost certainly be different from .63, the estimated value for the set of 16 quarters given in Table 16.1. The **standard error of beta** shown in Table 16.1 attempts to indicate the extent of such estimation errors. Given a number of necessary assumptions (for example, the true beta did not change during the 16-quarter estimation period), the chances are roughly two out of three that the "true" beta is within a standard error, plus or minus, of the estimated beta. Thus WM's true beta is likely to be larger than .35 (=.63 − .28) and smaller than .91 (=.63 + .28). Similarly, the **standard error of alpha** provides an indication of the magnitude of the possible sampling error that has been made in estimating alpha.

The *correlation coefficient* that is shown in Table 16.1 provides an indication of how closely the returns on WM were associated with the returns on the index. Because its range is between −1 and +1, the value for WM of .52 indicates a mildly strong positive relationship between WM and the index. This means that larger returns for WM seem to be associated with larger returns on the index.

The **coefficient of determination**, which equals the square of the correlation coefficient, represents the proportion of variation in the return on WM that is related to the variation in the return on the index. That is, it shows how much of the movements in WM's returns can be explained by movements in the returns on the index.

With a value of .27 it can be seen that 27% of the movements in the return on WM during the 16-quarter estimation period can be attributed to movements in the return on the index.

Because the **coefficient of nondetermination** is 1 minus the coefficient of determination, it represents the proportion of movements in the return on WM that is not due to movements in the return on the index. Thus 73% of the movements in WM cannot be attributed to movements in the index.

Figure 16.7 shows a page from the Security Risk Evaluation report prepared by Merrill Lynch, Pierce, Fenner & Smith Inc. Percentage price changes for many stocks, calculated for each of 60 months (when available), were compared by means of the corresponding percentage changes in the Standard & Poor's 500 using the market model in Table 16.1. Seven of the resulting values from this analysis are of interest for each stock. The values shown under "Beta" and "Alpha" indicate the slope and intercept, respectively, of the straight line that is the best fit for the scatter diagram of the percentage price changes for the stock and index.

The value of "R-Sqr," short for **R-squared**, is equivalent to the coefficient of determination shown in Table 16.1.[26]

The value for "Resid Std Dev-n" (**residual standard deviation**) corresponds to the standard deviation of the random error term in Table 16.1.

Ticker Symbol	Security Name	92/04 Close Price	Beta	Alpha	R-Sqr	Resid Std Dev-n	---Std. Err.--- of Beta	of Alpha	Adjusted Beta	Number of Observ
AOI	AOI COAL CO	0.500	1.11	−1.79	0.07	19.23	0.49	2.51	1.07	60
APAT	APA OPTICS INC	4.875	0.60	0.80	0.08	9.66	0.25	1.26	0.73	60
APIE	API ENTERPRISES INC	0.688	1.00	2.51	0.02	26.90	0.69	3.51	1.00	60
ASKI	ASK COMPUTER SYS INC	14.875	1.65	−0.06	0.37	10.82	0.28	1.41	1.43	60
ATV	ARC INTL CORP	0.813	1.22	−1.38	0.07	20.71	0.53	2.70	1.15	60
ASTA	AST RESEARCH INC	16.750	1.47	1.66	0.16	16.75	0.43	2.19	1.31	60
ARX	ARX INC	1.875	1.02	−1.90	0.07	17.02	0.43	2.22	1.01	60
ASAA	ASA INTL LTD	1.875	0.79	−1.03	0.01	23.55	0.60	3.07	0.86	60
RCH	ARCO CHEM CO	45.375	1.33	0.03	0.47	7.35	0.19	1.00	1.22	55
ANBC	ANB CORP	36.375	−0.02	1.80	0.10	1.90	0.13	0.56	0.32	12
ATCE	ATC ENVIRONMENTAL INC	2.813	−0.02	0.68	0.02	21.22	0.75	3.22	0.32	46
ATI	ATI MED INC	3.750	0.26	0.07	0.01	19.11	0.49	2.49	0.51	60
ATCIC	ATC INC	1.750	0.61	0.38	0.00	26.63	0.68	3.47	0.74	60
ATNN	ATNN INC	0.219	1.38	1.51	0.00	50.89	1.30	6.64	1.25	60
ATTNF	ATTN AVECA ENTERTAIN-MENT COR	1.750	2.81	0.39	0.05	42.49	1.59	6.97	2.20	39
AVSY	AVTR SYS INC	0.203	−0.54	6.23	0.06	55.49	3.33	14.41	−0.02	18
AWCSA	AW COMPUTER SYS INC CLASS A	5.875	1.23	7.08	0.01	71.41	1.85	9.29	1.15	60
ARON	AARON RENTS INC	13.125	0.92	−0.23	0.16	10.30	0.26	1.34	0.95	60
ABIX	ABATIX ENVIRONMENTAL CORP	1.750	0.00	0.36	0.03	17.54	0.67	2.96	0.34	37
ABT	ABBOTT LABS	66.000	0.87	0.87	0.51	4.31	0.11	0.56	0.92	60
ABERF	ABER RES LTD	0.969	1.53	3.52	0.02	29.18	1.11	4.93	1.35	37
AANB	ABIGAIL ADAMS NATL BANCORP I	11.000	−1.50	1.81	0.14	12.61	0.70	2.80	−0.66	24
ABBK	ABINGTON BANCORP INC	5.875	1.37	−0.15	0.09	20.09	0.51	2.62	1.24	60
ABD	ABIOMED INC	13.000	1.08	1.04	0.07	18.21	0.47	2.43	1.05	57
ABY	ABITIBI PRICE INC	12.625	0.65	−1.42	0.23	6.00	0.15	0.80	0.77	57
ABRI	ABRAMS INDS INC	4.313	1.28	1.90	0.07	20.91	0.53	2.73	1.18	60
ACAP	ACAP CORP	0.500	0.05	0.88	0.02	13.80	0.35	1.80	0.37	60
ACLE	ACCEL INTL CORP	6.750	1.12	−0.66	0.20	11.10	0.28	1.45	1.08	60
AKLM	ACCLAIM ENTHT INC	6.375	1.29	0.02	0.03	23.62	0.84	3.58	1.19	46
ACCU	ACCUHEALTH INC	5.438	0.53	0.60	0.00	13.47	0.49	2.17	0.69	41
	Based on S&P 500 Index, Using Straight Regression									Page 3

Figure 16.7

Sample Page from Security Risk Evaluation by Merrill Lynch, Pierce, Fenner & Smith Inc.

Source: Reprinted by permission. Copyright © Merrill Lynch, Pierce, Fenner & Smith Incorporated.

"Std. Err. of Beta" (standard error of beta) indicates that there is roughly a two out of three chance that the true beta is within one standard error, plus or minus, of the estimated beta. The term "Std. Err. of Alpha" can be interpreted similarly.

The seventh value in Figure 16.7, which is of particular interest, is the **adjusted beta** value, representing an estimate of the *ex ante* (or future) beta of the firm's stock. Typically, these values are obtained by simply adjusting the estimated *ex post* (or historical) beta by (1) multiplying the *ex post* value by .66 and (2) adding .34 to the product. Thus, a firm with an *ex post* beta of 1.5 would have an adjusted beta of $1.33 \left[= (1.5 \times .66) + .34 \right]$. Appendix B discusses procedures for adjusting *ex post* betas in more detail.

16.8 GROWTH VERSUS VALUE

Common stocks are often divided into two categories—**growth stocks** (sometimes called *glamour stocks*) and **value stocks**. Although there are no hard-and-fast rules on how they are divided and disagreement exists among investment professionals on what category certain stocks belong to, two financial measures are often used to distinguish growth stocks from value stocks. These are the book-value-to-market-value ratio (BV/MV) and the earnings-to-price ratio (E/P).[27]

16.8.1 Book-Value-to-Market-Value Ratio

The book-value-to-market-value ratio is typically calculated as follows. First, the book value of the firm's common stock is determined by using the most recent balance sheet data and calculating the total value of stockholders' equity. Second, the market capitalization of the firm's common stock is determined by taking the most recent market price for the firm's common stock and multiplying it by the number of shares outstanding. Last, the book value of stockholders' equity is divided by the market capitalization to arrive at the BV/MV ratio. Relatively low values of this ratio characterize growth stocks, and relatively high values characterize value stocks.[28]

An interesting question is whether there is a relationship between stock returns and the stocks' BV/MV ratios. Fama and French examined this issue and found that there was such a relationship.[29] Specifically, they found that on average the larger the size of the BV/MV ratio, the larger the rate of return. Table 16.2 presents their findings.

Table 16.2(a) was constructed as follows. First, at the end of June 1963, the book value was determined for each stock on the NYSE, AMEX, and Nasdaq using the annual financial statements that involved the fiscal year ending in 1962. This value was then divided by the market capitalization for each firm; the market capitalization was determined by using the market price for each firm as of the end of December 1962. Second, on the basis of these BV/MV ratios, the firms were ranked from smallest to largest and formed into 12 portfolios. Third, the return on each portfolio was tracked monthly from July 1963 through June 1964. Fourth, the entire process was updated by a year so that returns were calculated from July 1964 to June 1965 on 12 BV/MV-ranked portfolios that were formed on the basis of data as of the end of 1963. The process was repeated until a set of monthly returns was available from July 1963 through December 1990 for each of the 12 portfolios.

Table 16.2(a) shows a clear relationship between average monthly return and the BV/MV ratio; higher values of the ratio are associated with higher average returns. Because growth stocks tend to have low BV/MV ratios and value stocks tend to have

							Portfolio Number[a]					
Portfolio Basis	**1**	**2**	**3**	**4**	**5**	**6**	**7**	**8**	**9**	**10**	**11**	**12**
(a) BV/MV Ratio												
Return	.30	.67	.87	.97	1.04	1.17	1.30	1.44	1.50	1.59	1.92	1.83
BV/MV	.11	.22	.34	.47	.60	.73	.87	1.03	1.23	1.52	1.93	2.77
(b) E/P Ratio[b]												
Return	1.04	.93	.94	1.03	1.18	1.22	1.33	1.42	1.46	1.57	1.74	1.72
E/P	.01	.03	.05	.06	.08	.09	.11	.12	.14	.16	.20	.28
(c) Size												
Return	1.64	1.16	1.29	1.24	1.25	1.29	1.17	1.07	1.10	.95	.88	.90
ln(MV)	1.98	3.18	3.63	4.10	4.50	4.89	5.30	5.73	6.24	6.82	7.39	8.44

TABLE 16.2 Growth Versus Value Stocks

Source: Eugene F. Fama and Kenneth R. French, "The Cross-Section of Expected Stock Returns," *Journal of Finance*, 47, no. 2 (June 1992): table II, table IV.

[a] Portfolios formed on the basis of rankings of indicated financial measure for stocks from smallest (1) to largest (12); return indicates the average monthly return, in percent, from July 1963 through December 1990.

[b] The portfolio of stocks that had negative earnings had an average monthly return of 1.46.

high BV/MV ratios, this results suggests that over the period analyzed, value stocks tended to outperform growth stocks.

16.8.2 Earnings-to-Price Ratio

The earnings-to-price ratio is typically calculated as follows. First, the accounting value of the firm's earnings per share is determined by using the most recent income statement and dividing the firm's earnings after taxes by the number of shares outstanding. Second, the market price of the firm's common stock is determined by taking the most recent price at which the firm's common stock was traded. Last, the earnings per share figure is divided by the market price of the stock to arrive at the E/P ratio. Relatively low values of this ratio characterize growth stocks, and relatively high values characterize value stocks.

An interesting question is whether there is a relationship between stock returns and their E/P ratios. Fama and French also examined this issue and discovered such a relationship.[30] Specifically, they found that on average the larger the size of the E/P ratio, the larger the rate of return. Their results are shown in Table 16.2(b), which was constructed in the same manner as part (a) except that here, at the end of each June, firms were ranked and assigned to portfolios on the basis of their E/P ratios.

Except for portfolio 1, part (b) shows a clear relationship between average monthly return and the E/P ratio; higher values of the ratio are associated with higher average returns. Because growth stocks tend to have low E/P ratios and value stocks tend to have high E/P ratios, these data reinforce the conclusions drawn from the BV/MV data: namely, that value stocks tended to outperform growth stocks over the period analyzed.

There is one other interesting feature of this panel. When Fama and French assigned stocks to portfolios on the basis of their E/P ratios, they assigned those stocks that had negative earnings and hence a negative E/P ratio to a separate portfolio. This portfolio had an average monthly return of 1.46%. Thus if one considers a portfolio with a negative E/P ratio to be the lowest E/P portfolio (and thus a portfolio of growth stocks), then it can be seen from the table that as E/P gets larger, average returns at first decline and then rise. This finding led Fama and French to refer to the relationship between average returns and the E/P ratio as being "U-shaped."

16.8.3 Size

Although firm size is not generally used as a criterion for distinguishing growth from value stocks, it is often used to sort stocks. For example, many investment professionals think of stocks in terms of two dimensions as follows:

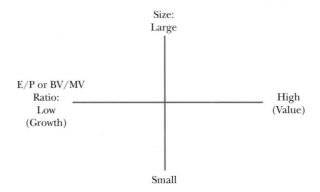

Hence stocks could be classified as growth or value using the BV/MV ratio and as large or small using their size. The result is that each stock could be located in one of the four quadrants of a diagram like the one shown here.

Typically a stock's market capitalization (the number of outstanding common shares times the current market price per share) is used as the measure of its size. Fama and French assigned stocks to one of 12 size portfolios after ranking them at the end of each June on the basis of market capitalization. Proceeding in a manner analogous to that discussed previously, they tracked the monthly returns for these 12 size-based portfolios from July 1963 to December 1990. Table 16.2(c) displays the average returns and sizes of these portfolios.

In contrast to parts (a) and (b), it can be seen that there is a clear inverse relationship between size and average return. That is, stocks of smaller firms tend to have higher returns than stocks of larger firms. Even more notable is the average return for the smallest portfolio (1). This return is significantly higher than for the next smallest portfolio (2) or for any other. Hence when some people refer to a **size effect** in stock returns, they are really referring to a "small firm effect."[31]

16.8.4 Interrelationships

The existence of a relationship between any one of three financial variables (BV/MV ratio, E/P ratio, and firm size) and stock returns suggests that there is at least one missing factor that is needed to explain the differences in returns.[32] Hence it is of interest to examine the interrelationships between the BV/MV ratio, the E/P ratio, firm size, and average returns. The joint effect of E/P ratio and firm size on stock returns is examined next.

E/P, Size, and Average Returns

In order to examine the joint effect of the two financial variables, E/P and, size on stock returns, one study identified at each year-end the break points formed by sorting NYSE and AMEX stocks in quintiles based on just size and then on just the E/P ratio.[33] Then, using both of these sets of break points, the study assigned stocks to one of 25 size-E/P portfolios for the next year. That is, each stock in the smallest size quintile was assigned to one of five E/P portfolios, then each stock in the next-to-smallest size quintile was assigned to one of five E/P portfolios, and so on until there were 25 (=5 sizes × 5 E/P ratios) size-E/P portfolios. The process was repeated year after year until a set of daily returns was available for each one of the 25 portfolios from 1963 through 1977.

Comparison of the average returns for the 25 portfolios showed a clear inverse relationship between size and average returns for any E/P quintile. For example, in the five size-ranked portfolios that were formed from the lowest E/P quintile, the larger the size, the smaller the average return.

However, there was no clear relationship between E/P ratios and average returns for any size quintile. For example, in the case of the five E/P-ranked portfolios that were formed from the smallest size quintile, the largest and third-largest average returns were associated with the lowest and next to lowest E/P portfolios. This result was contrary to previous observations of the relationship between E/P ratios and average returns. As a consequence, it appears that there is a missing factor that is needed to explain differences in stock returns, and that this factor is more closely related to size than to the E/P ratio.[34]

BV/MV, Size, and Average Returns

Fama and French were interested in the joint effect of the BV/MV ratio and firm size on stock returns.[35] Accordingly, they formed 100 portfolios annually based on the rankings of stocks using size and BV/MV ratio. Monthly returns on these portfolios were then recorded for the period from July 1963 through the end of 1990.

Comparison of the average returns for the 100 portfolios showed an inverse relationship between size and average return for almost every BV/MV decile. For example, for the ten size-ranked portfolios that were formed from the largest BV/MV decile, in general, the larger the size, the smaller the average return. The only exception was for the two smallest BV/MV deciles, where in each case there was no apparent relationship between size and return.

Furthermore, there was a clear direct relationship between BV/MV ratios and average returns for any size quintile. For example, in the comparison of the ten BV/MV-ranked portfolios that were formed from the smallest size decile, the larger the BV/MV ratio, the larger the average return. Consequently, Fama and French concluded that there are at least two missing factors that are needed to explain differences in stock returns and that those factors are closely related to size and the BV/MV ratio.

16.9   PRIMARY MARKETS

The discussion in this chapter and Chapter 13 (Fixed-Income Securities) has focused on secondary markets for stocks and bonds, where these securities that were initially issued at some previous point in time are traded. The focus will now shift to the **primary markets** for securities, which is the name given to the markets where the initial issuance itself takes place. Some issuers deal directly with purchasers in this market, but many rely on **investment bankers,** who serve as intermediaries between issuers and the ultimate purchasers of their securities.

16.9.1   Private Placements

Investment banking services are typically performed by brokerage firms and, to a limited extent, by commercial banks. In some instances only a few large institutional investors are solicited, and the entire issue is sold to one or a few of them. Indeed, such **private placements** are often announced only after the fact, via advertisements in the financial press. As long as relatively few potential buyers are contacted, requirements for detailed disclosure, SEC registration, public notice, and so on may be waived, considerably reducing the cost of floating an issue. However, such investments are illiquid because the investor is typically prohibited from selling the security within one year of the purchase date. This restriction has resulted in relatively few equities being sold in this manner. Instead, most private placements involve fixed-income securities that are purchased by investors who are attracted by their coupon payments, not by the prospect of capital gains.

16.9.2 Public Sale

When public sale is contemplated, much more must be done than with private placements. Many firms may serve as intermediaries in the process. One, acting as the "lead" investment banker, will put together a syndicate (or purchase group) and a selling group. The **syndicate** includes firms that purchase the securities from the issuing corporation and are thus said to **underwrite** the offering. The **selling group** includes firms that contact potential buyers and do the actual selling, usually on a commission basis.

The process begins with discussions between the issuing corporation and one or more investment bankers. Some issuers utilize **competitive bidding**, then select the investment banker offering the best overall terms. This procedure is used for many municipal bond issues and is required by law for securities issued by firms in certain regulated industries. However, many corporations maintain a continuing relationship with a single investment banker and negotiate the terms of each new offering with that firm. The investment banker is likely to be heavily involved in the planning of an offering, the terms involved, the amount to be offered, and so on, serving, in effect, as a financial consultant to the corporation.

Once the basic characteristics of an offering have been established, a **registration statement** is filed with the Securities and Exchange Commission, and a preliminary **prospectus** disclosing material relevant to the prospective buyer is issued. (This prospectus is often referred to as a **red herring,** because it has a disclaimer printed in red ink across the first page, which informs the reader that it is not an offer to sell.) The actual price of the security is not included in the preliminary prospectus, and no final sales may be made until the registration becomes effective and a final prospectus is issued, indicating the "offer" price at which the stock will be sold. The final prospectus may be issued as soon as, in the opinion of the Securities and Exchange Commission, there has been adequate disclosure and a reasonable waiting period has passed (usually 20 days). The commission, however, does not take a position regarding the investment merits of an offering or the reasonableness of the price.

A security issue may be completely underwritten by an investment banker and the other members of the syndicate. If it is, the issuing corporation receives the public offering price less a stated percentage spread [although underwriters will occasionally be compensated with some combination of shares and options to buy shares, known as warrants (see Chapter 19), perhaps in addition to a smaller spread]. The underwriters, in turn, sell the securities at the public offering price (or less) and may buy some of the securities themselves. Underwriters who provide this sort of **firm commitment** bear all the risk, because the public may not be willing to buy the entire issue.

Not all agreements are of this type. In the case of a rights offering (in which the current stockholders are given the opportunity to buy the new shares first, as mentioned earlier), an underwriter may agree to purchase at a fixed price all securities not taken by current stockholders. This arrangement is termed a **standby agreement**.

In the case of a nonrights offering (in which the shares are offered to the general public first), members of an investment banking group may serve as agents instead of dealers, agreeing to handle an offering only on a **best-efforts basis**.

During the period when new securities remain unsold, the investment banker is allowed to attempt to "stabilize" the price of the security in the secondary market by standing ready to make purchases at a particular price. There is a limit to the amount that can be purchased when engaged in such **pegging**, usually stated in the agreement under which the underwriting syndicate is formed, because the members typically share the cost of such transactions. If there is to be any pegging, a statement to that effect must be included in the prospectus.

In any security transaction there may be explicit and implicit costs. In a primary distribution, the explicit cost is the underwriting spread, and the implicit cost is any difference between the public offering price and the price that might have been obtained otherwise. The spread provides the investment banking syndicate with compensation for selling the issue and bearing the risk that the issue may not be completely sold to the public, thereby leaving it with ownership of the unsold shares. The lower the public offering price, the smaller the risk that the issue will not be sold quickly at that price. If an issue is substantially underpriced, the syndicate can be assured that the securities will sell rapidly, requiring little or no support in the secondary market. Because many corporations deal with only one investment banking firm and because the larger investment banking firms rely on one another for inclusion in syndicates, it has been alleged that issuers pay too much in spreads, given the prices at which their securities are offered. In other words, the returns to underwriting are alleged to be overly large relative to the risks involved owing to ignorance on the part of issuers or the existence of an informal cartel among investment banking firms.

16.9.3 Underpricing of Ipo's

Whether or not returns to underwriting are overly large, a number of **initial public offerings** (ipo's) do appear to have been underpriced. An ipo is a company's first offerings of shares to the public and is sometimes referred to as an **unseasoned offering.** The abnormal rates of return for a sample of ipo's are shown in Figure 16.8. Each one of the first 60 months after the initial offering is shown on the horizontal axis, and the corresponding average abnormal return (meaning the average return over and above that of stocks of equal risk) is shown on the vertical axis. The leftmost point indicates the average abnormal return obtained by an investor who purchased such a stock at its offering price and sold it for the bid price at the end of the month during which it was offered. The average abnormal return was substantial: 11.4%. The remaining points show the average abnormal returns that could have been obtained by an investor who purchased the security in the secondary market at the beginning of the month after its offering, which is indicated on the horizontal axis, and sold it at the end of that month. Some of these postoffering abnormal returns were positive, but most were negative.

A subsequent study found that the initial abnormal return, measured over the time period beginning with the offering and ending when the first closing price was reported, was 14.1%.[36] Although there is evidence that the average abnormal returns remained positive over the next two months, the average abnormal return over the three-year period after the first close was −37.4%. Three other interesting observations were that:

1. Offerings of smaller firms had lower three-year abnormal returns than those of larger firms.

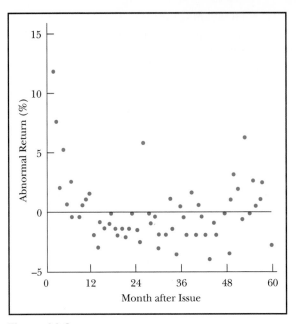

Figure 16.8

Average Abnormal Returns: 112 Common Stock Initial Public Offerings, 1960–1969

Source: Roger G. Ibbotson, "Price Performance of Common Stock New Issues," *Journal of Financial Economics* 2, no. 3 (September 1975): 252.

2. Firms that had the highest positive initial abnormal return had the worst performance over the subsequent three-year period.
3. Younger firms going public had both higher initial abnormal returns and lower subsequent three-year abnormal returns than older firms going public.

It would appear then that offerings of these unseasoned securities are typically underpriced (and then overpriced). Investors able to purchase a cross-section of such shares at their offering prices might thus expect better performance over the first two months than those holding other securities of equal risk. It is not surprising that such offerings are often rationed to "favored" customers by the members of the selling group. It is "not uncommon for underwriters to receive, prior to the effective date, 'public indication of interest' for five times the number of shares available."[37] Unfavored customers are presumably allowed to buy only the new issues that are not substantially underpriced. And, because costs may be incurred in becoming a favored customer, it is not clear that even such an investor obtains abnormally large returns overall.

Whereas the initial return obtained by the purchaser of a new issue may be substantial *on average*, the amount may be very good or very bad in any particular instance, as Figure 16.9 shows. Although the odds may be in the purchaser's favor, a single investment of this type is far from a sure bet.

16.9.4   Seasoned Offerings

Interestingly, the announcement of a seasoned stock offering seems to result in a decline of roughly 2% to 4% in the firm's stock price. This decline could be because managers tend to issue stock when they think it is overpriced in the marketplace. Thus

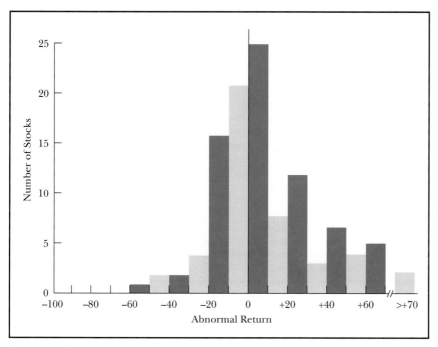

Figure 16.9

Average Abnormal Returns from Offering Date to End Month: 112 Common Stock Initial Public Offerings, 1960–1969

Source: Roger G. Ibbotson, "Price Performance of Common Stock New Issues," *Journal of Financial Economics* 2, no. 3 (September 1975): 248.

the announcement of the offering causes investors to revise downward their assessment of the value of the stock, leading to a price decline.[38] This decline is larger for stocks of industrial firms than for stocks of public utilities, probably because the typical utility issues seasoned offerings far more often than the typical industrial firm.[39]

Figure 16.10 displays the average post-issue abnormal price performance of a sample of seasoned equity offerings.[40] In particular, it shows the average abnormal return over the six-month and one-year periods beginning with the first post-issue price recorded on the exchange on which the security was listed. Also shown are the average abnormal returns for the second, third, fourth, and fifth year after issuance. As the figure shows, for the first six months after a seasoned equity offering, nothing unusual happened to the typical firm's stock price. However, over the first year there was a −6.3% abnormal return, suggesting that the stocks performed poorly during the second six-month period after the offering. The second, third, fourth, and fifth years showed continued poor performance. Overall, the seasoned equity offerings had an abnormal return of roughly −8% per year for the five years after the offering. This trend leaves a puzzle: Why do many firms issue equity when they ultimately provide investors with such low returns over the next five years? Equivalently, why do investors buy such offerings? Indeed, these two questions can be asked not only about seasoned offerings but also about ipo's.

16.9.5 Shelf Registration

A 1982 change in regulations made it possible for large corporations to foster greater competition among underwriters, when the Securities and Exchange Commission allowed firms to register securities in advance of issuance under Rule 415. With such **shelf registration**, securities may be sold up to two years later. With

---

Common Stocks

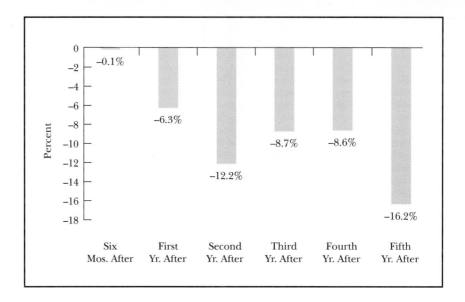

Figure 16.10
Average Abnormal Returns for Seasoned Equity Offerings
Source: Adapted from Tom Loughran and Jay R. Ritter, "The New Issues Puzzle," *Journal of Finance* 50, no. 1 (March 1995): 33.

securities "on the shelf," the corporation can require investment bankers to bid competitively, simply refusing to sell shares if desirable bids are not forthcoming. Thus one purpose of the SEC in allowing shelf registration was to reduce the costs of issuing securities. The evidence seems to suggest that indeed such costs have been reduced.[41]

16.9.6   Rule 144A Securities

Unregistered securities are issued via direct negotiations between issuers and investors. These securities are not registered with the Securities and Exchange Commission, and issuers do not have to satisfy the stringent financial disclosure requirements. Before 1990 all investors had to wait two years (now one year) before being permitted to trade private placements, making such securities highly illiquid.

In 1990 the Securities and Exchange Commission adopted Rule 144A, which permits privately placed securities issued under the provisions of the rule to be traded among large investors (those with assets in excess of $100 million; primarily institutional investors, including mutual funds) at any time after their initial purchase. By relaxing the time restriction for large investors, Rule 144A added liquidity to the private placement market, thereby increasing the attractiveness of these securities.

Historically, the private placement market has consisted predominantly of fixed-income securities. A large volume of high-yielding "junk" bonds have been issued under Rule 144A. In fact, in 1996, for the first time, more high-yield debt was issued under the rule than through the traditional public process. However, Rule 144A also applies to common stocks. Foreign corporations, who in many cases cannot or sometimes choose not to meet the SEC's disclosure rules, have been the primary issuers of common stock under Rule 144A. Whether the new rule will bring about an increase in private equity financing is still unclear.

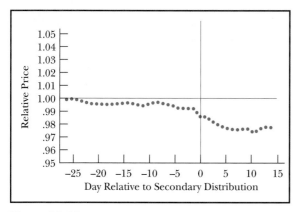

Figure 16.11
Prices for 345 Secondary Distributions, 1961–1965
Source: Myron S. Scholes, "The Market for Securities: Substitution versus Price Pressure and the Effects of Information on the Share Prices." *Journal of Business* 45, no. 2 (April 1972): 193.

16.9.7 Secondary Distributions

As mentioned earlier, an individual or institution wishing to sell a large block of stock can do so through a secondary distribution. An investment banking group buys the stock from the seller and then offers the shares to the public. Typically, the shares are first offered after normal trading hours at the day's closing price. The buyer often pays no commission, and the original seller receives the total proceeds less an underwriting spread.

The Securities and Exchange Commission requires that a secondary distribution be registered, with public announcement and disclosure and a 20-day waiting period, if the original seller has a "control relationship" with the issuer of the securities. Otherwise the distribution may be unregistered.

The impact of the sale of a large block on the market price of the stock provides information on the resiliency of the capital market. Figure 16.11 shows the average prices (adjusted for market changes) for 345 secondary distributions, with the price 25 days before the distribution taken as 1.0. On average, a secondary distribution leads to a 2% to 3% decline in price. Because there is no evidence of a subsequent price rebound, this decline is most likely due to the information contained in the fact that someone has decided to sell. Additional analysis of these results, as shown in Table 16.3, supports the assertion. The size of the decline was related to the identity of the seller, being greater for sellers likely to be information-motivated and smaller for sellers likely to be liquidity-motivated.[42]

TABLE 16.3 Average Price Decline Versus Type of Seller: 345 Secondary Distributions, 1961–1965	
Type of Seller	**Percentage Change in Adjusted Price from Ten Days before the Distribution to Ten Days after the Distribution**
Corporations and officers	2.9%
Investment companies and mutual funds	2.5
Individuals	1.1
Estates	.7
Banks and insurance companies	.3

Source: Myron S. Scholes, "The Market for Securities: Substitution versus Price Pressure and the Effects of Information on Share Prices," *Journal of Business* 45, no. 2 (April 1972): 202.

How Firms in the People's Republic of China Raise Funds

by Ann E. Sherman

Companies in the communist People's Republic of China (PRC) are very different from those of capitalist countries. Most large firms are State Owned Enterprises (SOEs), which traditionally have had to return all reported "profits" to the government each year. On the other hand, any losses could be covered by "loans" from the state-owned banks. The loans did not have to be repaid and were counted as profits by the firm. Accounting methods varied by industry, and the accounting records were prepared by the firm itself, without the help of an independent auditor. Any revenue shortfall for the enterprise would be offset by "loans," so that managers and employees would not lose anything because of low output, and they were not allowed to keep any of the profit from high output.

Reforming SOEs has been a top goal of the Chinese Communist Party since 1976. Many attempts have been made. In the early 1980s, managers were allowed some discretion and were allowed to keep part of any cost savings from greater efficiency. The cost savings could be used, for instance, to pay bonuses or to build better worker housing. In the mid-1980s, there was an attempt to make corporate taxes uniform across firms (at a rate of 55%). However, because managers had so much discretion in preparing accounting statements, they were easily able to avoid any taxable "profits." Beginning in 1987 target profit levels were set for each firm. Managers were allowed to keep any profits above the target. Managers were given much more discretion than before, and they can now do almost anything except fire workers or raise outside funds (except with permission, which has been hard to obtain).

China has chosen to go very slowly in its reforms of SOEs, "groping for stones to cross the river." Although the government has resisted following outside examples, viewing its problems as uniquely Chinese, these problems were easily predictable by anyone with a basic knowledge of managerial incentives. Despite the many reforms, managers of SOEs simply do not have an incentive to make companies profitable and efficient. They typically have no ownership stake, and their pay does not increase as corporate profits increase. One might guess that managing more efficiently would help them to keep their jobs, but in fact the truth is often the opposite. If a company is very profitable, then a Communist Party official may consider it easy to run and put a relative or a crony in charge. The manager of a troubled firm is less likely to lose his job, because it is less likely that someone else will want it.

Changes continue to be made, however. In 1992, the Communist Party adopted the goal of a "socialist market economy," although it insisted that state ownership was still the backbone of the economy and that the market system was a temporary stage in its communist evolution. In 1993, a new business model was established that should allow greater separation of ownership and control. It became possible to privatize some companies, giving the state limited liability (as a shareholder), although the state usually maintains majority control of the shares. In 1997, the move toward freer markets was continued. It was announced that roughly half (in terms of assets) of all state-owned firms would be privatized. By the number of firms, most SOEs should be privatized in the next few years. However, the largest firms will remain untouched, at least for now. The reasons for privatization are to raise funds for new investment and to transform management by using markets both to allocate capital efficiently and to give companies the right incentives.

There are already several ways in which a PRC firm can raise funds. Joint ventures have become common, although they usually involve forming a new corporation. Thus joint ventures allow an SOE to raise funds through a subsidiary to take on a new project, but they are not methods for transforming existing SOEs. Another popular method has been a "back door listing" on the Hong Kong market. PRC firms have bought controlling interests in shell companies already listed on the Stock Exchange of Hong Kong (SEHK). The companies picked are usually small and thinly traded (and thus cheap to purchase). The PRC parent can then issue new shares or debt through the subsidiary in order to raise funds. Funds are transferred through the sale of assets from parent to subsidiary or vice versa.

Back door listings are a relatively painless method of raising capital, because they do not require greater disclosure, reorganization, or the translation of the parent firm's accounting into international or Hong Kong standards. For that reason, however, they also do not improve the efficiency of the corporation, plus they enable firms to transfer assets out of the PRC. Back door listings are known as red chips (a play on the term "blue chips," since the companies are from "red," or communist, China). They typically sell at extremely low price/earnings ratios compared with other companies listed in Hong Kong, because investors are always hoping for future asset injections from the parent company.

Another way in which a PRC company can raise funds is through an A or B share listing on one of the country's two exchanges, in Shanghai or Shenzhen. For a PRC company to be listed on any exchange (local or foreign), it must first become a stock company, which is defined as an enterprise with legal person status that divides its capital into equal shares. Enterprises in areas such as national defense or strategic resources are not allowed to organize as stock companies; enterprises in priority industries such as energy, transportation, and communication can become stock companies only if the state still owns a majority of the shares. Equity in a stock company must be divided into four categories: state shares (purchased with state assets by government departments), legal person shares (held by a PRC "legal person," or corporation), individual shares (purchased by a PRC citizen), and foreign investment shares (purchased by foreigners). The first two categories are known as C shares and usually are not tradable. Shares held by PRC citizens and purchased in Reminbi (the Chinese currency) are called A shares, while shares held by foreign parties and denominated in U.S. dollars are known as B shares.

The fact that each type of share has a separate legal status means that there is a potential for discrimination; state shares may be treated better than individual shares, or A shareholders may be favored over B shareholders. Prices vary widely across the different share types, but it is virtually always true that B shares sell at a substantial discount to A shares. This relation reflects the fact that foreign investors have many choices, whereas PRC citizens have very few investment choices. The stock markets are still small relative to the amount of savings of PRC investors, but the government is trying to speed up listings. As a result of the huge excess demand for investments in the PRC, prices of A shares have been bid well above the prices of B shares in the same firms. With B shares selling at a substantial discount, PRC investors found ways to purchase them, despite the fact that they are not legally allowed to do so. This practice bid the prices up above levels that foreign investors were comfortable with, and now the B share market is primarily dominated by PRC investors. Occasionally, PRC officials threaten to crack down on the holding of B shares by PRC citizens. When the market takes these threats seriously, the prices of B shares fall dramatically, frightening regulators into backing off.

Listing standards for A or B shares on the Shanghai or Shenzhen exchanges are noticeably lower than for reputable foreign exchanges. For instance, B share firms have disclosed financial performance figures to analysts before revealing them to shareholders, failed to comply with disclosure obligations, failed to give adequate notice of shareholders' meetings, and failed to use funds in the manner specified in the prospectus. In direct contradiction to the plans outlined in prospectuses, a large portion of the funds raised so far have been used for property speculation.

A more prestigious funding choice for eligible firms is a foreign listing, for instance an H (Hong Kong) or N (New York) listing. H and N shares are Reminbi-denominated shares that may be purchased and traded in a foreign currency only by non-PRC residents. By June 1996, there were 226 A shares listed on the Shanghai Exchange and 155 A shares listed on the Shenzhen Exchange, in addition to 40 B listings, 50 H listings, and 2 listings of N shares. Firms are also seeking to list on the Singapore, Taiwan, and Vancouver exchanges. However, there are many adjustments for PRC firms wanting to list on an outside exchange. One problem is that many SOEs have several operating units, and it is difficult to decide which should be included in the public company. For instance, PRC firms in the past have been responsible for providing housing, medical care, education, and pensions to workers and their families. Thus they often provide and run hospitals, schools, dormitories, child care centers, and even recreational facilities, which do not generate revenues and are not normally part of, say, a steel-making company. Changing accounting standards is another major adjustment. For example, PRC accounting methods do not recognize "prudence concepts" such as making provisions for bad debt or writing off obsolescent inventory.

Finally, one of the biggest adjustments is in the attitude of managers toward stockholders. It is very difficult to convince PRC managers that they have obligations to shareholders, such as deploying funds in the way that they have promised. Of the first batch of H shares listed in Hong Kong in 1993, the most respected was Tsingtao Brewery. In its prospectus, Tsingtao stated that it would use the proceeds of its offering to build new breweries and to update equipment. When investors read the first annual report, more than a year after the listing, they were shocked to learn that Tsingtao had simply lent out most of the proceeds to other PRC firms. Tsingtao calmly announced that it was planning a rights issue to raise even more funds from stockholders, because it still wanted to expand and update its breweries at some point. From the standpoint of the company managers, they were simply responding to profitable investment opportunities as they arose. The fact that investors wanted to invest in a brewery, rather than a bank, was of no concern to them. Although it was upsetting to investors to learn how their funds had been used, at least holders of H shares were able to find out where their money went. Issuers of A and B shares in the PRC are not required to tell investors how their funds have been used, and most firms choose not to make such disclosures.

1. Common stock represents an ownership position in a corporation. Common stockholders possess a residual claim on the corporation's earnings and assets. Furthermore, their liability for the corporation's obligations is limited.

2. Common stockholders elect the corporation's directors through either a majority or a cumulative voting system.

3. Corporations may at times repurchase some of their outstanding stock either in the open market or through a tender offer. Such actions may involve an attempt to repel a takeover, a signal to shareholders that the stock is undervalued, or a tax-advantageous distribution of cash to shareholders.

4. Stock dividends and splits involve the issuance of additional shares of common stock to current stockholders, proportional to their ownership positions. No change in the total value of the corporation is caused by a stock dividend or split. Such actions may involve either an attempt to move the firm's stock price into a more favorable trading range or to signal favorable information to the firm's shareholders.

5. Preemptive rights give existing stockholders the right of first refusal to purchase new shares. Such shares are purchased in a rights offering.

6. Daily information regarding transactions in publicly traded stocks can be found in business newspapers and the business sections of most local newspapers.

7. A security's *ex post* beta can be estimated using historical return data for the security and a market index and can be adjusted to arrive at an estimate of the security's *ex ante* beta. The beta is the slope of the security's market model, calculated by using simple linear regression.

8. Firms that have either low book-value-to-market-value or low earnings-to-price ratios, or both, are generally referred to as growth stocks, whereas firms that have either high book-value-to-market-value or high earnings-to-price ratios, or both, are generally referred to as value stocks.

9. Firms that have high book-value-to-market-value ratios, high earnings-to-price ratios, or are of smaller firm size historically have had higher stock returns than have firms that have low ratios or are large.

10. When viewed jointly, stock returns and both firm size and the book-value-to-market-value ratio seem to be related.

11. The primary market involves the initial issuance of securities.

12. Although some issuers deal directly with investors, most hire investment bankers to assist them in the sale of securities.

QUESTIONS AND PROBLEMS

1. What is the significant advantage of the corporate form of business organization? Why would you expect that this advantage would be important to the success of a capitalist economy?

2. Fall Creek is conducting the annual election for its five-member board of directors. The firm has 1,500,000 shares of voting common stock outstanding.

   a. Under a majority voting system, how many shares must a stockholder own to ensure being able to elect his or her choices to each of the five director seats?

b. Under a cumulative voting system, how many shares must a stockholder own to ensure being able to elect his or her choices to two of the director seats?

c. Arlie Latham holds 20% of Fall Creek's outstanding stock. How many directors can Arlie elect under a cumulative voting system?

3. The issue of corporate ownership versus control has become quite controversial. Discuss the principal-agent problem as it is related to shareholder-management relations. Specifically, why is there a potential conflict between the two groups? What steps can be taken to mitigate this problem?

4. When a bidder makes a tender offer for a target firm, what types of defenses are often applied to fend off the bidder? Do these defenses generally seem to be in the best interests of the target firm's shareholders? Why?

5. Why might a corporation wish to issue more than one class of common stock?

6. With respect to the payment of corporate dividends, distinguish between declaration date, ex-dividend date, and date of record.

7. Theoretical arguments and empirical research support the case that stock dividends and splits do not enhance shareholder wealth. However, corporations continue to declare stock dividends and splits. Summarize the arguments for and against stock dividends and splits from the perspective of the shareholder.

8. Menomonie Publishing stock currently sells for $40 per share. The company has 1,200,000 shares outstanding. What would be the effect on the number of shares outstanding and on the stock price of the following:

a. 15% stock dividend

b. 4-for-3 stock split

c. Reverse 3-for-1 stock split

9. St. Paul Corporation is planning to raise $35,000,000 through the sale of new common stock under a rights offering. The subscription price is $70 per share. The stock currently sells for $80 per share, rights on. Total outstanding shares equal 10,000,000. Of this amount, Addie Joss owns 100,000 shares.

a. How many shares of stock will each right permit its owner to purchase?

b. What will be the total value of Addie's rights a day before the ex-rights date, assuming that the market price of St. Paul stock remains at $80 per share?

c. After the ex-rights date, if the market value of each St. Paul right equals $.20, what must be the ex-rights market price of St. Paul's stock?

10. Pep Clark owns stock in DeKalb Dairy. DeKalb is planning a rights offering in which seven shares must be owned to buy one additional share at a price of $15. DeKalb stock currently sells for $63 per share rights-on.

a. What is the value of a DeKalb right?

b. At the time of the offering announcement, Pep's assets consisted of $1,500 in cash and 490 shares of DeKalb. List and show the value of Pep's assets prior to the ex-rights date.

c. List and show the value of Pep's assets on the ex-rights date if DeKalb stock sells for $60 per share on that date.

d. List and show the value of Pep's assets if Pep sells the DeKalb rights on the ex-rights date.

11. Using a recent *Wall Street Journal* as a data source, select a NYSE-listed stock whose name begins with the same letter as the first letter of your last name. For this stock, calculate its rate of return for that day of the week. What was the stock's trading volume that day?

12. Tomah Electronics' stock price at the end of several quarters, along with the market index value for the same periods, is shown below. Tomah pays no dividends. Calculate the beta of Tomah's stock over the eight quarters.

Quarter	Quarter-End Tomah Stock Price	Quarter-End Market Index Value
0	60.000	210.00
1	62.500	220.50
2	64.375	229.87
3	59.875	206.88
4	56.875	190.33
5	61.500	209.36
6	66.500	238.67
7	69.750	257.76
8	68.375	262.92

13. Using the data from Problem 10 in Chapter 1, calculate the beta of the small stock portfolio over the 20-year period. Use the common stock returns from Table 1.1 as the returns on the market index.

14. Shown here are ten quarters of return data for Baraboo Associates stock, as well as return data over the same period for a stock market index. Using this information, calculate the following statistics for Baraboo Associates stock.
   a. Beta
   b. Alpha
   c. Standard deviation of random error term
   d. Coefficient of determination

Quarter	Baraboo Return	Market Return
1	3.8%	2.7%
2	5.3	3.1
3	−7.2	−4.9
4	10.1	9.9
5	1.0	2.7
6	2.5	1.2
7	6.4	3.8
8	4.8	4.0
9	6.0	5.5
10	2.2	2.0

15. Why are liquid and continuous secondary security markets important to the effective functioning of primary security markets?

16. Describe the role of an underwriting syndicate in a public security offering.

17. Distinguish between a competitive bid underwriting and a negotiated underwriting.

18. Investment bankers frequently attempt to stabilize the price of a newly issued security in the secondary market.
   a. How is this stabilization accomplished?
   b. What is the purpose of the stabilization?
   c. What can go wrong with the stabilization attempts?

19. Why must companies that publicly issue securities file a prospectus with the SEC? What does the SEC's acceptance of the prospectus imply?

20. Discuss why ipo's appear to generate abnormal returns for investors. Are these returns a "sure thing"? What are the economic implications of these high returns for ipo issuers?

21. (Appendix Question) The empirical regularities cited in this chapter have potentially troubling implications for the capital asset pricing model and the concept of highly efficient markets. Discuss some of these implications.

22. (Appendix Question) Boileryard Clarke, an astute investment observer, wrote, "Testing for empirical regularities is conceptually difficult because it is really a two-hypothesis test. One test is related to the validity of the underlying asset pricing model, and the other test is related to the existence of the empirical regularity." What does Boileryard mean by this statement?

23. (Appendix Question) Sugar Grove Technologies has debt and equity with total market values of $120 million and $230 million, respectively. With a 35% corporate tax, what is the firm's unlevered value?

24. (Appendix Question) The market value of Oswego Computers' total debt outstanding is $10 million. Further, the unlevered market value of Oswego is $40 million. The firm's average corporate tax rate is 35%.

    a. If the beta of the firm's debt is .40 and the beta of its equity is 1.20, what is the firm's beta?

    b. If the firm borrows another $10 million and uses the proceeds to purchase an equivalent amount of its own equity, what will be the effect on the beta of its equity?

25. (Appendix Question) Necedah Power is an electric utility company. Its historical beta is .70. Its stock offers a dividend yield of 7.6%. The market value of its equity is currently $140 million. On the basis of the data from Table 16.12, calculate Necedah's beta.

CFA EXAM QUESTIONS

26. You ask John Statdud, your research assistant, to analyze the relationship between the return on Coca-Cola Enterprises (CCE) common stock and the return on the market using the Standard & Poor's 500 Stock Index as a proxy for the market. The data include monthly returns for both CCE and S&P 500 over a recent five-year period. The results of the regression are indicated below:

$$R_{CCE,\,t} = .59 + .94(R_{S\&P,\,t}) + e_{CCE,\,t}$$

$$(.81) \qquad (3.10)$$

where:

$R_{CCE,\,t}$ = return on CCE common stock in month t

$R_{S\&P,\,t}$ = return on S&P 500 stock index in month t

$e_{CCE,\,t}$ = residual error in month t

The numbers in parentheses are the t-statistics (the .01 critical value is 2.66). The coefficient of determination R^2 for the regression is .215.

Statdud wrote the following summary of the regression results:

    a. The regression statistics indicate that during the five-year period under study, when the annual return on the S&P 500 was zero, CCE had an average annual return of 0.59%.

    b. The alpha value of .59 is a measure of the variability of the return on the market.

    c. The coefficient of .94 indicates CCE's sensitivity to the return on the S&P 500 and suggests that the return on CCE's common stock is less sensitive to market movements than the average stock.

    d. The t-statistic of 3.10 for the slope coefficient indicates that the coefficient is not statistically significant at the .01 level.

    e. The R^2 for the regression of .215 indicates that the average estimate deviates from the actual observation by an average of 21.5%.

    f. There is no concern that the slope coefficient lacks statistical significance since beta values tend to be less stable (and therefore less useful) than alpha values.

    g. The regression should be rerun using ten years of data. This would improve the reliability of the estimated coefficients while not sacrificing anything.

Identify which of the seven statements made by Statdud is (are) incorrect and justify your answer(s).

27. You are a portfolio manager meeting a client. During the conversation that followed your formal review of her account, your client asked the following question: "My granddaughter, who is studying investments, tells me that one of the best ways to make money in the stock market is to buy the stocks of small-capitalization firms on a Monday morning late in December and to sell the stocks one month later." What is she talking about?

    a. Identify the apparent market anomalies (empirical regularities) that would justify the proposed strategy.

    b. Explain why you believe such a strategy might or might not work in the future.

APPENDIX A

EMPIRICAL REGULARITIES IN THE STOCK MARKET

Researchers have uncovered certain **empirical regularities** in common stocks. That is, certain cross-sectional differences among stock returns have been found to occur with regularity. Some regularities should occur according to certain asset pricing models. For example, the CAPM asserts that different stocks should have different returns because different stocks have different betas. What makes the regularities that are about to be discussed of special interest is that they are not predicted by any of the traditional asset pricing models. Accordingly, they are sometimes also referred to as **anomalies.**

As was mentioned earlier, returns are related to a firm's size as well as to its book-value-to-market-value and earnings-to-price ratios. While these relationships are often used as examples of anomalies, Fama and French argue that they can be explained by a 3-factor APT model, and thus should not be viewed as anomalies.[43] This appendix will examine some calendar anomalies and present some international evidence that indicates that such anomalies also exist in other countries.

A.1   SEASONALITY IN STOCK RETURNS

The desire of individuals for liquidity may be thought to change from day to day and from month to month. If it does, there may be seasonal patterns in stock returns. One might presume that such patterns would be relatively unimportant. Indeed, accord-

TABLE 16.4	Seasonality in Stock Returns		
Time Period	Average Stock Return in January	Average Stock Return in Other Months	Difference in Returns
1904–1928	1.30%	.44%	.86%
1929–1940	6.63	−.60	7.23
1941–1974	3.91	.70	3.21
1904–1974	3.48	.42	3.06

Source: Michael S. Rozeff and William R. Kinney Jr., "Capital Market Seasonality: The Case of Stock Returns," *Journal of Financial Economics* 3, no. 4 (October 1976): 388.

ing to the notion of efficient markets, such patterns should be quite minor (if they exist at all), because they are not suggested by traditional asset pricing models. However, the evidence indicates that at least two are significant: the **January effect** and the **day-of-the-week effect.**[44]

A.1.1 January Effect

There is no obvious reason to expect stock returns to be higher in certain months than in others. However, in a study that looked at average monthly returns on NYSE-listed common stocks, significant seasonalities were found.[45] In particular, the average return in January was higher than the average return in any other month. Table 16.4 indicates the average stock return in January and the other 11 months for various time periods. Although the difference in returns was minor in the early part of the century, more recently it appears that the average return in January has been approximately 3% higher than the average monthly returns in February through December.[46]

A.1.2 Day-of-the-Week Effect

It is often assumed that the expected daily returns on stocks are the same for all days of the week. That is, the expected return on a given stock is the same for Monday as it is for Tuesday as it is for Wednesday as it is for Thursday as it is for Friday. However, a number of studies have uncovered evidence that refutes this belief. Two early studies looked at the average daily return on NYSE-listed securities and found that the return on Monday was quite different from returns on other days.[47] In particular, the average return on Monday was found to be much lower than the average return on any other day of the week. Furthermore, the average return on Monday was negative, whereas the other days of the week had positive average returns. Table 16.5 displays these findings.

TABLE 16.5	Analysis of Daily Returns				
	Monday	Tuesday	Wednesday	Thursday	Friday
French study: January 1953–December 1977	−.17%	.02%	.10%	.04%	.09%
Gibbons and Hess study: July 1962–December 1978	−.13%	.00	.10	.03	.08

Source: Kenneth R. French, "Stock Returns and the Weekend Effect," *Journal of Financial Economics* 8, no. 1 (March 1980): 58; and Michael R. Gibbons and Patrick Hess, "Day of the Week Effects and Asset Returns," *Journal of Business* 54, no. 4 (October 1981): 582–583.

The rate of return on a stock for a given day of the week is typically calculated by subtracting the closing price on the previous trading day from the closing price on that day, adding any dividends for that day to the difference, and then dividing the resulting number by the closing price as of the previous trading day:

$$r_t = \frac{(P_t - P_{t-1}) + D_t}{P_{t-1}} \tag{16.9}$$

where P_t and P_{t-1} are the closing prices on days t and $t-1$, and D_t is the value of any dividends paid on day t. This means that the return for Monday uses the closing price on Monday as P_t and the closing price on Friday as P_{t-1}. Thus the change in the price of a stock for Monday $(P_t - P_{t-1})$ actually represents the change in price *over the weekend*, as well as during Monday. This observation has caused some people to refer to the day-of-the-week effect as the *weekend effect*. Other people use the *weekend effect* to refer to price behavior from Friday close to Monday open, and the *Monday effect* to refer to price behavior from Monday open to Monday close.

A refinement of the day-of-the-week effect involved an examination of NYSE stock returns over 15-minute intervals during trading hours over the period of December 1, 1981, through January 31, 1983.[48] Figure 16.12 displays the results when

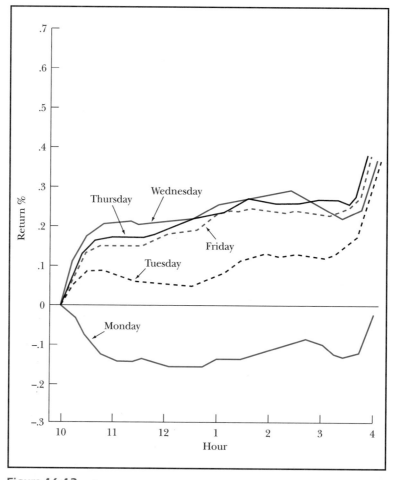

Figure 16.12
Cumulated 15-Minute Intraday Returns
Source: Lawrence Harris, "How to Profit from Intraday Stock Returns," *Journal of Portfolio Management* 12, no. 2 (Winter 1986): 63.

these returns were cumulated and examined on a day-of-the-week basis. Several observations can be made. First, the negative returns during trading hours on Monday occurred within an hour of the opening. Afterward, the behavior of stock prices on Monday was similar to that on the other days of the week. Second, on Tuesdays through Fridays there was a notable upward movement in prices in the first hour of trading. Third, on all days of the week there was a notable upward movement in prices during the last hour of trading.[49] Hence most of the daily price movement in a stock typically comes near the open and close.

Somewhat related to the day-of-the-week effect is the **holiday effect**. A study of this effect found that average stock returns on trading days around federal holidays (the market is closed on these holidays; there are eight each year) are 9 to 14 times as high as the average daily returns during the rest of the year.[50] Furthermore, this abnormally high return is spread out from the closing price two days before the holiday to the opening price on the day after the holiday. Tests indicate that it is unrelated to the size, January, or day-of-the-week effects.

A.2   INTERRELATIONSHIP OF SIZE AND JANUARY EFFECTS

Given the presence of these regularities as well as those mentioned earlier in the chapter, researchers have attempted to see whether there are any interrelationships among them. For example, is the January effect more pronounced for small firms than for large ones? A brief discussion of this interrelationship follows.[51]

Having observed that small firms have higher returns than large firms, and that returns are higher in January than in any other month of the year, one might wonder whether these two effects are somehow related. One study that examined this issue found that the two effects were strongly related.[52] All NYSE-listed and AMEX-listed stocks over the 17-year period of 1963 to 1979 were examined in this study. At the end of each year, each firm was ranked by market capitalization (that is, the year-end market price per share times the number of common shares outstanding). Ten portfolios were then formed on the basis of size, with portfolio 1 containing the smallest 10% of the firms, portfolio 2 the next smallest 10%, and so on.

Abnormal returns were calculated for each portfolio on a monthly basis over the 17-year period and averaged for each month. Figure 16.13, which displays the results, shows that the size effect was most pronounced in January, because the line for this month slopes down sharply from left to right. The other 11 months of the year appear to be quite similar to each other. In general, each one of these months displays a slight downward slope, indicating that the size effect also existed for these months, but only to a minor degree. Also of interest is the observation that large firms had a negative abnormal return in January. Thus the January effect has been due primarily to the behavior of small firms, and the size effect has been concentrated mainly in the month of January.

Further examination of this interrelationship between the size effect and the January effect has revealed that it is concentrated in the first five trading days of January.[53] In particular, the difference in returns between the smallest-firm portfolio and the largest-firm portfolio over these five days was 8.0%, whereas over the entire year it was 30.4%. Thus 26.3% (= 8.0%/30.4%) of the annual size effect occurred during these five days. (If the size effect had been spread evenly over the year, then .4% of it would have been attributed to these five days.)

Attempts have been made to explain this interrelationship between the January effect and the size effect. One explanation that appears to have some merit has to do

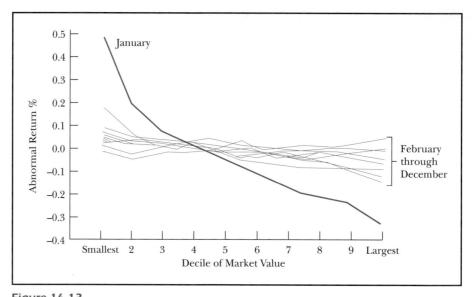

Figure 16.13
Relationship between the Size Effect and the January Effect
Source: Donald B. Keim, "Size-Related Anomalies and Stock Return Seasonality: Further Empirical Evidence," *Journal of Financial Economy* 12, no. 1 (June 1983): 21.

with "tax selling." This explanation begins by arguing that stocks that have declined during the year have downward pressure on their prices near year-end as investors sell them to realize capital losses in order to minimize tax payments. After the end of the year, this pressure is removed and the prices jump back to their "fair" values. A related argument asserts that some professional money managers wish to sell those stocks that have performed poorly during the past year in order to avoid their appearance on year-end reports. Such activity is often referred to as "window dressing." Note that these arguments fly in the face of the notion of efficient markets. (The notion of efficient markets would suggest that this behavior cannot happen, because if investors sensed that stocks were becoming undervalued at year-end, they would flood the market with buy orders, thereby preventing any substantive undervaluation from occurring.) Nevertheless, the arguments do appear to have some merit in that the stocks that declined during the previous year had the largest appreciation in January.[54] However, this association between January returns and previous year stock-price declines does not appear to be attributable solely to downward tax-selling price pressure because the biggest "losers" during a year appear to have abnormally high returns for as long as five Januaries thereafter. This finding contradicts tax-selling arguments, because according to them the abnormal price rebound should occur only in the first subsequent January.[55]

Contradictory evidence is also provided by noting that the January effect exists in Japan (as will be shown later), yet Japan has no capital gains tax and disallows any deduction for capital losses.[56] Rebutting this evidence, however, is the observation that the January effect apparently did not exist before the imposition of income taxes in the United States.[57]

A second possible explanation is that small stocks may be relatively riskier in January than during the rest of the year. If they are, then they should have a relatively higher average return in January. A study finding that the betas of small stocks tend to increase at the beginning of the year lends support to this explanation.[58]

Several people have investigated foreign stock markets in order to see whether similar anomalies exist outside the United States.[59] Because the Tokyo Stock Exchange is the largest non-U.S. exchange, evidence concerning anomalies there will be discussed next. Overall, the anomalies that have been observed in the United States also appear, for the most part, in Japan.

A.3.1   Size Effect

Table 16.6 presents evidence that suggests that the size effect also exists in Japan.[60] The data used in panel (a) were based on all stocks in the first section of the Tokyo Stock Exchange. (The Tokyo Stock Exchange has two "sections"; the second is less than 10% of the size of the first, measured by the market value of the securities traded on it.) Two indices were prepared and examined over the period from 1952 to 1980; they include the same stocks but are compiled differently. The EW index weights all the stocks equally, and the VW index weights the stocks by market value. Hence the EW index is influenced much more by the performance of small stocks than the VW index is. As the table indicates, the EW index returned 5.1% more, suggesting the presence of a size effect.

Panel (b) of Table 16.6 also indicates the presence of a size effect between 3.4% and 8.4% for the period from 1973 to 1987. Here the performance of small firms was measured with two indices. [Large stocks were measured by the TOPIX index, which is computed in a manner similar to the VW index in panel (a).] First, the smallest quintile of stocks in the first section was formed into a value-weighted index denoted TSEsmall. Second, the stocks in the second section were formed into a value-weighted index denoted TSE2. Interestingly, over the same time period the difference in the returns on the S&P 500 (a large stock-value-weighted index) and the returns on the smallest quintile of NYSE-listed stocks was 7.8%, comparable to the 8.4% difference in Tokyo.

A.3.2   January Effect

Table 16.7 shows the presence of a January effect in the Tokyo Stock Exchange.[61] The first two rows involve the same indices used in panel (a) of Table 16.6; panel (c) uses a value-weighted index published in *Morgan Stanley Capital International Perspective*. In all three panels the average return in January was clearly higher than the average monthly return in the remaining 11 months. Interestingly, June also had an unusually high average return, but not nearly as noticeable as January's.

TABLE 16.6	Size Effect on the Tokyo Stock Exchange		
	Small Stocks	Large Stocks	Difference
(a) 1952–1980: EW vs. VW[1]	22.7%	17.6%	5.1%
(b) 1973–1987: TSEsmall vs. TOPIX[2]	21.7	13.3	8.4
TSE2 vs. TOPIX[2]	16.7	13.3	3.4

Sources: The data are adapted from: 1. Kiyoshi Kato and James S. Schallheim, "Seasonal and Size Anomalies in the Japanese Stock Market," *Journal of Financial and Quantitative Analysis* 20, no. 2 (June 1985): 248. 2. Yasushi Hamao, "Fifteen-Year Performance of Japanese Capital Markets," in Edwin J. Elton and Martin J. Gruber (eds.), *Japanese Capital Markets* (New York: Ballinger, 1990), 10.

TABLE 16.7 January Effect on the Tokyo Stock Exchange

	Jan.	Feb.–Dec.	Difference	June	Feb.–May and July–Dec.	Difference
(a) 1952–1980: EW[1]	7.1%	1.4%	6.7%	2.8%	1.3%	1.5%
(b) 1952–1980: VW[1]	4.5	1.2	3.3	2.5	1.1	1.4
(c) 1959–1979: VW[2]	3.5	.7	2.8	2.1	.5	1.6

Sources: The data are adpted from: 1. Kiyoshi Kato and James S. Schallheim, "Seasonal and Size Anomalies in the Japanese Stock Market." *Journal of Financial and Quantitative Analysis* 20, no. 2 (June 1985): 248. 2. Mustafa N. Gultekin and N. Bulent Gultekin, "Stock Market Seasonality: International Evidence," *Journal of Financial Economics* 12, no. 4 (December 1983): 475.

TABLE 16.8 Day-of-the-Week Effect on the Tokyo Stock Exchange

	Monday	Tuesday	Wednesday	Thursday	Friday	Saturday
(a) 1970–1983: Nikkei Dow[1]	−.02%	−.09%	.15%	.03%	.06%	.12%
(b) 1970–1983: TOPIX[1]	−.01	−.06	.12	.03	.06	.10
(c) 1978–1987: TOPIX[2]	.00	−.09	.14	.06	.10	.14

Sources: The data are adapted from: 1. Jeffrey Jaffe and Randolph Westerfield, "Patterns in Japanese Common Stock Returns: Day of the Week and Turn of the Year Effects," *Journal of Financial and Quantitative Analysis* 20, no. 2 (June 1985): 263. 2. Kiyoshi Kato, Sandra L. Schwartz, and William T. Ziemba, "Day of the Week Effects in Japanese Stocks," in Edwin J. Elton and Martin J. Gruber (eds.), *Japanese Capital Markets* (New York: Ballinger, 1990), 253.

A.3.3 Day-of-the-Week Effect

Evidence regarding the day-of-the-week effect is provided in Table 16.8.[62] (The Tokyo Stock Exchange was open on Saturday mornings during the periods examined; hence there is an average return reported for Saturday as well as for Monday through Friday.) Two indices are involved. One is the TOPIX index, which is a value-weighted index based on all stocks listed in the first section. The other is the Nikkei Dow, which is based on 225 large, well-established companies on the Tokyo Stock Exchange and is a price-weighted index like the Dow Jones Industrial Average.

The table indicates that Monday returns are, in general, negative, just as in the United States (see Table 16.5 for comparisons).[63] Furthermore, Wednesday returns are the largest, again similar to the United States. Second largest is Saturday, the last trading day of the week in Japan. This behavior is similar to that in the United States in that the last trading day of the week is the second largest. What is surprising is that Tuesday is negative, and even more so than Monday. Otherwise the day-of-the-week effect in Japan is similar to that observed in the United States.[64]

A.3.4 Size and January Effects

Examination of average returns in Table 16.7 (a) and (b) reveals that the size effect occurs for the most part in January. Hence these two effects are interconnected in a manner similar to that in the United States. These panels show that there is a pronounced difference in the average returns between the equal-weighted and value-weighted indices of 2.6% (=7.1% − 4.5%) in January but a relatively small difference of .2% (=1.4% − 1.2%) during the other 11 months of the year. This difference is notable because the EW index gives much larger weights to small stocks than the VW index does, suggesting that the difference between the two indices can be attributed to the performance of the small stocks. In summary, it would appear that in Japan the size effect is primarily a January effect.

On balance, what do these regularities suggest that the investor should do? First, investors who want to buy stocks should avoid doing so late on Friday or early on Monday. Conversely, investors who want to sell stocks should try to sell late on Friday or early on Monday. Second, if the stocks of small firms are to be purchased, they should be purchased in late December or somewhat earlier. If the stocks of small firms are to be sold, they should be sold in mid-January or somewhat later. Third, if the stocks of large firms are to be purchased, they should be purchased in early February or somewhat later. If the stocks of large firms are to be sold, they should be sold in late December or somewhat earlier.[65]

Two words of caution are in order here. First, none of these empirical regularities is of a sufficient magnitude to suggest that riches are to be made by exploiting them. Indeed, transaction costs would devour most if not all of any profits that might be made.[66] All that they suggest is that if, for whatever reason, a buy or sell order is to be placed, there are some times when it may be more advantageous to do so. Second, although these regularities have been found to exist in the past, and in some instances for long periods of time and in several foreign markets, there is no guarantee that they will continue to exist in the future.[67] It may be the case that as more investors become aware of them and time their trades accordingly, such regularities will cease to exist.

APPENDIX B

ADJUSTMENTS TO HISTORICAL COMMON STOCK BETAS

Without any information at all it would be reasonable to estimate the beta of a stock to be equal to 1.0, the average size of beta. Given a chance to see how a stock moved relative to a market index over some past time period, a modification of this prior estimate would seem appropriate. Such a modification would sensibly produce a final estimate of beta that would lie between the value of 1.0 and its initially estimated value based purely on historical price changes.

Formal procedures for making such modifications have been adopted by most investment firms that estimate betas. The specific adjustments made typically differ from time to time and, in some cases, from stock to stock. In Figure 16.7 the adjusted beta values were obtained by giving approximately 34% weight to the average marketwide beta of 1.0 and approximately 66% weight to the historical estimate of beta for each stock. Thus the adjusted beta for a firm with a historical beta of 1.65 is $1.43 \left[= (.34 \times 1.0) + (.66 \times 1.65)\right]$. More generally,

$$\beta_a = (.34 \times 1.0) + (.66 \times \beta_h) \tag{16.10}$$

where β_a and β_h are the adjusted and historical betas, respectively.[68] Examination of Equation (16.10) indicates that this procedure takes the historical beta for a security and adjusts it by giving it a value closer to 1.0. Thus historical betas less than 1.0 are made larger, but will still be less than 1.0, and historical betas greater than 1.0 are made smaller, but will still be greater than 1.0. The adjustments are in these directions because the weights (.66 and .34) are positive and add up to 1.0, indicating that the adjustment procedure is an averaging technique. Hence, a stock's adjusted beta is a weighted average of the value of 1.0 and the stock's historical beta.

Table 16.9 shows the extent to which such a procedure anticipates differences between historical and future betas. The second column lists the unadjusted historical betas for eight portfolios of 100 securities each, based on monthly price changes from July 1947 through June 1954 (the portfolios were designed to have significantly different betas during this period). The third column of the table shows the values obtained when an adjustment of the type used by Merrill Lynch was applied. The betas in the fourth column are based on price changes over the subsequent seven years. For a majority of the portfolios, the adjusted betas are closer in magnitude to the subsequent historical betas than are the unadjusted betas. This finding suggests that the adjusted historical beta is a more accurate estimate of the future beta than is the unadjusted historical beta.

The fifth column of Table 16.9 shows the historical betas estimated using data from a third seven-year period. Comparing the unadjusted betas in columns 2, 4, and 5, one can see that there is a continuing tendency for betas to move toward the mean value of 1.0 over time. Thus adjustment procedures seem to have some usefulness when it comes to estimating betas for a future time period.

It seems plausible that "true" betas not only vary over time but also have a tendency to move back toward average levels, as extreme values are likely to be moderated over time. A firm whose operations or financing make the risk of its equity considerably different from that of other firms is more likely to move back toward the average than away from it over time. Such changes in betas are due to real economic phenomena; they are not simply an artifact of overly simple statistical procedures.

	July 1947–June 1954			
Portfolio (1)	**Unadjusted (2)**	**Adjusted (3)**	**July 1954–June 1961 (4)**	**July 1961–June 1968 (5)**
1	.36	.48	.57	.72
2	.61	.68	.71	.79
3	.78	.82	.88	.88
4	.91	.93	.96	.92
5	1.01	1.01	1.03	1.04
6	1.13	1.10	1.13	1.02
7	1.26	1.21	1.24	1.08
8	1.47	1.39	1.32	1.15

TABLE 16.9   Ex Ante and Ex Post Beta Values for Portfolios of 100 Securities

Source: Marshall E. Blume, "Betas and Their Regression Tendencies," *Journal of Finance* 30, no. 3 (June 1975): 792.

There is, however, no reason to expect all stocks' true betas to move to the same average in the same manner at the same speed. In this regard, some fundamental analysis of the firm may prove more useful than the adoption of more sophisticated statistical methods for processing past price changes in estimating beta.

Although historical betas for portfolios can provide useful information about future betas, historical betas for individual securities are subject to great error and should be treated accordingly. Their susceptibility to error can be seen by noting the magnitude of the standard errors of the betas shown earlier in Figure 16.7.

Table 16.10 provides another view. Every stock listed on the New York Stock Exchange was assigned to one of ten classes in each year from 1931 through 1967 on the basis of the magnitude of its historical beta calculated using data from the preceding five years. The stocks in the top 10% of each January's ranking were assigned to class 10, the next 10% to class 9, and so on. The table shows the percent of the stocks that were in the same class (column 1) and within one risk class (column 3) five years later. Also shown are the entries that would be expected if there were no relationship between such past and future beta classes. Examination of the table reveals that individual security betas have some but not a great deal of predictive value.

Figure 16.14 shows that the predictive ability of historical portfolio betas improves with the amount of diversification in a portfolio. The vertical axis plots the percentage of the differences in (measured) portfolio betas (based on weekly price changes) in one year that can be attributed to differences in their (measured) betas in the preceding year. The horizontal axis indicates the number of securities in each portfolio. It can be seen in the figure that the historical betas for portfolios containing roughly 10 to 20 securities or more have a high degree of predictive ability. Thus, individual security betas are worth estimating, even though they are rather inaccurate when viewed by themselves. Their individual inaccuracies seem to cancel out one another when the beta of a diversified portfolio is calculated, producing an accurate estimate of the portfolio's beta.

TABLE 16.10	Movement of Stocks Among Beta Classes			
Risk Class	**Percent of Stocks in the Same Beta Class Five Years Later**		**Percent of Stocks in the Same Beta Class or within One Risk Class Five Years Later**	
	Actual (1)	**Expected If There Were No Relationship (2)**	**Actual (3)**	**Expected If There Were No Relationship (4)**
10 (highest beta values)	35.2%	10%	69.3%	20%
9	18.4	10	53.7	30
8	16.4	10	45.3	30
7	13.3	10	40.9	30
6	13.9	10	39.3	30
5	13.6	10	41.7	30
4	13.2	10	40.2	30
3	15.9	10	44.6	30
2	21.5	10	60.9	30
1 (lowest beta values)	40.5	10	62.3	20

Source: William F. Sharpe and Guy M. Cooper, "Risk-Return Classes of New York Stock Exchange Common Stocks, 1931–1967," *Financial Analysts Journal* 28, no. 2 (March/April 1972): 53.

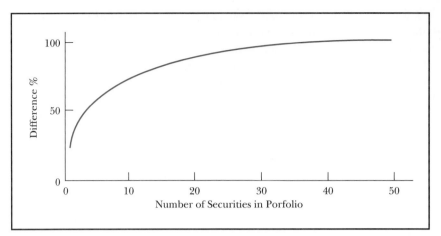

Figure 16.14
Percent of Differences in Beta Values Attributable to Differences in Prior Year's Betas
Source: Robert A. Levy, "On the Short-Term Stationary of Beta Coefficients," *Financial Analysts Journal* 27, no. 6 (November/December 1971): p. 57.

B.1   LEVERAGE AND BETA

The beta of a *firm* represents the sensitivity of the aggregate value of the firm to changes in the value of the market portfolio. It depends on both the demand for the firm's products and the firm's operating costs. However, most firms have both debt and equity outstanding. This means that the beta of a firm's *equity* (that is, stock) depends on the beta of the firm and the firm's financial leverage. For example, imagine that two firms are identical in every way except that firm A has debt while firm B is free of debt. This means that even though they have the same earnings before interest and taxes (EBIT), they will have different earnings after taxes (EAT) because A, unlike B, has to make interest payments. In this situation, the firm betas for A and B are the same, but the stock beta for A will be greater than the stock beta for B. The difference in their debt levels is the reason for the difference in their stock betas because the debt makes the earnings available to common stockholders more variable for A than for B. Thus the stock beta for A could be viewed as being equal to the stock beta it would have if it had no debt (that is, the beta of B) plus an adjustment for the amount of debt it actually has outstanding.

One method that has been suggested for determining the influence of debt on the beta of the stock of a firm involves a four-step procedure.[69] First, the current market values of the firm's outstanding debt D and equity E must be determined. Once those values have been determined, the current market value of the levered firm V_L can be determined:

$$V_L = D + E \qquad (16.11)$$

Second, the market value of the firm *if it were unlevered* can be determined by using the following formula:

$$V_u = V_L - \tau D \qquad (16.12)$$

where:

> V_u = market value of firm if it was unlevered
> τ = average corporate tax rate for the firm
> D = market value of firm's debt

Third, the beta of the firm can be calculated after estimating the betas of the firm's debt β_{debt} and equity β_{equity} by using the following formula:

$$\beta_{firm} = \beta_{debt} \frac{(1 - \tau)D}{V_u} + \beta_{equity} \frac{E}{V_u} \qquad (16.13)$$

Fourth, having used Equation (16.13) to estimate the beta of the firm, one can determine the effect of any degree of leverage on the equity beta of the firm by re-stating Equation (16.13). Specifically, solving Equation (16.13) for β_{equity} results in:[70]

$$\beta_{equity} = \beta_{firm} + (\beta_{firm} - \beta_{debt}) \frac{D}{E}(1 - \tau) \qquad (16.14)$$

In evaluating Equation (16.14) it should be noted that the value of β_{firm} does not change as the firm's debt-equity ratio D/E is changed. Assuming that the value of β_{debt} also does not change, one can see that increasing the firm's debt-equity ratio will increase the beta of the firm's equity. Intuitively this outcome makes sense, because a higher debt-equity ratio will make a firm's earnings after taxes more volatile. Conversely, lowering a firm's debt-equity ratio should lower the firm's equity beta because it makes earnings after taxes less volatile.

This property of beta can be useful in estimating the beta of a firm's equity if the firm has recently altered its debt-equity ratio (or is contemplating changing the ratio). For example, imagine that ABC Inc. had until last month $60 million of equity and $40 million of debt outstanding for a total firm value of $100 million; its tax rate is 30%. Using the market model shown in Table 16.2, but applied to data before the recent equity issuance, one can determine that the *ex post* equity and debt betas of ABC are 1.40 and .20, respectively. However, ABC has just issued $20 million of equity and used the proceeds to retire some of the debt so that the current values of ABC's equity and debt are $74 million and $20 million, respectively. (The $74 million value of equity represents the sum of $20 million in new equity and $54 million in old equity, which has decreased in value by $6 million owing to the loss of tax shields resulting from the $20 million reduction in ABC's debt.) What is the equity beta of ABC likely to be in the immediate future?

The previously described four-step procedure can be used to provide an answer. First, it is noted from Equation (16.11) that the value of ABC before the new equity issuance was $100 million. Second, it is noted from Equation (16.12) that the value of ABC if the firm were unlevered would be equal to $88 million [= $100 million − (.3 × $40 million)]. Third, the beta of the firm can be estimated using Equation (16.13):

$$\beta_{firm} = .20 \left[\frac{(1 - .3)\$40 \text{ million}}{\$88 \text{ million}} \right] + 1.40 \left(\frac{\$60 \text{ million}}{\$88 \text{ million}} \right)$$

$$= 1.02$$

Last, the current equity beta (that is, the equity beta after the recent issuance of $20 million of equity) can be estimated by using Equation (16.14),

$$\beta_{equity} = 1.02 + (1.02 - .20) \left(\frac{\$20 \text{ million}}{\$74 \text{ million}} \right)(1 - .3)$$

$$= 1.17$$

Hence the reduction in the amount of debt that ABC has outstanding has reduced the beta of the equity from 1.40 to 1.17.[71]

Firms in industries having highly cyclical demand or large fixed costs might be expected to have higher firm betas than those in industries with more stable demand or greater variable costs, because they will have greater variability in earnings before interest and taxes (EBIT). Differences in financial leverage could wholly offset such factors, leaving few, if any, differences among the equity betas of firms in different industries. However, it seems that they do not. Firms in certain industries tend to have higher equity betas than those in other industries, and, by and large, the classifications agree with prior expectations.

Table 16.11 shows the average equity betas for stocks in various industry classifications. Stock prices of firms whose products are termed "necessities" tend to respond less than the stock prices of most other firms when expectations about the future health of the economy are revised. That is, firms in necessities (such as utilities or food) tend to have low betas because they tend to have more stable earnings. Stock prices of firms that manufacture "luxuries" tend to respond more than most others when expectations about the future health of the economy are revised. That is, firms in luxuries (such as travel or electronics) tend to have high betas because they tend to have more cyclical earnings.

B.2.1   Forecasting Beta

Information of the type shown in Table 16.11 can be used to adjust historical equity betas. For example, the knowledge that a corporation is in the air transport indus-

TABLE 16.11   Average Values of Beta for Stocks in Selected Industries, 1966–1974

Industry	Beta Value	Industry	Beta Value
Air transport	1.80	Energy, raw materials	1.22
Real property	1.70	Tires, rubber goods	1.21
Travel, outdoor recreation	1.66	Railroads, shipping	1.19
Electronics	1.60	Forest products, paper	1.16
Miscellaneous finance	1.60	Miscellaneous, conglomerate	1.14
Nondurables, entertainment	1.47	Drugs, medicine	1.14
Consumer durables	1.44	Domestic oil	1.12
Business machines	1.43	Soaps, cosmetics	1.09
Retail, general	1.43	Steel	1.02
Media	1.39	Containers	1.01
Insurance	1.34	Nonferrous metals	.99
Trucking, freight	1.31	Agriculture, food	.99
Producer goods	1.30	Liquor	.89
Aerospace	1.30	International oil	.85
Business services	1.28	Banks	.81
Apparel	1.27	Tobacco	.80
Construction	1.27	Telephone	.75
Motor vehicles	1.27	Energy, utilities	.60
Photographic, optical	1.24	Gold	.36
Chemicals	1.22		

Source: Barr Rosenberg and James Guy. "Prediction of Beta from Investment Fundamentals, *Financial Analysts Journal* 32, no. 4 (July/August 1976): 66.

try suggests that a reasonable prior estimate of its equity beta is 1.8. Thus it makes more sense to adjust its historical equity beta toward a value of 1.8 than toward a value of 1.0, the average for all stocks, as was suggested in Equation (16.10).

The procedure used to adjust historical betas involves an implicit prediction equation for future betas. Equation (16.10) can be written more generally as:

$$\beta_a = a + b\beta_h \qquad (16.15)$$

where a and b are positive constants that sum to 1.0. One way to consider the differences in industry betas is to alter Equation (16.15) as follows:

$$\beta = a\beta_{ind} + b\beta_h \qquad (16.16)$$

where β_{ind} denotes the average equity beta of the industry to which the stock belongs.

For example, consider the values of .33 and .67 for a and b, respectively. Air Express is an air transport firm whose historical beta is 2.0. What is its adjusted beta? Noting that the average equity beta for stocks in the air transport industry is 1.8, its adjusted beta can be adjusted by using Equation (16.16) as follows:

$$\beta_a = (.33 \times 1.8) + (.67 \times 2.0)$$

$$= 1.93$$

Thus Air Express has an adjusted beta of 1.93, which lies between its historical beta of 2.0 and the average equity beta in its industry of 1.8. Indeed, this is what Equation (16.16) accomplishes: It alters a historical beta to give an adjusted beta lying between β_h and β_{ind}. Thus, with this model a stock's adjusted beta is a weighted average of its industry beta and the stock's historical beta.

B.2.2   Multiple-Industry Firms

What should be done if the firm has divisions that are in different industries? In a situation that involves two industries, Equation (16.16) could be modified as follows:

$$\beta_a = a\left(E_{ind1}\beta_{ind1} + E_{ind2}\beta_{ind2}\right) + b\beta_h \qquad (16.17)$$

where E_{ind1} and E_{ind2} denote the percentages of the firm's earnings that are from industries 1 and 2, respectively, and β_{ind1} and β_{ind2} are the betas for industries 1 and 2, respectively.[72]

As an example, consider Electrospace, a firm that has half of its earnings coming from a division that is in the electronics industry and half coming from a division that is in the aerospace industry. Assuming that a and b are equal to .33 and .67, respectively, and that the historical beta for Electrospace is 1.2, one can calculate its adjusted beta in two steps.

First, the value of $E_{ind1}\beta_{ind1} + E_{ind2}\beta_{ind2}$ needs to be calculated. Doing so produces a value of 1.45 $[= (.5 \times 1.6) + (.5 \times 1.3)]$. This can be interpreted as the average equity beta for any stock whose firm has equal business interests in the electronics and aerospace industries.

Second, the adjusted beta of Electrospace can be calculated using Equation (16.16) as 1.28 $[= (.33 \times 1.45) + (.67 \times 1.20)]$. Note that this value lies between the firm's historical beta of 1.20 and its "industry" beta of 1.45.

B.2.3 Adjustments Based on Financial Characteristics

Various financial characteristics can also be used to estimate an adjusted beta. For example, stocks with high dividend yields might have lower betas because more of their value is associated with near-term rather than far-term dividends. Equation (16.17) could thus be augmented to

$$\beta_a = a(E_{ind1}\beta_{ind1} + E_{ind2}\beta_{ind2}) + b\beta_h + cY + dS \qquad (16.18)$$

where c and d are constants, Y is the dividend yield of the firm's stock, and S is the market capitalization of the firm's equity. Now the constant a and b do not need to sum to 1.0.

Table 16.12 shows a beta prediction equation of this form, using historical data from 1928 through 1982.[73] To estimate the beta of a security using this prediction equation, start with a constant based on the industry (referred to as the "sector") in which the security is classified. Then add to this constant an amount equal to the security's historical beta times 0.576. [Note that this is similar to the adjustment to historical beta shown in Equation (16.10).] Finally, add (1) the security's dividend yield times −.019, and (2) the security's "size attribute" times −.105.[74] Algebraically, the model is:

$$\beta_a = a_s + (.576 \times \beta_h) + (-.019 \times Y) + (-.105 \times S) \qquad (16.19)$$

where a_s denotes the constant associated with the sector to which the stock belongs, β_h is the historical beta, Y is the dividend yield, and S is the size of the firm. With this formula, securities having higher yields are predicted to have lower betas, as are those with larger market values of equity outstanding.

TABLE 16.12 A Beta Prediction Equation Derived from a Factor Model

Constant Term

Sector	Value
Basic industry	.455
Capital goods	.425
Consumer staple	.307
Consumer cyclical	.443
Credit cyclical	.429
Energy	.394
Finance	.398
Transportation	.255
Utilities	.340

Variable Terms

Term	Value
Beta	.576
Yield	−.019
Size	−.105

Source: Blake Grossman and William F. Sharpe, "Factors in Security Returns," paper presented at the Center for the Study of Banking and Financial Markets, University of Washington, March 1984.

B.2.4 An Example

As an example, consider a stock that is classified as belonging to the "basic industry." It has a historical beta of 1.2, a dividend yield over the previous 12 months of 4%, and a market capitalization of $7 billion (that is, the firm has 100 million shares outstanding and the stock is selling for $70 per share). Using Equation (16.19), its adjusted beta is:

$$\beta_a = .455 + (.576 \times 1.2) + (-.019 \times 4) + \left[-.105 \times (\log 7) \right]$$

$$= .455 + .69 - .08 - .09$$

$$= .98.$$

Such prediction equations, based on multifactor models, fit historical data considerably better than do those that use only historical betas. One study reported an improvement of 86% over the simpler adjusted beta approach.[75] However, such figures describe only the extent to which the equations fit a given set of data. Because the true test of a prediction equation is its ability to *predict*, only extensive experience with such approaches can, in the final analysis, determine their relative accuracy.

B.3 BETA SERVICES

Services providing betas on a regular basis in published form are available in several countries. Many use only past price changes to form estimates. Some derive their estimates from more general factor models. One service uses weekly data for two years; another, monthly data for five years. One estimates betas for U.S. securities relative to Standard & Poor's 500; another, relative to the New York Stock Exchange composite index; and so on. In each case, estimates for individual securities are subject to error. Thus it is hardly surprising that estimated values for a given security obtained by different services using different procedures are not the same. These differences do not indicate that the various estimates are useless, only that they should be used appropriately and with caution.

ENDNOTES

[1] For more information on proxies, see Paul Jessup and Mary Bochnak, "Exercising Your Rights: How to Use Proxy Material," *AAII Journal* 14, no. 9 (October 1992): 8–11.

[2] For an interesting discussion of proxy fights, see David Ikenberry and Josef Lakonishok, "Corporate Governance through the Proxy Contest: Evidence and Implications," *Journal of Business* 66, no. 3 (July 1993): 405–435. In examining proxy contests that dealt with the election of directors, the authors found that such contests followed a period of below-average performance for both the firm's earnings and stock price. If management had its nominees elected, then afterward the firm's performance reverted to average. However, if the dissidents' nominees were elected, then the firm's performance continued its deterioration for another two years, with the deterioration being most acute if the dissidents took control of the board.

[3] Another form of a takeover is a **merger**. A merger occurs when two firms combine their operations, the result being that only one firm exists. Mergers usually are negotiated by the management of the two firms. Tender offers differ in that the management of the bidder makes a direct appeal to the stockholders of the target firm for their shares. Tender offers also differ in that afterward both firms will still exist, because most tender offers are not for all the shares of the target. **Management buyouts** are a special kind of tender offer, wherein the current management of the firm uses borrowed funds to buy the company. (Hence they are a

type of **leveraged buyout**, or "LBO." LBOs can be executed by anyone, including incumbent management.)

[4] See, for example, Michael C. Jensen and William H. Meckling, "Theory of the Firm: Managerial Behavior, Agency Costs and Ownership Structure," *Journal of Financial Economics* 3, no. 4 (October 1976): 305–360; Eugene F. Fama, "Agency Problems and the Theory of the Firm," *Journal of Political Economy* 88, no. 2 (April 1980): 288–307; Eugene F. Fama and Michael C. Jensen, "Separation of Ownership and Control," *Journal of Law and Economics* 26 (June 1983): 301–325; Eugene F. Fama and Michael C. Jensen, "Agency Problems and Residual Claims," *Journal of Law and Economics* 26 (June 1983): 327–349; the entire issues of vol. 11 (April 1983) and vol. 20 (January/March 1988) of the *Journal of Financial Economics*; Michael C. Jensen, "Eclipse of the Public Corporation," *Harvard Business Review* 89, no. 5 (September–October 1989): 61–74; and John Byrd, Robert Parrino, and Gunnar Pritsch, "Stockholder-Manager Conflicts and Firm Value," *Financial Analysts Journal* 54, no. 3 (May/June 1998). 14–30.

[5] An example of monitoring is having the firm's financial statements audited independently.

[6] For example, management may decide to procure lavishly furnished offices and an executive jet when the conduct of business suggests that these actions are not merited. Furthermore, management may invest in negative net present value investment projects when the firm has "free cash flow" instead of paying it to the shareholders. See Michael C. Jensen, "Agency Costs of Free Cash Flow, Corporate Finance and Takeovers," *American Economic Review* 76, no. 2 (May 1986): 323–329.

[7] Robert Comment and Gregg A. Jarrell, "The Relative Signalling Power of Dutch-Auction and Fixed-Price Self-Tender Offers and Open-Market Share Repurchases," *Journal of Finance* 46, no. 4 (September 1991): 1243–1271.

[8] Although in the study there were similar numbers of fixed-price and Dutch-auction tender offers, the Dutch-auction method is becoming increasingly popular, particularly among larger corporations.

[9] See Josef Lakonishok and Theo Vermaelen, "Anomalous Price Behavior around Repurchase Tender Offers," *Journal of Finance* 45, no. 2 (June 1990): 455–477.

[10] See David Ikenberry, Josef Lakonishok, and Theo Vermaelen, "Market Underreaction to Open Market Share Repurchases," *Journal of Financial Economics* 29, nos. 2, 3 (October–November 1995): 181–208.

[11] For more on "ex dates," see "Dividends and Interest: Who Gets Payments after a Trade?" *AAII Journal* 12, no. 4 (April 1990): 8–11.

[12] Some evidence in support of the optimal trading explanation is provided by Josef Lakonishok and Baruch Lev, "Stock Splits and Stock Dividends: Why, Who, and When," *Journal of Finance* 42, no. 4 (September 1987): 913–932. The tick size explanation has been put forth by James J. Angel in "Tick Size, Share Prices, and Stock Splits," *Journal of Finance* 52, no. 2 (June 1997): 655–681 and "Picking Your Tick: Toward a New Theory of Stock Splits," *Journal of Applied Corporate Finance* 10, no. 3 (Fall 1997): 59–68.

[13] David Ikenberry, Graeme Rankine, and Earl K. Stice, "What Do Stock Splits Really Signal?" *Journal of Financial and Quantitative Analysis* 31, no. 3 (September 1996): 357–375.

[14] Interestingly, a study of reverse stock splits found that for the typical firm, (1) the stock had average performance before the announcement, (2) the announcement was associated with an abnormal return of about −6%, and (3) the stock continued to perform somewhat poorly after the announcement. See J. Randall Woolridge and Donald R. Chambers, "Reverse Splits and Shareholder Wealth," *Financial Management* 12, no. 4 (Autumn 1983): 5–15.

[15] See Eugene F. Fama, Lawrence Fisher, Michael C. Jensen, and Richard Roll, "The Adjustment of Stock Prices to New Information," *International Economic Review* 10, no. 1 (February 1969): 1–21; Sasson Bar-Josef and Lawrence D. Brown, "A Re-examination of Stock Splits Using Moving Betas," *Journal of Finance* 32, no. 4 (September 1977): 1069–1080; and Guy Charest, "Split Information, Stock Returns and Market Efficiency—I," *Journal of Financial Economics* 6, no. 2/3 (June/September 1978): 265–296.

[16] See Thomas E. Copeland, "Liquidity Changes Following Stock Splits," *Journal of Finance* 34, no. 1 (March 1979): 115–141; and Robert M. Conroy, Robert S. Harris, and Bruce A. Benet,

"The Effects of Stock Splits on Bid-Ask Spreads," *Journal of Finance* 45, no. 4 (September 1990): 1285–1295.

[17] Mark S. Grinblatt, Ronald W. Masulis, and Sheridan Titman, "The Valuation Effects of Stock Splits and Stock Dividends," *Journal of Financial Economics* 13, no. 4 (December 1984): 461–490.

[18] Current stockholders may not be given this right if there is a provision in the charter denying it, or if it is denied by the stockholders at the annual meeting.

[19] The investor could simply let the rights expire, causing that investor's proportion in the corporation to decline as others are given ownership in the expanded firm in return for the provision of new capital. Sometimes an **oversubscription privilege** is given to the subscribing stockholders. Those stockholders who have exercised their rights will be given an opportunity to buy the shares that were not purchased, which can become important if the rights are not transferable.

[20] The subscription price is usually set at roughly 80% of the current market price of the stock.

[21] American Depositary Receipts (ADRs) for foreign stocks that are traded on Nasdaq are shown after the Small-Cap Issues under a heading of "ADRs." Exchange-listed ADRs are not shown separately. Instead, they are integrated into the tables with listed U.S. securities. ADRs are discussed in more detail in Chapter 25.

[22] It has been argued that roughly 300 months (25 years) of historical returns are needed in order for a simple averaging technique to produce useful estimates of expected returns, provided that the "true" but unobserved expected return is constant during this entire period. See J. D. Jobson and Bob Korkie, "Estimation for Markowitz Efficient Portfolios," *Journal of the American Statistical Association* 75, no. 371 (September 1980): 544–554, and "Putting Markowitz Theory to Work," *Journal of Portfolio Management* 7, no. 4 (Summer 1981): 70–74.

[23] In doing so, a number of researchers have uncovered certain "empirical regularities" in common stocks; Appendix A discusses a number of them. For a more detailed summary, see Donald B. Keim, "The CAPM and Equity Return Regularities," *Financial Analysts Journal* 42, no. 3 (May/June 1986): 19–34; Douglas K. Pearce, "Challenges to the Concept of Market Efficiency," *Federal Reserve Bank of Kansas City Economic Review* 72, no. 8 (September/October 1987): 16–33; and Robert A. Haugen and Josef Lakonishok, *The Incredible January Effect* (Homewood, IL: Dow Jones-Irwin, 1988).

[24] For an introduction to regression, see Chapters 10 and 11 of James T. McClave and P. George Benson, *Statistics for Business and Economics* (New York: MacMillan College Publishing, 1994); and Mark P. Kritzman, " ...About Regressions," *Financial Analysts Journal* 47, no. 3 (May/June 1991): 12–15.

[25] WM's beta and alpha would have been equal to .63 and .17%, respectively, if excess returns (that is, returns less the riskfree rate) had been used in the calculations instead of returns. Using returns or excess returns (as well as including or ignoring dividends in calculating returns) appears to make little difference in the estimated size of beta. However, there is a substantive difference in the estimated size of alpha. See William F. Sharpe and Guy M. Cooper, "Risk-Return Classes of New York Stock Exchange Common Stocks, 1931–1967," *Financial Analysts Journal* 28, no. 2 (March/April 1972): 46–54.

[26] R is used here to denote the correlation coefficient; sometimes (as in Chapter 7) the Greek letter rho (ρ) is used instead. Thus R-squared is equivalent to ρ-squared, or the square of the correlation coefficient.

[27] In general, growth stocks are stocks of companies that have experienced, or are expected to experience, rapid increases in earnings, whereas value stocks are stocks whose market price seems to be low relative to measures of their worth. Hence other ratios (such as dividend yield) are sometimes used in sorting out these two types of stocks.

[28] The S&P/BARRA Value Stock Index and the S&P/BARRA Growth Stock Index involve dividing the S&P 500 stocks into two groups based on the size of their BV/MV ratios every six months. The stocks in each group are then used to form these two market-capitalization-weighted indices. The construction of market indices is discussed in more detail in Chapter 24.

[29] Eugene F. Fama and Kenneth R. French, "The Cross-Section of Expected Stock Returns," *Journal of Finance* 47, no. 2 (June 1992): 427–465. Also see Barr Rosenberg, Kenneth Reid,

and Ronald Lanstein, "Persuasive Evidence of Market Inefficiency," *Journal of Portfolio Management* 11, no. 3 (Spring 1985): 9–16.

[30] Also see S. Basu, "Investment Performance of Common Stocks in Relation to Their Price-Earnings Ratios: A Test of the Efficient Market Hypothesis," *Journal of Finance* 32, no. 3 (June 1977): 663–682, and "The Relationship between Earnings' Yield, Market Value and Return for NYSE Common Stocks: Further Evidence," *Journal of Financial Economics* 12, no. 1 (June 1983): 129–156.

[31] Other studies of the size effect include Rolf Banz, "The Relationship between Return and Market Value of Common Stocks," *Journal of Financial Economics* 9, no. 1 (March 1981): 3–18; and Marc R. Reinganum, "Misspecification of Capital Asset Pricing: Empirical Anomalies Based on Earnings Yields and Market Values," *Journal of Financial Economics* 9, no. 1 (March 1981): 19–46. One explanation of the size effect is that small firms have higher discount rates because they are riskier than large firms, thereby causing them to have higher average returns over long time periods; see Jonathan Berk, "Does Size Really Matter?" *Financial Analysts Journal* 53, no. 5 (September/October 1997): 12-18 and "A Critique of Size-Related Anomalies," *Review of Financial Studies* 8, no. 2 (Summer 1995): 275–286.

[32] The missing variable apparently is not beta, because the relationship between these variables and stock returns has been found to exist independent of differences in beta. See Fama and French, "The Cross-Section of Expected Stock Returns." Also see the following three papers by Fama and French: "Common Risk Factors in the Returns on Stocks and Bonds," *Journal of Financial Economics* 33, no. 1 (February 1993): 3–56; "Size and Book-to-Market Factors in Earnings and Returns," *Journal of Finance* 50, no. 1 (March 1995): 131–155; and "Multifactor Explanations of Asset Pricing Anomalies," *Journal of Finance* 51, no. 1 (March 1996): 55–84.

[33] Reinganum, "Misspecification of Capital Asset Pricing." Also see Rolf W. Banz and William J. Breen, "Sample Dependent Results Using Accounting and Market Data: Some Evidence," *Journal of Finance* 41, no. 4 (September 1986): 779–793.

[34] This view is not universally held. See Jeffrey Jaffe, Donald B. Keim, and Randolph Westerfield, "Earnings Yields, Market Values, and Stock Returns," *Journal of Finance* 44, no. 1 (March 1989): 135–138.

[35] Fama and French, "The Cross-Section of Expected Stock Returns." Also see Peter J. Knez and Mark J. Ready, "On the Robustness of Size and Book-to-Market in Cross-Sectional Regressions," *Journal of Finance* 52, no. 4 (September 1997): 1355–1382; and Fama and French, "Multifactor Explanations of Asset Pricing Anomalies."

[36] Investors who quickly sell their shares in order to capture this price spurt are known as "flippers." Jay R. Ritter, "The Long-Run Performance of Initial Public Offerings," *Journal of Finance* 46, no. 1 (March 1991): 3–27. Also, see Roger G. Ibbotson, Jody L. Sindelar, and Jay R. Ritter, "Initial Public Offerings," *Journal of Applied Corporate Finance* 1, no. 2 (Summer 1988): 37–45. An interesting explanation for the initial underpricing is provided by Kevin Rock, "Why New Issues Are Underpriced," *Journal of Financial Economics* 15, no. 1/2 (January/February 1986): 187–212.

[37] Securities and Exchange Commission, *Report of Special Study on Security Markets* 1973. Also see Roger G. Ibbotson, "Price Performance of Common Stock New Issues," *Journal of Financial Economics* 2, no. 3 (September 1975): 235–272.

[38] See Stewart C. Myers and Nicholas S. Majluf, "Corporate Financing and Investment Decisions When Firms Have Information That Investors Do Not Have," *Journal of Financial Economics* 13, no. 2 (June 1984): 187–221, and Wayne H. Mikkelson and M. Megan Partch, "Valuation Effects of Security Offerings and the Issuance Process," *Journal of Financial Economics* 15, no. 1/2 (January/February 1986): 31–60.

[39] See Ronald W. Masulis and Ashok N. Korwar, "Seasoned Equity Offerings: An Empirical Investigation," *Journal of Financial Economics* 15, no. 1/2 (January/February 1986): 91–118.

[40] See Tim Loughran and Jay R. Ritter, "The New Issues Puzzle," *Journal of Finance* 50, no. 1 (March 1995): 23–51. This study also looked at 4,753 ipo's that were issued during 1970–1990, and found that they too had significant negative abnormal returns over the five-year period after issuance. Also see D. Katherine Spiess and John Affleck-Graves, "Underperformance in Long-Run Stock Returns Following Seasoned Equity Offerings," *Journal of Financial Economics* 38, no. 3 (July 1995): 243–267.

---

[41] See Sanjai Bhagat, M. Wayne Marr, and G. Rodney Thompson, "The Rule 415 Experiment: Equity Markets," *Journal of Finance* 40, no. 5 (December 1985): 1385–1401.

[42] A more recent study has confirmed these findings. See Wayne H. Mikkelson and M. Megan Partch, "Stock Price Effects and Costs of Secondary Distributions," *Journal of Financial Economics* 14, no. 2 (June 1985): 165–194.

[43] See "Multifactor Explanations of Asset Pricing Anomalies." Another possible anomaly involves financial leverage. More specifically, the stocks of firms with larger debt-to-equity ratios have, on average, larger stock returns. See Laxmi Chand Bhandari, "Debt/Equity Ratio and Expected Common Stock Returns: Empirical Evidence," *Journal of Finance* 43, no. 2 (June 1988): 507–528.

[44] There is also evidence of a "weather effect" in that NYSE stock returns appear to be related to the amount of cloud cover in New York City. More specifically, the average daily return was .13% when the cloud cover was 0% to 20% and .02% when the the cloud cover was 100%. This difference has been interpreted to mean that investor psychology influences asset prices. See Edward M. Saunders Jr., "Stock Prices and Wall Street Weather," *American Economic Review* 83, no. 5 (December 1993): 1337–1345.

[45] Michael S. Rozeff and William R. Kinney Jr., "Capital Market Seasonality: The Case of Stock Returns," *Journal of Financial Economics* 3, no. 4 (October 1976): 379–402. For an argument that the market does not have a January effect, see Jay R. Ritter and Navin Chopra, "Portfolio Rebalancing and the Turn-of-the-Year Effect," *Journal of Finance* 44, no. 1 (March 1989): 149–166.

[46] Interestingly, it appears that the returns over the first half of any month (defined to include the last day of the previous month) are significantly higher than the returns over the second half of the month. See Robert A. Ariel, "A Monthly Effect in Stock Returns," *Journal of Financial Economics* 18, no. 1 (March 1987): 161–174. Another study found this effect to be concentrated in the first three trading days (plus the last trading day of the previous month) and labeled it the **turn-of-the-month effect**. See Josef Lakonishok and Seymour Smidt, "Are Seasonal Anomalies Real? A Ninety-Year Perspective," *Review of Financial Studies* 1, no. 4 (Winter 1988): 403–425.

[47] Kenneth R. French, "Stock Returns and the Weekend Effect," *Journal of Financial Economics* 8, no. 1 (March 1980): 55–69; and Michael R. Gibbons and Patrick Hess, "Day of the Week Effects and Asset Returns," *Journal of Business* 54, no. 4 (October 1981): 579–596. It has been contended that the weekend effect was actually first discovered in the late 1920s. See Edwin D. Maberly, "Eureka! Eureka! Discovery of the Monday Effect Belongs to the Ancient Scribes," *Financial Analysts Journal* 51, no. 5 (Sepetember/October 1995): 10–11. For an argument that this effect disappeared in the mid-1970s, see Robert A. Connolly, "An Examination of the Robustness of the Weekend Effect," *Journal of Financial and Quantitative Analysis* 24, no. 2 (June 1989): 133–169. It has been observed that NYSE trading volume is lower on Monday than on any other day of the week but that trading by individuals is highest on Mondays (and thus institutional trading is much lower) and that individuals tend to be net sellers on Monday. This behavior is offered as a possible explanation for the day-of-the-week effect; see Josef Lakonishok and Edwin Maberly, "The Weekend Effect: Trading Patterns of Individual and Institutional Investors," *Journal of Finance* 45, no. 1 (March 1990): 231–243.

[48] Lawrence Harris, "How to Profit from Intradaily Stock Returns," *Journal of Portfolio Management* 12, no. 2 (Winter 1986): 61–64; and "A Transaction Data Study of Weekly and Intradaily Patterns in Stock Returns," *Journal of Financial Economics* 16, no. 1 (May 1986): 99–117.

[49] This rise in stock prices at the end of the day appears to be primarily due to a large price rise between the next to last and last trades; this observation appears to be widespread over firms and days of the week. See Lawrence Harris, "A Day-End Transaction Price Anomaly," *Journal of Financial and Quantitative Analysis* 24, no. 1 (March 1989): 29–45.

[50] Robert A. Ariel, "High Stock Returns before Holidays: Existence and Evidence on Possible Causes," *Journal of Finance* 45, no. 5 (December 1990): 1611–1626. Also see Paul Brockman, "A Review and Analysis of the Holiday Effect," *Financial Markets, Institutions & Instruments* 4, no. 5 (1995): 37–58 The holiday effect also exists in Japan and the United Kingdom. See Chan-Wang Kim and Jinwoo Park, "Holiday Effects and Stock Returns: Further Evidence," *Journal of Financial and Quantitative Analysis* 29, no. 1 (March 1994): 145–157.

[51] Other interrelationships are discussed in the 4th edition of this book (Englewood Cliffs, NJ: Prentice Hall, 1990), pp. 451–457.

[52] Donald B. Keim, "Size-related Anomalies and Stock Return Seasonality: Further Empirical Evidence," *Journal of Financial Economics* 12, no. 1 (June 1983): 13–32.

[53] Rogalski also found that the anomalous price behavior of stocks in January occurs mostly in the first five trading days. Roll has observed that the largest daily differences in the returns between small firms and large firms occur over the last trading day of the year and the first four trading days of the year. Furthermore, eight of the subsequent ten trading days also have notably large differences in returns. See Richard Rogalski, "New Findings Regarding Day-of-the-Week Returns over Trading and Non-Trading Periods: A Note," *Journal of Finance* 39, no. 5 (December 1984): 1603–1614; and Richard Roll, "Vas Ist Das?" *Journal of Portfolio Management* 9, no. 2 (Winter 1983): 18–28.

[54] See Roll, "Vas Ist Das?"; Edward A. Dyl, "Capital Gains Taxation and Year-End Stock Market Behavior," *Journal of Finance* 32, no. 1 (March 1977): 165–175; Ben Branch, "A Tax Loss Trading Rule," *Journal of Business* 50, no. 2 (April 1977): 198–207; Dan Givoly and Arie Ovadia, "Year-End Tax-Induced Sales and Stock Market Seasonality," *Journal of Finance* 38, no. 1 (March 1983): 171–185; Marc R. Reinganum, "The Anomalous Stock Market Behavior of Small Firms in January: Empirical Tests for Tax-Loss Selling Effects," *Journal of Financial Economics* 12, no. 1 (June 1983): 89–104; Josef Lakonishok and Seymour Smidt, "Capital Gain Taxation and Volume of Trading," *Journal of Finance* 41, no. 4 (September 1986): 951–974; Jay R. Ritter, "The Buying and Selling Behavior of Individual Investors at the Turn of the Year," *Journal of Finance* 43, no. 3 (July 1988): 701–717; Joseph P. Ogden, "Turn-of-Month Evaluations of Liquid Profits and Stock Returns: A Common Explanation for the Monthly and January Effects," *Journal of Finance,* 45, no. 4 (September 1990): 1259–1272; and Greggory A. Brauer and Eric C. Chang, "Return Seasonality in Stocks and Their Underlying Assets: Tax-Loss Selling versus Information Explanations," *Review of Financial Studies* 3, no. 2 (1990): 255–280.

[55] See K. C. Chan, "Can Tax-Loss Selling Explain the January Seasonal in Stock Returns?" *Journal of Finance* 41, no. 5 (December 1986): 1115–1128; Werner F. M. DeBondt and Richard Thaler, "Does the Stock Market Overreact?" *Journal of Finance* 40, no. 3 (July 1985), 793–805; and "Further Evidence on Investor Over-Reaction and Stock Market Seasonality," *Journal of Finance* 42, no. 3 (July 1987): 557–581.

[56] A similar observation has been made regarding Canada. See Angel Berges, John J. McConnell, and Gary G. Schlarbaum, "The Turn-of-the-Year in Canada," *Journal of Finance* 39, no. 1 (March 1984): 185–192.

[57] See Steven L. Jones, Winson Lee, and Rudolf Apenbrink, "New Evidence on the January Effect before Personal Income Taxes," *Journal of Finance* 46, no. 5 (December 1991): 1909–1924.

[58] Richard J. Rogalski and Seha M. Tinic, "The January Size Effect: Anomaly or Risk Mismeasurement?" *Financial Analysts Journal* 42, no. 6 (November/December 1986): 63–70. See also Avner Arbel, "Generic Stocks: An Old Product in a New Package," *Journal of Portfolio Management* 11, no. 4 (Summer 1985): 4–13; and K. C. Chan and Nai-Fu Chen, "Structural and Return Characteristics of Small and Large Firms," *Journal of Finance* 46, no. 4 (September 1991): 1467–1484.

[59] The BV/MV ratio anomaly was found to exist in other countries, particularly France, Switzerland, and Japan, suggesting that value stocks have outperformed growth stocks outside the United States. See Carlo Capaul, Ian Rowley, and William F. Sharpe, "International Value and Growth Stock Returns," *Financial Analysts Journal* 49, no. 1 (January/February 1993): 27–36.

[60] See Kiyoshi Kato and James S. Schallheim, "Seasonal and Size Anomalies in the Japanese Stock Market," *Journal of Financial and Quantitative Analysis* 20, no. 2 (June 1985): 243–260; and Yasushi Hamao, "Fifteen-Year Performance of Japanese Capital Markets," in Edwin J. Elton and Martin J. Gruber (eds.), *Japanese Capital Markets* (New York: Ballinger, 1990), pp. 3–26.

[61] See Kato and Schallheim, "Seasonal and Size Anomalies"; and Mustafa N. Gultekin and N. Bulent Gultekin, "Stock Market Seasonality: International Evidence," *Journal of Financial Economics* 12, no. 4 (December 1983): 469–481.

[62] See Jeffrey Jaffe and Randolph Westerfield, "Patterns in Japanese Common Stock Returns: Day of the Week and Turn of the Year Effects," *Journal of Financial and Quantitative Analysis*

20, no. 2 (June 1985): 261–272; "The Weekend Effect in Common Stock Returns: The International Evidence," *Journal of Finance* 40, no. 2 (June 1985): 433–454; and Kiyoshi Kato, Sandra L. Schwartz, and William T. Ziemba, "Day of the Week Effects in Japanese Stocks," in Martin and Gruber (eds.), *Japanese Capital Markets*, pp. 249–281.

[63] More recently there has been some evidence that the day-of-the-week effect has become much less noticeable in both the United States and Japan. See Connolly, "An Examination of the Robustness of the Weekend Effect"; and Eric C. Chang, J. Michael Pinegar, and R. Ravichandron, "International Evidence on the Robustness of the Day-of-the-Week Effect," *Journal of Financial and Quantitative Analysis* 28, no. 4 (December 1993): 497–513.

[64] Additional patterns have been discovered. Imagine splitting the set of Mondays in two with one set corresponding to Mondays that follow a week in which the market declined and the second set corresponding to Mondays that follow a week in which the market rose. Interestingly, in both the United States and Japan, the average return for the first set of Mondays is significantly negative (−.39% in the United States and −.18% in Japan), whereas the average return for the second set of Mondays is slightly positive (.06% in the United States and .11% in Japan). See Jeffrey F. Jaffe, Randolph Westerfield, and Christopher Ma, "A Twist on the Monday Effect in Stock Prices: Evidence from the U.S. and Foreign Stock Markets," *Journal of Banking and Finance* 13, no. 4/5 (September 1989): 641–650.

[65] These recommendations are based on studies that typically involved exchange-listed stocks. For over-the-counter stocks, Richard D. Fortin and O. Maurice Joy ["Buying and Selling OTC Stock: Fine-Tuning Your Trade Date," *AAII Journal* 15, no. 3 (March 1993): 8–10] recommend (1) buying just before and selling just after the end of the month, (2) buying on Tuesday and selling on Friday, and (3) buying within two days on either side of a holiday and avoiding selling during this period.

[66] See Donald B. Keim, "Trading Patterns, Bid-Ask Spreads, and Estimated Security Returns: The Case of Common Stocks at Calendar Turning Points," *Journal of Financial Economics* 25, no. 1 (November 1989): 75–97.

[67] The Appendix to Chapter 15 discusses regularities in the bond market.

[68] Adjusted betas are also published in the *Value Line Investment Survey*; their adjusted beta is equal to $(.35 \times 1.0) + (.67 \times \beta_h)$. Thus the adjustment procedures of Value Line and Merrill Lynch are quite similar. See Meir Statman, "Betas Compared: Merrill Lynch vs. Value Line," *Journal of Portfolio Management* 7, no. 2 (Winter 1981): 41–44; and Frank K. Reilly and David J. Wright, "A Comparison of Published Betas," *Journal of Portfolio Management* 14, no. 3 (Spring 1988): 64–69.

[69] The method is developed more fully in Stephen A. Ross, Randolph W. Westerfield, and Jeffrey Jaffe, *Corporate Finance* (Boston: Irwin McGraw-Hill, 1996), pp. 322, 469; Richard A. Brealey and Stewart C. Myers, *Principles of Corporate Finance* (New York: McGraw-Hill, 1991), pp. 191–192, 468–469; and Thomas E. Copeland and J. Fred Weston, *Financial Theory and Corporate Policy* (Reading, MA: Addison-Wesley, 1988), Chapter 13.

[70] To derive Equation (16.13), note that Equation (16.12) can be written as $V_u = D + E - \tau D$ since $V_L = D + E$. Hence the quantity $D + E - \tau D$ can be substituted for V_u in Equation (16.13), and then the altered equation can be solved for β_{equity} and simplified, resulting in Equation (16.14).

[71] It is assumed here that ABC's bond beta and average tax rate were unaffected by the new issuance of equity. More complex analyses are sometimes used to take into account the possible impact of capital structure changes upon bond betas and average tax rates.

[72] The term $(E_{ind1}\beta_{ind1} + E_{ind2}\beta_{ind2})$ would simply be expanded if more than two industries were involved.

[73] In this method, both historical and adjusted betas are calculated relative to a value-weighted index of the returns on all stocks listed on the New York Stock Exchange. All attributes were calculated using data available a full month prior to the beginning of the month in which stock returns are measured. This method avoids statistical problems and provides results that can be used for actual portfolio management.

[74] The dividend yield is measured in percent per year. The "size attribute" is calculated by taking the logarithm (to the base 10) of the total market value of equity outstanding (that is, price per share times shares outstanding), expressed in billions of dollars.

---

[75] Barr Rosenberg and Vinay Marathe, "The Prediction of Investment Risk: Systematic and Residual Risk," *Proceedings of the Seminar on the Analysis of Security Prices* University of Chicago, November 1975. Also see Barr Rosenberg, "Prediction of Common Stock Investment Risk," *Journal of Portfolio Management* 11, no. 1 (Fall 1984): 44–53, and "Prediction of Common Stock Betas," *Journal of Portfolio Management* 11, no. 2 (Winter 1985): 5–14.

KEY WORDS

common stock
limited liability
charter
transfer agent
registrar
proxy
proxy fight
cumulative voting system
majority voting system
takeover
tender offer
bidder
target firm
merger
management buyout
leveraged buyout
white knight
greenmail
repurchase offer
Pac-Man defense
crown jewel defense
poison pill defense
par value
book value of the equity
book value per share
treasury stock
restricted stock
letter stock
dividends
date of record
ex-dividend date
stock dividend
stock split
reverse stock split
ex-distribution date
preemptive rights
rights
oversubscription privilege
rights offering
subscription price
ex-rights date
closing price

dividend yield
ex ante
ex post
historical beta
simple linear regression
standard deviation of the random
 error term
standard error of beta
standard error of alpha
coefficient of determination
coefficient of nondetermination
R-squared
residual standard deviation
adjusted beta
growth stocks
value stocks
size effect
primary market
investment bankers
private placements
syndicate
underwrite
selling group
competitive bidding
registration statement
prospectus
red herring
firm commitment
standby agreement
best-efforts basis
pegging
initial public offerings
unseasoned offerings
shelf registration
size effect
empirical regularities
anomalies
January effect
day-of-the-week effect
turn-of-the-month effect
holiday effect

REFERENCES

1. Corporate governance issues are discussed in:

   Bevis Longstreth, "Corporate Governance: There's Danger in New Orthodoxies," *Journal of Portfolio Management* 21, no. 3 (Spring 1995): 47–52.

   Adrei Shliefer and Robert W. Vishny, "A Survey of Corporate Governance," *Journal of Finance* 52, no. 2 (June 1997): 737–783.

2. For a discussion of the motivations for takeovers and the associated consequences, see:

   Michael C. Jensen and Richard S. Ruback, "The Market for Corporate Control: The Scientific Evidence," *Journal of Financial Economics* 11, nos. 1–4 (April 1983): 5–50.

   Richard Roll, "The Hubris Hypothesis of Corporate Takeovers," *Journal of Business* 59, no. 1, pt. 2 (April 1986): 197–216.

   Michael C. Jensen, "Corporate Control and the Politics of Finance," *Journal of Applied Corporate Finance* 4, no. 2 (Summer 1991): 13–33.

   Andrei Shleifer and Robert W. Vishny, "The Takeover Wave of the 1980s," *Journal of Applied Corporate Finance* 4, no. 3 (Fall 1991): 49–56.

   Jack Treynor, "The Value of Control," *Financial Analysts Journal* 49, no. 5 (July/August 1993): 6–9.

   J. Fred Weston, Kwang S. Chung, and Susan E. Hoag, *Mergers, Restructuring, and Corporate Control* (Upper Saddle River, NJ: Prentice Hall, 1998).

3. For a study of how risk arbitrageurs (investors who buy and sell stocks of firms involved in takeovers and divestitures) are able to earn substantial returns, see:

   David F. Larcker and Thomas Lys, "An Empirical Analysis of the Incentives to Engage in Costly Information Acquisition: The Case of Risk Arbitrage," *Journal of Financial Economics* 18, no. 1 (March 1987): 111–126.

4. Some interesting studies of stock repurchases are:

   Larry Y. Dann, "Common Stock Repurchases: An Analysis of Returns to Bondholders and Stockholders," *Journal of Financial Economics* 9, no. 2 (June 1981): 113–138.

   Theo Vermaelen, "Common Stock Repurchases and Market Signaling: An Empirical Study," *Journal of Financial Economics* 9, no. 2 (June 1981): 139–183.

   Aharon R. Ofer and Anjan V. Thakor, "A Theory of Stock Price Reponses to Alternative Corporate Cash Disbursement Methods: Stock Repurchases and Dividends," *Journal of Finance* 42, no, 2 (June 1987): 365–394.

   George M. Constantinides and Bruce D. Grundy, "Optimal Investment with Stock Repurchase and Financing as Signals," *Review of Financial Studies* 2, no. 4 (1989): 445–465.

   Josef Lakonishok and Theo Vermaelen, "Anomalous Price Behavior around Repurchase Tender Offers," *Journal of Finance* 45, no. 2 (June 1990): 455–477.

   Robert Comment and Gregg A. Jarrell, "The Relative Signalling Power of Dutch-Auction and Fixed-Price Self-Tender Offers and Open-Market Share Repurchases," *Journal of Finance* 46, no. 4 (September 1991): 1243–1271.

   Laurie Simon Bagwell, "Dutch Auction Repurchases: An Analysis of Shareholder Heterogeneity," *Journal of Finance* 47, no. 1 (March 1992): 71–105.

   David Ikenberry, Josef Lakonishok, and Theo Vermaelen, "Market Underreaction to Open Market Share Repurchases," *Journal of Financial Economics* 39, nos. 2, 3 (October/November 1995): 181–208.

5. Stock splits and stock dividends are examined in:

   Eugene F. Fama, Lawrence Fisher, Michael C. Jensen, and Richard Roll, "The Adjustment of Stock Prices to New Information," *International Economic Review* 10, no. 1 (February 1969): 1–21.

   Sasson Bar-Yosef and Lawrence D. Brown, "A Re-examination of Stock Splits Using Moving Betas," *Journal of Finance* 32, no. 4 (September 1977): 1069–1080.

Guy Charest, "Split Information, Stock Returns, and Market Efficiency—I," *Journal of Financial Economics* 6, no. 2/3 (June/September 1978): 265–296.

Thomas E. Copeland, "Liquidity Changes Following Stock Splits," *Journal of Finance* 34, no. 1 (March 1979): 115–141.

J. Randall Woolridge, "Ex-Date Stock Price Adjustment to Stock Dividends: A Note," *Journal of Finance* 38, no. 1 (March 1983): 247–255.

J. Randall Woolridge and Donald R. Chambers, "Reverse Splits and Shareholder Wealth," *Financial Management* 12, no. 3 (Autumn 1983): 5–15.

Mark S. Grinblatt, Ronald W. Masulis, and Sheridan Titman, "The Valuation Effects of Stock Splits and Stock Dividends," *Journal of Financial Economics* 13, no. 4 (December 1984): 461–490.

Josef Lakonishok and Baruch Lev, "Stock Splits and Stock Dividends: Why, Who, and When," *Journal of Finance* 42, no. 4 (September 1987): 913–932.

Christopher G. Lamoureux and Percy Poon, The Market Reaction to Stock Splits," *Journal of Finance* 42, no. 5 (December 1987): 1347–1370.

Michael J. Brennan and Thomas E. Copeland, "Stock Splits, Stock Prices, and Transactions Costs," *Journal of Financial Economics* 22, no. 1 (October 1988): 83–101.

Maureen McNichols and Ajay Dravid, "Stock Dividends, Stock Splits, and Signaling," *Journal of Finance* 45, no. 3 (July 1990): 857–879.

Robert S. Conroy, Robert S. Harris, and Bruce A. Benet, "The Effects of Stock Splits on Bid-Ask Spreads," *Journal of Finance* 45, no. 4 (September 1990): 1285–1295.

David A. Dubofsky, "Volatility Increases Subsequent to NYSE and AMEX Stock Splits," *Journal of Finance* 46, no. 1 (March 1991): 421–431.

Michael J. Brennan and Patricia J. Hughes, "Stock Prices and the Supply of Information," *Journal of Finance* 46, no, 5 (December 1991): 1665–1691.

Michael T. Maloney and J. Harold Mulherin, "The Effects of Splitting on the Ex: A Microstructure Reconciliation," *Financial Management* 21, no. 4 (Winter 1992): 44–59.

H. Kent Baker, Aaron L. Phillips, and Gary E. Powell, "The Stock Distribution Puzzle: A Synthesis of the Literature on Stock Splits and Stock Dividends," *Financial Practice and Education* 5, no. 1 (Spring/Summer 1995): 24–37.

Eugene Pilotte and Timothy Manuel, "The Market's Response to Recurring Events: The Case of Stock Splits," *Journal of Financial Economics* 41, no. 1 (May 1996): 111–127.

David L. Ikenberry, Graeme Rankine, and Earl K. Stice, "What Do Stock Splits Really Signal?" *Journal of Financial and Quantitative Analysis* 31, no. 3 (September 1996): 357–375.

Chris J. Muscarella and Michael R. Vetsuypens, "Stock Splits: Signaling or Liquidity? The Case of ADR 'Solo Splits'," *Journal of Financial Economics* 42, no. 1 (September 1996): 3–26.

James J. Angel, "Tick Size, Share Prices, and Stock Splits," *Journal of Finance* 52, no. 2 (June 1997): 655–681.

James J. Angel, "Picking Your Tick: Toward a New Theory of Stock Splits," *Journal of Applied Corporate Finance* 10, no. 3 (Fall 1997): 59–68.

6. References for the relationship between size and return are contained in the endnotes. The characteristics of value and growth stocks are described in:

Ken Gregory, "Fund Investment Strategies: Growth vs. Value Investing," *AAII Journal* 11, no. 9 (October 1989): 22–25.

David E. Tierney and Kenneth J. Winston, "Using Generic Benchmarks to Present Manager Styles," *Journal of Portfolio Management* 17, no. 4 (Summer 1991): 33–36.

John Bajkowski, "A Question of Style: Growth and Value Investing," *AAII Journal* 14, no. 5 (June 1992): 33–37.

John Bajkowski, "Creating Stock Screens That Make Practical Sense," *AAII Journal* 15, no. 6 (July 1993): 34–37.

Louis K. C. Chan, Narasimhan Jegadeesh, and Josef Lakonishok, "Evaluating the Performance of Value versus Glamour Stocks: The Impact of Selection Bias," *Journal of Financial Economics* 38, no. 3 (July 1995): 269–296.

Rafael La Porta, Josef Lakonishok, Andrei Shleifer, and Robert Vishny, "Good News for Value Stocks: Further Evidence on Market Efficiency," *Journal of Finance* 52, no. 2 (June 1997): 859–874.

7. For more on investment banking, see the citations given in the endnotes and:

Richard A. Brealey and Stewart C. Myers, *Principles of Corporate Finance* (New York: McGraw-Hill, 1996), Chapter 15.

Stephen A. Ross, Randolph W. Westerfield, and Jeffrey F. Jaffe, *Corporate Finance* (Chicago: Irwin, 1996), Chapters 19–20.

8. Many of the studies conducted concerning various empirical regularities are cited in the endnotes. Also see:

Donald B. Keim, "The CAPM and Equity Return Regularities," *Financial Analysts Journal* 42, no. 3 (May/June 1986): 19–34.

Michael Smirlock and Laura Starks, "Day-of-the-Week and Intraday Effects in Stock Returns," *Journal of Financial Economics* 17, no. 1 (September 1986): 197–210.

Richard H. Thaler, "Anomalies: The January Effect," *Journal of Economic Perspectives* 1, no. 1 (Summer 1987): 197–201; and "Anomalies: Seasonal Movements in Security Prices II—Weekend, Holiday, Turn of the Month, and Intraday Effects," *Journal of Economic Perspectives* 1, no. 2 (Fall 1987): 169–177.

Douglas K. Pearce, "Challenges to the Concept of Market Efficiency," *Federal Reserve Bank of Kansas City Economic Review* 72, no. 8 (September/October 1987): 16–33.

Elroy Dimson (ed.), *Stock Market Anomalies* (Cambridge, England: Cambridge University Press, 1988).

Robert A. Haugen and Josef Lakonishok, *The Incredible January Effect* (Homewood, IL: Dow Jones-Irwin, 1988).

Burton G. Malkiel, *A Random Walk Down Wall Street* (New York: W. W. Norton, 1990), Chapter 8.

Eugene F. Fama, "Efficient Capital Markets: II," *Journal of Finance* 46, no. 5 (December 1991): 1575–1617.

Narasimhan Jegadeesh, "Does Market Risk Really Explain the Size Effect?" *Journal of Financial and Quantitative Analysis* 27, no. 3 (September 1992): 337–351.

Mark D. Griffiths and Robert W. White, "Tax-Induced Trading and the Turn-of-the-Year Anomaly: An Intraday Study," *Journal of Finance* 48, no. 2 (June 1993): 575–598.

Rick A. Cooper and Joel M. Shulman, "The Year-End Effect in Junk Bond Prices," *Financial Analysts Journal* 50, no. 5 (September/October 1994): 61–65.

Josef Lakonishok, Andrei Shliefer, and Robert W. Vishny, "Contrarian Investment, Extrapolation, and Risk," *Journal of Finance* 49, no. 5 (December 1994): 1541–1578.

David K. Musto, "Portfolio Disclosures and Year-End Price Shifts," *Journal of Finance* 52 no. 4 (September 1997): 1563–1588.

Richard W. Sias and Laura T. Starks, "Institutions and Individuals at the Turn-of-the-Year," *Journal of Finance* 52, no. 4 (September 1997): 1543–1562.

9. For a tongue-in-cheek article on anomalies that shows that market returns are influenced by superstition because returns on Friday the 13th are, on average, abnormally low, see:

Robert W. Kolb and Ricardo J. Rodriguez, "Friday the Thirteenth: 'Part VII'—A Note," *Journal of Finance* 42, no. 5 (December 1987): 1385–1387.

10. The behavior of beta coefficients has been extensively studied. See, for example:

Marshall Blume, "On the Assessment of Risk," *Journal of Finance* 26, no. 1 (March 1971): 1–10.

Robert A. Levy, "On the Short-Term Stationarity of Beta Coefficients," *Financial Analysts Journal* 27, no. 6 (November/December 1971): 55–62.

William F. Sharpe and Guy M. Cooper, "Risk-Return Classes of New York Stock Exchange Common Stocks, 1931–1967," *Financial Analysts Journal* 28, no. 2 (March/April 1972): 46–54.

Robert S. Hamada, "The Effect of the Firm's Capital Structure on the Systematic Risk of Common Stocks," *Journal of Finance* 27, no. 2 (May 1972): 435–452.

Marshall Blume, "Betas and Their Regression Tendencies," *Journal of Finance* 30, no. 3 (June 1975): 785–795.

Barr Rosenberg and Vinay Marathe, "The Prediction of Investment Risk: Systematic and Residual Risk," *Proceedings of the Seminar on the Analysis of Security Prices*, Center for Research in Security Prices, Graduate School of Business, University of Chicago, November 1975.

Barr Rosenberg and James Guy, "Prediction of Beta from Investment Fundamentals," *Financial Analysts Journal* 32, no. 3 (May/June 1976): 60–72, and no. 4 (July/August 1976): 62–70.

Meir Statman, "Betas Compared: Merrill Lynch vs. Value Line," *Journal of Portfolio Management* 7, no. 2 (Winter 1981): 41–44.

Diana R. Harrington, "Whose Beta Is Best?" *Financial Analysts Journal* 39, no. 5 (July/August 1983): 67–73.

Barr Rosenberg, "Prediction of Common Stock Investment Risk," *Journal of Portfolio Management* 11, no. 1 (Fall 1984): 44–53.

Barr Rosenberg, "Prediction of Common Stock Betas," *Journal of Portfolio Management* 11, no. 2 (Winter 1985): 5–14.

Gordon J. Alexander and Jack Clark Francis, *Portfolio Analysis* (Upper Saddle River, NJ: Prentice Hall, 1986): 185–192.

George Foster, *Financial Statement Analysis* (Upper Saddle River, NJ: Prentice Hall, 1986), Chapter 10.

Thomas E. Copeland and J. Fred Weston, *Financial Theory and Corporate Policy* (Reading, MA: Addison-Wesley, 1988), Chapter 13.

Frank K. Reilly and David J. Wright, "A Comparison of Published Betas," *Journal of Portfolio Management* 14, no. 3 (Spring 1988): 64–69.

Richard A. Brealey and Stewart C. Myers, *Principles of Corporate Finance* (New York: McGraw-Hill, 1991): 191–192, 468–469.

Louis K. C. Chan and Josef Lakonishok, "Robust Measurement of Beta Risk," *Journal of Financial and Quantitative Analysis* 27, no. 2 (June 1992): 265–282.

Stephon A Ross, Randolph W. Westerfield, and Jeffrey Jaffe, *Corporate Finance* (Chicago: Irwin, 1996): 322, 469.

THE VALUATION OF COMMON STOCKS

$\mathbf{I}$n Chapter 1 it was noted that one purpose of security analysis is to identify mispriced securities. Fundamental analysis was mentioned as one approach for conducting a search for such securities. With this approach the security analyst makes estimates of such things as the firm's future earnings and dividends. If these estimates are substantially different from the average estimates of other analysts but are felt to be more accurate, then from the viewpoint of the security analyst, a mispriced security has been identified. If it is also felt that the market price of the security will adjust to reflect these more accurate estimates, then the security will be expected to have an abnormal rate of return. Accordingly, the analyst will issue either a buy or a sell recommendation, depending on the direction of the anticipated price adjustment. Based on the capitalization of income method of valuation (also known as the *discounted cash flow* approach), dividend discount models have frequently been used by fundamental analysts as a means of identifying mispriced stocks.[1] This chapter will discuss dividend discount models and how they can be related to models based on price-earnings ratios.

17.1   CAPITALIZATION OF INCOME METHOD OF VALUATION

There are many ways to implement the fundamental analysis approach to identifying mispriced securities. Some of them are either directly or indirectly related to what is sometimes referred to as the **capitalization of income method of valuation**.[2] This method states that the "true," or "intrinsic," value of any asset is based on the cash flows that the investor expects to receive in the future from owning the asset. Because these cash flows are expected in the future, they are adjusted by a **discount rate** to reflect not only the time value of money but also the riskiness of the cash flows. Chapter 14 introduced the capitalization of income method of valuation and applied it to fixed-income securities. In this chapter the method is considered in more detail and then applied to common stocks.

Algebraically, the intrinsic value V of an asset is equal to the sum of the present values of the asset's expected cash flows:

$$V = \frac{C_1}{(1 + k)^1} + \frac{C_2}{(1 + k)^2} + \frac{C_3}{(1 + k)^3} + \cdots$$

$$= \sum_{t=1}^{\infty} \frac{C_t}{(1 + k)^t} \qquad (17.1)$$

where C_t denotes the expected cash flow associated with the asset at time t, and k is the appropriate discount rate for cash flows of this degree of risk. In this equation the discount rate is assumed to be the same for all periods. Because the symbol ∞ above the summation sign in the equation denotes infinity, all expected cash flows, from immediately after making the investment until infinity, will be discounted at the same rate in determining $V.$[3]

17.1.1   Net Present Value

For the sake of convenience, let the current moment in time be denoted as zero, or $t = 0$. If the cost of purchasing an asset at $t = 0$ is P, then its **net present value** (NPV) is equal to the difference between its intrinsic value and cost, or:

$$NPV = V - P$$

$$= \left[\sum_{t=1}^{\infty} \frac{C_t}{(1 + k)^t} \right] - P \qquad (17.2)$$

The NPV calculation shown here is conceptually the same as the NPV calculation made for capital budgeting decisions that has long been advocated in introductory finance textbooks. Capital budgeting decisions involve deciding whether a given investment project should be undertaken. (For example, should a new machine be purchased?) In making this decision, the decision–maker focuses on the NPV of the project. Specifically, an investment project is viewed favorably if its NPV is positive and unfavorably if its NPV is negative. For a simple project involving a cash outflow now (at $t = 0$) and expected cash inflows in the future, a positive NPV means that the present value of all the expected cash inflows is greater than the cost of making the investment. Conversely, a negative NPV means that the present value of all the expected cash inflows is less than the cost of making the investment.

The same views about NPV apply when financial assets (such as a share of common stock), instead of real assets (such as a new machine), are being considered for purchase. That is, a financial asset is viewed favorably and is said to be underpriced (or undervalued) if NPV > 0. Conversely, a financial asset is viewed unfavorably and is said to be overpriced or (overvalued) if NPV < 0. From Equation (17.2), this is equivalent to stating that a financial asset is underpriced if $V > P$:

$$\sum_{t=1}^{\infty} \frac{C_t}{(1 + k)^t} > P \qquad (17.3)$$

Conversely, the asset is overpriced if $V < P$:

$$\sum_{t=1}^{\infty} \frac{C_t}{(1 + k)^t} < P \qquad (17.4)$$

17.1.2   Internal Rate of Return

Another way of making capital budgeting decisions in a manner that is similar to the NPV method involves calculating the **internal rate of return** (IRR) associated with the investment project. In computing the IRR, the NPV in Equation (17.2) is set equal to zero, and the discount rate becomes the unknown that must be calculated. That is, the IRR for a given investment is the discount rate that makes the NPV of the investment equal to zero. Algebraically, the procedure involves solving the following equation for the internal rate of return $k*$:

$$0 = \sum_{t=1}^{\infty} \frac{C_t}{(1 + k*)^t} - P \qquad (17.5)$$

Equivalently, Equation (17.5) can be rewritten as:

$$P = \sum_{t=1}^{\infty} \frac{C_t}{(1 + k*)^t} \qquad (17.6)$$

The decision rule for IRR involves comparing the project's IRR (denoted by $k*$) with the required rate of return for an investment of similar risk (denoted by k). Specifically, the investment is viewed favorably if $k* > k$, and unfavorably if $k* < k$. As with NPV, the same decision rule applies if either a real asset or a financial asset is being considered for possible investment.[4]

17.1.3 Application to Common Stocks

This chapter is concerned with using the capitalization of income method to determine the intrinsic value of common stocks. Because the cash flows associated with an investment in any particular common stock are the dividends that are expected to be paid throughout the future on the shares purchased, the models suggested by this method of valuation are often known as **dividend discount models** (DDMs).[5] Accordingly, D_t will be used instead of C_t to denote the expected cash flow in period t associated with a particular common stock, resulting in the following restatement of Equation (17.1):

$$V = \frac{D_1}{(1 + k)^1} + \frac{D_2}{(1 + k)^2} + \frac{D_3}{(1 + k)^3} + \cdots$$

$$= \sum_{t=1}^{\infty} \frac{D_t}{(1 + k)^t} \qquad (17.7)$$

Usually the focus of DDMs is on determining the "true," or "intrinsic," value of one share of a particular company's common stock, even if larger purchases are being contemplated because it is assumed that larger purchases can be made at a cost that is a simple multiple of the cost of one share. (For example, the cost of 1,000 shares is usually assumed to be 1,000 times the cost of one share.) Thus the numerator in DDMs is the cash dividends per share that are expected in the future.

However, there is a complication in using Equation (17.7) to determine the intrinsic value of a share of common stock. In particular, in order to use this equation the investor must forecast *all* future dividends. Because a common stock does not have a fixed lifetime, a virtually infinite stream of dividends must be forecast. Although this may seem to be an impossible task, with the addition of certain assumptions, the equation can be made tractable (that is, usable).

These assumptions center on dividend growth rates. That is, the dividend per share at any time t can be viewed as being equal to the dividend per share at time $t - 1$ times a dividend growth rate of g_t,

$$D_t = D_{t-1}(1 + g_t) \qquad (17.8)$$

or, equivalently:

$$\frac{D_t - D_{t-1}}{D_{t-1}} = g_t \qquad (17.9)$$

For example, if the dividend per share expected at $t = 2$ is $4 and the dividend per share expected at $t = 3$ is $4.20, then $g_3 = (\$4.20 - \$4)/\$4 = 5\%$.

The different types of tractable DDMs reflect different sets of assumptions about dividend growth rates. The discussion begins with the simplest case, the zero-growth model.

17.2 THE ZERO-GROWTH MODEL

One assumption that could be made about future dividends is that they will remain at a fixed dollar amount. That is, the dollar amount of dividends per share that were paid over the past year D_0 will also be paid over the next year D_1, and the year after that D_2, and the year after that D_3, and so on; that is,

$$D_0 = D_1 = D_2 = D_3 = \ldots = D_\infty$$

This is equivalent to assuming that all the dividend growth rates are zero, because if $g_t = 0$, then $D_t = D_{t-1}$ in Equation (17.8). Accordingly, this model is often referred to as the **zero-growth** (or no-growth) **model**.

17.2.1 Net Present Value

The impact of this assumption on Equation (17.7) can be analyzed by noting what happens when D_t is replaced by D_0 in the numerator:

$$V = \sum_{t=1}^{\infty} \frac{D_0}{(1 + k)^t} \tag{17.10}$$

Fortunately, Equation (17.10) can be simplified by noting that D_0 is a fixed dollar amount, which means that it can be written outside the summation sign:

$$V = D_0 \left[\sum_{t=1}^{\infty} \frac{1}{(1 + k)^t} \right] \tag{17.11}$$

The next step involves using a property of infinite series from mathematics. If $k > 0$, then it can be shown that:

$$\sum_{t=1}^{\infty} \frac{1}{(1 + k)^t} = \frac{1}{k} \tag{17.12}$$

Applying this property to Equation (17.11) results in the following formula for the zero-growth model:

$$V = \frac{D_0}{k_0} \tag{17.13}$$

Because $D_0 = D_1$, Equation (17.13) is written sometimes as:

$$V = \frac{D_1}{k} \tag{17.14}$$

An Example

As an example of how this DDM can be used, assume that the Zinc Company is expected to pay cash dividends amounting to $8 per share into the indefinite future and has a required rate of return of 10%. Using either Equation (17.13) or Equation (17.14), one can see that the value of a share of Zinc stock is equal to $80 (=$8/.10). With a current stock price of $65 per share, Equation (17.2) would suggest that the

NPV per share is $15 (=$80 - $65). Equivalently, because $V = \$80 > P = \$65$, the stock is underpriced by $15 per share and would be a candidate for purchase.

17.2.2 Internal Rate of Return

Equation (17.13) can be reformulated to solve for the IRR on an investment in a zero-growth security. First, the security's current price P is substituted for V, and second, k^* is substituted for k. These changes result in:

$$P = \frac{D_0}{k^*}$$

which can be rewritten as:

$$k^* = \frac{D_0}{P} \tag{17.15a}$$

$$= \frac{D_1}{P} \tag{17.15b}$$

An Example

Applying this formula to the stock of Zinc indicates that $k^* = 12.3\%$ (=$8/$65). Because the IRR from an investment in Zinc exceeds the required rate of return on Zinc (12.3% > 10%), this method also indicates that Zinc is underpriced.[6]

17.2.3 Application

The zero-growth model may seem quite restrictive. After all, it seems unreasonable to assume that a given stock will pay a fixed dollar-size dividend forever. Although such a criticism has validity for common stock valuation, there is one particular situation in which this model is quite useful. Specifically, whenever the intrinsic value of a share of high-grade preferred stock is to be determined, the zero-growth DDM will often be appropriate because most preferred stock is nonparticipating. That is, it pays a fixed dollar-size dividend that will not change as earnings per share change. Furthermore, for high-grade preferred stock these dividends are expected to be paid regularly into the foreseeable future because preferred stock does not have a fixed lifetime. If the application of the zero-growth model is restricted to high-grade preferred stocks, the model is useful because the chance of a suspension of dividends is remote.[7]

| 17.3 | THE CONSTANT-GROWTH MODEL |

The next type of DDM to be considered is one that assumes that dividends will grow from period to period at the same rate forever and is therefore known as the **constant growth model**.[8] Specifically, the dividends per share that were paid over the previous year D_0 are expected to grow at a given rate g, so that the dividends expected over the next year D_1 are expected to be equal to $D_0(1 + g)$. Dividends the year after that are again expected to grow by the same rate g, meaning that $D_2 = D_1(1 + g)$. Stating that $D_1 = D_0(1 + g)$ and that the growth rate is constant is equivalent to assuming that $D_2 = D_0(1 + g)^2$ and, in general:

$$D_t = D_{t-1}(1 + g) \qquad (17.16a)$$

$$= D_0(1 + g)^t \qquad (17.16b)$$

17.3.1 Net Present Value

The impact of this assumption on Equation (17.7) can be analyzed by noting what happens when D_t is replaced by $D_0(1 + g)^t$ in the numerator:

$$V = \sum_{t=1}^{\infty} \frac{D_0(1 + g)^t}{(1 + k)^t} \qquad (17.17)$$

Similar to the zero-growth model, Equation (17.17) can be simplified by noting that D_0 is a fixed dollar amount, so it can be written outside the summation sign:

$$V = D_0 \left[\sum_{t=1}^{\infty} \frac{(1 + g)^t}{(1 + k)^t} \right] \qquad (17.18)$$

The next step involves using a property of infinite series from mathematics. If $k > g$, then it can be shown that:

$$\sum_{t=1}^{\infty} \frac{(1 + g)^t}{(1 + k)^t} = \frac{1 + g}{k - g} \qquad (17.19)$$

Substituting Equation (17.19) into Equation (17.18) results in the valuation formula for the constant-growth model:

$$V = D_0 \left(\frac{1 + g}{k - g} \right) \qquad (17.20)$$

Sometimes Equation (17.20) is rewritten as:

$$V = \frac{D_1}{k - g} \qquad (17.21)$$

because $D_1 = D_0(1 + g)$.

An Example

As an example of how this DDM can be used, assume that during the past year the Copper Company paid dividends amounting to $1.80 per share. The forecast is that dividends on Copper stock will increase by 5% per year into the indefinite future. Thus dividends over the next year are expected to equal $1.89 [=$1.80 × (1 + .05)]. Using Equation (17.20) and assuming a required rate of return k of 11%, shows that the value of a share of Copper stock is equal to $31.50 [=$1.80 × (1 + .05)/(.11 − .05) = $1.89/(.11 − .05)]. With a current stock price of $40 per share, Equation (17.2) would suggest that the NPV per share is −$8.50 (=$31.50 − $40). Equivalently, because $V = \$31.50 < P = \$40$, the stock is overpriced by $8.50 per share and would be a candidate for sale if currently owned.

17.3.2   Internal Rate of Return

Equation (17.20) can be reformulated to solve for the IRR on an investment in a constant-growth security. First, the current price of the security P is substituted for V, and then k^* is substituted for k. These changes result in:

$$P = D_0\left(\frac{1 + g}{k^* - g}\right) \tag{17.22}$$

which can be rewritten as:

$$k^* = \frac{D_0(1 + g)}{P} + g \tag{17.23a}$$

$$= \frac{D_1}{P} + g \tag{17.23b}$$

An Example

Applying this formula to the stock of Copper indicates that $k^* = 9.72\%$ $\{=[\$1.80 \times (1 + .05)/\$40] + .05 = (\$1.89/\$40) + .05\}$. Because the required rate of return on Copper exceeds the IRR from an investment in Copper ($11\% > 9.72\%$), this method also indicates that Copper is overpriced.

17.3.3   Relationship to the Zero-Growth Model

The zero-growth model can be shown to be a special case of the constant-growth model. In particular, if the growth rate g is assumed to be equal to zero, then dividends will be a fixed dollar amount forever, which is the same as saying that there will be zero growth. Letting $g = 0$ in Equations (17.20) and (17.23a) results in two equations that are identical to Equations (17.13) and (17.15a), respectively.

Even though the assumption of constant dividend growth may seem less restrictive than the assumption of zero dividend growth, it may still be viewed as unrealistic in many cases. However, as will be shown next, the constant-growth model is important because it is embedded in the multiple-growth model.

17.4   THE MULTIPLE-GROWTH MODEL

A more general DDM for valuing common stocks is the **multiple-growth model**. With this model, the focus is on a time in the future (denoted by T), after which dividends are expected to grow at a constant rate g. Although the investor is still concerned with forecasting dividends, these dividends do not need to have any specific pattern until time T, after which they will be assumed to have the specific pattern of constant growth. The dividends up to T ($D_1, D_2, D_3, \ldots, D_T$) will be forecast individually by the investor. (The investor also forecasts when this time T will occur.) Thereafter dividends are assumed to grow by a constant rate g that the investor must also forecast, meaning that:

$$D_{T+1} = D_T(1 + g)$$
$$D_{T+2} = D_{T+1}(1 + g) = D_T(1 + g)^2$$
$$D_{T+3} = D_{T+2}(1 + g) = D_T(1 + g)^3$$

and so on. Figure 17.1 presents a time line of dividends and growth rates associated with the multiple-growth model.

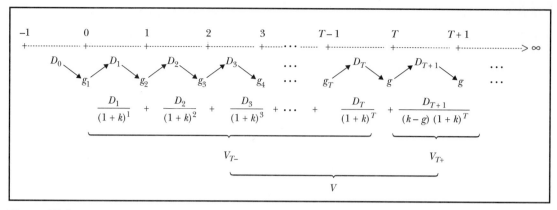

Figure 17.1
Time Line for Multiple-Growth Model

17.4.1 Net Present Value

Valuing a share of common stock with the multiple-growth model requires that the present value of the forecast stream of dividends be determined. This process can be facilitated by dividing the expected dividend stream into two parts, finding the present value of each part, and then adding these two present values together.

The first part consists of finding the present value of all the forecast dividends that will be paid up to and including time T. Denoting this present value by V_{T-}, it is equal to:

$$V_{T-} = \sum_{t=1}^{T} \frac{D_0}{(1+k)^t}$$

(17.24)

The second part consists of finding the present value of all the forecast dividends that will be paid after time T and involves the application of the constant-growth model. The application begins by imagining that the investor is not at time zero but is at time T and has not changed his or her forecast of dividends for the stock. As a result, the next period's dividend D_{T+1} and all those thereafter are expected to grow at the rate g. Because the investor would be viewing the stock as having a constant growth rate, its value at time T, V_T, can be determined with the constant-growth model of Equation (17.21):

$$V_T = D_{T+1}\left(\frac{1}{k-g}\right)$$

(17.25)

One way to view V_T is that it represents a lump sum that is just as desirable as the stream of dividends after T. That is, an investor would find a lump sum of cash equal to V_T, to be received at time T, to be equally desirable as the stream of dividends D_{T+1}, D_{T+2}, D_{T+3}, and so on. Now given that the investor is at time zero, not at time T, the present value at $t = 0$ of the lump sum V_T must be determined. This present value is found simply by discounting V_T for T periods at the rate k, resulting in the following formula for finding the present value at time zero for all dividends after T, denoted V_{T+}:

$$V_{T+} = V_T\left[\frac{1}{(1+k)^T}\right]$$

(17.26)

$$= \frac{D_{T+1}}{(k-g)(1+k)^T}$$

Having found the present value of all dividends up to and including time T with Equation (17.24), and the present value of all dividends after time T with Equation (17.26), the investor can determine the value of the stock by summing up these two amounts:

$$V = V_{T-} + V_{T+}$$

$$= \sum_{t=1}^{T} \frac{D_t}{(1+k)^t} + \frac{D_{T+1}}{(k-g)(1+k)^T} \tag{17.27}$$

Figure 17.1 illustrates the valuation procedure for the multiple-growth DDM that is given in Equation (17.27).

An Example

As an example of how this DDM can be used, assume that during the past year the Magnesium Company paid dividends amounting to $.75 per share. Over the next year, Magnesium is expected to pay dividends of $2 per share. Thus $g_1 = (D_1 - D_0)/D_0 = (\$2 - \$.75)/\$.75 = 167\%$. The year after that, dividends are expected to amount to $3 per share, indicating that $g_2 = (D_2 - D_1)/D_1 = (\$3 - \$2)/\$2 = 50\%$. At this time, the forecast is that dividends will grow by 10% per year indefinitely, indicating that $T = 2$ and $g = 10\%$. Consequently, $D_{T+1} = D_3 = \$3(1 + .10) = \$3.30$. Given a required rate of return on Magnesium shares of 15%, the values of V_{T-} and V_{T+} can be calculated as follows:

$$V_{T-} = \frac{\$2}{(1+.15)^1} + \frac{\$3}{(1+.15)^2}$$

$$= \$4.01$$

$$V_{T+} = \frac{\$3.30}{(.15-.10)(1+.15)^2}$$

$$= \$49.91$$

Summing V_{T-} and V_{T+} results in a value for V of $4.01 + $49.91 = $53.92. With a current stock price of $55 per share, Magnesium appears to be fairly priced. That is, Magnesium is not significantly mispriced because V and P are nearly of equal size.

17.4.2 Internal Rate of Return

The zero-growth and constant-growth models have equations for V that can be reformulated in order to solve for the IRR on an investment in a stock. Unfortunately, a convenient expression similar to Equations (17.15a), (17.15b), (17.23a), and (17.23b) is not available for the multiple-growth model. Note that the expression for IRR is derived by substituting P for V, and k^* for k in Equation (17.27):

$$P = \sum_{t=1}^{T} \frac{D_t}{(1+k^*)^t} + \frac{D_{T+1}}{(k^*-g)(1+k^*)^T} \tag{17.28}$$

This equation cannot be rewritten with k^* isolated on the left-hand side, so a closed-form expression for IRR does not exist for the multiple-growth model.

However, all is not lost. It is still possible to calculate the IRR for an investment in a stock conforming to the multiple-growth model by using an "educated" trial-and-error method. The basis for this method is in the observation that the right-hand side of Equation (17.28) is simply equal to the present value of the dividend stream, where k^* is used as the discount rate. Hence the larger the value of k^*, the smaller the value of the right-hand side of Equation (17.28). The trial-and-error method proceeds by initially using an estimate for k^*. If the resulting value on the right-hand side of Equation (17.28) is larger than P, then a larger estimate of k^* is tried. Conversely, if the resulting value is smaller than P, then a smaller estimate of k^* is tried. Continuing this search process, the investor can home in on the value of k^* that makes the right-hand side equal P on the left-hand side. Fortunately, it is a relatively simple matter to program a computer to conduct the search for k^* in Equation (17.28). Most spreadsheets include a function that does so automatically.

An Example

Applying Equation (17.28) to the Magnesium Company results in:

$$\$55 = \frac{\$2}{(1 + k^*)^1} + \frac{\$3}{(1 + k^*)^2} + \frac{\$3.30}{(k^* - .10)(1 + k^*)^2} \qquad (17.29)$$

Initially a rate of 14% is used in attempting to solve this equation for k^*. Inserting 14% for k^* in the right-hand side of Equation (17.29) results in a value of $67.54. Earlier 15% was used in determining V and resulted in a value of $53.92. This means that k^* must have a value between 14% and 15%, since $55 is between $67.54 and $53.92. If 14.5% is tried next, the resulting value is $59.97, suggesting that a higher rate should be tried. If 14.8% and 14.9% are subsequently tried, the respective resulting values are $56.18 and $55.03. Because $55.03 is the closest to P, the IRR associated with an investment in Magnesium is 14.9%. Given a required return of 15% and an IRR of approximately that amount, the stock of Magnesium appears to be fairly priced.

17.4.3 Relationship to the Constant-Growth Model

The constant-growth model can be shown to be a special case of the multiple-growth model. In particular, if the time when constant growth is assumed to begin is set equal to zero, then:

$$V_{T-} = \sum_{t=1}^{T} \frac{D_t}{(1 + k)^t} = 0$$

and

$$V_{T+} = \frac{D_{T+1}}{(k - g)(1 + k)^T} = \frac{D_1}{k - g}$$

because $T = 0$ and $(1 + k)^0 = 1$. Given that the multiple-growth model states that $V = V_{T-} + V_{T+}$, one can see that setting $T = 0$ results in $V = D_1/(k - g)$, a formula that is equivalent to the formula for the constant-growth model.

17.4.4 Two-Stage and Three-Stage Models

Two dividend discount models that investors sometimes use are the two-stage model and the three-stage model.[9] The two-stage model assumes that a constant growth rate g_1 exists only until some time T, when a different growth rate g_2 is assumed to begin and continue thereafter. The three-stage model assumes that a constant growth rate g_1 exists only until some time T_1, when a second growth rate is assumed to begin and last until a later time T_2, at which time a third growth rate is assumed to begin and last thereafter. Letting V_{T+} denote the present value of all dividends after the last growth rate has begun and V_{T-} denote the present value of all the preceding dividends, indicates that these models are just special cases of the multiple-growth model.

In the application of the capitalization of income method of valuation to common stocks, it might seem appropriate to assume that a particular stock will be sold at some point in the future. In this case the expected cash flows would consist of the dividends up to that point as well as the stock's expected selling price. Because dividends after the selling date would be ignored, the use of a dividend discount model may seem to be improper. However, as will be shown next, it is not.

17.5 VALUATION BASED ON A FINITE HOLDING PERIOD

The capitalization of income method of valuation involves discounting all dividends that are expected throughout the future. Because the simplified models of zero growth, constant growth, and multiple growth are based on this method, they too involve a future stream of dividends. Upon reflection one may think that such models are relevant only for an investor who plans to hold a stock forever, because only such an investor would expect to receive this stream of future dividends.

But what about an investor who plans to sell the stock in a year?[10] In such a situation, the cash flows that the investor expects to receive from purchasing a share of the stock are equal to the dividend expected to be paid one year from now (for ease of exposition, it is assumed that common stocks pay dividends annually) and the expected selling price of the stock. Thus it would seem appropriate to determine the intrinsic value of the stock to the investor by discounting these two cash flows at the required rate of return as follows:

$$V = \frac{D_1 + P_1}{(1 + k)}$$

$$= \frac{D_1}{(1 + k)} + \frac{P_1}{(1 + k)} \tag{17.30}$$

where D_1 and P_1 are the expected dividend and selling price at $t = 1$, respectively.

In order to use Equation (17.30), one must estimate the expected price of the stock at $t = 1$. The simplest approach assumes that the selling price will be based on the dividends that are expected to be paid after the selling date. Thus the expected selling price at $t = 1$ is:

$$P_1 = \frac{D_2}{(1 + k)^1} + \frac{D_3}{(1 + k)^2} + \frac{D_4}{(1 + k)^3} + \cdots$$

$$= \sum_{t=2}^{\infty} \frac{D_t}{(1 + k)^{t-1}} \tag{17.31}$$

Substituting Equation (17.31) for P_1 in the right-hand side of Equation (17.30) results in:

$$V = \frac{D_1}{(1 + k)^1} + \left[\frac{D_2}{(1 + k)^1} + \frac{D_3}{(1 + k)^2} + \frac{D_4}{(1 + k)^3} + \cdots \right] \left(\frac{1}{1 + k} \right)$$

$$= \frac{D_1}{(1 + k)^1} + \frac{D_2}{(1 + k)^2} + \frac{D_3}{(1 + k)^3} + \frac{D_4}{(1 + k)^4} + \cdots$$

$$= \sum_{t=1}^{\infty} \frac{D_t}{(1 + k)^t}$$

which is exactly the same as Equation (17.7). Thus valuing a share of common stock by discounting its dividends up to some point in the future and its expected selling price at that time is equivalent to valuing stock by discounting all future dividends.

Simply stated, the two are equivalent because the expected selling price is itself based on dividends to be paid after the selling date. Thus Equation (17.7), as well as the zero-growth, constant-growth, and multiple-growth models that are based on it, is appropriate for determining the intrinsic value of a share of common stock regardless of the length of the investor's planned holding period.

An Example

As an example, reconsider the common stock of the Copper Company. Over the past year Copper paid dividends of $1.80 per share and the investor forecasted that the dividends would grow by 5% per year forever. This means that dividends over the next two years (D_1 and D_2) are forecast to be $1.89 [=$1.80 × (1 + .05)] for the first year and $1.985 [=$1.89 × (1 + .05)] for the second. If the investor plans to sell the stock after one year, the selling price can be estimated by noting that, at $t = 1$, the forecast of dividends for the forthcoming year will be D_2, or $1.985. Thus the anticipated selling price at $t = 1$, denoted P_1, will be equal to $33.08 [= $1.985/(.11 − .05)]. Accordingly, the intrinsic value of Copper to such an investor would equal the present value of the expected cash flows, which are $D_1 = 1.89 and $P_1 = 33.08. Using Equation (17.30) and assuming a required rate of 11%, this value is equal to $31.50 [= ($1.89 + $33.08)/(1 + .11)]. Note that this is the same amount that was calculated earlier when all the dividends from now to infinity were discounted using the constant-growth model: $V = D_1/(k − g) = $1.89/(.11 − .05) = $31.50.

17.6 MODELS BASED ON PRICE-EARNINGS RATIOS

Despite the inherent sensibility of DDMs, many security analysts use a much simpler procedure to value common stocks. First, a stock's earnings per share over the forthcoming year E_1 are estimated, and then the analyst (or someone else) specifies a "normal" **price-earnings ratio** for the stock. The product of these two numbers gives the estimated future price P_1. Together with estimated dividends D_1 to be paid during the period and the current price P, the estimated return on the stock over the period can be determined:

$$\text{Expected return} = \frac{(P_1 − P) + D_1}{P} \qquad (17.32)$$

where $P_1 = (P_1/E_1) \times E_1$.

Some security analysts expand this procedure, estimating earnings per share and price-earnings ratios for optimistic, most likely, and pessimistic scenarios to produce a rudimentary probability distribution of a security's return. Other analysts determine whether a stock is underpriced or overpriced by comparing the stock's actual price-earnings ratio with its "normal" price-earnings ratio, as will be shown next.[11]

In order to make this comparison, one must rearrange Equation (17.7) and introduce some new variables. First, note that earnings per share E_t are related to dividends per share D_t by the firm's **payout ratio** p_t,

$$D_t = p_t E_t \qquad (17.33)$$

Furthermore, if an analyst has forecast earnings per share and payout ratios, then he or she has implicitly forecast dividends.

Equation (17.33) can be used to restate the various DDMs where the focus is on estimating what the stock's price-earnings ratio should be instead of on estimating the intrinsic value of the stock. In the restatement, $p_t E_t$ is substituted for D_t in the right-hand side of Equation (17.7), resulting in a general formula for determining a stock's intrinsic value that involves discounting earnings:

$$V = \frac{D_1}{(1+k)^1} + \frac{D_2}{(1+k)^2} + \frac{D_3}{(1+k)^3} + \cdots$$

$$= \frac{p_1 E_1}{(1+k)^1} + \frac{p_2 E_2}{(1+k)^2} + \frac{p_3 E_3}{(1+k)^3} + \cdots$$

$$= \sum_{t=1}^{\infty} \frac{p_t E_t}{(1+k)^t} \tag{17.34}$$

Earlier it was noted that dividends in adjacent time periods could be viewed as being "linked" to each other by a dividend growth rate g_t. Similarly, earnings per share in any year t can be "linked" to earnings per share in the previous year $t-1$ by a growth rate in earnings per share, g_{et},

$$E_t = E_{t-1}(1 + g_{et}) \tag{17.35}$$

This equation implies that

$$E_1 = E_0(1 + g_{e1})$$

$$E_2 = E_1(1 + g_{e2}) = E_0(1 + g_{e1})(1 + g_{e2})$$

$$E_3 = E_2(1 + g_{e3}) = E_0(1 + g_{e1})(1 + g_{e2})(1 + g_{e3})$$

and so on, where E_0 is the actual level of earnings per share over the past year, E_1 is the expected level of earnings per share over the forthcoming year, E_2 is the expected level of earnings per share for the year after E_1, and E_3 is the expected level of earnings per share for the year after E_2.

These equations relating expected future earnings per share to E_0 can be substituted into Equation (17.34), resulting in:

$$V = \frac{p_1[E_0(1 + g_{e1})]}{(1+k)^1} + \frac{p_2[E_0(1 + g_{e1})(1 + g_{e2})]}{(1+k)^2}$$

$$+ \frac{p_3[E_0(1 + g_{e1})(1 + g_{e2})(1 + g_{e3})]}{(1+k)^3} + \cdots \tag{17.36}$$

Because V is the intrinsic value of a share of stock, it represents what the stock would be selling for if it were fairly priced. It follows that V/E_0 represents what the price-earnings ratio would be if the stock were fairly priced and is sometimes referred to as the stock's "normal" price-earnings ratio. Both sides of Equation (17.36) can be divided by E_0 and the results simplified in the formula for determining the "normal" price-earnings ratio:

$$\frac{V}{E_0} = \frac{p_1(1 + g_{e1})}{(1+k)^1} + \frac{p_2(1 + g_{e1})(1 + g_{e2})}{(1+k)^2}$$

$$+ \frac{p_3(1 + g_{e1})(1 + g_{e2})(1 + g_{e3})}{(1+k)^3} + \cdots \tag{17.37}$$

This approach shows that, other things being equal, a stock's "normal" price-earnings ratio will be higher:

The *greater* the expected payout ratios ($p_1, p_2, p_3, \ldots$),
The *greater* the expected growth rates in earnings per share ($g_{e1}, g_{e2}, g_{e3}, \ldots$)
The *smaller* the required rate of return (k)

The qualifying phrase "other things being equal" should not be overlooked. For example, a firm cannot increase the value of its shares by simply making greater payouts. This will increase $p_1, p_2, p_3, \ldots$, but it will decrease the expected growth rates in earnings per share $g_{e1}, g_{e2}, g_{e3}, \ldots$. If the firm's investment policy is not altered, the effects of the reduced growth in its earnings per share will just offset the effects of the increased payouts, leaving its share value unchanged.

Earlier it was noted that a stock was viewed as underpriced if $V > P$ and as overpriced if $V < P$. Because dividing both sides of an inequality by a positive constant will not change the direction of the inequality, such a division can be done here to the two inequalities involving V and P, where the positive constant is E_0. The result is that a stock can be viewed as being underpriced if $V/E_0 > P/E_0$ and overpriced if $V/E_0 < P/E_0$. Thus a stock will be underpriced if its "normal" price-earnings ratio is greater than its actual price-earnings ratio, and overpriced if its "normal" price-earnings ratio is less than its actual price-earnings ratio.

Unfortunately, Equation (17.37) is intractable; it cannot be used to estimate the normal price-earnings ratio for any stock. However, simplifying assumptions can be made that result in tractable formulas for estimating normal price-earnings ratios. These assumptions, along with the formulas, parallel those made previously regarding dividends.

17.6.1   The Zero-Growth Model

The zero-growth model assumed that dividends per share remained at a fixed dollar amount forever. This situation is most likely to occur if earnings per share remain at a fixed dollar amount forever, with the firm maintaining a 100% payout ratio. Why 100%? Because the assumption that a lesser amount was being paid out would mean that the firm was retaining part of its earnings. These retained earnings would be put to some use and would thus be expected to increase future earnings and hence dividends per share.

Accordingly, the zero-growth model can be interpreted as assuming $p_t = 1$ for all time periods and $E_0 = E_1 = E_2 = E_3$, and so on. Consequently, $D_0 = E_0 = D_1 = E_1 = D_2 = E_2$, and so on. Thus, the valuation Equation (17.13) can be restated as:

$$V = \frac{E_0}{k} \tag{17.38}$$

Dividing Equation (17.38) by E_0 results in the formula for the normal price-earnings ratio for a stock having zero growth:

$$\frac{V}{E_0} = \frac{1}{k} \tag{17.39}$$

Earlier it was assumed that the Zinc Company was a zero-growth firm paying dividends of $8 per share, selling for $65 a share, and having a required rate of return of 10%. Because Zinc is a zero-growth company, it will be assumed that it has a 100% payout ratio which, in turn, means that $E_0 = \$8$. At this point Equation (17.38) can be used to calculate a normal price-earnings ratio for Zinc of $1/.10 = 10$. Because Zinc has an actual price-earnings ratio of $\$65/\$8 = 8.1$, and because $V/E_0 = 10 > P/E_0 = 8.1$, it can be seen that Zinc stock is underpriced.

17.6.2 The Constant-Growth Model

Previously, it was noted that dividends in adjacent time periods could be viewed as being connected to each other by a dividend growth rate g_t. Similarly, it was noted that earnings per share can be connected by an earnings growth rate g_{et}. The constant-growth model assumes that the growth rate in dividends per share will be the same throughout the future. An equivalent assumption is that earnings per share will grow at a constant rate g_e throughout the future, with the payout ratio remaining at a constant level p. These assumptions mean that:

$$E_1 = E_0(1 + g_e) = E_0(1 + g_e)^1$$

$$E_2 = E_1(1 + g_e) = E_0(1 + g_e)(1 + g_e) = E_0(1 + g_e)^2$$

$$E_3 = E_2(1 + g_e) = E_0(1 + g_e)(1 + g_e)(1 + g_e) = E_0(1 + g_e)^3$$

and so on. In general, earnings in year t can be connected to E_0 as follows:

$$E_t = E_0(1 + g_e)^t \tag{17.40}$$

Substituting Equation (17.40) into the numerator of Equation (17.34) and recognizing that $p_t = p$ results in:

$$V = \sum_{t=1}^{\infty} \frac{pE_0(1 + g_e)^t}{(1 + k)^t}$$

$$= pE_0 \left[\sum_{t=1}^{\infty} \frac{(1 + g_e)^t}{(1 + k)^t} \right] \tag{17.41}$$

The same mathematical property of infinite series given in Equation (17.19) can be applied to Equation (17.41), resulting in:

$$V = pE_0 \left(\frac{1 + g_e}{k - g_e} \right) \tag{17.42}$$

It can be noted that the earnings-based constant-growth model has a numerator that is identical to the numerator of the dividend-based constant-growth model, because $pE_0 = D_0$. Furthermore, the denominators of the two models are identical. Both assertions require that the growth rates in earnings and dividends be the same (that is, $g_e = g$). This equality can be seen by recalling that constant earnings growth means:

$$E_t = E_{t-1}(1 + g_e)$$

Now when both sides of this equation are multiplied by the constant payout ratio, the result is:

$$pE_t = pE_{t-1}(1 + g_e)$$

Because $pE_t = D_t$ and $pE_{t-1} = D_{t-1}$, this equation reduces to:

$$D_t = D_{t-1}(1 + g_e)$$

which indicates that dividends in any period $t - 1$ will grow by the earnings growth rate g_e. Because the dividend-based constant-growth model assumed that dividends in any period $t - 1$ would grow by the dividend growth rate g, the two growth rates must be equal for the two models to be equivalent.

Equation (17.42) can be restated by dividing each side by E_0, resulting in the following formula for determining the normal price-earnings ratio for a stock with constant growth:

$$\frac{V}{E_0} = p\left(\frac{1 + g_e}{k - g_e}\right) \tag{17.43}$$

An Example

Earlier it was assumed that the Copper Company had paid dividends of $1.80 per share over the past year, with a forecast that dividends would grow by 5% per year forever. Furthermore, it was assumed that the required rate of return on Copper was 11%, and the current stock price was $40 per share. Now assuming that E_0 was $2.70, one can see that the payout ratio was equal to $66\text{-}\frac{2}{3}\%$ (=$1.80/$2.70). So the normal price-earnings ratio for Copper, according to Equation (17.43), is equal to 11.7 [= .6667 × (1 + .05)/(.11 − .05)]. Because this is less than Copper's actual price-earnings ratio of 14.8 (=$40/$2.70), it follows that the stock of Copper Company is overpriced.

17.6.3 The Multiple-Growth Model

Earlier it was noted that the most general DDM is the multiple-growth model, wherein dividends are allowed to grow at varying rates until some point in time T, after which they are assumed to grow at a constant rate. In this situation the present value of all the dividends is found by adding the present value of all dividends up to and including T, denoted by V_{T-}, and the present value of all dividends after T, denoted by V_{T+}:

$$V = V_{T-} + V_{T+}$$

$$= \sum_{t=1}^{T} \frac{D_t}{(1 + k)^t} + \frac{D_{T+1}}{(k - g)(1 + k)^T} \tag{17.27}$$

In general, earnings per share in any period t can be expressed as being equal to E_0 times the product of all the earnings growth rates from time zero to time t:

$$E_t = E_0(1 + g_{e1})(1 + g_{e2}) \ldots (1 + g_{et}) \tag{17.44}$$

Because dividends per share in any period t are equal to the payout ratio for that period times the earnings per share, it follows from Equation (17.44) that:

$$D_t = p_t E_t$$
$$= p_t E_0 (1 + g_{e1})(1 + g_{e2}) \cdots (1 + g_{et}) \qquad (17.45)$$

Replacing the numerator in Equation (17.27) with the right-hand side of Equation (17.45) and then dividing both sides by E_0 gives the following formula for determining a stock's normal price-earnings ratio with the multiple-growth model:

$$\frac{V}{E_0} = \frac{p_1(1 + g_{e1})}{(1 + k)^1} + \frac{p_2(1 + g_{e1})(1 + g_{e2})}{(1 + k)^2} + \cdots$$
$$+ \frac{p_T(1 + g_{e1})(1 + g_{e2}) \cdots (1 + g_{eT})}{(1 + k)^T}$$
$$+ \frac{p(1 + g_{e1})(1 + g_{e2}) \cdots (1 + g_{eT})(1 + g)}{(k - g)(1 + k)^T} \qquad (17.46)$$

An Example

Consider the Magnesium Company again. Its share price is currently $55, and per share earnings and dividends over the past year were $3 and $.75, respectively. For the next two years, forecast earnings and dividends, along with the earnings growth rates and payout ratios, are:

$$D_1 = \$2.00 \quad E_1 = \$5.00 \quad g_{e1} = 67\% \quad p_1 = 40\%$$
$$D_2 = \$3.00 \quad E_2 = \$6.00 \quad g_{e2} = 20\% \quad p_2 = 50\%$$

Constant growth in dividends and earnings of 10% per year is forecast to begin at $T = 2$, which means that $D_3 = \$3.30$, $E_3 = \$6.60$, $g = 10\%$, and $p = 50\%$.

Given a required return of 15%, Equation (17.46) can be used as follows to estimate a normal price-earnings ratio for Magnesium:

$$\frac{V}{E_0} = \frac{.40(1 + .67)}{(1 + .15)^1} + \frac{.50(1 + .67)(1 + .20)}{(1 + .15)^2} + \frac{.50(1 + .67)(1 + .20)(1 + .10)}{(.15 - .10)(1 + .15)^2}$$
$$= .58 + .76 + 16.67$$
$$= 18.01$$

Because the actual price-earnings ratio of 18.33 (= $55/$3) is close to the normal ratio of 18.01, the stock of the Magnesium Company can be viewed as fairly priced.

17.7 **SOURCES OF EARNINGS GROWTH**

So far no explanation has been given as to why earnings or dividends will be expected to grow in the future. One way of providing such an explanation uses the constant-growth model. Assuming that no new capital is obtained externally and no shares are repurchased (meaning that the number of shares outstanding does not increase or decrease), the portion of earnings not paid to stockholders as dividends will be used to pay for the firm's new investments. Given that p_t denotes the payout ratio in year t, then $(1 - p_t)$ will be equal to the portion of earnings not paid out, known

---

as the **retention ratio**. Furthermore, the firm's new investments, stated on a per share basis and denoted by I_t, will be:

$$I_t = (1 - p_t)E_t \qquad (17.47)$$

If these new investments have an average return on equity of r_t in period t and every year thereafter, they will add $r_t I_t$ to earnings per share in year $t + 1$ and every year thereafter. If all previous investments also produce perpetual earnings at a constant rate of return, next year's earnings will equal this year's earnings plus the new earnings resulting from this year's new investments:

$$
\begin{aligned}
E_{t+1} &= E_t + r_t I_t \\
&= E_t + r_t(1 - p_t)E_t \qquad (17.48) \\
&= E_t[1 + r_t(1 - p_t)]
\end{aligned}
$$

Because it was shown earlier that the growth rate in earnings per share is:

$$E_t = E_{t-1}(1 + g_{et}) \qquad (17.35)$$

it follows that:

$$E_{t+1} = E_t(1 + g_{et+1}) \qquad (17.49)$$

A comparison of Equations (17.48) and (17.49) indicates that:

$$g_{et+1} = r_t(1 - p_t) \qquad (17.50)$$

If the growth rate in earnings per share g_{et+1} is to be constant over time, then the average return on equity for new investments r_t and the payout ratio p_t must also be constant over time. In this situation Equation (17.50) can be simplified by removing the time subscripts:

$$g_e = r(1 - p) \qquad (17.51a)$$

Because the growth rate in dividends per share g is equal to the growth rate in earnings per share g_e, Equation (17.51a) can be rewritten as:

$$g = r(1 - p) \qquad (17.51b)$$

From Equation (17.51b) it can be seen that the growth rate g depends on (1) the proportion of earnings that is retained, $1 - p$, and (2) the average return on equity for the earnings that are retained, r. Because it is expected to persist over the long term, g is sometimes referred to as the firm's rate of *sustainable growth*.

The constant-growth valuation formula given in Equation (17.20) can be modified by replacing g with the expression on the right-hand side of Equation (17.51b), resulting in:

$$
\begin{aligned}
V &= D_0\left(\frac{1 + g}{k - g}\right) \qquad (17.52) \\
&= D_0\left[\frac{1 + r(1 - p)}{k - r(1 - p)}\right] \\
&= D_1\left[\frac{1}{k - r(1 - p)}\right]
\end{aligned}
$$

Under these assumptions, a stock's value (and hence its price) should be greater, the greater its average return on equity for new investments, other things being equal.

Continuing with the Copper Company, recall that $E_0 = \$2.70$ and $p = 66\text{-}\frac{2}{3}\%$. This means that $33\text{-}\frac{1}{3}\%$ of earnings per share over the past year were retained and reinvested, an amount equal to $\$.90$ $(=.3333 \times \$2.70)$. The earnings per share in the forthcoming year E_1 are expected to be $\$2.835$ $[=\$2.70 \times (1 + .05)]$ because the growth rate g for Copper is 5%.

The source of the increase in earnings per share of $\$.135$ $(=\$2.835 - \$2.70)$ is the $\$.90$ per share that was reinvested at $t = 0$. The average return on equity for new investments r is 15%, because $\$.135/\$.90 = 15\%$. That is, the reinvested earnings of $\$.90$ per share can be viewed as having generated an annual increase in earnings per share of $\$.135$. This increase will occur not only at $t = 1$ but also at $t = 2$, $t = 3$, and so on. Equivalently, a $\$.90$ investment at $t = 0$ will generate a perpetual annual cash inflow of $\$.135$ beginning at $t = 1$.

Expected dividends at $t = 1$ can be calculated by multiplying the expected payout ratio p of $66\text{-}\frac{2}{3}\%$ times the expected earnings per share E_1 of $\$2.835$, or $.6667 \times \$2.835 = \$1.89$. They can also be calculated by multiplying 1 plus the growth rate g of 5% times the past amount of dividends per share D_0 of $\$1.80$, or $1.05 \times \$1.80 = \$1.89$.

It can be seen that the growth rate in dividends per share of 5% is equal to the product of the retention rate $\left(33\text{-}\frac{2}{3}\%\right)$ and the average return on equity for new investments (15%), an amount equal to $5\%(=.3333 \times .15)$.

Two years from now $(t = 2)$, earnings per share are anticipated to be $\$2.977$ $[=\$2.835 \times (1 + .05)]$, a further increase of $\$.142$ $(=\$2.977 - \$2.835)$ that is due to the retention and reinvestment of $\$.945$ $(=.3333 \times \$2.835)$ per share at $t = 1$. This expected increase in earnings per share of $\$.142$ is the result of earning (15%) on the reinvestment $(\$.945)$, because $.15 \times \$.945 = \$.142$.

The expected earnings per share at $t = 2$ can be viewed as having three components. The first is the earnings attributable to the assets held at $t = -1$, an amount equal to $\$2.70$. The second is the earnings attributable to the reinvestment of $\$.90$ at $t = 0$, earning $\$.135$. The third is the earnings attributable to the reinvestment of $\$.945$ at $t = 1$, earning $\$.142$. These three components, when summed, can be seen to equal $E_2 = \$2.977$ $(=\$2.70 + \$.135 + \$.142)$.

Dividends at $t = 2$ are expected to be 5% larger than at $t = 1$, or $\$1.985$ $(=1.05 \times \$1.89)$ per share. This amount corresponds to the amount calculated by multiplying the payout ratio by the expected earnings per share at $t = 2$, or $\$1.985$ $(=.6667 \times \$2.977)$. Figure 17.2 summarizes the example.

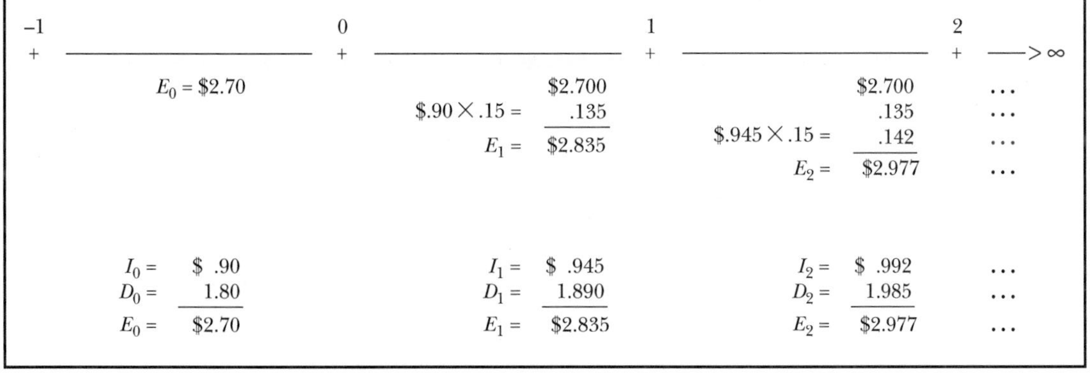

Figure 17.2
Growth in Earnings for Copper Company

Applying Dividend Discount Models

Since the late 1960s, dividend discount models (DDMs) have been used by various professional common stock investors. Although few investment managers rely solely on DDMs to select stocks, many have integrated some form of DDM into their security valuation procedures.

There are two reasons why DDMs warrant consideration. First, DDMs are based on a simple, widely understood concept: The fair value of any security should equal the discounted value of the cash flows expected to be produced by that security. Second, the basic inputs for DDMs are standard outputs for many large investment management firms; that is, these firms employ security analysts who are responsible for projecting corporate earnings.

Valuing common stocks with a DDM technically requires an estimate of future dividends over an infinite time horizon. Given that accurately forecasting dividends three years from today, let alone 20 years

in the future, is difficult, how do investment firms actually go about implementing DDMs?

One approach is to use constant or two-stage dividend growth models, as described in the text. However, although such models are relatively easy to apply, institutional investors typically view the assumed dividend growth assumptions as overly simplistic. Instead, these investors generally prefer three-stage models, believing that they provide the best combination of realism and ease of application.

Whereas many variations of the three-stage DDM exist, in general, the model is based on the assumption that companies evolve through three stages during their lifetimes. (Figure 17.3 portrays these stages.)

1. **Growth stage**. Characterized by rapidly expanding sales, high profit margins, and abnormally high growth in earnings per share. Because of highly profitable expected investment opportunities, the

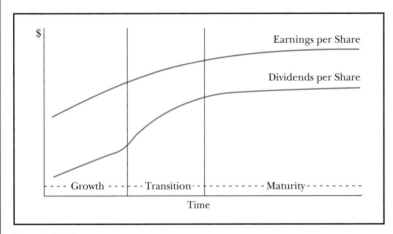

Figure 17.3
The Three Stages of the Multiple-Growth Model

A THREE-STAGE DDM

As *Institutional Issues: Applying Dividend Discount Models* discusses, the three-stage DDM is the most widely applied form of the general multiple-growth DDM. Consider analyzing the *ABC* Company.

17.8.1 Making Forecasts

Over the past year, *ABC* has had earnings per share of $1.67 and dividends per share of $.40. After carefully studying *ABC*, the security analyst has made the fol-

---

payout ratio is low. Competitors are attracted by the unusually high earnings, leading to a decline in the growth rate.

2. **Transition stage**. In later years, increased competition reduces profit margins, and earnings growth slows. With fewer new investment opportunities, the company begins to pay out a larger percentage of earnings.

3. **Maturity (steady-state) stage**. Eventually the company reaches a position at which its new investment opportunities offer, on average, only slightly attractive returns on equity. At that time its earnings growth rate, payout ratio, and return on equity stabilize for the remainder of its life.

The forecasting process of the three-stage DDM involves specifying earnings and dividend growth rates in each stage. Although one cannot expect a security analyst to be omniscient in his or her growth forecast for a particular company, one can hope that the forecast pattern of growth—in terms of magnitude and duration—resembles that actually realized by the company, particularly in the short run.

Investment firms attempt to structure their DDMs to make maximum use of their analysts' forecasting capabilities. Thus the models emphasize specific forecasts in the near term, when it is realistic to expect security analysts to project earnings and dividends accurately. Conversely, the models emphasize more general forecasts over the longer term, when distinctions between companies' growth rates become less discernible. Typically, analysts are required to supply the following for their assigned companies:

1. Expected annual earnings and dividends for the next several years
2. After these specific annual forecasts end, earnings growth and the payout ratio forecasts until the end of the growth stage

3. The number of years until the transition stage is reached
4. The duration (in years) of the transition stage: that is, once abnormally high growth ends, the number of years until the maturity stage is reached

Most three-stage DDMs assume that during the transition stage, earnings growth declines and payout ratios rise linearly to the maturity-stage steady-state levels. (For example, if the transition stage is ten years long, earnings growth at the maturity stage is 5% per year, and earnings growth at the end of the growth stage is 25%, then earnings growth will decline 2% in each year of the transition stage.) Finally, most three-stage DDMs make standard assumptions that all companies in the maturity stage have the same growth rates, payout ratios, and return on equity.

With analysts' inputs, plus an appropriate required rate of return for each security, all the necessary information for the three-stage DDM is available. The last step involves merely calculating the discounted value of the estimated dividends to determine the stock's "fair" value.

The seeming simplicity of the three-stage DDM should not lead one to believe that it is without its implementation problems. Investment firms must strive to achieve consistency across their analysts' forecasts. The long-term nature of the estimates involved, the substantial training required to make even short-term earnings forecasts accurately, and the coordination of a number of analysts covering many companies severely complicate the problem. Considerable discipline is required if the DDM valuations generated by a firm's analysts are to be sufficiently comparable and reliable to guide investment decisions. Despite these complexities, if successfully implemented, DDMs can combine the creative insights of security analysts with the rigor and discipline of quantitative investment techniques.

lowing forecasts of earnings per share and dividends per share for the next five years:

$$E_1 = \$2.67 \quad E_2 = \$4.00 \quad E_3 = \$6.00 \quad E_4 = \$8.00 \quad E_5 = \$10.00$$

$$D_2 = \$.60 \quad D_2 = \$1.60 \quad D_3 = \$2.40 \quad D_4 = \$3.20 \quad D_5 = \$5.00$$

These forecasts imply the following payout ratios and earnings-per-share growth rates:

$$p_1 = 22\% \quad p_2 = 40\% \quad p_3 = 40\% \quad p_4 = 40\% \quad p_5 = 50\%$$

$$g_{e1} = 60\% \quad g_{e2} = 50\% \quad g_{e3} = 50\% \quad g_{e4} = 33\% \quad g_{e5} = 25\%$$

Furthermore, the analyst believes that *ABC* will enter a transition stage at the end of the fifth year (that is, the sixth year will be the first year of the transition stage), and that the transition stage will last three years. Earnings per share and the payout ratio for year 6 are forecast to be $E_6 = \$11.90$ and $p_6 = 55\%$. {Thus $g_{e6} = 19\%$ [$= (\$11.90 - \$10.00)/\$10.00$] and $D_6 = \$6.55 (= .55 \times \$11.90)$}.

The last stage, known as the maturity stage, is forecast to have an earnings-per-share growth rate of 4% and a payout ratio of 70%. Now it was shown in Equation (17.51b) that with the constant-growth model, $g = r(1 - p)$, where r is the average return on equity for new investment and p is the payout ratio. Given that the maturity stage has constant growth, this equation can be reformulated and used to determine r:

$$r = g/(1 - p)$$

Thus r for *ABC* has an implied value of 13.33% [$=4\%/(100\% - 70\%)$], which is assumed to be consistent with the long-run growth forecasts for similar companies.

At this point only two missing pieces of information are needed to determine the value of *ABC*: the earnings-per-share growth rates and the payout ratios for the transition stage. Take earnings per share first; it has been forecast that $g_{e6} = 19\%$ and $g_{e9} = 4\%$. One method of determining how 19% will "decay" to 4% is to note that there are three years between the sixth and ninth years, and 15% between 19% and 4%. A "linear decay" rate would be determined by noting that 15%/3 years = 5% per year. This rate of 5% would be deducted from 19% to get g_{e7}, resulting in 14% ($= 19\% - 5\%$). Then it would be deducted from 14% to get g_{e8}, resulting in 9% ($=14\% - 5\%$). Finally, as a check it can be noted that 4% ($=9\% - 5\%$) is the value that was forecast for g_{e9}.

A similar procedure can be used to determine how the payout ratio of 55% in year 6 will grow to 70% in year 9. The "linear growth" rate will be $(70\% - 55\%)/3$ years = 15%/3 years = 5% per year, indicating that $p_7 = 60\%$ ($=55\% + 5\%$) and $p_8 = 65\%$ ($=60\% + 5\%$). Again a check indicates that 70% ($=65\% + 5\%$) is the value that was forecast for p_9.

With these forecasts of earnings-per-share growth rates and payout ratios in hand, one can now make forecasts of dividends per share:

$$D_7 = p_7 E_7$$
$$= p_7 E_6(1 + g_{e7})$$
$$= .60 \times \$11.90 \times (1 + .14)$$
$$= .60 \times \$13.57$$
$$= \$8.14$$

$$D_8 = p_8 E_8$$
$$= p_8 E_6(1 + g_{e7})(1 + g_{e8})$$
$$= .65 \times \$11.90 \times (1 + .14) \times (1 + .09)$$
$$= .65 \times \$14.79$$
$$= \$9.61$$

$$D_9 = p_9 E_9$$
$$= p_9 E_6(1 + g_{e7})(1 + g_{e8})(1 + g_{e9})$$
$$= .70 \times \$11.90 \times (1 + .14) \times (1 + .09) \times (1 + .04)$$
$$= .70 \times \$15.38$$
$$= \$10.76$$

17.8.2 Estimating the Intrinsic Value

Given a required rate of return on *ABC* of 12.4%, all the necessary inputs for the multiple-growth model have been determined. Hence it is now possible to estimate *ABC*'s intrinsic (or fair) value. To begin, it can be seen that $T = 8$, indicating that V_{T-} involves determining the present value of D_1 through D_8:

$$V_{T-} = \left[\frac{\$.60}{(1 + .124)^1}\right] + \left[\frac{\$1.60}{(1 + .124)^2}\right] + \left[\frac{\$2.40}{(1 + .124)^3}\right]$$

$$+ \left[\frac{\$3.20}{(1 + .124)^4}\right] + \left[\frac{\$5.00}{(1 + .124)^5}\right] + \left[\frac{\$6.55}{(1 + .124)^6}\right]$$

$$+ \left[\frac{\$8.14}{(1 + .124)^7}\right] + \left[\frac{\$9.61}{(1 + .124)^8}\right]$$

$$= \$18.89$$

Then V_{T+} can be determined using D_9:

$$V_{T+} = \frac{\$10.76}{(.124 - .04)(1 + .124)^8}$$

$$= \$50.28$$

Combining V_{T-} and V_{T+} results in the intrinsic value of *ABC*:

$$V = V_{T-} + V_{T+}$$

$$= \$18.89 + \$50.28$$

$$= \$69.17$$

Given a current market price for *ABC* of $50, it can be seen that its stock is underpriced by $19.17 (=\$69.17 - \$50) per share. Equivalently, it can be noted that the actual price-earnings ratio for *ABC* is 29.9 (=$50/$1.67) but that a normal price-earnings ratio would be higher, equal to 41.4 (=$69.17/$1.67), again indicating that *ABC* is underpriced.

17.8.3 Implied Returns

As shown with the previous example, once the analyst has made certain forecasts, it is relatively straightforward to estimate a company's stream of future dividends. Then the present value of these expected dividends can be calculated for a given required rate of return. However, many investment firms use a computerized trial-and-error procedure to determine the discount rate that equates the present value of the stock's expected dividends with its current price. Sometimes this long-run internal rate of return is referred to as the security's **implied return**. The implied return of *ABC* is 14.8%.

17.8.4 The Security Market Line

After implied returns have been estimated for a number of stocks, the associated beta for each stock can be estimated. Then, for all the stocks analyzed, this information can be plotted on a graph that has implied returns on the vertical axis and estimated betas on the horizontal axis, and hence corresponds to a graph of the security market line (SML).

At this point there are alternative methods for estimating the SML.[12] One method involves determining a line of best fit for this graph by using a statistical procedure known as simple linear regression (as discussed in Chapter 16). That is, the values of an intercept term and a slope term are determined from the data, thereby indi-

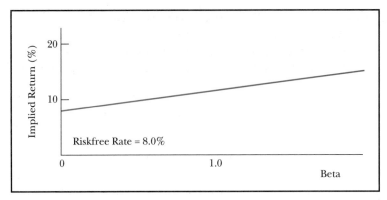

Figure 17.4
A Security Market Line Estimated from Implied Returns

cating the location of the straight line that best describes the relationship between implied returns and betas.[13]

Figure 17.4 provides an example of the estimated SML. In this case the SML has been determined to have an intercept of 8% and a slope of 4%, indicating that, in general, securities with higher betas are expected to have higher implied returns in the forthcoming period. Depending on the sizes of the implied returns, such lines can have steeper, flatter, or even negative slopes.

The second method of estimating the SML involves calculating the implied return for a portfolio of common stocks. This calculation is done by taking a value-weighted average of the implied returns of the stocks in the portfolio, with the resulting return being an estimate of the implied return on the "market" portfolio. Given this return and a beta of 1, the "market" portfolio can be plotted on a graph having implied returns on the vertical axis and betas on the horizontal axis. Next the riskfree rate, having a beta of zero, can be plotted on the same graph. Finally, the SML is determined by simply connecting these two points with a straight line.

Either of these SMLs can be used to determine the required return on a stock. However, they will likely result in different numbers, because the two lines will likely have different intercepts and slopes. For example, note that in the first method the SML may not go through the riskfree rate, whereas the second method forces the SML to go through this rate.

17.8.5   Alphas

Once a security's beta has been estimated, its required return can be determined from the estimated SML. For example, the equation for the SML shown in Figure 17.4 is:

$$k_i = 8 + 4\beta_i$$

Thus if *ABC* had an estimated beta of 1.1, then it would have a required return equal to 12.4% [=8 + (4 × 1.1)].

Once the required return on a stock has been determined, the difference between the stock's implied return (from the DDM) and this required return can be calculated. This difference is then viewed as an estimate of the stock's *alpha* and represents the degree to which a stock is mispriced. Positive alphas indicate undervalued securities and negative alphas indicate overvalued securities.[14] Because *ABC*'s implied and required returns were 14.8% and 12.4%, respectively, its estimated alpha would be 2.4% (= 14.8% − 12.4%) indicating that *ABC* is underpriced.

17.8.6 The Implied Return on the Stock Market

Another product of this analysis is that the implied return for a portfolio of stocks can be compared with the expected return on bonds. (The latter is typically represented by the current yield-to-maturity on long-term Treasury bonds.) Specifically, the difference between stock and bond returns can be used as an input for recommendations concerning asset allocation between stocks and bonds. That is, it can be used to form recommendations regarding what percent of an investor's money should go into stocks and what percent should go into bonds. For example, the greater the implied return on stocks relative to bonds, the larger the percentage of the investor's money that should be placed in common stocks.

17.9 DIVIDEND DISCOUNT MODELS AND EXPECTED RETURNS

The procedures described here are similar to those employed by a number of brokerage firms and portfolio managers.[15] A security's implied return, obtained from a DDM, is often treated as an expected return, which in turn can be divided into two components: the security's required return and alpha. However, the expected return on a stock over a given holding period may differ from its DDM-based implied return k^*. A simple set of examples will indicate why and when this difference exists.

Assume that a security analyst predicts that a stock will pay a dividend of $1.10 per year forever. On the other hand, the consensus opinion of "the market" (most other investors) is that the dividend will equal $1.00 per year forever. Thus, the analyst's prediction is a deviant, or nonconsensus, one.

Assume that both the analyst and other investors agree that the required rate of return for a stock of this type is 10%. The formula for the zero-growth model indicates that the value of the stock is $D_1/.10 = 10D_1$, meaning that the stock should sell for ten times its expected dividend. Because other investors expect to receive $1.00 per year, the stock has a current price P of $10 per share. The analyst feels that the stock has a value of $1.10/.10 = $11 and thus feels that it is underpriced by $11 - $10 = $1 per share.

17.9.1 Rate of Convergence of Investors' Predictions

In this situation the implied return according to the analyst is $1.10/$10 = 11%. If the analyst buys a share now with a plan to sell it a year later, what rate of return might the analyst expect to earn? The answer depends on what assumption is made regarding the *rate of convergence of investors' predictions*—that is, the answer depends on the expected market reaction to the mispricing that the analyst believes currently exists.

The cases shown in Table 17.1 are based on an assumption that the analyst is confident that his or her forecast of future dividends is correct. That is, in all of the cases, the analyst expects that at the end of the year, the stock will pay the predicted dividend of $1.10.

No Convergence

In column (A), it is assumed that other investors will regard the higher dividend as a fluke and steadfastly refuse to alter their projections of subsequent dividends from their initial estimate of $1.00. As a result, the security's price at $t = 1$ can be expected to remain at $10 (=$1.00/.10). In this case the analyst's total return is expected to be 11% (=$1.10/$10), which will be attributed entirely to dividends as no capital gains are expected.

TABLE 17.1 Alpha and the Convergence of Predictions

	Expected Amount of Convergence		
	0% (A)	100% (B)	50% (C)
Dividend predictions D_2			
Consensus of other investors	1.00	1.10	1.05
Analyst	1.10	1.10	1.10
Expected stock price P_1	10.00	11.00	10.50
Expected return			
Dividend yield D_1/P	11%	11%	11%
Capital gain $(P_1 - P)/P$	0	10	5
Total expected return	11%	21%	16%
Less required return	10	10	10
Alpha	1%	11%	6%

Note: P_1 is equal to the consensus dividend prediction at $t = 1$ divided by the required return of 10%. The example assumes that the current stock price P is $10, and dividends are forecast by the consensus at $t = 0$ to remain constant at $1.00 per share, whereas the analyst forecasts the dividends at $t = 0$ to remain constant at $1.10 per share.

The 11% expected return can also be viewed as consisting of the required return of 10% plus an alpha of 1% that is equal to the portion of the dividend unanticipated by other investors, $.10/$10. Accordingly, if it is assumed that there will be no convergence of predictions, the expected return will be set at the implied rate of 11% and the alpha will be set at 1%.

Complete Convergence

Column (B) shows a very different situation. Here it is assumed that the other investors will recognize their error and completely revise their predictions. At the end of the year, it is expected that they too will predict future dividends of $1.10 per year thereafter; thus the stock is expected to be selling for $11 (=$1.10/.10) at $t = 1$. Under these conditions, the analyst can expect to achieve a total return of 21% by selling the stock at the end of the year for $11, obtaining 11% (=$1.10/$10) in dividend yield and 10% (=$1/$10) in capital gains.

The 10% expected capital gains result directly from the expected repricing of the security because of the complete convergence of predictions. In this case the fruits of the analyst's superior prediction are expected to be obtained all in one year. Instead of an "extra" 1% per year forever, as in column (A), the analyst expects to obtain 1% (=$.10/$10) in extra dividend yield plus 10% (=$1/$10) in capital gains this year. By continuing to hold the stock in subsequent years, the analyst would expect to earn only the required return of 10% over those years. Accordingly, the expected return is 21% and the alpha is 11% for the forthcoming year when it is assumed that there is complete convergence of predictions.

Partial Convergence

Column (C) shows an intermediate case. Here the predictions of the other investors are expected to converge only halfway toward those of the analyst (that is, from $1.00 to $1.05 instead of to $1.10). Total return in the first year is expected to be 16%, consisting of 11% (=$1.10/$10) in dividend yield plus 5% (=$.50/$10) in capital gains.

Because the stock is expected to be selling for $10.50 (=$1.05/.10) at $t = 1$ but has an intrinsic value of $11 (=$1.10/.10) at that time, the analyst will still feel that

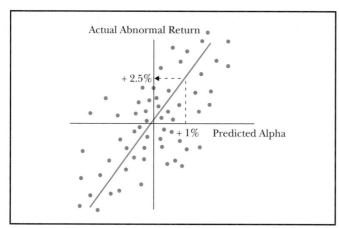

Figure 17.5
Adjusting Predictions

it is underpriced. To obtain the remainder of the "extra return" owing to this underpricing, the investor would have to hold the stock past $t = 1$. Accordingly, the expected return would be set at 16% and the alpha would be set at 6% for the forthcoming year when it is assumed that there is halfway convergence of predictions.

In general, a security's expected return and alpha will be larger, the faster the assumed rate of convergence of predictions.[16] Many investors use the implied rate (that is, the internal rate of return k^*) as a surrogate for a relatively short-term (for example, one year) expected return, as in column (A). In doing so, they are assuming that the dividend forecast is completely accurate but that there is no convergence. Alternatively, investors could assume that there is some degree of convergence, thereby raising their estimate of the security's expected return. Indeed, investors could further alter their estimate of the security's expected return by assuming that the security analyst's deviant prediction is less than perfectly accurate, as will be seen next.[17]

17.9.2 Predicted versus Actual Returns

An alternative approach does not simply use outputs from a model "as is" but *adjusts* them on the basis of relationships between previous predictions and actual outcomes. Figure 17.5 provides an example. Each point in Figure 17.5 plots a predicted alpha value for a security (on the horizontal axis) and the subsequent "abnormal return" for that period (on the vertical axis). Such a diagram can be made for a given security, or for all the securities that a particular analyst makes predictions about, or for all the securities that the investment firm makes predictions about. Again, a line of best fit can be drawn through the points. In this case, if the current prediction of a security's alpha is +1%, this relationship suggests that an "adjusted" estimate of +2.5% would be superior.

An important by-product of this type of analysis is the measure of correlation between predicted and actual outcomes, indicating the nearness of the points to the line. This **information coefficient** (IC) can serve as a measure of predictive accuracy. If it is too small to be significantly different from zero in a statistical sense, the value of the predictions is subject to considerable question.[18]

17.10   SUMMARY

1. The capitalization of income method of valuation states that the intrinsic value of any asset is equal to the sum of the discounted cash flows investors expect to receive from that asset.

Multiple Valuation Models

Despite the simple elegance and compelling logic of the dividend discount model (DDM), few investment management firms use it as a sole means of identifying mispriced common stocks. In general, managers have always been leery of the DDM approach. Many view with skepticism the notion that the market makes a long-term forecast of a company's dividends and then discounts that expected dividend stream at some appropriate discount rate to arrive at a "fair" value for the stock.

Some managers firmly believe that the market is highly inefficient and that any valuation method, including a DDM, that is based on the rationality of market participants will prove ineffective. They often rely on various technical stock selection tools (discussed in Chapter 22).

Most managers do concede that the market is very efficient, but they contend that enough inefficiencies exist to warrant the search for mispriced stocks. Yet rather than use a DDM to funnel their fundamental research into an objective estimate of a stock's intrinsic value, most of these managers prefer to use alternative methods of identifying mispricings that do not involve long-term forecasts. For example, some divide a stock's current price-earnings ratio by that of the market's price-earnings ratio. This *relative* price-earnings ratio is then compared with the stock's historical range of relative price-earnings. A stock whose relative price-earnings ratio is near or below the low end of its historical range is seen as undervalued.

Why do many managers prefer these alternative valuation methods to the DDM? Some believe that it is futile to forecast dividends for more than a few years in the future. In particular, they question the assumptions required to make a dividend growth forecast tractable (for example, the growth assumptions underlying the constant growth DDM or the three-stage DDM). Others are concerned that DDMs exhibit certain biases. Probably the most disconcerting problem is a tendency for DDMs to calculate high expected returns for stocks that currently pay high dividends and to calculate low expected returns for stocks that currently pay low or zero dividends. Because the earnings growth rates of companies with high current payout ratios tend to be lower than those with low current payout ratios, managers are naturally concerned that DDMs show a favorable bias toward low-growth, high-dividend stocks.

A small group of managers have responded to the problems of the DDM not by rejecting the concept but rather by incorporating DDMs into a broader framework of multiple valuation models. The basic idea behind this approach is that many different valuation models contain information about security mispricings. Some of these valuation models are based on perceived market anomalies, such as an overreaction to unexpected news about a company. Other models may be cousins of the DDM, such as relative price-earnings comparisons mentioned earlier. If DDMs and these models do contain mispricing information, and if their mispricing estimates are not perfectly correlated, then a combination of the models' forecasts can produce estimates of mispricings superior to any single model. A brief look at one investment manager gives a sense of how a multiple valuation model approach is applied.

Franklin Portfolio Associates (FPA) is a Boston-based investment management firm. It manages common stock portfolios for roughly two dozen clients, including some of the largest pension funds in the country such as General Motors, AT&T, and Amoco. The firm also manages the Growth and Income Fund for the Vanguard Group. Total assets under management exceed $13 billion. FPA has used a multiple valuation model approach for stock selection since the firm's formation in 1982.

2. Dividend discount models (DDMs) are a specific application of the capitalization of income method of valuation to common stocks.

3. To use a DDM, the investor must implicitly or explicitly supply a forecast of all future dividend that are expected to be generated by a security.

4. Investors typically make certain simplifying assumptions about the growth of common stock dividends. For example, a common stock's dividends may be assumed to exhibit zero growth or growth at a constant rate. More complex assumptions allow for multiple growth rates over time.

FPA divides its valuation models into four primary groups:

- Fundamental momentum
- Relative value
- Future cash flow
- Supplementary

The fundamental momentum models are based on data regarding earnings revisions and surprises. FPA purchases earnings estimates made by various brokerage house securities analysts. (Services that supply analysts' earnings estimates to firms such as FPA are the subject of Chapter 18's "Institutional Issues.") On a stock-by-stock basis, FPA computes the change (if any) in the average earnings estimate (called an *earnings revision*). The firm also compares a company's reported earnings against analysts' estimates. (The difference is called an *earnings surprise* and is discussed in Chapter 18.) Stocks with large earnings revisions or surprises are potentially misvalued. Relative value models compare a stock's current price with some base measure such as book value, dividends, or earnings. Future cash flow models are various versions of DDMs. The models differ in terms of the assumptions made about the path of dividend growth over time as well as the sources of dividend growth estimates. Finally, the supplementary models use measures of insider trading and relative strength to identify under and overvalued stocks. (See Chapter 22 for more on these two valuation indicators.)

In total, FPA uses over 30 different valuation models. Twice a month, each model is used to rank roughly 3,500 (primarily) U.S. common stocks by relative attractiveness. In order to create a composite rank, FPA assigns weights (or importance) to the individual models. One solution is to give all of the models an equal weight. (Thus with 30 models, each model would contribute one-thirtieth to a stock's composite rank.) FPA combines this approach with statistical techniques based on the past performance of the models to develop what it considers to be the most effective combination of model weights.

After calculating the composite rank of each stock, FPA divides the 3,500 stocks into deciles based on those ranks. Only the first-decile stocks are considered for purchase in the firm's portfolios, and any holdings that have slipped down below the fifth decile are considered to be sale candidates. Stocks in the second through fifth deciles can continue to be held if previously purchased. The composite rankings of the eligible stocks are then used as inputs into a portfolio "optimizer"—a statistical procedure for combining stocks to produce mean-variance efficient portfolios. FPA uses the optimizer to control the amount of expected variability in its portfolios' returns relative to the portfolios' assigned benchmarks.

Over the years, FPA's multiple valuation model methodology has successfully differentiated between high and low return stocks. For the 15-year period from 1982 through 1997, stocks ranked in the first decile by the FPA valuation process earned 29.5% per year; stocks ranked in the tenth decile earned a 7.0% annual return. In between the first and tenth deciles, returns were inversely related to the ranking deciles. The costs of transacting in securities makes it difficult to translate these differences in decile performance directly into portfolio returns. Nevertheless, in its flagship "core" accounts that are assigned a broad market index as the benchmark, FPA was able to outperform the benchmark in 32 out of 39 rolling three-year periods from April 1985 through September 1997, while taking on no more systematic risk than the benchmark. Cumulatively, during that period the firm's portfolios earned 18.6% per year versus 17.5% for the benchmark, a record that attests to the usefulness of the multiple model valuation approach to investing.

5. Instead of applying DDMs, many security analysts use an alternative method of security valuation that involves estimating a stock's "normal" price-earnings ratio and comparing it with the stock's actual price-earnings ratio.

6. The growth rate in a firm's earnings and dividends depends on its earnings retention rate and its average return on equity for new investments.

7. Determining whether a security is mispriced using a DDM can be done in one of two ways. First, the discounted value of expected dividends can be compared with the stock's current price. Second, the discount rate that equates the stock's

current price to the present value of forecast dividends can be compared with the required return for stocks of similar risk.

8. The rate of return that an analyst with nonconsensus dividend forecasts can expect to earn depends on both the analyst's accuracy and the rate of convergence of other investors' predictions to the predictions of the analyst.

QUESTIONS AND PROBLEMS

1. Consider five annual cash flows (the first occurring one year from today):

Year	Cash Flow
1	$5
2	6
3	7
4	8
5	9

Given a discount rate of 10%, what is the present value of this stream of cash flows?

2. Alta Cohen is considering buying a machine to produce baseballs. The machine costs $10,000. With the machine, Alta expects to produce and sell 1,000 baseballs per year for $3 per baseball, net of all costs. The machine's life is five years (with no salvage value). On the basis of these assumptions and an 8% discount rate, what is the net present value of Alta's investment?

3. Hub Collins has invested in a project that promised to pay $100, $200, and $300, respectively, at the end of the next three years. If Hub paid $513.04 for this investment, what is the project's internal rate of return?

4. Afton Products currently pays a dividend of $4 per share on its common stock.
   a. If Afton Products plans to increase its dividend at a rate of 5% per year indefinitely, what will be the dividend per share in 10 years?
   b. If Afton Products' dividend per share is expected to be $5.87 per share at the end of five years, at what annual rate is the dividend expected to grow?

5. Hammond Pipes has issued a preferred stock that pays $12 per share. The dividend is fixed, and the stock has no expiration date. What is the intrinsic value of Hammond preferred stock, assuming a discount rate of 15%?

6. Milton Information Services currently pays a dividend of $4 per share on its common stock. The dividend is expected to grow at 4% per year forever. Stocks with similar risk currently are priced to provide a 12% expected return. What is the intrinsic value of Milton stock?

7. Spring Valley Bedding stock currently sells for $53 per share. The stock's dividend is expected to grow at 6% per year indefinitely. Spring Valley just paid a dividend of $3 per share. Given this information, calculate the stock's internal rate of return.

8. Select a stock whose name begins with the first letter of your last name. From the *Value Line Investment Survey* find the average annual compounded growth rate in the stock's dividend over the last five years. Assume that this growth rate will continue indefinitely. Also from the *Value Line Investment Survey* find the beta of the stock. Using the current riskfree rate (90-day Treasury bills as found in *The Wall Street Journal*) and a 6% expected market risk premium, calculate the SML and the required return on the stock. Finally, using the dividend growth rate

and the required return, calculate the intrinsic value of the stock. (Note: If the data for your stock are incompatible with the constant-growth DDM, select another stock.) Compare this intrinsic value with the latest closing price for the stock. Is the stock underpriced or overpriced? What potential problems are involved with this approach to making investment decisions?

9. The constant-growth model is an overly simplistic means of valuing most corporations' stocks. However, a number of market analysts believe that it is a useful means of estimating a fair value for the stock market as a whole. Why might the constant-growth DDM be a more reasonable valuation tool for the market in aggregate as opposed to individual stocks?

10. This year Monona Air Cleaners Inc. will pay a dividend on its stock of $6 per share. The following year the dividend is expected to be the same, increasing to $7 the year after. From that point on, the dividend is expected to grow at 4% per year indefinitely. Stocks with similar risk are currently priced to provide a 10% expected return. What is the intrinsic value of Monona stock?

11. Knapp Carpet recently paid an annual dividend on its stock of $2 per share. The dividend is expected to grow at $1 per share for the next four years. Thereafter the dividend is expected to grow at 5% per year indefinitely. The required return on stocks with similar risk is 12%. What is the intrinsic value of Knapp stock?

12. Chief Medical Inc. is a little-known producer of heart pacemakers. The earnings and dividend growth prospects of the company are disputed by analysts. Albert Bender is forecasting 5% growth in dividends indefinitely. However, his brother John is predicting a 20% growth in dividends, but only for the next three years, after which the growth rate is expected to decline to 4% for the indefinite future. Chief dividends per share are currently $3. Stocks with similar risk are currently priced to provide a 14% expected return.

   a. What is the intrinsic value of Chief stock according to Albert?
   b. What is the intrinsic value of Chief stock according to John?
   c. Assume that Chief stock now sells for $39\frac{3}{4}$ per share. If the stock is fairly priced at the present time, what is the implied perpetual dividend growth rate? What is the implied P/E (price-earnings ratio) on next year's earnings, based on this perpetual dividend growth assumption and assuming a 25% payout ratio?

13. Elk Mound Candy Company currently pays a dividend of $3 per share. That dividend is expected to grow at a 6% rate indefinitely. Stocks with similar risk provide a 10% expected return. Calculate the intrinsic value of Elk Mound stock today using an interim computation based on the sale of the stock at its expected intrinsic value three years from now.

14. How would an increase in the perceived riskiness of a common stock's future cash flows affect its price-earnings ratio? Explain intuitively and mathematically.

15. Roberts Roofing currently earns $4 per share. Its return on equity is 20% and it retains 50% of its earnings (both figures are expected to be maintained indefinitely). Stocks of similar risk are priced to return 15%. What is the intrinsic value of Roberts' stock?

16. Osseo Operations recently paid an annual dividend of $4 per share. Earnings for the same year were $8 per share. The required return on stocks with similar risk is 11%. Dividends are expected to grow 6% per year indefinitely. Calculate Osseo's "normal" price-earnings ratio.

17. Reedsburg Associates is currently paying a dividend of $.40 per share on earnings of $4 per share. Its stock is selling for $200 per share. Stocks of similar risk are priced to return 15%. What kind of return on equity could explain investors' willingness to pay a price equal to 50 times earnings on this stock?

18. Rochelle Corp. is expected to pay out 40% of its earnings and to earn an average of 15% per year on its incremental reinvested earnings forever. Stocks with similar risk are currently priced to provide a 12% expected return. By what percentage can Rochelle's earnings be expected to grow each year? What is an appropriate price-earnings multiple for the stock? What portion of the return on Rochelle stock is expected to come from capital gains?

19. A three-stage DDM has become a popular common stock valuation model, used by institutional investors and brokerage firms. What advantages does it offer relative to a simple constant-growth DDM? Despite its increased sophistication compared with the constant-growth DDM, what disadvantages does it still retain?

20. What explanations can you offer for the fact that the SML shown in Figure 17.4 is so flat?

21. Fay Thomas, a financial analyst, once remarked: "Even if your dividend estimates and discount rate assumption are correct, dividend discount models identify stocks that will produce positive risk-adjusted returns only if other investors eventually come to agree with the DDM's valuation conclusions." Is this statement correct? Why?

22. Some people assert that a "true" growth company is one whose dividends grow at a rate greater than its required rate of return. Why is the constant-growth DDM incapable of valuing such a "true" growth stock?

CFA EXAM QUESTIONS

23. The constant-growth dividend discount model can be used for both the valuation of companies and the estimation of the long-term total return of a stock. Assume that

$$\$20 = \text{the price of a stock today}$$

$$8\% = \text{the expected growth rate of dividends}$$

$$\$0.60 = \text{the annual dividend one year forward}$$

a. Using only the above data, compute the expected long-term total return on the stock using the constant-growth dividend discount model. Show calculations.

b. Briefly discuss three disadvantages of the constant-growth dividend discount model in its application to investment analysis.

24. As a firm operating in a mature industry, Arbot Industries is expected to maintain a constant dividend payout ratio and constant growth rate of earnings for the foreseeable future. Earnings were $4.50 per share in the recently completed fiscal year. The dividend payout ratio has been a constant 55% in recent years and is expected to remain so. Arbot's return on equity (ROE) is expected to remain at 10% in the future, and you require an 11% return on the stock.

a. Using the constant-growth dividend discount model, calculate the current value of Arbot common stock. Show your calculations.

After an aggressive acquisition and marketing program, it now appears that Arbot's earnings per share and ROE will grow rapidly over the next two years. You are aware that the dividend discount model can be useful in estimating the value of common stock even when the assumption of constant growth does not apply.

b. Calculate the current value of Arbot's common stock, using the dividend discount model, assuming that Arbot's dividend will grow at a 15% rate for the next two years, returning in the third year to the historical growth rate and continuing to grow at the historical rate for the foreseeable future. Show your calculations.

[1] The usefulness of this method of valuation is shown in Steven N. Kaplan and Richard S. Ruback, "The Valuation of Cash Flow Forecasts: An Empirical Analysis," *Journal of Finance* 50, no. 4 (September 1995): 1059–1093.

[2] Some fundamental analysts use a model for identifying winners (that is, underpriced common stocks) that is not directly related to the capitalization of income method of valuation. Instead, stocks are identified as candidates for purchase if certain of their financial ratios exceed predetermined values. For example, the first screen might identify every stock whose price was less than 2/3 of its net current asset value (that is, the per share value of current assets less total debt) and the second screen might identify stocks that also had a debt-to-equity ratio greater than 1. Articles that discuss such screening methods include J. Ronald Hoffmeister and Edward A. Dyl, "Dividends and Share Value: Graham and Dodd Revisited," *Financial Analysts Journal* 41, no. 3 (May/June 1985): 77–78; and Lewis D. Johnson, "Dividends and Share Value: Graham and Dodd Revisited, Again," *Financial Analysts Journal* 41, no. 5 (September/October 1985): 79–80. For the most recent edition of the book, see Sidney Cottle, Roger F. Murray, and Frank E. Block, *Graham and Dodd's Security Analysis*, 5th ed. (New York: McGraw-Hill, 1988). For a brief discussion of their approach to investing, see Roger F. Murray, "Graham and Dodd: A Durable Discipline," *Financial Analysts Journal* 40, no. 5 (September/October 1984): 18–23; Paul Blustein, "Ben Graham's Last Will and Testament," *Forbes,* August 1, 1977: 43–45; and James B. Rea, "Remembering Benjamin Graham—Teacher and Friend," *Journal of Portfolio Management* 3, no. 4 (Summer 1977): 66–72; Henry R. Oppenheimer, "A Test of Ben Graham's Stock Selection Criteria," *Financial Analysts Journal* 40, no. 5 (September/October 1984): 68–74; Henry R. Oppenheimer, "Ben Graham's Net Current Asset Values: A Performance Update," *Financial Analysts Journal* 42, no. 6 (November/December 1986): 40–47; Marc R. Reinganum, "The Anatomy of Stock Market Winners," *Financial Analysts Journal* 44, no. 2 (March/April 1988): 16–28.

[3] Sometimes the expected cash flows after some time period will be equal to zero, meaning that the summation needs to be carried out only to that point. Even if they are never equal to zero, in many cases the denominator in Equation (17.1) will become so large as t gets large (for example, if $t = 40$ or more for a discount rate of 15%) that the present value of all expected cash flows past an arbitrary time in the future will be roughly zero and can be safely ignored. Furthermore, the discount rate may vary from period to period. It is assumed to be constant here for ease of exposition.

[4] With complex cash flows (such as a mix of positive and negative cash flows), the IRR method can be misleading. However, this is not a problem when it is applied to securities such as stocks and bonds. For a discussion of potential problems in other contexts, see Richard A. Brealey and Stewart C. Myers, *Principles of Corporate Finance* (New York: McGraw-Hill, 1996), Chapter 5.

[5] Because the focus of DDMs is on predicting dividends, there is a particular situation in which using DDMs to value common stocks is exceptionally difficult. This is the case where the firm has not paid dividends on its stock in the recent past, which results in a lack of historical record on which to base a prediction of dividends. Examples include valuing the stock of a firm being sold to the public for the first time (known as an *initial public offering,* or *ipo*), valuing the stock of a firm that has not paid dividends recently (perhaps the firm has never paid dividends, or perhaps it has suspended paying them), and valuing the stock of a closely held firm. A more extensive discussion of DDMs is contained in the entire November–December 1985 issue of the *Financial Analysts Journal.* For articles that describe some of the current applications of DDMs, see Barbara Donnelly, "The Dividend Discount Model Comes into Its Own," *Institutional Investor* 19, no. 3 (March 1985): 77–82; and Kent Hickman and Glen H. Petry, "A Comparison of Stock Price Predictions Using Court Accepted Formulas, Dividend Discount, and P/E Models," *Financial Management* 19, no. 2 (Summer 1990): 76–87.

[6] A share of common stock has a positive NPV if and only if it has an IRR greater than its required rate of return. Thus there can never be inconsistent signals given by the two ap-

proaches. That is, there will never be a situation in which one approach indicates that a stock is underpriced and the other approach indicates that it is overpriced. This is true not only for the zero-growth model, but for all DDMs.

[7] The formula for valuing *consols* (these are bonds that make regular coupon payments but have no maturity date) is identical to Equation (17.13), where the numerator now represents the annual coupon payment. Because it has been found that the price behavior of high-grade preferred stock is very similar to that of bonds, it is not surprising that the zero-growth model can be used to value high-grade preferred stocks. See John S. Bildersee, "Some Aspects of the Performance of Non-Convertible Preferred Stocks," *Journal of Finance* 28, no. 5 (December 1973): 1187–1201; and Enrico J. Ferreira, Michael F. Spivey, and Charles E. Edwards, "Pricing New-Issue and Seasoned Preferred Stock: A Comparison of Valuation Models," *Financial Management* 21, no. 2 (Summer 1992): 52–62. For another method of valuing preferred stock, see Pradipkumar Ramanlal, "A Simple Algorithm for the Valuation of Preferred Stock," *Financial Practice and Education* 7, no. 1 (Spring/Summer 1997): 11–19.

[8] For an extension of this model that introduces capital gains taxes, see Raymond Chiang and Ricardo J. Rodriguez, "Personal Taxes, Holding Period, and the Valuation of Growth Stocks," *Journal of Economics and Business* 42, no. 4 (November 1990): 303–309.

[9] For a discussion of these models, see Russell J. Fuller and Chi-Cheng Hsia, "A Simplified Common Stock Valuation Model," *Financial Analysts Journal* 40, no. 5 (September/October 1984): 49–56; Eric H. Sorensen and David A. Williamson, "Some Evidence on the Value of Dividend Discount Models," *Financial Analysts Journal* 41, no. 6 (November/December 1985): 60–69; Richard W. Taylor, "A Three-Phase Quarterly Dividend Discount Model," *Financial Analysts Journal* 44, no. 5 (September/October 1988): 79–80, and "A Three-Phase Quarterly Earnings Model, *Financial Analysts Journal* 45, no. 5 (September/October 1989): 79; and Michael S. Rozeff, "The Three-Phase Dividend Discount Model and the ROPE Model," *Journal of Portfolio Management* 16, no. 2 (Winter 1990): 36–42.

[10] The analysis is similar if it is assumed that the investor plans to sell the stock after some other length of time, such as six months or two years.

[11] Alternatively, some analysts focus on the **earnings-price ratio**, which is the reciprocal of the price-earnings ratio. Accordingly, the formulas for a stock's "normal" earnings-price ratio can be found by simply taking the reciprocal of the forthcoming formulas for determining a stock's "normal" price-earnings ratio. In cases in which earnings are close to zero, the earnings-price ratio is computationally preferred by analysts to the price-earnings ratio because it approaches zero in such a situation, whereas the price-earnings ratio approaches infinity.

[12] There are numerous methods besides those described here. Some of them are based on more complicated versions of the CAPM, whereas others are based on the APT (discussed in Chapter 11).

[13] There are ways of forcing the intercept of the line to go through the riskfree rate in order to agree with the implications of the traditional CAPM.

[14] A subsequent procedure divides the estimated alpha by an estimate of the security's unique risk (that is, nonmarket or unsystematic risk) to obtain a standardized alpha. Then, on the basis of the magnitude of the standardized alpha, the security is classified into one of ten "standardized alpha deciles." See also Marshall E. Blume, "The Use of 'Alphas' to Improve Performance," *Journal of Portfolio Management* 11, no. 1 (Fall 1984): 86–92.

[15] An example of a similar procedure formerly used by Wells Fargo Investment Advisors is described by George Foster in *Financial Statement Analysis* (Englewood Cliffs, NJ: Prentice Hall, 1986), pp. 428–430.

[16] In a perfectly efficient market (in the semistrong-form sense), these analysts would sometimes be right and sometimes be wrong, so on balance their predictions would be of no value. In such a situation, the expected return for any security would be its required return, and the alpha would be zero.

[17] As an example of how to estimate alpha if it is assumed that the analyst has less than perfect forecasting ability and there is less than 100% convergence, reconsider the example given in Table 17.1. First, assume that the forecast accuracy of the security analyst is 60%. Remembering

that the analyst's forecast of D_1 is $1.10, but the consensus forecast is $1.00, then 60% accuracy means that the forecast that should be used is $1.06 [= $1.00 + .60 × ($1.10 − $1.00)]. Second, assume that there will be 50% convergence. This means that the security's price at $t = 1$ is expected to be $10.30 {= [$1.00 + .50 × ($1.06 − $1.00)]/.10}. Hence the expected return under 60% forecast accuracy and 50% convergence is 13.6% {= [($10.30 − $10) + $1.06]/$10}, which translates into an alpha of 3.6% (= 13.6% − 10%).

[18] It has been argued that a value of .15 for an IC is indicative of good performance with regard to stock forecasting and that several different forecasters have recorded ICs of this magnitude (a value of zero would be expected in a perfectly efficient market). See Keith P. Ambachtsheer, "Profit Potential in an 'Almost Efficient' Market," *Journal of Portfolio Management* 1, no. 1 (Fall 1974): 84–87, and "Where Are the Customers' Alphas?" *Journal of Portfolio Management* 4, no. 1 (Fall 1977): 52–56; Keith P. Ambachtsheer and James L. Farrell Jr., "Can Active Management Add Value?" *Financial Analysts Journal* 35, no. 6 (November/December 1979): 39–47; and S. D. Hodges and R. A. Brealey, "Portfolio Selection in a Dynamic and Uncertain World," *Financial Analysts Journal* 29, no. 2 (March/April 1973): 50–65.

KEY TERMS

capitalization of income method of valuation
discount rate
net present value
internal rate of return
dividend discount model
zero-growth model
constant-growth model

multiple-growth model
price-earnings ratio
earnings-price ratio
payout ratio
retention ratio
implied return
information coefficient

REFERENCES

1. The foundation for dividend discount models was laid out in:

   John Burr Williams, *The Theory of Investment Value* (Amsterdam: North-Holland Publishing, 1964). The original edition was published in 1938.

2. The constant-growth and multiple-growth models were subsequently developed by:

   M. J. Gordon, "Dividends, Earnings, and Stock Prices," *Review of Economics and Statistics* 41, no. 2 (May 1959): 99–105.

   Nicholas Molodovsky, Catherine May, and Sherman Chottiner, "Common Stock Valuation: Principles, Tables and Application," *Financial Analysts Journal* 21, no. 2 (March/April 1965): 104–123.

3. For interesting extensions of the multiple-growth DDM, see:

   Patricia M. Fairfield, "P/E, P/B and the Present Value of Future Dividends," *Financial Analysts Journal* 50, no. 4 (July/August 1994): 23–31.

   Joseph R. Gordon and Myron J. Gordon, "The Finite Horizon Expected Return Model," *Financial Analysts Journal* 53, no. 3 (May/June 1997): 52–61.

   William J. Hurley and Lewis D. Johnson, "Stochastic Two-Phase Dividend Discount Models," *Journal of Portfolio Management* 23, no. 4 (Summer 1997): 91–98.

   Yulin Yao, "A Trinomial Dividend Valuation Model," *Journal of Portfolio Management* 23, no. 4 (Summer 1997): 99–103.

4. For more on DDMs, see the entire November/December 1985 issue of the *Financial Analysts Journal* and *Damodaran on Valuation: Security Analysis for Investment and Corporate Finance* by Aswath Damodaran (New York: Wiley, 1994), particularly chapter 6. Some of the problems involved in using dividend discount models are discussed in:

   Richard O. Michaud and Paul L. Davis, "Valuation Model Bias and the Scale Structure of Dividend Discount Returns," *Journal of Finance* 38, no. 2 (May 1982): 563–573.

Adam K. Gehr Jr., "A Bias in Dividend Discount Models," *Financial Analysts Journal* 48, no. 1 (January/February 1992): 75–80.

5. For a discussion of how to estimate the discount rate k used with DDMs, see the entire issue of *Financial Markets, Institutions & Instruments* 3, no. 3 (1994) and:

Eugene F. Fama and Kenneth R. French, "Industry Costs of Equity," *Journal of Financial Economics* 43, no. 2 (February 1997): 153–193.

Bradford Cornell, John I. Hirshleifer, and Elizabeth P. James, "Estimating the Cost of Equity Capital," *Contemporary Finance Digest* 1, no. 1 (Autumn 1997): 5–26.

6. For more on how to measure and use P/E ratios, see:

John Markese, "Will the Real P/E Please Stand Up?" *AAII Journal* 11, no. 9 (October 1989): 32–34.

Robert J. Angell and Alonzo Redman, "How to Judge a P/E? Examine the Expected Growth Rate," *AAII Journal* 12, no. 3 (March 1990): 16–17.

John Baijkowski, "Price-Earnings Ratios and Fundamental Stock Valuation," *AAII Journal* 13, no. 6 (July 1991): 33–36.

7. The issue of market volatility has been studied by use of dividend discount models. In essence, these studies compare the actual levels of various stock market indices with their intrinsic values, calculated by determining the present value of rational forecasts of subsequent dividends paid on the stocks in the indices. The main observation is that the actual levels fluctuate far more over time than the intrinsic values. A conclusion that some people draw from these studies is that there is excess volatility in stock prices and hence markets are not efficient. This hotly debated topic was introduced in:

Stephen F. LeRoy and Richard D. Porter, "The Present-Value Relation: Tests Based on Implied Variance Bounds," *Econometrica* 49, no. 3 (May 1981): 555–574.

Robert J. Shiller, "Do Stock Prices Move Too Much to Be Justified by Subsequent Changes in Dividends?" *American Economic Review* 71, no. 3 (June 1981): 421–436.

8. For more on market volatility, see:

Robert J. Shiller, "Theories of Aggregate Stock Price Movements," *Journal of Portfolio Management* 10, no. 2 (Winter 1984): 23–37.

Robert J. Shiller, *Market Volatility* (Cambridge, MA: MIT Press, 1989).

Stephen F. LeRoy, "Efficient Capital Markets and Martingales," *Journal of Economic Literature* 27, no. 4 (December 1989): 1583–1621.

Stephen F. LeRoy, "Capital Market Efficiency: An Update," *Federal Reserve Bank of San Francisco Economic Review* (Spring 1990): 29–40.

Lucy F. Ackert and Brian F. Smith, "Stock Price Volatility, Ordinary Dividends, and Other Cash Flows to Shareholders," *Journal of Finance* 48, no. 4 (September 1993): 1147–1160.

Bong-Soo Lee, "The Response of Stock Prices to Permanent and Temporary Shocks to Dividends," *Journal of Financial and Quantitative Analysis* 30, no. 1 (March 1995): 1–22.

EARNINGS

Chapter 17 discussed how the intrinsic value of a share of common stock can be determined by discounting expected dividends per share at a rate of return that is appropriate for a security of similar risk. Alternatively, the implied return on a share of common stock can be determined by finding the discount rate that makes the present value of all the expected dividends equal to the current market price of the stock. In either case, a forecast of dividends per share is necessary. Because dividends per share are equal to earnings per share times a payout ratio, dividends can be forecast by forecasting earnings per share and payout ratios. Currently there are numerous methods that are used by security analysts for forecasting either earnings or dividends. This chapter presents a discussion of some of the important features of dividends and earnings that the analyst should be aware of in making such forecasts. It begins with a discussion of the relationship among earnings, dividends, and investment.

18.1   STOCK VALUATION BASED ON EARNINGS

A continual controversy in the investment community concerns the relevance of dividends versus earnings as the underlying source of value of a share of common stock. Clearly, earnings are important to stockholders because earnings provide the cash flow necessary for paying dividends.[1] However, dividends are also important because dividends are what stockholders actually receive from the firm, and they are the focus of the dividend discount models discussed in Chapter 17. Indeed, it would seem that if management increased the proportion of earnings per share paid out as dividends, they could make their stockholders wealthier, suggesting that the **dividend decision** (deciding on the amount of dividends to pay) is a very important one.

Considerable light was shed on this controversy in 1961 when Merton Miller and Franco Modigliani (both are recipients of the Nobel Prize in Economic Science) published a seminal paper arguing that the underlying source of value of a share of common stock was earnings, not dividends. An implication of this conclusion is that the dividend decision is relatively unimportant to the stockholders, because it will not affect the value of their investment in the firm.

In the course of a year, a firm generates revenues and incurs costs. With cash accounting, the difference between revenues and costs would be termed *cash flow*. With accrual accounting, used by almost all firms, both revenues and costs are likely to include estimates made by accountants of the values of noncash items. Items such as depreciation charges are deducted from cash flow to obtain earnings. Moreover, each year some amount is invested in the business. Of the total (gross) investment, a portion will be equal in value to the estimated depreciation of various real assets (such as machines and buildings); the rest is new (net) investment.

The dollar amount of new investment each year should be based on the investment opportunities that are available to the firm and should be unaffected by the dollar amount of dividends that are to be paid out. In particular, any investment opportunity whose net present value (NPV) is positive should be undertaken. This means that the future prospects of the firm can be described by a stream of expected earnings $(E_1, E_2, E_3, \dots)$ and the expected net investment required to produce such earnings $(I_1, I_2, I_3, \dots)$. When these two streams are taken as given, it can be shown that management can set the total dollar amount of current dividends (D_0) at any level without making the current stockholders either better or worse off.[2] This will be done next, with the focus on earnings and how they can be used to pay for new investments and dividends.

18.1.1   Earnings, Dividends, and Investment

Figure 18.1(a) shows one way that the firm can use total earnings for the current year (E_0). In this situation, new investment (I_0) is financed out of earnings, and the firm uses the remainder of the earnings to pay dividends (D_0) to its stockholders. For example, if the Plum Company has just earned \$5,000 and has new investments it would like to make that cost \$3,000, then Plum could pay for these investments out of earnings and declare a dividend of \$2,000.

Issuing Stock

Whereas earnings are exactly equal to dividends and investment $(E_0 = D_0 + I_0)$ in Figure 18.1(a), this need not be the case. In the situation shown in Figure 18.1(b), earnings are less than dividends and investment $(E_0 < D_0 + I_0)$. Because the amount of investment has been determined by the number of positive NPV projects available to the firm, the reason for this inequality is that the firm has decided to pay its current stockholders a higher dividend than was paid in Figure 18.1(a). However, in order for the higher dividend to be paid, additional funds must be obtained from outside the firm. Additional funds are obtained by a new sale of common stock (it is assumed that the flotation costs associated with a new sale of common stock are negligible).

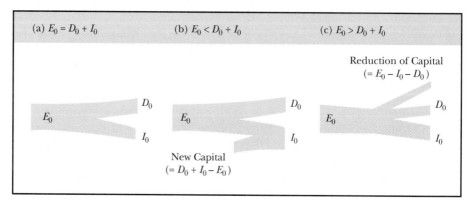

Figure 18.1
Earnings, Dividends, and Investment

The reason the funds are obtained through a new sale of common stock instead of through a new sale of debt is a desire to avoid the confounding effects of a change in the firm's debt-equity ratio. That is, if debt financing is to be allowed, then two things will be changing at the same time: the amount of the dividend and the debt-equity ratio for the firm. As a result, if stockholders appear to be made better off by a change in the amount of the dividend, their betterment may actually be due to a change in the debt-equity ratio. If debt financing is prohibited, the debt-equity ratio will remain constant and only the amount of the dividend will be allowed to change. That is, each additional dollar in equity funds raised by issuing new stock is offset by a dollar in dividend payments. Thus if stockholders appear to be better off, it has to be due to the change in the amount of the dividend, because everything else (specifically, the amount of investment and the debt-equity ratio) has remained fixed.

Note that if investment is financed out of earnings, as in Figure 18.1(a), then it has been financed with equity obtained *internally*. In Figure 18.1(b), investment has also been financed with equity, but here some of the equity has been obtained *externally*. As a result, the debt-equity ratio for the firm is the same in both situations.

In the case of Plum, instead of paying dividends amounting to $2,000, the firm could decide to pay dividends amounting to $3,000. Because investment is equal to $3,000, Plum will have a cash outflow of $6,000 (=$3,000 + $3,000), with earnings amounting to only $5,000. This means that Plum will have to sell $1,000 (=$6,000 − $5,000) of new common stock.

Repurchasing Stock

In Figure 18.1(c), the situation is reversed from Figure 18.1(b); earnings are now greater than dividends and investment $(E_0 > D_0 + I_0)$. Given that the amount of investment has been determined by the number of positive NPV projects available to the firm, the reason for this inequality is that the firm has decided to pay its stockholders a lower dividend than was paid in Figure 18.1(a). In paying this smaller dividend, the firm will be left with excess cash. It is assumed that the firm will use this cash to repurchase some of its outstanding shares in the marketplace (and that the transaction costs associated with such repurchases are negligible). The reason for this assumption is the desire to keep the situation comparable to the two earlier ones. Allowing the firm to keep the excess cash would be tantamount to letting the firm invest the cash, an investment decision that was not made in the two earlier cases and therefore does not have a positive NPV (remember that I_0 consists of all positive NPV projects). Allowing the firm to keep the excess cash would also mean that the firm has made a decision to lower its debt-equity ratio because retention of the excess cash would increase the amount of equity for the firm, thereby decreasing the amount of debt outstanding relative to the amount of equity.

The Plum Company could set dividends at $1,000 instead of $2,000 or $3,000. In this case, the firm would have a cash outflow for dividends and investment amounting to $4,000 (=$1,000 + $3,000). With earnings of $5,000, there would then be $1,000 (=$5,000 − $4,000) of cash left for the firm to use to repurchase its own stock.

The Dividend Decision

The firm has a decision to make regarding the size of its current dividends. The amount of current earnings E_0 and the amount of new investment I_0 have been determined. What is left to be decided is the amount of dividends, D_0. They can be set equal to earnings less investment [as in Figure 18.1(a)], or greater than that amount [as in Figure 18.1(b)], or less than that amount [as in Figure 18.1(c)]. The question that remains to be answered is this: Will one of these three levels of dividends make the current stockholders better off than the other two? That is, which level of dividends—$1,000, $2,000, or $3,000—will make the current stockholders better off?

The simplest way to answer that question is to consider a stockholder who presently holds 1% of the common stock of the firm and is determined to maintain this percentage ownership in the future.[3] If the firm follows a dividend policy as shown in Figure 18.1(a), the stockholder's current dividends will equal $.01D_0$ or, equivalently, $.01(E_0 - I_0)$. Similarly, the stockholder's future dividends will be equal to $.01D_t$ or, equivalently, $.01(E_t - I_t)$. Because the stockholder wants to be certain of receiving this amount regardless of the level of current dividends, he or she will take whatever actions are necessary to maintain a 1% ownership position in the firm. When the situation is analyzed in this manner, there is only one variable that can affect the stockholder's current wealth—the amount of the current dividend.

If the firm follows a dividend policy as shown in Figure 18.1(b), the stockholder must invest additional funds in the firm's common stock in order to avoid a diminished proportional ownership position in the firm. Why? Because in this situation the firm must raise funds by selling additional shares in order to pay for the larger cash dividends. Because $E_0 < D_0 + I_0$, the total amount of funds that the firm needs to raise is the amount F_0 such that:

$$E_0 + F_0 = D_0 + I_0 \tag{18.1}$$

or:

$$F_0 = D_0 + I_0 - E_0 \tag{18.2}$$

The amount of the additional investment that the stockholder needs to make in order to maintain a 1% position in the firm is $.01F_0$, which from Equation (18.2) is equal to $.01(D_0 + I_0 - E_0)$. Because the stockholder receives 1% of the dividends, the net amount the stockholder receives at time zero is equal to $.01D_0 - .01F_0$, or:

$$.01D_0 - .01(D_0 + I_0 - E_0) = .01E_0 - .01I_0 \tag{18.3}$$

Interestingly, the net amount the stockholder receives, $.01E_0 - .01I_0$, is the same as in the first situation. The amount of the extra cash dividend received is exactly offset by the amount the stockholder needs to spend to maintain his or her ownership position in the firm.

If the firm follows a dividend policy as shown in Figure 18.1(c), then the firm will repurchase shares. Accordingly, the stockholder must sell some shares back to the firm in order to avoid having an increased ownership position in the firm. Because $E_0 > D_0 + I_0$, the total amount of funds that the firm will spend on repurchasing its own shares is the amount R_0 such that:

$$E_0 = D_0 + I_0 + R_0 \tag{18.4}$$

or:

$$R_0 = E_0 - D_0 - I_0 \tag{18.5}$$

The amount of stock that the stockholder needs to sell back to the firm to maintain a 1% position in the firm is $.01R_0$, which from Equation (18.5) is equal to $.01(E_0 - D_0 - I_0)$. Because the stockholder receives 1% of the dividends, the net amount the stockholder receives at time zero is equal to $.01D_0 + .01R_0$, or:

$$.01D_0 + .01(E_0 - D_0 - I_0) = .01E_0 - .01I_0 \tag{18.6}$$

Again this net amount, $.01E_0 - .01I_0$, is the same as in the first situation. That is, in the third situation, the smaller amount of the cash dividend received by the stockholder is exactly made up for by the amount of cash received from the repurchase of shares by the firm.

Thus no matter what the firm's dividend policy, a stockholder choosing to maintain a constant proportional ownership will be able to spend the same amount of money on consumption at time zero. This amount will be equal to the proportion times the quantity $E_0 - I_0$. Furthermore, this will also be true in the future. That is, in any year t the stockholder will be able to spend on consumption an amount that is equal to the proportion times the quantity $E_t - I_t$.

18.1.2 Earnings Determine Market Value

In determining the value of 1% of the current shares outstanding, remember that the firm is about to declare and pay current dividends. Regardless of the magnitude of these dividends, the stockholder will be able to spend on consumption only an amount equal to $.01(E_0 - I_0)$. Furthermore, the stockholder will be able to spend on consumption an amount equal to $.01(E_t - I_t)$ in any future year t. Discounting these expected amounts by a (constant) rate k reveals that the value V of 1% of the current shares outstanding will be:

$$.01V = \frac{.01(E_0 - I_0)}{(1 + k)^0} + \frac{.01(E_1 - I_1)}{(1 + k)^1} + \frac{.01(E_2 - I_2)}{(1 + k)^2} + \cdots$$

Multiplying both sides of this equation by 100 results in the following expression for the total market value of all shares outstanding:

$$V = \frac{(E_0 - I_0)}{(1 + k)^0} + \frac{(E_1 - I_1)}{(1 + k)^1} + \frac{(E_2 - I_2)}{(1 + k)^2} + \cdots \tag{18.7}$$

Equation (18.7) shows that the aggregate market value of equity is equal to the present value of expected earnings net of investment. Note that the size of the dividends does not enter into the formula. This fact indicates that the market value of the stock is *independent* of the dividend decision made by the firm, meaning that the dividend decision is irrelevant to stock valuation. Instead, the market value of the firm is related to the earnings prospects of the firm, along with the required amounts of new investment needed to produce those earnings.[4]

Dividend Discount Models

In Chapter 17 it was shown that the value of a share of common stock was equal to the present value of all dividends expected in the future. Hence it is tempting to believe that, contrary to the assertion above, the market value of a firm's stock is *dependent* on the dividend decision. However, it turns out that there is nothing inconsistent between valuation based on dividend discount models and the irrelevancy of the dividend decision.

The dividend irrelevancy argument suggests that if the firm decides to increase its current dividend, then new shares will need to be sold. In turn, future dividends will be smaller because the aggregate amount of dividends will have to be divided among an increased number of shares outstanding. Ultimately, the current stockholders will be neither better off nor worse off, because the increased current dividend will be exactly offset by the decreased future dividends. Conversely, if the firm decides to decrease its current dividend, then shares will be repurchased and future dividends will be increased because there will be fewer shares outstanding. Ultimately, the decreased current dividend will be exactly offset by the increased future dividends, again leaving current stockholders neither better off nor worse off.

An Example

These situations can be illustrated with the example of the Plum Company. Because Plum currently has reported earnings of $5,000 and investments totaling $3,000, if dividends amounting to $2,000 were paid, then the stockholder owning 1% of the firm would receive cash amounting to $20 (=.01 × $2,000).

Alternatively, if dividends amounting to $3,000 were paid, then Plum would have to raise $1,000 from the sale of new common stock. The stockholder would receive $30 (=.01 × $3,000) in dividends but would have to pay $10 (=.01 × $1,000) to purchase 1% of the new stock, thereby maintaining his or her 1% ownership position. Consequently, the net cash flow to the stockholder would be $20 (=$30 − $10), the same amount as in the previous situation.

Last, if dividends amounting to $1,000 were paid, then Plum would have cash amounting to $1,000 to use to repurchase common stock. The stockholder, desirous of maintaining a 1% position, would thus sell shares amounting to $10 (=.01 × $1,000). As a result, the stockholder would have a cash inflow totaling $20 (=$10 + $10), again the same amount as in the two previous situations.

Under all three situations, the 1% stockholder would receive the same cash flow at the present time (=$20) and would have the same claim on the future earnings of Plum $\left[= .01(E_t - I_t)\right]$. That is, in all three cases, the stockholder would still own 1% of Plum and would therefore receive the same amount of dividends in the future. Accordingly, the 1% stockholder (and all the others) would be neither better off nor worse off if Plum pays a dividend amounting to $1,000, $2,000, or $3,000. In summary, the dividend decision is a nonevent; whatever the level of dividends, current stockholders will be neither better off nor worse off. This result is sometimes referred to as the *dividend irrelevancy theorem*.

18.2   DETERMINANTS OF DIVIDENDS

Few firms attempt to maintain a constant ratio of dividends to current earnings; doing so would result in a fluctuating dollar amount of dividends. The dividends would fluctuate because earnings on a year-to-year basis are likely to be quite variable. Instead, firms attempt to maintain a desired ratio of dividends to earnings over some relatively long period, meaning that there is a target payout ratio of dividends to long-run or sustainable earnings. As a result, dividends are usually kept at a constant dollar amount and are increased only when management is confident that it will be relatively easy to keep paying this increased amount in the future.[5] Nonetheless, larger earnings are likely to be accompanied by some sort of increase in dividends, as Table 18.1 shows.

18.2.1   Changes in Earnings and Dividends

The first two lines of Table 18.1 indicate that 59.3% of the time the earnings of the firms examined rose, and the remaining 40.7% of the time earnings fell. The majority of the times when current earnings rose, firms increased their current dividends. However, whenever current earnings fell, firms would increase their current dividends as frequently as they would decrease their current dividends (note that, roughly speaking, $42.8\% \cong 39.5\%$).

The next two lines of the table suggest that firms are more likely to increase current dividends if they have had two consecutive years of rising earnings than if they have had falling and then rising earnings (74.8% > 54.1%). The last two lines of the table suggest that firms are more likely to decrease current dividends if they have had two consecutive years of falling earnings than if they have had rising and then

TABLE 18.1 **Earnings and Dividend Changes of 392 Firms, 1946–1964**

Earnings Changes		Percent of Cases	Percent of Cases in Which Firms		
Current Year	Previous Year		Increased Dividends	Did Not Change Dividends	Decreased Dividends
+		59.3%	65.8%	13.9%	20.3%
−		40.7	42.8	17.9	39.5
+	+	33.4	74.8	11.4	13.8
+	−	25.9	54.1	17.2	28.7
−	+	24.7	49.7	16.9	33.4
−	−	16.0	31.8	19.4	48.8

Source: Eugene F. Babiak, "Dividend Policy: An Empirical Analysis," *Journal of the American Statistical Association* 63, no. 324 (December 1968): 1134.

falling earnings (48.8% > 33.4%). Overall, the table shows that firms in general are more likely to increase dividends than to decrease them.

18.2.2   The Lintner Model

A formal representation of the kind of behavior implied by a constant long-run target payout ratio begins by assuming that the goal of the firm is to pay out p^* (for example, $p^* = 60\%$) of long-run earnings. If this target ratio were maintained every year, total dividends paid in year t would be:

$$D_t^* = p^* E_t \tag{18.8}$$

where D_t^* denotes the target amount for dividends to be paid in year t, and E_t is the amount of earnings in year t. The difference between target dividends in year t and the previous year's actual dividends is determined by subtracting D_{t-1} from both sides of Equation (18.8), resulting in:

$$D_t^* - D_{t-1} = p^* E_t - D_{t-1} \tag{18.9}$$

Although firms would like to change their dividends from D_{t-1} to D_t^*, few (if any) firms would actually change their dividends by this amount. Instead, the actual change in dividends will be a proportion of the desired change:

$$D_t - D_{t-1} = a\left(D_t^* - D_{t-1}\right) \tag{18.10}$$

where a is a "speed of adjustment" coefficient, a number between 0 and 1.

For example, if a firm has just earned \$5 million $\left(E_t = \$5 \text{ million}\right)$ and has a target payout ratio of 60%, then it would like to pay dividends amounting to \$3 million $(=.6 \times \$5 \text{ million})$. If it paid dividends of \$2 million last year, this amount represents an increase of \$1 million (=\$3 million − \$2 million). However, if $a = 50\%$, then the firm will actually increase the dividends by \$500,000 (=.5 × \$1 million). Thus actual dividends will be equal to \$2.5 million (=\$2 million + \$500,000), an amount equal to last year's dividends plus the change in dividends from last year to this year.

This model can be summarized by substituting $p^* E_t$ for D_t^* in Equation (18.10) and then solving the resulting expression for D_t:

$$D_t = ap^* E_t + (1 - a)D_{t-1} \tag{18.11}$$

Equation (18.11) indicates that the amount of current dividends is based on the amount of current earnings and the amount of last year's dividends.[6] In the previous example, $a = 50\%$, $p^* = 60\%$, $E_t = \$5$ million, and $D_{t-1} = \$2$ million. Thus actual dividends D_t would be equal to $2.5 million [= (.5 × .6 × $5 million) + (1 − .5) × $2 million)].

Subtracting D_{t-1} from both sides of Equation (18.11) shows that the change in dividends is equal to:

$$D_t - D_{t-1} = ap^* E_t - aD_{t-1} \qquad (18.12)$$

When written in this form, the model suggests that the size of the *change* in dividends will be positively related to the current amount of earnings (because ap^* is a positive number) and negatively related to the amount of the previous period's dividends (because $-aD_{t-1}$ is a negative number). Thus the larger current earnings are, the larger the change in dividends; but the larger the previous period's dividends, the smaller the change in dividends.

18.2.3 Test Results

Statistical analysis has been used to test how well this model describes the way a sample of firms set the amount of their dividends. Table 18.2 summarizes some of the values obtained in one such study. The average firm had a target payout ratio of 59.1% and adjusted dividends 26.9% of the way toward its target each year. However, most firms' dividends varied substantially from the pattern implied by their targets and adjustment factors. Somewhat less than half (42%) of the annual variance in the typical firm's dividends could be explained in this manner. This result means that the model, although explaining a portion of the changes in dividends that occurred, leaves a substantial portion unexplained.

A refinement of the model presented in Equation (18.12) uses an alternative definition of earnings. Specifically, the term E_t in Equation (18.8) can be defined as the *permanent* earnings of the firm in year *t* instead of total earnings. Here total earnings can be thought of as having two components: permanent earnings, which are likely to be repeated, and transitory earnings, which are not likely to be repeated. Accordingly, the refinement is based on the idea that management ignores the transitory component of earnings in arriving at its target amount of dividends. Hence, the target amount is based on the permanent earnings of the firm, not on the total earnings, and the change in dividends shown in Equation (18.12) is related to the past

TABLE 18.2 Target Payout Ratios and Speed of Dividend Adjustment Factors of 298 Firms, 1946–1968					
Speed of Adjustment Coefficient		Target Payout Ratio		Percent of Variance Explained	
Value	Percent of Firms with Smaller Value	Value	Percent of Firms with Smaller Value	Value	Percent of Firms with Smaller Value
.104	10%	.401	10%	11%	10%
.182	30	.525	30	32	30
.251	50	.584	50	42	50
.339	70	.660	70	54	70
.470	90	.779	90	72	90
Average .269		Average .591		Average 42	

Source: Eugene F. Fama, "The Empirical Relationship between the Dividend and Investment Decisions of Firms," *American Economic Review* 64, no. 3 (June 1974): 310.

level of dividends and permanent earnings. A test of this model found that it described changes in dividends better than the previously described model that was based on total earnings.[7]

18.3 THE INFORMATION CONTENT OF DIVIDENDS

It is reasonable to believe that management has more information about the future earnings of the firm than does the public (which includes its own stockholders). This situation of **asymmetric information** suggests that managers will seek to convey the information to the public if they have an incentive to do so. If they do have such an incentive, one way of conveying information is to announce a change in the amount of the firm's dividends. When used in this manner, dividend announcements are said to be a signaling device.[8]

18.3.1 Signaling

A relatively simple view of dividend changes is that an announced increase in dividends is a signal that management has increased its assessment of the firm's future earnings. The announced increase in dividends is therefore good news and will, in turn, cause investors to raise their expectations regarding the firm's future earnings. Conversely, an announced decrease in dividends is a signal that management has decreased its assessment of the firm's future earnings. The announced decrease in dividends is therefore bad news and will, in turn, cause investors to lower their expectations regarding the firm's future earnings. An implication is that an announced increase in dividends will cause the firm's stock price to rise, and an announced decrease will cause it to fall.

This simple model of dividend changes can be thought of as a special case of the model given in Equation (18.12), where the speed of adjustment, a, is zero. With this model, the expected change in dividends, $D_t - D_{t-1}$, is zero, suggesting that a simple increase in dividends will be viewed as good news. Conversely, a simple decrease in dividends will be viewed as bad news.

One way of testing to see if dividend changes do indeed convey information to the public is to see how stock prices react to announcements of changes in dividends. However, care must be exercised in conducting such a study because the firm's announcement of dividends is often made at the same time that the firm announces its earnings. When such announcements are made at the same time, any price change in the firm's common stock may be attributable to either (or both) announcements.

One study attempted to avoid this problem of contamination by looking only at cases in which the announcement of earnings was at least 11 trading days apart from the announcement of dividends. Figure 18.2 illustrates the average abnormal return associated with a firm's dividend announcement for firms that announced their dividends 11 or more days after they announced their earnings. (Similar results were obtained when the authors of the study examined cases in which dividend announcements preceded earnings announcements.)

In cases in which firms announced an increase in their dividends, there was a significant positive reaction in their stock prices. Conversely, for firms that announced a decrease in their dividends, there was a significant negative reaction in their stock prices. These findings strongly support the **information content of dividends hypothesis**, which asserts that dividend announcements contain inside information about the firm's future prospects.

It should be noted that there is nothing inconsistent with dividends being used as a signal and with the dividend irrelevancy argument of Miller and Modigliani that

---

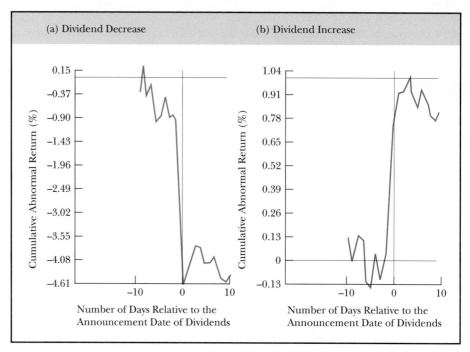

Figure 18.2
Cumulative Abnormal Returns Starting Ten Days before a Dividend Announcement
Source: Joseph Aharony and Itzhak Swary, "Quarterly Dividend and Earnings Announcements and Stockholders' Returns: An Empirical Analysis," *Journal of Finance* 35, no. 1 (March 1980): 8.

was made earlier. In particular, stockholders will be neither better off nor worse off if the *level* of dividends, relative to earnings, is high or low. *Changes* in dividends may, however, be important because they convey information to the public about the future earnings prospects for the firm.

18.3.2 Dividend Initiations and Omissions

One study looked at the relationship between dividend changes and past, current, and future changes in earnings.[9] Specifically, it focused on the most dramatic dividend announcements possible—dividend initiations and omissions—because the information being conveyed in these announcements is unambiguous.

That is, if the information content of dividends hypothesis is correct, then firms that start to pay dividends for the first time in at least ten years must be signaling that they believe that earnings have recently increased to a permanently higher level and that earnings may increase even more in the near future. The question to be addressed is this: Have firms actually experienced notably higher earnings around the time of such initiations and afterward?

Conversely, firms that have paid dividends for at least ten years and that suddenly stop paying any dividends must believe that their earnings have recently decreased to a permanently lower level and that earnings may decrease even more in the future. For them the question is this: Have firms actually experienced notably lower earnings around the time of such omissions and afterward?

After examining 131 dividend-initiating and 172 dividend-omitting stocks on the NYSE and Amex from 1969–1980, support was found for the information content of dividends hypothesis. Specifically, the study found that earnings tended to increase for at least one year leading up to dividend initiations and to decrease for up to two years leading up to dividend omissions. Furthermore, earnings continued to increase for at least one year after initiations and to decrease for one year after omissions, and such changes appear to be permanent. Interestingly, the larger the change in the firm's stock price when the dividend initiation or omission was announced, the larger the change in the firm's earnings in both the year of the announcement and the year thereafter. Thus it seems that dividends do indeed convey information about earnings.

A second study also focused on the stock price movements of firms around the time that they either initiated or omitted dividends.[10] In this study, which examined a sample of firms listed on the New York Stock Exchange and the American Stock Exchange, 887 occurrences of dividend omissions and 561 initiations were uncovered during 1964–1988. The following observations were made:

1. Firms that initiated dividends had on average an abnormal rise of 15.1% in their stock price over the year up to the time of the dividend announcement. The corresponding figure for firms that omitted dividends was −31.8%. Hence, firms that initiated dividends seem to have been prior "winners," whereas firms that omitted dividends seem to have been prior "losers."
2. Over the three-day period centered on the initial announcement of a dividend, the average firm had its stock rise by an abnormal 3.4%. The corresponding figure for omissions was −7.0%.
3. The average stock of firms that initiated a dividend rose by an abnormal 24.8% in the three years afterward, whereas the average stock price of firms that omitted a dividend fell by an abnormal 15.0% over the subsequent two years, and thereafter had normal returns. Because of the lagged response to the dividend initiations and omissions, it appears that the market underreacts to these dividend announcements, implying a market inefficiency.
4. The average dividend yield at the time a dividend was initiated was .9%; the average dividend yield just before an omission was 6.7%.

18.3.3   Dividends and Losses

In a similar vein to dividend initiations and omissions, it is interesting to examine situations in which firms that have had a string of at least ten years of positive earnings and dividend payments suddenly experience negative earnings. In particular, do dividends in such a situation convey information about future earnings?

One study examined this situation by looking at firms that had at least one year of negative earnings during the 1980–1985 period but previously had at least ten consecutive years of positive earnings and dividend payments; 167 firms ("loss" firms) were uncovered that met those criteria.[11] A comparison sample of 440 firms ("non-loss" firms) that had positive earnings during the 1980–1985 period as well as during a previous ten-year period was also formed.

Approximately half the loss firms reduced or omitted their dividends in the four subsequent quarters after the fiscal year-end of the loss. In comparison, fewer than 1% of the non-loss firms either reduced or omitted their dividends during the six-year period of 1980–1985. Further examination revealed that:

1. The loss firms that did not reduce their dividends were likely to have unusual income items, indicating that their earnings problems were likely to be temporary.
2. The loss firms that reduced their dividends had deeper losses than the loss firms that did not reduce their dividends.
3. The loss firms that reduced their dividends were much more likely to have negative earnings in the next two years than the nonreducing loss firms.

Hence knowing what happened to dividends for a loss firm tends to make it easier to predict its future earnings, thereby indicating that dividends have information content when a firm suddenly has negative earnings.

Because the prediction of earnings is of critical importance in security analysis and investment research, a review of what is known about earnings and the relationship between earnings and security prices is essential. At a fundamental level, consideration of the concept of earnings itself is needed. Specifically, just what is meant by "earnings" to those who produce the figures, and how does its meaning affect the valuation process?

18.4.1 Accounting Earnings

A firm's accountants operate under constraints and guidelines imposed by regulatory authorities and professional organizations such as the Securities and Exchange Commission (SEC) and the Financial Accounting Standards Board (FASB).[12] In cooperation with management, the accountants produce, on a quarterly basis, a set of financial statements for the firm that ends with a figure for the firm's **accounting earnings** (also known as the firm's reported earnings). In a broad sense, such earnings represent the difference between revenues and expenses, including the expenses associated with nonequity sources of funds (such as debt). This difference, the "total earnings available for common stock," is divided by the number of shares outstanding to calculate **earnings per share** (EPS). It may also be divided by the book value per share to calculate the **return on equity** (ROE).

A basic principle of accounting makes the book value of a firm's equity at the end of a period (such as a quarter or a year) equal to (1) its value at the end of the previous period plus (2) the portion of accounting earnings for the period that is retained by the firm (here it is assumed that there has been no change in the number of shares outstanding during the period).[13] Letting B_t denote the book value of the equity of the firm at the end of period t, E_t^a denote the accounting earnings for period t, and D_t denote the dividends paid during period t, this relationship can be expressed algebraically as:

$$B_t = B_{t-1} + E_t^a - D_t \qquad (18.13)$$

From Equation (18.13), it can be seen that accounting earnings equal the change in book value of equity plus dividends paid:

$$E_t^a = B_t - B_{t-1} + D_t \qquad (18.14)$$

This is equivalent to noting that accounting earnings are equal to the change in retained earnings plus dividends paid.

18.4.2 Economic Earnings

Economic earnings $\left(E_t^e\right)$ may be defined as the amount that would be obtained in Equation (18.14) if the change in the book value of the firm equaled the change in the **economic value of the firm**:

$$E_t^e = V_t - V_{t-1} + D_t \qquad (18.15)$$

Here the change in the economic value of the firm during period t, $V_t - V_{t-1}$, is defined as the change in the market value of the firm's common stock (assuming that there is no change in the market value of the firm's other securities).[14]

It is easy to show that reported book values and market values (that is, economic values) of stocks are often considerably different. Figure 18.3 shows the ratio of (1) the year-end market price per share for Standard & Poor's Industrial Stock Index to

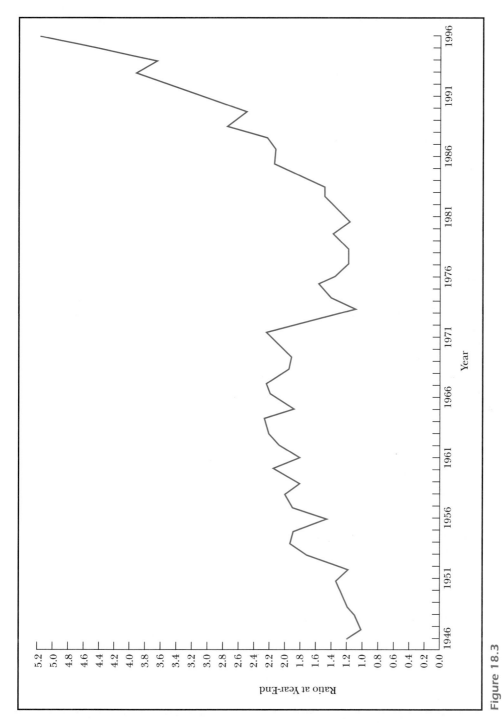

Figure 18.3
Ratio of Market Price to Book Value: Standard & Poor's Industrial Stock Index, 1946–1996

Source: Standard & Poor's Statistical Service: *Current Statistics*, various issues.

(2) the corresponding year-end book value per share. It can be seen that the ratio is typically greater than 1.0 and has fluctuated considerably from year to year.

Figure 18.3 indicates that there can be sizable differences between market and book values. Because Equations (18.14) and (18.15) show that accounting and economic earnings will be equal only if market and book values are equal, the evidence suggests that accounting and economic earnings differ by varying amounts for different firms.

It is sometimes contended that investors estimate the value of a firm's common stock by directly applying a formula to the firm's current and past accounting earnings.[15] Such a belief may tempt a firm's managers to try to "manage" such earnings in order to make a firm appear more valuable than it is, thereby fooling investors, at least temporarily. This "managing" is possible because the **generally accepted accounting principles** (GAAP) set by the regulatory authorities (such as FASB) allow a large amount of discretion in how certain items are accounted for (examples include methods for depreciation and inventory valuation). As a result, management may pressure accountants to use those principles that maximize the level of reported earnings, or that result in a high growth rate of reported earnings, or that "smooth" earnings by reducing the year-to-year variability of earnings around a growth rate.[16] Some of these activities can be continued for only a limited number of years; others can go on indefinitely.

To obtain a truly independent estimate of value, analysts must dissect reported earnings. In doing so, they should not be fooled by any accounting illusions, meaning that they should ignore any manipulations that may have been made by the accountants at management's request.[17] Anyone who estimates value by applying a formula (no matter how complex) to reported earnings is not producing an estimate that is completely free from all possible manipulations by management. This is not to say that reported earnings are irrelevant for security valuation. Instead, they should be viewed as one source of information about the future prospects of a firm.

18.5 PRICE-EARNINGS RATIOS

Chapter 17 discussed how dividend discount models could be used to determine if stocks were either underpriced or overpriced. One means of making this determination was to compare the actual price-earnings ratio for a firm with what the security analyst had determined it should be. In view of this use of price-earnings ratios, some evidence on the behavior of overall earnings, prices, and price-earnings ratios will now be presented.

18.5.1 The Historical Record

Figure 18.4(a) presents a plot of the year-end price-earnings ratios for the Standard & Poor's 500. It can be seen from this plot that the variation in the ratio on a year-to-year basis is considerable, suggesting that investors do not simply apply a standard multiple to earnings in order to determine an appropriate value.

Figure 18.4(b) presents a plot of earnings per share (the lower line) and price (the upper line) for the Standard & Poor's 500.[18] Both lines generally move upward to the right, showing a general trend for both earnings per share and prices to increase over time. However, the two lines are not parallel. This means that earnings per share and prices do not move together in a lockstep manner, an observation that is also apparent in panel (a).

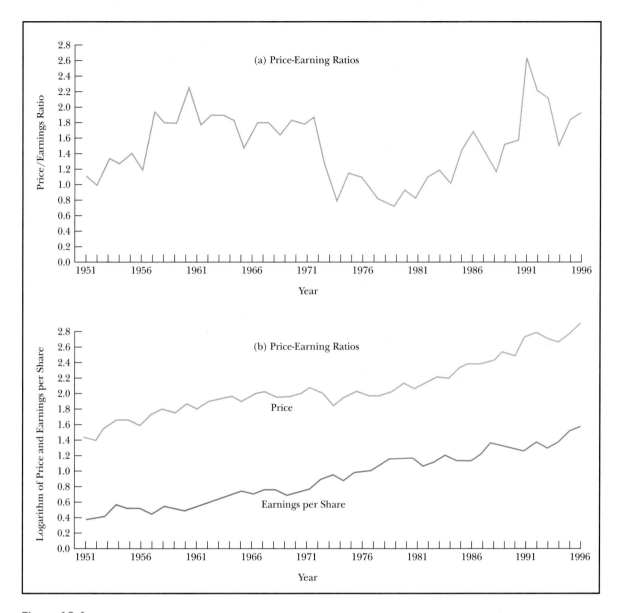

Figure 18.4
Price, Earnings, and Price-Earnings Ratios, Standard & Poor's 500. Year-End, 1951–1996
Source: Standard & Poor's *Statistical Service: Current Statistics*, various issues.

18.5.2   Permanent and Transitory Components of Earnings

When individual common stocks are analyzed, they too show considerable variation in their price-earnings ratios over time. Furthermore, their ratios are quite different from each other at any point in time. One possible explanation notes that reported total earnings can be viewed as having two components, as noted earlier. The *permanent component* is the component that is likely to be repeated in the future, whereas the *transitory component* is not likely to be repeated.

Earlier, it was argued that the intrinsic value of a stock depends on the firm's earnings prospects. This idea suggests that changes in a stock's intrinsic value, and in turn its price, will be correlated with changes in the permanent component of its

---

earnings but not with changes in the transitory component. If the transitory component is positive, then the price-earnings ratio will be relatively low owing to a relatively large number in the denominator. Conversely, if the transitory component is negative, then the price-earnings ratio will be relatively high owing to a relatively small number in the denominator.

As an example, consider a firm whose current stock price is $30 per share. Its permanent component of earnings per share over the past year is $4, and its transitory component is $1, resulting in reported earnings of $5 (=$4 + $1) and a price-earnings ratio of 6 (=$30/$5). Remember that this stock's current price is based on its future prospects, which are in turn based on the permanent component of earnings per share over the past year. Thus if the firm had had the same permanent component of $4 but had had a transitory component of −$1 instead of +$1, the stock would still have had a current price of $30 per share. However, its reported earnings would have been $3 (=$4 − $1) and its price-earnings ratio would have been 10 (=$30/$3).

The permanent component of earnings will change over time, causing investors to revise their forecasts. The revision of forecasts will lead to a change in a firm's stock price and, in turn, its price-earnings ratio. However, changes in the transitory component will have an even greater effect on the price-earnings ratio because this component will sometimes be positive and sometimes be negative. As a result, a firm's price-earnings ratio will be variable over time, as was shown in Figure 18.4(a) for the S&P 500. In addition, at any point in time, the transitory component of earnings for a group of firms will have varying sizes, some being positive and some being negative. As a result, at any point in time, firms will have a range of different price-earnings ratios.

If this were a complete explanation for the considerable variation in price-earnings ratios over time and among firms, then most of the variation in a firm's price-earnings ratio would itself be transitory. That is, the ratio would vary over time around some average value. However, the evidence suggests that it does not. Figure 18.5 shows the behavior over time of price-earnings ratios for two groups of stocks. The first group includes stocks with high price-earnings ratios at the beginning of the period (that is, during a portfolio formation period). The other group includes stocks with low price-earnings ratios at the beginning of the period.

Over time, the price-earnings ratios tend to revert to an average ratio for the market as a whole. The changes are substantial in the first two years, owing undoubtedly to the influence of transitory components of earnings. That is, those stocks in the high price-earnings ratio group apparently had, on average, a negative transitory component in their earnings in the portfolio formation period. (Remember that such a component would tend to give a stock a high price-earnings ratio.) Conversely, those stocks in the low price-earnings ratio group apparently had, on average, a positive transitory component. (Remember that such a component would tend to give a stock a low price-earnings ratio.) Over future periods, each group of stocks would tend to have an equal number of stocks with positive and negative transitory components, resulting in an average transitory component for each group of roughly zero.

However, Figure 18.5 shows that the two groups of stocks have convergent but still different price-earnings ratios for many years after the portfolio formation period. Three explanations can be offered for this persistent difference.

1. Appropriate discount rates (that is, required returns) differ because of differences in security attributes. For two firms with the same current and expected future earnings, the firm with the lower discount rate will have a higher stock price and hence a higher price-earnings ratio.

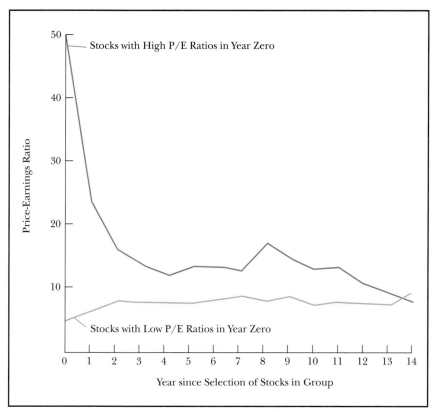

Figure 18.5
Price-Earnings Ratios over Time for Two Groups of Stocks
Source: William Beaver and Dale Morse, "What Determines Price-Earnings Ratios?" *Financial Analysts Journal* 34, no. 4 (July/August 1978): 68.

2. There may be permanent differences between economic and reported earnings owing to the use of different accounting methods. As mentioned earlier, there is evidence that the market sees through such differences in reported earnings.

3. There may be persistent differences in the forecasts of long-term permanent earnings growth rates by security analysts. That is, firms with high price-earnings ratios may have long-term permanent earnings growth rates that are forecast to be high, and hence relatively high prices. Conversely, firms with low price-earnings ratios may have long-term permanent earnings growth rates that are forecast to be low, and hence have relatively low prices.[19] If such forecasts persisted over time, then firms with high price-earnings ratios would tend to continue having high ratios over time, while firms with low ratios would tend to continue having low ratios over time. Evidence suggests that indeed this is the case.

18.6   RELATIVE GROWTH RATES OF FIRMS' EARNINGS

Because security analysis typically involves forecasting earnings per share, it is useful to examine the historical record to see how earnings per share have changed over time. An interesting question about growth rates in firm earnings over time focuses on "growth stocks" (growth stocks were discussed in Chapter 16). The very idea of a growth stock suggests that growth in some firms' earnings will exceed the average growth of all firms' earnings in most years, while other firms' earnings will grow less than the average.

18.6.1 Earnings Growth Rates

The results of a study of the earnings growth rates for 610 industrial companies from 1950 to 1964 are shown in Table 18.3. For every year, each firm's earnings were compared with its earnings in the previous year, and the percentage change was calculated. The year was counted as "good" for the firm if its percentage change was in the top half of the changes for all firms that year and as "bad" if it was in the bottom half. Fairly long runs of good years should occur for firms that tend to experience above-average earnings growth rates. Conversely, fairly long runs of bad years should occur for firms that tend to experience below-average earnings growth rates.

The middle two columns of Table 18.3 indicate the actual number of runs of various lengths. The right-hand column shows the number that would be expected if there were a 50-50 chance of either a good year or a bad year. The three columns are remarkably similar. Above-average earnings growth in the past does not appear to indicate above-average growth in the future, and below-average growth in the past does not appear to indicate below-average growth in the future. Flipping a coin seems to be as reliable a predictor of future growth as looking at past growth rates.

A study using longer time periods for measuring growth reached generally similar conclusions.[20] For each of 323 companies with positive earnings in each year from 1946 through 1965, average growth rates were computed for (1) the period from 1946 through 1955 and (2) the period from 1956 through 1965. Differences among firms' earnings growth rates in the first period accounted for less than 1% of the variation in the differences among their earnings growth rates in the second period.

TABLE 18.3	Earnings Growth Rates of 610 Firms, 1950–1964		
Length of Run	Actual Number of Good Runs	Actual Number of Bad Runs	Number of Good or Bad Runs Expected If the Odds Each Year Were 50-50 Regardless of Past Performance
1	1,152	1,102	1,068
2	562	590	534
3	266	300	267
4	114	120	133
5	55	63	67
6	24	20	33
7	23	12	17
8	5	6	8
9	3	3	4
10	6	0	2
11	2	0	1
12	1	0	1
13	0	0	0
14	0	1	0

Source: Richard A. Brealey, *An Introduction to Risk and Return from Common Stocks* (Cambridge, MA: MIT Press, 1983), p. 89.

18.6.2 Annual Earnings

The results of these and other studies suggest that *annual reported earnings* follow what is known in statistics as a **random walk model**. That is, annual earnings for the forthcoming year (E_t) can be thought of as being equal to annual earnings over the past year (E_{t-1}) plus a random error term. (Remember that a random error term can be thought of as a roulette wheel with the numbers distributed around zero.) Accordingly, next year's earnings can be described by the following statistical model:

$$E_t = E_{t-1} + \varepsilon_t \tag{18.16}$$

where ε_t is the random error term. With this model, the estimate of next year's earnings is simply the past year's earnings, E_{t-1}. Another way of viewing a random walk model for earnings is that the change in earnings is independent and identically distributed:

$$E_t - E_{t-1} = \varepsilon_t \tag{18.17}$$

This means that the change in earnings, $E_t - E_{t-1}$, is unrelated to past changes in earnings and can be thought of as a spin from a roulette wheel that is perhaps unique to the firm but, more important, is used year after year. Because the expected outcome from a spin of the roulette wheel is zero, the expected change in earnings is zero. This relation implies that the expected level of earnings is equal to the past year's earnings, as was suggested earlier.[21]

18.6.3 Quarterly Earnings

In terms of *quarterly reported earnings*, consideration must be given to the fact that there is typically a seasonal component to a firm's earnings (for example, many retailing firms have high earnings during the quarter that includes Christmas). As a result, a slightly different model appears to be best for forecasting purposes. This model forecasts the growth in earnings for the forthcoming quarter relative to the same quarter one year ago, a quantity denoted $QE_t - QE_{t-4}$. It does so by relating this growth to the growth during the most recent quarter relative to the comparable quarter one year before it, $QE_{t-1} - QE_{t-5}$. Formally, the model for the "seasonally differenced series" of quarterly earnings is known as an *autoregressive model of order one* and is as follows:

$$QE_t - QE_{t-4} = a(QE_{t-1} - QE_{t-5}) + b + e_t \tag{18.18}$$

where a and b are constants and e_t is a random error term.

Alternatively, the model can be rewritten by moving the term QE_{t-4} to the right-hand side:

$$QE_t = QE_{t-4} + a(QE_{t-1} - QE_{t-5}) + b + e_t \tag{18.19}$$

When the constants a and b are estimated, this model can be used to forecast quarterly earnings.[22] For example, assuming estimates for a and b of .4 and .05, respectively, the forecast of a firm's earnings for the next quarter would be equal to $QE_{t-4} + .4(QE_{t-1} - QE_{t-5}) + \$.05$. Thus if a firm had earnings per share for the last quarter $(t-1)$ of \$3, for four quarters ago $(t-4)$ of \$2, and for five quarters ago $(t-5)$ of \$2.60, then its forecast earnings for the forthcoming quarter would be equal to \$2.21 [$=\$2 + .4(\$3 - \$2.60) + \$.05$]. Note that the forecast consists of three components: a component equal to last quarter's earnings (\$2); a component that considers the year-to-year quarterly growth in earnings [$\$.16 = .4(\$3 - \$2.60)$]; and a component that is a constant (\$.05).[23]

A number of studies have shown large price changes for stocks of companies that report earnings that differ substantially from consensus expectations. One study looked at three groups of 50 stocks.[24] The first group consisted of the 50 stocks listed on the New York Stock Exchange (NYSE) that experienced the greatest price rise during 1970. The second group consisted of 50 stocks chosen randomly from all those listed on the NYSE during 1970. The third group consisted of the 50 stocks listed on the NYSE that experienced the greatest price decline during 1970. As shown in Figure 18.6, the median changes in the prices of the stocks in the top, random, and bottom groups were 48.4%, −3.2%, and −56.7%, respectively.

Next, the study looked at the actual change in earnings per share from 1969 to 1970 for each stock in each group. As shown in Figure 18.6, the median changes in actual earnings per share for the top, random, and bottom groups were 21.4%, −10.5%, and −83.0%, respectively.

Last, the study determined the forecast change in earnings per share at the beginning of 1970 for each stock in each group. The investigators used the predictions contained in Standard & Poor's *Earnings Forecaster*, which reports estimates made by several investment research organizations. The median forecast changes in earnings per share for the top, random, and bottom groups are shown in Figure 18.6 to be 7.7%, 5.8%, and 15.3%, respectively.

Interestingly, the forecasts of earnings per share hardly correspond to the price movements of the stocks. In fact, the earnings of the stocks in the bottom group were expected to increase more than the earnings of the stocks in the top group (15.3%, compared with 7.7%). However, the prediction for the bottom group was disastrously wrong, with a median earnings per share decline of 83.0%. And, as Figure

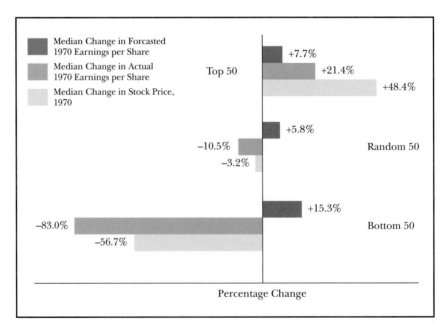

Figure 18.6
Earnings and Price Changes: Selected Stocks Listed on the New York Stock Exchange during 1970

Source: Victor Niederhoffer and Patrick J. Regan, "Earnings Changes, Analysts' Forecasts, and Stock Prices," *Financial Analysts Journal* 28, no. 3 (May/June 1972): 67.

18.6 shows, prices definitely followed suit. Overall, it appears that unexpected changes in earnings do indeed affect security prices.[25]

But do earnings surprises affect prices before or after their announcement? In a completely efficient market, such information would be reflected in prices as soon as it had been disseminated to a few major market participants. The reaction of security prices around the time of earnings announcements has been examined by a number of authors and will be discussed next.

18.7.1 Deviations from Time-Series Models of Earnings

A comprehensive study involving 2,053 firms from 1974 through 1981 provided evidence concerning the speed of response of security prices to earnings announcements.[26] For each company, an expected earnings figure was computed for each quarter by using the model of the time-series behavior of earnings shown in Equation (18.19). With this model, the expected earnings for a firm during period t was equal to $QE_{t-4} + a(QE_{t-1} - QE_{t-5}) + b$. For example, the earnings expected for the firm in the second quarter of 1999 would equal (1) the firm's earnings in the second quarter of 1998, plus (2) the change in earnings from the first quarter of 1998 to the first quarter of 1999 times the parameter a, plus (3) the parameter b. The values of a and b would be determined by analysis of the behavior of earnings prior to the second quarter of 1999.

Given actual earnings and an estimate of expected earnings, a forecast error (FE_t) can be computed for the firm:

$$FE_t = QE_t - \overline{QE_t} \qquad (18.20)$$

where QE_t is the actual earnings for quarter t and $\overline{QE_t}$ is the expected earnings for quarter t, forecast at time $t-1$. Simply stated, Equation (18.20) indicates that the forecast error for a quarter is the difference between actual earnings for that quarter and expected earnings.

The forecast error provides a measure of the "surprise" in the quarterly earnings announcement, but it fails to differentiate between stocks for which large forecast errors are routine and those for which they are rare. The important surprises are those associated with forecast errors that are large by historical standards. Surprises are accounted for by relating a forecast error to previous errors to obtain a measure of **standardized unexpected earnings** (SUE):

$$SUE_t = \frac{FE_t}{\sigma_{FE_t}} \qquad (18.21)$$

where σ_{FE_t} is the standard deviation of forecast errors over the 20 quarterly earnings of the firm prior to t. (That is, forecast errors were determined for each one of the 20 quarters before t, then the standard deviation for this set of 20 errors was estimated.)

For example, a firm with a forecast of earnings per share of $3 that subsequently reports actual earnings of $5 will have a forecast error of $2 (=$5 − $3). That is, the earnings announcement will surprise people by $2. If the standard deviation of past errors is $.80, this surprise will be notable, because the standardized unexpected earnings (SUE) equal 2.50 (=$2/$.80).[27] However, if the standard deviation is $4, then this surprise will be minor, because SUE will equal .50 (=$2/$4). Thus, a large positive value for SUE would indicate that the earnings announcement contained significant good news, whereas a large negative SUE would indicate that the earnings announcement contained significant bad news.

In the study, the SUEs associated with all the earnings announcements for all the sampled firms were ranked from smallest to largest. Then they were divided into

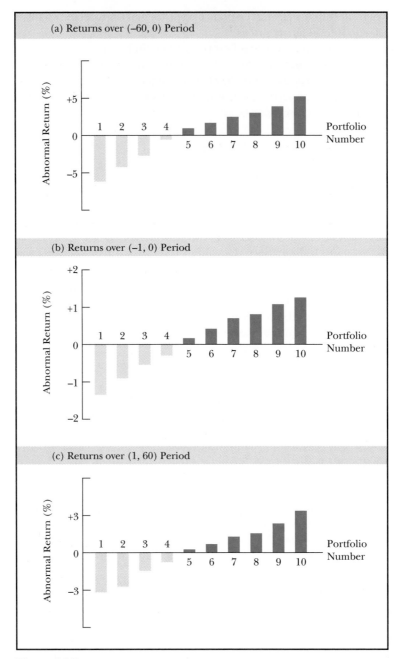

Figure 18.7

Security Returns in Periods Surrounding Earnings Announcements

Source: George Foster, Chris Olsen, and Terry Shevlin, "Earnings Releases, Anomalies, and the Behavior of Security Returns," *Accounting Review* 59, no. 4 (October 1984): 587.

ten equal-sized groups based on the ranking. Group 1 consisted of those announcements resulting in the most negative SUEs, and group 10 consisted of those with the most positive SUEs.

After these ten groups were formed, the stock returns for each firm in each group were measured for the period from 60 days before its earnings announcement through 60 days after its announcement. Figure 18.7 shows the **abnormal return** for the average firm in each of the ten groups for three different time periods.

Figure 18.7(a) shows the average abnormal return for the period from 60 days before the earnings announcement through the day the announcement appeared in *The Wall Street Journal*. This period is denoted (−60, 0).

Figure 18.7(b) shows the average abnormal return for the two-day period consisting of the day before the announcement appeared in *The Wall Street Journal* and the day the announcement appeared, a period that is denoted (−1, 0). Because day 0 is the day the announcement appeared in *The Wall Street Journal*, day −1 is the day the announcement was made to the public. If this announcement was made after trading hours on day −1, investors could not have bought or sold the stock until the next day, day 0. If the announcement was made during trading hours on day −1, then investors could have acted on that day. Because the hour of the announcement could not be pinpointed, the return over the two-day period was examined to see the immediate impact of the announcement on the price of the security.

Figure 18.7(c) shows the average abnormal return for the period from the day after the announcement through 60 days after the announcement, a period that is denoted (1, 60).

Figure 18.7(a) shows that prices of firms that announced unexpectedly high earnings (such as SUE group 10) tended to *increase before* the announcement (day 0), suggesting that information relevant to the earnings announcement was becoming available to the market before the actual announcement. Conversely, prices of firms that announced unexpectedly low earnings (such as SUE group 1) tended to *decrease before* the announcement, undoubtedly for the same reason. In general, there seems to be a strong direct correspondence between the size of the unexpected earnings and the size of the abnormal return. Note that an investor who knew what the earnings were going to be 60 days before the announcement could exploit this information by either buying the stock if the firm was going to announce unexpected large earnings or short selling the stock if the firm was going to announce unexpected low earnings. However, because investors typically do not have prior access to earnings, such exploitation is generally impossible. Thus the existence of abnormal returns before the announcement date does not necessarily indicate some sort of market inefficiency.

Figure 18.7(b) shows that the larger the size of the unexpected earnings, the larger the price movement during the two-day period surrounding the announcement. For example, firms in SUE group 1 had an abnormal return of −1.34%, whereas those in SUE group 10 had an abnormal return of 1.26%. As in panel (a), there is a direct relationship between the size of the unexpected earnings and the abnormal stock return.[28] Thus it appears that the market reacted in a predictable fashion, pushing up the stock prices of those firms announcing good news and pushing down the stock prices of those firms announcing bad news.

As shown in Figure 18.7(c), the changes in stock prices after the announcement dates are quite remarkable in that they appear to suggest a market inefficiency. Prices of stocks of firms announcing unexpectedly high earnings tended to *increase for many days after* the announcement (the average abnormal return over the 60-day period after the announcement was 3.23% for SUE group 10). Conversely, the prices of firms announcing unexpectedly low earnings tended to *decrease for many days after* the announcement (the average abnormal return over the 60-day period subsequent to the announcement was −3.08% for SUE group 1).

As was shown in panels (a) and (b), there seems to be a strong direct correspondence between the size of the unexpected earnings and the size of the abnormal return. This observation suggests that an investor could make abnormal returns by simply looking at quarterly earnings announcements and, on the basis of the magnitude and sign of the unexpected component, acting appropriately. That is, if the firm announces earnings that are notably above expectations, the investor should immediately purchase some of the firm's stock. In contrast, if the announced earnings are notably below expectations, the investor should immediately sell any holdings and perhaps even short sell the firm's stock; announcements of earnings that are reasonably close to expectations will not motivate either a buy or a sell order. Accordingly, the "post-earnings-announcement drift" can be viewed as an empirical anomaly that is inconsistent with the notion of semistrong efficient markets.[29]

18.7.2 Unexpected Earnings and Abnormal Returns

One possible explanation for the abnormal returns associated with large SUEs that is inconsistent with the notion of efficient markets concerns the cost of information transfer. "New news" must reach a large number of investors before the appropriate new equilibrium price can be completely established (In an efficient market, investors would immediately exploit the mispricing causing it to rapidly disappear). Although large institutional investors can obtain news quickly, it may take some time before it reaches smaller institutional investors and individuals. Thus after an earnings announcement there can be a period of abnormal price movement that is related in sign and magnitude to the nature of the announcement.

Alternatively, perhaps the measurement of "abnormal" returns has been in error. When such a measurement is made, a determination of what is a "normal" return must be made. Such a determination is not straightforward but instead is fraught with difficulty. The estimated abnormal returns could actually be due to measurement errors, leaving open the possibility that a more accurate measure of normal return would have resulted in no significant abnormal returns.

Nevertheless, there appear to be striking differences in subsequent stock returns for firms with different SUEs. Although the magnitudes of the return differences may be too small to warrant extensive trading, they do suggest the consideration of such things as SUE values and forecast revisions when money must be invested or a portion of an existing portfolio must be liquidated.

18.7.3 Security Analysts' Forecasts of Future Earnings

It was mentioned earlier that, when only the historical record of past earnings is used to forecast future earnings, an autoregressive model of order one, as shown in Equation (18.19), seems to work about as well as any other model. However, security analysts do not restrict themselves to just past earnings when developing their forecasts. Instead, they look at many different pieces of information. How well can analysts forecast earnings? And do their forecasts actually incorporate information other than that contained in past earnings? The results of two studies that provide some answers to those questions are shown in Tables 18.4 and 18.5.

Forecasts of Analysts

In one study, illustrated in Table 18.4, two sets of forecasts were examined for the quarterly earnings of 50 firms over the period from 1971 through 1975.[30] The first set was obtained by applying sophisticated mechanical models to each firm's previous earnings history [such as the autoregressive model of Equation (18.19)]. The second set was obtained from the earnings forecasts of security analysts as reported in the *Value Line Investment Survey*.[31] The results suggest that the analysts outperformed the mechanical model. For example, 63.5% of the analysts' forecasts were within 25% of the actual earnings values, whereas only 54.4% of the forecasts made

TABLE 18.4 Accuracy of Mechanical and Judgmental Earnings Forecasts

Earnings Forecast Error as a Percent of Actual Earnings	Percent of Forecasts with a Smaller Error	
	Mechanical Model	Analysts' Forecasts
5%	15.0%	18.0%
10	26.5	32.0
25	54.5	63.5
50	81.0	86.5
75	87.5	90.5
100	89.5	92.0

Source: Lawrence D. Brown and Michael S. Rozeff, "The Superiority of Analyst Forecasts As Measures of Expectations: Evidence from Earnings," *Journal of Finance* 33, no. 1 (March 1978): 7–8.

by means of mechanical models came as close. Analysts appear to base their forecasts on both past earnings and other information, and the latter appears to help.

In another study, forecasts of annual earnings made by security analysts approximately 240, 180, 120, and 60 days before the announcement date of actual annual earnings were examined.[32] Typically these days correspond to dates in each of the year's fiscal quarters before the announcement date. Hence, 240 days falls roughly between last year's earnings announcement and this year's first-quarter earnings announcement; 180 days falls roughly between the first-quarter and second-quarter earnings announcement, and so on. These forecasts, made over the period from 1975 to 1982 by analysts at between 50 and 130 brokerage firms, were obtained from the Institutional Brokers Estimate System (I/B/E/S) database developed by the brokerage firm of Lynch, Jones, & Ryan.

Table 18.5 presents a comparison of the accuracy of four forecasts. The first forecast is the annual forecast generated by using a model like the random walk model of Equation (18.16). The second is the annual forecast produced by using an autoregressive model like the one shown in Equation (18.19). The third is the average forecast published by I/B/E/S, and the fourth is the single most current individual forecast published by I/B/E/S.

Forecast accuracy for a particular model and firm is measured by absolute forecast error (*FE*), or:

$$FE = |A - F| \qquad (18.22)$$

where *F* denotes the forecast and *A* denotes the subsequent actual earnings of the firm.

TABLE 18.5 Earnings Forecast Errors of Time-Series Models and Security Analysts

Model	Number of Days before Annual Announcement Date			
	240	180	120	60
Random walk	$.963	$.781	$.620	$.363
Autoregressive	.975	.780	.592	.350
Average analyst	.747	.645	.516	.395
Current analyst	.742	.610	.468	.342

Source: Adapted from Patricia C. O'Brien, "Analysts' Forecasts as Earnings Expectations," *Journal of Accounting and Economics* 10, no. 1 (January 1988): table 4.

There are several interesting observations to be made from Table 18.5. First, as the announcement date gets closer, all of the forecasting models become more accurate. This result is hardly surprising, because more information is available as the announcement date gets closer. Second, for long horizons both the average and most current forecasts are more accurate than either of the time-series models. Third, the current forecast is more accurate than any of the other models. However, subsequent examination of the forecasts indicates that the average forecast was more accurate than the most current forecast, provided that none of the individual forecasts used to determine the average was "stale" (that is, more than roughly a week old). The reason is that such averaging reduces the forecast error by having individual forecast errors offset each other (that is, positive errors will offset negative errors, resulting in a smaller error for the average forecast). In summary, it appears that analysts on average are better forecasters of earnings than are sophisticated mechanical models.[33]

Another interesting observation that has been uncovered about security analysts' forecasts is that they tend to be too optimistic, meaning that they tend to have an upward bias (more on this shortly). Hence most of the typical analysts' revisions are downward. One interpretation of this observation is that many of the analysts work for brokerage firms and thus find it in their employers' best interest (and thus their own) to avoid antagonizing any corporation that is or might become an investment banking client.[34]

All-American Analysts

The monthly publication *Institutional Investor* announces each October its All-American Research Team after querying 2,000 money managers.[35] These managers are asked to evaluate security analysts on the basis of (1) stock recommendations, (2) earnings forecasts, (3) written reports, and (4) overall performance. From these evaluations, analysts are selected for the Team (there is a First Team, a Second Team, a Third Team, and Runners-up) in over 60 industries as well as in such areas as portfolio strategy, quantitative analysis, economics, and market timing.

One study looked at the relative forecasting ability of All-American and non-All-American industry analysts for the fiscal years 1981–1985. In doing so, the investigators matched each EPS forecast of an All-American with a forecast by a non-All-American for the same firm, with each forecast having been made an identical number of days before the fiscal year-end as all the other forecasts. Forecast accuracy was measured by using Equation (18.22). Table 18.6(a) indicates that the average forecast error for All-Americans was $.95, and non-All-Americans had an error of $.98. Hence, All-American EPS forecasts were more accurate by approximately $.03 per share.

Also examined in the study were the records of analysts in the three-year period before they became All-Americans ("future" All-Americans) and the records of All-Americans in the three-year period before they lost their exalted status and became non-All-Americans ("former" All-Americans).[36] This examination was done as follows.

1. The track records of future All-Americans were matched with those of analysts who were and remained non-All-Americans. Table 18.6(b) indicates that future All-Americans were only slightly more accurate {by $.01 [= ($.00 + $.01 + $.02)/3] per share, on average} than non-All-Americans in the three-year period before they became All-Americans.
2. The track records of former All-Americans were matched with those of All-Americans who maintained their team membership ("remaining"

TABLE 18.6   Eps Forecast Errors of All-American and Non-All-American Analysts

	Average Absolute Forecast Error		
	Non-All-Americans	All-Americans	Difference
(a) While on team:	$.98	$.95	$.03
	(3.7%)	(3.6%)	(.1%)
(b) Before gaining membership			
One year before	$.97	$.97	$.00
	(3.1%)	(3.1%)	(.0%)
Two years before	.95	.94	.01
	(3.2%)	(3.2%)	(.0%)
Three years before	.96	.94	.02
	(3.5%)	(3.5%)	(.0%)
(c) Before losing membership			
One year before	$1.03	$1.01	$.02
	(3.8%)	(3.7%)	(.1%)
Two years before	.91	.88	.03
	(3.3%)	(3.3%)	(.0%)
Three years before	.91	.87	.04
	(2.8%)	(2.7%)	(.1%)

Note: The numbers parentheses below the average absolute forecast error represent the average of the percentage absolute forecast errors, where the percentage is calculated as $|A - F|/A$ where A = actual and F = forecast.

Source: Scott E. Stickel, "Reputation and Performance among Security Analysts," *Journal of Finance* 47, no. 5 (December 1992): 1818, 1819, 1821.

All-Americans). Table 18.6(c) indicates that former All-Americans were less accurate than the remaining All-Americans by between $.04 and $.02 per share in the three-year period before removal.

Given the nearly indistinguishable differences in earnings forecasting performance between All-Americans and non-All-Americans, the reasons for Team membership appear to be explained by other factors, such as high-quality company research or good personal relationships with money managers.

The study also documented the existence of forecast bias. This bias was measured by the average forecast error, where the forecast error for a given analyst is:

$$FE = A - F \tag{18.23}$$

As before, F denotes the forecast, and A denotes the subsequent actual earnings of the firm. Note that Equation (18.23) is identical to Equation (18.22), except that absolute values are no longer used. The average forecast error for All-Americans was −$.73 per share (or 2.9% of the actual EPS). For non-All-Americans the comparable figure was −$.74 (or 3.0%). Given that the average *FE* was negative, both types of analysts tended to overestimate the level of EPS. This is clear evidence that both All-Americans' and non-All-Americans' are too optimistic in forecasting EPS.

18.7.4   Management Forecasts of Future Earnings

Often management itself will make a forecast of next year's earnings for the firm. In general, the forecasts of security analysts are not as accurate as the forecasts of management when the two sets of forecasts are made at about the same time, as shown in Table 18.7.[37] Here average security analysts' forecasts, as reported weekly by Zacks

TABLE 18.7 Security Analyst and Management Forecast Errors

Week	Average Analyst Forecast Error	Average Analyst Forecast Error − Average Management Forecast Error[a]
−12	.224	.074
−11	.222	.072
−10	.221	.071
−9	.221	.071
−8	.214	.064
−7	.221	.071
−6	.222	.072
−5	.216	.066
−4	.210	.060
−3	.208	.058
−2	.211	.061
−1	.209	.059
0	.195	.045
+1	.186	.036
+2	.177	.027
+3	.174	.024
+4	.171	.021
+5	.166	.016
+6	.160	.010
+7	.153	.003
+8	.150	.000
+9	.141	−.009
+10	.133	−.017
+11	.129	−.021
+12	.124	−.026

[a] The size of the average management forecast error was .150.

Source: Adapted from John M. Hassell and Robert H. Jennings, "Relative Forecast Accuracy and the Timing of Earnings Forecast Announcements," *Accounting Review* 61, no. 1 (January 1986): Tables 2 and 3.

Investment Research's Icarus Service, were compared with corresponding management forecasts.[38] The objective was to see who was the more accurate forecaster. Forecast error (*FE*) was calculated for both sets of forecasts as:

$$FE = |(F - A)/A| \tag{18.24}$$

where *F* is the earnings forecast and *A* is the actual earnings subsequently reported by the firm. Hence an earnings forecast of $3 per share that subsequently turned out to be $4 would have $FE = |(\$3 - \$4)/\$4| = .25$, or 25%.

Letting $t = 0$ denote the date that the management forecast is released, analysts' forecasts were collected weekly from 12 weeks before to 12 weeks after $t = 0$. As Table 18.7 shows at the bottom, the average forecast error for management was .150. Analyst forecast errors ranged from .224 at week −12 (meaning 12 weeks before the date of the management forecast) to .124 at week +12. Hence, as was shown in Table 18.6, analysts' forecasts became more accurate the closer they were to the date the actual earnings were announced, because the size of the average forecast error decreases fairly steadily from $t = -12$ to $t = +12$.

Most important, however, is the observation that management forecasts were more accurate than analyst forecasts from $t = -12$ to $t = +8$ (the difference was found to be statistically significant through $t = +4$). That is, forecasts issued by analysts before, coincident to, or up to four months after management's forecast were less accurate. This observation is not surprising up to $t = 0$, because management has private information about the firm that is not available to the analysts. However, it is surprising that management forecasts were statistically superior from $t = +1$ through $t = +4$ because it suggests that analysts could have improved their accuracy simply by using management's previously released forecast. After $t = +4$, the analysts' forecasts were more accurate (the difference was statistically significant beginning nine weeks after the release date of the management forecast), a finding that is not surprising, because the analysts probably had access to more timely information upon which to base their forecasts.

These results leave a question: Why does management occasionally produce an earnings forecast for the firm? Is it to reduce *information asymmetry* in the marketplace? That is, management might want to tell investors about the firm's prospects when it feels the prevailing view of the investing public is in serious error. One way to examine this issue is to look at the firm's bid-ask spread. In Chapter 3 it was noted that specialists tend to widen the bid-ask spread if they sense an increase in information asymmetry, because they tend to sustain losses from trading with informed investors. One study examined the bid-ask spreads of firms whose management issued forecasts and a matching sample of firms whose management did not issue forecasts.[39] Interestingly, the study found that the firms issuing forecasts had significantly wider spreads than those that did not issue forecasts before the forecasts were made and that afterward the spreads of the two were equivalent. Thus, it appears that the management tends to issue forecasts when it senses an increased level of information asymmetry and that the forecast reduces the amount of the asymmetry.

18.7.5   Sources of Errors in Forecasting

Because security analysts' forecasts are not perfect, it is interesting to consider the major source of their errors. One study examined the I/B/E/S database and attempted to break down the forecast errors into three components: (1) errors that could be traced to misjudgments about the economy, (2) errors that could be traced to misjudgments about the firm's particular industry, and (3) errors that were purely due to misjudgments about the firm.[40] The results indicated the following: Less than 3% of the typical error was due to a misjudgment about the economy; roughly 30% of the typical error was due to a misjudgment about the industry; and over 65% of the typical error was due to a misjudgment about the firm.

18.8   SUMMARY

1. Assuming that a firm undertakes positive NPV projects and maintains a constant debt-equity ratio, shareholders will be indifferent to the level of dividends.
2. If dividends and new investment are greater than earnings, the firm may issue new equity. If dividends and new investment are less than earnings, the firm may repurchase equity. In either case, a stockholder maintaining constant proportional ownership will be able to spend the same amount on consumption, regardless of the level of dividends.
3. Earnings, not dividends, are the source of a firm's value.
4. Few firms attempt to maintain a constant ratio of dividends to current earnings. It is often assumed that firms establish a long-run payout ratio and adjust current

Consensus Earnings Expectations

Reference is frequently made in the financial press to "market" or "consensus" expectations. We may read that the "market" expects inflation to remain stable or that the "market" expects the Fed to raise interest rates. Given that the market is the amalgam of a large, diverse group of investors, how does anyone determine what the market really expects?

Of course, the most important market expectations are established and published daily—that is, the expected values of corporate assets as reflected in security prices. But what about market expectations regarding economic and financial variables that underlie security prices? In general, these expectations are reported anecdotally, perhaps through interviews with prominent investors or through a variety of surveys.

Investing based on such ambiguous information is problematic. Abnormal returns can be earned only by staking out positions based on expectations contrary to those of the market. Superior investors will consistently identify securities for which market expectations are somehow in error. But unless these investors can correctly interpret the market's expectations, they will not know whether their expectations are significantly different from those of the market.

As the text discusses, earnings expectations are the most important determinant of common stock prices. An investor who can identify companies for which the market is under- or overestimating future earnings can appropriately buy and sell these stocks to produce portfolio returns superior to those of the market on a risk-adjusted basis.

Many organizations publish earnings estimates, including Standard & Poor's, Value Line, and brokerage houses. However, individually these estimates do not represent market expectations; they are merely the opinions of specific analysts. What is needed is a means to collect the earnings estimates of many analysts following a particular company. That need has been satisfied for over 20 years by a firm called Institutional Brokers Estimate System, or I/B/E/S.

Although I/B/E/S is not the only company collecting earnings expectations data (Zacks Investment Research and First Call are prominent competitors), it was the first and it remains a leader in the field. I/B/E/S was formed in 1971. Its initial objectives were modest: to collect timely earnings estimates from brokerage firms on several hundred large, well-followed companies. These estimates were then compiled and the distributions of earnings estimates (high, low, median, measure of dispersion) were periodically reported to subscribers.

For example, suppose that an institutional investment firm was estimating earnings next year of $2.50 per share for *XYZ* company and $3.30 per share for *ABC* company. Through I/B/E/S, the institutional investor might find that the consensus earnings estimates for *XYZ* and *ABC* were currently $1.50 and $3.50, respectively. Further, the coefficient of variation (standard deviation divided by mean—a measure of the estimates' relative dispersion) was .20 for *XYZ* and 0.80 for *ABC*. If the institutional investor has confidence in its own estimates, then it should expect

actual dividends on the basis of the difference between current target dividends and the last period's actual dividends.

5. Corporate management may use dividend changes as a signaling device, raising or lowering dividends on the basis of its assessment of the firm's future earnings.

6. A firm has considerable discretion in calculating its accounting earnings. These accounting earnings may differ substantially from the firm's economic earnings. Similarly, a firm's book value may differ considerably from its market value.

7. Firms initiate paying dividends after a period during which their stock price has risen by an abnormally large amount and earnings have increased. The announcement of the initiation is associated with an abnormal increase in the stock's price, with earnings and the price continuing to move upward afterward.

8. Firms omit paying dividends after a period during which their stock price has fallen by an abnormally large amount and earnings have decreased. The announcement of the omission is associated with an abnormal decrease in the stock's price, with earnings and the price continuing to move downward afterward.

XYZ stock to perform relatively well. The market's earnings expectations are clustered tightly around the $1.50 level, which is $1.00 less than the investor's estimate. If the market comes to realize that $2.50 is the actual level of XYZ earnings, it will likely bid the company's stock price up.

ABC stock is much less attractive. The institutional investor's estimate is less than the consensus by $0.20, so it might wish to sell ABC out of its portfolio if it owns the stock or perhaps even short sell the stock. However, the relatively high dispersion of estimates around the median indicates that the market's expectations are not firm. If ABC's earnings actually come in at $3.30, the result may not be a particularly unpleasant surprise to the market, and therefore may have little impact on ABC's stock price.

The advantages of using consensus earnings expectations in common stock analysis quickly caught on among institutional investors. Today, I/B/E/S receives, compiles, and distributes earnings estimates from over 6,000 equity analysts in nearly 600 research departments in over 33 countries. Although by far the most intense analyst earnings coverage is for U.S. companies, the contributing I/B/E/S analysts now cover over 13,000 companies in 39 equity markets around the world. Even companies in emerging equity markets such as the People's Republic of China, Sri Lanka, and Chile have attracted institutional analysts' coverage and have been included in the I/B/E/S service.

I/B/E/S collects earnings estimates in a number of ways, including faxes, diskettes, telephone calls, and printed reports. Many research firms now pro-vide I/B/E/S with data directly by computer. Upon receipt of analysts' earnings estimates, I/B/E/S staffers perform several quality checks to ensure the integrity of the data. At that point, the estimates are entered into the firm's database. Summary consensus numbers are updated daily and made available to I/B/E/S subscribers.

The original I/B/E/S reports were simply printed books containing summary data on individual company earnings estimates. Although the original printed format is still available, I/B/E/S now provides data through a variety of electronic vendors. For example, I/B/E/S data can be accessed through an optical disk data delivery system that can easily bring earnings expectation data into an electronic spreadsheet for detailed analysis.

Customers can now receive I/B/E/S data diced and sliced in a number of ways. The firm makes available to subscribers analyst-by-analyst data, daily alerts of analyst changes, and custom-designed reports. The firm also provides commentaries and analyses of market trends that it discerns from the earnings estimate data.

The systematic collection of earnings estimates is an excellent example of the forces that have been increasing the efficiency of security markets. Before I/B/E/S collected such data, consensus earnings estimates were difficult to obtain and highly ambiguous. Now those estimates are rigorously quantified and widely distributed, decreasing the likelihood of investors' acting on incomplete or erroneous information.

9. Earnings can be divided into permanent and transitory components. A firm's intrinsic value will be based on the permanent component of earnings. The transitory component is a significant factor in short-run changes in a firm's price-earnings ratio.

10. Stocks with the highest returns typically have earnings that are substantially greater than expected, whereas those with the lowest returns have earnings substantially below expectations.

11. Stock prices tend to correctly anticipate earnings announcements by moving in the appropriate direction beforehand.

12. Stock prices tend to react correctly but not fully to earnings announcements immediately afterward.

13. Stock prices continue to move in a direction similar to their initial reaction for several months afterward. This phenomenon is known as post-earnings-announcement drift.

14. Analysts appear to forecast earnings better than sophisticated mechanical models.

15. Analysts tend to overestimate when forecasting earnings per share.

16. Management earnings forecasts are generally more accurate than analysts' forecasts.

QUESTIONS AND PROBLEMS

1. For a given level of earnings (E), net new investment (I), and dividends (D), explain why a firm must issue new stock if $E < D + I$ and it desires to maintain a constant debt-equity ratio. Similarly, why must it repurchase shares if $E > D + I$ and it desires to maintain a constant debt-equity ratio?

2. Merrillan Motors had earnings of $8 million last year. It made $5 million of investments in projects with positive net present values. Pat Collins owns 20% of the firm's common stock. Assume that Pat desires no change in proportional ownership of Merrillan and the firm wishes to maintain a constant debt-equity ratio. What will be Pat's action in response to:
   a. Merrillan's paying out dividends of $5 million?
   b. Merrillan's paying out dividends of $1 million?
   c. Merrillan's paying out dividends of $3 million?

3. Why is an individual stockholder indifferent between the firm's retaining $1 of earnings and its paying out the $1 of earnings as a dividend, assuming that the firm and the stockholder maintain a constant debt-equity ratio and a constant proportional ownership position, respectively?

4. If the dividend decision is irrelevant to the valuation of a firm, then are not dividend discount models irrelevant to valuing a share of common stock? Why?

5. Scoops Cooney, a confused investment student, commented, "I understand the irrelevance of the dividend decision to the value of the firm. As a result, I calculate the value of a firm's stock on the basis of the present value of the firm's expected earnings per share." Is Scoops correct? Why?

6. Why do most corporations not maintain a constant payout ratio? What payout strategy do most firms pursue?

7. Hixton Farms has a target payout ratio of 50%. Dividends paid last year amounted to $10 million. Its earnings were $20 million. Hixton's "speed of adjustment" factor for dividends is 60%. What will be its dividend payments over the next five years if its earnings display the following path:

Year	Earnings
1	$30 million
2	35 million
3	30 million
4	25 million
5	30 million

Draw a graph of Hixton's actual dividends paid versus the desired dividend payments over this five-year period.

8. Rockton Plastics has made changes to its dividends over the last 14 years. On the basis of a target payout ratio of 30%, according to the Lintner model, the firm would have preferred to make a different set of dividend changes. Both the actual and the preferred dividend changes are shown on the following table. What "speed of adjustment" factor is implied by these two dividend change series?

(Use of a regression program, such as one provided with a compute spreadsheet, is recommended.)

Year	Actual Change in Dividends	Preferred Change in Dividends
1	−$.28	−$.47
2	−.09	−.16
3	−.05	−.08
4	−.01	−.02
5	.01	.02
6	.04	.07
7	.01	.01
8	.03	.05
9	.03	.05
10	.01	.02
11	.04	.07
12	.03	.06
13	.03	.05

9. How are dividends used as a signaling device by corporate management? To the extent that dividends are a signaling device, how are dividend changes related to stock prices?

10. Discuss why there generally does not exist a one-to-one relationship between corporations' book values and their market values.

11. The price per share of the Dells Deli Corporation is less than its book value. Does this difference indicate that the firm's present shareholders have lost money in the past? Does it indicate that they are likely to lose money in the future? Does it indicate that the Dells Deli should not undertake any further capital investment? Explain your answers.

12. Why might a steady trend in a firm's reported earnings from year to year suggest that the figures do not represent the firm's economic earnings?

13. Reported earnings typically differ, sometimes considerably, from economic earnings. Nevertheless, it is often argued that reported earnings are intended simply to provide a "source of information" to investors about the value of the firm. If that is true, might there not be many alternative accounting procedures of equal use to investors? How might one go about evaluating the usefulness of such procedures?

14. Distinguish between permanent and transitory earnings. Would you expect companies across industries to differ in terms of the relative importance of transitory earnings to total earnings? Explain.

15. Price-earnings ratios for individual companies vary over time and among firms. Discuss some of the possible reasons for this variability.

16. Harlond Clift once wrote in a market newsletter, "I focus my research on consensus earnings forecasts. Those companies that the consensus believes will produce the largest earnings increases next year are most likely to produce the best returns." Is Harlond's opinion consistent with empirical evidence? Explain why or why not.

17. Calculate the relationship between the following series of quarterly earnings using an autoregressive model of order one (use of a computer regression program is recommended). What is your forecast for earnings in quarter 21?

Quarter	Earnings	Quarter	Earnings
1	$4.00	11	$4.25
2	4.10	12	4.49
3	3.95	13	4.59
4	4.20	14	4.58
5	4.30	15	4.39
6	4.29	16	4.63
7	4.11	17	4.73
8	4.35	18	4.72
9	4.44	19	4.54
10	4.43	20	4.78

18. Oakdale Orchards has produced the following earnings over the last nine quarters:

Quarter	Earnings per Share
1	$2.00
2	1.95
3	2.05
4	2.10
5	2.40
6	2.24
7	2.67
8	2.84
9	2.64

The expected earnings for the current quarter are based on the equation $QE_t = QE_{t-4} - .75(QE_{t-1} - QE_{t-5})$. Calculate the standardized unexpected earnings in each of the last four quarters, given a standard deviation of $.35.

19. Why might the price of a stock react only partially to an "earnings surprise" on the first day or two after the earnings announcement?

ENDNOTES

[1] Although earnings and cash flow are typically highly correlated, they are not perfectly correlated. Thus, there can be instances in which earnings rise and cash flow falls. Hence, earnings do not always provide the cash flow necessary for paying dividends. For more on cash flow analysis, see Chapter 22.

[2] In Chapter 17, D_0 denoted the *per share* dividends that had been paid over the past year. Now D_0 is used to denote the *aggregate* amount of dividends that are about to be paid. Similarly, the quantities of earnings (E_t) and new investment (I_t) are measured for the firm on an aggregate basis, not a per share basis. Note that dividends cannot be set at an arbitrarily high value relative to earnings (for example, earnings of $10 million and dividends of $100 million), because the firm would then find it practically impossible to obtain the necessary funds to pay the dividends.

[3] The use of such a stockholder is for ease of exposition. The same answer would be obtained if other types of stockholders (such as those who are not interested in maintaining a constant proportional ownership position in the firm in the future) are considered.

[4] It has been argued that if the tax rate on dividends is greater than the tax rate on capital gains, then stockholders will earn more on an after-tax basis if the firm has a relatively low payout ratio. An additional benefit to stockholders if the firm has a low payout ratio is that capital gains taxes are paid only when the stock is sold and can therefore be deferred. Thus

it appears that stockholders will be better off if the firm has a relatively low payout ratio. For a more detailed discussion of the issue, along with the relevant citations, see pp. 128–135 of Gordon J. Alexander and Jack Clark Francis, *Portfolio Analysis* (Upper Saddle River, NJ: Prentice Hall, 1986). Also see James S. Ang, David W. Blackwell, and William L. Megginson, "The Effect of Taxes on the Relative Valuation of Dividends and Capital Gains: Evidence from Dual-Class British Investment Trusts," *Journal of Finance* 46, no. 1 (March 1991): 383–399.

[5] In addition to a regular dividend, sometimes a firm will declare a "special" or "extra" dividend, usually at year-end. By calling it a special dividend, the firm is conveying a message to its stockholders that such a dividend is a one-time event.

[6] Looking backward in time, one can see that current dividends D_t are a linear function of past earnings E_{t-1}, E_{t-2}, E_{t-3}, and so on. More specifically, it can be shown that:

$$D_t = ap^* \left[(1-a)^0 E_{t-0} + (1-a)^1 E_{t-1} + (1-a)^2 E_{t-2} + (1-a)^3 E_{t-3} + \dots \right]$$

Because the quantity $(1-a)$ is a positive fraction (for example, $1/3$), when it is raised to a power it becomes smaller in value, with larger powers resulting in values closer to zero. Thus current dividends depend more on recent past earnings than on distant past earnings, and the equation can be approximated by using an arbitrary number of past earnings (the accuracy of the approximation depends on the number used).

[7] See Bong-Soo Lee, "Time Series Implications of Aggregate Dividend Behavior," *Review of Financial Studies* 9, no. 2 (Summer 1996): 589–618.

[8] Other signaling devices include changes in the firm's capital structure (for example, announcing an issuance of debt with the proceeds being used to repurchase stock). It has been argued that in order for the signal to be useful to the public, (1) management must have an incentive to send a truthful signal; (2) the signal cannot be imitated by competitors in different financial positions; and (3) there cannot be a cheaper means of conveying the same information. See Stephen A. Ross, "The Determination of Financial Structure: The Incentive Signalling Approach," *Bell Journal of Economics* 8, no. 1 (Spring 1977): 23–40.

[9] Paul M. Healy and Krishna G. Palepu, "Earnings Information Conveyed by Dividend Initiations and Omissions," *Journal of Financial Economics* 21, no. 2 (September 1988): 149–175.

[10] See Roni Michaely, Richard H. Thaler, and Kent L. Womack, "Price Reactions to Dividend Initiations and Omissions: Overreaction or Drift?" *Journal of Finance* 50, no. 2 (June 1995): 573–608.

[11] Harry DeAngelo, Linda DeAngelo, and Douglas J. Skinner, "Dividends and Losses," *Journal of Finance* 47, no. 5 (December 1992): 1837–1863. Also see Harry DeAngelo and Linda DeAngelo, "Dividend Policy and Financial Distress: An Empirical Investigation of Troubled NYSE Firms," *Journal of Finance* 45, no. 5 (December 1990): 1415–1431.

[12] The Securities Exchange Act of 1934 gives the SEC the authority to set accounting standards for firms that must register with it. In turn, the SEC has delegated this responsibility to FASB while retaining final authority if any disagreements arise. See Robert Van Riper *Setting Standards for Financial Reporting: FASB and the Struggle for Control of a Critical Process* (Westport, CT: Quorum Books, 1994) for more on the history of FASB and its relationship to the SEC.

[13] Book value of the firm's equity is also called stockholders' equity, particularly when the discussion refers to a company's balance sheet. Stockholders' equity is discussed further in Chapter 22.

[14] Sir John R. Hicks, winner in 1972 of the Nobel Prize in Economics, defined the weekly economic income of an individual as "the maximum value which he can consume during a week and still be as well off at the end of the week as he was at the beginning" (*Value and Capital*, London: Oxford University Press, 1946, p. 172). The definition of the economic earnings of a firm that is given in Equation (18.15) can be viewed as an extension of Hicks's definition for an individual.

[15] Two assertions that have been made in regard to what investors look at when valuing stocks are known as the *mechanistic hypothesis* and the *myopic hypothesis*. The former asserts that investors look only at reported earnings, and the latter asserts that investors look only at the short-term future. Both these assertions seem to be invalid when data are analyzed. For an

in-depth discussion, see George Foster, *Financial Statement Analysis* (Englewood Cliffs, NJ: Prentice Hall, 1986), 443–445.

[16] For a discussion of a number of related issues, see Ross Watts, "Does It Pay to Manipulate EPS?" in *Issues in Corporate Finance* (New York: Stern Stewart Putnam & Macklis, 1983).

[17] There is evidence that investors in publicly held firms are not fooled by such manipulations. See, for example, John R. M. Hand and Patricia Hughes, "The Motives and Consequences of Debt-Equity Swaps and Defeasances: More Evidence That It Does Not Pay to Manipulate Earnings," *Journal of Applied Corporate Finance* 3, no. 3 (Fall 1990): 77–81.

[18] The vertical axis of this figure actually measures the logarithm of earnings per share and of the price index. In this type of diagram, a given vertical distance represents the same percentage change, no matter where it appears. If prices, for example, changed by the same percentage every year (such as $10 to $20 to $40 to $80), then the plot of log prices would be a straight line sloping upward to the right whereas the plot of prices would curve upward.

[19] This explanation suggests that firms will have high price-earnings ratios if they have either negative transitory current earnings or high forecasted long-term permanent earnings, or both. The converse holds for firms with low price-earnings ratios.

[20] John Lintner and Robert Glauber, "Higgledy Piggledy Growth in America," in James Lorie and Richard Brealey (eds.), *Modern Developments in Investment Management* (Hinsdale, IL: Dryden Press, 1978). However, a more recent study came to a different conclusion concerning the predictability of earnings changes. This study divided a large number of companies into five groups based on their earnings-to-price (E/P) ratios and found that lower E/P stock groups exhibited consistently higher long-term earnings growth rates. See two articles by Russell J. Fuller, Lex C. Huberts, and Michael Levinson, "It's Not Higgledy-Piggledy Growth!" *Journal of Portfolio Management* 18, no. 2 (Winter 1992): 38–45, and "Predictability Bias in the U.S. Equity Market," *Financial Analysts Journal* 51, no. 2 (March/April 1995): 12–28. Also see H. Bradlee Perry, "Analyzing Growth Stocks: What's a Good Growth Rate?" *AAII Journal* 13, no. 9 (October 1991): 7–10.

[21] Some people [for example, Jane Ou and Stephen H. Penman, "Financial Statement Analysis and the Prediction of Stock Returns," *Journal of Accounting and Economics* 11, no. 4 (November 1989): 295–329] think that a "random walk with drift" model as follows is more accurate:

$$E_t - E_{t-1} = \delta + \varepsilon_t$$

where δ is a positive constant that represents the "drift" term. With this model, the expected change in earnings is equal to δ. Note that the random walk model given in Equation (18.17) is a special case where $\delta = 0$.

[22] This model can also be used to forecast annual earnings by working forward one quarter at a time and then adding up the forecasts for the forthcoming four quarters. Doing so would result in a forecast of annual earnings (E_t) equal to $E_{t-1} + c(QE_{t-1} - QE_{t-5}) + d$, where $c = a^1 + a^2 + a^3 + a^4$ and $d = 4b + 3ab + 2a^2b + a^3b$. Note that the random walk model is a special case where a and b are equal to zero, thereby making c and d equal to zero.

[23] It has been argued that an improvement can be made in this model by either (1) adding to the right-hand side the term $k(QE_{t-4} - QE_{t-8})$ where k is a constant or (2) by multiplying the constant b term by the random error term that occurred four quarters ago (e_{t-4}). See P. A. Griffin, "The Time-Series Behavior of Quarterly Earnings: Preliminary Evidence," *Journal of Accounting Research* 15, no. 1 (Spring 1977): 71–83; Lawrence D. Brown and Michael S. Rozeff, "Univariate Time-Series Models of Quarterly Accounting Earnings per Share: A Proposed Model," *Journal of Accounting Research* 17, no. 1 (Spring 1979): 179–189; and Allen W. Bathke Jr. and Kenneth S. Lorek, "The Relationship between Time Series Models and the Security Market's Expectations of Quarterly Earnings," *Accounting Review* 59, no. 2 (April 1984): 163–176.

[24] One of the original studies was Victor Niederhoffer and Patrick J. Regan, "Earnings Changes, Analysts' Forecasts, and Stock Prices," *Financial Analysts Journal* 28, no. 3 (May/June 1972): 65–71. Also the entire June/September 1992 issue of the *Journal of Accounting and Economics* is devoted to an examination of how stock prices are related to earnings and other financial statement information.

[25] Another study using data from 1980 and 1981 reached similar conclusions. That is, the top 50 stocks had forecasted and actual earnings growth rates of 14.3% and 31.3%, respectively. For the bottom 50 stocks the respective rates were 17.4% and –10.3%. See Gary A. Benesh and Pamela P. Peterson, "On the Relation between Earnings Changes, Analysts' Forecasts and Stock Price Fluctuations," *Financial Analysts Journal* 42, no. 6 (November/December 1986): 29–39, 55.

[26] George Foster, Chris Olsen, and Terry Shevlin, "Earnings Releases, Anomalies, and the Behavior of Security Returns," *Accounting Review* 59, no. 4 (October 1984): 574–603. For a related paper, see Roger Kormendi and Robert Lipe, "Earnings Innovations, Earnings Persistence, and Stock Returns," *Journal of Business* 60, no. 3 (July 1987): 323–345.

[27] Assume that a firm's earnings are normally distributed and that this distribution remains unchanged over time. Accordingly, 67% of the actual earnings should fall within one standard deviation of the firm's expected earnings. Equivalently, 67% of the SUEs should fall between +1.0 and –1.0. Similarly, 95% of the SUEs should fall between +2.0 and –2.0. One study has argued that most forecast errors are too large for the forecast to be useful; see David N. Dreman and Michael A. Berry, "Analyst Forecasting Errors and Their Implications for Security Analysis," *Financial Analysts Journal* 51, no. 3 (May/June 1995): 30–41. For a refutation, see Lawrence D. Brown, "Analyst Forecasting Errors and Their Implications for Security Analysis: An Alternative Perspective," *Financial Analysts Journal* 52, no. 16 (January/February 1996): 40–47.

[28] Studies have shown that earnings announcements containing good news are often made earlier than expected, whereas those containing bad news are often made later than expected. These studies also show that the "timeliness" (defined as the difference between the actual announcement date and the expected announcement date) affects the size of the abnormal return. Interestingly, around the time of earnings announcements there appears to be both increased trading volume and increased variability in security returns. See George Foster, *Financial Statement Analysis* (Englewood Cliffs, NJ: Prentice Hall, 1986): 377–386; and V. V. Chari, Ravi Jagannathan, and Aharon Ofer, "Seasonalities in Security Returns: The Case of Earnings Announcements," *Journal of Financial Economics* 21, no. 1 (May 1988): 101–121.

[29] One article argues that the post-earnings announcement drift should be listed with the set of empirical regularities described in Appendix A to Chapter 16. See Charles P. Jones and Bruce Bublitz, "The CAPM and Equity Return Regularities: An Extension," *Financial Analysts Journal* 43, no. 3 (May/June 1987): 77–79.

[30] Lawrence D. Brown and Michael S. Rozeff, "The Superiority of Analyst Forecasts As Measures of Expectations: Evidence from Earnings," *Journal of Finance* 33, no. 1 (March 1978): 1–16.

[31] Value Line also ranks stocks in terms of their relative attractiveness as investments. For a discussion of the usefulness of the Value Line rankings, see Table 22.8 and the end-of-chapter references in Chapter 22.

[32] Patricia C. O'Brien, "Analysts' Forecasts As Earnings Expectations," *Journal of Accounting and Economics* 10, no. 1 (January 1988): 53–83.

[33] In one study it was found that sophisticated investors (such as big institutional investors) placed more weight on analysts' forecasts than on mechanical models in forming their expectations about earnings. See Beverly R. Walther, "Investor Sophistication and Market Earnings Expectations," *Journal of Accounting Research* 35, no. 2 (Autumn 1997): 157–179.

[34] The observation that analysts (1) tend to be too optimistic in their EPS forecasts, (2) tend to revise these forecasts downward, and (3) issue far more buy than sell recommendations has been documented in several places. See, for example, the studies cited in Table 22.8 of Chapter 22 as well as John C. Groth, Wilbur G. Lewellen, Gary Schlarbaum, and Ronald C. Lease, "An Analysis of Brokerage House Recommendations," *Financial Analysts Journal* 35, no. 1 (January/February 1979): 32–40; and Werner F. De Bondt and Richard H. Thaler, "Do Security Analysts Overreact?" *American Economic Review* 80, no. 2 (May 1990): 52–57. For a counterview, see Michael P. Keane and David E. Runkle, "Are Financial Analysts' Forecasts of Corporate Profits Rational?" *Journal of Political Economy* 106, no. 4 (August 1998): 768–805.

[35] The discussion that follows draws from Scott E. Stickel, "Reputation and Performance among Security Analysts," *Journal of Finance* 47, no. 5 (December 1992): 1811–1836.

[36] The study also found that the median number of firms analyzed by All-Americans and non-All-Americans was 14 and 8, respectively, and that All-Americans revised their forecasts within a given fiscal year on average every 86 days, whereas non-All-Americans revised them every 93 days.

[37] John M. Hassell and Robert H. Jennings, "Relative Forecast Accuracy and the Timing of Earnings Forecast Announcements," *Accounting Review* 61, no. 1 (January 1986): 58–75.

[38] Similar to I/B/E/S, Zacks Investment Research provides weekly summaries of earnings forecasts for thousands of firms that are provided by analysts at roughly 50 brokerage firms. Whereas Zacks dates forecasts by the date of issuance by the analysts' employers, I/B/E/S dates forecasts by when they receive them.

[39] Maribeth Collier and Teri Lombardi Yohn, "Management Forecasts and Information Asymmetry: An Examination of Bid-Ask Spreads," *Journal of Accounting Research* 35, no. 2 (Autumn 1997): 181–191.

[40] Edwin J. Elton, Martin J. Gruber, and Mustafa N. Gultekin, "Professional Expectations: Accuracy and Diagnosis of Errors," *Journal of Financial and Quantitative Analysis* 19, no. 4 (December 1984): 351–363.

KEY TERMS

dividend decision
asymmetric information
information content of dividends
   hypothesis
accounting earnings
earnings per share
return on equity
economic earnings

economic value of the firm
generally accepted accounting
   principles
random walk model
market beta
standardized unexpected earnings
abnormal return

REFERENCES

1. The seminal paper on dividend policy that established both the "dividend irrelevancy theorem" and the notion that earnings are the basis for the market value of the firm was written by two Nobel laureates in economics:

   Merton H. Miller and Franco Modigliani, "Dividend Policy, Growth, and the Valuation of Shares," *Journal of Business* 34, no. 4 (October 1961): 411–433.

2. The Lintner model of dividend behavior and some studies that empirically tested it are:

   John Lintner, "Distribution of Incomes of Corporations among Dividends, Retained Earnings, and Taxes," *American Economic Review* 46, no. 2 (May 1956): 97–113.

   John A. Brittain, *Corporate Dividend Policy* (Washington, DC: The Brookings Institution, 1966).

   Eugene F. Fama and Harvey Babiak, "Dividend Policy: An Empirical Analysis," *Journal of the American Statistical Association* 63, no. 324 (December 1968): 1132–1161.

   Eugene F. Fama, "The Empirical Relationship between the Dividend and Investment Decisions of Firms," *American Economic Review* 64, no. 3 (June 1974): 304–318.

   Terry A. Marsh and Robert C. Merton, "Dividend Behavior for the Aggregate Stock Market," *Journal of Business*, 60, no. 1 (January 1987): 1–40.

   Bong-Soo Lee, "Time-Series Implications of Aggregate Dividend Behavior," *Review of Financial Studies* 9, no. 2 (Summer 1996): 589–618.

3. The determinants of recent dividend behavior appear to be similar to those in the Lintner model from the 1950s, according to:

   H. Kent Baker, Gail E. Farrelly, and Richard B. Edelman, "A Survey of Management Views on Dividend Policy," *Financial Management* 14, no. 3 (Autumn 1985): 78–84.

4. A summary of the literature on signaling can be found in:

Thomas E. Copeland and J. Fred Weston, *Financial Theory and Corporate Policy* (Reading, MA: Addison-Wesley, 1988), 501–507, 584–588.

5. The information content of dividends hypothesis, closely linked to the signaling literature, has been the subject of much research. Some of the more important papers are:

R. Richardson Pettit, "Dividend Announcements, Security Performance, and Capital Market Efficiency," *Journal of Finance* 27, no. 5 (December 1972): 993–1007.

Ross Watts, "The Information Content of Dividends," *Journal of Business* 46, no. 2 (April 1973): 191–211.

Joseph Aharony and Itzak Swary, "Quarterly Dividend and Earnings Announcements and Stockholders' Returns: An Empirical Analysis," *Journal of Finance* 35, no. 1 (March 1980): 1–12.

Clarence C. Y. Kwan, "Efficient Market Tests of the Informational Content of Dividend Announcements: Critique and Extension," *Journal of Financial and Quantitative Analysis* 16, no. 2 (June 1981): 193–206.

Paul Asquith and David W. Mullins Jr., "The Impact of Initiating Dividend Payments on Shareholders' Wealth," *Journal of Business* 56, no. 1 (January 1983): 77–96.

James A. Brickley, "Shareholder Wealth, Information Signaling and the Specially Designated Dividend: An Empirical Study," *Journal of Financial Economics* 12, no. 2 (August 1983): 187–209.

J. Randall Woolridge, "Dividend Changes and Stock Prices," *Journal of Finance* 38, no. 5 (December 1983): 1607–1615.

Terry E. Dielman and Henry R. Oppenheimer, "An Examination of Investor Behavior During Periods of Large Dividend Changes," *Journal of Financial and Quantitative Analysis* 19, no. 2 (June 1984): 197–216.

Paul M. Healy and Krishna G. Palepu, "Earnings Information Conveyed by Dividend Initiations and Omissions," *Journal of Financial Economics* 21, no. 2 (September 1988): 149–175.

P. C. Venkatesh, "The Impact of Dividend Initiation on the Information Content of Earnings Announcements and Returns Volatility," *Journal of Business* 62, no. 2 (April 1989): 175–197.

Larry H. P. Lang and Robert H. Litzenberger, "Dividend Announcements: Cash Flow Signalling vs. Free Cash Flow Hypothesis," *Journal of Financial Economics* 24, no. 1 (September 1989): 181–191.

Harry DeAngelo, Linda DeAngelo, and Douglas J. Skinner, "Dividends and Losses," *Journal of Finance* 47, no. 5 (December 1992): 1837–1863.

Keith M. Howe, Jia He, and G. Wenchi Kao, "One-Time Cash Flow Announcements and Free Cash-Flow Theory: Share Repurchases and Special Dividends," *Journal of Finance* 47, no. 5 (December 1992): 1963–1975.

Roni Michaely, Richard H. Thaler, and Kent L. Womack, "Price Reactions to Dividend Initiations and Omissions: Overreaction or Drift?" *Journal of Finance* 50, no. 2 (June 1995): 573–608.

6. The relationship between economic and accounting earnings is discussed in:

Fischer Black, "The Magic in Earnings: Economic Earnings versus Accounting Earnings," *Financial Analysts Journal* 36, no. 6 (November/December 1980): 19–24.

7. For a study on the timing of dividend announcements as well as a listing of other studies concerning dividend announcements, see:

Avner Kalay and Uri Loewenstein, "The Informational Content of the Timing of Dividend Announcements," *Journal of Financial Economics* 16, no. 3 (July 1986): 373–388.

Aharon R. Ofer and Daniel R. Siegel, "Corporate Financial Policy, Information, and Market Expectations: An Empirical Investigation of Dividends," *Journal of Finance* 42, no. 4 (September 1987): 889–911.

8. For a review of the literature dealing with dividends, see:

James S. Ang, *Do Dividends Matter? A Review of Corporate Dividend Theories and Evidence*, Monograph Series in Finance and Economics 1987–2, (New York University Salomon Center, Leonard N. Stern School of Business, 1987).

9. For a discussion of price-earnings ratios, see:

William Beaver and Dale Morse, "What Determines Price-Earnings Ratios?" *Financial Analysts Journal* 34, no. 4 (July/August 1978): 65–76.

William H. Beaver, *Financial Reporting: An Accounting Revolution* (Englewood Cliffs, NJ: Prentice Hall, 1981), Chapters 4 and 5.

George Foster, *Financial Statement Analysis* (Englewood Cliffs, NJ: Prentice Hall, 1986), 437–442.

Paul Zarowin, "What Determines Earnings-Price Ratios: Revisited," *Journal of Accounting, Auditing, and Finance* 5, no. 3 (Summer 1990): 439–454.

Peter D. Easton and Trevor S. Harris, "Earnings as an Explanatory Variable for Returns," *Journal of Accounting Research* 29, no. 1 (Spring 1991): 19–36.

William H. Beaver, Mary Lea McAnally, and Christopher H. Stinson, "The Information Content of Earnings and Prices: A Simultaneous Equations Approach," *Journal of Accounting and Economics* 23, (1997): 53–81.

10. Time-series models of annual and quarterly earnings per share are discussed in:

George Foster, "Quarterly Accounting Data: Time-Series Properties and Predictive-Ability Results," *Accounting Review* 52, no. 1 (January 1977): 1–21.

George Foster, *Financial Statement Analysis* (Englewood Cliffs, NJ: Prentice Hall, 1986), Chapter 7.

Ross L. Watts and Jerold L. Zimmerman, *Positive Accounting Theory* (Englewood Cliffs, NJ: Prentice Hall, 1986), Chapter 6.

11. The relationship between earnings announcements and stock prices has been documented in many studies. See the following as well as their citations:

Ray Ball and Philip Brown, "An Empirical Evaluation of Accounting Income Numbers," *Journal of Accounting Research* 6, no. 2 (Autumn 1968): 159–178.

William H. Beaver, "The Information Content of Annual Earnings Announcements," *Empirical Research in Accounting: Selected Studies*, Supplement to *Journal of Accounting Research* 6 (1968): 67–92.

Leonard Zacks, "EPS Forecasts—Accuracy Is Not Enough," *Financial Analysts Journal* 35, no. 2 (March/April 1979): 53–55.

Dale Morse, "Price and Trading Volume Reaction Surrounding Earnings Announcements: A Closer Examination," *Journal of Accounting Research* 19, no. 2 (Autumn 1981): 374–383.

James M. Patell and Mark A. Wolfson, "The Ex Ante and Ex Post Effects of Quarterly Earnings Announcements Reflected in Stock and Option Prices," *Journal of Accounting Research* 19, no. 2 (Autumn 1981): 434–458.

Richard J. Rendleman Jr., Charles P. Jones, and Henry A. Latane, "Empirical Anomalies Based on Unexpected Earnings and the Importance of Risk Adjustments," *Journal of Financial Economics* 10, no. 3 (November 1982): 269–287.

James M. Patell and Mark A. Wolfson, "The Intraday Speed of Adjustment of Stock Prices to Earnings and Dividend Announcements," *Journal of Financial Economics* 13, no. 2 (June 1984): 223–252.

George Foster, Chris Olsen, and Terry Shevlin, "Earnings Releases, Anomalies, and the Behavior of Security Returns," *Accounting Review* 59, no. 4 (October 1984): 574–603.

Catherine S. Woodruff and A. J. Senchack Jr., "Intradaily Price-Volume Adjustments of NYSE Stocks to Unexpected Earnings," *Journal of Finance* 43, no. 2 (June 1988): 467–491.

The entire issue of the *Journal of Accounting and Economics* 15, no. 2/3 (June/September 1992).

Anthony Bercel, "Consensus Expectations and International Equity Returns," *Financial Analysts Journal* 50, no. 4 (July/August 1994): 76–80.

Beverly R. Walther, "Investor Sophistication and Market Earnings Expectations," *Journal of Accounting Research* 35, no. 2 (Autumn 1997): 157–179.

12. Some of the studies that have examined possible explanations for the "post-earnings-announcement drift" in stock prices are:

Richard J. Rendleman Jr., Charles P. Jones, and Henry A. Latane, "Further Insight into the Standardized Unexpected Earnings Anomaly: Size and Serial Correlation Effects," *Financial Review* 22, no. 1 (February 1987): 131–144.

Victor L. Bernard and Jacob K. Thomas, "Post-Earnings-Announcement Drift: Delayed Price Response or Risk Premium?" *Journal of Accounting Research* 27 (Supplement 1989): 1–36.

Robert N. Freeman and Senyo Tse, "The Multiperiod Information Content of Accounting Earnings: Confirmations and Contradictions of Previous Earnings Reports," *Journal of Accounting Research* 27 (Supplement 1989): 49–79.

Victor L. Bernard and Jacob K. Thomas, "Evidence That Stock Prices Do Not Fully Reflect the Implications of Current Earnings for Future Earnings," *Journal of Accounting and Economics* 13, no. 4 (December 1990): 305–340.

Richard R. Mendenhall, "Evidence on the Possible Underweighting of Earnings-Related Information," *Journal of Accounting Research* 29, no. 1 (Spring 1991): 170–179.

Ray Ball, "The Earnings-Price Anomaly," *Journal of Accounting and Economics* 15, no. 2/3 (June/September 1992): 319–345.

Jeffery S. Abarbanell and Victor L. Bernard, "Tests of Analysts' Overreaction/Underreaction to Earnings Information As an Explanation for Anomalous Stock Price Behavior," *Journal of Finance* 47, no. 3 (July 1992): 1181–1207.

Ray Ball and Eli Bartov, "How Naïve Is the Stock Market's Use of Earnings Information?" *Journal of Accounting and Economics* 21, no. 3 (June 1996): 319–337.

13. There have been numerous studies concerning the earnings forecasts made by security analysts and management. Some of the studies are:

Lawrence D. Brown and Michael S. Rozeff, "The Superiority of Analyst Forecasts as Measures of Expectations: Evidence from Earnings," *Journal of Finance* 33, no. 1 (March 1978): 1–16.

Lawrence D. Brown and Michael S. Rozeff, "Analysts Can Forecast Accurately!" *Journal of Portfolio Management* 6, no. 3 (Spring 1980): 31–34.

John G. Cragg and Burton G. Malkiel, *Expectations and the Structure of Share Prices* (Chicago: University of Chicago Press, 1982), particularly pp. 85–86 and 165.

Dan Givoly and Josef Lakonishok, "Properties of Analysts' Forecasts of Earnings: A Review and Analysis of the Research," *Journal of Accounting Literature* 3 (Spring 1984): 117–152.

Dan Givoly and Josef Lakonishok, "The Quality of Analysts' Forecasts of Earnings," *Financial Analysts Journal* 40, no. 5 (September/October 1984): 40–47.

Philip Brown, George Foster, and Eric Noreen, *Security Analyst Multi-Year Earnings Forecasts and the Capital Markets* (Sarasota, FL: American Accounting Association, 1985).

John M. Hassell and Robert H. Jennings, "Relative Forecast Accuracy and the Timing of Earnings Forecast Announcements," *Accounting Review* 61, no. 1 (January 1986): 58–75.

Gary A. Benesh and Pamela P. Peterson, "On the Relation between Earnings Changes, Analysts' Forecasts and Stock Price Fluctuations," *Financial Analysts Journal* 42, no. 6 (November/December 1986): 29–39, 55.

Lawrence D. Brown, Robert L. Hagerman, Paul A. Griffin, and Mark Zmijewski, "Security Analyst Superiority Relative to Univariate Time-Series Models in Forecasting Quarterly Earnings," *Journal of Accounting and Economics* 9, no. 1 (April 1987): 61–87.

Robert Conroy and Robert Harris, "Consensus Forecasts of Corporate Earnings: Analysts' Forecasts and Time-Series Methods," *Management Science* 33, no. 6 (June 1987): 725–738.

Lawrence D. Brown, Robert L. Hagerman, Paul A. Griffin, and Mark Zmijewski, "An Evaluation of Alternative Proxies for the Market's Assessment of Unexpected Earnings," *Journal of Accounting and Economics* 9, no. 2 (July 1987): 159–193.

Patricia C. O'Brien, "Analysts' Forecasts as Earnings Expectations," *Journal of Accounting and Economics* 10, no. 1 (January 1988): 53–83.

Werner F. De Bondt and Richard H. Thaler, "Do Security Analysts Overreact?" *American Economic Review* 80, no. 2 (May 1990): 52–57.

Lawrence D. Brown and Kwon-Jung Kim, "Timely Aggregate Analyst Forecasts As Better Proxies for Market Earnings Expectations," *Journal of Accounting Research* 29, no. 2 (Autumn 1991): 382–385.

Ashiq Ali, April Klein, and James Rosenfeld, "Analysts' Use of Information about Permanent and Transitory Earnings Components in Forecasting Annual EPS," *Accounting Review* 67, no. 1 (January 1992): 183–198.

Scott E. Stickel, "Reputation and Performance among Security Analysts," *Journal of Finance* 47, no. 5 (December 1992): 1811–1836.

David N. Dreman and Michael A. Berry, "Analyst Forecasting Errors and Their Implications for Security Analysis," *Financial Analysts Journal* 51, no. 3 (May/June 1995): 30–41.

David N. Dreman, "Analyst Forecasting Errors," *Financial Analysts Journal* 52, no. 3 (May/June 1995): 77–80.

Lawrence D. Brown, "Analyst Forecasting Errors and Their Implications for Security Analysis: An Alternative Perspective," *Financial Analysts Journal* 52, no. 16 (January/February 1996): 40–47.

Robert A. Olsen, "Implications of Herding Behavior for Earnings Estimation, Risk Assessment, and Stock Returns," *Financial Analysts Journal*, 52, no. 4 (July/August 1996): 37–41.

Maribeth Collier and Teri Lombardi Yohn, "Management Forecasts and Information Asymmetry: An Examination of Bid-Ask Spreads," *Journal of Accounting Research* 35, no. 2 (Autumn 1997): 181–191.

Lawrence D. Brown, "Analyst Forecasting Errors: Additional Evidence," *Financial Analysts Journal* 53, no. 6 (November/December 1997): 81–88.

Maribeth Coller and Teri Lombardi Yohn, "Management Forecasts: What Do We know?" *Financial Analysts Journal* 54, no. 1 (January/February 1998): 58–62.

OPTIONS

In the world of investments, an **option** is a type of contract between two people wherein one person grants the other person the right to buy a specific asset at a specific price within a specific time period. Alternatively, the contract may grant the other person the right to sell a specific asset at a specific price within a specific time period. The person who has received the right, and thus has a decision to make, is known as the *option buyer* because he or she must pay for this right. The person who has sold the right, and thus must respond to the buyer's decision, is known as the *option writer*.

The variety of contracts containing an option feature is enormous. Even within the domain of publicly traded securities, many types can be found. Traditionally only certain instruments are referred to as options; the others, though similar in nature, are designated differently. This chapter introduces the institutional features of option contracts along with some basics regarding how they are valued and used in the marketplace.

19.1   TYPES OF OPTION CONTRACTS

The two most basic types of option contracts are known as calls and puts. Such contracts are traded on many exchanges around the world, and many are created privately (that is, "off exchange" or "over the counter"). Privately created calls and puts typically involve financial institutions or investment banking firms and their clients.

19.1.1   Call Options

The most prominent type of option contract is the **call option** for stocks. It gives the buyer the right to buy ("call away") a specific number of shares of a specific company from the option writer at a specific purchase price at any time up to and including a specific date. Note that the contract specifies four items:

1. The company whose shares can be bought
2. The number of shares that can be bought
3. The purchase price for those shares, known as the **exercise price** (or striking price)
4. The date when the right to buy expires, known as the **expiration date**

An Example

Consider a simple hypothetical example in which investors B and W are thinking about signing a call option contract. This contract will allow B to buy 100 shares of Widget from W for $50 per share at any time during the next six months. Currently Widget is selling for $45 per share on an organized exchange. Investor B, the potential option buyer, believes that the price of Widget's common stock will rise substantially over the next six months. Investor W, the potential option writer, has a different opinion about Widget, believing that its stock price will not rise above $50 over this time period.

Will investor W be willing to sign this contract without receiving something in return from investor B? No. W is running a risk by signing the contract and will demand compensation for doing so. The risk is that Widget's stock price will rise above $50 per share, in which case W will have to buy the shares at the market price and then turn them over to B for only $50 per share. Perhaps the stock will rise to $60, costing W $6,000 ($=60×100 shares) to buy the stock. Then W will give the 100 shares to B and receive in return $5,000 ($=50×100 shares). Consequently W will have lost $1,000 ($=$6,000 - $5,000$).

The point is that the buyer of a call option will have to pay the writer something in order to get the writer to sign the contract. The amount paid is known as the **premium**, although option price is a more appropriate term. In the example, perhaps the premium is $3 per share; investor B will pay $300 ($=3×100 shares) to investor W in order to induce W to sign the contract. Because investor B expects Widget's stock price to rise in the future, B expects to make money by purchasing shares of Widget today at $45 per share. The attraction of purchasing call options instead of shares is that investor B can apply a high degree of leverage; only $3 per share needs to be spent in order to purchase the option.

At some point in time after investors B and W have signed the call option contract, investor W might like to get out of the contract, but breaching the contract is illegal. Investor W could buy the contract back from investor B for a negotiated amount of money and then destroy the document. If Widget rises in one month to $55 per share, perhaps the amount will be $7 per share [or, in total, $700 ($=7×100 shares)]. In this case, W will have lost $400 ($=$300 - 700) and B will have made $400. Alternatively, if Widget falls to $40 per share, perhaps the amount will be $.50 per share [or, in total, $50 ($=$.50 \times 100$ shares)], in which case W will have made $250 ($=$300 - 50) and B will have lost $250.

Another way that W can get out of the contract is to find someone else to take his or her position in the contract (assuming that the contract has a provision that allows this transfer to be made). For example, if Widget has risen to $55 per share after one month, perhaps investor W will find an investor, denoted WW, who is willing to become the option writer if W will pay him or her $7 per share (or $700 in total). If they agree, the contract will be amended so that WW is now the option writer, with W no longer being a party in the contract.

What if investor B wants to get out of the contract? Analogous to W's actions, B could look for someone who is willing to pay an agreed-upon sum of money to possess the right to buy Widget stock under the terms of the contract; that is, B could try to sell the contract to someone else. Perhaps investor B will find another investor, denoted BB, who is willing to pay B $7 per share (or $700 in total) in return for the right to buy Widget under the terms of the call option contract. If B agrees on that amount, the call option contract will be sold to BB and amended, making BB the option buyer.

In this example, both of the original parties, W and B, "closed out" (or "offset" or "unwound") their positions and are no longer involved in the call option contract. However, the example suggests that the original writer and buyer must meet face to face in order to draw up the terms of the contract. It also suggests that if either the original writer or the original buyer wants to get out of the contract, then he or she must reach an agreeable price with the other original party or, alternatively, find a third investor to whom he or she can transfer the position in the contract. Thus it would appear that there is a great amount of effort involved if an investor wants to deal in options.

Role of Exchanges

Fortunately this is not the case in the United States because of the introduction of *standardized contracts* and the maintenance of a relatively liquid marketplace by organized exchanges for listed options.[1] The Options Clearing Corporation (OCC), a company that is jointly owned by several exchanges, greatly facilitates trading in these options. It does so by maintaining a computer system that keeps track of all these contracts by recording the position of each investor in each one. Although the mechanics are rather complex, the principles are simple enough. As soon as a buyer and a writer decide to trade a particular option contract and the buyer pays the agreed-upon premium, the OCC steps in, becoming the effective writer as far as the buyer is concerned and the effective buyer as far as the writer is concerned. Thus at this time all direct links between original buyer and writer are severed. If a buyer chooses to exercise an option, the OCC will randomly choose a writer who has not closed his or her position and assign the exercise notice accordingly. The OCC also guarantees delivery of stock if the writer is unable to come up with the shares.

The OCC makes it possible for buyers and writers to close out their positions at any time. If a buyer subsequently becomes a writer of the same contract, meaning that the buyer later "sells" the contract to someone else, the OCC computer will note the offsetting positions in this investor's account and will simply cancel both entries. Consider an investor who buys a contract on Monday and then sells it on Tuesday. The computer will note that the investor's net position is zero and will remove both entries. The second trade is a **closing sale** because it serves to close out the investor's position from the earlier trade. Closing sales thus allow buyers to sell options rather than exercise them.

A similar procedure allows a writer to pay to be relieved of the potential obligation to deliver stock. Consider an investor who writes a contract on Wednesday and buys an identical one on Thursday. The latter is a **closing purchase** and, analogous to a closing sale, serves to close out the investor's position from the earlier trade.

Stock Split and Dividend Protection

Call options are protected against stock splits and stock dividends on the underlying stock. In the example in which the option was on 100 shares of Widget stock with an exercise price of $50, a two-for-one stock split would cause the contract to be altered so that it was for 200 shares at $25 per share. The reason for this protection has to do with the effect that stock splits and stock dividends have on the share price of the firm. Because either of these events will cause the share price to fall below what it otherwise would have been without adjustment they would work to the disadvantage of the call option buyer and to the advantage of the call option writer.

In terms of cash dividends, there is no protection for listed call options.[2] That is, the exercise price and the number of shares are unaffected by the payment of cash dividends. For example, the terms of the Widget call option would remain the same if Widget declared and paid a $4 per share cash dividend.

19.1.2 Put Options

A second type of option contract for stocks is the **put option**. It gives the buyer the right to sell ("to put away") a specific number of shares of a specific company to the option writer at a specific selling price at any time up to and including a specific date. Note that the contract specifies four items that are analogous to those for call options:

1. The company whose shares can be sold
2. The number of shares that can be sold
3. The selling price for those shares, known as the exercise price (or striking price)
4. The date when the right to sell expires, known as the expiration date

An Example

Consider an example in which investors B and W are thinking about signing a put option contract. This contract will allow B to sell 100 shares of XYZ Company to W for $30 per share at any time during the next six months. Currently XYZ is selling for $35 per share on an organized exchange. Investor B, the potential option buyer, believes that the price of XYZ's common stock will fall substantially over the next six months. Investor W, the potential option writer, has a different opinion about XYZ, believing that its stock price will not fall below $30 over this time period.

As with the call option on Widget, investor W would be running a risk by signing the contract and would demand compensation for doing so. The risk is that XYZ's stock price will subsequently fall below $30 per share, in which case W will have to buy the shares at $30 per share from B when they are not worth that much in the marketplace. Perhaps XYZ will fall to $20, costing W $3,000 (=$30 $\times$ 100 shares) to buy stock that is worth only $2,000 (=$20 $\times$ 100 shares). Consequently W would have lost $1,000 (=$3,000 − $2,000). In this case B would make $1,000, purchasing XYZ in the marketplace for $2,000 and then selling the shares to W for $3,000.

As with a call option, the buyer of a put option will have to pay the writer an amount of money known as a premium in order to get the writer to sign the contract and assume this risk. Also as with call options, the buyer and writer may close out (or offset or unwind) their positions at any time by simply entering an offsetting transaction. As with calls, this is easily done for listed put options in the United States because these contracts are standardized.

Again, the OCC facilitates trading in listed puts, as these contracts exist only in the memory of its computer system. As with calls, as soon as a buyer and a writer decide to trade a particular put option contract and the buyer pays the agreed-upon premium, the OCC steps in, becoming the effective writer as far as the buyer is concerned and the effective buyer as far as the writer is concerned. If a buyer chooses to exercise an option, the OCC will randomly choose a writer who has not closed his or her position and will assign the exercise notice accordingly. The OCC also guarantees delivery of the exercise price if the writer is unable to come up with the necessary cash.

Like calls, puts are protected against stock splits and stock dividends on the underlying stock. In the example in which the option was on 100 shares of XYZ stock with an exercise price of $30, a two-for-one stock split would cause the contract to be altered so that it was for 200 shares at $15 per share. In terms of cash dividends, there is no protection for listed puts.

Exchanges begin trading a new set of options on a given stock every three months. The newly created options have roughly nine months before they expire.[3] For example, options on Widget might be introduced in January, April, July, and October, with expiration dates in, respectively, September, December, March, and June. Furthermore, the exchange might decide to introduce long-term options on Widget, dubbed *LEAPS* by the exchanges for *long-term equity anticipation securities*, that expire as far into the future as two years. They might also allow the creation of customized options on Widget, dubbed *FLEX* options for *flexible exchange options*, that have exercise prices and expiration dates of the investor's choosing (FLEX options are discussed later in the chapter).

In general, two call options on a stock are introduced at the same time, the two being identical in all respects except for the exercise price. In terms of the exercise price, if the stock is selling for $200 or less at the time the options are to be introduced, then the two exercise prices will be set at $5 intervals bracketing the stock price.[4] Furthermore, a pair of put option contracts may also be introduced at the same time. For example, if Widget is selling for $43 in January, then two September call options may be introduced that have exercise prices of $40 and $45. Similarly, two September put options with exercise prices of $40 and $45 may also be introduced.

After an option has been introduced, new options having the same terms as the existing ones but with different exercise prices may be introduced when the stock price of the company moves up or down so much that it is substantially outside of the initial bracket. In terms of Widget, if its stock price rises in the next month to $49, perhaps September put and call options having a $50 exercise price will be introduced.

Once listed, an option remains listed until its expiration date. Specifically, listed options on common stocks generally expire on the third Friday of the specified month.

19.2.1 Trading Activity

Common stock options are currently traded on the Chicago Board Options Exchange (CBOE) and on the American, Pacific, and Philadelphia stock exchanges. Figure 19.1 shows a portion of the daily listing of the trading activity on the CBOE. The first column lists the name of the company and, indented below it, the closing price on its common stock. The next column lists the exercise price for the option contracts on the company, followed by a column giving the expiration date. The next two columns give the trading volume and last trade premium for call options having the exercise price and expiration date shown on the left. The last two columns give the trading volume and last trade premium for the matching put option.

For example, AT&T common stock closed at $45.50 on October 7, 1997. By the end of that day, 234 AT&T call option contracts having an exercise price of $40 per share that expire on the third Friday of January of 1998 had been traded. The closing trade that day took place at $6-$\frac{1}{2}$ per share (or $650 per contract). Similarly, 74 AT&T put option contracts with the same exercise price ($40) and expiration date (January 1998) had been traded. The closing trade was at $\$\frac{11}{16}$ per share (or $68.75 per contract).

Some options are not traded during a given day and are indicated by three periods "...". Others, although included because of the format of the report, have not been introduced and are therefore unavailable for trading. These contracts are also indicated by the three periods. Hence when nothing is reported (see, for example,

Tuesday, October 7, 1997

Composite volume and close for actively traded equity and LEAPS, or long-term options, with results for the corresponding put or call contract. Volume figures are unofficial. Open interest is total outstanding for all exchanges and reflects previous trading day. Close when possible is shown for the underlying stock on primary market. **CB**-Chicago Board Options Exchange. **AM**-American Stock Exchange. **PB**-Philadelphia Stock Exchange. **PC**-Pacific Stock Exchange. **NY**-New York Stock Exchange. **XC**-Composite. **p**-Put.

Option/Strike		Exp.	Call Vol.	Call Last	Put Vol.	Put Last
ADC Tel	35	Nov	247	3 1/8	50	1 3/4
A M R	120	Oct	547	1 1/16	20	4 5/8
APL Ltd	30	Oct	...	...	350	5/8
A S A	30	Oct	288	1 1/4	...	...
31 3/16	30	Nov	1510	2	10	5/8
31 3/16	35	Nov	...	...	385	4 1/4
AT&T	40	Jan	234	6 1/2	74	11/16
45 1/2	45	Oct	1114	1 5/16	168	3/4
45 1/2	45	Nov	233	2 1/8	15	1 1/2
45 1/2	45	Jan	1940	3 3/8	40	2 1/4
45 1/2	50	Oct	245	3/16	...	...
45 1/2	50	Nov	477	9/16	...	...
Abbt L	65	Nov	489	2 7/8	10	2 1/8
Acuson	30	Nov	285	1	...	...
Adaptc	50	Oct	351	3 5/8	34	1/2
53 3/16	55	Nov	262	2 3/4	1	3 7/8
AdobeS	45	Jan	6	8 1/2	6000	2
51 1/16	55	Nov	909	1 3/4	...	...
51 1/16	60	Jan	7040	2 3/8	...	...
51 1/16	75	Jan	505	1/2	...	...
Adtran	45	Nov	506	2 7/8	5	5 3/4
A M D	25	Oct	13	5 1/4	245	3/16
30	27 1/2	Oct	172	3 1/8	799	1/2
30	27 1/2	Nov	37	4	861	1 3/8
30	30	Oct	1733	1 3/8	1417	1 3/8
30	30	Nov	1136	2 9/16	87	2 7/16
30	32 1/2	Oct	582	1/2	76	3 1/4
30	35	Oct	401	3/16	696	5 1/8
30	35	Nov	250	7/8	31	5 1/4
30	35	Apr	291	3 5/8	10	7 1/2
Aetna	75	Oct	321	5 3/8	44	5/16
80 1/4	80	Oct	600	2	20	1 7/8
Agourn	45	Oct	235	8 5/8	80	1/2
53 1/4	45	Feb	10	13	287	4 1/4
53 1/4	47 1/2	Oct	414	6 7/8	20	13/16
53 1/4	47 1/2	Feb	335	11 3/4	100	5 1/8
53 1/4	50	Oct	547	4 7/8	238	1 1/4
53 1/4	50	Nov	355	7 1/4	105	3 3/8
53 1/4	50	Feb	521	10 3/8	1	5 7/8
53 1/4	55	Oct	1050	2	83	3 3/8
53 1/4	55	Nov	370	4 7/8	...	...
53 1/4	60	Nov	279	2 5/8	...	...

Option/Strike		Exp.	Call Vol.	Call Last	Put Vol.	Put Last
36	37 1/2	Oct	320	15/16	...	...
36	40	Oct	241	3/8	...	...
Autoimu	5	Oct	503	1/8	...	...
AutoZn	35	Mar	555	1	...	...
BakrHu	5	Nov	2231	2	...	...
45 15/16	40	Oct	271	5 7/8	...	...
45 15/16	45	Oct	272	1 7/8	25	1 1/8
BancOne	50	Oct	500	9 3/8	...	...
59 13/16	60	Oct	270	1	...	...
BncoFrn	35	Nov	255	1 7/16	...	...
BankNY	45	Oct	240	7 1/4	102	3/16
51 7/8	50	Jan	302	4 3/8	...	...
51 7/8	55	Jan	1306	2 1/16	...	...
BankAm	60	Oct	500	19 7/8	...	...
80 5/8	70	Jan	102	13 1/8	6019	1 1/8
80 5/8	75	Nov	2	7 1/2	228	1 3/8
80 5/8	80	Oct	328	2 1/8	47	1 3/8
80 5/8	80	Jan	5949	6 3/8	20	4 1/4
BkrsTr	110	Oct	230	17	...	...
127 3/8	125	Oct	222	4	...	...
Baxter	55	Nov	28	3	497	1 3/8
56 3/16	60	Nov	300	7/8	...	...
BayNwk	35	Oct	1823	5 3/8	3	5/16
39 15/16	37 1/2	Oct	326	3 1/8	60	7/8
39 15/16	37 1/2	Nov	...	...	617	2
39 15/16	40	Oct	958	1 5/8	882	1 1/2
39 15/16	42 1/2	Oct	345	11/16	...	...
39 15/16	42 1/2	Nov	4682	2	15	3 3/4
39 15/16	45	Nov	225	1 7/16	1	5 1/8
BellAtl	55	Oct	400	29	...	...
84 3/4	60	Oct	2200	24	...	...
84 3/4	65	Oct	608	19 3/4	...	...
84 3/4	70	Oct	5595	14 7/8	...	...
84 3/4	75	Oct	4418	9 1/2	...	...
BellSo	50	Nov	2598	1 3/8	40	2 5/16
BergBrun	45	Nov	270	1 3/16	...	...
39 5/8	50	Dec	2000	1 1/4	...	...
Bindly	30	Oct	390	1	...	...
Biogen	30	Oct	20	3 1/8	560	1/2
33	35	Oct	137	5/8	447	3 1/8
33	35	Nov	918	1 3/4	305	3 3/4
BioTcG	15	Oct	45	5/16	255	1 3/8

Option/Strike		Exp.	Call Vol.	Call Last	Put Vol.	Put Last
81 11/16	75	Jan	350	11 3/4	796	3 7/8
81 11/16	80	Oct	2728	3	1192	1 3/16
81 11/16	80	Nov	561	6	520	3 1/2
81 11/16	80	Jan	632	8 5/8	100	5 5/8
81 11/16	80	Apr	207	12	212	8 1/8
81 11/16	85	Oct	1980	11/16	295	3 7/8
81 11/16	85	Nov	1605	3 1/2	303	6 1/8
81 11/16	85	Jan	669	6 1/4	81	8 1/8
81 11/16	90	Nov	805	1 15/16	2	9 1/4
81 11/16	90	Jan	731	4 1/8	125	11 1/8
Citicp	140	Oct	610	1 3/4	312	2 5/8
CitrixS	50	Oct	223	5	27	1 1/4
54 1/2	55	Oct	453	1 3/4	...	...
Clarify	15	Oct	299	5/16	...	...
Coke	60	Oct	449	4 1/8	152	3/16
63 7/8	60	Nov	353	5	514	1
63 7/8	65	Oct	1104	11/16	148	1 7/8
63 7/8	65	Nov	1926	2 1/16	156	3
63 7/8	70	Feb	392	2 3/16	5	8 1/4
ColumHCA	40	Nov	277	1/16	...	...
ColLb	17 1/2	Oct	235	1/2	50	15/16
CmpUSA	35	Oct	218	1 1/8	...	...
35 1/8	40	Nov	4642	7/8	...	...
Compaq	65	Oct	223	11 1/4	288	5/16
76	65	Nov	17	12 5/8	373	1 1/2
76	70	Oct	1397	6 3/4	907	7/8
76	70	Nov	32	9 1/8	231	2 3/4
76	75	Oct	1861	3 1/4	695	2 3/16
76	75	Nov	1387	6 3/8	2040	5
76	80	Oct	2744	1 5/16	302	5 3/4
76	80	Nov	854	4 1/8	60	8
76	80	Jan	464	7 1/4	230	9 7/8
76	85	Oct	333	1/2	10	9 1/8
76	85	Nov	318	2 1/2	10	11
Cmpuwr	55	Nov	105	14	1000	1 3/8
CorTher	17 1/2	Oct	321	4	10	1/8
CoramH	5	Oct	218	1/8	...	...
CoreFn	65	Nov	145	9 1/2	213	1 5/16
72	70	Oct	287	3 3/4	20	1 1/4
72	75	Nov	230	4	...	...
CntwCrd	35	Jan	9	5 1/8	352	3/4

Figure 19.1

Listed Options Quotations (Excerpts)

Source: Reprinted by permission of *The Wall Street Journal,* Dow Jones & Company, Inc., October 8, 1997, p. C24. All rights reserved worldwide.

AT&T October 50 puts in Figure 19.1), it cannot be determined whether the reason is that there was no trading or the contracts simply did not exist at the time.

While not shown in Figure 19.1, at the bottom of the listings, the total volume (that is, the number of contracts traded) and the open interest (the number of contracts outstanding) for calls and puts are displayed for each exchange and overall.

19.2.2 Most Active Options

Additional information besides the trading activity for options that is shown in Figure 19.1 is provided every day for the "most active" options. Figure 19.2 provides an example of the most active options on October 7, 1997. After the name of the company and the contract specifications come the trading volume on the contract on that day, the exchange on which the option is traded, the closing price on the contract, the change this price represents from the previous day's closing price, the closing price on the underlying stock, and the open interest in that contract.

For example, WorldCom November 40 calls that are traded on the Pacific Stock Exchange were the most active issue on October 7, 1997. On that day, 8,664 of these contracts were traded. The premium on the last trade was $\$\frac{3}{4}$ per share (or \$75.00 per contract). This represents an decrease of $\frac{1}{4}$ from the last trade premium on the previous trading day. On October 7, 1997 the closing price on the common stock of WorldCom was \$36.75 per share.

MOST ACTIVE CONTRACTS

Option/Strike	Vol	Exch	Last	Net Chg	a-Close	Open Int	Option/Strike	Vol	Exch	Last	Net Chg	a-Close	Open Int
WorldCm Nov 40	8,664	PC	3/4	− 1/4	36 3/4	5,993	BellAtl Oct 75	4,418	CB	9 1/2	+ 1 1/2	84 3/4	956
WorldCm Nov 40 p	8,440	PC	3 7/8	+ 1/2	36 3/4	4,989	AscendC Oct 35	4,396	XC	7/8	+ 7/16	33 3/8	16,794
I B M Jan 75 p	7,600	XC	9/16	...	106 13/16	10,638	I B M Oct 110	4,283	XC	1 1/8	+ 1/2	106 13/16	16,049
AdobeS Jan 60	7,040	PC	2 3/8	+ 3/16	51 11/16	5,002	Intel Oct 90 p	4,157	AM	1 1/8	− 5/8	95 1/4	32,163
M C I Nov 37 1/2	6,304	CB	3/4	− 3/8	34 3/4	22,084	Iomega Oct 25	3,834	XC	9/16	− 15/16	22 7/8	9,566
Intel Oct 100	6,027	AM	1 1/4	+ 5/16	95 1/4	39,067	I B M Jan 85 p	3,826	XC	13/16	− 5/16	106 13/16	4,482
Intel Oct 95	6,026	AM	3 1/8	+ 5/8	95 1/4	30,903	Micsft Oct 135	3,670	PC	3 3/4	+ 3/4	136 1/2	10,237
BankAm Jan 70 p	6,019	CB	1 1/8	− 5/8	80 5/8	6,729	3Com Oct 55	3,481	PC	1 9/16	+ 1/16	55	23,463
AdobeS Jan 45 p	6,000	PC	2	− 3/16	51 11/16	5,705	US Airwy Oct 45	3,443	PC	3 1/4	+ 1/2	47 13/16	3,384
BankAm Jan 80	5,949	CB	6 3/8	...	80 5/8	6,754	US Airwy Oct 40	3,419	PC	7 1/2	+ 1/2	47 13/16	5,616
BellAtl Oct 70	5,595	CB	14 7/8	+ 2 3/8	84 3/4	1,113	Motorola Oct 70 p	3,317	AM	1/2	− 7/8	73 3/16	11,911
L S I Oct 30 p	5,176	CB	1 5/8	+ 9/16	29 5/8	12,589	Micsft Oct 130 p	3,095	PC	5/8	− 7/16	136 1/2	13,293
Intel Oct 90	4,754	AM	6 3/8	+ 1	95 1/4	19,298	Intel Jan 90	2,762	AM	11 7/8	+ 1 3/8	95 1/4	14,746
BayNwk Nov 42 1/2	4,682	XC	2	− 1/4	39 15/16	297	M C I Oct 40	2,759	CB	1/16	− 1/16	34 3/4	11,217
I B M Oct 105	4,657	XC	3 3/8	+ 1 1/8	106 13/16	15,043	Compaq Oct 80	2,744	PC	15/16	− 1/16	76	15,102
CmpUSA Nov 40	4,642	XC	7/8	− 1/4	35 1/8	378	Cisco Oct 80	2,728	XC	3	+ 1 1/8	81 11/16	18,406
L S I Oct 30	4,601	CB	1 1/16	− 1/2	29 5/8	4,530	PepsiCo o Jan 40	2,657	CB	3 1/2	+ 3/4	38 3/4	...
TelBrasl Apr 150	4,572	XC	14 1/2	− 1 1/8	142 1/4	251	I B M Oct 100	2,617	XC	7 3/8	+ 1 5/8	106 13/16	12,153
TelBrasl Jan 160	4,530	XC	5 3/4	− 3/4	142 1/4	7,992	US OfcP Feb 40	2,604	XC	3	+ 1 1/2	36 5/8	2,955
M C I Nov 35	4,489	CB	1 3/4	− 1/2	34 3/4	28,769	AscendC Nov 35	2,603	XC	2 1/4	+ 1/2	33 3/8	2,917

Figure 19.2

Most Active Options Quotations

Source: Reprinted by permission of *The Wall Street Journal*, Dow Jones & Company, Inc., October 8, 1997, p. C24. All rights reserved worldwide.

Investors may place the same kinds of orders for options as for stocks: market, limit, stop, and stop limit orders. (These orders were discussed in Chapter 2.) However, the way that the orders for options are executed on the exchanges is, in some cases, different from the way that orders for stocks are executed.

19.2.3 Trading on Exchanges

There are two types of exchange-based mechanisms in the United States for trading option contracts. The focal point for trading involves either specialists or market-makers, as will be discussed next. However, it should be kept in mind that many options are created and traded in the over-the-counter market, where the terms are negotiated between the buyer and writer, who are typically financial institutions, corporations, and large institutional investors.

Use of Specialists

As was mentioned in Chapter 3, trading on stock exchanges centers on specialists. These people serve two functions, acting as both dealers and brokers. As dealers they keep an inventory of the stocks that are assigned to them and buy and sell from that inventory at bid and asked prices, respectively. As brokers they keep the limit order book and execute the orders in it as market prices move up and down. Some option markets, such as the American Stock Exchange, function in a similar manner. These markets have specialists who are assigned specific option contracts, and these specialists act as dealers and brokers in their assigned options. As with the stock exchanges, there may also be **floor traders**, who trade solely for themselves, hoping to buy low and sell high, and **floor brokers**, who handle orders from the public.

Use of Market-Makers

Other option markets, such as the Chicago Board Options Exchange, do not involve specialists. Instead they involve **market-makers**, who act solely as dealers, and **order book officials** (previously known as board brokers), who keep the limit order book. The market-makers quote bid and asked prices and must trade with floor brokers, who are members of the exchange who handle orders from the public. Whereas typically one and only one specialist is assigned to a stock, usually more than one market-

Open Outcry

Is it a scene from a Fellini movie? Or perhaps the crowd at a 90%-off sale at Bloomingdale's? No, it is simply the members of the Chicago Board Options Exchange (CBOE) participating in the time-honored tradition of open outcry.

As the text describes, at the CBOE and other option exchanges (as well as futures exchanges; see Chapter 20), members come together in various trading pits to conduct transactions in specific option contracts. Like the trading posts of the New York Stock Exchange (see Chapter 3), the CBOE trading pits serve as central locations where market-clearing prices for option contracts are continuously determined through an auction process. Unlike the NYSE trading posts, however, the CBOE and most other option exchanges do not use a specialist system. No one individual acts as a monopolistic dealer and auctioneer, ensuring the setting of market-clearing prices. Instead, those prices are established through *open outcry*, a public auction method involving verbal bids and offers initiated by the exchange members in the pit.

Open outcry is a raucous and colorful trading mechanism that combines the mental gymnastics of rapid-fire decision making with a set of physical skills ranging from strategic positioning in the trading pit to shouting instructions to frenetic hand signaling.

To describe the open outcry system as "the pits" is no exaggeration. The process begins in the trading pits, large depressions in the exchange floor surrounded by several levels of stairs on which the members stand. Although no formal rules are involved, traders generally behave very territorially in the pit. Floor traders usually have certain market-makers with whom they prefer to trade, and these individuals position themselves to make convenient contact with one another. Further, the most senior and important traders take positions in the pit where they have most efficient access to their counterparts. Junior members must stand in less desirable positions, where they are less likely to catch the attention of other traders.

The trading pits are often crowded, noisy, and uncomfortable. Members may jostle each other for position. Hence such attributes as voice strength and physical endurance are important. The pits are dominated by men, and the disadvantages endured by women in this physical environment are not lost on critics of the open outcry system.

Members deliver their trading intentions through a system of verbal orders and hand signals. For example, a floor broker may enter the IBM trading pit and verbally announce his or her intention to purchase June IBM call option contracts at a specified price. At the same time, he or she will typically re-

maker is assigned to the options on a given stock. Furthermore, a market-maker is prohibited from handling public orders in his or her assigned options but may handle public orders in other options. That is, market-makers can also act as floor brokers, but only in unassigned options.

The order book official, in keeping the limit order book, is not allowed to engage in any trading. Unlike the specialist, the order book official can show the limit order book to other members of the exchange. The order book official stands at the trading post for those options that are his or her responsibility. All orders must be executed by means of an auction at the trading post with "open outcry," meaning that the auction is conducted orally.

Like the organized stock exchanges in the United States, all option exchanges are continuous markets, meaning that orders can be executed at any time when the exchanges are open. However, actual trading in options is, on occasion, far from continuous. In the financial press it is not unusual to find prices for various options that appear to be out of line with one another or with the price of the underlying stock. It should be remembered that each listed price is that of the last trade of the day and that these trades may have taken place at different times. Apparent price disparities may simply reflect trades that occurred before and after major news, rather than concurrent values at which obviously profitable trades could have been made.

peat the buy order and desired price through hand signals. A market-maker who wishes to sell at that price will signal the desired quantity by hand.

To the uninitiated, the hand gestures used by members appear wild and unintelligible. In actuality, the signals are simple and highly efficient. Buy and sell orders are indicated by the position of the trader's palm(s). If the trader's palms are facing him or her, a buy is signaled. The trader signals a sell by keeping his or her palms pointed outward.

The trader indicates the bid or asked price by holding his or her hand in a vertical position and using fingers to indicate the fraction of a dollar involved. For example, one finger indicates an eighth of a dollar, whereas a closed fist indicates a full dollar.

Traders likewise display their quantity intentions with their hands. In this case, however, fingers pointed vertically indicate one through five contracts, while fingers pointed horizontally indicate six through nine contracts. One finger to the forehead indicates ten contracts.

At any given time, members in the pit may be trading in different option contracts, shouting in an attempt to make their voices heard above the din, and flailing their arms about to signal their trading intentions. Add to this scene runners milling about the edge of the pit, time and sale clerks, price reporters, order book officials keeping track of transactions, and persons situated away from the pit signaling in orders to the floor brokers, and pandemonium hardly seems an adequate description of the trading process.

Open outcry is a controversial trading mechanism. It has been criticized as an archaic method designed primarily to perpetuate control over lucrative option trading by the exchanges' members. In an age of advanced electronics, there are readily available computer systems that could facilitate electronic auctions and permit wider access to the auction process. (For example, the three major U.S. futures exchanges operate electronic after-hours trading systems. Volume on those systems has been growing more rapidly than has regular hours trading volume. Further, the major European futures exchanges are rapidly moving toward "screen" trading.) The benefits of such electronic auction systems would appear to be lower trading costs and greater liquidity.

Defenders of the open outcry system claim that it is the most efficient method of price discovery. They believe that the system's face-to-face contact permits traders to better ascertain the "true" intentions of buyers and sellers. Moreover, the defenders contend that price manipulation is less likely in an open environment. Whether this contention is true remains an open question.

19.2.4 Commissions

Although a commission must be paid to a stockbroker whenever an option is either written, bought, or sold, the size of the commission has been reduced substantially since options began to be traded on organized exchanges in 1973. Furthermore, this commission is typically smaller than the commission that would have been paid if the underlying stock had been purchased instead of the option. This difference is probably due to two reasons: (1) clearing and settling are easier with options than with stocks (with options there are no share certificates that have to change hands with every trade) and (2) the order size is smaller for options than stocks (the total dollar amount paid for the option is much less than the total dollar amount of the underlying stock).[5] However, the investor should be aware that exercising an option will typically result in the buyer's having to pay a commission equivalent to the commission that would be incurred if the stock itself were being bought or sold.

19.3 MARGIN

Any buyer of an option would like some assurance that the writer can deliver as required if the option is exercised. Specifically, the buyer of a call option would like some assurance that the writer is capable of delivering the requisite shares, and the buyer of a put option would like some assurance that the writer is capable of delivering the necessary cash. Because all option contracts are with the OCC, it is actually the OCC that is concerned with the ability of the writer to fulfill the terms of the contract.

To relieve the OCC of this concern, the exchanges where the options are traded have set margin requirements. However, brokerage firms are allowed to impose even stricter requirements if they so desire, because they are ultimately liable to the OCC for the actions of their investors.

In the case of a call, shares are to be delivered by the writer in return for the exercise price. In the case of a put, cash is to be delivered in return for shares. In either case the net cost to the option writer will be the absolute difference between the exercise price and the stock's market value at the time of exercise. The OCC is at risk if the writer is unable to bear this cost, so it is not surprising that the OCC would have a system in place to protect itself from the actions of the writers. This system is known as margin, and it is similar to the notion of margin associated with stock purchases and short sales that was discussed in Chapter 2.[6]

19.4 VALUATION OF OPTIONS

19.4.1 Valuation at Expiration

The value of an option is related to the value of the underlying security in a manner that is most easily seen just before expiration (which for simplicity will be referred to as "at expiration"). Figure 19.3(a) relates the value of a call option with an exercise price of $100 to the price of the underlying stock at expiration. If the stock price is below $100, the option will be worthless when it expires. If the price is above $100, the option can be exercised for $100 to obtain a security with a greater value, resulting in a net gain to the option buyer that will equal the difference between the security's market price and the $100 exercise price. However, there is no need for the option buyer to actually exercise the option. Instead, the option writer can simply pay the buyer the difference between the security price and the $100 exercise price, thereby allowing both parties to avoid the inconvenience of exercise. This practice is commonly used for listed options (by using the services of the OCC), although a minority of investors choose to exercise their options, possibly for tax purposes.

Figure 19.3(b) shows the value at expiration of a put option with an exercise price of $100. If the stock price is above $100, the option will be worthless when it expires. If the price is below $100, the option can be exercised to obtain $100 for stock

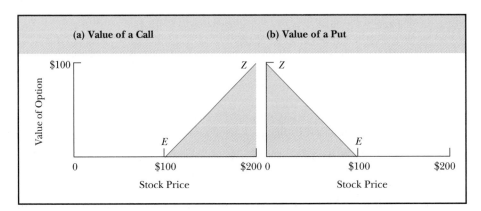

Figure 19.3
Values of Options at Expiration

having a lower value, resulting in a net gain to the option buyer that will equal the difference between the $100 exercise price and the stock's market price. As with a call option, neither the put option buyer nor the writer need actually deal in the stock. Instead, the writer of any put option that is worth exercising at expiration can simply pay the buyer of the option the difference between the stock price and the $100 exercise price.

In both panels of Figure 19.3, the lines indicating the value of a call and a put at expiration can also be interpreted to be the *exercise value* of a call or a put, meaning it is the option's value at the moment it is exercised, no matter when that occurs during the life of the option. In particular, for calls, the kinked line connecting points 0, *E*, and *Z* is known as the **intrinsic value** of the call. Similarly, for puts, the kinked line connecting points *Z*, *E*, and $200 is known as the intrinsic value of the put.

The kinked lines representing the intrinsic values of calls and puts such as those shown in Figure 19.3 can be expressed as IV_c and IV_p, respectively, as follows:

$$IV_c = \max \left\{ 0, P_s - E \right\} \tag{19.1a}$$

$$IV_p = \max \left\{ 0, E - P_s \right\} \tag{19.1b}$$

where P_s denotes the market price of the underlying stock and E denotes the exercise price of the option. (Here *max* means to use the larger of the two values in braces.)

Consider the call option in Figure 19.3(a). Its intrinsic value, according to Equation (19.1a), is $\max \left\{ 0, P_s - \$100 \right\}$ because its exercise price is $100. Note that for any market price of the stock below $100, such as $50, the intrinsic value of the call option is max {0, $50 − $100} = 0. Hence $IV_c = 0$ in such situations. Next imagine that the market price of the stock is above $100, for example, $150. In this situation the call option's intrinsic value is max {0, $150 − $100} = $50. Hence $IV_c = \$50$. Thus the kinked intrinsic value line has its kink at *E*, because it has two components that meet there: a horizontal line going through the origin out to the value *E* and then a 45 degree line (and therefore having a slope of one) going northeast from *E*. Similar analysis reveals that the kinked intrinsic value line for the put also has its kink at *E*, as shown in Figure 19.3(b).

Calls and puts will not sell for less than their intrinsic values, owing to the actions of shrewd investors. If an option sold for less than its intrinsic value, then such investors could instantaneously make riskless profits. For example, if the stock price was $150 and the call was selling for $40, which is $10 less than its intrinsic value of $50, then these investors would simultaneously buy these calls, exercise them, and sell the shares received from the writers. In doing so they would spend a total of $140 on each call ($40) and exercise price ($100) and get $150 in return for each share sold, resulting in a net riskless profit of $10 per call. As a consequence, the call will not sell for less than $50 if the stock price is $150.

19.4.2 Profits and Losses on Calls and Puts

Figure 19.3 shows the values of call and put options at expiration. However, in order to determine profits and losses from buying or writing these options, one must take into consideration the premiums involved.[7] Figure 19.4 accounts for premiums in some of the more complicated option strategies. Each strategy assumes that the underlying stock is selling for $100 at the time an option is initially bought or written. It is also assumed that closing transactions are made just before the expiration date for the option being considered. Outcomes are shown for each of ten strategies. Because the profit obtained by a buyer is the writer's loss and vice versa, each diagram in the figure has a corresponding mirror image.

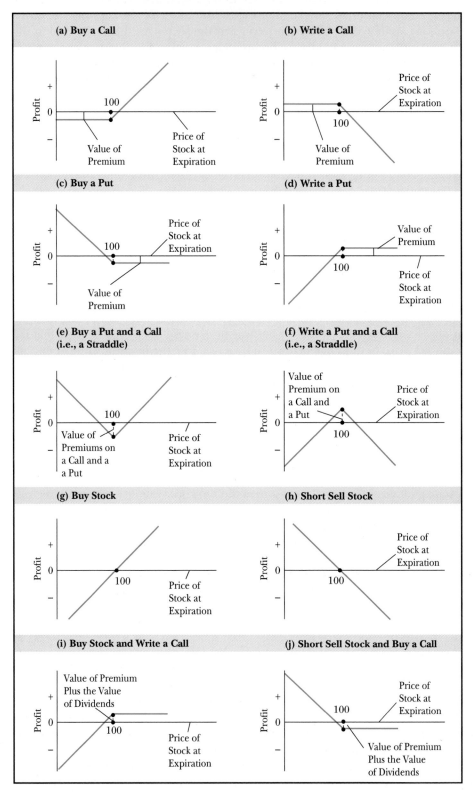

Figure 19.4
Profits and Losses from Various Strategies

Panels (a) and (b) in Figure 19.4 show the profits and losses associated with buying and writing a call, respectively. Similarly, panels (c) and (d) show the profits and losses associated with buying and writing a put, respectively.

Consider panels (a) and (c) first. The kinked lines representing profits and losses in these two panels are simply graphs of the intrinsic value equations, Equations (19.1a) and (19.1b), shown in Figure 19.3, less the premiums on the options. Thus they are graphs of the following equations:

$$\pi_c = IV_c - P_c \tag{19.2a}$$
$$= \max \{0, P_s - E\} - P_c$$
$$= \max \{-P_c, P_s - E - P_c\}$$

$$\pi_p = IV_p - P_p \tag{19.2b}$$
$$= \max \{0, E - P_s\} - P_p$$
$$= \max \{-P_p, E - P_s - P_p\}$$

where π_c and π_p denote the profits associated with buying a call and a put, and P_c and P_p denote the premiums on the call and the put, respectively. This means that the kinked profit line for the call is simply the same kinked line for the intrinsic value but lowered by an amount equal to the call premium P_c. Similarly, the kinked profit line for the put is simply the kinked intrinsic value line for the put, lowered by an amount equal to the put premium P_p.

If the premium on the call and put options shown in Figure 19.3 were $5, then their profit lines would be graphs of the following two equations:

$$\pi_p = \max \{-\$5, P_s - \$100 - \$5\}$$
$$= \max \{-\$5, P_s - \$105\}$$
$$\pi_p = \max \{-\$5, \$100 - P_s - \$5\}$$
$$= \max \{-\$5, \$95 - P_s\}$$

Therefore the kinked line for the call would be a horizontal line intersecting the vertical axis at −$5, and it would have a kink at a stock price of $100, where it would turn upward to intersect the horizontal axis at $105. This graph indicates that the call buyer would not make a profit unless the stock price was above the breakeven point of $105 at expiration. Each dollar that the stock price is above $105 represents an additional dollar of profit. (Hence a price of $108 would represent a profit of $3, because the call buyer pays a premium of $5 and an exercise price of $100 to procure a share of stock that is worth $108.)

Similarly, the kinked line for the put would be a downward-sloping line that would have a kink at a stock price of $100 after intersecting the horizontal axis at $95. At the kink the line would become horizontal so that if this part of the line were extended leftward to the vertical axis, it would intersect it at −$5. This graph indicates that the put buyer would not make a profit unless the stock price was below the breakeven point of $95 at expiration. Each dollar that the stock price is below $95 represents an additional dollar of profit. (Hence a price of $92 would represent a profit of $3, because the put buyer pays a premium of $5 and gives up a share of stock worth $92 in order to receive $100 in return.)

Panels (b) and (d) of Figure 19.4 are mirror images of panels (a) and (c), respectively, because options are zero-sum games, where the profits to one party occur at the expense of the other party. Hence if the stock price is at $108 so that the call buyer has a $3 profit, then the call writer has a $3 loss (because the writer receives the $5 premium and $100 exercise price but must give up a share of stock worth

Option Overwriting

Option overwriting is one of the oldest options-related portfolio management strategies. In its basic form it is a relatively simple technique that conveniently illustrates certain fundamental aspects of options and demonstrates how options can be used to control the shape of a portfolio's distribution of returns.

Option overwriting is a type of covered call writing. The owner of an asset (for purposes of discussion, assume that asset is a portfolio of common stocks) writes out-of-the-money or at-the-money calls on the asset and receives premium income in exchange. The option overwriter stands to gain relative to a strategy of merely holding the portfolio if the portfolio should either decline in value or not rise in value significantly. In that case, the premium helps to either cushion the decline in the portfolio's value or enhance any small price appreciation. On the other hand, the option overwriter loses if the portfolio's value rises above the option's exercise price by more than the amount of the premium received. In that case, the option will be exercised at a loss to the overwriter.

Option overwriting can be done on an individual security basis. However, writing one index option on an entire common stock portfolio is more cost effective than writing many options on individual stocks. Further, index options provide for cash settlement, a feature that eliminates the risk that the overwritten asset will be called away. Consequently, it was the introduction of equity index options in 1983 that encouraged institutional investors to first engage in option overwriting programs on their common stock portfolios.

Option overwriting serves two principle objectives: risk reduction and return enhancement. The first objective is unambiguous; an overwritten port-folio has less risk than the portfolio without option overwriting. The premium reduces potential downside returns, while the existence of the call limits upside price appreciation for the overwriter. The second objective is more controversial. In an efficient market, an option overwriter should not stand to gain on a risk-adjusted basis. The lower risk of option overwriting should be offset by a lower expected return. However, if option markets are not perfectly efficient, then the opportunity may exist for enhanced returns if the option overwriter can identify situations when index calls are overvalued. In that case, the option overwriter would selectively sell calls when they appear overpriced and buy them back when they appear underpriced.

There are many variations on the option overwriting theme. A passively managed index fund (see Chapter 23), designed to match the performance of an index on which options are actively traded is the ideal underlying asset for option overwriting. Out-of-the-money index call options (with exercise prices usually at least 1% to 5% above the current level of the index) are often used to reduce the likelihood of call losses if market prices should rise, although at-the-money options may be sold because they offer higher premiums. Short-term options (usually three months to expiration) are used to maximize the capture of time value decay. That is, the time value of an option (the difference between the option's market value and its intrinsic value) declines most rapidly near expiration. Thus a seller captures the greatest amount of time value decay by selling near expiration. Some option overwriters may sell calls against the entire value of the portfolio; others may overwrite only a fraction. Some overwriters continuously sell calls against the portfolio; others are more selective in their timing. Because American options are more ex-

---

$108). Similarly, if the put buyer has a $3 profit, then the put writer has a loss of $3. Panel (b) corresponds to what is known as **naked call writing**, and panel (d) to **naked put writing**. The term *naked* indicates that the option writer does not own the stock on which the option is written.

19.4.3 Profits and Losses from Some Option Strategies

Panels (e) and (f) of Figure 19.4 illustrate a more complicated options strategy known as a **straddle**. This strategy involves buying (or writing) both a call and a put on the same stock, with the options having the same exercise price and expiration date.[8]

---

pensive than European options (they can be exercised any time up to expiration), and because the option writer does not expect to have the call exercised, American options are the preferred instrument, where appropriate.

Option overwriters typically estimate the relative attractiveness of selling covered calls by examining the implied volatility of the available options. (As the text discusses, implied volatility is the standard deviation of a stock's return that equates the "fair" value of an option to its current market price.) Option values vary directly with the volatility of the underlying asset. Overwriters contend that the market is prone to periods of overreaction, usually around times of market instability, such as October 1987 and the 1990 Gulf War. The overwriters hope to benefit from a mean reversion effect, selling calls when implied volatilities (and prices) are abnormally high and buying when implied volatilities (and prices) have fallen back to "normal" levels. Overwriters will often compare an option's implied volatility with a historical range of volatility for the index. If the implied volatility lies outside of that range, the option may be significantly mispriced.

Consider a hypothetical institutional investor XYZ who has hired manager ABC to conduct an option overwriting program on XYZ's $300 million portfolio of common stocks. Examination of XYZ's portfolio indicates that it most closely resembles the S&P 500, so ABC decides to concentrate on S&P 500 index options. The S&P 500 is currently at 950, and March options (the contract with three months to expiration) with an exercise price of 1000 (5% out-of-the-money) are selling for $2,450 per contract. Assuming a riskfree rate of 5%, ABC calculates an implied volatility for the S&P 500 of 21%. The historical average volatility is 17%, with a standard deviation of

3% around that mean, so it appears that the market is overvaluing the March option. ABC decides to overwrite 25% of XYZ's common stock portfolio, or $75 million. ABC sells 790 contracts and receives $1,935,500 in premiums, equal to .65% of XYZ's total common stock portfolio's value. Three months later, implied volatilities have declined to 18% and the S&P 500 has risen in value to 980, still below the exercise price of the option, which expires worthless. ABC chooses not to roll over the option and to let the portfolio remain unwritten for the time being. Consequently, the option overwriting program has boosted the return on XYZ's portfolio by .65%.

The biggest risk to an options overwriting program is that the stock market might rise sharply for an extended period of time. The relatively small amount of premium income can quickly be overwhelmed by the losses incurred when the market moves against the overwriting strategy. In fact, that situation occurred in the mid-1990s. Option overwriting strategies generally worked well from 1990 through 1994, when the market had several down or modestly positive return years. The success of those strategies led a number of institutional investors to enter into option overwriting programs. Overwritten assets were estimated to be more than $17 billion at their peak in 1995. However, these programs generally produced disappointing results as stock prices rose sharply from 1995 through 1997. As a result, most of the institutional investors who had entered into option overwriting in the early 1990s had abandoned the strategy by 1997. In hindsight, one is left to conclude that many of these investors either did not understand the risk-reward tradeoffs involved in option overwriting or overestimated the active management skills of overwriting managers.

Note that panel (e) can be derived by adding the profits and losses shown in panels (a) and (c), whereas panel (f) can be derived by adding the profits and losses shown in panels (b) and (d). It can also be seen that panels (e) and (f) are mirror images of each other, again reflecting the fact that the profits to buyers equal the losses to writers and vice versa.

Panel (g) of Figure 19.4 shows the profit or loss made by an investor who avoids options entirely but buys a share of the underlying stock (at $100) at the same time that others buy or write options and sells the stock when the options expire. If no dividends are paid in the interim, the relationship is that shown by the solid line.[9] Similarly, panel (h) shows the profit or loss obtained by an investor who short sells the stock at the initial date and then buys it back at the expiration date.

Panel (i) of Figure 19.4 shows the results obtained by an investor who buys one share of stock and simultaneously writes a call on it, a strategy known as **covered call writing**. These results can be derived by adding the profits and losses shown in panels (b) and (g).

Panel (j) of Figure 19.4 shows the results obtained by an investor who short sells one share of stock and simultaneously buys a call option, and can be derived by adding the profits and losses in panels (a) and (h). Note that this panel is the mirror image of panel (i).

Comparison of the diagrams in Figure 19.4 suggests that similar results can be obtained via alternative strategies. Panels (c) and (j) are similar, as are (d) and (i). Neither the premiums involved nor the initial investments required need be equal in every case. Nonetheless, the similarity of the results obtained with different "packages" of securities suggests that the total market values of the packages will be similar.

Now that the value of options (and option-based strategies) when they expire has been discussed, it is appropriate to discuss next the value of options before they expire. Specifically, what is the fair (or true) value of an option today if it expires at some future date? A method utilizing the binomial option pricing model can be used to answer such a question. It is presented next.

19.5 THE BINOMIAL OPTION PRICING MODEL

The binomial option pricing model (BOPM) can be used to estimate the fair value of a call or put option. It is best presented through an example in which it is assumed that the options are **European options**, meaning that they can be exercised only on their expiration dates. In addition, it is assumed that the underlying stock does not pay any dividends during the life of the option. The model can be modified to value **American options**, which are options that can be exercised at any time during their life and can also be used to value options on stocks that pay dividends during the life of the option.

19.5.1 Call Options

Assume that the price of Widget stock today ($t = 0$) is $100, and that after one year ($t = T$) its stock will be selling for either $125 or $80, meaning that the stock will either rise by 25% or fall by 20% over the year. In addition, the annual riskfree rate is 8% compounded continuously. Investors are assumed to be able to either lend (by purchasing these 8% bonds) or borrow (by short selling the bonds) at this rate.

Now consider a call option on Widget that has an exercise price of $100 and an expiration date of one year from now. On the expiration date the call will have a value of either $25 (if Widget is at $125) or $0 (if Widget is at $80). Figure 19.5(a) illustrates the situation by use of a "price tree." It can be seen from this tree why this is called a binomial model; there are only two branches that represent prices at the expiration date.

Valuation

The question that arises is this: What is a fair value for the call at time 0? The binomial option pricing model is designed to answer that question.

Three investments are of interest here: the stock, the option, and a riskfree bond. The prices and payoffs for the stock are known. It is also known that $100 invested

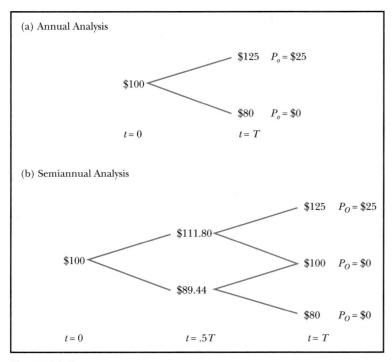

(a) Annual Analysis

$100 → $125 $P_o = \$25$
$100 → $80 $P_o = \$0$

$t = 0$ $t = T$

(b) Semiannual Analysis

$100 → $111.80 → $125 $P_O = \$25$
$111.80 → $100 $P_O = \$0$
$100 → $89.44 → $100 $P_O = \$0$
$89.44 → $80 $P_O = \$0$

$t = 0$ $t = .5T$ $t = T$

Figure 19.5
Binomial Model of Prices for Widget

in a riskfree bond will grow to approximately $108.33 given that interest is continuously compounded at an annual rate of 8%.[10] Finally, the end-of-period payoffs associated with the option are known. What is to be determined is a fair price that the option should sell for now.

The key to understanding the situation is the observation that there are two possible future *states of nature.* The stock's price may go up or down. For simplicity, these two states are called the "up state" and the "down state," respectively. This essential information is summarized as follows:

Security	Payoff in Up State	Payoff in Down State	Current Price
Stock	$125.00	$80.00	$100.00
Bond	108.33	108.33	100.00
Call	25.00	0.00	???

Note that at this juncture the current price of the call is unknown.

Replicating Portfolios

Although the Widget call option may seem exotic, its characteristics can in fact be replicated with an appropriate combination of the Widget stock and the riskfree bond. Moreover, the cost of this *replicating portfolio* constitutes the fair value of the option. Why? Because otherwise there would be an *arbitrage opportunity;* an investor could buy the cheaper of the two alternatives and sell the more expensive one, thereby achieving a guaranteed profit. (Just how this is done will be shown shortly.)

The composition of a portfolio that will precisely replicate the payoffs of the Widget call option needs to be determined. Consider a portfolio with N_s shares of

Widget stock and N_b riskfree bonds. In the up state such a portfolio will have a payoff of $\$125N_s + \$108.33N_b$, whereas in the down state it will have a payoff of $\$80N_s + \$108.33N_b$. The call option is worth $25 in the up state. Thus N_s and N_b need to have values so that:

$$\$125N_s + \$108.33N_b = \$25 \tag{19.3a}$$

On the other hand, the call option is worthless in the down state. Thus N_s and N_b need to have values so that:

$$\$80N_s + \$108.33N_b = \$0 \tag{19.3b}$$

These two linear equations, (19.3a) and (19.3b), have two unknowns and can easily be solved. Subtracting the second equation from the first gives:

$$(\$125 - \$80)N_s = \$25 \tag{19.3c}$$

so that N_s equals .5556. Substituting this value in either Equation (19.3a) or Equation (19.3b) gives the remainder of the solution, $N_b = -.4103$.

What does this mean in financial terms? It means that an investor can replicate the payoffs from the call by *short selling* $41.03 of the riskfree bonds (note that investing $-.4103$ in $100 bonds is equivalent to short selling $41.03 of the bonds or borrowing $41.03 at the riskfree rate) and *purchasing* .5556 shares of Widget stock. This is indeed the case, as can be seen here:

Portfolio Component	Payoff in Up State	Payoff in Down State
Stock investment	.5556 × $125	.5556 × $80
	=$69.45	=$44.45
Loan repayment	−$41.03 × 1.0833	−$41.03 × 1.0833
	=−$44.45	=−$44.45
Net payoff	$25.00	$0.00

Because the replicating portfolio provides the same payoffs as the call, only its cost needs to be calculated in order to find the fair value of the option. To obtain the portfolio, the investor must spend $55.56 to purchase .5556 shares of Widget stock (at $100 per share). However, $41.03 of this amount is provided by the proceeds from the short sale of the bond. Thus only $14.53 ($55.56 − $41.03) of the investor's own funds must be spent. Accordingly, this is the fair value of the call option.

More generally, the value of the call option will be:

$$V_o = N_s P_s + N_b P_b \tag{19.4}$$

where V_o represents the value of the option, P_s is the price of the stock, P_b is the price of a riskfree bond, and N_s and N_b are the number of shares and riskfree bonds required to replicate the option's payoffs.

Overpricing

To see that equilibrium will be attained if the call is selling for $14.53, consider what a shrewd investor would do if the call were selling for either more or less than this amount. Imagine that the call is selling for $20, so it is overpriced. In this case the investor would consider writing one call, buying .5556 shares, and borrowing $41.03. The net cash flow when this is done (that is, at $t = 0$) would be $5.47 [= $20 − (.5556 × $100) + $41.03], indicating that the investor has a net cash inflow. At the end of the year (that is, at $t = T$) the investor's net cash flow will be as follows:

Portfolio Component	Payoff in Up State	Payoff in Down State
Written call	−$25.00	$0.00
Stock investment	.5556 × $125 = $69.45	.5556 × $80 = $44.45
Loan repayment	−$41.03 × 1.0833 = −$44.45	−$41.03 × 1.0833 = −$44.45
Net payoff	$0.00	$0.00

Because the net aggregate value is zero regardless of the ending stock price, the investor has no risk of loss from this strategy. Thus the investor currently has a means for generating free cash as long as the call is priced at $20, because the investment strategy does not require any cash from the investor later on. This situation cannot represent equilibrium, as anyone can get free cash by investing similarly.

Underpricing

Next imagine that the call is selling for $10 instead of $20, so it is underpriced. In this case the investor would consider buying one call, short selling .5556 shares, and investing $41.03 at the riskfree rate. The net cash flow (that is, at $t = 0$) would be $4.53 [=−$10 + (.5556 × $100) − $41.03], indicating that the investor has a net cash inflow. At the end of the year (that is, at $t = T$) the investor's net cash flow will be as follows:

Portfolio Component	Payoff in Up State	Payoff in Down State
Call investment	$25.00	$0.00
Repay shorted stock	−.5556 × $125 = −$69.45	−.5556 × $80 = −$44.45
Riskfree investment	$41.03 × 1.0833 = $44.45	$41.03 × 1.0833 = $44.45
Net payoff	$0.00	$0.00

Once again, the net aggregate value is zero regardless of the ending stock price, indicating that the investor has no risk of loss from this strategy. Hence the investor currently has a means for generating free cash as long as the call is priced at $10. This situation cannot represent equilibrium, however, because anyone can get free cash by investing similarly.

The Hedge Ratio

To replicate the Widget call option, imagine borrowing $41.03 and purchasing .5556 shares of Widget stock. Now consider the effect of a change in the price of the stock tomorrow (not a year from now) on the value of the replicating portfolio. Because .5556 shares of stock are included in the portfolio, the value of the portfolio will change by $.5556 for every $1 change in the price of Widget stock. But because the call option and the portfolio should sell for the same price, it follows that the price of the call should also change by $.5556 for every $1 change in the price of the stock. This relationship is defined as the option's **hedge ratio**, denoted h. It is equal to the value of N_s that was determined in Equation (19.3c).

In the case of the Widget call option, the hedge ratio was equal to .5556, which equals the value of ($25 − $0)/($125 − $80). Note that the numerator equals the difference between the option's payoffs in the up and down states, and the denominator equals the difference between the stock's payoffs in the two states. More generally, in the binomial model the hedge ratio is:

$$h = \frac{P_{ou} - P_{od}}{P_{su} - P_{sd}} \tag{19.5}$$

where P represents the end-of-period price and the subscripts indicate the instrument (o for option, s for stock) and the state of nature (u for up, d for down).

To replicate a call option in a binomial world, an investor must purchase h shares of stock and risklessly borrow an amount B by short selling bonds. The amount to be borrowed is:

$$B = \text{PV}\left(hP_{sd} - P_{od}\right) \tag{19.6}$$

where PV refers to taking the present value of the figure calculated in the following parentheses. (Note that the figure in parentheses is the value of the bond at the end of the period.)[11]

To summarize, the value of a call option is given to be:

$$V_o = hP_s - B \tag{19.7}$$

where h and B are the hedge ratio and the current value of a short bond position in a portfolio that replicates the payoffs of the call, and they are calculated by using Equations (19.5) and (19.6).

More Than Two Prices

At this juncture it is reasonable to wonder about the accuracy of the BOPM if it is based on an assumption that the price of Widget stock can assume only one of two values at the end of a year. Realistically, Widget stock can assume any one of a great number of prices at year-end. It turns out that this is not a problem, because the model can be extended in a straightforward manner.

In the case of Widget, divide the year into two six-month periods. In the first period, assume that Widget can go up to $111.80 (an 11.80% increase) or down to $89.44 (a 10.56% decrease). For the second six-month period, the price of Widget can again go either up by 11.80% or down by 10.56%. Hence the price of Widget will follow one of the paths of the price tree shown in Figure 19.5(b) over the forthcoming year. Note that Widget can now assume one of three prices at year-end: $125, $100, or $80. The associated value of the call option is also given in the figure for each of these stock prices.

How can the value of the Widget call option at time 0 be calculated from the information given in the figure? The answer is remarkably simple. All that is done is that the problem is broken down into three parts, each of which is solved in a manner similar to that shown earlier when panel (a) was discussed. The three parts must be approached sequentially by working backward in time.

First, imagine that six months have passed and the price of Widget stock is $111.80. What is the value of the call option at this node in the price tree? The hedge ratio h is calculated to be 1.0 [= ($25 − $0)/($125 − $100)], and the amount of the borrowing B is calculated to be $96.08 [= (1 × $100 − $0)/1.0408]. (The 8% riskfree rate compounded continuously corresponds to a discrete discount rate of 4.08% for the six-month period.) With Equation (19.7), the value of the call is determined to be $15.72 (=1 × $111.80 − $96.08).

Second, again imagine that six months have passed, but the price of Widget is $89.44. Equations (19.5), (19.6), and (19.7) could be used to determine the value of the call at this node in the price tree, but intuition gives the answer in this example more quickly: The call has to be selling for $0. In six months the price of Widget will be either $100 or $80, and regardless of which it is, the call will still be worthless. That is, investors will realize that the call will be worthless at the end of the year if the stock price is at $89.44 after six months, and hence they will be unwilling to pay anything for the call option.

Third, imagine that no time has elapsed, so that it is time 0. In this case the price tree can be simplified to:

$$
\$100 \begin{cases} \$111.80 \qquad P_o = \$15.72 \\ \$89.44 \qquad P_o = \$0 \end{cases}
$$

Applying Equations (19.5) and (19.6) indicates that the hedge ratio h is equal to .7030 [= ($15.72 − $0)/($111.80 − $89.44)], and the amount of borrowing B is equal to $60.41 [= (.7030 × $89.44 − $0)/1.0408]. Applying Equation (19.7) results in a value for the call at $t = 0$ of $9.89 [= (.7030 × $100) − $60.41].

There is no need to stop here. Instead of analyzing two six-month periods, four quarterly periods can be analyzed, or 12 monthly periods. Note that the number of year-end stock prices for Widget is equal to one more than the number of periods in a year. Hence, when annual periods were used in Figure 19.5(a), there were two year-end prices, and when semiannual prices were used, there were three year-end prices. It follows that if quarterly or monthly periods had been used, there would have been 5 or 13 year-end prices, respectively.

19.5.2 Put Options

Can the BOPM be used to value puts? Because the formulas cover any set of payoffs, they can be applied directly. Consider Widget once again from an annual perspective, where the put option has an exercise price of $100 and an expiration date of one year. Its price tree will be:

$$
\$100 \begin{cases} \$125 \qquad P_o = \$0 \\ \$80 \qquad P_o = \$20 \end{cases}
$$

Applying Equation (19.5) gives the hedge ratio for the put option as −.4444 [= ($0 − $20)/($125 − $80)]. Note that this is a negative number, indicating that Widget stock is to be sold short and that a rise in the price of the stock will lower the price of the put.

Applying Equation (19.6) shows that B equals −$51.28, which is the present value of the year-end value of −$55.55. Because these are negative numbers, they denote the amount of bonds to be purchased (that is, the negative value of a short position should be interpreted as the value of a long position).

To replicate the put option, then, one *sells short* .4444 shares of Widget and *lends* (that is, invests in the riskfree bond) $51.28. The short sale will generate $44.44 while the bond purchase will cost $51.28, so the net cost of the replicating portfolio will be $6.84 (=$51.28 − $44.44). Accordingly, this is the fair value of the put.

This is the same value that is obtained when Equation (19.7) is used: $6.84 [= −.4444 × $100 − (−$51.28)], where $h = −.4444$, $B = −$51.28$, and $P_s = 100. Hence Equations (19.5), (19.6), and (19.7) can be used to value not only calls but also puts. Furthermore, the procedure for extending the valuation of puts to the situation in which there are two or more periods between now and the expiration date is analogous to the one that was given for calls.

19.5.3 Put-Call Parity

Earlier it was shown that the call on Widget had a hedge ratio of .5556. Note that .5556 − 1 = −.4444, the hedge ratio for the put. This is not a coincidence. The hedge ratios of a European put and call having the same exercise price and expiration date are related in the following manner:

$$h_c - 1 = h_p \tag{19.8}$$

where h_c and h_p denote the hedge ratios for the call and the put, respectively.

Of even greater interest is the relationship between the market prices of a call and a put on a given stock that have the same exercise price and expiration date. Again consider the example involving Widget options that have an exercise price of $100 and an expiration date of one year. Two investment strategies need to be compared. Strategy A involves buying a put and a share of stock. (This strategy is sometimes known as a "protective put" or a "married put.") Strategy B involves buying a call and investing an amount of money in the riskfree asset that is equal to the present value of the exercise price.

At the expiration date the values of these two investment strategies can be calculated under two scenarios: the price of Widget being below its exercise price of $100, and the price of Widget being above its exercise price. (The case in which it is exactly equal to its exercise price can be added to either scenario without affecting the results.) Table 19.1 shows the calculations for both scenarios. Note that if the stock of Widget is selling for less than the $100 exercise price on the expiration date, both strategies have a payoff of $100 in cash. Alternatively, if the price of Widget stock is above $100, both strategies result in the investor's having possession of a share of stock that is worth more than $100. Hence, because the two strategies have the same payoffs, they must cost the same amount in equilibrium:

$$P_p + P_s = P_c + \frac{E}{e^{RT}} \tag{19.9}$$

where P_p and P_c denote the current market prices of the put and the call, respectively. This equation represents what is known as **put-call parity**. In Table 19.1 it can be seen that the cost of each strategy is $106.84, just as was suggested previously by the calculations using Equations (19.5), (19.6), and (19.7).

Strategy	Initial Cost	Value at Expiration Date	
		$P_s < E = \$100$	$E = \$100 > P_s$
A: Buy put Buy share of stock	$P_p + P_s$ =$6.84 + $100 =$106.84	Exercise put, get $100	Throw away put, have stock worth P_s
B: Buy call Invest present value of E in riskfree asset	$P_c + E/e^{RT}$ =$14.53 + $92.31 =$106.84	Throw away call, get $100 from riskfree asset	Exercise call, get stock worth P_s

TABLE 19.1 Put-Call Parity Involving Widget

Consider what would happen with the binomial option pricing model if the number of periods before the expiration date were allowed to increase. For example, with Widget's option for which the expiration date was a year in the future, there could be a price tree with periods for each one of the approximately 250 trading days in a year. Hence there would be 251 possible year-end prices for Widget stock. Needless to say, the fair value of any call associated with such a tree would require a computer to perform calculations such as those shown earlier for Widget. If the number of periods were even larger, with each one representing a specific hour of each trading day, then there would be about 1,750 ($=7 \times 250$) hourly periods (and 1,751 possible year-end prices). Note that the number of periods in a year gets larger as the length of each period gets shorter. In the limit there will be an infinite number of infinitely small periods (and, consequently, an infinite number of possible year-end prices). In this situation the BOPM given in Equation (19.7) reduces to the Black-Scholes model, so named in honor of its originators.[12]

19.6.1   The Formula

In a world not bothered by taxes and transaction costs, the fair value of a call option can be estimated by using the valuation formula developed by Black and Scholes. It has been widely used by those who deal with options to search for situations in which the market price of an option differs substantially from its fair value. A call option that is found to be selling for substantially less than its Black-Scholes value is a candidate for purchase, whereas one that is found to be selling for substantially more is a candidate for writing. The Black-Scholes formula for estimating the fair value of a call option V_c is:

$$V_c = N(d_1)P_s - \frac{E}{e^{RT}} N(d_2) \tag{19.10}$$

where:

$$d_1 = \frac{\ln(P_s/E) + (R + .5\sigma^2)T}{\sigma\sqrt{T}} \tag{19.11}$$

$$d_2 = \frac{\ln(P_s/E) + (R - .5\sigma^2)T}{\sigma\sqrt{T}} \tag{19.12a}$$

$$= d_1 - \sigma\sqrt{T} \tag{19.12b}$$

and where:

P_s = current market price of the underlying stock

E = exercise price of the option

R = continuously compounded riskfree rate of return expressed on an annual basis

T = time remaining before expiration, expressed as a fraction of a year

σ = risk of the underlying common stock, measured by the standard deviation of the continuously compounded annual rate of return on the stock and commonly referred to as **volatility**

Note that E/e^{RT} is the present value of the exercise price where a continuous discount rate is used. The quantity $\ln(P_s/E)$ is the natural logarithm of P_s/E. Finally,

TABLE 19.2		Values of N(d) for Selected Values of d			
d	**N(d)**	**d**	**N(d)**	**d**	**N(d)**
		−1.00	.1587	1.00	.8413
−2.95	.0016	−.95	.1711	1.05	.8531
−2.90	.0019	−.90	.1841	1.10	.8643
−2.85	.0022	−.85	.1977	1.15	.8749
−2.80	.0026	−.80	.2119	1.20	.8849
−2.75	.0030	−.75	.2266	1.25	.8944
−2.70	.0035	−.70	.2420	1.30	.9032
−2.65	.0040	−.65	.2578	1.35	.9115
−2.60	.0047	−.60	.2743	1.40	.9192
−2.55	.0054	−.55	.2912	1.45	.9265
−2.50	.0062	−.50	.3085	1.50	.9332
−2.45	.0071	−.45	.3264	1.55	.9394
−2.40	.0082	−.40	.3446	1.60	.9452
−2.35	.0094	−.35	.3632	1.65	.9505
−2.30	.0107	−.30	.3821	1.70	.9554
−2.25	.0122	−.25	.4013	1.75	.9599
−2.20	.0139	−.20	.4207	1.80	.9641
−2.15	.0158	−.15	.4404	1.85	.9678
−2.10	.0179	−.10	.4602	1.90	.9713
−2.05	.0202	−.05	.4801	1.95	.9744
−2.00	.0228	.00	.5000	2.00	.9773
−1.95	.0256	.05	.5199	2.05	.9798
−1.90	.0287	.10	.5398	2.10	.9821
−1.85	.0322	.15	.5596	2.15	.9842
−1.80	.0359	.20	.5793	2.20	.9861
−1.75	.0401	.25	.5987	2.25	.9878
−1.70	.0446	.30	.6179	2.30	.9893
−1.65	.0495	.35	.6368	2.35	.9906
−1.60	.0548	.40	.6554	2.40	.9918
−1.55	.0606	.45	.6736	2.45	.9929
−1.50	.0668	.50	.6915	2.50	.9938
−1.45	.0735	.55	.7088	2.55	.9946
−1.40	.0808	.60	.7257	2.60	.9953
−1.35	.0885	.65	.7422	2.65	.9960
−1.30	.0968	.70	.7580	2.70	.9965
−1.25	.1057	.75	.7734	2.75	.9970
−1.20	.1151	.80	.7881	2.80	.9974
−1.15	.1251	.85	.8023	2.85	.9978
−1.10	.1357	.90	.8159	2.90	.9981
−1.05	.1469	.95	.8289	2.95	.9984

$N(d_1)$ and $N(d_2)$ denote the probabilities that outcomes of less than d_1 and d_2, respectively, will occur in a normal distribution that has a mean of 0 and a standard deviation of 1.

Table 19.2 provides values of $N(d_1)$ for various levels of d_1.[13] Only this table and a pocket calculator are needed to use the Black-Scholes formula for valuing a call option. With this formula the interest rate R and the stock volatility σ are assumed to be constant over the life of the option. (More recently formulas have been developed where those assumptions are relaxed.)

For example, consider a call option that expires in three months and has an exercise price of $40 (thus $T = .25$ and $E = \$40$). Furthermore, the current price and volatility of the underlying common stock are $36 and 50%, respectively, whereas the riskfree rate is 5% (thus $P_s = \$36$, $R = .05$, and $\sigma = .50$). Solving Equations (19.11) and (19.12b) provides the following values for d_1 and d_2:

$$d_1 = \frac{\ln(36/40) + [.05 + .5(.50)^2].25}{.50\sqrt{.25}} = -.25$$

$$d_2 = -.25 - .50\sqrt{.25} = -.50$$

Now Table 19.2 can be used to find the corresponding values of $N(d_1)$ and $N(d_2)$:

$$N(d_1) = N(-.25) = .4013$$

$$N(d_2) = N(-.50) = .3085$$

Finally, Equation (19.10) can be used to estimate the fair value of this call option:

$$V_c = (.4013 \times \$36) - \left(\frac{\$40}{e^{.05 \times .25}} \times .3085\right)$$

$$= \$14.45 - \$12.19 = \$2.26$$

If this call option is currently selling for $5, the investor should consider writing some of them because they are overpriced (according to the Black-Scholes model), suggesting that their price will fall in the near future. Thus the writer would receive a premium of $5 and would expect to be able to enter a closing buy order later for a lower price, making a profit on the difference. Conversely, if the call option were selling for $1, the investor should consider buying some of them because they are underpriced and can be expected to rise in value in the future.

19.6.2 Comparison with the Binomial Option Pricing Model

At this juncture the BOPM formula [given in Equation (19.7) where V_0 is now denoted V_c] can be compared with the Black-Scholes option pricing formula [given in Equation (19.10)]:

$$V_c = hP_s - B \tag{19.7}$$

$$V_c = N(d_1)P_s - \frac{E}{e^{RT}} N(d_2) \tag{19.10}$$

Comparison of the two equations shows the quantity $N(d_1)$ in Equation (19.10) corresponds to h in Equation (19.7). Remember that h is the hedge ratio, so the quantity $N(d_1)$ in the Black-Scholes formula can be interpreted in a similar manner. That is, it corresponds to the number of shares that an investor would need to purchase in executing an investment strategy that was designed to have the same payoffs as a call option. Similarly, the quantity $EN(d_2)/e^{RT}$ corresponds to B, the amount of money that the investor borrows as the other part of the strategy. Consequently, the quantity $EN(d_2)$ corresponds to the face amount of the loan, because it is the amount that must be paid back to the lender at time T, the expiration date. Hence e^{RT} is the discount (or present value) factor, indicating that the interest rate on the loan is R

per period and that the loan is for T periods. Thus the seemingly complex Black-Scholes formula can be seen to have an intuitive interpretation. It simply involves calculating the cost of a buy-stock-and-borrow-money investment strategy that has the same payoffs at T as a call option.

In the example, $N(d_1)$ was equal to .4013 and $EN(d_2)/e^{RT}$ was equal to $12.19. Hence an investment strategy that involves buying .4013 shares and borrowing $12.19 at time 0 will have payoffs exactly equal to those associated with buying the call.[14] Because this strategy costs $2.26, it follows that in equilibrium the market price of the call must also be $2.26.

19.6.3 Static Analysis

Close scrutiny of the Black-Scholes formula reveals some interesting features of European call option pricing. In particular, the fair value of a call option is dependent on five inputs: the market price of the common stock P_s, the exercise price of the option E, the length of time until the expiration date T, the riskfree rate R, and the volatility of the common stock σ. What happens to the fair value of a call option when one of these inputs is changed while the other four remain the same?

1. The higher the price of the underlying stock P_s, the higher the value of the call option.
2. The higher the exercise price E, the lower the value of the call option.
3. The longer the time to the expiration date T, the higher the value of the call option.
4. The higher the riskfree rate R, the higher the value of the call option.
5. The greater the volatility σ of the common stock, the higher the value of the call option.

Of these five factors, the first three $(P_s, E,$ and $T)$ are readily determined. The fourth factor, the riskfree rate R, is often estimated by using the yield-to-maturity on a Treasury bill having a maturity date close to the expiration date of the option. The fifth factor, the volatility of the underlying stock σ, is not readily observed; consequently various methods for estimating it have been proposed. Two of these methods are presented next.

19.6.4 Estimating a Stock's Volatility from Historical Prices

One method for estimating the volatility of the underlying common stock associated with a call option involves analyzing historical prices of the stock. Initially a set of $n + 1$ market prices on the underlying stock must be obtained from either financial publications or a computer database. These prices are then used to calculate a set of n continuously compounded returns as follows:

$$r_t = \ln \left(\frac{P_{st}}{P_{st-1}} \right) \tag{19.13}$$

where P_{st} and P_{st-1} denote the market price of the underlying stock at times t and $t - 1$, respectively. Here, ln denotes taking the natural logarithm of the quantity P_{st}/P_{st-1}, which thus results in a continuously compounded return.

For example, the set of market prices for the stock might consist of the closing price at the end of each of 53 weeks. If the price at the end of one week was $105 and the price at the end of the next week was $107, then the continuously compounded return for that week r_t will be equal to 1.886% [$=\ln(107/105)$]. Similar calculations will result in a set of 52 weekly returns.

Once a set of n returns on the stock has been calculated, the next step involves using them to estimate the stock's average return:

$$r_{av} = \frac{1}{n} \sum_{t=1}^{n} r_t \qquad (19.14)$$

The average return is then used in estimating the per period variance: that is, the square of the per period standard deviation:

$$s^2 = \frac{1}{n-1} \sum_{t=1}^{n} (r_t - r_{av})^2 \qquad (19.15)$$

This is called the per period variance because its size is dependent on the length of time over which each return is measured. In the example, weekly returns were calculated and would lead to the estimation of a weekly variance. Alternatively, daily returns could have been used, leading to a daily variance that would be of smaller magnitude than the weekly variance. However, what is needed is not a weekly or a daily variance but an annual variance. This is obtained by multiplying the per period variance by the number of periods in a year. Thus an estimated weekly variance would be multiplied by 52 in order to estimate the annual variance σ^2 (that is, $\sigma^2 = 52s^2$).[15]

Alternative methods of estimating a stock's volatility exist. One such method involves subjectively estimating the probabilities of possible future stock prices. Another method involves combining the historical and subjective estimates of volatility. For any estimate of future uncertainty, historical data are likely to prove more helpful than definitive. And because recent data may prove more helpful than older data, some analysts study daily price changes over the most recent 6 to 12 months, sometimes giving more weight to more recent data than to earlier ones. Others take into account the price histories of related stocks and the possibility that a stock whose price has recently decreased may be more volatile in the future than it was in the past. Still others make explicit subjective estimates of the future, taking into account changes in uncertainty concerning the economy in general as well as uncertainty in specific industries and in stocks. In some cases an analyst's estimate of a stock's volatility over the next three months may differ from that for the following three months, leading to the use of different values of σ for call options on the same stock that have different expiration dates.

19.6.5 The Market Consensus of a Stock's Volatility

Another way to estimate a stock's volatility is based on the assumption that a currently outstanding call option is fairly priced in the marketplace. Because this means that $P_c = V_c$, the current market price of the call P_c can be entered on the left-hand side of Equation (19.10) in place of the fair value of the call V_c. Next all the other factors except for σ are entered on the right-hand side, and a value for σ, the only unknown variable, is found that satisfies the equation. The solution for σ can be interpreted as representing a consensus opinion in the marketplace on the size of the stock's volatility, and it is sometimes known as the stock's **implied volatility**.[16]

For example, assume that the riskfree rate is 6% and that a six-month call option with an exercise price of $40 sells for $4 when the price of the underlying stock is $36. Different estimates of σ can be "plugged into" the right-hand side of Equation (19.10) until a value of $4 for this side of the equation is obtained. In this example an estimated value of .40 (that is, 40%) for σ will result in a number for the right-hand side of Equation (19.10) that is equal to $4, the current market price of the call option that is on the left-hand side.

The procedure can be modified by applying it to several call or put options on the same stock. For example, σ can be estimated for each of several call options on the same stock that have different exercise prices but the same expiration date. Then the resulting estimates for σ can be averaged and, in turn, used to determine the fair value of another call option on the same stock having yet another exercise price but a similar expiration date.

In the example, σ can be estimated not only for a six-month option having an exercise price of $40, but also for six-month options having exercise prices of $35 and $45. Then the three estimates of σ can be averaged to produce a "best estimate" of σ that is used to value a six-month $50 option on the same stock.

Alternatively, the procedure can be modified by averaging the estimates for σ associated with each of several expiration dates. In the example, σ can be estimated not only for a six-month option having an exercise price of $40 but also for a three-month and a nine-month option that each have an exercise price of $40. The three estimates of σ can be averaged to produce a best estimate of σ that will subsequently be used to determine the fair value of a one-month $40 option on the same stock.

There are other ways of using a set of estimates of σ that correspond to different call options on the same stock. Perhaps σ will be estimated for a set of calls having different expiration dates and different exercise prices, and then averaged. Perhaps σ will be estimated from historical returns using Equation (19.15), with the resulting figure averaged with one or more estimates of the stock's implied volatility. Although the evidence is still unclear, it appears that methods based on calculating implied volatility are better than methods based on historical returns.[17] It should be remembered, however, that all of these methods assume that volatility remains constant over the life of the option—an assumption that can be challenged.

19.6.6 More on Hedge Ratios

The slope of the Black-Scholes value curve at any point represents the expected change in the value of the option for each dollar change in the price of the underlying common stock. This amount corresponds to the hedge ratio of the call option and is equal to $N(d_1)$ in Equation (19.10). As can be seen in Figure 19.6 (assuming that the market price of the call is equal to its Black-Scholes value), the slope (that

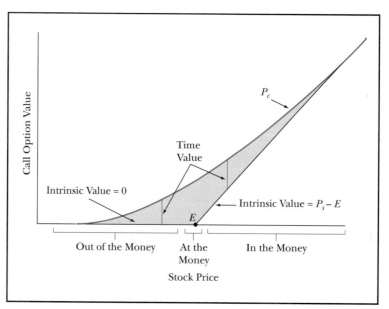

Figure 19.6
Option Terminology for Calls

is, the hedge ratio) of the curve is always positive. Note that if the stock has a relatively low market price, the slope will be near zero. For higher stock prices the slope increases and ultimately approaches a value of 1 for relatively high prices.

Because the hedge ratio is less than 1, a $1 increase in the stock price will typically result in an increase in a call option's value of less than $1. However, the percentage change in the value of the call option will generally be much greater than the percentage change in the price of the stock. It is this relationship that leads people to say that options offer high leverage.

The reason for referring to the slope of the Black-Scholes value curve as the hedge ratio is that a "hedge" portfolio, meaning a nearly riskfree portfolio, can be formed by simultaneously writing one call option and purchasing a number of shares equal to the hedge ratio, $N(d_1)$. For example, assume that the hedge ratio is .5, indicating that the hedge portfolio consists of writing one call and buying .5 shares of stock. Now if the stock price rises by $1, the value of the call option will rise by approximately $.50. The hedge portfolio would lose approximately $.50 on the written call option but gain $.50 from the rise in the stock's price. Conversely, a $1 decrease in the stock's price would result in a $.50 gain on the written call option but a loss of $.50 on the half-share of stock. Overall, it can be seen that the hedge portfolio will neither gain nor lose value when the price of the underlying common stock changes by a relatively small amount.[18]

Even if the Black-Scholes model is valid and all the inputs have been correctly specified, risk is not permanently eliminated in the hedge portfolio when the portfolio is first formed (or, for that matter, at any time). There will still be risk because the hedge ratio will change as the stock price changes and as the life of the option decreases with the passage of time. In order to eliminate risk from the hedge portfolio, the investor will have to alter its composition continuously. Altering it less often will reduce but not completely eliminate risk.

19.6.7 Limitations on Use of the Black-Scholes Model

At first the Black-Scholes model might seem to have limited use, because almost all options in the United States are American options that can be exercised at any time up to their expiration date, whereas the Black-Scholes model applies only to European options. Furthermore, strictly speaking, the model is applicable only to options on stocks that will not pay any dividends over the life of the option. However, most of the common stocks on which options are written do in fact pay dividends.

The first drawback of the Black-Scholes model—that it is applicable only to European options—can be dispensed with rather easily when the option is a call and the underlying stock does not pay dividends. The reason is that it is unwise for an investor holding an American call option on a non-dividend-paying stock to exercise it before maturity.[19] Because there is no reason for exercising such an option before maturity, the opportunity to do so is worthless. Consequently there will be no difference in the values of an American and a European call option. In turn, the Black-Scholes model can be used to estimate the fair value of American call options on non-dividend-paying stocks.

The reason can be seen in Figure 19.6, but first some terminology must be introduced. A call option is said to be **at the money** if the underlying stock has a market price roughly equal to the call's exercise price. If the stock's market price is below the exercise price, the call is said to be **out of the money**, and if the market price is above the exercise price, the call is said to be **in the money**. Occasionally, finer gradations are invoked, and one hears of "near the money," "deep in the money," or "far out of the money."

As mentioned earlier, the value of an option if it were exercised immediately is known as its intrinsic value. This value is equal to zero if the option is out of the money. However, it is equal to the difference between the stock price and the exercise price if the option is in the money. The excess of the option's price over its intrinsic value is the option's **time value** (or time premium). As shown in Figure 19.3(a), for call options at expiration the time value is zero. However, before then the time value is positive. Note that a call option's premium is simply the sum of its intrinsic and time values.

An investor considering exercising a call option on a non-dividend-paying stock before its expiration date will always find it cheaper to sell the call option and purchase the stock in the marketplace. Exercising the call would result in the investor's losing the time value of the option (hence the expression that call options are "worth more alive than dead").

For example, consider a stock that has a current price of $110. If this stock has a call option with an exercise price of $100 that is selling for $14, then the intrinsic and time values of this option are $10 (=$110 − $100) and $4 (=$14 − $10), respectively. An investor who owns one of these calls could exercise it by spending an additional $100. However, it would be cheaper for the investor to get the share of stock by selling the call option and buying the share of stock in the marketplace, because the additional cost would be only $96 (=$110 − $14).

The second drawback of the Black-Scholes model—that it is applicable only to non-dividend-paying stocks—cannot be easily dismissed, because many call options are written on stocks that will pay dividends over the life of the option. Some procedures have been suggested for amending this formula to value call options on such stocks.[20] As will be seen shortly, European options on dividend-paying stocks can generally be valued using the Black-Scholes formula by making one simple alteration, but American options are more problematic.

19.6.8 Adjustments for Dividends

Thus far the issue of dividend payments on the underlying stock during the life of an option has been avoided. Other things being equal, the greater the amount of the dividends to be paid during the life of a call option, the lower the value of the call option because the greater the dividend that a firm declares, the lower its stock price will be. Options are not "dividend-protected," so this lower stock price will result in a lower value for the call option (and a higher value for put options).

The simplest case is valuing European call options on dividend-paying stocks when the future dividends can be accurately forecast, both in size and date. An accurate forecast is often possible, because most options have an expiration date that is within nine months. In such cases, all that is done in valuing European call options is to take the current stock price, subtract from it the discounted value of the dividends (using the ex-dividend date and the riskfree rate for discounting), and insert the resulting adjusted price in the Black-Scholes call option formula along with the other inputs. The reason is quite straightforward. The current stock price can be viewed as consisting of two components: the present value of the known dividends that will be paid over the life of the option and the present value of all the dividends thereafter (see the discussion of dividend discount models in Chapter 17). Because the option is exercisable only at expiration, it is applicable to only the second component, whose current value is just the adjusted price. Thus, if the stock previously discussed that is currently priced at $36 will pay a dividend in six months of $1, its adjusted price is $35.025 given a riskfree rate of 5% $\left[\$35.025 = \$36 - \left(\$1/e^{.05 \times .5}\right)\right]$. Consequently any European calls that expire in more than six months but before the next ex-dividend date can be valued by using the Black-Scholes call option formula and a current price of $35.025.

When it comes to American call options, things are much more complicated because it may pay to exercise such an option just before an ex-dividend date. Earlier it was mentioned that, in the absence of dividends, an American call option would be worth at least as much "alive" (not exercised) as "dead" (exercised). When dividends are involved, however, the situation may be different. This difference is shown in Figure 19.7.

The call option's value if exercised immediately, referred to as the option's intrinsic value, lies along the lower boundary $0EZ$. If the option is allowed to live, its value will lie along the higher Black-Scholes curve, as shown in the figure. Imagine that the stock is currently priced at P_{s1} and is about to go ex-dividend for the last time before the option's expiration. Afterward it can be expected to sell for a lower price P_{s2}. The Black-Scholes formula can be used to estimate the option's value if it

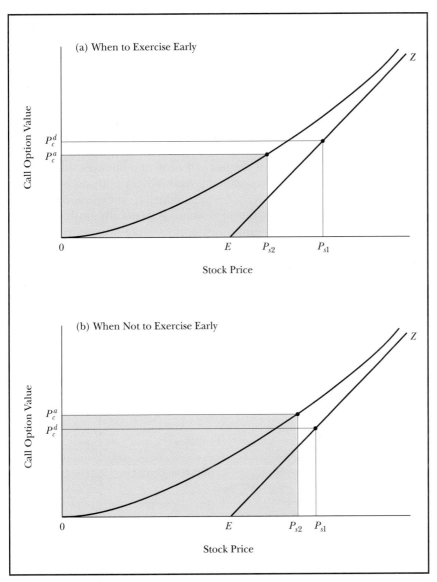

Figure 19.7
Option Values before and after an Ex-Dividend Date

remains alive just after the ex-dividend date. In Figure 19.7, this alive value is P_c^a. If instead the option is exercised just before the ex-dividend date while the stock price is still P_{s1}, the investor will obtain the dead value (that is, the intrinsic value) of P_c^d. Because the investor is interested in maximizing the value of the option, exercising earlier or not involves comparing P_c^a and P_c^d. If P_c^d is greater than P_c^a [as is the case in panel (a)], the option should be exercised now, just before the ex-dividend date; if P_c^d is less than P_c^a [as is the case in panel (b)], the option should not be exercised. Hence for an American call option on a dividend-paying stock, the possibility of early exercise must be taken into consideration.[21] Fortunately, the BOPM is capable of handling such a situation.

19.7 THE VALUATION OF PUT OPTIONS

Similar to a call option, a put option is said to be at the money if the underlying stock has a market price roughly equal to the put's exercise price. However, the terms *out of the money* and *in the money* have, in one sense, *opposite meanings* for puts and calls. In particular, a put option is out of the money if the underlying stock has a market price above the exercise price and is in the money if the market price is below the exercise price. Figure 19.8 provides an illustration of how these terms apply to a put option.

An option's intrinsic value equals zero if the option is out of the money and equals the difference between the exercise price and the stock price if the stock is in the money. Thus, in another sense, the terms *out of the money* and *in the money* have *similar meanings* for puts and calls.

As mentioned earlier, the excess of the price of a call or a put over this intrinsic value is the option's time value (or time premium). As shown for calls and puts in panels (a) and (b) of Figure 19.3, respectively, the time value is 0 at expiration. However, Figures 19.6 and 19.8 show that the time value is generally positive before expiration. Note that an option's premium is simply the sum of its intrinsic value and its time value.

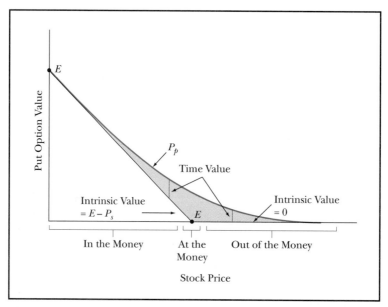

Figure 19.8
Option Terminology for Puts

19.7.1 Put-Call Parity

Consider a put and a call on the same underlying stock that have the same exercise price and expiration date. Earlier it was shown in Equation (19.9) that their market prices should be related, with the nature of the relationship known as put-call parity. However, this relationship is valid only for European options on non-dividend-paying stocks. Equation (19.9) can be rearranged in the following manner so that it can be used to estimate the value of European put options:

$$P_p = P_c + \frac{E}{e^{RT}} - P_s \tag{19.16}$$

Thus the value of a put can be estimated by using either the BOPM or the Black-Scholes formula to estimate the value of a matching call option, then adding an amount equal to the present value of the exercise price to this estimate, and finally subtracting from this sum an amount that is equal to the current market price of the underlying common stock.

For example, consider a put option that expires in three months and has an exercise price of $40, while the current market price and the volatility of the underlying common stock are $36 and 50%, respectively. It was shown earlier that, if the riskfree rate is 5%, the Black-Scholes estimate of the value for a matching call option is $2.26. Because the 5% riskfree rate is a continuously compounded rate, the present value of the exercise price equals $39.50 $\left[= \$40/\left(e^{.05 \times .25}\right)\right]$. At this point, because it has been determined that $P_c = \$2.26$, $E/e^{RT} = \$39.50$, and $P_s = \$36$, Equation (19.16) can be used to estimate the value of the put option as being equal to $5.76 $(=\$2.26 + \$39.50 - \$36)$.

Alternatively, the Black-Scholes formula for estimating the value of a call given in Equation (19.10) can be substituted for P_c in Equation (19.16). After the substitution the resulting equation can be used directly to estimate the value of a put. That is:

$$P_p = \frac{E}{e^{RT}} N(-d_2) - P_s N(-d_1) \tag{19.17}$$

where d_1 and d_2 are given in Equations (19.11) and (19.12a), respectively.

In the previous example, $d_1 = -.25$ and $d_2 = -.50$; thus $N(-d_1) = N(.25) = .5987$ and $N(-d_2) = N(.50) = .6915$. With the application of Equation (19.17), the value of this put can be estimated directly:

$$P_p = \left(\frac{\$40}{e^{.05 \times .25}} \times .6915 \right) - (\$36 \times .5987)$$

$$= \$27.31 - \$21.55 = \$5.76$$

which is the same estimated value as indicated earlier when Equation (19.16) was used.

19.7.2 Static Analysis

Close scrutiny of the put-call parity equation reveals some interesting features of European put option pricing. In particular, the value of a put option is dependent on the values of the same five inputs used for call valuation: the market price of the common stock P_s, the exercise price of the option E, the length of time until the expiration date T, the riskfree rate R, and the volatility of the common stock σ. What happens to the value of a put option when one of these inputs is changed while the other four remain the same?

1. The higher the price of the underlying stock P_s, the lower the value of the put option.

2. The higher the exercise price E, the higher the value of the put option.

3. In general, but not always, the longer the time to the expiration date T, the higher the value of the put option.

4. The higher the riskfree rate R, the lower the value of the put option.

5. The greater the volatility σ of the common stock, the higher the value of the put option.

The relationships for the underlying stock price P_s, exercise price E, and riskfree rate R are in the opposite direction from those shown earlier for call options; the relationships for the time to the expiration date T and volatility σ are in the same direction. Exceptions can occur with T when the put is deep in the money. In such a situation a longer time to expiration could actually decrease the value of the put.

19.7.3 Early Exercise and Dividends

Equations (19.16) and (19.17) apply to a European put on a stock that will not pay dividends before the option's expiration. As with call options, it is straightforward to handle European puts if there are dividends that will be paid on the underlying common stock during the option's life, provided they can be accurately forecast. All that needs to be done is to follow the same procedure as described earlier for calls: Reduce the current stock price by the present value of the dividends that are to be paid during the option's life, and then use this adjusted price in the Black-Scholes put option formula along with the other inputs. However, complications arise when it is recognized that most put options are American, meaning that they can be exercised before expiration, and that often dividends on the underlying common stock will be paid before the expiration date.

Consider first the ability to exercise a put option at any time up to its expiration date. Earlier it was shown that if there were no dividends on the underlying stock, then a call option was worth more alive than dead, meaning that call options should not be exercised before expiration. Such an argument does *not* hold for put options.

Specifically, if a put option is in the money, meaning that the market price of the stock is less than the exercise price, then the investor may want to exercise the put option. In doing so, the investor will receive an additional amount of cash equal to $E - P_s$. In turn, this cash can be invested at the riskfree rate to earn money over the remaining life of the option. Because these earnings may be greater than any additional profits received by the investor if the put option were held, it may be advantageous to exercise the put early and thereby receive the earnings.

An example can be used to illustrate the point. Consider a put option on Widget that has a year left until its expiration date. The exercise price on the put is $100, and the annual riskfree rate is 10%. Imagine that the stock price of Widget is now at $5 per share, having recently plunged in value. If an investor owned such a deep-in-the-money option, it would be in his or her best interest to exercise it immediately. The logic is as follows.

The intrinsic value of the put is currently $95 (=$100 − $5), indicating that if the put is exercised immediately, the buyer will receive $95. That is, the buyer will spend $5 to buy a share of Widget and then turn the share and the put over to the writer in return for the exercise price of $100. The net cash inflow to the put buyer of $95 could be invested in the riskfree asset so that in one year it would be worth $104.50 (= $95 × 1.10). Alternatively, if the put is held, what is the best that the buyer can hope to earn at year-end? If the stock price of Widget drops to $0, the buyer will receive $100 at expiration from the put writer. Clearly the buyer would be better off exercising the put now instead of holding onto it. Hence early exercise is merited in such a situation.

What will happen to the market price of the put in such a situation? In equilibrium it will be equal to the put's intrinsic value $E - P_s$ (in this instance, $95). Hence the put's time premium would be zero because nobody would pay more than the intrinsic value for the put, knowing that a better return could be obtained by investing in the riskfree asset. In addition, nobody would be willing to sell a put for less than its intrinsic value because doing so would open up the opportunity for immediately earning riskfree profits by purchasing the put and exercising it right away. Hence the only price that the put could sell for would be its intrinsic value.

Consider next the impact of dividends on put valuation. Previously it was shown that the owner of a call may find it optimal to exercise just *before* an ex-dividend date, because doing so allowed the investor to receive the forthcoming dividends on the stock. With respect to a put, the owner may find it optimal to exercise just *after* the ex-dividend date, because the corresponding drop in the stock price will cause the value of the put to rise.[22] In summary, the uncertainty of when to exercise makes American puts difficult to value regardless of whether the underlying stock pays dividends. Fortunately, as it is for calls, the BOPM is capable of handling such situations.

19.8   INDEX OPTIONS

Not all options are written on individual issues of common stock. In recent years many new options have been created that have as an underlying asset something other than the stock of a particular company. One of them—index options—is discussed here. The appendix discusses others, and the next chapter discusses what are known as futures options.

19.8.1   Cash Settlement

A call option on General Motors stock is a relatively simple instrument. Upon exercise, the call buyer literally calls away 100 shares of GM stock. The call writer is expected to physically deliver the shares. In practice, both the buyer and the writer may find it advantageous to close their positions in order to avoid the costs associated with the physical transfer of shares. In this event the buyer may expect a gain (and the seller a loss) approximately equal to the difference between the current market price of the security and the option's exercise price, with a net gain equal to this amount less the premium that was paid to purchase the call.

It would be entirely feasible to use only a "cash settlement" procedure upon expiration for any option contract. The writer would be required to pay the buyer an amount equal to the difference between the current price of the security and the call option's exercise price (provided that the current price is larger than the exercise price). Similarly for puts, the writer could be expected to pay the buyer an amount equal to the difference between the option's exercise price and the current market price (provided that the exercise price is larger than the current price). Although listed options on individual securities retain the obligation to "deliver," the realization that cash settlement can serve as a substitute has allowed the creation of index options.

19.8.2   The Contract

An index option is based on the level of an index of stock prices and thus allows investors to take positions in the market that the index represents. Some indices are designed to reflect movements in the stock market, broadly construed. Other "specialized" indices are intended to capture changes in the fortunes of particular industries or sectors. Figure 19.9 shows two of the major indices on which options

Tuesday, October 7, 1997

Volume, last, net change and open interest for all contracts. Volume figures are unofficial. Open interest reflects previous trading day. p-Put c-Call

CHICAGO

Strike		Vol.	Last	Net Chg.	Open Int.
		DJ INDUS AVG(DJX)			
Nov	72c	2	10 1/8	...	...
Nov	72p	3	1/4	...	...
Dec	72c	10	10 5/8	...	...
Jan	72c	80	12 1/4	+ 3/4	79
Jan	72p	21	1 3/8	...	...
Dec	74c	7	8 7/8	...	...
Dec	74p	10	7/8	− 1/8	100
Jan	74c	12	10 3/4	+ 5/8	4
Oct	76p	148	1/16	− 1/8	25
Nov	76c	20	6 3/8	...	...
Jan	76c	2	9	...	...
Oct	77p	5	1/4	...	60
Nov	77p	127	3/4	− 1/4	1,000
Oct	78c	2	3 1/2	+ 1/8	5
Oct	78p	61	3/16	...	...
Nov	78p	5	1	− 1/8	563
Dec	78c	2	5 3/4	+ 1/4	34
Dec	78p	51	1 5/8	− 3/16	15
Jan	78p	30	2 3/4	− 3/8	2
Oct	79c	20	2 9/16	...	123
Oct	79p	40	5/16	...	...
Nov	79c	1	3 7/8	+ 1/4	2
Oct	80c	9,952	2 1/4	+ 1/2	718
Oct	80p	1,362	3/8	− 5/16	676
Nov	80c	10,457	3 1/2	+ 1/4	2,831
Nov	80p	34	1 9/16	− 1/4	741
Dec	80c	43	4 1/2	+ 1/2	2,102
Dec	80p	50	2 3/16	− 1/4	36
Jan	80p	5	3 1/2	− 3/8	8
Oct	81c	10,251	1 9/16	+ 1/2	1,576
Oct	81p	1,040	5/8	− 3/8	1,110
Nov	81c	135	2 11/16	+ 1/8	1,084
Nov	81p	89	1 13/16	− 5/16	2,747
Oct	82c	14,818	13/16	+ 3/16	205
Oct	82p	1,052	1	− 5/8	1,263
Nov	82c	20,306	2 3/8	+ 7/16	433
Nov	82p	26	2 3/16	− 7/16	950
Dec	82c	58	3 3/8	+ 1/2	33
Jan	82c	100	5	...	...
Oct	83c	295	7/16	+ 1/8	50
Oct	83p	40	1 13/16	− 7/16	6
Nov	83c	100	1 9/16	+ 1/16	35
Nov	83p	11	2 13/16	− 7/16	1,000
Oct	84c	5,010	3/16	+ 1/16	150
Oct	84p	14	2 3/8	− 7/8	2
Nov	84c	10,055	1 1/4	+ 3/16	5
Dec	84c	12	2 3/16	+ 5/16	30
Jan	84c	37	4	...	...
Nov	85p	20	4 1/8	− 1/4	10
Nov	88c	51	5/16	...	...
Dec	88c	38	7/8	+ 3/16	600
Dec	88p	10	6 7/8	...	...
Call Vol.		**81,890**	**Open Int.**		**10,655**
Put Vol.		**4,254**	**Open Int.**		**11,272**
		S & P 100 INDEX(OEX)			
Oct	780c	1	166 7/8	+ 10 1/4	155
Oct	780p	92	1/8	...	9,395
Oct	790p	2	1/8	...	3,966
Oct	800c	8	146	+ 31	62
Oct	800p	734	1/8	− 1/8	7,323
Nov	800c	5	146 1/4	+ 17 1/4	33
Nov	800p	342	1 3/4	− 1/2	6,181
Dec	800c	9	156	+ 9 7/8	43
Dec	800p	3	4 1/2	− 3/8	1,929
Oct	810p	59	1/4	− 1/16	4,789
Nov	810p	27	2 1/8	− 9/16	758
Dec	810p	2	5 3/4	− 1/4	1,511
Oct	820p	782	1/4	− 1/8	6,007
Nov	820c	1	130	+ 8 1/8	39
Nov	820p	108	2 9/16	− 13/16	1,211
Dec	820p	2	5 7/8	− 2 1/4	1,111
Jan	820p	104	9 3/4	− 1 5/8	504
Oct	830c	10	117 7/8	+ 26 1/8	32
Oct	830p	600	1/4	− 1/4	4,047
Nov	830p	32	2 7/8	− 7/8	1,109
Dec	830p	58	6 1/8	− 1 7/8	822
Oct	840c	69	106 1/4	+ 9 3/8	525
Oct	840p	1,032	1/4	− 3/8	4,949
Nov	840p	17	3 3/8	− 1 5/8	849
Dec	840p	150	7 1/2	− 1 1/8	1,832
Oct	845p	50	7/16	− 1/4	2,676
Oct	850p	2,005	7/16	− 7/16	7,471
Nov	850p	36	4	− 2	2,227
Dec	850p	252	9	− 1 5/8	2,813
Oct	855p	170	1/2	− 1/2	1,339
Oct	860c	10	80 3/4	+ 3 3/4	402
Oct	860p	734	5/8	− 3/8	7,721
Nov	860p	93	5 1/4	− 1 1/2	1,358
Dec	860p	22	10 1/8	− 1 7/8	330

Figure 19.9
Index Options Quotations (Excerpts)
Source: Reprinted by permission of *The Wall Street Journal*, Dow Jones & Company, Inc., October 8, 1997, p. C15. All rights reserved worldwide.

were offered in 1997, along with their quotations. Some indices are highly specialized, consisting of only a few stocks. Others are broadly representative of major portions of the stock market. Roughly one-half are European and the other half are American. In general, the options expire within a few months, but a few expire in up to two years.

Contracts for index options are not stated in terms of numbers of shares. Instead, the size of a contract is determined by multiplying the level of the index by a *multiplier* specified by the exchange on which the option is traded. The premium (price) of an index option times the applicable multiplier indicates the total amount paid.

Consider, for example, the Dow Jones Industrial Average (DJX) index call option that is traded on the Chicago Board Options Exchange with an exercise price of 80 and expiring in December 1997. Note that it had an indicated premium of $4\frac{1}{2}$ on October 7, 1997. Because the multiplier for these contracts is 100, an investor would have to pay $450 (=4.5 \times 100$) for this contract (plus a commission).

After purchasing this contract, the investor could later sell it or exercise it for its cash settlement value. Perhaps in November 1997 the Dow will be at 8500. In this case the investor could exercise the call, receiving its intrinsic value of $500 [= (85 - 80) \times 100]$ for doing so. Alternatively, the investor could simply sell the call on the exchange. In doing so, the investor would almost certainly receive an amount greater than $500 because the call would sell for an amount equal to the sum of its intrinsic and time values (see Figure 19.6).

19.8.3 Flex Options

In an effort to counteract the growing off-exchange over-the-counter market for customized call and put options, the CBOE now lists "flexible option contracts," called "flex options" for short. These contracts are on individual stocks or indices, and they allow an investor (typically an institution) to specify the exercise price and expiration date. In addition, the investor can specify whether the option is American (exercisable at any time) or European (exercisable only at expiration). Once the investor has placed the order, it is executed on the CBOE, where someone else takes the other side of the contract. Because the OCC is in the middle between the buyer and the writer, there is little risk of default on the contract. This is an advantage to these customized options, because options created off-exchange (say between investors A and B) are only as good as the creditworthiness of the parties themselves. (The possibility that the writer of one of these off-exchange options may default on his or her obligations is referred to as **counterparty risk**.[23])

19.9 PORTFOLIO INSURANCE

In the mid-1980s one of the more popular uses of options was a strategy called **portfolio insurance**, which is a way of synthetically creating a put on a given portfolio. Consider an investor who holds a highly diversified portfolio. This investor would like to be able to benefit from any upward movements that may subsequently occur in the stock market but would also like to be protected from any downward movements.[24] There are, in principle, at least two ways this goal might be accomplished.[25]

19.9.1 Purchase a Protective Put

Assume that the investor's portfolio is currently worth $100,000 and that a put option is available on a stock market index that closely resembles the investor's portfolio. The investor's portfolio will have a value indicated by the line $0BC$ in Figure 19.10(a) if

---

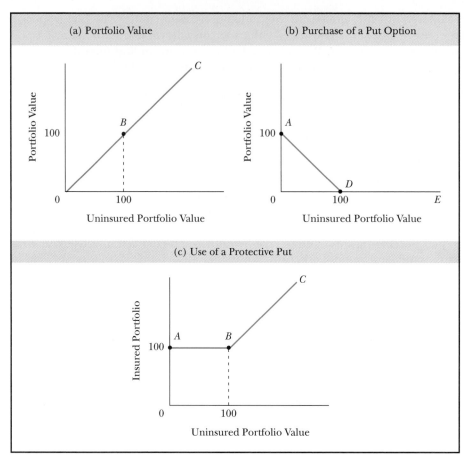

Figure 19.10
Portfolio Insurance

nothing is done. The kinked line *ADE* in Figure 19.10(b) shows the value to a buyer of the index put at the expiration date, where the put has an exercise price of $100,000. What would happen to an investor who (1) held the portfolio and (2) purchased this put? Figure 19.10(c) shows the answer. The value of the portfolio (*ABC*) is simply the sum of the values 0*BC* and *ADE* shown in Figures 19.10(a) and (b).

In this case the purchase of a put provides protection against declines in portfolio value. In this role it is termed a protective put (or "married put"). In practice, stock indices may not closely correspond with an investor's portfolio. Thus the purchase of a put on a stock index may provide only imperfect insurance. In a graph such as that shown in Figure 19.10(c), the resulting curve would be somewhat fuzzy owing to the possible divergence of values of the portfolio and the index. For example, the portfolio may decline in value by $25,000, whereas the index might decline by only $10,000. In this case the portfolio would be insured for only 40% (=$10,000/$25,000) of its decline in value.

What if an appropriate put were not available? Can something still be done to insure the portfolio's value against market declines? Yes, if the allocation of funds between the portfolio and a riskless security can be altered frequently enough (and at reasonable cost). This type of portfolio insurance involves the creation of a **synthetic put**, and its application involves the use of a dynamic strategy for asset allocation, which will be discussed next.

19.9.2   Create a Synthetic Put

Insuring a portfolio by creating a synthetic put can most easily be described with an example.[26] Assume that the investor has $100,000 and is considering the purchase of a portfolio of common stocks. It is believed that the market value of this portfolio will either increase to $125,000 or decrease to $80,000 in six months. If it does increase to $125,000, then it will end up being worth either $156,250 or $100,000 after another six months. Alternatively, if it decreases to $80,000, then it will subsequently end up being worth either $100,000 or $64,000. Each one of these possible states of nature is indicated by a letter in Figure 19.11(a), with the current state being denoted as state A.

Figure 19.11(a) also shows two sets of terminal portfolio values (that is, portfolio values after 12 months) on the assumption that the common stock portfolio is purchased. The first set gives the values of the portfolio if it is uninsured. The second shows the desired portfolio values—that is, the values of an insured portfolio. In this example the investor wants to be certain that the ending portfolio is worth at least $100,000, while also being able to earn the returns associated with state D, should that state occur.[27]

What should the investor do initially in order to be certain of this outcome? Clearly, the investor cannot simply purchase the portfolio of stocks because the portfolio would be worth only $64,000 if state G occurs. However, the investor could purchase portfolio insurance—that is create a synthetic put—by investing in both the stock portfolio and riskfree bonds.

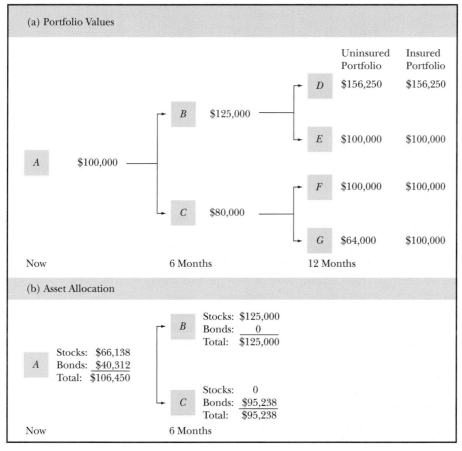

Figure 19.11
Creation of a Synthetic Put

The way this is done is to imagine that six months have passed and that state B has occurred. In this situation, how might one be certain to have \$156,250 if the final state is D and \$100,000 if the state is E? The answer is simple; if state B occurs, make sure that the portfolio at that point is worth \$125,000. Thus an initial investment strategy is required that will provide \$125,000 if the six-month state turns out to be state B.

It is also possible that after the first six months state C will occur. In this situation, how might one be certain to have \$100,000 regardless of the final state? If risk-free bonds return 5% (compounded discretely) per six months, the investor should purchase \$95,238 (=\$100,000/1.05) of these bonds if state C occurs. Consequently, an initial investment strategy is required that will provide \$95,238 if the six-month state turns out to be state C.

Figure 19.11(b) shows the investments and the amounts required in situations B and C. It remains only to determine an appropriate initial set of investments (at point A).

An amount of \$1 invested in the common stock portfolio at A will grow to \$1.25 after six months if the state at that time is B. More generally, s invested in the common stock portfolio at A will grow to $1.25s$ if the six-month state is B. Similarly, b invested in bonds at A will grow to $1.05b$ after six months. Thus, a set of initial investments s and b that will provide \$125,000 if state B occurs must solve the following equation:

$$1.25s + 1.05b = \$125,000 \qquad (19.18)$$

If the six-month state is C, then s invested in the common stock portfolio will be worth $.8s$, while b invested in bonds will be worth $1.05b$. Thus the set of initial investments s and b that will provide \$95,238 if state C occurs must solve the following equation:

$$.8s + 1.05b = \$95,238 \qquad (19.19)$$

Actual solutions for s and b can now be found because there are two equations and two unknowns. The solution, shown in Figure 19.11(b), is that the investor should initially put \$66,138 in common stocks and \$40,312 in bonds (that is, $s = \$66,138$ and $b = \$40,312$), for a total initial investment of \$106,450 (=\$66,138 + \$40,312).

Making this initial investment is equivalent to investing \$100,000 in the common stock portfolio and buying a protective put option (or an insurance policy) for \$6,450. Indeed, this analysis could be used to determine the appropriate price for such an option. Equivalently, the actions of the investor have resulted in the creation of a synthetic put for which the stocks being held are the underlying asset.

By design, this initial investment will provide precisely the desired ending values but only if the "mix" is altered as values change. The goal is achieved by using a dynamic strategy in which investments are bought and sold at intermediate points, depending on the returns of the underlying assets.

In the example, if state B occurs, the stocks will be worth \$82,672 (=\$66,138 × 1.25), and the bonds will be worth \$42,328 (=\$40,312 × 1.05), for an aggregate value of \$125,000. In this situation the \$42,328 of bonds would be sold and the proceeds used to make an additional investment in the common stock portfolio so that the investor is entirely invested in common stocks for the last six months.

However, if state C occurs, the stocks will be worth \$52,910 (=\$66,138 × .8), and the bonds will be worth \$42,328 (=\$40,312 × 1.05), for an aggregate value of \$95,238. In this situation the \$52,910 of stocks would be sold and the proceeds used to make an additional investment in the riskfree bonds for the last six months.

Thus more money is invested in common stocks if the initial portfolio rises in value, with the money obtained by selling bonds. However, if the initial portfolio falls in value, more money is invested in bonds, with the money obtained by selling stocks. In this example the percentage invested in stocks is initially 62.13% (=$66,138/$106,450) and subsequently goes to either 100% (if stocks go up) or 0% (if stocks go down) with the reverse happening to the initial 37.87% investment in bonds.

More realistic applications involve many time intervals within the one-year period, with smaller stock price movements in each interval. Consequently, there would be more changes in the mix of stocks and bonds after each interval, but the changes would be of smaller magnitude. Nevertheless, the essential nature of the strategy would be the same:

When stock prices rise, sell some bonds and buy more stocks.
When stock prices fall, sell some stocks and buy more bonds.

Often, computers are used to monitor stock price movements of investors who have obtained portfolio insurance in this manner. When these movements are of sufficient magnitude, the computer is used to place the requisite buy and sell orders electronically. Because much of this monitoring and ordering is programmed into a computer, portfolio insurance is often referred to as a form of **program trading**.[28]

If there are only two states of nature in each interval, and reallocation is possible after every interval, and there are no transaction costs, then the values associated with any desired "insured portfolio" can be replicated exactly with a dynamic strategy. In practice, however, the results are likely to be only approximately equal. First there are transaction costs associated with buying and selling securities for the dynamic strategy.[29] Second, if an interval is defined as a length of time over which only two alternative states may occur, then the amount of time to an interval may be so short that reallocation is impossible after each interval.

In practice, arbitrary rules are applied to avoid frequent revisions and the associated high level of transaction costs while being reasonably certain of providing the portfolio with the desired level of insurance.[30] Unfortunately these arbitrary rules did not work very well on Black Monday (October 19, 1987). During these two days stock prices moved downward so fast that reallocation could not be performed in a timely fashion, resulting in a situation in which portfolio insurance did not provide the protection that had been anticipated. As a result, dynamic strategies have been used much less frequently and to some extent have been replaced by index puts.[31]

19.10 SUMMARY

1. An option is a contract between two investors that grants one investor the right (but not the obligation) to sell to or buy from the other investor a specific asset at a specific price within a specific time period.
2. A call option for a stock gives the buyer the right to buy a specific number of shares of a specific company from the option writer at a specific price at any time up to and including a specific date.
3. A put option for a stock gives the buyer the right to sell a specific number of shares of a specific company to the option writer at a specific price at any time up to and including a specific date.
4. Option trading is facilitated by standardized contracts traded on organized exchanges. These exchanges employ the services of a clearing corporation, which maintains records of all trades and acts as a buyer from all option writers and a writer to all option buyers.

5. Option writers are required to deposit margin to ensure performance of their obligations. The amount and form of the margin will depend on the particular option strategy involved.

6. The intrinsic value of a call option equals the difference between the stock's price and the option's exercise price, if this difference is positive. Otherwise the option's intrinsic value is zero.

7. The intrinsic value of a put option equals the difference between its exercise price and the stock's price, if this difference is positive. Otherwise, the option's intrinsic value is zero.

8. Calls and puts will not sell for less than their intrinsic values. However, they may sell for more than their intrinsic values owing to their time values.

9. The binomial option pricing model can be used to determine the fair value of an option based on the assumption that the underlying asset will attain one of two possible known prices at the end of each of a finite number of periods, given its price at the start of each period.

10. An option's hedge ratio indicates the change in the option's value resulting from a one dollar change in the value of the underlying asset.

11. The Black-Scholes option valuation model shows that the fair value of an option is determined by five factors: the market price of the stock, the exercise price, the life of the option, the riskfree rate, and the volatility of the common stock. It assumes that the riskfree rate and common stock volatility are constant over the option's life.

12. Put-call parity states that buying both a put option on a stock and a share of the stock will produce the same payoff as buying both a call option on the stock and a riskfree bond (assuming that both options have the same exercise price and expiration date).

13. In addition to put and call options on individual common stocks, options on other assets are traded, such as options on stock indices, debt instruments, and foreign currency.

14. Synthetic options can be created by holding the underlying asset and a riskfree asset in relative amounts that vary with the market price of the underlying asset.

QUESTIONS AND PROBLEMS

1. Why have organized options exchanges been so important to the growth in options trading?

2. How do organized options exchanges permit option buyers and writers to open and close positions without having to contact one another directly?

3. Consider the following stocks selling for the prices listed below:

Stock	Current Price
A	$ 26
B	73
C	215

Specify the likely exercise prices that will be set for newly created options on these stocks.

4. From the latest two consecutive issues of *The Wall Street Journal*, find the price of the General Motors call option with the nearest expiration date and the exercise price closest to the current price of GM stock. What is the premium on the call option? What has been the percentage change in the option's price from the previous day? From another part of the *Journal*, calculate the percentage change in

the price of GM stock from the previous day. Compare this number with the option's percentage price change.

5. Draw a profit-loss graph for the following option strategies:
   a. Buy a put, $2 premium, $70 exercise price
   b. Write a call, $3 premium, $40 exercise price
   c. Buy a stock for $80 and buy a put on the same stock, $1 premium, $70 exercise price

6. Elizabeth Stroud had only a few hours left to decide whether to exercise a call option on Carson Company stock. The call option has an exercise price of $54. Elizabeth originally purchased the call six months ago for $400 (or $4 per share).
   a. For what range of stock prices should Elizabeth exercise the call on the last day of the call's life?
   b. For what range of stock prices would Elizabeth realize a net loss (including the premium paid for the call)?
   c. If Elizabeth had purchased a put instead of a call, how would your answers to parts (a) and (b) change?

7. On November 18, three call options on Eden Prairie Associates stock, all expiring in December, sold for the following prices:

Exercise Price	Option Price
$50	$7-$\frac{1}{2}$
60	3
70	1-$\frac{1}{2}$

Firpo Marberry is considering a "butterfly spread" that involves the following positions:
Buy 1 call at $50 exercise price.
Sell (write) 2 calls at $60 exercise price.
Buy 1 call at $70 exercise price.
   a. What would be the values at expiration of Firpo's spread if Eden Prairie Associates' stock price is below $50? Between $50 and $60? Between $60 and $70? Above $70?
   b. What dollar investment would be required of Firpo to establish the spread?

8. What is the time value of an option? Why does an option's time value decline as the option approaches expiration?

9. Shorewood Systems stock currently sells for $50 per share. One year from today the stock will be worth either $58.09 or $43.04. The continuously compounded riskfree rate is 5.13% for one year. On the basis of the binomial option pricing model, what is the fair value for a call option on Shorewood stock with one year to expiration and a $50 exercise price?

10. Hopkins Pharmaceuticals stock is currently priced at $40 per share. Six months from now its price will be either $44.21 or $36.19. If the price rises to $44.21, then six months later the price will be either $48.86 or $40. If, however, the price initially falls to $36.19, then six months later the price will be either $40 or $32.75. The riskfree rate (continuously compounded) is 3.05% over each six-month period. Use the binomial option pricing model to determine the fair value of a one-year call option on Hopkins stock.

11. Given the information below, calculate the three-month call option price that is consistent with the Black-Scholes model:

$$P_s = 47, \quad E = 45, \quad R = .05, \quad \sigma = .40$$

12. If the premium on a call option has recently declined, does this decline indicate that the option is a better buy than it was previously? Why?

---

13. List the variables needed to estimate the value of a call option. Describe how a change in the value of these variables affects the value of a call option.

14. Calculate the hedge ratio of a call option for a stock with a current price of $40, an exercise price of $45, a standard deviation of 34%, and a time to expiration of six months, given a riskfree return of 7% per annum.

15. Using the Black-Scholes model, calculate the implicit volatility of a stock with a three-month call option currently selling for $8.54 and:

$$P_s = \$83, \quad E = \$80, \quad R = .05$$

16. Blondy Ryan owns 20,000 shares of Merrimac Monitoring Equipment stock. This stock makes up the bulk of Blondy's wealth. Concerned about the stock's near-term prospects, Blondy wishes to fully hedge the risk of the stock. Given a hedge ratio of .37 and a premium of $2.50 for the near Merrimac put option, how many put options should Blondy buy?

17. A six-month call option with an exercise price of $40 is selling for $5. The current price of the stock is $41.25. The hedge ratio of the option is .65.
    a. What percentage change in the option's price is likely to accompany a 1% change in the stock's price?
    b. If the beta of the stock is 1.10, what is the beta of the option? (Hint: Recall what the beta of a stock implies about the relationship between the stock's price and that of the market.)

18. The fair value of a three-month call option on Portage Industries stock is $1.50. The exercise price of the call option is $30. The riskfree rate is 5%, and the stock price of Portage is currently $28 per share. What is the fair value of a three-month put option on Portage stock with the same exercise price as the call option?

19. Given the following information, calculate the three-month put option price that is consistent with the Black-Scholes model:

$$P_s = \$32, \quad E = \$45, \quad R = .06, \quad \sigma = .35$$

20. Explain why call options on non-dividend-paying stocks are "worth more alive than dead."

21. In February Gid Gardner sold a September 55 call on Dane Corporation stock for $4.375 per share and simultaneously bought a September 55 put on the same stock for $6 per share. At the time, Treasury bills coming due in September were priced to yield 12.6%, and Dane stock sold for $53 per share.
    a. What value would put-call parity suggest was appropriate for the Dane put?
    b. Dane was expected to make three dividend payments between February and September. Could that account for the discrepancy between your answer to part (a) and the actual price of the put? Why or why not?
    c. If Dane stock were to fall to a very low value before September, might it pay for Gid to exercise the put? Why?

22. Why does a stock index option sell at a lower price than the cost of a portfolio of options on the constituent stocks (assuming that the index call option and the portfolio of call options control the same dollar value of stocks)?

23. Distinguish between portfolio insurance implemented through a protective put and through dynamic asset allocation.

24. (Appendix Question) What is the primary advantage to an investor of a warrant compared with a call option?

25. (Appendix Question) Wheeling Corp. has a 10% subordinated convertible debenture outstanding, maturing in eight years. The bond's face value is $1,000. It currently sells for 99 of par. The bond is convertible into 15 shares of common stock. The company's common stock currently sells for $50 per share. Nonconvertible bonds of similar risk have a yield of 12%.

a. What is the bond's conversion value?

b. What is the bond's conversion premium?

c. What is the bond's investment value?

APPENDIX

SECURITIES WITH OPTIONLIKE FEATURES

Many securities have features that are similar to stock options, particularly call options. In some cases the optionlike features are explicit. Examples include options on stock market indices (discussed earlier in the chapter), debt instruments, and foreign currencies.[32] These options let investors take positions based on their forecasts of movements of the stock market, interest rates, and foreign exchange rates. In other cases more subtle optionlike features are involved. This appendix discusses some of these securities.

A.1 WARRANTS

A stock purchase warrant (or, more simply, a warrant) is a call option issued by the firm whose stock serves as the underlying security. At the time of issue, a warrant usually has a longer time to expiration (for example, five or more years) than a typical call option or even a LEAP option. Some perpetual warrants, with no expiration date, have also been issued. In general, warrants may be exercised before expiration—that is, they are like American call options—but some require an initial waiting period.

The exercise price may be fixed, or it may change during the life of the warrant, usually increasing in steps. The initial exercise price is typically set to exceed the market price of the underlying security at the time the warrant is issued, often by a substantial amount.

At the time of issue, one warrant typically entitles the holder to purchase one share of stock for the appropriate exercise price. However, most warrants are protected against stock splits and stock dividends. This means that any warrant with such protection will enable the investor to buy more or less than one share at an altered exercise price if a stock dividend or stock split is declared. For example, a two-for-one stock split would allow the warrant holder to purchase two shares at one-half the original exercise price, whereas a one-for-two reverse stock split would allow the warrant holder to purchase one-half share at twice the original exercise price.

Warrants may be distributed to stockholders in lieu of a stock or cash dividend or sold directly as a new security issue. Alternatively, warrants may be issued in order to "sweeten" an offering of some other kind of security. For example, a bond may be sold by the firm with warrants attached to it. In some cases, the warrants are nondetachable, except upon exercise; if an investor wants to sell one of the bonds, the warrants must be either exercised or sold with the bond. In other cases the warrants are detachable, meaning that after the initial sale of the bonds an investor may sell either the bonds or the warrants (or both).

Terms associated with a warrant are contained in a warrant agreement, which serves the same function as an indenture for a bond issue. In this agreement the scope of the warrant holder's protection is defined (for example, the treatment of warrants in the event of a merger). It may also specify certain restrictions on corporate behavior.

Some warrants that are issued with bonds have an additional attribute. Although they may be detached and exercised by paying cash to the corporation, an alternative method of payment is provided. This alternative allows bonds from the initial issue to be used in lieu of cash to pay the exercise price, with the bonds being valued at par for this purpose.

One difference between warrants and call options is the limitation on the amount of warrants that are outstanding. A specific number of warrants of a particular type will be issued. The total generally cannot be increased and typically will be reduced as the warrants are exercised. In contrast, a call option can be created whenever two people wish to create one. Thus the number outstanding is not fixed. Exercise of a call option on its stock has no more effect on a corporation than a transaction in its stock on the secondary market. However, the exercise of a warrant does have an effect. In particular, it leaves the corporation with more cash, fewer warrants outstanding, and more stock outstanding.

Warrants are traded on major stock exchanges and on the over-the-counter market. Quotations for those with active markets are provided in the financial press in the sections devoted primarily to stocks.

A.2   RIGHTS

A right is similar to a warrant in that it also is like a call option issued by the firm whose stock serves as the underlying security. Rights, also known as subscription warrants, are issued to give existing stockholders their preemptive right to subscribe to a new issue of common stock before the general public is given an opportunity. Each share of stock receives one right. A stated number of rights plus cash equal to a specified subscription price are required in order to obtain one new share. The sale of the new stock is ensured by setting the subscription price below the stock's market price at the time the rights are issued. New subscribers do not get a bargain, however; they must pay old stockholders for the required number of rights, which become valuable as a result.

Rights generally have short lives (from two to ten weeks when issued) and may be freely traded before exercise. Up to a specified date, old shares of the stock trade *cum rights*, meaning that the buyer of the stock is entitled to receive the rights when issued. Afterward the stock trades *ex rights* at a correspondingly lower price. Rights for popular issues of stock are sometimes traded on exchanges; others are available in the over-the-counter market. Often trading begins before actual availability, with the rights sold for delivery on a *when-issued* basis.

A right is, in effect, a warrant, although one with a rather short time before expiration. It also differs with regard to exercise price, which is typically set above the stock's market price at issuance for a warrant and below it for a right. Because of their short lives, rights need not be protected against stock splits and stock dividends. Otherwise they have all the attributes of a warrant and can be valued in a similar manner.[33]

Many firms issue bonds with call provisions that allow the firm to repurchase the bonds before maturity, usually at a price above par value. This amounts to the simultaneous sale of a straight bond and purchase of a call option that is paid by the corporation in the form of a relatively lower selling price for the bond. The writer of the option is the bond purchaser.

Bond call provisions usually can be exercised only after some specified date (for example, five years after issue). Moreover, the exercise price, known as the call premium, may be different for different exercise dates (typically shrinking in size the longer the bond is outstanding). The implicit call option associated with such a bond is thus both longer-lived and more complex than those traded on the listed option markets.[34]

A.4   CONVERTIBLE SECURITIES

A particularly popular financial instrument is a security that can be converted into a different security of the same firm under certain conditions. The typical case involves a bond or a preferred stock convertible into shares of the firm's common stock, with a stated number of shares received for each bond or share of preferred stock. Usually no cash is involved: the old security is simply traded in, and the appropriate number of new securities is issued in return. Convertible preferred stocks are issued from time to time, but tax effects make them, like other preferred stock, attractive primarily to corporate investors. For other investors, issues of convertible bonds are more attractive.

If a $1,000 par value bond can be converted into 20 shares of common stock, the *conversion ratio* is 20. Alternatively, the *conversion price* may be said to be $50 (=$1,000/20), because $50 of the bond's par value must be given up to obtain one common share. Neither the conversion ratio nor the conversion price is affected by changes in a bond's market value. Conversion ratios and conversion prices are typically set so that conversion will not prove attractive unless the stock price increases substantially from its value at the time the convertible security was first issued. This is similar to the general practice used in setting exercise prices for warrants.

A convertible bond's *conversion value*, obtained by multiplying the conversion ratio by the stock's current market price, is the value that would be obtained by conversion; it is the bond's current "value as stock." The *conversion premium* is the amount by which the bond's current market price exceeds its conversion value, expressed as a percent of the latter. A related amount is the convertible's *investment value*. This value is an estimate based on the convertible's maturity date, coupon rate, and credit rating of the amount for which the bond might sell if it were not convertible. Equivalently, it is the convertible's "value as a straight bond."

Consider a $1,000 par value bond convertible into 20 shares of stock. If the market price of the stock is $60 per share, then the conversion value of the bond is $1,200 (=$60 × 20). If the current market price of the convertible bond is $1,300, then its conversion premium is $100 (=$1,300 − $1,200). Its investment value might be estimated to be, say, $950, meaning that the bond would sell for this much if it did not provide the investor with the option of convertibility.

Convertible securities of great complexity can be found in the marketplace. Some may be converted only after an initial waiting period. Some may be converted at any time up to the bond's maturity date; others, only for a stated, shorter period. Some have different conversion ratios for different years. A few can be converted

---

into packages of two or more different securities; others require the additional payment of cash upon conversion.

Convertible bonds are usually protected against stock splits and stock dividends via adjustment in the conversion ratio. For example, a bond with an initial conversion ratio of 20 could be adjusted to have a ratio of 22 following a 10% stock dividend. Protection against cash dividends is not generally provided, but some indentures require that the holders of convertible bonds be notified prior to payment of cash dividends so that they may convert before the resultant fall in the stock's market price.

Convertible securities often contain a call provision, which may be used by the corporation to force conversion when the stock's market price is sufficiently high to make the value of the stock obtained on conversion exceed the call price of the bond. For example, if the conversion value of the bond is $1,200 (the bond is convertible into 20 shares of stock that are currently selling for $60 per share) and the call price is $1,100, the firm can force conversion by calling the bond. The reason this provision forces conversion is that a bondholder faces two choices when the call is received—either convert and receive 20 shares collectively worth $1,200 or receive cash of $1,100—and should choose the shares because they have a higher value.

A convertible bond is, for practical purposes, a bond with nondetachable warrants plus the restriction that *only* the bond is usable (at par) to pay the exercise price. If the bond were not callable, the value of this package would equal the value of a straight noncallable bond (that is, the estimated investment value) plus that of the warrants. However, most convertible bonds are callable and thus involve a double option: The holder has an option to convert the bond to stock, and the issuing corporation has an option to buy the bond back from the investors.

ENDNOTES

[1] Before 1973, options were traded over the counter through the efforts of dealers and brokers in a relatively illiquid market. These dealers and brokers brought buyers and writers together, arranged terms, helped with the paperwork, and charged fees for their efforts.

[2] However, there is protection for any cash dividend that is formally designated a "return of capital." Furthermore, options that are traded over the counter typically are protected from any type of cash dividend. In both cases the protection is in the form of a reduction in the exercise price.

[3] For some active stocks, options may be introduced that have only one or two months to expiration.

[4] If the stock sells for less than $25, then the interval may be $2.50 (for example, at $15 and $17.50 for a stock selling at $16). If the stock sells for more than $200, the interval will be $10 (or perhaps even $20). Exchange officials have discretion in setting the terms of the options.

[5] For more on commissions, see John C. Hull, *Options, Futures and Other Derivatives*, (Upper Saddle River, NJ, Prentice Hall, 1997), pp. 147–148.

[6] A call or put buyer is not allowed to use margin. Instead, the option buyer is required to pay 100% of the option's purchase price. In contrast, the stock buyer can use margin, where part of the cost of purchasing the stock is borrowed. For the specifics on margin requirements, see the option textbooks cited at the end of the chapter.

[7] Because the premium is paid by the buyer to the writer at the time the option is created, its value should be compounded to the expiration date using an appropriate rate of interest when calculating profits and losses.

[8] *Strips* and *straps* are option strategies similar to a straddle. The former involves combining two puts with one call, and the latter involves combining two calls with one put. Another kind of strategy is known as a *spread*, where one call is bought while another is written on the same underlying security. Specifically, a price spread involves two calls having the same expiration date but different exercise prices. A time spread involves two calls having the same exercise price but different expiration dates.

[9] If there are dividends, they should be expressed as a compounded value at the expiration date associated with the options (as they would have been previously received) and added to the line, thereby shifting it upward.

[10] In general, \$1 will grow to $\$1e^{RT}$ at the end of T periods if it is continuously compounded at a rate of R per period. Here e represents the base of the natural logarithm, which is equal to approximately 2.71828. For a more detailed discussion, see the Appendix to Chapter 5.

[11] Equations (19.5) and (19.6) can be derived by solving the set of Equations (19.3a) and (19.3b) using symbols instead of numbers.

[12] Fischer Black and Myron Scholes, "The Pricing of Options and Corporate Liabilities," *Journal of Political Economy* 81, no. 3 (May/June 1973): 637–654. Also see Fischer Black, "How We Came Up with the Option Formula," *Journal of Portfolio Management* 15, no. 2 (Winter 1989): 4–8, and "How to Use the Holes in Black-Scholes," *Journal of Applied Corporate Finance* 1, no. 4 (Winter 1989): 67–73. For an intuitive explanation of the Black-Scholes formula, see Dwight Grant, Gautam Vora, and David Weeks, "Teaching Option Valuation: From Simple Discrete Distributions to Black/Scholes via Monte Carlo Simulation," *Financial Practice and Education* 5, no. 2 (Fall/Winter 1995): 149–155. Scholes and Robert Merton were the co-recipients of the 1997 Nobel Prize in Economic Science, largely for their contributions in this area. Undoubtedly, Black would have shared the Prize with them had he not suffered an untimely death.

[13] Table 19.2 is an abbreviated version of a standard cumulative normal distribution table. More detailed versions can be found in most statistics textbooks.

[14] The investment strategy is more complicated than it might appear because the number of shares that are to be held will change over time as the stock price changes and the expiration date gets closer. Similarly, the amount of the loan will change over time. Hence it is a *dynamic strategy*.

[15] If daily data are used, it is best to multiply the daily variance by 250 instead of 365 because there are about 250 trading days in a year. See Mark Kritzman, "About Estimating Volatility: Part I," *Financial Analysts Journal* 47, no. 4 (July/August 1991): 22–25; and "About Estimating Volatility: Part II," *Financial Analysts Journal* 47, no. 5 (September/October 1991): 10–11. For a method of estimating σ that uses high, low, opening, and closing prices as well as trading volume, see Mark B. Garman and Michael J. Klass, "On the Estimation of Security Price Volatilities from Historical Data," *Journal of Business* 53, no. 1 (January 1980): 67–78.

[16] Alternatively, Equation (19.10) could be solved for the interest rate R; doing so gives an estimate of the *implied interest rate*. See Menachem Brenner and Dan Galai, "Implied Interest Rates," *Journal of Business* 59, no. 3 (July 1986): 493–507.

[17] For a further discussion of these methods, see any of the options textbooks cited at the end of the chapter, or see Menachem Brenner and Marti Subrahmanyam, "A Simple Formula to Compute the Implied Standard Deviation," *Financial Analysts Journal* 44, no. 5 (September/October 1988): 80–83; and Charles J. Corrado and Thomas W. Miller Jr., "A Note on a Simple Accurate Formula to Compute Implied Standard Deviations," *Journal of Banking and Finance* 20, no. 3 (April 1996): 595–603.

[18] This explanation of a hedge ratio follows from the BOPM-based interpretation of the Black-Scholes formula that was given earlier. That is, if a call's payoffs can be duplicated by buying stock and borrowing at the riskfree rate, it follows that buying stock and writing a call will duplicate investing in the riskfree asset.

[19] See Robert C. Merton, "Theory of Rational Option Pricing," *Bell Journal of Economics and Management Science* 4, no. 1 (Spring 1973): 141–183.

[20] These procedures are reviewed in the options textbooks cited at the end of the chapter.

[21] See Thomas J. Finucane, "An Empirical Analysis of Common Stock Call Exercise: A Note," *Journal of Banking and Finance* 21, no. 4 (April 1997): 563–571.

[22] See Robert Geske and Kuldeep Shastri, "The Early Exercise of American Puts," *Journal of Banking and Finance* 9, no. 2 (June 1985): 207–219.

[23] For a discussion of how the possibility of default by the writer affects the prices of options, see Herb Johnson and Rene Stulz, "The Pricing of Options with Default Risk," *Journal of Finance* 42, no. 2 (June 1987): 267–280.

Options

[24] In an efficient market, investors with "average" attitudes toward risk should not purchase portfolio insurance. Those who are especially averse to "downside risk" (relative to "upside potential") may find it useful to buy insurance. The key is the investor's attitude toward risk and return. See Hayne E. Leland, "Who Should Buy Portfolio Insurance?" *Journal of Finance* 35, no. 2 (May 1980): 581–594.

[25] Some people would argue that the use of stop orders or getting an insurance company to sell the investor a policy represent two other ways.

[26] For an exposition, see Mark Rubinstein and Hayne E. Leland, "Replicating Options with Positions in Stock and Cash," *Financial Analysts Journal* 37, no. 4 (July/August 1981): 63–72; Mark Rubinstein, "Alternative Paths to Portfolio Insurance," *Financial Analysts Journal* 41, no. 4 (July/August 1985): 42–52; Robert Ferguson, "How to Beat the S&P 500 (Without Losing Sleep)," *Financial Analysts Journal* 42, no. 2 (March/April 1986): 37–46; and Thomas J. O'Brien, "The Mechanics of Portfolio Insurance," *Journal of Portfolio Management* 14, no. 3 (Spring 1988): 40–47.

[27] In this example, portfolio insurance is sought for a one-year horizon with a floor of 0% (meaning that the investor does not want to lose any of the initial investment over the next 12 months). Other horizons and floors, such as a two-year horizon with a floor of −5% (meaning that the investor does not want to lose more than 5% of the initial investment over the next 24 months), are possible. Note the parallel to the discussion of the BOPM, which provides a theoretical basis for the development of portfolio insurance.

[28] The next chapter discusses another form of program trading that is known as index arbitrage.

[29] There is another dynamic strategy for insuring the portfolio that is often preferred because it has smaller transaction costs. It involves index futures, which are a type of financial contract that is discussed in the next chapter. For a survey of dynamic trading strategies, see Robert R. Trippi and Richard B. Harriff, "Dynamic Asset Allocation Rules: Survey and Synthesis," *Journal of Portfolio Management* 17, no. 4 (Summer 1991): 19–26.

[30] For a discussion of transaction costs, see John E. Gilster Jr., and William Lee, "The Effects of Transactions Costs and Different Borrowing and Lending Rates on the Option Pricing Model: A Note," *Journal of Finance* 39, no. 4 (September 1984): 1215–1222; Hayne E. Leland, "Option Pricing and Replication with Transactions Costs," *Journal of Finance* 40, no. 5 (December 1985): 1283–1301; Fischer Black and Robert Jones, "Simplifying Portfolio Insurance," *Journal of Portfolio Management* 14, no. 1 (Fall 1987): 48–51; and Phelim P. Boyle and Ton Yorst, "Option Replication in Discrete Time with Transactions Costs," *Journal of Finance* 47, no. 1 (March 1992): 271–293.

[31] See Mark Rubinstein, "Portfolio Insurance and the Market Crash," *Financial Analysts Journal* 44, no. 1 (January/February 1988): 38–47. For a discussion of various types of dynamic strategies, see André F. Perold and William F. Sharpe, "Dynamic Strategies for Asset Allocation," *Financial Analysts Journal* 44, no. 1 (January/February 1988): 16–27; and Philip H. Dybvig, "Inefficient Dynamic Portfolio Strategies or How to Throw Away a Million Dollars in the Stock Market," *Review of Financial Studies* 1, no. 1 (Spring 1988): 67–88.

[32] See the textbooks cited at the end of the chapter for more on these types of options. For more on foreign exchange options, see Ian Giddy, "The Foreign Exchange Option As a Hedging Tool," *Midland Corporate Finance Journal* 1, no. 3 (Fall 1983): 32–42; Niso Abauf, "Foreign Exchange Options: The Leading Hedge," *Midland Corporate Finance Journal* 5, no. 2 (Summer 1987): 51–58; and Mark Kritzman, "About Option Replication," *Financial Analysts Journal* 48, no. 1 (January/February 1992): 21–23.

[33] Rights are also discussed in Chapter 16. Valuation of rights is relatively simple if it is assumed that there is no chance that they will end up being out of the money on the expiration date and the time value of money is ignored (meaning that the riskfree rate is assumed to be zero).

[34] Bond call and put provisions are discussed in Chapters 13 and 14.

option	straddle
call option	covered call writing
exercise price	European options
expiration date	American options
premium	hedge ratio
closing sale	put-call parity
closing purchase	implied volatility
put option	at the money
floor traders	out of the money
floor brokers	in the money
market-makers	time value
order book officials	counterparty risk
intrinsic value	portfolio insurance
naked call writing	synthetic put
naked put writing	program trading

REFERENCES

1. Investment strategies involving options are discussed in many papers. Here are three of the most notable ones:

   Robert C. Merton, Myron S. Scholes, and Mathew L. Gladstein, "The Returns and Risk of Alternative Call Option Portfolio Investment Strategies," *Journal of Business* 51, no. 1 (April 1978): 183–242.

   Robert C. Merton, Myron S. Scholes, and Mathew L. Gladstein, "The Returns and Risk of Alternative Put-Option Portfolio Investment Strategies," *Journal of Business* 55, no. 1 (January 1982): 1–55.

   Aimee Gerberg Ronn and Ehud I. Ronn, "The Box Spread Arbitrage Conditions: Theory, Tests, and Investment Strategies," *Review of Financial Studies* 2, no. 1 (1989): 91–107.

2. A description and comparison of the specialist and market-maker systems for trading options are presented by:

   Robert Neal, "A Comparison of Transaction Costs between Competitive Market-Maker and Specialist Structures," *Journal of Business* 65, no. 2 (July 1992): 317–334.

3. The binomial option pricing model was initially developed in:

   William F. Sharpe, *Investments* (Englewood Cliffs, NJ: Prentice Hall, 1978), Chapter 14.

4. A short while later the following two papers expanded upon Sharpe's model:

   John C. Cox, Stephen A. Ross, and Mark Rubinstein, "Option Pricing: A Simplified Approach," *Journal of Financial Economics* 7, no. 3 (September 1979): 229–263.

   Richard J. Rendleman Jr., and Brit J. Bartter, "Two-State Option Pricing," *Journal of Finance* 34, no. 5 (December 1979): 1093–1110.

5. For more on the theory of binomial models, see:

   Daniel B. Nelson and Krishna Ramaswamy, "Simple Binomial Processes As Diffusion Approximations in Financial Models," *Review of Financial Studies* 3, no. 3 (1990): 393–430.

6. Two seminal papers on option pricing are:

   Robert C. Merton, "Theory of Rational Option Pricing," *Bell Journal of Economics and Management Science* 4, no. 1 (Spring 1973): 141–183.

   Fischer Black and Myron Scholes, "The Pricing of Options and Corporate Liabilities," *Journal of Political Economy* 81, no. 3 (May/June 1973): 637–654.

7. The Black-Scholes option pricing model assumes that the riskfree rate is constant over the life of the option. Four interesting papers that relax this assumption are:

   Ramon Rabinovitch, "Pricing Stock and Bond Options When the Default-Free Rate Is Stochastic," *Journal of Financial and Quantitative Analysis* 24, no. 4 (December 1989): 447–457.

Stuart M. Turnbull and Frank Milne, "A Simple Approach to Interest-Rate Option Pricing," *Review of Financial Studies* 4, no. 1 (1991): 87–121.

Jason Z. Wei, "Valuing American Equity Options with a Stochastic Interest Rate: A Note," *Journal of Financial Engineering* 2, no. 2 (June 1993): 195–206.

T. S. Ho, Richard C. Stapleton, and Marti G. Subrahmanyam, "The Valuation of American Options with Stochastic Interest Rates: A Generalization of the Geske-Johnson Technique," *Journal of Finance* 52, no. 2 (June 1997): 827–840.

8. The Black-Scholes model also assumes that the volatility of the underlying asset is constant over the life of the option. For papers that relax this assumption, see:

Andrew A. Christie, "The Stochastic Behavior of Common Stock Variances: Value, Leverage, and Interest Rate Effects," *Journal of Financial Economics* 10, no. 4 (December 1982): 407–432.

John Hull and Alan White, "The Pricing of Options on Assets with Stochastic Volatilities," *Journal of Finance* 42, no. 2 (June 1987): 281–300.

Herb Johnson and David Shanno, "Option Pricing When the Variance Is Changing," *Journal of Financial and Quantitative Analysis* 22, no. 2 (June 1987): 143–151.

Louis O. Scott, "Option Pricing When the Variance Changes Randomly: Theory, Estimation, and an Application," *Journal of Financial and Quantitative Analysis* 22, no. 4 (December 1987): 419–438.

James B. Wiggins, "Option Values under Stochastic Volatility: Theory and Empirical Estimates," *Journal of Financial Economics* 19, no. 2 (December 1987): 351–372.

Marc Chesney and Louis Scott, "Pricing European Currency Options: A Comparison of the Modified Black-Scholes Model and a Random Variance Model," *Journal of Financial and Quantitative Analysis* 24, no. 3 (September 1989): 267–284.

Thomas J. Finucane, "Black-Scholes Approximations of Call Option Prices with Stochastic Volatilities: A Note," *Journal of Financial and Quantitative Analysis* 24, no. 4 (December 1989): 527–532.

Steven L. Heston, "A Closed-Form Solution for Options in Stochastic Volatility with Applications to Bond and Currency Options," *Review of Financial Studies* 6, no. 2 (1993): 327–343.

Stephen Figlewski, "Forecasting Volatility," *Financial Markets, Institutions & Instruments* 6, no. 1 (1997): 1–88.

9. For an interesting paper on static analysis of calls, see:

Don M. Chance, "Translating the Greek: The Real Meaning of Call Option Derivatives," *Financial Analysts Journal* 50, no. 4 (July/August 1994): 43–49.

10. Portfolio insurance has received much attention. In addition to the citations given in the chapter, see:

M. J. Brennan and R. Solanki, "Optimal Portfolio Insurance," *Journal of Financial and Quantitative Analysis* 16, no. 3 (September 1981): 279–300.

Ethan S. Etzioni, "Rebalance Disciplines for Portfolio Insurance," *Journal of Portfolio Management* 13, no. 1 (Fall 1986): 59–62.

Richard J. Rendelman Jr. and Richard McEnally, "Assessing the Costs of Portfolio Insurance," *Financial Analysts Journal* 43, no. 3 (May/June 1987): 27–37.

C. B. Garcia and F. J. Gould, "An Empirical Study of Portfolio Insurance," *Financial Analysts Journal* 43, no. 4 (July/August 1987): 44–54.

Robert Ferguson, "A Comparison of the Mean-Variance and Long-Term Return Characteristics of Three Investment Strategies," *Financial Analysts Journal* 43, no. 4 (July/August 1987): 55–66.

Fischer Black and Robert Jones, "Simplifying Portfolio Insurance," *Journal of Portfolio Management* 14, no. 1 (Fall 1987): 48–51.

Yu Zhu and Robert C. Kavee, "Performance of Portfolio Insurance Strategies," *Journal of Portfolio Management* 14, no. 3 (Spring 1988): 48–54.

Fischer Black and Robert Jones, "Simplifying Portfolio Insurance for Corporate Pension Plans," *Journal of Portfolio Management* 14, no. 4 (Summer 1988): 33–37.

Thomas J. O'Brien, *How Option Replicating Portfolio Insurance Works: Expanded Details*, Monograph Series in Finance and Economics No. 1988–4 (New York University Salomon Center, Leonard N. Stern School of Business, 1988).

Erol Hakanoglu, Robert Koppraseh, and Emmanuel Roman, "Constant Proportion Portfolio Insurance for Fixed-Income Investment," *Journal of Portfolio Management* 15, no. 4 (Summer 1989): 58–66.

Michael J. Brennan and Eduardo Schwartz, "Portfolio Insurance and Financial Market Equilibrium," *Journal of Business* 62, no. 4 (October 1989): 455–472.

Sanford J. Grossman and Jean-Luc Vila, "Portfolio Insurance in Complete Markets: A Note," *Journal of Business* 62, no. 4 (October 1989): 473–476.

Robert R. Trippi and Richard B. Harriff, "Dynamic Asset Allocation Rules: Survey and Synthesis," *Journal of Portfolio Management* 17, no. 4 (Summer 1991): 19–26.

Charles J. Jacklin, Allan W. Kleidon, and Paul Pfleiderer, "Underestimation of Portfolio Insurance and the Crash of October 1987," *Review of Financial Studies* 5, no. 1 (1992): 35–63.

11. A great deal has been written on warrants and convertibles. For an introduction to this literature, see:

Richard A. Brealey and Stewart C. Myers, *Principles of Corporate Finance* (New York: McGraw-Hill, 1996), Chapter 22.

Stephen A. Ross, Randolph W. Westerfield, and Jeffrey Jaffe, *Corporate Finance* (Boston: Irwin McGraw Hill, 1996), Chapter 22.

12. Many textbooks are devoted exclusively to options or have options as one of their primary subjects. Most cover everything discussed in this chapter but in more detail and with a more complete list of citations. Here are a few:

Robert A. Jarrow and Andrew Rudd, *Option Pricing* (Homewood, IL: Richard D. Irwin, 1983).

John C. Cox and Mark Rubinstein, *Options Markets* (Englewood Cliffs, NJ: Prentice Hall, 1985).

Richard M. Bookstaber, *Option Pricing and Investment Strategies* (Chicago: Probus Publishing, 1987).

Peter Ritchken, *Options: Theory, Strategy, and Applications* (Glenview, IL: Scott, Foresman, 1987).

Robert W. Kolb, *Options: An Introduction* (Miami: Kolb Publishing, 1991).

Alan L. Tucker, *Financial Futures, Options, and Swaps* (St. Paul, MN: West Publishing, 1991).

David A. Dubofsky, *Options and Financial Futures* (New York: McGraw-Hill, 1992).

Hans R. Stoll and Robert E. Whaley, *Futures and Options* (Cincinnati: South-Western Publishing, 1993).

Don M. Chance, *An Introduction to Derivatives* (Fort Worth: Dryden Press, 1995).

Fred D. Arditti, *Derivatives* (Boston: Harvard Business School Press, 1996).

Robert Jarrow and Stuart Turnbull, *Derivative Securities* (Cincinnati: South-Western Publishing, 1996).

John C. Hull, *Options, Futures, and Other Derivative Securities* (Upper Saddle River, NJ: Prentice Hall, 1997).

13. The various exchanges where options are traded all have Web sites containing useful information about their products (the New York Stock Exchange withdrew from the option trading business in 1997):

American Stock Exchange: ⟨www.amex.com⟩.

Chicago Board Options Exchange: ⟨www.cboe.com⟩.

Pacific Exchange: ⟨www.pacificex.com⟩.

Philadelphia Stock Exchange: ⟨www.phlx.com⟩.

FUTURES

Consider a contract that involves the delivery of some specific asset by a seller to a buyer at an agreed-upon future date. Such a contract also specifies the purchase price, but the asset is not to be paid for until the delivery date. However, the buyer and the seller will both be requested to make a security deposit at the time the contract is signed. The purpose of this deposit is to protect each person from experiencing any losses should the other person renege on the contract. Hence the size of the deposit is checked daily to see that it provides sufficient protection. If it is insufficient, it will have to be increased. If it is more than sufficient, the excess can be withdrawn.

These contracts are often referred to as **futures** (short for futures contract), and in the United States they involve assets such as agricultural goods (for example, wheat), natural resources (for example, copper), foreign currencies (for example, Swiss francs), fixed-income securities (for example, Treasury bonds), and market indices (for example, the Standard & Poor's 500).[1] As with options, standardization of the terms in these contracts makes it relatively easy for anyone to create and subsequently trade the contracts.

20.1 | HEDGERS AND SPECULATORS

There are two types of people who deal in futures (and options): speculators and hedgers. **Speculators** buy and sell futures for the sole purpose of making a profit by closing out their positions at a price that is better than the initial price (or so they hope). Such people neither produce nor use the asset in the ordinary course of business. In contrast, **hedgers** buy and sell futures to offset an otherwise risky position in the spot market. In the ordinary course of business, they either produce or use the asset.

20.1.1 Example of Hedging

For example, consider wheat futures. A farmer might note today that the market price for a wheat futures contract with delivery around harvest time is $4 per bushel, a price that is high enough to ensure a profitable year. The farmer could sell wheat futures today. Alternatively the farmer could wait until harvest and at that time sell the wheat on the **spot market** (which involves the immediate exchange of an asset for cash). However, waiting until harvest entails risk because the **spot price** (the purchase price of an asset) of wheat could fall by then, perhaps to $3 per bushel. Such a fall would bring financial ruin to the farmer. In contrast, selling wheat futures today will allow the farmer to "lock in" a $4 per bushel selling price. Doing so would remove an element of risk from the farmer's primary business of growing wheat. Thus a farmer who sells futures is known as a hedger or, more specifically, a **short hedger**.

Perhaps the buyer of the farmer's futures contract is a baker who uses wheat in making bread. Currently the baker has enough wheat in inventory to last until harvest season. In anticipation of the need to replenish the inventory at that time, the baker could buy a wheat futures contract today at $4 per bushel. Alternatively, the baker could simply wait until the inventory runs low and then buy wheat in the spot market. However, there is a chance that the spot price will be $5 per bushel at that time. If it were, the baker would have to raise the selling price of bread and perhaps lose sales in doing so. Alternatively, by purchasing wheat futures, the baker can "lock in" a $4 per bushel purchase price, thereby removing an element of risk from the bread business. Thus a baker who buys futures is also known as a hedger or, more specifically, a **long hedger**.

20.1.2   Example of Speculating

The farmer and the baker can be compared to a speculator—a person who buys and sells wheat futures, based on the forecast price of wheat, in the pursuit of relatively short-term profits. As mentioned earlier, such a person neither produces nor uses the asset in the ordinary course of business.

A speculator who thinks that the price of wheat is going to rise substantially will buy wheat futures. Later this person will enter a **reversing trade** by selling wheat futures. If the forecast was accurate, a profit will have been made on an increase in the wheat futures price.

For example, consider a speculator expecting at least a $1 per bushel rise in the spot price of wheat. Whereas this person could buy wheat, store it, and hope to sell it later at the anticipated higher price, it would be easier and more profitable to buy a wheat futures contract today at $4 per bushel. Later, if the spot price of wheat did rise by $1, the speculator would enter a reversing trade by selling the wheat futures contract for perhaps $5 per bushel. (A $1 rise in the spot price of wheat will cause the futures price to rise by about $1.) Thus the speculator will make a profit of $1 per bushel, or $5,000 in total, because these contracts are for 5,000 bushels. As will be shown later, the speculator might need to make a security deposit of $1,000 at the time the wheat futures contract is bought. This deposit is returned when the reversing trade is made, so the speculator's rate of return is quite high (500%) relative to the percentage rise in the price of wheat (25%).

Alternatively, if a speculator forecasts a substantial price decline, then initially wheat futures would be sold. Later the person would enter a reversing trade by purchasing wheat futures. If the forecast was accurate, a profit will have been made on the decrease in the wheat futures price.

20.2   THE FUTURES CONTRACT

Futures contracts are standardized in terms of delivery as well as the type of asset that is permissible for delivery. For example, the Chicago Board of Trade specifies the following requirements for its July wheat contract:

1. The seller agrees to deliver 5,000 bushels of either no. 2 soft red wheat, no. 2 hard red winter wheat, no. 2 dark northern spring wheat, or no. 1 northern spring wheat at the agreed-upon price. Alternatively, a number of other grades can be delivered at specified premiums or discounts from the agreed-upon price. In any case, the seller is allowed to decide which grade shall be delivered.

2. The grain will be delivered by registered warehouse receipts issued by approved warehouses in Chicago or Toledo, Ohio. (Toledo deliveries are discounted $.02 per bushel.)

3. Delivery will take place during the month of July, with the seller allowed to decide the actual date.

4. Upon delivery of the warehouse receipt from the seller to the buyer, the latter will pay the former the agreed-upon price in cash.

After an organized exchange has set all the terms of a futures contract except for its price, the exchange will authorize trading in the contract.[2] Buyers and sellers (or their representatives) meet at a specific place on the floor of the exchange and try to agree on a price at which to trade. If they succeed, one or more contracts will be created, with all the standard terms plus an additional one—the price involved. Prices are normally stated on a per unit basis. Thus if a buyer and a seller agree to a price of $4 per bushel for a contract of 5,000 bushels of wheat, the amount of money involved is $20,000.

Figure 20.1 shows a set of daily quotations giving the prices at which some popular futures contracts were traded and the total volume of sales for each type of contract. Such listings of active futures markets are published regularly in the financial press, with each item for delivery (such as corn) having a heading that indicates the number of units per contract (5,000 bushels) and the terms on which prices are stated (cents per bushel).

Below the heading for the asset are certain details for each type of contract. Moving from left to right in Figure 20.1, the first column shows the delivery dates for the contracts. For example, there are six different futures contracts for corn, each one involving the same item but having different delivery dates. Next comes *open*, denoting the price at which the first transaction was made on that day; *high* and *low*, representing the highest and lowest prices during the day; and **settle** (short for settlement price), a price that is a representative price (for example, the average of the high and low prices) during the "closing period" designated by the exchange in question (for example, the last two minutes of trading). After *change* from the previous day's settlement price come the highest and lowest prices recorded during the lifetime of the contract. The last column on the right shows the **open interest** (the number of outstanding contracts) on the previous day.

For each futures contract, summary figures are given below the figures for the last delivery date. (In the case of corn, these summary figures are below the December 1998 delivery date figures.) They indicate the total volume (that is, the number of contracts) traded on that day and on the previous trading day as well as the total open interest in such contracts on that day and the change in total open interest from the previous day.

20.3   FUTURES MARKETS

The futures contracts shown in Figure 20.1 are traded on various organized exchanges. The Chicago Board of Trade (CBT) was the earliest one, founded in 1848, and currently is the largest futures exchange in the world. Other futures exchanges are listed in the lower right-hand corner of Figure 20.1.

Figure 20.1

Quotations for Futures Prices (Excerpts)

Source: Reprinted by permission of *The Wall Street Journal*, Dow Jones & Company, Inc., October 9, 1997, p. C16.

The method of trading futures on organized exchanges is in some ways similar to and in other ways different from the way stocks and options are traded. As with stocks and options, customers can place market, limit, and stop orders with a **futures commission merchant** (FCM), which is simply a firm that carries out orders involving futures (much as a brokerage firm carries out orders involving stocks; often brokerage firms are also FCMs). Furthermore, once an order is transmitted to an exchange floor, it must be taken to a designated spot for execution by a member of the exchange, just as is done for stocks and options. This spot is known as a *pit* because of its shape, which is circular with a set of interior descending steps on which members stand. What happens in the pit is what distinguishes trading in futures from trading in stocks and options.

First, there are no specialists or market-makers on futures exchanges. Instead, members can be floor brokers, meaning that they execute customers' orders. In doing so, they (or their phone clerks) each keep a file of any stop or limit orders that cannot be immediately executed. Alternatively, members can be floor traders (those with very short holding periods, of less than a day, are known as **locals** or scalpers), meaning that they execute orders for their own personal accounts in an attempt to make profits by "buying low and selling high." Floor traders are in some ways similar to market-makers, because a floor trader may have an inventory of futures contracts and may act as a dealer. However, unlike a market-maker, a floor trader is not required to do so.

Second, all futures orders must be announced by "open outcry," meaning that any member wishing to buy or sell any futures contract must verbally announce the order and a price at which the member is willing to trade. This way, the order is exposed to everyone in the pit, thereby enabling an auction to take place that will lead to the order being filled at the best possible price.

20.3.1 The Clearinghouse

Each futures exchange has an associated clearinghouse that becomes the "seller's buyer" and the "buyer's seller" as soon as a trade is concluded. The procedure is similar to that used for options. This is not surprising, because the first market in listed options was organized by people associated with a futures exchange. (Specifically, the Chicago Board Options Exchange was set up by the Chicago Board of Trade.)

In order to understand how a clearinghouse operates, consider the futures market for wheat. Assume that on the first day of trading in July wheat, buyer B agrees to purchase 5,000 bushels (one contract) from seller S for $4 per bushel, or $20,000 in total. (Actually, what happens is that a floor broker working for B's brokerage firm and a floor broker working for S's brokerage firm meet in the wheat pit and agree on a price.) In this situation, B might believe that the price of wheat is going to rise whereas S might believe that it is going to fall.

After B and S reach their agreement, the clearinghouse will immediately step in and break the transaction apart; that is, B and S no longer deal directly with each other. Now it is the obligation of the clearinghouse to deliver the wheat to B and to accept delivery from S. At this point there is an open interest of one contract (5,000 bushels) in July wheat, because only one contract exists at this time. (Technically there are two, because the clearinghouse has separate contracts with B and S.) Figure 20.2 summarizes the creation of this contract.

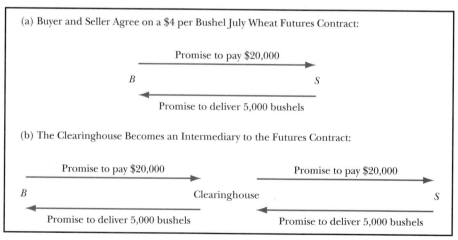

Figure 20.2
Creating a Futures Contract

It is important to realize that if nothing else is done at this point, the clearinghouse is in a potentially risky position. For example, if the price of wheat rises to $5 per bushel by July, what will happen if S does not deliver the wheat? The clearinghouse will have to buy the wheat on the spot market for $25,000 ($=5,000 \times \$5$) and then deliver it to B. Because the clearinghouse will receive the selling price of $20,000 ($=5,000 \times \$4$) from B in return, it will have lost $5,000. Even though the clearinghouse has a claim on S for the $5,000, it faces protracted legal battles in trying to recover this amount and may end up with little or nothing from S.

Alternatively, if the price of wheat falls to $3 per bushel by July, then B will be paying $20,000 for wheat that is worth only $15,000 ($=5,000 \times \$3$) on the spot market. What will happen if B refuses to make payment? In this case the clearinghouse will not deliver the wheat that it received from S. Instead, it will have to sell the wheat for $15,000 on the spot market. Because the clearinghouse paid $20,000 to S for the wheat, it will have lost $5,000. Again, although the clearinghouse has a claim on B for the $5,000, it may end up with little or nothing from B.

The procedures that protect the clearinghouse from such potential losses involve having brokers:

- Impose initial margin requirements on both buyers and sellers
- Mark to market the accounts of buyers and sellers every day
- Impose daily maintenance margin requirements on both buyers and sellers

20.3.2 Initial Margin

In order to buy and sell futures, an investor must open a futures account with a brokerage firm. This type of account must be kept separate from other accounts (such as a cash account or a margin account) that the investor might have. Whenever a futures contract is signed, both buyer and seller are required to post initial margin. That is, both buyer and seller are required to make security deposits that are intended to guarantee that they will in fact be able to fulfill their obligations; accordingly, initial margin is often referred to as **performance margin**. The amount of this margin is roughly 5% to 15% of the total purchase price of the futures contract. However, it is often stated as a given dollar amount regardless of the purchase price.[3]

For example, a July wheat futures contract for 5,000 bushels at $4 per bushel would have a total purchase price of $20,000 ($=5,000 \times \$4$). With a 5% initial margin requirement, buyer B and seller S would each have to make a deposit of $1,000 ($=.05 \times \$20,000$). This deposit can be made in the form of cash, cash equivalents (such as Treasury bills), or a bank line of credit, and it forms the equity in the account on the first day.

Whereas initial margin provides some protection to the clearinghouse, it does not provide complete protection. As indicated earlier, if the futures price of wheat rises to $5 per bushel by July, the clearinghouse faces a potential loss of $5,000, only $1,000 of which can be quickly recovered owing to the margin deposit. This is where the use of marking to market, coupled with a maintenance margin requirement, provides the requisite amount of additional protection.

20.3.3 Marking to Market

In order to understand marking to market, consider the previous example in which B and S were, respectively, a buyer and a seller of a 5,000-bushel wheat futures contract at $4 per bushel. Assume now that on the second day of trading the settlement price of July wheat is $4.10 per bushel. In this situation, S has "lost" $500 owing to the rise in the price of wheat from $4 to $4.10 per bushel, while B has "made" $500

(=\$.10 $\times$ 5,000). Thus the equity in the account of S is reduced by \$500, and the equity in the account of B is increased by \$500. Because the initial equity was equal to the initial margin requirement of \$1,000, S has equity of \$500 whereas B has equity of \$1,500. This process of adjusting the equity in an investor's account in order to reflect the change in the settlement price of the futures contract is known as *marking to market*. It should also be noted that as part of the marking-to-market process, the clearinghouse every day replaces each existing futures contract with a new one that has as the purchase price the settlement price as reported in the financial press.

In general, the equity in either a buyer's or a seller's account is the initial margin deposit and the sum of all daily gains, less losses, on open positions in futures. Because the amount of the gains (less losses) changes every day, the amount of equity changes every day.

In the example, if the settlement price of the July wheat futures contract had fallen to \$3.95 per bushel the third day (that is, the day after rising to \$4.10), then B would have "lost" \$750 [=5,000 $\times$ (\$4.10 − \$3.95)] whereas S would have "made" \$750 on that day. When their accounts were marked to market at the end of the day, the equity in B's account would have dropped from \$1,500 to \$750, whereas S's equity would have risen from \$500 to \$1,250.

20.3.4   Maintenance Margin

Another key concept is maintenance margin. According to the maintenance margin requirement, the investor must keep the account's equity equal to or greater than a certain percentage of the amount deposited as initial margin. Because this percentage is roughly 65%, the investor must have equity equal to or greater than 65% of the initial margin. If this requirement is not met, the investor will receive a margin call from his or her broker. This call is a request for an additional deposit of cash (nothing else can be deposited for this purpose) known as **variation margin** to bring the equity up to the initial margin level. If the investor does not (or cannot) respond, then the broker will close out the investor's position by entering a reversing trade in the investor's account.

For example, reconsider investors B and S, who had, respectively, bought and sold a July wheat futures contract at \$4 per bushel. Each investor had made a deposit of \$1,000 in order to meet the initial margin requirement. The next day the price of the wheat futures contract rose to \$4.10 per bushel, or \$20,500. Thus the equity of B increased to \$1,500 while the equity of S decreased to \$500. If the maintenance margin requirement is 65% of initial margin, both B and S are required to have equity of at least \$650 (=.65 $\times$ \$1,000) in their accounts every day. Because the actual level of equity for B clearly exceeds that amount, B does not need to do anything. Indeed, B may withdraw an amount of cash equal to the amount by which the equity exceeds the initial margin; in this example, B can withdraw cash of \$500.

However, S is undermargined and will be asked to make a cash deposit of at least \$500, because this will increase the equity from \$500 to \$1,000, the level of the initial margin. In the event that S refuses to make this deposit, the broker will enter a reversing trade for S by purchasing a July wheat futures contract. The result is that S will simply receive an amount of money approximately equal to the account's equity, \$500, and the account will be closed. Because S initially deposited \$1,000, S will have sustained a loss of \$500.

On the third day the price of the July wheat futures contract is assumed to settle at \$3.95 per bushel, representing a \$750 loss for B and a \$750 gain for S (see Table 20.1). As a consequence, B is now undermargined and will be asked to deposit \$750 so that the equity in B's account will be \$1,000. (This example assumes that B had withdrawn the \$500 in excess margin that had accumulated from the previous day's price change.) Conversely, S can withdraw $750, because the equity in S's account is over the $1,000 initial margin requirement by that amount. (Remember that S had added $500 to bring the account's equity up to $1,000 at the end of the previous day.)

20.3.5   Reversing Trades

Suppose that on the next day B finds that people are paying $4.15 per bushel for July wheat. This represents daily profit to B of $.20 per bushel, because the price was $3.95 the previous day. If B believes that the price of July wheat will not go any higher, then B might sell a July wheat futures contract for $4.15 to someone else. (Conversely, S might buy a July wheat futures contract because S's equity has been reduced to zero.) In this situation B has made a reversing trade, because B now has offsetting positions with respect to July wheat. (Equivalently, B is said to have unwound or closed out or offset his or her position in July wheat.)

At this point the benefit to B of having a clearinghouse involved can be seen. Nominally, B is obligated to deliver 5,000 bushels of wheat to the clearinghouse in July, which in turn is obligated to deliver it back to B. Why? Because B is involved in two July wheat contracts, one as a seller and one as a buyer. However, the clearinghouse will note that B has offsetting positions in July wheat, and it will immediately cancel both of them. Furthermore, once the reversing trade has been made, B will be able to withdraw $2,000, consisting of:

- The initial margin of $1,000
- A net variation margin deposit owing to the daily marking to market of $250 [$=5,000 \times (\$4 - \$3.95)$]
- The $750 [$=5,000 \times (\$4.15 - \$4)$] net profit that has been made

Table 20.1 illustrates the effect these events have had on the equity in the account of B (and that of S). In effect, a futures contract is replaced every day by adjusting the equity in the investor's account and drawing up a new contract that has a purchase price equal to the current settlement price. This daily marking-to-market

	Price		Buyer B		Seller S	
Day	of Wheat	Event	Amount	Equity in Account	Amount	Equity in Account
TABLE 20.1		**Margin Requirements for a Futures Contract**				
(a) If Maintenance Margin Were Not Required						
1	$4	Deposit initial margin	$1,000	$1,000	$1,000	$1,000
2	$4.10	Mark to market	+500	1,500	−500	500
3	$3.95	Mark to market	−750	750	+750	1,250
4	$4.15	Mark to market	+1,000	1,750	−1,000	250
(b) With Required Maintenance Margin						
1	$4	Deposit initial margin	$1,000	$1,000	$1,000	$1,000
2	$4.10	Mark to market:	+500	1,500	−500	500
		Buyer withdraws cash	−500	1,000	—	—
		Seller deposits cash	—	—	+500	1,000
3	$3.95	Mark to market:	−750	250	+750	1,750
		Buyer deposits cash	+750	1,000	—	—
		Seller withdraws cash	—	—	−750	1,000
4	$4.15	Mark to market:	+1,000	2,000	−1,000	0
		Reversing trade and withdrawal of cash	−2,000	0	—	—

procedure, coupled with margin requirements, results in the clearinghouse's always having a security deposit of sufficient size to protect it from losses owing to the actions of the individual investors.[4]

These rather complex arrangements make it possible for futures traders to think in very simple terms. In the example, B bought a contract of July wheat at $4 and sold it on day 4 for $4.15, making a profit of $.15 per bushel. If S, having initially sold a contract of July wheat at $4, later made a reversing trade for $4.25, then S's position can also be thought of in simple terms; specifically, S sold July wheat for $4 and later bought it back for $4.25, suffering a loss of $.25 per bushel in the process.

20.3.6 Futures Positions

In the previous example, B was the person who initially bought a July wheat futures contract. Accordingly, B now has a long position and is said to be *long* one contract of July wheat. In contrast S, having initially sold a July wheat futures contract, has a short position and is said to be *short* one contract of July wheat.

The process of marking to market every day means that changes in the settlement price are realized as soon as they occur. When the settlement price rises, investors with long positions realize profits equal to the change and those who are short realize losses. Conversely, when the settlement price falls, those with long positions realize losses, while those with short positions realize profits. In either event, total profits always equal total losses. Thus either the buyer gains and the seller loses, or the seller gains and the buyer loses because both parties are involved in a "zero-sum game" (as was also the case with buyers and writers of options, discussed in Chapter 19).

20.3.7 Open Interest

When trading is first allowed in a contract, there is no open interest because no contracts are outstanding. Subsequently, as people begin to make transactions, the open interest grows. At any time open interest equals the amount that those with short positions (the sellers) are currently obligated to deliver. It also equals the amount that those with long positions (the buyers) are obligated to receive.

Open interest figures are typically shown with futures prices in the financial press. For example, Figure 20.1 indicates that on October 8, 1997, a total of 203,184 contracts in December 1997 corn were outstanding on the Chicago Board of Trade (CBT). Note the substantial differences in the open interest figures for the other corn contracts on the Chicago Board of Trade on that day. This disparity is quite typical. Figure 20.3 shows why. Open interest in the December 1997 corn contract is shown for every month from the preceding January until the contract expired at the end of the delivery month, December. From January until the end of October, more trades were generally made to open new positions than to reverse old ones, and open interest continued to increase. As the delivery month came closer, reversing trades began to outnumber trades intended to open new positions, and the open interest began to decline.[5] The amount remaining at the beginning of December was the number of bushels of corn that could have been delivered against futures contracts at that time, but most of these contracts were also settled by reversing trades instead of delivery.

Relatively few futures positions—less than 3% of the total—end in actual delivery of the asset involved.[6] However, the fact that delivery is a possibility makes a contract's value in the delivery month differ only slightly, if at all, from the spot price (that is, the current market price) of the asset.

If not reversed, most futures contracts require delivery of the corresponding asset. Notable exceptions are market index futures; they do not require delivery of

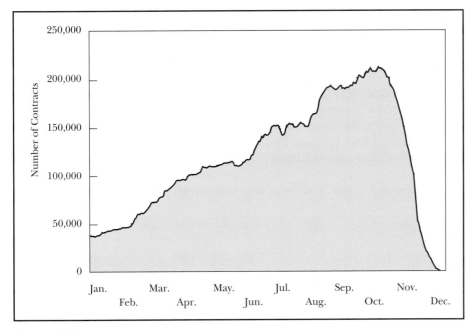

Figure 20.3
Open Interest, December 1997 Chicago Board of Trade
Corn Futures Contract: January 2, 1997 through December 29, 1997

the set of securities constituting the corresponding index. Instead, *cash settlement* is required; an amount equal to the difference between the level of the index and the purchase price must be paid in cash on the delivery date. Nevertheless, similar to other types of futures, most positions in market index futures are closed out with reversing trades before the date at which delivery (in cash) is required.

20.3.8   Price Limits

The futures exchanges, subject to approval by the **Commodity Futures Trading Commission** (CFTC), place dollar limits on the extent to which futures prices are allowed to vary from day to day. For example, if July wheat closed at $4 on the previous day and the daily price limit is $.20, then on the following day contracts at prices outside the range from $3.80 to $4.20 would not be allowed to be traded on the exchange. If a major piece of news during the day led traders to consider $4.25 a reasonable price for the contract, they would have to:

1. trade privately, forgoing the advantages offered by the exchange; or
2. trade on the exchange at the limit price of $4.20; or
3. let the contract settle at $4.20 and then wait until the next day, when the range of acceptable prices would be from $4 to $4.40.

One result of the "limit move" to $4.20 is that it is entirely possible that no contracts will be traded at all on that day. Nobody will want to sell these wheat contracts for a below-market price of $4.20, preferring to wait until the next day when the range of acceptable prices is raised. Indeed, if the news is important enough (such as a massive freeze in Florida, destroying many orange trees and dramatically affecting orange juice futures), there can be limit moves for a number of successive days, with no trading taking place for several days.

The futures exchanges impose price limits on futures because of a belief that traders may overreact to major news and should be "protected" from voluntarily entering into agreements under such conditions. Interestingly, initial margins are usually set at an amount that is roughly equal to the price limit times the size of the contract. In the case of wheat having a $.20 price limit and a contract for 5,000 bushels, the initial margin is usually about $1,000 (=$.20 × 5,000). Thus if the price of wheat moves the limit against the investor, no more than the initial margin of $1,000 will be lost on the day of the adverse limit move. In a sense, the price limit has "protected" the investor (and the clearinghouse) from losing more than $1,000 on that day. However, it is possible that the investor cannot enter a reversing trade as soon as prices have moved the limit, meaning that much larger losses can be incurred later (as in the case of the "Florida freeze" and orange juice futures).

20.4   BASIS

The difference between the current spot price on an asset (that is, the price of the asset for immediate delivery) and the corresponding futures price (that is, the purchase price stated in the futures contract) is known as the **basis** for the futures:

$$\text{Basis} = \text{current spot price} - \text{futures price} \qquad (20.1)$$

20.4.1   Speculating on the Basis

Because the futures price will equal the spot price on the delivery date, the basis will ultimately narrow and disappear on the delivery date. However, before then it can widen or narrow, opening up the opportunity for profitable investing if such changes in the basis can be accurately forecasted. Typically, depending on whether the basis is positive or negative and on whether the basis is forecasted to widen or narrow, an investor will want to either be (1) short in the futures contract and long in the underlying deliverable asset or (2) long in the futures contract and short in the underlying deliverable asset. The risk that the basis will narrow or widen, causing gains or losses to these investors, is known as **basis risk**. The only type of uncertainty they face concerns the difference between the spot price of the deliverable asset and the price of the futures contract. Such a person is said to be *speculating on the basis*.[7]

20.4.2   Spreads

It is quite possible to take a long position in a futures contract and a short position in another futures contract in the same asset but with a different delivery date. The person who does this is speculating on changes in the difference between the prices of the two contracts, a difference that constitutes the "basis" for these particular positions.

Others attempt to profit from temporary imbalances among the prices of futures contracts on different but related assets. For example, one might take a long position in soybeans along with a short position in an item produced from soybeans, such as soybean meal. Another possibility involves a position in wheat with an offsetting position in corn, which serves as a substitute for wheat in many applications.

Such people are known as *spreaders*, and, like those who speculate on the basis, they reduce or eliminate the risk associated with general price moves. Instead, they take on the risk associated with changes in price *differences* in the hope that their alleged superior knowledge will enable them to consistently make profits from such changes.

For the period from 1950 through 1976, a portfolio made up of positions in 23 different commodity futures contracts was compared with a diversified portfolio of common stocks.[8] The average rates of return and risk level of the two portfolios were found to be of similar magnitude:

Portfolio	Average Annual Return	Standard Deviation
Futures	13.83%	22.43%
Common stocks	13.05	18.95

Given these results, an investor might view the two alternatives as equally desirable. Better yet, during the period from 1950 to 1976, a combination of the two portfolios was found to be more desirable than either portfolio by itself. The returns of the commodity futures and stock portfolios were negatively correlated, suggesting that the return on a combined portfolio would have had considerably less variation than the return on either portfolio separately. Specifically, the correlation coefficient was −.24, resulting in the following standard deviations for portfolios with different combinations:

Percent in Stocks	Percent in Futures	Average Annual Return	Standard Deviation
0%	100%	13.83%	22.43%
20	80	13.67	17.43
40	60	13.52	13.77
60	40	13.36	12.68
80	20	13.20	14.74
100	0	13.05	18.95

Whereas there was little difference in the average returns of the various portfolios, there was a noticeable difference in their risks. In particular, the portfolio with roughly 60% in stocks and 40% in futures seems to have had much less risk than the others.

Also of interest was the observation that commodity futures have been at least a partial hedge against inflation. During the period from 1950 to 1976, the returns on the portfolio of 23 futures were positively correlated with changes in the Consumer Price Index, having a correlation coefficient of .58. In contrast, the returns on the portfolio of common stocks were negatively correlated with changes in the Consumer Price Index, having a correlation coefficient of −.43. (See this chapter's *Institutional Issues: Commodity Futures: The Selling of an Asset Class* for a further discussion of commodity futures returns.)

At this point it is appropriate to discuss the pricing of futures contracts. Specifically, what is the relationship between the futures price and investors' expectations of what the spot price will be on the delivery date? And what is the relationship between the futures price and the current spot price of the deliverable asset? The next two sections explore these relationships.

20.6.1 Certainty

If future spot prices could be predicted with certainty, there would be no reason for anyone to be either a buyer or a seller of a futures contract. To understand why, imagine what a futures contract would look like in a world of certainty. First, the purchase price of the futures contract would simply equal the (perfectly predictable) expected spot price on the delivery date. Neither buyers nor sellers would be able to make profits from the existence of futures. Second, the purchase price would not change as the delivery date got closer.[9] Finally, no margin would be necessary because there would not be any unexpected "adverse" price movements.

20.6.2 Uncertainty

Although it is useful to know something about the way in which futures prices and expected spot prices are related to each other in a world of certainty where forecasting is done with complete accuracy, the real world is uncertain. Given this fact, how are futures prices related to expected spot prices? There are several possible explanations, but no definitive answer has been provided.

Expectations Hypothesis

One possible explanation is given by the **expectations hypothesis**: The current purchase price of a futures contract equals the consensus expectation of the spot price on the delivery date. In symbols:

$$P_f = \overline{P}_s$$

where P_f is the current purchase price of the futures contract and $\overline{P}_s$ is the expected spot price of the asset on the delivery date. Thus if a July wheat futures contract is currently selling for $4 per bushel in March, then it can be inferred that the consensus opinion in March is that in July the spot price of wheat will be $4.

If the expectations hypothesis is correct, a speculator should not expect to either win or lose from a position in the futures market, be it long or short. Neglecting margin requirements, a speculator who takes a long position in futures agrees to pay P_f at the delivery date for an asset that is expected to be worth $\overline{P}_s$ at that time. Thus the long speculator's expected profit is $\overline{P}_s - P_f$, which equals zero. Conversely, a speculator with a short position will have sold an asset at a price of P_f and will expect to enter a reversing trade at $\overline{P}_s$ on the delivery date. Thus the short speculator's expected profit is $P_f - \overline{P}_s$, which also equals zero.

The expectations hypothesis is often defended on the grounds that speculators are indifferent to risk and are thus happy to accommodate hedgers without any compensation in the form of the risk premium. The reason for their indifference has to do with the belief that the impact of a specific futures position on the risk of a diversified portfolio that includes many types of assets will be very small. Thus speculators holding diversified portfolios may be willing to take over some risk from hedgers with little (if any) compensation in the form of a risk premium. Figure 20.4 shows the pattern of futures prices implied by the expectations hypothesis, given that the expected spot price $\overline{P}_s$ does not change during the life of the contract.

Normal Backwardation

The famous economist John Maynard Keynes felt that the expectations hypothesis did not correctly explain futures prices.[10] He argued that, on balance, hedgers will want to be short in futures, and therefore they will have to entice the speculators to be long

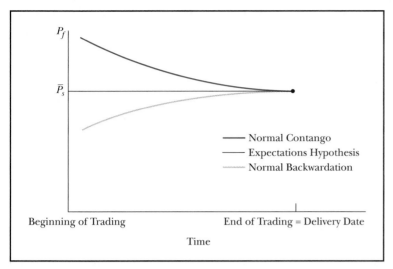

Figure 20.4
Price of a Futures Contract through Time When the Spot Price Expected
at the Time of Delivery Does Not Change

in futures. Because there are risks associated with being long, Keynes hypothesized
that the hedgers would have to entice the speculators by making the expected return
from a long position greater than the riskfree rate. Doing so requires the futures
price to be less than the expected spot price:

$$P_f < \overline{P}_s$$

Thus a speculator who bought a futures contract at a price P_f would expect to
be able to sell it on (or near) the delivery date at a higher price, $\overline{P}_s$. This relationship between the futures price and the expected spot price has been referred to as
normal backwardation and implies that the price of a futures contract can be expected to rise during its life, as shown in Figure 20.4.

Normal Contango

A contrary hypothesis holds that, on balance, hedgers will want to be long in futures
and therefore they will have to entice speculators to be short in futures. Because
there are risks associated with being short, it can be hypothesized that the hedgers
will have to entice the speculators by making the expected return from a short position greater than the riskfree rate. Doing so requires the futures price to be greater
than the expected spot price:

$$P_f > \overline{P}_s$$

Thus a speculator who short sold a futures contract at a price P_f would expect to be
able to buy it back on (or near) the delivery date at a lower price, $\overline{P}_s$. This relationship between the futures price and the expected spot price has been referred to as
normal contango and implies that the price of a futures contract can be expected to
fall during its life, as shown in Figure 20.4.[11]

20.7   FUTURES PRICES AND CURRENT SPOT PRICES

The previous section discussed the relationship between the futures price associated with an asset and the expected spot price of the asset on the delivery date given
in the futures contract. What about the relationship between the futures price and
the current spot price of the asset? In general, they will be different, but is there

some explanation for why these prices are different? Is there some model that can be used to forecast how the size of the difference will change over time? This section attempts to answer those questions.[12]

20.7.1 Introducing the Problem

Consider the owner of a circa 1910 Honus Wagner baseball card who is getting ready to sell the card. The owner knows that the card's current market price is $100,000 because there are very few (reputedly fewer than five) of these cards available. (One actually sold for $451,000 in 1990.) Furthermore, an investor has offered to buy it but wants to pay for it a year from now. The buyer is willing to take delivery of the card then and wants to sign the contract for sale today. More specifically, he or she would like to sign a futures contract with the owner in which the delivery date is one year from now.

20.7.2 No Costs or Benefits of Ownership

What price should the owner ask for in the futures contract? Assume that there is no risk that either party will default on the contract, and that there are no benefits (such as from showing the card) or costs (such as insurance) associated with owning the card. Given that the current one-year interest rate is 4%, the owner could sell the card today on the spot market for $100,000, put the proceeds in the bank to earn 4%, and have $104,000 in one year. Hence the owner would not be willing to sign the futures contract for any futures price that is less than $104,000. The buyer, on the other hand, is unwilling to pay more than $104,000 because he or she could pay $100,000 now and get the card immediately but forgo $4,000 of interest that would have been paid had the $100,000 been left in the bank where it earned 4%. Because the seller wants to receive at least $104,000 and the buyer will pay no more than $104,000, they will settle at a futures price of $104,000.

To generalize, let P_s denote the current spot price of the asset (in this case, $100,000) and I the dollar amount of interest corresponding to the period of time from the present to the delivery date (in this case, $4,000). If P_f denotes the futures price, then:

$$P_f = P_s + I \tag{20.2}$$

This equation shows that the futures price will be greater than the spot price by the amount of the interest that the owner forgoes by holding onto the asset, provided that there are no costs or benefits associated with ownership.

20.7.3 Benefits from Ownership

To add a complication to the model, imagine that a baseball card exhibition will be held in 12 months, just before the delivery date. The exhibitor is willing to pay the card owner $1,000 in order to have the card displayed at the exhibition. How will this benefit of ownership affect the futures price?

As mentioned earlier, if the owner sells the card now, then he or she will receive $100,000 immediately, which could be invested right away and be worth $104,000 in 12 months. Alternatively, the owner could hold on to the card and receive the $1,000 exhibitor fee as well as the futures price. Hence the futures price must be at least $103,000 in order for the owner to be as well off financially by selling the card by means of a futures contract as by selling it immediately in the spot market. On the other side, the buyer will agree to a futures price of no more than $103,000 because he or she could buy the card on the spot market for $100,000, thereby forgoing $4,000 of interest but receiving the $1,000 exhibitor fee. Consequently, the futures price will be $103,000; this is the only price that is agreeable to both buyer and seller.

What if the exhibition were to be held in six months instead of one year? In that case the owner of the card would receive the $1,000 exhibitor fee in six months and would be able to invest it risklessly at 2% for the remaining six months until the delivery date. Thus the $1,000 in six months would be equivalent to $1,020 in 12 months, and the futures price would be $102,980 (=$100,000 + $4,000 − $1,020).

Let B denote the value of the benefits of ownership (sometimes known as the *convenience yield* of the asset) as of the delivery date (in this case, $1,020). When such benefits are present, the futures price can be calculated as:

$$P_f = P_s + I - B \qquad (20.3)$$

This equation shows that the futures price can be greater or less than the spot price, depending on whether the net amount of interest forgone less benefits received is positive or negative and provided that there are no costs associated with ownership of the asset.

20.7.4 Costs of Ownership

What if the owner of the baseball card decides that it must be insured at an annual cost of $100? How will insuring the card affect the futures price? The easiest way to think of such costs of ownership as insurance and storage is to view them as the opposite of benefits of ownership. Because the benefits of ownership result in cash inflows to the owner, the costs of ownership result in cash outflows. Hence the previously calculated futures price of $102,980 would have to be increased by the $100 cost of insurance (assuming the insurance is paid in 12 months) to $103,080. If C denotes the costs of ownership (in this example, $100), then the futures price will be:

$$P_f = P_s + I - B + C \qquad (20.4)$$

The total value of interest less benefits received plus cost of ownership, $I - B + C$, is known as the **cost of carry** associated with the futures contract. Note that the futures price can be greater or less than the spot price, depending upon whether the cost of carry is positive or negative.

20.8 FINANCIAL FUTURES

Until the 1970s, futures contracts were limited to those on agricultural goods and natural resources. Since then, financial futures based on foreign currencies, fixed-income securities, and market indices have been introduced on major exchanges. Indeed, in terms of trading volume, they are now far more important than both the underlying assets and traditional futures contracts. Unlike other types of futures that permit delivery any time during a given month, most financial futures have a specific delivery date. (The exceptions involve some fixed-income futures.)

20.8.1 Foreign Currency Futures

Anyone who has crossed a national border knows that there is an active spot market for foreign currency and that the rate at which one currency can be exchanged for another varies over time. At any particular point in time, however, all such rates must be in conformance or else a riskless profit-making situation may arise. For example, it is usually possible to exchange U.S. dollars for British pounds, then exchange the British pounds for French francs, and, finally, exchange the French francs for U.S.

Commodity Futures: The Selling of an Asset Class

When institutional investors discuss investments in futures, we can safely assume that they are referring to *financial futures:* that is, futures contracts on, for example, stock market indices or Treasury bonds. Commodity futures, on the other hand, play only an insignificant role in institutional investors' portfolios.

Given the history of the futures markets, this situation might seem somewhat surprising. After all, financial futures are mere fledglings compared with commodity futures. The oldest futures exchange, the Chicago Board of Trade, was organized in 1848 for the sole purpose of trading futures contracts on agricultural commodities. The first financial futures contracts (a futures contract on foreign currencies) were established in 1972. The most popular financial futures contract today, S&P 500 futures, was not created until 1981.

The dollar volume of trading in financial futures contracts now far exceeds the trading volume in commodity futures. Traditional users of commodity futures contracts have not become less enamored with those products. Rather, directly and indirectly institutional investors have helped create a gigantic market for financial futures.

The question then is not why institutional investors have become extensively involved in financial futures. The application of financial futures to the activities of institutional investors, in terms of both hedging and speculating, are obvious. More intriguing is why institutional investors have not entered the commodity futures market in any substantial way.

Institutional investors, particularly pension funds, in recent years have expanded the range of asset types (or classes) in which they invest. Whereas once they restricted themselves to domestic common stocks, high-grade bonds, and cash equivalents, institutional investors now own foreign securities, high-yield bonds, real estate, and oil and gas properties, to mention just a few. With some notable exceptions, however, institutional investors have been unwilling to add commodity futures to their asset class toolboxes.

Financial services providers have recognized the tremendous profit potential if institutional investors could be enticed to invest in commodities. If those investors chose to place just 2% to 3% of their immense wealth in commodities, the accompanying fees to brokers and money managers would easily run into the hundreds of millions of dollars.

How to convince institutional investors to trade in commodities? One potential means is to help publicize the risk-reward opportunities historically offered by investments in commodities. Institutional investors have generally shown a reluctance to become involved in investments lacking a quantifiable track record. If an index of a diversified investment in commodity futures were developed, institutional investors would have performance data that could be compared against the results of investments in other asset classes. Furthermore, institutional investors would be able to construct simulated past portfolios that included commodity futures, thus emphasizing the diversification benefits of this asset class.

Beyond the industrywide benefit of stimulating institutional investor interest in commodity futures, a unique benefit accrues to the creator of an investable commodity futures index. If that index were to become widely accepted, the creator would have a considerable advantage in designing and trading products based on that index. That advantage could translate into significant revenue.

In 1991 Goldman Sachs, a large New York brokerage firm, with considerable fanfare introduced its own commodity futures index. Other organizations had previously developed such indices. Goldman Sachs, however, directly targeted institutional investors by designing its index to be truly reflective of the commodity futures investment opportunities available to large investors. Furthermore, Goldman Sachs developed detailed simulated performance data for the index extending back to 1970.

The Goldman Sachs Commodities Index (GSCI) is composed of "near" futures prices for which active liquid markets exist. ("Near" refers to the contract in a given commodity with the shortest time remaining until delivery.) This liquidity requirement allows large investors to replicate the index by buying its individual components. Weights in the index are based on world production of the respective commodities. Thus the most economically important commodities receive the most weight in the index.

Currently 18 commodities constitute the index, which is dominated by various energy, livestock, and grain futures (with weights of roughly 50%, 25%, and 15%, respectively). Historically the composition of the index has changed over time as new commodity futures contracts were created or met the GSCI liquidity requirements. In the 1970s the livestock and grain futures made up most of the index. Energy-related futures did not begin trading until 1983 and were not added to the index until 1987.

The reported historical performance of the GSCI has been impressive in terms of both return and risk. Ibbotson Associates reported the following returns, standard deviations, and correlations for the GSCI and comparative asset classes over the period of 1970 through the first quarter of 1992:

	Annual Return	Annual Standard Deviation	Correlation with GSCI
GSCI	14.8%	18.3	1.00
U.S. stocks	11.5	16.2	−.42
Foreign stocks	13.1	17.6	−.27
U.S. long-term bonds	9.0	11.5	−.32
U.S. Treasury bills	7.5	0.8	−.20
U.S. inflation	6.0	1.4	.26

The GSCI has produced returns exceeding those of U.S. and foreign stocks while offering only slightly more variability. Also impressive has been the GSCI's negative correlation with other asset classes and its positive correlation with inflation. The conclusions one draws from these data are that commodities offer equity-like returns, are excellent portfolio diversifiers, and are a good inflation hedge.

How Goldman Sachs has calculated the GSCI returns has generated some controversy. Those returns have three components: the spot return, the Treasury bill return, and the roll yield. The first two components are straightforward. The spot return reflects how much the price of the underlying commodity changes. The Treasury bill return reflects the interest earned if the investor were to post as collateral the full dollar value (that is, *the notional principal*) of the investment in the commodities at the time of the futures contract purchase.

The roll yield is more complicated. It represents the change in the futures price over the life of the contract. If futures are priced according to normal backwardation (discussed in this chapter), then futures prices are expected to rise toward the spot price of the commodity over time. Therefore the process of "rolling" over expiring futures will be profitable on average.

Which is the correct explanation of the relationship between futures and expected spot prices: the expectations hypothesis, normal backwardation, or normal contango? Because historically about one-third of the GSCI's return has come from roll yield, this question is more than academic. Goldman Sachs argues that the markets for commodities that are normally consumed as they are produced (such as energy or livestock) are typically subject to backwardation. Only if this will be the case in the future can a positive roll yield for the GSCI (and the resulting high GSCI total returns) be expected to persist.

Equally problematic is whether institutional investors can be expected to increase their investments in commodities. Current indications are that institutions are beginning to dip their toes into commodity futures through accounts called *managed futures*. In these accounts money managers actively take long and short positions in commodity and financial futures. The accounts gain only if their managers are adept at anticipating the direction of various futures price changes. Over $2 billion is now invested in managed futures accounts. Are these investments the harbingers of increased institutional activity or a mere passing fancy? The jury is still out.

dollars. If all three exchange rates were not in line, an investor might end up with more dollars at the end of this chain of transactions than at the beginning. Such an opportunity would attract large amounts of money, placing pressure on exchange rates and rapidly restoring balance. Although transaction costs and certain exchange restrictions might limit the ability of people to exploit such imbalances among exchange rates, they would nevertheless force the rates into being closely aligned.

The familiar market in foreign currency, operated by banks, travel agents, and others, is in effect a spot market, because both the agreement on terms and the actual exchange of currencies occur at the same time. There are also markets for agreements involving the future delivery of foreign currency.

The largest such market is operated by banks and specialized brokers that maintain close communications with each other throughout the world. Corporations, institutions, and some individuals deal in this market via large banks. Substantial amounts of money are involved, and every agreement is negotiated separately. Typical rates are quoted daily in the financial press, as shown in Figure 20.5. This network of large institutions is generally termed the *market for forward exchange* because there is no marking to market. Furthermore, because the contracts are not standardized, no organized secondary market for them exists. However, there is a market that deals in standardized futures contracts for foreign currency.[13] Procedures are similar to those used for commodity futures.

For example, one of the currency futures contracts traded on the International Monetary Market (IMM) of the Chicago Mercantile Exchange requires the seller to deliver 12,500,000 Japanese yen to the buyer on a specific date for a number of U.S. dollars agreed upon in advance. Only the price of the transaction (expressed in both dollars per yen and yen per dollar) is negotiated by the parties involved; all other terms are standard. Clearing procedures allow positions to be covered by reversing trades, and few contracts result in the actual delivery of foreign currency. As shown in Figure 20.1, prices and volumes for such contracts are quoted daily in the financial press along with those for other futures.

Markets for foreign currency futures attract both hedgers and speculators. Hedgers wish to reduce or possibly eliminate the risk associated with planned future transfers of funds from one country to another.

An Example

For example, an American importer might know on October 8, 1997, that he or she will have to make a payment of 50 million yen to a Japanese exporter in March 1998. Figure 20.5 shows that the current exchange rate is $.008258 per yen (or, equivalently, 121.10 yen per dollar), so the anticipated dollar size of the payment is $412,900 (=$.008258 × 50,000,000). The risk the importer faces by simply waiting until March to make this payment is that the exchange rate will change in an unfavorable manner—perhaps rising to $.01 per yen, in which case the dollar cost to the importer will have risen to $500,000 (=$.01 × 50,000,000). The importer can hedge this risk by purchasing four March futures contracts for yen. Figure 20.1 indicates that the settlement price on October 8, 1997, for these contracts was $.008441, meaning that the dollar cost of one contract is $422,050 (=$.008441 × 50,000,000). Thus the importer can remove the risk of the yen's appreciating by more than $.000183 (=$.008441 − $.008258) against the dollar before the payment date by purchasing the four (=50,000,000/12,500,000) yen futures contracts.

Speculators are attracted to the foreign currency futures market when they believe that the current price of the futures contract is substantially different from what they expect the spot rate to be on the delivery date. For example, a speculator might

---

CURRENCY TRADING

EXCHANGE RATES

Wednesday, October 8, 1997

The New York foreign exchange selling rates below apply to trading among banks in amounts of $1 million and more, as quoted at 4 p.m. Eastern time by Dow Jones and other sources. Retail transactions provide fewer units of foreign currency per dollar.

Country	U.S. $ equiv. Wed	Tue	Currency per U.S. $ Wed	Tue
Argentina (Peso)	1.0014	1.0014	.9986	.9986
Australia (Dollar)	.7285	.7242	1.3727	1.3808
Austria (Schilling)	.08096	.08087	12.352	12.366
Bahrain (Dinar)	2.6525	2.6525	.3770	.3770
Belgium (Franc)	.02765	.02762	36.167	36.209
Brazil (Real)	.9113	.9115	1.0973	1.0972
Britain (Pound)	1.6220	1.6225	.6165	.6163
1-month forward	1.6199	1.6204	.6173	.6171
3-months forward	1.6158	1.6162	.6189	.6187
6-months forward	1.6094	1.6099	.6213	.6212
Canada (Dollar)	.7287	.7287	1.3723	1.3723
1-month forward	.7300	.7300	1.3699	1.3698
3-months forward	.7323	.7323	1.3655	1.3655
6-months forward	.7353	.7353	1.3599	1.3600
Chile (Peso)	.002418	.002414	413.60	414.30
China (Renminbi)	.1203	.1203	8.3100	8.3145
Colombia (Peso)	.0008016	.0007994	1247.51	1250.95
Czech. Rep. (Koruna)	....	....	....	....
Commercial rate	.03041	.03048	32.885	32.805
Denmark (Krone)	.1499	.1494	6.6690	6.6920
Ecuador (Sucre)	....	....	....	....
Floating rate	.0002424	.0002424	4125.00	4125.00
Finland (Markka)	.1903	.1901	5.2560	5.2609
France (Franc)	.1702	.1693	5.8750	5.9055
1-month forward	.1706	.1697	5.8627	5.8928
3-months forward	.1712	.1703	5.8399	5.8713
6-months forward	.1721	.1712	5.8095	5.8409
Germany (Mark)	.5718	.5690	1.7490	1.7575
1-month forward	.5729	.5702	1.7454	1.7539
3-months forward	.5752	.5723	1.7386	1.7472
6-months forward	.5783	.5753	1.7292	1.7383
Greece (Drachma)	.003629	.003606	275.53	277.30
Hong Kong (Dollar)	.1293	.1293	7.7363	7.7357
Hungary (Forint)	.005127	.005133	195.05	194.81
India (Rupee)	.02762	.02763	36.201	36.195
Indonesia (Rupiah)	.0002734	.0002747	3657.50	3640.50
Ireland (Punt)	1.4590	1.4639	.6854	.6831
Israel (Shekel)	.2867	.2867	3.4881	3.4885
Italy (Lira)	.0005831	.0005799	1715.00	1724.50
Japan (Yen)	.008258	.008160	121.10	122.55
1-month forward	.008296	.008196	120.53	122.02
3-months forward	.008369	.008268	119.49	120.95
6-months forward	.008477	.008374	117.97	119.41
Jordan (Dinar)	1.4094	1.4094	.7095	.7095
Kuwait (Dinar)	3.2862	3.2862	.3043	.3043
Lebanon (Pound)	.0006524	.0006524	1532.75	1532.75
Malaysia (Ringgit)	.3157	.3087	3.1678	3.2398
Malta (Lira)	2.5674	2.5707	.3895	.3890
Mexico (Peso)	....	....	....	....
Floating rate	.1289	.1292	7.7560	7.7400
Netherland (Guilder)	.5078	.5055	1.9692	1.9784
New Zealand (Dollar)	.6414	.6399	1.5591	1.5627
Norway (Krone)	.1415	.1415	7.0653	7.0673
Pakistan (Rupee)	.02496	.02496	40.070	40.070
Peru (new Sol)	.3797	.3810	2.6338	2.6248
Philippines (Peso)	.02809	.02793	35.600	35.800
Poland (Zloty)	.2936	.2931	3.4055	3.4118
Portugal (Escudo)	.005616	.005582	178.06	179.16
Russia (Ruble) (a)	.0001703	.0001704	5870.50	5869.00
Saudi Arabia (Riyal)	.2666	.2666	3.7505	3.7505
Singapore (Dollar)	.6421	.6402	1.5575	1.5620
Slovak Rep. (Koruna)	.02980	.02980	33.558	33.558
South Africa (Rand)	.2142	.2144	4.6695	4.6635
South Korea (Won)	.001093	.001093	914.85	914.55
Spain (Peseta)	.006771	.006738	147.69	148.41
Sweden (Krona)	.1324	.1328	7.5512	7.5295
Switzerland (Franc)	.6930	.6904	1.4430	1.4485
1-month forward	.6954	.6929	1.4380	1.4432
3-months forward	.7003	.6974	1.4280	1.4338
6-months forward	.7073	.7042	1.4138	1.4201
Taiwan (Dollar)	.03511	.03509	28.485	28.495
Thailand (Baht)	.02797	.02789	35.750	35.850
Turkey (Lira)	.00000570	.00000572	175580.00	174840.00
United Arab (Dirham)	.2723	.2723	3.6725	3.6725
Uruguay (New Peso)	....	....	....	....
Financial	.1024	.1024	9.7700	9.7700
Venezuela (Bolivar)	.002008	.002008	497.98	497.93
SDR	1.3676	1.3681	.7312	.7309
ECU	1.1206	1.1151	....	....

Special Drawing Rights (SDR) are based on exchange rates for the U.S., German, British, French, and Japanese currencies. Source: International Monetary Fund.

European Currency Unit (ECU) is based on a basket of community currencies.

a-fixing, Moscow Interbank Currency Exchange.

The Wall Street Journal daily foreign exchange data for 1996 and 1997 may be purchased through the Readers' Reference Service (413) 592-3600.

Figure 20.5
Quotations for Foreign Exchange
Source: Reprinted by permission of *The Wall Street Journal*, Dow Jones & Company, Inc., October 9, 1997, p. C20.

believe that the price of the March futures contract for Japanese yen is too high. Perhaps a speculator might believe that when March comes around, the exchange rate will be $.008 per yen (or, equivalently, 125 yen per dollar). By selling (that is, short selling) a March futures contract for yen, the speculator will be selling yen for $.008441, the settlement price on October 8, 1997. At the time delivery has to be made, the speculator believes that yen can be bought on the spot market for $.008, thereby allowing a profit to be made on the difference between the selling and buying prices.[14] Specifically, the speculator expects to be able to make a profit of $5,512.50 [= ($.008441 − $.008) × 12,500,000)] per futures contract.

Pricing

Futures contracts involving foreign currencies are priced according to the notion of **interest-rate parity**, which is merely a special application of the model of futures pricing given in Equation (20.4). Imagine that it is October 1997 and you are planning to invest some money for one year. You could simply invest in a one-year U.S. riskfree security and then receive the principal and interest a year later in the form of U.S. dollars. Alternatively, you could exchange the dollars for German marks and use the marks to buy a one-year German riskfree security. In addition, you would short sell the requisite number of one-year German mark futures contracts so that a year later, when you receive the principal and interest in the form of German marks, you would know exactly how many U.S. dollars you would receive for them.

Neither of these strategies—investing in U.S. riskfree securities or investing in German riskfree securities—has any risk associated with it in that you know exactly how many U.S. dollars each will yield after one year. If the German strategy had a higher return per dollar invested, Americans would not buy the U.S. riskfree securities because they could earn the same amount for a smaller investment by buying the German riskfree securities. Similarly, if the U.S. strategy had a higher return per dollar invested, Germans would not buy the German riskfree securities because they could earn the same amount for a smaller investment by buying U.S. dollars in the spot market, purchasing U.S. riskfree securities, and buying a one-year German mark futures contract. As a consequence, in equilibrium the two strategies must have the same cost if they have the same dollar payoffs.

Consider what would happen to each dollar invested. The strategy of investing \$1 in a U.S. riskfree security that has a return of R_{US} will provide a cash inflow of $\$1(1 + R_{US})$ after one year. The strategy of investing \$1 in a German riskfree security that has a return of R_G, where the current spot rate of exchange is P_s and the futures price is P_f, will provide a dollar cash inflow of $(\$1/P_s)(1 + R_G)P_f$ after one year. (Here both P_s and P_f are stated in dollars per mark.) Given that these two strategies cost the same (\$1), their payoffs must be equal:

$$\$1(1 + R_{US}) = \left(\frac{\$1}{P_s}\right)(1 + R_G)P_f \tag{20.5}$$

Hence the futures price of the mark can be determined by rewriting Equation (20.5) as the interest-rate parity equation:

$$P_f = P_s\left(\frac{1 + R_{US}}{1 + R_G}\right) \tag{20.6}$$

Thus if the current spot rate of exchange for the German mark is \$.60, and the U.S. and German one-year riskfree rates are 4% and 5%, respectively, then the one-year futures price of the mark will be \$.5943 [=\$.60 × (1.04/1.05)].

In relation to Equation (20.4), the cost of carry is −\$.0057 (=\$.5943 − \$.60). In the case of foreign currency, the costs of ownership C are zero. However, the net benefits of ownership $I − B$ amount to the −\$.0057 cost of carry. More generally, the cost of carry, denoted *carry*, will equal:

$$Carry = P_s\left(\frac{R_{US} - R_G}{1 + R_G}\right) \tag{20.7}$$

for foreign currency futures, where R_G now denotes the riskfree rate in the foreign currency under consideration. From Equation (20.7) it can be seen that because $Carry = I − B$, it follows that:

$$I = \frac{P_s R_{US}}{1 + R_G} \tag{20.8a}$$

$$B = \frac{P_s R_G}{1 + R_G} \tag{20.8b}$$

Hence in the example I, the amount of interest forgone by the owner by selling marks in the futures market instead of the spot market, equals \$.0229 (=\$.60 × .04/1.05), whereas B, the benefit of owning marks instead of selling them, equals \$.0286 (=\$.60 × .05/1.05). Consequently, the cost of carry equals −\$.0057 (=\$.0229 − \$.0286), as shown earlier.

Equation (20.4) indicates that the futures price will be less than the current spot price when the cost of carry is negative. This will occur when the U.S. riskfree rate is less than the foreign riskfree rate because the numerator on the right-hand side of

Equation (20.7) will be negative whereas the denominator is positive in such a situation. Conversely, the futures price will be greater than the current spot price when the cost of carry is positive, which will occur when the U.S. riskfree rate is greater than the foreign riskfree rate. Hence the reason why futures prices are different from spot prices is that riskfree interest rates between countries are different.

20.8.2 Interest-Rate Futures

Futures involving fixed-income securities are often referred to as interest-rate futures because their prices are greatly influenced by the current and forecast interest rates. More specifically, their pricing can be related to the term structure of interest rates, which in turn is related to the concept of forward rates.[15]

An Example

Just how the pricing of interest-rate futures is related to the concept of forward rates can be illustrated with an example. Consider the futures market for Treasury bonds, which is the most popular long-term interest rate futures contract in the United States. As Figure 20.1 indicates, on October 8, 1997, any purchaser of a futures contract calling for delivery in December 1997 of a $100,000 face value Treasury bond would have paid a settlement price of 115-29, meaning $115\text{-}\frac{29}{32}$ of par, or $115,906.25.[16] However, the actual amount that the purchaser would pay equals the settlement price times a *conversion factor*, plus accrued interest. The conversion factor varies depending on which Treasury bond is delivered to satisfy the contract, because the contract calls for delivery of a Treasury bond that either (1) if not callable, has a maturity of at least 15 years from the December 1; or (2) if callable, has a first call date of at least 15 years after December 1.[17] Specifically, the conversion factor is the proportion of par the delivered Treasury bond would be selling for on the first day of the delivery month if it had a yield-to-maturity of 8%. Thus, deliverable bonds with coupons of less than 8% will have a conversion factors of less than 1 (because they would be selling at discount), and those with coupons of greater than 8% will have conversion factors of greater than 1 (because they would be selling at a premium).

As an example, a noncallable 7% coupon Treasury bond that matures 20 years after the delivery month would be selling for $90.10 per $100 of par value [=$20.83 (the present value of the $100 par value of the bond) plus $69.27 (the present value of a stream of 40 semi-annual coupon payments of $3.50 each)]. Thus, the conversion value for this bond is .9010 (=$90.10/$100). Given there is no accrued interest on this bond on the delivery date, the purchaser of the futures would pay $104,432 (=$115,906.25 × .9010) for this Treasury bond on the December delivery date. This price corresponds with a 6.60% yield-to-maturity. If the market yield on this bond on the delivery date is less than 6.60%, then the purchaser of the futures will have made a profit because his or her purchase price is less than the spot price of the bond.

As with commodity futures, neither the buyers nor the sellers of such contracts must maintain their positions until the delivery date. Reversing trades can be made at any time, and relatively few contracts result in actual delivery.

Actively traded interest rate futures involve underlying securities ranging from short term (such as 90-day Treasury bills) to intermediate term (such as 10-year Treasury notes) to long term (such as the 20-year Treasury bonds just described). Prices are generally stated in terms of percentages of par values for the corresponding securities. Yields-to-maturity (or discounts) associated with the settlement prices are also given.

In general, pricing of interest rate futures contracts involves applying the cost of carry model given in Equation (20.4). As an example, consider a 90-day Treasury bill futures contract that calls for delivery in six months. Note that nine-month Treasury bills will be equivalent to 90-day Treasury bills after six months have passed. Hence they could be delivered as the underlying assets in 90-day Treasury bill futures contracts where the delivery date is six months from now. What futures price is fair for these contracts?

Assume that the current market price of a nine-month Treasury bill is $95.24, providing a yield of 5% (=$4.76/$95.24) over the nine months. (This yield and those that follow are not annualized.) Furthermore, assume that six-month yield on Treasury bills is 6%. This owner should not short sell a futures contract calling for delivery in six months of a 90-day Treasury bill where the price to be received is less than $98.10 (=$95.24 × 1.03). For example, if the price of the futures contract was $97, then the owner would be making only 1.85% on his or her initial investment of $95.24 over the subsequent six months. This is less than the 3% that could be earned by selling the nine-month Treasury bill now and investing in a six-month Treasury bill.

Conversely, the buyer should not agree to a price that is more than $98.10. The buyer could buy the nine-month Treasury bill in the spot market today for $95.24 and receive $100 in nine months, or the buyer could risklessly invest the $95.24 for six months at 3% and then use the $98.10 proceeds to pay the futures price for a 90-day Treasury bill that pays $100 at maturity. If the futures price were greater than $98.10 (for example, $99), then the buyer would have to invest more than $95.24 today [for example, $96.12 (=$99/1.03) would have to be invested today] so that the principal plus 3% interest for six months would be sufficient to pay the futures price of $99 after six months. In such a situation, nobody would choose to be long in the futures contract, because he or she would be better off buying a nine-month Treasury bill in the spot market for $95.24 instead of investing more at 3% for six months in order to be able to pay the futures price upon delivery of the Treasury bill. Consequently, the futures price must be $98.10, because this is the only price that is acceptable to both parties to the futures contract.

Generalizing, the futures price P_f must equal the spot price P_s plus the forgone interest I, just as shown in Equation (20.2), because the benefits B and costs C of ownership are zero with such assets. Equivalently, letting R denote the riskfree interest rate that exists on Treasuries that mature on the delivery date, the futures price is:

$$P_f = P_s(1 + R) \tag{20.9}$$

Notice that the futures price will be greater than the spot price as long as the riskfree rate R is positive. Similarly, note that the cost of carry equals:

$$Carry = P_s R \tag{20.10}$$

because both B and C are equal to zero. In this example, $Carry = \$2.86$ (=$95.24 × .03). Note that the difference between the futures price of $98.10 and the spot price of $95.24 also equals $2.86.

20.8.3 Market Index Futures

Figure 20.1 shows a set of quotations for futures contracts on the Standard & Poor's 500 market index. This contract involves the payment of *cash* on the delivery date of an amount equal to a *multiplier* times the difference between the value of the index at the close of the last trading day of the contract and the purchase price of the futures contract. If the index is above the futures price, those with short positions pay those with long positions. If the index is below the futures price, those with long positions pay those with short positions.

In practice, a clearinghouse is used, and all contracts are marked to market every day. In a sense, the delivery day differs from other days in only one respect; all open positions are marked to market for the last time and then closed.

Cash settlement provides results similar to those associated with the delivery of all the securities in the index. It avoids the effort and transaction costs associated with (1) the purchase of securities by people who have taken short futures positions, (2) the delivery of these securities to people who have taken long futures positions, and (3) the subsequent sale of the securities by those who receive them.

Major Contracts

Several U.S. stock market index futures were available in 1997, with the most popular one in terms of both trading volume and open interest being the S&P 500. This contract is traded on the Chicago Mercantile Exchange (CME). Also of note are futures contracts on the Dow Jones Industrial Average, which began trading on October 6, 1997 at the Chicago Board of Trade.

For the S&P 500, the multiplier is $250 (previously, it was $500), and for the Dow it is $10. Thus the purchase of an S&P 500 contract when the index is 1100 would cost $275,000 (=$250 × 1100). The subsequent sale of this contract when the index is 1120 would result in proceeds of $280,000 (=$250 × 1120) and a profit of $5,000 (=$280,000 − $275,000). Similarly, if the Dow is at 8700, a Dow Jones Industrial Average futures contract would cost $87,000 (=$10 × 8700). If the investor executed a reversing trade with the Dow at 8800, a profit of $1,000 would result [=$10 × (8800 − 8700)].

Trading Volume

The volume of trading in futures contracts is very large. Its relative size can be assessed by multiplying the number of contracts by the total dollar value represented by one contract. As shown in Figure 20.1, the estimated volume on October 8, 1997, for S&P 500 futures was 90,005 contracts. At a value of 982.35 for the lowest-priced S&P 500 contract, the total dollar value is in excess of $44 billion (=90,005 × 982.50 × $500). In comparison, the average daily dollar value of all trades of shares on the New York Stock Exchange during 1997 was approximately $23 billion per day—a figure that is much less than the dollar size of the S&P futures on October 8, 1997. This situation is not unusual. On many days the dollar value involved in trades of S&P 500 futures exceeds that all of trades of individual stocks.

Hedging

What accounts for the popularity of market index futures in general and the S&P 500 in particular? Simply stated, they provide relatively inexpensive and highly liquid positions similar to those obtained with diversified stock portfolios.

For example, instead of purchasing 500 stocks in anticipation of a market advance, one can invest an equivalent amount of money in Treasury bills and take a long position in S&P 500 futures. Alternatively, instead of trying to take short positions in 500 stocks in anticipation of a market decline, one can take a short position in S&P 500 futures, using Treasury bills as margin.

Another important use of market index futures involves allowing broker-dealers to hedge the market risk that is associated with the temporary positions they often take in the course of their business.[18] This hedging ultimately benefits investors by providing them with greater liquidity than they would have otherwise.

For example, consider an investor who wants to sell a large block of stock. In this situation a broker-dealer might agree to purchase the stock immediately at an agreed-upon price and then spend time "lining up" buyers. In the interim, however, economic news might cause the market to fall, and with it the price of the stock. The broker-dealer would experience a loss, because the broker-dealer owns the stock during the period between purchasing it from the investor and lining up the ultimate buyers. One traditional way that broker-dealers protect themselves (at least partially) from this risk is to pay the investor a relatively low price for the stock. However, the broker-dealer can now hedge this risk (at least partially) by short selling S&P 500 futures at the time the stock is bought from the investor and later on reversing this position when the ultimate buyers are found.

Given competition among broker-dealers, the existence of S&P 500 futures will lead them to provide higher bid prices and lower asked prices. Because of this reduced bid-ask spread the existence of S&P 500 futures provides the associated spot market for stocks with greater liquidity.

It should be pointed out that the use of S&P 500 futures (or any index futures) in such situations does not remove all risk from the position of the broker-dealer. All that it removes is market risk, because these futures contracts involve a broad market index, not an individual stock. Thus it is possible for the broker-dealer to experience a loss even if an appropriate position has been taken in futures. Specifically, the individual stock with which the broker-dealer is involved may move up or down in price while the S&P 500 is stable, or the S&P 500 may move up or down while the individual stock is stable. In either case, the broker-dealer who has hedged with S&P 500 futures may still experience a loss. The possibility of this happening will be substantial when the broker-dealer has little diversification, with the greatest possibility associated with a one-stock portfolio.

Index Arbitrage

When stock index futures were first proposed, a number of people predicted that at long last there would be an indicator of investors' expectations about the future course of the stock market. It was said that the market price of such a futures contract would indicate the consensus opinion of investors concerning the future level of the associated index. In times of optimism, the futures price might be much higher than the current level of the market, whereas in times of pessimism, the futures price might be much lower.

Such predictions have since been found to be quite off the mark because the price of a futures contract on an asset will not diverge by more than the cost of carry from the spot price of the asset. Should a relatively large divergence occur, clever investors known as **arbitrageurs** can be expected to make trades designed to capture riskless (that is, "arbitrage") profits.

What effect does the presence of these arbitrageurs have on the pricing of stock index futures? Their actions will force the price of a stock index futures contract to stay close to an "appropriate" relationship with the current level of the associated index. To find out just what is meant by appropriate, consider a hypothetical example. Today is a day in June when the Standard & Poor's 500 is at 1000 and a December Standard & Poor's 500 futures contract is selling for 1100. The following investment strategies will be compared:

1. Purchase the stocks in the S&P 500, hold them until December, and then sell them on the delivery date of the December S&P 500 contract.

2. Purchase a December S&P 500 futures contract along with Treasury bills that mature in December. Hold them until the delivery date of the futures contract in December.

Strategy 1 would cost $1,000 (in "index terms") at the outset. In return, it would provide the investor with (1) an amount of money equal to the value of the S&P 500 on the delivery date and (2) dividends on those stocks that went ex-dividend before the delivery date. That is, by denoting the level the S&P 500 will have on the delivery date by P_d and assuming that the dividend yield over the six-month time period from June to December is 3%, the investor following strategy 1 will receive in December a net cash inflow that is equal to $P_d + \$30$ [that is, $P_d + (.03 \times \$1,000)$].[19]

Assume that $1,000 is invested in Treasury bills in strategy 2. Because Treasury bills can be used as margin on futures, the total cost of strategy 2 is $1,000, which is the same as the cost of strategy 1. In return, strategy 2 would provide the investor with (1) an amount of money equal to the difference between the value of the S&P 500 and $1,100 on the delivery date and (2) the face value of the Treasury bills on the delivery date. That is, by assuming that the six-month yield on the Treasury bills is 5%, the investor following strategy 2 will receive in December a net cash inflow that is equal to $P_d - \$50$ [that is, $(P_d - \$1,100) + (1.05 \times \$1,000)$].

By design, the two strategies require the same initial outlay. Furthermore, both strategies are subject to precisely the same uncertainty: the unknown level of the S&P 500 on the future delivery date, P_d. However, the December net cash inflows are not equal, indicating that an opportunity exists for **index arbitrage**.[20]

In this example, the way index arbitrage would work is for an investor to go "long" strategy 1 and "short" strategy 2. Why? Because strategy 1 has a higher payoff than strategy 2 (note that $P_d + \$30 > P_d - \$50$). Going long strategy 1 means that the investor is to do exactly what was indicated earlier—purchase the stocks in the S&P 500 and hold them until the December delivery date. Going short strategy 2 means to do exactly the opposite of what was indicated earlier. Specifically, the investor is to short (that is, sell) a December S&P 500 futures contract and sell Treasury bills that mature in December. (It is assumed that the investor has these in his or her current portfolio.) The net cash outflow of going long strategy 1 and short strategy 2 is zero; $1,000 is spent buying the stocks in going long strategy 1, which is obtained by selling $1,000 worth of December Treasury bills when the investor goes short strategy 2. The margin necessary for being short the futures contract is met by having purchased the underlying stocks. Thus no additional cash needs to be committed in order to engage in index arbitrage; all that is necessary is for the investor to own Treasury bills that mature in December.

Next, consider the investor's position on the delivery date in December. First of all, the investor "bought" the individual stocks in the S&P 500 at $1,000 and "sold" them at $1,100 by being short the S&P 500 futures contract. Thus the investor has made $100 from being long the individual stocks and short the futures on the index. Second, the investor will have received dividends totaling $30 ($=.03 \times \$1,000$) from owning the stocks from June to December. Third, the investor will have given up $50 ($=.05 \times \$1,000$) in interest that would have been earned on the December Treasury bills. This interest is forgone because the investor sold $1,000 of these Treasury bills in June in order to get the requisite cash to buy the individual stocks. Overall, the investor has increased the dollar return that would have been made on the Treasury bills by $80 ($=\$100 + \$30 - \$50$). Furthermore, this increase is certain, meaning that it will be received regardless of what happens to the level of the S&P 500. Thus by going long strategy 1 and short strategy 2 the investor will not have increased the risk of his or her portfolio but will have increased the dollar return.

Earlier it was mentioned that an investor going long strategy 1 would receive cash of P_d + $30 in December, whereas an investor going long strategy 2 would receive cash of P_d − $50. It can now be seen that going long strategy 1 and short strategy 2 will provide a net dollar return of $80 [that is, ($P_d$ + $30) − ($P_d$ − $50)], just as was shown in the previous paragraph. However, if enough investors do this, the opportunity for making the $80 profit will disappear. The reason is that (1) going long will push the prices of the individual stocks up, thereby raising the current level of the S&P 500 from 1000, and (2) going short the S&P 500 futures will push the price of the futures down from 1100. These two adjustments will continue until it is no longer profitable to go long strategy 1 and short strategy 2.

What if the price of the S&P 500 December futures contract is $900 instead of $1,100? The net cash inflow from being long strategy 1 is still equal to P_d + $30. However, the net cash inflow from being long strategy 2 will be different. In particular, purchasing Treasury bills and the futures contract will provide the investor with P_d + $150 [that is, ($P_d$ − $900) + (1.05 × $1,000)] on the delivery date. Because these two inflows are not equal, again there is an opportunity for index arbitrage. However, it would involve the investor's going short strategy 1 and long strategy 2. Why? Because strategy 1 now has a lower payoff than strategy 2 (note that P_d + $30 < P_d + $150). By doing this, the investor will, without risk, earn $120 [that is, ($P_d$ + $150) − ($P_d$ + $30)]. Furthermore, being short the individual stocks and long the futures will push the current level of the S&P 500 down from 1000 and the price of the futures up from 900.

In equilibrium, because these two strategies cost the same to implement, prices will adjust so that their net cash inflows are equal. Letting y denote the dividend yield on the stocks in the index, P_f the current price of the futures contract on the index, and P_s the current spot price of the index (that is, P_s denotes the current level of the index), the net cash inflow from strategy 1 is:

$$P_d + yP_s$$

Letting R denote the interest rate on Treasury bills, the net cash inflow from strategy 2 is:

$$\left(P_d - P_f\right) + \left[(1 + R) \times P_s\right]$$

Setting these two inflows equal to each other results in:

$$P_d + yP_s = \left(P_d - P_f\right) + \left[(1 + R) \times P_s\right] \tag{20.11}$$

Simplifying this equation results in:

$$P_f - P_s = (R - y)P_s \tag{20.12}$$

or:

$$P_f = P_s + RP_s - yP_s \tag{20.13}$$

Equation (20.12) indicates that the difference between the price of the futures contract and the current level of the index should depend only on (1) the current level of the index P_s and (2) the difference between the interest rate on Treasury bills and the dividend yield on the index $R − y$. As the delivery date nears, the difference between the interest rate and the dividend yield diminishes, converging to zero on the delivery date. Thus as the delivery date approaches, the futures price P_f should converge to the current spot price P_s.

Equation (20.13) shows that index futures are priced according to the cost of carry model given earlier in Equation (20.4), where the costs of ownership C are zero. Here the interest forgone by ownership I is equal to RP_s, whereas the benefit of ownership B is the dividend yield yP_s. Hence the cost of carry is:

$$Carry = RP_s - yP_s \qquad (20.14)$$

which will be positive as long as the riskfree interest rate R is greater than the dividend yield on the index y—a situation that exists nearly all the time.

In the example the interest rate was 5%, the dividend yield was 3%, and the current level of the S&P 500 was 1000. This means that the difference between the S&P 500 December futures contract and the current level of the S&P 500 should be 20 [$=(.05 - .03) \times 1000$]. Equivalently, the equilibrium price of the futures contract when the S&P 500 is 1000 would be 1020 because the cost of carry is 20. Note that when three of the six months have passed, the interest rate and the dividend yield will be 2.5% ($=5\%/2$) and 1.5% ($=3\%/2$), respectively. Thus the difference should be about 10 [$=(.025 - 015) \times 1000$], assuming that the S&P 500 is still at 1000 at that time.

In practice, the situation is not this simple for a number of reasons. Positions in futures, stocks, and Treasury bills involve transaction costs.[21] Consequently, arbitrage will not take place unless the difference diverges far enough from the amount shown in Equation (20.12) to warrant incurring such costs. The futures price, and hence the difference, can be expected to move within a band around the "theoretical value," with the width of the band determined by the costs of those who can engage in transactions most efficiently.

To add to the complexity, both the dividend yield and the relevant interest rate on Treasury bills are subject to some uncertainty. Neither the amounts of dividends to be declared nor their timing can be specified completely in advance. Furthermore, because futures positions must be marked to market daily, the amount of cash required for strategy 2 may have to be varied by means of additional borrowing (if short this strategy) or lending (if long this strategy). Also, on occasion market prices may be reported with a substantial time lag, making the current level and the futures price of the index appear to be out of line when they actually are not. (An extreme example of this situation occurred on Black Monday, October 19, 1987.) Thus an investor may enter into the transactions necessary for index arbitrage when actual prices are in equilibrium, thereby incurring useless transaction costs. Nevertheless, index arbitrage is still actively pursued, most notably by brokerage firms, as shown in Figure 20.6.

Stock index futures are also used extensively by other professional money managers. As a result, prices of such contracts are likely to track their underlying indices very closely, taking into account both dividends and current interest rates. It is unlikely that a private investor will be able to exploit "mispricing" of such a contract by engaging in index arbitrage. Nevertheless, stock index futures can provide inexpensive ways to take positions in the stock market or to hedge portions of the risk associated with other positions. Furthermore, their use can lower transaction costs by reducing the size of the bid-ask spread in individual securities, thereby benefiting investors who may never take direct positions in futures contracts.

20.9 FUTURES VERSUS OPTIONS

People occasionally make the mistake of confusing a futures contract with an options contract.[22] With an options contract there is the possibility that both parties involved will have nothing to do at the end of the life of the contract. In particular, if

PROGRAM TRADING

NEW YORK — Program trading in the week ended Oct. 3, accounted for 19.1%, or an average 105.8 million daily shares, of New York Stock Exchange volume.

Brokerage firms executed an additional 51.7 million daily shares of program trading away from the Big Board, mostly on foreign markets. Program trading is the simultaneous purchase or sale of at least 15 different stocks with a total value of $1 million or more.

Of the program total on the Big Board, 13.9% involved stock index arbitrage, down from 15.6% the prior week. In this strategy, traders dart between stocks and stock-index options and futures to capture fleeting price differences.

Some 76.6% of program trading was executed by firms for their customers, while 19.9% was done for their own accounts, or principal trading. Another 3.5% was designated as customer facilitation, in which firms use principal positions to facilitate customer trades.

The report includes a special profile of trading whenever the Dow Jones Industrial Average moves more than 50 points in a single direction during any one hour period. There were six such periods in the past week. Unless otherwise specified, all firms listed here executed both buy and sell orders.

The first period occurred on Monday when the DJIA moved up more than 50 points. The following firms reported making program trades during 10:15 a.m. to 11:15 a.m.: BNP Securities (mostly buying), Natwest (mostly buying), Lawrence Helfant, Bridge Trading (buying) and RBC Dominion (buying).

The second period occurred on Tuesday when the DJIA moved down more than 50 points. The following firms reported making program trades during 10 a.m. to 11 a.m.: BNP Securities, Donaldson Lufkin, Natwest, Merrill Lynch, and Susquehanna Brokerage Services.

The third period occurred on Wednesday when the DJIA moved up more than 50 points. The following firms reported making program trades during 9:30 a.m. to 10:30 a.m.: Merrill Lynch (mostly selling), Interactive Brokers, BNP Securities, Natwest, and Salomon Brothers.

The fourth period also occurred on Wednesday. The following firms reported making program trades during 2:30 p.m. to 4 p.m. when the DJIA moved up more than 50 points: BNP Securities, Morgan Stanley, Natwest, W&D Securities (mostly buying), and Salomon Brothers.

The last two periods occurred on Friday. The following firms reported making program trades during 9:30 a.m. to 10:30 a.m. when the DJIA moved up more than 50 points: BNP Securities, Interactive Brokers (buying), Salomon Brothers, Merrill Lynch, and Susquehanna Brokerage Services.

The following firms reported making program trades during 2 p.m. to 3:30 p.m. when the DJIA moved down more than 50 points: BNP Securities, Goldman Sachs (mostly selling), Nomura Securities, Natwest, and First Boston.

Of the five most active firms, Natwest and Interactive Brokers executed all of their program activity for customers as agent. BNP Securities, Morgan Stanley, and Salomon Brothers executed most of their program trading for customers as agent.

NYSE PROGRAM TRADING
Volume (in millions of shares) for the week ending October 3, 1997

Top 15 Firms	Index Arbitrage	Derivative- Related*	Other Strategies	Total
BNP Securities	...	....	146.5	146.5
NatWest	16.2	0.5	50.7	67.4
Morgan Stanley	1.9	0.7	40.8	43.4
Salomon Bros.	...	....	32.7	32.7
Interactive Brokers	...	....	29.1	29.1
First Boston	5.4	....	15.2	20.6
Merrill Lynch	...	3.6	16.9	20.5
Susquehanna Bkrg Svcs	10.6	....	8.0	18.6
W&D Securities	...	....	16.8	16.8
Lehman Brothers	1.9	3.0	7.7	12.6
Nomura Securities	6.5	....	5.2	11.7
Smith Barney	...	....	11.0	11.0
Goldman Sachs	...	....	8.8	8.8
Societe Generale	...	....	7.9	7.9
RBC Dominion	7.3	....	0.2	7.5
OVERALL TOTAL	**73.8**	**7.9**	**447.3**	**529.0**

*Other derivative-related strategies besides index arbitrage
Source: New York Stock Exchange

Figure 20.6

Index Arbitrage as a Form of Program Trading

Source: Reprinted by permission of *The Wall Street Journal*, Dow Jones & Company, Inc., October 10, 1997, p. C17.

the option is out of the money on the expiration date, then the options contract will be worthless and can be thrown away. However, with a futures contract, both parties involved must do something at the end of the life of the contract. The parties are obligated to complete the transaction, either by a reversing trade or by actual delivery.

Figure 20.7 contrasts the payoffs for the buyer and the seller of a call option with the payoff for the buyer and the seller of a futures contract. Specifically, payoffs for

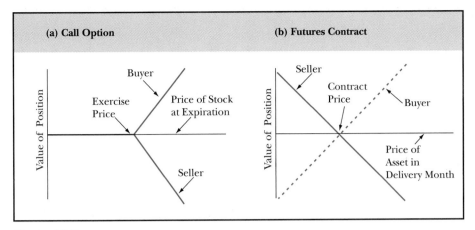

Figure 20.7
Terminal Values of Positions in Calls and Futures

buyers and sellers are shown at the last possible moment—the expiration date for the option and the delivery date for the futures contract.

As shown in Figure 20.7(a), no matter what the price of the underlying stock, an option buyer cannot lose and an option seller cannot gain on the expiration date. Option buyers compensate sellers for putting sellers in this position by paying them a premium when the contract is signed.

The situation is quite different with a futures contract. As shown in Figure 20.7(b), the buyer may gain or lose, depending on the price of the asset in the delivery month. Whatever the buyer gains or loses, an exactly offsetting loss or gain will be registered by the seller. The higher the contract price (that is, the price of the futures contract when the buyer purchased it from the seller), the greater the likelihood that the buyer will lose and the seller will gain. The lower the contract price, the greater the likelihood that the seller will lose and the buyer will gain.

20.10 SYNTHETIC FUTURES

For some assets, futures contracts are unavailable, but both put and call options are available. In such cases, an investor can create a **synthetic futures contract**.

The clearest example involves European options on common stocks. As shown in the previous chapter, the *purchase* of a European call option and the *sale* of a European put option at the same exercise price and with the same expiration date will provide a value at expiration that will be related, dollar for dollar, to the stock price at that time. This relation is shown in Figure 20.8.

Panel (a) shows the payoff associated with the purchase of a call at an exercise price E, whereas panel (b) shows the payoff associated with the sale of a put at the same exercise price. The results obtained by taking *both* positions are shown by the solid line in panel (c).

Depending on the prices (that is, premiums) of the call and the put, this strategy may initially either require a net outflow of cash or provide a net inflow. For comparability with the purchase of a futures contract, this cash flow may be offset with borrowing or lending as required to bring the net investment to zero. The dashed line in panel (c) shows a case in which the call option costs more than is provided by the sale of the put option. The difference is borrowed, requiring the loan repayment shown in the figure. The dashed line thus indicates the net end-of-period payoffs for a strategy requiring no initial outlay. Because these payoffs are equivalent to

Transportable Alpha

Years ago trustees of the multi-billion General Mills pension fund adopted a disciplined approach to allocating assets among various broad categories was accomplished by establishing specific long-run allocation targets: 60% to common stocks and 40% to fixed-income securities. The trustees believe that this *policy asset allocation* provides an optimal balance of expected return and risk, given their collective tolerance for possible adverse outcomes. The trustees expect the fund's staff, which handles the fund's day-to-day investment operations, to stick closely to this policy asset allocation. In turn, the staff follows a procedure of reducing exposure to any asset category that has appreciated in relative value and increasing exposure to any asset category that has depreciated in relative value.

To manage the pension fund's assets, the staff had retained what the trustees considered to be a superior group of domestic common stock managers. Over a ten-year period, those managers, in aggregate, had outperformed the S&P 500 by 1.5% annually (after all fees and expenses)—an exceptional amount by the standards of the investment management business. The trustees and staff expected such superior performance to continue in the future.

More recently the trustees found themselves facing a dilemma: The trustees would have liked to have assigned more than 60% of the fund's assets to the common stock managers. However, the trustees were also committed to the discipline of their asset allocation process. Could the trustees have their proverbial cake and eat it too? The answer was yes, through a concept called *transportable alpha.*

Consider three strategies through which General Mills could have maintained its policy asset allocation yet taken advantage of its common stock managers' skills. Each strategy involves allocating more than 60% of the pension fund's assets to the common stock managers, while simultaneously reducing the pension fund's common stock exposure and increasing its fixed-income exposure in order to comply with the fund's asset allocation targets.

1. *Long-short strategy.* The managers, in aggregate, purchase long positions in stocks as they typically would with their assigned assets. However, they also short sell stocks (see Chapter 2) equal in value to the pension fund's overweighting of domestic equity assets. The cash generated by these short sales is used to buy fixed-income securities that are held as margin but nevertheless provide returns through interest income and price changes. The particular long-short transactions result from the managers' investment research, which identifies under- and overpriced securities.

2. *Futures strategy.* The managers purchase long stock positions with their assigned assets. At the same time the pension fund's staff sells futures contracts on a stock market index and buys futures contracts on Treasury bonds in sufficient amounts to compensate for the over- and underweighting of common stocks and fixed-income securities, respectively.

3. *Swap strategy.* The managers purchase long stock positions with their assigned assets. Through a financial intermediary (such as a bank or a broker) the pension fund "swaps" (exchanges) with another institutional investor the return on a common stock index in order to receive the return on a fixed-income index. These swaps (see Chapter 23) are based on dollar amounts equal to the over- and underweightings of the common stocks and fixed-income securities, respectively.

In general, these strategies can be characterized as allowing the pension fund to earn (1) the total return generated by a 40% allocation to fixed-income securities, (2) the total return produced by a 60% allocation to common stocks (that is, the normal plus abnormal returns of the common stock managers), and (3) the abnormal returns earned by the common stock managers associated with the allocation in excess of 60% to common stocks. The common stock managers' abnormal returns (known as *alphas*) are effectively "transported" to the fixed-income asset category.

the payoffs from a futures contract with a contract price equal to F, a synthetic futures contract has been created.

In practice, the equivalence is not perfect. Most listed options are American, not European, raising the possibility that the buyer of the put will exercise it before ma-

In the final analysis, General Mills chose to implement the second strategy. The pension fund's staff believed that listed futures contracts provided the cheapest and administratively least cumbersome means of carrying out its alpha transport program. Nevertheless, the ability to customize the other strategies to specific situations may make those strategies attractive at times to certain institutional investors.

These strategies highlight fundamental changes in the financial markets that began in the 1980s and have rapidly gathered momentum in the 1990s. Through the development of derivative financial instruments (options, futures, and swaps) and the technological advancements in communications and computing power, financial markets have become highly integrated and fungible. Investors are increasingly able to exploit perceived profit opportunities and simultaneously maintain desired risk positions.

Pacific Investment Management Company (PIMCO) provides another example of the transportable alpha concept. PIMCO is one of the largest fixed-income managers in the world, with assets under management exceeding $120 billion. Over the years, the firm has produced an enviable track record, earning positive risk-adjusted returns under a variety of fixed-income investment assignments.

Since 1986, PIMCO has transported its fixed-income management skills to the U.S. stock market through a product called StocksPlus. PIMCO's process is simple. The firm purchases S&P 500 futures contracts equal to a specified *notional principal*. (Notional principal is the market exposure of the futures contracts; that is, the number of contracts purchased times the contracts' price times the contract multiplier.) At the same time PIMCO sets aside cash reserves equal to the notional principal. The cash reserves serve as collateral for the futures contracts.

As the text discusses, futures prices are set by investors on the assumption that they can hold a combination of futures contracts and the riskfree asset. PIMCO uses its investment skills to create a short-term fixed-income portfolio with the cash reserves that has substantially outperformed 90-day Treasury bills with little incremental risk. As a result, the firm's combination of S&P 500 futures contracts and short-term fixed-income investments has consistently exceeded the returns on the S&P 500.

PIMCO uses a variety of cash management strategies to add value relative to a portfolio of 90-day Treasury bills. The firm takes advantage of the most consistently upward-sloping portion of the yield curve—that is, maturities between zero days and one year. Because the StocksPlus strategy needs liquidity from only a small portion of its fixed-income portfolio to meet margin requirements, PIMCO extends roughly one-half of its portfolio to maturities past 90 days. Further, the firm accepts some credit risk by purchasing nongovernment securities such as commercial paper. PIMCO also takes advantage of certain securities that offer little credit risk but relatively high yields. At times these securities have included short-term tranches of collateralized mortgage obligations, floating-rate notes, and foreign government short-term securities (with currency risk fully hedged).

Transportable alpha involves investors' capturing inefficiencies in certain markets while maintaining desired exposure to markets beyond those in which the superior performance is earned. Transportable alpha is not a free lunch. Investors must pay commissions on their trades in stocks, options, futures, and swaps either directly or through bid-ask spreads. Real-world frictions such as collateral requirements and even custodial accounting difficulties still complicate the smooth implementation of the alpha transport strategies. Further, investors must take active management risk in order to earn their alphas. For example, General Mills's common stock managers, in aggregate, may underperform the stock market, or PIMCO's short-term portfolio may underperform 90-day Treasury bills. However, institutional investors applying the transportable alpha concept believe that their active management investment strategies possess sufficiently positive expected returns that more than compensate for the additional risk assumed.

turity. Moreover, the synthetic future is not marked to market on a daily basis. Despite these differences, the existence of well-functioning markets for call and put options will enable investors to synthetically create arrangements that have payoffs that are similar to those of futures on the underlying asset.

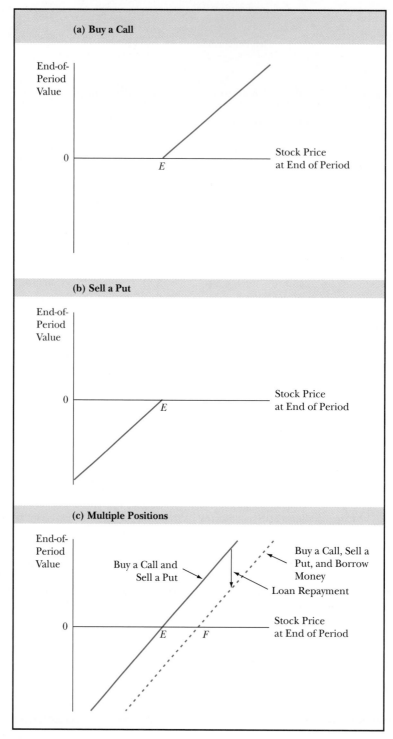

Figure 20.8
Creating a Synthetic Futures Contract

1. A futures contract involves the delivery of a specific type of asset at a specific location at a given future date.

2. People who buy and sell futures can be classified as either hedgers or speculators. Hedgers transact in futures primarily to reduce risk because these people either produce or use the asset in their ordinary course of business. Speculators transact in futures in pursuit of relatively short-term profits.

3. Futures are bought and sold on organized exchanges. Futures are standardized in terms of the type of asset, time of delivery, and place of delivery.

4. Each futures exchange has an associated clearinghouse that becomes the "seller's buyer" and the "buyer's seller" as soon as the trade is concluded.

5. A futures investor is required to deposit initial margin in order to guarantee fulfillment of his or her obligations.

6. A futures investor's account is marked to market daily, with the equity in the investor's account adjusted to reflect the change in the futures contract's settlement price.

7. A futures investor must maintain his or her account's equity equal to or greater than a certain percentage of the amount deposited as initial margin. If this requirement is not met, the investor will be requested to deposit variation margin in the account.

8. The basis for futures is the difference between the current spot price of the asset and the corresponding futures price.

9. There are three possible relationships between the current futures price and the expected spot price: the expectations hypothesis (futures price equal to expected spot price), normal backwardation (futures price less than expected spot price), and normal contango (futures price greater than expected spot price).

10. The current futures price should equal the current spot price plus the cost of carry. The cost of carry equals (1) the amount of interest that the owner forgoes by holding onto the asset less (2) the benefits of owning the asset plus (3) the costs of owning the asset.

11. If the price of a futures contract becomes too far removed from the current spot price of the asset plus the cost of carry, arbitrageurs will enter into transactions that generate riskless profits from the perceived price discrepancy. Their actions will cause prices to adjust until the opportunity to make such profits disappears.

QUESTIONS AND PROBLEMS

1. Distinguish between a speculator and a hedger. Give an example of a short hedger and a long hedger.

2. Using the latest *Wall Street Journal*, for the near futures contracts in corn, orange juice, and gasoline, calculate the percentage change in the settlement price from the previous day. Find the open interest in these contracts. Into how many units of the commodities do these open interest figures translate?

3. How do organized futures exchanges ensure that the obligations incurred as various parties enter into futures contracts are ultimately satisfied?

4. What is the purpose of initial and maintenance margins? How does marking to market affect the amount of funds held in the futures investor's margin account?

5. Chicken Wolf sells ten June 5000–bushel corn futures at $2 per bushel. Chicken deposits $5,000 in performance margin. If the price of corn rises to $2.20 per bushel, how much equity is in Chicken's margin account? What if corn falls to $1.80 per bushel?

6. Zack Wheat has just bought four September 5000–bushel corn futures contracts at $1.75 per bushel. The initial margin requirement is 3%. The maintenance margin requirement is 80% of the initial margin requirement.

   a. How many dollars in initial margin must Zack put up?

   b. If the September price of corn rises to $1.85, how much equity is in Zack's commodity account?

   c. If the September price of corn falls to $1.70, how much equity is in Zack's commodity account? Will Zack receive a margin call?

7. How does a futures contract differ from a forward contract?

8. Do exchange-imposed price limits protect futures traders from losses that would result in the absence of such limits? Explain.

9. Corky Withrow is long a stock market futures contract and short a diversified portfolio of stocks. Would Corky prefer the basis to widen or to narrow? Why?

10. A publication used by farmers such as Mordecai Brown provides diagrams of the typical annual patterns of cash prices for a number of seasonal commodities. Should Mordecai expect that the price of a futures contract will follow the same pattern? Why?

11. In the market for a particular agricultural or natural resource commodity, what kind of market forces might lead to normal backwardation or normal contango?

12. Consider a futures contract on mangoes that calls for the delivery of 2,000 pounds of the fruit three months from now. The spot price of mangoes is $2 per pound. The three-month riskfree rate is 2%. It costs $.10 per pound to store mangoes for three months. What should be the price of this futures contract?

13. Byrd Lynn owns a famous Renoir painting that has a current market value of $5,000,000. It costs Byrd $200,000 annually to insure the painting, payable at the start of the year. Byrd is able to loan the painting to a local art gallery for $300,000 per year, paid at the end of the year. Byrd is considering selling the painting under a futures contract arrangement that calls for delivery one year from today. If the one-year riskfree rate is 5%, what is the fair value of the futures contract?

14. Tuck Turner is planning a trip in six months to Germany, where Tuck plans to purchase a BMW for 80,000 German marks (DM). Using a recent *Wall Street Journal*, calculate how much the purchase would cost in U.S. dollars at the current exchange rate. Given the recent settlement price of a six-month DM futures contract, how much would Tuck have to pay to hedge the cost of the BMW purchase?

15. Assume that the exchange rate between British pounds and U.S. dollars is currently $1.80 per pound. If the six-month riskfree rate is 3% in the United States and 3.5% in Great Britain, what should the six-month futures price of U.S. dollars in British pounds be? Why is the futures exchange rate greater or less than the current spot exchange rate?

16. The one-year futures price of the Utopian currency darmas is $2.03 per darma. The interest forgone by selling darmas in the futures market instead of the spot market is $.0591. The benefit of owning darmas instead of selling them is $.0788. If the U.S. one-year riskfree rate is 3%, according to interest-rate parity, what should be the Utopian one-year riskfree rate?

17. What should be the price of a three-month 90-day Treasury bill futures contract if the spot price of a six-month Treasury bill is currently $98 and the three-month riskfree rate is 1%?

18. Estel Crabtree believes that the spread between long-term and short-term interest rates is going to narrow in the next few months but does not know in which direction interest rates in general will move. What financial futures position would permit Estel to profit from this forecast if it is correct?

19. Sleeper Sullivan bought ten S&P 500 December futures contracts at 310. If the S&P 500 index rises to 318, what is Sleeper's dollar profit?

20. Why does hedging a common stock portfolio using stock index futures work best if the portfolio being hedged is very similar to the underlying stock index of the futures contract?

21. Assume that the S&P 500 currently has a value of 200 (in "index" terms). The dividend yield on the underlying stocks in the index is expected to be 4% over the next six months. New-issue six-month Treasury bills now sell for a six-month yield of 6%.

    a. What is the theoretical value of a six-month futures contract on the S&P 500?

    b. What potential problems are inherent in this calculation?

22. In December 19X1 Granny Hamner bought a January 19X2 gold futures contract on the New York Commodity Exchange for $487.50 per ounce. Simultaneously, Granny sold an October 19X3 contract for $614.80. At the time, yields on Treasury notes with 1.75 years to maturity were 10.50%. Will this transaction be profitable for Granny? What factors are relevant to making this calculation?

23. In each of the following situations, discuss how Hippo Vaughn might use stock index futures to protect a well-diversified stock portfolio:

    a. Hippo expects to receive a sizable bonus check next month and would like to invest in stocks, believing that current stock market prices are extremely attractive (but realizing they may not remain so for long).

    b. Hippo expects the stock market to decline dramatically very soon and realizes that selling a stock portfolio quickly would result in significant transaction costs.

    c. Hippo has a large, unrealized gain and for tax purposes would like to defer the gain until the next tax year, which is several weeks away.

24. Does the fair value of a stock index futures contract depend on investors' expectations about the future value of the underlying stock index? Why?

25. Swats Swacina, a futures investor who has lost considerable sums in futures investments, said, "Even though I don't directly borrow to invest in futures, the performance of my investments acts as if I were highly leveraged." Is Swats correct? Why?

26. (Appendix Question) Distinguish between futures contracts and options on futures contracts.

27. (Appendix Question) Pinky Swander buys a call option on a March 5000–bushel soybean futures contract. The call costs $.50 per bushel and has an exercise price of $5.25 per bushel. If Pinky exercises the option in February at a price of $5.55 per bushel, what is Pinky's return on investment in the option?

CFA EXAM QUESTIONS

28. Robert Chen, CFA, is reviewing the characteristics of derivative securities and their use in portfolios.

    a. Chen is considering the addition of either a short position in stock index futures or a long position in stock index (put) options to an existing well-diversified portfolio of equity securities. Contrast the way in which each of these two alternatives would affect the risk and return of the resulting combined portfolios.

    b. Four factors affect the value of a futures contract on a stock index. Three of these factors are the current price of the stock index, the time remaining until the contract maturity (delivery) date, and the dividends on the stock index. Identify the fourth factor and explain how and why changes in this factor affect the value of the futures contract.

    c. Six factors affect the value of call options on stocks. Three of these factors are the current price of the stock, the time remaining until the option expires, and the dividend on the stock. Identify the other three factors and explain how and why changes in each of these three factors affect the value of call options.

29. The foundation's grant-making and investment policy issues have been finalized. Receipt of the expected $45 million Franklin cash gift will not occur for 90 days, yet the committee believes current stock and bond prices are unusually attractive and wishes to take advantage of this perceived opportunity.

   a. Briefly describe two strategies that utilize derivative financial instruments and could be implemented to take advantage of the committee's market expectations.

   b. Evaluate whether it is appropriate for the foundation to undertake a derivatives-based hedge to bridge the expected 90-day time gap, considering both positive and negative factors.

APPENDIX

FUTURES OPTIONS

The previous chapter described options, and this chapter has described futures. Interestingly, there are contracts currently in existence that are known as **futures options** (or options on futures). As might be expected, these contracts are, in a sense, combinations of futures and options contracts. In particular, a futures option is an option in which the underlying asset is a specific futures contract, with the expiration date on the option normally being shortly before the delivery date on the futures contract.[23] Figure 20.9 provides a set of quotations on some of the more frequently traded ones. As the figure shows, there are both put and call options on futures. Thus an investor can be either a buyer or a writer of either a put or a call option on a futures contract.[24]

CALL OPTIONS ON FUTURES CONTRACTS

If a call option on a futures contract is exercised, then the writer must deliver the appropriate futures contract to the buyer; that is, the writer must assume a short position in the futures contract while the buyer assumes the long position. For example, consider the buyer of a call option on May corn futures where the exercise price is 300 (that is, $3) per bushel. Because the futures contract is for 5,000 bushels, the total exercise price is $15,000 ($=5,000 \times \$3$). If the buyer purchased this option at the settle price on October 8, 1997, which is given in Figure 20.9, then the buyer would have paid the writer a premium of $18\frac{3}{8}$ (that is, $.18375) per bushel, or $918.75 ($=5,000 \times \$.18375$) in total.

FUTURES OPTIONS PRICES

Wednesday, October 8, 1997.

AGRICULTURAL

CORN (CBT)
5,000 bu.; cents per bu.

Strike Price	Calls-Settle Dec	Mar	May	Puts-Settle Dec	Mar	May
260	25¼	34½	40⅜	2½	3½	4½
270	17⅜	27	33¼	4¾	6¼	7
280	11¼	21½	27	8⅝	10	10
290	7	16½	21¾	14½	15	14¾
300	4⅜	12¾	18⅜	21½	21	20¾
310	2½	9½	15	29¾	27¾	....

Est vol 30,000 Tu 17,855 calls 18,430 puts
Op int Tues 221,814 calls 203,566 puts

SOYBEANS (CBT)
5,000 bu.; cents per bu.

Strike Price	Calls-Settle Nov	Jan	Mar	Puts-Settle Nov	Jan	Mar
625	44⅞	52½	62	2⅝	7¼	11
650	24⅛	35	46½	6⅞	14½	20
675	10½	22¾	34	18	27	32
700	4⅛	14¼	24½	36⅝	43	47
725	1¾	8¾	18	59	63	65
750	⅞	5½	12	83	....	....

Est vol 30,000 Tu 24,480 calls 25,318 puts
Op int Tues 158,720 calls 131,323 puts

OIL

CRUDE OIL (NYM)
1,000 bbls.; $ per bbl.

Strike Price	Calls-Settle Nov	Dec	Jan	Puts-Settle Nov	Dec	Jan
2100	1.31	1.59	1.65	.13	.46	.69
2150	.94	1.27	1.37	.26	.64	.90
2200	.63	.99	1.11	.45	.86	1.14
2250	.39	.77	.91	.71	1.14	....
2300	.24	.59	.73	1.06	1.46	....
2350	.14	.44	.59	1.46	....	....

Est vol 44,853 Tu 20,935 calls 13,099 puts
Op int Tues 282,491 calls 191,174 puts

METALS

COPPER (CMX)
25,000 lbs.; cents per lb.

Strike Price	Calls-Settle Nov	Dec	Jan	Puts-Settle Nov	Dec	Jan
90	4.60	6.05	6.75	.85	1.80	2.25
92	3.25	4.75	5.55	1.50	2.50	3.05
94	2.15	3.75	4.50	2.40	3.50	3.95
96	1.35	2.70	3.60	3.60	4.45	5.00
98	.80	2.10	2.80	5.05	5.85	6.25
100	.45	1.50	2.20	6.65	7.25	7.60

Est vol 300 Tu 320 calls 39 puts
Op int Tues 7,715 calls 2,802 puts

GOLD (CMX)
100 troy ounces; $ per troy ounce

Strike Price	Calls-Settle Nov	Dec	Feb	Puts-Settle Nov	Dec	Feb
325	10.50	11.90	14.50	.20	1.60	2.90
330	5.70	8.00	10.20	.40	2.70	4.10
335	1.80	4.80	8.20	1.50	4.50	6.20
340	.50	3.00	5.30	5.10	7.70	10.10
345	.20	1.70	3.60	9.90	11.40	11.40
350	.10	1.00	2.60	14.70	15.70	16.30

Est vol 4,000 Tu 3,553 calls 942 puts
Op int Tues 307,846 calls 124,693 puts

INTEREST RATE

T-BONDS (CBT)
$100,000; points and 64ths of 100%

Strike Price	Calls-Settle Nov	Dec	Mar	Puts-Settle Nov	Dec	Mar
113	3-01	....	....	0-07	....	....
114	2-09	2-32	3-26	0-15	0-38	1-53
115	1-26	....	....	0-32	....	....
116	0-53	1-18	2-23	0-59	1-24	2-49
117	0-27	....	....	1-33	....	....
118	0-11	0-34	1-36	2-17	2-40	....

Est. vol. 260,000;
Tu vol. 71,872 calls; 52,430 puts
Op. int. Tues 659,726 calls; 416,052 puts

EURODOLLAR (CME)
$ million; pts. of 100%

Strike Price	Calls-Settle Oct	Nov	Dec	Puts-Settle Oct	Nov	Dec
9375	0.44	....	0.44	0.00	0.00	0.00
9400	0.20	0.20	0.21	0.01	0.01	0.02
9425	0.00	0.02	0.03	0.07	0.08	0.09
9450	0.00	0.00	0.00	....	....	0.31
9475	....	....	0.00	....	....	0.56
9500	....	....	0.00	....	....	0.81

Est. vol. 244,657;
Tu vol. 62,195 calls; 37,324 puts
Op. int. Tues 1,229,825 calls; 1,223,-667 puts

INDEX

DJ INDUSTRIAL AVG (CBOT)
$100 times premium

Strike Price	Calls-Settle Nov	Dec	Mar	Puts-Settle Nov	Dec	Mar
80	32.00	39.00	59.00	16.15	23.15	....
81	25.70	32.75	....	19.70	27.00	....
82	20.10	27.25	....	24.15	31.50	....
83	15.25	22.50	....	....	....	....
84	11.25	18.40	....	....	....	....
85	8.00	14.60	33.00	....	....	....

Est vol 2,000 Tu 1,338 calls 1,635 puts
Op int Tues 2,869 calls 3,531 puts

S&P 500 STOCK INDEX (CME)
$500 times premium

Strike Price	Calls-Settle Oct	Nov	Dec	Puts-Settle Oct	Nov	Dec
970	19.05	32.70	41.10	6.70	20.45	28.90
975	15.60	29.60	38.15	8.25	22.30	30.90
980	12.45	26.65	35.35	10.10	24.30	33.00
985	9.65	23.95	32.65	12.30	26.45	35.25
990	7.30	21.35	30.10	14.95	28.85	37.65
995	5.25	18.90	27.65	17.90	31.45	....

Est vol 13,758 Tu 6,723 calls 7,456 puts
Op int Tues 54,658 calls 125,559 puts

CURRENCY

JAPANESE YEN (CME)
12,500,000 yen; cents per 100 yen

Strike Price	Calls-Settle Nov	Dec	Jan	Puts-Settle Nov	Dec	Jan
8250	1.54	1.95	....	0.74	1.16	....
8300	1.25	1.68	....	0.95	1.38	....
8350	1.00	1.42	....	1.20	1.62	....
8400	0.79	1.21	....	1.49	1.90	....
8450	0.62	1.02	....	1.81	2.21	....
8500	0.49	0.85	....	2.18	2.53	....

Est vol 6,643 Tu 4,568 calls 2,347 puts
Op int Tues 39,866 calls 35,692 puts

DEUTSCHEMARK (CME)
125,000 marks; cents per mark

Strike Price	Calls-Settle Nov	Dec	Jan	Puts-Settle Nov	Dec	Jan
5650	1.24	1.43	....	0.31	0.51	....
5700	0.90	1.13	....	0.47	0.70	....
5750	0.63	0.88	....	0.70	0.95	....
5800	0.43	0.68	....	....	1.24	....
5850	0.28	0.51	....	....	....	....
5900	0.18	0.37	....	....	1.93	....

Est vol 2,432 Tu 984 calls 1,323 puts
Op int Tues 30,041 calls 39,017 puts

Figure 20.9
Quotations for Futures Options (Excerpts)

Source: Reprinted by permission of *The Wall Street Journal*, Dow Jones & Company, Inc., October 9, 1997, p. C17.

Now if the buyer subsequently decides to exercise this option, then the writer of this option must deliver a May corn futures contract to the buyer. Furthermore, this futures contract will be fully marked to market at the time it is delivered. In the example, assume that the option is exercised in February when May corn futures are selling for $4 per bushel. In February the call writer must provide the call buyer with a May corn futures contract that has a delivery price of $3 which has been marked to market. This can be accomplished in two steps. First, the writer must purchase a May corn futures contract and deliver it to the call buyer. Because the cost of the futures will be $4 per bushel (the current market price of May corn futures), this purchase is costless to the call writer. Second, the futures contract that has been delivered must be marked to market, which is done by having the call writer pay the call buyer an amount of cash equal to $1 (=$4 − $3) per bushel, or $5,000 (=5,000 × $1) in aggregate. Thus the call writer has lost $4,081.25 (=$5,000 − $918.75) while the call buyer has made an equivalent amount.

Whereas this example has shown what happens when the call is exercised, it should be noted that most futures options are not exercised. Instead, just as with most options and futures, buyers and writers of futures options typically make reversing trades before the expiration date.

A.2   PUT OPTIONS ON FUTURES CONTRACTS

If a put option on a futures contract is exercised, then the writer must accept delivery of the appropriate futures contract from the buyer; that is, the writer must assume a long position in the futures contract while the buyer assumes the short position. For example, consider the buyer of a put option on May corn where the exercise price is 300, meaning $3 per bushel or $15,000 in total because the futures contract is for 5,000 bushels. If the buyer purchased this put at the settlement price on October 8, 1997 that is given in Figure 20.9, then the buyer would have paid the writer a premium of $20\frac{3}{4}$ per bushel, or $1,037.50 (=5,000 × $.2075) in total.

Now if the buyer subsequently decides to exercise this option, then the writer of this option must accept delivery of a May corn futures contract from the buyer. Furthermore, this futures contract must be fully marked to market at the time it is delivered. In the example, assume that the option is exercised in April when May corn futures are selling for $2 per bushel. In April the put buyer will become the seller of a May corn futures contract where the purchase price is $2 per bushel. That is, when this contract is marked to market, the put writer must pay the put buyer an amount of cash equal to $1 (=$3 − $2) per bushel, or $5,000 (=5,000 × $1) in aggregate. Thus the put writer has lost $3,962.50 (=$5,000 − $1,037.50), whereas the put buyer has made an equivalent amount.

Again, it should be kept in mind that most put options on futures are not exercised. Instead, these option buyers and writers typically enter reversing trades at some time before the expiration date.

In summary, the positions of futures options buyers and writers in the futures contracts upon exercise by the buyer are as follows:

	Buyer	Seller
Call	Long	Short
Put	Short	Long

As mentioned earlier, neither a writer nor a buyer needs to maintain his or her position. Both are free to enter into offsetting trades at any time, even after the buyer has exercised the option (but then the offsetting trade would be made in the futures market).

A.3 COMPARISON WITH FUTURES

At this point it is worthwhile to think about the distinctions between futures and futures options. In doing so, consider an investor who is contemplating *buying* a futures contract. If this contract is purchased, the investor can potentially make or lose a great deal of money. In particular, if the price of the asset rises substantially, then so will the price of the futures, and the investor will have made a sizable profit. In contrast, if the price of the asset drops substantially, then the investor will have lost a sizable amount of money.

In comparison, if the investor had bought a futures call option on the asset, then the investor would also make a sizable profit if the price of the asset rose substantially. Unlike with futures, however, if the price of the asset dropped, then the investor need not worry about incurring a sizable loss. Instead, only the premium (the price paid to buy the futures option) would be lost. Nevertheless, purchasing a futures call option is not a better (or worse) strategy than purchasing a futures contract. Why? Because the protection on the downside that an investor gets from buying a futures call option is paid for in the form of the premium. This premium would not be present if the investor had bought a futures contract instead.

Consider next an investor who is contemplating *selling* a futures contract. In doing so, the investor can potentially make a great deal of money if the price of the asset declines substantially. However, if the price of the asset rises substantially, then the investor will have lost a sizable amount of money.

In comparison, the investor could buy a futures put option on the asset. In this case, the investor would make a sizable profit if the price of the asset declined substantially. However, if the price of the asset rose, then the investor need not worry about incurring a sizable loss. Instead, only the premium would be lost. Again, this does not mean that purchasing a futures put option is better (or worse) strategy than selling a futures contract.

A.4 COMPARISON WITH OPTIONS

Having established that futures options can exist if futures already exist, one may wonder why futures options exist if options already exist. The commonly given reason why futures options exist in such a situation is that it is easier to make or take delivery of a futures contract on the asset as required by the futures options contract than to make or take delivery in the asset itself as required by the options contract. In addition, there is sometimes more timely price information on the deliverable asset for the futures option contract (namely, price information on the futures contract) than on the deliverable asset for the options contract (namely, price information in the spot market). For these reasons (although they are not compelling for certain contracts), futures, futures options, and options can exist simultaneously with the same underlying asset.

ENDNOTES

[1] The term *commodity futures* is often used to refer to futures on agricultural goods and natural resources. The term *financial futures* is typically used in reference to futures on financial instruments such as Treasury bonds, foreign currencies, and stock market indices.

[2] For a relatively complete description of the terms for many exchange-traded futures contracts, see the *Commodity Trading Manual* (Chicago Board of Trade, 1989); and Malcolm J. Robertson, *Directory of World Futures and Options* (Upper Saddle River, NJ: Prentice Hall, 1990). These two books also contain descriptions of various futures exchanges.

[3] Since Black Monday and Terrible Tuesday (October 19 and 20, 1987), a number of people have advocated an increase in the size of the initial margin deposit for certain futures contracts (particularly stock index futures, which will be discussed later). The levels of initial and maintenance margins are set by each exchange, with brokers being allowed to set them higher. Typically, higher amounts of margin are required on futures contracts that have greater price volatility because the clearinghouse faces larger potential losses on such contracts.

[4] Actually, only brokerage firms belong to a clearinghouse, and it is *their* accounts that are settled by the clearinghouse at the end of every day. Each brokerage firm acts in turn as a clearinghouse for its own clients. For more information on clearing procedures, see Chapter 6 of the *Commodity Trading Manual.*

[5] Interestingly, it has been observed that typically the volatility of the futures price changes increases as the contract approaches its delivery date. This phenomenon is known as the "Samuelson hypothesis"; see Paul A. Samuelson, "Proof That Properly Anticipated Prices Fluctuate Randomly," *Industrial Management Review* 6, no. 2 (Spring 1965): 41–49. Also see Hendrik Bessembinder, Jay F. Coughenour, Paul J. Seguin, and Margaret Monroe Smoller, "Is There a Term Structure of Futures Volatilities? Reevaluating the Samuelson Hypothesis," *Journal of Derivatives* 4, no. 2 (Winter 1996): 45–58.

[6] Merrill Lynch, Pierce, Fenner & Smith, Inc., *Speculating on Inflation: Futures Trading in Interest Rates, Foreign Currencies and Precious Metals,* July 1979.

[7] For more on the relationship between spot and futures prices as reflected in the basis, see the *Commodity Trading Manual*, Chapter 8. Sometimes basis is defined as the futures price less the current spot price—the reverse of what is shown in Equation (20.1).

[8] The futures contracts consisted of agricultural goods and natural resources. See Zvi Bodie and Victor Rosansky, "Risk and Return in Commodity Futures," *Financial Analysts Journal* 36, no. 3 (May/June 1980): 27–39. Similar conclusions were reached when the period from 1978 to 1981 was examined. See Cheng F. Lee, Raymond M. Leuthold, and Jean E. Cordier, "The Stock Market and the Commodity Futures Market: Diversification and Arbitrage Potential," *Financial Analysts Journal* 41, no. 4 (July/August 1985): 53–60.

[9] These first two points do not mean that the current spot price will not change as time passes. For futures involving a seasonal commodity (such as wheat), the spot price will sometimes be greater than and sometimes be less than the futures price during the life of the contract. Furthermore, sometimes a futures contract involving a more distant delivery date will sell for more than one with a nearer delivery date, whereas at other times it will sell for less.

[10] J. M. Keynes, *Treatise on Money*, vol. 2 (London: Macmillan, 1930), 142–144.

[11] There are other hypotheses regarding the relationship between futures prices and expected spot prices. See, for example, Paul H. Cootner, "Speculation and Hedging," Stanford University, *Food Research Institute Studies*, Supplement, 1967.

[12] This section and the next one borrow from Kenneth R. French, "Pricing Financial Futures Contracts: An Introduction," *Journal of Applied Corporate Finance* 1, no. 4 (Winter 1989): 59–66. It ignores the apparently minor effect that daily marking to market has on the futures price that is stated in futures contracts (see p. 65 and footnotes 5 and 6 in French's paper).

[13] The prices of foreign currency forward and futures contracts appear to be quite similar. See Bradford Cornell and Marc Reinganum, "Forward and Futures Prices: Evidence from the Foreign Exchange Market," *Journal of Finance* 36, no. 5 (December 1981): 1035–1045. Their findings are challenged by Michael A. Polakoff and Paul C. Grier, "A Comparison of Foreign Exchange Forward and Futures Prices," *Journal of Banking and Finance* 15, no. 6 (December 1991): 1057–1079, but they are supported by Carolyn W. Chang and Jack S. K. Chang, "Forward and Futures Prices: Evidence from the Foreign Exchange Markets," *Jour-*

nal of Finance 45, no. 4 (September 1990): 1333–1336. See Kenneth R. French, "A Comparison of Futures and Forward Prices," *Journal of Financial Economics* 12, no. 3 (November 1983): 311–342 for a discussion of the difficulties encountered when testing to see whether the prices of forward and futures contracts are similar.

[14] Actually the typical speculator will plan to realize this profit by entering a reversing trade instead of buying yen on the spot market and then making delivery. Similarly, the previously mentioned hedging importer will typically plan to enter a reversing trade.

[15] See Chapter 5 for a discussion of term structure and forward rates.

[16] Delivery on Treasury bond futures can take place on any business day in the delivery month even though the trading ceases when there are seven business days left in the month.

[17] For this and certain other interest-rate futures contracts there is flexibility in just what the seller has to deliver, known as the *quality option*. The short position in the contract will usually decide on the *cheapest-to-deliver* Treasury bond and will deliver it to the long position. Sometimes there is also some flexibility regarding when during a business day that an intention to deliver must be announced, known as the *wild card option*.

[18] Similarly, interest-rate futures are often used by financial institutions to hedge interest-rate risk to which they may be exposed; that is, when a large movement in interest rates would cause a large loss, these institutions will seek protection by either buying or selling interest-rate futures.

[19] The 3% dividend yield is actually the accumulated December value of the dividends divided by the purchase price of the stocks. Hence the dividends might be received in three months and amount to 2.93% of the purchase price of the index. Putting them in a riskfree asset that returns 2.47% for the last three months results in a yield of 3%, or $3, in December.

[20] Index arbitrage is one of two major forms of program trading. The other form, known as portfolio insurance, was discussed in the previous chapter. For a discussion and example of how futures can be used to procure portfolio insurance, see Stephen R. King and Eli M. Remolona, "The Pricing and Hedging of Market Index Deposits," *Federal Reserve Bank of New York Quarterly Review* 12, no. 2 (Summer 1987): 9–20; or Thomas J. O'Brien, *How Option Replicating Portfolio Insurance Works: Expanded Details*, Monograph Series in Finance and Economics, 1988-4 (New York University Salomon Center, Leonard N. Stern School of Business, 1988).

[21] People involved in index arbitrage need to be able to quickly make a large number of transactions in individual stocks. In order to do this, they often have their computers send in their orders through the SuperDOT system (discussed in Chapter 3). For a discussion of some of the complications involved in successfully executing index arbitrage strategies, see David M. Modest, "On the Pricing of Stock Index Futures," *Journal of Portfolio Management* 10, no. 4 (Summer 1984): 51–57.

[22] Adding to the confusion is the existence of a contract known as a futures option, which is an option that has a futures contract instead of a stock as its underlying asset. Futures options are discussed in more detail in the appendix.

[23] The near-simultaneous quarterly expiration of (1) options on individual stocks and market indices, (2) futures on market indices, and (3) options on market index futures has been referred to as the **triple witching hour**. When it occurs, the stock market is allegedly roiled, particularly in the latter part of the day. See Hans R. Stoll and Robert E. Whaley, "Program Trading and Expiration Day Effects," *Financial Analysts Journal* 43, no. 2 (March/April 1987): 16–28; Arnold Kling, "How the Stock Market Can Learn to Live with Index Futures and Options," *Financial Analysts Journal* 43, no. 5 (September/October 1987): 33–39; and G. J. Santoni, "Has Programmed Trading Made Stock Prices More Volatile?" *Federal Reserve Bank of St. Louis Review* 69, no. 5 (May 1987): 18–29.

[24] For more on futures options, see Chapter 12 of the *Commodity Trading Manual*. For a computer program that can be used to determine the "true" value of these complex contracts, see Chapter 8 of Stuart M. Turnbull, *Option Valuation* (Holt, Rinehart and Winston of Canada, 1987).

futures
speculators
hedgers
spot market
spot price
short hedger
long hedger
reversing trade
settle
open interest
futures commission merchant
locals
performance margin
marking to market
variation margin

Commodity Futures Trading
    Commission
basis
basis risk
expectations hypothesis
normal backwardation
normal contango
cost of carry
interest-rate parity
arbitrageurs
index arbitrage
synthetic futures contract
futures options
triple witching hour

REFERENCES

1. Many books either are devoted exclusively to futures or have futures as one of their primary subjects. Most cover everything discussed in this chapter in more detail and with a more complete list of citations. Here are a few:

Stephen Figlewski, *Hedging with Financial Futures for Institutional Investors* (Cambridge, MA: Ballinger, 1986).

Edward W. Schwarz, Joanne M. Hill, and Thomas Schneeweis, *Financial Futures* (Homewood, IL: Richard D. Irwin, 1986).

Commodity Trading Manual (Chicago: Chicago Board of Trade, 1989).

Darrell Duffie, *Futures Markets* (Englewood Cliffs, NJ: Prentice Hall, 1989).

Daniel R. Siegel and Diane F. Siegel, *Futures Markets* (Hinsdale, IL: Dryden Press, 1990).

Alan L. Tucker, *Financial Futures, Options, & Swaps* (St. Paul, MN: West, 1991).

David A. Dubofsky, *Options and Financial Futures* (New York: McGraw-Hill, 1992).

Hans R. Stoll and Robert E. Whaley, *Futures and Options* (Cincinnati: South-Western Publishing, 1993).

Robert T. Daigler, *Financial Futures and Markets: Concepts and Strategies* (New York: Harper-Collins, 1994).

Robert W. Kolb, *Understanding Futures Markets* (Miami, FL: Kolb, 1994).

Don M. Chance, *An Introduction to Derivatives* (Fort Worth: Dryden Press, 1995).

Fred D. Arditti, *Derivatives* (Boston: Harvard Business School Press, 1996).

Robert Jarrow and Stuart Turnbull, *Derivative Securities* (Cincinnati: South-Western Publishing, 1996).

John C. Hull, *Options, Futures, and Other Derivative Securities* (Upper Saddle River, NJ: Prentice Hall, 1997).

2. For a discussion of the market structure of futures exchanges, see:

Sanford J. Grossman and Merton H. Miller, "Liquidity and Market Structure," *Journal of Finance* 43, no. 3 (July 1988): 617–633.

Michael J. Fishman and Francis A. Longstaff, "Dual Trading in Futures Markets," *Journal of Finance* 47, no. 2 (June 1992): 643–671.

3. For a more complete discussion of margin and marking to market, see:

Robert W. Kolb, Gerald D. Gay, and William C. Hunter, "Liquidity Requirements for Financial Futures Investments," *Financial Analysts Journal* 41, no. 3 (May/June 1985): 60–68.

Don M. Chance *The Effect of Margins on the Volatility of Stock and Derivative Markets: A Review of the Evidence* Monograph Series in Finance and Economics 1990–2 (New York University Salomon Center, Leonard N. Stern School of Business, 1990).

Ann Kremer, "Clarifying Marking to Market," *Journal of Financial Education* 20 (November 1991): 17–25.

4. The concepts of spreads and basis are discussed in:

Martin L. Leibowitz *The Analysis of Value and Volatility in Financial Futures* Monograph Series in Finance and Economics 1981–3 (New York University Salomon Center, Leonard N. Stern School of Business, 1981).

5. Foreign currency markets are discussed in:

J. Orlin Grabbe *International Financial Markets* (Upper Saddle River, NJ: Prentice Hall, 1996), Part 2.

6. Interest-rate futures were shown to be useful in immunizing bond portfolios by:

Robert W. Kolb and Gerald D. Gay, "Immunizing Bond Portfolios with Interest Rate Futures," *Financial Management* 11, no. 2 (Summer 1982): 81–89.

Jess B. Yawitz and William J. Marshall, "The Use of Futures in Immunized Portfolios," *Journal of Portfolio Management* 11, no. 2 (Spring 1985): 51–58.

7. Using futures to hedge bond portfolios is discussed in:

Richard Bookstaber and David P. Jacob, "The Composite Hedge: Controlling the Credit Risk of High-Yield Bonds," *Financial Analysts Journal* 42, no. 2 (March/April 1986): 25–35.

Robin Grieves, "Hedging Corporate Bond Portfolios," *Journal of Portfolio Management* 12, no. 4 (Summer 1986): 23–25.

8. Stock index futures and their relationship to the market crash in October 1987 have been heavily researched. Some of the papers are:

Paula A. Tosini, "Stock Index Futures and Stock Market Activity in October 1987," *Financial Analysts Journal* 44, no. 1 (January/February 1988): 28–37.

F. J. Gould, "Stock Index Futures: The Arbitrage Cycle and Portfolio Insurance," *Financial Analysts Journal* 44, no. 1 (January/February 1988): 48–62.

Lawrence Harris, "The October 1987 S&P 500 Stock–Futures Basis," *Journal of Finance* 44, no. 1 (March 1989): 77–99.

Marshall E. Blume, A. Craig MacKinlay, and Bruce Terker, "Order Imbalances and Stock Price Movements on October 19 and 20, 1987," *Journal of Finance* 44, no. 4 (September 1989): 827–848.

Lawrence Harris, "S&P 500 Cash Stock Price Volatilities," *Journal of Finance* 44, no. 5 (December 1989): 1155–1175.

Hans R. Stoll and Robert E. Whaley, "The Dynamics of Stock Index and Stock Index Futures Returns," *Journal of Financial and Quantitative Analysis* 25, no. 4 (December 1990): 441–468.

Kolak Chan, K. C. Chan, and G. Andrew Karolyi, "Intraday Volatility in the Stock Index and Stock Index Futures Markets," *Review of Financial Studies* 4, no. 4 (1991): 657–684.

Avanidhar Subrahmanyam, "A Theory of Trading in Stock Index Futures," *Review of Financial Studies* 4, no. 1 (1991): 17–51.

Kolak Chan, "A Further Analysis of the Lead–Lag Relationship between the Cash Market and Stock Index Futures Market," *Review of Financial Studies* 5, no. 1 (1992): 123–152.

9. Papers on index arbitrage and program trading include:

A. Craig MacKinlay and Krishna Ramaswamy, "Index-Futures Arbitrage and the Behavior of Stock Index Futures Prices," *Review of Financial Studies* 1, no. 2 (Summer 1988): 137–158.

Michael J. Brennan and Eduardo S. Schwartz, "Arbitrage in Stock Index Futures," *Journal of Business* 63, no. 1, part 2 (January 1990): S7–S31.

Hans R. Stoll and Robert E. Whaley, "Program Trading and Individual Stock Returns: Ingredients of the Triple–Witching Brew," *Journal of Business* 63, no. 1, part 2 (January 1990): S165–S192.

Gary L. Gastineau, "A Short History of Program Trading," *Financial Analysts Journal* 47, no. 5 (September/October 1991): 4–7.

10. Forward and futures prices were shown to be equal when interest rates are constant over time in:

John C. Cox, Jonathan E. Ingersoll, and Stephen A. Ross, "The Relation between Forward Prices and Futures Prices," *Journal of Financial Economics* 9, no. 4 (December 1981): 320–346.

11. The performance of commodity funds, which are investment companies that speculate in futures, has not been attractive, according to:

Edwin J. Elton, Martin J. Gruber, and Joel C. Rentzler, "Professionally Managed, Publicly Traded Commodity Funds," *Journal of Business* 60, no. 2 (April 1987): 175–199.

12. Construction and performance of the Goldman Sachs Commodity Index is described in:

Scott L. Lummer and Lauence B. Siegel, "GSCI Collateralized Futures: A Hedging and Diversification Tool for Institutional Portfolios," *Journal of Investing* 2, no. 2 (Summer 1993): 75–82.

13. The relationships among futures, options, and futures options are discussed in:

Clifford W. Smith Jr., Charles W. Smithson, and D. Sykes Wilford, "Managing Financial Risk," *Journal of Applied Corporate Finance* 1, no. 4 (Winter 1989): 27–48.

Charles W. Smithson, Clifford W. Smith Jr., and D. Sykes Wilford *Managing Financial Risk: A Guide to Derivative Products, Financial Engineering, and Value Maximization* (Homewood, IL: Irwin Professional Publishing, 1995).

14. The seminal paper on the pricing of futures options is:

Fischer Black, "The Pricing of Commodity Contracts," *Journal of Financial Economics* 3, nos. 1/2 (January/March 1976): 167–179.

15. For a thought–provoking book that covers futures markets, among other subjects, see:

Merton H. Miller *Financial Innovations and Market Volatility* (Cambridge, MA: Blackwell, 1991).

16. The various exchanges where futures are traded all have Web sites containing useful information about their products:

Chicago Board of Trade: <www.cbot.com>.

Chicago Mercantile Exchange: <www.cme.com>.

Coffee, Sugar & Cocoa Exchange: <www.csce.com>.

Kansas City Board of Trade: <www.kcbt.com>.

MidAmerica Commodity Exchange: <www.midam.com>.

Minneapolis Grain Exchange: <www.mgex.com>.

New York Cotton Exchange/New York Futures Exchange: <www.nyce.com>.

New York Mercantile Exchange/Commodity Exchange: <www.nymex.com>.

17. The Commodity Futures Trading Commission, the federal regulator of trading in futures contracts that was established in 1974, has a Web site at:

<www.cftc.gov>.

INVESTMENT COMPANIES

Investment companies are a type of financial intermediary. They obtain money from investors and use it to purchase financial assets such as stocks and bonds. In return, the investors receive certain rights regarding the financial assets that the investment company has bought and any earnings that the company may generate. In the simplest and most common situation, the investment company has only one type of investor—stockholders. These stockholders own the investment company directly and thus own indirectly the financial assets that the company itself owns.

For an individual there are two advantages to investing in such companies instead of investing directly in the financial assets that these companies own. Specifically, the advantages arise from (1) economies of scale and (2) professional management. Consider an individual with moderate financial resources who wishes to invest in the stock market. In terms of economies of scale, the individual could buy stocks in odd lots and thus have a diversified portfolio. However, the brokerage commissions on odd lot transactions are relatively high. Alternatively, the individual could purchase round lots but would be able to afford only a few different securities. Unfortunately the individual would then be giving up the benefits of owning a well-diversified portfolio. In order to receive the benefits of both diversification and substantially reduced brokerage commissions, the individual could invest in the shares of an investment company. Economies of scale make it possible for an investment company to provide diversification at a lower cost per dollar of investment than would be incurred by a small individual investor.

In terms of professional management, the individual investing directly in the stock market would have to go through all the details of investing, including making all buying and selling decisions as well as keeping records of all transactions for tax purposes. In doing so, the individual would have to be continually on the lookout for mispriced securities in an attempt to find undervalued ones for purchase, while selling any that were found to be overvalued. Simultaneously, the individual would have to keep track of the overall risk level of the portfolio so that it did not deviate from some desired level. However, by purchasing shares of an investment company, the individual can turn over all of these details to a professional money manager.

Many of these managers hope to identify areas of mispricing in the market, exploit them, and share the resultant abnormal gains with investors by charging them for a portion of the gains. However, it appears that most managers cannot find mispriced situations frequently enough to recoup more than the additional costs they have incurred, costs that take the form of increased operating expenses and transaction costs owing to the continual buying and selling of securities. Nevertheless, other potential advantages to be gained from investing in an investment company may still outweigh any disadvantages, particularly for smaller investors.

Investment companies differ in many ways, and classification is difficult. Common practice will be followed here, where the term *investment company* will be restricted to those financial intermediaries that do not obtain money from "depositors." Thus the traditional operations of savings and loan companies and banks, for example, will be excluded. However, the process of deregulation is rapidly breaking down barriers that previously prevented financial intermediaries from competing with traditional investment companies. The future will likely find many different types of organizations offering investment company services.

21.1 NET ASSET VALUE

An important concept in understanding how investment companies operate is **net asset value**. Given that an investment company has assets consisting of various securities, it is often (but not always) easy to determine the market value of all the assets held by the investment company at the end of each business day. For example, an investment company that holds various common stocks traded on the New York Stock Exchange, the American Stock Exchange, and Nasdaq could easily find out what the closing prices of those stocks were at the end of the day and then simply multiply these prices by the number of shares that it owns. After adding up these figures, the investment company would subtract any liabilities that it had outstanding. Dividing the resulting difference by the number of outstanding shares of the investment company produces its net asset value.

Equivalently, an investment company's net asset value at the end of day t, NAV_t, can be determined by using the following equation:

$$NAV_t = \frac{MVA_t - LIAB_t}{NSO_t} \qquad (21.1)$$

where MVA_t, $LIAB_t$, and NSO_t denote the market value of the investment company's assets, the dollar amount of the investment company's liabilities, and the number of shares the investment company has outstanding, respectively, as of the end of day t.

As an example, consider an investment company with 4,000,000 shares outstanding whose assets consisted of common stocks with an aggregate market value of $102,000,000 and whose liabilities amounted to $2,000,000 as of November 15. This company would report a net asset value on that date of $25 [= ($102,000,000 − $2,000,000)/4,000,000] per share. This amount will change every day, because the values of MVA_t, $LIAB_t$, or NSO_t (or of some combination of the three) will typically change daily.

Investors should note that calculating NAV_t can be difficult if some of the assets do not trade frequently or involve foreign securities that trade in vastly different time zones. In such situations, estimates of their fair market value are often used. Continuing with the previous example, what if, in on November 16 there were still 4,000,000 shares outstanding, the liabilities were still $2,000,000, but the common stocks had not been traded on any market since November 15? In this situation MVA_t is often calculated by using the last bid prices for the stocks on November 16, which in this example is assumed to result in a value for MVA_t of $106,000,000.[1] Hence the net asset value on November 16 is $26 [= ($106,000,000 − $2,000,000)/4,000,000] per share.

The Investment Company Act of 1940 classifies investment companies as follows:[2]

1. Unit investment trusts
2. Managed investment companies
   a. Closed-end investment companies
   b. Open-end investment companies

These types of investment companies are discussed next.

21.2.1   Unit Investment Trusts

A **unit investment trust** is an investment company that owns a fixed set of securities for the life of the company.[3] That is, the investment company rarely alters the composition of its portfolio over the life of the company.

Formation

To form a unit investment trust, a sponsor (often a brokerage firm) purchases a specific set of securities and deposits them with a trustee (such as a bank). Then a number of shares known as redeemable trust certificates are sold to the public. These certificates provide their owners with proportional interests in the securities that were previously deposited with the trustee. All income received by the trustee on these securities is subsequently paid out to the certificate holders, as are any repayments of principal. Changes in the original set of securities (that is, selling some of them and buying different ones) are made only under exceptional circumstances. Because there is no active management of a unit investment trust, the annual fees charged by the sponsor are correspondingly low (perhaps equal to .15% of the net asset value per year).

Most unit investment trusts hold fixed-income securities and expire after the last one has matured (or, possibly, sold). Life spans range from six months for unit investment trusts of money market instruments to over 20 years for trusts of bond market instruments. Unit investment trusts usually specialize in certain types of securities. Some trusts include only federal government bonds, others only corporate bonds, others only municipal bonds, and so on.

Not surprisingly, the sponsor of a unit investment trust will seek compensation for the effort and risk involved in setting up the trust by setting a selling price for the shares that exceeds the cost of the underlying assets. For example, a brokerage firm might purchase $10,000,000 worth of bonds, place them in a unit investment trust, and issue 10,000 shares. Each share might be offered to the public for $1,035. When all the shares have been sold, the sponsor will have received $10,350,000 (= $1,035 × 10,000). This is enough to cover the $10,000,000 cost of the bonds, leaving $350,000 for selling expenses and profit. Markups (or load charges) of this sort range from less than 1% for short-term trusts to 3.5% for long-term trusts.

Secondary Market

Typically an investor who purchases shares of a unit investment trust is not required to hold the shares for the entire life of the trust. Instead the shares usually can be sold back to the trust at net asset value, calculated on the basis of bid prices for the assets in the portfolio; that is, the market value of the securities in the portfolio is determined, using dealers' bid quotations. Because unit investment trusts have no liabilities, this amount is divided by the number of shares outstanding to obtain the net asset value per share. Having determined the per share price, the trustee may sell one or more securities to raise the required cash for the repurchase.

Alternatively, it is possible that a secondary market is maintained by the sponsor of the trust. In this situation investors can sell their shares back to the sponsor. Afterward, other investors (including those who did not participate in the initial sale) can purchase these shares. Typically the sponsor's selling price in the secondary market is equal to the net asset value of the securities in the portfolio (based on dealers' asked prices) plus a markup charge equal to that in effect at the time the trust was created.

21.2.2 Managed Companies

Whereas a unit investment trust has no board of directors and no portfolio manager, **managed investment companies** have both. Because they are organized as corporations or trusts (a few are limited partnerships), a managed investment company will have a board of directors or trustees that is elected by its shareholders. In turn, the board will commonly hire a firm—the management company—to manage the company's assets for an annual fee that is typically based on the total market value of the assets.

These management companies may be independent firms, investment advisers, firms associated with brokers, or insurance companies. Often the management company is the business entity (for example, a subsidiary of a brokerage firm) that started and promoted the investment company. A management company may have contracts to manage a number of investment companies, each of which is a separate organization with its own board of directors or trustees.

Annual management fees (also known as advisory fees) usually range from .50% to 1% of the average market value of the investment company's total assets, with the percentage sliding downward as the dollar value of the assets increases. Some funds provide "incentive compensation," where the better the fund's investment performance, the higher the fee paid to the management company.

In addition to the fee paid by an investment company to its management company, there are administrative expenses that cover record keeping and services to shareholders. (Sometimes these are embedded in the management fee.) Such annual expenses usually range from .20% to .40% of the average market value of total assets.

Last, there are other operating expenses that the investment company incurs annually for such things as state and local taxes, legal and auditing expenses, and directors' fees. These annual expenses usually range from .10% to .30% of the average market value of total assets. The combination of management fees, administrative expenses, and other operating expenses results in total annual operating expenses typically ranging from .80% to 1.70% of the average total assets.[4] This figure is referred to as a fund's **operating expense ratio**. During 1996 the average bond and equity fund had an operating expense ratio of 1.12% and 1.51%, respectively.[5]

Closed-End Investment Companies

Unlike unit investment trusts, **closed-end investment companies** (or closed-end funds) do not stand ready to purchase their own shares whenever one of their owners decides to sell them. Instead their shares are traded either on an organized exchange or in the over-the-counter market. Thus an investor who wants to buy or sell shares of a closed-end fund would simply place an order with a broker, just as if the investor wanted to buy or sell shares of IBM.

Most closed-end funds have unlimited lives. Dividends and interest received by a closed-end fund from the securities in its portfolio are paid out to its shareholders, as are any net realized capital gains. However, most funds allow (and encourage) the reinvestment of such payments. The fund keeps the money and sends the investor additional shares based on the lower of net asset value or market price per share at that time. For example, consider a closed-end fund whose shares are selling for $20 that has just declared a dividend of $1 per share. If its net asset value were $15 per share, a holder of 30 shares would have a choice of receiving either $30 (=30 × $1) or two shares (=$30/$15). However, if the shares were selling for $10, then the choice would be between $30 and three shares.

Being a corporation, a closed-end fund can issue new shares not only through reinvestment plans but also with public stock offerings. However, this is done infrequently, and the fund's capitalization is "closed" most of the time. Furthermore, the fund's capitalization will have little or no interest-bearing debt in it because of certain restrictions imposed by the Investment Company Act of 1940.

In general, a closed-end fund's shares are initially offered to the public at a price that is nearly 10% above its net asset value because of investment banking fees charged to the fund. This practice suggests that the shares are overpriced because most funds' shares sell for a price below their net asset value in the aftermarket. Evidence indicates that there are no unusual movements in the price of a typical fund on the offering day but that in the 100 days thereafter its price declines relative to the market to the point at which it sells for roughly 10% below its net asset value. This movement is in sharp contrast to the price behavior of non-fund initial public offerings, where the stocks, on average, experience a substantial price jump on the offering day of about 14% and no notable price movements in roughly the following 100 days.[6] Left unanswered is why an investor would want to be involved in the initial public offering of a closed-end fund.[7]

Most closed-end funds can repurchase their own shares in the open market, although they seldom do. Whenever a fund's market price falls substantially below its net asset value, a repurchase will increase the fund's net asset value per share. For example, if the net asset value were $20 per share at a time when the fund's shares could be purchased in the open market (say, on the New York Stock Exchange) for $16 per share, the managers of the fund could sell $20 worth of securities from the fund's portfolio, buy back one of the fund's outstanding shares, and have $4 left over. If the $4 were used to buy securities for the fund, the net asset value per share would increase, with the size of the increase depending on the number of remaining shares, the number of shares repurchased, and their repurchase price.

Quotations

The market prices of the shares of closed-end funds are published daily in the financial press, provided that the funds are listed on an exchange or traded actively in the over-the-counter market. However, their net asset values are published only weekly, on the basis of closing market prices for securities in their portfolios as of the previous Friday. Figure 21.1 provides an example. The first column indicates where a fund's shares are traded (N = NYSE, A = AMEX, O = Nasdaq, C = Chicago Stock Exchange, T = Toronto Stock Exchange). Both the net asset value and the last price at which the fund's shares traded on the day in question are shown next, followed by the percentage of net asset value that the difference between the two figures represents.

If this percentage is positive (meaning that the stock price is greater than the net asset value), then the fund's shares are said to be selling at a premium. Conversely, if this difference is negative (meaning that the stock price is less than the net asset value), then the fund's shares are said to be selling at a discount. For example, Figure 21.1 indicates that the India Growth Fund was selling at a 13.0% discount while the Indonesia Fund was selling for an 90.7% premium. (These two investment companies are known as "country funds," as they specialize in Indian and Indonesian

---

Investment Companies   **703**

Fund Name (Symbol)	Stock Exch	NAV	Market Price	Prem /Disc	52 week Market Return
Friday, March 20, 1998					
General Equity Funds					
Adams Express (ADX)	♣N	31.97	27	− 15.5	43.9
Alliance All-Mkt (AMO)	N	36.72	36 5/8	− 0.3	84.5
Avalon Capital (MIST)	O	N/A	N/A	N/A	N/A
Baker Fentress (BKF)	♣N	23.77	20 5/8	− 13.2	30.9
Bergstrom Cap (BEM)	A	175.82	155 1/2	− 11.6	40.0
Blue Chip Value (BLU)	♣N	11.12	11 1/4	+ 1.2	53.1
Central Secs (CET)	A	31.00	30 1/2	− 1.6	20.8
Corp Renaissance (CREN)-c	O	9.32	7 11/16	− 17.5	9.8
Engex (EGX)	A	12.91	10 1/8	− 21.6	− 4.7
Equus II (EQS)	♣A	31.58	28	− 11.3	68.9
Gabelli Equity (GAB)	N	N/A	11 15/16	N/A	40.3
General American (GAM)	♣N	32.56	28 3/4	− 11.7	47.6
Librty AllStr Eq (USA)-g	♣N	14.74	14 1/16	− 4.6	37.2
Librty AllStr Gr (ASG)	♣N	14.29	13 13/16	− 3.3	45.9
MFS Special Val (MFV)	N	15.98	19 1/16	+ 19.3	120.1
Morgan FunShares (MFUN)-c	O	N/A	N/A	N/A	N/A
Morgan Gr Sm Cap (MGC)	♣N	12.89	11 9/16	− 10.3	46.0
NAIC Growth (GRF)-c	C	12.15	16 5/16	+ 34.3	37.6
Royce Micro-Cap (OTCM)	♣O	11.75	10 15/16	− 6.9	50.4
Royce Value (RVT)	♣N	18.12	17 1/2	− 3.4	52.8
Royce,5.75 '04Cv-w	N	N/A	N/A	N/A	N/A
Royce,5.75 '04Cv-w	N	N/A	N/A	N/A	N/A
Salomon SBF (SBF)	N	20.56	18 1/2	− 10.0	35.8
Source Capital (SOR)	N	53.87	55 15/16	+ 3.8	39.5
Tri-Continental (TY)-a	♣N	36.01	29 11/16	− 17.6	34.2
Zweig (ZF)-g	♣N	13.54	13 13/16	+ 2.0	35.2
Specialized Equity Funds					
C&S Realty (RIF)	♣A	10.86	11 1/2	+ 5.9	3.5
C&S Total Rtn (RFI)	♣N	16.97	16 5/8	− 2.0	12.8
Delaware Gr Div (DDF)	N	18.30	18 7/8	+ 3.1	26.2
Delaware Grp Gl (DGF)	N	17.56	17 13/16	+ 1.4	26.6
Duff&Ph Util Inc (DNP)	N	10.51	10 1/2	− 0.1	25.1
Emer Mkts Infra (EMG)	♣N	15.18	12 1/4	− 19.3	4.4
Emer Mkts Tel (ETF)	♣N	17.70	14 9/16	− 17.7	10.7
First Financial (FF)	N	18.92	21 13/16	+ 15.3	63.0
Gabelli Gl Media (GGT)	N	N/A	10 1/8	N/A	62.6
H&Q Health Inv (HQH)	♣N	20.60	17	− 17.5	9.5
H&Q Life Sci Inv (HQL)	♣N	17.01	14 1/8	− 17.0	13.3
INVESCO Gl Hlth (GHS)	♣N	21.03	18 7/16	− 12.3	35.1
J Han Bank (BTO)	♣N	13.73	13 3/8	− 2.6	79.9
J Han Pat Globl (PGD)	♣N	15.59	13 9/16	− 13.0	15.7
J Han Pat Sel (DIV)	♣N	17.21	15 9/16	− 9.6	20.0
Nations Bal Tgt (NBM)	N	10.47	9 7/8	− 5.7	26.9
Petroleum & Res (PEO)	♣N	42.94	38 1/16	− 11.4	21.5
SthEastrn Thrift (STBF)	♣O	29.02	30	+ 3.4	85.0
Thermo Opprtunty (TMF)	A	13.10	10 5/8	− 18.9	− 7.6
Preferred Stock Funds					
J Han Pat Pref (PPF)	♣N	14.57	14 3/4	+ 1.2	20.0
J Han Pat Prm (PDF)	♣N	10.75	10 1/8	− 5.8	14.7
J Han Pat Prm II (PDT)-a	♣N	13.55	12 1/4	− 9.6	17.7
Preferred Inc Op (PFO)	♣N	N/A	N/A	N/A	N/A
Preferred IncMgt (PFM)	♣N	N/A	N/A	N/A	N/A
Preferred Income (PFD)	♣N	N/A	N/A	N/A	N/A
Putnam Divd Inc (PDI)-a	N	11.74	10 11/16	− 9.0	15.7
Convertible Sec's. Funds					
Bancroft Conv (BCV)	♣A	29.27	28 5/8	− 2.2	45.5
Castle Conv (CVF)	A	29.06	26 1/8	− 10.1	17.8
Ellsworth Conv (ECF)	♣A	12.55	11 1/2	− 8.4	38.0
Gabelli Conv Sec (GCV)	N	11.89	10 15/16	− 8.0	26.1
Lincoln Conv (LNV)-c	♣N	19.59	18	− 8.1	18.1
Putnam Conv Opp (PCV)	N	27.99	27 1/8	− 3.1	26.5
Putnam Hi Inc Cv (PCF)-a	N	10.04	10 7/8	+ 8.3	17.5
TCW Conv Secs (CVT)-g	♣N	10.14	10 1/2	+ 3.6	26.3
VKAC Cv Sec (ACS)	N	25.74	22 9/16	− 12.3	25.9
World Equity Funds					
ASA Limited (ASA)-cv	N	18.89	20 1/8	+ 6.5	− 39.6
Anchor Gold&Curr (GCT)	C	4.67	4 9/16	− 2.3	− 27.0
Argentina (AF)	N	15.92	13 1/16	− 17.9	2.4
Asia Pacific (APB)	N	9.33	8 13/16	− 5.5	− 18.3
Global Small Cap (GSG)	A	19.33	15 7/8	− 17.9	27.0
Growth Fd Spain (GSP)	♣N	22.78	20 7/8	− 8.4	80.6
Herzfeld Caribb (CUBA)	O	6.64	7 1/4	+ 9.2	30.9
India Fund (IFN)	N	8.45	7 3/16	− 14.9	− 10.2
India Growth (IGF)-d	N	10.71	9 5/16	− 13.0	− 23.2
Indonesia (IF)	♣N	3.08	5 7/8	+ 90.7	− 39.7
Irish Inv (IRL)	N	24.60	23 1/4	− 5.5	61.5
Italy (ITA)	N	17.31	14 5/8	− 15.5	67.4
Jakarta Growth (JGF)	N	2.24	3 7/8	+ 73.0	− 56.1
Japan Equity (JEQ)	♣N	6.18	7 9/16	+ 22,4	− 19.3
Japan OTC Equity (JOF)	N	4.52	5 5/16	+ 17.5	− 12.0
Jardine Fl China (JFC)	♣N	11.77	9 13/16	− 16.6	− 15.3
Jardine Fl India (JFI)-gc	♣N	8.18	6 15/16	− 15.2	− 15.9
Korea (KF)	N	7.64	8 3/16	+ 7.2	− 39.5
Korea Equity (KEF)	N	3.20	3 1/2	+ 9.4	− 41.7
Korean Inv (KIF)	N	3.95	4 1/4	+ 7.6	− 41.4
Latin Am Sm Companies (LLF)	♣N	11.21	9 1/4	− 17.5	− 10.0
Latin Amer Disc (LDF)	N	13.04	12	− 8.0	26.9
Latin Amer Eq (LAQ)	♣N	16.86	13 13/16	− 18.1	1.5
Latin Amer Inv (LAM)	♣N	18.03	14 5/8	− 18.9	0.8
Malaysia (MF)	N	6.12	8 1/8	+ 32.8	− 50.0
Mexico (MXF)-c	N	22.71	17 3/4	− 21.8	15.1
Mexico Eqty&Inc (MXE)-c	N	11.64	9 11/16	− 16.8	27.7
Morgan St Africa (AFF)	N	16.62	13 3/16	− 20.7	− 5.3
Morgan St Asia (APF)	N	8.84	7 3/4	− 12.3	− 19.2
Morgan St Em (MSF)	N	14.31	12 3/4	− 10.9	− 5.9
Morgan St India (IIF)	N	9.11	7 7/8	− 13.6	− 26.7
Morgan St Russia (RNE)	N	27.21	24 3/16	− 11.1	15.5
New South Africa (NSA)	♣N	17.49	14 3/4	− 15.7	11.7
Pakistan Inv (PKF)	N	5.22	4 7/16	− 15.0	− 15.3
Portugal (PGF)	♣N	25.56	21 7/16	− 16.1	69.1
ROC Taiwan (ROC)	N	10.20	8 13/16	− 13.6	0.2
Royce Global Trust (FUND)	♣O	6.64	5 1/2	− 17.2	27.0
Schroder Asian (SHF)-cs	N	8.78	N/A	N/A	N/A
Scud Spain & Por (IBF)	N	19.02	17 5/8	− 7.3	84.6
Scudder New Asia (SAF)	N	12.33	10 7/8	− 11.8	− 12.1
Scudder New Eur (NEF)	N	22.98	19	− 17.3	44.9
Singapore (SGF)-c	♣N	7.97	7 11/16	− 3.5	− 34.6
Southern Africa (SOA)	N	18.18	15 1/16	− 17.1	10.4
Spain (SNF)	N	21.31	18 9/16	− 12.9	88.2
Swiss Helvetia (SWZ)	♣N	37.65	31 3/8	− 16.7	55.4
Taiwan (TWN)-c	N	21.07	18 1/8	− 14.0	− 9.1
Taiwan Equity (TYW)-c	♣N	15.36	13	− 15.4	8.3
Templeton China (TCH)-c	N	10.33	8 9/16	− 17.1	− 30.1
Templeton Dragon (TDF)	N	13.59	11 1/2	− 15.4	− 12.2
Templeton Em App (TEA)-c	N	13.16	12 5/16	− 6.4	7.1
Templeton Em Mkt (EMF)	N	16.69	18 1/16	+ 8.2	− 2.4
Templeton Russia (TRF)-c	N	28.66	36	+ 25.6	16.8
Templeton Vietnm (TVF)	N	9.38	8 3/8	− 10.7	− 24.0
Thai (TTF)	N	6.15	8 7/8	+ 44.3	− 43.5
Thai Capital (TC)	♣N	4.18	5 3/8	+ 28.6	− 39.4
Third Canadian (THD)-cy	T	24.49	20	− 18.3	7.9
Turkish Inv (TKF)	N	7.55	6 1/4	− 17.2	0.2
United Corps Ltd (UNC)-cy	T	75.75	60	− 20.8	51.1
United Kingdom (UKM)	♣N	17.35	15 3/8	− 11.4	28.8
Z-Seven (ZSEV)	O	8.38	8 1/2	+ 1.4	5.6

Fund Name (Symbol)	Stock Exch	NAV	Market Price	Prem /Disc	12 Mo. Yield 2/28/98
U.S. Gov't. Bond Funds					
ACM Govt Inc (ACG)	N	10.78	11 5/16	+ 4.9	7.9
ACM Govt Oppty (AOF)	N	8.65	8 1/8	− 6.1	7.7
ACM Govt Secs (GSF)	N	10.67	10 1/8	− 5.1	8.8
ACM Govt Spec (SI)	N	7.22	6 5/8	− 8.2	8.9
Amer Govt Income (AGF)-c	N	5.87	5 5/8	− 4.2	6.3
Amer Govt Port (AAF)-c	N	6.97	6 11/16	− 4.1	6.3
Bull&Bear US Gvt Sec (BBG)-a	♣A	14.73	13 1/2	− 8.4	6.1
Dean Witter Govt (GVT)	♣N	9.44	8 5/8	− 8.6	6.9
Excelsior Income (EIS)-c	♣N	18.80	17	− 9.6	6.9
Kemper Int Govt (KGT)	♣N	7.84	7 1/2	− 4.3	8.4

Figure 21.1

Listing of Closed-End Funds (Excerpts)

Source: Reprinted by permission of *Barron's*, Dow Jones & Company, Inc., March 23, 1998, p. MW91. All rights reserved worldwide.

stocks, respectively.) Most closed-end funds that invest in stocks (other than a few country funds) sell at a discount.[8]

Finally, the last column in the figure shows the rate of return over the past 12 months for funds investing primarily in stocks and the past 12-month yield for funds investing primarily in fixed-income securities.

Open-End Investment Companies

An investment company that stands ready at all times to purchase its own shares at or near their net asset value is termed an **open-end investment company** (or open-end fund). Most of these companies, commonly known as **mutual funds**, also continuously offer new shares to the public for a price at or near their net asset values. Hence their capitalization is "open," with the number of shares outstanding changing on a daily basis.

There are two methods used by mutual funds to sell their shares to the public: direct marketing and the use of a sales force. With direct marketing the mutual fund sells shares directly to investors without the use of a sales organization. In such a situation the open-end companies, known as **no-load funds**, sell their shares at a price equal to their net asset value. The other method of selling shares involves the use of a sales force that is paid a commission based on the number of shares it sells. This sales force often involves brokers, financial planners, and employees of insurance companies and banks. The open-end companies that use this method are known as **load funds**, because the commission involves adding a percentage load charge to the net asset value.

The percentage **load charge** by law cannot exceed 8.5% of the amount invested. For example, a selling organization receiving $1,000 to be invested in a fund might retain as much as $85, leaving $915 to purchase the fund's shares at the current net asset value per share. Although this is usually described as a load charge of 8.5%, it is actually equal to 9.3% (= $85/$915) of the amount ultimately invested. Load charges of this magnitude are levied by some funds for small purchases, but typically they are reduced for larger purchases. Furthermore, some funds have loads of less than 3.5% for purchases of all sizes and are hence dubbed **low-load funds**.[9]

When mutual fund shareholders want to sell their shares, they usually receive an amount equal to the fund's net asset value times the number of shares sold. However, a few funds charge a **redemption fee**, which usually is no more than 1% of the fund's net asset value and typically is not levied if the investor has owned the shares for more than a specified time, such as one year. Hence its basic purpose is to discourage investors from selling their shares right after buying them. By discouraging such in-and-out trading the fund avoids the transaction costs associated with having to sell securities frequently in order to satisfy some investors' desires to sell their mutual fund shares rapidly.[10]

In addition, mutual funds may charge current shareholders a **distribution fee** annually. This 12b-1 fee (named for an SEC ruling involving a section of the Investment Company Act of 1940) is legally not allowed to exceed 1% of the average market value of the total assets. It pays for advertising, promoting, and selling the fund to prospective purchasers as well as for providing certain services to existing investors.[11] Sometimes the fee is coupled with a load charge that is paid when shares are initially purchased. One alleged benefit of the 12b-1 fee to the current owners of the fund is that the subsequent increased size of the portfolio will bring with it certain economies of scale.

Some mutual funds have different classes of stock. In such a situation an investor can choose the class that he or she wants to purchase. For example, class A stock might involve a 5% load charge but no annual 12b-1 fee, whereas class B stock might not have a load charge. Instead this class might have a 12b-1 fee of .5% per year plus a **contingent deferred sales charge** (paid when the investor sells shares) that starts at 5% if the investor sells his or her shares within a year of purchase and declines thereafter by 1% a year for each year that the stock is held, reaching zero after the fifth year. In addition, the class B shares might be set up so that they convert to class A shares after five years (when the contingent deferred sales charge has declined to zero). This feature allows investors who initially bought class B shares to avoid 12b-1 fees after five years. There might also be class C stock for which the investor pays an annual 12b-1 fee of 1% for as long as the shares are held.

In summary, there are many different methods that mutual funds use to get the cash needed to pay for sales commissions and other selling costs. Some methods (such as the class C stock) are more attractive to investors who plan to hold their investment only for the short term. Others (such as the class B stock) are more attractive to investors who plan to hold their investment for the long term.

As will be discussed later, the investment performance of no-load funds as a whole does not differ in any notable way from that of load funds. This fact is not surprising. The load charge (roughly 30% to 50% of which goes to the individual who sold the shares, with the selling organization keeping the rest) represents the cost of advertising, education, and persuasion. Mail-order firms often sell items for less than stores charge. Sales representatives who work in stores and those who sell mutual funds provide a service and require compensation. Buyers who consider such services worth less than their cost can and should avoid paying for them.

Quotations

Figure 21.2 shows a portion of the quotations for mutual funds provided in *The Wall Street Journal* for each business day except Friday. Funds that are listed under a name in boldface type have a common management company that is associated with that name. For example, note all the funds listed under AARP Invst. (AARP Invst stands for AARP Investment Program from Scudder, an investment program sponsored by the American Association of Retired People that involves mutual funds run by the management company of Scudder, Stevens & Clark.) After the abbreviated name of the mutual fund comes its net asset value, based on closing prices for the fund's securities on the day in question. The third column displays the change in net asset value from the close of the previous trading day, and the fourth column indicates the fund's rate of return for the year so far.

On Friday of each week, *The Wall Street Journal* presents much more detailed information on mutual funds. Besides presenting net asset value, its change from the previous day, and the year-to-date return for each fund, the following additional information is presented:

1. Investment objective
2. Four-week return
3. Total return for the last year, three years, and five years, along with an indication of the fund's pentile rank relative to other funds with the same investment objective (top 20% = A, next 20% = B, middle 20% = C, next 20% = D, bottom 20% = E) for each of these time periods
4. Front-end load charge
5. Operating expense ratio

Figure 21.3 shows the weekly quotations that appear for a special type of mutual fund known as a money market fund. These funds invest in short-term, fixed-income securities, such as Treasury bills, commercial paper, and bank certificates of deposit. A special type of money market fund that invests primarily in short-term municipal

LIPPER INDEXES

Friday, October 3, 1997

Equity Indexes	Prelim. Close	Percentage chg. since Prev.	Wk ago	Dec. 31
Capital Appreciation ...	1937.65	+ 0.57	+ 2.05	+ 24.48
Growth Fund	6332.15	+ 0.61	+ 2.14	+ 29.43
Small Cap Fund	674.73	+ 0.66	+ 2.22	+ 23.50
Growth & Income	6064.80	+ 0.51	+ 1.94	+ 27.52
Equity Income Fd	3217.23	+ 0.38	+ 1.77	+ 25.96
Science and Tech Fd ...	600.10	+ 0.84	+ 1.37	+ 29.21
International Fund	665.79	+ 0.88	+ 2.02	+ 17.81
Gold Fund	119.10	+ 0.45	+ 6.78	− 18.05
Balanced Fund	3669.49	+ 0.33	+ 1.46	+ 19.74
Emerging Markets	104.26	+ 0.15	+ 1.16	+ 12.81
Bond Indexes				
Corp A-Rated Debt	730.61	+ 0.01	+ 0.49	+ 7.05
US Government	275.48	+ 0.02	+ 0.45	+ 6.35
GNMA	299.09	− 0.04	+ 0.25	+ 6.62
High Current Yield	756.41	+ 0.19	+ 0.88	+ 11.85
Intmdt Inv Grade	201.01	+ 0.04	+ 0.44	+ 6.54
Short Inv Grade	185.22	+ 0.03	+ 0.22	+ 4.91
General Municipal	527.59	+ 0.03	+ 0.33	+ 6.38
High Yield Municipal ..	255.94	+ 0.01	+ 0.31	+ 6.71
Short Municipal	114.11	+ 0.02	+ 0.11	+ 3.35
Global Income	200.68	+ 0.32	+ 0.59	+ 3.94
International Income ...	126.50	+ 0.58	+ 0.68	+ 2.22

OVERSEAS FUND INDEXES-a

Friday, October 3, 1997

LOFT GL Eqty Idx	591.93	N/A	+ 0.97	+ 14.65
LOFT GL Bond Idx	203.99	N/A	− 0.11	− 2.58

Indexes are based on the largest funds within the same investment objective and do not include multiple share classes of similar funds. The Yardsticks table, appearing with Friday's listings, includes all funds with the same objective.

Source: Lipper Analytical Services, Inc. The Lipper Funds Inc. are not affiliated with Lipper Analytical Services.

Ranges for investment companies, with daily price data supplied by the National Association of Securities Dealers and performance and cost calculations by Lipper Analytical Services Inc. The NASD requires a mutual fund to have at least 1,000 shareholders or net assets of $25 million before being listed. NAV-Net Asset Value. Detailed explanatory notes appear elsewhere on this page.

Name	NAV	Net Chg	YTD %ret
AAL Mutual A:			
Bond p	9.94	−0.01	+ 6.6
CGrowth p	26.17	+0.20	+28.6
HiYBdA	10.49	+0.02	NS
Intl p	12.17	+0.02	+11.0
MidCap p	17.03	+0.09	+25.4
MuniBd p	11.47	...	+ 7.0
SmCap p	14.19	+0.12	+26.7
EqInc p	12.78	−0.01	+14.3
AAL Mutual B:			
CGrowth p	26.05	+0.19	NS
Intl p	12.09	+0.02	NS
MidCap	16.93	+0.08	NS
SmCap p	14.11	+0.12	NS
AARP Invst:			
BalS&B	21.68	+0.08	+21.5
BdInc	15.29	+0.02	NS
CaGr	58.83	+0.37	+39.8
DivGr	17.62	+0.08	NS
DivInc	16.08	+0.03	NS
GiniM	15.17	−0.01	+ 5.9
GlblGr	19.67	+0.18	+20.7
GthInc	59.27	+0.38	+32.8
HQ Bd	16.21	+0.01	+ 6.0
IntlSkt	17.62	+0.18	NS
SmCoStk	20.27	+0.06	NS
TxFBd	18.44	...	+ 6.4
USStkI	18.31	+0.08	NS
AHA Funds:			
Balan	16.17	+0.05	+22.6
DivrEq	23.17	+0.12	+33.5
Full	9.99	...	+ 7.1
Lim	10.22	+0.01	+ 5.0
AIM Funds A:			
Agrsv p	53.71	+0.26	+25.3
Bal p	26.99	+0.12	+25.7
BlChp p	32.66	+0.14	+32.1
CapDev p	15.28	+0.10	+31.6
Chart p	14.27	+0.09	+30.1
Const p	31.72	+0.25	+25.6
GlAgGr	19.22	+0.07	+17.3
GlGr p	18.26	+0.16	+22.1
GlInc p	11.00	+0.04	+ 6.7
GlUtil p	18.53	−0.01	+18.3
Grth p	18.97	+0.13	+28.3
HYld p	10.26	+0.01	+11.1
Inco p	8.58	+0.02	+ 9.6
IntGov p	9.39	...	+ 6.6
IntlEq p	18.48	+0.19	+16.5
LimM p	10.07	+0.01	+ 4.6
Muni p	8.29	+0.01	+ 5.4
Sumit	16.18	+0.13	+33.2
TeCt p	11.02	...	+ 5.3
TFInt	10.98	...	+ 5.4
Valu p	37.56	+0.38	+28.9
Weing p	24.23	+0.18	+30.9

Name	NAV	Net Chg	YTD %ret
MuPAB t	10.36	...	+ 7.2
NtlMuB t	10.93	...	+ 7.0
NEurB t	19.14	+0.26	+22.1
NAGvB t	8.40	...	+15.5
PrGrthB t	22.61	+0.22	+39.0
QusarB t	28.15	+0.06	+25.2
ReEInvB t	14.29	+0.16	+23.3
ST MIb t	7.67	...	+ 3.9
StrBalB t	16.77	+0.11	+13.4
TechB t	60.61	+0.60	+26.5
WldPrivB t	13.94	+0.15	+25.6
Alliance Cap C:			
CpBdC t	14.82	...	+12.4
GlbDIGvC p	11.18	+0.06	+18.9
GovtC t	7.53	...	+ 5.3
GrInc t	3.66	+0.01	+28.9
GwthC t	38.05	+0.24	+26.8
InBldC t	13.01	+0.03	+19.0
InsMuC t	10.49	...	+ 6.4
IntlC t	18.19	+0.22	+11.9
LtdMtGC t	9.41	...	+ 4.4
MrtgC t	8.62	...	+ 6.0
MuCA C t	11.02	−0.01	+ 7.1
MuFLC t	10.16	...	+ 7.1
MuNJC t	10.18	...	+ 6.9
MuNYC t	10.10	...	+ 7.8
MuOHC t	10.19	...	+ 8.2
NtlMuC t	10.93	...	+ 7.0
NAGvC t	8.40	...	+15.5
PrGrthC t	22.64	+0.22	+39.0
QuasarC t	28.16	+0.05	+25.2
ReEInvC t	14.29	+0.16	+23.3
TechC t	60.60	+0.59	+26.4
AmanaIncome	18.12	−0.01	+22.7
AmUtlFd	27.01	...	+10.8
Amer AAdvant Funds:			
Bal	16.61	+0.03	+18.7
BalPlan	16.46	+0.03	+18.4
BdInst	10.12	...	NA
GrInc	22.80	+0.07	+27.4
GrInPlan	22.54	+0.08	+27.1
IntlEq	18.26	+0.13	+18.9
LtdTr	9.65	...	+ 5.0
Amer Century:			
Balanced	20.17	+0.15	+18.5
EqGro	21.39	+0.15	+35.3
EqInc	7.80	+0.01	+26.6
GlGold	9.63	+0.05	−14.5
IncGro	26.58	+0.15	+33.5
NatRes	13.86	+0.13	+17.7
Real	16.85	+0.10	+26.4
StrAgg	6.53	+0.04	+19.8
StrConv	5.62	+0.02	+12.9
StrMod	6.14	+0.03	+16.7
Util	13.25	−0.01	+18.2
Value	8.37	+0.01	+28.6

Name	NAV	Net Chg	YTD %ret
LtdMat	10.42	...	NA
MuniBd	10.13	+0.01	NA
RegEq	29.92	+0.08	NA
AmeriStar Funds:			
CapGro	14.51	+0.08	+28.5
CoreInc	10.16	...	+ 6.0
DivGr	11.73	+0.05	NS
LimDurInc	10.00	+0.01	+ 5.0
LimDurTn	10.07	+0.01	NS
LimDurUS	10.10	...	NS
TnTEBd	10.05	...	+ 4.7
Amway	9.50	+0.03	+24.7
Analytic Funds:			
MstrFixI	10.63	...	+ 8.0
Def Eq	16.92	+0.09	+18.2
ShTmGv	9.84	...	+ 4.4
AnchrCa	30.46	+0.29	+15.8
AnchrInBd	7.54	+0.06	− 9.4
ApexMCapGr	7.56	+0.13	+ 7.1
Aon Funds:			
AstAllo	17.20	+0.10	+32.5
GovSec	10.41	+0.01	+ 7.0
IntlEq	12.21	+0.06	+14.6
REIT	14.27	+0.13	+18.6
S&P500	14.92	+0.07	+31.7
Aquila Funds:			
AZ TF	10.76	...	+ 6.1
CO TF	10.55	...	+ 5.2
HI TF	11.60	...	+ 5.4
KY TF	10.70	...	+ 5.6
Nrgnst TF	10.36	...	+ 6.1
OR TF	10.70	...	+ 5.4
TxFUT	10.12	...	+ 6.2
Aquinas:			
Balance	13.45	+0.03	+18.8
EqGrth	17.34	+0.10	+28.9
EqInc	16.67	+0.02	+27.4
FxInc	10.10	+0.01	+ 6.4
Arch Funds:			
Bal	13.46	+0.07	+18.1
BdIdx	10.14	+0.01	NS
EqIdxA p	12.06	+0.06	NS
EqInc	11.67	+0.10	NS
SmCap	16.17	+0.07	+28.6
GovCorp	10.32	+0.01	+ 5.8
GroInc	21.71	+0.17	+29.1
IntlEqInv	13.26	+0.07	+13.7
IntmCorBd	10.10	+0.01	NS
MoTF	11.86	...	+ 5.8
NatlMuBd	10.28	...	+ 7.2
ShIntmMu	10.11	...	+ 3.8
US Gov	10.62	...	+ 4.8
ARMADA FUNDS:			
CorEqI	10.07	+0.07	NA
EnhIncI p	10.07	...	+ 5.0
EqGroI p	21.86	+0.16	+36.1
EqGroR p	21.90	+0.16	+35.9
EqInI p	16.97	+0.08	+28.1
FxdIncI p	10.56	...	+ 5.5
GNMA I p	10.37	...	+ 7.3
IntEqI	10.11	+0.07	NA
IntmGvI p	10.21	+0.01	+ 6.2
MidCapI p	18.51	+0.05	+35.9
OH TE I p	11.07	...	+ 5.2
PA MuI p	10.40	...	+ 4.9
TotAdvI p	10.23	+0.01	+ 7.4
Ariel Mutual Funds:			
Apprec p	34.03	−0.01	+30.5
BondInst	10.34	−0.01	+ 6.8
Growth p	41.86	−0.07	+31.0
Amstng	12.03	+0.08	+18.9
Arrow Funds:			
Equity	19.19	+0.14	+28.7
FxdIncm	10.00	...	+ 5.5
Muni	10.45	...	+ 4.6
ArtisanIntl	15.01	+0.16	+12.7
ArtisanSmCp	17.43	+0.18	+27.8
Astra Group:			
AUS I-A	5.65	...	+ 5.9
ARS I	3.11	...	+ 2.6
ARS I-A	3.09	...	+ 1.8
AdjUSI	5.63	...	+ 5.9
AdjUSII	5.70	+0.01	+ 6.1
Atlas Funds:			
BalancA p	14.20	+0.04	+19.6
CaInsA p	10.55	...	+ 4.9
CaMuniA p	11.36	...	+ 5.6
GlbGroA	14.42	+0.20	+31.6
GvtScA p	10.21	...	+ 6.6
GroIncA p	22.09	+0.15	+24.3
GroIncB p	22.03	+0.15	+24.0
NaMuniA p	11.47	...	+ 6.0
StrGroA p	18.94	+0.05	+35.2
StrIncA p	5.26	+0.01	+ 8.4
AVESTA Trust:			
Balanced	29.03	+0.11	+22.7
CoreEq	21.02	+0.10	+31.9
EqGro	38.34	+0.24	+37.2
EqIncm	36.53	+0.14	+29.5
Income	19.76	+0.01	+ 6.5
ShTmGv	12.23	+0.01	+ 4.9
SmCap	23.02	+0.14	+31.2
BB&T:			
BalA p	13.76	+0.04	+17.8
BalT	13.73	+0.04	+18.0
GroIncA p	20.28	+0.09	+30.0
GroIncB p	20.22	+0.08	+29.2
GroIncT	20.32	+0.09	+30.3
IntGovT	9.91	...	+ 6.0

Name	NAV	Net Chg	YTD %ret
EmgMkt	9.65	+0.07	+10.7
IntrFx	8.15	+0.01	+ 5.9
IntlEq	11.36	+0.07	+12.5
IntlFx	8.47	+0.05	− 1.9
LgGrw	18.52	+0.11	+30.6
LgVal	16.04	+0.10	+30.7
LTBnd	8.52	...	+ 8.8
MtgBkd	8.04	...	+ 6.8
Muni	8.72	...	+ 6.4
SmGrw	20.16	+0.14	+23.1
SmVal	15.75	+0.10	+35.2
CGM Funds:			
AmerTF	9.62	−0.05	NE
CapDv	41.69	+0.25	+43.4
Focus	11.06	+0.04	NA
FxdInc	12.06	−0.02	+ 8.7
Mutl	37.75	+0.15	+21.4
Realty	18.20	+0.20	+28.1
C&OMktOpp	18.18	+0.05	+24.1
CRARealty	12.03	+0.11	+23.7
CRMSmCapV	18.06	+0.24	+28.8
California Trust:			
CalIncTF	13.03	...	+ 6.8
CalInsTF	10.81	...	+ 5.1
CalUS	10.61	...	+ 5.6
S&P500	21.36	+0.10	+31.7
S&PMidCap	19.83	+0.10	+32.6
Calmos	16.86	+0.05	+21.0
Calvert Group:			
CapAccm p	27.75	+0.10	+24.5
Inco p	17.31	...	+ 8.0
IntlEqA p	22.14	+0.12	+16.0
IntlEqC p	21.46	+0.11	+15.2
MuBdCAI	10.55	+0.01	+ 4.6
MunInt	10.68	...	+ 4.8
Social p	35.39	+0.16	+19.5
SocBd p	16.75	+0.01	+ 7.4
SocEq p	28.23	+0.22	+25.9
SocGr p	35.02	+0.15	+18.5
StrGwthA p	17.40	+0.03	− 7.7
StrGwthC p	17.04	+0.02	− 8.1
TxF Lt	10.71	+0.01	+ 3.2
TxF Lg p	17.08	+0.01	+ 5.7
TxF VT	16.29	+0.01	+ 4.5
CapValEqSel	13.78	+0.11	+18.2
CapValTotSel	11.46	+0.05	+12.4
Cappiello-Rushmore:			
EmgGr	17.16	+0.03	+28.4
Grwth	23.03	+0.25	+35.1
Util	11.15	+0.04	+11.0
Capstone Group:			
GvtInc p	24.78	...	+ 3.5
Grth p	17.57	+0.07	+27.9
NJapan p	5.56	−0.03	− 9.6
NZland p	12.56	−0.08	− 4.6
The Cardinal Group:			
Aggr Grth	14.97	+0.13	+26.9
Balanced	13.42	+0.07	+20.7
Fund	16.93	+0.06	+31.2
Govt Oblg	8.21	...	+ 6.7
CarilCa	13.63	+0.01	+ 7.9
Centura Funds:			
EqGrC	19.08	+0.04	+27.0
EqIncmC	13.05	−0.01	+24.6
FedSecC	10.13	...	+ 5.2
NC TxFr	10.31	...	+ 5.8
Cnt Shs	43.81	+0.42	+40.7
ChaconiaInGr p	12.53	+0.04	+20.0
Chesapeake Funds:			
Class A	21.56	+0.14	+36.4
Growth	24.56	+0.11	+37.7
Insti	21.71	+0.14	+36.7
SupInsti	21.77	+0.15	+36.9
Chestnt	300.15	+1.42	+24.4
Chicago Trust:			
Balncd p	11.24	+0.05	+18.1
Bond	10.10	+0.01	+ 6.9
GroInc	20.43	+0.14	+24.3
Talon p	18.20	−0.24	NE
ChubbGrIn	27.92	+0.23	+36.2
ChubbTR	21.80	+0.12	+27.7
CitiSelect:			
Folio200 p	11.52	+0.03	NA
Folio300 p	12.03	+0.04	NA
Folio400 p	12.50	+0.07	NA
Folio500 p	12.68	+0.07	NA
Citizens Trust:			
CitEmGro	16.55	+0.12	+23.6
CitInc	10.85	+0.01	+ 8.0
CitIndx	20.25	+0.14	+34.9
CitGbl	15.47	+0.11	+25.8
Clipper	84.28	+0.48	+24.7
Colonial Funds Cl A:			
CA TEx	7.62	−0.01	+ 6.7
CT TEx	7.70	...	+ 6.8
FedSec	10.70	...	+ 7.0
FL TEx	7.63	...	+ 6.2
ColFund	11.69	+0.08	+27.5
GlEqty	15.45	+0.15	+19.6
GlUtil	14.55	+0.02	+17.5
HiYld	7.28	+0.01	+12.2
HYMu p	10.31	−0.01	+ 6.9
Income p	6.53	+0.02	+ 7.4
IntlGr	10.87	+0.07	+11.1
IntlHz	16.39	+0.10	+18.1
MA TEx	8.04	...	+ 6.7
MI TEx	7.17	+0.01	+ 6.7
MN TEx	7.39	...	+ 6.9
NY TEx	7.22	...	+ 6.3

Figure 21.2

Listing of Mutual Funds (Excerpts)

Source: Reprinted by permission of *The Wall Street Journal*, Dow Jones & Company, Inc., October 6, 1997, p. C21.

The following quotations, collected by the National Association of Securities Dealers Inc., represent the average of annualized yields and dollar-weighted portfolio maturities ending Wednesday, October 8, 1997. Yields don't include capital gains or losses.

Fund	Avg. Mat.	7 Day Yield	Assets	Fund	Avg. Mat.	7 Day Yield	Assets
Money Market:				GoldenOK-PC	58	5.27	105
AARP HQ	52	4.66	472	GovTxMgSS	43	5.07	541
AAdMileP	45	4.67	47	GovOb IS	41	5.42	3416
AAdvGovP	44	4.60	75	GovOb SS	41	5.17	1023
AAdvMMPlat	45	4.83	470	GovTxMgIS	43	5.32	682
AIM MM C	18	4.66	277	GradisonGvtRv	56	4.84	1653
AIM MMA	18	4.59	264	GrtHallGv	49	4.97	236
ARK GvIn II	40	5.19	94	GrtHallPr	46	5.01	3273
ARK MMIn II	50	5.30	90	Griffin	49	4.86	233
ARKMM A	50	5.40	331	GrdCMA	26	4.74	115
ARKMM B	50	5.09	158	GrdCsFd	29	5.06	360
ARKUSG A	40	5.29	1173	HSBC Csh	47	5.06	178
ARKUST A	85	4.94	244	HSBC Gvt	49	4.95	72
ARKUST C	85	4.84	88	HSBC USTrea	60	4.95	23
AVESTA Tr	50	5.13	126	Harbor	61	5.19	64
AccUSGov	74	5.01	51	HarrisCashA	66	5.25	597
ActAsGv	69	4.93	690	HarrisCashC	66	5.54	933
ActAsMny	80	5.21	10129	HTInsgtGv p	61	5.05	255
Advantus a	43	4.68	55	HarrisGovtC	61	5.37	71
AetnaAdvs	49	5.32	151	HtgCshA	43	4.87	2094
Aetna Sel	49	5.32	271	HiMrkUSFid	39	5.02	209
AlexBwn	47	4.93	2956	HiMrkTrsFid	67	4.95	255
AlxBTr	53	4.64	661	HiMrkTrsRtl p	67	4.70	632
AlgerMM	20	4.71	173	HiMrkDvFid	37	5.12	1052
AlliaGenMu	65	2.93	152	HiMrkDvRtl p	37	4.87	872
AlliaGov	35	4.58	127	HiMrkUSRtl p	39	4.78	50
AlliaPrime	53	4.73	3347	HilrdGovt	52	5.01	617
Alli TrResv	37	4.68	714	HmestdDiv	63	4.86	54
AlliaCpRs	58	4.72	6295				
AliaGvR	41	4.60	4078				
AlliMny	62	4.71	1101	**Tax Exempt:**			
AmAAdGvl	44	5.32	33	AARPHTe	54	2.89	103
AmAAdMMI	45	5.53	1353	AAdvMunP	10	2.82	67
AmCRes	51	4.86	297	AIMTx	41	3.11	50
AmPerCsh	47	5.01	313	ARKTaxFr A	80	3.44	110
AmPerTrs	1	4.81	340	ActAsCal	40	2.70	537
Amcore Gv	53	4.73	146	ActAstTx	49	3.06	1805
AmAAdMMP	45	5.23	160	ALMuni	44	3.38	230
AmAAdGvM	44	4.98	29	AlxB TF	49	3.12	740
AmAAdMMM	45	5.09	105	AllMuNJ	77	2.76	142
AmStarPr I	28	4.83	58	AllMunCal	47	2.78	406
AmerStarPrT	28	5.08	42	AllMuCT	64	2.83	115
AmStarUST I	45	4.73	74	AlliMuFL	42	3.00	106
AmStarUST T	45	4.98	118	AllianMuVA	27	3.00	96
AmSouthPrC	55	4.91	118	AllMuNY	44	2.81	471
AmSouthPrP	55	5.01	508	AlliaMun	52	2.88	1118
AmSouthUSC	57	4.58	10	AmAAdMuM	10	3.22	25
AmSouthUSP	57	4.68	273	AmCBnCA Mu	56	3.17	170
AonMMktY	58	5.43	846	AmCBn CATF	56	3.17	421
ArchFd	50	4.90	152	AmCBn FL	56	3.24	81
Armada Gvl	48	5.14	940	AmCBn NatTF	51	3.78	114
ArmadaGvR	48	5.04	200	AmSouthTEC	46	2.97	23
Armada MMI	45	5.24	1996	AmSouthTEP	46	3.07	57
Armada MMR	45	5.14	412	ArchFd	25	2.73	11
Armada Trsyl	52	4.75	274	ArmadaPA Txl	43	3.30	66
ArrowGovt	13	4.77	140	Armada TER	41	3.26	67
AMF MM Pt	3	5.17	48	Armada TEI	41	3.36	370
Atlas USTrs	53	4.77	60	AtlasCA	55	2.94	49
AutCsh	41	5.09	1459	BT InvNY	40	2.78	107
AutGvt	39	4.96	2294				
AuGvSvc	42	4.94	619				
AutCshCII	41	4.92	635				
AutTreasC	47	4.58	290				
BB&T UST Tr	46	4.69	255				
BNYHam TrHm	2	4.93	82				
BNYHmltTrPr	2	4.68	126				
BNY Hmltn	49	5.37	809				
BNY HmltnPr	49	5.10	593				

Figure 21.3

Listing of Money Market Mutual Funds (Excerpts)

debt is also shown in the lower right-hand part of the figure. Next to the name of such a fund are shown the average maturity of its holdings, the annual yield based on what was earned over the last seven days, and the aggregate market value of its assets. Not shown, but an important factor in selecting a money market fund, is the degree of safety (that is, default risk) associated with the assets held by each fund.

An Example

In order to highlight the differences in purchasing shares of closed-end funds, no-load funds, and load funds, consider the following example. An investor has $1,000 to use in purchasing shares of a fund and is considering the following funds, all of which have the same net asset value (NAV) of $10 per share.

Closed-end fund *E* is selling for a market price that equals its NAV, whereas closed-end fund *D* is selling at a 20% discount, or $8 (= $10 × .80). The broker charges a commission equal to 2% of the market price for each share purchased. Mutual fund N is a no-load fund, whereas mutual fund L charges an $8\text{-}\frac{1}{2}\%$ load. How many shares does the investor end up with in each case?

Closed-end fund E: cost per share $= \$10 + \$.20$ commission $= \$10.20$
number of shares $= \$1,000/\$10.20 = 98.04$

Closed-end fund D: cost per share $= \$8 + \$.16$ commission $= \$8.16$
number of shares $= \$1,000/\$8.16 = 122.55$

Mutual fund N: cost per share $= \$10$
number of shares $= \$1,000/\$10 = 100$

Mutual Fund L: cost per share $= \$10 + \$.93$ load $= \$10.93$
(note: $8.5\% \times \$10.93 = \$.93$)
number of shares $= \$1,000/\$10.93 = 91.50$

Thus the largest number of shares would be received when buying the shares of discounted closed-end fund D; the fewest shares would be received when buying the shares of load fund L.

21.3   INVESTMENT POLICIES

Different investment companies have different investment objectives (also termed investment styles). Some companies are designed as substitutes for their shareholders' entire portfolio; others expect their shareholders to own other securities. Some restrict their domain or selection methods severely; others give their managers wide latitude. Many engage in highly active management, with substantial portfolio changes designed to exploit perceived superior investment predictions. Others are more passive, concentrating instead on tailoring a portfolio to serve the interests of a particular clientele.

Although categorization is difficult, broad classes of investment objectives are often defined. As mentioned earlier, money market funds hold short-term (typically less than one year) fixed-income instruments, such as bank certificates of deposit, commercial paper, and Treasury bills. The fund manager will extract an annual fee for this service, usually between .25% and 1% of the average value of total assets. There are usually no load charges, and investors may add or remove money from their accounts at almost any time. Dividends are usually declared daily. Arrangements with a cooperating bank often make it possible to write a check on an account, where the bank obtains the amount involved by redeeming "shares" in the fund when the check clears.

Bond funds invest in fixed-income securities. Some go further, specifying that only particular types will be purchased. There are corporate bond funds, U.S. government bond funds, GNMA (or Ginnie Mae) funds, convertible bond funds, and so on. Some are organized as open-end investment companies, others as closed-end investment companies.

As indicated earlier, the predominant type of unit investment trust in the United States is the bond unit investment trust. Some purchase only government issues, others purchase only corporate issues, and still others specialize to an even greater extent. Municipal bond unit investment trusts often make it easier for those in high tax brackets to obtain diversification and liquidity while taking advantage of the exemption of such securities from personal income taxation. Bond unit investment trusts typically hold securities with different coupon payment schedules and pay roughly equal-size dividends every month.

Many open-end companies consider themselves managers for the bulk of the investment assets of their clients. Those that hold both equity and fixed-income securities particularly fit this description. CDA/Wiesenberger Investment Companies Service refers to such companies as *balanced funds*, provided that at least 25% of their portfolios are invested in bonds. These funds seek to "minimize investment risks without unduly sacrificing possibilities for long-term growth and current income."[12] Somewhat similar to balanced funds are *flexible income funds*. These funds seek to "provide liberal current income."[13] Whereas balanced funds typically hold relatively constant mixes of bonds, preferred stock, convertible bonds, and common stocks, flexible income funds often alter the proportions periodically in attempts to "time the market." Similar to these flexible funds are *asset allocation funds*, which also attempt to time the market but, in doing so, focus on total return instead of current income.

A diversified common stock fund invests most of its assets in common stocks, although some short-term money market instruments may be held to accommodate irregular cash flows or to engage in market timing. In 1997 CDA/Wiesenberger classified the majority of diversified common stock funds as having one of three types of objectives: (1) capital gain, (2) growth, or (3) growth and income.[14] Two factors appear to be involved in this classification: the relative importance of dividend income versus capital gains and the overall level of risk taken. The classifications are arranged in decreasing order of emphasis the funds place on capital appreciation but in increasing order of emphasis the funds place on current income and relative price stability. Because high-dividend portfolios are generally less risky than portfolios with low dividends, relatively few major conflicts arise, although two rather different criteria are involved. There is also another class, *equity income funds*, that CDA/Wiesenberger describes as seeking to generate a stream of current income by investing in stocks with sizable dividend yields.

Borderline cases remain in which the difference between a capital gain fund and a growth fund is a matter of degree, which, in some cases, can be small. Similarly, the differences between a growth fund and a growth-income fund can be small. Classification is difficult because the official statement of investment objectives in a fund's prospectus is often fuzzy.

A few specialized investment companies concentrate on the securities of firms in a particular industry or sector; these are known as *sector funds*. For example, there are chemical funds, aerospace funds, technology funds, and gold funds. Others deal in securities of a particular type; examples include funds that hold restricted (that is, "letter") stock, funds that invest in over-the-counter stocks, and funds that invest in the stocks of small companies. Still others provide a convenient means for holding the securities of firms in a particular country, such as the previously mentioned India and Indonesia funds. There are also investment companies that, by design, invest more widely internationally, purchasing stocks and bonds from a variety of countries. (From a U.S. viewpoint, international funds are those investing in non-U.S. securities, whereas global funds invest in both U.S. and non-U.S. securities.)[15]

Although municipal bond unit investment trusts have been available for many years, open-end municipal bond funds were first offered in 1976. Some municipal bond funds hold long-term issues from many states. Others specialize in the long-term issues of governmental units in one state ("single-state" funds) in order to provide an investment vehicle for residents of that state who wish to avoid paying state taxes (as well as federal taxes) on the income. Still others buy short-term municipal securities (as noted in Figure 21.3), with some specializing in the short-term issues of governmental units in one state.

An index fund attempts to provide results similar or identical to those computed for a specified market index. For example, the Vanguard Index 500 Trust, a no-load open-end investment company, provides a vehicle for small investors who wish

TABLE 21.1 Mutual Fund Classifications as of Year-end 1996

Classification	Number of Funds	Total Net Assets (billions)
(a) Classification by assets		
Equity	2,626	$1,751
Bond and income	2,679	886
Taxable money market	665	762
Tax-exempt money market	323	140
Total	6,293	$3,539
(b) Classification by investment objectives		
Aggressive growth		$275
Growth		482
Growth and Income		589
Precious metals		5
International		177
Global-equity		107
Income-equity		116
Flexible portfolio		63
Balanced		99
Income-mixed		88
Income-bond		101
U.S. government income		80
Ginnie Mae		51
Global bond		37
Corporate bond		36
High-yield bond		78
National municipal bond—long-term		136
State municipal bond—long-term		117
Taxable money market		762
Tax-exempt money market		140
Total		$3,539

Source: Adapted from *1997 Mutual Fund Fact Book* (Washington, DC: Investment Company Institute, 1997), pp. 60–61, 64, 84–85. Used with permission of the Investment Company Institute.

to obtain results matching those of the Standard & Poor's 500 stock index, less operating expenses. Similarly, a number of banks have established commingled index funds, and corporations and other organizations have set up index funds for their own employee retirement trust funds.

Table 21.1 provides an indication of the number of mutual funds pursuing various kinds of investment objectives, along with the amount of assets under their control. In total there were nearly 6,300 mutual funds in existence at year-end 1996. At that time these funds had nearly $3.6 trillion invested in a variety of financial assets. Both the number of funds and the dollars invested in them have continued to rise rapidly as investors, ranging from individuals to large institutions, have come to appreciate the advantages of investing through mutual funds.

21.4 MUTUAL FUND TAXATION

The U.S. Internal Revenue Code allows an investment company to avoid corporate income taxation, provided it meets certain standards and pays at least 90% of its net income to its stockholders. Instead, its stockholders must pay taxes on the income that they receive. Most investment companies choose to distribute their net income by making two kinds of cash payments to their shareholders—one for income (from dividends and interest that the fund has received) and one for net realized capital gains. These two payments are then taxed at the shareholder level as ordinary income and capital gains, respectively.

This practice creates a potential problem for investors near the end of the year that can best be seen with an example. Imagine on December 15 an investor pays $10,000 in a no-load fund whose shares are selling for $20, thus receiving 500 shares. On December 16 the fund declares and pays a dividend of $2 per share, thereby lowering its net asset value by $2 per share to $18. When the new year arrives, the investor will have to report $1,000 of taxable income, because he or she received a dividend check for $1,000 (=$2 × 500), even if the shares are still selling for $18 at the end of the year. Thus, the investor has not seen his or her investment increase in value but will still owe income taxes on the investment. Consequently, most financial advisers suggest that investors avoid investing in a taxable mutual fund near year-end. (Investors who buy mutual funds with their tax-exempt accounts such as IRAs would escape such taxation at this time, as mentioned in Chapter 12.)

21.5 MUTUAL FUND PERFORMANCE

Mutual funds are required to compute and publicize their net asset values daily. Because their income and their capital gain distributions are also publicized, they are ideal candidates for studies of the performance of professionally managed portfolios. Thus it is hardly surprising that mutual funds have frequently been the subject of extensive study.

21.5.1 Calculating Returns

In studies of performance, the rate of return on a mutual fund for period t is calculated by adding the change in net asset value to the amount of income and the capital gains distributions made during the period, denoted by I_t and G_t, respectively, and dividing this total by the net asset value at the beginning of the period:

$$r_t = \frac{\left(NAV_t - NAV_{t-1}\right) + I_t + G_t}{NAV_{t-1}} \qquad (21.2)$$

For example, a mutual fund that had a net asset value of $10 at the beginning of month t, made income and capital gain distributions of, respectively, $.05 and $.04 per share during the month, and then ended the month with a net asset value of $10.03 would have a monthly return of:

$$r_t = \frac{(\$10.03 - \$10.00) + \$.05 + \$.04}{\$10.00}$$

$$= 1.20\%.$$

Returns calculated in this manner can be used to evaluate the performance of the portfolio manager of a mutual fund because this method reflects the results of the manager's investment decisions. However, it does not necessarily indicate the return earned by the shareholders in the fund because a load charge may have been involved. In the example, perhaps the investor paid $10.50 at the beginning of the month for one share of this fund, with $.50 being a front-end load. If this were the case, the investor's return for this month is calculated using Equation (21.2), where NAV_{t-1} is $10.50, not $10.00:

$$r_t = \frac{(\$10.03 - \$10.50) + \$.05 + \$.04}{\$10.50}$$

$$= -3.62\%$$

Thus the return for the investor who bought one share at the beginning of the month and paid a \$.50 per share load charge at that time would be -3.62%. However, the portfolio manager was only given \$10.00 per share to invest, because the load charge was paid to certain people who were responsible for getting the investor to buy the share. Accordingly, the portfolio manager should be evaluated on the basis of the return provided on the \$10.00, which in this example was 1.20%.

Recently, data on professionally managed pension funds and bank commingled funds have become available. The performance of the managers of such funds appears to be similar to that of mutual fund managers: They do reasonably well tailoring portfolios to meet clients' objectives, but few seem to be able to consistently "beat the market." Although the following sections deal only with U.S. mutual funds, many of the results apply to other investment companies, both in the United States and in other countries. A more detailed discussion of certain risk-adjusted measures of performance and their application to mutual funds is deferred to Chapter 24.

21.5.2 Average Return

Some organizations have established two kinds of indices based on the net asset values of mutual funds that have similar investment objectives. One kind of index includes nearly all of the U.S.-based mutual funds, whereas the second kind uses a much smaller sample. As shown in Figure 21.4, both types of indices are presented every week (and, more extensively, every quarter) in *Barron's*, where mutual fund indices that have been prepared by Lipper Analytical Services are published.

Many studies have compared the performance of investment companies that have invested primarily in common stocks with the performance of a **benchmark portfolio** that generally consisted of a combination of (1) a market index, such as Standard & Poor's 500 stock index; (2) a riskfree asset, such as Treasury bills; and sometimes other indices, such as (3) an index to account for the difference in performance between large and small capitalization stocks and (4) an index to account for the difference in performance between high and low book-to-market price stocks. Each particular combination was chosen so that the benchmark portfolio had a risk level that was equal to that of the investment company. Thus an investment company that had a beta of .80 would be compared with a benchmark portfolio that had 80% invested in the market index and 20% in the riskfree asset (provided these were the only indices used to construct the benchmark portfolio).[16] Alternatively, sometimes *style analysis* is used to arrive at the appropriate benchmark. With this approach, a fund's returns are matched with those of a set of indices, such as the Standard & Poor's/BARRA Value and Growth indices, the Wilshire 4500 index (for small-cap stocks), and various others in order to arrive at a combination of the indices that seem to best describe the investment style of the fund (for more on style analysis, see *Institutional Issues: Custom Benchmark Portfolios* in Chapter 24).

One way of determining whether a mutual fund has had superior performance is to subtract the average return on the benchmark portfolio from the average return of the mutual fund. This abnormal return, known as the fund's *ex post* **alpha**, is denoted α_p:

$$\alpha_p = ar_p - ar_{bp} \tag{21.3}$$

where ar_p is the average return on portfolio p and ar_{bp} is the average return on the benchmark portfolio associated with portfolio p. Note that if $\alpha_p > 0$, then the

Variable Annuities

Variable annuities have become one of the hottest products to hit the institutional investment market in the 1990s. Despite the rather incongruous name, assets invested in variable annuities have grown to over $500 billion.

What is a variable annuity? To start, perhaps a better question is, "What is an annuity?" In the world of financial services, an annuity is a tax-advantaged form of investment made through an insurance company. The insurer makes certain promises about how and in what amounts the proceeds of the investment will be returned to the investor (or the investor's beneficiaries). There are two types of annuities: fixed and variable. A familiarity with fixed annuities is helpful in understanding variable annuities.

With a fixed annuity, you as the investor enter into a contract with an insurance company, agreeing to pay a stated amount known as the *premium*, which represents the cost of the annuity. This premium is usually paid in a lump sum. In exchange for the premium, the insurance company sets an interest rate that it will credit your investment with over a specified *guarantee period* of time. You choose the length of the guarantee period, with rates usually higher for longer periods. At the end of the guarantee period, the insurance company will establish new rates and you must again choose a guarantee period.

The commitment involved in a fixed annuity is a two-way street. In the early years of your contract, withdrawing more than a small proportion (usually up to 10%) of your investment annually invokes a *surrender penalty*. Over several years, the size of the penalty declines to zero. Further, if at the end of a rate guarantee period, the newly offered rate is materially lower (as defined by the annuity contract) than the previous rate, you can withdraw from the contract penalty-free and move the balance to another annuity provider.

Fixed annuities are similar in many respects to bank certificate of deposits (CDs). There are several distinctions however. Most important, your investment is allowed to accumulate interest on a tax-deferred basis. Only when you withdraw from the annuity must you pay tax on the earned interest. In the case of a CD, you pay taxes annually on your earnings. In exchange for this tax advantage, however, you cannot withdraw funds from your annuity until age 59.5 (un-less you transfer to another annuity) without being assessed a 10% penalty by the IRS.

Fixed annuities are also different from CDs in that you have the option to "annuitize" the distribution of your accumulated investment. There are many different annuity variations. Payments are typically monthly or quarterly. You can receive payments for a specified period of time, or you can have the payments continue over your entire life, ending only when you die. You can even have your payments go to your beneficiary after you die. The size of your annuity payments will depend on the selected payout option.

Variable annuities are really not much more complicated than fixed annuities. Essentially the word *variable* refers to the rate of return earned on the premiums that you invest with the insurance company. Instead of offering a fixed interest rate guaranteed over a specified period of time, the annuity provider offers you a set of investment options into which your premiums can be invested, such as a portfolio of growth stocks. You make the decision as to where to place your investment and if, and when, to switch those choices. The value of your accumulated earnings will respond commensurately (up or down) with the returns on your investment selection.

Variable annuities are different from fixed annuities in two other key ways. First, you can add more funds to a variable annuity at any time before starting to receive annuitized distributions. In the case of fixed-rate annuities, adding additional funds requires purchasing a new contract at possibly a different interest rate. Second, the insurance company promises your beneficiaries a "death benefit" equal to the greater of your paid premiums (less any withdrawals) or the value of your investments at the time of your death. Thus, variable annuities offer an insured "floor" on the value of your investments. (Because of the guaranteed interest rate, fixed-rate annuities have no need for such a provision.)

The remainder of the variable annuity contract is essentially no different from the fixed annuity contract. Your earnings compound on a tax-deferred basis. Withdrawals are subject to surrender penalties depending on the terms of your contract. IRS penalties are charged on withdrawals before age 59.5. And when you move from the accumulation phase to the distribution phase, you can annuitize your distributions in a similar variety of ways.

Variable annuities have been around since the early 1950s. The explosion in variable annuity popularity has come in recent years as the federal government has vastly reduced the ability of investors to shelter investment income from taxes. Especially for people without access to employer-sponsored 401(k) retirement plans or who make contributions to either IRAs or Keogh Plans that are by law capped (see Chapter 12), variable annuities offer the only means to easily make large tax-deferred investments.

Traditionally, insurance companies offered their variable annuity customers only investment options managed by the insurance companies themselves. Today, many insurance companies have made arrangements with mutual fund providers to offer versions of the mutual funds to variable annuity investors, with the insurers handling the death benefits. Although variable annuity investments must be kept in legally separate portfolios (known as "separate accounts"), mutual fund providers in many cases create "clone" versions of their popular funds specifically for variable annuity clients. More recently, an increasing number of mutual fund companies have turned the tables on the insurance companies by offering their own variable annuity products and making arrangements with insurance companies to provide the death benefits.

Should you invest in mutual funds on a taxable basis or in variable annuities on a tax-deferred basis? The answer is not as clear-cut as many proponents of variable annuities might contend. Certainly if you are under age 59.5 and may need access to your funds soon, you should factor in the IRS 10% withdrawal penalty and any insurance company surrender charges into your calculations.

Suppose though that you are investing for the long haul. The tax-deferred benefits of variable annuities appear attractive compared with the alternative of facing annual taxation of distributed income and realized capital gains that investors in taxable mutual funds must pay. However, these tax benefits may be overwhelmed by two adverse aspects of variable annuities. The first is their cost. Variable annuity investors not only must pay standard management and administrative expense fees similar to those paid by mutual fund shareholders, but they must also pay a fee to cover the death benefit. That fee typically runs in the range of 1% to 1.5% per year. Only you can decide whether the option to redeem your investment at its original value is worth this expense. (It is true that variable annuities do not involve explicit sales commissions, but an informed mutual fund investor generally should not purchase a load fund.)

Further, when assets are ultimately withdrawn from a variable annuity, the investor must pay taxes at ordinary income tax rates. The mutual fund investor, on the other hand, has annually been paying taxes primarily on realized capital gains at capital gains tax rates which are currently much lower than ordinary income tax rates (see Chapter 12). Depending on how quickly capital gains in the taxable mutual funds are realized and the amount of dividend and interest income earned, it is possible that the combination of no death benefit expenses and lower taxes paid at capital gains tax rates may be better than deferring ordinary income taxes until distribution. In general, the longer your investment horizon, the more the tax-deferred aspects of variable annuities are able to overcome their higher costs relative to taxable mutual funds.

If you are an investor who likes to move among funds (for example, between stock and bond funds) within a family of funds, variable annuities do offer a significant advantage over taxable mutual funds in rising markets. Within a variable annuity's fund family, switches occur without triggering a taxable event. With taxable mutual funds, a switch among funds will require payment of capital gains taxes on any appreciation in fund share values, regardless of whether the funds belong to a family of funds.

Finally, in terms of estate planning, variable annuities are at a disadvantage compared with taxable mutual funds. The death proceeds from a variable annuity bypass probate, easing administration of your estate. However, those proceeds are taxable to your beneficiaries as ordinary income. Conversely, the cost basis of taxable mutual funds will be stepped up to their market value at the time of your death—potentially a huge tax benefit.

LIPPER MUTUAL FUND PERFORMANCE AVERAGES

Weekly Summary Report: Thursday, March 19, 1998
Cumulative Performances With Dividends Reinvested

Net Asset	No. Funds		12/31/97– 03/19/98	03/12/98– 03/19/98	02/19/98– 03/19/98	12/18/97– 03/19/98	03/20/97– 03/19/98
General Equity Funds:							
107,074.8	258	Capital Appreciation	+ 10.76%	+ 1.47%	+ 5.26%	+ 14.37%	+ 33.41%
609,120.4	979	Growth Funds	+ 11.77%	+ 1.51%	+ 5.37%	+ 14.59%	+ 36.60%
89,436.1	302	Mid Cap Funds	+ 10.94%	+ 1.46%	+ 5.73%	+ 15.68%	+ 36.51%
140,082.7	577	Small Cap Funds	+ 9.15%	+ 1.54%	+ 4.90%	+ 13.77%	+ 37.73%
3,270.7	45	Micro Cap Funds	+ 8.94%	+ 1.26%	+ 5.15%	+ 12.88%	+ 45.86%
549,876.0	721	Growth and Income	+ 10.80%	+ 1.52%	+ 5.46%	+ 12.87%	+ 35.19%
123,675.8	88	S&P 500 Objective	+ 12.54%	+ 1.83%	+ 6.04%	+ 14.34%	+ 40.77%
142,015.0	219	Equity Income	+ 9.38%	+ 1.40%	+ 5.33%	+ 11.30%	+ 33.76%
1,764,551.5	3,189	Gen. Equity Funds Avg.	+ 10.73%	+ 1.51%	+ 5.34%	+ 13.88%	+ 36.21%
Other Equity Funds:							
14,906.0	43	Health/Biotechnology	+ 11.43%	+ 0.69%	+ 4.25%	+ 14.71%	+ 32.04%
6,289.6	59	Natural Resources	+ 0.13%	− 0.05%	+ 2.54%	+ 3.03%	+ 0.52%
24,520.5	72	Science & Technol.	+ 15.25%	+ 1.30%	+ 3.07%	+ 21.15%	+ 35.13%
3,847.7	16	Telecommunication Funds	+ 20.47%	+ 3.60%	+ 11.17%	+ 23.20%	+ 55.88%
22,690.2	105	Utility Funds	+ 8.29%	+ 2.54%	+ 6.84%	+ 11.14%	+ 35.79%
20,648.2	45	Financial Services	+ 10.54%	+ 2.76%	+ 7.61%	+ 12.23%	+ 49.43%
12,893.5	87	Real Estate Fund	− 2.40%	− 0.16%	− 0.90%	+ 0.46%	+ 14.64%
3,130.1	63	Specialty/Misc.	+ 6.52%	+ 0.61%	+ 3.37%	+ 8.51%	+ 32.62%
2,785.2	44	Gold Oriented Funds	− 1.65%	− 2.98%	− 1.88%	+ 1.67%	− 42.71%
102,907.6	216	Global Funds	+ 11.69%	+ 1.73%	+ 5.98%	+ 13.02%	+ 25.08%
20,911.9	35	Global Small Cap Funds	+ 11.04%	+ 1.72%	+ 6.01%	+ 13.45%	+ 18.54%
162,712.1	515	International Funds	+ 12.50%	+ 1.96%	+ 6.29%	+ 12.51%	+ 19.99%
4,324.6	50	Int'l Small Cap Funds	+ 15.69%	+ 2.49%	+ 8.60%	+ 15.32%	+ 13.59%
14,621.4	92	European Region Fds	+ 17.45%	+ 2.63%	+ 9.16%	+ 17.54%	+ 35.76%
4,836.6	50	Pacific Region Funds	+ 2.32%	+ 1.47%	+ 0.43%	+ 1.03%	− 22.23%
1,694.4	35	Japanese Funds	+ 1.32%	− 0.98%	− 4.11%	− 1.02%	− 7.19%
4,496.1	82	Pacific Ex Japan Funds	+ 4.98%	+ 3.58%	+ 4.30%	+ 3.70%	− 31.12%
1,002.8	22	China Region Funds	+ 2.84%	+ 3.91%	+ 6.17%	+ 1.12%	− 18.99%
19,178.4	153	Emerging Markets Funds	+ 3.53%	+ 1.28%	+ 5.98%	+ 5.95%	− 8.28%
3,903.7	43	Latin American Funds	− 0.60%	+ 2.06%	+ 7.90%	+ 5.12%	+ 8.34%
113.4	5	Canadian Funds	+ 1.93%	− 2.34%	+ 3.19%	+ 8.72%	− 7.89%
343,488.2	1,342	World Equity Funds Avg.	+ 9.50%	+ 1.76%	+ 5.62%	+ 10.16%	+ 9.53%
2,216,965.5	5,021	All Equity Funds Avg.	+ 10.05%	+ 1.55%	+ 5.28%	+ 12.53%	+ 28.35%
Other Funds:							
62,767.8	218	Flexible Portfolio	+ 7.81%	+ 1.02%	+ 3.69%	+ 9.35%	+ 25.37%
24,039.7	92	Global Flex Port.	+ 7.68%	+ 1.14%	+ 3.87%	+ 8.69%	+ 18.83%
144,885.4	391	Balanced Funds	+ 7.19%	+ 0.91%	+ 3.36%	+ 8.61%	+ 24.98%
1,206.3	15	Balanced Target	+ 5.24%	+ 0.42%	+ 1.45%	+ 6.35%	+ 18.40%
7,586.7	57	Conv. Securities	+ 6.70%	+ 0.89%	+ 3.77%	+ 8.71%	+ 23.07%
26,767.5	74	Income Funds	+ 4.93%	+ 0.73%	+ 2.60%	+ 6.04%	+ 20.24%
22,745.6	266	World Income Funds	+ 2.43%	+ 0.24%	+ 0.84%	+ 2.62%	+ 8.09%
416,625.8	1,814	Fixed Income Funds	+ 1.84%	+ 0.07%	+ 0.25%	+ 2.05%	+ 10.32%
2,923,590.3	7,948	Long-Term Average	+ 7.61%	+ 1.10%	+ 3.79%	+ 9.38%	+ 22.87%
N/A		Long-Term Median	+ 8.23%	+ 1.17%	+ 4.37%	+ 10.37%	+ 24.48%
N/A		Funds with a % Change	+ 7,686	+ 7,381	+ 7,644	+ 7,650	+ 6,898

Securities Market Indexes

Value	U.S. Equities:					
474.30	Russell 2000 Index xd	+ 8.53%	+ 1.40%	+ 4.42%	+ 12.83%	+ 34.63%
567.38	NYSE Composite xd	+ 10.99%	+ 1.70%	+ 6.05%	+ 13.09%	+ 37.79%
1,260.82	S&P Industrials	+ 12.43%	+ 1.41%	+ 5.27%	+ 14.32%	+ 37.82%
1,089.74	S&P 500 xd	+ 12.29%	+ 1.85%	+ 5.98%	+ 14.07%	+ 39.24%
8,803.05	Dow Jones Ind. Avg. xd	+ 11.31%	+ 1.66%	+ 5.10%	+ 12.19%	+ 29.07%
Value	**International Equities:**					
1,667.90	Nikkei 225 Average xd	+ 9.31%	+ 0.63%	+ 0.38%	+ 3.20%	− 9.81%
5,997.90	FT S-E 100 Index	+ 16.79%	+ 3.50%	+ 4.89%	+ 16.05%	+ 40.86%
4,936.32	DAX Index	+ 16.16%	+ 2.00%	+ 7.72%	+ 18.48%	+ 51.20%

Fund Management Companies

Value:						
3,376.12	Stock-price Index	+ 15.91%	+ 1.22%	+ 6.62%	+ 16.72%	+ 52.52%

xd-Price only index. Calculated without reinvestment of dividends. The Nikkei index value is divided by 10 due to space limitation. Source: Lipper Analytical Services Inc., Summit, New Jersey 07901

Figure 21.4
Mutual Fund Indices

Source: Reprinted by permission of *Barron's*, Dow Jones & Company, Inc., March 23, 1998, p. MW92. All rights reserved worldwide.

portfolio will have performed well because it will have had positive risk-adjusted returns. Conversely, if $\alpha_p < 0$, then the portfolio will have had inferior returns.

In addition to examining portfolio performance to see if some group of mutual funds has earned abnormally high (or low) returns, it also important to examine the persistence of funds' performance. That is, do the funds that have had the highest returns (or abnormal returns) over some time period continue to have the highest returns (or abnormal returns) over a succeeding time period? Do poor performers in one time period continue to be poor performers in the next time period? Alternatively, does a fund's performance in one time period provide any indication of how it will perform in the next time period? The next two sections examine portfolio performance and persistence of performance for equity funds and bond funds.

21.5.3   Equity Funds

A major study published in 1997 examined the performance of 1,892 diversified equity funds over the 32-year period of 1962–1993.[17] This study first sorted funds on January 1 of each year by their returns the previous year and then put the top 10% into portfolio 1, the next 10% into portfolio 2, and so on through portfolio 10, which consisted of the 10% worst performers the previous year. The portfolio's returns were then tracked over the next year. Thus, there is a series of monthly returns from 1963 to 1993 for each of the ten portfolios. In addition, the funds were similarly sorted into ten portfolios on January 1 of each year on the basis of their *abnormal* returns over the previous three years.

Figure 21.5 shows the average monthly *excess* return (that is, the average monthly return over the monthly Treasury bill rate) on the ten portfolios formed by sorting them on their previous year's returns. Note that the returns clearly decrease with the ranking, with portfolio 1 having the highest average excess return of .68% per month and portfolio 10, at .01%, having the lowest. Similarly, Figure 21.6 shows the average excess returns when the portfolios were sorted on the basis of their abnormal returns over the previous three years. While, again, there is a clear relationship between return and portfolio rank, the difference in the average excess return between portfolios 1 and 10 is not as extreme as in Figure 21.5.

Figures 21.5 and 21.6 also show the average monthly *abnormal* returns earned by the ten portfolios *subsequent* to their formation. Three observations can be made.

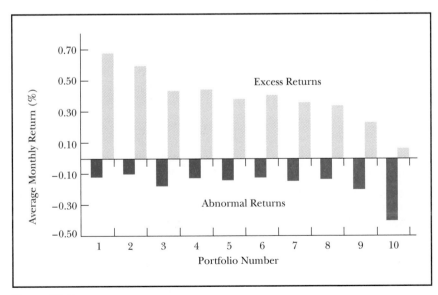

Figure 21.5
Average Monthly Returns of Mutual Fund Portfolios That Were Based
on Previous One-Year Returns
Source: Adapted from Mark M. Carhart, "On Persistence in Mutual Fund Performance," *Journal of Finance* 52, no. 1 (March 1997): 77.

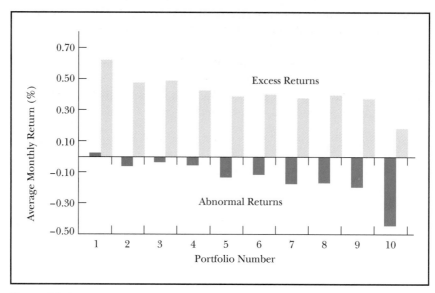

Figure 21.6
Average Monthly Returns of Mutual Fund Portfolios That Were Based
on Previous Three-Year Abnormal Returns

Source: Adapted from Mark M. Carhart, "On Persistence in Mutual Fund Performance," *Journal of Finance* 52, no. 1 (March 1997): 64.

First, note that all of the abnormal returns are negative except one, portfolio 1 in Figure 21.6. Because the exception has an abnormal return that is not statistically significantly greater than zero, this result would appear to be consistent with the argument that the typical mutual fund cannot beat the market. Second, there is still dispersion in the returns, with portfolio 1 having the highest (or nearly the highest) and portfolio 10 having the lowest abnormal return. Third, the bottom decile portfolio stands out for having by far the lowest abnormal return.

Each fund's abnormal return was related to certain of the fund's characteristics in order to see if an explanation could be found for the differing levels of abnormal returns. Measures of the following fund characteristics were used:

1. Operating expense ratio
2. Portfolio turnover rate (A fund's **portfolio turnover rate** is the ratio of the smaller of purchases or sales during a time period divided by the average total asset value during the period, and hence is a measure of how much trading was done during that period.)
3. Maximum load charge
4. Average total net assets

The results indicated that there was a strong negative relationship between abnormal return and the first two of these characteristics. That is, funds with higher expense ratios and turnover had lower abnormal returns. Although a negative relationship between load charges and abnormal returns was observed, it was likely due to the fact that load funds tend to have higher turnover rates, and thus the existence of higher loads does not, by itself, lead to lower performance. Larger funds tended to have slightly lower abnormal returns, but the relationship was not statistically significant. There is also evidence that transaction costs are inversely related to fund performance, as funds with lower abnormal returns tend to hold more illiquid stocks that cost more to trade.

Further analysis of the rankings of funds in the first year ("Subsequent Ranking") after they are sorted into portfolios ("Initial Ranking") used one year of *gross returns* for ranking purposes, where each fund's operating expense ratio was added back into its return.[18] If a fund did not survive the year after it was assigned to a decile, it was put in a "dead fund" category. The results weakly indicated that winners were likely to remain winners in the next year, and losers were likely to remain losers. In addition, the number of funds that become "dead" in the year after they were assigned to a portfolio increased monotonically with the fund's Initial Ranking, meaning that funds with lower gross returns were more likely to subsequently become dead than were funds with higher gross returns. Thus, for the most part the rankings of funds in the year after they are assigned to a portfolio decile appear to be random. Subsequent analysis of those top-decile funds that tended to remain in the top decile indicated that their high ranking was short-lived; it disappeared in the second year after the Initial Ranking period.

Similar observations were made when the Initial Ranking was based on each fund's abnormal return over a three-year period. That is, relatively few funds remained in their portfolio decile in the Subsequent Ranking period, with only a few more than chance remaining in the top and bottom deciles.

Aside from concluding that the evidence suggests that markets are efficient, the study provides three rules of thumb for the investor:

1. Do not purchase funds that have persistently poor performance.
2. Expect funds that had high returns in the last year to at most have high returns in only the next year.
3. Expect high expense ratios, load fees, and transaction costs to hinder fund performance.

Another study reached similar conclusions.[19] The returns from 1965 through 1984 were examined for 143 equity mutual funds that were divided into two groups based on whether they had a load charge. The average abnormal return of the load funds was −1.6%; for no-load funds it was −.8%. This difference suggests that funds with load charges do not on average earn sufficiently higher returns to justify investors' buying their shares.

The 143 funds were also divided into five groups based on the size of their operating expense ratios. Then the average abnormal return was calculated for each group. From the highest to the lowest expense group, these values were equal to −3.9%, −1.7%, −.7%, −1.2%, and −.6%. Note that with one exception there is a perfect ordering between performance and expenses; lower expenses are associated with better (but still negative) performance.

The mutual funds were again divided into five groups, but this time the division was based on the size of their turnover ratios. Again the average abnormal return was calculated for each group. From the highest to the lowest turnover group, these values were equal to −2.2%, −1.9%, −2.2%, −1.1%, and −.6%. Similar to the expense ratio results, there is a perfect ordering (again with one exception) between performance and turnover; lower turnover is associated with better performance.

One reasonable explanation for these observations is that, in an efficient market, higher expense ratios and more frequent revisions will cause a fund to incur more costs but without being able to consistently earn gains from the purchase of underpriced securities as an offset. Furthermore, whereas revisions in a fund's portfolio may be desirable so as to maintain a desired risk level or dividend yield, the evidence indicates that revisions intended to exploit supposed market inefficiencies generally prove unproductive because of the associated transaction costs.

These results suggest that the average equity mutual fund has not significantly outperformed an equal-risk passive alternative over any extended period.[20] This outcome is not surprising. After all, the market's performance is itself an average of the performance of all investors. If, on average, mutual funds had beaten the market, then some other group of investors would have "lost" to the market. With the substantial amount of professional management in today's stock market, it is difficult to think of a likely group of victims.

21.5.4 Bond Mutual Funds

All of the results reported so far focus on mutual funds that have at least a large part of their assets invested in common stocks. This leaves open the question of bond mutual funds: Is their performance similar to that of stock funds? One study looked at a sample of 41 bond funds over the period from 1979 through 1988.[21]

A variety of models were used to produce benchmark returns. The average abnormal return ranged from −.023% to −.069% per month. Furthermore, regardless of the model, at least two-thirds of the funds had negative abnormal returns. Expanding the sample to cover 223 bond funds over the period of 1987 to 1991 produced similar results. It was determined that there was an inverse relationship between the size of a fund's expense ratio and its performance; that is, higher expenses tended to be associated with worse performance. In summary it appears that the results regarding stock funds are also applicable to bond funds.

In a more recent study of 123 bond funds (excluding high-yield funds) over the six-year period of 1986 to 1991 revealed that no matter which one of four methods was used to estimate benchmark returns, the average bond fund had a negative abnormal return, and in three of the cases it was significantly negative. Specifically, the four average abnormal returns were −.12%, −.06%, −.10%, and −.08% per month. Average abnormal returns calculated using gross returns were −.04%, .02%, −.02%, and .00% per month, with none of these values being significantly different from zero.[22] Thus, apparently, the average fund approximately matches the returns on a similar-risk benchmark, but, owing to expenses, it underperforms its benchmark. This outcome suggests that investors in bond mutual funds should choose low-expense funds, unless they are confident in the forecasting ability of a particular fund's manager.

21.6 EVALUATING MUTUAL FUNDS

Along with the rapid growth in money invested in mutual funds in recent years has come a corresponding increase in the number and diversity of mutual funds offered to investors. Not surprisingly then, various organizations have created businesses devoted to evaluating mutual funds. One of the most prominent of these organizations is Morningstar, Inc., located in Chicago. Besides providing a wealth of information on a given fund, it also provides an in-depth analysis of past returns.

The best way to understand the breadth of Morningstar's mutual fund evaluations is to consider an analysis of a specific fund. An example involving the Fidelity Magellan Fund, an equity fund, is shown in Figure 21.7 and explained next. Where different, a description of the analysis is also given for a fixed-income fund.

21.6.1 Performance

In the left-hand side of Figure 21.7 is a section with the heading "Performance." Displayed here are, first, the quarterly returns over the last five years and second, the average returns earned by the fund over various time periods ending March 31, 1997, ranging from the past three months to the past 15 years. These returns are calculated net of operating expenses and 12b-1 fees, although load charges are ignored.

Performance 03-31-97

	1st Qtr	2nd Qtr	3rd Qtr	4th Qtr	Total
1993	8.62	6.42	8.21	−0.34	24.66
1994	−1.59	−4.49	5.43	−0.90	−1.81
1995	8.44	15.77	10.60	−1.46	36.82
1996	1.79	1.00	1.67	6.85	11.69
1997	−0.56	—	—	—	—

Trailing	Total Return%	+/− S&P 500	+/− Wil Top 750	% Rank All	% Rank Cat	Growth of $10,000
3 Mo	−0.56	−3.24	−2.44	63	88	9,944
6 Mo	6.25	−4.99	−3.45	26	77	10,625
1 Yr	9.11	−10.71	−8.01	36	95	10,911
3 Yr Avg	14.88	−7.40	−6.43	23	89	15,163
5 Yr Avg	14.92	−1.49	−0.28	13	34	20,045
10 Yr Avg	13.79	0.42	0.98	7	6	36,391
15 Yr Avg	21.02	3.44	4.18	1	1	174,946

Risk Analysis

Time Period	Load-Adj Return %	Risk %Rank[1] All	Risk %Rank[1] Cat	Morningstar Return	Morningstar Risk	Morningstar Risk-Adj Rating
1 Yr	5.84					
3 Yr	13.72	83	95	0.89	1.11	★★★
5 Yr	14.22	74	79	1.20	0.93	★★★
10 Yr	13.44	72	78	1.57	0.96	★★★★

Average Historical Rating (136 months). 4.8★s

[1] 1=low, 100=high

Category Rating (3 Yr)

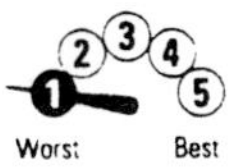

Return	Below Avg
Risk	High

Other Measures	Standard Index S&P 500	Best Fit Index SPMid400
Alpha	−5.9	0.2
Beta	0.99	0.94
R-Squared	68	75
Standard Deviation		13.13
Mean		14.61
Sharpe Ratio		0.85

Historical Profile

Return	Above Avg
Risk	Average
Rating	★★★★ Above Avg

Current Investment Style

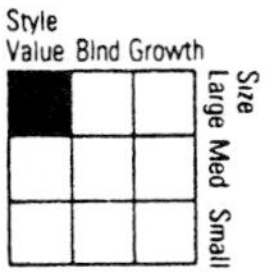

	Stock Port Avg	Relative S&P 500 Current	Relative S&P 500 Hist	Rel Cat
Price/Earnings Ratio	22.7	0.96	1.1	0.97
Price/Book Ratio	3.8	0.72	0.9	0.77
4 Yr Earnings Gr%	23.9	1.33	1.6	1.25
Price/Cash Flow	12.7	0.90	1.1	0.92
Debt % Total Cap	32.6	1.03	1.0	1.04
Med Mkt Cap $mil	10,201	0.4	0.8	0.60
Foreign %	12.5	—	—	1.88

Figure 21.7
Performance and Risk Analysis of the Magellan Fund (Excerpts)
Source: Excerpts from *Morningstar Mutual Funds.* Morningstar, Inc. 225 W. Wacker Dr., Chicago, IL 60606. 312-696-6000. September, 25, 1997, p. 118.

Thus the average returns reflect what an investor would have earned after having bought the fund's shares.[23] Next to each average return is an indication of how it compares with the average return on the S&P 500 and Wilshire 750 indices over the same time period. For fixed-income funds these indices are replaced by the Lehman Brothers Aggregate Bond Index and another fixed-income bond index that best matches the fund's holdings.

In the fourth and fifth columns from the left are the percentile ranks of the fund's average return relative to all mutual funds and relative to those funds identified by Morningstar as having a similar stated investment objective. (For classification purposes, Morningstar refers to investment objectives as *categories*.)[24] Here a rank of 1 places a fund at the top and a rank of 100 places a fund at the bottom. The sixth column shows the amount a $10,000 dollar investment in the fund would have grown to over the applicable time period (ignoring taxes and load charges).

Over the three months ending March 31, 1997, Magellan had a return of −.56%, which was 3.24% lower than the S&P 500 and 2.44% lower than the Wilshire 750. This return caused the fund to be ranked at the 63rd percentile of all funds and the 88th percentile of those funds in the same category. Notably, over the past 15 years it can be seen that the Magellan Fund did substantially better than both indices, placing it in the first percentile overall and in its category. Note that a $10,000 investment in the Magellan Fund that was made on March 31, 1982, would have grown to $174,946 on March 31, 1997, 15 years later.

21.6.2 Ratings

In the "Risk Analysis" section of Figure 21.7 are columns under Load-Adj Return, Risk % Rank: All and Cat, Morningstar: Return and Risk, and Morningstar Risk-Adj Rating. The three columns labeled Load-Adj Return, Morningstar: Return and Risk need to be explained first. It is easiest to focus on the ten-year row; the other rows are straightforward extensions of it. First, the average return for Magellan and all other portfolios in the same category are determined for the past ten years. The actual net return is adjusted for any load charges that the fund levies on investors, producing a return of 13.44% in the Load-Adj Return column. Second, the average ten-year returns for all funds in the same category are averaged. Third, Magellan's average return is divided by this overall average. Hence a return measure of greater than 1 means that the fund did better than average, whereas a return measure of less than 1 indicates that the fund did worse than average. In Magellan's case the Morningstar Return measure of 1.57 indicates that its average return was 57% better than the overall average.

For the ten-year Morningstar Risk entry, the appropriate monthly Treasury bill return is subtracted from each of the previous 120 monthly net returns to calculate the fund's excess returns. Then only the negative excess returns are summed, and the absolute value is divided by 120 to provide a measure of the fund's downside risk. (This risk measure is similar to the risk measure known as mean shortfall, which was discussed in *Institutional Issues: Alternative Risk Measures* in Chapter 6.)

For example, imagine that this risk measure is calculated over six months instead of 120 months and that the following returns are observed:

Month	Fund Return	T-Bill Return	Fund Return Less T-Bill Return
1	4.0%	.5%	3.5%
2	−2.0	.5	−2.5
3	.4	.6	−0.2
4	5.0	.6	4.4
5	−3.0	.6	−3.6
6	1.0	.7	.3

The three negative excess returns of −2.5%, −.2%, and −3.6% sum to −6.3%. Dividing this sum by 6, the total number of months, results in a downside risk measure of 1.05 (=6.3/6).

Downside risk measures are calculated by Morningstar for funds in the same category, and an overall average for these funds is determined. Then the fund's downside risk measure is divided by this overall measure; the resulting number is Morningstar's measure of the fund's relative risk. In the case of Magellan, it is .96, indicating that it had 4% less downside risk than the average similar fund over the ten-year period.

Under the heading "Risk % Rank" the percentile rankings are found for the fund's downside risk measure against all funds ("All") and funds in the same category ("Cat"). Here a percentile rank of 1 indicates that the fund had the least risk, whereas a rank of 100 indicates that the fund had the most risk. In the case of Magellan, its ranks of 72 and 78 over ten years indicate that it had more risk than 72% of all the other funds and 78% of the other funds in the same category.

Morningstar's rating system has five ranks, as follows:

Stars	Percentile	Return Category	Risk Category
*****	1–10	Highest or high	Lowest or low
****	11–32.5	Above average	Below average
***	33.5–67.5	Average	Average
**	68.5–90	Below average	Above average
*	91–100	Lowest or low	Highest or high

Hence the percentile rank, based on the set of funds in the same category, determines how many stars the fund is given and the category in which it is placed.[25]

The Morningstar Risk-Adj Rating is determined by subtracting the fund's downside risk measure from its return measure. In the case of Magellan, its ten-year risk-adjusted measure is .59 (= 1.57 − .98). This measure is also determined for all the other funds in the same category, and then percentile ranks are determined. Magellan ranked somewhere between 11 and 32.5, causing it to receive a four-star rating.[26]

21.6.3 Historical Profile

Summary performance measures are contained in the "Historical Profile" part of Figure 21.7. Consider the return measure first. The previously described return measures for three, five, and ten years are averaged using weights of 20%, 30%, and 50% to arrive at a weighted-average return. After this calculation has been made for each of the other funds in the same category, the fund is given a percentile rank and then a rating, as indicated before. Magellan's percentile rank was somewhere between 11 and 32.5, giving it an *above average* ranking. Similar weighted-average calculations are done for the fund's downside risk measure and risk-adjusted measure, resulting in Magellan's receiving an *average* risk rating and a four-star *above average* risk-adjusted rating.

21.6.4 Category Rating and Other Measures

Just below the "Risk Analysis" section of the figure is a gauge that can point to one of five numbers based on the fund's returns over the last three years. This simply indicates the overall performance of the fund over the past three years but uses a gauge instead of the star-based system as described earlier. Thus, over the past three years Fidelity Magellan received a rating of 1, the lowest possible overall rating. This rating is undoubtedly due to its having received a rating of *below average* for its three-year return, and a rating of *high* for its level of risk over the past three years, as indicated directly below the gauge. These two ratings are the equivalent of two and one stars, respectively.

Next to the "Category Rating" in Figure 21.7 is the section that Morningstar refers to as "Other Measures." The top part provides values for alpha, beta, and R-squared. They correspond to the statistics related to a portfolio's *ex post* characteristic line, which is a regression model like the market model that was discussed in chapter 7.[27] The only difference between the two is that the *ex post* characteristic line uses excess returns instead of returns. Hence Morningstar reports the results from regressing the previous 36 monthly excess returns of the mutual fund (that is, the fund's net returns less the corresponding Treasury bill rates) on the previous 36 monthly excess returns of the S&P 500 (that is, the index's returns less the corresponding Treasury bill rates). As a result the fund's *ex post* alpha ("Alpha") and beta ("Beta") are estimated. Similarly, R-squared is the coefficient of determination (multiplied by 100) that is determined when the 36 excess returns of the fund are compared with those of the S&P 500. Morningstar also reports the regression results for the index that produced the highest R-squared from a set of indices. For example, if the R-squared of a fund is higher with the Russell 2000 than with the S&P 500, this result would indicate that the fund follows an investment objective of investing in small companies.

It can be seen that Magellan had a beta of .99 and .94 when regressed against the the S&P 500 and S&P MidCap 400 index, respectively. Its *ex post* alpha of −5.9% and .2% indicates that it did much worse than the S&P 500 but about the same as the S&P MidCap 400 index, respectively, over the last 36 months on a risk-adjusted basis. The R-squared values of 68 and 75 mean that roughly 68% and 75% of the variation in the excess returns of the fund could be attributed to variations in the excess returns on the two S&P indices.

The second part of this section provides values for the fund's standard deviation, mean, and Sharpe ratio. These three values are also based on the previous 36 monthly rates of return on the fund. Standard deviation and mean are the standard deviation and the average return (annualized) for the portfolio, which for Magellan are 13.13% and 14.61%, respectively. The Sharpe ratio, discussed more fully in Chapter 24, gives a risk-adjusted measure of performance. Here Morningstar takes the fund's average excess return over the previous 12 months and divides it by the fund's standard deviation over the previous 36 months. Hence it is the ratio of excess return to risk, which for Magellan equals .85.

21.6.5 Investment Style

The Current Investment Style section appears in the lower right part of Figure 21.7. On the right are seven descriptive measures of the average stock held by the fund using the most recently available data. For example, the average price/earnings ratio of the stocks held in the Magellan Fund was 22.7 as of March 31, 1997. This number is divided by the average price-earnings ratio of the stocks in the S&P 500, indicating a value of .96, or 4% less than the average ratio in the index. Furthermore, the average price-earnings ratio for the past three years for the stocks in the fund's portfolio was 1.1. Last, the current value of the ratio, when divided by the average for all funds in the same category, was .97, indicating that the ratio was 3% less than the current average. The ratios shown here are weighted averages, where the weight for each security is based on the relative proportion of the fund that is invested in the security. In the case of a fund that invests in fixed-income securities, these seven measures are replaced by average measures such as effective duration, effective maturity, credit quality, coupon interest rate, and price.

Also in this part of Figure 21.7 is a 3 by 3 matrix, which Morningstar calls a *style box*. The two extreme columns represent the investment styles of value and growth, with the middle column representing a mixture of the two. A fund's style is determined by summing the fund's price-earnings ratio and price-book ratio, where both are expressed relative to the S&P 500. Note that this sum for the S&P 500 itself is 2.00 (since each ratio is, by definition, equal to 1.00). Morningstar has decided that if the sum for a fund is less than 1.75, then the fund follows a *value style*; the fund has invested in stocks that collectively have relatively low valuation ratios and hence are viewed as value stocks. On the other hand, if the sum is greater than 2.25, the fund is deemed to follow a *growth style* because it has invested in stocks with relatively high valuation ratios. Sums between 1.75 and 2.25 indicate that the fund follows a *blended style*, investing in stocks that in aggregate have no distinct style. Magellan's sum is 1.68 (=.96 + .72), indicating that it currently follows a value style. The value of this sum for the S&P 500 itself is 2.00, so the Magellan Fund tends to purchase stocks that have price-earnings and price-book ratios that on average are lower than the two valuation ratios of stocks in the S&P 500.

The three rows of the style box are based on the size of the stocks held by the fund, where size is measured by the Median Market Capitalization figure for the fund. If this figure is less than $1 billion, the fund is deemed to be *small*, and if it is greater than $5 billion, then the fund is deemed to be *large* and between $1 billion and $5 billion the fund is deemed medium. Because the median size of Magellan's holdings is $10.201 billion the fund is categorized as *large*.

In Chapter 16 it was mentioned that stocks can be classified along the two dimensions of value-growth and size. Now it can be seen that investment companies investing primarily in stocks can be similarly classified. Morningstar does this by use of the style box, thereby allowing investors to quickly understand a fund's investment strategy. Nine combinations of the three levels of value-growth and size are possible. Morningstar indicates its classification of a fund by darkening one of the nine sections of the style box. In the case of Magellan the upper left box is darkened, indicating that its investment strategy involves purchases of large value stocks.

In the case of fixed-income funds, the columns of the style box are based on the average duration of the securities in the fund, and hence the style box focuses on the fund's interest rate sensitivity. The column headings are "Short Term" (if the average duration is between one and 3.5 years), "Intermediate Term" (if the average duration is between 3.5 and six years), and "Long Term" (if the average duration is greater than six years). The rows are based on the average credit quality of the securities in the fund, and hence measure default risk. The credit quality row headings are "High" (if the average bond rating is at least AA), "Average" (if the average is between BBB and AA), and "Low" (if the average is less than BBB); federal government securities are treated as being AAA.

In general, when Morningstar assigns a stock or bond fund to a category, it is based on where the fund is located in the style box. Hence, there are nine categories of stock funds and nine categories of bond funds for the two style boxes. In addition, there are special categories for sector and international stock funds as well as municipal and international bond funds.[28]

21.6.6 Caveats

Morningstar's performance measures are useful in giving an investor a quick reading of how a mutual fund has performed in the past relative to other funds. However, several things should be kept in mind.

1. Performance comparisons are made with the S&P 500 and Lehman Brothers Aggregate Bond Index for all equity and bond funds, respectively, but these indices may not be appropriate for certain funds. For example, a fund that invests primarily in securities listed on Nasdaq might more appropriately be compared with an over-the-counter index. Morningstar attempts to overcome this problem by making performance comparisons within categories composed of funds with similar investment objectives.

2. As will be discussed in Chapter 23, portfolio managers can attempt to earn abnormal returns by trying to (1) buy underpriced securities and then profit from their subsequent abnormal price appreciation or (2) if a stock fund, shift funds out of the stock market just before it goes down and then back into the stock market just before it rises or, if a bond fund, shift funds between long-term and short-term bonds depending on the forecast for interest rates, or (3) do both. Morningstar's performance measures do not indicate which approach the fund is using in its quest for abnormal returns.

3. The use of peer group comparisons to evaluate performance has several serious conceptual and practical shortcomings. For example, the set of similar funds may not be entirely appropriate (even though they may be the best match that Morningstar can provide), causing the ratings to be misleading. One fund may be restricted to buying just NYSE-listed common stock whereas another is free to purchase stocks that are listed on the NYSE, AMEX, or Nasdaq. Furthermore, similar funds may differ considerably in the amount of risk that they take on. Morningstar has attempted to minimize this problem by its use of more narrowly defined categories for comparison purposes, but such categorization is far from perfect.

4. Finally, *survivorship bias* (the tendency for poorly performing funds to go out of business and hence leave the peer group) hampers comparisons with similar funds.

CLOSED-END FUND PREMIUMS AND DISCOUNTS

Several studies have shown that the performance of diversified closed-end investment company managers in the United States is similar to that of open-end investment company managers.[29] When returns are measured by changes in net asset values (plus all distributions), closed-end investment companies appear to be neither better nor worse than open-end ones. Again, there is little evidence that portfolio managers can, on average, either select underpriced securities or time the market successfully.

21.7.1 Pricing of Shares

However, there is more to be said about closed-end funds. An investor can purchase an open-end fund's shares for their net asset value (plus any required load charge) and sell them later at the subsequent net asset value. Except for any operating expenses, load charges and 12b-1 fees, the performance of the *management* of such a fund, based on net asset values, corresponds exactly to the returns provided to the *shareholders*. This is not the case for closed-end investment companies, because investors buy and sell shares of investment companies at prices determined on the open (secondary) market. Whereas some companies have share prices that are above their net asset values (such shares are said to sell at a *premium*), many have share prices below their net asset values (such shares are said to sell at a *discount*).

This situation has resulted in several "puzzles" concerning the typical pricing of closed-end fund shares. Three of the most prominent are as follows. First, as mentioned earlier, the shares sell at a premium of roughly 10% of their net asset value when initially sold and then fall to a discount of roughly 10% of their net asset value shortly thereafter. Why would investors buy such shares when they are initially offered for sale, knowing that their price is going to fall substantially afterward? Second, the size of this discount fluctuates widely over time.[30] Figure 21.8 shows the price behavior of a sample of 16 closed-end funds. Note that the average fund sold at a discount that ranged from roughly 3% to 12% over the previous four quarters. What causes these fluctuations? Third, it appears possible to earn abnormally high returns by purchasing funds with the biggest discounts. One study that examined closed-end funds from 1965 to 1985 found that buying a portfolio of roughly seven or eight funds with the biggest discounts and holding them until their discounts shrank so that there were about 15 funds with larger discounts resulted in an inexplicable average abnormal monthly return of .8% (or about 10% per year).[31] How can such a simple investment strategy exist in an efficient market?

21.7.2 Investing in Fund Shares

The fact that the share price of a closed-end investment company differs from its net asset value, with the magnitude of the difference varying over time, introduces an added source of risk and potential return to investors. By purchasing shares at a discount, an investor may be able to earn more than just the change in the company's net asset value. Even if the company's discount remains constant, the effective dividend yield will be greater than that of an otherwise similar no-load, open-end investment company, because the purchase price will be less. If the discount is substantial when the shares are purchased, it may subsequently narrow and the re-

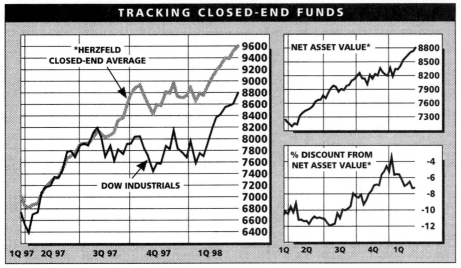

TRACKING CLOSED-END FUNDS

The Herzfeld Closed-End Average measures 16 equally-weighted closed-end funds based in the U.S. that invest principally in American equities. The net asset value is a weighted average of the funds' NAVs. *The net asset value and % discount charts lag the market by one week. Source: Thomas J. Herzfeld Advisors Inc., Miami. 305-271-1900

Figure 21.8
Closed-End Fund Performance
Source: Reprinted by permission of *Barron's*, Dow Jones & Company, Inc., March 23, 1998, p. MW91. All rights reserved worldwide.

turn will be even greater.[32] On the other hand, if the discount increases, the investor's overall return may be less than that of an otherwise comparable open-end investment company.

Consider a closed-end fund that at the beginning of the year has a net asset value of $10 per share but is selling at a 10% discount for $9 per share. Over the year it receives cash dividends amounting to $.50 per share, which it distributes to its shareholders. Hence its dividend yield is 5.6% (=$.50/$9.00), which is larger than the 5% yield (=$.50/$10) that it would pay if it were an open-end fund. Furthermore, if its net asset value at year-end remains at $10 per share but its discount shrinks to 4% so that it is selling at $9.60 per share, then its annual return of 12.2% [=($.60 + $.50)/$9] will be notably larger than the 5% return of its open-end counterpart. Of course, if its discount widened to 20% so that it was selling at $8 per share, then its annual return of −5.6% [=(−$1 + $.50)/$9] would be notably lower than the counterpart's 5% return.

Some of the risk associated with varying discounts can be reduced by holding a portfolio of shares in several closed-end investment companies. Discounts on different companies move together, but not perfectly. For example, past data suggest that the standard deviation of the percentage change in the ratio of market price to net asset value for a *portfolio* of 10 to 12 closed-end investment companies is likely to be approximately half that of a typical investment in the shares of a *single* closed-end investment company.[33]

21.7.3 Open-Ending Closed-End Funds

Explaining the puzzling behavior of prices of closed-end investment companies is a challenge for anyone who believes that capital markets are highly efficient. For anyone not firmly committed to such a view, the purchase of shares of closed-end investment companies at prices sufficiently below net asset values may provide an opportunity for superior returns.[34] One way of realizing superior returns is for the closed-end investment company to convert to an open-end one.[35] If the company

---

Investment Companies

Real Estate Investment Trusts

Real estate provides attractive investment opportunities for most institutional investors. Notwithstanding its 1980s boom-and-bust cycle, real estate offers long-lived assets with steady cash flows and a huge, diversified market. The returns on real estate exhibit relatively low correlations with those of stocks and bonds and a positive correlation with inflation.

Insurance firms, particularly life insurance companies, have long maintained large real estate holdings. Most of their investments consist of "direct deals," where the investor has sole ownership of the properties, perhaps assisted in certain functions by various third parties. Pension funds, both public and private, entered into real estate primarily in the late 1970s and early 1980s. (Cynics will note that this entry coincided with the peak of the real estate pricing cycle.) Although some pension funds engaged in direct deals, most invested through *commingled funds*. These commingled funds are essentially partnerships with other investors. A management firm organizes the partnership and serves as the adviser and manager of the partnership's properties.

The earliest *commingled real estate funds* (CRFs) were open-end in that participants were permitted to enter and depart at prices based on the appraised value of the CRFs' assets, as determined by the funds' managers. Closed-end funds appeared later and quickly proved more popular. Those CRFs were created with a finite life and an initial subscription amount. Once the fund was formed, no new participants were accepted, nor were existing participants able to liquidate their holdings.

Institutional investors placed billions of dollars in CRFs and smaller amounts in direct deals. Commingled real estate funds seemed particularly efficient investment vehicles as real estate prices continued to rise. However, as real estate prices began to tumble in the late 1980s, the primary weakness of the CRF structure became readily apparent—very limited or nonexistent liquidity.

Institutional investors found that they could not move out of their real estate investments. Directly owned properties were difficult to sell in a declining market. Closed-end CRFs, of course, never promised that liquidity would be available to participants until the end of the funds' lives. Moreover, secondary markets in participation interests have been frustratingly slow to develop.

Most disappointing were the open-end CRFs. Investors were required to queue up for withdrawals. Few new participants were entering, and the funds' managers were not required to sell properties to meet withdrawal requests unless such sales were in the best interests of the remaining investors. Perhaps more troubling were the prices at which the lucky investors were allowed to withdraw. As appraised property prices tend to lag market prices, in a downward market outgoing investors benefited at the expense of the remaining investors.

The liquidity and valuation problems faced by institutional real estate investors in the late 1980s begged the question: Was there a way that these investors might own real estate through a liquid vehicle with market-determined prices? The answer may lie with an instrument known as *real estate investment trusts* (REITs).

Real estate investment trusts have existed for over 30 years. They are essentially (although not legally) closed-end investment companies that invest in real estate instead of financial assets. Similar to true investment companies, as long as 95% of their income is distributed to shareholders, that income is free from taxation. Further, at least 75% of their assets and income must be derived from real estate equity or mortgages. Real estate investment trusts must also

converted, the discount on the shares would have to disappear because conversion would result in the investment company's offering its shareholders the right to redeem their shares for their net asset value.

In one study, a sample of 138 closed-end funds was examined from 1979 to 1989 by determining the amount of concentrated ownership in each fund. Shareholdings of officers and directors as well as others who owned 5% or more of a fund's shares were determined and aggregated for each fund in the sample. After eight funds in which at least some shareholders were actively involved in attempting to open up the fund had been discarded, the remaining funds were examined. It was observed that those with blockholdings sold at an average discount of 14.2%, whereas those without blockholdings sold at a discount of only 4.1%. Subsequent analysis revealed

have at least 100 shareholders. Their portfolios must be diversified, and no more than 30% of their income may come from selling properties held for less than four years. (This last requirement is designed to prevent REITs from becoming vehicles for real estate speculation.)

Real estate investment trusts engage in a common financial intermediation process known as *securitization*. (Mortgage participation pools—see Chapter 13–are another example.) A REIT manager converts (securitizes) properties into financial assets by purchasing properties (typically 35 to 40) for the REIT. In order to finance the purchases, the REIT manager issues freely tradable ownership shares. Returns to REIT investors come from rental income, which is passed on to shareholders, and from property value changes, which are reflected in REIT prices.

Real estate investment trusts offer investors several benefits over direct investments or CRFs. Most important, because their shares can be traded on the open market (both through exchanges and over the counter), they provide liquidity and market-determined prices.

Further, REIT boards of directors must have a majority composed of independent outsiders, and REIT shareholders can remove directors if they are dissatisfied with their funds' results. In addition, REIT managers may enter into profit-sharing arrangements with REIT shareholders. As a result, the interests of REIT managers may be better aligned with those of shareholders than is the case under the CRF structure.

Like investment companies that own financial assets, REITs come in many different varieties. Some invest in real estate mortgages; others make equity investments. Most own specific types of properties, such as apartments or retail facilities, in specific geographic areas. Some employ leverage to boost expected returns, whereas others avoid debt financing. Some are traded publicly, whereas others have their shares exchanged on a privately arranged basis.

One important difference between investment companies specializing in financial assets and REITs is that most REITs today are really operating companies. The managers of financial asset investment companies generally do not participate in the operation of the firms whose securities they own. On the other hand, REIT managers often have extensive real estate management capabilities and oversee the acquisition, property management, and disposition of a portfolio of real estate properties.

Although REITs offer institutional investors many advantages, the key question is whether the REIT market will offer sufficient trading volume to attract large investors. Currently, publicly traded REITs have a total market capitalization over $125 billion. (By comparison, the market capitalization of several U.S. companies is greater than that of the entire REIT market.) Thus even though REIT shares are freely tradable, a large investor may displace the market for a particular REIT's shares if the investor attempts to make a sizable transaction. Trading in REITs has historically not been large enough to accommodate a substantial influx of institutional investors. Instead, the REIT market has been geared toward retail investors.

Nevertheless, if demand increases, ultimately more REIT offerings will occur. Property development firms will package more properties into REITs to finance growth. Some CRFs have already converted to a REIT format. Insurance companies and pension funds may create REITs to dispose of unwanted properties. Interestingly, a growing list of mutual funds has been established to invest solely in REITs, thereby producing a situation in which financial investment companies invest in real estate "investment companies."

that the larger the size of the blockholdings, the larger the discount. An explanation put forth is that the funds with blockholdings were less likely to be opened up. It was determined that large investors in such funds were receiving a variety of private benefits (for example, being involved with firms that execute the fund's trades, being involved with the management firm that receives the fund's management fees, being able to find employment at the fund for close friends and relatives) that were not available to small investors.

Given their voting power, these large investors apparently gain more from these benefits than they would gain from opening up the fund, and hence vote against any effort to do so.[36] Needless to say, this finding leaves open the question of why small investors hold shares in such funds.

1. Investment companies are financial intermediaries that obtain money from investors and use it to purchase financial assets.
2. Investment companies offer investors the advantages of economies of scale and professional management.
3. The net asset value of an investment company is the difference between the market value of its assets and its liabilities divided by the number of outstanding shares.
4. The operating expense ratio of an investment company represents the annual percentage of total assets that are spent in operating the fund. Typically these expenses consist of fees paid to the management company as well as administrative and other operating expenses.
5. The three major types of investment companies are unit investment trusts, closed-end investment companies, and open-end investment companies.
6. Unit investment trusts typically make a set of initial investments in fixed-income securities and then hold those securities until they mature.
7. Closed-end investment companies issue shares initially to capitalize the fund. After that, new shares are rarely issued (or repurchased). Closed-end investment company shares trade on organized exchanges or on the over-the-counter market at prices determined by the market.
8. Open-end investment companies have a variable capitalization, standing ready to issue new shares or to repurchase existing shares at prices based on their net asset values.
9. Different investment companies follow different investment policies. These policies determine such characteristics as the asset classes in which the investment companies invest, the degree of active management (if any), and the emphasis on income as opposed to capital appreciation.
10. Owing to data availability, mutual funds have been the subject of many performance studies. The results show that the typical fund has not been able to produce superior rates of return consistently.
11. There is mild evidence that the superior results of the top-performing and the inferior results of the bottom-performing mutual funds persist over time. However, this evidence is not strong, indicating that many top and bottom performers subsequently become middle-of-the-pack performers.
12. Closed-end investment companies typically sell at premiums to their net asset values at their initial offerings. Later they typically sell at discounts to their net asset values, and these discounts tend to vary over time. Why investors buy initial public offerings of closed-end investment companies, why the discounts of these companies vary over time, and why an investment strategy that involves buying a portfolio of roughly seven or eight funds with the deepest discounts produces abnormally high returns are puzzles for proponents of market efficiency.

QUESTIONS AND PROBLEMS

1. The Neptune Value Fund has sold 150,000 shares to investors. Currently the fund has accrued investment management fee obligations of $50,000. The fund's portfolio is shown below. Calculate the fund's net asset value.

Stock	Shares	Price/Share
A	50,000	$ 10
B	20,000	7
C	35,000	30
D	10,000	100

2. Using a recent *Wall Street Journal*, find the NAV for the following funds:
   a. The Magellan Fund (Fidelity Investments)
   b. The Wellington Fund (Vanguard Group)
   c. The New Horizons Fund (Price Funds)
   What is the percentage change in each fund's NAV over the previous day? Calculate each fund's load as a percentage of its NAV.
3. Wildfire Schulter, a veteran mutual fund investor, argued: "I can compute the monthly rate of return on a mutual fund by calculating the percentage change in the fund's NAV from the beginning to the end of the month (assuming no distributions to shareholders)." Is Wildfire correct? Why?
4. The X Fund, a closed-end investment company, has a portfolio of assets worth $500 million. It has liabilities of $2 million. It also has 40 million shares outstanding.
   a. What is the fund's NAV?
   b. If the fund trades at an 8% discount from its NAV, what is the market price of the fund's shares?
5. Discuss the advantages and disadvantages of unit investment trusts compared with managed investment companies.
6. Distinguish between closed-end and open-end investment companies.
7. Why do some mutual funds have load charges whereas others do not? Why are investors willing to pay load charges?
8. Assume that you placed a $1,000 investment with a mutual fund that charged an 8.5% load. Management and other fees charged by the fund total 1.10% per annum. Ignoring other costs, over five years, what annual return would the fund have to produce to equal the value that your initial investment would have earned in a savings account paying 5% interest? (Assume annual compounding of income and no taxes.)
9. In recent years so-called families of funds that offer a wide range of investment policies through narrowly focused mutual funds have become popular. Discuss why these funds have achieved such popularity.
10. There are literally thousands of mutual funds available for purchase. Describe what criteria you might use in selecting from among these many funds.
11. At the beginning of the year, the Saturn Fund's NAV was $18.50. At the end of the year its NAV was $16.90. At year-end the fund paid out $1.25 in income and capital gains. What was the return to an investor in the Saturn Fund during the year?
12. Over the last three years, the Pluto Fund produced the following per share financial results. Calculate the annual returns on an investment in the Pluto Fund over this period.

	Year 1	Year 2	Year 3
NAV at beginning of year	$13.89	$14.40	$15.95
NAV at end of year	14.40	15.95	15.20
Income distribution	.29	.33	.36
Capital gains distribution	.12	.25	.05

13. Analysis of mutual fund performance has been extensive. What does the evidence indicate about the ability of mutual fund managers, as a group, to produce positive abnormal returns consistently?
14. Lip Pike is attempting to select a superior-performing mutual fund. On the basis of the evidence presented in the text, discuss how much importance Lip should attach to the past performance of mutual funds in making decisions.
15. What is the purpose of Rule 12b-1? Does it seem designed to serve the interests of existing shareholders? Explain.

16. Why do the stated percentage load charges of mutual funds not fully reflect the percentage costs of these sales fees?

17. Distinguish between a common stock fund and a balanced fund. In particular, compare their expected return and risk characteristics.

18. If most investment managers appear unable to "beat the market" on a risk-adjusted basis, should an investor still consider investing in investment companies? Why?

19. Consider three individuals: a young, well-educated woman just beginning a career with high expected future earnings; a middle-aged man with a young family who has a secure job but modest expected future earnings growth; a widow in her seventies, living comfortably but not richly off a pension. Referring to Table 21.1, prescribe and explain an investment strategy for these persons involving investments in the various funds listed. (Feel free to introduce other assumptions regarding such things as the individuals' risk tolerances and consumption preferences.)

20. Assuming that certain conditions are satisfied, an investment company does not have to pay federal tax on the income it earns. Why?

21. Why do the market prices of closed-end investment company shares represent a "mystery" to proponents of market efficiency?

ENDNOTES

[1] As mentioned in Chapter 3, dealers in securities generally quote both bid and asked prices. The bid price is the amount the dealer will pay for a security; the asked price is the amount a dealer will sell a security for.

[2] Another classification covers certain companies that issue "face-amount certificates" promising specific payments. This type of company is rare and will not be discussed here.

[3] In some countries (such as the United Kingdom), the term *unit trust* refers to an open-end investment company.

[4] Many investment companies require their management companies to cover all expenses over a specified amount, effectively limiting total expenses. All of these fees are discussed extensively in Chapter 10 of John Bogle, *Bogle on Mutual Funds* (Burr Ridge, IL: Richard D. Irwin, 1994).

[5] CDA/Wiesenberger Investment Companies Service, *Investment Companies Yearbook 1997* (Rockville, MD: CDA Investment Technologies, 1997), p. 21. These percentages also include distribution fees, also known as 12b-1 fees, which will be discussed shortly. It should be noted that, in general, larger funds have smaller operating expense ratios. Hence, the average *dollar* invested in bond or equity funds will pay a slightly lower percent than those indicated here.

[6] See Jay R. Ritter, "The Long-Run Performance of Initial Public Offerings," *Journal of Finance* 46, no. 1 (March 1991): 3–27. Over the three years following the initial offering date, non-fund initial public offerings underperformed a matching sample of firms by roughly 27%.

[7] Closed-end funds that have received permission from foreign governments to invest in their securities do not show the type of price behavior described here and hence may be initially attractive to investors. See John W. Peavey III, "Returns on Initial Public Offerings of Closed-End Funds," *Review of Financial Studies* 3, no. 4 (1990): 695–708. For more information about closed-end investment companies, see Albert J. Fredman and George Cole Scott, "Analyzing and Finding Data on Closed-End Funds," *AAII Journal* 13, no. 8 (September 1991): 15–19, and "Guidelines for Handling Closed-End Fund Transactions," *AAII Journal* 14, no. 5 (June 1992): 18–22.

[8] **Real estate investment trusts** (REITs), although not classified as investment companies for legal purposes, are similar to closed-end funds in that they serve as a conduit for earnings on investments in real estate or loans secured by real estate, passing earnings on to their shareholders and avoiding corporate taxation. They are discussed in this chapter's *Institutional Issues: Real Estate Investment Trusts*.

[9] Investing in a **wrap account** is similar to investing in a mutual fund. This type of account is sponsored by a brokerage firm and involves brokers helping investors identify suitable money managers (or mutual funds) that will manage some of the investors' wealth. All of the fees for financial planning, investment management, and securities trading are "wrapped up" into one annual fee that typically amounts to 3% of assets. See John Bogle, *Bogle on Mutual Funds*, p. 54, for a discussion of the analogy between wrap accounts and mutual funds.

[10] For more on mutual fund load charges and redemption fees, see Tarun Chordia, "The Structure of Mutual Fund Charges," *Journal of Financial Economics* 41, no. 1 (May 1996): 3–39. Typically, redemption fees are paid to the fund, not to the fund's manager. Thus departing shareholders effectively compensate remaining shareholders for the costs of liquidating a portion of the fund's assets.

[11] To be precise, the limit is .75% for advertising, promoting, and selling the fund and .25% for servicing existing investors.

[12] CDA/Wiesenberger, *Investment Companies Yearbook 1997*, p. 25.

[13] CDA/Wiesenberger, *Investment Companies Yearbook 1997*, p. 25. Equity income and fixed-income funds are other types of income funds that invest in common stocks and fixed-income securities, respectively.

[14] Sometimes the capital gain category is referred to as "maximum capital gain" or "aggressive growth." A fourth category ("specialized") consists of funds that, by design, are not highly diversified. One interesting kind of fund (typically organized as a limited partnership) is a hedge fund, where the manager will often engage in short selling and margin purchases of securities (see *Institutional Issues: Hedge Funds* in Chapter 2 for more on hedge funds).

[15] For more information about mutual funds that specialize in investing in foreign stocks, see Ken Gregory, "Traveling Overseas via No-Load Mutual Funds," *AAII Journal* 13, no. 9 (October 1991): 22–25.

[16] Benchmarks can be calculated in many different ways. For example, the benchmark may be based on the investment company's standard deviation relative to that of a market index, such as the S&P 500. Thus if the investment company's standard deviation has been 60% of the index's standard deviation, then the mix would consist of 60% invested in the index and 40% invested in the riskfree asset. The results from evaluating mutual fund performance using this type of benchmark are very similar to the results when beta-based benchmarks are used. See, for example, Hany A. Shawky, "An Update on Mutual Funds: Better Grades," *Journal of Portfolio Management* 8, no. 2 (Winter 1982): 29–34. Portfolio performance evaluation and benchmarks are discussed in detail in Chapter 24.

[17] See Mark M. Carhart, "On Persistence in Mutual Fund Performance," *Journal of Finance* 51, no. 1 (March 1997): 57–82. Sector, balanced, and international equity funds were excluded from the sample.

[18] By adding operating expenses to a fund's rate of return, one can obtain an estimate of a fund's gross performance (that is, its performance based solely on what happened to the securities it bought and sold). This calculation is done by adding the per share values of such expenses to the numerator of Equation (21.2). In the example shown earlier, perhaps the fund had paid expenses of this nature totaling $.02 per share during month t. In such a situation the net return of 1.20% (= $.12/$10.00) corresponds to a gross return of 1.40% [= ($.12 + $.02)/$10.00].

[19] Edwin J. Elton, Martin J. Gruber, Sanjiv Das, and Matthew Hlavka, "Efficiency with Costly Information: A Reinterpretation of Evidence from Managed Portfolios," *Review of Financial Studies* 6, no. 1 (1993): 1–22.

[20] Similar conclusions can be drawn regarding pension and endowment funds. See Eugene F. Fama, "Efficient Capital Markets: II," *Journal of Finance* 46, no. 5 (December 1991): 1575–1617, particularly pp. 1605–1607, and Josef Lakonishok, Andrei Shleifer, and Robert W. Vishny,"The Structure and Performance of the Money Management Industry," *Brookings Papers on Economic Activity: Microeconomics 1992*, (Washington, DC: Brookings Institute, 1992), pp. 339–379. Also see T. Daniel Coggin, Frank J. Fabozzi, and Shafiqur Rahman, "The Investment Performance of U.S. Equity Pension Fund Managers: An Empirical Investigation," *Journal of Finance* 48, no. 3 (July 1993): 1039–1055.

[21] Christopher R. Blake, Edwin J. Elton, and Martin J. Gruber, "The Performance of Bond Mutual Funds," *Journal of Business* 66, no. 3 (July 1993): 371–403.

[22] Edwin J. Elton, Martin J. Gruber, and Christopher R. Blake, "Fundamental Economic Variables, Expected Returns, and Bond Fund Performance," *Journal of Finance* 50, no. 4 (September 1995): 1229–1256, particularly pp. 1251–1252. All of these studies finding persistence have been challenged by other investigators on methodological grounds.

[23] Morningstar's average return referred to here and elsewhere is calculated using compounding. For example, the one-year return is calculated by compounding the four previous quarterly returns and subtracting one; the three-year average return is calculated by compounding the 12 previous quarterly returns, taking the cube root of the result, and then subtracting one.

[24] Since 1996, Morningstar has defined its own set of investment objectives. These are different from the CDA/Weisenberger investment objectives discussed earlier. Morningstar determines a fund's investment objective on the basis of a set of variables related to the composition of the fund's portfolio. For U.S. common stock funds, these variables include the market value and the price-earnings and price-book ratios of the fund's holdings. For U.S. bond funds, these variables include duration and credit quality of the fund's holdings. The Morningstar approach is more complex than the CDA/Weisenberger approach, but it allows an investor to more finely differentiate among funds.

[25] Similar ratings are provided in *The Individual Investor's Guide to No-Load Mutual Funds* (Chicago: American Association of Individual Investors, 1997).

[26] For more on Morningstar's risk-adjusted ratings, see William F. Sharpe, "Morningstar's Risk-Adjusted Ratings," *Financial Analysts Journal*, 54, no. 4 (July/August 1998): 21–33.

[27] The *ex post* characteristic line is discussed more fully in Chapter 24.

[28] For more on mutual fund styles, see Stephen J. Brown and William N. Goetzmann, "Mutual Fund Styles," *Journal of Financial Economics* 43, no. 3 (March 1997): 373–399.

[29] See, for example, William F. Sharpe and Howard B. Sosin, "Closed-End Investment Companies in the United States: Risk and Return," *Proceedings, 1974 Meeting of the European Finance Association* ed. B. Jacquillat (Amsterdam: North-Holland Publishing, 1975): 37–63; Antonio Vives, "Analysis of Forecasting Ability of Closed-End Fund's Management" (unpublished working paper, Carnegie-Mellon University, September 1975), and "Discounts and Premiums on Closed-End Funds: A Theoretical and Empirical Analysis" (unpublished Ph.D. thesis, Carnegie-Mellon University, 1975).

[30] These two puzzles are presented and investigated in Charles M. C. Lee, Andrei Shleifer, and Richard H. Thaler, "Investor Sentiment and the Closed-End Fund Puzzle," *Journal of Finance* 46, no. 1 (March 1991): 75–109. In the June 1991 issue of *Journal of Finance* there is a contentious debate about their findings. For a comparison of the volatility of closed-end fund share prices and the volatility of the underlying securities in their portfolios, see Jeffrey Pontiff, "Excess Volatility and Closed-End Funds," *American Economic Review* 87, no. 1 (March 1997): 155–169.

[31] See Jeffrey Pontiff, "Closed-End Fund Premia and Returns: Implications for Financial Market Equilibrium," *Journal of Financial Economics* 37, no. 3 (March 1995): 341–370, especially the appendix. Also see Rex Thompson, "The Information Content of Discounts and Premiums on Closed-End Fund Shares," *Journal of Financial Economics* 6, no. 2/3 (June/September 1978): 151–186.

[32] There is evidence that this is what happens to those funds with the greatest discounts; see Pontiff, "Closed-End Fund Premia and Returns." There is also some evidence that discounts narrow during "down markets" and widen during "up markets" and that the size of discounts and premiums increases as interest rates increase. See R. Malcolm Richards, Donald R. Fraser, and John C. Groth, "Premiums, Discounts, and the Volatility of Closed-End Mutual Funds," *Financial Review* (Fall 1979): 26–33, and "The Attractions of Closed-End Bond Funds," *Journal of Portfolio Management* 8, no. 2 (Winter 1982): 56–61; and Jeffrey Pontiff, "Costly Arbitrage: Evidence from Closed-End Funds," *Quarterly Journal of Economics* 111, no. 4 (November 1996): 1135–1151.

[33] Sharpe and Sosin, "Closed-End Investment Companies in the United States."

[34] Burton G. Malkiel advocated such an investment strategy in the 1973, 1975, and 1981 editions of *A Random Walk Down Wall Street* (New York: W. W. Norton), but not in his more recent editions. The basis for his initial advocacy can be found in two studies: Burton Malkiel, "The Valuation of Closed-End Investment Company Shares," *Journal of Finance* 32, no. 3 (June 1977): 847–859, and Thompson, "The Information Content of Discounts and Premiums on Closed-End Fund Shares." Pontiff's more recent study supports these two earlier studies; see Pontiff, "Closed-End Fund Premia and Returns."

[35] For an analysis of the "open-ending" of closed-end investment companies, see Greggory A. Brauer, "'Open-Ending' Closed-End Funds," *Journal of Financial Economics* 13, no. 4 (December 1984): 491–507.

[36] See Michael Barclay, Clifford Holderness, and Jeffrey Pontiff, "Concentrated Ownership and Discounts on Closed-End Funds," *Journal of Applied Corporate Finance* 8, no. 1 (Spring 1995): 32–42 (an expanded version of this paper appears in the June 1993 issue of the *Journal of Financial Economics*).

KEY TERMS

investment companies	load funds
net asset value	load charge
unit investment trust	low-load funds
managed investment companies	wrap account
operating expense ratio	redemption fee
closed-end investment companies	distribution fee
real estate investment trusts	contingent deferred sales charge
open-end investment company	benchmark portfolio
mutual funds	*ex post* alpha
no-load funds	portfolio turnover rate

REFERENCES

1. Good reference sources for information on investment companies are:

   William J. Baumol, Stephen M. Goldfeld, Lilli A. Gordon, and Michael F. Koehn, *The Economics of Mutual Fund Markets: Competition versus Regulation* (Boston: Kluwer Academic Publishers, 1990).

   Investment Companies Yearbook 1993 (to order, write: CDA Investment Technologies, Inc., 1355 Piccard Drive, Rockville, MD 20850).

   1997 Mutual Fund Fact Book (to order, write: Investment Company Institute, 1401 H Street, N.W., Suite 1200, Washington, DC 20005-2148). Also see the Investment Company Institute's Web site at ⟨www.ici.org⟩.

   John C. Bogle, *Bogle on Mutual Funds* (Burr Ridge, IL: Richard D. Irwin, 1994).

   The Individual Investor's Guide to No-Load Mutual Funds (to order, write: American Association of Individual Investors, 625 North Michigan Avenue, Research Department, Chicago, IL 60611-3110).

   Morningstar Mutual Funds (to order this biweekly publication, write: Morningstar, Inc., 225 West Wacker Drive, Chicago, IL 60606).

   Peter Fortune, "Mutual Funds, Part I: Reshaping the American Financial System," *New England Economic Review* Federal Reserve Bank of Boston (July/August 1997): 45–72.

2. Although annual management fees of investment companies are usually a given percentage of the market value of the assets under management, performance-based fees are

allowed. In addition to the January/February 1987 issue of the *Financial Analysts Journal*, which is devoted to this topic, see:

Laura T. Starks, "Performance Incentive Fees: An Agency Theoretic Approach," *Journal of Financial and Quantitative Analysis* 22, no. 1 (March 1987): 17–32.

Mark Grinblatt and Sheridan Titman, "How Clients Can Win the Gaming Game," *Journal of Portfolio Management* 13, no. 4 (Summer 1987): 14–23.

Joseph H. Golec, "Do Mutual Fund Managers Who Use Incentive Compensation Outperform Those Who Don't?" *Financial Analysts Journal* 44, no. 6 (November/December 1988): 75–78.

Mark Grinblatt and Sheridan Titman, "Adverse Risk Incentives and the Design of Performance-Based Contracts," *Management Science* 35, no. 7 (July 1989): 807–822.

Jeffery V. Bailey, "Some Thoughts on Performance-Based Fees," *Financial Analysts Journal* 46, no. 4 (July/August 1990): 31–40.

Philip Halpern and Isabelle I. Fowler, "Investment Management Fees and Determinants of Pricing Structure in the Industry," *Journal of Portfolio Management* 17, no. 2 (Winter 1991): 74–79.

Keith C. Brown, W. V. Harlow, and Laura T. Starks, "Of Tournaments and Temptations: An Analysis of Managerial Incentives in the Mutual Fund Industry," *Journal of Finance* 51, no. 1 (March 1996): 85–110.

Tarun Chordia, "The Structure of Mutual Fund Charges," *Journal of Financial Economics* 41, no. 1 (May 1996): 3–39.

Robert Ferguson and Dean Leistikow, "Investment Management Fees: Long-Run Incentives," *Journal of Financial Engineering* 6, no. 1 (March 1997): 1–30.

Peter Tufano and Matthew Sevick, "Board Structure and Fee-Setting in the U.S. Mutual Fund Industry," *Journal of Financial Economics* 46, no. 3 (December 1997): 321–355.

3. The imposition of 12b-1 distribution fees by mutual funds has been contentious. See:

Stephen P. Ferris and Don M. Chance, "The Effect of 12b-1 Plans on Mutual Fund Expense Ratios: A Note," *Journal of Finance* 42, no. 4 (September 1987): 1077–1082.

Charles Trzcinka and Robert Zweig, *An Economic Analysis of the Cost and Benefits of S.E.C. Rule 12b-1*, Monograph Series in Finance and Economics, 1990-1 (New York University Salomon Center, Leonard N. Stern School of Business, 1990).

4. For a discussion of the distribution feed associated with the various classes of mutual fund shares, see:

Miles Livingston and Edward S. O'Neal, "The Cost of Mutual Fund Distribution Fees," *Journal of Financial Research*, 21, no. 2 (Summer 1998): 205–218.

5. Closed-end investment companies known as "country funds" have been examined by:

Catherine Bonser-Neal, Greggory Brauer, Robert Neal, and Simon Wheatley, "International Investment Restrictions and Closed-End Country Fund Prices," *Journal of Finance* 45, no. 2 (June 1990): 523–547.

Gordon Johnson, Thomas Schneeweis, and William Dinning, "Closed-End Country Funds: Exchange Rate and Investment Risk," *Financial Analysts Journal* 49, no. 6 (November/December 1993): 74–82.

6. Real estate investment trusts (REITs) are discussed in:

William L. Burns and Donald R. Epley, "The Performance of Portfolios of REITs Stocks," *Journal of Portfolio Management* 8, no. 3 (Spring 1982): 37–42.

Robert H. Zerbst and Barbara R. Cambon, "Real Estate: Historical Returns and Risks," *Journal of Portfolio Management* 10, no. 3 (Spring 1984): 5–20.

Paul M. Firstenburg, Stephen A. Ross, and Randall C. Zisler, "Real Estate: The Whole Story," *Journal of Portfolio Management* 14, no. 3 (Spring 1988): 22–34.

Stephen E. Roulac, "How to Value Real Estate Securities," *Journal of Portfolio Management* 14, no. 3 (Spring 1988): 35–39.

Steven D. Kapplin and Arthur L. Schwartz Jr., "Investing in REITs: Are They All They're Cracked Up to Be?" *AAII Journal* 13, no. 5 (May 1991): 7–11.

Joeseph Gyourko and Donald B. Keim, "Risk and Return in Real Estate: Evidence from a Real Estate Stock Portfolio," *Financial Analysts Journal* 49, no. 5 (September/October 1993): 39–46.

7. For evidence on the performance of international funds, see:

Andre L. Farber, "Performance of Internationally Diversified Mutual Funds," in Edwin J. Elton and Martin J. Gruber (eds.), *International Capital Markets* (Amsterdam: North-Holland Publishing, 1975); pp. 298–309.

R. S. Woodward, "The Performance of U.K. Investment Trusts as Internationally Diversified Portfolios over the Period 1968 to 1977," *Journal of Banking and Finance* 7, no. 3 (September 1983): 417–426.

Jess H. Chua and Richard S. Woodward, *Gains from Market Timing*, Monograph Series in Finance and Economics 1986-2 (New York University Salomon Center, Leonard N. Stern School of Business, 1986).

Robert E. Cumby and Jack D. Glen, "Evaluating the Performance of International Mutual Funds," *Journal of Finance* 45, no. 2 (June 1990): 497–521.

Cheol S. Eun, Richard Kolodny, and Bruce G. Resnick, "U.S.-Based International Mutual Funds: A Performance Evaluation," *Journal of Portfolio Management* 17, no. 3 (Spring 1991): 88–94.

8. Studies of mutual fund performance are discussed and cited in:

Gordon J. Alexander and Jack Clark Francis, *Portfolio Analysis* (Upper Saddle River, NJ: Prentice Hall, 1986), Chapter 13.

Bruce N. Lehmann and David M. Modest, "Mutual Fund Performance Evaluation: A Comparison of Benchmarks and Benchmark Comparisons," *Journal of Finance* 42, no. 2 (June 1987): 233–265.

Richard A. Ippolito, "Efficiency with Costly Information: A Study of Mutual Fund Performance," *Quarterly Journal of Economics* 104, no.1 (February 1989): 1–23.

Mark Grinblatt and Sheridan Titman, "Mutual Fund Performance: An Analysis of Quarterly Portfolio Holdings," *Journal of Business* 62, no. 3 (July 1989): 393–416.

Cheng-Few Lee and Shafiqur Rahman, "Market Timing, Selectivity, and Mutual Fund Performance: An Empirical Investigation," *Journal of Business* 63, no. 2 (April 1990): 261–278.

Cheng F. Lee and Shafiqur Rahman, "New Evidence on Timing and Security Selection Skill of Mutual Fund Managers," *Journal of Portfolio Management* 17, no. 2 (Winter 1991): 80–83.

John C. Bogle, "Selecting Equity Mutual Funds," *Journal of Portfolio Management* 18, no. 2 (Winter 1992): 94–100.

Ravi Shukla and Charles Trzcinka, "Performance Measurement of Managed Portfolios," *Financial Markets, Institutions & Instruments* 1, no. 4 (1992).

Mark Grinblatt and Sheridan Titman, "The Persistence of Mutual Fund Performance," *Journal of Finance* 47, no. 5 (December 1992): 1977–1984.

Mark Grinblatt and Sheridan Titman, " Performance Measurement without Benchmarks: An Examination of Mutual Fund Returns," *Journal of Business* 66, no. 1 (January 1993): 47–68.

Edwin J. Elton, Martin J. Gruber, Sanjiv Das, and Matthew Hlavka, "Efficiency with Costly Information: A Reinterpretation of Evidence from Managed Portfolios," *Review of Financial Studies* 6, no. 1 (1993): 1–22.

Richard A. Ippolito, "On Studies of Mutual Fund Performance," *Financial Analysts Journal* 49, no. 1 (January/February 1993): 42–50.

Darryll Hendricks, Jayendu Patel, and Richard Zeckhauser, "Hot Hands in Mutual Funds: Short-Run Persistence of Relative Performance, 1974–1988," *Journal of Finance* 48, no. 1 (March 1993): 93–130.

Christopher R. Blake, Edwin J. Elton, and Martin J. Gruber, "The Performance of Bond Mutual Funds," *Journal of Business* 66, no. 3 (July 1993): 371–403.

William N. Goetzmann and Roger G. Ibbotson, "Do Winners Repeat?" *Journal of Portfolio Management* 20, no. 2 (Winter 1994): 9–18.

Mark Grinblatt and Sheridan Titman, "A Study of Monthly Mutual Fund Returns and Performance Evaluation Techniques," *Journal of Financial and Quantitative Analysis* 29, no. 3 (September 1993): 419–444.

John Bogle, *Bogle on Mutual Funds* (Burr Ridge, IL: Richard D. Irwin, 1994), Chapter 4.

Edwin J. Elton and Martin J. Gruber, *Modern Portfolio Theory and Investment Analysis* (New York: Wiley, 1995), Chapter 24.

Burton G. Malkiel, "Returns from Investing in Equity Mutual Funds," *Journal of Finance* 50, no. 2 (June 1995): 549–572.

Stephen J. Brown and William N. Goetzmann, "Performance Persistence," *Journal of Finance* 50, no. 2 (June 1995): 679–698.

Edwin J. Elton, Martin J. Gruber, and Christopher R. Blake, "Fundamental Economic Variables, Expected Returns, and Bond Fund Performance," *Journal of Finance* 50, no. 4 (September 1995): 1229–1256.

Ronald N. Kahn and Andrew Rudd, "Does Historical Performance Predict Future Performance?" *Financial Analysts Journal* 51, no. 6 (November/December 1995): 43–52.

Mark Grinblatt, Sheridan Titman, and Russ Wermers, "Momentum Strategies, Portfolio Performance, and Herding: A Study of Mutual Fund Behavior," *American Economic Review* 85, no. 5 (December 1995): 1088–1105.

Edwin J. Elton, Martin J. Gruber, and Christopher R. Blake, "The Persistence of Risk-Adjusted Mutual Fund Performance," *Journal of Business* 69, no. 2 (April 1996): 133–157.

Wayne E. Ferson and Rudi W. Schadt, "Measuring Fund Strategy and Performance in Changing Economic Conditions," *Journal of Finance* 51, no. 2 (June 1996): 425–461.

Mark M. Carhart, "On Persistence in Mutual Fund Performance," *Journal of Finance* 51, no. 1 (March 1997): 57–82.

9. *Survivorship bias* refers to the problems incurred in mutual fund studies due to the fact that unskilled portfolio managers are usually fired whereas the skilled ones stay around. These problems are examined in:

Stephen J. Brown, William Goetzmann, Roger G. Ibbotson, and Stephen A. Ross, "Survivorship Bias in Performance Studies," *Review of Financial Studies* 5, no. 4 (1992): 553–580.

Edwin J. Elton, Martin J. Gruber, and Christopher R. Blake, "Survivorship Bias and Mutual Fund Performance," *Review of Financial Studies* 9, no. 4 (Winter 1996): 1097–1120.

10. For a discussion of Morningstar's risk-adjusted ratings and style analysis of mutual funds, see:

William F. Sharpe, "Morningstar's Performance Measures," *Financial Analysts Journal*, 54, no. 4 (July/August 1998): 21–33.

William F. Sharpe, "Morningstar's Risk-Adjusted Ratings," *Financial Analysts Journal*, 54, no. 2 (July/August 1998): 21–33.

Marshall Blume, "An Anatomy of Morningstar Ratings," *Financial Analysts Journal* 54, no. 2 (March/April 1998): 19–27.

11. For a discussion and extensive set of references regarding closed-end funds, see, along with the citations given in the chapter, the following papers:

Rex Thompson, "The Information Content of Discounts and Premiums on Closed-End Fund Shares," *Journal of Financial Economics* 6, no. 2/3 (June/September 1978): 151–186.

Greggory A. Brauer, "'Closed-End Fund Shares' Abnormal Returns and the Information Content of Discounts and Premiums," *Journal of Finance* 43, no. 1 (March 1988): 113–127.

Kathleen Weiss, "The Post-Offering Price Performance of Closed-End Funds," *Financial Management* 18, no. 3 (Autumn 1989): 57–67.

Charles M. C. Lee, Andrei Shleifer, and Richard H. Thaler, "Anomalies: Closed-End Mutual Funds," *Journal of Economic Perspectives* 4, no. 4 (Fall 1990): 153–164.

John W. Peavey III, "Returns on Initial Public Offerings of Closed-End Funds," *Review of Financial Studies* 3, no. 4 (1990): 695–708.

Charles M. C. Lee, Andrei Shleifer, and Richard H. Thaler, "Investor Sentiment and the Closed-End Fund Puzzle," *Journal of Finance* 46, no. 1 (March 1991): 75–109.

Albert J. Fredman and George Cole Scott, "An Investor's Guide to Closed-End Fund Discounts," *AAII Journal* 13, no. 5 (May 1991): 12–16.

James Brickley, Steven Manaster, and James Schallheim, "The Tax-Timing Option and Discounts on Closed-End Investment Companies," *Journal of Business* 64, no. 3 (July 1991): 287–312.

J. Bradford DeLong and Andrei Shleifer, "Closed-End Fund Discounts," *Journal of Portfolio Management* 18, no. 2 (Winter 1992): 46–53.

Nai-Fu Chen, Raymond Kan, and Merton H. Miller, "Are the Discounts on Closed-End Funds a Sentiment Index?" and "A Rejoinder," *Journal of Finance* 48, no. 2 (June 1993): 795–800 and 809–810.

Navin Chopra, Charles M. C. Lee, Andrei Shleifer, and Richard H. Thaler, "Yes, Discounts on Closed-End Funds Are a Sentiment Index," and "Summing Up," *Journal of Finance* 48, no. 2 (June 1993): 801–808 and 811–812.

Jeffrey Pontiff, "Closed-End Fund Premia and Returns: Implications for Financial Market Equilibrium," *Journal of Financial Economics* 37, no. 3 (March 1995): 341–370.

Michael Barclay, Clifford Holderness, and Jeffrey Pontiff, "Concentrated Ownership and Discounts on Closed-End Funds," *Journal of Applied Corporate Finance* 8, no. 1 (Spring 1995): 32–42.

Jeffrey Pontiff, "Excess Volatility and Closed-End Funds," *American Economic Review* 87, no. 1 (March 1997): 155–169.

12. Open-ending of closed-end investment companies is discussed in:

Greggory A. Brauer, "'Open-Ending' Closed-End Funds," *Journal of Financial Economics* 13, no. 4 (December 1984): 491–507.

James A. Brickley and James S. Schallheim, "Lifting the Lid on Closed-End Investment Companies: A Case of Abnormal Returns," *Journal of Financial and Quantitative Analysis* 20, no. 1 (March 1985): 107–117.

Jeffrey Pontiff, "Costly Arbitrage: Evidence from Closed-End Funds," *Quarterly Journal of Economics* 111, no. 4 (November 1996): 1135–1151.

FINANCIAL ANALYSIS

In a broad sense, financial analysis involves determining the levels of risk and expected return of individual financial assets as well as groups of financial assets. For example, financial analysis involves both individual common stocks such as IBM and groups of common stocks such as the computer industry or, on an even larger basis, the stock market itself. In this case, financial analysis would result in a decision of how to split the investor's money between the stock, bond, and money markets as well as a decision of whether to buy or sell computer stocks in general and IBM in particular.

An alternative definition of financial analysis is more pragmatic: the *Financial Analyst's Handbook*[1] defines the term **financial analyst** as synonymous with **security analyst** or investment analyst—"one who analyzes securities and makes recommendations thereon."[2] According to this definition, financial analysis can be viewed as the activity of providing inputs to the portfolio management process. This chapter (as well as Chapters 17 and 18) takes such a view in discussing the financial analysis of common stocks. Chapter 23 subsequently discusses how financial analysis can be used by **portfolio managers**, also known as investment managers.

22.1   PROFESSIONAL ORGANIZATIONS

In the United States, individuals who belong to one of 65 local societies of financial analysts automatically belong to a national organization known as the Association for Investment Management and Research (AIMR). The local societies offer members the opportunity to meet as a group with corporate managements, consultants, money managers, and academics to discuss issues of relevance to the investment management business.

The AIMR organization acts as an advocate for the financial analyst profession, presenting unified positions before regulators and Congress. It also hosts conferences and workshops designed to enhance the investment knowledge of its members. In addition, AIMR publishes the *Financial Analysts Journal,* a major source of information on basic research conducted by analysts and by members of the academic community. In 1997 there were over 32,000 members of AIMR.

In 1962 the Institute of Chartered Financial Analysts (ICFA) was formed by the Financial Analysts Federation (the precursor to AIMR) to award the professional designation of Chartered Financial Analyst (CFA). In 1997 over 23,000 analysts (or over 70% of the AIMR membership) held the CFA designation. The CFA program is designed to establish a common set of investment knowledge and ethical standards for the various types of investment professionals. The ICFA attempts to accomplish the first objective by requiring that prospective CFAs pass a series of three exams and attain several years of investment experience. It attempts to achieve the second objective by disseminating and enforcing a set of professional conduct guidelines. (The CFA program is discussed further in this chapter's *Institutional Issues: The Chartered Financial Analyst Program.*)[3]

Societies of financial analysts have been formed around the world. For example, the European Federation of Financial Analysts draws its membership from many European countries. Other societies are located in countries such as Canada, Australia, Japan, and Brazil.

22.2   REASONS FOR FINANCIAL ANALYSIS

There are two primary reasons for engaging in financial analysis. The first is to try to determine certain characteristics of securities. The second is to attempt to identify mispriced securities.[4] These reasons are discussed next.

22.2.1   Determining Security Characteristics

According to modern portfolio theory, a financial analyst will want to estimate a security's future sensitivity to major factors and unique risk because this information is needed to determine the risk (measured by standard deviation) of a portfolio. Perhaps the analyst will also want to estimate the dividend yield of a security over the next year in order to determine its suitability for portfolios in which dividend yield is relevant. Careful analysis of such matters as a company's dividend policy and likely future cash flows may lead to better estimates than can be obtained by simply extrapolating last year's dividend yield.

In many cases it is desirable to know something about the sources of a security's risk and return. If a portfolio is being managed for a person who is in the oil business, one might want to minimize the sensitivity of the portfolio's return to changes in oil prices because it is likely that if oil prices are in a decline, the person's income from the oil business will also be in a decline. If the portfolio were sensitive to oil prices (which would be the case if it contained a substantial investment in securities of businesses directly or indirectly involved in the energy sector), then it too would be in a decline, thereby reinforcing the deterioration of the person's financial position.[5]

22.2.2   Attempting to Identify Mispriced Securities

The search for mispriced securities typically involves the use of **fundamental analysis**. In essence, this process entails identifying situations in which the financial analyst's estimates of such things as a firm's future earnings and dividends:

    1. differ substantially from consensus (that is, average) estimates of others;
    2. are viewed as being closer to the correct values than the consensus estimates; and
    3. are not yet currently reflected in the market price of the firm's securities.

Two rather different approaches may be taken in the search for mispriced securities using fundamental analysis. The first approach involves valuation, wherein an attempt is made to determine the appropriate "intrinsic" or "true" value for a

---

The Chartered Financial Analyst Program

The investment profession encompasses a wide range of activities. Investment bankers, brokers, portfolio managers, traders, security analysts, salespeople, consultants, and pension fund administrators all fall under the rubric of investment professionals. These individuals, and the organizations for which they work, directly or indirectly affect the financial well-being of millions of people.

The Chartered Financial Analyst (CFA) program was born of a need to bring a common set of investment management concepts and standards of professional conduct to the diverse membership of the investment industry. From its modest beginnings in 1963, when 268 professionals were effectively "grandfathered" as chartered members, the CFA program has grown to a worldwide organization, with over 23,000 CFA charters awarded and more than 30,000 candidates currently enrolled. Although the CFA charter is far from a prerequisite for employment in the investment industry, many organizations are encouraging or even requiring new employees to participate in the CFA program.

From its inception, the Institute of Chartered Financial Analysts (ICFA), which administers the CFA program, has pursued three explicit objectives:

1. To compile a comprehensive set of currently accepted concepts and techniques relevant to the investment decision-making process (the CFA "Body of Knowledge").
2. To establish a uniform set of ethical standards to guide the activities of investment professionals.
3. To ensure that CFA charterholders have demonstrated satisfactory understanding of the Body of Knowledge and that they adhere to the established ethical standards.

Of course, like any other professional certification organization, the ICFA has multiple motives for promoting the CFA designation. By setting difficult hurdles for prospective members to clear, the CFA certification process enhances the monetary value of the charter to existing holders. Further, by demonstrating a responsible and comprehensive education and ethics program, the ICFA helps the investment industry ward off onerous government regulation and provides the industry with wider latitude to police itself.

To enroll in the CFA program, an individual must hold a bachelor's degree (or equivalent work experience), provide three acceptable character references, and pay the required registration fee. Once accepted into the program, to earn the CFA designation a candidate must pass three exams, possess three years of investment-related work experience, be a member of (or have applied to) a constituent financial analyst society, demonstrate a high level of professional conduct, and abide by the Code of Ethics and Standards of Practice of the Association for Investment Management and Research.

The CFA course of study and examinations are the cornerstone of the CFA certification process. Candidates must pass three six-hour exams. The ICFA administers these exams once a year in June at 140 locations, primarily in the United States and Canada. Because candidates may take only one exam a year, a minimum of three years is required to complete the examination sequence.

The ICFA specifies a set of review materials and assigned readings for candidates to use in preparation for the exams. The study program has evolved over the years as new concepts have been introduced into the exams. The ICFA estimates that candidates average 200 hours in individual study time for each exam. Many candidates also participate in independently sponsored study groups.

The CFA examinations are designed in a progressive format. The exam levels become increasingly comprehensive, building on previous levels. The

security. After this determination has been made, the intrinsic value is compared with the security's current market price. If the market price is substantially greater than the intrinsic value, the security is said to be overpriced or overvalued. If the market price is substantially less than the intrinsic value, the security is said to be underpriced or undervalued.

Instead of comparing price with value, the analyst sometimes estimates a security's expected return over a specified period, given its current market price and intrinsic value. This estimate is then compared with the "appropriate" return for securities with similar attributes.

CFA curriculum underwent a major change in 1993. The exams are divided into four major subject areas and several subtopics within each major subject:

1. Ethical and Professional Standards
   a. Applicable laws and regulations
   b. Professional standards of practice
   c. Ethical conduct and professional obligations
   d. International ethical and professional considerations
2. Tools for Inputs for Investment Valuation and Management
   a. Quantitative methods and statistics
   b. Macroeconomics
   c. Microeconomics
   d. Financial statements and accounting
3. Investment (Asset) Evaluation
   a. Overview of the valuation process
   b. Applying economic analysis in investment valuation
   c. Applying industry analysis in investment valuation
   d. Applying company analysis in investment valuation
   e. Equity securities
   f. Fixed-income securities
   g. Other investments
   h. Derivative securities
4. Portfolio Management
   a. Capital market theory
   b. Portfolio policies
   c. Expectational factors
   d. Asset allocation
   e. Fixed-income portfolio management
   f. Equity portfolio management
   g. Real estate portfolio management
   h. Specialized asset portfolio management
   i. Implementing the investment process
   j. Performance measurement

The CFA exams are rigorous and difficult. A high number of the candidates fail at least one exam, although exams can be retaken. In 1997, a total of 30,627 candidates sat for the exams. Only 53%, 59%, and 59% of the candidates taking the first, second, and third exams, respectively, passed.

The CFA program experienced tremendous growth in the 1980s. The number of candidates sitting for the exams has increased over 15-fold since 1980. Given this past success, where does the CFA program go from here?

Clearly, the ICFA desires to continue to enhance the prestige and uniqueness of its CFA certification. In recent years, however, the ICFA has also begun to strongly emphasize the continuing education aspect of its mission. Technological obsolescence is a serious problem in the rapidly changing investment industry. (For example, organized financial futures markets—see Chapter 20—did not even exist in 1980.) Many professionals who received the CFA designation just a decade ago might find it difficult to pass an exam now. Current charterholders are encouraged (although not yet required) to participate in a self-administered continuing education program. Further, to enhance the investment knowledge of its membership, the ICFA publishes conference proceedings and research monographs covering a wide range of topics.

The ICFA also sees a role for itself globally. With the investment industry becoming increasingly international in scope, the ICFA has moved to administer its program abroad. (Twenty percent of the current CFA candidates reside outside of the United States.) It has also begun to join forces with analyst societies in other countries to develop means of jointly recognizing one another's certification programs. In fact, the CFA program has become the de facto global standard for investment education.

Determining a security's intrinsic value may be done in great detail, using estimates of all major factors that influence security returns (for example, gross domestic product of the economy, industry sales, firm sales and expenses, and capitalization rates). Alternatively, shortcuts may be taken whereby, for example, an estimate of earnings per share may be multiplied by a "justified" or "normal" price-earnings ratio to determine the intrinsic value of a share of common stock. (To avoid complications arising when seeking the intrinsic value of a stock that has negative earnings per share, some analysts estimate sales per share and multiply this figure by a "normal" price-sales ratio.)

A second approach involves estimating only one or two financial variables and then comparing these estimates directly with consensus estimates. For example, next year's earnings per share for a stock may be estimated. If the analyst's estimate substantially exceeds the consensus of other analysts' estimates, the stock may be considered an attractive investment because the analyst expects the actual earnings to provide a pleasant surprise for the market when announced. In turn, there will be an increase in the stock's price at that time, resulting in the investor's receiving a greater-than-normal return. Conversely, when an analyst's estimate of earnings per share is substantially below that of the other analysts, then the analyst expects that the market will receive an unpleasant surprise. The resulting decrease in the stock's price will lead to a smaller-than-normal return.

At an aggregate level, an analyst may be more optimistic about the economy than the consensus of other analysts. This view would suggest that a larger-than-normal investment in stocks be taken, offset perhaps by a smaller-than-normal investment in fixed-income securities. Conversely, a relatively pessimistic view would suggest a smaller-than-normal investment in stocks, offset perhaps by a larger-than-normal investment in fixed-income securities.

Alternatively, the analyst might agree with the consensus view on both the economy and the individual characteristics of specific securities but feel that the consensus view of the prospects for a certain group of securities in a particular industry is in error. In such a case, a larger-than-normal investment may be made in stocks from an industry having prospects about which the analyst feels relatively optimistic. Conversely, a smaller-than-normal investment would be made in stocks from an industry about which the analyst feels relatively pessimistic.

The use of fundamental analysis to identify mispriced common stocks and fixed-income securities was discussed in previous chapters. This chapter will discuss the subject in more detail and compare it with the method of technical analysis.

22.2.3   Conveying Advice on Beating the Market

Many books and articles have been written that allegedly show how financial analysis can be used to "beat the market," meaning that they purport to show how to make abnormally high returns by investing in the stock market.

It is interesting to ponder whether advice regarding how to beat the market will remain useful after becoming public. It seems logical that any such prescription that has been in print for long is not likely to allow the investor to continue to beat the market consistently. Just because someone asserts that an approach has worked in the past does not mean that it, in fact, has worked. Moreover, even if it did work in the past, as more and more investors apply it, prices will be driven to levels at which the approach will not work in the future. Any system designed to beat the market, once known to more than a few people, carries the seeds of its own destruction.

There are two reasons for not including advice on "guaranteed" ways to beat the market in this book. First, to do so would make a successful system public and hence unsuccessful. Second, the authors know of no such system. Some apparent anomalies and possible inefficiencies have been described previously. But any book that purports to open the door to the *certainty* of making abnormally high returns for those who follow its advice should be regarded with the greatest skepticism.

This does not mean that financial analysis is useless. Although individuals should be skeptical when others tell them how to use financial analysis to *beat* the market, individuals can try to *understand* the market with the use of financial analysis.

22.2.4 Financial Analysis and Market Efficiency

The concept of an efficient market (discussed in Chapter 4) may appear to be based on a paradox. Financial analysts carefully evaluate the prospects for companies, industries, and the economy in the search for mispriced securities. If an undervalued security is found, then it will be purchased. However, the act of purchasing the security will tend to push its price upward toward its intrinsic value, thereby making it no longer undervalued. That is, financial analysis tends to result in security prices that reflect intrinsic values, and hence it tends to make markets efficient. But if this is the case, why would anyone perform financial analysis in an attempt to identify mispriced securities?

There are two responses to that question. First, there are costs associated with performing financial analysis. Consequently, financial analysis may not be conducted on all securities all the time. As a result, not all the prices of all securities will reflect intrinsic values all the time. Pockets of opportunity may arise from time to time, thereby opening the possibility for added benefits from financial analysis. The implication is that people should engage in financial analysis only to the point at which the added benefits cover the added costs.[6] Ultimately, in a highly competitive market, prices would be close enough to intrinsic values to make it worthwhile for only the most skillful analysts to search for mispriced securities. Thus the market would be nearly, but not perfectly, efficient. Skilled investors will be able to earn abnormally high gross returns, but after the costs of gathering and processing information and then making the requisite trades are taken into consideration, they will end up with a net return that is not abnormal.[7]

The other response to the question focuses on the first reason given earlier for engaging in financial analysis: to determine relevant characteristics of securities. This reason is appropriate even in a perfectly efficient market. Because investors differ in their circumstances (consider the person in the oil business, discussed earlier), portfolios should be tailored to accommodate such differences. Successful performance of this task generally requires estimation of certain characteristics of securities, thereby justifying the use of financial analysis.

22.2.5 Needed Skills

To understand and estimate the risk and return of individual securities as well as groups of securities (such as industries), one must understand financial markets and the principles of valuation. Much of the material required for such an understanding can be found in this book. However, even more is required. Future prospects must be estimated and interrelationships assessed. This process requires the skills of an economist and an understanding of industrial organization. Some command of quantitative methods is needed, along with an understanding of the nuances of accounting, to process relevant historical data.

This book cannot provide all the material one needs to become a successful financial analyst. Books on accounting, economics, industrial organization, and quantitative methods are required. Instead, some techniques used by financial analysts will be discussed, along with some of the pitfalls involved. In addition, sources of investment information will be presented.

One of the major divisions in the ranks of financial analysts is between those using fundamental analysis (known as fundamental analysts or fundamentalists) and those using **technical analysis** (known as technical analysts or technicians). The fundamentalist tends to look forward; the technician backward. The fundamentalist is concerned with such matters as future earnings and dividends, whereas the technician thinks little (if at all) about such matters.

> *Technical analysis is the study of the internal stock exchange information as such. The word "technical" implies a study of the market itself and not of those external factors which are reflected in the market.... [A]ll the relevant factors, whatever they may be, can be reduced to the volume of the stock exchange transactions and the level of share prices; or more generally, to the sum of the statistical information produced by the market.*[8]

The technician usually attempts to predict short-term price movements and thus makes recommendations concerning the *timing* of purchases and sales of either specific stocks or groups of stocks (such as industries) or stocks in general. It is sometimes said that fundamental analysis is designed to answer the question What? and technical analysis to answer the question When?

The concept of technical analysis is completely at odds with the notion of efficient markets:

> *The methodology of technical analysis ... rests upon the assumption that history tends to repeat itself in the stock exchange. If a certain pattern of activity has in the past produced certain results nine times out of ten, one can assume a strong likelihood of the same outcome whenever this pattern appears in the future.* It should be emphasized, however, that a large part of the methodology of technical analysis lacks a strictly logical explanation.[9] *[Emphasis added.]*

Thus technicians assert that the study of past patterns of variables such as prices and volumes will allow the investor to accurately identify times when certain specific stocks (or groups of stocks, or the market in general) are either overpriced or underpriced. Most (but not all) technical analysts rely on charts of stock prices and trading volumes. The appendix describes some of the more frequently used tools.

Early studies found little evidence showing technical analysis to be useful in enabling investors to "beat the market."[10] Many "proofs" of the ability of technical analysis to beat the market were offered, but most committed serious analytical errors that invalidated their results. However, several recent studies have indicated that technical analysis may be useful to investors.[11] The evidence presented in these studies can be divided into two groups based on the strategies involved. The first group, consisting of momentum and contrarian strategies, simply examines the returns on stocks over a time period that just ended in order to identify candidates for purchase and sale. The second group, consisting of moving average and trading range breakout strategies, makes such an identification on the basis of the relationship of a security's price over a relatively short time period that just ended to its price over a relatively longer time period.

22.3.1 Momentum and Contrarian Strategies

Consider ranking a group of stocks on the basis of the size of their returns over some time period that just ended. *Momentum investors* seek out for purchase those stocks that have recently risen significantly in price on the belief that they will continue to rise owing to an upward shift in their demand curves. Conversely, those stocks that have recently fallen significantly in price are sold on the belief that their demand curves have shifted downward.

Investors who call themselves *contrarians* do just the opposite of what most other investors are doing in the market: They buy stocks that others have shunned and think of as losers, and they sell stocks that others have feverishly pursued and think of as winners. They do so in the belief that investors tend to overreact to news. That is, stocks that have plunged in price because of some recent piece of bad news (such as recently announced weak earnings) are thought to have fallen too far in price. Hence such stocks are viewed as being ready for a price rebound as investors realize that they have overreacted to the bad news associated with the stock and subsequently drive the price upward toward the stock's fundamental value.

Similarly, stocks that have risen rapidly in price because of some recent piece of good news (such as recently announced strong earnings) are thought to have risen too far in price. Hence such stocks are viewed as being ready for a price drop as investors realize that they have overreacted to the good news associated with the stock and subsequently drive the price downward toward the stock's fundamental value. Researchers have tested strategies of this type. Their overall test design is discussed first, followed by the results.

The Test Design

Consider the following investment strategy:

1. Identify those stocks that have been listed on either the NYSE or AMEX (or just the NYSE). This step focuses the technician's attention on established stocks.
2. Rank these stocks on the basis of the size of their returns over a just-ending time period, referred to as the portfolio "formation period."
3. Assign some of those stocks that have the lowest average return in the formation period to the "loser" portfolio and some of those stocks that have the highest average return in this period to the "winner" portfolio.
4. Determine the returns on the winner and loser portfolios over a just-starting subsequent time period, referred to as the portfolio "test period."
5. Repeat the analysis all over again, starting with step 1, but moving forward one time period. Stop after several repetitions.
6. Determine the abnormal returns on the winner portfolio by subtracting the returns on a benchmark portfolio having a comparable level of risk (see Chapters 21 and 24); calculate the average of these abnormal returns. Similarly, determine the average abnormal returns on the loser portfolio.

If a momentum strategy works, then the winner portfolio should have a significantly positive average abnormal return and the loser portfolio a significantly negative one. Conversely, if a contrarian strategy works, then the loser portfolio should have a significantly positive abnormal return and the winner portfolio a significantly negative one.

However, if stocks are priced efficiently, then their past price behavior is useless in terms of its predictive value. Neither momentum nor contrarian strategies should "work," in that winner portfolios should perform no differently from loser portfolios. Both portfolios should have average abnormal returns of approximately zero.

Test Results

Table 22.1 presents test results of various momentum and contrarian strategies. In part (a), portfolios were formed on the basis of their returns during the past week. All stocks with an above-average return were put into a winner portfolio and those with a below-average return put into a loser portfolio. Then the returns on these

TABLE 22.1   Returns from Momentum and Contrarian Strategies

Length of Portfolio Formation and Test Period	Annualized Abnormal Returns	
	Winner Portfolio	Loser Portfolio
(a) Weekly, 1962–1986		
Top 50% and bottom 50% of NYSE		
and AMEX stocks	−24.9%	89.8%
(b) Monthly, 1929–1982		
Top 10% and bottom 10% of all		
NYSE and AMEX stocks	−11.6	12.1
(c) Semiannually, 1962–1989		
Top 10% and bottom 10% of all		
NYSE and AMEX stocks	8.7	−3.5
(d) Annually, 1929–1982		
Top 10% and bottom 10% of all		
NYSE and AMEX stocks*	5.0	−16.1
(e) Three years, 1926–1982		
Top 35 and bottom 35 NYSE stocks	−1.7	6.5
(f) Five years, 1926–1982		
Top 50 and bottom 50 NYSE stocks	−12.4	7.2

Sources: Adapted from (a) Bruce N. Lehmann, "Fads, Martingales, and Market Efficiency," *Quarterly Journal of Economics* 105, no. 1 (February 1990): 16. (b, d) Narasimhan Jegadeesh, "Evidence of Predictable Behavior of Security Returns," *Journal of Finance* 45, no. 3 (July 1990): 890–891. (c) Narasimhan Jegadeesh and Sheridan Titman, "Returns to Buying Winners and Selling Losers: Implications for Stock Market Efficiency," *Journal of Finance* 48, no. 1 (March 1993): 79. (e) Werner F. M. De Bondt and Richard Thaler, "Does the Stock Market Overreact?" *Journal of Finance* 40, no. 3 (July 1985): 799. (f) Werner F. M. De Bondt and Richard Thaler, "Further Evidence on Investor Overreaction and Stock Market Seasonality," *Journal of Finance* 42, no. 3 (July 1987): 561.
* Abnormal returns were measured over one month subsequent to the portfolio formation date.

two portfolios were tracked for the next week. When this process was repeated week by week from 1962 through 1986, marked differences were found in the annualized average abnormal returns on the two portfolios. Specifically, the returns were nearly −25% for the winners and +90% for the losers, with both returns (as well as the other returns in the table) being significantly different from zero. Note that a similar but not as extreme observation is apparent in part (b), where the time frame is one month instead of a week.[12] Overall, this evidence indicates that short-term contrarian strategies hold promise. Interestingly, the correction for the overreaction is asymmetric in part (a) because the losers rebound by a much larger percentage than the winners fall. Perhaps contrarians should concentrate more on identifying losers than on identifying winners if they are going to focus on weekly returns.

In part (c) of Table 22.1, portfolios were formed on the basis of their returns over the past six months. The 10% of stocks with the highest returns were put in the winner portfolio, whereas the 10% with the lowest returns were put in the loser portfolio. Tracking their returns over the next six months revealed that now the winners had significantly positive abnormal returns and the losers had significantly negative abnormal returns. This result, which is in complete contrast to parts (a) and (b), suggests that momentum strategies have promise. Stocks that shot up in price over six months continued to rise during the next six months, whereas those that plunged over six months continued their fall. Although not quite as strong, similar results were observed when the top 10% and bottom 10% were identified on the basis of a full year's returns, as shown in part (d).[13]

Oddly, part (e) shows that the momentum strategy would not work if the winner and loser portfolios were formed on the basis of three-year stock returns. Instead, the contrarian strategy appears to have worked once again. Note that the average annual abnormal return on the loser portfolio was +6.5%. Conversely, the average annual abnormal return on the winner portfolio was −1.7%. Part (f) shows that similar results were obtained when portfolios were formed on the basis of returns over the previous five years.[14] As in part (a), the correction for the overreaction is asymmetric in that losers rebound by a much larger percentage than the winners fall.

In summary, there does appear to be some merit to the contrarian strategy for both very short (a week or a month) and very long (three or five years) time periods.[15] Surprisingly, for intermediate periods such as six months and one year, an exact opposite strategy—momentum—seems to have merit. Unfortunately, both strategies involve a high degree of turnover, because portfolios are reconstituted frequently—particularly for the weekly contrarian strategy.[16] The strategies would incur substantial transaction costs, so it remains to be seen whether they would be profitable after such costs were fully accounted for.

22.3.2 Moving Average and Trading Range Breakout Strategies

Consider the following investment strategy:

1. Calculate the average closing price of a given stock over the last 200 trading days.
2. Take today's closing price and divide it by the 200-day average to form a short-to-long price ratio.
3. A ratio greater than 1 is a buy signal that indicates that the stock is to be bought tomorrow. A ratio of less than 1 is a sell signal that indicates that the stock is to be sold tomorrow.
4. Tomorrow after closing, repeat the above process.
5. At the end of a test period, calculate the average daily return during both the "buy" days and the "sell" days.

If the stock market is efficient, the average return during the buy days should be approximately the same as the average return during the sell days. That is, the difference in their returns should be approximately zero. However, technical analysis might have merit if they are significantly different.

A study examined this strategy using daily data from 1897 to 1986, a total of over 25,000 trading days. The daily closing level of the Dow Jones Industrial Average (DJIA) was used instead of daily closing prices for individual stocks. As shown in part (a) of Table 22.2, this strategy resulted in markedly different returns on buy and sell days. In particular, the annualized average return on buy days was 10.7%, whereas the

TABLE 22.2 Returns from Moving Average and Trading Range Breakout Strategies			
	Annualized Average Returns		
	Buy Signal	Sell Signal	Buy Return Less Sell Return
(a) Moving average tests			
Variable length	10.7%	−6.1%	16.8%
Fixed length	13.8	−4.8	18.6
(b) Trading range breakout tests	11.8	−5.8	17.6

Source: Adapted from William Brock, Josef Lakonishok, and Blake LeBaron, "Simple Technical Trading Rules and the Stochastic Properties of Stock Returns," *Journal of Finance* 47, no. 5 (December 1992): 1739, 1741, 1742. Based on one-day short and 200-day long periods during 1897 to 1986 with no filter; annualized assuming that there are 260 trading days in a year and 26 ten-day trading periods in a year.

return on sell days was −6.1%. The difference of 16.8% was significantly different from zero (as were the differences in the other parts of the table).

Because this strategy classifies every day as either a buy day or a sell day, thereby allowing a given stock to be bought on consecutive days, it is referred to as a variable-length moving average strategy. However, it can result in many trades over the course of a year, because an investor using it could be "whipsawed" into buying and selling repeatedly. The frequency of changing positions from buying to selling, or from selling to buying, can be reduced by modifying the strategy as follows to make it a fixed-length moving average strategy. Buy signals are now generated only when the ratio *changes* from less than 1 to greater than 1, and sell signals are generated only when the ratio *changes* from greater than 1 to less than 1. Furthermore, when a buy signal is generated, the stock is bought the next day and then held for ten days. Similarly, when a sell signal is generated, the stock is sold and not bought for ten days. In either case, when the ten days are over, the investor starts looking again for a buy or a sell signal. Whereas the variable-length strategy classified every day as either a buy or a sell day, there can be days that are not classified as either buy or sell with the fixed-length strategy.

Part (a) of Table 22.2 shows that the fixed-length moving average strategy performed similarly to the variable-length one. The annualized average return on buy days was 13.8%, and on sell days it was −4.8%, resulting in a significant difference of 18.6%. On average there were about 1.3 buy and 1.7 sell signals per year.

The trading range breakout strategy is similar to the fixed-length moving average strategy. Here the high and low prices over the past 200 trading days are noted. A buy signal is generated on a given day only when that day's closing price is greater than the high, provided that the previous day's closing price was less than the high. Conversely, a sell signal arises when the closing price moves from being above the low on one day to being below the low on the next day. When a buy signal is generated, the stock is repurchased the next day and then held for ten days. Similarly, when a sell signal is generated, the stock is sold and not bought for ten days. In either case, when the ten days are over, the investor starts looking again for a buy or a sell signal.

Part (b) of Table 22.2 shows that the trading range breakout strategy performed similarly to the two moving average strategies. The annualized average returns on buy days was 11.8%, and on sell days it was −5.8%, with a significant difference of 17.6%. On average there were about 5.2 buy and 2.0 sell signals per year.

22.3.3 The Bottom Line

What is the bottom line? The four strategies reported in Tables 22.1 and 22.2 have been rigorously tested, avoiding procedural pitfalls that have tainted the results of many studies. Furthermore, although not reported, slight variations among the strategies had only a minor effect on their results. However, the usefulness of such technical strategies remains an open question subject to much debate. Although the strategies appear to be profitable, even after transaction costs have been considered, it is quite possible that a more complete accounting of these costs (including such aspects as the impact of bid-ask spreads) will reveal that the strategies are incapable of generating abnormal profits. Hence evaluating investment systems will not always provide unambiguous answers on their potential usefulness. Furthermore, it has been speculated that the commonplace usage of computerized trading programs designed to implement technical strategies will ultimately eliminate any potential such strategies have for generating abnormal profits.[17] Nevertheless, the apparent success of these strategies offers a challenge to those who contend that the U.S. stock market is highly efficient.

The rest of this chapter is concerned with the principles of fundamental analysis of common stocks. Although technical analysis is used by many investors, fundamental analysis is far more prevalent. Furthermore, unlike technical analysis, it is an essential activity if capital markets are to be efficient.

22.4.1   Top-Down versus Bottom-Up Forecasting

Fundamental analysts forecast, among other things, future levels of the economy's gross domestic product, future sales and earnings for a number of industries, and future sales and earnings for an even larger number of firms. Eventually such forecasts are converted to estimates of expected returns of specific stocks and, perhaps, certain industries and the stock market itself. In some cases the conversion is made explicitly. For example, an estimate of next year's earnings per share for a firm may be multiplied by a projected price-earnings ratio in order to estimate the expected price of the firm's stock a year hence. Or an estimate of future dividends may be supplied to a dividend discount model. Both approaches allow the analyst to make an direct forecast of the stock's expected return. In other cases the conversion is implicit. For example, stocks with projected earnings substantially exceeding consensus estimates may be placed on an "approved" list.

Some investment organizations that employ financial analysts follow a sequential **top-down forecasting approach**. With this approach, the financial analysts are first involved in making forecasts for the economy, then for industries, and finally for companies. The industry forecasts are based on the forecasts for the economy, and, in turn, a company's forecasts are based on the forecasts for both its industry and the economy.

Other investment organizations begin with estimates of the prospects for companies and then build to estimates of the prospects for industries and ultimately the economy. Such **bottom-up forecasting** may unknowingly involve inconsistent assumptions. For example, one analyst may use one forecast of foreign exchange rates in projecting the foreign sales of company A, while another analyst may use a different forecast in projecting the foreign sales of company B. Top-down systems are less susceptible to this danger because all the analysts in the organization would use the same forecast of exchange rates.

In practice, a combination of the two approaches is often employed. For example, forecasts are made for the economy in a top-down manner. These forecasts then provide a setting within which financial analysts make bottom-up forecasts for individual companies. The sum of the individual forecasts should be consistent with the original economywide forecast.[18] If it is not, the process is repeated (perhaps with additional controls) to ensure consistency.

22.4.2   Probabilistic Forecasting

Explicit **probabilistic forecasting** often focuses on economywide forecasts, because uncertainty at this level is of the greatest importance in determining the risk and expected return of a well-diversified portfolio. A few alternative economic scenarios may be forecast, along with their respective probability of occurrence. Then accompanying projections are made of the prospects for industries, companies, and stock prices. Such an exercise provides an idea of the likely sensitivities of different stocks to surprises concerning the economy and hence is sometimes referred to as "what-if" analysis. Risks may also be estimated by assigning probabilities to the different scenarios.

22.4.3 Econometric Models

An **econometric model** is a statistical model that provides a means of forecasting the levels of certain variables, known as **endogenous variables**. In order to make these forecasts, the model relies on assumptions that have been made in regard to the levels of certain other variables supplied by the model user, known as **exogenous variables**. For example, the level of next year's car sales may be specified by an econometric model to be related to next year's level of gross domestic product and interest rates. The values of next year's gross domestic product and interest rates, the exogenous variables, must be provided in order to forecast next year's car sales, the endogenous variable.

An econometric model may be extremely complex or it may be a simple formula that can be implemented with a calculator. In either case, it should involve a blend of economics and statistics, where first economics is used to suggest the forms of relevant relationships and then statistical procedures are applied to historical data to estimate the exact nature of the relationships involved.

Some investment organizations use large-scale econometric models to translate predictions about such factors as the federal budget, expected consumer spending, and planned business investment into predictions of future levels of gross domestic product, inflation, and unemployment. Several firms and nonprofit organizations maintain such models, selling either the forecasts or the computer program itself to investment organizations, corporate planners, public agencies, and others.

The developers of such large-scale models usually provide several "standard" predictions, based on different sets of assumptions about the exogenous variables. Some also assign probabilities to the alternative predictions. In some cases, users can substitute their own assumptions and subsequently examine the resulting predictions.

Large-scale econometric models of this type employ many equations that describe many important relationships. Although estimates of the magnitudes of such relationships are obtained from historical data, these estimates may or may not enable the model to work well in the future. When predictions turn out to be poor, it is sometimes said that there has been a structural change in the underlying economic relationships. However, the failure may result from the influence of factors omitted from the model. Either situation necessitates changes in either the magnitudes of the estimates or the basic form of the econometric model, or both. Rare indeed is the user who does not "fine-tune" (or completely overhaul) such a model from time to time as further experience is accumulated.

22.5   FINANCIAL STATEMENT ANALYSIS

For some, the image of a typical financial analyst is that of a gnome, fully equipped with green eyeshade, poring over financial statements in a back room. While the physical description is rarely accurate, it is true that many analysts do study financial statements in an attempt to predict the future.

A company's financial statements can be regarded as the output of a model of the firm—a model designed by management, the company's accountants, and (indirectly) the tax authorities. Different companies use different models, meaning that they treat similar events in different ways. One reason this is possible is because generally accepted accounting principles (GAAP) allow a certain degree of latitude in how to account for various events. Examples include the method of depreciating assets (straight-line or accelerated) and the method of valuing inventory (FIFO or LIFO).

To fully understand a company and to compare it with others that use different accounting procedures, the financial analyst must be a financial detective, looking for clues in footnotes and the accompanying text that discuss how the financial statements were prepared. Those who take bottom-line figures such as earnings per share on faith may be more surprised by future developments than those who try to look behind the accounting veil.

The ultimate goal of fundamental analysis is to determine the values of the outstanding claims on a firm's income (claimants include the firm's bondholders and stockholders). The firm's income must first be projected, then the possible distributions of that income among the claimants must be considered, with relevant probabilities assessed.

In practice, shortcut procedures are often used. Many analysts focus on reported accounting figures, even though such numbers may not adequately reflect true economic values. In addition, simple measures are often used to assess complex relationships. For example, some analysts attempt to estimate the probability that short-term creditors will be paid in full and on time by examining the ratio of liquid assets to the amount of short-term debt (known as the *quick ratio*). Similarly, the probability that interest will be paid to bondholders in a timely fashion may be estimated by examining the ratio of earnings before interest and taxes to the periodic amount of such interest payments (known as *times interest earned*). Often the value of a firm's common stock is estimated by examining the ratio of earnings after taxes to the book value of equity (known as *return on equity*).

Financial statement analysis can help an analyst understand a company's current situation, where it may be going, what factors affect it, and how those factors affect it. If others are doing such analysis and doing it well, it will be difficult to find mispriced securities in this manner. However, it should be possible to identify firms likely to go bankrupt, firms with higher or lower betas, and firms with greater or lesser sensitivities to major factors. Increased understanding of such aspects may well provide ample rewards.

Analysts who regularly work with financial statements develop a keen sense of what items are important to their research. Those items will vary depending on the type of security being examined (for example, the common stock of a company as opposed to its debt securities). Furthermore, the list of critical items may vary from industry to industry and from company to company. Moreover, one analyst may approach the analysis of a particular company's financial statements differently than another analyst. Despite these differences, certain standard techniques are commonly applied and are discussed next. Understanding the analysis of financial statements is facilitated by applying the process to a specific example. In the discussion below, general steps and observations are presented along with reference to Dayton Hudson Corporation, a large retailing company whose stock is both listed on the New York Stock Exchange and is a constituent of the Standard and Poor's 500 index.

22.5.1 Company Background

The analysis of a company's financial statements in a security analyst's research report typically begins with an overview of the company. Although the reporting analyst presumably knows the company well, the purpose of the overview is to acquaint readers of the research with the company. Among other topics that this discussion may include are a short corporate history, a description of the company's lines of business, a listing of its primary competitors, a description of the key business challenges facing the company, and a summary of basic financial information.

Dayton Hudson Corporation is one of the largest general merchandise retailers in the United States. The company has its roots in the department store business, even though today the vast majority of its sales and profits are derived from discount retailing. The J.L. Hudson Company was founded in Detroit in 1881, and the Dayton Department Store Company was established in 1902 in Minneapolis. Both companies were predominately department stores with long and storied traditions in their Midwestern markets when they merged in 1969 to form the Dayton Hudson Corporation. In 1963 the Dayton Company opened its first Target store, an initial entrance into the low-margin merchandising business. In 1978, the Dayton Hudson Corporation acquired Mervyn's, a West Coast moderate-priced promotional department store chain. In 1990, the company purchased Chicago-based Marshall Field & Company, thereby establishing its dominance in the department store business in the upper Midwest.

Today, Dayton Hudson Corporation operates three lines of retailing business: Target, Mervyn's, and the Department Stores Division. Target is an upscale discount store business with a high-volume, low-margin orientation. Target offers high-quality merchandise, convenience, and competitive prices. Mervyn's is a moderate-priced family department store, specializing in national brand and private-label clothing and other soft goods. The Department Stores Division operates stores that emphasize fashion leadership and quality merchandise in the moderate to high price range supported by superior customer service.

Due to its multiline business, Dayton Hudson Corporation encounters a number of different retail competitors. Its Target stores compete primarily against Wal-Mart and Kmart on a national level. Mervyn's competes against J.C. Penney and Sears, Roebuck and Company, and to a lesser extent against Kohl's, a rapidly growing regional chain. Finally, in the Midwest, the Department Stores Division faces Federated Department Stores, May Department Stores Company, and Nordstrom.

Dayton Hudson confronts a number of imposing business challenges, including:

- Can the company sustain the rebound in earnings that occurred in 1996 following a poor year in 1995? Further, can it meet its goal of 15% long-run annual earnings growth in a highly competitive industry?
- Can it maintain the extraordinary growth of its Target stores?
- Can stagnant sales growth at its Mervyn's and Department Stores be regenerated?
- Can the multidivision corporation become better organized to take advantage of synergies between its operations and achieve increased economies of scale?

Statistical Abstract			
Ticker/Exchange	DH/NYSE	Dividend	$0.64
Price (31-Aug-97)	$57.000	Dividend Yield	1.05%
52-Week Price Range	$30.750–$64.625	Book Value per Share	$17.33
Earnings per Share (1996) (Fully diluted)	$1.95	Market Capitalization	$13.1 billion
Sales (1996)	$25.4 billion	Net Income (1996)	$463 million

22.5.2   Review of Accounting Statements

From an investment perspective, the analysis of a company's accounting statements is not an end in itself. Rather it is a means to identify financial aspects of a company that may have direct relevance to understanding the intrinsic values and risks of the company's securities. The analyst will want to obtain access to a wide range of financial information about the company under review. Much of that information is found in three primary accounting statements issued by the company in its annual report: the balance sheet, the income statement, and the statement of cash flows.

Balance Sheet

The balance sheet (also called the statement of financial position) presents a snapshot of the company's financial position at a point in time. The statement describes amounts or levels of various items. In particular, the balance sheet presents a listing of the company's *assets, liabilities,* and *stockholders' equity.*

Assets represent the company's economic resources. An asset is an item that has the potential to generate economic benefits (that is, cash inflows) for the company in the future. For example, plant and equipment can produce goods and services that can be sold to customers for cash. Liabilities are claims on the company's economic resources. These claims are usually of a specified amount and must be satisfied as of a certain date in the future. Both assets and liabilities are classified on the balance sheet as either current or long-term. Current assets consist of cash or other assets, such as marketable securities, inventory, and accounts receivable, that are expected to be turned into cash in the near future. Current liabilities are expected to be (or are at risk of being) discharged shortly, usually within one year. Long-term assets are held and used for several years, whereas long-term liabilities are due more than a year in the future. Stockholders' equity (or *net worth*) is a residual claim of the owners of the company on the company's assets, after all liabilities have been extinguished.

The balance sheet does not show all of a company's assets and liabilities. For example, the capabilities of its management team are often the company's most valuable asset, yet the value of those capabilities is nowhere to be found on the balance sheet. On the liability side, the value of operating leases signed by the company may be large, yet are relegated to footnotes in the company's annual report.

Because the balance sheet represents the resources of the company and the claims on those resources, it must be the case that assets equal liabilities plus stockholders' equity. In this sense, the components of the balance sheet must balance. In fact, a balance sheet is often presented with assets and their values listed on the left-hand side and liabilities and stockholders' equity and their values listed on the right-hand side. Balance sheet items are generally reported at their unadjusted or adjusted acquisition costs. For example, a building will be carried on the balance sheet at its purchase price plus the value of any physical improvements less accumulated depreciation. Accounts receivable will be reported as the actual amount of the account less an allowance for doubtful accounts.

Dayton Hudson Corporation

Table 22.3 presents the fiscal year-end consolidated balance sheets of the Dayton Hudson Corporation over the period 1990 to 1996.

A look at the company's balance sheets confirms that Dayton Hudson Corporation is a large company and is growing at a fairly rapid pace. The company's assets total over $13 billion and have grown at almost an 8% annual rate since 1990. Property and equipment, composed primarily of the company's stores and fixtures, represents the largest asset, making up 56% of 1996 total assets. Inventories, at 23% of 1996 total assets, are also a prominent asset. Somewhat surprisingly, accounts receivable, at 13% of 1996 total assets, have grown much more slowly than total assets. This slow growth is due in part to the company's policy of selling off a portion of its

TABLE 22.3 Dayton Hudson Corporation Consolidated Balance Sheets (millions)

	1990	1991	1992	1993	1994	1995	1996
Assets							
Cash & equivalents	$92	$96	$117	$321	$147	$175	$201
Receivables	1,407	1,430	1,514	1,536	1,810	1,510	1,720
Inventories	2,016	2,381	2,618	2,497	2,777	3,018	3,031
Other	143	125	165	157	225	252	488
Total Current Assets	$3,658	$4,032	$4,414	$4,511	$4,959	$4.955	$5,440
Property & equipment (net)	4,525	5,102	5,563	5,947	6,385	7,294	7,467
Other assets	341	351	360	320	353	321	482
Total Assets	$8,524	$9,485	$10,337	$10,778	$11,697	$12,570	$13,389
Liabilities and Stockholders' Equity							
Short-term debt	$357	$453	$394	$373	$209	$182	$233
Accounts payable	1,267	1,324	1,596	1,654	1,961	2,247	2,528
Accrued liabilities	638	705	849	903	1,045	957	1,168
Taxes payable	160	98	125	145	175	137	182
Total Current Liabilities	$2,422	$2,580	$2,964	$3,075	$3,390	$3,523	$4,111
Long-term debt	3,682	4,227	4,330	4,279	4,488	4,959	4,808
Deferred taxes and other	372	447	557	687	626	685	680
Total Liabilities	$6,476	$7,254	$7,851	$8,041	$8,504	$9,167	$9,599
Stockholders' Equity	$2,048	$2,231	$2,486	$2,737	$3,193	$3,403	$3,790
Total Liabilities and Stockholders' Equity	$8,524	$9,485	$10,337	$10,778	$11,697	$12,570	$13,389

receivables to investors through a securitization process similar to that used to create mortgage-backed securities. (Asset-backed securities are discussed in Chapter 13.) It is also due to the increasing importance of Target in the company's total financial picture; as a discount retailer, Target tends to carry a relatively low level of receivables.

On the liability side, the company's long-term debt relative to total assets is almost 36% in 1996. That debt has been declining as a proportion of total assets after reaching a high of 45% following the 1990 acquisition of Marshall Field & Company. Stockholders' equity represents about 28% of total assets. Net working capital (current assets less current liabilities) is almost 10% of total assets, down from over 14% in 1990. Again, this decline is due to the growth of Target, which has a higher asset turnover than the other two operating divisions.

Income Statement

The income statement (also called the statement of earnings) indicates the *earnings* (or *profits* or *net income*) of the company. Instead of presenting levels at a point in time, the income statement reports flows that occur over a period of time. A company's net income is the difference between its sales (or revenues) and expenses. Sales measure the inflow of assets from selling goods and services to the company's customers. Expenses measure the outflow of assets (or the increase in liabilities) associated with generating sales. Ultimately, the success of a company is directly related to producing a sufficient surplus of sales over expenses.

The income statement provides a breakdown of the sources of sales and expenses for the company. Sales are reported net of returns and allowances. Expenses are divided into two groups. The first group are those expenses—such as costs of goods sold;

selling, general, and administrative (S, G, & A) expenses; and depreciation and amortization—that are directly associated with producing and selling the company's goods and services. These are called *operating expenses*. The second group are costs associated with financing and taxes on the company's income. These are called *non-operating expenses*. Thus, the income statement has the following general format:

Sales
−Operating expenses
=Operating income (or earnings before interest and taxes, *EBIT*)
−Interest expense
=Pre-tax income (or earnings before taxes, *EBT*)
−Taxes
=Net income (or earnings after taxes, *EAT*)

The income statement is related to the beginning and end-of-period balance sheets. Net income that is not distributed to shareholders in the form of dividends increases retained earnings. On the balance sheet it increases the end-of-period stockholders' equity and reflects an increase in one or more asset items and (or) decrease of one or more liability items.

Earnings are often presented on a "per share" basis. As Chapter 17 discussed, analysts commonly use the ratio of a stock's market price to the company's earnings per share as a measure of the stock's relative valuation. Earnings per share is calculated by dividing net income by the average number of common shares outstanding over the period. Comparisons with current numbers are made relevant by adjusting historical earnings per share for any stock splits or stock dividends that may have occurred after the earnings were originally reported. For example, if last year's income statement shows earnings per share of $6 and this year's of $4, it would be tempting to believe that the firm was less profitable this year. However, suppose that a two-for-one stock split took place right after the last year's earnings were announced. Consequently, in this year's financial statements, last year's earnings per share would be reported as $3 (=$6/2), thereby revealing that the firm has actually been more, not less, profitable this year.

A company may issue securities, such as convertible bonds, convertible preferred stock, stock options, and warrants, that at some future date can be converted into common stock at the discretion of the company or the securityholder, or sometimes both. Companies that issue these convertible securities must calculate per share earnings on both a primary and a fully diluted basis. The primary basis assumes no conversion of the securities into common shares; the fully diluted basis assumes full conversion. Because the existence of additional common shares "dilutes," or reduces, the net income available to existing common stockholders, fully diluted earnings per share will generally be less than or equal to primary earnings per share, with the difference depending on the existence and the terms of the dilutive securities.[19]

Sometimes a company will report nonrecurring (or one-time) expenses or income. Although these transactions may be intended to enhance the future operating profitability of the company, they are not expected to appear again on the company's income statement. The analyst generally will want to exclude these transactions in evaluating the company's operating performance.

Confusingly, some nonrecurring transactions are categorized as extraordinary items. Companies that incur these transactions must report them separately. The result is two sets of net income and earnings per share calculations: both before and after consideration of the extraordinary items. However, not all nonrecurring transactions are deemed extraordinary items. Nonrecurring transactions that are not deemed extraordinary enter the income statement as operating items, and consequently only one set of net income and earnings per share will be reported. In summary:

Nonrecurring Items	
Extraordinary	Not extraordinary
1. reported separately	1. not reported separately
2. two sets of income figures	2. one set of income figures

Certain companies regularly report large transactions identified as nonrecurring. For example, from 1985 to 1994, AT&T reported four nonrecurring restructuring charges totaling $14.2 billion. The company's total reported net income over this period was only $10.3 billion. The high frequency of nonrecurring transactions at some companies has led analysts to question the reporting companies' motives and to wonder just how "nonrecurring" the transactions truly are.

Dayton Hudson Corporation

Table 22.4 shows the annual consolidated income statements for Dayton Hudson Corporation from 1990 to 1996.

Dayton Hudson Corporation's revenues have grown at a 9.5% annual rate over the last six years. Earnings, on the other hand, have not kept pace, increasing only 2.5% per year on average. In the mid-1990s, the company's net income stagnated. In fact, in 1995 it was lower than in 1990. The primary explanation for the slow growth in earnings was the company's lack of pricing power to expand revenues relative to operating expenses as well as insufficiently tight controls over S, G, & A expenses. As a result, operating expenses grew from 93% of sales in 1990 to 96% of sales in 1995. Note, however, that in 1996 the company experienced a significant rebound in net income, in part due to a concerted cost control campaign. In addition, note that in

TABLE 22.4 Dayton Hudson Corporation Consolidated Income Statements (millions)							
	1990	1991	1992	1993	1994	1995	1996
Revenues (Sales)	$14,739	$16,115	$17,927	$19,233	$21,311	$23,516	$25,371
Expenses							
Cost of goods sold	$10,652	$11,751	$13,129	$14,164	$15,636	$17,527	$18,628
S, G, & A expenses	2,478	2,801	2,978	3,175	3,614	4,043	4,289
Depreciation and amortization	369	410	459	498	548	594	650
Other taxes	256	283	313	343	373	409	445
Nonrecurring operating expenses	0	0	0	0	0	0	134
Total Operating Expenses	$13,755	$15,245	$16,879	$18,180	$20,171	$22,573	$24,146
Operating Income (EBIT)	$984	$870	$1,048	$1,053	$1,140	$943	$1,225
Interest expense	325	398	437	446	426	442	442
Pre-tax Income (EBT)	$659	$472	$611	$607	$714	$501	$783
Taxes	249	171	228	232	280	190	309
Net Income (EAT)	410	301	383	375	434	311	$474
Extraordinary items	0	0	0	23	0	0	11
Net Income after Extraordinary Items	$410	$301	$383	$352	$434	$311	$463
Earnings per Share (Fully diluted)	$1.72	$1.24	$1.61	$1.59	$1.84	$1.30	$2.00
Extraordinary charges	0.00	0.00	0.00	(0.18)	0.00	0.00	(0.05)
Earnings per Share (Fully diluted)	$1.72	$1.24	$1.61	$1.41	$1.84	$1.30	$1.95

both 1993 and 1996, Dayton Hudson reported charges to earnings related to earthquake damage and an early redemption of long-term debt, respectively. Hence, in both years extraordinary charges were reported, resulting in two sets of net income and earnings per share figures. In addition, in 1996 the company reported a large nonrecurring, operating expense related to the closing of stores in several states. This expense, however, was not classified as an extraordinary item.

Statement of Cash Flows

Analysts are concerned with the amount of cash that a company generates. In the long-run, a company can afford to make payments to its securityholders only if it produces surplus cash flow from its operations. Even profitable companies may find themselves facing cash shortages that, in the extreme, can lead to bankruptcy. In the short run, dwindling cash balances may be recharged by borrowing or through the sales of assets. However, those strategies may adversely affect the company's future profitability.

The statement of cash flows shows how a company's cash balance changed from one year to the next. It assists the analyst in evaluating the ability of the company to meet its obligations for cash, its needs for future external financing, and the effectiveness of its financing and investing strategies. The statement of cash flows is divided into three parts:

1. Cash flow from operating activities
2. Cash flow from investing activities
3. Cash flow from financing activities

Construction of the statement of cash flows begins with a comparison of balance sheets from one period to another. Each activity of the corporation is classified into either operating, investing, or financing categories and identified as either inflows or outflows. For example, an increase in inventory constitutes an operating outflow of cash, whereas an increase in long-term debt represents an inflow of financing cash.

Cash flows from operating activities are obtained by adding the company's operating cash inflows to net income and substracting the operating cash outflows from it. Cash from investing activities are primarily calculated from changes in the property, plant, and equipment accounts. Cash flows from financing are associated with raising or reducing capital through debt or equity offerings or refinancings and the payment of dividends.

Closely related to these measures of cash flows is a company's *free cash flow*, which takes two forms. First of all, there is *free cash flow to the firm*, determined as:

After-tax operating income
+Depreciation, amortization, and deferred taxes
−Increase in working capital
−Investment in fixed assets
=Free cash flow to the firm

Here after-tax operating earnings are equal to operating earnings times the quantity of 1 minus the tax rate, that is, $EBIT(1 - t)$, or equivalently $EAT + tI$. Investment in fixed assets involves spending on items such as property, plant, and equipment. Thus, free cash flow to the firm is the cash generated by the company's operations that is available to all of the company's debt- and equityholders. Note that it is equivalent to the sum of cash flow from operating activities, cash flow from investing activities, and the after-tax cost of any interest and preferred stock dividend payments.

The second type of free cash flow is *free cash flow to equity*, defined as:

Net income
+Depreciation, amortization, and deferred taxes
−Increase in working capital
−Investment in fixed assets
−Principal repayments
+New debt issued
=Free cash flow to equity

Thus, free cash flow to equity represents cash flow generated by the company's operations that is left after the company has covered all its financial obligations, working capital needs, and fixed asset needs. Accordingly, it is what is left for the company to pay out as dividends, although most companies do not use the entire amount for this purpose. Note that it is equal to the sum of cash flow from operations, cash flow from investing, cash flow from financing, and dividends. It is also equal to free cash flow to the firm less principal repayments plus new debt issued.[20]

Dayton Hudson Corporation

Table 22.5 shows the annual consolidated statements of cash flows for Dayton Hudson Corporation from 1990 to 1996.

Dayton Hudson Corporation has a large need for cash to finance its capital expenditures program, a need that is primarily related to the rapid growth of its Target stores and is indicated by its reported total investing cash flow figures. The company meets much of these cash requirements through its net income and noncash expenses (principally depreciation), as indicated by its total operating cash flow figures. Since 1992, cash from financing sources has generally been negative as indicated by its total financing cash flow figures, as the company has reduced its long-term debt outstanding as a proportion of total assets. Also interesting is the steady increasing pattern in aggregate dividends paid, while free cash flow to equity has been much more volatile, being sometimes above and sometimes below the amount of dividends paid.

Additional Financial Statement Information

The balance sheet, income statement, and statement of cash flows contain much of the financial statement information required by the analyst. However, considerable detail about the financial performance of the company also can be found in other parts of a company's annual report. Thus, as part of his or her research, the analyst will want to examine:

- Notes to the financial statements
- Management discussion and analysis
- Auditor's report

The notes to the financial statements contain supplemental information regarding particular accounts, such as the company's method of valuing inventory and a listing of its long-term debts outstanding. Furthermore, the notes will present information regarding major acquisitions or divestitures, officer and employee retirement and stock options plans, leasing arrangements, legal proceedings, and changes in accounting procedures, among other issues.

Management discussion and analysis provide an interpretation by the company's senior officers of financial trends and significant events affecting the company, particularly as they affect the company's liquidity, financial resources, and results of

	1990	1991	1992	1993	1994	1995	1996
Cash from Operating Activities							
Net income	$410	$301	$383	$375	$434	$311	$474
Depreciation and amortization	372	410	459	498	548	594	650
Deferred taxes and other	(18)	60	59	89	(3)	46	(96)
Changes in Working Capital							
Receivables	(116)	(23)	(84)	(22)	(274)	300	(210)
Inventories	(36)	(365)	(237)	121	(280)	(241)	(13)
Accounts payable	8	57	272	58	307	286	281
Accrued liabilities	(15)	59	142	63	147	(88)	275
Income taxes payable	(13)	(62)	27	20	30	(38)	55
Other	33	0	(37)	17	(17)	(9)	42
Total Operating Cash Flow	$625	$437	$984	$1,219	$892	$1,161	$1,458
Cash from Investing Activities							
Capital expenditures	$(1,732)	$(1,009)	$(918)	$(969)	$(1,095)	$(1,522)	$(1,301)
Proceeds from disposals, etc.	2	19	10	79	89	17	103
Total Investing Cash Flow	$(1,730)	$(990)	$(908)	$(890)	$(1,006)	$(1,505)	$(1,198)
Cash from Financing Activities							
Change in notes payable	$(130)	$161	$(242)	$(23)	$247	$501	$416
Change in long-term debt	1,337	476	260	(53)	(199)	(60)	(286)
Equity issuance	0	0	0	0	0	0	0
Dividends	(116)	(128)	(133)	(138)	(144)	(148)	(155)
Other	3	48	60	89	36	79	51
Total Financing Cash Flow	$1,094	$557	$(55)	$(125)	$(60)	$372	$(234)
Change in Cash	$(11)	$4	$21	$204	$(174)	$28	$(26)
Beginning Cash	$103	$92	$96	$117	$321	$147	$175
Ending Cash	$92	$96	$117	$321	$147	$175	$201
Free Cash Flow Analysis							
Total operating cash flow	$625	$437	$984	$1,219	$892	$1,161	$1,458
Total investing cash flow	(1,730)	(990)	(908)	(890)	(1,006)	(1,505)	(1,198)
After-tax interest expense	123	144	163	170	167	168	174
Free Cash Flow to the Firm	$(982)	$(409)	$239	$499	$53	$(176)	$434
Total operating cash flow	$625	$437	$984	$1,219	$892	$1,161	$1,458
Total investing cash flow	(1,730)	(990)	(908)	(890)	(1,006)	(1,505)	(1,198)
Total financing cash flow	1,094	557	(55)	(125)	(60)	372	(234)
Dividends	116	128	133	138	144	148	155
Free Cash Flow to Equity	$105	$132	$154	$342	$(30)	$176	$181

operations. In preparing this report, some corporate managements are more forthcoming than others. Consequently, the value of the report to the analyst varies widely among companies.

The auditor's report presents the opinion of the company's independent auditor regarding the "fairness" of the company's financial statements. In the vast majority of cases, the auditor issues an unqualified opinion, stating that over the accounting period the company's financial statements fairly present, in all material respects, the financial position, results of operations, and the cash flows in conformance with generally accepted accounting principles (GAAP). A qualified opinion, indicating material departures from GAAP, is a rarity and may signal serious problems with the company's disclosures. The mere threat that the auditor might issue a qualified opinion is usually sufficient to prevent a company from releasing intentionally incorrect reports. Note, however, that an unqualified opinion is related merely to the fairness of the disclosures; it does not imply any endorsement on the part of the auditor as to the quality of the company's business operations or the value of the company's securities.

22.5.3 Ratio Analysis

Ratio analysis is a technique commonly employed by analysts examining a company's financial statements. Standing alone, the values of various financial statement items are difficult to interpret. They display more meaning when they are considered relative to one another. For example, a growing firm will generally increase the amount of its debt outstanding. Such increases are expected and appropriate. However, when that debt relative to total assets or stockholders' equity increases significantly, a red flag is raised for analysts. They will want to know the reasons for, and ramifications of, such an increase in leverage.

Ratios may be used in several ways. Some analysts apply absolute standards, on the grounds that a substandard ratio indicates a potential weakness that merits further analysis. Other analysts compare a company's ratios with those of the "average" firm in the same industry in order to detect differences that may need further consideration. Others analyze trends in a company's ratios over time, perhaps in comparison with industry trends, hoping that these past data will help them predict future changes. Still others combine ratios with technical analysis (discussed in this chapter's appendix) in order to arrive at investment decisions.

Ratio analysis can be very sophisticated, but it can also be overly simplistic. Routine extrapolation of a ratio (or its recent trend) may produce a poor estimate of its future value. (For example, there is no reason for a firm to maintain a constant ratio of inventory to sales.) Moreover, a series of simple projections may produce inconsistent financial statements. For example, projections of ratios imply predictions of the levels of various balance sheet items. However, it may be that when these levels are looked at together, the resulting balance sheet does not balance. Furthermore, comparisons of one company's ratios with those of its competitors can be fraught with problems. In many industries, competitors' lines of business do not precisely match up. Even very similar companies may use different accounting procedures. The result is often an apples and oranges situation that diminishes the value of peer comparisons.

The types of ratios considered depends on the purpose of the analysis. In general, analysts concerned with a company's equity securities will look at ratios relating to the firm's return on equity. Analysts viewing the company from a creditor's perspective will focus on measures of debt capacity and liquidity.

Equity Ratio Analysis

Stock prices are ultimately determined by expected growth in corporate earnings. Analysts, therefore, are naturally concerned with identifying the elements that cause a company's long-run earnings growth rate to increase or decrease. Equation (17.51b) demonstrated that the long-run (or *sustainable*) growth rate (g) of a company's earnings depends on (1) the proportion of earnings that is retained $(1 - p)$ and (2) the average return on equity for the earnings that are retained (r). That is:

$$g = r(1 - p) \qquad (17.51b)$$

Ratio analysis is used to plumb the past return on equity for clues as to improvements or deterioration in the return on equity in the future. Ratio analysis breaks down the return on equity into its various components, which in turn are examined for trends and relative position versus competing companies. The simplest expression for return on equity (ROE) is to view it as the product of profit margin (net income divided by sales) and equity turnover (sales divided by stockholders' equity).[21] That is:

$$ROE = \frac{\text{net income}}{\text{stockholders' equity}} = \frac{\text{net income}}{\text{sales}} \times \frac{\text{sales}}{\text{stockholders' equity}}$$

Although it is a useful starting point, this expression aggregates considerable detail concerning the company's financial performance. A better understanding is gained by recognizing that the profit margin reflects not only the operating results of the company but non-operating factors as well. Disaggregating those two elements allows for a more intensive analysis. Similarly, equity turnover reflects not only the company's operating efficiency but also how it finances its operations.

Operating Results.   Operating results measure the performance of the company's underlying business. That is, how profitable and efficient has the company been in producing (or acquiring) and selling its goods and services to its customers? A company's (pre-tax) return on assets (ROA) is expressed in a manner similar to its return on equity. That is, it is a function of operating margin (operating income divided by sales) and asset turnover (sales divided by total assets). However, in the definition of operating margin, operating income replaces net income and total assets replaces stockholders' equity. That is:

$$ROA = \frac{\text{operating income}}{\text{total assets}} = \frac{\text{operating income}}{\text{sales}} \times \frac{\text{sales}}{\text{total assets}}$$

Operating margin can be further disaggregated. Operating expenses in turn are composed of three primary components: cost of goods sold (primarily labor and materials); selling, general, and administrative (S, G, & A) expenses; and depreciation. The difference between sales and costs of goods sold is called gross income, and the ratio of the two items is known as gross margin. Subtracting the other operating expenses from gross income yields operating income. An analyst will consider the extent to which changes in operating margin have been related to changes in the company's control over pricing (as reflected in gross margin) and its management of operating expenses.[22]

Asset turnover can likewise be further disaggregated. The analyst will explore how the use of those assets relative to sales has changed over time and thus increased or lowered the return on assets. Furthermore, the analyst will examine how the company's use of its assets compares with that of other similar companies.

Non-operating Factors.   Operating results translate into total financial performance through the interaction of two non-operating factors: leverage and taxes. Whereas operating results are a measure of how effective management has been in producing and selling the goods and services of the company, another critical aspect of management policy is how the company finances its business activities. Common stock and long-term debt are the principal sources of financing for most businesses. Although leverage causes the return on equity to become more variable, effective use of debt financing can enhance shareholder returns. Return on equity (pre-tax) can be expressed as:

$$(\text{Pre-tax})\ ROE = \frac{\text{pre-tax income}}{\text{stockholders' equity}} =$$

$$\frac{\text{operating income}}{\text{total assets}} \times \frac{\text{total assets}}{\text{stockholders' equity}} - \frac{\text{interest}}{\text{stockholders' equity}}$$

Finally, taxes reduce the return to shareholders. Multiplying the pre-tax return on equity by 1 minus the tax rate yields the after-tax return on equity, ROE:

$$(\text{After-tax})\ ROE = \frac{\text{net income}}{\text{stockholders' equity}} = \frac{\text{pre-tax income}}{\text{stockholders' equity}} \times (1 - \text{tax rate})$$

Summarizing the relationship between the various financial ratios yields the expression for ROE:

$$(\text{After-tax})\ ROE =$$

$$\left[\frac{\text{operating income}}{\text{sales}} \times \frac{\text{sales}}{\text{total assets}} \times \frac{\text{total assets}}{\text{stockholders' equity}} - \frac{\text{interest}}{\text{stockholders' equity}} \right]$$

$$\times (1 - \text{tax rate})$$

Effectively, the company can influence its after-tax return on equity through three primary factors: (1) expenses relative to sales (operating margin), (2) sales relative to assets (asset turnover), and (3) the cost of debt used to support the company's capital structure (interest divided by stockholders' equity). The effect of these factors is magnified by financial leverage (total assets divided by stockholders' equity) and is reduced by taxes. The interaction of the various ratios to derive the after-tax return on equity is shown in Figure 22.1.

Dayton Hudson Corporation

Table 22.6 contains various relevant financial ratios for the Dayton Hudson Corporation over the period 1990 through 1996. From the company's income statement,

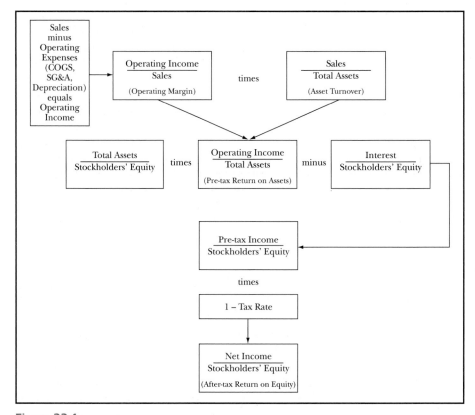

Figure 22.1
Interaction of Financial Ratios to Derive After-tax Return on Equity

TABLE 22.6	Dayton Hudson Corporation Selected Financial Ratios						
	1990	**1991**	**1992**	**1993**	**1994**	**1995**	**1996**
Profit margin	2.8%	1.9%	2.1%	2.0%	2.0%	1.3%	1.9%
Equity turnover	7.8	7.5	7.6	7.4	7.2	7.1	7.1
Return on equity	21.6%	14.1%	16.2%	14.4%	14.6%	9.4%	13.2%
Operating margin	6.7%	5.4%	5.9%	5.5%	5.4%	4.0%	5.4%
Asset turnover	1.9	1.8	1.8	1.8	1.9	1.9	2.0
Return on operating assets	12.9%	9.7%	10.6%	10.0%	10.1%	7.8%	10.5%
Cost of goods sold/sales	72.3%	72.9%	73.2%	73.6%	73.4%	74.5%	73.4%
S, G, & A/sales	16.8%	17.4%	16.6%	16.5%	17.0%	17.2%	16.9%
Depreciation/sales	2.5%	2.5%	2.6%	2.6%	2.6%	2.5%	2.6%
Interest expense/sales	2.2%	2.5%	2.4%	2.3%	2.0%	1.9%	1.7%
Sales/cash	151.2	171.4	168.3	87.8	91.1	146.1	135.0
Sales/accounts receivable	11.6	11.4	12.2	12.6	12.7	14.2	15.7
Sales/inventories	7.7	7.3	7.2	7.5	8.1	8.1	8.4
Sales/current assets	4.4	4.2	4.3	4.3	4.5	4.7	4.9
Sales/net plant & equipment	3.7	3.4	3.4	3.3	3.5	3.4	3.4
Total assets/stockholders' equity	4.0	4.2	4.2	4.0	3.8	3.7	3.6
Interest/stockholders' equity	17.1%	18.6%	18.5%	17.1%	14.4%	13.4%	12.3%
Pre-tax income/stockholders' equity	34.5%	22.1%	25.9%	23.2%	24.1%	15.2%	25.5%
Tax rate	37.8%	36.2%	37.3%	38.2%	39.2%	37.9%	39.5%
Total debt/stockholders' equity	3.00	3.21	3.20	3.04	2.79	2.68	2.61
Current assets/current liabilities	1.47	1.54	1.52	1.48	1.46	1.43	1.36
Operating income/interest expense	3.03	2.19	2.40	2.36	2.68	2.13	3.07

the variability in the earnings per share is readily apparent. That variability is even more noticeable looking at the company's return on equity. Return on equity reached a high of 21.6% in 1990, declining to 9.4% in 1995 and rebounding to 13.2% in 1996. Examining the principal components of Dayton Hudson's return on equity reveals two observations. The first observation is that throughout the period the company's equity turnover (sales divided by stockholders' equity) steadily declined, from 7.8 times in 1990 to 7.1 times in 1996. This trend largely represents a deliberate effort by the company to reduce its debt-to-stockholders' equity ratio. The resulting relative increase in equity in its capital structure had the effect of reducing equity turnover. That this decline was not caused by a less efficient use of company resources is confirmed by noting that the company's asset turnover shows a fairly constant value of roughly 1.9 times over the period and actually increased slightly in recent years. Presumably then, the equity turnover ratio will flatten out as the company approaches its desired debt level.

The second observation is that the profit margin (net income divided by sales) mirrored the up and down nature of the company's financial results. In 1990, Dayton Hudson's profit margin was 2.8%. In 1995, the profit margin fell to 1.3%, but improved to 1.9% in 1996.

Dayton Hudson's operating margin (operating income divided by total assets) displayed less variability than the profit margin, as leverage tends to magnify the effects of variations in operating results on bottom-line financial performance. However, despite some interim fluctuations, the company's operating margin was lower in 1996 than it was in 1990. In part, this decline was due to the fact that 1990 was an exceptional year for the company. Further, the decline was also a result of the growing importance of the Target division in Dayton Hudson's overall financial picture. In 1990, Target's sales represented 56% of the company's total sales. By 1996, that figure had increased to 70%. Because Target's discount retailing operations involve lower operating margins than either Mervyn's or particularly the Department Stores Division, the increasing prominence of Target reduces the company's total operating margin.

Breaking down the operating margin further, the ratio of both costs of goods sold and S, G, & A expenses relative to sales had been on an upward trend, in combination peaking in 1995. Some of that increase is again related to the lower margin business of Target. However, the company still can act to control costs, which it did in 1996. In total, operating expenses as a percent of sales declined from 94.3% in 1995 to 92.9% in 1996—a 1.4 percentage point improvement—which was a critical component of Dayton Hudson's improved financial performance. This improvement was due both to a more favorable experience in terms of the company's gross margin (cost of goods sold divided by sales) and to lower S,G, & A and interest expenses as a percent of sales. In terms of asset turnover, the key items of accounts receivable and inventories both have demonstrated improved operating efficiency (higher sales to asset ratios), while the ratio of sales to net plant and equipment has changed little.

Examining non-operating factors, as discussed, the company has made a concerted effort to decrease leverage on its balance sheet. This is evidenced by the decline in the company's debt-to-stockholders' equity ratio from 3.21 in 1991 to 2.61 in 1996. This reduced debt load has decreased the company's relative interest expense. Interest payments relative to sales fell from 2.5% in 1991 to 1.7% in 1996. The reduction in leverage will ultimately lower the variability of the company's return on equity. However, it will also give less of a boost to net income in periods of high operating margins. In terms of taxes, the company's tax rate has remained fairly constant over the period at approximately 38%.

Being a national multiline retailer, Dayton Hudson faces a wide range of competitors. The diversity of its competition tends to limit the validity of comparing its financial ratios with those of its competitors. Nevertheless, Table 22.7 lists various year-end 1996 ratios for five of the company's competitors: Wal-Mart, Kmart, Sears, J.C. Penney, and Federated Department Stores.

TABLE 22.7   Large U.S. Retailers vs. Dayton Hudson 1996 Selected Financial Ratios

	Wal-Mart	Kmart	Sears	J.C. Penney	Federated	Average	Dayton Hudson
Profit margin	2.9%	0.7%	3.3%	2.4%	1.8%	2.2%	1.9%
Equity turnover	5.8	5.2	6.1	3.9	3.3	4.8	7.1
Return on equity	16.8%	3.8%	20.2%	9.4%	5.7%	11.2%	13.2%
Operating margin	4.2%	2.5%	9.0%	6.6%	7.9%	6.0%	5.4%
Asset turnover	2.7	2.2	1.1	1.1	1.1	1.6	2.0
Return on assets	11.1%	5.4%	9.5%	7.1%	8.4%	8.3%	10.5%
Cost of goods sold/sales	79.8%	77.6%	65.2%	71.2%	61.0%	71.0%	73.4%
S, G, & A/sales	16.0%	20.0%	25.8%	22.2%	31.1%	23.0%	16.9%
Interest expense/sales	0.8%	1.4%	3.6%	1.5%	3.3%	2.1%	1.7%
Sales/current assets	5.8	4.1	1.3	2.0	2.4	3.1	4.9
Sales/net plant & equipment	5.2	5.5	6.5	3.6	2.3	4.6	3.4
Total assets/stockholders' equity	2.2	2.4	5.7	3.7	3.1	3.4	3.6
Interest/stockholders' equity	4.7%	7.5%	21.7%	6.0%	10.7%	10.1%	12.3%
Pre-tax income/stockholders' equity	19.3%	5.3%	33.0%	20.0%	15.0%	18.5%	25.5%
Tax rate	37.0%	n.a.	39.6%	37.8%	39.8%	38.6%	39.5%
Total debt/stockholders' equity	1.18	1.35	4.74	2.66	2.05	2.40	2.61
Current assets/current liabilities	1.64	2.14	1.90	1.47	1.79	1.79	1.36
Operating income/interest expense	5.22	1.71	2.53	4.36	2.41	3.25	3.07

Wal-Mart and Sears are the largest U.S. retailers, and both have earned returns on equity much higher than their competitors, including Dayton Hudson, as shown in Table 22.7. Wal-Mart accomplishes this result with low amounts of leverage, whereas Sears, with its large and profitable credit card business, carries more debt relative to its equity. Comparing Dayton Hudson's financial ratios with the five-company average shows a slightly below-average profit margin more than offset by efficient use of stockholders' equity to produce an above-average return on equity. At the operating level, Dayton Hudson's operating margin and asset turnover interact to produce a comparatively strong return on assets. Operating expense relative to sales and sales relative to current assets both indicate superior performance by Dayton Hudson. Further, the company has accomplished these results while at the same time bringing its debt to total assets ratio down very near that of its competitors.

In summary, through its improved gross margin and its cost-cutting efforts in 1996, Dayton Hudson managed to increase its profit margin and continued to make efficient use of company assets. It also was able to continue its reduction in balance sheet leverage. These accomplishments put it in a strong financial position relative to its competitors. In turn, those improvements were associated with a 57.0% surge in the company's stock price in 1996 as compared with an 18.7% average increase for its competitors. Dayton Hudson's challenge and the question confronting investors in its common stock is whether the company can continue its rapid revenue growth while maintaining and even building on the 1996 profit margin expansion.

Fixed-Income Ratio Analysis

Holders of a company's debt are primarily concerned with being paid their interest and principal in a full and timely manner. Some lenders want to know about the company's short-run ability to service its debt. For example, a banker making a short-term loan will want to examine financial ratios that indicate the company's liquidity. Holders of the company's long-term debt, on the other hand, will place more emphasis on the company's long-run earnings power, somewhat akin to an equity analyst.

Liquidity ratios measure the company's ability to quickly discharge its near-term obligations. The most commonly used liquidity ratios are the *current ratio* (current assets divided by current liabilities) and the *quick ratio* (current assets less inventory, divided by current liabilities). The greater are these liquidity ratios, the greater is the company's capacity to generate cash that can be used to pay off its short-term obligations.

Leverage ratios indicate the extent to which the company's capital was financed through debt as opposed to equity. Higher leverage ratios indicate that more financing came from debt sources. As a result, more risk of the business is placed on creditors. Moreover, the higher is the company's leverage, the more variable will be the company's earnings, because a larger fixed expense (that is, interest payments) must be paid before earnings can flow through to the company's owners. The most widely recognized leverage ratio is the ratio of *total-debt-to-stockholders' equity*. Coverage ratios, such as *times interest earned* (operating income divided by interest expense), measure the extent to which interest expense is covered by the company's operating income.

Dayton Hudson Corporation

As shown in Tables 22.6 and 22.7, Dayton Hudson's current ratio has remained fairly constant over the last six years, and is somewhat lower than that of its peers' due in part to the company's previously mentioned program of selling off its accounts re-

---

Financial Analysis **767**

ceivables to investors. Although this program has the effect of lowering its available liquidity, the company apparently believes that it can make more efficient use of those assets through investments in its capital projects and paying down debt. In fact, the company's current asset turnover (sales divided by current assets) has increased in recent years and is far above most of its competitors. Again, the increasing importance of Target, which has exceptionally high inventory turnover, is largely responsible for this result.

Dayton Hudson appears to be managing its debt effectively. As noted, it has managed to bring down its total debt-to-stockholders' equity ratio considerably over the last several years and is now near the average of its competitors. Furthermore, the company's times interest earned ratio (operating income divided by interest expense) has also improved in recent years, and it too is very close to that of its competitors.

22.6 ANALYSTS' RECOMMENDATIONS AND STOCK PRICES

When a security analyst decides that a stock is mispriced and informs certain clients, some of the clients may act on the information. As they do so, the price of the security may be affected. As news of the analyst's recommendation spreads, more investors may act, and the price may react even more. At some point, the analyst's information will be "fully reflected" in the stock price.

If the analyst decides that a stock is underpriced and clients subsequently purchase it, the stock's price will tend to rise. Conversely, if the analyst decides that a stock is overpriced and clients subsequently sell it, the stock's price will tend to decline. If the analyst's views were well founded, no subsequent counterreaction in the stock's price would be expected. Otherwise, the price is likely to return to its prerecommendation level at some later time.

Table 22.8 summarizes six studies of publicly available analysts' recommendations. Two of the studies deal with recommendations that appeared in *First Call* and *Zach's Investment Research*, which are large computer databases that provide up-to-date records of analysts' recommendations from a number of different brokerage firms for a large number of securities.[23] The third study deals with recommendations that appeared annually in *Barron's*, a weekly publication, and involves eight to twelve prominent money managers who had been invited to participate in their "Roundtable," referring to them as "Wall Street Superstars." The next two studies deal with recommendations that appeared in columns in *The Wall Street Journal*. One of these columns, "Heard on the Street," appears daily and involves a changing group of a variable number of analysts who discuss a variety of stocks.[24] The "Dartboard" is the second column; it appears monthly and presents "Pros Picks," provided by a changing panel of four analysts who each recommend one stock. The last study involves recommendations made by *Value Line* analysts that appeared weekly in the *Value Line Investment Survey*, reputed to be the largest stock investment advisory service in the United States.[25]

In terms of how soon the analysts' recommendations appear publicly, *First Call* is the quickest because the brokerage firms generally send them in promptly. *Barron's* and *The Wall Street Journal* are probably the slowest; their analysts may have disclosed their recommendations to their clients at some point before publication (in the case of *Barron's*, the Roundtable meets on average about two weeks before publication). *Zach's* and *Value Line* are probably somewhere in the middle.

Whereas the recommendations in *The Wall Street Journal* and *Barron's* are simple recommendations to buy or sell, those in *First Call*, *Zach's*, and *Value Line* are more

TABLE 22.8   A Summary of Studies That Have Evaluated the Performance of Security Analysts

Source	Before	Announcement	Around	Announcement	After	Announcement
	Time Period	Abnormal Return	Time Period	Abnormal Return	Time Period	Abnormal Return
(a) Buy Recommendations						
First Call[1]	6 months	1.2%	−1 to +1	3.0%*	1 month	2.4%*
Zach's[2]	10 days	.7*	0 to +10	.9*	20 days	.6*
Barron's Roundtable[3]	25 days	2.7†	0	1.0*	25 days	.3
Dartboard[4]	25 days	.6	0 to +1	4.1*	24 days	−2.1
Heard on the Street[5]	28 days	.4	−2 to +1	2.1*	29 days	−.5
Value Line[6]	50 days	8.7*	0 to +2	2.4*	48 days	.7
(b) Sell Recommendations						
First Call[1]	6 months	−2.1%	−1 to +1	−4.7%*	6 months	−9.2%*
Zach's[2]	10 days	−1.1*	0 to +10	−.8*	20 days	−.3
Barron's Roundtable[3]	25 days	−1.8†	0	−1.2*	25 days	.1
Heard on the Street[5]	28 days	.4	−2 to +1	−3.6*	29 days	1.3
Value Line[6]	50 days	−7.0*	0 to −2	−.3*	48 days	−1.3*

Sources: The data are adapted from: 1. Kent L. Womack, "Do Brokerage Analysts' Recommendations Have Investment Value?" *Journal of Finance* 51, no. 1 (March 1996): 148–149. 2. Scott E. Stickel, "The Anatomy of the Performance of Buy and Sell Recommmendations," *Financial Analysts Journal* 51, no. 5 (September/October 1995): 28. 3. Hemang Desai and Prem C. Jain, "An Analysis of the Recommendations of the 'Superstar' Money Managers at *Barron's* Annual Roundtable," *Journal of Finance* 50, no, 4 (September 1995): 1264, 1270. 4. Brad M. Barber and Douglas Loeffler, "The 'Dartboard' Column: Second-Hand Information and Price Pressure," *Journal of Financial and Quantitative Analysis* 28, no. 2 (June 1993): 276. 5. Messod D. Beneish, "Stock Prices and the Dissemination of Analysts' Recommendations," *Journal of Business* 64, no. 3 (July 1991): 403, 406–407. 6. Scott E. Stickel, "The Effect of Value Line Investment Survey Rank Changes on Common Stock Prices," *Journal of Financial Economics* 14, no. 1 (March 1985): 130–131.

* The number was found to be statistically significantly different from zero at the 5% level.

† A test of statistical significance was neither presented in the study nor could be conducted by an outside reader from the data provided.

complicated. Usually an analyst following a stock gives it a rating on a five-point scale, where 1 = strong buy, 2 = buy, 3 = hold, 4 = sell, and 5 = strong sell, or some similar metric. Thereafter, the rating will be either changed or confirmed at irregular intervals. In the *First Call* study, buy recommendations were defined as those recommendations that represented a rating upgrade to a 1 and sell recommendations were defined as a rating downgrade to a 5. In contrast, the *Zach*'s study defined buys as those recommendations that were upgraded to a 1 or 2. Similarly, sells were those recommendations that were downgraded to a 3, 4, or 5. In the *Value Line* study, the results shown in Table 22.8 focus on those stocks that were upgraded to a 1 and those that were downgraded to a 5.

Overall, the table reveals the following about analysts' recommendations:

1. It appears that the buy recommendations are associated with a slight abnormal price rise in the period before the recommendations are widely published, perhaps because the recommendations are released early to certain special clients or perhaps because analysts change their recommendations after a notable upward price movement by the stocks under analysis. Sell recommendations are associated with a slight abnormal price decline in the period before publication.

2. Around the time of the announcement (that is, day 0, with −1 and +1 referring to the day before and the day after the announcement) the buys jumped up in price and the sells slumped in price. This movement indicates that investors immediately acted on the recommendations when they were published.

3. There is mixed evidence regarding what happened after the announcement. The evidence that recommended buys keep rising for a month after *First Call* publishes a buy recommendation and that their recommended sells keep falling for six months after publication is compelling because *First Call* has the "freshest" recommendations. These results appear to be inconsistent with the notion of efficient markets, because it suggests that an investor might be able to earn abnormal returns by reacting promptly to *First Call* recommendations (note that, because transaction costs have not been accounted for, it is entirely possible that these postannouncement abnormal returns are illusory). Nevertheless, at a minimum the absence of a subsequent correction to the announcement day's abnormal stock price movement for the other studies suggests that the recommendations in all of the studies contained information of value.[26]

4. Although not shown in the table, most of the recommendations were buys of large firms. One reason given for the predominance of buys is that there are several costs associated with sells, perhaps the biggest one being possible lost investment banking opportunities. That is, an analyst who issues a sell recommendation about a firm's stock may be fearful of annoying management of the firm to such an extent that they will not use the analyst's firm for any investment banking activities in the future. Hence, there is an incentive to not say anything negative about a firm's stock unless it is particularly obvious.

5. Also not shown in the table is the observation that analysts' recommendations are often made public around the same time that earnings forecasts are released. Hence it is possible that one of these two pieces of information dominates the other by making the other valueless when both are provided to the investor. For example, a significant upward revision in the earnings forecast of a firm by a prominent analyst might cause the firm's stock price to jump up, while the issuance of a buy recommendation two days later might not result in any notable price change. However, a study found that this is not the case; both announcements were found to be associated with notable stock price movements.[27] Furthermore, stock recommendations were found to be more valuable when they represent a change of position instead of a reiteration of a position. Most interesting, it appears that earnings forecast revisions are of more value when the analyst's report contains a buy recommendation than a sell recommendation. Apparently, this is because the known bias for analysts to issue buy recommendations means that investors tend to look at other things in the analyst's report when such a recommendation is made.

22.7   ANALYST FOLLOWING AND STOCK RETURNS

An interesting issue involves the relationship between the amount of attention devoted by analysts to individual stocks and the price behavior of those stocks. Do stocks that are intensively followed have significantly different returns from those stocks that are relatively neglected by analysts? One study examined all stocks in the S&P 500 for the period from 1970 to 1979 to answer such a question. Table 22.9 summarizes the results.

Column (1) shows that the stocks followed by the largest number of analysts had the lowest average returns. However, the stocks followed by the fewest analysts had the highest average returns, thereby suggesting the presence of a **neglected-firm effect**.

It is possible that this effect is simply a reflection of the size effect, because the average return on small-sized firms has been shown to be larger than the average return on larger firms.[28] The reason for this possibility is that the number of analysts following a stock is generally related to the size of the underlying firm. However, columns (2), (3), and (4) show that this effect is not simply another manifestation of the size effect.[29] It can be seen that the neglected-firm effect exists for all firm

Amount of Following	All Stocks (1)	Small Firms (2)	Medium Firms (3)	Large Firms (4)
High	7.5%	5.0%	7.4%	8.4%
Moderate	11.8%	13.2%	11.0	10.2%
Low	15.4	15.8	13.9%	15.3
Low-high	7.9%	10.8%	6.5%	6.9%
Average return	11.0	13.5	10.7	9.8

TABLE 22.9   Analyst Following and Stock Returns

Source: Adapted from Avner Arbel and Paul Strebel, "Pay Attention to Neglected Firms!" *Journal of Portfolio Management* 9, no. 2 (Winter 1983): 39.

sizes. Furthermore, it is most pronounced for small firms; note that the difference between the high and low categories is largest in column (2).

What are the implications of the neglected-firm effect? First, it could be that the higher average return associated with neglected firms is a reward for investing in securities that have less available information. Second, because the neglected-firm effect exists across all sizes of firms, large institutional investors that are prohibited from investing in small firms can still take advantage of this effect, because it also exists for medium and large firms (although it is notably less significant). Finally, whether such a simple rule will be useful in the future is debatable. Why? If investors increase their purchases of neglected firms, then such firms will no longer be neglected and hence will no longer provide abnormally high returns.

22.8   INSIDER TRADING

The Securities and Exchange Commission requires the officers and directors of a corporation whose securities are traded on an organized exchange to report any transactions they have made in the firm's shares. Such a report, known as form 4, must be filed within ten days following the month in which the transaction takes place. This reporting requirement is also applicable to any stockholder who owns 10% or more of a firm's shares.[30] Such stockholders, officers, and directors are often referred to as **insiders**. The information they provide about their trading is subsequently reported in the Securities and Exchange Commission's monthly *Official Summary of Insider Transactions*.[31] For example, the summary of trades made in January (and reported by early February) is published early in March. Thus up to two months may elapse before knowledge of such trades becomes widespread.

The Securities Exchange Act of 1934 prohibits corporate insiders from short selling (discussed in Chapter 2). Furthermore, it requires them to return all short-term profits from security transactions in their own stocks to the corporation. For this purpose, *short term* is defined as less than six months, meaning that the shares were both bought and sold within a six-month period.[32] As a result of this requirement, few insiders buy and sell within a six-month period. Instead, most prefer to spread their buy-and-sell orders over longer time periods so that they do not have to return their profits.

In the United States it is illegal for anyone to enter into a security transaction if he or she has taken advantage of material "inside" information (that is, substantive

---

Inside Information

In 1990, Michael Milken pleaded guilty to six felony charges. He was fined an astounding $600 million and sentenced to ten years in prison. Milken's conviction brought to a close a saga involving criminal behavior by a number of highly influential individuals and organizations on Wall Street. The common thread tying together all of the defendants: rampant trading on inside information.

Insider trading has always been a controversial subject. The concept itself is rife with paradox. At the heart of our prosperous capital markets is the proposition that certain participants should not possess significant, unfair advantages over others. If you believe that the game is rigged against you, that the people with whom you trade consistently have ready access to valuable inside information, then you will soon take your investments to a fairer playing field.

Conversely, without inside information, there would be little rationale for trading to occur. Unless you believe that you know something many others do not, why trade? (This question ignores the occasional portfolio adjustments necessitated by changing financial situations or rebalancing holdings back to target positions.) Further, how would information relevant to security values be transmitted to stock prices unless someone who knew more than others traded on that information?

Thus an overdose or a dearth of inside information trading would seem detrimental to security markets. But how much inside information trading is optimal? No one knows the answer, but to better understand the issues involved we have to be more specific about what we mean by "inside information."

Justice Potter Stewart once wrote about pornography: "I can't define it. But I know what it is when I see it." A similar attitude must be taken in defining inside information. The Association for Investment Management and Research, the representative organization for investment professionals, defines inside information (or more formally, material non-public information) as

> *any information about a company or the market for the company's securities, that has not been generally disclosed to the marketplace, the dissemination of which is likely to affect significantly the market price of the company's securities or is likely to be considered important by reasonable investors in determining whether to trade in such securities.* (*AIMR Standards of Practice Handbook,* 5th ed. p.)

Although that definition provides a useful starting point, it involves several vague concepts. Does "generally disclosed" mean that everyone knows the information or that it is available simply by contacting the company? Similarly, how large a price impact is implied by the term "affect significantly"? Further, who are the "reasonable investors" who determine the importance of the information? Unfortunately, neither Congress, the courts, nor the Securities and Exchange Commission has been able or willing to

nonpublic information) about the corporation that is unavailable to other people involved in the transaction. This proscription includes not only insiders but also those to whom they give such secret information. (The recipient of such a "tip" is termed the "tippee.")

Legally there are two types of nonpublic information: that which is "private" (that is, legal) and that which is "inside" (that is, possibly illegal). Unfortunately, the distinction between the two types is highly ambiguous, causing continuous problems for security analysts.

Legal issues aside, two questions of relevance to outside investors may be posed: (1) Do insiders make unusual profits on transactions in their own stocks? and (2) If they do, can others profit by following their example as soon as it becomes public knowledge?

Insiders trade their stock for many reasons. For example, some purchases result from the exercise of options, and some sales result from the need for cash. Moreover, it is not unusual to find some insiders purchasing a stock during a month in which other insiders are selling it. However, when a major piece of inside information sug-

operationally define inside information. The issue has been handled on a case-by-case basis, à la Justice Stewart.

If defining inside information has proved troublesome, enforcing the laws against trading on inside information has been much more difficult, even in some flagrant cases. As the concept has evolved in the courts, for an "insider" to have violated insider trading laws through the disclosure of inside information, that person must:

1. Be in possession of inside information.
2. Be in a position of trust and confidence.
3. Stand to gain from the disclosure; for example, monetarily or through an exchange with someone or as a "gift" to another person.

An individual receiving and trading on inside information (the "tippee") may also violate the law if (1) the "tipper" had a fiduciary duty to the client; (2) the tipper breached that duty through the disclosure; and (3) the tippee had knowledge of that breach. Proving all three points makes it difficult to prosecute may tippees, especially those who have received inside information third- or fourth-hand.

Security analysts are placed in a precarious position with respect to inside information. One can view their jobs as the creation of inside information. Security analysts examine the prospects for companies and their securities, attempting to identify mispriced securities. If they are successful, their information is unique, non-public, and material—clearly inside information. The courts have generally recognized the legality of trading on inside information derived in this manner. But security analysts maintain frequent contact with corporate insiders as part of their jobs. This contact potentially exposes them to inside information of the illegal, if unintentional, kind. Most investment firms and the AIMR have guidelines for dealing with these situations. Nevertheless, the ambiguity can cause confusion and the situation may be difficult to control.

The interrelated nature of many large investment firms makes the dissemination of inside information a potentially serious problem. For example, investment banking firms typically operate divisions that trade for the firms' own accounts. Investment bankers have access to valuable inside information concerning corporate mergers and acquisitions. If traders at an investment banking firm acquired this information, they would be in a position to profit handsomely. To prevent such conflicts, investment firms establish "Chinese Walls"; that is, regulations against information transfers, rules against trading on inside information, and policies against personnel serving in multiple capacities in various departments. Unfortunately, these precautions are not always effective. The insider trading scandals of the 1980s were largely a result of the ample opportunities for inside information abuse existing at investment banking firms.

gests that a stock's value differs significantly from its current market price, it is reasonable to expect a preponderance of insider trades on one side of the market (that is, either purchases or sales). This is a situation in which there is *asymmetric information* in the marketplace, because insiders know more than others and are trading on the basis of this information.

One way to search for such situations is to examine the *Official Summary* and count the number of days during a month that each insider traded his or her firm's stock (excluding the exercise of options).[33] If the number of days on which purchases were made exceeded those on which sales were made, the individual can be counted as a net purchaser during that month; and if the converse held, the individual would be a net seller. Next the number of net purchasers and sellers for the firm's stock can be considered. If there were at least, say, three more net purchasers than net sellers, it might be inferred that, on balance, favorable insider information motivated the insider trades during the month. Conversely, if there were at least three more net sellers than net purchasers, it might be inferred that, on balance, unfavorable insider information motivated the insider trades.

Different cutoff levels could be used in this process to reflect the intensity of insider trading. A cutoff of 1 would require a simple majority of trades of one type, whereas a cutoff of 5 would require a "supermajority" of trades of one type.

Such a procedure was used in a detailed study of insider transactions during the 1950s and 1960s.[34] Table 22.10 summarizes the key results. The two columns on the

TABLE 22.10 Abnormal Returns Associated with Insider Trading				
Sample Cutoff (No. of Net Purchasers or Sellers)	No. of Cases	Period	Average Abnormal Return (%) Over Eight Months Following	
			Month of Transaction	Month Information Became Publicly Available
1	362	1960s	1.36	.70
3	861	1960s	5.07	4.94
4	293	1950s	5.14	4.12
5	157	1950s	4.48	4.08

Source: Jeffrey F. Jaffe, "Special Information and Insider Trading," *Journal of Business* 47, no. 3 (July 1974): 421, 426.
© 1974, The University of Chicago.

right-hand side of the table indicate the "abnormal" returns over an eight-month period on securities that exceeded the cutoff level for insider trading. For example, during the 1960s, if an investor purchased every stock in the sample for which there were three or more net purchasers, and sold every stock for which there were three or more net sellers during a month, more or less coincident with the transactions of the insiders themselves, then the investor would have earned, on average, an abnormal return of 5.07% over the subsequent eight months. If the transactions had been made instead at roughly the time the information was published in the *Official Summary*, an average abnormal return of 4.94% would have been earned over the next eight months.

As the first row in the table shows, a bare majority of insider trades does not appear to isolate possible effects of insider information. But a majority of 3, 4, or 5 does seem to do so. The figures shown are gross of any transaction costs; but even so, it appears that insiders can and do make money from their special knowledge of their companies. This outcome is not surprising, because if anyone can know the true value of a firm, it should be the insiders. The information these insiders presumably are using is nonpublic in nature, so these findings suggest that markets are not strong-form efficient. (The notion of market efficiency was introduced in Chapter 4.)

On the other hand, the abnormal returns associated with transactions that could have been made by outsiders, using only publicly available information on insider trading, are quite surprising. After all, once the *Official Summary* is made public, for all practical purposes information is no longer asymmetric, so investors should not be able to invest profitably on the basis of its contents. Those abnormal returns associated with cutoffs of 3, 4, or 5 pass statistical tests designed to see if they might result simply from chance. After transaction costs, trades designed to capitalize on such information appear to still produce abnormal returns (although not highly so), suggesting that markets are not even semistrong-form efficient. However, more recent studies have found that outsiders cannot use the publicly available information about insider trading to make abnormal profits, and thus support the notion that markets are semistrong-form efficient.[35] With such conflicting evidence it appears that whether insider trading information can be profitably used by outsiders remains an open question.

22.9 SOURCES OF INVESTMENT INFORMATION

Because information affects the values of investments, the serious financial analyst must be well informed. There is a staggering array of such "investment information," some of it published on paper ("hard copy") and some of it appearing in electronic form.

22.9.1 Publications

Every investor should read *The Wall Street Journal.* It provides extensive statistical data, financial news, and even a bit of humor. An alternative is the financial section of *The New York Times* or the *Investors Business Daily.* Most other daily newspapers contain financial information, but much less than the *Journal* or the *Times.* A weekly publication with a wealth of statistical data (particularly in the "Market Laboratory" section) is *Barron's.* Another weekly publication that contains reports prepared by security analysts at various brokerage firms is *The Wall Street Transcript.*

A useful source of daily stock price and volume figures is the *Daily Stock Price Record,* published by Standard & Poor's Corporation. Each issue covers one calendar quarter, and all values for a given stock are listed in a single column. Standard & Poor's also publishes forecasts of company earnings in the weekly *Earnings Forecaster* and dividend information in the *Dividend Record.* Furthermore, some brokerage houses provide their major clients with copies of Standard & Poor's monthly *Stock Guide* and *Bond Guide,* which are illustrated in Figures 22.2 and 22.3.

6 AAM-ADO Standard & Poor's

¶ S&P 500 # MidCap 400 ✣ SmallCap 600 • Options

Index	Ticker	Name of Issue (Call Price of Pfd. Stocks)	Market	Com. Rank. & Pfd. Rating	Inst. Hold Cos	Inst. Hold Shs. (000)	Principal Business	Price Range 1971-95 High	1971-95 Low	1996 High	1996 Low	1997 High	1997 Low	Nov. Sales in 100s	November, 1997 Last Sale Or Bid High	Low	Last	%Div Yield	P-E Ratio	EPS 5 Yr Growth	% Annualized Total Return 12 Mo	36 Mo	60 Mo
1	SPSC	S&P Super Composite 1500 Index		NR	..	...	U.S. equity performance indicator	134.43	111.17	163.88	128.92	207.27	157.41	....	....	....	204.92	1.6	21	...	28.3	...	...
2•[1]	SPIC	S&P 500 Index		NR	..	...	Broad large-cap indicator	622.88	60.96	762.12	597.29	983.12	729.55	....	964.55	900.61	955.40	1.7	20	17	28.5	31.1	20.2
3•[1]	SPMC	S&P MidCap 400 Index		NR	..	...	Broad mid-cap indicator	220.73	119.43	259.29	206.34	340.40	247.27	....	327.29	309.21	321.25	1.4	19	15	27.5	26.1	17.7
4•[1]	SPYC	S&P SmallCap 600 Index		NR	..	...	Broad small-cap indicator	122.69	92.45	146.14	114.44	192.98	134.15	....	184.68	174.03	177.71	0.9	23	18	24.5	25.7	17.9
5•[2]	AAM	✓Aames Financial	NY,P	NR	174	17453	Mortgage brokerage svcs	16⅜	1 15/16	40¾	10⅞	32⅜	9⅝	58546	16¼	12⅜	13½	1.0	11	20	−52.7	56.1	36.1
6	AAON	✓AAON Inc	NNM	NR	8	748	Mfr air-condition'g/heat'g eqp	16⅝	7/16	6⅜	4¼	9¾	4¾	1585	7⅞	6¾	7⅝	...	18	2	48.8	−9.9	49.1
✣7•[3]	AIR	✓AAR Corp	NY,Ch,Ph	B+	157	14677	Mkts aviation parts/service	37½	1¼	31¼	17¾	39⅜	24¼	8860	39⅜	35¾	38½	1.2	26	NM	31.7	48.2	30.8
8	ABDR	✓Abacus Direct	NNM	NR	76	7235	Direct mktg svcs	....	....	32½	14	44¼	17	21752	44¼	36¾	41¾	...	63	...	72.2	..	...
9•[4]	ABACF	Abacan Resource	NNM,To	NR	92	45285	Intl oil/gas explor'n,devlp	3	2⅛	9⅝	2½	11¾	1 13/16	78582	3⅛	1 13/16	2 5/16	...	..	...	−73.6	...	...
10	ABAX	✓Abaxis Inc	NNM	NR	12	1310	Dvlp stge:blood analyzer sys	17½	3	7¼	2⅝	5¼	2 7/16	7200	3⅛	2 7/16	2⅝	...	d	27	−23.6	−13.1	−16.6
¶11•[5]	ABT	✓Abbott Laboratories	NY,B,C,Ch,P,Ph	A+	1403	365349	Diversified health care prod	44¾	½	57⅞	38⅛	69¾	49¾	206219	66½	61⅛	65⅛	1.7	24	12	18.8	29.4	18.4
12	ABCR	✓ABC Rail Products	NNM	NR	53	6207	Mfr orig'l&replace'mt rail prd	27⅝	12	25½	14⅜	22⅜	13½	5490	21½	19	20 3/16	...	47	−16	8.7	−2.5	...
13•[6]	ANF	✓Abercrombie & Fitch Co'A'	NY,Ch,Ph	NR	71	5615	Retail casual apparel	....	....	27	15¾	36⅛	12½	33421	36⅛	25½	29⅞	...	40	...	62.9	...	...
14•[3]	ABY	✓Abitibi-Consolidated	NY,To,Mo,P,Vc	B–	71	45359	Newsprint,paper prods	28⅝	2 5/16	17¼	12¼	21	12½	42033	14½	12½	13	◆2.2	d	NM	−10.4	3.2	5.4
✣15	ABM	✓ABM Industries Inc	NY,B,Ch,P,Ph	A	85	10213	Janitorial & building maint	14¼	¾	20¼	13½	29⅛	17⅜	2037	27⅞	25⅞	27⅞	1.4	24	11	65.8	42.9	27.0
16	AAN	✓ABN AMRO Holding ADS[52]	NY,Ph	NR	36	11358	Bank'g operations, Netherlands	....	....	....	....	24⅜	18¼	10063	20⅞	18½	19⅛	2.4	15	...	...	...	...
17	ABRX	✓ABR Information Services	NNM	NR	143	17325	Healthcare benefits svcs	14⅝	2 3/16	38¾	13	33	16	17709	25⅞	22	24	...	55	51	12.9	92.0	...
18	ABRI	✓Abrams Industries	NNM	B−	13	505	Construct'n/mfg, real estate	7⅞	¾	5	3¼	8⅜	4¾	674	8⅜	6	7½B	e2.1	4	30	66.3	23.6	15.9
19	AXAS	✓Abraxas Petroleum	NNM	NR	29	2344	Oil & gas explorn,dvlp,prod'n	13½	2½	10½	4⅛	19½	8⅞	12373	19½	15⅞	16	...	d	NM	107	15.1	16.4
20	ABTC	✓ABT Building Products	NNM	NR	62	4045	Mfr special build'g products	30	11⅞	26¾	14¼	27¼	16½	3391	18¾	17¼	18	...	13	14	−22.6	9.4	...
21	ANA	✓Acadiana Bancshares	AS	NR	10	586	Savings bank, Louisiana	....	....	15¼	11⅜	24¾	14⅞	1227	23¾	22⅝	23¾	1.5	..	...	61.3	...	...
✣22•[7]	ACCC	✓ACC Corp[55]	NNM	B	119	8390	Full-svc telecommun'n co	17½	½	54¾	14⅞	47¼	14¼	142003	47¼	41⅜	46¾	...	48	17	58.4	64.7	40.3
23	ACLE	✓Accel Intl	NNM	C	12	776	Insurance:credit life/disab	14⅜	1 11/16	3⅞	2⅜	4¼	2¾	993	4	3¾	3¾	...	9	NM	30.4	16.4	−3.6
24	AIF	✓Acceptance Insur Cos	NY,B,Ch,P,Ph	B−	70	6863	Hldg co: prop & casualty insur	54⅝	6	22½	13⅞	28⅝	17¾	3652	24⅜	22⅜	24¼	...	11	NM	18.6	22.4	15.1
✣25•	ACCS	✓Access Health	NNM	NR	97	12543	Healthcare ind market'g svcs	30⅜	1 15/16	65½	27½	45¼	11½	50043	37½	29½	29¾	...	..	43	−22.2	35.1	57.6
26•[4]	AKLM	✓Acclaim Entertainment	NNM	C	54	17419	Dvlp video game cartridges	31¾	1 15/16	13⅞	3	6⅛	2⅞	98542	4¾	3⅝	4	...	d	Neg	−21.7	−36.8	−17.2
27	ACMI	✓AccuMed Intl	NNM	NR	14	2767	Hlthcare diagnostic/screen pd	5⅜	5/16	9⅜	1 1/16	4⅜	1¾	20621	2 7/16	1¾	1 15/16	...	d	...	−42.6	41.3	...
28•[4]	ASI	✓AccuStaff Inc	NY	NR	330	84412	Temporary personnel service	14¾	1¾	38	11⅝	32	15¾	65165	30¾	27⅛	29½	...	44	...	46.9	148	...
29	ACL	✓ACE Limited	NY,Ph	NR	..	...	Provides liability insurance	40	20¾	60¼	37¾	101	56⅛	25791	100	89	99¼	1.0	12	NM	74.2	68.6	...
30	ACET	✓Aceto Corp	NNM	B+	38	1951	Mfrs & dstr chemicals	16⅜	5/16	17½	12¼	20¾	12½	960	20¾	18⅞	19¾	1.8	13	24	50.0	22.5	10.0
31	AK	✓Ackerley Group	AS	B−	47	5730	Brdcstg:pro basketball:adv	8	⅝	17	7⅝	18½	10	1916	17⅝	15⅜	16	0.1	28	26	23.3	69.5	68.5
32	ACE	✓Acme Electric	NY,P	B−	16	943	Pwr conv eq: transformers	38¾	⅜	13⅞	6	10⅜	6⅛	1678	6⅞	6⅛	6¼	...	..	NM	−11.4	−21.4	4.8
✣33	AMI	✓Acme Metals	NY	B−	58	5258	Producer steel/steel prod	27¼	8	21⅜	13¾	19⅝	12¼	8688	13⅜	12¼	12⅜	...	d	−35	−39.0	−7.8	1.1
34	ACU	✓Acme United	AS,Ch	C	12	526	Medic eq:shears,scissors	19½	1⅜	5½	2⅞	8⅛	4½	334	6½	5¾	5½B	...	..	17	22.2	22.4	−1.8
#35•[8]	ART	✓ACNielsen Corp	NY	NR	260	45205	Marketing/info analysis	....	....	20⅛	14½	24⅝	14	24344	23½	22⅛	22⅜	...	42	...	26.4	...	...
36	ACRG	ACR Group	NSC	NR	2	15	Dstr heating & cooling equip	20⅞	5/16	2	½	4⅛	1¾	1525	2¾	2⅛	2¾	...	31	77	57.1	58.8	46.6
37	ACRO	✓Acrodyne Communications	NSC	NR	3	220	Dvlp,mfr transmitter equip	5⅜	1⅞	7¾	3⅝	6¼	3	3546	4¾	3	3⅝	...	d	...	−34.1	...	...
38•[4]	ANET	✓ACT Networks	NNM	NR	51	3852	Mfr data commun ntwk prd	22½	5¾	48½	9¾	37¼	8⅛	20134	10⅛	8⅛	8⅛	...	d	−19	−72.0	...	...
39•[9]	ACTL	✓Actel Corp	NNM	NR	96	13047	Dvlp programmable gate arrays	21	7¼	24⅝	9	29⅛	12⅝	31621	15⅜	14¼	14¾	..	18	87	−31.8	21.4	...
40	ACZ	✓Action Indus[59]	AS,B	C	3	79	Merchandising programs	18¼	7/16	2¾	5/16	....	....	....	....	....	....	...	..	...	77.9	−14.9	−31.7
41	ACTN	✓Action Performance Cos	NNM	NR	107	10328	Motorsports replicas/merch	9⅞	1½	20½	6⅜	36⅛	16½	59181	29	24¾	29	...	42	NM	71.9	121	...
42	ACVC	✓Active Voice	NNM	NR	22	502	Mfr voice messaging softwr sys	33	15	28½	9½	15⅝	9⅝	1049	14⅞	13¼	13¾	...	66	−16	17.0	−11.7	...
#43•[10]	ACN	✓Acuson Corp	NY,P	B−	161	16742	Medical ultrasound imaging	40	5	24¾	12	29¾	17	27286	20	17¾	19	...	27	Neg	−12.9	7.1	1.4
44	ACX	✓ACX Technologies	NY,Ch	NR	105	8672	Mfr packag'g ceramic,alum'n pd	31⅜	5⅜	22½	14⅝	27½	17⅝	5706	27⅜	25⅞	26¾	...	d	Neg	49.0	15.6	...
✣45	ACXM	✓Acxiom Corp	NNM	B+	150	21171	Computer-based mkting svcs	16⅛	1	25	11	24	11⅛	17285	17¾	15½	17⅛	...	33	30	−25.3	38.3	35.9
✣46•[8]	ADAC	✓ADAC Laboratories	NNM	B	112	12402	Nuclear medicine comput sys	82⅛	1½	25¼	11⅝	27¾	15⅜	32156	22½	18⅞	20⅞	...	24	−2	−4.0	39.9	11.4
47	AE	✓Adams Res & Energy	AS,B,Ch,Ph	B	10	472	Oil&gas explor,dev,prod'n	70½	1¾	13⅞	5⅝	18⅜	11⅝	1309	16¾	13½	14⅝B	0.7	10	47	47.2	20.5	21.5
48•[11]	ADPT	✓Adaptec Inc	NNM	B	475	91569	Mfr computer data flow sys	24¼	9/16	41⅛	17½	54¼	30⅛	223436	52½	44	49½	...	23	27	32.4	63.2	52.5
#49•[12]	ADCT	✓ADC Telecommunications	NNM	B	413	89333	Telecommunications equip	24¾	1/64	40¼	14¼	45	21¼	147632	37⅞	34	37⅛	...	45	32	0.2	49.8	46.3
50	ASF	✓Administaff Inc	NY,Ch,Ph	NR	40	4064	Professional employment svcs	....	....	....	....	26½	13¾	1758	23	21⅝	22¼	...	48	68	...	...	...
51	PVD	✓Administradora de Fondos ADS[60]	[13]NY	NR	30	1911	Pension fund administ'r/Chile	28¾	12¾	27⅝	17⅝	24½	16¼	15737	18⅜	16¼	17⅛	5.3	12	3	−7.7	3.7	...
¶52•[10]	ADBE	✓Adobe Systems	NNM,Ch	B+	443	52381	Print,graphic software sys	74¼	1 7/16	64¼	28½	53⅛	32½	214940	49¼	40½	42	0.5	19	33	...	...	...

Uniform Footnote Explanations-See Page 1. Other: [1]CBOE. [2]CBOE:Cycle 3. [3]Ph:Cycle 1. [4]CBOE:Cycle 1. [5]Ph:Cycle 2. [6]CBOE:Cycle 2. [7]Ph:Cycle 3. [8]ASE:Cycle 2. [9]P,Ph:Cycle 3. [10]P:Cycle 1. [11]ASE:Cycle 1. [12]P:Cycle 2. [13]Ph,P [51]5 Mo Dec'95. [52]Ea ADS rep 1 ord 1.25NLG. [53]Approx. [54]5 Mo Dec'96. [55]Tel-Save Holdings prop acq,$50 in stk. [56]®$1.96,'96. [57]3 Mo Dec'95:Fiscal Sep'95 earned d$0.59. [58]Redemption of stk purch rt. [59]ASE trading halted 10-21-96. [60]Ea ADS rep 1 com, no par.

Figure 22.2
Standard & Poor's *Stock Guide,* December 1997

Source: Standard & Poor's *Stock Guide* (New York: Standard & Poor's, December 1997), p. 6.

Title-Industry Code & Co. Finances (In Italics) / Individual Issue Statistics, Exchange	Ind / Interest Dates	Fixed Charge Coverage 1994 / S&P Rating	1995 / Date of Last Rating Change	1996 / Prior Rating	Eligible	Year End / Bond Form	Cash & Equiv. (Million $) / Redemption Provisions: Regular Price	Curr. Assets / Regular (Begins) Thru	Curr. Liab. / Sinking Fund Price	Balance Sheet Date / Sinking Fund (Begins) Thru	L. Term Debt (Mil $) / Refund/Other Restriction Price	Refund/Other Restriction (Begins) Thru	Capital-ization (Mil $) / Outst'g (Mil $)	Total Debt % Capital / Underwriting Firm	Underwriting Year	Price Range 1998 High	Price Range 1998 Low	Mo. End Price Sale(s) or Bid	Curr. Yield	Yield to Mat.
A I M Management Gr	*62*	*2.78*	*5.14*	*11.44*		*Dc*	*59.40*			*6-30-97*	*97.10*		*180.0*	*53.9*						
Sr[1]Sec[2]Nts 9s 2003	mN15	NR	1/98	BBB–	X	R	104.50	(11-15-98)	....	....	....	....	110	M2	'93	106⅝	106⅜	106⅜	8.46	7.60
AAF-McQuay Inc	*42b*	*Δn/a*	*Δ2.40*	*Δ1.54*		*Je*	*14.00*	*381.0*	*290.0*	*9-30-97*	*214.0*		*432.0*	*52.3*						
Sr Nts[3] 8⅞s 2003	Fa15	B+			Y	R	NC	....	....	....	....	....	125	C4	'96	99	98½	98½	9.01	9.26
Aames Financial	*25h*	*Δ6.35*	*Δ6.73*	*Δ2.01*		*Je*				*9-30-97*	*391.0*		*672.0*	*58.2*						
• Sr Nts 10½s 2002	[4]Feb	NR				R	■100	(2-1-00)	100	(2-1-99)	....	....	23.0	P2	'95	105½	102⅝	103¾	10.12	9.33
Sr Nts[2] 9⅛s 2003	mN	BB–	11/96	NR	Y	BE	104.562	(11-1-00)	....	....	[5]Z110	10-31-99	150	B7	'96	100	96	100	9.13	9.12
AAR Corp	*3a*	*Δ2.35*	*Δ3.15*	*Δ4.06*		*My*	*6.99*	*437.0*	*138.0*	*11-30-97*	*119.0*		*425.0*	*33.4*						
Nts[6] 9½s 2001	mN	BBB	7/97	BBB–	X	R	NC	....	....	....	....	....	65.0	G1	'89	109¾	108⅛	108¼	8.78	6.92
Nts 7¼s 2003	aO15	BBB	7/97	BBB–	X	R	NC	....	....	....	....	....	50.0	G1	'93	102⅞	100⅝	101½	7.14	6.92
Nts 6⅞s 2007	jD15	BBB			X	BE	NC	....	....	....	....	....	60.0	G1	'97	102⅞	101¾	102⅞	6.68	6.47
[7]***Abbey Healthcare Group***	*30a*	*1.55*	*2.36*	*2.06*		*Dc*	*26.60*	*420.0*	*138.0*	*9-30-97*	*574.0*		*896.0*	*65.1*						
Sr[3]Sub Nts 9½s 2002	mN	BB+	7/95	B–	Y	R	104.75	(11-1-98)	....	....	....	....	200	D6	'93	105⅜	103½	104¾	9.07	8.25
Abbott Laboratories	*21a*	*44.34*	*35.72*	*29.11*		*Dc*	*166.0*	*4653*	*4721*	*9-30-97*	*939.0*		*7420*	*34.7*						
Nts 5.60s 2003	aO	AAA			X	BE	NC	....	....	....	....	....	200	G1	'93	100¼	98	98⅞	5.66	5.84
Nts 6.80s 2005	Mn15	AAA			X	BE	NC	....	....	....	....	....	150	G1	'95	106⅝	104¼	104¾	6.49	5.98
Nts 6.40s 2006	jD	AAA			X	BE	NC	....	....	....	....	....	250	G1	'96	104½	102⅛	102⅝	6.24	6.01
Acme Metals	*66b*	*3.72*	*1.74*	*3.43*		*Dc*	*6.72*	*164.0*	*94.60*	*9-28-97*	*354.0*		*576.0*	*61.5*						
• Sr Sec[8]Disc[9]Nts 13½s 2004	fA	B			Y	R	106.75	(8-1-99)	....	....	....	....	[10]118	L3	'94	No Sale		114¾	11.76	10.30
• Sr Sec[2]Nts[11] 12½s 2002	fA	B			Y	R	106.25	(8-1-98)	....	....	....	....	125	L3	'94	115	105⅛	106½	11.74	10.62
Act III Theatres	*24b*	*1.20*	*1.35*	*1.26*		*Dc*	*4.65*	*9.07*	*38.50*	*9-30-97*	*303.0*		*290.0*	*105.0*						
Sr Sub Nts[2] 11⅞s 2003	Fa	NR	5/96	B–		R	105.938	1-31-99	100	(2-1-02)	....	....	85.0	K2	'93	107	106⅜	106⅜	11.16	10.19
Adelphia Communications	*12a*	*0.66*	*0.66*	*0.50*		*Mr*				*12-31-97*	*2544*		*1333*	*191.0*						
Sr Deb 11⅞s 2004	mS15	B			Y	R	104.50	(9-15-99)	....	....	....	....	125	S1	'92	110¾	108¾	110	10.80	9.77
Sr Nts 12½s 2002	Mn15	B			Y	R	106	5-14-98	....	....	....	....	400	S1	'92	106	105	106	11.79	10.68
ADT Operations	*63*	*Merged into Tyco Intl, see*																		
Sr Nts[2] 8¼s 2000	fA	A–	7/97	BBB–	X	R	NC	....	....	....	....	....	250	M2	'93	105⅜	104¼	104¼	7.91	6.33
Sr[2]Sub Nts[12] 9¼s 2003	fA	BBB+	7/97	BB+	X	R	103.75	(8-1-98)	....	....	....	....	317	M2	'93	105⅜	105⅛	105⅛	8.80	8.06
Advanced Micro Dev	*23h*	*38.27*	*12.07*	*d13.07*		*Dc*	*441.0*	*1134*	*622.0*	*9-28-97*	*677.0*		*2766*	*26.1*						
Sr Sec Nts[2] 11s 2003	fA	BB–			Y	BE	105.50	(8-1-01)	....	....	....	....	400	D6	'96	108¾	107	108¾	10.11	8.93
ADVANTA Corp	*25e*	*4.16*	*3.27*	*2.45*		*Dc*				*9-30-97*	[13]*2518*		*3498*	*72.0*						
M-T Nts 'C'[14] 6.384s '98	fA7	BB–	2/98	BB	Y	BE	NC	....	....	....	....	....	16.0	M2	'96	99½	99¼	99¼	6.43	8.10
F/R[15]M-T[14]Nts 'C' 5.925s '98	QAug10	BB–	2/98	BB	Y	BE	NC	....	....	....	....	....	15.0	U1	'96	100	99⅞	99⅞	5.93	....
M-T Nts 'C' 6.97s '99	jJ30	BB–	2/98	BB	Y	BE	NC	....	....	....	....	....	5.00	D6	'96	98¾	97¼	97¼	7.17	9.06
F/R[16]M-T Nts 'C'[14] 5.975s '99	[17]Qaug7	BB–	2/98	BB	Y	BE	NC	....	....	....	....	....	5.00	P4	'96	98⅜	98⅛	98⅜	6.07	....
M-T Nts[14]'C' 7⅜s 2000	aO16	BB–	2/98	BB	Y	BE	NC	....	....	....	....	....	25.0	B7	'97	98¼	95⅞	95⅞	7.69	9.16
M-T Nts 'D' 7½s 2000	fA28	BB–	2/98	BB	Y	BE	NC	....	....	....	....	....	50.0	M2	'97	98⅜	96⅜	96⅜	7.78	9.15
Nts 7s 2001	Mn	BB–	2/98	BB	Y	BE	NC	....	....	....	....	....	200	S1	'96	96½	94	94	7.45	9.21
Aeroquip-Vickers Inc	*41h*	*5.81*	*7.68*	*6.94*		*Dc*	*31.10*	*729.0*	*451.0*	*9-30-97*	*258.0*		*831.0*	*40.8*						
M-T Nts 7.58s 2012	[18]mn	BBB+	6/97	BBB	X	BE	NC	....	....	....	....	....	10.0	M6	'97	110½	107	108⅛	7.01	6.69
M-T Nts 7.09s 2018	[19]mn	BBB+			X	BE	NC	....	....	....	....	....	25.0	M6	'97	105⅛	100⅛	100½	7.05	7.04
Aetna Services Inc[20]	*35d*	*7.66*	*7.26*	*3.01*		*Dc*	*1333*			*9-30-97*	*2374*		*14273*	*20.4*						
Deb 6¾s 2013	mS15	A	7/97	A–	X	BE	NC	....	....	....	....	....	200	G1	'93	99⅞	96⅜	96¾	6.98	7.10
Deb 8s 2017	Jj15	A	7/97	A–	X	R	103.60	1-14-99	100	....	....	....	200	M2	'87	102⅛	101¾	101⅞	7.85	7.81
Deb 7¼s 2023	fA15	A	7/97	A–	X	BE	NC	....	....	....	....	....	200	G1	'93	104⅜	100	100⅛	7.24	7.24
Deb[21] 7⅝s 2026	fA15	A	7/97	A–	X	BE	NC	....	....	....	....	....	450	M2	'96	107½	103¾	104½	7.30	7.25
[22]Deb[21] 6.97s 2036	fA15	A	7/97	A–	X	BE	NC	....	....	....	....	....	300	M2	'96	107	103⅝	103⅝	6.73	6.71
Nts 8⅝s '98	Ms	A	7/97	A–	X	R	NC	....	....	....	....	....	100	M6	'88	100⅜	100	100	8.63	Mat.

Uniform Footnote Explanations-See Page 1. Other: [1] Gtd by AIM Advisors Inc. [2] (HRO)On Chge of Ctrl at 101. [3] Co must offer repurch at 101 on Chge of Ctrl. [4] Int pd monthly. [5] Max $45M red w/proceeds of Pub Eq Off'gs. [6] (HRO)For Trigger Event at 100. [7] Now Apria Healthcare Group. [8] Int accrues at 13.5% fr 8-1-97. [9] (HRO)On Chge of Ctrl at 101(Accreted Val). [10] Incl disc. [11] Purch offer to Dec 12. [12] Gtd by ADT Ltd. [13] Incl amts. [14] Issued in min denom $100T. [15] Int to 5-11-98,adj qtrly(3 MO LIBOR&0.30%). [16] Int to 5-7-98,adj qtrly aft(3 MO LIBOR&0.35%). [17] Due 8-9-99. [18] Due 6-6-12. [19] Due 1-5-18. [20] Was Aetna Life & Casualty,now Aetna Inc. [21] Gtd by Aetna Inc. [22] (HRO)On 8-15-04 at 100.

Figure 22.3
Standard & Poor's *Bond Guide,* March 1998
Source: Standard & Poor's *Bond Guide* (New York: Standard & Poor's, March 1998), p. 26.

Standard & Poor's *Corporation Records* are a major reference source for the financial history of individual companies. They consist of six alphabetical volumes and are periodically updated. A second major reference source is provided by Moody's Investor Services, Inc. Their *Manuals* are published annually, with periodic updates, and cover various fields: *Bank & Finance, Industrial, International, Municipal & Government, OTC Industrial, OTC Unlisted, Public Utility,* and *Transportation* are the titles of various volumes. In addition, both Standard & Poor's and Moody's also provide a number of other publications to subscribers.

Historical data and analyses for approximately 1,700 stocks and most major industries can be found in the *Value Line Investment Survey.* Adjusted betas are also shown for the individual stocks in the *Survey.* The *Value Line Options* and *Convertibles* manuals, along with the *Survey,* offer estimates of the relative attractiveness of these investments.

Publications of major security analysts' societies include the *Financial Analysts Journal* (United States); *Analyse Financière* (France); and the *Investment Analyst* (United Kingdom). Academic journals that include articles on financial markets and various aspects of investing include the *Journal of Business,* the *Journal of Finance,* the *Journal of Financial and Quantitative Analysis,* the *Journal of Financial Economics, Journal of Financial Intermediation,* and the *Review of Financial Studies.*

Anyone interested in the management of money for institutional or corporate investors (especially pension funds) should consider reading the *Journal of Portfolio Management,* the *Journal of Fixed Income,* the *Journal of Investing, Journal of Futures Markets,* and the *Journal of Derivatives,* all of which publish the views of both practitioners and academicians. A biweekly periodical that covers current industry news and that is widely read by institutional investors and money managers is *Pensions and Investment Age*. *Institutional Investor*, a periodical full of feature stories on the investment industry, is published monthly. *Plan Sponsor* is a monthly publication directed at institutional investors managing pension funds. Individual investors will find the articles in the monthly issues of the *AAII Journal*, published by the Chicago-based American Association of Individual Investors, to be informative. Also of interest are *Business Week* (a weekly publication) and two biweeklies, *Forbes* and *Fortune*.

Data on mutual funds is published in a number of places. Morningstar provides extensive information in both hard copy and computer-readable forms. Other sources include publications put out by Lipper Analytical Services, William E. Donoghue, American Association of Individual Investors, Value Line, Micropal, and CDA/Wiesenberger Financial Services.

Although a company's annual and quarterly reports provide useful information, the annual (10-K) and quarterly (10-Q) business and financial reports filed with the Securities and Exchange Commission usually include more details. Whereas the annual reports are audited, it should be noted that quarterly reports are unaudited.

A source of macroeconomic data such as monetary aggregates (like the money supply) and other monetary items is the *Federal Reserve Bulletin*, a monthly publication by the Board of Governors of the Federal Reserve System. The Department of the Treasury publishes quarterly the *Treasury Bulletin*, which contains data on government debt and interest rates. Data on national income and production are published monthly by the U.S. Department of Commerce in the *Survey of Current Business*. The Department of Commerce also publishes on a monthly basis the *Business Conditions Digest*, where various economic indicators can be found.

22.9.2 Electronically Delivered Data

The rapid increase in the use of personal computers by those who invest money for others, as well as by those who invest for themselves, has led to a major expansion in the availability of computer-readable investment data. Large amounts of financial and economic data, such as common stock prices, mutual fund information, and financial statements, are provided on computer disks that are made available to investors for a fee by Standard & Poor's Compustat Services, Value Line, Inc., Morningstar, and Lipper Analytical Services, among others.

The Internet has the potential to revolutionize the delivery of investment information. Virtually every organization involved in investment management maintains a Web site. In many cases, information that just a few years ago would have cost thousands of dollars to obtain is now available for free on demand over the Internet. The Internet simply is too dynamic to make it worthwhile listing attractive Web sites here. Nevertheless, students are encouraged to explore for themselves the immense investment resources now available to them on the Internet.[36]

22.10 SUMMARY

1. Financial analysts are investment professionals who evaluate securities and then make investment recommendations. Those recommendations may be used by professional money managers (portfolio managers) or by certain clients of the analysts.
2. There are two primary reasons for engaging in financial analysis: to determine certain characteristics of securities and to attempt to identify mispriced securities.
3. To understand and estimate the risks and returns of individual securities as well as groups of securities, one must understand both financial markets and the principles of security valuation.

4. Technical analysis involves short-term predictions of security price movements based on past patterns of prices and trading volumes. Fundamental analysis concerns estimates of the basic determinants of security values, such as future sales, expenses, and earnings for firms.

5. Many financial analysts focus their research efforts on analyzing company financial statements. Such research permits an analyst to better understand a company's business operations, its plans for future growth, what factors affect its profitability, and how those factors affect its profitability.

6. When prominent analysts publish favorable reports on a stock, its price tends to immediately rise by an abnormal amount. Conversely, when they publish unfavorable reports on a stock, its price tends to immediately fall. Neither of these price movements is subsequently reversed.

7. Stocks that are neglected by analysts tend to have abnormally high returns.

8. In the United States, trading on inside information is illegal in public security markets. However, defining inside information is difficult.

9. Many printed sources of information about investing in general and firms in particular are available to the public. However, currently the fastest-growing source is an electronic one—the Internet.

QUESTIONS AND PROBLEMS

1. If security markets are highly efficient, what role is there for financial analysts?

2. If an analyst can correctly forecast a company's next year earnings, does that necessarily imply that the analyst can correctly forecast how the company's stock will perform? Why?

3. Compare the price reaction to the purchase of stocks that have been identified with a system that previously has been able to "beat the market" with the reactions to (a) the accurate prediction of rainfall and (b) the accurate prediction of the locations of enemy submarines.

4. Despite the arguments and evidence offered by proponents of efficiency market many investors pay attention to technical analysis in some form. Speculate as to why these investors use this kind of investment research.

5. Describe the types of behavior that must be exhibited by investors as a group if momentum and contrarian investment strategies are to be successful. In what ways do those behaviors run counter to how the efficient markets hypothesis assumes investors will act?

6. Distinguish between "top-down" and "bottom-up" approaches to financial forecasting. What are the primary advantages and disadvantages of each approach?

7. Last year both Hudson Homes and Baldwin Construction earned $1 million in net income. Both companies have assets of $10 million. However, Hudson generated a return on equity of 11.1%, whereas Baldwin produced a return on equity of 20.0%. What can explain the differences in return on equity between the two companies?

8. Last fiscal year, Afton Machinery had the following financial statement data:

Sales/assets	2.10
Net income/EBIT	.65
EBIT/sales	.10
Assets/equity	3.00

Calculate Afton's return on assets and return on equity.

9. Augusta Ironworks reported the following fiscal year-end financial data (stated in 000s).

Assets	$1,500
Liabilities	$900
Stockholders' equity	$600
Net income	$200
Dividends per share	$.50
Stock price	$30.00
Average shares outstanding	100

Given this information, calculate Augusta's:

a. Price-earnings ratio

b. Book value per share

c. Price-book ratio

d. Dividend yield

e. Payout ratio

10. Is it true that, when comparing the reported earnings of corporations, "a dollar is a dollar?"

11. Obtain an annual report for a corporation of your choosing. Using the financial statements contained in the report, compute the company's most recent year's return on equity by first calculating:

a. Operating margin

b. Asset turnover

c. Total assets-to-stockholders' equity

d. Interest-to-stockholders' equity

e. Tax rate

12. If Company A has a higher return on equity than Company B, does that necessarily mean that Company A's earnings should grow faster than Company B's earnings? Why?

13. Why does financial statement analysis typcially rely heavily on examining financial ratios as opposed to absolute numbers (for example, net income-to-sales as opposed to just net income)?

14. What are some of the drawbacks of comparing a company's financial ratios with those of other companies within the same industry?

15. From the perspective of a proponent of market efficiency, why is it surprising that trades based on insider trading data found in the SEC's *Official Summary of Insider Transactions* appear to produce significant abnormal profits?

16. (Appendix Question) Technical analysis is predicated on stock prices' moving in repetitive patterns. What would one have to believe about the timing of the receipt of information by financial markets' participants in order to believe in the existence of such patterns?

17. (Appendix Question) The closing, high, and low prices for Fort McCoy Packaging stock over a ten-day interval are shown below. Construct a bar chart for Fort McCoy Packaging stock over this period of time.

Day	Closing Price	High	Low
1	20	21	19
2	$20\frac{1}{4}$	$20\frac{1}{4}$	18
3	21	22	$20\frac{1}{2}$
4	$21\frac{1}{8}$	$22\frac{7}{8}$	$21\frac{1}{8}$
5	21	$23\frac{1}{4}$	20
6	$21\frac{3}{4}$	22	$20\frac{3}{4}$
7	22	$23\frac{1}{2}$	$20\frac{1}{8}$
8	$20\frac{1}{8}$	22	$19\frac{1}{4}$
9	$19\frac{1}{8}$	$21\frac{1}{2}$	19
10	$18\frac{1}{4}$	$21\frac{7}{8}$	$17\frac{1}{8}$

18. (Appendix Question) Calculate the relative strength of Fort McCoy Packaging stock versus the S&P 500 over the ten-day period referred to in Problem 17, given the following closing prices for the S&P 500:

	Day									
	1	**2**	**3**	**4**	**5**	**6**	**7**	**8**	**9**	**10**
S&P 500 closing price	300	302	306	310	320	315	330	325	325	330

CFA EXAM QUESTION

19. The duPont formula defines the net return on shareholders' equity as a function of the following components:
- Operating margin
- Asset turnover
- Interest burden
- Financial leverage
- Income tax rate

Using only the data in the table shown below:
a. Calculate each of the five components listed above for 1985 and 1989, and calculate the return on equity (ROE) for 1985 and 1989, using all of the five components. Show calculations.
b. Briefly discuss the impact of the changes in asset turnover and financial leverage on the change in ROE from 1985 to 1989.

	1985	1989
Income Statement Data		
Revenues	$542	$979
Operating income	38	76
Depreciation and amortization	3	9
Interest expense	3	0
Pretax income	32	67
Income taxes	13	37
Net income after tax	19	30
Balance Sheet Data		
Fixed assets	$41	$70
Total assets	245	291
Working capital	123	157
Total debt	16	0
Total shareholders' equity	159	220

APPENDIX

TECHNICAL ANALYSIS

As mentioned earlier, most (but not all) technical analysts rely on charts of stock prices and trading volumes. Virtually all employ colorful, and sometimes even mystical, terminology. For example, a significant price rise on relatively large trading volume might be described as an accumulation. The stock is said to be moving from "weak hands" to "strong hands" because a rising stock price on large trading volume is viewed as a situation in which demand is stronger than supply. In contrast, a significant price decline on relatively large trading volume may be described as a distribution. The stock is said to be moving from "strong hands" to "weak hands" because a declining stock price on large trading volume is viewed as a situation in which supply is stronger than demand. In both situations, relatively large trading volume might be considered a sign of a sustainable change in the stock's price, whereas relatively small trading volume indicates a transitory change.

What if there is a period during which a stock's price does not move significantly? If the stock's price movements are within a narrow band, the stock is said to be in a consolidation phase. A price level that a stock has difficulty rising above is known as a *resistance level*, and a price level that a stock does not seem to fall below is known as a *support level*.

Such statements may sound meaningful, but a proponent of market efficiency would argue that they fail to pass the tests of simple logic. First, changes in a stock's price occur when the consensus opinion concerning its value changes. This observation means that large volume associated with a price change only reflects a substantial difference of opinion concerning the impact of new information on the stock's value; small volume reflects smaller differences of opinion. Second, if price or volume data could be used to predict future short-term price movements, investors would rush to exploit such information, moving prices rapidly enough to make the information useless. However, as shown in Tables 22.1 and 22.2, some evidence suggests that there may be some technical trading rules that have merit. Whether they will be useful after transaction costs are fully taken into account is difficult to determine. Even if they do pass muster with respect to transaction costs, it is uncertain whether they will be useful in the future.

A.1   CHARTS

Chartists (technicians who rely on chart formations) nonetheless believe that certain patterns carry great significance, although they often disagree among themselves on the significance of a pattern or even on the existence of a pattern. Three basic types of charts are used: bar charts, line charts, and point and figure charts.

On a *bar chart* the horizontal axis is a time line, and the vertical axis measures a particular stock's price. More specifically, corresponding to a given day on the horizontal axis will be a vertical line, the top and bottom of which represent the high and low price for that stock on that day. Somewhere on this vertical line will be a small horizontal line representing the closing price for the day. As an example, consider the following hypothetical stock, whose trading background over the last five days is as follows:

Day	High Price	Low Price	Closing Price	Volume
$t - 5$	11	9	10	200
$t - 4$	12	9	11	300
$t - 3$	13	12	12	400
$t - 2$	11	10	11	200
$t - 1$	14	11	12	500

Figure 22.4(a) presents a bar chart for this stock. Figure 22.4 (b) indicates how such a bar chart of prices can be augmented by adding trading volume at the bottom.

Figure 22.5(a) shows a bar chart exhibiting a pattern that is known as "head and shoulders." As time passed, the stock's price initially rose, hit a peak at *A*, and then fell to a bottom at *B*. Recovering from this fall, it went up to an even higher peak at *C*, but then fell again to a bottom at *D*. Next it rose to a peak at *E* that was not as high as the previous peak, *C*, and then it started to fall. As soon as the price went down past its previous low, *D*, a forecast was immediately made that the stock was going to plunge much lower (if the stock had not reached a level equal to *D*, no such forecast would have been made). Figure 22.5(b) shows a bar chart pattern known as "inverted head and shoulders," which results in a forecast that the stock is going to quickly rise by a substantial amount.[37]

On a *line chart*, the axes are the same as on a bar chart. However, only closing prices are presented, and they are connected to each other successively with straight lines, as illustrated in Figure 22.4(c). Although it is not shown, line charts are also frequently augmented with volume data in a manner identical to bar charts.

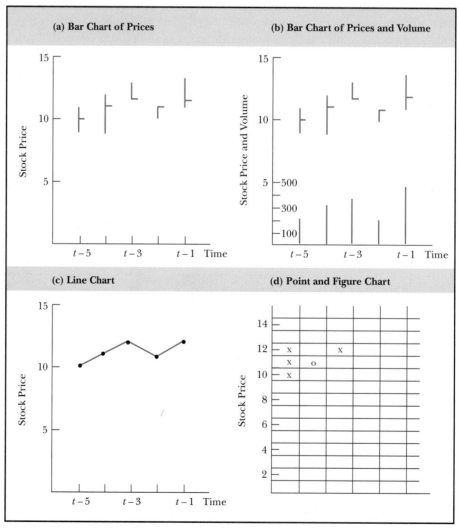

Figure 22.4
Types of Charts

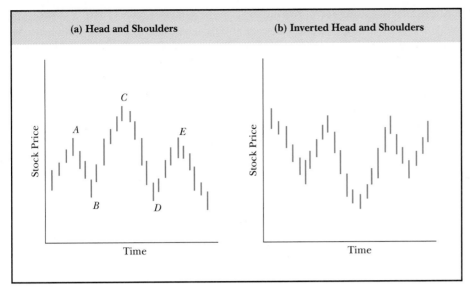

Figure 22.5
Bar Chart Patterns

Details of construction of *point and figure charts* vary, but the idea is to plot closing prices that form a trend in a single column, moving to the next column only when the trend is reversed. For example, closing prices might be rounded to the nearest dollar and the chart begun by plotting a beginning rounded price on a certain day. As long as the (rounded) price does not change, nothing is done. When a different price is recorded, it is plotted on the chart. A price higher than the initial price is indicated with an *X*, with any gaps between the prices also marked with an *X*. A price below the initial price is marked with an *O* in a similar fashion. Then when a price that is different from the last one is recorded, it is plotted in the same column only if it is in the same direction. (In general, *X*s denote advancing prices and *O*s denote declining prices.)

For example, if the first different price is above the beginning price, it is plotted above the beginning one. Then, if a price is recorded that is above the second one, it is plotted in the same column, but if it is below the second one, it is plotted in a new column to the right of the first column. Continuing, as long as new prices are in the same direction, they are plotted in the same column. Whenever there is a reversal, a new column is started. Figure 22.4(d) presents a point and figure chart for the same hypothetical stock used in the other panels.

Point and figure enthusiasts look for all sorts of patterns in their charts. As with all chartist techniques, the idea is to recognize a pattern early enough to profit from one's ability to foresee the course of prices—a neat trick, if one can do it.

A.2   MOVING AVERAGES

Many other procedures are used by technicians. Some construct moving averages to try to detect "intermediate" and "long-term" trends. With this procedure, a set number of the most recent closing prices on a security are averaged each day. (For example, daily closing prices over the previous 200 days may be used.) This means that each day, the oldest price is replaced with the most recent price in the set of closing prices that will be averaged. Frequently a line chart of these moving averages is plotted, along with a line chart of daily closing prices. Each day the charts are updated and then examined for trends to see if there is a buy or a sell signal present somewhere.

Financial Analysis   **783**

Alternatively, a long-term moving average may be compared with a short-term moving average (the distinction between the two averages is that the long-term average uses a substantially larger set of closing prices in its calculations than the short-term average). When the short-term average crosses the long-term average, a "signal" is said to have been given. The action recommended will depend on such things as whether the averages have been rising or falling, as well as the direction from which the short-term average crossed the long-term average (it may have been below and now is above, or it may have been above and now is below). A moving average trading rule was used to generate the returns shown in part (a) of Table 22.2.

A.3 RELATIVE STRENGTH MEASURES

Another procedure used by technicians involves measuring what they call relative strength. For example, a stock's price may be divided by a price index of its industry each day to indicate the stock's movement relative to its industry. Similarly, an industry index may be divided by a market index to indicate the industry's movement relative to the market, or a stock's price may be divided by a market index to indicate a stock's movement relative to the market. The idea is to examine changes in these relative strength measures with the hope of finding a pattern that can be used to accurately predict the future.

The momentum trading rules used in preparing Table 22.1 were based on the notion of relative strength in its simplest form. Stock returns over a just-ended holding period were calculated, and then portfolios of winners and losers were formed. When semiannual or annual returns were used, the momentum trading rules seemed to have merit.

Some procedures of technical analysts focus on relationships among different indexes. For example, the Dow Theory requires that a pattern in the Dow Jones Industrial Average be "confirmed" by a certain movement in the Dow Jones Transportation Average before action be taken.[38] Another example involves computing the difference between the number of issues advancing and the number declining each day. A chart of the differences cumulated over time, known as the *advance-decline line*, may then be compared with a market index such as the Dow Jones Industrial Average.

A.4 CONTRARY OPINION

Many technical procedures are based on the idea of contrary opinion. The idea is to determine the consensus opinion and then do the opposite. Two examples that were discussed earlier involved (1) buying stocks that had recently dropped in price and selling stocks that had recently risen in price and (2) buying stocks with low P/E ratios and selling stocks with high P/E ratios. For a third example, one might see whether the "odd-lotters" (those with trade orders involving less than 100 shares) are buying and then sell any holdings of these stocks. If "the little investor is usually wrong," this procedure will usually be right. However, the basic premise about the little investor has yet to be factually established.

The widespread availability of personal computers and on-line services with data on stock prices and trading volumes has made it possible for individual investors to engage in technical analysis in the privacy of their own homes. Producers of software have been quick to provide programs to perform such analysis, complete with multicolored graphs. Nevertheless, the number of investors using fundamental analysis is much larger than the number using technical analysis.

---

[1] Sumner N. Levine (ed.), *Financial Analyst's Handbook I* (Homewood, IL: Dow Jones-Irwin, 1975).

[2] William C. Norby, "Overview of Financial Analysis," in Levine, *Financial Analyst's Handbook I*, p. 3.

[3] To obtain more information about becoming a CFA, contact the Institute of Chartered Financial Analysts. Their mailing address is P.O. Box 3668, Charlottesville, VA 22903, and their telephone number is (804) 980-3668. Information can also by obtained by contacting the AIMR Web site at ⟨www.aimr.org⟩.

[4] Some would add a third reason for conducting financial analysis: monitoring the firm's management in order to prevent managers from consuming an excessive amount of perquisites and making inappropriate decisions to the detriment of the firm's shareholders. See Michael C. Jensen and William H. Meckling, "Theory of the Firm: Managerial Behavior, Agency Costs and Ownership Structure," *Journal of Financial Economics* 3, no. 4 (October 1976): 305–360.

[5] For a discussion regarding portfolio selection by an investor who has earned income (for example, from wages or from running a business), see Edward M. Miller, "Portfolio Selection in a Fluctuating Economy," *Financial Analysts Journal* 34, no. 3 (May/June 1978): 77–83.

[6] If the added benefits exceeded the added costs, then it would be profitable to perform more financial analysis, because the incremental benefits from doing so would cover the associated costs. If, on the other hand, the added costs exceeded the added benefits, then it would be profitable to cut back on the amount of financial analysis, because costs would be reduced by an amount greater than benefits.

[7] For an interesting argument on why the existence of trading costs results in some investors' performing financial analysis in an efficient market, see Sanford J. Grossman, "On the Efficiency of Competitive Stock Markets Where Traders Have Diverse Information," *Journal of Finance* 31, no. 2 (May 1976): 573–585; Sanford J. Grossman and Joseph E. Stiglitz, "On the Impossibility of Informationally Efficient Markets," *American Economic Review* 70, no. 3 (June 1980): 393–408; and Bradford Cornell and Richard Roll, "Strategies for Pairwise Competitions in Markets and Organizations," *Bell Journal of Economics* 12, no. 1 (Spring 1981): 201–213.

[8] Felix Rosenfeld (ed.), *The Evaluation of Ordinary Shares*, is a summary of the proceedings of the Eighth Congress of the European Federation of Financial Analysts Societies (Paris: Dunod, 1975), p. 297.

[9] Rosenfeld, *The Evaluation of Ordinary Shares*, pp. 297–298. For an argument that technical analysis can be of value in an efficient market, see David P. Brown and Robert H. Jennings, "On Technical Analysis," *Review of Financial Analysis* 2, no. 4 (1989): 527–551. Also see Jack L. Treynor and Robert Ferguson, "In Defense of Technical Analysis," *Journal of Finance* 40, no. 3 (July 1985): 757–773; and Lawrence Blume, David Easley, and Maureen O'Hara, "Market Statistics and Technical Analysis: The Role of Volume," *Journal of Finance* 49, no. 1 (March 1994): 153–181.

[10] See, for example, Eugene F. Fama, "Efficient Capital Markets: A Review of Theory and Empirical Work," *Journal of Finance* 25, no. 2 (May 1970): 383–417.

[11] See, for example, Eugene F. Fama, "Efficient Capital Markets: II," *Journal of Finance* 46, no. 5 (December 1991): 1575–1617.

[12] Other studies present evidence that is consistent with these results. See Barr Rosenberg, Kenneth Reid, and Ronald Lanstein, "Persuasive Evidence of Market Inefficiency," *Journal of Portfolio Management* 11, no. 3 (Spring 1985): 9–16; John S. Howe, "Evidence on Stock Market Overreaction," *Financial Analysts Journal* 42, no. 4 (July/August 1986): 74–77; and Andrew W. Lo and A. Craig MacKinlay, "When Are Contrarian Profits Due to Stock Market Overreaction?" *Review of Financial Studies* 3, no. 2 (1990): 175–205.

[13] One explanation for these results that has been offered is that investors underreact to quarterly earnings announcements. See Chapter 18, particularly section 18.7, and Victor L.

Bernard, Jacob K. Thomas, and Jeffery S. Abarbanell, "How Sophisticated Is the Market in Interpreting Earnings News?" *Journal of Applied Corporate Finance* 6, no. 2 (Summer 1993): 54–63. Another related observation involving one-year formation periods concerns the Dow dividend strategy. This strategy requires buying the ten highest-dividend-yielding stocks in the Dow Jones Industrial Average (DJIA) and holding them for one year, at which point the portfolio is revised accordingly for another year. From 1973 through 1992 this strategy outperformed the DJIA by 5.15% per year, on average. Interestingly, it turns out that the stocks purchased in any year had a return that was 5.99% less than the DJIA the previous year, on average. Thus the strategy actually involves buying last year's "losers" among the Dow Jones 30. See Dale L. Domian, David A. Louton, and Irene M. Seahawk, "The Dow Dividend Strategy: How It Works and Why," *AAII Journal* 16, no. 4 (May 1994): 7–10.

[14] A puzzling observation associated with part (f) was that 5% of the 7.2% abnormal return for the loser portfolio was earned during the Januaries that occurred during the test period. Conversely, −.8% of the −2.4% abnormal return for the winners was earned during Januaries. Hence the January anomaly (discussed in Appendix A to Chapter 16) appears to somehow be intertwined with the long-term contrarian strategy.

[15] Other studies have examined contrarian strategies and have been unable to confirm the usefulness of such strategies. In two of these studies it was argued that the benchmark portfolio returns were incorrectly determined. This means that the abnormal returns were not calculated correctly because by definition they are equal to the difference between the returns on the portfolio and its benchmark. In a third study, the alleged cause of the overreaction—security analysts' underpredicting earnings on losers and overpredicting earnings on winners—was contested. A fourth study suggested that the size effect (discussed in Appendix A to Chapter 16) was largely responsible for the results because losers tend to be smaller than winners. Last, a fifth study argued that incorrect prices were used when the costs of buying and selling stocks were determined in arriving at the results reflected in parts (e) and (f) of Table 22.1. However, these studies have, in turn, been contested in a sixth study. Specifically, after their objections had been taken into consideration it was found that losers outperform winners by 5% to 10% per year, with the difference being the largest when only small firms were classified into winners and losers. The six studies are, respectively, K. C. Chan, "On the Contrarian Investment Strategy," *Journal of Business* 61, no. 2 (April 1988): 147–163; Ray Ball and S. P. Kothari, "Nonstationary Expected Returns: Implications for Tests of Market Efficiency and Serial Correlations in Returns," *Journal of Financial Economics* 25, no. 1 (November 1989): 51–74; April Klein, "A Direct Test of the Cognitive Bias Theory of Share Price Reversals," *Journal of Accounting and Economics* 13, no. 2 (July 1990): 155–166; Paul Zarowin, "Size, Seasonality, and Stock Market Overreaction," *Journal of Financial and Quantitative Analysis* 25, no. 1 (March 1990): 113–125; Jennifer Conrad and Gautam Kaul, "Long-Term Overreaction or Biases in Computed Returns?" *Journal of Finance* 48, no. 1 (March 1993): 39–63; and Navin Chopra, Josef Lakonishok, and Jay R. Ritter, "Measuring Abnormal Performance: Do Stocks Overreact?" *Journal of Financial Economics* 31, no. 2 (April 1992): 235–268.

Adding to the puzzle is the behavior of Canadian stocks. For one-year test periods the results were similar to those in the United States in that a momentum strategy seemed to work (as in part (d) of Table 22.1). For three-year and five-year test periods, neither a momentum nor a contrarian strategy worked [unlike parts (e) and (f) of Table 22.1]. See Lawrence Kryzanowski and Hao Zhang, "The Contrarian Investment Strategy Does Not Work in Canadian Markets," *Journal of Financial and Quantitative Analysis* 27, no. 3 (September 1992): 383–395.

[16] Apparently significant returns can be earned from the weekly strategy if transaction costs are small (such as for large institutional investors). However, larger transaction costs result in negative net returns. See Bruce N. Lehmann, "Fads, Martingales, and Market Efficiency," *Quarterly Journal of Economics* 105, no. 1 (February 1990): 1–28. For an argument that Lehmann underestimated the size of transaction costs, see Jennifer Conrad, Mustafa N. Gultekin, and Gautam Kaul, "Profitability of Short-Term Contrarian Portfolio Strategies," unpublished paper, University of Michigan, 1991.

[17] Lehmann, "Fads, Martingales, and Market Efficiency," p. 26.

[18] Input-output analysis is sometimes used to ensure consistency between various industries and the economy in aggregate. This type of analysis is based on the notion that the output of certain industries (for example, the steel industry) is the input for certain other industries (for example, the household appliance industry).

[19] In 1997, the Financial Accounting Standards Board proposed rule no. 128, which would affect how earnings per share are reported. The rule would replace *primary earnings per share*, which factors in some dilution for certain common-stock equivalents, with an entirely undiluted measure of earnings per share called *basic earnings per share*. *Fully diluted earnings per share* would remain calculated in almost the same manner as before but would now be called *diluted earnings per share*. Financial analysts will have two distinct measures of earnings per share: one with no dilution and one with full dilution. For many companies, the change will be insignificant. For some companies, however, the change will highlight the large impact that dilutive securities, such as warrants and employee stock options, potentially can have on earnings per share.

[20] For more on free cash flow and how it can be used to value a firm and its equity, see Aswath Damodaran, *Corporate Finance: Theory and Practice* (New York: Wiley, 1997), pp. 170–171, 634–646.

[21] Analysts typically calculate an average value for balance sheet items used in financial ratios. This approach facilitates comparisons of point-in-time levels on the balance sheet with period flows on the income statement. In the Dayton Hudson example, the financial ratios were computed using an average of beginning-of-year and year-end values for balance sheet items.

[22] In recent years analysts have increasingly come to view earnings before interest, taxes, depreciation, and amortization (EBITDA) relative to the total market value of the firm (its equity and debt) as a more effective measure of operating performance than pre-tax ROA. EBITDA is essentially a measure of the company's pre-tax cash flow.

[23] Similar observations have been made in regard to other studies of the recommendations made by major brokerage houses. See John C. Groth, Wilbur G. Lewellen, Gary G. Schlarbaum, and Ronald C. Lease, "An Analysis of Brokerage House Securities Recommendations," *Financial Analysts Journal* 35, no. 1 (January/February 1979): 32–40; James H. Bjerring, Josef Lakonishok, and Theo Vermaelen, "Stock Prices and Financial Analysts' Recommendations," *Journal of Finance* 38, no. 1 (March 1983): 187–204; and Philip Heitner, "Isn't It Time to Measure Analysts' Track Records?" *Financial Analysts Journal* 47, no. 3 (May/June 1991): 5–6. For a comment on the first study, see the Letter to the Editor in the May/June 1980 issue by Clinton M. Bidwell, with a responding Letter to the Editor in the July/August 1980 issue by Wilbur G. Lewellen. Also see endnote 1 in Chapter 23.

[24] Two other studies of "Heard on the Street" recommendations reached similar conclusions to those shown here. See Peter Lloyd-Davies and Michael Canes, "Stock Prices and the Publication of Second-Hand Information," *Journal of Business*, 51, no. 1 (January 1978): 43–56; and Pu Liu, Stanley D. Smith, and Azmat A Syed, "Stock Price Reactions to *The Wall Street Journal's* Securities Recommendations," *Journal of Financial and Quantitative Analysis* 25, no. 3 (September 1990): 399–410. Interestingly, a former author of the "Heard on the Street" column, R. Foster Winans, was convicted of fraud and theft in 1985 for leaking the contents of his column to four brokers and subsequently sharing in the associated trading profits.

[25] Value Line has a service called Value Line Investment Survey for Windows to which investors can subscribe that involves software and periodic updates of their rankings as well as other data. Besides its stock recommendations, Value Line also provides a measure of the risk of individual securities that is known as Safety Rank. This risk measure was found to be more highly correlated with subsequent returns than either beta or standard deviation, suggesting that it is a more useful measure of risk. See Russell J. Fuller and G. Wenchi Wong, "Traditional versus Theoretical Risk Measures," *Financial Analysts Journal* 44, no. 2 (March/April 1988): 52–57, 67, and the Value Line Web site ⟨www.valueline.com⟩.

[26] One study of Value Line recommendations found that most rank changes occur shortly after earnings announcements are made. Subsequent investigation revealed that Value

Line's superior performance was attributable to the "post-earnings-announcement drift" (this phenomenon was discussed in Chapter 18). Hence the two anomalies appear to be related. See John Affleck-Graves and Richard R. Mendenhall, "The Relation between the Value Line Enigma and Post-Earnings-Announcement Drift," *Journal of Financial Economics* 31, no. 1 (February 1992): 75–96.

[27] Jennifer Francis and Leonard Soffer, "The Relative Informativeness of Analysts' Stock Recommendations and Earnings Forecast Revisions," *Journal of Accounting Research* 35, no. 2 (Autumn 1997): 193–211. Chapter 18 contains a discussion of analysts' forecasts of earnings.

[28] See Appendix A in Chapter 16 for a discussion of the size effect.

[29] The presence of the size effect can be seen by noting that the average return for small firms of 13.5% is much larger than the average return for medium and large firms of 10.7% and 9.8%, respectively. It should be noted, however, that the existence of the neglected-firm effect has been contested; see Craig G. Beard and Richard W. Sias, "Is There a Neglected-Firm Effect?" *Financial Analysts Journal* 53, no. 5 (September/October 1997): 19–23.

[30] This reporting requirement should not be confused with SEC Rule 13d, which requires investors to disclose their holdings in a company once they are equal to 5% or more of the company's stock. Unlike form 4 investors, Rule 13d investors are not viewed as insiders by the SEC, and they do not have to report every transaction they subsequently make.

[31] The *Value Line Investment Survey* (published by Value Line, Inc., New York, NY) reports an "index of insider decisions" for each stock covered in its weekly service. In essence, this is a cumulative index of the net number of purchasers (including those who exercise options) and sellers. The *Weekly Insider Report* (published by Vickers Stock Research Corp., Brookside, NJ) reports a ratio of total insider buying to total insider selling. For an article about what constitutes insider trading, see Gary L. Tidwell, "Here's a Tip—Know the Rules of Insider Trading," *Sloan Management Review* 28, no. 4 (Summer 1987): 93–98.

[32] If the insider bought the stock by exercising an option that was given to him or her as part of his or her compensation, then the six-month period is measured from the day the option was granted.

[33] An alternative method is to examine stock returns on days of illegal insider trading. Looking at 183 SEC cases from 1980 to 1989, one study found that stock prices had an average abnormal return of 3.0% on each day that illegal insider buying took place and −3.5% on each day that illegal insider selling took place. See Lisa K. Meulbroek, "An Empirical Analysis of Illegal Insider Trading," *Journal of Finance* 47, no. 5 (December 1992): 1661–1699.

[34] Jeffrey F. Jaffe, "Special Information and Insider Trading," *Journal of Business* 47, no. 3 (July 1974): 410–428. Also see Joseph E. Finnerty, "Insiders and Market Efficiency," *Journal of Finance* 31, no. 4 (September 1976): 1141–1148; and Aaron B. Feigen, "Information Opportunities from Insider Trading Laws," *AAII Journal* 11, no. 8 (September 1989): 12–15.

[35] See Herbert S. Kerr, "The Battle of Insider Trading and Market Efficiency," *Journal of Portfolio Management* 6, no. 4 (Summer 1980): 47–58; Wayne Y. Lee and Michael E. Solt, "Insider Trading: A Poor Guide to Market Timing," *Journal of Portfolio Management* 12, no. 4 (Summer 1986): 65–71; H. Nejat Seyhun, "Insiders' Profits, Costs of Trading, and Market Efficiency," *Journal of Financial Economics* 16, no. 2 (June 1986): 189–212; Michael S. Rozeff and Mir A. Zaman, "Market Efficiency and Insider Trading: New Evidence," *Journal of Business* 61, no. 1 (January 1988): 25–44; and Ji-Chai Lin and John S. Howe, "Insider Trading in the OTC Market," *Journal of Finance* 45, no. 4 (September 1990): 1273–1284.

[36] Such information can become quickly outdated, but a comprehensive list of useful investment-related Web sites is found in Jean Henrich, "The Individual Investor's Guide to Investment Web Sites," *AAII Journal* 19, no. 8 (September 1997): 15–23. Also see the following three articles in the Fall/Winter 1996 issue (vol. 6, no. 2) of *Financial Practice and Education*: "An Introduction to Finance on the Internet" by Russ Ray; "A Guide to Locating Financial Information on the Internet" by James B. Pettijohn; and "The Ways in Which the Financial Engineer Can Use the Internet" by Anthony F. Herbst.

[37] For details on many kinds of patterns, see Alan R. Shaw, "Technical Analysis," in Levine, *Financial Analyst's Handbook I*, pp. 944–988; Chapter 8 in Jerome B. Cohen, Edward D. Zinbarg,

and Arthur Zeikel, *Investment Analysis and Portfolio Management* (Homewood, IL: Richard D. Irwin, 1987); and Richard L. Evans, "Chart Basics Using Bars, Point & Figure and Candlesticks," *AAII Journal*, 15, no. 4 (April 1993): 24–28.

[38] For more on the Dow Theory, see Richard L. Evans, "Dow's Theory and the Averages: Relevant... or Relics?" *AAII Journal* 15, no. 1 (January 1993): 27–29.

KEY TERMS

financial analyst	probabilistic forecasting
security analyst	econometric model
portfolio managers	endogenous variables
fundamental analysis	exogenous variables
technical analysis	neglected-firm effect
top-down forecasting	insiders
bottom-up forecasting	chartists

REFERENCES

1. For a discussion of contrarian investment strategies, see, in addition to the references in Table 22.1 and endnotes 12 and 15, the following:

   David Dremen, *Contrarian Investment Strategies* (New York: Random House, 1979).

   Paul Zarowin, "Short-Run Market Overreaction: Size and Seasonality Effects," *Journal of Portfolio Management* 15, no. 3 (Spring 1989): 26–29.

   Paul Zarowin, "Does the Stock Market Overreact to Corporate Earnings Information?" *Journal of Finance* 44, no. 5 (December 1989): 1385–1399.

   Jennifer Conrad, Mustafa N. Gultekin, and Gautam Kaul, "Profitability of Short-Term Contrarian Portfolio Strategies," unpublished paper, University of Michigan, 1991.

   Victor L. Bernard, Jacob K. Thomas, and Jeffery S. Abarbanell, "How Sophisticated Is the Market in Interpreting Earnings News?" *Journal of Applied Corporate Finance* 6, no. 2 (Summer 1993): 54–63.

   Josef Lakonishok, Andrei Shleifer, and Robert W. Vishny, "Contrarian Investment, Extrapolation, and Risk," *Journal of Finance* 49, no. 5 (December 1994): 1541–1578.

   Ray Ball, S. P. Kothari, and Charles E. Wasley, "Can We Implement Research on Stock Trading Rules?" *Journal of Portfolio Management* 21, no. 2 (Winter 1995): 54–63.

   Ray Ball, S. P. Kothari, and Jay Shanken, "Problems in Measuring Portfolio Performance: An Application to Contrarian Investment Strategies," *Journal of Financial Economics* 38, no. 1 (May 1995): 79–107.

   Tim Loughran and Jay Ritter, "Long-Term Market Overreaction: The Effect of Low-Priced Stocks," *Journal of Finance* 51, no. 5 (December 1996): 1959–1970.

   S. P. Kothari and Jerold Warner, "Measuring Long-Horizon Security Price Performance," *Journal of Financial Economics* 43, no. 3 (March 1997): 301–339.

2. Closely related to the issue of contrarian investment strategies is the issue of how stock price levels in one period are related to stock price levels in a subsequent period. This issue, like the usefulness of contrarian strategies, has been open to debate. Two of the earliest papers and two recent ones that contradict them are:

   Eugene F. Fama and Kenneth R. French, "Permanent and Temporary Components of Stock Prices," *Journal of Political Economy* 96, no. 2 (April 1988): 246–273.

   James M. Poterba and Lawrence H. Summers, "Mean Reversion in Stock Prices: Evidence and Implications," *Journal of Financial Economics* 22, no. 1 (October 1988): 27–59.

Myung Jig Kim, Charles R. Nelson, and Richard Startz, "Mean Reversion in Stock Prices? A Reappraisal of the Empirical Evidence," *Review of Economic Studies* 58, no. 3 (May 1991): 515–528.

Grant McQueen, "Long-Horizon Mean-Reverting Stock Prices Revisited," *Journal of Financial and Quantitative Analysis* 27, no. 1 (March 1992): 1–18.

3. Momentum strategies are discussed in:

Narasimhan Jegadeesh and Sheridan Titman, "Returns to Buying Winners and Selling Losers: Implications for Stock Market Efficiency," *Journal of Finance* 48, no. 1 (March 1993): 65–91.

4. Moving average and trading range breakout strategies are discussed in:

William Brock, Josef Lakonishok, and Blake LeBaron, "Simple Technical Trading Rules and the Stochastic Properties of Stock Returns," *Journal of Finance* 47, no. 5 (December 1992): 1731–1764.

5. The reaction of stock prices to the publication of analysts' recommendations is discussed in the sources given in Table 22.8 and in:

Peter Lloyd-Davies and Michael Canes, "Stock Prices and the Publication of Second-Hand Information," *Journal of Business* 51, no. 1 (January 1978): 43–56.

John C. Groth, Wilbur G. Lewellen, Gary G. Schlarbaum, and Ronald C. Lease, "An Analysis of Brokerage House Securities Recommendations," *Financial Analysts Journal* 35, no. 1 (January/February 1979): 32–40.

Clark Holloway, "A Note on Testing an Aggressive Investment Strategy Using Value Line Ranks," *Journal of Finance* 36, no. 3 (June 1981): 711–719.

Thomas E. Copeland and David Mayers, "The Value Line Enigma (1965–1978): A Case Study of Performance Evaluation Issues," *Journal of Financial Economics* 10, no. 3 (November 1982): 289–321.

James H. Bjerring, Josef Lakonishok, and Theo Vermaelen, "Stock Prices and Financial Analysts' Recommendations," *Journal of Finance* 38, no. 1 (March 1983): 187–204.

Gur Huberman and Shmuel Kandel, "Value Line Rank and Firm Size," *Journal of Business* 60, no. 4 (October 1987): 577–589.

Gur Huberman and Shmuel Kandel, "Market Efficiency and Value Line's Record," *Journal of Business* 63, no. 2 (April 1990): 187–216.

Pu Liu, Stanley D. Smith, and Azmat A Syed, "Stock Price Reactions to *The Wall Street Journal*'s Securities Recommendations," *Journal of Financial and Quantitative Analysis* 25, no. 3 (September 1990): 399–410.

Philip Heitner, "Isn't It Time to Measure Analysts' Track Records?" *Financial Analysts Journal* 47, no. 3 (May/June 1991): 5–6.

Donna R. Philbrick and William E. Ricks, "Using Value Line and IBES Analyst Forecasts in Accounting Research," *Journal of Accounting Research* 29, no. 2 (Autumn 1991): 397–417.

John Affleck-Graves and Richard R. Mendenhall, "The Relation between the Value Line Enigma and Post-Earnings-Announcement Drift," *Journal of Financial Economics* 31, no. 1 (February 1992): 75–96.

John Markese, "The Role of Earnings Forecasts in Stock Price Behavior," *AAII Journal* 14, no. 4 (April 1992): 30–32.

Rajiv Sant and Mir A. Zaman, "Market Reaction to *Business Week* 'Inside Wall Street' Column: A Self-Fulfilling Prophecy," *Journal of Banking and Finance* 20, no. 4 (May 1996): 617–643.

Jennifer Francis and Leonard Soffer, "The Relative Informativeness of Analysts' Stock Recommendations and Earnings Forecast Revisions," *Journal of Accounting Research* 35, no. 2 (Autumn 1997): 193–211.

6. The "Heard on the Street" column also sometimes discusses takeover rumors. For an analysis of the effects these rumors have on stock prices, see:

John Pound and Richard Zeckhauser, "Clearly Heard on the Street: The Effect of Takeover Rumors on Stock Prices," *Journal of Business* 63, no. 3 (July 1990): 291–308.

7. For a discussion of the neglected firm effect, see:

Avner Arbel and Paul Strebel, "Pay Attention to Neglected Firms!" *Journal of Portfolio Management* 9, no. 2 (Winter 1983): 37–42.

Avner Arbel, Steven Carvel, and Paul Strebel, "Giraffes, Institutions, and Neglected Firms," *Financial Analysts Journal* 39, no. 3 (May/June 1983): 57–63.

Craig G. Beard and Richard W. Sias, "Is There a Neglected-Firm Effect?" *Financial Analysts Journal* 53, no. 5 (September/October 1997): 19–23.

8. Insider trading has been examined in a number of studies. Some of the major ones are:

Jeffrey F. Jaffe, "Special Information and Insider Trading," *Journal of Business* 47, no. 3 (July 1974): 410–428.

Joseph E. Finnerty, "Insiders and Market Efficiency," *Journal of Finance* 31, no. 4 (September 1976): 1141–1148.

Herbert S. Kerr, "The Battle of Insider Trading and Market Efficiency," *Journal of Portfolio Management* 6, no. 4 (Summer 1980): 47–58.

Wayne Y. Lee and Michael Solt, "Insider Trading: A Poor Guide to Market Timing," *Journal of Portfolio Management* 12, no. 4 (Summer 1986): 65–71.

H. Nejat Seyhun, "Insiders' Profits, Costs of Trading, and Market Efficiency," *Journal of Financial Economics* 16, no. 2 (June 1986): 189–212.

H. Nejat Seyhun, "The Information Content of Aggregate Insider Trading," *Journal of Business* 61, no. 1 (January 1988): 1–24.

Michael S. Rozeff and Mir A. Zaman, "Market Efficiency and Insider Trading: New Evidence," *Journal of Business* 61, no. 1 (January 1988): 25–44.

Ji-Chai Lin and John S. Howe, "Insider Trading in the OTC Market," *Journal of Finance* 45, no. 4 (September 1990): 1273–1284.

Lisa K. Meulbroek, "An Empirical Analysis of Illegal Insider Trading," *Journal of Finance* 47, no. 5 (December 1992): 1661–1699.

Mustafa Chowdhury, John S. Howe, and Ji-Chai Lin, "The Relation between Aggregate Insider Transactions and Stock Market Returns," *Journal of Financial and Quantitative Analysis* 28, no. 3 (September 1993): 431–437.

9. Leading books on technical analysis, financial statement analysis, and fundamental analysis are, respectively:

Robert D. Edwards and John Magee, *Technical Analysis of Stock Trends* (Boston: John Magee, 1966).

George Foster, *Financial Statement Analysis* (Englewood Cliffs, NJ: Prentice Hall, 1986).

Sidney Cottle, Roger Murray, and Frank Block, *Graham and Dodd's Security Analysis* (New York: McGraw-Hill, 1988).

10. The new FASB reporting rules for earnings per share are discussed in: Ross Jennings, Marc J. Le Clere, and Robert B. Thompson II, "Evidence on the Usefulness of Alternative Earnings per Share Measures," *Financial Analysts Journal* 53, no. 6 (November/December 1997): 24–33.

11. Information sources for investing are described in:

Maria Crawford Scott and John Bajkowski, "Sources of Information for the Simplified Approach to Valuation," *AAII Journal* 16, no. 3 (April 1994): 29–32.

John Markese, "Picking Common Stocks: What Seems to Work, At Least Sometimes," *AAII Journal* 16, no. 5 (June 1994): 24–27.

INVESTMENT MANAGEMENT

Investment management, also known as portfolio management, is the process by which money is managed. It may (1) be active or passive, (2) use explicit or implicit procedures, and (3) be relatively controlled or uncontrolled. The trend is toward highly controlled operations consistent with the notion that capital markets are relatively efficient. However, approaches vary, and many different ones can be found. This chapter will discuss investment management, and in doing so it will present various types of investment styles.

<table>
<tr><td>**23.1**</td><td>**TRADITIONAL INVESTMENT MANAGEMENT ORGANIZATIONS**</td></tr>
</table>

Few people or organizations like to be called "traditional." However, some investment management organizations follow procedures that have changed little from those that were popular decades ago and thus deserve the title. Figure 23.1 shows the major characteristics of a traditional investment management organization.

Projections concerning the economy and the financial markets are made by economists, technicians, fundamentalists, or other market experts within or outside the organization. The projected economic environment is communicated by means of briefings and written reports—usually in a rather implicit and qualitative manner—to the organization's security analysts. Each analyst is responsible for a group of securities, often those in one or more industries (in some organizations, analysts are called industry specialists). A group of analysts may report to a senior analyst responsible for a sector of the economy or market.

The analysts, often drawing heavily on reports of others (for example, "street analysts" in brokerage houses), make predictions about the securities for which they are responsible. In a sense, such predictions are conditional on the assumed economic and market environments, although the relationship is typically quite loose.

Analysts' predictions seldom specify an expected rate of return or the time over which predicted performance will take place. Instead, an analyst's feelings about a security may be summarized by assigning it one of five codes, such as where a 1 represents a buy and a 5 represents a sell, as indicated in Figure 23.1.[1] In many organizations, a simple buy-hold-sell designation is given.

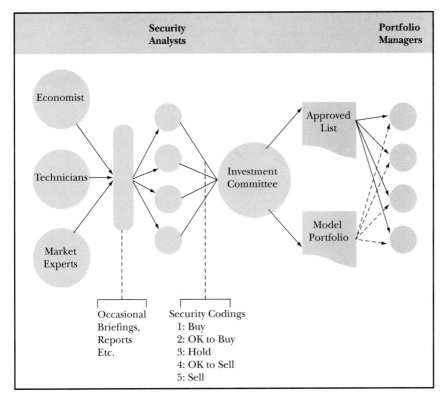

Figure 23.1
A Traditional Investment Management Organization

These security codings and various written reports constitute the information formally transmitted to an **investment committee**, which typically includes the senior management of the organization. In addition, analysts occasionally brief the investment committee on their feelings about various securities. The investment committee's primary formal output is often an **approved** (or authorized) **list**, which consists of the securities deemed worthy of accumulation in a given portfolio. The rules of the organization typically specify that any security on the list may be bought, whereas those not on the list should be either held or sold, barring special circumstances.

The presence or absence of a security on the approved list constitutes the major information transmitted explicitly from the investment committee to a **portfolio manager**. In some organizations, senior management supervises a "model portfolio" (for example, a bank's major commingled equity fund), the composition of which indicates to portfolio managers the relative intensity of senior management's feelings regarding different securities.

In many ways, this description is a caricature of an investment organization—even one run along traditional lines. Nevertheless, most of these attributes can be observed in practice in one form or another.

In recent years, specialty investment firms have gained considerable popularity. As opposed to traditional investment firms that invest in a broad spectrum of securities, these organizations concentrate their investment efforts on a particular asset class, such as stocks or bonds. They often specialize even further, focusing on a narrow segment of a particular asset class, such as the stocks of small start-up companies.

Although these specialty investment firms may follow many of the security analysis procedures of the traditional investment organizations, they usually employ few security analysts. Often the portfolio managers serve jointly as analysts. Furthermore, their decision-making processes are typically more streamlined, often avoiding investment committee structures entirely, thereby permitting portfolio managers considerable discretion to research securities and construct portfolios. Whether this less hierarchical approach to investing actually produces superior results is open to question.

23.2 INVESTMENT MANAGEMENT FUNCTIONS

In Chapter 1 a five-step procedure was outlined for making investment decisions. These steps can all be viewed as functions of investment management, and they must be undertaken for each client whose money is being managed. They are as follows:

1. *Set investment policy.* Identify the client's investment objectives, particularly as regards his or her attitude toward the tradeoff between expected return and risk.
2. *Perform security analysis.* Scrutinize individual securities or groups of securities in order to identify mispriced situations.
3. *Construct a portfolio.* Identify specific securities in which to invest, along with the proportion of investable wealth to be put into each security.
4. *Revise the portfolio.* Determine which securities in the current portfolio are to be sold and which securities are to be purchased to replace them.
5. *Evaluate the performance of the portfolio.* Determine the actual performance of a portfolio in terms of risk and return, and compare the performance with that of an appropriate "benchmark" portfolio.

The remainder of this chapter deals with how an investment management organization could perform the first four functions; the next chapter deals with the fifth function.

23.3 SETTING INVESTMENT POLICY

An investment manager who is in charge of a client's entire portfolio must be concerned with the client's risk-return preferences. Investors who use more than one manager can select one to help in this important phase, or they may employ the services of a consultant or financial planner. In any event, one of the key characteristics that differentiates clients from one another concerns their investment objectives. These objectives are reflected in the client's attitude toward risk and expected return. As discussed in Chapter 6, specifying indifference curves is one method of describing these objectives. However, determining a client's indifference curves is not a simple task. In practice, it can be done in an indirect and approximate fashion by estimating the client's level of **risk tolerance**, defined as the largest amount of risk that the client is willing to accept for a given increase in expected return.

23.3.1 Estimating Risk Tolerance

The starting point in making such an estimation is to provide the client with a set of risks and expected returns for different combinations of two hypothetical portfolios. For example, imagine that the client is told that the expected return on a stock portfolio is 12%, while the return on a riskfree portfolio consisting of Treasury bills is 7.5% (that is, $\bar{r}_S = 12\%$ and $r_f = 7.5\%$). Similarly, the client is told that the standard

TABLE 23.1 Combinations of Stock and Riskfree Treasury Bill Portfolios

Proportion In		Expected Return	Standard Deviation	Implied Level of Risk Tolerance
Stock	Bills			
0%	100%	7.50%	0.0%	0
10	90	7.95	1.5	10
20	80	8.40	3.0	20
30	70	8.85	4.5	30
40	60	9.30	6.0	40
50	50	9.75	7.5	50
60	40	10.20	9.0	60
70	30	10.65	10.5	70
80	20	11.10	12.0	80
90	10	11.55	13.5	90
100	0	12.00	15.0	100
110	−10	12.45	16.5	110
120	−20	12.90	18.0	120
130	−30	13.35	19.5	130
140	−40	13.80	21.0	140
150	−50	14.25	22.5	150

deviation of the stock portfolio is 15%, while the standard deviation of the riskfree portfolio is, by definition, 0.0% (that is, $\sigma_S = 15\%$ and $\sigma_f = 0.0\%$).[2] In addition, the client is told that all combinations of these two portfolios lie on a straight line that connects them. (The reason is that the covariance between these two portfolios is 0.0, meaning that $\sigma_{Sf} = 0.0$.) Some combinations of these two portfolios are shown in Table 23.1.

Note that the investor is being presented with the efficient set that arises when there is a set of stocks and a riskfree borrowing and lending rate. As shown in Chapter 8, this efficient set is linear, meaning that it is a straight line that emanates at the riskfree rate and goes through a tangency portfolio that consists of a certain combination of securities. (In this case those securities are common stocks.) Hence negative percentages in Treasury bills (shown at the bottom of Table 23.1) represent riskfree borrowing in order to purchase greater amounts of stocks.

At this point, the client is asked to identify the combination that appears to be most desirable, in terms of expected return and standard deviation. Note that asking the investor to identify the most desirable combination is equivalent to asking the investor to locate where one of his or her indifference curves is tangent to the linear efficient set; this point will represent the most desirable portfolio.[3]

After the client has selected the best mix of stocks and Treasury bills, what can be said about his or her risk tolerance? One would, of course, like to identify all the indifference curves that represent a client's attitude toward risk and expected return. However, in practice a more modest goal is usually adopted: to obtain a reasonable representation of the shape of such curves in the region of risk and expected return within which the client's optimal choices will most likely fall.

The points in Figure 23.2 plot the alternative mixes presented to the client that were given in Table 23.1. Curve *fCS* shows the risk-return characteristics of all possible mixes, and point *C* identifies the attributes of the mix chosen by the client. Note

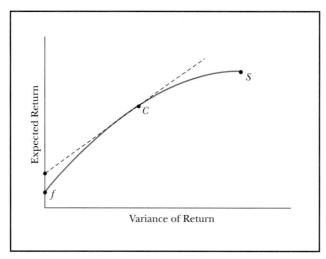

Figure 23.2
Inferring Client Risk Tolerance.

that in this figure expected return is measured on the vertical axis and *variance* on the horizontal axis. Although the combinations available to the client plot on a straight line when standard deviation is measured on the horizontal axis, the combinations plot on a concave curve when variance is used (as in this figure).

If all the possible mixes have been presented to the client and point *C* has been chosen, it can be inferred that the slope of the client's indifference curve going through *C* is precisely equal to that of curve *fCS* at this point. As mentioned earlier, this inference follows from the observation that the portfolio on the efficient set that a client identifies as being the "best" corresponds to the one where the client's indifference curves are just tangent to the efficient set.

23.3.2   Constant Risk Tolerance

In principle, the choice of a mix provides information about the slope of an indifference curve at only one point. To go beyond this inference, the analyst must make an assumption about the general shape of the client's indifference curves. An assumption commonly made is that the client has constant risk tolerance over a range of alternative portfolios in the neighborhood of the point originally chosen. Figure 23.3 shows the nature of this assumption. As indicated in panel (a), indifference curves in a diagram with variance on the horizontal axis are linear when it is assumed that the client has *constant risk tolerance*. This means that the equation for an indifference curve of such an investor is equivalent to the equation for a straight line, where the variable on the horizontal axis is variance $\left(\sigma_p^2\right)$ and the variable on the vertical axis is expected return $\left(\bar{r}_p\right)$. Given that the equation of a straight line takes the form of $Y = a + bX$, where a is the vertical intercept and b is the slope, the equation for an indifference curve can be written as:

$$\bar{r}_p = a + b\sigma_p^2$$

or:

$$\bar{r}_p = u_i + \frac{1}{\tau}\sigma_p^2 \tag{23.1}$$

where u_i is the vertical intercept for indifference curve i and the slope of the indifference curve is $1/\tau$.[4] Any two indifference curves for a client differ from one another

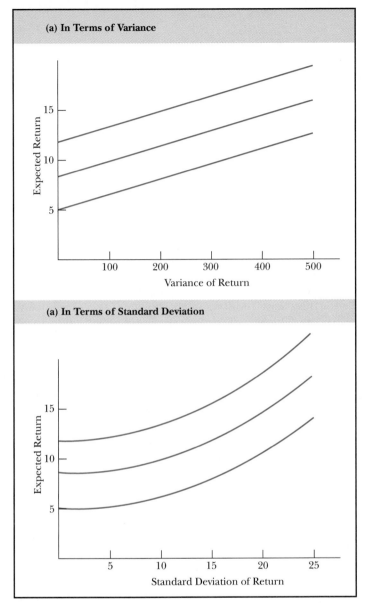

(a) In Terms of Variance

Expected Return (vertical axis): 5, 10, 15

Variance of Return (horizontal axis): 100, 200, 300, 400, 500

(a) In Terms of Standard Deviation

Expected Return (vertical axis): 5, 10, 15

Standard Deviation of Return (horizontal axis): 5, 10, 15, 20, 25

Figure 23.3
Constant Risk Tolerance

only by the value of the vertical intercept because the indifference curves are parallel, meaning that they have the same slope, $1/\tau$.

Figure 23.3(b) plots the same indifference curves in a more familiar manner—with standard deviation on the horizontal axis. Note that the curves have the conventional shape; they indicate that the investor requires more return to compensate for an additional unit of standard deviation as the risk of the portfolio increases. That is, the curves are convex when standard deviation is measured on the horizontal axis.

In the estimation of the client's level of risk tolerance τ, as was mentioned, the slope of the indifference curve, $1/\tau$, would be set equal to the slope of the efficient set at the location of the portfolio that was selected, denoted portfolio *C*. Doing so results in the following formula for estimating τ:

$$\tau = \frac{2\left[(\bar{r}_C - r_f)\sigma_S^2\right]}{(\bar{r}_S - r_f)^2} \tag{23.2}$$

where $\bar{r}_C$ denotes the expected return of the portfolio that the client selected, $\bar{r}_S$ and r_f denote the expected return of the stock portfolio and riskfree rate, respectively, and σ_S^2 denotes the variance of the stock portfolio. (A detailed presentation of how this formula was derived is presented in the appendix.)

In the example, the client was given a choice between S, f, and various combinations of S and f where $\bar{r}_S = 12\%$, $r_f = 7.5\%$, and $\sigma_S^2 = 15^2 = 225$. Now, by using Equation (23.2), the level of risk tolerance τ inferred from the choice of portfolio C can be determined to equal:

$$\tau = \frac{2\left[(\bar{r}_C - 7.5)225\right]}{(12 - 7.5)^2} \tag{23.3}$$

$$= 22.22\,\bar{r}_C - 166.67$$

Assuming the choice of a portfolio consisting of a 50% investment in stocks and a 50% investment in riskfree Treasury bills, the client in this example has chosen a portfolio C with an expected return of 9.75%. Accordingly, Equation (23.3) can be used to determine the value of τ for this client, resulting in an estimated level of τ equal to $50 = (22.22 \times 9.75) - 166.67$. This means that the client will accept up to an additional 50 units of variance, in order to receive an extra 1% in expected return. Thus, the client's indifference curves are estimated to have the form of:

$$\bar{r}_p = u_i + \frac{1}{50}\,\sigma_p^2 \tag{23.4}$$

Table 23.1 shows the inferred level of risk tolerance if a different portfolio had been chosen by the client [these levels were determined by substituting the appropriate values for $\bar{r}_C$ into the right-hand side of Equation (23.3) and then solving for τ]. First, note that the level of risk tolerance is the same as the percentage invested in the stock portfolio associated with C. That is, Equation (23.3) can be rewritten as $\tau = 100X_S$, where X_S is the proportion invested in the stock portfolio associated with C. It can be shown that this will always be the case when $\bar{r}_S - r_f = 4.5\%$ and $\sigma_S = 15\%$. Other estimates would give different expressions for τ, but the relationship between X_S and τ would still be linear.

Second, note that the level of risk tolerance is lower if the selected portfolio is more conservative (that is, when the selected level of expected return and standard deviation is lower). Thus more conservative risk-averse clients will have lower levels of risk tolerance (and thus steeper indifference curves) than less conservative risk-averse clients.

Having estimated the client's indifference curves, recall from Chapter 6 that the objective of investment management is to identify the portfolio that lies on the indifference curve farthest to the northwest because such a portfolio will offer the investor the level of expected return and risk that is preferable to what is offered by all the other portfolios. Identifying this portfolio is the same as identifying the portfolio that lies on the indifference curve that has the highest vertical intercept, u_i. This equivalence can be seen graphically in both panels of Figure 23.3, where the indifference curves have been extended to the vertical axis.

23.3.3 Certainty Equivalent Return

The term u_i can be thought of as the **certainty equivalent return** for any portfolio that lies on indifference curve i.[5] Thus portfolio C in Figure 23.2 is as desirable for this particular client as a hypothetical portfolio with an expected return of u_i and no risk—that is, one providing a return of u_i with certainty. When viewed in this manner, the job of the portfolio manager is to identify the portfolio with the highest certainty equivalent return.

Equation (23.1) can be rewritten so that the certainty equivalent return u_i appears on the left-hand side. Doing so results in:

$$u_i = \bar{r}_p - \frac{1}{\tau} \sigma_p^2 \qquad (23.5)$$

This equation shows that the certainty equivalent return can be thought of as a risk-adjusted expected return because a risk penalty that depends on both the portfolio's variance and the client's risk tolerance must be subtracted from the portfolio's expected return in determining u_i.

In the example, the investor selected the portfolio with $\bar{r}_p = 9.75\%$ and $\sigma_p^2 = 56.25(\ = 7.5^2)$. Thus the certainty equivalent return for this portfolio is 8.625% $\left[= 9.75 - (56.25/50)\right]$. Equivalently, the *risk penalty* for the portfolio that was selected was 1.125% $(=56.25/50)$. If the certainty equivalent return for any other portfolio shown in Table 23.1 is calculated, it will have a lower value $\{\left[\text{for example, the } 80/20 \text{ portfolio has a certainty equivalent return of } 8.22\% \left[= 11.1 - (144/50)\right]\right]\}$. Thus the goal of investment management can be thought of as identifying the portfolio that has the maximum value of $\bar{r}_p - (\sigma_p^2/\tau)$, because it will provide the client with the maximum certainty equivalent return.

23.4 SECURITY ANALYSIS AND PORTFOLIO CONSTRUCTION

23.4.1 Passive and Active Management

Within the investment industry, a distinction is often made between **passive management**—holding securities for relatively long periods with small and infrequent changes—and **active management.** Passive managers generally act as if the security markets are relatively efficient. Put somewhat differently, their decisions are consistent with the acceptance of consensus estimates of risk and return. The portfolios they hold may be surrogates for the market portfolio that are known as **index funds**, or they may be portfolios that are tailored to suit clients with preferences and circumstances that differ from those of the average investor.[6] In either case, passive portfolio managers do not try to outperform their designated benchmarks.

For example, a passive manager might only have to choose the appropriate mixture of Treasury bills and an index fund that is a surrogate for the market portfolio. The best mixture would depend on the shape and location of the client's indifference curves. Figure 23.4 provides an illustration.

Point f plots the riskfree return offered by Treasury bills, and point M plots the risk and expected return of the surrogate market portfolio, using consensus forecasts. Mixtures of the two investments plot along line fM. The client's attitude toward risk and return is shown by the set of indifference curves, and the optimal mixture of f and M lies at the point O^*, where an indifference curve is tangent to line fM. In this example, the best mixture uses both Treasury bills and the surrogate market portfolio. In other situations, the surrogate market portfolio might be "levered up" by borrowing (that is, money might be borrowed and added to the client's own investable funds, with the total being used to purchase the surrogate market portfolio).

When management is passive, the optimal mixture is altered only when:

- the client's preferences change; or
- the riskfree rate changes; or
- the consensus forecast about the risk and return of the benchmark portfolio changes.

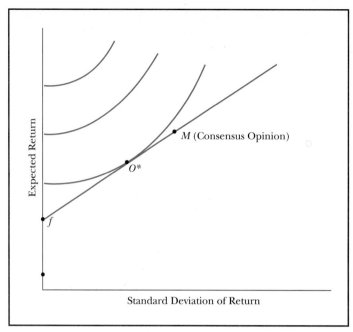

Figure 23.4
Passive Investment Management

The manager must continue to monitor the last two variables and keep in touch with the client concerning the first one. No additional activity is required.

Active managers believe that from time to time there are mispriced securities or groups of securities. They do not act as if they believe that security markets are efficient. Put somewhat differently, they use deviant predictions; that is, their forecasts of risks and expected returns differ from consensus opinions. Whereas some managers may be more bullish than average about a security, others may be more bearish. The former will hold "more-than-normal" proportions of the security; the latter will hold "less-than-normal" proportions.

It is useful to think of a portfolio as having two components: (1) a benchmark portfolio and (2) deviations designed to take advantage of security mispricing. For example, a portfolio can be broken down as follows:

Name of Security (1)	Proportion in Actual Portfolio (2)	Proportion in Benchmark Portfolio (3)	Active Position (4)
S1	.30	.45	−.15
S2	.20	.25	−.05
S3	.50	.30	+.20
	1.00	1.00	.00

The second column shows the actual proportions in the actively managed portfolio. The third column indicates the percentages in a benchmark portfolio. The **active positions** can be represented by the differences between the proportions in the actual and benchmark portfolios. Such differences arise because active managers disagree with the consensus forecast about expected returns or risks. When expressed as differences of this sort, the actual portfolio can be viewed as an investment in the benchmark portfolio with a series of *bets* being placed on certain securities (such as *S3*) and against certain other securities (such as $S1$ and $S2$). Note that the bets are "balanced" in that the amount of the negative bets exactly counters the amount of the positive bets.

23.4.2 Security Selection, Asset Allocation, and Market Timing

Security Selection

In principle, the investment manager should make forecasts of expected returns, standard deviations, and covariances for all available securities. These forecasts will allow an efficient set to be generated, upon which the indifference curves of the client can be plotted. The investment manager should then invest in those securities that form the optimal portfolio (that is, the portfolio indicated by the point at which an indifference curve is tangent to the efficient set) for the client in question. Such a one-stage **security selection** process is illustrated in Figure 23.5(a).

In practice, this is rarely (if ever) done. Excessive costs would be incurred to obtain detailed forecasts of the expected returns, standard deviations, and covariances for all the individual securities under consideration. Instead, the decision on which securities to purchase is made in two or more stages.

Figure 23.5(b) illustrates a two-stage procedure in which the investment manager has decided to consider investing in common stocks and corporate bonds for a client. In this case, the expected returns, standard deviations, and covariances are forecast for all common stocks under consideration. Then, on the basis of just these common stocks, the efficient set is formed and the optimal stock portfolio identified. Next the same analysis is performed for all corporate bonds under consideration, resulting in the identification of the optimal bond portfolio. The security selection process used in each of these two **asset classes** can be described as being myopic. That is, covariances between the individual common stocks and corporate bonds have not been considered in the identification of the two optimal portfolios.

Although this example has only two asset classes—stocks and bonds—the number of asset classes can be relatively large. Other asset classes that are often used consist of money market securities ("cash"), foreign stocks, foreign bonds, venture capital, and real estate.

Asset Allocation

The second stage of the process divides the client's funds among two (or more) asset class portfolios and is known as **asset allocation**.[7] In this stage, forecasts of the expected return and standard deviation are needed for both the optimal stock portfolio and the optimal bond portfolio, along with the covariance between the two portfolios. This information will allow the expected return and standard deviation to be determined for all combinations of these two portfolios. Finally, after the efficient set has been generated, the indifference curves of the client can be used to determine which portfolio should be chosen.[8]

Some people refer to two types of asset allocation. *Strategic asset allocation* refers to how a portfolio's funds would be divided, given the portfolio manager's long-term forecasts of expected returns, variances, and covariances, whereas *tactical asset allocation* refers to how these funds are to be divided at any particular moment, given the investor's short-term forecasts. Hence the former reflects what the portfolio manager would do for the long term, and the latter reflects what he or she would do under current market conditions.

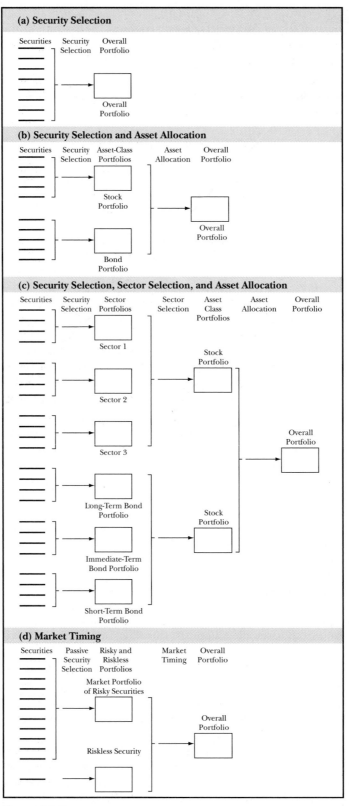

Figure 23.5
Investment Styles

For example, the first stage might have indicated that the investor should hold the proportions of stocks $S1$, $S2$, and $S3$ given earlier (that is, the optimal stock portfolio has proportions of .30, .20, and .50, respectively). Similarly, the first stage might have indicated that the investor should hold a proportion of .35 in bond $B1$ and .65 in bond $B2$. Then under tactical asset allocation, the second stage might indicate that the client's funds should be split so that 60% goes into stocks and 40% into bonds because of current market conditions (whereas under strategic asset allocation these percentages might have been 70% and 30%, respectively). This decision translates into individual investments of the following magnitudes:

Stocks	
$S1$	$.60 \times .30 = .18$
$S2$	$.60 \times .20 = .12$
$S3$	$.60 \times .50 = .30$
Bonds	
$B1$	$.40 \times .35 = .14$
$B2$	$.40 \times .65 = .26$
	1.00

The two-stage process just discussed can be extended by introducing **sectors**. Figure 23.5(c) illustrates a three-stage process. In the first stage, known as security selection, the investment manager would exercise discretion in identifying sectors of securities in each asset class. Then having identified the sectors, the investment manager would determine the optimal portfolio for each one. For example, within the asset class of common stocks, it could be that the investment manager has identified all industrial stocks as the first sector, all utility stocks as the second sector, and all transportation stocks as the third sector. Within the asset class of bonds, sectors of long-term, intermediate-term, and short-term bonds have been identified. Then, the investment manager would proceed to identify six optimal portfolios, one for each sector of securities.

In the second stage, known as **sector selection** (or sector rotation), the investment manager determines the appropriate combination of sectors within each asset class. For example, the manager may have decided that the appropriate combination is 70% industrials, 10% utilities, and 20% transportation stocks. Similarly, the manager may have decided that the appropriate combination of bonds is 100% in long-term, with nothing in either intermediate-term or short-term bonds. Thus in this stage the manager will determine the composition of an optimal stock portfolio and an optimal bond portfolio but will not know how much to allocate to each one.

The third and final stage makes this allocation and, as noted previously, is referred to as asset allocation. It is performed in a manner that is identical to the second stage of the two-stage procedure illustrated in Figure 23.5(b).

Active or passive management may be used in any stage. For example, *active bets* might be placed on individual securities but with funds allocated among asset classes on the basis of consensus long-term forecasts of expected returns for such classes. That is, the investment manager may decide to stick to a long-term mix of 70% stocks and 30% bonds. However, the choice of individual stocks and bonds in which to invest will change with time on the basis of the manager's forecasts.

Alternatively, passive portfolios of individual securities might be constructed, with deviant predictions of asset class returns used to allocate funds actively among the asset classes. For example, the investment manager may decide to always hold common stocks in the same relative proportions they have in the S&P 500, which is often used as a surrogate for the U.S. stock market portfolio. However, the proportion of funds invested in the S&P 500 will change at the start of every period, on the

Evaluating Investment Systems

Institutional investors are constantly in search of the holy grail: an investment system that can produce high returns with low risk and without the expense of retaining a team of skilled analysts. This search has led down many and varied paths. Over the years, numerous individuals and organizations have claimed to have developed mechanical investment systems that use only available historical data and a set of objective analytical procedures to produce results superior to passive management. Some mechanical systems simply provide predictions of how the market will behave; others prescribe a complete set of instructions for investing in individual securities. Almost all of them present impressive statistics based on tests using data from some past evaluation period.

Advocates of such mechanical investment systems may sincerely believe that they have found the path to instant affluence. However, their proofs often rest on shaky ground. In the evaluation of any system, it is imperative that several possible errors be avoided.

Failure to Adjust for Risk.   Any investment system that results in the selection of high-beta stocks is likely to produce above-average returns in bull markets and below-average returns in bear markets. Because the stock market over the long term has trended upward, on balance such a system will tend to produce above-average returns over the long run (as will systems that involve purchasing either small-capitalization stocks or stocks with high book-to-market ratios; see Chapter 16). Therefore, an evaluation of the performance of any investment system should involve not only measuring the resulting average return but also determining the amount of risk incurred. Then the average return from a passive management benchmark of similar risk can be computed for comparison. Techniques for making such comparisons are presented in Chapter 24.

Failure to Consider Transaction Costs.   Systems that rely on frequent, high-volume trading may produce *gross* returns that exceed those of a similar risk passive management benchmark. However, if transaction costs have not been included in the analysis, the results may be invalid. *Net* returns are calculated by adding transaction costs to the purchase price of an investment and deducting them from the investment's selling price. After inclusion of realistic transaction costs, most high-turnover investment systems produce negative risk-adjusted performance.

Failure to Consider Dividends.   When the performance of a mechanical system is compared with that of a passive management benchmark, dividends (and interest payments) are often ignored. Failure to consider dividends may seriously bias the results. For example, a system may be advocated that, in effect, selects low-yield stocks. The prices of such stocks should increase at a faster rate than those of high-yield stocks with the same amount of risk because a stock's return consists of both dividends and capital appreciation. Two stocks with the same risk should have the same return, meaning that the stock with a smaller yield will have a larger capital appreciation. Thus if just capital appreciation is examined, a system that selects low-yield stocks would tend to show a more rapid rate of capital appreciation than a passive management benchmark involving a well-diversified portfolio consisting of both low- and high-yield stocks. Consequently, when yields of systems differ significantly from average yields, it is important to examine *total* returns, not just the rate of capital appreciation.

Non-operational Systems.   Although obvious, it still must be mentioned: To be useful, a system must not require knowledge about the future. For example, many systems require action after some time series of values (such as a stock's price) has reached a "peak" or a "trough." But it is rarely apparent until well afterward that in fact a peak or trough has been reached. Hence such a system is non-operational. Similarly, an investigator might use a database prepared

basis of the overall prognosis for the stock and bond markets. Thus during one period the manager may have as much as 100% of the client's funds in stocks, on the strong belief that the stock market is going to rise rapidly in the near future. Conversely, during another period the manager may have as much as 100% of the client's funds in bonds on the strong belief that the stock market will soon decline sharply.

Market Timing

Figure 23.5(d) portrays a manager following an investment style that is known as **market timing**. The only active decision concerns the appropriate allocation of funds

in 1998 with stock price data relating to the period from 1987 through 1997. The stocks included in the database may have been chosen because they existed and were important in 1998 (for example, they may have been considered important because they were listed on the NYSE in 1998). A superior investment system based on an analysis of this database is a type of non-operational system involving **ex post selection bias** (or survivorship bias). That is, the system discovered in 1998 was based on an analysis of those stocks that were certain to be alive and important in 1998. Accordingly, it should have done well over the period of 1987 to 1997. However, these systems require some information not available in advance. In particular, they require knowledge before 1998 of which stocks will be around in 1998.

Spurious Fits. When a set of data from a past period is used, it is not difficult to discover a investment system that works quite well when tested on the same data. One simply has to test enough systems. However, this does not mean that it would be useful to the investor. If 100 seemingly irrelevant systems are tried with a set of data, owing to the laws of probability one of them is likely to give results that are "statistically significant at the 1% level." This result should not cause undue excitement because it would not necessarily have any notable predictive power in the future. For example, stock prices in the United States have been shown to be correlated with both sunspot activity and the length of skirts. However, these correlations are unlikely to demonstrate actual causal relationships. Instead, they are likely to have been "spurious," meaning that they probably were coincidental. Without solid reasons to believe that a relationship is due to underlying forces, it would be unwise to predict its continuation in the future.

Reliance on Misleading Visual Comparisons. Occasionally the proponent of a system will produce a graph that plots both the level of an indicator intended to predict market moves and the levels of the market itself. Visual comparison of the two curves may suggest that the indicator does indeed predict changes in the market. However, the eye cannot easily differentiate between a situation in which changes in a market "predictor" *lead* the market and one in which the changes *lag* behind the market. This is a crucial distinction because only a leading indicator can bring superior investment performance.

Failure to Use Out-of-Sample Data. Can any evidence concerning a system's ability to beat the market be persuasive? Probably not to those who believe absolutely in market efficiency. But there are appropriate tests that can be undertaken. The search for a system should be conducted using one set of data, and the test of the system's predictive ability should be performed using an entirely different set of data. The latter set of data is sometimes known as **out-of-sample data**, or a holdout sample. To be complete, such a test should involve the (simulated) management of a portfolio and be designed so that each investment decision is based solely on information available at the time the decision is made. Finally, the performance of the system should be evaluated in the way one would evaluate the performance of any investment manager (to be discussed in Chapter 24). This evaluation involves, among other things, attempting to determine the probability that the investment results were due to chance rather than skill.

Despite the increasing popularity of passive management, the search for successful investment systems will continue. As always the most useful advice to investors considering such systems is *caveat emptor* (buyer beware). Checking for the errors described above will make for more intelligent evaluations of prospective investment systems.

between a surrogate market portfolio (usually consisting of either stocks or long-term bonds) and a riskfree asset, such as Treasury bills. An investment organization following this style changes its mixture of risky and riskfree assets on the basis of its own forecasts of the risk and expected return of "the market" relative to the riskfree rate, even if there is no change in consensus forecasts or in the client's attitude toward risk and return.

Investment organizations that engage in the type of management that places active bets on individual securities are said to have a *security selection style*. Those that engage in the type of management that places active bets on asset classes are said to have an *asset allocation style*, with market timing being one specific example. Last, investment organizations that place active bets on certain sectors of securities are said to employ a *sector rotation style*. Some organizations use relatively pure **investment styles**, meaning that they use basically just one of the three styles previously mentioned. Others employ various combinations, making it difficult to classify them into neat categories.

Although these styles have been described in terms of capital market theory, it should be pointed out that other procedures could be used to implement them. For example, capital market theory states that an optimal stock portfolio [as in Figure 23.5(b)] is to be identified by use of forecast expected returns, standard deviations, and covariances in conjunction with indifference curves. Once it has been identified, the portfolio manager will have determined the appropriate relative investments in individual common stocks. However, such an identification could be made using some other procedure. Often it is done on a much less formal and more qualitative basis.

23.4.3 International Investing

An interesting extension of the previous discussion of investment styles involves international investing (which is the subject of Chapter 25). Consider security selection first. This style, when applied internationally, would involve determining the efficient set associated with a number of stocks found around the world. Alternatively, a security selection style could be combined with an asset allocation style. For example, the portfolio manager could first determine the optimal portfolios associated with just Japanese stocks, just U.S. stocks, and just German stocks. Then, using these optimal portfolios, the manager would decide how much to allocate to each of the three countries.

Imagine that the optimal Japanese portfolio consisted of two stocks, J_1 and J_2, in proportions of 70% and 30%, respectively, and half of the portfolio's funds were to be devoted to Japanese stocks. As a result, 35% ($=.50 \times 70\%$) would be invested in J_1 and 15% ($=.50 \times 30\%$) in J_2. Similar calculations could be done for the sets of U.S. and German stocks.

Analogous procedures to those previously described could be followed for the security selection, sector rotation, asset allocation, and market timing styles in an international setting. However, the issue of foreign currency risk adds a confounding element to this comparison.[9]

23.5   PORTFOLIO REVISION

With the passage of time, a previously purchased portfolio that is currently held will often be viewed as suboptimal by the investment manager, meaning that the portfolio is no longer viewed as the best one for the client. Either the weights in the different securities have changed as their market prices have changed, or the client's attitude toward risk and return has changed or, more likely, the manager's forecasts have changed. In response, the manager could identify a new optimal portfolio and then make the necessary revisions to the current portfolio so that subsequently the new optimal portfolio will be held. However, this process is not as straightforward as it might seem at first because transaction costs will have to be paid when any revisions are made. Such costs must be compared with the perceived benefits associated with the revision in order to determine what course of action to take.

23.5.1 Cost-Benefit Analysis

Transaction costs were discussed in Chapter 3. They include brokerage commissions, price impacts, and bid-ask spreads. A security would have to increase in value by a certain amount just to pay these costs in order to leave the investor neither better nor worse off. This necessary increase in value may exceed 1% for many securities and can range as high as 5% to 10% or more for others, particularly small stocks.

The existence of transaction costs greatly complicates the life of any investment manager, and the more active the manager, the greater the complications. The hoped-for advantage of any revision must be weighed against the cost of making that revision. That is, a revision can be viewed as bringing certain kinds of benefits; either it will increase the expected return of the portfolio or it will reduce the standard deviation of the portfolio, or it will do both. To be weighed against these benefits are the transaction costs that will be incurred if the revision is made. As a result, some of the revisions in the holdings of individual securities that the manager may initially want to make will be dropped from consideration because of the transaction costs involved. The goal of the manager is to identify the set of individual revisions that collectively maximizes the improvement, after transaction costs, in the risk-return characteristics of the current portfolio.

Identifying the appropriate set of individual revisions requires sophisticated procedures (for example, quadratic programming) to compare the relevant costs and benefits. Fortunately, improvements in procedures and dramatic decreases in computing costs have made such approaches economically feasible for many investment managers.

In some situations investors may find it economically more attractive to revise their portfolios by transacting in entire asset classes instead of individual securities. Buying or selling futures contracts (see Chapter 20) on stock market indices or Treasury bonds is one such approach.[10] A potentially more flexible strategy makes use of the swaps market.

23.5.2 Swaps

Consider a situation in which a portfolio manager wants to make major changes in the proportions of funds that are invested in different asset classes. He or she recognizes that substantial transaction costs will be incurred if the traditional method of selling certain securities and replacing them with others is used to make the changes. Indeed, these costs can be so large that most of the changes, if conducted in this manner, should not be made. One relatively new method that has become very popular in allowing such changes to be made at relatively low transaction costs involves the use of swaps.[11]

Although the unique features of swaps can become quite complicated, their general nature is quite simple. Such "plain-vanilla" swaps are contracts that typically involve two parties (in the language of swaps the two parties are referred to as *counterparties*) exchanging sets of cash flows over a predetermined period of time.[12] Two types of swaps—equity and interest rate—are considered here.

Equity Swaps

With an **equity swap**, one counterparty agrees to pay a second counterparty a stream of variable-size cash payments that is based on the rate of return of an agreed-upon stock market index. In return, the second counterparty agrees to pay the first counterparty a stream of fixed-size cash payments that is based on current interest rates.

Both sets of payments are to be made for a given time period and are based on a certain percentage (the percentage is variable for one counterparty and fixed for the other) of an underlying *notional principal.* Through an equity swap the first counterparty has, in essence, sold stocks and bought bonds while the second counterparty has sold bonds and bought stocks. Both of them have effectively restructured their portfolios without having to pay any transaction costs, other than a relatively small fee to a **swap bank** (usually a commercial or investment bank) that set up the contract.

Consider the example that is shown in Figure 23.6(a). Ms. Bright, a pension fund manager, thinks that the stock market is going to move upward sharply in the next three years. In contrast, Mr. Gloom, who also runs a pension fund, thinks that the stock market is likely to move downward in the next three years. Ms. Bright is considering selling $100 million of bonds and investing the proceeds in common stocks, whereas Mr. Gloom is thinking of selling $100 million of common stocks and using the proceeds to purchase bonds. However, both portfolio managers realize that such changes will involve the payment of substantial transaction costs. Consequently, both of them contact a swap bank.

The swap bank sets up the following contract for Ms. Bright and Mr. Gloom. Shortly after the end of each quarter Mr. Gloom is to pay Ms. Bright an amount that is equal to the rate of return on the S&P 500 for the quarter times the notional principal. At the same time, Ms. Bright is to pay Mr. Gloom an amount that is equal to 2% of the notional principal. Both Ms. Bright and Mr. Gloom agree that the notional principal will be equal to $100 million and that the contract will last for three years. Each pays the swap bank a relatively small fee for setting up the contract.

Imagine that the quarterly rates of return on the S&P 500 during the first year of the swap contract are equal to 3%, −4%, 1%, and 5%, as shown in Figure 23.6(b). Ms. Bright must pay $2 million (=.02 × $100 million) to Mr. Gloom each quarter; in return, Mr. Gloom must pay Ms. Bright the following amounts:

First quarter:	.03 × $100 million = $3 million
Second quarter:	−.04 × $100 million = −$4 million
Third quarter:	.01 × $100 million = $1 million
Fourth quarter:	.05 × $100 million = $5 million

(a) The Contract

(b) The Cash Flows

		Ms. Bright's Cash Flows*			Mr. Gloom's Cash Flows*		
Quarter	S&P 500 Return	Payment from Gloom	Payment to Gloom	Net	Payment from Bright	Payment to Bright	Net
First	3%	$3	$2	$1	$2	$3	−$1
Second	−4	−4	2	−6	2	−4	6
Third	1	1	2	−1	2	1	1
Fourth	5	5	2	3	2	5	−3

* All cash flows are in millions as the notional principal is $100 million.

Figure 23.6
Equity Swap

Hence it appears that in the first quarter Ms. Bright pays $2 million to Mr. Gloom and in return Mr. Gloom pays $3 million to Ms. Bright. However, the way the contract is structured, only the net amount is paid; in this case, Mr. Gloom will pay $1 million (=$3 million − $2 million) to Ms. Bright. In the second quarter it appears that Mr. Gloom must pay −$4 million to Ms. Bright. What the minus sign means is that Ms. Bright must pay Mr. Gloom $4 million plus the fixed payment of $2 million, for a total payment of $6 million. In the third period, Ms. Bright must pay Mr. Gloom $1 million (=$2 million − $1 million), and in the fourth quarter Mr. Gloom must pay Ms. Bright $3 million (=$5 million − $2 million). In summary, the net payments are:

First quarter:	Mr. Gloom pays $1 million to Ms. Bright
Second quarter:	Ms. Bright pays $6 million to Mr. Gloom
Third quarter:	Ms. Bright pays $1 million to Mr. Gloom
Fourth quarter:	Mr. Gloom pays $3 million to Ms. Bright

These amounts reflect what would have happened (roughly) if Mr. Gloom had sold stocks and bought bonds and Ms. Bright had sold bonds and bought stocks, and both had incurred relatively low transaction costs. Consider the first quarter. If Mr. Gloom had sold the stocks and replaced them with 2% bonds, he would have earned $2 million. Instead, he kept the stocks and earned $3 million on them (remember that the S&P 500 went up 3%) but had to pay Ms. Bright a net amount of $1 million, leaving him with $2 million, the same amount.[13]

There are many ways that equity swaps can be modified. For example, a foreign stock market index such as the Nikkei 225 could be used instead of the S&P 500. Using this index would allow one counterparty to cheaply achieve the benefits of international diversification. Alternatively, the swap could involve two stock market indices, say, a large stock index such as the S&P 500 and a small stock index such as the Russell 2000. There are many other variations, limited only by investors' imaginations and their ability to periodically determine the value of the swaps.

Interest Rate Swaps

With an **interest rate swap**, one counterparty agrees to pay a second party a stream of cash payments whose size is reset regularly on the basis of the current level of a highly visible interest rate. A popular one is the London Interbank Offered Rate (LIBOR), which is an interest rate set daily in London that applies to loans made among large international banks. In return, the second counterparty agrees to pay the first counterparty a stream of fixed-size cash payments that is based on the level of interest rates in existence at the time the contract is signed. As in equity swaps, both sets of payments are to be made for a certain number of years and are based on a certain percentage of an underlying notional principal. (The percentage is variable—or "floating"—for one counterparty and fixed for the other.) Through the interest rate swap the first counterparty has, in essence, sold short-term fixed-income securities and bought long-term bonds while the second counterparty has sold these bonds and bought the short-term fixed-income securities. As in equity swaps, both of them have effectively restructured their portfolios without having to pay any transaction costs other than a relatively small fee to a swap bank that set up the contract.

Consider the example that is shown in Figure 23.7(a). Ms. Uppe, a fixed-income mutual fund manager, thinks that interest rates are going to move upward in the near future. In contrast, Mr. Downe, who also runs a fixed-income mutual fund, thinks that interest rates are likely to soon move downward. Consequently, Ms. Uppe is considering selling $100 million of long-term bonds and investing the proceeds in money market securities, whereas Mr. Downe is thinking of selling $100 million of

		Ms. Uppe's Cash Flows*			Mr. Downe's Cash Flows*		
Quarter	LIBOR	Payment from Downe	Payment to Downe	Net	Payment from Uppe	Payment to Uppe	Net
First	1.5%	$1.5	$2	–$.5	$2	$1.5	$.5
Second	1.8	1.8	2	–.2	2	1.8	.2
Third	2.1	2.1	2	.1	2	2.1	–.1
Fourth	2.4	2.4	2	.4	2	2.4	–.4

* All cash flows are in millions as the notional principal is $100 million.

Figure 23.7
Interes Rate Swap

money market securities and using the proceeds to purchase long-term bonds.[14] As with the case of an equity swap, both of them contact a swap bank to help them make such changes without the payment of substantial transaction costs.

The swap bank sets up the following contract for the two of them. Shortly after the end of each quarter Mr. Downe is to pay Ms. Uppe an amount that is equal to the end-of-quarter three-month LIBOR times the notional principal. At the same time Ms. Uppe is to pay Mr. Downe an amount that is equal to 2% of the notional principal. Both Ms. Uppe and Mr. Downe agree that the notional principal will be equal to $100 million and that the contract will last for five years. Each pays the swap bank a fee for setting up the contract.

Imagine that the three-month LIBOR at the beginning of each of the next four quarters equals, successively, 1.5%, 1.8%, 2.1%, and 2.4%. This means that the following amounts are to be paid by Mr. Downe to Ms. Uppe:

First quarter:	.015 × $100 million = $1.5 million
Second quarter:	.018 × $100 million = $1.8 million
Third quarter:	.021 × $100 million = $2.1 million
Fourth quarter:	.024 × $100 million = $2.4 million

In return, Ms. Uppe must pay $2 million (= .02 × $100 million) to Mr. Downe each quarter.

The payments from Ms. Uppe and Mr. Downe are netted against each other, so the net payments are:

First quarter:	Ms. Uppe pays $.5 million to Mr. Downe
Second quarter:	Ms. Uppe pays $.2 million to Mr. Downe
Third quarter:	Mr. Downe pays $.1 million to Ms. Uppe
Fourth quarter:	Mr. Downe pays $.4 million to Ms. Uppe

These amounts reflect what would have happened (roughly) if Ms. Uppe had sold bonds and bought money market securities and Mr. Downe had sold money market securities and bought bonds and both had incurred relatively low transaction costs. Consider the first quarter. If Ms. Uppe had sold the bonds and replaced them with money market securities yielding roughly LIBOR, she would have earned $1.5 million in interest. Instead, she kept the bonds and earned $2 million on them but had to pay Mr. Downe a net amount of $.5 million, leaving her with $1.5 million, the same amount.[15]

As with equity swaps, there are many variations on this plain-vanilla type of interest rate swap. For example, the notional principal could change over time. Or one variable-rate stream of cash flows based on one interest rate (such as LIBOR) could be swapped for a variable rate stream of cash flows based on another interest rate (such as Treasury bills). In addition, there can be caps or floors or collars on the size of the variable payments.

Swaps Market

The swaps market is an unregulated market in that no governmental agency has oversight responsibilities. As a consequence, there has been a high degree of innovation in the types of swap contracts that have been created.[16] Furthermore, there is privacy for all parties involved, because no reporting requirements exist other than those imposed by accountants. In addition, it means that anyone involved in a swap must be concerned with *counterparty risk*. That is, each counterparty to a swap must pay close attention to the creditworthiness of the other counterparty in order to reduce the risk that the other counterparty will default in making his or her required payments under the terms of the contract.

At the heart of the swaps market are swap banks. These "banks" facilitate the creation of swaps for their clients, and they will often take the other side of the contract if another counterparty is not available at the moment. In such situations they are acting as *swap dealers*, and they will use various kinds of techniques (such as taking positions in futures or contacting other swap banks) to hedge their exposure to financial risk. In such a situation no fee is typically charged to the counterparty. Instead, the terms of the swap are set in the swap dealer's favor, thereby allowing the dealer to make a profit after hedging his or her position.

What happens if at some point during the life of the swap one counterparty wants to get out of the contract? In such a situation the counterparty has a choice of contacting either the other counterparty or a swap bank. In the first case, it is possible that the swap contract can be canceled if a mutually acceptable cash payment is made from one counterparty to the other. In the interest rate swap example, if interest rates have risen high enough (as in the third and fourth quarter), then Ms. Uppe will be in a favorable position because the swap's net cash flows will be going from Mr. Downe to her. Hence, regardless of who wants to get out of the swap, Ms. Uppe would want to be compensated for the loss of the anticipated future cash flows. This means that Mr. Downe would give her a lump sum payment when the contract is canceled.

Similarly, if a swap bank is contacted, then either it will assume the counterparty's position in the contract or it will search for someone else to do so. (Note that the counterparty that wants to get out of the contract can conduct such a search without using a swap bank.) In the previous example, if Ms. Uppe wants to get out of the contract, then the swap bank will pay her a lump sum. Conversely, if Mr. Downe wants to get out, then he will have to pay a lump sum to the swap bank. In either case, the contract remains in force afterward for the other counterparty.

Manager Structuring

Administrators of pension and endowment funds might be surprised to find themselves referred to as investment engineers. Yet these institutional investors (who are often called "plan sponsors") face the complex problem of efficiently allocating their assets among various investment managers so as to best achieve their stated investment objectives. The disciplined process through which this manager "structuring" problem can best be resolved is analogous to the process through which an engineer designs a building or a machine.

When plan sponsors choose to invest in a particular asset class, especially a well-defined and liquid one such as the U.S. common stock market, they typically choose a market index to characterize the expected return and risk opportunities of the asset class and to serve as a benchmark against which to evaluate the subsequent performance of their investments. In this context, the selected market index is called an *asset class target*. For example, a plan sponsor might specify the Standard & Poor's 500 and the Lehman Aggregate Bond Index as the asset class targets for its U.S. common stock and fixed-income investments, respectively. In a sense these market indices represent the portfolios that the plan sponsors would own if all of their investments in these asset classes were passively managed.

Plan sponsors rarely opt to conduct all of their investments in an asset class on a strictly passive basis. Instead, they typically hire a number of active investment managers (possibly in addition to using an index fund). In aggregate, these active managers are expected to exceed the performance of the asset class target on a risk-adjusted basis.

For various reasons most active investment managers pursue distinct investment styles, focusing their efforts in particular niches of the marketplace. For example, some common stock managers concentrate on small-capitalization growth stocks, whereas some bond managers invest primarily in mortgage-backed securities.

Just as an investment manager will diversify within a portfolio to avoid unintended risks, a plan sponsor will diversify among investment managers. (The text refers to this approach as *split-funding*.) This manager diversification reduces the possibility that one manager's mistakes will seriously harm the plan sponsor's total portfolio. Further, it avoids the risk that the total portfolio will be excessively exposed to the results of a specific investment style. In particular, it is this "diversification of style" that underlies the plan sponsor's investment engineering problem.

The goal of efficient style diversification is to be *style-neutral* relative to the asset class target. That is, in aggregate, the investment styles of a plan sponsor's managers should exhibit exposures to factors of risk and return (see Chapter 10) similar to those of the asset class target.

Suppose that a plan sponsor decision maker, who had selected the S&P 500 as the asset class target for his or her U.S. common stock investments, were to hire only investment managers that invested in large capitalization, high-dividend-yield stocks. The aggregate of the managers' investment styles would display investment characteristics quite different from those of the S&P 500. For example, relative to the S&P 500, the aggregate manager style would heavily emphasize utility stocks, which pay high dividends, and deemphasize technology stocks, which pay little or no dividends.

In some periods, such as during an economic downturn, these large high-yield stocks would perform well relative to the S&P 500. In other periods, they might perform relatively poorly. This relative performance difference would occur regardless of whether the large-capitalization, high-yield managers were good or bad stock pickers within their area of

It is also possible that the swap bank will arrange for the party that wants to get out to agree to a second swap contract that effectively cancels the first one. For example, if after one year Ms. Uppe wants to get out of the contract where she "pays fixed and receives floating," then the swap bank could construct a four-year swap where she "pays floating and receives fixed" for the same amount of notional principal. With the first contract she pays 2% and receives LIBOR, and with the second

expertise. The aggregate style of these managers does not "fit" with the asset class target. Therefore the risk that the aggregate manager style will perform differently from the asset class target is known as *style bias* or *misfit risk*. Style diversification seeks to limit misfit risk.

Unfortunately, simply hiring many active managers with differing investment styles is not a cost-effective means of controlling misfit risk. Investment skill is a rare commodity. A plan sponsor decision maker may not be able to identify what he or she believes to be skillful managers in sufficient quantity to provide a diverse group of investment styles. Because the costs of active management are much higher than those of passive management, a strategy of hiring a large number of active managers with different investment styles within an asset category is likely to produce nothing more than an expensive index fund.

Plan sponsors would prefer to allocate their assets only to those managers who they believe can perform best relative to the managers' investment styles, without concern for how those investment styles in aggregate compare with the asset class target. How can plan sponsors accommodate this preference and at the same time control misfit risk? That question is the essence of the investment engineering problem.

Consider a plan sponsor who has identified certain managers that he or she believes will be the strongest risk-adjusted performers. Upon examining the managers' aggregate investment style, the plan sponsor finds that it heavily emphasizes smaller companies and companies expected to produce high relative earnings growth. The plan sponsor has selected the S&P 500 as the asset class target, which tends to be dominated by large, mature companies. Thus considerable misfit risk exists.

The plan sponsor could reduce this misfit risk by also investing in a specially designed, passively managed portfolio. This portfolio, called a *completeness fund*, would hold long positions in securities underrepresented by the managers' aggregate investment style relative to the asset class target. Conversely, it would contain short positions in overrepresented securities. In our example, the completeness fund would purchase large-capitalization, low-growth stocks and sell short smaller, high-growth stocks.

Properly constructed, the completeness fund will eliminate misfit risk and create a style-neutral total portfolio. If the active managers exceed the performance of their respective investment style benchmarks, then the total portfolio will outperform the asset class target.

Complicating the issue is the fact that the active managers' investment styles may have non-zero covariances with one another. If they do, various allocations among them will produce different levels of misfit risk. Moreover, the plan sponsor may have more confidence in some managers than in others and therefore wish to allocate more funds to the former than to the latter. These active manager allocation decisions directly affect the aggregate manager investment style and thus the composition of the completeness fund.

Determining desired allocations to the active managers and the composition of the resulting completeness fund requires a disciplined, quantitative approach. Further, the problem is dynamic, with the appropriate solution shifting over time as the investment characteristics of securities evolve and plan sponsors' estimates of the relative skills of their current and prospective managers change. Each plan sponsor faces a unique misfit problem. Effective solutions typically require specialized risk control computer software and experience in manipulating the inputs to and understanding the output from that software. The task of manager structuring is truly one of investment engineering.

contract she will pay LIBOR and receive 2.3%. The fixed rate is higher with the second contract (2.3% > 2%) because interest rates have risen since the first contract was signed. Now Ms. Uppe both receives and pays LIBOR, so those two cash streams effectively cancel each other out. She also pays 2% and receives 2.3%, meaning that, on balance, she receives .3%, or $300,000 (=.003 × $100 million). Thus for the next four years she will receive $300,000 quarterly.

The larger the amount of money managed, the more communication there is likely to be between investment manager and client. Not surprisingly, corporate, union, and government officials responsible for pension funds spend a great deal of time with those who manage their money. Such officials also concern themselves with a number of questions: Who should manage the money, how should it be managed, and how should the managers be instructed and constrained?

Many of the aspects of manager-client relations can be characterized as responses to a difference of opinion concerning the manager's abilities to make "good bets." Often clients will divide their funds among two or more managers. This type of **split-funding** is used by most pension funds. Two reasons are given. First, it allows the employment of managers with different skills or different styles. Second, the impact of erroneous "bets" can be reduced by diversifying among different managers because the managers are the "bettors." However, if a client were to broadly diversify among managers without regard to the managers' investment abilities, the overall portfolio would likely produce results similar to those of the market portfolio. Thus excessive use of split-funding is like explicitly investing in a passive fund, but at considerably greater cost to the client, owing to the expenses associated with transaction costs and fees charged by the investment managers.

Whether or not split-funding is used, a client who feels that a manager is "betting" too much would like to simply reduce the size of the "bets." For example, the client might ask a manager to diverge only half as much as he or she normally would from passive proportions of individual securities. Thus, if the market proportion in $S1$ were 45%, a manager who decided that the optimal proportion is 30% would ultimately invest only a proportion equal to 37.5% $\left[= (30\% + 45\%)/2 \right]$. However, there is no simple way to monitor compliance. In the example, the manager could buy 30% of $S1$ and state that he or she originally wanted to invest 15% in it but settled for 30%, even though truthfully he or she originally wanted 30%. Instead, a simpler approach is often employed: Limits are placed on the holdings in any single security.[17]

Institutional investors (for example, pension and endowment funds) often use more than one investment manager and provide each with a set of objectives and a set of constraints on allowed divergences from specified target positions.[18] Individual investors who employ investment managers tend to give such instructions only implicitly, if at all. This timidity may reflect less sophistication, a less formal relationship with the manager, or the fact that the management fee for a small account is not large enough to cover the cost of dealing with a series of client-specific objectives and constraints.

23.7 SUMMARY

1. Investment decisions are made through a five-step procedure: (1) set investment policy; (2) perform security analysis; (3) construct a portfolio; (4) revise the portfolio; and (5) evaluate the performance of the portfolio.

2. To set investment policy, an investor should specify his or her risk tolerance—that is, the maximum amount of additional risk that the investor will accept for a given increase in expected return.

3. One means of establishing an investor's risk tolerance is for the investor to identify the most desirable portfolio from a set of portfolios. Once this identification has been made, the slope of the investor's indifference curve, and hence the investor's attitude toward risk and expected return, can be estimated.

4. Passive management rests on the belief that markets are efficient and typically involves investing in an index fund. Active management, conversely, involves a belief that mispriced situations occur and can be identified with reasonable consistency.

5. There are many forms of active management. They can involve security selection, sector selection, asset allocation, and market timing.

6. Portfolio revision involves both realizing that the currently held portfolio is not optimal and specifying another portfolio to hold with superior risk-return characteristics. The investor must balance the costs of moving to the new portfolio against the benefits of the revision.

7. Swaps often provide a low-cost method of restructuring a portfolio's funds across various asset classes.

8. Most large investors use split-finding to spread their investments across various managers with different styles and to protect themselves against incorrect active management decisions by a single manager.

QUESTIONS AND PROBLEMS

1. Describe the functioning of a "traditional" investment management organization. Much of the decision making in these organizations is "qualitative" in nature. What types of "quantitative" decision-making techniques might be introduced?

2. Technological changes have decreased the cost and increased the speed of information dissemination in security markets. Why might one suspect that firms following a "traditional" approach to investment management would find it increasingly difficult to generate "positive alphas" (that is, to identify and acquire underpriced securities) in this environment?

3. Consider Table 23.1. If your investment adviser presented you with these data, which stock–Treasury bill combination would you choose? Describe your thought process in making this choice.

4. Why is it difficult to specify the risk-return preferences of investment management clients? Why are these problems particularly acute in the case of institutional investor clients (for example, pension and endowment funds)?

5. Consider a portfolio whose asset mix can vary between stocks and Treasury bills. Given the historical returns on these two assets that is provided in Chapter 1, describe the distribution of possible portfolio returns as the proportion of the portfolio invested in stocks increases and that invested in Treasury bills decreases. What causes the distribution to change as the asset mix changes?

6. Explain the meaning of the slope of an investor's indifference curve at any particular point. For a "typical" risk-averse investor, describe how the investor's risk-return tradeoff changes at different points along one of his or her indifference curves.

7. Assume that the expected return on stocks is 12%, the standard deviation of stocks is 18%, and the riskfree rate is 5%. Given this information, an investor selects a portfolio comprising a 70% allocation to stocks and a 30% allocation to the riskfree asset. According to the derivation of risk tolerance found in Equation (23.2), what risk tolerance is indicated by this choice?

8. Buzz Arlett, a portfolio manager for an investment management firm, has estimated the following risk-return characteristics for the stock and bond markets.

	Expected Return	Standard Deviation
Stocks	18%	22%
Bonds	10	5

The correlation between stocks and bonds is estimated to be .50.

Using these estimates, Buzz ran a number of simulations, tracing out the implications of different bond-stock mixes for the financial situation of Zinn Beck, a client. After much thought, Zinn indicated that, of the mixes considered, the most desirable was the allocation of 60% to stocks and 40% to bonds. Given this information, calculate Zinn's risk tolerance. [Hint: To solve this problem algebraically, write Equation (23.5) using the 60:40 stock-bond allocation. Do the same for a 61:39 allocation. Finally, set these two formulas equal to each other and solve for the risk tolerance.] Is this answer likely to represent Zinn's risk tolerance over all possible stock-bond allocations?

9. Should an "overpriced" stock definitely be excluded from an investor's portfolio? Why?

10. Studies that simulate the value of an investment portfolio under alternative mixes of stocks and bonds invariably demonstrate that higher stock allocations produce higher returns, particularly as the holding period increases. If you as an investor have a time horizon that is reasonably long, say over ten years, and you have no current income needs, could you justify holding any bonds in your portfolio?

11. Assume a riskfree return of 7%, an expected stock return of 18%, and a standard deviation of 21%. Under these conditions, if Birdie Cree chooses a portfolio composed of a 40% investment in stocks and a 60% investment in a riskfree asset, what is Birdie's risk tolerance? In words, describe what this value means.

12. Dee Cousineau can earn a riskfree return of 6%. Dee expects the stock market to return 15% and exhibit a standard deviation of 20%. If Dee chooses a portfolio of 60% stocks and 40% riskfree asset, calculate Dee's certainty equivalent return.

13. The portfolio manager's job can be defined as identifying the portfolio with the highest certainty equivalent return. Explain.

14. Despite its obvious simplicity and potential benefits, common stock passive management is a relatively "new" investment tool. Yet in the last 25 years, assets under passive management have grown from essentially zero to hundreds of billions of dollars. What are some possible reasons for the tremendous growth in passive management?

15. It is often argued (especially by active managers) that passive management implies settling for "mediocre" performance. Is this statement necessarily true? Why?

16. Gavvy Cravath, an astute investor, once commented, "With the stock market composed of about 8,000 actively traded securities, I view my portfolio as about 7,950 short positions and 50 long positions." Explain what Gavvy means.

17. Why is the "one-stage" approach to security selection theoretically superior to the "two-stage" approach? Why is the "two-stage" approach preferred by most investment managers?

18. Why should investment portfolios, even those that are passively managed, be periodically revised? What factors weigh against making such revisions?

19. A typical money management firm, particularly one specializing in stocks or bonds, invests in essentially the same portfolio for all of its clients, regardless of the clients' individual risk-return preferences. Speculate as to why money managers often operate in this manner. What can clients do to ensure that their portfolios reflect their own specific risk-return preferences?

20. Many investment management clients split their assets among a number of managers. Two rationales for this approach have been described as "diversification of judgment" and "diversification of style." Explain the meaning of these two terms.

CFA Exam Questions

21. Adviser 1: "Long-term asset allocation should be determined using an efficient frontier. Returns, risks (standard deviations), and correlations can be deter-

mined for each asset class from historical data. After calculating the efficient frontier for various allocations, you should select the asset mix on the efficient frontier that best meets your fund's risk tolerance."

Adviser 2: "History gives no guide to the future. For example, everybody agrees that bond risk has increased above historical levels as a result of financial deregulation. A far better approach to long-term asset allocation is to use your best judgment about expected returns on the various asset classes, based on current market conditions. You should rely on your experience to determine the best asset mix and avoid being influenced by computer printouts."

Adviser 1 Rebuttal: "Current market conditions are not likely to persist into the future and are not appropriate for long-term asset allocation decisions. Moreover, your use of judgment and experience can be influenced by biases and emotions and is not as rigorous a method as my efficient frontier approach."

Evaluate the strengths and weaknesses of each of the two approaches presented above. Recommend and justify an alternative process for asset allocation that draws from the strengths of each approach and corrects their weaknesses.

22. Colinos Associates is an investment management firm utilizing a very rigorous and disciplined asset allocation methodology as a key element of its investment approach. Twice a year, three or four economic scenarios are developed, based on the judgment of Colinos' most senior people. Probabilities are then assigned to the scenarios; return forecasts for U.S. stocks, bonds, and cash equivalents (the only asset types used by the firm) are generated; and expected values are computed for each asset category. These expected values are then combined with historical standard deviations and covariances to produce forecasts of results from various combinations of the three asset classes.

From this range of possible outcomes, senior staff selects what it regards as the best asset combinations, defined as those combinations promising the highest three-year returns with a 90% probability of achieving a pre-set minimum annual return requirement. These optimal allocations (sample output in the following table) are then presented to all clients for discussion and implementation. The process is repeated in roughly six months' time, when new allocations are developed.

Minimum Annual Required Return (90% Probability)	Anticipated 3–Year Compound Annual Return	Recommended Asset Allocation		
		Cash	Bonds	Stock
16%	12.0%	10%	30%	60%
14	11.0	20	40	40
12	10.0	30	40	30
0	9.0	50	30	20
2	8.5	60	30	10
4	8.0	70	20	10
6	7.5	80	15	5

a. Discuss the strengths and weaknesses of Colinos' asset allocation approach.
b. Recommend and justify an alternative asset allocation approach for wealthy individuals.

APPENDIX

DETERMINING THE RISK TOLERANCE OF AN INVESTOR

The purpose of this appendix is to derive in some detail the formula for determining the risk tolerance τ of an investor. As mentioned earlier, the equation for an indifference curve of an investor having constant risk tolerance is of the form:

$$\bar{r}_p = u_i + \frac{1}{\tau}\sigma_p^2 \tag{23.1}$$

where u_i and $1/\tau$ are the vertical intercept and slope for indifference curve i when variance is measured on the horizontal axis. As the equation shows, an indifference curve will be a straight line because u_i and $1/\tau$ are constants (thus the equation is of the general form $Y = a + bX$, which is a straight line). Furthermore, any two indifference curves for an investor will have the same slope $(1/\tau)$ but will have different vertical intercepts (u_i).

In the estimation of the investor's level of risk tolerance τ, as was mentioned, the slope of the indifference curve, $1/\tau$, would be set equal to the slope of the efficient set at the location of the portfolio that was selected, denoted portfolio C. The reason is that the indifference curve is tangent to the efficient set at this point, so the two must have the same slope. Thus the slope of the efficient set at point C must be determined in order to estimate τ.

Let X_S denote the proportion invested in the stock portfolio S and $(1 - X_S)$ denote the proportion invested in a riskfree Treasury bill portfolio f. The expected return of any portfolio consisting of S and f is simply:

$$\bar{r}_p = X_S\bar{r}_S + (1 - X_S)r_f \tag{23.6}$$

where $\bar{r}_S$ and r_f are the expected return of the stock portfolio and the riskfree rate, respectively. This equation can be solved for X_S, resulting in:

$$X_S = \frac{\bar{r}_p - r_f}{\bar{r}_S - r_f} \tag{23.7}$$

The equation for the variance of portfolio p is equal to:

$$\sigma_p^2 = X_S^2\sigma_S^2 + (1 - X_S)^2\sigma_f^2 + 2X_S(1 - X_S)\sigma_{Sf} \tag{23.8}$$

where σ_S^2 and σ_f^2 are the variances of the stock and riskfree portfolios, respectively, and σ_{Sf} is the covariance between these two portfolios. However, because f is the riskfree portfolio, by definition, σ_f^2 and σ_{Sf} are equal to zero. Thus, Equation (23.8) reduces to:

$$\sigma_p^2 = X_S^2\sigma_S^2 \tag{23.9}$$

Next, the right-hand side of Equation (23.7) can be substituted for X_S in Equation (23.9), resulting in:

$$\sigma_p^2 = \frac{(\bar{r}_p - r_f)^2}{(\bar{r}_S - r_f)^2} \sigma_S^2 \qquad (23.10)$$

This equation can be viewed as describing the functional relationship between the expected return and variance of any portfolio p that can be formed by combining the stock portfolio S and the riskfree portfolio f. That is, for a particular S and f, it gives the variance for a portfolio consisting of S and f with expected return $\bar{r}_p$. Equivalently, it represents the slope of the curved line in Figure 23.2 that connects S and f. Using calculus, the slope of this line can be shown to be equal to:[19]

$$Slope = \frac{(\bar{r}_S - r_f)^2}{2[(\bar{r}_p - r_f)\sigma_S^2]} \qquad (23.11)$$

The next step in estimating the slope of the client's indifference curves is to note that the portfolio on the curve connecting S and f that is of concern is the tangency portfolio C. Thus, the slope of the curve at C is determined by substituting $\bar{r}_C$ for $\bar{r}_p$ in Equation (23.11) and equating this value with the slope of the indifference curves, $1/\tau$. Doing this results in the following equation:

$$\frac{1}{\tau} = \frac{(\bar{r}_S - r_f)^2}{2[(\bar{r}_C - r_f)\sigma_S^2]} \qquad (23.12)$$

Finally, Equation (23.12) ca be solved for τ:

$$\tau = \frac{2[(\bar{r}_C - r_f)\sigma_S^2]}{(\bar{r}_S - r_f)^2} \qquad (23.13)$$

Note that this is the same formula that was given earlier in Equation (23.2) for estimating τ, given the client's choice of portfolio C.[20]

After substituting $\bar{r}_C$ for $\bar{r}_p$, Equation (23.7) can be rewritten as:

$$(\bar{r}_S - r_f)X_S = \bar{r}_C - r_f \qquad (23.14)$$

Thus, $(\bar{r}_S - r_f)X_S$ can be substituted for $\bar{r}_C - r_f$ in the numerator of Equation (23.13). Doing so and simplifying results in:

$$\tau = \frac{2[X_S \sigma_S^2]}{(\bar{r}_S - r_f)} \qquad (23.15)$$

In the example given earlier in the chapter, $\sigma_S = 15\%$ and $\bar{r}_S - r_f = 4.5\%$. Substituting these values into Equation (23.15) and simplifying results in:

$$\tau = \frac{2[X_S \times 15^2]}{4.5} \qquad (23.16)$$

$$= 100 X_S$$

as was previously mentioned and illustrated in Table 23.1.

ENDNOTES

[1] One study found that a firm's stock price tended to move upward when analysts upgraded its coding and downward when analysts downgraded its coding. See Edwin J. Elton, Martin J. Gruber, and Seth Grossman, "Discrete Expectational Data and Portfolio Performance," *Journal of Finance* 41, no. 3 (July 1986): 699–713.

[2] This example is taken from William F. Sharpe, *Asset Allocation Tools* (Redwood City, CA: Scientific Press, 1987), p. 38.

[3] If such a decision is made on behalf of the client (for example, by a trustee for one or more beneficiaries), the task is much more difficult, but a decision is still required.

[4] Note that the reciprocal of risk tolerance $1/\tau$ appears in Equation (23.1). This is necessitated by having risk on the horizontal axis in Figure 23.3. That is, the slope of a line is "rise over run" or the change in the y-axis value for a given change in the x-axis value. As the variable τ indicates variance per unit of expected return, its reciprocal must be used to indicate the slope of the indifference curve.

[5] The term u_i is also known as the expected utility of indifference curve i. It represents the level of satisfaction associated with all portfolios plotting on indifference curve i. For more about utility theory, indifference curves, and certainty equivalent returns, see Mark Kritzman, "...About Utility," *Financial Analysts Journal* 48, no. 3 (May/June 1992): 17–20. In considering an investor's utility of wealth function, Chapter 6 discussed a closely related concept, the certainty equivalent of wealth.

[6] An example of a tailored portfolio would be one consisting of stocks with high dividend yields. Such a portfolio might be purchased for a corporate investor because 80% of all dividends received by a corporate investor are exempt from corporate income tax.

[7] For evidence suggesting that asset allocation is the most important decision an investor has to make, see Gary P. Brinson, L. Randolph Hood, and Gilbert L. Beebower, "Determinants of Portfolio Performance," *Financial Analysts Journal* 42, no. 4 (July/August 1986): 39–44; and Gary P. Brinson, Brian D. Singer, and Gilbert L. Beebower, "Determinants of Portfolio Performance II: An Update," *Financial Analysts Journal* 47, no. 3 (May/June 1991): 40–48.

[8] One study examined four prominent sources who provided recommendations for how investors should allocate their money and found that all of them recommended that the ratio of bonds to stocks should be higher for conservative investors relative to more aggressive investors. According to the separation theorem (see Chapter 9), this ratio should not change because capital market theory says that investors should purchase the market portfolio, which is a fixed blend of stocks and bonds, and then either invest or borrow money at the riskfree rate. Consequently, they refer to this as the "asset allocation puzzle." See Niko Canner, N. Gregory Mankiw, and David N. Weil, "An Asset Allocation Puzzle," *American Economic Review* 87, no. 1 (March 1997): 181–191.

[9] An intriguing description of how to use equilibrium models (such as the CAPM, discussed in Chapter 9) and portfolio optimizers (see *Institutional Issues: The Trouble with Optimizers*, in Chapter 7) to make asset allocation decisions in a global setting is presented in Fischer Black and Robert Litterman, "Global Portfolio Optimization," *Financial Analysts Journal* 48, no. 5 (September/October 1992): 28–43. Black and Litterman's model includes foreign currencies as one of the assets; see Chapter 25 for a discussion of foreign currencies and their risks.

[10] The American Stock Exchange has available for purchase and sale two securities known as Standard & Poor's Depositary Receipts (or "spiders") and Diamonds. These two securities are designed to represent ownership in the Standard & Poor's 500 and Dow Jones Industrial Average, respectively. Hence, they allow an investor to "buy" and "sell" either index, with the investor's gain or loss very closely tracking the index's gain or loss. Similar securities exist for the S&P MidCap 400 Index and Morgan Stanley Capital International's indices on 17 countries. For more information on these unique securities, see the AMEX's home page at <www.amex.com>.

[11] The discussion of swaps here should not be confused with the discussion of bond swaps in Chapter 15.

[12] For a discussion of many of the complicating features present in swaps, see Robert H. Litzenberger, "Swaps: Plain and Fanciful," *Journal of Finance* 47, no. 3 (July 1992): 831–850. He notes that over 2/3 of swaps are of the "plain vanilla" variety, and that the first major swap took place in 1981. The International Swaps and Derivatives Association (an industry association for participants in swaps and other privately negotiated derivatives transactions) reports on its Web site that at June 30, 1997, the notional amount of interest rate and currency swaps outstanding were $22.1 trillion and $1.6 trillion, respectively.

[13] Swaps can be compared to a series of forward contracts (forward contracts were discussed in Chapter 5). In this case, Ms. Bright has a swap position equivalent to having long positions in a series of equity forward contracts, whereas Mr. Gloom has short positions in these

contracts. Consider the swap contract's first quarterly payment. Imagine that instead of the swap contract Ms. Bright had taken a long position in a forward contract. In general, forward contracts involve the exchange of a stated amount of cash for a given asset at a specified future date. Ms. Bright has agreed to pay $2 million one quarter later for delivery of an asset that can be thought of as shares in an S&P 500 index fund (the number of shares will be determined on the delivery date and will be equal to $100 million times the quarterly return on the S&P 500, divided by the fund's net asset value at the end of the quarter).

[14] By convention, the counterparty that makes the fixed payments (Ms. Uppe) is known as the *swap buyer*, and the counterparty that makes the variable payments (Mr. Downe) is known as the *swap seller*. Hence the swap buyer "pays fixed and receives floating," and the swap seller "pays floating and receives fixed."

[15] In this case, Ms. Uppe has a swap position equivalent to having long positions in a series of money market forward contracts, whereas Mr. Downe has short positions in these contracts. For example, the first quarterly payment is identical to what would happen if Ms. Uppe signed a forward contract agreeing to pay $2 million in exchange for the delivery of shares in a money market mutual fund (the number of shares will be determined on the delivery date, and will be equal to $100 million times the LIBOR, divided by the fund's net asset value at the end of the quarter). See endnote 13.

[16] One interesting innovation is the *swaption*, a contract that combines an option (usually European) with an interest rate swap (or some other kind of swap). Call swaptions involve the right to "pay fixed and receive floating" and put swaptions involve the right to "pay floating and receive fixed." The notional principal, fixed rate, source of the floating rate, and swap life are all set when the swaption is created, as is the life of the swaption itself. If the owner of either type of swaption decides to exercise the option, then the writer (usually a swap bank) must become the other counterparty to the swap. In return for this right, the owner pays the writer a premium. Owners of calls will exercise their options if interest rates rise because then the fixed payment cash outflows will be less than the floating rate cash inflows. Conversely, put owners will exercise their options if interest rates fall. See David R. Smith, "A Simple Method for Pricing Interest Rate Swaptions," *Financial Analysts Journal* 47, no. 3 (May/June 1991): 72–76.

[17] There are other kinds of limits frequently imposed on the manager, such as limits on the holdings of bonds versus stocks or on the amount invested in a single industry.

[18] Sometimes these objectives and constraints are stated vaguely; in other cases they are specified precisely.

[19] Note that the slope of this line $\mathrm{d}\bar{r}_p/\mathrm{d}\sigma_p^2$ is equal to $1/(\mathrm{d}\sigma_p^2/\mathrm{d}\bar{r}_p)$. Thus the slope can be determined by taking the derivative of σ_p^2 with respect to $\bar{r}_p$ in Equation (23.10) and then inverting the resulting expression.

[20] Risk tolerance, along with a procedure for estimating the value of τ, is presented in William F. Sharpe, *Asset Allocation Tools* (Redwood City, CA: Scientific Press, 1987), pp. 33–39.

KEY TERMS

investment committee	asset allocation
approved list	sector selection
portfolio manager	market timing
risk tolerance	investment styles
certainty equivalent return	*ex post* selection bias
passive management	out-of-sample data
active management	equity swaps
index funds	swap bank
active positions	interest rate swap
security selection	split-funding
asset classes	

REFERENCES

1. Investment management is discussed in:

   William F. Sharpe, "Decentralized Investment Management," *Journal of Finance* 36, no. 2 (May 1981): 217–234.

   Jeffery V. Bailey and Robert D. Arnott, "Cluster Analysis and Manager Selection," *Financial Analysts Journal* 42, no. 6 (November/December 1986): 20–28.

   Richard A. Brealey, "Portfolio Theory versus Portfolio Practice," *Journal of Portfolio Management* 16, no. 4 (Summer 1990): 6–10.

   William F. Sharpe, "The Arithmetic of Active Management," *Financial Analysts Journal* 47, no. 1 (January/February 1991): 7–9.

   Robert H. Jeffery, "Do Clients Need So Many Portfolio Managers?" *Journal of Portfolio Management* 18, no. 1 (Fall 1991): 13–19.

   C. B. Garcia and F. J. Gould, "Some Observations on Active Manager Performance and Passive Indexing," *Financial Analysts Journal* 47, no. 6 (November/December 1991): 11–13.

   Richard C. Grinold and Ronald N. Kahn, *Active Portfolio Management* (Chicago: Probus Publishing, 1995).

2. Investment management for an individual investor is discussed in:

   Burton G. Malkiel, *A Random Walk Down Wall Street* (New York: W. W. Norton, 1996), particularly Chapter 12.

3. Assessment of investor risk tolerance is discussed in:

   Gail Farrelly and Dean LeBaron, "Assessing Risk Tolerance Levels: A Prerequisite for Personalizing and Managing Portfolios," *Financial Analysts Journal* 45, no. 1 (January/February 1989): 14–16.

   W. V. Harlow and Keith C. Brown, "Understanding and Assessing Financial Risk Tolerance: A Biological Perspective," *Financial Analysts Journal* 46, no. 6 (November/December 1990): 50–62.

   William B. Riley Jr., and K. Victor Chow, "Asset Allocation and Individual Risk Aversion," *Financial Analysts Journal* 48, no. 6 (November/December 1992): 32–37.

   Karen Hube, "Time for Investing's Four-Letter Word," *The Wall Street Journal,* January 23, 1998, pp. C1, C17.

4. An extensive discussion of risk tolerance is included in:

   William F. Sharpe, *Asset Allocation Tools* (Redwood City, CA: Scientific Press, 1987), Chapter 2.

   William F. Sharpe, "Integrated Asset Allocation," *Financial Analysts Journal* 43, no. 5 (September/October 1987): 25–32.

5. Market timing, asset allocation, and investment styles are discussed in the preceding article and in:

   Keith P. Ambachtsheer, "Portfolio Theory and the Security Analyst," *Financial Analysts Journal* 28, no. 6 (November/December 1972): 53–57.

   Jack L. Treynor and Fischer Black, "How to Use Security Analysis to Improve Portfolio Selection," *Journal of Business* 46, no. 1 (January 1973): 66–86.

   William F. Sharpe, "Likely Gains From Market Timing," *Financial Analysts Journal* 31, no. 2 (March/April 1975): 60–69.

   William F. Sharpe, "Major Investment Styles," *Journal of Portfolio Management* 4, no. 2 (Winter 1978): 68–74.

   Keith P. Ambachtsheer and James L. Farrell Jr., "Can Active Management Add Value?" *Financial Analysts Journal* 35, no. 6 (November/December 1979): 39–47.

   Robert D. Arnott and James N. von Germeten, "Systematic Asset Allocation," *Financial Analysts Journal* 39, no. 6 (November/December 1983): 31–38.

   Jess H. Chua and Richard S. Woodard, *Gains from Market Timing* Monograph Series in Finance and Economics 1986-2, (New York University Salomon Center, Leonard N. Stern School of Business, 1986).

Richard A. Brealey, "How to Combine Active Management with Index Funds," *Journal of Portfolio Management* 12, no. 2 (Winter 1986): 4–10.

André F. Perold and William F. Sharpe, "Dynamic Strategies for Asset Allocation," *Financial Analysts Journal* 44, no. 1 (January/February 1988): 16–27.

William F. Sharpe, "Asset Allocation," in John L. Maginn and Donald L. Tuttle (eds.), *Managing Investment Portfolios: A Dynamic Process* (Boston, MA: Warren, Gorham & Lamont, 1990), Chapter 7.

David E. Tierney and Kenneth Winston, "Defining and Using Dynamic Completeness Funds to Enhance Total Fund Efficiency," *Financial Analysts Journal* 46, no. 4 (July/August 1990): 49–54.

Craig B. Wainscott, "The Stock-Bond Correlation and Its Implications for Asset Allocation," *Financial Analysts Journal* 46, no. 4 (July/August 1990): 55–60, 79.

John Markese, "All Eggs in One Basket, or A Basket for Each Egg?" *AAII Journal* 12, no. 7 (August 1990): 31–33.

David E. Tierney and Kenneth Winston, "Using Generic Benchmarks to Present Manager Styles," *Journal of Portfolio Management* 17, no. 4 (Summer 1991): 33–36.

P. R. Chandy and William Reichenstein, "Timing Strategies and the Risk of Missing Bull Markets," *AAII Journal* 13, no. 7 (August 1991): 17–19.

William F. Sharpe, "Asset Allocation: Management Style and Performance Measurement," *Journal of Portfolio Management*, 18, no. 2 (Winter 1992): 7–19.

P. R. Chandy and William Reichenstein, "Stock Market Timing: A Modest Proposal," *AAII Journal* 14, no. 4 (April 1992): 7–10.

Mark Hulbert, "Market Timing Strategies: Taxes Are a Drag," *AAII Journal* 14, no. 7 (August 1992): 18–20.

Maria Crawford Scott, "Asset Allocation among the Three Major Categories," *AAII Journal* 15, no. 4 (April 1993): 13–16.

Mark Hulbert, "Bond Market Timing: Even More Tough Than Timing the Stock Market," *AAII Journal* 16, no. 3 (April 1994): 11–13.

Joseph B. Ludwig, "The Market Timing Approach: A Guide to the Various Strategies," *AAII Journal* 16, no. 4 (May 1994): 11–14.

Richard Bernstein, *Style Investing* (New York: John Wiley, 1995).

T. Daniel Coggin, Frank J. Fabozzi, and Robert Arnott (eds.), *The Handbook of Equity Style Management* (New Hope, PA: Frank J. Fabozzi Associates, 1997).

6. Investing in an international context is discussed in Chapter 25 (see the references listed there) and in:

Robert D. Arnott and Roy D. Henriksson, "A Disciplined Approach to Global Asset Allocation," *Financial Analysts Journal* 45, no. 2 (March/April 1989): 17–28.

Carlo Capaul, Ian Rowley, and William F. Sharpe, "International Value and Growth Stock Returns," *Financial Analysts Journal* 49, no. 1 (January/February 1993): 27–36.

Jess Lederman and Robert A. Klein (eds.), *Global Asset Allocation: Techniques for Optimizing Portfolio Management* (New York: Wiley, 1994).

Lucie Chaumeton, Gregory Connor, and Ross Curds, "A Global Stock and Bond Model," *Financial Analysts Journal* 52, no. 6 (November/December 1996): 65–74.

7. For a discussion of portfolio revision procedures, see:

Gordon J. Alexander and Jack Clark Francis, *Portfolio Analysis* (Upper Saddle River, NJ: Prentice Hall, 1986), pp. 221–228.

William F. Sharpe, *Asset Allocation Tools* (Redwood City, CA: Scientific Press, 1987), pp. 65–68.

8. Swaps are discussed in many of the textbooks on options and futures listed in the references for Chapters 19 and 20. Also see the following and their lists of references:

Robert H. Litzenberger, "Swaps: Plain and Fanciful," *Journal of Finance* 47, no. 3 (July 1992): 831–850.

John F. Marshall and Vipul K. Bansal, *Financial Engineering* (Boston: Blackwell Publishing, 1995).

Charles W. Smithson, Clifford W. Smith Jr., and D. Sykes Wilford, *Managing Financial Risk: A Guide to Derivative Products, Financial Engineering, and Value Maximization* (Burr Ridge, IL: Irwin Professional Publishing, 1995).

Frank J. Fabozzi, Franco Modigliani, and Michael G. Ferri, *Foundations of Financial Markets and Institutions* (Upper Saddle River, NJ: Prentice Hall, 1998).

Robert W. Kolb, *Futures, Options, and Swaps* (Boston: Blackwell Publishing, 1998).

Also see the Web site for the International Swaps and Derivatives Association, an industry association for the participants in swaps and other privately negotiated derivatives transactions, at <www.isda.org>.

9. For more or completeness funds, see:

David E. Tierney and Kenneth J. Winston, "Defining and Using Dynamic Completeness Funds to Enhance Total Fund Efficiency," *Financial Analysts Journal* 46, no. 4 (July/August 1990), 49–54.

Jeffery V. Bailey and David E. Tierney, *Controlling Misfit Risk in Multiple-Manager Investment Programs* (Charlottesville: The Research Foundation of the Institute of Chartered Financial Analysts, 1998).

PORTFOLIO PERFORMANCE EVALUATION

An investor who has been paying someone to actively manage his or her portfolio has every right to insist on knowing what sort of performance was obtained. Such information can be used to alter the constraints placed on the manager, the investment objectives given to the manager, or the amount of money allocated to the manager. Perhaps more important, by evaluating performance in specified ways, a client can forcefully communicate his or her interests to the investment manager and, in all likelihood, affect the way in which his or her portfolio is managed in the future. Moreover, an investment manager, by evaluating his or her own performance, can identify sources of strength or weakness. Although the previous chapter indicated that portfolio performance evaluation was the last stage of the investment management process, it can also be viewed as simply part of a continuing operation. More specifically, it can be viewed as a feedback and control mechanism that can make the investment management process more effective.

Superior performance in the past may have resulted from good luck, in which case such performance should not be expected to continue in the future. On the other hand, superior performance in the past may have resulted from the actions of a highly skilled investment manager. Conversely, inferior performance in the past may have been the result of bad luck, but it may also have resulted from excessive turnover, high management fees, or other costs associated with an unskilled investment manager. These possibilities suggest that the first task in performance evaluation is to try to determine whether past performance was superior or inferior. Once that task has been done, the second task is to try to determine whether such performance was due to skill or luck. Unfortunately, there are difficulties associated with carrying out both of these tasks. Accordingly, this chapter will present not only certain methods that have been advocated and used for evaluating portfolio performance but also a discussion of the difficulties encountered with their use.

Frequently portfolio performance is evaluated over a time interval of at least four years, with returns measured for a number of periods within the interval—typically monthly or quarterly. This approach provides a fairly adequate sample size for statistical evaluation (for example, if returns are measured quarterly for four years, there will be 16 observations). Sometimes, however, a shorter time interval must be used in order to avoid examining a portfolio's returns that were earned by a different investment manager. The examples to follow will involve 16 quarterly observations for tractability. In practice, one would prefer monthly observations if only four years were to be analyzed.

In the simplest situation, in which the client neither deposits nor withdraws money from the portfolio during a time period, calculation of the portfolio's periodic return is straightforward. All that is required is that the market value of the portfolio be known at two points in time—the beginning and the end of the period.

In general, the market value of a portfolio at a point in time is determined by adding the market values of all the securities held at that particular time. For example, the value of a common stock portfolio at the beginning of a period is calculated by (1) noting the market price per share of each stock held in the portfolio at that time, (2) multiplying each of these stock prices by the corresponding number of shares held, and (3) adding up the resulting products. The market value of the portfolio at the end of the period is calculated in the same way, only using end-of-period prices and shares.

With the beginning and ending portfolio values in hand, the return on the portfolio (r) can be calculated by subtracting the beginning value (V_b) from the ending value (V_e) and then dividing the difference by the beginning value:

$$r = \frac{V_e - V_b}{V_b} \tag{24.1}$$

For example, if a portfolio had a market value of \$40 million at the beginning of a quarter and a market value of \$46 million at the end of the quarter, then the return on this portfolio for the quarter would be 15% [= (\$46 million − \$40 million)/\$40 million].

Measurement of portfolio returns is complicated by the fact that the client may either add to or withdraw money from the portfolio. If the client did either, the percentage change in the market value of the portfolio during a period would not be an accurate measurement of the portfolio's return during that period.

For example, consider a portfolio that at the beginning of a quarter has a market value of \$100 million. Just before the end of the quarter the client deposits \$5 million with the investment manager, and subsequently at the end of the quarter the market value of the portfolio is \$103 million. If the quarterly return was measured without consideration of the \$5 million deposit, the reported return would be 3% [= (\$103 million − \$100 million)/\$100 million]. However, this return would be incorrect because \$5 million of the ending \$103 million market value did not result from the investment actions of the manager. Consideration of the deposit would suggest that a more accurate measure of the quarterly return would be −2% {= [(\$103 million − \$5 million) − \$100 million]/\$100 million}.

Identification of exactly *when* any deposits or withdrawals occur is important in accurately measuring portfolio returns. If a deposit or withdrawal occurs just *before* the end of the period, then the return on the portfolio should be calculated by adjusting the ending market value of the portfolio. In the case of a deposit, the ending value should be reduced by the dollar amount (as was done in the previous example). In the case of a withdrawal, the ending value should be increased by the dollar amount.

If a deposit or withdrawal occurs just *after* the start of the period, then the return on the portfolio should be calculated by adjusting the beginning market value of the portfolio. In the case of a deposit, the beginning value should be increased by the dollar amount. In the case of a withdrawal, the beginning value should be decreased by the dollar amount. For example, if the $5 million deposit in the earlier example had been received just after the start of the quarter, the return for the quarter should be calculated as -1.90% {= [$103 million $-$ ($100 million $+$ $5 million)]/($100 million $+$ $5 million)}.

24.1.1 Dollar-Weighted Returns

Difficulties are encountered, however, when deposits or withdrawals occur sometime *between* the beginning and end of the period. One method that has been used for calculating a portfolio's return in this situation is the **dollar-weighted return** (or internal rate of return). For example, if the $5 million deposit in the earlier example was made in the middle of the quarter, the dollar-weighted return would be calculated by solving the following equation for r:

$$\$100 \text{ million} = \frac{-\$5 \text{ million}}{(1 + r)} + \frac{\$103 \text{ million}}{(1 + r)^2} \tag{24.2}$$

The solution to this equation, $r = -.98\%$, is a semiquarterly rate of return. It can be converted into a quarterly rate of return by adding 1 to it, squaring this value, and then subtracting 1 from the square, resulting in a quarterly return of -1.95% $\{= [1 + (-.0098)]^2 - 1\}$.[1]

24.1.2 Time-Weighted Returns

Alternatively, the **time-weighted return** on a portfolio can be calculated when cash flows occur between the beginning and end of the period. This method involves using the market value of the portfolio just before each cash flow occurs. In the earlier example, assume that in the middle of the quarter the portfolio had a market value of $96 million, so that right after the $5 million deposit the market value was $101 million (=$96 million $+$ $5 million). In this case, the return for the first half of the quarter would be -4% [= ($96 million $-$ $100 million)/$100 million], and the return for the second half of the quarter would be 1.98% [= ($103 million $-$ $101 million)/$101 million]. Next these two semiquarterly returns can be converted into a quarterly return by adding 1 to each return, multiplying the sums, and then subtracting 1 from the product. In the example, this procedure results in a quarterly return of -2.1% {= [(1 $-$ .04) $\times$ (1 $+$ .0198)] $-$ 1}.

24.1.3 Comparing Dollar-Weighted and Time-Weighted Returns

Which method is preferable for calculating the return on a portfolio? In the example given here, the dollar-weighted return was -1.95%, whereas the time-weighted return was -2.1%, suggesting that the difference between the two methods may not be very important. Although this may be true in certain situations, examples can be given to show that such differences can be quite large and that the time-weighted return method usually is preferable.

Consider a hypothetical portfolio that starts a quarter with a market value of $50 million. In the middle of the quarter, it has fallen to a market value of $25 million, at which point the client deposits $25 million with the investment manager. At the end of the quarter the portfolio has a market value of $100 million. The semiquarterly dollar-weighted return for this portfolio is equal to the value of r in the following equation:

$$\$50 \text{ million} = \frac{-\$25 \text{ million}}{(1 + r)} + \frac{\$100 \text{ million}}{(1 + r)^2} \tag{24.3}$$

Solving this equation for r results in a value of 18.6%, which in turn equals a quarterly dollar-weighted return of 40.66% $\left[= (1.186)^2 - 1\right]$. However, its quarterly time-weighted return is 0% because its return for the first half of the quarter was −50% and its return for the second half of the quarter was 100% [note that $(1 - .5) \times (1 + 1) - 1 = 0\%$].

Comparing these two returns—40.66% and 0%—indicates that a sizable difference exists. However, the time-weighted return figure of 0% is more meaningful for performance evaluation than the dollar-weighted return figure of 40.66%. The reason can be seen by considering the return over the entire quarter on each dollar that was in the portfolio at the start of the quarter. Each dollar lost half of its value over the first half of the quarter, but then the remaining half-dollar doubled its value over the second half. Consequently, a dollar at the beginning was worth a dollar at the end, suggesting that a return of 0% on the portfolio is a more accurate measure of the investment manager's performance than the 40.66% figure.

In general, the dollar-weighted return method of measuring a portfolio's return for purposes of evaluation is regarded as inappropriate. The reason behind this view is that the return is strongly influenced by the size and timing of the cash flows (namely, deposits and withdrawals), over which the investment manager typically has no control. In the example, the dollar-weighted return was 40.66% because the client fortuitously made a big deposit just before the portfolio appreciated rapidly in value. Thus the 40.66% return figure results at least partly from the actions of the client, not of the manager.

24.1.4 Annualizing Returns

The previous discussion focused on calculating quarterly returns. Such returns may be added or multiplied to obtain an annual measure of return. For example, if the returns in the first, second, third, and fourth quarters of a given year are denoted r_1, r_2, r_3, and r_4, respectively, then the annual return can be calculated by adding the four figures:

$$\text{Annual return} = r_1 + r_2 + r_3 + r_4 \tag{24.4}$$

Alternatively, the annual return could be calculated by adding 1 to each quarterly return, then multiplying the four figures, and finally subtracting 1 from the resulting product:

$$\text{Annual return} = \left[(1 + r_1)(1 + r_2)(1 + r_3)(1 + r_4)\right] - 1 \tag{24.5}$$

This return is more accurate because it reflects the value that one dollar would have at the end of the year if it were invested at the beginning of the year and grew *with compounding* at the rate of r_1 for the first quarter, r_2 for the second quarter, r_3 for the third quarter, and r_4 for the fourth quarter. That is, it assumes reinvestment of both the dollar and any earnings at the end of each quarter.

The essential idea behind performance evaluation is to compare the returns obtained by the investment manager through active management with the returns that could have been obtained for the client if one or more appropriate alternative portfolios had been chosen for investment. The reason for this comparison is straightforward; performance should be evaluated on a relative basis, not on an absolute basis.

As an example, consider a client who is told that his or her portfolio, invested in a diversified common stocks portfolio of average risk, had a return of 20% last year. Does this return suggest superior or inferior performance? If a broad stock market index (such as the Wilshire 5000) went up by 10% last year, then the return on the portfolio suggests superior performance and is good news. However, if the index went up by 30% last year, then the return on the portfolio suggests inferior performance and is bad news. The returns on "similar" portfolios are needed for comparison in order to infer whether the manager's performance is superior or inferior.

Such comparison portfolios are often referred to as **benchmark portfolios**. In selecting them, the client should be certain that they are relevant, feasible, and known in advance, meaning that they should represent alternative portfolios that could have been chosen for investment instead of the portfolio being evaluated. That is, the benchmark should reflect the objectives of the client. Hence, if the objective is to earn superior returns by investing in small stocks, then the S&P 500 would be an inappropriate benchmark. Instead, an index such as the Russell 2000 would be more suitable. *Return* is a key aspect of performance, of course, but some way must be found to account for the portfolio's exposure to *risk*. The choice of benchmark portfolios may be restricted to portfolios perceived to have similar levels of risk, thereby permitting a direct comparison of returns.

Figure 24.1 illustrates such a comparison for a hypothetical common stock (or "equity") portfolio referred to as Fund 07632. In this figure, Fund 07632's performance for each year is represented by a diamond. The hypothetical comparison portfolios are other common stock portfolios that are represented by the box surrounding the diamond (hence such a representation is known as a *box plot* or a *floating bar chart*). The top and bottom lines of the box indicate the returns of the 5th and 95th percentile comparison portfolios, respectively. Similarly, the top and bottom dashed lines represent the 25th and 75th percentiles, respectively. The solid line in the middle represents the median (that is, the 50th percentile) portfolio. This particular evaluation technique presumes that the comparison portfolios exhibit risk similar to Fund 07632 and that they represent feasible alternatives for Fund 07632's owner. Failing to meet these conditions (as is often the case in such peer group comparisons) will generally invalidate the performance evaluation.

Alternatively, risk may be explicitly measured so that a single measure of performance taking both return and risk into account can be employed. This method will allow benchmark portfolios of varying degrees of risk to be compared with the portfolio being evaluated. One such approach is to compare the portfolio with a market index that is constructed from the same set of securities that the portfolio manager evaluates in making investments. Hence, it is useful to understand just how market indices are constructed.

What did the market do yesterday? How much would an unmanaged common stock portfolio have returned last year? Such questions are often answered by examining

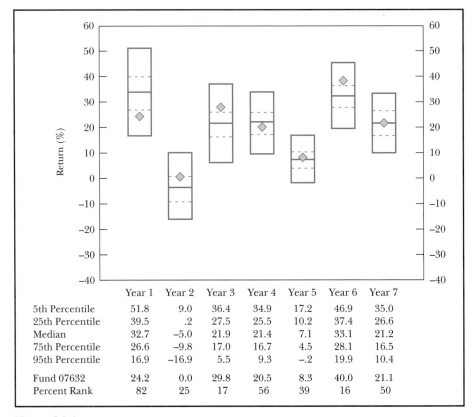

	Year 1	Year 2	Year 3	Year 4	Year 5	Year 6	Year 7
5th Percentile	51.8	9.0	36.4	34.9	17.2	46.9	35.0
25th Percentile	39.5	.2	27.5	25.5	10.2	37.4	26.6
Median	32.7	–5.0	21.9	21.4	7.1	33.1	21.2
75th Percentile	26.6	–9.8	17.0	16.7	4.5	28.1	16.5
95th Percentile	16.9	–16.9	5.5	9.3	–.2	19.9	10.4
Fund 07632	24.2	0.0	29.8	20.5	8.3	40.0	21.1
Percent Rank	82	25	17	56	39	16	50

Figure 24.1

Comparing Returns of Equity Portfolios

Source: Adapted from SEI, *Funds Evaluation Service.*

the performance of a **market index**. Figure 24.2 displays many stock market indices that are commonly referenced. These indices differ from one another with respect to (1) the securities included in the index and (2) the method employed in calculating the value of the index.[2]

In order to understand how some of the most popular indices are computed, consider a simple example in which the market index is based on two stocks, referred to as *A* and *B*. At the end of day 0, their closing prices are, respectively, $10 and $20 per share. Furthermore, at this time *A* has 1,500 shares outstanding and *B* has 2,000 shares outstanding.

24.3.1 Price Weighting

There are three weighting methods that are most often used in computing a market index. The first method, involving **price weighting**, begins by summing the prices of the stocks that are included in the index and ends by dividing this sum by a constant (the "divisor") in order to calculate an average price. If the index includes only stocks *A* and *B* and was started on day 0, the divisor would be equal to the number of stocks in the average, 2. Thus on day 0 the average price would be 15 [=(10 + 20)/2], and this would denote the level of the index. The divisor is adjusted thereafter whenever there is a stock split in order to avoid giving misleading indications of the "market's" direction (it is also adjusted in a similar manner whenever the composition of the index changes, meaning whenever one stock is substituted for another).

For example, assume that on day 1, *B* splits two-for-one and closes at $11 per share, while *A* closes at $13. In this situation, it is clear that the market has risen be-

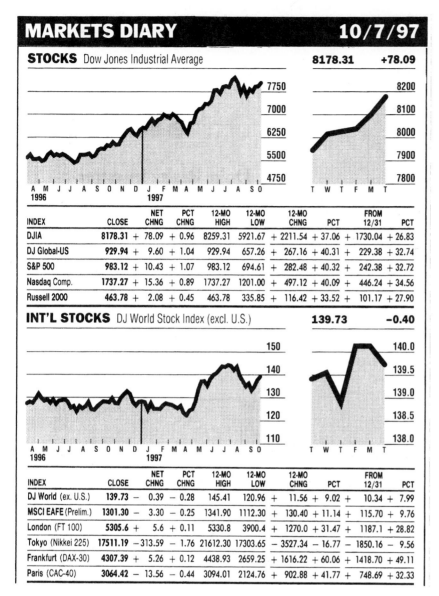

Figure 24.2

Stock Marke Indices Published in the *Wall Street Journal,* October 8, 1997

Source: Reprinted by permission of *The Wall Street Journal,* Dow Jones & Company, Inc., October 8, 1997, pp. C1, C4. All rights reserved worldwide.

cause both stocks have a higher price than on day 0 after adjusting *B* for the split. If nothing were done in computing the index, its value on day 1 would be 12 [$= (13 + 11)/2$], a drop of 20% [$= (12 - 15)/15$] from day 0 that falsely suggests that the market went down on day 1. In reality, the index went up to 17.5 {$= [13 + (11 \times 2)]/2$}, a gain of 16.67% [$= (17.5 - 15)/15$].

A stock split is accounted for in a price-weighted index by adjusting the divisor whenever a split takes place. In the example, the divisor is adjusted by examining the index on day 1, the day of the split. More specifically, the following equation would be solved for the unknown divisor *d*:

$$\frac{13 + 11}{d} = 17.5 \tag{24.6}$$

MAJOR INDEXES

†12-MO HIGH	LOW		DAILY HIGH	LOW	CLOSE	NET CHG	% CHG	†12-MO CHG	% CHG	FROM 12/31	% CHG
DOW JONES AVERAGES											
8259.31	5921.67	30 Industrials	8181.75	8088.92	8178.31 +	78.09 +	0.96	+ 2211.54 +	37.06	+ 1730.04 +	26.83
3281.20	2049.63	20 Transportation	3284.05	3236.35	3281.20 +	31.25 +	0.96	+ 1205.03 +	58.04	+ 1025.53 +	45.46
245.52	209.47	15 Utilities	245.68	243.96	245.52 +	1.29 +	0.53	+ 22.84 +	10.26	+ 12.99 +	5.59
2616.33	1863.88	65 Composite	2617.09	2589.06	2616.33 +	23.33 +	0.90	+ 736.91 +	39.21	+ 590.50 +	29.15
929.94	657.44	DJ Global-US	929.94	919.76	929.94 +	9.60 +	1.04	+ 266.98 +	40.27	+ 229.38 +	32.74
NEW YORK STOCK EXCHANGE											
514.21	370.35	Composite	514.22	509.13	514.21 +	4.51 +	0.88	+ 140.70 +	37.67	+ 121.91 +	31.08
643.81	469.02	Industrials	643.81	637.23	643.81 +	5.78 +	0.91	+ 169.54 +	35.75	+ 149.43 +	30.23
310.70	246.53	Utilities	310.71	307.42	310.70 +	3.06 +	0.99	+ 60.69 +	24.28	+ 50.79 +	19.54
471.20	326.50	Transportation	471.29	464.79	471.20 +	4.73 +	1.01	+ 141.58 +	42.95	+ 118.90 +	33.75
493.08	320.41	Finance	493.09	488.50	493.08 +	3.68 +	0.75	+ 169.57 +	52.42	+ 141.91 +	40.41
STANDARD & POOR'S INDEXES											
983.12	694.61	500 Index	983.12	971.95	983.12 +	10.43 +	1.07	+ 282.48 +	40.32	+ 242.38 +	32.72
1146.82	820.70	Industrials	1146.82	1133.67	1146.82 +	12.73 +	1.12	+ 319.47 +	38.61	+ 276.85 +	31.82
209.13	180.93	Utilities	209.13	208.08	209.13 +	0.75 +	0.36	+ 15.80 +	8.17	+ 10.32 +	5.19
339.84	240.49	400 MidCap	339.84	337.84	339.84 +	1.66 +	0.49	+ 95.97 +	39.35	+ 84.26 +	32.97
191.74	134.54	600 SmallCap	191.79	190.94	191.74 +	0.78 +	0.41	+ 52.65 +	37.85	+ 46.26 +	31.80
212.04	150.18	1500 Index	212.04	209.84	212.04 +	2.06 +	0.98	+ 60.67 +	40.08	+ 52.23 +	32.68
NASDAQ STOCK MARKET											
1737.27	1201.00	Composite	1739.86	1721.91	1737.27 +	15.36 +	0.89	+ 497.12 +	40.09	+ 446.24 +	34.56
1145.07	731.21	Nasdaq 100	1144.92	1125.93	1140.74 +	14.81 +	1.32	+ 387.50 +	51.44	+ 319.38 +	38.88
1402.84	971.06	Industrials	1402.87	1396.42	1402.84 +	8.12 +	0.58	+ 296.94 +	26.85	+ 293.21 +	26.42
1884.02	1321.01	Insurance	1885.48	1864.73	1884.02 +	18.41 +	0.99	+ 526.37 +	38.77	+ 418.59 +	28.56
1935.82	1168.79	Banks	1936.38	1926.28	1935.82 +	9.04 +	0.47	+ 764.11 +	65.21	+ 662.36 +	52.01
727.69	460.65	Computer	729.82	719.58	727.69 +	10.44 +	1.46	+ 246.59 +	51.26	+ 208.90 +	40.27
305.69	198.06	Telecommunications	306.01	303.32	305.69 +	1.72 +	0.57	+ 89.72 +	41.54	+ 89.78 +	41.58
OTHERS											
721.90	541.20	Amex Composite*	721.90	716.80	721.90 +	5.10 +	0.71	+ 143.74 +	24.86	+ 149.56 +	26.13
518.94	370.19	Russell 1000	518.94	513.46	518.94 +	5.22 +	1.02	+ 145.55 +	38.98	+ 125.19 +	31.79
463.78	335.85	Russell 2000	463.82	461.70	463.78 +	2.08 +	0.45	+ 116.42 +	33.52	+ 101.17 +	27.90
551.24	394.25	Russell 3000	551.24	545.80	551.24 +	5.23 +	0.96	+ 153.07 +	38.44	+ 131.80 +	31.42
477.08	355.32	Value-Line(geom.)	477.09	475.07	477.08 +	1.49 +	0.31	+ 117.62 +	32.72	+ 101.76 +	27.11
9486.69	6792.59	Wilshire 5000	...	...	9486.69 +	80.85 +	0.86	+ 2617.77 +	38.11	+ 2288.40 +	31.79

†-Based on comparable trading day in preceding year. *-I.eplaced previous index eff. 1/02/97.

Figure 24.2 (continued)

The value of d that solves this equation is 1.37. The new divisor will continue in use after day 1 until there is another split, when it will again be recalculated.

If it is desired to have the index begin at a given level, such as 100 on day 0, then updating it is straightforward. First the percentage change in average price is calculated. In the example, this was determined to be 16.67%. Second this percentage is multiplied by the previous day's index value in order to determine the change in the index. In the example, the index level on day 0 was 100, so the change from day 0 to day 1 would be 16.67 (= 16.67% $\times$ 100), resulting in a level on day 1 of 116.67. This is equivalent to dividing the average price on day 1 (17.5) by the average price on the beginning date (15) and then multiplying the result by the index's level on the beginning day (100). Mathematically the formula is:

$$I_t = I_0 \times \frac{AP_t}{AP_0} \tag{24.7}$$

where AP_t denotes the average price on day t and I_t denotes the index level on day t.

The Dow Jones Industrial Average, one of the most widely followed indices, is a price-weighted index. It involves the prices of 30 stocks that generally represent large-size firms. Other Dow Jones Averages, for example one involving 20 transportation stocks and another involving 15 utility stocks, are similarly calculated. Furthermore,

Dow Jones calculates stock market indices for each of several countries as well as an Asia/Pacific index and two World Indices, one with and one without the United States. Levels of several of these Dow Jones Averages are reported in almost every daily newspaper. Historical data on the Averages, including quarterly dividends and earnings figures, are published from time to time in *Barron's* and other periodicals. Some bond market indices are also calculated in this manner and will be discussed later on in this chapter.

24.3.2 Value Weighting

A second weighting method is known as **value weighting** or capitalization weighting. In this method, the prices of the stocks in the index are multiplied by their respective number of shares outstanding and then added up in order to arrive at a figure equal to the aggregate market value for that day. This figure is then divided by the corresponding figure for the day the index was started, with the resulting value being multiplied by an arbitrarily determined beginning index value.

Continuing with the example, assume that the start-up day for the index is day 0 and that the index will be assigned a beginning value of 100. First note that the aggregate market value on day 0 is equal to $55,000 [= ($10 × 1,500) + ($20 × 2,000)]. Next note that the aggregate market value on day 1 is equal to $63,500 [=($13 × 1,500) + ($11 × 4,000)]. Dividing $63,500 by $55,000 and then multiplying the result by 100 gives the index value for day 1 of 115.45 [= ($63,500/$55,000) × 100]. Thus the market would be reported as having risen by 15.45% [=(115.45 − 100)/100] from day 0 to day 1. Note that no special procedures are needed to handle stock splits, because the resulting increased number of shares for a company is automatically used after a split in calculating its market value. In general, the total market value of the securities in the index on day t (MV_t) is divided by the total market value on the beginning date (MV_0) and then multiplied by the index's level on the beginning day in order to get its value on day t. Mathematically the formula is:

$$I_t = I_0 \times \frac{MV_t}{MV_0} \tag{24.8}$$

The Standard & Poor's 500 (the S&P 500), widely used by institutional investors, is a value-weighted average of 500 large-size stocks. Standard & Poor's also computes value-weighted indices for industrial, transportation, utility, and financial stocks, as well as other sized-based indices. Industry indices are also calculated. Values for all indices, along with quarterly data on dividends, earnings, and sales, may be found in Standard & Poor's *Analysts' Handbook* (annual), *Trade and Securities Statistics* (annual), and *Analysts' Handbook Supplement* (monthly).

More comprehensive value-weighted indices for U.S. stocks are computed by other organizations. The New York Stock Exchange publishes a composite index of all stocks listed on that exchange, as well as four subindices (industrials, utilities, transportation, and finance). The American Stock Exchange computes an index of its stocks. The National Association of Securities Dealers (NASD), using its automated quotation service (Nasdaq), computes indices based on the market value of over 5,000 over-the-counter stocks. In addition to this composite index, NASD calculates indices for six categories representing industrials, banks, insurance, other finance, transportation, and utilities. NASD also publishes four indices that are based on just those stocks in their National Market System (the previously mentioned NASD indices are based on both NMS and non-NMS stocks).

The broadest value-weighted index is calculated by Wilshire Associates. Their index, known as the Wilshire 5000 Equity Index, is based on all stocks listed on the

New York and American Stock Exchanges plus those "actively traded over-the-counter." The Russell 1000, 2000, and 3000 are also broad value-weighted indices, covering the largest 1,000 U.S. stocks; the next 2,000; and the sum of the two. Various value-weighted U.S. stock indices are also produced to represent certain investment styles, as were discussed in Chapter 16. For example, the S&P 500 is split into a value stock index and a growth stock index. Stocks in the S&P 500 are first ordered by their book-value-to-market-value (BV/MV) ratios. Then the index is divided into two segments with equal aggregate market value; the low BV/MV stocks constitute the S&P/BARRA 500 Growth Index, and the high BV/MV stocks constitute the S&P/BARRA 500 Value Index. A similar procedure is used to construct growth and value indices for Standard & Poor's middle-capitalization stocks (the S&P 400) and small-capitalization stocks (the S&P 600).

In terms of international indices, *Morgan Stanley Capital International Perspective* publishes value-weighted indices using various combinations of over 1,000 stocks from many different countries, resulting in a "world market index" (these, and other international indices, are discussed in Chapter 25). Levels of many of these indices are published weekly in *Barron's*, with *The Wall Street Journal* providing daily values for several of them.

24.3.3 Equal Weighting

The third method of weighting is known as **equal weighting**. This index is computed daily by multiplying the level of the index on the previous day by the arithmetic mean of the daily **price relatives** (today's price divided by yesterday's price) of the relevant stocks in the index. For example, the value of the index consisting of A and B on day 1 would be calculated by first determining the price relatives to be equal to 1.3 ($=13/10$) for A and 1.1 [$=(11 \times 2)/20$] for B. Note that an adjustment was made in calculating the price relative for B because of its stock split. All that was required was to multiply the postsplit price of 11 by 2, the split ratio.

Once the price relatives have been determined, then their arithmetic mean can be calculated as:

$$(1.3 + 1.1)/2 = 1.20.$$

If the value of the index on day 0 was 100, then the value on day 1 would be reported as 120 ($=100 \times 1.20$), an increase of 20% ($=1.20 - 1$). (When the index is created, its value on that day can be set at any arbitrary starting value, such as 100.) The Value Line Composite (Arithmetic) Index, based on over 1,500 stocks, is prepared in this manner.

24.3.4 Geometric Mean

Value Line also prepares a popular index that does not involve price weighting, value weighting, or equal weighting. This index is computed daily by multiplying the previous day's index by the *geometric mean* of the daily price relatives of the relevant stocks in the index. It is referred to as the Value Line Composite (Geometric) Index and is based on the same stocks that are used in the arithmetic version of the index.

In the example, the geometric index for day 1 is calculated in the following manner. First, the geometric mean of the daily price relatives of stocks A and B is calculated:

$$(1.3 \times 1.1)^{1/2} = 1.1958$$

Second, given that the value of the index on the previous day (day 0) was 100, then the value on day 1 would be reported as 119.58 ($=100 \times 1.1958$). Note that this represents an increase of 19.58% ($=1.1958 - 1$). More generally, if there are N

stocks in the index, then the geometric index is calculated by multiplying their price relatives, taking the Nth root of the resulting product, and multiplying the level of the index on the previous day by this root.

In summary, four types of indices have been presented. Investors often use these indices interchangeably when they refer to how "the market" has done. However, the indices can give notably different answers. In the example shown here, the market was calculated to have risen by either 16.67%, 15.45%, 20%, or 19.58%, depending on the index used. In practice, most professional money managers use a value-weighted index such as the S&P 500 as the barometer of the stock market because such an index, by weighting larger companies more heavily than smaller companies, represents the performance of the average dollar invested in the corresponding part of the market.

24.4 RISK-ADJUSTED MEASURES OF PERFORMANCE

Once the periodic returns for a portfolio during a time interval (say, quarterly returns for a four years) have bean measured, the next step is to determine whether these returns represent superior or inferior performance. This step reguires an estimate of the portfolio's risk level during the time interval. Two kinds of risk can be estimated: the portfolio's market (or systematic) risk, measured by its beta, and the portfolio's total risk, measured by its standard deviation.

It is important to analyze risk appropriately. The key issue here is determining the impact of the portfolio on the client's overall level of risk. If the client has many other assets, then the market risk of the portfolio provides the relevant measure of the portfolio's impact on the client's overall level of risk. If, however, the portfolio provides the client's sole support, then its total risk is the relevant measure of risk. Risk-adjusted performance evaluation is generally based on one of these two viewpoints, taking either market risk or total risk into consideration.

Assume that there are T time periods in the time interval (for example, $T = 16$ when there are four years of quarterly data) and let r_{pt} denote the return on the portfolio during period t. The average return on the portfolio, denoted ar_p, is simply:

$$ar_p = \frac{\sum_{t=1}^{T} r_{pt}}{T} \qquad (24.9)$$

Once ar_p has been calculated, the *ex post* (that is, "after the fact," or historical) standard deviation σ_p can be calculated as:

$$\sigma_p = \left[\frac{\sum_{t=1}^{T} \left(r_{pt} - ar_p\right)^2}{T - 1} \right]^{1/2} \qquad (24.10)$$

This estimate of the portfolio's standard deviation can be used as an indication of the amount of total risk that the portfolio had during the time interval.[3] It can be compared directly with the standard deviations of other portfolios, as illustrated in Figure 24.3. (This figure is to be interpreted in the same manner as Figure 24.1.)

The returns of a portfolio may also be compared with those of a substitute for the market portfolio, such as Standard & Poor's 500, in order to determine the portfolio's *ex post* beta during the time interval. With the *excess return* on the portfolio during period t denoted as $er_{pt} = r_{pt} - r_{ft}$, the return on the S&P 500 (or some other market substitute) during period t denoted as r_{Mt}, and the excess return on the S&P 500 during period t denoted as $er_{Mt} = r_{Mt} - r_{ft}$, this beta can be estimated as follows:

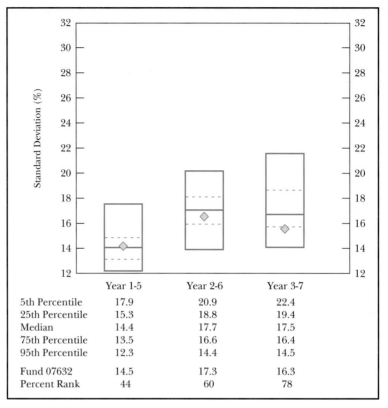

	Year 1-5	Year 2-6	Year 3-7
5th Percentile	17.9	20.9	22.4
25th Percentile	15.3	18.8	19.4
Median	14.4	17.7	17.5
75th Percentile	13.5	16.6	16.4
95th Percentile	12.3	14.4	14.5
Fund 07632	14.5	17.3	16.3
Percent Rank	44	60	78

Figure 24.3

Comparing Standard Deviations of Equity Portfolios

Source: Adapted from SEI, *Funds Evaluation Service.*

$$\beta_p = \frac{\left(T\sum_{t=1}^{T} er_{Mt}\,er_{pt}\right) - \left(\sum_{t=1}^{T} er_{pt}\sum_{t=1}^{T} er_{Mt}\right)}{\left(T\sum_{t=1}^{T} er_{Mt}^2\right) - \left(\sum_{t=1}^{T} er_{Mt}\right)^2}. \tag{24.11}$$

This estimate of the portfolio's beta can be used as an indication of the amount of market risk that the portfolio had during the time interval.[4] It can be compared directly with the betas of other portfolios, as illustrated in Figure 24.4. (This figure is to be interpreted in the same manner as Figures 24.1 and 24.3.)

Although a portfolio's return and a measure of its risk can be compared individually with those of other portfolios, as in Figures 24.1, 24.3, and 24.4, it is often not clear how the portfolio performed on a risk-adjusted basis relative to these other portfolios. For the fund shown in the figures, the average percentile rank for the portfolio's return over years 3 through 7 is 36 [= (17 + 56 + 39 + 16 + 50)/5]. Over the same period, its standard deviation put it in the 78th percentile rank. How would a client who is concerned with total risk interpret these percentile ranks? In terms of the return, the portfolio was slightly above average. In terms of standard deviation, it was less risky than approximately three-quarters of the other portfolios. Overall, this result suggests that the portfolio did better on a risk-adjusted basis than the others, but it does not give the client a clear and precise sense of how much better.

Such a sense can be conveyed by certain CAPM-based measures of portfolio performance. Each one of these measures provides an estimate of a portfolio's risk-adjusted performance, thereby allowing the client to see how the portfolio performed relative to other portfolios and relative to the market.

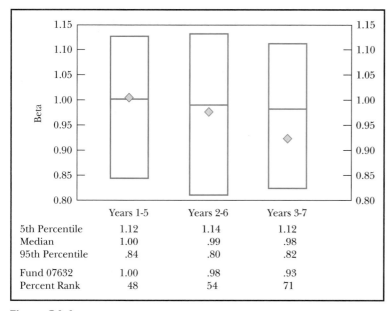

	Years 1-5	Years 2-6	Years 3-7
5th Percentile	1.12	1.14	1.12
Median	1.00	.99	.98
95th Percentile	.84	.80	.82
Fund 07632	1.00	.98	.93
Percent Rank	48	54	71

Figure 24.4
Comparing Betas of Equity Portfolios
Source: Adapted from SEI, *Funds Evaluation Service.*

24.4.1 *Ex Post* Characteristic Lines

Over a time interval, an *ex post* security market line (SML) can be estimated by determining the average riskfree rate and market return:

$$ar_f = \frac{\sum_{t=1}^{T} r_{ft}}{T} \tag{24.12}$$

$$ar_M = \frac{\sum_{t=1}^{T} r_{Mt}}{T} \tag{24.13}$$

Once these averages have been calculated, the *ex post* SML is simply the equation of the line going through the points $(0, ar_f)$ and $(1, ar_M)$. The return given by the *ex post* SML for a portfolio with a beta of β_p can be used as a benchmark return, ar_{bp}, for that portfolio. That is:

$$ar_{bp} = ar_f + (ar_M - ar_f)\beta_p \tag{24.14}$$

Panel (a) of Table 24.1 presents an example by using the quarterly returns for the S&P 500 over a 16-quarter time interval, along with corresponding returns on 90-day Treasury bills. Equations (24.12) and (24.13) show that the average riskfree return and market return were, respectively, 2.23% and 4.88%. These values can be inserted into Equation (24.14) to obtain the *ex post* SML for this time interval:

$$ar_{bp} = 2.23\% + (4.88\% - 2.23\%)\beta_p \tag{24.15}$$

$$= 2.23\% + 2.65\%\beta_p$$

TABLE 24.1 The *Ex Post* Characteristic Line for the First Fund

(a) Data

Quarter	Treasury Bill Return	First Fund Return	First Fund Excess Return	S&P 500 Return	S&P 500 Excess Return
1	2.97%	−8.77%	−11.74%	−5.86%	−8.83%
2	3.06	−6.03	−9.09	−2.94	−6.00
3	2.85	14.14	11.29	13.77	10.92
4	1.88	24.96	23.08	14.82	12.94
5	1.90	3.71	1.81	11.91	10.01
6	2.00	10.65	8.65	11.55	9.55
7	2.22	−.22	−2.44	−.78	−3.00
8	2.11	.27	−1.84	.02	−2.09
9	2.16	−3.08	−5.24	−2.52	−4.68
10	2.34	−6.72	−9.06	−1.85	−4.19
11	2.44	8.58	6.14	8.73	6.29
12	2.40	1.15	−1.25	1.63	−.77
13	1.89	7.87	5.98	10.82	8.93
14	1.94	5.92	3.98	7.24	5.30
15	1.72	−3.10	−4.82	−2.78	−4.50
16	1.75	13.61	11.86	14.36	12.61

(b) Calculations[a]

Quarter	First Fund Excess Returns $ Y (1)	S&P 500 Excess Returns $ X (2)	Y^2 (3)	X^2 (4)	$Y \times X$ (5)
1	−11.74%	−8.83%	137.83	77.93	103.66
2	−9.09	−6.00	82.63	36.05	54.54
3	11.29	10.92	127.46	119.26	123.29
4	23.08	12.94	532.69	167.53	298.66
5	1.81	10.01	3.28	100.11	18.12
6	8.65	9.55	74.82	91.28	82.61
7	−2.44	−3.00	5.95	8.97	7.32
8	−1.84	−2.09	3.39	4.35	3.85
9	−5.24	−4.68	27.46	21.94	24.52
10	−9.06	−4.19	82.08	17.54	37.96
11	6.14	6.29	37.70	39.53	38.62
12	−1.25	−.77	1.56	.60	.96
13	5.98	8.93	35.76	79.82	53.40
14	3.98	5.30	15.84	28.07	21.09
15	−4.82	−4.50	23.23	20.25	21.69
16	11.86	12.61	140.66	158.93	149.56
Sum (S)	27.31	42.49	1,332.34	972.16	1,039.85
	$= \Sigma Y$	$= \Sigma X$	$= \Sigma Y^2$	$= \Sigma X^2$	$= \Sigma XY$

Thus, after a portfolio's *ex post* beta has been estimated and this value entered on the right-hand side of Equation (24.15), a benchmark return for the portfolio can be determined. For example, a portfolio with a beta of .8 during the 16-quarter time interval would have a benchmark return of 4.35% [=2.23 + (2.65 × .8)]. Figure 24.5 presents a graph of the *ex post* SML given by Equation (24.15).

TABLE **24.1** (continued)   The *Ex Post* Characteristic Line for the First Fund

1. Beta:

$$\frac{(T \times \Sigma XY) - (\Sigma Y \times \Sigma X)}{(T \times \Sigma X^2) - (\Sigma X)^2} = \frac{(16 \times 1{,}039.85) - (27.31 \times 42.49)}{(16 \times 972.16) - (42.49)^2} = 1.13$$

2. Alpha:

$$[\Sigma Y/T] - [\text{Beta} \times (\Sigma X/T)] = [42.49/16] - [1.13 \times (42.49/16)] = -1.29$$

3. Standard Deviation of Random Error Term:

$$\{[\Sigma Y^2 - (\text{Alpha} \times \Sigma Y) - (\text{Beta} \times (\Sigma XY)]/[T-2]\}^{1/2}$$
$$= \{[1{,}332.34 - (-1.29 \times 27.31) - (1.13 \times 1{,}039.85)]/[16-2]\}^{1/2} = 3.75$$

4. Standard Error of Beta:

$$\text{Standard Deviation of Random Error Term}/\{\Sigma X^2 - [(\Sigma X)^2/T]\}^{1/2}$$
$$= 3.75/\{972.16 - [(42.49)^2/16]\}^{1/2} = .13$$

5. Standard Error of Alpha:

$$\text{Standard Deviation of Random Error Term}/\{T - [(\Sigma X)^2/\Sigma X^2]\}^{1/2}$$
$$= 3.75/\{16 - [(42.49)^2/972.16]\}^{1/2} = 1.00$$

6. Correlation Coefficient:

$$\frac{(T \times \Sigma XY) - (\Sigma Y \times \Sigma X)}{\{[(T \times \Sigma Y^2) - (\Sigma Y)^2] \times [(T \times \Sigma X^2) - (\Sigma X)^2]\}^{1/2}} =$$
$$\frac{(16 \times 1{,}039.85) - (27.31 \times 42.49)}{\{[(16 \times 1{,}332.34) - (27.31)^2] \times [(16 \times 972.16) - (42.49)^2]\}^{1/2}} = .92$$

7. Coefficient of Determination:

$$(\text{Correlation Coefficient})^2 = (.92)^2 = .85$$

8. Coefficient of Nondetermination:

$$1 - \text{Coefficient of determination} = 1 - .85 = .15$$

[a] All summations are to be carried out over *t*, where *t* goes from 1 to *T* (in this example, *t* = 1,..., 16).

As shown in Chapter 21, one measure of a portfolio's risk-adjusted performance is the difference between its average return (ar_p) and the return on its corresponding benchmark portfolio, denoted ar_{bp}. This difference is generally referred to as the portfolio's *ex post* **alpha** (or differential return), and is denoted α_p:

$$\alpha_p = ar_p - ar_{bp} \qquad (21.3)$$

A positive value of α_p for a portfolio would indicate that the portfolio had an average return greater than the benchmark return, suggesting that its performance was superior. On the other hand, a negative value of α_p would indicate that the portfolio had an average return less than the benchmark return, suggesting that its performance was inferior.

By substituting the right-hand side of Equation (24.14) for ar_{bp} in Equation (21.3), one can see that a portfolio's *ex post* alpha based on the *ex post* SML is equal to:[5]

$$\alpha_p = ar_p - [ar_f + (ar_M - ar_f)\beta_p] \qquad (24.16)$$

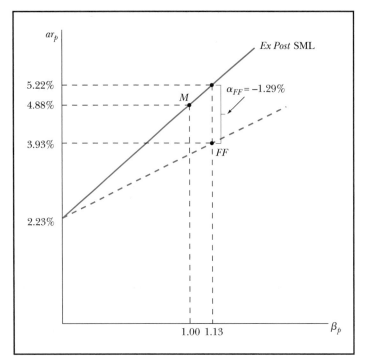

Figure 24.5
Performance Evaluation Using the *Ex Post* SML.

After the values for α_p and β_p for a portfolio have been determined, the *ex post* **characteristic line** for the portfolio can be written as:

$$r_p - r_f = \alpha_p + \beta_p(r_M - r_f) \tag{24.17}$$

The characteristic line is similar to the market model (introduced in Chapter 7) except that the portfolio's returns and the market index's returns are expressed in excess of the riskfree return. Graphically, the characteristic line formulation is the equation of a straight line where $(r_M - r_f)$ is measured on the horizontal axis and $(r_p - r_f)$ is measured on the vertical axis. Furthermore, the line has a vertical intercept of α_p and a slope of β_p.

As an example, consider the performance of the hypothetical portfolio "First Fund," indicated in panel (a) of Table 24.1, for the given 16-quarter time interval. During this interval, the First Fund had an average quarterly return of 3.93%. Equation (24.11), shows that First Fund had a beta of 1.13. Having an average beta over the 16 quarters that is greater than the market portfolio's beta of 1 indicates that First Fund was relatively *aggressive* (if its average beta had been less than 1, it would have been relatively *defensive*).

Given these values for its beta and average return, the location of First Fund in Figure 24.5 is represented by the point having coordinates (1.13, 3.93), denoted *FF*. The exact vertical distance from *FF* to the *ex post* SML can be calculated by using Equation (24.16):

$$\alpha_p = ar_p - \left[ar_f + \left(ar_M + ar_f\right)\beta_p\right]$$
$$= 3.93\% - \left[2.23\% + (4.88\% - 2.23\%)1.13\right]$$
$$= -1.29\%$$

Because *FF* lies below the *ex post* SML, its *ex post* alpha is negative, and its performance would be viewed as inferior.[6] Using Equation (24.17), the *ex post* characteristic line for First Fund would be:

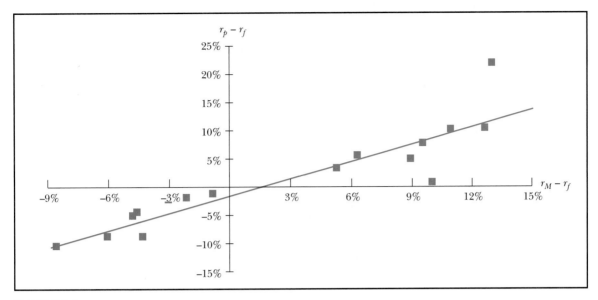

Figure 24.6
Ex Post Characteristic Line for First Fund.

$$r_p - r_f = -1.29\% + 1.13(r_M - r_f)$$

Figure 24.6 provides an illustration of this line.[7]

The method for determining a portfolio's *ex post* alpha, beta, and characteristic line suggests the use of a five-step procedure:

1. Determine the periodic rates of return for the portfolio and market index over the time interval, as well as the corresponding riskfree rates.
2. Determine the average market return and riskfree rate by using the formulas in Equations (24.12) and (24.13).
3. Determine the portfolio's *ex post* beta by using the formula in Equation (24.11).
4. Determine the portfolio's *ex post* alpha by using the formula given in Equation (24.16).
5. Insert these values for alpha and beta in Equation (24.17) in order to determine the portfolio's *ex post* characteristic line.

However, there is a simpler method for determining a portfolio's *ex post* alpha, beta, and characteristic line that also provides a number of other pieces of information relating to the portfolio's performance. This method involves the use of **simple linear regression**, and corresponds to the method presented in Chapters 7 and 16 for estimating the market model for an individual security.

With this method, the excess return on portfolio *p* in a given period *t* is viewed as having three components. The first component is the portfolio's alpha; the second component is a risk premium equal to the excess return on the market times the portfolio's beta; and the third component is a random error term.[8] These three components can be seen on the right-hand side of the following equation:

$$r_{pt} - r_{ft} = \alpha_p + \beta_p(r_{Mt} - r_{ft}) + \varepsilon_{pt} \qquad (24.18)$$

Because α_p and β_p are assumed to be constant during the time interval, Equation (24.18) can be viewed as a regression equation. Accordingly, there are certain standard formulas for estimating α_p, β_p, and a number of other statistical parameters associated with the regression equation.

Panel (b) of Table 24.1 presents these formulas, with First Fund being used as an example. As can be seen, the formulas indicate that First Fund's *ex post* alpha and beta were equal to −1.29 and 1.13, respectively, over the 16-quarter time interval. These values are the same as those arising when Equations (24.11) and (24.16) were used earlier. Indeed, they will always result in the same values.

Figure 24.6 presents a scatter diagram of the excess returns on First Fund and the S&P 500. Based on Equation (24.18), the regression equation for First Fund is:

$$r_{FF} - r_f = -1.29\% + 1.13(r_M - r_f) + \varepsilon_{FF} \tag{24.19}$$

where −1.29 and 1.13 are the estimated *ex post* alpha and beta for First Fund over the 16-quarter time interval. As mentioned earlier, also shown in the figure is the *ex post* characteristic line for First Fund, a line that is derived by the use of simple linear regression:

$$r_{FF} - r_f = -1.29\% + 1.13(r_M - r_f) \tag{24.20}$$

The vertical distance between each point in the scatter diagram and the regression line represents an estimate of the size of the random error term for the corresponding quarter. The exact distance can be found by rewriting Equation (24.19) as:

$$\varepsilon_{FF} = (r_{FF} - r_f) - [-1.29\% + 1.13(r_M - r_f)] \tag{24.21}$$

For example, in the 11th quarter the excess return on First Fund and the S&P 500 were 6.14% and 6.29%, respectively. The value of ε_{FF} for that quarter can be calculated by using Equation (24.21) as follows:

$$\varepsilon_{FF} = (6.14\%) - [-1.29\% + 1.13(6.29\%)]$$

$$= .32\%$$

The value of ε_{FF} can be calculated similarly for the other 15 quarters of the time interval. The standard deviation of the resulting set of 16 numbers is an estimate of the standard deviation of the random error term (also known as the residual standard deviation) and is shown in panel (b) of Table 24.1 to be equal to 3.75%. This number can be viewed as an estimate of the *ex post* unique (or unsystematic or non-market) risk of First Fund.

The regression line for First Fund that is shown in Figure 24.6 is the line of best fit for the scatter diagram and corresponds to First Fund's *ex post* characteristic line. What is meant by "best fit"? Given that a straight line is defined by its intercept and slope, it means that there are no other values for alpha and beta that fit the scatter diagram any better than this one. In terms of simple linear regression, this means that there is no line that could be drawn such that the resulting standard deviation of the random error term would be smaller than the one of best fit.

A portfolio's "true" *ex post* beta cannot be observed; all that can be done is to estimate its value. Thus, even if a portfolio's true beta remained the same forever, its estimated value, obtained in the manner illustrated in Table 24.1 and Figure 24.6, would still change from time to time because of errors (known as sampling errors) in estimating it. For example, if a different set of 16 quarters were examined, with the first quarter being replaced by a more recent quarter, the resulting estimated beta for First Fund would almost certainly be different from 1.13.

The standard error of beta shown in Table 24.1 attempts to indicate the extent of such estimation errors. Given a number of necessary assumptions (for example, the "true" beta did not change during the 16-quarter estimation period), the chances are roughly two out of three that the true beta is within one standard error, plus or minus, of the estimated beta. Thus First Fund's true beta is likely to be between the values of 1.00 (=1.13 − .13) and 1.26 (=1.13 + .13). Similarly, the value under standard error of alpha provides an indication of the magnitude of the possible sampling error that has been made in estimating the portfolio's alpha.

The value under correlation coefficient provides an indication of how closely the excess returns on First Fund were associated with the excess returns on the S&P 500. Because its range is between -1 and $+1$, the value for First Fund of .92 indicates a strong positive relationship between First Fund and the S&P 500. That is, larger excess returns for First Fund seem to have been closely associated with larger excess returns for the S&P 500.

The coefficient of determination is equal to the squared value of the correlation coefficient; it represents the proportion of variation in the excess return on First Fund that is related to the variation in the excess return on the S&P 500. That is, it shows how much of the movement in First Fund's excess returns can be explained by movements in the excess returns on the S&P 500. The a value of .85 shows that 85% of the movement in the excess return on First Fund over the 16 quarters can be attributed to movement in the excess return on the S&P 500.

Because the coefficient of nondetermination is 1 minus the coefficient of determination, it represents the proportion of movement in the excess return on First Fund that does not result from movement in the excess return on the S&P 500. Thus 15% of the movement in First Fund cannot be attributed to movement in the S&P 500.

Although Table 24.1 shows the formulas for calculating all these values, it should be pointed out that there are many different software packages that can quickly carry out these calculations. The only substantive effort involves gathering all the return data shown in panel (a) of Table 24.1 and then entering it into a computer spreadsheet.

24.4.2 The Reward-to-Volatility Ratio

Closely related to the *ex post* alpha measure of portfolio performance is a measure known as the **reward-to-volatility ratio**.[9] This measure, denoted $RVOL_p$, also uses the *ex post* security market line to form a benchmark for performance evaluation, but in a somewhat different manner. The calculation of the reward-to-volatility ratio for a portfolio involves dividing its average excess return by its market risk as follows:

$$RVOL_p = \frac{ar_p - ar_f}{\beta_p} \qquad (24.22)$$

Here the beta of the portfolio can be determined using the formula in Equation (24.11).

In the example of First Fund, it was noted earlier that its average return for the 16-quarter time interval was 3.93%. Furthermore, it was noted that the average Treasury bill rate was 2.23%. Thus the average excess return for First Fund was 1.70% ($=3.93\% - 2.23\%$) and, given a beta of 1.13, its reward-to-volatility ratio was 1.50% ($=1.70\%/1.13$).

The reward-to-volatility ratio corresponds to the slope of a line originating at the average riskfree rate and going through the point (β_p, ar_p). This correspondence can be seen by noting that the slope of a line is easily determined if two points on the line are known; it is simply the vertical distance between the two points ("rise") divided by the horizontal distance between the two points ("run"). In this case, the vertical distance is $ar_p - ar_f$ and the horizontal distance is $\beta_p - 0$, so the slope is $(ar_p - ar_f)/\beta_p$ and thus corresponds to the formula for $RVOL_p$ given in Equation (24.22). Note that the value being measured on the horizontal axis is β_p and the value being measured on the vertical axis is ar_p, suggesting that the line can be drawn on the same diagram as the *ex post* SML.

In the First Fund example, remember that the *ex post* SML for the 16-quarter time interval was shown by the solid line in Figure 24.5. Also appearing in this figure was the point denoted *FF*, corresponding to $(\beta_p, ar_p) = (1.13, 3.93\%)$ for First Fund. The dashed line in this figure originates from the point $(0, ar_f) = (0, 2.23\%)$, goes through *FF*, and has a slope of 1.50% $[= (3.93\% - 2.23\%)/1.13]$ that corresponds to the value noted earlier for $RVOL_p$.

The benchmark for comparison with this measure of performance is the slope of the *ex post* SML. Because this line goes through the points $(0, ar_f)$ and $(1, ar_M)$, its slope is simply $(ar_M - ar_f)/(1 - 0) = (ar_M - ar_f)$ If $RVOL_p$ is greater than this value, the portfolio lies above the *ex post* SML, indicating that it has outperformed the market. Alternatively, if $RVOL_p$ is less than this value, the portfolio lies below the *ex post* SML, indicating that it has not performed as well as the market.

In the case of First Fund, the benchmark is 2.65% $[= (ar_M - ar_f) = (4.88\% - 2.23\%)]$. Because $RVOL_p$ for First Fund is less than the benchmark $(1.50\% < 2.65\%)$, according to this measure of portfolio performance, First Fund did not perform as well as the market.

In the comparison of the two measures of performance that are based on the *ex post* SML, α_p and $RVOL_p$, it should be noted that they will *always* give the same assessment of a portfolio's performance relative to the market portfolio. That is, if one measure indicates that the portfolio outperformed the market, so will the other. Similarly, if one measure indicates that the portfolio did not perform as well as the market, the other measure will show the same thing. This correspondence can be seen by noting that any portfolio with a positive *ex post* alpha (an indication of superior performance) lies *above* the *ex post* SML and thus must have a slope *greater* than the slope of the *ex post* SML (also an indication of superior performance). Similarly, any portfolio with a negative *ex post* alpha (an indication of inferior performance) lies *below* the *ex post* SML and thus must have a slope *less* than the slope of the *ex post* SML (also an indication of inferior performance).

However, it should also be noted that it is possible for the two measures to *rank* portfolios differently on the basis of performance simply because the calculations are different. For example, if Second Fund had a beta of 1.5 and an average return of 4.86%, its *ex post* alpha would be -1.34% $\{=4.86\% - [2.23 + (4.88 - 2.23) \times 1.5]\}$. Thus its performance appears to be worse than that of First Fund because it has a smaller *ex post* alpha $(-1.34\% < -1.29\%)$. However, its reward-to-volatility ratio of 1.75% $[= (4.86\% - 2.23\%)/1.5]$ is larger than the reward-to-volatility of 1.50% for First Fund, suggesting that its performance was better than First Fund's.

24.4.3   The Sharpe Ratio

Both measures of risk-adjusted performance described so far, *ex post* alpha (that is, differential return) and the reward-to-volatility ratio, use benchmarks that are based on the *ex post* security market line (SML). Accordingly, they measure returns relative to the market risk of the portfolio. In contrast, the **Sharpe ratio** (or *reward-to-variability ratio*) is a measure of risk-adjusted performance that uses a benchmark based on the *ex post* capital market line (CML).[10] It measures returns relative to the total risk of the portfolio, where total risk is the standard deviation of portfolio returns.

In order to use the Sharpe ratio (SR_p), one must determine the location of the *ex post* CML. This line goes through two points on a graph that measures average return on the vertical axis and standard deviation on the horizontal axis. The first point is the vertical intercept of the line and corresponds to the average riskfree rate during the 16-quarter time interval. The second point corresponds to the location of the market portfolio, meaning that its coordinates are the average return and standard deviation of return for the market portfolio during the evaluation interval, or

(σ_M, ar_M). Because the *ex post* CML goes through these two points, its slope can readily be calculated as the vertical distance between the two points divided by the horizontal distance between the two points, or $(ar_M - ar_f)/(\sigma_M - 0) = (ar_M - ar_f)/\sigma_M$. The return given by the *ex post* CML for a portfolio with total risk σ_p can be used as a benchmark return, ar_{bp}, for that portfolio. That is, given a vertical intercept of ar_f, the equation of this line is:

$$ar_{bp} = ar_f + \frac{ar_M - ar_f}{\sigma_M} \sigma_p \qquad (24.23)$$

In the example shown in Table 24.1, the average return and standard deviation for the S&P 500, calculated using Equations (24.9) and (24.10), were 4.88% and 7.39%, respectively. The average return on Treasury bills was 2.23%, so the *ex post* CML during these 16 quarters was:

$$ar_{bp} = 2.23\% + \frac{4.88\% - 2.23\%}{7.39\%} \sigma_p \qquad (24.24)$$

$$= 2.23\% + .36\sigma_p$$

Figure 24.7 presents a graph of this line.

Once the location of the *ex post* CML has been determined, the average return and standard deviation of the portfolio being evaluated can be calculated next by using Equations (24.9) and (24.10). When these values are known, the portfolio can be located on the same graph as the *ex post* CML. In the case of First Fund, its average return and standard deviation were 3.93% and 9.08%, respectively. Thus in Figure 24.7 its location corresponds to the point having coordinates (9.08%, 3.93%), which is denoted *FF*.

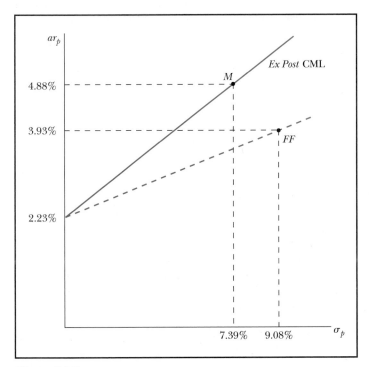

Figure 24.7
Performance Evaluation Using the *Ex Post* CML.

The calculation of the Sharpe ratio SR_p is analogous to the calculation of the reward-to-volatility ratio $RVOL_p$ described earlier. Specifically, $RVOL_p$ involves dividing the portfolio's average excess return by its beta, whereas SR_p involves dividing the portfolio's average excess return by its standard deviation:

$$SR_p = \frac{ar_p - ar_f}{\sigma_p} \tag{24.25}$$

Note that SR_p corresponds to the slope of a line originating at the average riskfree rate and going through a point having coordinates of (σ_p, ar_p). This correspondence can be seen by noting that the slope of this line is simply the vertical distance between the two points divided by the horizontal distance between the two points, or $(ar_p - ar_f)/(\sigma_p - 0) = (ar_p - ar_f)/\sigma_p$, which corresponds to the formula for SR_p given in Equation (24.25).

In the First Fund example, recall that the *ex post* CML was shown by the solid line in Figure 24.7. Also appearing in this figure was the point denoted *FF*, corresponding to $(\sigma_p, ar_p) = (9.08\%, 3.93\%)$ for First Fund. The dashed line in this figure originates from the point $(0, ar_f) = (0, 2.23\%)$ and goes through *FF*. The slope of this line is simply .19 [$= (3.93 - 2.23)/9.08$].

Because the *ex post* CML represents various combinations of riskfree lending or borrowing with investing in the market portfolio, it can be used to provide a benchmark for the Sharpe ratio in a manner similar to the SML-based benchmark for the reward-to-volatility ratio. As noted earlier, the slope of the *ex post* CML is $(ar_M - ar_f)/\sigma_M$. If SR_p is greater than this value, the portfolio lies above the *ex post* CML, indicating that it has outperformed the market. Alternatively, if SR_p less than this value, the portfolio lies below the *ex post* CML, indicating that it has not performed as well as the market.

In the case of First Fund, the benchmark is .36 [$= (4.88 - 2.23)/7.39$]. Because SR_p is less than the benchmark (.19 < .36), First Fund did not perform as well as the market according to this risk-adjusted measure of portfolio performance.

24.4.4 *M²*

The measure **M-squared** uses standard deviation as the relevant measure of risk.[11] Thus, like the Sharpe ratio, it is based on the *ex post* CML. This measure simply takes a portfolio's average return and determines what it would have been if the portfolio had had the same degree of total risk as the market portfolio (in the case of a common stock portfolio usually represented by the S&P 500). Consider a line that goes through the average riskfree rate and the average return on the portfolio, where standard deviation is being used as the measure of risk, such as the line going through the average riskfree rate of 2.23% and First Fund (FF) in Figure 24.7. The following equation describes such a line:

$$ar_i = ar_f + \left(\frac{ar_p - ar_f}{\sigma_p} \right) \sigma_i \tag{24.26}$$

because the line has a vertical intercept of ar_f and a slope of $(ar_p - ar_f)/\sigma_p$. This equation indicates the average return, ar_i, that would have been earned by investing in portfolio p and either investing or borrowing at the riskfree rate to such a degree that the resulting standard deviation was σ_i. The risk-adjusted return M_p^2 is the average return that would have been earned if the amount of riskfree investing or lending had resulted in the standard deviation of the portfolio being equal to that of the market portfolio. Hence, setting σ_i equal to σ_M in Equation (24.26) results in the value of M_p^2 for portfolio p:

$$M_p^2 = ar_f + \left(\frac{ar_p - ar_f}{\sigma_p} \right) \sigma_M \qquad (24.27)$$

Accordingly, M_p^2 measures the return an investor would have earned if the portfolio had been altered by use of the riskfree rate through borrowing or lending in order to match the market portfolio's risk level as measured by standard deviation.

For example, First Fund had on a quarterly basis an average return of 3.93% and a standard deviation of 9.08%. Because the average riskfree rate was 2.23%, the equation describing the dashed line in Figure 24.7 can be determined by using Equation (24.26) to be:

$$ar_i = 2.23 + \left(\frac{3.93 - 2.23}{9.08} \right) \sigma_i$$

$$= 2.23 + .19\sigma_i \qquad (24.28)$$

The standard deviation of the market portfolio (estimated by using the S&P 500) was 7.39%, so it follows that M_p^2 for the First Fund was 3.61%. That is, by investing $7.39/9.08 = 81.4\%$ in First Fund and 18.6% in the riskfree rate, the investor would have had a portfolio that had the same standard deviation as the market portfolio. In this example, M^2 effectively "de-levers" First Fund's return to bring its risk level down to that of the market portfolio and then proportionately reduces First Fund's return by the degree of de-leveraging. If the market portfolio's standard deviation had been greater than that of First Fund, then M^2 would have leveraged First Fund's return by borrowing at the riskfree rate to increase its standard deviation to that of the market portfolio. This action would have proportionately increased First Fund's return by the degree of leveraging.

M_p^2 can be compared directly with the average return on the market portfolio ar_M in order to see if the portfolio outperformed or underperformed the market portfolio on a risk-adjusted basis. In the case of First Fund, the market portfolio had an average return of 4.88%, suggesting underperformance on the fund's part since $M_{FF}^2 = 3.61\% < 4.88\% = ar_M$.

When the two measures of risk-adjusted performance that are based on the *ex post* CML, SR_p and M_p^2, are compared, they will always give the same assessment of a portfolio's performance relative to the market portfolio.[12] Hence, it is impossible for one measure to indicate that a portfolio performed better than the market and the other to indicate that it performed worse. This correspondence can be seen by noting that if a portfolio plots below the *ex post* CML, then (1) the slope of the line going through the portfolio (SR_p) will be less than the slope of the *ex post* CML, and (2) M_p^2 will lie on the line going through the portfolio at a point that is directly below the location of the market portfolio on the *ex post* CML. The converse is also true if the portfolio plots above the *ex post* CML.

Furthermore, the two measures will rank a set of portfolios exactly the same, because comparing slopes of lines that all go through the average riskfree rate will rank portfolios exactly the same as comparing the average returns on all of these lines at a given level of standard deviation. Equivalently, Equations (24.25) and (24.27) can be combined to show that:

$$M_p^2 = ar_f + SR_p \sigma_M \qquad (24.29)$$

Thus, the value of M_p^2 for any portfolio is simply equal to a positive constant plus the portfolio's reward-to-variability ratio multiplied by a positive constant. Because these

Custom Benchmark Portfolios

Investment management has become increasingly specialized. Many managers have chosen not only to concentrate on specific asset classes (for example, stocks or bonds), but within those asset classes they have further focused their efforts on certain types of securities. This specialization has been particularly prevalent among managers owning U.S. common stocks. For example, some managers specialize in small, emerging growth company stocks. Others select only from certain industries, such as health care. These specializations have come to be known as "investment styles." Investment styles have significant ramifications for the evaluation of investment manager performance.

Investment management can be viewed as a fishing contest. Each angler has his or her own fishing hole (investment style). No one fishing hole is assumed to be any better than another, although from year to year the sizes and quantity of fish fluctuate independently in each hole. The anglers attempt to catch the largest fish from their fishing holes. How should institutional investor clients evaluate the proficiency of these anglers on the basis of their catches? It would make little sense to directly compare the anglers' respective catches. If Angler *A*'s fishing hole was extremely well stocked this year and Angler *B*'s was not, Angler *B* would be at a tremendous disadvantage. More appropriately, clients would like to compare what each angler caught against the opportunities available in their respective fishing holes. In other words, the clients should want to take into account

the impact of managers' investment styles on their performance.

Investment styles tend to dominate the performance of investment managers within a particular asset class. For example, suppose that the domestic common stock market was split along two dimensions similar to those discussed in Chapter 16: market capitalization (share price times shares outstanding) and growth prospects. In 1997, for example, the best-performing group was small value stocks, which returned 32%. Conversely, small growth stocks returned 13%, a difference of 19 percentage points. Differences between investment styles of similar magnitudes can be found in other years. These differences are typically large enough so that no investment manager can hope to consistently overcome the performance effect of his or her investment style. Therefore to evaluate a manager's investment skill, how the manager has performed relative to his or her investment style should be considered explicitly.

One means of dealing with this issue is to develop a comparison portfolio that specifically represents the manager's investment style. This comparison portfolio is referred to as a *custom benchmark portfolio*. The custom benchmark contains the types of securities from which the manager typically selects. Further, these securities are weighted in the custom benchmark in a manner similar to weights typically assigned by the manager. Moreover, the custom benchmark displays portfolio characteristics (for example, price-earnings ratios, earnings growth rates, and market

---

two constants are the same for all portfolios, the ranking for M_p^2 will be exactly the same as the ranking for SR_p.

24.4.5 Comparing the Risk-Adjusted Measures of Performance

The measures of performance that are based on the *ex post* SML, α_p and $RVOL_p$, can be compared with the measure of performance that is based on the *ex post* CML, SR_p. Because the *ex post* CML-based measure M_p^2 evaluates portfolios exactly the same as SR_p, there is no need to compare α_p and $RVOL_p$ with it.

It should be noted that in certain situations, $RVOL_p$ and SR_p can give different assessments of a portfolio's performance relative to the market portfolio. (The comparison also applies to α_p and SR_p.) In particular, if $RVOL_p$ indicates that the portfolio outperformed the market, it is possible for SR_p to indicate that the portfolio did not perform as well as the market. The reason is that the portfolio may have a rela-

capitalizations) consistent with the manager's actual portfolio.

Consider a manager whose investment style entails investing in large-capitalization, high-dividend-yield stocks. In building portfolios, the manager follows certain rules, some explicitly, others implicitly. For example, the manager does not buy stocks with less than $5 billion in market capitalization. All stocks in the manager's portfolio must display at least a 3% dividend yield. The manager assigns each stock an equal weight in the portfolio. Further, to avoid overconcentrations, no industry may constitute more than 10% of the portfolio's market value.

A custom benchmark can be designed to reflect these characteristics of the manager's investment style. The custom benchmark might be composed of 300 stocks, as opposed to the manager's portfolio, which might contain only 30 stocks. The manager, in effect, has searched through his or her fishing hole and selected the 30 stocks that he or she thinks will perform the best. An evaluation of the manager's performance will be based over time on how these 30 stocks perform relative to the 300 stocks.

This performance evaluation process takes advantage of a powerful paired-comparison test. Given a group of stocks, can the manager consistently identify the best-performing issues? The question is simple and the results easy to interpret. No special risk-adjusted performance measures are required. If the custom benchmark has been properly constructed, it exhibits a risk level consistent with that exhibited on average by the manager.

The primary drawback of custom benchmarks is the effort required to design them. Each manager's investment style has unique aspects, and not all of them are as explicit as those of the large-capitalization, high-yield manager discussed above. Typically, identifying those unique aspects involves examining past portfolios and engaging in lengthy discussions with the manager.

Recently a number of analysts have adopted a method in which a benchmark made up of combinations of standard indices is constructed on the basis of statistical analysis of a manager's past returns. The use of this procedure, known as *style analysis*, can in many cases provide some of the advantages of more elaborate custom benchmark portfolios at a fraction of the cost, time, and effort. (For details on this approach, see the references listed at the end of the chapter.)

Custom benchmarks, whether derived via detailed analyses or using style analysis, can provide effective performance evaluations. Moreover, they have uses outside of performance evaluation. For example, as discussed in Chapter 23's *Institutional Issues: Manager Structuring*, clients who hire more than one investment manager can use custom benchmarks to examine how various investment styles fit together into an aggregate portfolio. This type of analysis permits a client to better understand and control the investment risks present in the client's total portfolio.

tively large amount of unique risk. Such risk would not be a factor in determining the value of $RVOL_p$ for the portfolio, because only *market risk* is in the denominator. However, such risk would be included in the denominator of SR_p for the portfolio because this measure is based on *total risk* (that is, both market and unique risk). Thus a portfolio with a low amount of market risk could have a high amount of total risk, resulting in a relatively high $RVOL_p$ (due to the low amount of market risk) and a low SR_p (due to the high amount of total risk). Accordingly, $RVOL_p$ could indicate that the portfolio outperformed the market at the same time that SR_p indicated that it did not perform as well as the market.[13]

As an example, consider Third Fund, which had an average return of 4.5%, a beta of .8, and a standard deviation of 18%. Accordingly, $RVOL_{TF} = 2.71\%$ [= (4.5% − 2.23%)/.8], indicating that Third Fund outperformed the market portfolio because the benchmark is 2.65% [= (4.88% − 2.23%)/1.0]. However, $SR_{TF} = .12$ [= (4.5% − 2.23%)/18%], indicating that Third Fund did not perform as well as the market portfolio because the benchmark is .36 [= (4.88% − 2.23%)/7.39%]. The reason for the difference can be seen by noting Third Fund's low beta relative to the market

(.8 < 1.0) but high standard deviation relative to the market (18% > 7.39%). This outcome suggests that Third Fund had a relatively high level of unique risk.

It also follows that it is possible for $RVOL_p$ and SR_p to rank two or more portfolios differently on the basis of their performance because these two measures of risk-adjusted performance use different types of risk. Recall that earlier it was shown that First Fund had an average return of 3.93%, a beta of 1.13, and a standard deviation of 9.08%. Thus, $RVOL_{FF} = 1.50\%$ [= (3.93% − 2.23%)/1.13], which is less than $RVOL_{TF} = 2.65\%$, thereby indicating that First Fund ranked lower than Third Fund. However, $SR_{FF} = .13$ [=(3.93% − 2.23%)/9.08%], which is greater than $SR_{TF} = .12$, thereby indicating that First Fund ranked higher than Third Fund.

Did Third Fund do better or worse than the market on a risk-adjusted basis? And did Third Fund perform better or worse than First Fund? The answer to those two questions lies in identifying the appropriate measure of risk for the client. If the client has many other assets, then beta is the relevant measure of risk, and performance should be based on $RVOL_p$. To such a client, Third Fund should be viewed as a superior performer relative to both the market and First Fund. However, if the client has few other assets, then standard deviation is the relevant measure of risk, and performance should be based on SR_p. To such a client, Third Fund should be viewed as an inferior performer relative to both the market and First Fund.

24.5   MARKET TIMING

A market timer structures a portfolio to have a relatively high beta when he or she expects the market to rise and a relatively low beta when a market drop is anticipated. Why? Because, as noted earlier, the expected return on a portfolio is a linear function of its beta:

$$\bar{r}_p = \alpha_p + r_f + \left(\bar{r}_M - r_f \right)\beta_p \qquad (24.30)$$

This means that the market timer will want to have a high-beta portfolio when he or she expects the market to have a higher return than the riskfree rate because such a portfolio will have a higher expected return than a low-beta portfolio. Conversely, the market timer will want to have a low-beta portfolio when he or she expects the market to have a lower return than the riskfree rate because it will have a higher expected return than a high-beta portfolio. Simply put, the market timer will want to:

1. Hold a high-beta portfolio when $\bar{r}_M > r_f$, and
2. Hold a low-beta portfolio when $\bar{r}_M < r_f$.

If the timer is accurate in his or her forecasts of the expected return on the market, then his or her portfolio will outperform a benchmark portfolio that has a constant beta equal to the average beta of the timer's portfolio.

For example, if the market timer set the portfolio beta at 0.0 when $\bar{r}_M < r_f$ and at 2.0 when $\bar{r}_M > r_f$, the return on the portfolio would be higher than the return on a portfolio having a beta constantly equal to 1.0, provided that the timer is accurate in forecasting $\bar{r}_M$. Unfortunately, if the market timer's forecast are inaccurate and consequently alters the portfolio's beta in ways unrelated to subsequent market moves, then the timer's portfolio will not perform as well as a constant-beta portfolio. For example, if the timer sometimes sets the portfolio's beta equal to 0 when the market is forecast to fall but actually rises and at other times sets the beta equal to 2 when the market is forecast to rise but actually falls, then the portfolio will have an average return that is less than what a portfolio with a constant beta of 1 would have earned.

To "time the market," one must change either the average beta of the risky securities held in the portfolio or the relative amounts invested in the riskfree asset and risky securities. For example, the beta of a portfolio could be increased by selling bonds or low-beta stocks and using the proceeds to purchase high-beta stocks. Alternatively, Treasury bills in the portfolio could be sold (or the amount of borrowing increased), with the resulting proceeds being invested in stocks or stock index futures. Because of the relative ease of buying and selling derivative instruments such as stock index futures, most investment organizations specializing in market timing prefer the latter approach.

In Figure 24.8, the excess returns of two hypothetical portfolios are measured on the vertical axis and those of a market index are on the horizontal axis. Straight lines, fit via standard regression methods, reveal positive *ex post* alpha values in each case. However, the scatter diagrams tell a different story.

The scatter diagram for the portfolio shown in panel (a) seems to indicate that the relationship between the portfolio's excess returns and the market's excess returns was linear, because the points cluster close to the regression line. This result suggests that the portfolio consisted of securities in a manner such that the beta of the portfolio was roughly the same at all times. Because the *ex post* alpha was positive, it appears that the investment manager successfully identified and invested in some underpriced securities.

The scatter diagram for the portfolio shown in panel (b) seems to indicate that the relationship between this portfolio's excess returns and the market's excess returns was not linear because the points in the middle lie below the regression line and those at the ends lie above the regression line. This diagram suggests that the portfolio consisted of high-beta securities during periods when the market return was high and low-beta securities during periods when the market return was low. Upon examination, it appears that the portfolio has a positive *ex post* alpha because of successful market timing by the investment manager.

24.5.1 Quadratic Regression

Measuring the ability of an investment manager to successfully time the market requires that something more complex than a straight line be "fit" to scatter diagrams such as those shown in Figure 24.8. One procedure fits a curve to the data; statistical methods are used to estimate the parameters a, b, and c in the following *quadratic regression equation*:

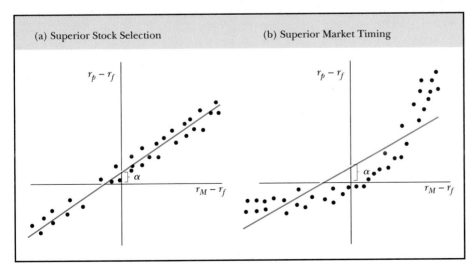

Figure 24.8
Superior Fund Performance.

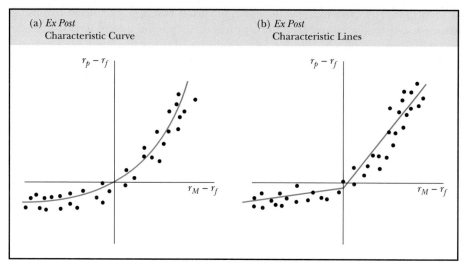

Figure 24.9
Ex Post Characteristic Curve and Line.

$$r_{pt} - r_{ft} = a + b(r_{Mt} - r_{ft}) + c\left[(r_{Mt} - r_{ft})^2\right] + \varepsilon_{pt} \qquad (24.31)$$

where ε_{pt} is the random error term.

The *ex post characteristic curve* shown in Figure 24.9(a) is simply the following quadratic function, where the values of *a*, *b*, and *c* for the portfolio have been estimated by standard regression methods:

$$r_{pt} - r_{ft} = a + b(r_{Mt} - r_{ft}) + c\left[(r_{Mt} - r_{ft})^2\right] \qquad (24.32)$$

If the estimated value of *c* is positive [as it is for the portfolio depicted in Figure 24.9(a)], the slope of the curve will increase as one moves to the right. This change in slope would indicate that the portfolio manager successfully timed the market. Note that this equation corresponds to the equation for the *ex post* characteristic line if *c* is approximately equal to zero. In such a situation, *a* and *b* would correspond to the portfolio's *ex post* alpha and beta, respectively.[14]

24.5.2 Dummy Variable Regression

An alternative procedure fits two *ex post* characteristic lines to the scatter diagram, as shown in Figure 24.9(b). Periods when risky securities outperform riskfree securities (that is, when $r_{Mt} > r_{ft}$) can be termed *up markets*. Periods when risky securities do not perform as well as riskfree securities (that is, when $r_{Mt} < r_{ft}$) can be termed *down markets*. A successful market timer would select a high up-market beta and a low down-market beta. Graphically, the slope of the *ex post* characteristic line for positive excess market returns (up markets) is greater than the slope of the *ex post* characteristic line for negative excess market returns (down markets).

Such a relationship can be estimated by using standard regression methods to determine the parameters *a*, *b*, and *c* in the following *dummy variable regression equation*:

$$r_{pt} - r_{ft} = a + b(r_{Mt} - r_{ft}) + c\left[D_t(r_{Mt} - r_{ft})\right] + \varepsilon_{pt} \qquad (24.33)$$

Here, ε_{pt} is the random error term, and D_t is a "dummy variable" that is assigned a value of zero for any past time period *t* when $r_{Mt} > r_{ft}$ and a value of −1 for any past time period t when $r_{Mt} < r_{ft}$. To see how this procedure works, consider the effective equations for different values of $r_{Mt} - r_{ft}$.

Value of $r_{Mt} - r_{ft}$	Equation
> 0	$r_{pt} - r_{ft} = a + b(r_{Mt} - r_{ft}) + \varepsilon_{pt}$
$= 0$	$r_{pt} - r_{ft} = a + \varepsilon_{pt}$
< 0	$r_{pt} - r_{ft} = a + (b - c)(r_{Mt} - r_{ft}) + \varepsilon_{pt}$

Note that the parameter b corresponds to the portfolio's up-market beta, while $(b - c)$ corresponds to the portfolio's down-market beta. Thus the parameter c indicates the difference between the two betas and will be positive for the successful market timer.

For the portfolio shown in Figure 24.9(b), the *ex post* characteristic line on the right side of the graph corresponds to the equation

$$r_{pt} - r_{ft} = a + b(r_{Mt} - r_{ft}) \tag{24.34a}$$

whereas the *ex post* characteristic line shown on the left side of the graph corresponds to the equation

$$r_{pt} - r_{ft} = a + (b - c)(r_{Mt} - r_{ft}) \tag{24.34b}$$

In this example, the investment manager has successfully engaged in market timing, because the slope of the line on the right side (that is, b) is greater than the slope of the line on the left side (that is, $b - c$).

In either regression Equation (24.31) or (24.33), the value of the parameter a provides an estimate of the investment manager's ability to identify mispriced securities (that is, security selection ability), and the value of the parameter c provides an estimate of the manager's market timing ability. The difference between the two equations is that the quadratic equation indicates that the portfolio's beta fluctuated over many values, depending on the size of the market's excess returns. This fluctuation can be seen graphically by noting that the slope of the quadratic curve continually increases from left to right in Figure 24.9(a). On the other hand, the dummy variable equation indicates that the portfolio's beta fluctuated between just two values, depending on whether r_{Mt} was less than or greater than r_{ft}. Note that the slope of the equation increases from one value (that is, $b - c$) to a second value (that is, b) when moving from left to right in Figure 24.9(b).

As an example, again consider First Fund. Table 24.2 presents the results from applying regression Equations (24.31) and (24.33) to this portfolio over the 16-quarter time interval. The table indicates that the portfolio manager has neither selectivity nor market timing ability because the parameter a is negative whereas the parameter c is near zero.[15] Further evidence is provided regarding the lack of market timing ability by the fact that the correlation coefficient is higher for the *ex post* characteristic line than for either of the other equations.

24.6   CRITICISMS OF RISK-ADJUSTED PERFORMANCE MEASURES

The previously mentioned risk-adjusted measures of portfolio performance have been criticized on several grounds. Some of the major criticisms are described in this section.

TABLE 24.2	Market Timing Test Results for First Fund		
Parameter Being Estimated[a]	Ex Post Characteristic Line	Quadratic Equation	Dummy Variable Equation
a	−1.29%	−2.12%	−1.33%
	(1.00)	(1.65)	(2.54)
b	1.13	1.03	1.13
	(.13)	(.20)	(.28)
c	—	.02	.02
	—	(.03)	(.78)
Correlation[b]	.92	.91	.91

[a] Standard errors are shown in parentheses below the respective parameters.

[b] The correlation coefficient for the quadratic and dummy variable equations has been adjusted for the number of independent variables.

24.6.1 Use of a Market Surrogate

Because all of the measures other than the reward-to-variability ratio require the identification of a market portfolio surrogate, whatever is used can be criticized as being inadequate. Indeed, it has been shown that when slight changes are made in the surrogate, the performance rankings of a set of portfolios can be completely reversed (that is, the top-ranked portfolio with one surrogate could be the bottom-ranked portfolio if a slightly different surrogate were used). However, it also has been noted that when commonly used NYSE-based surrogates are involved, such as the Dow Jones Industrial Average, the S&P 500, and an index comparable to the New York Stock Exchange Composite, the performance rankings of common stock portfolios appear to be quite similar.[16]

A related criticism of using a market index such as the S&P 500 to determine the benchmark portfolio's return is that it is nearly impossible for an investor to form a portfolio whose returns replicate those on such an index over time. Transaction costs will be encountered in initially forming the portfolio, in restructuring the portfolio when stocks are replaced in the index, and in purchasing more shares of the stocks when cash dividends are received.[17] Hence it has been argued that the returns on an index overstate the returns that a passive investor could earn, meaning that the returns on the benchmark portfolio are too high.[18]

24.6.2 Distinguishing Skill from Luck

A very long time interval is needed in order to be able to obtain a measure of performance that can distinguish skill from luck on the part of the investment manager. That is, it would be useful to know if an apparently successful manager was skilled or just lucky because skill can be expected to have a favorable impact on the portfolio's performance in the future, whereas luck cannot be expected to continue. Unfortunately, too many years' worth of data are generally needed to make such a determination. (This issue is discussed further in this chapter's *Institutional Issues: Assessing Manager Skill.*)[19]

24.6.3 Measuring the Riskfree Rate

The use of Treasury bills for measuring the riskfree rate in determining benchmark portfolios based on either the *ex post* SML or CML can be criticized. Consider a benchmark portfolio that involves an investment in both Treasury bills and the market portfolio. Such a benchmark portfolio can be criticized for having too low a rate of return, making it easier for a portfolio to show superior performance, because Treasury bills may provide excessively low returns to compensate for their high degree of liquidity. If a higher riskfree rate (such as the commercial paper rate) is used, then any benchmark portfolio that lies between this riskfree rate and the market portfolio on either the *ex post* SML or the *ex post* CML will have a higher rate of return and thus will represent a higher but more appropriate standard.

Furthermore, consider a benchmark portfolio that involves leveraging a positive investment in the market portfolio by borrowing at the riskfree rate. Use of the Treasury bill rate can be criticized because realistic borrowing alternatives typically involve a higher rate and are thus less attractive. Accordingly, benchmarks that involve borrowing at the Treasury bill rate have too high a rate of return, making it more difficult for a portfolio to show superior performance. If a higher riskfree borrowing rate (such as the call money rate plus a small premium) is used, then any benchmark portfolio involving riskfree borrowing will have a lower rate of return and thus will represent a lower but more appropriate standard.

In summary, measures of portfolio performance based on either the *ex post* SML or the *ex post* CML that use Treasury bills to determine the riskfree rate are alleged to discriminate in favor of conservative portfolios and against aggressive ones.

24.6.4   Validity of the CAPM

The measures of portfolio performance that involve beta (namely, the *ex post* alpha and reward-to-volatility measures) are based on the CAPM, yet the CAPM may not be the correct asset pricing model. That is, perhaps assets are priced according to some other model. If they are, the use of beta-based performance measures will be inappropriate.

Interestingly, a measure analogous to *ex post* alpha has been shown to be a meaningful gauge of performance if the arbitrage pricing theory (APT) model of asset pricing is believed to be more appropriate.[20] In such a situation, APT is used to estimate the benchmark portfolio's return ar_{bp} that is used in Equation (21.3) to calculate α_p.

It should also be noted that the reward-to-variability ratio cannot be considered inapppropriate on these grounds because it uses standard deviation as a measure of risk and does not rely on the validity of the CAPM or the identification of a market portfolio or APT.

24.6.5   Performance Attribution

The previously mentioned risk-adjusted measures of performance concentrate on the question of *how* a portfolio did relative to both a benchmark and a set of other portfolios. The use of quadratic and dummy variable regression is an attempt to evaluate separately the manager's ability at selectivity and timing. However, the client might want to know more about *why* the portfolio had a certain return over a particular interval of time. **Performance attribution** using a *factor model* is one method that has been used to try to make such a determination. An example is presented in the appendix.

| 24.7 | BOND PORTFOLIO PERFORMANCE EVALUATION |

The performance of portfolios of bonds and other types of fixed-income securities is often evaluated by comparing their total returns (consisting of coupon payments plus capital gains or losses) with those of an index representing a comparable class of securities over some interval of time. Hence, a portfolio that invested in investment-grade long-term corporate bonds would be compared with an investment-grade long-

Assessing Manager Skill

Perhaps no issue elicits more frustration among institutional investors than the evaluation of manager investment skill. The problem stems from the inherent uncertainty of manager investment performance. Even the most talented managers can underperform their benchmarks during any given quarter, year, or even multiyear period. Conversely, ineffective managers at times may make correct decisions and outperform their benchmarks simply by good fortune.

The odds that a "skillful" manager will underperform his or her benchmark over what most observers would consider to be acceptably long evaluation intervals are surprisingly high (under reasonable assumptions about expected return and return volatilty, roughly one out of four over a three-year evaluation period). The chances that an "unskillful" manager will outperform his or her benchmark are likewise considerable (roughly one out of three over a three-year evaluation period). Even when we extend the evaluation period to five years (an eternity in the investment management business), the possibility of confusing skillful with unskillful managers decreases only slightly.

Let us step back for a moment and define the term *investment skill*. It as the ability to outperform a passive risk-adjusted benchmark consistently over time. In other words, the skillful manager is capable of generating a statistically significant "alpha." Because no manager is omniscient, every manager's alpha, regardless of skill, will be positive in some periods and negative in others. Nevertheless, a skillful manager will produce a larger alpha more frequently than his or her less talented peers.

Note that a skillful manager may produce a small alpha very frequently or a larger alpha less frequently. It is the magnitude of the alpha relative to the volatility around that alpha value that determines a manager's skill (the ratio of these two variables is a form of the Sharpe ratio discussed in the text). Yet when plan sponsors evaluate their managers, most focus solely on the level of alpha produced, while ignoring volatility around the alpha. As a consequence, superior managers may be terminated (or not hired) and inferior managers may be retained (or hired), on the basis of statistically questionable performance data.

Attempting to evaluate manager skill strictly by consulting past performance data is a problem in statistical inference. Essentially, we want to test whether the manager's alpha is positive enough to be considered unlikely a result of mere chance. To undertake this analysis, we must make three key assumptions concerning the shape and dispersion of the manager's returns around his or her benchmark. Somewhat paradoxically, we first assume that the manager has no investment skill. That is, we begin with a *null hypothesis* that the manager's alpha is zero on average over time. It is actually this assumption of no skill that we want to test. Second, we assume that the manager's alpha is normally distributed around the average (or mean) value of zero (that is, the alpha distribution is in the form of the familiar bell-shaped curve, with zero as its center). Third, we assume that the volatility of the manager's returns around the benchmark in the future will be the same as that that occurred in the past. That is, we will assume that the standard deviation of the manager's alpha is constant over time. (Recall that a normally distributed random variable will have two-thirds of its outcomes fall within one standard deviation from the mean.)

Statistical inference by its nature can be a baffling exercise in double negatives. For example, we do not accept the null hypothesis. Rather, we fail to reject it. Conversely, although we may reject the null hypothesis, that does not necessarily mean that we accept an alternative hypothesis. Nevertheless, the equivocal nature of this type of analysis is well suited to the world of investments, where luck often masquerades as skill, and skill is frequently overwhelmed by random events.

Consider a manager whose alpha exhibits an annual standard deviation of 4.0%. Assuming a normal distribution and a mean alpha of 0.0, the expected distribution of the manager's alpha over a three-year period should appear as in the accompanying graph. (Note that as time passes the normal distribution will become tighter around the mean of zero because the longer the evaluation period the more likely that the manager's random positive and negative alphas will offset one another, gradually converging on the mean value. Specifically, the three-year annualized standard deviation is 2.3% or $1/\sqrt{3}$ times the one-year standard deviation of 4.0%.) Now suppose, on the basis of monthly observations, that the manager actually produced an alpha of 3% per year over the three years. What are we to make of that outcome? If our null hypothesis of no skill is correct, then there is only a 10-in-100 chance that this result would have occurred by luck. It is up to us to decide whether we want to believe that luck was the cause of this outcome or whether we should reject the null hypothesis. That is, do we believe that the manager actually does have skill and that his or her true expected alpha is not zero but some positive number? This would make the 3% realized alpha seem much more plausible.

Unfortunately, it is the rare manager who demonstrates sufficiently strong results to allow us to comfortably reject the null hypothesis. Most managers live in a statistical netherworld, producing neither sufficiently large positive nor sufficiently large negative alphas to warrant definitive conclusions. For example, few U.S. common stock managers can hope to outperform their benchmarks by more than 1% per year on average after accounting for all fees and expenses. With an alpha standard deviation of 4%, it would take over 40 years before our statistical test would indicate that there is less than a 5 in 100 chance that such an outcome was due to luck.

As a result of these nebulous statistical answers, it should not be surprising that institutional investors turn to various qualitative decision rules to help them identify manager skill. For example, they will intensively examine the manager's process for selecting securities and want to understand the pedigree of the firm's portfolio managers. Whether such investigations actually help to uncover skillful managers is a highly debatable proposition.

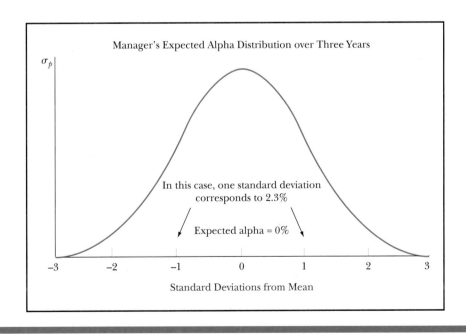

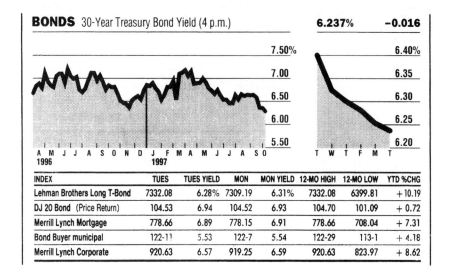

BONDS 30-Year Treasury Bond Yield (4 p.m.)				6.237%		−0.016
INDEX	TUES	TUES YIELD	MON	MON YIELD	12-MO HIGH	12-MO LOW	YTD %CHG
Lehman Brothers Long T-Bond	7332.08	6.28%	7309.19	6.31%	7332.08	6399.81	+ 10.19
DJ 20 Bond (Price Return)	104.53	6.94	104.52	6.93	104.70	101.09	+ 0.72
Merrill Lynch Mortgage	778.66	6.89	778.15	6.91	778.66	708.04	+ 7.31
Bond Buyer municipal	122-11	5.53	122-7	5.54	122-29	113-1	+ 4.18
Merrill Lynch Corporate	920.63	6.57	919.25	6.59	920.63	823.97	+ 8.62

Figure 24.10

Bond Indices Published in *The Wall Street Journal,* October 8, 1997

Source: Reprinted by permission of *The Wall Street Journal,* Dow Jones & Company, Inc., October 8, 1997, p. C1. All rights reserved worldwide.

term corporate bond index; a portfolio invested in mortgage-backed securities would be compared with a mortgage-backed securities index, and a high-yield bond fund would be compared with a high-yield bond index.

24.7.1   Bond Indices

Bond indices typically represent either the average total return or the average price on a portfolio of bonds that have certain similar characteristics. Figure 24.10 presents various bond indices that are published daily in *The Wall Street Journal.*[21] The Lehman Brothers Long Treasury Bond Index is typical of many bond market indices. This index is a total return index, reflecting interest income and changes in prices from one day to the next of nearly all Treasury securities with maturities between 10 and 30 years. It is value-weighted in that price changes and interest income for each bond in the index are weighted by the bond's issue size relative to the combined size of all the securities in the index. It was set at a level of 1,000 at year-end 1980, and each day since then it has changed by the average total return measured from the previous day. Note that the way this index is constructed makes it easy to determine the return on long-term Treasuries over any time period by simply looking up the value of the index on a previous date. For example, Figure 24.10 indicates that on Tuesday, October 7, 1997, the index was at 7332.08. A year before then the index was at 6457.64 (= 7332.08 − 874.44; in another place in *The Wall Street Journal* readers are told the change in the value of the index from a year earlier), so the annual return was 13.54% [= (7332.08 − 6457.64)/6457.64].

There is a yield figure also presented for the Lehman Brothers Long Treasury Bond Index. In the calculation of this index, the annual interest payments for each bond are divided by its current market price, and then these interest yields are averaged by using value weighting. Hence it is an index of *current yields.*

The second index shown in Figure 24.10 is the Dow Jones 20 Bond Index, where the prices of 20 bonds (10 utilities and 10 industrials) are simply added together and then divided by 20. Similarly, the yield on this index is an average of the yields on the 20 bonds. In Figure 24.10 this index was at 104.53, indicating that the average bond was selling at an 4.53% premium on October 7, 1997, with a yield of 6.94%.

The third index is the Merrill Lynch mortgage-backed bond index. It is based on conventional mortgage pass-through securities as well as those issued by GNMA, FHLMC, FNMA, and FHA. Like the Lehman Brothers Long Treasury Bond Index, it is a total return index standardized to equal 100 at year-end 1979.

The fourth index is the *Bond Buyer* municipal bond index. It is based on a set of long-term investment-grade general obligation and revenue bonds whose prices and yields are averaged in a manner similar to those of the Dow Jones 20 Bond Index.

The fifth index is the Merrill Lynch corporate bond index. It is based on a set of corporate bonds, including industrial, utility, financial, and transportation bonds, of all maturities. It is a total return index, like the Lehman Brothers Long Treasury Bond Index, except that its base of 100 was set at year-end 1972.

24.7.2 Time-Series and Cross-Sectional Comparisons

Figure 24.11 illustrates two ways of evaluating the returns on a bond portfolio by comparing them with the returns on a bond index over a time interval. In part (a), a time-series comparison is made; the bond portfolio's quarterly returns (for example, the last 16 quarters) during the time interval are graphed along with those of a comparable bond index.

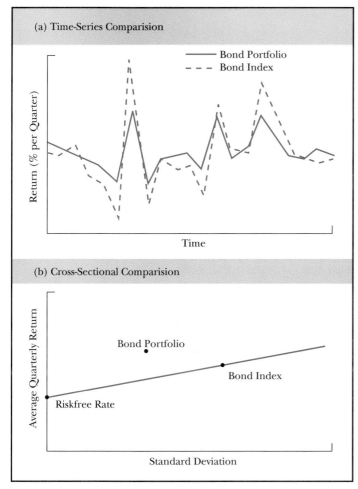

Figure 24.11
Bond Portfolio Performance Evaluation

In part (b), a cross-sectional comparison is made in a manner similar to the equity performance measures that were based on the *ex post* CML. Here the bond portfolio's average return and standard deviation are graphed and compared with a line that goes through the average riskfree rate and the average return and standard deviation of the bond index (instead of a common stock index), based on quarterly returns during the time interval.

A variation of this procedure involves estimating the bond portfolio's *ex post* alpha by using the *ex post* characteristic line approach described earlier. That is, a figure similar to Figure 24.6 would be prepared, but now the excess returns on a bond portfolio would be measured on the vertical axis and the excess returns on a bond index would be measured on the horizontal axis.[22] Many analysts use as the market index the returns on the Lehman Government/Corporate bond index, which is a value-weighted index of government and corporate investment-grade bonds that have more than one year remaining until maturity. Others use the returns on a bond index that most closely fits with the investment objectives and policies of the portfolio under scrutiny. In both cases, an *ex post* alpha would be calculated and used as a measure of portfolio performance.[23]

24.8 SUMMARY

1. Performance measurement is an integral part of the investment management process. It is a feedback and control mechanism that can make the investment management process more effective.
2. In evaluating performance, there are two major tasks: determine whether the performance is superior or inferior, and determine whether the performance is due to luck or skill.
3. Without intraperiod contributions or withdrawals, measurement of periodic portfolio returns is simple: the difference between ending and beginning portfolio values divided by beginning portfolio value.
4. Intraperiod cash flows complicate the calculation of periodic portfolio returns. Two methods have been developed to calculate returns when these cash flows occur: dollar-weighted and time-weighted returns.
5. The dollar-weighted return is influenced by the size and timing of cash flows, whereas the time-weighted return is not. As a result, the time-weighted return is generally the preferred method when evaluating portfolio performance.
6. The essential idea behind performance evaluation is to compare an actively managed portfolio's returns against the returns of an alternative benchmark portfolio. An appropriate benchmark should be relevant and feasible, and it should exhibit risk similar to that of the actively managed portfolio.
7. Risk-adjusted performance measures involve both a portfolio's *ex post* return and its *ex post* risk.
8. *Ex post* alpha (differential return) and the Sharpe ratio involve analysis of a portfolio's excess return and systematic risk. The reward-to-variability ratio and M^2 involve analysis of a portfolio's excess return and total risk.
9. Successful equity market timers will hold portfolios with relatively high betas during market rises and relatively low betas during market declines. Successful bond market timers will hold portfolios with relatively long durations during periods when interest rates drop and relatively short durations during periods when interest rates rise. Quadratic regression and dummy variable regression are two methods designed to measure market timing performance.
10. Risk-adjusted measures of performance have been criticized for using a market surrogate instead of the "true" market portfolio; being unable to statistically distinguish luck from skill except over very long periods of time; using an inappropriate riskfree rate; and relying on the validity of the CAPM.

1. Crungy Patrick owns a portfolio of three stocks. Crungy's holdings and the prices of the stocks at the end of Year 1 and Year 2 are shown below. Assuming no contributions, withdrawals, or dividends paid, what is the return on Crungy's portfolio in Year 2?

Stock	Shares Owned	Year 1 Price	Year 2 Price
A	100	$10	$15
B	300	5	4
C	250	12	14

2. Why do cash inflows and outflows between the beginning and end of a performance evaluation period complicate the measurement of portfolio returns?

3. At the beginning of the year, Lave Cross's portfolio was worth $39,000. At year-end, Lave received a gift of $4,000, which was invested in the portfolio. The portfolio's value at year-end was $42,000. What was the return on Lave's portfolio during the year?

4. New Lisbon Laundry's pension fund was worth $30 million at the end of Year 1. On the first day of Year 2 the firm made a $2 million contribution to the fund. At the end of Year 2, the pension fund was valued at $38 million. What was the return on the New Lisbon pension fund during Year 2?

5. At the beginning of the year, Con Daily's portfolio was worth $9,000. At the end of each of the next four quarters, Con received a gift of $500, which was invested in the portfolio. At the end of each quarter, Con's portfolio was worth, respectively, $9,800, $10,800, $11,200, and $12,000. What was the time-weighted rate of return on Con's portfolio during the year?

6. Dell Darling's portfolio was worth $12,000 at the beginning of a 30-day month. On day 10 of the month, Dell received a contribution to the portfolio of $800. At the end of the month, Dell's portfolio was worth $13,977.71. What was the dollar-weighted return on Dell's portfolio for the month?

7. Ginger Beaumont began the year with a portfolio valued at $10,000 and made a contribution to and a withdrawal from this portfolio over the next three months. Information regarding amounts and dates of these cash flows and the portfolio's market value at various dates is shown below.

Date	Contribution (−) or Withdrawal (+)	Portfolio Value
12/31	$ 0	$10,000
1/31	+956	9,000
2/28	−659	12,000
3/31	0	13,000

   a. Calculate the dollar-weighted return for the three-month period. (Hint: Unless you have a suitable calculator, you will have to use trial and error to find the dollar-weighted return. To begin, the monthly dollar-weighted return is less than 10%.)
   b. Calculate the time-weighted return for the three-month period.
   c. Why is the time-weighted return for the quarter less than the dollar-weighted return in this particular problem?

8. Distinguish between time-weighted and dollar-weighted rates of return. Under what performance measurement circumstances might the dollar-weighted return be preferred to the time-weighted?

9. Oats DeMaestri's portfolio was valued at $22,000 at the beginning of a 31-day month. During the month, Oats withdrew $1,500 from the portfolio on day 12 and contributed $600 on day 21. At month-end, the portfolio was worth $21,769.60. What was Oats's dollar-weighted return for the month?

10. At the beginning of a 30-day month, Buttercup Dickerson owned a portfolio valued at $5,000. On day 10, Buttercup's portfolio was worth $7,300 after a $2,000 contribution had been made on that day. At the end of the month, the portfolio was worth $9,690.18. Calculate both the time-weighted and dollar-weighted returns on Buttercup's portfolio for the month. Why do the two returns differ so substantially?

11. Why does performance evaluation require an appropriate benchmark in order to be meaningful? How would you define the term *appropriate* in this context?

12. It is common practice for performance evaluation services to compare the returns on a common stock portfolio with a distribution of returns obtained from a large sample of other common stock portfolios. What potential problems are involved in this sort of analysis?

13. Using a recent *Wall Street Journal*, find the closing value of the Dow Jones Industrial Average. On the same date, find the closing prices of the DJIA's component stocks. (The names of those stocks are usually listed on page 3 of the *Journal's* third section.) Calculate the value of the DJIA's divisor.

14. Consider a price-weighted market index composed of two securities, A and B, with prices of $16 and $30, respectively. The index divisor is currently 2.0. Calculate the value of the divisor when:
    a. Stock A issues a 5% stock dividend.
    b. Stock B undergoes a 3-for-1 stock split.
    c. Stock A undergoes a 4-for-1 stock split.

15. It is often argued that the S&P 500 is a better indicator than the Dow Jones Industrial Average of the performance of the entire U.S. stock market. Explain the reasoning behind this contention.

16. Assume that the market is composed of the following three securities:

Security	Current Price	Shares Outstanding
A	$20	20,000
B	35	40,000
C	30	40,000

   a. What is the aggregate value of the market?
   b. If security C's price increases by 20%, what is the percentage change in the market's aggregate value?
   c. If security B splits 2-for-1, what is the percentage change in the market's aggregate value?

17. Consider three stocks, X, Y, and Z, with the following closing prices on two particular dates:

Stock	Date 1	Date 2
X	$16	$22
Y	5	4
Z	24	30

   On date 1 there are 100 shares of stock X, 200 shares of stock Y, and 100 shares of stock Z outstanding.

a. Construct a price-weighted market index using the three stocks, X, Y, and Z. What is the index's value on date 1?

b. What is the price-weighted index's value on date 2?

c. Assume that, on date 2, stock X splits 4-for-1. What is the price-weighted index's value on that date?

d. Construct a value-weighted index using the three stocks. Assign the value-weighted index a value of 100 on date 1. What is the index's value on date 2?

18. According to Ferris Fain, "The success of a stock market index depends on its ability to measure the performance of stocks not included in the index." Explain what Ferris means.

19. Consider an equal-weighted market index composed of three securities. The market prices of those securities on three dates are shown below.

	Market Price		
Security	Date 1	Date 2	Date 3
A	$50	$55	$60
B	30	28	30
C	70	75	73

a. What is the return on the index from date 1 to date 2?

b. What is the return on the index from date 2 to date 3?

20. Consider a market index based on three securities and their associated prices on three dates.

	Market Price		
Security	Date 1	Date 2	Date 3
L	$20	$23	$30
M	27	30	31
N	40	35	29

If the index's value is 200 on date 1, calculate its value on date 2 and date 3 if the index return is computed on a geometric mean basis.

21. Pickles Dillhoefer owns a portfolio that over the last five years has produced a 16.8% annual return. During that time the portfolio produced a 1.10 beta. Further, the riskfree return and market return averaged 7.4% and 15.2% per year, respectively. What was the *ex post* alpha on Pickles's portfolio over this time period? Draw the *ex post* SML and the position of Pickles's portfolio.

22. The performance of the Venus Fund, a common stock mutual fund, compared with that of the S&P 500 over a ten-year period, is as follows:

	Venus Fund	S&P 500
Average quarterly excess return	0.6%	0.5%
Standard deviation of quarterly excess returns	9.9%	6.6%
Beta	1.10	1.00

Dazzy Vance is considering investing in either the Venus Fund or another mutual fund whose objective is to track the performance of the S&P 500. Which fund would you recommend that Dazzy select, assuming that your decision is based solely on past performance? Justify your answer using various measures of risk-adjusted performance.

23. Why is the sharpe ratio a more appropriate measure of performance than the *ex post* alpha if the portfolio being assessed represents the entire wealth of the portfolio's owner?

24. Can the *ex post* alpha, the reward-to-volatility ratio, and the Sharpe ratio and *M*-squared give conflicting answers to the question of whether a particular portfolio has outperformed a market index on a risk-adjusted basis? If so, which of these measures can conflict with the others, and why can this conflict occur?

25. Does a portfolio's *ex post* alpha measure gains and losses due to security selection, market timing, or both? Explain.

26. Assume that broad stock market indices, such as the S&P 500, are not good surrogates for the "true" market portfolio. What potential problems does this cause for performance evaluation using the *ex post* alpha measure?

27. You are given the following historical performance information on the capital markets and the Jupiter Fund, a common stock mutual fund.

Year	Jupiter Fund Beta	Return on Jupiter Fund	Return on Market Index	Return on Treasury Bills
1	.90	−2.99%	−8.50%	6.58%
2	.95	.63	4.01	6.53
3	.95	22.01	14.31	4.39
4	1.00	24.08	18.98	3.84
5	1.00	−22.46	−14.66	6.93
6	.90	−25.12	−26.47	8.00
7	.80	29.72	37.20	5.80
8	.75	22.15	23.84	5.08
9	.80	.48	−7.18	5.12
10	.85	6.85	6.56	7.18

a. Compute the Jupiter Fund's average beta over the ten-year period. What investment percentages in the market index and Treasury bills are required in order to produce a beta equal to the fund's average beta?

b. Compute the year-by-year returns that would have been earned on a portfolio invested in the market index and Treasury bills in the proportions calculated in part (a).

c. Compute the year-by-year returns that would have been earned on a portfolio invested in the market index and Treasury bills in the proportions needed to match Jupiter's beta year by year. (Note: These proportions will change yearly as the fund's beta changes yearly.)

d. One measure of a fund's market timing ability is the average difference between (1) what the fund would have earned annually by investing in the market index and Treasury bills so that the year-by-year beta equals the fund's actual year-by-year beta and (2) what the fund would have earned annually by investing in the market index and Treasury bills so that the year-by-year beta equals the fund's average beta. Given your previous calculations, evaluate the market timing ability of Jupiter's manager.

e. One measure of a fund's security selection ability is the average difference between (1) the fund's annual returns and (2) what the fund would have earned annually by investing in the market index and Treasury bills so that the year-by-year beta equals the fund's actual year-by-year beta. Calculate Jupiter's average return and then, using your previous calculations, evaluate the security selection ability of Jupiter's manager.

28. Consider the following annual returns produced by a MiniFund, a mutual fund investing in small stocks:

1971	16.50%	1976	57.38%	1981	13.88%	1986	6.85%
1972	4.43	1977	25.38	1982	28.01	1987	−9.30
1973	−30.90	1978	23.46	1983	39.67	1988	22.87
1974	−19.95	1979	43.46	1984	−6.67	1989	10.18
1975	52.82	1980	39.88	1985	24.66	1990	−21.56

Referring to Table 1.1, use the Treasury bill returns as the riskfree return and the common stock returns as the market return, and calculate the following risk-adjusted return measures for the small stock mutual fund:

a. *Ex post* alpha

b. Reward-to-volatility ratio

c. Reward-to-variability ratio

Comment on the mutual fund's risk-adjusted performance. What problems are associated with using a large capitalization index such as the S&P 500 (the source of the common stock returns) as the benchmark in evaluating this small company mutual fund?

29. In an article in the *Journal of Finance* (March 1983), Jess Chua and Richard Woodward investigated the investment skill of the legendary economist John Maynard Keynes. A portfolio managed by Keynes had the following returns:

	Keynes's Return	Market Return	Riskfree Return
1928	−3.4%	7.9%	4.2
1929	.8	6.6	5.3
1930	−32.4	−20.3	2.5
1931	−24.6	−25.0	3.6
1932	44.8	−5.8	1.6
1933	35.1	21.5	.6
1934	33.1	−.7	.7
1935	44.3	5.3	.6
1936	56.0	10.2	.6
1937	8.5	−.5	.6
1938	−40.1	−16.1	.6
1939	12.9	−7.2	1.3
1940	−15.6	−12.9	1.0
1941	33.5	12.5	1.0
1942	−.9	.8	1.0
1943	53.9	15.6	1.0
1944	14.5	5.4	1.0
1945	14.6	.8	1.0

Chua and Woodward concluded that Keynes demonstrated superior investment abilities. They did not, however, distinguish between his market timing and security selection skills. Using the quadratic regression and dummy variable techniques, evaluate Keynes's market timing skills. (Hint: Use of a regression package found in a standard personal computer spreadsheet program is highly recommended.)

---

30. (Appendix Question) What is the purpose of performance attribution? What types of problems can hinder performance attribution?

31. (Appendix Question) Assume that security returns are explained by a sector-factor model. Eugene Stephens has been asked to develop a performance attribution report analyzing the returns on portfolio A versus those of a market index for the latest year, and he has collected the following information:

	Portfolio *A*	Market Index	Sector-Factor Values
Return	12.50%	5.50%	—
Beta	1.10	1.00	−.50
Size	1.30	6.00	−.60
% Industrial	40%	80%	8.00
% Nonindustrial	60%	20%	16.00

Unfortunately, Eugene is confused by the subject of performance attribution. Carry out the analysis for him.

CFA EXAM QUESTIONS

32. As a corporate treasurer, you are responsible for evaluating prospective investment managers for your company's pension fund. You have interviewed three managers, examined their reported investment performances, and identified clear-cut differences in their investment approaches.

Manager A has developed a very appealing and apparently successful investment process based on extensive research and back-testing, but she has not yet managed money using this process.

Manager B has been investing relatively small amounts of money over only the past two years, producing what appears to be extraordinary investment performance. His process is based on exploiting what he believes to be a market inefficiency (or anomaly) to produce superior returns.

Manager C is a global investment counselor who emphasizes active selection of stocks and bonds across the major world markets. He has a long track record and uses a well-established and widely accepted process for selecting securities.

a. Discuss the usefulness of historical investment performance in evaluating investment managers.

b. For each of the three managers, identify and discuss the two most important factors that you would consider in assessing the manager's performance.

APPENDIX

PERFORMANCE ATTRIBUTION

With performance attribution, an attempt is made to ascertain why a portfolio had a given return over a particular time period. One procedure for making such a determination involves assuming that security returns are related to a number of pre-specified factors as well as to sector factors.[24] For example, there may be a beta factor, a size factor, and two sector factors that indicate whether a stock is issued by an industrial company. With such a model, the returns for a stock during a given time period are related to these factors and sector factors in the following manner:

$$r_i = \beta_i F_1 + s_i F_2 + c_{i1} SF_1 + c_{i2} SF_2 + \varepsilon_i \qquad (24.35)$$

Here each stock has four attributes: β_i, s_i, and c_{i2}. The attributes β_i and s_i are, respectively, the beta and firm size of stock i in a given time period; and c_{i1} and c_{i2} are sector-factor attributes that have values of one and zero, respectively, if stock i is an industrial firm, and values of zero and one if stock i is not an industrial firm. (For example, it may be a utility or a transportation company such as Northern States Power or Delta Air Lines.)

The factors and sector factors F_1, F_2, SF_1, and SF_2 are parameters that can be estimated using a statistical technique known as multiple linear regression. For example, the annual returns for each one of 500 firms for 1997 could be calculated. Then, the betas for each stock could be estimated using 16 quarters of returns ending with the last quarter of 1996 (by using the *ex post* characteristic line equation given earlier). The firm size for each stock could be measured by taking the market price per share as of December 31, 1996, multiplying it by the number of shares outstanding at that time, and then taking the logarithm of the product (expressed in billions). Last, each firm can be classified as either an industrial or a nonindustrial, resulting in a zero or one value assigned to c_{i1} and c_{i2}. This will result in four columns of 500 numbers representing security attributes—one column with the betas for each stock, one column for the firm sizes of each stock, and two columns of zeros and ones corresponding to whether the firms are industrials or nonindustrials—upon which will be regressed the column of annual returns for the 500 stocks during 1997.

Suppose that the resulting regression produced estimated values for F_1, F_2, SF_1, and SF_2 of 1.20, −.40, 10.00, and 9.00, respectively. Thus Equation (24.35) for 1997 would be:

$$r_i = 1.20\beta_i - .40s_i + 10.00c_{i1} + 9.00c_{i2} + \varepsilon_i \qquad (24.36)$$

Because the estimated value of F_1 (= 1.20) is positive, the year of 1997 was one in which high-beta stocks tended to outperform low-beta stocks. Furthermore, because the estimated value of F_2 (= −.40) is negative, the year 1997 was one in which the

---

stocks of small firms tended to outperform the stocks of large firms. With an estimated value for SF_1 that is greater than the estimated value of SF_2 $(10.00 > 9.00)$, 1997 also appears to have been a year when industrials tended to outperform nonindustrials.

Equation (24.36) can be used to analyze the 1997 return on a stock. Consider, for example, a hypothetical industrial stock that had a return of 12.13%, a beta of .8, and a size of 4.00. (Its market value was $54.6 billion, so s_i = natural logarithm of $54.6 = \ln 54.6 = 4.00$.) According to Equation (24.36), the "normal" return on such a stock is 9.36% $[=(1.20 \times .8) - (.40 \times 4.00) + (10.00 \times 1) + (9.00 \times 0)]$. Thus, for this stock, its "nonfactor return" ε_i for 1997 was 2.77% $(=12.13\% - 9.36\%)$, suggesting that this particular stock did relatively well in comparison with other stocks having comparable attributes.

Similar analysis can be conducted on a portfolio's return for 1997. Consider a hypothetical portfolio that had a return of 10.03% in 1997. Upon close examination, it has been determined that this portfolio had an average beta of 1.3 and an average size of 3.2 (that is, the average value of s_i for all the stocks held was 3.2). Furthermore, 67% of the stocks in the portfolio were industrials and 33% were nonindustrials. According to Equation (24.36), the normal return on such a portfolio is 9.95% $[=(1.20 \times 1.30) - (.40 \times 3.20) + (10.00 \times .67) + (9.00 \times .33)]$. Because the nonfactor return on this portfolio was .08% $(=10.03\% - 9.95\%)$, this portfolio shows little evidence of successful security selection.

Such absolute performance evaluation with a factor model is interesting, but in many cases comparative performance is more relevant. A manager may do poorly in a bad market. But if he or she provides a higher return than would have been obtained otherwise, the client is clearly better off. With comparative performance, the overall return of a portfolio is compared with that of one or more other benchmark portfolios in order to determine the *differences* in the returns. Then the *sources* of the differences can be determined with **comparative performance attribution**.

Assume that the i in Equation (24.35) refers to the portfolio under evaluation. Letting j refer to the return on a benchmark portfolio with which it is to be compared, the difference in their returns for the year is simply $r_i - r_j$. Using Equation (24.35), this difference can be expressed as:

$$r_i - r_j = \left(\beta_i F_1 + s_i F_2 + c_{i1} SF_1 + c_{i2} SF_2 + \varepsilon_i\right) \tag{24.37}$$
$$- \left(\beta_j F_1 + s_j F_2 + c_{j1} SF_1 + c_{j2} SF_2 + \varepsilon_j\right)$$

Gathering similar terms, this equation can be rewritten as:

$$r_i - r_j = F_1\left(\beta_i - \beta_j\right) + F_2\left(s_i - s_j\right) \tag{24.38}$$
$$+ SF_1\left(c_{i1} - c_{j1}\right) + SF_2\left(c_{i2} - c_{j2}\right) + \left(\varepsilon_i - \varepsilon_j\right)$$

Each of the first four terms represents a differential effect equal to the product of (1) the difference in the attributes of the two portfolios and (2) the actual value of the related factor. The last term in the equation indicates the difference in the nonfactor returns of the two portfolios.

Table 24.3 provides an example in which portfolio i is the one mentioned earlier that had a return in 1997 of 10.03%. It is being compared with a benchmark portfolio that had a return in 1997 of 11.21%. This benchmark portfolio had a beta of 1.50, and the average size of the firms whose stocks it held was 1.40. Furthermore, 80% of the portfolio's funds were invested in industrials, with the remaining 20% being invested in nonindustrials. Using Equation (24.36), the normal return on such a portfolio in 1997 was 11.04% $[=(1.20 \times 1.50) - (.40 \times 1.40) + (10.00 \times .80) + (9.00 \times .20)]$, indicating that the portfolio had a nonfactor return of .17% $(=11.21\% - 11.04\%)$.

TABLE 24.3   Comparative Performance Attribution

	Attribute				
	Portfolio *i* (1)	Portfolio *j* (2)	Differential Difference (3) = (1) − (2)	Factor (4)	Effect (5) = (3) × (4)
(a) Factors					
Common factor					
Beta	1.30	1.50	−.20	1.20	−.24%
Size	3.20	1.40	1.80	−.40	−.72
Sector-factors					
Industrials	.67	.80	−.13	10.00	−1.30
Nonindustrials	.33	.20	.13	9.00	1.17
					−1.09

	Return		
	Portfolio *i* (1)	Portfolio *j* (2)	Difference (3) = (1) − (2)
(b) Returns			
Factor return	9.95%	11.04%	−1.09%
Nonfactor return	.08	.17	−.09
Total return	10.03%	11.21%	−1.18%

A direct comparison of the two portfolios reveals a difference in returns of −1.18% ($r_i - r_j = 10.03\% - 11.21\%$). That is, portfolio *i* performed worse than the benchmark by 1.18%. Security selection played a small role because the nonfactor returns were both quite low (.08% for portfolio *i* and .17% for the benchmark). On balance, sector selection lowered returns for portfolio *i* relative to the benchmark slightly; the sum of the values in the last column for the two sector factors was −0.13%. In portfolio *i*, industrials were underweighted relative to the benchmark, whereas nonindustrials were overweighted. A successful "sector picker" would have placed bets on (that is, overweighted) the sector with a relatively high factor value (industrials) and placed bets against (that is, underweighted) the sector with a relatively low factor value (nonindustrials), leading to a net positive "sector bet effect." In 1998 the investment manager for portfolio *i* was not a successful sector picker relative to the benchmark.

The major sources of the relatively lower performance of portfolio *i* were those associated with common factors. The manager had lower-beta stocks than those in the benchmark during a period when high-beta stocks tended to do better than low-beta stocks. That is, the manager placed a bet against high-beta stocks in favor of low-beta stocks and lost. He or she also had invested in stocks that were larger than those in the benchmark during a period when larger stocks tended to do poorly. That is, the manager placed a bet against smaller firms in favor of larger firms and lost. Both differences lowered returns relative to the benchmark portfolio, with the "size bet" being more detrimental than the "beta bet."

ENDNOTES

[1] This procedure provides a quarterly return with "quarterly compounding." Alternatively, the semiquarterly return could be doubled, resulting in a quarterly return with "semiquarterly compounding" of −1.96% (=−.98% × 2).

[2] For more on the construction of market indices, see Mary M. Cutler, "Market Indices: A Learning Exercise Using Warsaw Stock Exchange Prices," *Financial Practice and Education* 5, no. 2 (Fall/Winter 1995): 99–106.

[3] Sometimes the excess return for a portfolio, which is equal to its return minus the riskfree rate $(= r_{pt} - r_{ft})$, is used instead of r_{pt} in Equation (24.9) to determine the average excess return (denoted aer_p). Then, the summation in the numerator of Equation (24.10) is carried out using $[(r_{pt} - r_{ft}) - aer_p]^2$ instead of $(r_{pt} - ar_p)^2$. The resulting number is the standard deviation of excess returns, which is sometimes used as an estimate of the total risk of the portfolio. Typically, the two standard deviations are quite similar in numerical value.

[4] Equation (24.11) corresponds to the formula for estimating the slope term in a simple regression model where the independent variable is er_{Mt} and the dependent variable is er_{pt}. Sometimes returns are used in Equation (24.11), where er_{Mt} is replaced by r_{Mt} and er_{pt} is replaced by r_{pt}. In this situation, the beta corresponds to the slope term in the market model for the portfolio (as discussed in Chapter 7). Typically, the two betas are quite similar in numerical value.

[5] This measure of performance is sometimes known as the *Jensen coefficient* (or *Jensen alpha*) because it was developed by Michael C. Jensen in "The Performance of Mutual Funds in the Period 1945–1964," *Journal of Finance* 23, no. 2 (May 1968): 389–416.

[6] Alternatively, if *FF*'s average return had been 6%, then its coordinates would have been (1.13, 6.00), placing it above the *ex post* SML. In this situation, *FF*'s *ex post* alpha would have been .78%, and its performance would have been viewed as superior.

[7] An alternative measure of performance involves dividing the *ex post* alpha by an estimate of the *ex post* unique (or unsystematic) risk of the portfolio. This measure, known as the *appraisal* (or *information*) *ratio*, would be equal to $-.34$ $(=-1.29/3.75)$ for First Fund. Comparisons can be made with the value of the appraisal ratio for the market portfolio (its value is defined to be zero) and other portfolios. Note that a positive value indicates superior performance and that the larger the value, the better the performance. See Jack L. Treynor and Fischer Black, "How to Use Security Analysis to Improve Portfolio Selection," *Journal of Business* 46, no. 1 (January 1973): 66–86.

[8] The random error term can be viewed as a number that arises from a spin of a roulette wheel, where the numbers on the wheel are symmetrically distributed around zero. That is, the expected outcome from a spin of the roulette wheel is zero. The standard deviation associated with the wheel is denoted $\sigma_{\varepsilon p}$.

[9] This measure of performance is sometimes known as the *Treynor ratio* because it was developed by Jack L. Treynor in "How to Rate Management of Investment Funds," *Harvard Business Review* 43, no. 1 (January/February 1965): 63–75.

[10] This measure of performance is known as the *Sharpe ratio* because it was developed by William F. Sharpe in "Mutual Fund Performance," *Journal of Business* 39, no. 1 (January 1966): 119–138. Chapter 21 mentioned that it is used by Morningstar, Inc. in its evaluation of mutual fund performance.

[11] The popular use of "M^2" to refer to this measure of performance can be attributed to the fact that the measure was put forth by Nobel laureate Franco Modigliani and his granddaughter, Leah Modigliani in "Risk-Adjusted Performance," *Journal of Portfolio Management* 23, no. 2 (Winter 1997): 45–54.

[12] There is a third measure of portfolio performance that is based on the *ex post* CML. This measure, called the *ex post total risk alpha*, is simply the vertical distance the portfolio lies above or below the *ex post* CML. It is similar to the measure referred to earlier as *ex post* alpha, except that it is based on a different risk measure (total risk instead of market risk) and uses a different benchmark (the *ex post* CML instead of the *ex post* SML). It also gives the same assessment of a portfolio's performance relative to the market as the Sharpe ratio and M^2, but it can lead to a different ranking for the portfolio.

[13] The market portfolio does not have any unique risk. Thus it can be shown that if $RVOL_p$ indicates that a portfolio did not perform as well as the market, then SR_p must also indicate that the portfolio did not perform as well as the market because a portfolio with a relatively high amount of market risk will also have a relatively high amount of total risk.

[14] The quadratic regression equation (24.31), originally suggested by Jack Treynor and Kay Mazuy, has been refined by Sudipto Bhattacharya and Paul Pfleiderer in a 1983 Stanford University unpublished paper (Technical Report 714) whose principal results are described in T. Daniel Coggin, Frank J. Fabozzi, and Shafiqur Rahman, "The Investment Performance of U.S. Equity Pension Fund Managers: An Empirical Investigation," *Journal of Finance* 48, no. 3 (July 1993): 1040–1043.

[15] The size of parameter c (as well as the parameters a and b) should be judged relative to its standard error. In both of the equations shown here, it is quite small relative to both zero and the respective standard errors. Most standard statistical textbooks have an introductory discussion of the regression procedures that are used here. See, for example, Chapters 10 and 11 in James T. McClave and P. George Benson, *Statistics for Business and Economics*, 6th ed. (New York: Macmillan College Publishing, 1994).

[16] See Richard Roll, "Ambiguity When Performance Is Measured by the Security Market Line," *Journal of Finance* 33, no. 4 (September 1978): 1051–1069; David Peterson and Michael L. Rice, "A Note on Ambiguity in Portfolio Performance Measures," *Journal of Finance* 35, no. 5 (December 1980): 1251–1256; and Heinz Zimmermann and Claudia Zogg-Wetter, "On Detecting Selection and Timing Ability: The Case of Stock Market Indexes," *Financial Analysts Journal* 48, no. 1 (January/February 1992): 80–83.

[17] The problem is much more severe when the index is equal-weighted, because periodically part of the holdings of those stocks that had risen the most would have to be sold and the proceeds invested in additional shares of those stocks that had risen the least in order to keep equal weights in each stock.

[18] With the widespread use of index funds and index futures (discussed in Chapters 23 and 20, respectively), this criticism has lost much of its validity.

[19] See Dan W. French and Glenn V. Henderson Jr., "How Well Does Performance Evaluation Perform?" *Journal of Portfolio Management* 11, no. 2 (Winter 1985): 15–18.

[20] Under APT (discussed in Chapter 11), there is another measure of portfolio performance that is analogous to the CAPM-based *appraisal ratio* mentioned in endnote 7. It involves dividing the APT-based *ex post* alpha by the *ex post* standard deviation of the APT-based random error term.

[21] Like the equity indices described earlier, many of these and other bond indices are published in *Barron's* and *The Wall Street Journal*. For more on bond indices, see John Markese, "The Complexities of Bond Market Indicators," *AAII Journal* 14, no. 9 (October 1992): 34–36.

[22] As discussed in Chapter 21, this method is used by Morningstar, Inc. in evaluating bond mutual fund performance. It is also used by Christopher R. Blake, Edwin J. Elton, and Martin J. Gruber in "The Performance of Bond Mutual Funds," *Journal of Business* 66, no. 3 (July 1993): 371–403. These authors also used multiple regression where the excess returns on more than one bond index were the explanatory variables.

[23] Bond portfolio performance evaluation is also discussed in Peter O. Dictz and Jeannette R. Kirschman, "Evaluating Portfolio Performance," *Managing Investment Portfolios: A Dynamic Process*, John L. Maginn and Donald L. Tuttle (eds.), (Boston, MA: Warren, Gorham & Lamont, 1990), Chapter 14.

[24] For a discussion of factor models, see Chapter 10 and William F. Sharpe, "Factors in New York Stock Exchange Security Returns, 1931–1979," *Journal of Portfolio Management* 8, no. 4 (Summer 1982): 5–18.

dollar-weighted return	*ex post* alpha
time-weighted return	characteristic line
benchmark portfolios	reward-to-volatility ratio
market index	Sharpe ratio
price weighting	*M*-squared
value weighting	performance attribution
equal weighting	comparative performance attribution
price relatives	

REFERENCES

1. The use of portfolio benchmarks for performance evaluation is discussed in:

    Richard Roll, "Performance Evaluation and Benchmark Errors (I)," *Journal of Portfolio Management* 6, no. 4 (Summer 1980): 5–12.

    Richard Roll, "Performance Evaluation and Benchmark Errors (II)," *Journal of Portfolio Management* 7, no. 2 (Winter 1981): 17–22.

    Gary P. Brinson, Jeffrey J. Diermeier, and Gary G. Schlarbaum, "A Composite Portfolio Benchmark for Pension Plans," *Financial Analysts Journal* 42, no. 2 (March/April 1986): 15–24.

    Mark P. Kritzman, "How to Build a Normal Portfolio in Three Easy Steps," *Journal of Portfolio Management* 13, no. 4 (Summer 1987): 21–23.

    Jeffery V. Bailey, Thomas M. Richards, and David E. Tierney, "Benchmark Portfolios and the Manager/Plan Sponsor Relationship," *Journal of Corporate Finance* 4, no. 4 (Winter 1988): 25–32.

    Arjun Divecha and Richard C. Grinold, "Normal Portfolios: Issues for Sponsors, Managers, and Consultants," *Financial Analysts Journal* 45, no. 2 (March/April 1989): 7–13.

    Edward P. Rennie and Thomas J. Cowhey, "The Successful Use of Benchmark Portfolios: A Case Study," *Financial Analysts Journal* 46, no. 5 (September/October 1990): 18–26.

    Jeffery V. Bailey, "Are Manager Universes Acceptable Performance Benchmarks?" *Journal of Portfolio Management* 18, no. 3 (Spring 1992): 9–13.

    Jeffery Bailey,"Evaluating Benchmark Quality," *Financial Analysts Journal* 48, no. 3 (May/June 1992): 33–39.

    Martin L. Leibowitz, Lawrence N. Bader, Stanley Kogelman, and Ajay R. Dravid, "Benchmark Departures and Total Fund Risk: A Second Dimension of Diversification," *Financial Analysts Journal* 51, no. 5 (September/October 1995): 40–48.

2. The four measures of risk-adjusted performance were initially developed in:

    Jack L. Treynor, "How to Rate Management of Investment Funds," *Harvard Business Review* 43, no. 1 (January/February 1965): 63–75.

    William F. Sharpe, "Mutual Fund Performance," *Journal of Business* 39, no. 1 (January 1966): 119–138 and "The Sharpe Ratio," *Journal of Portfolio Management* 21, no. 1 (Fall 1994): 49–58.

    Michael C. Jensen, "The Performance of Mutual Funds in the Period 1945–1964," *Journal of Finance* 23, no. 2 (May 1968): 389–416 and "Risk, the Pricing of Capital Assets, and the Evaluation of Investment Portfolios," *Journal of Business* 42, no. 2 (April 1969): 167–185.

    Franco Modigliani and Leah Modigliani, "Risk-Adjusted Performance," *Journal of Portfolio Management* 23, no. 2 (Winter 1997): 45–54.

3. More sophisticated measures of portfolio performance that also measure market timing ability were initially developed by:

    Jack L. Treynor and Kay K. Mazuy, "Can Mutual Funds Outguess the Market?" *Harvard Business Review* 44, no. 4 (July/August 1966): 131–136.

Robert C. Merton, "On Market Timing and Investment Performance I. An Equilibrium Theory of Value for Market Forecasts," *Journal of Business* 54, no. 3 (July 1981): 363–406.

Roy D. Henriksson and Robert C. Merton, "On Market Timing and Investment Performance II. Statistical Procedures for Evaluating Forecasting Skill," *Journal of Business* 54, no. 4 (October 1981): 513–533.

4. There have been many criticisms leveled at the various measures of portfolio performance that are presented in this chapter. One of the most formidable critiques was:

Richard Roll, "Ambiguity When Performance Is Measured by the Security Market Line," *Journal of Finance* 33, no. 4 (September 1978): 1051–1069.

5. APT-based measures of portfolio performance have been developed by:

Gregory Connor and Robert Korajczyk, "Performance Measurement with the Arbitrage Pricing Theory: A New Framework for Analysis," *Journal of Financial Economics* 15, no. 3 (March 1986): 373–394.

Bruce N. Lehmann and David M. Modest, "Mutual Fund Performance Evaluation: A Comparison of Benchmarks and Benchmark Comparisons," *Journal of Finance* 42, no. 2 (June 1987): 233–265.

Nai-Fu Chen, Thomas E. Copeland, and David Mayers, "A Comparison of Single and Multifactor Portfolio Performance Methodologies," *Journal of Financial and Quantitative Analysis*, 22, no. 4 (December 1987): 401–417.

Edwin J. Elton, Martin J. Gruber, and Christopher R. Blake, "Fundamental Economic Variables, Expected Returns, and Bond Fund Performance," *Journal of Finance* 50, no. 4 (September 1995): 1229–1256.

6. Developments in measuring portfolio performance are discussed in the end-of-chapter references in Chapter 21 and in:

Stanley J. Kon, "The Market-Timing Performance of Mutual Fund Managers," *Journal of Business* 56, no. 3 (July 1983): 323–347.

Anat R. Admati and Stephen A. Ross, "Measuring Investment Performance in a Rational Expectations Equilibrium Model," *Journal of Business* 58, no. 1 (January 1985): 1–26.

Philip H. Dybvig and Stephen A. Ross, "Differential Information and Performance Measurement Using a Security Market Line," *Journal of Finance* 40, no. 2 (June 1985): 383–399.

Philip H. Dybvig and Stephen A. Ross, "The Analytics of Performance Measurement Using a Security Market Line," *Journal of Finance* 40, no. 2 (June 1985): 401–416.

Mark Kritzman, "How to Detect Skill in Management Performance," *Journal of Portfolio Management* 12, no. 2 (Winter 1986): 16–20.

Ravi Jagannathan and Robert A. Korajczyk, "Assessing the Market Timing Performance of Managed Portfolios," *Journal of Business* 59, no. 2, pt. 1 (April 1986): 217–235.

Anat R. Admati, Sudipto Bhattacharya, Paul Pfleiderer, and Stephen A. Ross, "On Timing and Selectivity," *Journal of Finance* 41, no. 3 (July 1986): 715–730.

Gary P. Brinson, L. Randolph Hood, and Gilbert L. Beebower, "Determinants of Portfolio Performance," *Financial Analysts Journal* 42, no. 4 (July/August 1986): 39–44.

William Breen, Ravi Jagannathan, and Aharon R. Ofer, "Correcting for Heteroscedasticity in Tests for Market Timing Ability," *Journal of Business* 59, no. 4, pt. 1 (October 1986): 585–598.

Robert E. Cumby and David M. Modest, "Testing for Market Timing Ability: A Framework for Forecast Evaluation," *Journal of Financial Economics* 19, no. 1 (September 1987): 169–189.

Larry J. Lockwood and K. Rao Kadiyala, "Measuring Investment Performance with a Stochastic Parameter Regression Model," *Journal of Banking and Finance* 12, no. 3 (September 1988): 457–467.

Alex Kane and Gary Marks, "Performance Evaluation of Market Timers: Theory and Evidence," *Journal of Financial and Quantitative Analysis* 23, no. 4 (December 1988): 425–435.

Mark Grinblatt and Sheridan Titman, "Portfolio Performance Evaluation: Old Issues and New Insights," *Review of Financial Studies* 2, no. 3 (1989): 393–421.

Portfolio Performance Evaluation

Cheng-few Lee and Shafiqur Rahman, "Market Timing, Selectivity, and Mutual Fund Performance: An Empirical Investigation," *Journal of Business* 63, no. 2 (April 1990): 261–278.

Michel Gendron and Christian Genest, "Performance Measurement under Asymmetric Information and Investment Constraints," *Journal of Finance* 45, no. 5 (December 1990): 1655–1661.

Cheng-Few Lee and Shafiqur Rahman, "New Evidence on Timing and Security Selection Skill of Mutual Fund Managers," *Journal of Portfolio Management* 17, no. 2 (Winter 1991): 80–83.

Gary P. Brinson, Brian D. Singer, and Gilbert L. Beebower, "Determinants of Portfolio Performance II: An Update," *Financial Analysts Journal* 47, no. 3 (May/June 1991): 40–48.

Chris R. Hensel, D. Don Ezra, and John H. Ilkiw, "The Importance of the Asset Allocation Decision," *Financial Analysts Journal* 47, no. 4 (July/August 1991): 65–72.

Eric J. Weigel, "The Performance of Tactical Asset Allocation," *Financial Analysts Journal* 47, no. 5 (September/October 1991): 63–70.

G. L. Beebower and A. P. Varikooty, "Measuring Market Timing Strategies," *Financial Analysts Journal* 47, no. 6 (November/December 1991): 78–84, 92.

L. R. Glosten and R. Jagannathan, "A Contingent Claim Approach to Performance Evaluation," *Journal of Empirical Finance* 1, no. 2 (January 1994): 133–160.

Wayne E. Ferson and Rudi Schadt, "Measuring Fund Strategy and Performance in Changing Economic Conditions," *Journal of Finance* 51, no. 2 (June 1996): 425–461.

Zhiwu Chen and Peter Knez, "Portfolio Performance Measurement: Theory and Applications," *Review of Financial Studies* 9, no. 2 (Summer 1996): 511–555.

Jeffery V. Bailey, "Evaluating Investment Skill with a VAM Graph," *Journal of Investing* 5, no. 2 (Summer 1996): 64–71.

7. An alternative approach to portfolio performance evaluation that is called style analysis is described in the end-of-chapter references in Chapter 23 and in:

William F. Sharpe, "Major Investment Styles," *Journal of Portfolio Management* 4, no. 2 (Winter 1978): 68–74.

William F. Sharpe, "Determining a Fund's Effective Asset Mix," *Investment Management Review* (December 1988): 59–69.

William F. Sharpe, "Asset Allocation," in John L. Maginn and Donald L. Tuttle eds. *Managing Investment Portfolios: A Dynamic Process* (Boston: Warren, Gorham & Lamont, 1990), Chapter 7.

William F. Sharpe, "Asset Allocation: Management Style and Performance Measurement," *Journal of Portfolio Management* 18, no. 2 (Winter 1992): 7–19.

Richard Bernstein, *Style Investing* (New York: Wiley, 1995).

T. Daniel Coggin, Frank J. Fabozzi, and Robert Arnott (eds.), *The Handbook of Equity Style Management* (New Hope, PA: Frank J. Fabozzi Associates, 1997).

Angelo Lobosco and Dan Di Bartolomeo, "Approximating the Confidence Intervals for Sharpe Style Weights, *Financial Analysts Journal* 53, no. 4 (July/August 1997): 80–85.

Dan diBartolomeo and Erik Witkowski, "Mutual Fund Misclassification: Evidence Based on Style Analysis," *Financial Analysts Journal* 53, no. 5 (September/October 1997): 32–43.

8. Bond portfolio performance evaluation is discussed in:

Wayne H. Wagner and Dennis A. Tito, "Definitive New Measures of Bond Performance and Risk," *Pension World* 13, no. 5 (May 1977): 10–12.

Wayne H. Wagner and Dennis A. Tito, "Is Your Bond Manager Skillful?" *Pension World* 13, no. 6 (June 1977): 9–13.

Peter O. Dietz, H. Russell Fogler, and Donald J. Hardy, "The Challenge of Analyzing Bond Portfolio Returns," *Journal of Portfolio Management* 6, no. 3 (Spring 1980): 53–58.

Mark Kritzman, "Can Bond Managers Perform Consistently?" *Journal of Portfolio Management* 9, no. 4 (Summer 1983): 54–56.

Robert N. Anthony, "How to Measure Fixed-Income Performance Correctly," *Journal of Portfolio Management* 11, no. 2 (Winter 1985): 61–65.

Peter O. Dietz and Jeannette R. Kirschman, "Evaluating Portfolio Performance," in John L. Maginn and Donald L. Tuttle (eds.), *Managing Investment Portfolios: A Dynamic Process* (Boston: Warren, Gorham & Lamont, 1990), Chapter 14.

Ronald N. Kahn, "Bond Performance Analysis: A Multi-Factor Approach," *Journal of Portfolio Management* 18, no. 1 (Fall 1991): 40–47.

Christopher R. Blake, Edwin J. Elton, and Martin J. Gruber in "The Performance of Bond Mutual Funds," *Journal of Business* 66, no. 3 (July 1993): 371–403.

Edwin J. Elton, Martin J. Gruber, and Christopher R. Blake, "Fundamental Economic Variables, Expected Returns, and Bond Fund Performance," *Journal of Finance* 50, no. 4 (September 1995): 1229–1256.

9. Performance attribution was initially developed and then expanded in:

Eugene F. Fama, "Components of Investment Performance," *Journal of Finance* 27, no. 3 (June 1972): 551-567.

H. Russell Fogler, "Common Stock Management in the 1990s," *Journal of Portfolio Management* 16, no. 2 (Winter 1990): 26–35.

Ernest M. Ankrim, "Risk-Adjusted Performance Attribution," *Financial Analysts Journal* 48, no. 2 (March/April 1991): 74–82.

Peter J. Higgs and Stephen Goode, "Target Active Returns and Attribution Analysis," *Financial Analysts Journal* 49, no. 3 (May/June 1993): 77–80.

Ernest M. Ankrim and Chris R. Hansel, "Multicurrency Perfoemance Attribution," *Financial Analysts Journal* 50, no. 2 (March/April 1994): 29–35.

Brian D. Singer and Denis S. Karnosky, "The General Framework for Global Investment Management and Performance Attribution," *Journal of Portfolio Management* 21, no. 2 (Winter 1995): 84–92.

INTERNATIONAL INVESTING

One of the major themes of capital market theory concerns the merits of diversification: In an efficient capital market, sensible investment strategies will include holdings of many different assets. Previous chapters have generally considered traditional domestic securities, such as stocks and bonds, and some less traditional ones, such as options and futures. However, an investor should also consider holding foreign securities, thereby diversifying his or her portfolio internationally. (Some people also believe that investing in tangible assets brings additional diversification benefits; see the appendix for a discussion.)

If the world were under one political jurisdiction, with one currency and complete freedom of trade, then "the market portfolio" could be thought of as including all securities in the world, each in proportion to its market value. In such a situation, limiting one's investments to securities representing firms located in only one part of the world would most likely result in a relatively low rate of return per unit of risk. After all, few people would advocate that Californians own only securities issued by California firms. And in a world without political boundaries, few people would advocate that Americans own only securities issued by American firms.

Unfortunately, there are political boundaries, different currencies, varying disclosure rules and accounting procedures, and restrictions on trade and currency exchange. Such irritants diminish, but do not destroy, the advantages to be gained from international investment. This chapter discusses international investing, giving consideration to these "irritants" in the process

25.1   THE TOTAL INVESTABLE CAPITAL MARKET PORTFOLIO

Figure 25.1 provides a 1997 year-end estimate of the size of the total investable capital market portfolio in the world, which can be thought of as representing the set of investments that are available to U.S. portfolio managers. Many problems are encountered in the construction of such a portfolio. It is almost impossible to adequately represent *all* security markets, because undoubtedly certain classes of assets have been omitted (such as foreign real estate) and double counting is involved in that some firms own parts of other firms.[1]

The figure indicates that non-U.S. bond and equity markets amount to U.S. $24.9 trillion (=$7.4 + $2.3 + $0.7 + $8.7 + $1.0 + $3.8 + $1.0) and constitute about one-half the value of the entire $49 trillion world portfolio (there are seven foreign categories: Japan Equity, Other Equity, Emerging Markets Equity, Other Bonds, Emerging Market Debt, Japan Bonds, and Dollar Bonds; the last category consists of foreign and Eurobonds denominated in U.S. dollars). Also of interest is the observation that fixed-income securities amount to $25.7 trillion (=$8.8 + $.3 + $2.1 + $8.7 + $1.0 + $3.8 + $1.0) and make up slightly more than one-half of the portfolio's value.[2] About one-half of this total is non-U.S. fixed-income securities. Similarly, about one-half of the $20.9 trillion (= $7.4 + $10.4 + $0.7 + $2.3 + $0.1) equity market consists of non-U.S. stocks.

A more detailed breakdown of the stock market capitalization at the end of January 1998 in the countries followed by Morgan Stanley Capital International is provided in columns (2) and (3) of Table 25.1. The largest market for common stocks is the United States, followed by Japan. In total, these two countries make up 61.9% of the total. In the third position is the United Kingdom, and then notably behind the United Kingdom comes Germany. These four countries represent 77.1% of the total. It will be shown next how Morgan Stanley calculates international stock market indices involving these countries.

25.1.1 International Equity Indices

In most countries, there are indices of overall stock values and of the values of stocks within various industry or economic sectors. Such indices can be used for assessing "market moves" within the country and, more important, for comparative performance measurement. Important indices include the Financial Times-Stock Exchange 100 Index (often referred to as FT-SE, or the "Footsie") for the London Stock Exchange, the Nikkei 225 Average for the Tokyo Stock Exchange, and the TSE 300

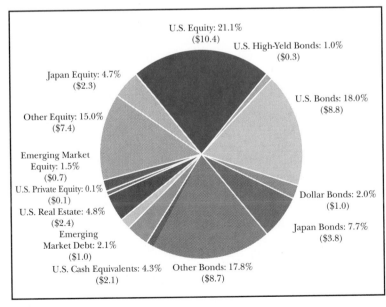

Figure 25.1
Total Investable Capital Market Portfolio, Year-End 1997, Preliminary (trillions of U.S. dollars)
Source: Brinson Partners, Inc. (Chicago, 1998).

TABLE 25.1 World Stock Market Capitalization, January 1998

Country (1)	Market Capitalization	
	Dollars (billion U.S.) (2)	Percentage (3)
Austria	23.8	.2
Belgium	78.2	.6
Denmark	63.3	.5
Finland	48.0	.4
France	490.9	3.8
Germany	602.5	4.7
Ireland	24.7	.2
Italy	262.1	2.0
Netherlands	339.6	2.7
Norway	29.2	.2
Portugal	36.4	.3
Spain	170.9	1.3
Sweden	158.3	1.2
Switzerland	483.0	3.8
U.K.	1,343.7	10.5
Total Europe	4,154.6	32.4
Australia	174.9	1.4
Hong Kong	143.1	1.1
Japan	1,631.5	12.8
Malaysia	43.4	.3
New Zealand	17.7	.1
Singapore	44.6	.3
Total Pacific	2,055.2	16.0
Canada	299.8	2.4
U.S.	6,283.6	49.1
Total North America	6,583.4	51.5
Total World	$12,793.2	100.0

Source: Adapted from *Morgan Stanley Capital International Global Investment Monitor*, January 30, 1998, p. 3.

Composite Index for the Toronto Stock Exchange. As shown in Figure 25.2(a), these and other indices are published daily in *The Wall Street Journal*.[3]

On the international level, the indices produced by Morgan Stanley Capital International are also widely used for such purposes.[4] Each index is based on a value-weighted portfolio of stocks (using total shares outstanding) in a particular country. Nearly all of these stocks can be purchased by foreigners. Values for each of the national indices (plus various industry indices for each country) are given both in the local currency and in U.S. dollars on the basis of the exchange rates at the time. The stocks selected for each index are designed to represent about 60% of the aggregate market value of the particular country's equity markets.[5] A listing of the countries with the largest and most mature stock markets is presented in Table 25.1.

The individual country indices are combined into various regional indices. Furthermore, all of these indices are also used to compute a "World" index based on 23 countries with well-developed capital markets (see Table 25.1), an "Emerging Markets" index based on 26 countries, and an "All-Country World" index based on the combined 48 countries (Malaysia is in both the World and Emerging Markets in-

(a) Foreign Stock Market Indices

EXCHANGE	INDEX	10/6/97 CLOSE	NET CHG	PCT CHG	YTD NET CHG	YTD PCT CHG
Argentina	Merval Index	837.60	+ 3.51	+ 0.42	+ 188.23	+ 28.99
Australia	All Ordinaries	2769.70	+ 6.60	+ 0.24	+ 345.10	+ 14.23
Belgium	Bel-20 Index	2515.28	+ 8.15	+ 0.33	+ 619.79	+ 32.70
Brazil	Sao Paulo Bovespa	12688.00	+ 148.00	+ 1.18	+ 5648.10	+ 80.23
Britain	London FT 100-share	5300.00	− 30.80	− 0.58	+ 1181.50	+ 28.69
Britain	London FT 250-share	4867.40	− 16.50	− 0.34	+ 377.00	+ 8.40
Canada	Toronto 300 Comp.	7168.38	+ 76.51	+ 1.08	+ 1241.35	+ 20.94
Chile	Santiago IPSA	125.70	− 1.22	− 0.96	+ 25.70	+ 25.70
China	Dow Jones China 88	141.05	+ 0.13	+ 0.09	+ 28.83	+ 25.69
China	Dow Jones Shanghai	147.01	+ 0.26	+ 0.18	+ 32.16	+ 28.00
China	Dow Jones Shenzhen	150.00	− 0.10	− 0.07	+ 21.48	+ 16.71
France	Paris CAC 40	3077.98	− 16.03	− 0.52	+ 762.25	+ 32.92
Germany	Frankfurt DAX	4302.13	+ 28.42	+ 0.66	+ 1413.44	+ 48.93
Germany	Frankfurt IBIS DAX	4326.35	+ 60.18	+ 1.41	+ 1446.28	+ 50.22
Hong Kong	Hang Seng	14776.78	− 351.24	− 2.32	+ 1325.33	+ 9.85
India	Bombay Sensex	3857.34	+ 9.61	+ 0.25	+ 772.14	+ 25.03
Italy	Milan MIBtel	15458.00	− 77.00	− 0.50	+ 4887.00	+ 46.23
Japan	Tokyo Nikkei 225	17824.78	+ 177.33	+ 1.00	− 1536.57	− 7.94
Japan	Tokyo Nikkei 300	276.31	+ 2.56	+ 0.94	− 3.95	− 1.41
Japan	Tokyo Topix Index	1391.06	+ 12.91	+ 0.94	− 79.88	− 5.43
Mexico	I.P.C. All-Share	5315.96	+ 1.78	+ 0.03	+ 1954.93	+ 58.16
Netherlands	Amsterdam AEX	961.81	− 1.51	− 0.16	+ 313.57	+ 48.37
Singapore	Straits Times	1880.58	− 21.46	− 1.13	− 336.21	− 15.17
South Africa	Johannesburg Gold	1058.80	+ 16.70	+ 1.60	− 447.20	− 29.69
South Korea	Composite	644.21	− 1.94	− 0.30	− 7.01	− 1.08
Spain	Madrid General Index	622.14	− 11.48	− 1.81	+ 177.37	+ 39.88
Sweden	Affaersvaerlden	3262.49	− 17.52	− 0.53	+ 859.55	+ 35.77
Switzerland	Zurich Swiss Market	5897.40	− 31.60	− 0.53	+ 1955.20	+ 49.60
Taiwan	Weighted Index	8392.59	+ 11.76	+ 0.14	+ 1458.65	+ 21.04

na-Not available

(b) Morgan Stanley Indices

	Oct. 3	Oct. 2	% FROM 12/31/96
U.S.	917.3	912.6	+ 30.1
Britain	1592.0	1582.1	+ 28.5
Canada	776.0	771.5	+ 20.0
Japan	887.6	879.4	− 2.0
France	990.2	978.0	+ 31.6
Germany	560.3	560.3	+ 45.0
Hong Kong	9144.7	9119.8	+ 5.7
Switzerland	742.0	730.2	+ 49.4
Australia	538.8	543.4	+ 10.8
World Index	**976.0**	**970.8**	**+ 19.0**
EAFE MSCI	**1304.3**	**1297.5**	**+ 10.0**

As calculated by Morgan Stanley Capital International Perspective, Geneva. Each index, calculated in local currencies, is based on the close of 1969 equaling 100.

Figure 25.2
International Equity Indices on October 6, 1997
Source: Reprinted by permission of *The Wall Street Journal*, Dow Jones & Company, Inc., October 7, 1997, p. C16. All rights reserved worldwide.

dexes). These indices are formed using weights that are based on market capitalization, thus producing value-weighted indices. In addition, alternative versions of these indexes are calculated using gross domestic product (GDP) to form weights. Some countries with well-established stock markets but relatively small economies (such as the United Kingdom) have less weight in a GDP-weighted index than in a market capitalization–weighted index compared with countries with large economies but relatively smaller stock markets (such as Germany).

Morgan Stanley also calculates the "Europe, Australia, Far East" (EAFE) index, which is widely used by U.S. investors as a benchmark when evaluating the performance of international portfolio managers. The index excludes the United States and Canada and is currently based on the stock performance in the remaining 21 countries listed in Table 25.1. Several of the Morgan Stanley individual country indices are published daily in *The Wall Street Journal*, as shown in Figure 25.2(b), with the World and EAFE indices at the bottom.

25.1.2 Emerging Markets

In recent years many countries have initiated organized stock exchanges or highly active over-the-counter stock markets. In general, these countries have in common a relatively low (compared with Western countries) level of per capita gross domestic product, improving political and economic stability, a currency convertible into Western countries' currencies (or at least some means for foreigners to repatriate income and capital gains), and most important, securities available for investment by foreigners. Such countries have what are referred to as **emerging markets**.

Investments in emerging market stocks have proven attractive to a number of institutional investors, who in many cases have invested directly in those securities, or when that is not possible, through country funds, (such as the Indonesia Fund; see Chapter 21). Because many emerging market economies at various times have undergone rapid growth, and because their stock markets are not highly developed and therefore are less efficient, there is considerable opportunity for relatively high returns from emerging market investments. However, there is also a relatively high level of risk involved as witnessed by the meltdown of several Asian emerging stock markets in 1997 and 1998.

As mentioned earlier, Morgan Stanley Capital International currently defines 26 countries as emerging markets and publishes stock market indices for each one of these countries as well as various regional stock market indices and an overall emerging markets index.[6] Also popular are various country, regional and composite indices produced by the International Financial Corporation (IFC), including the IFC Global and Investable emerging markets indices.

25.2 RISK AND RETURN FROM FOREIGN INVESTING

Investing in a foreign security involves all the risks associated with investing in a domestic security plus additional risks. The investor expects to receive cash flows in the future from the foreign security. However, these cash flows will be in a foreign currency and thus will be of relatively little use to the investor if they cannot be converted into the investor's domestic currency. The additional risks associated with foreign investing arise from uncertainties associated with converting these foreign cash flows into domestic currency. They are known as **political risk** and **exchange (or currency) risk**.[7]

Political risk refers to uncertainty about the *ability* of an investor to convert the foreign currency into domestic currency. Specifically, a foreign government might restrict, tax, or completely prohibit the exchange of one currency for another. Because such policies change from time to time, the ability of an investor to repatriate foreign cash flows may be subject to some uncertainty. There may even be a possibility of complete expropriation, making the political risk very large.

Exchange risk refers to uncertainty about the *rate* at which a foreign currency can be converted for the investor's domestic currency in the future. That is, at the time a foreign security is bought, the rate at which future foreign cash flows can be converted into domestic currency is uncertain, and it is this uncertainty that is known as exchange risk.

25.2.1 Managing Exchange Risk

To an extent, exchange risk can be reduced by hedging in the forward (or futures) market for foreign currency. In the case of default-free fixed-income securities, it may be possible to completely eliminate such risk in this way. For example, assume that a one-year pure-discount bond paying 1,000 British pounds at maturity can be purchased for 850 British pounds. Furthermore, assume that a forward contract can be signed whereby the investor will receive $1,300 for delivering 1,000 British pounds a year from now since the *forward exchange rate* is $1.30 per pound. In this situation, the rate of return *in British pounds* on this security is 17.65% [= (1,000 − 850)/850].

If the *spot* (that is, current) *exchange rate* were $1.35 per pound, then the cost of this bond to an American investor would be $1,147.50 (=850 × $1.35). Thus the rate of return *in U.S. dollars* on this British security would be 13.29% [= ($1,300 − $1,147.50)/$1,147.50]. Except for political risk, this is a certain return, because exchange risk has been completely removed by hedging with a forward contract.

Unfortunately, it is not possible to completely hedge the exchange risk associated with risky investments. Forward contracts can be made to cover expected cash flows, but if the actual cash flows are larger or smaller than expected, then some of the foreign currency may have to be exchanged at the spot rate prevailing at the time that the cash is received. Because future spot rates usually cannot be predicted with complete certainty, overall risk will be affected. As a practical matter, this "unhedgeable" risk is likely to be small in many cases involving fixed-income securities, but it can be rather large in the case of equities. Nevertheless, the cost of hedging foreign investments, regardless of whether they are fixed-income securities or equities, may exceed the benefit (see this chapter's *Institutional Issues: Currency Risk: To Hedge or not to Hedge*).

It is important to differentiate between two very different approaches to managing exchange risk. The first approach is *passive currency management*, which involves a strategy of permanently controlling a portfolio's exposure to currency risk. For example, a foreign stock manager may choose to use forward contracts to consistently remove half of the portfolio's currency exposure. Although an attempt might be made initially to examine the effect such a strategy has on the portfolio's level of risk, afterward, all decisions with respect to currency management are mechanical. The second approach is *active currency management*, which involves a strategy of frequently changing currency exposures to take advantage of perceived short-run mispricings among currencies. In this approach, the effect of such a strategy on the portfolio's level of risk is constantly being taken into consideration.

Passive currency management requires the investor to set a policy concerning the desired level of exchange risk. This acceptable risk level is predicated on the investor's risk tolerance as well as the investor's assumptions about the long-run levels of volatilities and correlations of the currencies in the portfolio. Active currency management, on the other hand, involves moving away from the investor's

Currency Risk: To Hedge or Not to Hedge

Investors in securities denominated in currencies other than those of their home country incur a risk not borne by their domestic investor counterparts: currency risk. For investors in foreign assets, currency (or exchange) risk is the variability in portfolio returns caused by fluctuations in the rate at which foreign currencies can be converted into their home currency. Whether investors in foreign securities should attempt to minimize currency risk in their portfolios has become a topic of considerable controversy in recent years. Among institutional investors, the issue has taken on increased importance as these investors have expanded their foreign investments.

As the text describes, the return on an investor's foreign portfolio can be divided into two components: a domestic (also called local) return and a currency (also called foreign exchange) return. Likewise, foreign portfolio risk can be decomposed into domestic risk, currency risk, and any possible interaction between the two. Most studies indicate that currency risk can increase total portfolio risk by anywhere from 15% to 100% of the underlying domestic risk.

Investors have a choice of whether to bear currency risk. Through a variety of techniques, currency risk can be "hedged" and almost eliminated. The most popular means of hedging currency risk is to purchase units of the investor's home currency in the forward market equal to the expected value of the foreign investment. For example, consider a U.S. investor holding 1,000 shares of a Japanese company selling for 4,000 yen per share. He or she can purchase dollars for delivery six months from today at a rate of 125 yen per dollar. (The forward market is quite similar to the futures market; see Chapter 20. Both forward and futures contracts involve a promise to deliver something

of value on a specified future date at a currently agreed-upon price. The forward market, however, does not involve a standardized contract traded on an organized exchange with a third-party clearinghouse that ensures that contracts are honored. Moreover, forward contracts, unlike futures contracts, are not marked to market daily.) By purchasing $32,000 for delivery six months from today to be paid for with 4 million yen, the investor insulates himself or herself from changes in the exchange rate between the yen and the dollar over the next six months.

Despite the availability of effective hedging tools, why do many investors in foreign securities choose not to hedge their currency risks and instead remain exposed to exchange rate fluctuations? Considered next are the primary arguments in support of and in opposition to currency risk hedging.

Proponents of hedging currency risk contend that a no-hedge policy violates one of the basic laws of capital market theory: Only accept risks for which adequate compensation is expected to be earned. They view currencies as having zero expected returns. That is, in a world in which capital is free to flow across borders, there is no reason to expect the value of foreign currencies to move systematically in one direction relative to an investor's home currency. However, exchange rates do fluctuate, generating additional risk for an investor in foreign securities. Proponents view currency risk as uncompensated and believe that risk-averse investors should seek its minimization. Investors who do not hedge would seem to be passing up an opportunity to reduce portfolio risk while not diminishing portfolio returns. Proponents point out that the reduction in portfolio variability gained by hedging currency risk can be substantial.

normally desired levels of currency exposures. It assumes that currency markets are at times in disequilibrium. Further, it assumes that the investor can add value by appropriately altering the portfolio's currency exposures as the disequilibrium corrects or shifts.

Unfortunately, both currency management approaches have come to be known as "hedging." Yet only passive currency management is truly hedging in the sense of attempting to eliminate or reduce unwanted risk. Active currency management, like any other active management strategy, might very well add risk to a portfolio, not reduce it.[8]

If an investor chooses to actively manage the currency exposure of a diversified foreign portfolio, there are several ways of doing so. First, the investor could manage the currency exposures directly or hire a *currency specialist* to perform that func-

Opponents of currency hedging generally concede that forgoing hedging means accepting additional uncompensated risks. (However, there is a school of thought that contends that currency risk should be systematically rewarded by the market.) Nevertheless, they believe that market "frictions" cause the costs of currency hedging to outweigh the risk reduction benefits. That is, significant expenses are likely to be incurred by an investor managing currency risk. Currency dealers must be compensated for facilitating hedging transactions. Custodian banks must be paid for record keeping. Investment managers charge fees for maintaining the hedge. Estimates of the total cost of hedging typically range from .25% to .50% per year of the value of the hedged assets, enough to convince opponents that currency risk hedging may not be cost-effective.

In addition, some hedging opponents have questioned the wisdom of hedging for an investor who spends a high percentage of his or her income on goods produced abroad. Suppose the value of foreign currencies declines relative to the investor's home currency (thereby negatively affecting the investor's foreign portfolio returns, other things being equal). The declining relative value of the foreign currencies also reduces the effective cost of foreign-produced goods to the investor. In a sense the investor's own consumption basket serves as a hedge against currency risk in his or her portfolio.

Of additional importance to the discussion is the fact that the total risk (variance) of a portfolio containing foreign securities increases with the square of the amount of unhedged currency risk (assuming zero correlation between currency and domestic returns). On the other hand, the cost of hedging increases linearly. Thus, within a total portfolio of home country and foreign securities, there is some foreign allocation threshold (some observers have argued 15%) below which there should be no currency hedging and above which all incremental foreign positions should be completely hedged. Moreover, the longer is the investor's time horizon, the higher will be this threshold. This is because as the time horizon increases, currency risk declines due to mean reversion (that is, the tendency for currencies to move back toward "normal" relationships over time).

In the final analysis, an investor's optimal currency hedge will depend on a number of factors, including the following:

1. correlations between currencies,
2. correlations between domestic returns and currency returns,
3. the cost of hedging,
4. the portions of the investor's portfolio allocated to foreign securities,
5. the variability of foreign asset returns,
6. the variability of currency returns,
7. the investor's consumption basket,
8. the investor's level of risk aversion,
9. the investor's time horizon, and
10. the premium earned (if any) for holding foreign currencies.

These factors are difficult to quantify, making it hard to build a strong case for or against currency hedging. Moreover, as investors differ in both their financial circumstances and their beliefs about the characteristics of currencies and security markets, it is not surprising that everything from zero hedges to fully hedged positions is observed.

tion. Second, after deciding who is to manage these exposures, the investor must determine how integrated the currency management and security selection decisions are to be. At one extreme, the currency management and security selection decisions are made independently. In that case, if a currency specialist is used, that manager is often referred to as a *currency overlay* manager (that is, the currency management is *overlaid* on top of the foreign security portfolio). Here judgments on the amount and types of currency exposures to put in place are made without any consideration of which foreign securities are in the portfolio. This type of currency management is not likely to result in reducing the risk of a portfolio. At the other extreme, the currency management and security selection decisions are made jointly and hence do not involve the use of a separate currency manager. That is, decisions of which securities to purchase and how to manage the resulting currency exposures are made at the same time by one manager, keeping in mind how the two decisions affect each other. This type of currency management is likely to reduce the risk of a portfolio. A middle course involves making such decisions sequentially; the foreign investor selects the portfolio of securities first and then a currency specialist chooses the make up of the portfolio's currency exposures on the basis of the securities selected. Not surprisingly, one study found that the best approach was the joint-decision approach and that the least desirable one was the one in which decisions were made independently.[9]

25.2.2 Foreign and Domestic Returns

Changes in exchange rates can cause major differences between the returns obtained by domestic investors and the returns obtained by unhedged foreign investors. Consider an American investor and a Swiss investor, both of whom purchase shares of a Swiss company whose stock is traded only in Switzerland. Let the price of the stock in Swiss francs be P_0 at the beginning of a period and P_1 at the end of the period. The **domestic return**, denoted r_D, is:

$$r_D = \frac{P_1 - P_0}{P_0} \tag{25.1}$$

For example, if $P_0 = 10$ Swiss francs and $P_1 = 12$ Swiss francs, then $r_D = 20\%$ [$= (12 - 10)/10$].

For the Swiss investor, r_D is the stock's return. Not so for the U.S. investor. Assume that at the beginning of the period the price (in dollars) of one Swiss franc is $.50. Denoting this exchange rate (that is, the exchange rate at the beginning of the period) as X_0, the cost of a share to the American investor will be $X_0 P_0$. In the example, this cost will be $5 (=$.50 \times 10$).

Now assume that the exchange rate rises to $.55 per Swiss franc at the end of the period. Denoting this by X_1, the ending value of the stock for the American investor will be $X_1 P_1$. In the example, this value will be $6.60 (=$.55 \times 12$).

The **foreign return** (that is, the return to a foreign investor), denoted r_F, is:

$$r_F = \frac{X_1 P_1 - X_0 P_0}{X_0 P_0} \tag{25.2}$$

In the example, the foreign investor (an American) would have earned a return of $r_F = 32\%$ [$= ($6.60 - $5.00)/$5.00$] on an investment in the Swiss firm's stock.

In effect, the American made two investments: (1) an investment in a Swiss stock and (2) an investment in the Swiss franc. Accordingly, the overall return to the American can be decomposed into a return on the investment in the Swiss stock and a return on the investment in the Swiss franc. This can be illustrated by considering an American who had purchased a Swiss franc at the beginning of the period. If the American subsequently sold the franc at the end of the period, the return on foreign currency, denoted r_C, would be:

$$r_C = \frac{X_1 - X_0}{X_0} \tag{25.3}$$

In the example, $r_C = 10\%$ [$= ($.55 - $.50)/$.50$].

From Equations (25.1), (25.2), and (25.3), it can be shown that:

$$1 + r_F = (1 + r_D)(1 + r_C) \tag{25.4}$$

---

which can be rewritten as:

$$r_F = r_D + r_C + r_D r_C \qquad (25.5)$$

In the example, Equation (25.5) reveals that $r_F = 32\%\ [=.20 + .10 + (.20 \times .10)]$.

The last term in this equation $(r_D r_C)$ will generally be smaller than the two preceding ones because it equals their product, and both are generally less than 1.0. Thus Equation (25.5) can be restated as an approximation:

$$r_F \cong r_D + r_C \qquad (25.6)$$

It can now be seen that the return on a foreign security (r_F) can be approximated by summing the domestic return on the security (r_D) and the return on foreign currency (r_C). In the example, the precise value for r_F was shown earlier to be 32%. Use of the approximation indicates its value is equal to 30% (=.20 + .10). Thus the approximation is in error by 6% (=2/32), a relatively small amount.

25.2.3   Expected Returns

Equation (25.6) leads directly to the proposition that the expected return on a foreign security will approximately equal the expected domestic return plus the expected return on foreign currency:

$$\bar{r}_F \cong \bar{r}_D + \bar{r}_C \qquad (25.7)$$

It might be tempting for an investor to purchase a foreign security that has a high expected return in its host country on the belief that the security will have a high expected return to the foreign investor. However, Equation (25.7) reveals this type of logic to be flawed. Just because a foreign security has a high value for $\bar{r}_D$ does not mean that it has a high value for $\bar{r}_F$, because $\bar{r}_C$ can be negative. This can be shown by considering the case of bonds. The expected domestic returns of fixed-income securities in countries with high expected inflation rates will typically be high. However, a foreign investor in a country with a lower expected inflation rate should expect a *negative* return on foreign currency, because his or her currency can be expected to *appreciate* relative to that of the country with the higher expected inflation rate. Thus in evaluating the expected return on the foreign security, there is good news (a high expected domestic return $\bar{r}_D$) and bad news (a negative expected return on foreign currency $\bar{r}_C$). On balance, the expected foreign return $\bar{r}_F$ might not be as exceptional as first thought when just $\bar{r}_D$ was considered. Indeed, if markets were completely integrated, it would be reasonable to expect the values of $\bar{r}_D$ and $\bar{r}_C$ to roughly sum to an amount $\bar{r}_F$ that is equal to the expected return on an equivalent bond in the investor's own country. When government securities are involved, this is known as the **interest-rate parity** (Chapter 20 also discussed interest-rate parity).

As an example, assume that an investor can buy either one-year Treasuries in the United States that have a yield of 5% or similar one-year German governments that are at 7%, where both securities have no coupons before they mature. Both securities are free from default risk, call risk, and political risk. Interest-rate parity states that the expected return from owning either security is the same. Interest-rate parity exists because, in the market's view, the German mark is expected to depreciate against the dollar so that at the end of the year, the 2% extra return a U.S. investor would earn from holding the German security will be exactly offset by a currency loss when it is exchanged for dollars. Applying equation (25.5) to this situation results in the following equation:

$$.05 = .07 + \bar{r}_C + .07\bar{r}_C$$

which has the solution: $\bar{r}_C = -1.87\%$ [or, using Equation (25.6) as an approximation, −2%]. Accordingly, interest-rate parity would say that the reason the German security has a 2% higher yield is that the mark is expected to fall by roughly 2%. Indeed, the one-year dollar-mark forward rate should be roughly 2% lower than the spot rate, meaning if the spot rate is $.60 per mark, then the one-year forward rate should be about $.5888 [=.60 × (1 − .0187)] per mark. In sum, an investor should not expect to make more by investing in fixed-income securities of a country that has higher interest rates than in the investor's home country.

Columns (2) and (3) of Table 25.2(a) indicate what the average excess returns [that is, returns over the London Interbank Offered Rate (LIBOR), an estimate of the riskfree rate] were for the stocks and bonds of six countries as well as the United States for the 200-month period ending August 1991. These averages were measured from the perspective of a U.S. investor and hence represent the historical average value of r_F. The table indicates that, although the stock and bond averages for the six countries are very similar to the U.S. averages, there are some notable differences among individual countries. For both stocks and bonds, the Canadian market had an average return that was much lower than the U.S. average, whereas the U.K. and Japanese averages were notably higher.[10]

25.2.4 Foreign and Domestic Risks

Having seen in Equation (25.7) that the expected return on a foreign security consists of two components, it is appropriate that the risk of the foreign security be evaluated next. As before, consider an American investor and a Swiss investor who have purchased shares of a Swiss company. The domestic variance, denoted σ_D^2, is the risk that the Swiss investor faces with respect to the Swiss stock. Correspondingly, the foreign variance, denoted σ_F^2, is the risk that the American investor faces with respect to the Swiss stock. On the basis of Equation (25.5), it can be shown that the foreign variance consists of three components:

$$\sigma_F^2 = \sigma_D^2 + \sigma_C^2 + 2\rho_{DC}\sigma_D\sigma_C \tag{25.8}$$

where σ_C^2 is the variance associated with the currency return to an American from investing in Swiss francs and later exchanging them for American dollars, and ρ_{DC} is the correlation coefficient between the return on the Swiss stock and the return on Swiss francs.[11]

For example, assume that the domestic variance is 225 (meaning that the domestic standard deviation, σ_D, is $\sqrt{225}$, or 15%) and the currency variance is 25 (meaning that the currency standard deviation, σ_C, is $\sqrt{25}$, or 5%). If $\rho_{DC} = 0$, then Equation (25.8) indicates that the foreign variance is 250 (= 225 + 25). Accordingly, the foreign standard deviation is 15.8% (= $\sqrt{250}$), which is only slightly greater than the domestic standard deviation of 15%.

Columns (4) and (5) of Table 25.2(a) provide the standard deviations of the excess returns for six foreign countries along with the United States from the perspective of a U.S. investor. Hence it provides estimates of the value of σ_F for the 200-month period ending in August 1991. The six-country average standard deviation for both stocks and bonds is similar to the respective U.S. values, with the United Kingdom having notably larger values for both stocks and bonds.

Table 25.3 provides evidence on the relative magnitudes of the three types of risk. Standard deviations of monthly values over the period from December 1970 through December 1980 are shown for domestic risk (corresponding to σ_D), currency risk (corresponding to σ_C), and foreign risk (corresponding to σ_F), where the latter two types of risk have been measured from the perspective of an American investor. The last column represents the ratio of foreign risk to domestic risk. Thus a

TABLE 25.2 Security Returns, January 1975–August 1991[a]

(a) Excess Returns and Standard Deviations

Country (1)	Average Excess Return (%)		Standard Deviation (%)	
	Stocks (2)	Bonds (3)	Stocks (4)	Bonds (5)
Australia	4.5	−.8	21.9	5.5
Canada	.9	−1.5	18.3	7.8
France	4.8	−.1	22.2	4.5
Germany	4.7	.9	18.3	4.5
Japan	7.3	2.1	17.8	6.5
U.K.	8.6	1.2	24.7	9.9
U.S.	5.2	−.3	16.1	6.8
Average (excluding U.S.)	5.1	.3	20.5	6.4
Average	5.1	.2	19.9	6.5

(b) Correlations between Foreign and U.S. Stocks and Bonds[b]

Country (1)	U.S. Stocks with Foreign		U.S. Bonds with Foreign	
	Stocks (2)	Bonds (3)	Stocks (4)	Bonds (5)
Australia	.48	.24	−.05	.20
Canada	.74	.31	.18	.82
France	.50	.21	.20	.31
Germany	.43	.23	.17	.50
Japan	.41	.12	.11	.28
U.K.	.58	.23	.12	.28
Average	.52	.22	.12	.40

[a] Results are given from U.S. investor perspective and are in excess of the London Interbank Offered Rate (LIBOR).

[b] Correlation of U.S. stocks with U.S. bonds was .32.

Source: Adapted from Fischer Black and Robert Litterman, "Global Portfolio Optimization," *Financial Analysts Journal* 48, no. 5 (September/October 1992): 30–31.

ratio greater than 1 can be taken as an indication that the risk to an American investor is greater than the risk to a domestic investor. Indeed, with the exception of Hong Kong stocks, all the ratios are greater than 1, suggesting that fluctuations in currency exchange rates increased the risk an American investor would have faced in buying foreign securities. Although the exact values of these ratios have undoubtedly changed since the study was conducted, in general, the conclusion—that exchange risk in general increases the risk to American investors from buying foreign securities—remains valid today.

The importance of currency risk can easily be exaggerated. Calculations such as those in Table 25.3 assume that investors purchase only domestic goods and services and thus convert all proceeds from foreign investments into their own currency before engaging in any spending for consumption purposes. But most people buy foreign goods and many buy foreign services as well (for example, as tourists). The cheaper another country's currency relative to one's own, the more attractive purchases of its goods and services will be. Other things being equal, it may make sense to invest more in countries whose products and scenery are admired, for the effective currency risk is likely to be smaller there than elsewhere.

		TABLE 25.3	Risks for Domestic and U.S. Investors Based on Historical Values, December 1970–December 1980		
		Domestic Risk (1)	Currency Risk (2)	Foreign Risk (3)	Foreign Domestic Risk (4)
(a) Stocks					
	Australia	24.62%	9.15%	27.15%	1.10
	Belgium	13.28	11.02	18.76	1.41
	Canada	18.92	4.16	20.29	1.07
	Denmark	15.41	10.28	17.65	1.15
	France	22.00	10.24	25.81	1.17
	Germany	13.87	11.87	18.39	1.33
	Hong Kong	47.95	5.63	45.80	.96
	Italy	24.21	8.58	26.15	1.08
	Japan	16.39	10.42	19.55	1.19
	Netherlands	16.37	10.97	18.91	1.16
	Norway	28.61	8.89	29.92	1.05
	Singapore	35.82	6.52	36.03	1.01
	Spain	16.71	9.10	20.26	1.21
	Sweden	15.05	8.89	18.06	1.20
	Switzerland	16.80	14.67	21.40	1.27
	U.K.	28.94	8.84	31.61	1.09
	U.S.	16.00	.00	16.00	1.00
(b) Bonds					
	Canada	6.16	4.16	7.93	1.29
	France	4.39	10.24	11.80	2.69
	Germany	6.91	11.87	14.35	2.08
	Japan	6.53	10.42	14.36	2.20
	Netherlands	7.16	10.97	13.61	1.90
	Switzerland	4.33	14.67	15.33	3.54
	U.K.	12.30	8.84	16.29	1.32
	U.S.	8.96	.00	8.96	1.00

Source: Adapted from Bruno **Solnik** and Bernard Noetzlin, "Optimal International Asset Allocation," *Journal of Portfolio Management* 9, no. 1 (Fall 1982) 13.

25.3 INTERNATIONAL LISTINGS

The common stocks of many firms are traded not only on the major stock exchange in their home country but also on an exchange in at least one foreign country. For this reason foreign investors no longer have to engage in foreign currency transactions when buying and selling the firm's stock. It is also possible that foreign investors can escape certain taxes and regulations to which they would be subject if the security were to be bought in the firm's home country. There are two methods of trading such internationally listed foreign securities in the United States. They involve the use of ordinary shares and American Depositary Receipts (ADRs).

The first way foreign securities may be traded in the United States is for the shares of the firm to be traded directly, just as the shares of a typical U.S. firm are. Canadian firms generally are traded in this manner in the United States; at year-end 1996, none of the 55 Canadian firms that had their stock listed on the NYSE involved ADRs. Stocks traded in this form are referred to as *ordinary shares* or simply *ordinaries*.

The second way foreign securities may be traded in the United States is with **American Depositary Receipts** (ADRs).[12] American Depositary Receipts are financial assets that are issued by U.S. banks and represent indirect ownership of a certain number of shares of a specific foreign firm that are held on deposit in a bank in the firm's home country. The advantage of ADRs over direct ownership is that the investor need not worry about the delivery of the stock certificates or converting dividend payments from a foreign currency into U.S. dollars. The depository bank automatically does the converting for the investor and also forwards all financial reports from the firm. The investor pays the bank a relatively small fee for these services. Typically, non-Canadian firms use ADRs. For example, Mexican firms are traded in this manner in the United States; at year-end 1996, all 25 Mexican firms with their stock listed on the NYSE used ADRs.

Table 25.4 displays the extent of foreign stock listings in the United States at year-end 1996. As the table shows, about 900 foreign issues were listed on either the NYSE, AMEX, or Nasdaq, and nearly 45% of them were in the form of ADRs. Interestingly, the NYSE has nearly 70% of its foreign issues in the form of ADRs, whereas for Nasdaq the percentage is about half of this amount, due in large part to the 162 Canadian firms that are traded on Nasdaq without the use of ADRs.

One study that examined the diversification implications of investing in ADRs found that such securities were of notable benefit to U.S. investors.[13] Specifically, a sample of 45 ADRs was examined and compared with a sample of 45 U.S. securities over the period from 1973 to 1983. When an index based on all NYSE-listed stocks was used, the betas of the ADRs had an average value of .26, which was much lower than the average beta of 1.01 for the U.S. securities. Furthermore, the correlation of the ADRs' returns with those of the NYSE market portfolio averaged .33, whereas U.S. securities had a notably higher average correlation of .53.

Given these two observations, it is not surprising that portfolios formed from U.S. securities and ADRs had much lower standard deviations than portfolios consisting of just U.S. securities. For example, portfolios consisting of ten U.S. securities had an average monthly standard deviation of 5.50%, whereas a ten-security portfolio split evenly between U.S. securities and ADRs had an average monthly standard deviation of 4.41%. Thus, it seems that investing in ADRs brings significant benefits in terms of risk reduction.[14]

The SEC currently requires that foreign firms prepare their financial statements using U.S. generally accepted accounting principles (GAAP) if they want their shares

TABLE 25.4	Foreign Company Listings in the United States, Year-end 1996		
	Number of Issues	ADR Issuers Number	Percent
NYSE	365	247	67.7%
AMEX	65	7	10.8%
Nasdaq	460	142	30.9%
Total	890	396	44.5%

Source: *The Nasdaq Stock Market 1997 Fact Book & Company Directory* (Washington, DC: National Association of Security Dealers, 1997), p. 28.

The Stock Exchange of Hong Kong: Another Asian Exchange Switches to Automated Matching

by Ann Guenther Sherman
Hong Kong University of Science and Technology

As the unrelenting march toward integration of the world's security markets continues, the competitive pressures on national stock exchanges to adopt efficient and low-cost trading mechanisms have grown stronger. The Stock Exchange of Hong Kong (SEHK) provides an interesting example of the conflict between entrenched business practices and external competition, and the ultimate resolution of that conflict.

Stock trading has a long history in Hong Kong, with informal trading dating back to 1866 and a formal exchange established in 1891 (the second in Asia, after Japan's). By 1973 four exchanges operated in the tiny city-state, far too many to justify from an economic perspective. Despite considerable controversy, the four exchanges were merged into the SEHK in 1986.

The newly created SEHK had many potential models for a trading system. It could have built on CATS (Computer-Assisted Trading System) of the Toronto Stock Exchange, which was the world's first fully automated trading system. The SEHK could also have learned from CORES (Computer-Assisted Order Routing and Execution System), a modified version of CATS instituted by the Tokyo Stock Exchange. Other models include Nasdaq (National Association of Securities Dealers Automated Quotations), which was used as the basis for the Big Bang reorganization of the London Stock Market. Or, of course, Hong Kong could have followed one of the many auction/modified open-outcry systems in use around the world, including that of the New York Stock Exchange (NYSE).

Instead, the SEHK chose an unusual way of arranging trades. Each member of the exchange has a booth or a desk on the exchange floor, at which it can have up to two representatives. Each booth has two telephones (an internal and an external line) and up to two computer terminals, only one of which operates in an interactive mode while the other is in display-only mode. Members enter buy and sell orders into the computer, and the orders are shown on the screen for that stock. The orders include price but not quantity. If another member of the exchange wishes to trade with the person who input the order, then he or she telephones that person. If the lines are full and the call cannot get through, then the trader may choose to get up and go to the other person's booth. The member who input the order is under no obligation to deal with the first person who calls or dashes over, and the quantity of any trade must be negotiated. After a trade has been made, the seller must enter the details into the system within 15 minutes. There is no order-matching facility, no designated market-maker, and no priority assigned to orders at the same price.

One of the system's weaknesses is that a person entering an order has less information than he or she would have in a simple open-outcry system. When a trader standing at a post on the NYSE shouts out an order, he or she can see how many other people at the post are ready to respond to the order and may even be able to judge how anxious they are to trade. When a trader enters an order into a terminal on the SEHK, he or she can only wait for the phone to ring. While talking to the first person who calls, the trader cannot tell how many others are also trying to get through—the only way to learn this is to hang up and wait for the phone to ring again, a method that may prove costly if in fact no one else is interested. This weakness is partially offset by the habit of traders' running over to each other's desks, a feature that was not in the original plan.

Another potential problem, especially during busy times, is that each order takes longer to arrange than in an automated order-matching system. Rather than simply entering a limit order into an automated system and receiving confirmation when the order is filled, traders must enter the order, wait for someone to contact them, negotiate a quantity, and then (if they are selling) enter the details into the computer. Most exchanges, such as those in Malaysia and Singapore, experienced sharp rises in turnover after they introduced automated trading systems. Taiwan, with fully automated trading, has handled daily volume levels close to Tokyo's (even though Tokyo's market capitalization at the time was around 30 times larger). In spite of the possible reduction in trading capacity, however, the Hong Kong system may appeal to those who prefer private negotiation when arranging deals, rather than the impersonality of an order-matching system or the open competition of an open-outcry system.

A key disadvantage (or advantage, depending on your outlook) to the Hong Kong system is that it may facilitate manipulation of stock prices. Efficient and cheap price manipulation requires coordination on the part of the manipulators. The manipulators want to create a series of fake trades among themselves at ever increasing (or decreasing) prices, in order to artificially drive a stock price up (or down). In an automated matching system, price manipulators can still buy shares at above-market prices, but they cannot determine who gets those high prices, because orders are filled based on price and time priority. With the Hong Kong system, a price manipulator need only tell an accomplice when he or she plans to enter the order and make sure that the accomplice is ready to dial quickly. If the accomplice is not the first person to call, the manipulator can refuse to trade.

Although the SEHK fell behind many other Asian countries in updating trading methods, its members eventually recognized the necessity for reform. The Hong Kong securities industry was heavily influenced by the October 1987 crash, in which the Hong Kong stock and futures exchanges performed embarrassingly poorly. During the crash, the SEHK closed for four days, October 20–23 (the only stock exchange in the world to close for so long), and the chairman of the exchange was later arrested and convicted for accepting bribes in connection with a new listing on the exchange. In the aftermath of the crash, there have been major changes in Hong Kong, including the formation of the Securities and Futures Commission, which has tightened regulation of the market. Among other changes, some forms of insider trading are now illegal, and stock price manipulation is now prosecuted.

At the SEHK a new clearing system was adopted in 1992, and an automated order-matching system began operating on November 1, 1993, although it initially handled only a few stocks on an experimental basis. The order-matching system was originally expected to be introduced two years earlier, but complications in the replacement of the clearing system and the resistance of vested interests delayed its implementation. Since January 1996, members have been allowed to trade from terminals in their offices. Exchange officials expect the trading floor to eventually be deserted, as happened in London after the Big Bang. The SEHK has also introduced short selling and stock options in the last few years.

There has been pressure to extend the trading hours, which are currently from 10:00 to 12:30 and 14:30 to 15:55. Many stocks listed on the SEHK are cross-listed in London or New York, and Hong Kong over the years has lost much of the trading volume in these stocks to the overseas exchanges. Extension of the trading hours might allow the exchange to recapture some of the lost trades, since extended afternoon hours could overlap with the business day in London. Extended hours, like many of the earlier changes, have been fought by small brokers in Hong Kong, who are finding it hard to compete with larger, more efficient major brokerages. It is the very fact that share trading in Hong Kong was so well developed, relative to newer markets in Shanghai and Shenzhen, and in other Asian countries, that delayed Hong Kong's adoption of new technology. The well-established Hong Kong market was full of vested interests which fought any changes that they thought would not help them personally.

In 1997, Hong Kong went from being a colony of the United Kingdom to being a Special Administrative Region (SAR) of the People's Republic of China (PRC). For many years, the SEHK's plans for expansion have involved the listing of mainland companies, which it began in 1993. If the economic opening and development of the PRC continues, Hong Kong may be able to greatly enlarge its position as an international financial center. On the other hand, Hong Kong's stock market has a close rivalry with Singapore's. Even before the 1997 handover, there were signs of deterioration in two of Hong Kong's key competitive advantages, the rule of law and press freedom. Further, the PRC's interest in promoting the SEHK relative to the mainland stock exchange in Shanghai is unclear. As a result, it remains to be seen whether the Hong Kong SAR will remain competitive.

or ADRs to be listed on a U.S. exchange or on Nasdaq. There are two consequences of this requirement. First, many foreign firms have their shares and ADRs traded in the segment of the over-the-counter market that does not involve Nasdaq.[15] Second, many large and actively traded foreign firms have decided against listing their shares in the United States. This decision has caused U.S. exchanges to fear that certain foreign exchanges that do not have such reporting requirements (particularly London) will gain trading business at the expense of the U.S. exchanges. In response to the complaints of the exchanges, the SEC argues that this requirement is necessary to protect U.S. investors and that it would be patently unfair to U.S. firms if they had to meet such requirements but their foreign competitors did not have to do so. One thing is certain; this conflict between the exchanges and the SEC over this issue will not soon go away.[16]

25.4   CORRELATIONS BETWEEN MARKETS

If all economies were completely integrated (and there were no specialization by countries in terms of industries, products, and so on), then stock markets in different countries would move together, and little advantage could be gained through international diversification. However this is not the case. Table 25.2(b) shows the correlations of returns on stocks and bonds in six countries with the returns of stocks and bonds in the United States. There are three general observations to be made:

1. With the exception of Canada, the correlations of foreign stocks with U.S. stocks are less than .60; see column (2).[17] This observation, along with the results in panel (a) of Table 25.2, suggests that there are sizable potential diversification advantages to a U.S. stock investor of investing in the stocks of these five countries.
2. Similarly, the correlations of foreign bonds with U.S. bonds are .50 or less with the exception of Canadian bonds; see column (5).[18] Again, this observation, combined with the observations in panel (a), suggests that there are sizable potential diversification advantages to a U.S. bond investor of investing in the bonds of these five countries.
3. The correlations of foreign bonds with U.S. stocks—column (3)—and the correlations of foreign stocks with U.S. bonds—column (4)—are almost all less than roughly .30. Once again, there are sizable potential advantages to diversification; but now the advantages are in diversifying across both asset classes and countries. That is, for a given level of risk, a U.S. stock investor would find it advantageous to buy foreign bonds, and a U.S. bond investor would find it advantageous to buy foreign stocks.

The bottom line is that international diversification is beneficial. Earlier, Figure 7.10 showed how diversification in general reduces the total risk of a portfolio. Similarly, Figure 25.3 shows that internationally well-diversified portfolios will have lower levels of risk than will those that are diversified just among domestic securities. Investors can either increase their expected return without increasing their risk or decrease their risk without decreasing their expected return by judiciously adding foreign securities to their portfolios.[19] Consequently, the efficient set of domestic securities, denoted *DD* in Figure 25.4, is dominated by the efficient set constructed from both domestic and foreign securities, denoted *FF*.

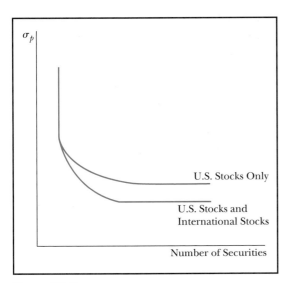

Figure 25.3
The Effects of International Diversification on Total Portfolio Risk

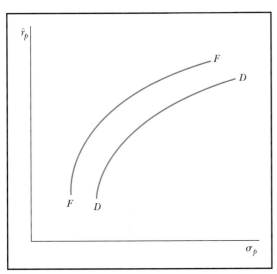

Figure 25.4
Efficient Set with (*FF*) and without (*DD*) International Diversification

---

25.5   SUMMARY

1. Investing in a foreign security involves all the risks associated with investing in a domestic security, plus political and exchange (currency) risks associated with converting foreign cash flows into domestic currency.
2. The return on a foreign security can be decomposed into a domestic return and a return on the currency in which the security is denominated.
3. Passive currency management refers to the process of controlling a portfolio's exposure to exchange risk on a long-term policy basis. Active currency management refers to the process of altering a portfolio's exposure to foreign currencies on the basis of a near-term forecast of relative valuations among currencies.
4. Owing to interest-rate parity, the expected return from owning government securities of either one of two countries is the same, provided they are both free from political and default risk.

---

5. The standard deviation of return on a foreign security is a function of the security's domestic return standard deviation, the foreign currency return standard deviation, and the correlation between the two returns.

6. Exchange risk can be reduced by hedging in the forward or futures market for foreign currency.

7. Investments in ADRs appear to bring U.S. investors significant risk reduction benefits similar to the benefits obtained by investing directly in foreign securities.

8. Purchasing domestic and foreign securities typically results in an efficient frontier whose portfolios have more favorable risks and returns than those associated with the efficient frontier resulting from purchasing just domestic securities.

QUESTIONS AND PROBLEMS

1. What types of political risks are relevant only for foreign investors? What types are relevant for both foreign and domestic investors? To what extent and in what manner would you expect the current prices of securities in a particular country to reflect these types of political risk?

2. Using a recent *Wall Street Journal*, find the exchange rate between German marks, British pounds, and U.S. dollars. Lyle Luttrell, a British citizen, is planning a trip to Germany and has budgeted expenses of 30 pounds per day. At current exchange rates, into how many dollars and marks does 30 pounds translate?

3. Why would an investor wish to hedge the currency risk in a portfolio of foreign securities? What considerations are relevant to making the decision whether to hedge?

4. Smead Jolly is a U.S. investor who has the opportunity to convert $1 into 130 Japanese yen and 1.90 German marks. Given this information, into how may yen should Smead be able to convert one mark?

5. How might a U.S. citizen or company use currency futures to hedge against exchange-rate risk?

6. Wickey McAvoy, a U.S. citizen, holds a portfolio of French common stocks. Last year the portfolio produced an 8% return, denominated in French francs. Over that year the franc appreciated 20% against the U.S. dollar. What was Wickey's return measure in U.S. dollars?

7. Jigger Statz, a U.S. investor, owns a portfolio of Argentinean securities that earned a return of 14.0% last year, measured in U.S. dollars. If the portfolio also earned 19.7% measured in Argentinean pesos, what must have been the currency return in Jigger's portfolio?

8. Tris Speaker bought a Japanese stock one year ago when it sold for 280 yen per share and the exchange rate was $0.008 per yen. The stock now sells for 350 yen and the exchange rate is $0.010 per yen. The stock paid no dividends over the year. What was Tris's rate of return on this stock? What would be the rate of return on the stock to a Japanese investor?

9. Why is international diversification attractive to an investor who already has a well-diversified domestic portfolio?

10. Ownie Carroll owns a portfolio composed of U.S. stocks and bonds. Interested in further diversifying the portfolio, Ownie decides to add investments in Canadian common stocks. Ownie's broker, Slick Castleman, voices the opinion that the Canadian securities would not be particularly effective risk-reducing investments. Discuss the logic behind Slick's opinion.

11. Peek-A-Boo Veach, a U.S. citizen, estimates that a diversified portfolio of Norwegian common stocks has a standard deviation of 24%. Peek-A-Boo also estimates that the standard deviation of the U.S. and Norwegian currency return is 7%. Finally, Peek-A-Boo estimates the correlation between the dollar-krone cur-

rency return and the Norwegian stock market return to be 0.20. Given this information, what should Peek-A-Boo conclude is the standard deviation for a U.S. investor investing solely in the Norwegian stock market?

12. When a U.S. citizen is attempting to estimate the expected return and standard deviation for a foreign security, what factors, in addition to those recognized in domestic security analysis, should be considered?

13. Why is it the case that a foreign security with a high expected *domestic* return relative to what an investor could earn in his or her home country does not necessarily have a high expected *foreign* return for that investor?

14. Assume that the one-year U.S. riskfree rate is 6%. Moon Gibson, an investor knowledgable concerning the implications of interest-rate parity, expects the U.K. pound to appreciate by 3% next year relative to the U.S. dollar. What does that expectation imply about the current one-year U.K. riskfree rate?

15. Lin Storti, a U.S. citizen, is considering investing in both U.S. and Zanistan common stock index funds. Lin estimates the following market characteristics:

U.S. market expected return	20%
U.S. market standard deviation	18%
Zanistan market expected return	30%
Zanistan market standard deviation	30%
U.S.-Zanistan expected currency return	0%
U.S.-Zanistan currency return standard deviation	10%
Zanistan domestic return and U.S.-Zanistan currency return correlation	.15

Further, Lin estimates that the U.S. and Zanistan markets are uncorrelated as is the U.S. market return (or the Zanistan market return) and the U.S.-Zanistan currency exchange rate. Given that Lin is planning to hold a portfolio 60% invested in the U.S. index fund and 40% invested in the Zanistan index fund, what are the expected return and standard deviation of Lin's portfolio?

16. Eva Lange wants the diversification benefits of international investments but does not want to own foreign securities directly. Would investing in ADRs be an effective substitute for Eva? Explain.

17. Discuss why mutual funds are a particularly cost-effective means for small investors to own foreign securities.

18. Is a low correlation between the price movements of two countries' market indices a sufficient condition to ensure that a portfolio containing securities of both countries dominates a portfolio containing only domestic securities?

19. (Appendix Question) What practical difficulties prevent collectible assets from playing a major role in most investors' portfolios?

CFA EXAM QUESTIONS

20. Robert Devlin and Neil Parish are portfolio managers at the Broward Investment Group. At their regular Monday strategy meeting, the topic of adding international bonds to one of their portfolios came up. The portfolio, an ERISA-qualified pension account for a U.S. client, was currently 90% invested in U.S. Treasury bonds, and 10% invested in ten-year Canadian government bonds. Devlin suggested buying a position in ten-year German government bonds; Parish argued for a position in ten-year Australian government bonds.

    a. Briefly discuss the three major issues that Devlin and Parish should address in their analysis of the return prospects for German and Australian bonds relative to those of U.S. bonds.

Having made no changes to the original portfolio, Devlin and Parish hold a subsequent strategy meeting and decide to add positions in the government bonds of Japan, United Kingdom, France, Germany, and Australia.

    b. Identify and discuss two reasons for adding a broader mix of international bonds to the pension portfolio.

21. Adviser 1: A currency cannot consistently appreciate or depreciate relative to an investor's local currency, since some local or global economic adjustment must eventually redress the currency change. Therefore, having currency exposure in a portfolio increases risk but does not increase long-term expected returns. Since you are not compensated for taking currency risk, you should always hedge a portfolio's currency exposure back to your local currency.

Adviser 2: I completely disagree, except as to the implication that economic changes are related to currency changes. Because economic changes affect international stocks, bonds, and currencies, as well as domestic stocks and bonds in ways that often offset each other, currency exposure improves diversification in a portfolio. Portfolios should never hedge their currency exposures; otherwise, they would be less diversified.

Adviser 1 Rebuttal: "I have evidence which would appear to refute your claim of improved diversification resulting from currency exposure. My studies of hedged and unhedged international bond portfolios show very little difference between either their risks or returns over the past ten years.

Evaluate the strengths and weaknesses of each of the two approaches presented above. Recommend and justify an alternative currency strategy that draws from the strengths of each approach and corrects their weaknesses.

APPENDIX

TANGIBLE ASSETS

In the first half of the 1970s, marketable securities such as stocks and bonds provided returns that were relatively disappointing, especially after adjusting for inflation. And, as shown in Chapter 12, neither bonds nor stocks have served as good hedges against unanticipated inflation in recent years. Overall, tangible assets have been better hedges against inflation. One example, real estate, was shown in Chapter 12 to have been an attractive inflation hedge.[20] Other examples, such as collectible assets and precious metals (for instance, gold and silver), provide various degrees of protection against inflation.

A.1   COLLECTIBLE ASSETS

Not surprisingly, periodic disenchantment with returns on marketable securities has led some investors to examine a host of tangible assets that are normally considered only by "collectors." The average returns on *collectibles* such as Chinese ceramics, coins, diamonds, paintings, and stamps have on occasion been quite high, but generally such assets also experience periods of negative returns. This fluctuation is not surprising because if one (or more) type of collectible had provided consistently high returns, many investors would have been attracted to it and would have bid its price up to a level where high returns would no longer have been possible. Indeed, more recent studies of prints and paintings have concluded that their risk and return characteristics make them relatively unattractive investments for risk-averse investors.[21]

In a sense, a collectible asset often provides income to the owner in the form of consumption. For example, an investor can admire a Roberto Clemente rookie baseball card, sit on a Chippendale chair, gaze upon a Georgia O'Keefe painting, play a Stradivarius violin, and drive a Stutz Bearcat automobile. Value received in this manner is not subject to income taxation and is thus likely to be especially attractive for those in high tax brackets. However, the value of such consumption depends strongly on one's preferences.

If markets are efficient, collectible assets will be priced so that those who enjoy them most will find it desirable to hold them in greater-than-market-value proportions, whereas those who enjoy them least will find it desirable to hold them in less-than-market-value proportions (or, in many cases, not at all).

Institutional funds and investment pools have been organized to own collectibles of one type or another. These arrangements are subject to serious question if they involve locking such objects in vaults where they cannot be seen by those who derive pleasure from this sort of consumption. On the other hand, if the items are rented to others, the only loss may be that associated with the transfer of a portion of the consumption value to the government in the form of a tax on income.

Investors in collectibles should be aware of two especially notable types of risk. The first is that the bid-ask spread is often very large. Thus an investor must see a large price increase just to recoup the spread and break even. The second is that collectibles are subject to fads (this risk has been referred to as *stylistic risk*).[22] For example, Chinese ceramics may be actively sought by many investors today, leading to high prices, and big returns for earlier purchasers. However, they may fall out of favor later on and plunge in value. Unlike financial assets, there is no such thing as fair value for collectibles that can act as a kind of anchor for the market price.

A.2 GOLD

In the United States, private holdings of gold bullion were illegal before the 1970s. In other countries, investment in gold has long been a tradition. According to one estimate, at the end of 1984 gold represented over 6% of the world market wealth portfolio.[23]

History suggests gold has performed like other types of collectibles in that it has had periods of high returns but also periods of low returns (particularly since the early 1980s). Furthermore, gold has had a high standard deviation, suggesting that by itself it has been a risky investment. However, for any single investment, risk and return are only parts of the story. Correlations of an asset's return with the returns on other assets are also relevant. In general, gold price changes have a near-zero correlation with stock returns. Gold thus appears to be an effective diversifying asset for an equity investor.[24] Furthermore, gold prices generally have been highly correlated with the rate of inflation in the United States as measured by changes in the Consumer Price Index. This is consistent with gold's traditional role as a hedge against inflation, because higher inflation generally brings higher gold prices.

Investors interested in gold need not restrict themselves to bullion. Other possibilities range from stocks of gold mining companies to gold futures to gold coins and commemoratives. Furthermore, there are other types of precious metals, such as silver, that investors may want to consider.

Alternative Investments

Institutional investors have long acknowledged the wisdom of holding well-diversified portfolios. For many years, however, they focused their investments almost exclusively on U.S. common stocks, bonds, and short-term securities. The spectrum of investable asset categories extends well beyond these three (for example, see the discussion of the world capital market portfolio in this chapter). Thus for a considerable time institutional investors overlooked fertile opportunities to reduce their portfolios' risks and perhaps even enhance returns as well.

That myopia receded in the 1980s. Institutional investors began to take significant positions in international stocks and bonds. Furthermore, they made sizable commitments to a variety of asset categories commonly grouped under the rubric *alternative investments.*

Although there is no precise definition of the term, in practice institutional investors consider alternative investments to be virtually any type of asset not actively traded in the public markets. In terms of their relative importance in institutional investors' portfolios, the most prominent types of alternative investments are:

Venture capital, which involves investments in young companies, ranging from start-up firms to developed businesses preparing to initially offer their stock in the public market.

Resource investments, which involve primarily holdings of properties producing or expected to produce crude oil and natural gas. In recent years, timber properties have gained in relative importance as a resource investment.

Leveraged buy-outs, which involve acquisitions of existing companies using large amounts of debt and little equity to finance the deal. Typically, these companies are restructured, with various divisions sold off to retire debt and other divisions consolidated or otherwise altered to improve efficiency for later reissuance of equity in the public market.

Real estate, which involves investments in income-producing physical structures, including retail shopping centers, office buildings, apartments, and commercial warehouses.

Each type of alternative investment exhibits its own distinct risk and return characteristics. As a result, treating them as one monolithic category leads to faulty analysis. Yet each of these asset types has several similar features:

- Illiquidity
- Difficulty in determining current market values
- Limited historical return and risk data
- Extensive investment analysis required.

The primary distinguishing characteristic of alternative investments is their illiquidity. Institutional investors typically participate in alternative investments through a limited partnership structure (although sometimes direct investments are made with the issuing entity). In a limited partnership, a general partner (or partners) negotiates a deal with the issuing entity. The general partner then solicits limited partners to provide the financing for the deal. The general partners exercise complete control over the investment, while limited partners absorb the risk of failure and share any profits with the general partners.

ENDNOTES

[1] For a discussion of the difficulties in measuring the size of the world market, see Roger G. Ibbotson, Laurence B. Siegel, and Kathryn S. Love, "World Wealth: Market Values and Returns," *Journal of Portfolio Management* 12, no. 1 (Fall 1985): 4–23.

[2] A more detailed study of bonds outstanding at the end of 1989 found that 57% was government debt, 22% was local corporate debt, 9% was "crossborder" debt (that is, foreign bonds and Eurobonds), and 12% was "other domestic" debt. See Roger G. Ibbotson and Laurence B. Siegel, "The World Bond Market: Market Values, Yields, and Returns," *Journal of Fixed Income* 1, no. 1 (June 1991): 90–99.

[3] *The Wall Street Journal* also publishes daily a set of Dow Jones stock market indices for 31 countries. These country indices are combined into three regional indices (Americas; Europe/Africa; Asia/Pacific; there are other regional indices that exclude certain countries)

With rare exceptions, limited partnerships are not registered with the Securities and Exchange Commission. Thus the limited partners cannot freely trade their ownership interests in the public market. Some secondary markets for limited partnership interests have begun to form, but their volume is extremely small. Essentially, institutional investors participating in alternative investments must be prepared to hold those investments until they expire.

For similar reasons, little pricing data is available for alternative investments. General partners periodically (at most quarterly, often annually) supply estimates of a partnership's current market value. Limited partners, however, have few practical means of independently verifying those prices.

Because of the relative newness of alternative investments and the paucity of market prices, virtually no historical return and risk data on these investments is available. Such questions as, "How can the standard deviation of my existing portfolio be expected to change if I place 10% of my funds in venture capital?" are essentially unanswerable. Thus when making portfolio allocation decisions, institutional investors must rely on highly subjective estimates of alternative investments' expected returns, standard deviations, and correlations with other asset categories.

Finally, alternative investments require considerable analysis on the part of institutional investors. Information on potential investments is not readily available. Investors must carefully study partnership agreements, consider the management fees and other operating costs, and investigate the capabilities of the general partners. Unlike common stocks and bonds, investors cannot rely on the market to provide efficient pricing. Although these less efficient markets present many potential pitfalls, conversely they offer the opportunity for relatively high returns.

Each of the alternative investment categories described previously has seen dramatic highs and lows over the last 20 years. All these categories produced high returns in the late 1970s and early 1980s, followed soon after by disappointing results. Venture capital returns declined in the poor market for small capitalization stocks in the mid- and late-1980s. Real estate suffered staggering losses in the late 1980s. Oil and gas prices plummeted in the mid-1980s. By the early-1990s, leveraged buy-out deals had fallen in terms of volume and profitability after the most obvious targets were purchased in the 1980s. The mid- and late-1990s, on the other hand, have been much kinder to alternative investments of all types. For venture capital and leveraged buy-out deals, returns have attained or surpassed their 1980s highwater marks. Real estate returns have been more subdued, but have rebounded to double-digit levels. Resource investment returns have at least stabilized.

What the near future holds for alternative investment returns as always is unclear. Nevertheless, the diversification argument seems to have remained intact. Bearing in mind the questionable quality of much alternative investment pricing data, over the last two decades, returns on alternative investments have apparently exhibited low or even negative correlations with those of the stock and bond markets. Those features combined with seemingly attractive long-run return prospects would argue for the inclusion of alternative investments in most institutional investors' portfolios.

and a World Stock Index that are also reported daily. For a discussion of European stock markets, see Gabriel Hawawini, *European Equity Markets: Price Behavior and Efficiency*, Monograph Series in Finance and Economics 1984-4/5 (New York University Salomon Center, Leonard N. Stern School of Business, 1984). Also see Victor A. Canto, "Everything You Always Wanted to Know about the European Monetary System, the ECU and ERM, But Didn't Know Who to Ask," *Financial Analysts Journal* 47, no. 6 (November/December 1991): 22–25.

[4] For a discussion of the Morgan Stanley indices, see Campbell R. Harvey, "The World Price of Covariance Risk," *Journal of Finance* 46, no. 1 (March 1991): 111–157.

[5] For more on these and other indices, see Chapter 5 in Bruno Solnik, *International Investments* (Reading, MA: Addison-Wesley, 1991); and John Markese, "An Investor's Guide to the International Marketplace," *AAII Journal* 14, no. 7 (August 1992): 29–32.

[6] For more on emerging markets, see Vihang Errunza, "Emerging Markets: A New Opportunity for Improving Global Portfolio Performance," *Financial Analysts Journal* 39, no. 5 (Sep-

tember/October 1983): 51–58; Vihang Errunza and Etienne Losq, "How Risky Are Emerging Markets? Myths and Perceptions versus Theory and Evidence," *Journal of Portfolio Management* 14, no. 1 (Fall 1987): 62–67; Vihang Errunza and Prasad Padmanabhan, "Further Evidence on the Benefits of Portfolio Investments in Emerging Markets," *Financial Analysts Journal* 44, no. 4 (July/August 1988): 76–78; Christopher B. Barry, John W. Peavy III, and Maurico Rodriguez, "Performance Characteristics of Emerging Capital Markets," *Financial Analysts Journal* 54, no. 1 (January/February 1998): 72–80.

[7] The effects these types of risk have on asset pricing has been considered by a number of people. For a discussion and list of references, see Chapters 1 and 5 in Solnik, *International Investments.*

[8] The relationship of passive currency management to active currency management is quite similar to the relationship between strategic asset allocation and tactical asset allocation discussed in Chapter 23.

[9] See Philippe Jorion, "Mean/Variance Analysis of Currency Overlays," *Financial Analysts Journal* 50, no. 3 (May/June 1994): 48–56. The integration issue of managing a foreign portfolio's currency exposures and security holdings is essentially the same as the integration of the security selection and asset allocation decisions discussed in Chapter 23.

[10] In a study of monthly stock returns from February 1970 through May 1989 using the Morgan Stanley indices, it was found that the return on Japanese stocks was inexplicably high. See Harvey, "The World Price of Covariance Risk."

[11] The importance of accurately estimating the correlations between asset and currency returns in determining whether to hedge a portfolio is stressed in Victor S. Filatov and Peter Rappoport, "Is Complete Hedging Optimal for International Bond Portfolios?" *Financial Analysts Journal* 48, no. 4 (July/August 1992): 37–47.

[12] The London Stock Exchange began trading many of these ADRs in August 1987, with prices quoted in U.S. dollars.

[13] Dennis T. Officer and J. Ronald Hoffmeister, "ADRs: A Substitute for the Real Thing?" *Journal of Portfolio Management* 13, no. 2 (Winter 1987): 61–65. See also Leonard Rosenthal, "An Empirical Test of the Efficiency of the ADR Market," *Journal of Banking and Finance* 7, no. 1 (March 1983): 17–29. For a summary article, see Amar Gande, "American Depositary Receipts: Overview and Literature Survey," *Financial Markets, Institutions & Instruments* 6, no. 5 (1997): 61–84.

[14] One might expect that investment in the stocks of multinational firms could serve as a good substitute for investment in stocks of foreign firms. A study of U.S multinationals found that the percentage of a firm's sales that were overseas varied directly with a measure of how sensitive the firm's stock price was to an index of the dollar's value. That is, the greater the percentage, the larger the positive effect of dollar depreciations on the firm's profits and hence on its stock returns. Accordingly, investing in U.S. firms that have a large percentage of their sales overseas may be beneficial. See Philippe Jorion, "The Exchange-Rate Exposure of U.S. Multinationals," *Journal of Business* 63, no. 3 (July 1990): 331–345; and "The Pricing of Exchange Rate Risk in the Stock Market," *Journal of Financial and Quantitative Analysis* 26, no. 3 (September 1991): 363–376.

[15] An article published in 1993 stated that at that time there were 722 ADRs listed in the U.S. over-the-counter market. (Large bid-ask spreads are commonplace for these thinly traded ADRs, thereby limiting the ability to invest profitably in them.) In comparison, at year-end 1993, there were 536 foreign companies (with 213 of them being ADRs) that had their shares listed on a U.S. exchange. See Franklin R. Edwards, "Listing of Foreign Securities on U.S. Exchanges," *Journal of Applied Corporate Finance* 5, no. 4 (Winter 1993): 28–36.

[16] Rule 144A (see Chapters 3 and 16), which permits the issuance of unregistered securities on a private placement basis, was intended in part to accommodate foreign issuers of stock that did not want to meet the SEC's financial reporting requirements. For more on the reporting requirements for foreign firms that want to have their securities traded in the United States see Frederick D. S. Choi, "Financial Reporting Requirements for Non-U.S. Registrants: International Market Perspectives," *Financial Markets, Institutions & Instruments* 6, no. 5 (December 1997): 23–44.

[17] Over the period 1960–1980, another study found that stocks in Austria and Spain had slightly negative correlations with U.S. stocks, whereas stocks in Norway had a correlation of .01; see Roger G. Ibbotson, Richard C. Carr, and Anthony W. Robinson, "International Bond and Equity Portfolios," *Financial Analysts Journal* 38, no. 4 (July/August 1982): 61–83. Yet another study of 349 stocks in 11 countries revealed an average intercountry correlation coefficient of .234 for the period from January 1973 to December 1983; see D. Chinhyung Cho, Cheol S. Eun, and Lemma W. Senbet, "International Arbitrage Pricing Theory: An Empirical Investigation," *Journal of Finance* 41, no. 2 (June 1986): 313–329. A third study of ten equity markets found that the average correlation was .43 and the largest correlation of any of the countries with the U.S was .52 (the U.K.); see Gary L. Gastineau, "The Currency Hedging Decision: A Search for Synthesis in Asset Allocation," *Financial Analysts Journal* 51, no. 3 (May/June 1995): 8–17. In addition, the correlations between emerging markets and the United States have historically been near zero; see the references given in endnote 6. For a multiperiod approach that indicates the benefits from international diversification, particularly for highly risk-averse investors, see Robert R. Grauer and Nils H. Hakansson, "Gains from International Diversification: 1968–85 Returns on Portfolios of Stocks and Bonds," *Journal of Finance* 42, no. 3 (July 1987): 721–739. Although the correlations between the U.S. and foreign stock markets is surely much less than 1, the actual values are highly dependent on the time period studied.

[18] Similar results were found in another study involving the period of 1960 to 1980. A negative correlation between the bonds in Italy and the United States was observed. See Ibbotson, Carr, and Robinson, "International Bond and Equity Portfolios."

[19] Unfortunately, a study has found that the benefits from international diversification are lessened just when these benefits are most needed by investors. Specifically, the low correlations between market returns appear to increase when markets become more volatile. See Patrick Odier and Bruno Solnik, "Lessons for International Asset Allocation," *Financial Analysts Journal* 49, no. 2 (March/April 1993): 63–77. Another study found that the diversification benefits from international investing was due more to the fact that different countries have unique sources causing their returns to vary than that they have different industrial structures. Hence, international diversification efforts should be aimed more at investing in different countries than in different industries. See Steven L. Heston and K. Geert Rouwenhorst, "Does Industrial Structure Explain the Benefits of International Diversification?" *Journal of Financial Economics* 36, no. 1 (August 1994): 3–27.

[20] Although not a tangible asset, commodity futures were shown in Chapter 20 to have also been an attractive inflation hedge.

[21] See James E. Pesando, "Art As an Investment: The Market for Modern Prints," *American Economic Review* 83, no. 5 (December 1993): 1075–1089. See also William N. Goetzmann, "Accounting for Taste: Art and the Financial Markets over Three Centuries," *American Economic Review* 83, no. 5 (December 1993): 1370–1376.

[22] The term *stylistic risk* was coined by William N. Goetzmann in "Accounting for Taste," p. 1371.

[23] Ibbotson, Siegel, and Love, "World Wealth," p. 9. This study is an example of one that provides empirical evidence supporting the assertions that follow about the statistical properties of gold.

[24] For a view against investing in gold, see James B. Cloonan, "Goodbye Gold: It's Now Just Another Commodity," *AAII Journal* 14, no. 9 (October 1992): 25–26.

KEY TERMS

emerging markets	foreign return
political risk	interest-rate parity
exchange risk	American Depositary Receipts
domestic return	

1. Three books devoted to understanding international financial markets and investing are:

    Bruno Solnik, *International Investments* (Reading, MA: Addison-Wesley, 1991), particularly Chapter 5.

    Roger G. Ibbotson and Gary P. Brinson, *Global Investing* (New York, NY McGraw-Hill, 1993).

    Piet Sercu and Raman Uppal, *International Financial Markets and the Firm* (Cincinnati: South-Western, 1995).

    J. Orlin Grabbe, *International Financial Markets* (Upper Saddle River, NJ: Prentice Hall, 1996).

2. Foreign stock market indices are studied in:

    Campbell R. Harvey, "The World Price of Covariance Risk," *Journal of Finance* 46, no. 1 (March 1991): 111–157.

    Richard Roll, "Industrial Structure and the Comparative Behavior of International Stock Market Indices," *Journal of Finance* 47, no. 1 (March 1992): 3–41.

    Seth J. Masters, "The Problem with Emerging Markets Indexes," *Journal of Portfolio Management,* 24, no. 2 (Winter 1998): 93–100.

3. Investing internationally in bonds has been studied by:

    Kenneth Cholerton, Pierre Pieraerts, and Bruno Solnik, "Why Invest in Foreign Currency Bonds?" *Journal of Portfolio Management* 12, no. 4 (Summer 1986): 4–8.

    Haim Levy and Zvi Lerman, "The Benefits of International Diversification of Bonds," *Financial Analysts Journal* 44, no. 5 (September/October 1988): 56–64.

    Paul Burik and Richard M. Ennis, "Foreign Bonds in Diversified Portfolios: A Limited Advantage," *Financial Analysts Journal* 46, no. 2 (March/April 1990): 31–40.

    Roger G. Ibbotson and Laurence B. Siegel, "The World Bond Market: Market Values, Yields, and Returns," *Journal of Fixed Income* 1, no. 1 (June 1991): 90–99.

    Victor S. Filatov, Kevin M. Murphy, Peter M. Rappoport, and Russell Church, "Foreign Bonds in Diversified Portfolios: A Significant Advantage," *Financial Analysts Journal* 47, no. 4 (July/August 1991): 26–32.

    Mark Fox, "Different Ways to Slice the Optimization Cake," *Financial Analysts Journal* 47, no. 4 (July/August 1991): 32–36.

    Richard M. Ennis and Paul Burik, "A Response from Burik and Ennis," *Financial Analysts Journal* 47, no. 4 (July/August 1991): 37.

    Fischer Black and Robert Litterman, "Asset Allocation: Combining Investors Views with Market Equilibrium," *Journal of Fixed Income* 1, no. 2 (September 1991): 7–19.

    Shmuel Hauser and Azriel Levy, "Effect of Exchange Rate and Interest Rate Risk on International Fixed-Income Portfolios," *Journal of Economics and Business* 43, no. 4 (November 1991): 375–388.

    Mark R. Eaker and Dwight M. Grant, "Currency Risk Management in International Fixed-Income Portfolios," *Journal of Fixed Income* 1, no. 3 (December 1991): 31–37.

    Steven Dym, "Global and Local Components of Foreign Bond Risk," *Financial Analysts Journal* 48, no. 2 (March/April 1992): 83–91.

    John Markese, "Foreign Bond Funds: What Are You Buying Into?" *AAII Journal* 14, no. 10 (November 1992): 28–31.

    Kent G. Becker, Joseph E. Finnerty, and Kenneth J. Kopecky, "Economic News and Intraday Volatility in International Bond Markets," *Financial Analysts Journal* 49, no. 3 (May/June 1993): 65, 81–86.

    Richard M. Levich and Lee R. Thomas, "The Merits of Active Currency Risk Management: Evidence from International Bond Portfolios," *Financial Analysts Journal* 49, no. 5 (September/October 1993): 63–70.

    Claude B. Erb, Campbell R. Harvey, and Tadas E. Viskanta, "National Risk in Global Fixed-Income Allocation," *Journal of Fixed Income* 4, no. 2 (September 1994): 17–26.

Antti Ilmanen, "Time-Varying Expected Returns in International Bond Markets," *Journal of Finance* 50, no. 2 (June 1995): 481–506.

Claude B. Erb, Campbell R. Harvey, and Tadas E. Viskanta, "The Influence of Political, Economic, and Financial Risk on Expected Fixed-Income Returns," *Journal of Fixed Income* 6, no. 2 (June 1996): 7–30.

Richard Cantor and Frank Packer, "Determinants and Impacts of Sovereign Ratings," *Journal of Fixed Income* 6, no. 3 (December 1996): 76–91.

4. Investing internationally in stocks has also been studied by:

Jeff Madura and Wallace Reiff, "A Hedge Strategy for International Portfolios," *Journal of Portfolio Management* 12, no. 1 (Fall 1985): 70–74.

Lee R. Thomas III, "Currency Risks in International Equity Portfolios," *Financial Analysts Journal* 44, no. 2 (March/April 1988): 68–71.

Fischer Black, "Universal Hedging: Optimizing Currency Risk and Reward in International Equity Portfolios," *Financial Analysts Journal* 45, no. 4 (July/August 1989): 16–22.

Warren Bailey and Rene M. Stulz, "Benefits of International Diversification: The Case of Pacific Basin Stock Markets," *Journal of Portfolio Management* 16, no. 4 (Summer 1990): 57–61.

Mark R. Eaker and Dwight Grant, "Currency Hedging Strategies for Internationally Diversified Equity Portfolios," *Journal of Portfolio Management* 17, no. 1 (Fall 1990): 30–32.

John E. Hunter and T. Daniel Coggin, "An Analysis of the Diversification Benefit from International Equity Investment," *Journal of Portfolio Management* 17, no. 1 (Fall 1990): 33–36.

Martin L. Leibowitz and Stanley Kogelman, "Return Enhancement from 'Foreign' Assets: A New Approach to the Risk Return Trade-off," *Journal of Portfolio Management* 17, no. 4 (Summer 1991): 5–13.

Mark Eaker, Dwight Grant, and Nelson Woodard, "International Diversification and Hedging: A Japanese and U.S. Perspective," *Journal of Economics and Business* 43, no. 4 (November 1991): 363–374.

Wayne E. Ferson and Campbell R. Harvey, "The Risk and Predictability of International Equity Returns," *Review of Financial Studies* 6, no. 3 (1993): 527–566.

Steven L. Heston and K. Geert Rouwenhorst, "Does Industrial Structure Explain the Benefits of International Diversification?" *Journal of Financial Economics* 36, no. 1 (August 1994): 3–27.

Wayne E. Ferson and Campbell R. Harvey, "Sources of Risk and Expected Returns in Global Equity Markets," *Journal of Banking and Finance* 18, no. 4 (September 1994): 775–803.

Claude B. Erb, Campbell R. Harvey, and Tadas E. Viskanta, "Inflation and World Equity Selection," *Financial Analysts Journal* 51, no. 6 (November/December 1995): 28–42.

Claude B. Erb, Campbell R. Harvey, and Tadas E. Viskanta, "Political Risk, Economic Risk, and Financial Risk," *Financial Analysts Journal* 52, no. 6 (November/December, 1996): 29–46.

Rex A. Sinquefield, "Where are the Gains from International Diversification?" *Financial Analysts Journal* 52, no. 1 (January/February 1996): 8–14.

Claude B. Erb, Campbell R. Harvey, and Tadas E. Viskanta, "Expected Returns and Volatility in 135 Countries," *Journal of Portfolio Management* 22, no. 3 (Spring 1996): 46–59.

Bruno Solnik, Cyril Boucrelle, and Yann Le Fur, "International Market Correlation and Volatility," *Financial Analysts Journal* 52, no. 5 (September/October 1996): 17–34.

5. Many of the previously cited papers include a discussion of hedging foreign exchange risk. For additional discussion see:

Andre F. Perold and Evan C. Schulman, "The Free Lunch in Currency Hedging: Implications for Investment Policy and Performance Standards," *Financial Analysts Journal* 44, no. 3 (May/June 1988): 45–50.

Fischer Black, "Universal Hedging: Optimizing Currency Risk and Reward in International Equity Portfolios," *Financial Analysts Journal* 45, no. 4 (July/August 1989): 16–22.

Fischer Black, "Equilibrium Exchange Rate Hedging," *Journal of Finance* 45, no. 3 (July 1990): 899–907.

Stephen L. Nesbitt, "Currency Hedging Rules for Plan Sponsors," *Financial Analysts Journal* 47, no. 2 (March/April 1991): 73–81.

Ira G. Kawaller, "Managing the Currency Risk of Non-Dollar Portfolios," *Financial Analysts Journal* 47, no. 3 (May/June 1991): 62–64.

Evi Kaplanis and Stephen M. Schaefer, "Exchange Risk and International Diversification in Bond and Equity Portfolios," *Journal of Economics and Business* 43, no. 4 (November 1991): 287–307.

Michael Adler and Bhaskar Prasad, "On Universal Currency Hedges," *Journal of Financial and Quantitative Analysis* 27, no. 1 (March 1992): 19–38.

Mark Kritzman, "…About Currencies," *Financial Analysts Journal* 48, no. 2 (March/April 1992): 27–30.

Kenneth Froot, "Currency Hedging over Long Horizons," *NBER Working Paper No. 4355*, May 1993.

Mark Kritzman, "The Minimum-Risk Currency Hedge Ratio and Foreign Asset Exposure," *Financial Analysts Journal* 49, no. 5 (September/October 1993): 77–79.

Ira G. Kawaller, "Foreign Exchange Hedge Management Tools: A Way to Enhance Performance," *Financial Analysts Journal* 49, no. 5 (September/October 1993): 79–80.

Jack Glen and Philippe Jorion, "Currency Hedging for International Portfolios," *Journal of Finance* 48, no. 5 (December 1993): 1865–1886.

John Markese, "How Currency Exchange Rates Can Affect Your International Returns," *AAII Journal* 16, no. 2 (February 1994): 29–31.

Bernard Dumas and Bruno Solnik, "The World Price of Foreign Exchange Risk," *Journal of Finance*, 50, no. 2 (June 1995): 445–479.

Gary L. Gastineau, "The Currency Hedging Decision: A Search for Synthesis in Asset Allocation," *Financial Analysts Journal* 51, no. 3 (May/June 1995): 8–17.

Kenneth J. Winston and Jeffery V. Bailey, "Investment Policy Implications of Currency Hedging," *Journal of Portfolio Management* 22, no. 4 (Summer 1996): 50–57.

6. International asset allocation has been studied by:

Philippe Jorion, "Asset Allocation with Hedged and Unhedged Foreign Stocks and Bonds," *Journal of Portfolio Management* 15, no. 4 (Summer 1989): 49–54.

Fischer Black and Robert Litterman, "Global Portfolio Optimization," *Financial Analysts Journal* 48, no. 5 (September/October 1992): 28–43.

Patrick Odier and Bruno Solnik, "Lessons for International Asset Allocation," *Financial Analysts Journal* 49, no. 2 (March/April 1993): 63–77.

Bruno Solnik, "The Performance of International Asset Allocation Strategies Using Conditional Information," *Journal of Empirical Finance* 1, no. 1 (June 1993): 33–55.

Philippe Jorion, "Mean/Variance Analysis of Currency Overlays," *Financial Analysts Journal* 50, no. 3 (May/June 1994): 48–56.

7. For an interesting paper that examines the market crash of October 1987 from a world-wide perspective, and three subsequent related papers, see:

Richard Roll, "The International Crash of October 1987," *Financial Analysts Journal* 44, no. 5 (September/October 1988): 19–35.

Mervyn A. King and Sushil Wadhwani, "Transmission of Volatility between Stock Markets," *Review of Financial Studies* 3, no. 1 (1990): 5–33.

Yasushi Hamao, Ronald W. Masulis, and Victor Ng, "Correlations in Price Changes and Volatility across International Stock Markets," *Review of Financial Studies* 3, no. 2 (1990): 281–307.

C. Sherman Cheung and Clarence C. Y. Kwan, "A Note on the Transmission of Public Information across International Stock Markets," *Journal of Banking and Finance* 16, no. 4 (August 1992): 831–837.

(The following paper attempts to find an explanation for the crash in the United States): Jeremy J. Siegel, "Equity Risk Premia, Corporate Profit Forecasts, and Investor Sentiment around the Stock Market Crash of October 1987," *Journal of Business* 65, no. 4 (October 1992): 557–570.

8. In addition to the references provided in endnote 6, emerging markets are also discussed in:

W. Scott Bauman, "Investment Research Analysis in an Emerging Market: Singapore and Malaysia," *Financial Analysts Journal* 45, no. 12 (November/December 1989): 60–67.

Jarrod W. Wilcox, "Global Investing in Emerging Markets," *Financial Analysts Journal* 48, no. 1 (January/February 1992): 15–19.

Warren Bailey and Joseph Lim, "Evaluating the Diversification Benefits of the New Country Funds," *Journal of Portfolio Management* 18, no. 3 (Spring 1992): 74–80.

Arjun B. Divecha, Jamie Drach, and Dan Stefek, "Emerging Markets: A Quantitative Perspective," *Journal of Portfolio Management* 18, no. 1 (Fall 1992): 41–50.

Mark Mobius, *The Investor's Guide to Emerging Markets* (Burr Ridge, IL: Irwin, 1995).

Christopher B. Barry and Larry J. Lockwood, "New Directions in Research on Emerging Capital Markets," *Financial Markets, Institutions & Instruments* 4, no. 5 (1995): 15–36.

Campbell R. Harvey, "Predictable Risk and Returns in Emerging Markets," *Review of Financial Studies* 8, no. 3 (Fall 1995): 773–816.

Jonathan M. Kelly, Luis F. Martins, and John H. Carlson, "The Relationship Between Bonds and Stocks in Emerging Countries," *Journal of Portfolio Management* 24, no. 3 (Spring 1998): 110–122.

9. Discussions of international and global factor models can be found in some of the previously cited papers and in:

Richard Grinold, Andrew Rudd, and Dan Stefek, "Global Factors: Fact or Fiction?" *Journal of Portfolio Management* 15, no. 1 (Fall 1989): 79–88.

Martin Drummen and Heinz Zimmermann, "The Structure of European Stock Returns," *Financial Analysts Journal* 48, no. 7 (July/August 1992): 15–26.

Claude B. Erb, Campbell R. Harvey, and Tadas E. Viskanta, "Country Risk and Global Equity Selection," *Journal of Portfolio Management* 21, no. 2 (Winter 1995): 74–83.

Steven L. Heston and K. Geert Ronwenhorst, "Industry and Country Effects in International Stock Returns," *Journal of Portfolio Management* 21, no. 3 (Spring 1995): 53–58.

Stan Beckers, Gregory Connor, and Ross Curds, "National versus Global Influences on Equity Returns," *Financial Analysts Journal* 52, no.2 (March/April 1996): 31–39.

10. For some general thoughts on investing in collectibles and three studies of collectibles (stamps, prints, and paintings), see:

Burton G. Malkiel, *A Random Walk Down Wall Street* (New York: W. W. Norton, 1990): pp. 304–309.

William M. Taylor, "The Estimation of Quality-Adjusted Auction Returns with Varying Transaction Intervals," *Journal of Financial and Quantitative Analysis* 27, no. 1 (March 1992): 131–142.

James E. Pesando, "Art As an Investment: The Market for Modern Prints," *American Economic Review* 83, no. 5 (December 1993): 1075–1089.

William N. Goetzmann, "Accounting for Taste: Art and the Financial Markets over Three Centuries," *American Economic Review* 83, no. 5 (December 1993): 1370–1376.

11. Alternative investments are discussed:

George W. Fenn, Nellie Liang, and Stephen Prowse, "The Economics of the Private Equity Market," Staff Study 168, Board of Governors of the Federal Reserve System, December 1995.

Josh Lerner, "Venture Capitalists and the Oversight of Private Firms," *Journal of Finance* 50, no. 1 (March 1995): 301–318.

Thomas J. Healey and Donald J. Hardy, "Growth in Alternative Investments," *Financial Analysts Journal* 53, no. 4 (July/August 1997): 58–65.

Stephen L. Nesbitt and Hal W. Reynolds, "Benchmarks for Private Market Investments, *Journal of Portfolio Management* 23, no. 4 (Summer 1997): 85–90.

Glossary

Abnormal Return   The return earned on a financial asset in excess of that required to compensate for the risk of the asset.

Account Executive (alternatively, **Registered Representative**)   A representative of a brokerage firm whose primary responsibility is servicing the accounts of individual investors.

Accounting Beta   A relative measure of the sensitivity of a firm's accounting earnings to changes in the accounting earnings of the market portfolio.

Accounting Earnings (alternatively, **Reported Earnings**)   A firm's revenues less its expenses. Equivalently, the change in the firm's book value of the equity plus dividends paid to shareholders.

Accrued Interest   Interest earned but not yet paid.

Active Efficient Set   The combinations of securities that offer investors both maximum expected active return for varying levels of active risk and minimum active risk for varying levels of expected active return.

Active Management   A form of investment management that involves buying and selling financial assets with the objective of earning positive abnormal returns.

Active Position   The difference between the percentage of an investor's portfolio invested in a particular financial asset and the percentage of a benchmark portfolio invested in that same asset.

Actual Margin   The equity in an investor's margin account expressed as a percentage of the account's total market value (for margin purchases) or total debt (for short sales).

Adjusted Beta   An estimate of a security's future beta, derived initially from historical data, but modified by the assumption that the security's "true" beta has a tendency over time to move toward the market average of 1.0.

Adverse Selection   A problem in pricing insurance in that persons with above-average risk are more likely to purchase insurance than are those with below-average risk.

Aggressive Stocks   Stocks that have betas greater than 1.

Allocationally Efficient Market   A market for securities in which those firms with the most promising investment opportunities have access to the needed funds.

Alpha   The difference between a security's expected return and its benchmark return.

American Depositary Receipts (ADRs)   Financial assets issued by U.S. banks that represent indirect ownership of a certain number of shares of a specific foreign firm. These shares are held on deposit in a bank in the firm's home country.

American Option   An option that can be exercised at any time until and including its expiration date.

Annual Percentage Rate (APR)   With respect to a loan, the APR is the yield-to-maturity of the loan, computed using the most frequent time between payments as the compounding interval.

Anomaly   An empirical regularity that is not predicted by any known asset pricing model.

Approved List   A list of securities that an investment organization deems worthy of accumulation in a given portfolio. In an organization that uses an approved list, typically, any security on the list may be purchased by the organization's portfolio managers without additional authorization.

Arbitrage   The simultaneous purchase and sale of the same, or essentially similar, security in two different markets for advantageously different prices.

Arbitrage Portfolio   A portfolio that requires no investment, has no sensitivity to any factor, and has a positive expected return. More strictly, a portfolio that provides inflows in some circumstances and requires no outflows under any circumstances.

Arbitrage Pricing Theory   An equilibrium model of asset pricing that states that the expected return on a security is a linear function of the security's sensitivity to various common factors.

Arbitrageur   A person who engages in arbitrage.

Asked (or Ask) Price (alternatively, **Offer Price**)   The price at which a market-maker is willing to sell a specified quantity of a particular security.

Asset Allocation   The process of determining the optimal division of an investor's portfolio among available asset classes.

Asset Class   A broadly defined generic group of financial assets, such as stocks or bonds.

Asymmetric Information   A situation in which one party has more information than another party.

At the Money   An option whose exercise price is roughly equal to the market price of its underlying asset.

Attribute   See **Factor Loading**.

Automated Bond System (ABS)   A computer system established by the New York Stock Exchange to facilitate the trading of bonds.

Average Tax Rate   The amount of taxes paid expressed as a percentage of the total income subject to tax.

Bank Discount Basis   A method of calculating the interest rate on a pure-discount fixed-income security that uses the principal of the security as the security's cost.

Bankers' Acceptance   A type of money market instrument. It is a promissory note issued by a business debtor, with a stated maturity date, arising out of a business transaction. A bank, by endorsing the note, assumes the obligation. If this obligation becomes actively traded, it is referred to as a bankers' acceptance.

Basis   The difference between the spot price of an asset and the futures price of the same asset.

Basis Point   1/100 of 1%.

Basis Risk   The risk to a futures investor that the basis will widen or narrow.

Bearer Bond   A bond that has attached coupons representing the right to receive interest payments. The owner submits each coupon on its specified date to receive payment. Ownership is transferred simply by the seller's endorsing the bond over to the buyer.

Benchmark Portfolio   A portfolio against which the investment performance of an investor can be compared for the purpose of determining investment skill. A benchmark portfolio represents a relevant and feasible alternative to the investor's actual portfolio and, in particular, is similar in terms of risk exposure.

Best-Efforts Basis   A security underwriting in which the members of the investment banking group serve as agents instead of dealers, agreeing only to obtain for the issuer the best price that the market will pay for the security.

Beta (alternatively, **Beta Coefficient** or **Market Beta**)   A relative measure of the sensitivity of an asset's return to changes in the return on the market portfolio. Mathematically, the beta coefficient of a security is the security's covariance with the market portfolio divided by the variance of the market portfolio.

Bid-Ask Spread   The difference between the price that a market-maker is willing to pay for a security and the price at which the market-maker is willing to sell the same security.

Bidder   In the context of a corporate takeover, the firm making a tender offer to the target firm.

Bid Price   The price at which a market-maker is willing to purchase a specified quantity of a particular security.

Block   A large order (usually 10,000 shares or more) to buy or sell a security.

Block House   A brokerage firm with the financial capacity and the trading expertise to deal in block trades.

Bond Rating   An indicator of the creditworthiness of specific bond issues. These ratings are often interpreted as an indication of the relative likelihood of default on the part of the respective bond issuers.

Bond Swapping   A form of active bond management that entails the replacement of bonds in a portfolio with other bonds so as to enhance the return of the portfolio.

Book Value of the Equity   The sum of the retained earnings and other balance sheet entries classified under stockholders' equity, such as common stock and capital contributed in excess of par value.

Book Value per Share   A corporation's book value of the equity divided by the number of its common shares outstanding.

Bottom-Up Forecasting   A sequential approach to security analysis that entails first making forecasts for individual companies, then for industries, and finally for the economy. Each level of forecasts is conditional on the previous level of forecasts made.

Broker   An agent, or "middleman," who facilitates the buying and selling of securities for investors.

Call Market   A security market in which trading is allowed only at certain specified times. At those times, persons interested in trading a particular security are physically brought together and a market clearing price is established.

Call Money Rate   The interest rate paid by brokerage firms to banks on loans used to finance margin purchases by the brokerage firm's customers.

Call Option   A contract that gives the buyer the right to buy a specific number of shares of a company from the option writer at a specific purchase price during a specific time period.

Call Premium   The difference between the call price of a bond and the par value of the bond.

Call Price   The price that an issuer must pay bondholders when an issue is retired before its stated maturity date.

Call Provision   A provision in some bond indentures that permits an issuer to retire some or all of the bonds in a particular bond issue before the bonds' stated maturity date.

Capital Asset Pricing Model (CAPM)   An equilibrium model of asset pricing that states that the expected return on a security is a positive linear function of the security's sensitivity to changes in the market portfolio's return.

Capital Gain (or Loss)   The difference between the current market value of an asset and the original cost of the asset, with the cost adjusted for any improvement or depreciation in the asset.

Capitalization of Income Method of Valuation   An approach to valuing financial assets. It is based on the concept that the "true" or intrinsic value of a financial asset is equal to the discounted value of future cash flows generated by that asset.

Capitalization-Weighted Market Index See **Value-Weighted Market Index**.

Capital Market Line   The set of portfolios obtainable by combining the market portfolio with riskfree borrowing or lending. Assuming homogeneous expectations and perfect markets, the capital market line represents the efficient set.

Capital Markets   Financial markets in which financial assets with a term to maturity of typically more than one year are traded.

Cash Account   An account maintained by an investor with a brokerage firm in which deposits (cash and the proceeds from security sales) must fully cover withdrawals (cash and the costs of security purchases).

Cash Matching   A form of immunization that involves the purchase of bonds that generate a stream of cash inflows identical in amount and timing to a set of expected cash outflows over a given period of time.

Certainty Equivalent Return   For a particularly risky investment, the return on a riskfree investment that makes the investor indifferent between the risky and riskfree investments.

Certificate of Deposit   A form of time deposit issued by banks and other financial institutions.

Certificate of Incorporation See **Charter**.

Characteristic Line   A simple linear regression model expressing the relationship between the excess return on a security and the excess return on the market portfolio.

Charter (alternatively, **Certificate of Incorporation**)   A document issued by a state to a corporation that specifies the rights and obligations of the corporation's stockholders.

Chartist   A technical analyst who relies primarily on stock price and volume charts when evaluating securities.

Circuitbreakers   Established by the New York Stock Exchange, a set of upper and lower limits on the market price movements as measured by the Dow Jones Industrial Average. Depending on the magnitude of the price change, breaking through those limits, particularly on the downside, results initially in restrictions on program trading and ultimately in closing the exchange.

Clearinghouse   A cooperative venture among banks, brokerage firms, and other financial intermediaries that maintains records of transactions made by member firms during a trading day. At the end of the trading day, the clearinghouse calculates net amounts of securities and cash to be delivered among the members, permitting each member to settle once with the clearinghouse.

Close See **Closing Price**.

Closed-End Investment Company   A managed investment company, with an unlimited life, that does not stand ready to purchase its own shares from its owners and rarely issues new shares beyond its initial offering.

Closing Price (alternatively, **Close**)   The price at which the last trade of the day took place in a particular security.

Closing Purchase   The purchase of an option contract by an investor that is designed to offset, and thereby cancel, the previous sale of the same option contract by the investor.

Closing Sale   The sale of an option contract by an investor that is designed to offset, and thereby cancel, the previous purchase of the same option contract by the investor.

Coefficient of Determination   (alternatively, *R*-**Squared**)   In the context of a linear regression, the proportion of the variation in the dependent variable that is related to (that is, "is explained by") variation in the independent variables.

Coefficient of Nondetermination   In the context of a linear regression, the proportion of the variation in the dependent variable that is not related to (that is, "is not explained by") variation in the independent variables. Equivalently, one minus the coefficient of determination.

Coincident Indicators   Economic variables that have been found to change at the same time that the economy is changing.

Collateral Trust Bond   A bond that is backed by other financial assets.

Commercial Paper   A type of money market instrument. It represents unsecured promissory notes of large, financially sound corporations.

Commission   The fee an investor pays to a brokerage firm for services rendered in the trading of securities.

Commission Broker   A member of an organized security exchange who takes orders that the public has placed with brokerage firms and sees that these orders are executed on the exchange.

Commodity Fund   An investment company that speculates in futures.

Commodity Futures Trading Commission (CFTC)   A federal agency established by the Commodity Futures Trading Commission Act of 1974 that approves (or disapproves) the creation of new futures contracts and regulates the trading of existing futures contracts.

Common Factor   A factor that affects the return on virtually all securities to a certain extent.

Common Stock   Legal representation of an equity (or ownership) position in a corporation.

Comparative Performance Attribution   Comparing the performance of a portfolio with that of one or more other portfolios (or market indices) in order to determine the sources of the differences in their returns.

Competitive Bidding   With respect to selecting an underwriter, the process of an issuer soliciting bids on the underwriting and choosing the underwriter offering the best overall terms.

Competitive Trader See **Floor Trader**.

Complete Market   A market in which there are enough unique securities so that for any given contingency an investor can construct a portfolio that will produce a payoff if that contingency occurs.

Composite Stock Price Tables   Price information provided on all stocks traded on the national exchanges, the regional stock exchanges, the Nasdaq system, and the Instinet system.

Compounding   The payment of interest on interest.

Computer-Assisted Order Routing and Execution System (CORES)   A computer system for trading all but the 150 most active stocks on the Tokyo Stock Exchange.

Computer-Assisted Trading System (CATS)   A computer system for trading stocks on the Toronto Stock Exchange that involves a computer file containing a publicly accessible limit order book.

Consolidated Quotations System   A system that lists current bid and asked prices of specialists on the national and regional stock exchanges and of certain over-the-counter dealers.

Consolidated Tape   A system that reports trades that occur on the national stock exchanges, the regional stock exchanges, the Nasdaq system, and the Instinet system.

Constant-Growth Model   A type of dividend discount model in which dividends are assumed to exhibit a constant growth rate.

Consumer Price Index   A cost-of-living index that is representative of the goods and services purchased by U.S. consumers.

Contingent Deferred Sales Charge   A fee charged by a mutual fund to its shareholders if they sell their shares within a specified time after initially purchasing them.

Contingent Immunization   A form of bond management that entails both passive and active elements. Under contingent immunization, as long as favorable results are obtained, the bond portfolio is actively managed. However, if unfavorable results occur, then the portfolio is immediately immunized.

Continuous Market   A security market in which trades may occur at any time during business hours.

Contrarian   An investor who has opinions opposite those of most other investors, leading to actions such as buying recent losers and selling recent winners.

Convertible Bond   A bond that may, at the holder's option, be exchanged for other securities, often common stock.

Convexity   The tendency for bond prices to change asymmetrically relative to yield changes. Typically, for a given yield change, a bond will rise in price more if the yield change is negative than it will fall in price if the yield change is positive.

Corner Portfolio   An efficient portfolio possessing the property that, if it is combined with any adjacent corner portfolio, the combination will produce another efficient portfolio.

Correlation Coefficient   A statistical measure similar to covariance, in that it measures the degree of mutual variation between two random variables. The correlation coefficient rescales covariance to facilitate comparison among pairs of random variables. The correlation coefficient is bounded by the values $+1$ and -1.

Cost of Carry   The differential between the futures and spot prices of a particular asset. It equals the interest forgone less the benefits plus the costs of ownership.

Cost-of-Living Index   A collection of goods and services, and their associated prices, designed to reflect changes over time in the cost of making normal consumption expenditures.

Counterparty Risk   The risk posed by the possibility that the person or organization with which an investor has entered into a financial arrangement may fail to make required payments.

Coupon Payments   The periodic payment of interest on a bond.

Coupon Rate   The annual dollar amount of coupon payments made by a bond expressed as a percentage of the bond's par value.

Coupon Stripping   The process of separating and selling the individual cash flows of Treasury notes or bonds.

Covariance   A statistical measure of the relationship between two random variables. It measures the extent of mutual variation between two random variables.

Covered Call Writing   The process of writing a call option on an asset owned by the option writer.

Cross-Deductibility   An arrangement among federal and state tax authorities that permits state taxes to be deductible expenses for federal tax purposes and federal taxes to be deductible expenses for state tax purposes.

Crown Jewel Defense   A strategy used by corporations to ward off hostile takeovers. The strategy entails the target company's selling off its most attractive assets to make itself less attractive to the acquiring firm.

Cumulative Dividends   A common feature of preferred stock that requires that the issuing corporation pay all previously unpaid preferred stock dividends before any common stock dividends may be paid.

Cumulative Voting System   In the context of a corporation, a method of voting in which a stockholder is permitted to give any one candidate for the board of directors a maximum number of votes equal to the number of shares owned by that shareholder times the number of directors being elected.

Currency Risk See **Exchange Risk**.

Current Yield   The annual dollar amount of coupon payments made by a bond expressed as a percentage of the bond's current market price.

Customer's Agreement See **Hypothecation Agreement**.

Date of Record   The date, established quarterly by a corporation's board of directors, on which the stockholders of record are determined for the purpose of paying a cash or stock dividend.

Day Order   A trading order for which the broker will attempt to fill the order only during the day on which it was entered.

Day-of-the-Week Effect (alternatively, **Weekend Effect**)   An empirical regularity whereby stock returns appear to be lower on Mondays than on other days of the week.

Dealer (alternatively, **Market-Maker**)   A person who facilitates the trading of financial assets by maintaining an inventory in particular securities. The dealer buys for and sells from this inventory, profiting from the difference in the buying and selling prices.

Dealer's Spread   The bid-ask spread quoted by a security dealer.

Debenture   A bond that is not secured by specific property.

Debit Balance   The dollar amount borrowed from a broker as the result of a margin purchase.

Debt Refunding   The issuance of new debt for the purpose of paying off currently maturing debt.

Dedicated Portfolio   A portfolio of bonds that provides its owner with cash inflows that are matched against a specific stream of cash outflows.

Default Premium   The difference between the promised and expected yield-to-maturity on a bond arising from the possibility that the bond issuer might default on the bond.

Defensive Stocks   Stocks that have betas less than 1.

Delist   The process of removing a security's eligibility for trading on an organized security exchange.

Delta See **Hedge Ratio**.

Demand-to-Buy Schedule   A description of the quantities of a security that an investor is prepared to purchase at alternative prices.

Demand Deposit   A checking account at a financial institution.

Depository Trust Company   A central computerized depository for securities registered in the names of member firms. Members' security certificates are immobilized and computerized records of ownership are maintained. This arrangement permits electronic transfer of the securities from one member to another as trades are conducted between the members' clients.

Discount Broker   An organization that offers a limited range of brokerage services and charges fees substantially below those of brokerage firms that provide a full range of services.

Discount Factor   The present value of $1 to be received in a specified number of years.

Discounting   The process of calculating the present value of a given stream of cash flows.

Discount Rate   The interest rate used in calculating the present value of future cash flows. The discount rate reflects not only the time value of money but also the riskiness of the cash flows.

Discretionary Order   A trading order that permits the broker to set the specifications for the order.

Disintermediation   A pattern of funds flow whereby investors withdraw funds from financial intermediaries, such as banks and savings and loans, because market interest rates exceed the maximum interest rates that these organizations are permitted to pay. The investors reinvest their funds in financial assets that pay interest rates not subject to ceilings.

Distribution (12b-1) Fee   An annual fee charged by a mutual fund to its shareholders to pay for advertising, promoting, and selling the fund to new investors.

Diversification   The process of adding securities to a portfolio in order to reduce the portfolio's unique risk and, thereby, the portfolio's total risk.

Dividend Decision   The process of determining the amount of dividends that a corporation will pay its shareholders.

Dividend Discount Model   The term used for the capitalization of income method of valuation as applied to common stocks. All variants of dividend discount models assume that the intrinsic value of a share of common stock is equal to the discounted value of the dividends forecast to be paid on the stock.

Dividends   Cash payments made to stockholders by the corporation.

Dividend Yield   The current annualized dividend paid on a share of common stock, expressed as a percentage of the current market price of the corporation's common stock.

Dollar-Weighted Return   A method of measuring the performance of a portfolio over a particular period of time. It is the discount rate that makes the present value of cash flows into and out of the portfolio, as well as the portfolio's ending value, equal to the portfolio's beginning value.

Domestic Return   The return on an investment in a foreign financial asset, excluding the impact of exchange rate changes.

Double Auction   Bidding among both buyers and sellers for a security that may occur when the specialist's bid-ask spread is large enough to permit sales at one or more prices within the spread.

Duration   A measure of the average maturity of the stream of payments generated by a financial asset. Mathematically, duration is the weighted average of the lengths of time until the asset's remaining payments are made. The weights in this calculation are the proportion of the asset's total present value represented by the present value of the respective cash flows.

Earnings per Share   A corporation's accounting earnings divided by the number of its common shares outstanding.

Earnings-Price Ratio   The reciprocal of the price-earnings ratio.

Econometric Model   A statistical model designed to explain and forecast certain economic phenomena.

Economic Earnings The change in the economic value of the firm plus dividends paid to shareholders.

Economic Value of the Firm The aggregate market value of all securities issued by the firm.

Effective Duration A measure of a bond's duration that accounts for the ability of either the bond's issuer or the bondholder to cause the actual stream of cash payments to differ from that which would be received if the bond were paid off as promised over its entire life.

Efficient Diversification The process of creating diversification in a portfolio by selecting securities in a manner that explicitly considers the standard deviations and correlations of the securities.

Efficient Market A market for securities in which every security's price equals its investment value at all times, implying that a specified set of information is fully and immediately reflected in market prices.

Efficient Portfolio A portfolio within the feasible set that offers investors both maximum expected return for varying levels of risk and minimum risk for varying levels of expected return.

Efficient Set (Frontier) The set of efficient portfolios.

Efficient Set Theorem The proposition that investors will choose their portfolios only from the set of efficient portfolios.

Emerging Markets Financial markets in countries that have a relatively low level of per capita gross domestic product, improving political and economic stability, a currency that is convertible into Western countries' currencies, and securities available for investment by foreigners.

Empirical Regularities Differences in returns on securities that occur with regularity from period to period. See also **Anomaly**.

Endogenous Variable In the context of an econometric model, an economic variable that represents the economic phenomena explained by the model.

Equal-Weighted Market Index A market index in which all the component securities contribute equally to the value of the index, regardless of the various attributes of those securities.

Equilibrium Expected Return The expected return on a security assuming that the security is correctly priced by the market. This "fair" return is determined by an appropriate asset pricing model.

Equipment Obligation (alternatively, **Equipment Trust Certificate**) A bond that is backed by specific pieces of equipment that, if necessary, can be readily sold and delivered to a new owner.

Equipment Trust Certificate See **Equipment Obligation**.

Equity Premium The difference between the expected rate of return on common stocks and the riskfree return.

Equity Swap A contract between two counterparties wherein one pays the other a fixed stream of cash flows and in return receives a varying stream whose cash flows are regularly reset on the basis of the performance of a given stock or a given stock market index.

Equivalent Yield The annualized yield-to-maturity on a fixed-income security sold on a discount basis.

Eurobond A bond that is offered outside of the country of the borrower and usually outside of the country in whose currency the security is denominated.

Eurodollar Certificate of Deposit A certificate of deposit denominated in U.S. dollars and issued by banks domiciled outside of the United States.

Eurodollar Deposit A U.S. dollar-denominated time deposit held at a bank domiciled outside of the United States.

European Option An option that can be exercised only on its expiration date.

Ex Ante Before the fact; future.

Excess Return The difference between the return on a security and the return on the riskfree asset.

Exchange Distribution or Acquisition   A trade involving a large block of stock on an organized security exchange whereby a brokerage firm attempts to execute the order by finding enough offsetting orders from its customers.

Exchange Risk (alternatively, **Currency Risk**)   The uncertainty in the return on a foreign financial asset owing to unpredictability regarding the rate at which the foreign currency can be exchanged into the investor's own currency.

Ex-Distribution Date   The date on which ownership of stock is determined for purposes of paying stock dividends or issuing new shares due to stock splits. Owners purchasing shares before the ex-distribution date receive the new shares in question. Owners purchasing shares on or after the ex-distribution date are not entitled to the new shares.

Ex-Dividend Date   The date on which ownership of stock is determined for purposes of paying cash dividends. Owners purchasing shares before the ex-dividend date receive the dividend in question. Owners purchasing shares on or after the ex-dividend date are not entitled to the dividend.

Exercise Price (alternatively, **Striking Price**)   In the case of a call option, the price at which an option buyer may purchase the underlying asset from the option writer. In the case of a put option, the price at which an option buyer may sell the underlying asset to the option writer.

Exogenous Variable   In the context of an econometric model, an economic variable taken as given and used in the model to explain the model's endogenous variables.

Expectations Hypothesis   A hypothesis that the current futures price of an asset equal the expected spot price of the asset on the delivery date of the futures contract.

Expected Rate of Inflation   That portion of inflation experienced over a given period of time that was anticipated by investors.

Expected Return   The return on a security (or portfolio) that an investor anticipates receiving over a holding period.

Expected Return Vector   A column of numbers that correspond to the expected returns for a set of securities.

Expected Value See **Mean**.

Expected Yield-to-Maturity   The yield-to-maturity on a bond calculated as a weighted average of all possible yields that the bond might produce under different scenarios of default or late payments, where the weights are the probabilities of each scenario occurring.

Expiration Date   The date on which the right to buy or sell a security under an option contract ceases.

Ex Post   After the fact; historical.

Ex Post **Alpha**   A portfolio's alpha calculated on an *ex post* basis. Mathematically, over an evaluation interval, it is the difference between the average return on the portfolio and the average return on a benchmark portfolio.

Ex Post **Selection Bias**   In the context of constructing a security valuation model, the use of securities that have performed well and the avoidance of securities that have performed poorly, thus making the model appear more effective than it truly is.

Ex-Rights Date   The date on which ownership of stock is determined for purposes of granting rights to purchase new stock in a rights offering. Owners purchasing shares before the ex-rights date receive the rights in question. Owners purchasing shares on or after the ex-rights date are not entitled to the rights.

Externally Efficient Market   A market for securities in which information is quickly and widely disseminated, thereby allowing each security's price to adjust rapidly in an unbiased manner to new information so that the price reflects investment value.

Face Value See **Principal**.

Factor (alternatively, **Index**)   An aspect of the investment environment that influences the returns of financial assets. To the extent that a factor influences a significant number of financial assets, it is termed common or pervasive.

Factor Beta   A relative measure of the mutual variation of a particular common factor with the return on the market portfolio. Mathematically, a factor beta is the covariance of the factor with the market portfolio, divided by the variance of the market portfolio.

Factor Loading (alternatively, **Attribute** or **Sensitivity**)   A measure of the responsiveness of a security's returns to a particular common factor.

Factor Model (alternatively, **Index Model**)   A return-generating process that attributes the return on a security to the security's sensitivity to the movements of various common factors.

Factor Risk   That part of a security's total risk that is related to moves in various common factors and, hence, cannot be diversified away.

Factor Risk Premium   The expected return over and above the riskfree rate on a portfolio that has unit sensitivity to a particular factor and zero sensitivity to all other factors.

Fail to Deliver   A situation in which a seller's broker is unable to deliver the traded security to the buyer's broker on or before the required settlement date.

Fallen Angel   A high-yield bond that was of investment grade when originally issued.

Feasible Set (alternatively, **Opportunity Set**)   The set of all portfolios that can be formed from the group of securities being considered by an investor.

Federally Sponsored Agency   A privately owned organization with government backing that issues securities and uses the proceeds to support the granting of various types of special-purpose loans.

Fill-or-Kill Order   A trading order that is canceled if the broker is unable to execute it immediately.

Financial Analyst (alternatively, **Security Analyst** or **Investment Analyst**)   An individual who analyzes financial assets in order to determine the investment characteristics of those assets and to identify mispricings among those assets.

Financial Asset See **Security**.

Financial Institution See **Financial Intermediary**.

Financial Intermediary (alternatively, **Financial Institution**)   An organization that issues financial claims against itself and uses the proceeds of the issuance primarily to purchase financial assets issued by individuals, partnerships, corporations, government entities, and other financial intermediaries.

Financial Investment   An investment in financial assets.

Financial Leverage   The use of debt to fund a portion of an investment.

Financial Market (alternatively, **Security Market**)   A mechanism designed to facilitate the exchange of financial assets by bringing orders from buyers and sellers of securities together.

Firm Commitment   An arrangement between underwriters and a security issuer whereby the underwriters agree to purchase, at the offering price, all of the issue not bought by the public.

Floating Rate (alternatively, **Variable Rate**)   A rate of interest on a financial asset that may vary over the life of the asset, depending on changes in a specified indicator of current market interest rates.

Floor Broker (alternatively, **Two-Dollar Broker**)   A member of an organized security exchange who assists commission brokers when there are too many orders flowing into the market for the commission brokers to handle alone.

Floor Order Routing and Execution System (FORES)   A computer system for trading the 150 most active stocks on the Tokyo Stock Exchange.

Floor Trader (alternatively, **Competitive Trader** or **Registered Competitive Market-Maker** or **Registered Trader**)   A member of an organized security exchange who trades solely for his or her own account and is prohibited by exchange rules from handling public orders.

Foreign Return   The return on an investment in a foreign financial asset, including the impact of exchange rate changes.

Forward Rate   The interest rate that links the current spot interest rate over one holding period to the current spot interest rate over a longer holding period. Equivalently, the interest rate agreed to at a point in time at which the associated loan will be made at a future date.

Fourth Market   A secondary security market in which investors (typically, financial institutions) trade securities directly with one another, bypassing the brokers and dealers on organized security exchanges and the over-the-counter market.

Fundamental Analysis   A form of security analysis that seeks to determine the intrinsic value of securities on the basis of underlying economic factors. These intrinsic values are compared with current market prices to estimate current levels of mispricing.

Futures (Futures Contract)   An agreement between two investors under which the seller promises to deliver a specific asset on a specific future date to the buyer for a predetermined price to be paid on the delivery date.

Futures Commission Merchant (FCM)   A firm that carries out customers' orders involving futures.

Futures Option (alternatively, **Option on Futures**)   An option contract for which the deliverable asset is a specific futures contract.

Generally Accepted Accounting Principles (GAAP)   Accounting rules established by recognized U.S. authorities, such as the Financial Accounting Standards Board (FASB).

General Obligation Bond   A municipal bond that is backed by the full faith and credit of the issuing agency.

Geometric Mean Return   The compounded per period average rate of return on a financial asset over a specified time interval.

Good-Till-Canceled Order See **Open Order**.

Greenmail   An offer by the management of a corporation that is the target of an attempted hostile takeover to repurchase its shares from the hostile bidder at an above-market price.

Growth Stock   A stock that has experienced or is expected to experience rapidly increasing earnings per share and is often characterized as having low earnings-to-price and book-value-to-market-value ratios.

Guaranteed Bond   A bond issued by one corporation but backed by another corporation.

Hedger   An investor in futures contracts whose primary objective is to offset an otherwise risky position.

Hedge Ratio (alternatively, **Delta**)   The expected change in the value of an option for each dollar change in the market price of the underlying asset.

High-Yield Bonds See **Speculative-Grade Bonds**.

Historical Beta   An estimate of a security's beta, derived solely from historical returns. Equivalently, the slope of the market model or the *ex post* characteristic line.

Holding Period   The length of time over which an investor is assumed to invest a given sum of money.

Holding-Period Return   The rate of return on an investment over a given holding period.

Holdout Sample See **Out-of-Sample Data**.

Holiday Effect   The observation that average stock returns have been abnormally high around federal holidays.

Homogeneous Expectations   A situation in which all investors possess the same perceptions with regard to the expected returns, standard deviations, and covariances of securities.

Horizon Analysis   A form of active bond management whereby a single holding period is selected for analysis, and possible yield structures at the end of the period are considered. Bonds with the most attractive expected returns under the alternative yield structures are selected for the portfolio.

Hypothecation Agreement (alternatively, **Customer's Agreement**)   A legal arrangement between a brokerage firm and an investor that permits the brokerage firm to pledge the investor's securities as collateral for bank loans, provided that the securities were purchased through the investor's margin account.

Idiosyncratic Risk See **Nonfactor Risk**.

Immunization   A bond portfolio management technique that permits an investor to meet a promised stream of cash outflows with a high degree of certainty.

Implied Volatility   The risk of an asset derived from an options valuation model, assuming that an option on the asset is fairly priced by the market.

Implied Return See **Internal Rate of Return**.

Income Bond   A bond for which the size of the interest payments varies on the basis of the income of the issuer.

Indenture   A legal document formally describing the terms of the legal relationship between a bond issuer and bondholders.

Index See **Factor**.

Index Arbitrage   An investment strategy that involves buying a stock index futures contract and selling the individual stocks in the index, or selling a stock index futures contract and buying the individual stocks in the index. The strategy is designed to take advantage of a mispricing between the stock index futures contract and the underlying stocks.

Indexation   A method of linking the payments associated with a bond to the price level in order to provide a certain real return on the bond.

Index Fund   A passively managed investment in a diversified portfolio of financial assets designed to mimic the investment performance of a specific market index.

Index Model See **Factor Model**.

Indifference Curve   All combinations of portfolios, considered in terms of expected returns and risk, that provide an investor with an equal amount of satisfaction.

Individual Retirement Account   A tax-advantaged means for people to set aside income (either on a before-tax or an after-tax basis) and avoid taxes on the subsequent earnings until those earnings and the original funds are withdrawn.

Industrial Development Bond (IDB)   A form of revenue bond used to finance the purchase or construction of industrial facilities that are leased by the issuing municipality to firms on a favorable basis.

Inefficient Portfolio   A portfolio that does not satisfy the criteria of an efficient portfolio and, hence, does not lie on the efficient set.

Inflation   The rate of change in a price index over a certain period of time. Equivalently, the percentage change in the purchasing power of a unit of currency over a certain period of time.

Inflation Hedge   An asset that preserves the value of its purchasing power over time despite changes in the price level.

Inflation-indexed security   A type of fixed-income security that offers investors a promised (pretax) real rate of return by adjusting the security's principal and coupon payments for changes in a specified price index.

Information Coefficient   The correlation coefficient between a security analyst's predicted returns and subsequent actual returns that is used to measure the accuracy of the analyst's predictions.

Information Content of Dividends Hypothesis   The proposition that dividend announcements contain inside information about a corporation's future prospects.

Initial Margin Requirement   The minimum percentage of a margin purchase (or short sale) price that must come from the investor's own funds.

Initial Public Offering (ipo) (alternatively, **Unseasoned Offering**)   The first offering of the shares of a company to the public.

Initial Wealth   The value of an investor's portfolio at the beginning of a holding period.

Inside Quotes (alternatively, **NBBO**)   The highest bid price and the lowest asked price for a given stock offered by a group of dealers in a particular stock.

Insider   Narrowly defined, a stockholder, officer, or director of a corporation who owns a "significant" proportion of a corporation's stock. More broadly defined, anyone who has access to information that is both "materially" related to the value of a corporation's securities and unavailable to the general public.

Instinet   Acronym for Institutional Network. A computerized communications system that provides price quotations and order execution for fourth market participants.

Interest-Rate Parity   An explanation for why spot and futures exchange rates differ. It asserts that such differences result from different interest rates in the two countries.

Interest-Rate Risk   The uncertainty in the return on a fixed-income security caused by unanticipated fluctuations in the value of the asset owing to changes in interest rates.

Interest Rate Swap   A contract between two counterparties wherein one pays the other a fixed stream of cash flows and in return receives a varying stream whose cash flows are regularly reset on the basis of the level of a given market-determined interest rate.

Intermarket Spread Swap   A type of bond swap whereby an investor moves out of one market segment and into another because the investor believes that one segment is significantly underpriced relative to the other.

Intermarket Trading System   An electronic communications network that links the national and regional organized security exchanges and certain over-the-counter dealers. The network provides market-maker price quotes and allows participating brokers and dealers to route orders to market-makers offering the best prices.

Internal Rate of Return (alternatively, **Implied Return**)   The discount rate that equates the sum of the present value of future cash flows expected to be received from a particular investment to the cost of that investment.

Internalization   A form of preferencing whereby broker-dealers who are members of the New York Stock Exchange take their customers' orders and fill them internally instead of sending them to an exchange floor for execution.

Internally Efficient Market   A market for securities in which brokers and dealers compete fairly so that the cost of transacting is low and the speed of transacting is high.

In the Money   In the case of a call option, an option whose exercise price is less than the current market price of its underlying asset. In the case of a put option, an option whose exercise price is greater than the current market price of its underlying asset.

Intrinsic Value of an Option   The value of an option if it were exercised immediately. Equivalently, the market price of the asset upon which a call option is written less the exercise price of the option (or the exercise price less the market price of the asset, in the case of a put option).

Investment   The sacrifice of certain present value for (possibly uncertain) future value.

Investment Adviser   An individual or organization that provides investment advice to investors.

Investment Analyst See **Financial Analyst**.

Investment Banker (alternatively, **Underwriter**)   An organization that acts as an intermediary between issuers and the ultimate purchasers of securities in the primary security market.

Investment Banking   The process of analyzing and selecting a means of procuring financing on behalf of an issuer of securities.

Investment Committee   In a traditional investment organization, a group of senior management responsible for establishing the organization's broad investment strategy.

Investment Company   A type of financial intermediary that obtains money from investors and uses that money to purchase financial assets. In return, the investors receive shares in the investment company and thus indirectly own a proportion of the financial assets that the company itself owns.

Investment Environment   The financial structure in which investors operate, consisting of the kinds of marketable securities available for purchase or sale and how and where those securities are bought and sold.

Investment-Grade Bonds   Bonds that possess bond ratings that permit them to be purchased by the vast majority of institutional investors, particularly regulated financial institutions. Usually, investment-grade bonds have a BBB (Standard & Poor's) or Baa (Moody's) or higher bond rating.

Investment Policy   A component of the investment process that involves determining an investor's objectives, particularly as regards his or her attitude toward the tradeoff between expected return and risk.

Investment Process   The set of procedures by which an investor decides what marketable securities to invest in, how extensive those investments should be, and when the investments should be made.

Investment Style   The method an investor uses to take active positions in certain types of securities.

Investment Value   The present value of a security's future prospects as estimated by well-informed market participants.

January Effect   An empirical regularity whereby stock returns appear to be higher in January than in other months of the year.

Junk Bonds See **Speculative-Grade Bonds**.

Keogh Plan   A tax-advantaged means by which people who are self-employed (or otherwise have no access to an employer-sponsored retirement plan) can set aside income on a before-tax basis and invest tax-free until the original funds and subsequent earnings are withdrawn.

Lagging Indicators   Economic variables that have been found to follow movements in the economy.

Lambda   The expected return premium (above the riskfree rate of interest) per unit of sensitivity to a particular common factor. Also, the sensitivity of the price of an option to changes in its volatility.

Leading Indicators   Economic variables that have been found to signal future changes in the economy.

Letter Stock (alternatively, **Restricted Stock**)   Stock that is unregistered and sold directly to the purchaser, rather than through a public offering. Such stock must be held at least one year and cannot be sold even at that time unless certain information on the company is available and the amount sold is a relatively small percentage of the total shares outstanding.

Leveraged Buyout   A situation in which a private investment group, using substantial amounts of debt financing, buys all of the shares of a publicly held firm, thereby gaining complete control of the firm.

Limited Liability   An aspect of the corporate form of organization that prevents common stockholders from losing more than their investment if the corporation should default on its obligations.

Limit Order   A trading order that specifies a limit price at which the broker is to execute the order. The trade will be executed only if the broker can meet or better the limit price.

Limit Order Book (alternatively, **Specialist's Book**)   The records kept by the specialist identifying the unfilled limit, stop, and stop limit orders that brokers want to execute in a particular security.

Limit Price   The price specified when a limit order is placed with a broker, defining the maximum purchase price or minimum selling price at which the order can be executed.

Liquidity (alternatively, **Marketability**)   The ability of investors to convert securities to cash at a price similar to the price of the previous trade in the security, assuming that no significant new information has arrived since the previous trade. Equivalently, the ability to sell an asset quickly without having to make a substantial price concession.

Liquidity Preference (Premium) Theory   An explanation of the term structure of interest rates. It holds that the term structure is a result of the preference of investors for short-term securities. Investors can be induced to hold longer-term securities only if they expect to receive a higher return.

Liquidity Premium   The expected incremental return of longer-term securities over shorter-term securities that compensates investors for the greater interest rate risk entailed in holding longer-term securities.

Listed Security   A security that is traded on an organized security exchange.

Load Charge   A sales charge levied by a mutual fund when an investor buys its shares.

Load Fund   A mutual fund that has a load charge.

Local (alternatively, **Scalper**)   A member of an organized futures exchange who trades for his or her own account and has a very short holding period.

Long Hedger   A hedger who offsets risk by buying futures contracts.

Low-Load Fund   A mutual fund that has a small load charge, usually 3.5% or less.

Maintenance Margin Requirement   The minimum actual margin that a brokerage firm requires investors to keep in their margin accounts.

Majority Voting System (alternatively, **Straight Voting System**)   In the context of a corporation, a method of voting in which a stockholder is permitted to give any one candidate for the board of directors a maximum number of votes equal to the number of shares owned by that shareholder.

Managed Investment Company   An investment company with a portfolio that may be altered at the discretion of the company's portfolio manager.

Management Buyout   A situation in which the existing management of a publicly owned firm, perhaps joined by an outside investment group, buys all the shares of the existing stockholders, thereby gaining complete control of the firm.

Margin Account   An account maintained by an investor with a brokerage firm in which securities may be purchased by borrowing a portion of the purchase price from the brokerage firm or may be sold short by borrowing the securities from the brokerage firm.

Marginal Tax Rate   The amount of taxes, expressed as a percentage, paid on each additional dollar of taxable income received.

Marginal Utility   The extra utility that a person derives from engaging in an extra unit of economic activity such as work, consumption, or investment.

Margin Call   A demand upon an investor by a brokerage firm to increase the equity in the investor's margin account. The margin call is initiated when the investor's actual margin falls below the maintenance margin requirement.

Margin Purchase   The purchase of securities financed by borrowing a portion of the purchase price from a brokerage firm.

Markdown   The difference in prices between what an investor's broker receives and what the investor receives for a security sold in the over-the-counter market.

Marked (or Marking) to the Market   The process of calculating, usually on a daily basis, the actual margin in an investor's account. Equivalently, the process of adjusting the equity in an investor's account to reflect the changes in the market value of the account's assets and liabilities.

Marketability See **Liquidity**.

Market Beta See **Beta**.

Market Capitalization   The aggregate market value of a security, equal to the market price per unit of the security multiplied by the total number of outstanding units of the security.

Market Discount Bond   A bond issued at par, but currently selling that sells in the secondary market at a price below its par value.

Market Discount Function   The set of discount factors on all default-free bonds across the spectrum of terms-to-maturity.

Market Index   A collection of securities whose prices are averaged to reflect the overall investment performance of a particular market for financial assets.

Market-Maker See **Dealer**.

Market Model   A simple linear model that expresses the relationship between the return on a security and the return on a market index.

Market Order   A trading order that instructs the broker to buy or sell a security immediately at the best obtainable price.

Market Portfolio   A portfolio consisting of an investment in all securities. The proportion invested in each security equals the percentage of the total market capitalization represented by the security.

Market Risk (alternatively, **Systematic Risk**)   The portion of a security's total risk that is related to moves in the market portfolio and, hence, cannot be diversified away.

Market Segmentation Theory An explanation of the term structure of interest rates. It holds that various investors and borrowers are restricted by law, preference, or custom to certain maturity ranges. Spot rates in each market segment are determined by supply and demand conditions there.

Market Timing A form of active management that entails shifting an investor's funds between a surrogate market portfolio and the riskfree asset, depending on the investor's perception of their relative near-term prospects.

Markup The difference in prices between what an investor pays and what the investor's broker pays for a security purchased in the over-the-counter market.

Maturity Date The date upon which a bond issuer promises to repay investors the principal of the bond.

May Day The date (May 1, 1975) that the New York Stock Exchange ended its fixed-commission rate requirement and permitted member firms to negotiate commission rates with customers.

Mean (alternatively, **Expected Value**) A measure of central tendency of the probability distribution of a random variable that equals the weighted average of all possible outcomes using their probabilities as weights.

Median The outcome of a random variable where there is an equal probability of observing a value greater or less than it.

Member Corporation See **Member Firm.**

Member Firm (alternatively, **Member Corporation** or **Member Organization**) A brokerage firm with one or more memberships in an organized security exchange.

Member Organization See **Member Firm**.

Merger A form of corporate takeover in which two firms combine their operations and become one firm. Mergers are usually negotiated by the management of the two merging corporations.

Minus Tick A trade in a security made at a price lower than the price of the previous trade in that same security.

Mispriced Security A security that is trading at a price substantially different from its investment value.

Mode The outcome of a random variable that has the highest probability of occurring.

Modified Duration The duration of a bond divided by the quantity 1 plus the bond's yield. For a 1% change in yields, it measures the percentage change (in the opposite direction) of the bond's price.

Money Market Deposit A short-term fixed income security.

Money Markets Financial markets in which financial assets with a term to maturity of typically one year or less are traded.

Moral Hazard A problem in pricing insurance where the likelihood of the insured event's occurring increases after insurance is purchased.

Mortgage Bond A bond that is secured by the pledge of specific property. In the event of default, bondholders are entitled to obtain the property in question and to sell it to satisfy their claims on the issuer.

M-Squared (M^2) An *ex post* risk-adjusted measure of portfolio performance that compares a portfolio's average return with what it would have earned if the portfolio had been invested with the same degree of total risk as the market portfolio.

Multinational Firm A corporation that carries on a substantial portion of its business in countries other than the country in which it is domiciled.

Multiple-Growth Model A type of dividend discount model in which dividends are assumed to grow at different rates over specifically defined time periods.

Municipal Bond A bond issued by a state or local unit of government.

Mutual Fund See **Open-End Investment Company**.

Naked Call Writing The process of writing a call option on a stock that the option writer does not own.

Naked Put Writing   The process of writing a put option on a stock when the writer does not have sufficient cash (or securities) in his or her brokerage account to purchase the stock.

Nasdaq International   An early morning system for trading NYSE, AMEX, and Nasdaq securities through the use of a dealer network.

National Association of Securities Dealers (NASD)   A self-regulatory agency that establishes rules and regulations and monitors the activities of brokers and dealers in the over-the-counter market.

National Association of Securities Dealers Automated Quotations (Nasdaq)   An automated nationwide communications network operated by the NASD that connects dealers and brokers in the over-the-counter market. Nasdaq provides current market-maker bid and asked price quotes to market participants.

National Best Bid or Offer (NBBO) See **Inside Quotes**.

National Market System (Nasdaq/NMS)   A segment of the over-the-counter market composed of issues with relatively large trading volumes. More detailed trading information is provided on stocks included in Nasdaq/NMS than on other over-the-counter stocks.

Neglected-Firm Effect   An empirical observation that firms followed by relatively few security analysts have had abnormally high returns.

Net Asset Value   The market value of an investment company's assets, less any liabilities, divided by the number of shares outstanding.

Net Present Value   The present value of future cash flows expected to be received from a particular investment less the cost of that investment.

No-Growth Model See **Zero-Growth Model**.

No-Load Fund   A mutual fund that does not have a load charge.

Nominal Return   The percentage change in the value of a financial asset, where the beginning and ending values of the asset are not adjusted for inflation over the time of the investment.

Nonfactor Risk (alternatively, **Idiosyncratic Risk**)   The portion of a security's total risk that is not related to moves in various common factors and, hence, can be diversified away.

Non-Market Risk See **Unique Risk**.

Nonsatiation   A condition whereby investors are assumed to always prefer higher levels of terminal wealth to lower levels of terminal wealth.

Normal Backwardation   A relationship between the futures price of an asset and the expected spot price of the asset on the delivery date of the contract. Normal backwardation states that the futures price should be less than the expected spot price.

Normal Contango   A relationship between the futures price of an asset and the expected spot price of the asset on the delivery date of the contract. Normal contango states that the futures price should be greater than the expected spot price.

Normal Distribution   A symmetric bell-shaped probability distribution, completely described by its mean and standard deviation.

Normative Economics   A form of economic analysis that is prescriptive in nature, dealing with what "ought to be."

Odd Lot   An amount of stock that is less than the standard unit of trading, generally from 1 to 99 shares.

Offer Price See **Asked Price**.

On-the-Run Issue   The most recently issued Treasury security of a particular maturity.

Open See **Opening Price**.

Open-End Investment Company (alternatively, **Mutual Fund**)   A managed investment company, with an unlimited life, that stands ready at all times to purchase its shares from its owners and usually will continuously offer new shares to the public.

Opening Price (alternatively, **Open**)   The price at which the first trade of the day took place in a particular stock.

Open Interest   The number of a particular futures contract that are outstanding at a particular point in time.

Open Order (alternatively, **Good-Till-Canceled Order**) A trading order that remains in effect until it is either filled or canceled by the investor.

Operating Expense Ratio The percentage of an investment company's assets that were used to pay for management fees, administrative expenses, and other operating expenses in a given year.

Opportunity Set See **Feasible Set**.

Optimal Portfolio The feasible portfolio that offers an investor the maximum level of satisfaction. This portfolio represents the tangency between the efficient set and an indifference curve of the investor.

Option A contract between two investors in which one investor grants the other the right to buy (or sell) a specific asset at a specific price within a specific time period.

Option on Futures See **Futures Option**.

Order Book Officials The people who keep the limit order book in those option markets that involve market-makers instead of specialists.

Order Specification The investor's instructions to a broker regarding the particular characteristics of a trading order, including the name of the security's issuing firm, whether to buy or sell, order size, maximum time the order is to be outstanding, and the type of order to be used.

Ordinary Least Squares See **Simple Linear Regression**.

Organized Exchange A central physical location where trading of securities is done under a set of rules and regulations.

Original Issue Discount (OID) Security A bond that was originally issued at a price below its par value.

Out of the Money In the case of a call option, an option whose exercise price is greater than the market price of its underlying asset. In the case of a put option, an option whose exercise price is less than the market price of its underlying asset.

Out-of-Sample Data (alternatively, **Holdout Sample**) In the context of constructing a security valuation model, information that is obtained from periods different from those used to estimate the valuation model. Out-of-sample data can be used to test the model's validity.

Over-the-Counter Market (OTC Market) A secondary market for securities distinct from an organized security exchange.

Overmargined (alternatively, **Unrestricted**) A situation in which the actual margin in a margin account has risen above the initial margin requirement.

Overpriced Security (alternatively, **Overvalued Security**) A security whose expected return is less than its equilibrium expected return. Equivalently, a security with a negative alpha.

Oversubscription Privilege The opportunity given shareholders who have exercised their rights in a rights offering to buy shares that were not purchased in the offering.

Overvalued Security See **Overpriced Security**.

Pac-Man Defense A strategy used by corporations to ward off hostile takeovers. The targeted company reverses the takeover effort and seeks to acquire the firm making the initial takeover attempt.

Participating Bond A bond that promises to pay a stated rate of interest to its owner but may also pay additional interest if the issuer's earnings exceed a specified level.

Participation Certificate A bond that represents an ownership interest in a pool of fixed-income securities. The holders of the certificates receive the interest and principal payments on the pooled securities in proportion to their ownership of the pool.

Par Value of Stock The nominal value of shares of common stock as legally carried on the books of a corporation.

Par Value of Bond See **Principal**.

Passive Investment System (alternatively, **Passive Management**) The process of buying and holding a well-diversified portfolio.

Passive Management See **Passive Investment System**.

Payment for Order Flow A form of preferencing whereby a dealer pays cash to a broker in order to receive trades from the broker for execution.

Payout Ratio The percentage of a firm's earnings paid to shareholders in the form of cash dividends.

Pegging The process by which investment bankers attempt to stabilize the price of an underwritten security in the secondary market for a period of time after the initial offering date.

Perfect Markets Security markets in which no impediments to investing exist. These impediments include finite divisibility of securities, taxes, transaction costs, and costly information.

Performance Attribution The identification of sources of returns for a portfolio or security over a particular evaluation interval of time.

Performance Margin The initial margin that must be posted by a futures buyer or seller.

Pink Sheets Written published quotations on over-the-counter stocks that are not listed on Nasdaq.

Plus Tick See **Up Tick**.

Poison Pill Defense A strategy used by corporations to ward off hostile takeovers. The targeted company gives its shareholders certain rights that can be exercised only in the event of a hostile takeover, and that, once exercised, will be extremely onerous to the acquirer.

Political Risk The uncertainty in the return on a foreign financial asset owing to the possibility that the foreign government might take actions that are detrimental to the investor's financial interests.

Portfolio Construction (alternatively, **Security Selection**) A component of the investment process that involves identifying which assets to invest in and determining the proportion of funds to invest in each of the assets.

Portfolio Insurance An investment strategy designed to earn a minimum rate of return while allowing the investor to benefit substantially from the positive returns generated by an investment in a risky portfolio.

Portfolio Manager An individual who uses the information provided by financial analysts to construct a portfolio of financial assets.

Portfolio Performance Evaluation A component of the investment process involving periodic analysis of how a portfolio performed in terms of both returns earned and risk incurred.

Portfolio Revision A component of the investment process, involving periodically repeating the process of setting investment policy, conducting security analysis, and constructing a portfolio.

Portfolio Turnover Rate A measure of how much buying and selling occurs in a portfolio over a given period of time.

Positive Economics A form of economic analysis that is descriptive in nature, dealing with "what is."

Preemptive Rights When a corporation plans an issuance of new common shares, the right of existing shareholders to purchase the new shares in proportion to the number of shares that they currently own.

Preferencing A standing arrangement on the part of a broker of taking trade orders from customers and sending those orders for execution to a specific dealer.

Preferred Habitat Theory An explanation of the term structure of interest rates. Similar to the market segmentation theory, it holds that various investors and borrowers have segments of the market in which they prefer to operate. However, these investors are assumed to be willing to leave their desired maturity segments if there are significant differences in yields between the various segments.

Preferred Stock A hybrid form of security that has characteristics of both common stocks and bonds.

Premium The price of an option contract.

Price-Earnings Ratio A corporation's current stock price divided by its earnings per share.

Price Impact The effect on the price of a security resulting from a trade in that security. Price impact is the result of several factors, including size of the trade, demand for immediate liquidity, and presumed information of the individual or organization placing the order.

Price-Relative   The price of a security at the end of one period divided by its price at the end of the previous period.

Price-Weighted Market Index   A market index in which the contribution of a security to the value of the index is based solely on the security's current market price.

Primary Market   The market in which securities are sold at the time of their initial issuance.

Principal (alternatively, **Face Value** or **Par Value of Bond**)   The nominal value of a bond that is promised to be repaid to bondholders at the maturity date.

Private Placement   The direct sale of a newly issued security to a small number of institutional or high networth investors.

Probabilistic Forecasting   A form of security analysis that begins with a series of economic scenarios, along with their respective probabilities of occurrence. Under each of these scenarios, accompanying projections are made as to the prospects for various industries, companies, and stock prices.

Probability Distribution   A model describing the relative frequency of possible values that a random variable can assume.

Professional Money Manager   An individual or organization that invests funds on behalf of others.

Program Trading   The purchase or sale of a collection of securities as if the collection were one security. Program trades are prominently employed in portfolio insurance and index arbitrage strategies.

Promised Yield-to-Maturity   The yield-to-maturity on a bond calculated on the assumption that all promised cash flows are received on a full and timely basis.

Prospectus   The official selling circular that must be given to purchasers of new securities registered with the Securities and Exchange Commission. The prospectus provides various information about the issuer's business, its financial condition, and the nature of the security being offered.

Proxy   The signing by a shareholder of a power of attorney, thereby authorizing a designated party to cast all of the shareholder's votes on any matter brought up at the corporation's annual meeting.

Proxy Fight   An attempt by dissident shareholders to solicit proxies to vote against corporate incumbents.

Purchasing Group See **Syndicate**.

Purchasing-Power Risk   The risk experienced by investors in financial assets owing to uncertainty concerning the impact of inflation on the real returns produced by those financial assets.

Pure-Discount Security (alternatively, **Zero-Coupon Security**)   A security that promises to make only one payment to its owner at the security's maturity date.

Pure Factor Play See **Pure Factor Portfolio**.

Pure Factor Portfolio (alternatively, **Pure Factor Play**)   A portfolio that possesses a unit sensitivity to one factor and no sensitivity to any other factor and has zero nonfactor risk.

Pure Yield Pickup Swap   A type of bond swap whereby an investor exchanges one bond for another to obtain a higher yield over the long term, with little attention paid to the near-term outlook for the bonds' respective market segments or for the market as a whole.

Putable Bond   A bond that offers the owner the option to present the bond to the issuer in exchange for cash equal to the bond's face value during a time period stated in the indenture.

Put-Call Parity   The relationship between the market price of a put and a call that have the same exercise price, expiration date, and underlying stock.

Put Option   A contract that gives the buyer the right to sell a specific number of shares of a company to the writer at a specific price within a specific time period.

Random Diversification   The process of creating diversification in a portfolio by randomly selecting securities without regard to the standard deviations and correlations of the securities.

Random Error Term   The difference between the actual value of a random variable and the predicted value based on some model.

Random Variable   A variable that takes on alternative values according to chance.

Random Walk (or **Random Walk Model**)   In general, a situation in which changes in the value of a random variable are independent and identically distributed. When applied to common stocks, it refers to a situation in which security price changes are independent and identically distributed, meaning that the size of a security's price change from one period to the next can be viewed as being determined by the spin of a roulette wheel.

Random Walk with Drift   A situation in which security prices follow a random walk, except that those prices are expected to rise over time.

Rate Anticipation Swap   A type of bond swap whereby an investor exchanges bonds that are expected to perform relatively poorly for those that are expected to perform relatively well, given an anticipated movement in interest rates.

Rate of Return   The percentage change in the value of an investment in a financial asset (or portfolio of financial assets) over a specified time period.

Real Estate Investment Trust (REIT)   An investment fund, similar to an investment company, whose investment objective is to hold primarily real estate–related assets, either through mortgages, construction and development loans, or equity interests.

Real Investment   An investment involving some kind of tangible asset, such as land, equipment, or buildings.

Realized Capital Gain (or Loss)   A capital gain (or loss) on an asset that is recognized, for tax purposes, through the sale or exchange of the asset.

Real Return   The percentage change in the value of an investment in a financial asset, where the beginning and ending values of the asset are adjusted for inflation over the time of the investment.

Redemption Fee   A fee levied by an investment company when an investor sells his or her shares back to the investment company within a specified period of time after the purchase.

Red Herring   A preliminary prospectus that provides much of the information in the final prospectus but is not an offer to sell the security, nor does it display an actual offering price.

Regional Brokerage Firm   An organization offering brokerage services that specializes in trading the securities of companies located in a particular region of the country.

Regional Exchange   An organized exchange that specializes in trading the securities of companies located in a particular region of the country.

Registered Bond   A bond for which the owner is registered with the issuer. The bondholder receives coupon payments directly from the issuer. Ownership changes require notification of the issuer.

Registered Competitive Market-Maker See **Floor Trader**.

Registered Representative See **Account Executive**.

Registered Trader See **Floor Trader**.

Registrar   A designated agent of a corporation responsible for canceling and issuing shares of stock in the corporation as these shares are issued or traded.

Registration Statement   A document filed with the Securities and Exchange Commission prior to initiating a public security offering.

Reinvestment-Rate Risk   The uncertainty in the return on a fixed-income asset caused by unanticipated changes in the interest rate at which cash flows from the asset can be reinvested.

Replacement Cost Accounting   The use of estimated replacement costs instead of historical book-value costs when calculating corporate earnings.

Repo Rate   The rate of interest involved in a repurchase agreement.

Reported Earnings See **Accounting Earnings**.

Repurchase Agreement   A type of money market instrument that involves the sale of a financial asset from one investor to another. The investor selling the asset simultaneously agrees to repurchase it from the purchaser on a stated future date at a predetermined price, which is higher than the original transaction price.

Repurchase Offer An offer by the management of a corporation to buy back some of its own stock.

Residual Standard Deviation See **Standard Deviation of the Random Error Term**.

Restricted Account A margin account in which the actual margin has fallen below the initial margin requirement but remains above the maintenance margin requirement.

Restricted Stock See **Letter Stock**.

Retention Ratio The percentage of a firm's earnings that are not paid to shareholders but instead are retained by the firm. Equivalently, one minus the payout ratio.

Return on Equity The earnings of a firm divided by the firm's book value.

Return-Generating Process A statistical model that describes how the returns on a security are produced.

Revenue Bond A municipal bond that is backed solely by the revenues from a designated project, authority, or agency or by the proceeds from a specific tax.

Reverse Stock Split A form of stock split whereby the number of shares is reduced and the par value per share is increased.

Reversing Trade The purchase or sale of a futures or options contract designed to offset, and thereby cancel, the previous sale or purchase of the same contract.

Reward-to-Variability Ratio See **Sharpe Ratio**.

Reward-to-Volatility Ratio (Treynor Ratio) An *ex post* risk-adjusted measure of portfolio performance where risk is defined as the market risk of the portfolio. Mathematically, over an evaluation period, it is the excess return of a portfolio divided by the beta of the portfolio.

Right An option issued to existing shareholders that permits them to buy a specified number of new shares at a designated subscription price. For each shareholder this number is proportional to the number of existing shares currently owned by the shareholder.

Rights Offering The sale of new stock conducted by offering the stock to existing shareholders in proportion to the number of shares owned by each shareholder.

Risk The uncertainty associated with the end-of-period value of an investment.

Risk-Adjusted Return The return on an asset or portfolio, modified to explicitly account for the risk to which the asset or portfolio is exposed.

Risk-Averse Investor An investor who prefers an investment with less risk over one with more risk, assuming that the two investments offer the same expected return.

Riskfree Asset An asset whose return over a given holding period is certain and known at the beginning of the holding period.

Riskfree Borrowing The act of borrowing funds that are to be repaid with interest calculated at the riskfree rate.

Riskfree Lending (or **Riskfree Investing**) The act of investing in a riskfree asset.

Risk-Neutral Investor An investor who has no preference between investments with varying levels of risk, assuming that the investments offer the same expected return.

Risk Premium The difference between the expected yield-to-maturity of a risky bond and the expected yield-to-maturity of a same-maturity default-free bond.

Risk-Seeking Investor An investor who prefers an investment with more risk over one with less risk, assuming that the two investments offer the same expected return.

Risk Structure The set of yields-to-maturity among bonds that possess different degrees of default risk but are similar with respect to other attributes.

Risk Tolerance The tradeoff between risk and expected return demanded by a particular investor.

Round Lot An amount of stock that is equal to a standard unit of trading, generally 100 shares or a multiple of 100 shares.

R-**Squared** See **Coefficient of Determination**.

Savings Foregone consumption. Also, the difference between current income and current consumption.

Scalper See **Local**.

SEAQ Automated Execution Facility (SAEF) A small-order execution system, similar to the Small Order Execution System of Nasdaq, that is used on the London Stock Exchange.

Seat The designation of membership in an organized exchange. By holding a seat, the member has the privilege of being able to execute trades using the facilities provided by the exchange.

Secondary Distribution A means of selling a block of stock whereby the shares are sold away from an organized exchange after the close of trading in a manner similar to the sale of new issues of common stock.

Secondary Market The market in which securities are traded that have been issued at some previous point in time.

Sector In the context of a specific asset class, or collection of financial assets that have common distinguishing financial characteristics.

Sector Factor A factor that affects the return on securities within a particular sector.

Sector-Factor Model A special kind of multiple-factor model in which some of the factors are particular industries or economic sectors.

Sector Selection A component of the security selection process involving the identification of desirable combinations of sectors within an asset class.

Securities and Exchange Commission (SEC) A federal agency established by the Securities Exchange Act of 1934 that regulates the issuance of securities in the primary market and the trading of securities in the secondary market.

Securities Investor Protection Corporation (SIPC) A quasigovernmental agency that insures the accounts of brokerage firms against loss owing to any of the firms' failure.

Securities Lending The process of making available securities owned by one investor to another investor in the form of a loan. The borrower provides collateral to the lender to secure the loan and pays the lender a fee.

Security (alternatively, **Financial Asset**) A legal representation of the right to receive future benefits under stated conditions.

Security Analysis A component of the investment process that involves determining the prospective future benefits of a security, the conditions under which such benefits will be received, and the likelihood that such conditions will occur.

Security Analyst See **Financial Analyst**.

Security Market See **Financial Market**.

Security Market Line Derived from the capital asset pricing model, a linear relationship between the expected returns on securities and the risk of those securities, with risk expressed as the security's beta (or equivalently, the security's covariance with the market portfolio).

Security Selection See **Portfolio Construction**.

Selectivity An aspect of security analysis that entails forecasting the price movements of individual securities.

Self-Regulation A method of governmental regulation whereby the rules and standards of conduct in security markets are set by firms that operate in these markets, subject to the oversight of various federal agencies such as the SEC and CFTC.

Selling Group A group of investment banking organizations that, as part of a security underwriting, are responsible for selling the security.

Semistrong-Form Market Efficiency A level of market efficiency in which all relevant publicly available information is fully and immediately reflected in security prices.

Sensitivity See **Factor Loading**.

Separation Theorem A feature of the capital asset pricing model that states that the optimal combination of risky assets for an investor can be determined without any knowledge about the investor's preferences toward risk and return.

Serial Bond A bond issue with different portions of the issue maturing at different dates.

Settle (or Settlement) Price The representative price for a futures contract determined during the closing period of the futures exchange.

Settlement Date   The date after a security has been traded on which the buyer must deliver cash to the seller and the seller must deliver the security to the buyer.

Sharpe Ratio (alternatively, **Reward-to-Variability Ratio**)   An *ex post* risk-adjusted measure of portfolio performance where risk is defined as the standard deviation of the portfolio's returns. Mathematically, over an evaluation period, it is the excess return of a portfolio divided by the standard deviation of the portfolio's returns.

Shelf Registration   Under Securities and Exchange Commission Rule 415, issuers may register securities in advance of their issuance and sell these securities up to a year later.

Short Hedger   A hedger who offsets risk by selling futures contracts.

Short Interest   The number of shares of a given company that have been sold short and, as of a given date, have loans outstanding.

Short Sale   The sale of a security that is not owned by an investor but rather is borrowed from a broker. The investor eventually repays the broker in kind by purchasing the same security in a subsequent transaction.

Simple Linear Regression (alternatively, **Ordinary Least Squares**)   A statistical model of the relationship between two random variables in which one variable is assumed to be linearly related to the other. This relationship is depicted by a regression line, which is a straight line, "fitted" to pairs of values of the two variables, so that the sum of the squared random error terms is minimized.

Sinking Fund   Periodic payments made by a bond issuer to reduce, in an orderly manner, the amount of outstanding principal on a bond issue over the life of the bond.

Size Effect (alternatively, **Small Firm Effect**)   An empirical regularity whereby stock returns appear to differ consistently across the spectrum of market capitalization. Over extended periods of time, smaller-capitalization stocks have outperformed larger-capitalization stocks on a risk-adjusted basis.

Small Cap Issues   Less active stocks that are listed on Nasdaq.

Small Firm Effect See **Size Effect**.

Small Order Execution System (SOES)   A computer system associated with Nasdaq that provides for automatic order execution of as many as 1,000 shares.

Soft Dollars   Brokerage commissions ostensibly paid for having a brokerage firm execute a trade and indirectly designated, in part, as payment for non-trade-related services rendered.

Specialist   A member of an organized exchange who has two primary functions. First, the specialist maintains an orderly market in assigned securities by acting as a dealer, buying and selling from his or her inventory of securities to offset temporary imbalances in the number of buy and sell orders. Second, the specialist facilitates the execution of limit, stop, and stop limit orders by acting as a broker, maintaining a limit order book and executing these orders as they are triggered.

Specialist Block Purchase or Sale   The accommodation of a relatively small block trade by a specialist who buys or sells from his or her inventory at a price negotiated with the seller or buyer.

Specialist's Book See **Limit Order Book**.

Special Offering or Bid   A trade involving a large block of stock on an organized security exchange whereby a number of brokerage firms attempt to execute the order by soliciting offsetting orders from their customers.

Speculative-Grade Bonds (alternatively, **Junk Bonds** or **High-Yield Bonds**)   Bonds that are not investment-grade bonds. Usually, speculative bonds have a BB (Standard & Poor's) or Ba (Moody's) or lower rating.

Speculator   An investor in futures contracts whose primary objective is to make a profit from buying and selling these contracts.

Split-Funding   A situation in which an institutional investor divides its funds among two or more professional money managers.

Spot Market   The market for an asset that involves the immediate exchange of the asset for cash.

Spot Price   The purchase price of an asset in the spot market.

Spot Rate   The annual yield-to-maturity on a pure-discount security.

Standard Deviation   A measure of the dispersion of possible outcomes around the expected value of a random variable.

Standard Deviation of the Random Error Term (alternatively, **Residual Standard Deviation**)   In the context of simple linear regression, a measure of the dispersion of the random error term.

Standard Error of Alpha   The standard deviation of a security's estimated alpha, as derived from the *ex post* characteristic line.

Standard Error of Beta   The standard deviation of a security's estimated beta, as derived from the *ex post* characteristic line.

Standardized Unexpected Earnings   The difference between a firm's actual earnings over a given period and an estimate of the firm's expected earnings, with this quantity divided by the standard deviation of the firm's previous earnings forecast errors.

Standby Agreement   An arrangement between a security issuer and an underwriter as part of a rights offering. The underwriter agrees to purchase at a fixed price all securities not purchased by current stockholders.

State-Preference Method   A method of valuing securities that is based on analyzing a security's payoffs in different states of the world (outcomes) and the probabilities of those states occurring.

Stochastic Process Risk   In the context of immunization, the risk that the yield curve will shift in a way that prevents an immunized bond portfolio from producing its expected cash inflows.

Stock Dividend   An accounting transaction that distributes stock to existing shareholders in proportion to the number of shares currently owned by the shareholders. A stock dividend entails a transfer from retained earnings to the capital stock account of a dollar amount that is equal to the market value of the distributed stock.

Stock Exchange Automated Quotations (SEAQ)   A computer system, similar to Nasdaq, that is used to trade stocks on the London Stock Exchange.

Stock Split   Similar to a stock dividend, an accounting transaction that increases the amount of stock held by existing shareholders in proportion to the number of shares currently owned by the shareholders. A stock split entails a reduction in the par value of the corporation's stock and the simultaneous exchange of a multiple number of new shares for each existing share.

Stop Limit Order   A trading order that specifies both a stop price and a limit price. If the security's price reaches or passes the stop price, then a limit order is created at the limit price.

Stop Loss Order See **Stop Order**.

Stop Order (alternatively, **Stop Loss Order**)   A trading order that specifies a stop price. If the security's price reaches or passes the stop price, then a market order is created.

Stop Price   The price specified by an investor when a stop order or a stop limit order is placed that defines the price at which the market order or limit order for the security is to become effective.

Straddle   An options strategy that involves buying (or writing) both a call and a put on the same asset, with the options having the same exercise price and expiration date.

Straight Voting System See **Majority Voting System**.

Street Name   An arrangement between an investor and a brokerage firm whereby the investor maintains an account in which the investor's securities are registered with the issuer in the name of the brokerage firm.

Striking Price See **Exercise Price**.

Strong-Form Market Efficiency   A level of market efficiency in which all relevant information, both public and private, is fully and immediately reflected in security prices.

Subordinated Debenture   A debenture whose claims, in the event of bankruptcy, are junior to other debentures issued by the firm.

Subscription Price   The price at which holders of rights are permitted to purchase shares of stock in a rights offering.

Substitution Swap   A type of bond swap whereby an investor exchanges one bond with a lower yield for another with a higher yield, yet the two bonds have essentially the same financial characteristics.

Super Designated Order Turnaround (SuperDOT)   A set of special procedures established by the New York Stock Exchange to handle routine small trading orders. Through these procedures, participating member firms can route orders directly to the specialist for immediate execution.

Supply-to-Sell Schedule   A description of the quantities of a security that an investor is prepared to sell at alternative prices.

Sustainable Earnings   The amount of earnings that a firm could pay out each year as dividends, with the result that the firm's future earnings would neither increase nor decrease.

Swap Bank   Typically a commercial or investment bank that sets up equity, interest rate, and other kinds of swaps between interested counterparties.

Syndicate (alternatively, **Purchasing Group**)   A group of investment banking organizations that, as part of a security underwriting, are responsible for purchasing the security from the issuer and reselling it to the public.

Synthetic Futures (Synthetic Futures Contract)   The creation of a position equivalent either to the purchase of a futures contract by buying a call option and writing a put option on the asset or to the sale of a futures contract by buying a put option and writing a call option on the asset.

Synthetic Put   A form of portfolio insurance that emulates the investment outcomes of a put option through the use of a dynamic asset allocation strategy.

Systematic Risk See **Market Risk**.

Takeover   An action by an individual or a firm to acquire controlling interest in a corporation.

Target Firm   A firm that is the subject of a takeover attempt.

Taxable Municipal Bond   A municipal bond whose income is fully taxable by the federal government.

Tax-Exempt Bond   A security whose income is not taxable by the federal government.

Technical Analysis   A form of security analysis that attempts to forecast the movement in the prices of securities primarily on the basis of historical price and volume trends in those securities.

Tender Offer   A form of corporate takeover in which a firm or individual offers to buy some or all of the shares of a target firm at a stated price. This offer is publicly advertised, and material describing the bid is mailed to the target's stockholders.

Term Bond   A bond issue wherein all of the bonds mature on the same date.

Terminal Wealth   The value of an investor's portfolio at the end of a holding period. Equivalently, the investor's initial wealth multiplied by 1 plus the rate of return earned on the investor's portfolio over the holding period.

Term Structure   The yields-to-maturity among bonds that possess different terms-to-maturity but are similar with respect to other attributes.

Term-to-Maturity   The time remaining until a bond's maturity date.

Third Market   A secondary security market where exchange-listed securities are traded over the counter.

Time Deposit   A savings account at a financial institution.

Time Value (Time Premium)   The excess of the market price of an option over its intrinsic value.

Time-Weighted Return   A method of measuring the performance of a portfolio over a particular period of time. Effectively, it is the return on one dollar invested in the portfolio at the beginning of the measurement period.

Timing   An aspect of security analysis that entails forecasting the price movements of asset classes relative to one another.

Top-Down Forecasting   A sequential approach to security analysis that entails first making forecasts for the economy, then for industries, and finally for individual companies. Each level of forecasts is conditional on the previous level of forecasts made.

Total Risk   The standard deviation of the return on a security or portfolio.

Trading Halt   A temporary suspension in the trading of a security on an organized exchange.

Trading Post   The physical location on the floor of an organized exchange where a specialist in a particular stock is located and where all orders involving the stock must be taken for execution.

Transfer Agent   A designated agent of a corporation, usually a bank, that administers the transfer of shares of a corporation's stock between old and new owners.

Treasury Bill   A pure-discount security issued by the U.S. Treasury with a maximum term-to-maturity of one year.

Treasury Bond   A security issued by the U.S. Treasury with a term-to-maturity of over seven years. Interest is paid semiannually, and principal is returned at maturity.

Treasury Note   A security issued by the U.S. Treasury with a term-to-maturity between one and seven years. Interest is paid semiannually, and principal is returned at maturity.

Treasury Stock   Common stock that has been issued by a corporation and then later purchased by the corporation in the open market or through a tender offer. This stock does not have voting rights or rights to receive dividends as long as it is held by the corporation, and is equivalent economically to unissued stock.

Triple Witching Hour   The date when options on individual stocks and market indices, futures on market indices, and options on market index futures expire simultaneously.

Trustee   An organization, usually a bank, that serves as the representative of bondholders. The trustee acts to protect the interests of bondholders and facilitates communication between them and the issuer.

Turn-of-the-Month Effect   The observation that average stock returns have been abnormally high during a four-day period beginning on the last trading day of the month.

Two-Dollar Broker See **Floor Broker**.

Unbiased Expectations Theory   An explanation of the term structure of interest rates. It holds that a forward rate represents the average opinion of the expected future spot rate for the time period in question.

Undermargined   A situation in which the actual margin in a margin account has fallen below the maintenance margin requirement.

Underpriced Security (alternatively, **Undervalued Security**)   A security whose expected return is greater than its equilibrium expected return. Equivalently, a security with a positive expected alpha.

Undervalued Security See **Underpriced Security**.

Underwrite   The process by which investment bankers bring new securities to the primary security market.

Underwriter See **Investment Banker**.

Unexpected Rate of Inflation   That portion of inflation experienced over a given period of time that was not anticipated by investors.

Unique Risk (alternatively, **Non-Market Risk** or **Unsystematic Risk**)   The portion of a security's total risk that is not related to moves in the market portfolio and, hence, can be diversified away.

Unit Investment Trust   An unmanaged investment company with a finite life that raises an initial sum of capital from investors and uses the proceeds to purchase a fixed portfolio of securities (typically bonds).

Unrealized Capital Gain (or Loss)   A capital gain (or loss) on an asset that has not yet been recognized for tax purposes through the sale or exchange of the asset.

Unrestricted See **Overmargined**.

Unseasoned Offering See **Initial Public Offering (ipo)**.

Unsystematic Risk See **Unique Risk**.

Upstairs Dealer Market   An adjunct to organized exchanges, where block houses that are member firms handle large block trades. The block houses act as both agents and principals, lining up trading partners to take the other side of the block orders.

Up Tick (alternatively, **Plus Tick**)   A trade in a security made at a price higher than the price of the previous trade in that same security.

Utility   The relative enjoyment or satisfaction that a person derives from economic activity such as work, consumption, or investment.

Value-Relative   The holding period return for a security, plus one.

Value Stock   Typically, a stock that has experienced relatively poor past price performance, or whose issuing company has experienced relatively poor past earnings results. It is often characterized as having high earnings-to-price and book-value-to-market-value ratios.

Value-Weighted Market Index (alternatively, **Capitalization-Weighted Market Index**)   A market index in which the contribution of a security to the value of the index is a function of the security's market capitalization.

Variable Rate See **Floating Rate**.

Variance   The squared value of the standard deviation.

Variance-Covariance Matrix   A table that symmetrically arrays the covariances between a number of random variables. Variances of the random variables lie on the diagonal of the matrix, whereas covariances between the random variables lie above and below the diagonal.

Variation Margin   The amount of cash that an investor must provide to meet a margin call on a futures contract.

Voting Bond   A bond that gives its holder a voice in the management of the issuer.

Warrant   A type of call option issued by the firm whose stock serves as the underlying security. Typically warrants have longer times to expiration than listed or over-the-counter call options.

Wash Sale   The sale and subsequent purchase of a "substantially identical" security solely for the purpose of generating a tax-deductible capital loss.

Weak-Form Market Efficiency   A level of market efficiency in which all previous security price and volume data are fully and immediately reflected in current security prices.

Weekend Effect See **Day-of-the-Week Effect**.

White Knight   Another firm, favorably inclined toward a target firm's current management, that during the process of a hostile takeover of that corporation agrees to make a better offer to the corporation's stockholders.

Wrap Account   A type of account at a brokerage firm that involves having a broker provide the investor with advice. All fees for financial planning, investment management, and securities trading are "wrapped" into one annual fee.

Yield   The yield-to-maturity of a bond.

Yield-to-Call   The yield-to-maturity of a callable bond calculated on the assumption that the bond is called at the earliest possible time.

Yield-to-Maturity   For a particular fixed-income security, the single interest rate (with interest compounded at some specified interval) that, if paid by a bank on the amount invested in the security, would enable the investor to obtain all the payments made by that security. Equivalently, the discount rate that equates the present value of future promised cash flows from the security to the current market price of the security.

Yield Curve   A visual representation of the term structure of interest rates.

Yield Spread   The difference in the promised yields-to-maturity of two bonds.

Yield Structure   The set of yields-to-maturity among bonds differing in terms of attributes that include term-to-maturity, coupon rate, call provisions, tax status, marketability, and likelihood of default.

Zero-Coupon Security See **Pure-Discount Security**.

Zero-Growth Model (alternatively, **No-Growth Model**)   A type of dividend discount model in which dividends are assumed to maintain a constant value in perpetuity.

Zero-Minus Tick   A trade in a security made at a price equal to that of the previous trade in that security but lower than that of the last trade made in the security at a different price.

Zero-Plus Tick   A trade in a security made at a price equal to that of the previous trade in that security but higher than that of the last trade made in the security at a different price.

Selected Solutions to End-of-Chapter Questions and Problems

Chapter 1

3. 18.2%
4. 8.0%
5. a. 30.0%
   b. −13.3%
   c. 4.0%
9. First period average return: .67%
   First period standard deviation: .45%
   Second period average return: 2.08%
   Second period standard deviation: .72%
10. Small stock average return: 21.23%
    Small stock standard deviation: 19.94%
    Common stock average return: 15.37%
    Common stock standard deviation: 13.65%

Chapter 2

2. Five round lots and one 11-share odd lot
5. Total assets: $15,000
   Total liabilities: $6,750
6. a. 62.5%
   b. 75.0%
   c. 57.1%
8. 40.0%
9. $8.00
10. $30,000
12. 17.1%
13. 74.0%, −26.0%
14. a. 56.0%
    b. −65.2%
    c. 36.7%, −30.0%
16. Total assets: $18,750
    Total liabilities: $12,500
17. a. 25.0%
    b. 72.6%
18. Actual margin: 39.5%
19. $45.00
21. −20.0%
22. a. −27.6%
    b. 43.6%
25. a. $5,400
    b. $5,500
26. Total assets: $12,750
    Total liabilities: $7,600

Chapter 3

14. Asked price: $45.19
    Bid price: $42.66

Chapter 5

1. 5.0%
3. −5.6%
4. a. 7.0%
   b. 9.0%
5. $939.26, $1,066.23
7. 10.0%
8. One-year spot rate: 7.5%
   Two-year spot rate: 4.0%
   Three-year spot rate: 2.8%
9. Three-year discount factor: .810
   Four-year discount factor: .731
   Five-year discount factor: .650
11. Forward rate from year 1 to year 2: 6.0%
    Forward rate from year 2 to year 3: 8.5%
    Forward rate from year 3 to year 4: 8.5%
12. One-year spot rate: 10.0%
    Two-year spot rate: 9.8%
    Three-year spot rate: 9.5%
    Four-year spot rate: 9.2%
13. $994.45
14. a. One-year discount factor: .909
       Two-year discount factor: .819
       Three-year discount factor: .749
    b. Forward rate from today to year 1: 10.0%
       Forward rate from year 1 to year 2: 11.0%
       Forward rate from year 2 to year 3: 9.4%
    c. $1,470.20
15. a. 6.1%
    b. 6.2%
16. a. $39.916.80
    b. $40,195.58
17. 9.0%, 9.9%
23. Yield on one-year pure-discount bond: 10.0%
    Yield on two-year pure discount bond: 12.0%
24. .54%
25. 10.2 years
26. a. .234
    b. −30.5
27. 13.37% or 4.27% per year

28. 6.2%, $40,495.76
29. $923.36

Chapter 6

12. 18.3%
13. 35.0%
14. Expected return: 8.5%
Standard deviation: 10.1%
15. Expected return: 17.0%
Standard deviation: 15.4%
18. Covariance: −52.1
Correlation: −.98
19. Correlation (A,B): .53
Correlation (A,C): .71
Correlation (B,C): .21
20. 11.6%
21. Expected return: 5.3%
Standard deviation: 4.7%
24. a. 34.1%
b. 25.0%
c. 9.2%
25. a. 8.8%
b. 4.7%
c. Weight in security A: .556
Weight in security B: .444
26. Expected return: 21.6%
Mode: 0%
Median: between +15% and +30%
27. $.06
28. −10.3
29. −.90

Chapter 7

7. Minimum standard deviation: 9.2%
Maximum standard deviation: 23.3%
9. 12.3%
15. 1.03%
17. 19.7%
18. Portfolio 1 standard deviation: 25.0%
Portfolio 2 standard deviation: 22.1%
21. .80
22. a. 1,325
b. 152

Chapter 8

4. a. 17.0%
b. 14.0%
c. 12.5%
5. Risky portfolio weight: 1.46

6. a. 26.0%
b. 18.0%
c. 14.0%
7. 11.0%
14. b. Expected return: 9.0%
Standard deviation: 10.2%
c. Expected return: 8.0%
Standard deviation: 7.7%
19. Riskfree asset weight: .50
Security 1 weight: .09
Security 2 weight: .15
Security 3 weight: .12
Security 4 weight: .14

Chapter 9

10. $5.0\% + .39\,\sigma_p$
12. 15.8%
16. 12.7%
19. $\beta_A = 1.30$
$\beta_B = 0.80$
$\beta_C = 1.00$
20. 1.03
21. 25.2%
22. c. Security A expected return: 9.4%
Security B expected return: 10.8%
23. b. $\beta_1 = 1.50$
$\beta_2 = .60$
25. $\beta_A = .74$
$\beta_B = 1.17$

Chapter 10

6. 82% factor related, 18% nonfactor related
7. a. 1,069.3
b. 43.8
c. 33.4%
8. 866.1
b. 35.5
c. 30.0%
9. 22.4%
10. Standard deviation of security A: 28.9%
Standard deviation of security B: 26.3%
11. 22.5, 2.25, 0.225
13. 220, 20
15. Sensitivity to factor 1: .28
Sensitivity to factor 2: 4.60
Sensitivity to factor 3: .24
17. Expected return: 15.5%
Standard deviation: 15.8%
20. −3.2
21. Earnings yield factor value: .243%
Book-price factor value: 4.286%

22. Security A standard deviation: 64.8%
Security B standard deviation: 30.2%
Covariance (A,B): 1,936.5

Chapter 11

4. $X_2 = .15$
$X_3 = -.35$
6. Weight of security B: $-.10$
Weight of security C: $-.10$
10. 26.0%
12. $r_f = 5.0\%$
14. 13.6%
15. a. $b_{p1} = .0$
$b_{p2} = .5$
b. $b_{p1} = .0$
$b_{p2} = 1.0$
c. 17.0%
d. 7.0%
16. a. Weight of security A: .05
Weight of security C: $-.60$
Weight of security D: .82
21. a. $\beta_A = .65$
$\beta_B = 1.02$
b. Security A expected return: 9.9%
Security B expected return: 12.1%
22. $\beta_A = 2.08$
$\beta_B = 1.56$

Chapter 12

3. Preferred stock after-tax return: 6.2%
Corporate bond after-tax return: 6.5%
5. $13,735.50
8. a. 6.7%
b. 8.3%
c. 9.0%
9. Municipal bond tax-equivalent yield: 7.1%
10. Tax bill if assets held for 13 months: $21,187
11. a. 6.1%
b. 23.5%
c. 29.6%
13. a. 20.0%
b. 13.4%
c. -7.4%
14. Arithmetic average inflation rate:
1926–33: -3.7%
1934–52: 3.9%
1953–65: 1.4%
1966–81: 7.1%
1982–96: 3.6%

15. a. $.78
b. $.62
c. $.50
16. $20,286.85
17. 8.1%
19. Nominal value triples in 12.8 years
Real value triples in 29.5 years

Chapter 13

1. 16.9%
2. a. 13.0%
b. 13.6%
10. 12.8%
19. Corporate bond after-tax return: 6.3%
24. a. 14.9%
b. 10.4%

Chapter 14

1. $5,583.95
2. Bond's intrinsic value: $937.82
3. Bond's intrinsic value: $9,358.16
4. a. $9,366.03
b. 12.0%
5. Change in five-year bond's price: -7.6%
Change in ten-year bond's price: -12.3%
7. 107 basis points
8. a. 9.0%
b. 12.8%
9. 12.9%
10. Actual yield with 15% reinvestment rate: 9.7%
Actual yield with 0% reinvestment rate: 8.0%
15. 7.6%

Chapter 15

1. $10,000.00, $8,770.68, $12,316.36
2. Price of bond A: $10,912.50
Price of bond B: $10,388.70
3. Five year bond's price: $713.00
Ten-year bond's price: $508.30
Twenty-year bond's price: $258.40
4. Four-year bond's price change: -11.7%
Fifteen-year bond's price change: -24.6%
5. -7.2%, 8.0%
6. Proportion of five-year bond's price increase due to change in present value of principal: 79.1%

Proportion of twenty-year bond's price increase due to change in present value of principal: 42.4%

7. 10% coupon bond's price increase: 14.1%
   8% coupon bond's price increase: 14.7%
8. 2.8 years
9. 2.6 years
10. 2.7 years
12. 3.4 years
15. −.98%
24. Overall rate of return: 50.9%

Chapter 16

2. **a.** 750,001
   b. 500,001
   c. 1
8. **a.** 1,380,000, $34.78
   b. 1,600,000, $30.00
   c. 400,000, $120.00
9. **a.** .05
   b. $.476
   c. $74.00
10. **a.** $6.00
    b. $35,310
    c. $34,051
    d. $34,051
12. .67
13. .84
14. **a.** 1.18
    b. −.05
    c. 1.45
    d. .906
23. $308 million
24. **a.** 1.07
    b. 1.39
25. .69

Chapter 17

1. $25.82
2. $1,978.10
3. 7.0%
4. **a.** $6.52
   b. 8.0%
5. $80.00
6. $52.00
7. 12.0%
10. $106.83
11. $70.44
12. **a.** $35.00
    b. $46.34
    c. 3.13
13. $73.03
15. $44.00

16. 10.60
17. 16.41%
18. 14.53

Chapter 18

2. **a.** Purchase $400,000 of new equity
   b. Sell $400,000 of existing equity
   c. No action
7. D1 = $13.0 million
   D2 = $15.7 million
   D3 = $15.3 million
   D4 = $13.6 million
   D5 = $14.4 million
8. .59
17. $4.88
18. SUE6 = −.03
    SUE7 = +1.14
    SUE8 = +0.77
    SUE9 = −.91

Chapter 19

9. $4.87
10. $3.27
11. $5.08
14. .41
15. .40
16. 216 contracts
17. **a.** 5.4%
    b. 5.94
18. $3.13
19. $12.40
21. $2.19
25. **a.** $750.00
    b. $240.00
    c. $900.66

Chapter 20

5. $.00, $15,000
6. **a.** $1,050
   b. $3,050
   c. $50
12. $4,280
13. $5,164,286
15. $1.79
16. 4.0%
17. $98.98
19. $20,000
21. **a.** 204
27. −40.0%

Chapter 21

1. $17.60
4. a. $12.45
   b. $11.45
8. 8.0%
11. −1.9%
12. Year 1: 6.6%
    Year 2: 14.8%
    Year 3: −2.1%

Chapter 22

8. ROA = 13.7%
   ROE = 41.1%
9. a. 15.0
   b. $6.00
   c. 5.0
   d. 1.7%
   e. 25.0%

Chapter 23

7. 64.8
8. 54.0
11. 32.1
12. 8.7%

Chapter 24

1. 12.7%
3. −2.6%
4. 18.8%
5. 10.5%

6. 9.4%
7. a. 26.0%
   b. 22.5%
9. 3.1%
10. 40.7%, 43.0%
14. a. 1.967
    b. 1.130
    c. 1.478
16. a. $3,000,000
    b. 8.0%
    c. No change
17. a. 15.0
    b. 18.7
    c. 18.7
    d. 120.0
19. a. 3.5%
    b. 4.5%
20. 207.6, 215.3
21. .8%
22. .05, .55, .06
27. d. −.51%
    e. 1.11%
28. 3.50, 8.24, .35

Chapter 25

4. 68.42 yen/DM
6. 29.6%
7. −4.76%
8. 56.3%
11. 26.3%
14. 2.9%
15. 17.0%

Options (cont.)
  futures vs., 681–83
  index options, 635–37
    cash settlement, 635
    contract, 635–37
    flex options, 637
  margin, 609–10
  naked call writing, 614
  naked put writing, 614
  option contracts, types of, 601–4
  option overwriting, 614–15
  option trading, 605–9
  portfolio insurance, 637–41
    creating a synthetic put, 639–41
    purchasing a protective put, 637–38
  time value, 630
  valuation of, 610–16
    at expiration, 610–11
    profits/losses on calls and puts, 611–14
    profits/losses from option strategies, 614–16
  valuation of put options, 632–35
Option trading, 605–9
  commissions, 609
  market-makers, 607–8
  most active options, 606–7
  open outcry, 608–9
  specialists, 607
  trading activity, 605–6
  trading on exchanges, 607–9
Option writer, 601
Order book officials, 607–8
Order handling rules, SEC, 68
Orders, 23–26
  day, 23
  discretionary, 23
  fill-or-kill (FOK) orders, 23
  good-till-canceled (GTC), 23
  limit orders, 24
  market orders, 24
  open, 23
  stop limit orders, 25
  stop orders, 24–25
  Super Designated Order Turnaround system (SuperDOT), 54–55
Order size, 23
Order specifications, 23
Ordinary least squares (OLS), 476
Organized exchanges, 48
Original issue discount securiteis (OID), 353
OTC Bulletin Board, 59
Out of the money, 629, 632
Out-of-sample data, 805
Overmargined accounts, 28
Oversubscription privilege, 513fn
Over-the-counter market, 57–59
  National Association of Securities Dealers Automated Quotatons system (Nasdaq), 57–58
  OTC Bulletin Board, 59
  Pink Sheets stocks, 59
  Small Order Execution System (SOES), 58–59
Overwriting, options, 614–15
Owner of a corporation, 2

P

Pacific Investment Management Company (PIMCO), 685
Pac-Man defense, 460
Participating bonds, 369
Participating preferred stock, 377
Participation certificates (pass-throughs), 357–58
  innovations, 358
  prepayment risk, 357–58
Par value, 461
Passive currency managment, 881
Passive management, 799–801
  bond portfolio, 442–43
Passive managers, 188–89
Pass-throughs, 357–58
Payment for order flow, 60–61
Payout ratio, 534
Pegging, 485
Pension funds, 11, 434
  administrators, 15
  taxing, 310–11
Pensions and Investment Age, 777
People's Republic of China (PRC), firms' fund raising in, 490–91
Perfectly efficient markets:
  observations about, 96–97
  with transaction costs, observations about, 97
Perfect markets, 228
Performance:
  examining, 102
  mutual funds, 712–20
  portfolio performance evaluation, 14, 825–75
  See also Bond portfolio performance evaluation; Portfolio performance evaluation; Risk-adjusted performance measures
Performance attribution, 855, 867–69
  comparative, 868
Performance margin, 659
Personal income taxes, 309–19
  capital gains/losses, 315–19
  tax-exempt bonds, 313–15
  tax rates, 309–13
Pink Sheets stocks, 59
Plan Sponsor, 777
Poison pills, 460
Policy asset allocation, 684
Policy asset mix, 13
Porfolios, manager, 740, 856–57
Portfolio analysis, 171–203
  concavity of efficient set, 175–80
    actual locations of portfolios, 179–80
    bounds on location of portfolios,175–79
  diversification, 184–90
    portfolio market risk, 186
    portfolio total risk, 185–86
    portfolio unique risk, 186–87
    random vs. efficient, 190
    three-security portfolio example, 189–90
    two-security portfolio example, 187–88
  efficient set, defined, 171
  efficient set theorem, 171–74
    applied to feasible set, 172–73
    defined, 171